Handbook of Industrial
and Organizational Psychology

Contributors

Arthur Brief, *Tulane University*
Philippe Byosiere, *University of Michigan*
Gerald F. Davis, *Northwestern University*
René V. Dawis, *University of Minnesota*
Barry Gerhart, *Cornell University*
Richard A. Guzzo, *University of Maryland*
J. Richard Hackman, *Harvard University*
Joy Fisher Hazucha, *Personnel Decisions, Inc.*
Lowell W. Hellervik, *Personnel Decisions, Inc.*
Wayne Hoyer, *University of Texas, Austin*
Jacob Jacoby, *New York University*
G. Douglas Jenkins, Jr., *University of Arkansas*
Robert L. Kahn, *University of Michigan*
Edward D. Lawler III, *University of Southern California*
David Lubinski, *Iowa State University*
D. Douglas McKenna, *Seattle Pacific University*
George T. Milkovich, *Cornell University*
Michael D. Mumford, *George Mason University*
Jerry I. Porras, *Stanford University*
Walter W. Powell, *University of Arizona*
Robert D. Pritchard, *Texas A & M University*
Peter J. Robertson, *University of Southern California*
Robert J. Schneider, *Personnel Decisions, Inc.*
Garnett S. Stokes, *University of Georgia*
Gregory P. Shea, *University of Pennsylvania*
Ronald N. Taylor, *Rice University*
Kenneth W. Thomas, *Naval Postgraduate School*
David D. Van Fleet, *Arizona State University West*
Patrick M. Wright, *Texas A & M University*
Gary Yukl, *State University of New York at Albany*

Handbook of Industrial and Organizational Psychology

SECOND EDITION

Volume 3

Marvin D. Dunnette and Leaetta M. Hough
Editors

Consulting Psychologists Press, Inc.
Palo Alto, California

Library of Congress Cataloging-in-Publication Data
(Revised for vol. 3)

Handbook of industrial and organizational psychology

    Spine title: Handbook of industrial & organizational psychology.
    Includes bibliographical references and index.
    1. Psychology, Industrial. 2. Organizational behavior. I. Dunnette, Marvin D. II. Hough, Leaetta M. III. Title. IV. Title: Handbook of industrial & organizational psychology.
HF 5548.8.H265   1990   158.7   90-2294 CIP
ISBN 0-89106-041-3 (v. 1)
ISBN 0-89106-042-1 (v. 2)
ISBN 0-89106-043-X (v. 3)

Printed in the United States of America

Dedicated to our fathers,
Rodney A. Dunnette, attorney,
and
Mervin B. Hough, master builder.
They set standards of
quiet excellence and uncommon wisdom
that challenge us still.

Contents

Figures

Tables

Preface

As we mentioned in our preface to the first two volumes of this *Handbook*, the basic topic structure has not changed much from that of the first edition published in 1976.

The similarity of structure was retained because we wanted to preserve a continuity between the content of the first *Handbook* and the present one. In approaching possible authors for contributions to the present *Handbook*, we emphasized that they should not be constrained by what was in the first edition, but neither should they feel compelled to make their contributions so new and different that no links with the first were recognizable. The hope was that the content of the two editions of the *Handbook* would play an important role in reflecting the nature of the growth and development of industrial and organizational psychology during the last 35 to 40 years of this century.

Although the basic structure of the two editions has been retained, changes in content were inevitable. Several chapters have been added to reflect the emergence of new areas of knowledge and concern in industrial and organizational psychology. These are reviewed briefly below:

- *Theory in Industrial and Organizational Psychology*
  This section was expanded to include chapters on individual differences theory, decision-making theory, and cognitive theory. Volume 1 of the *Handbook* contains five chapters focusing on theory: "The Role of Theory in Industrial and Organizational Psychology" by J. P. Campbell, "Motivation Theory" by R. Kanfer, "Learning Theory" by H. M. Weiss, "Individual Differences Theory" by P. L. Ackerman and L. G. Humphreys, and "Judgment and Decision-making Theory" by M. Stevenson, J. R. Busemeyer, and J. C. Naylor. "Cognitive Theory" by R. G. Lord and K. J. Maher is contained in volume 2.

- *Measurement and Method in Industrial and Organizational Psychology*
  A separate chapter on item response theory has been added. Two chapters on research strategy have been included—one on the process of *discovery* as it influences research methods, and the other on the broad domain of research strategies and tactics in industrial and

organizational psychology. Thus, volume 1 of the *Handbook* contains six chapters focusing on measurement and method: "Research Methods in the Service of Discovery" by M. W. McCall and P. Bobko, "Research Strategies and Tactics" by P. R. Sackett and J. R. Larson, Jr., "Quasi Experimentation" by T. D. Cook, D. T. Campbell, and L. Peracchio, "Item Response Theory" by F. Drasgow and C. L. Hulin, "Multivariate Correlational Analysis" by P. Bobko, and "Modeling the Performance Prediction Problem" by J. P. Campbell.

- *Individual Behavior and Organizational Practices*
New chapters have been included on work structure and the design of jobs and roles, recruitment and organizational entry processes, and methods of utility estimation in human resources practices and functions. Issues related to job satisfaction are considered within the somewhat broader context of organizational socialization and persistence.

Accordingly, volume 2 of the *Handbook* contains the topics specified in the following nine chapters: "Job Analysis" by R. J. Harvey, "The Structure of Work" by D. R. Ilgen and J. R. Hollenbeck, "Human Factors" by W. C. Howell, "Job Behavior, Performance and Effectiveness" by W. C. Borman, "Personnel Assessment, Selection, and Placement" by R. M. Guion, "Recruitment, Job Choice, and Post-hire Consequences" by S. L. Rynes, "Organizational Adaptation, Persistence, and Commitment" by C. L. Hulin, "Training in Work Organizations" by I. L. Goldstein, and "Utility Analysis" by J. W. Boudreau.

- *Attributes of Individuals in Organizations*
In addition to chapters on vocational interests, personality, aptitudes and abilities, and background information, all of which were included in the first *Handbook*, a new chapter on physical abilities has been added.

Thus, volume 2 of the *Handbook* includes the following chapters: "Physical Abilities" by J. C. Hogan, "Vocational Interests, Values, and Preferences" by R. V. Dawis, and "Personality and Measurement" by R. T. Hogan.

Two additional chapters on individual attributes make up the first two chapters of the present volume, volume 3. They are "Aptitudes, Abilities, and Skills" by D. Lubinski and R. V. Dawis, and "Background Data Measures" by M. D. Mumford and G. S. Stokes.

The remaining 14 chapters in this volume of the *Handbook* are organized as follows:

- *Organizational Behavior: Individual, Group, and Environmental Influences*
Four of the six topics in this section—leadership, group influences on individuals, organization-environment relations, and consumer psychology—contained counterparts in the first *Handbook*. These

chapters are "Theory and Research on Leadership" by G. Yukl and D. D. Van Fleet, "Group Influences on Individuals" by J. R. Hackman, "Organization-Environment Relations" by G. F. Davis and W. W. Powell, and "Consumer Psychology" by J. Jacoby, W. Hoyer, and A. Brief. The other two chapters in section 1 cover issues not dealt with explicitly in the first *Handbook.* These are "Group Performance and Intergroup Relations" by R. A. Guzzo and G. P. Shea, and "Organizational Productivity" by R. D. Pritchard.

- *Individual and Group Responses and Behavior Change in Organizations*
  Two areas have been added to the present edition that were not covered in the first *Handbook*—employee compensation and individual behavioral change. Thus, the five chapters covered in this section are "Employee Compensation" by B. Gerhart and G. Milkovich, "Stress in Organizations" by R. L. Kahn and P. Byosiere, "Conflict and Negotiation Processes" by K. W. Thomas, "Organizational Development" by J. I. Porras and P. J. Robertson, and "Behavior Change" by L. W. Hellervik, J. Fisher Hazucha, and R. J. Schneider.

- *Organization Design and Strategy*
  Each of the three chapters in this section were represented in the first *Handbook.* They are "Alternative Metaphors for Organization Design" by D. D. McKenna and P. M. Wright, "Strategic Decision Making" by R. N. Taylor, and "Strategic Reward Systems" by E. E. Lawler III and G. D. Jenkins, Jr.

An overview of what is contained in volumes 1, 2, and 3 and what this knowledge may mean for the future of industrial and organizational psychology is being prepared by Ray Katzell. His chapter, currently titled "Implications for the Future of Past and Current Issues in Industrial and Organizational Psychology," is slated to be the lead chapter in volume 4. The remainder of volume 4 is devoted to issues of diversity and to the cross-cultural context of industrial and organizational psychology. As was mentioned in the preface to volume 2, Harry Triandis has joined us as a coeditor of volume 4. Each of the contributors to volume 4 has been asked to write about his or her own research interests and activities and to present them in the context of issues seen as most salient to organizational psychology in her or his particular country.

Thus, in addition to the chapter by Katzell and two chapters by Triandis (one on diversity and the other on cross-cultural issues in the field), chapters in volume 4 will include contributions by authors from Australia, France, Germany, Hong Kong, India, Israel (two), Japan (two), the Netherlands, the People's Republic of China, Russia, Spain, Sweden, and the United Kingdom.

Procedures used to designate content for chapters of this second edition and to designate particular candidates as authors were described in our prefaces for volumes 1 and 2. Ultimately, a total of 64 scholars agreed to author or coauthor one or more chapters for the first three volumes of the new *Handbook*. These 64 authors include scholars of diverse training and institutional affiliation. They are from 40 different institutions; 61 are in academic departments (33 in psychology, 26 in schools of business, and 2 in sociology), and 3 are with consulting firms. The 23 additional authors of chapters in volume 4 represent 18 different institutions in 13 different countries.

As mentioned in our prefaces to the previous two volumes, the level of scholarship shown by all these contributors has been superb. It is apparent that each author worked hard and long to produce the best possible statement of current research and thinking in his or her area of expertise. We believe that the hundreds of industrial and organizational psychologists who have joined our ranks over the last 15 years, as well as the next several generations of entering students of industrial and organizational psychology and organizational behavior, will profit from what is contained in the pages of these volumes.

As with the previous two volumes, Kim Downing has provided indispensable assistance. She has handled the mountain of correspondence with authors of these chapters and with a vast number of other authors and publishers during the process of obtaining required permissions. She most certainly deserves a medal of honor for diligence and perspicacity. Kim tackled problems as they appeared and solved them quickly and efficiently. The editorial "struggle" was eased considerably by her quickness, her persistence, and on occasion, her friendly audacity in being able to cope with the occasional contentious individual who seemed to be standing in the way of the *Handbook*'s progress.

We have been gratified that we had the opportunity to work with Consulting Psychologists Press as our publisher. We appreciate the helpfulness of Bob Most, John Black, and in particular, CPP's president and CEO, Lorin Letendre, for their support and enthusiasm in choosing this project as a major vehicle for their expansion into publishing state-of-the-art contributions in industrial and organizational psychology.

A very special advantage in working with Consulting Psychologists Press has been the privilege of working with the director of their book division, Lee Langhammer Law, who has managed the publication of volumes 1 and 2. For the present volume, Lee has been joined by Kathleen Hummel. Together, they have handled all phases of production. They have carefully and delightfully edited these manuscripts from beginning to end. This has been done with wisdom and patience and without rancor. They have been more helpful to both the contributing authors and to us than we could have ever expected. There is no way in which one could properly acknowledge the level of excellence they have demonstrated throughout this process.

The so-called incidental expenses involved in a project of this magnitude can grow far beyond what one would ever reasonably estimate. Hundreds of phone calls, thousands of pages of copying costs, and a seemingly endless stream of letters and packages requiring substantial amounts of postage, air express fees, and other special delivery charges accumulate over the days, weeks, months, and years. These costs have been borne by grants made to the project by Personnel Decisions Research Institute. It is fair to say that the financial feasibility of this undertaking would be difficult to justify purely on the basis of sound business reasoning. The generosity of PDRI's Board of Trustees is deeply appreciated for their willingness to grant facilities and funds to help in handling the substantial incidental expenses accumulated over the lifetime of this effort.

MARVIN D. DUNNETTE
LEAETTA M. HOUGH
St. Paul, Minnesota
March 1992

CHAPTER 1

Aptitudes, Skills, and Proficiencies

David Lubinski
Iowa State University

René V. Dawis
University of Minnesota

This chapter deals with the role of human abilities or response capabilities as determinants of work behavior. Some definitions are offered for conceptualizing labels used to classify these attributes (e.g., abilities, achievements, aptitudes, and skills) and indices thereof. Particular attention is devoted to cognitive/intellectual abilities and to the optimal utilization of contrasting dimensions generated by factor analytic research. Throughout this treatment, the criterion of scientific significance is employed to evaluate both well-known and contemporary ability parameters. Although the scientific significance of general intelligence and its central role in industrial and organizational psychology as well as psychology in general is quite robust, it is without question that multiple ability dimensions are worthy of both applied and theoretical attention. The importance of setting expectations on how much predictive power to expect solely from ability attributes is addressed. We also suggest how new assessment procedures may be compared and evaluated against existing techniques in terms of an empirically based form of competitive support. In this vein, the importance of using multiple criteria for assessing performance (including the aggregation of distinct criteria) is recommended.

We suggest that personal qualities not typically considered in conventional treatments of human abilities (e.g., personality dimensions) may be construed as instrumental response capabilities. The causal status of these entities as determinants of proficient work behavior is developed, and suggestions are offered on how these attributes might be incorporated into future research. Meta-analytic studies of validity generalization are reviewed. And two topics concerning group differences in abilities are discussed in detail. First, a new methodology is offered for predicting group differences in performance; and second, the importance of assessing group differences in variability (ability dispersion) is examined. The chapter closes by explicating the importance of achievement as opposed to topographical accounts of behavior for measuring human attributes and for future developments in both applied and theoretical psychology. It is suggested that the role of normal science and the importance of systematically accumulating knowledge (using existing techniques) might be underappreciated.

Introduction

THE WORLD IS a continually changing place. Familiar situations recur, but all situations contain components that are new. Familiar tasks change as they take on unfamiliar dimensions. The demands people encounter are becoming more complex. To function successfully in this world, people must be able to change behaviorally in effective ways. To deal with change effectively, old behavior patterns must be modified and new, more sophisticated behaviors must be learned. In a real way, life is a series of actions and reactions to varying degrees of novelty in a variety of contexts. But because future events often share important features with past circumstances, people are able to adapt to new situations—if they have profited from their experience. In many ways, what we call *talent* or *competence* is the ability to produce more effective and more efficient behavior in novel situations. In this sense, every instrumental act is, quite literally, a creative happening.

The way people cope with change reflects both history and disposition—their tendencies to assimilate and accommodate to ever changing environmental demands. The behavior people manifest tells us how they may have acted and reacted in the past and how facile they are likely to be at dealing with unfamiliar tasks in the future. Because behavior is repeated, even when modified to suit the changing context, people can be characterized in terms of their behavioral attributes.

The present chapter is about an important class of behavior attributes: human capabilities. In industrial and organizational psychology, human capabilities are assessed in order to predict work performance. Assessing human capabilities involves sampling the behavioral repertoire for classes of behavior that are related to work performance. These behavior classes also factor into other important facets of a person's psychological world. We will devote particular attention to human capabilities manifested in careers and occupations, but our discussion will necessarily touch on other domains of human conduct.

To understand the human capabilities that make for career and occupational effectiveness, we have also to understand the settings in which behavior takes place—in particular, the school and work settings. It is useful to construe such settings as *environmental ecologies*, following Brunswik (1956), wherein various contingencies operate to structure the behavior classes that are required to achieve prescribed goals. School and work settings are loosely standardized environmental ecologies. Because the behaviors, contingencies, and goals are often highly specialized, if one is to perform successfully in these ecologies, the requisite behaviors must be in place.

This, basically, is why we assess human capabilities—to find out if individuals have the required behaviors in their repertoires.

Whether an individual's current level of behavioral effectiveness is linked primarily to personal gifts or environmental privilege may be an interesting question, but applied psychologists are more interested in the behavioral phenotype—what it is that a person can do. Furthermore, to predict future behavior—whether it be the likelihood that currently available behavior will be manifested or the probability that new behavior will be acquired—assessment is always based on behavior. The significance of these points will become clearer as our discussion unfolds.

Definitions

Assessment means collecting information for a purpose, and the purpose of psychological assessment is to make behavioral predictions. *Psychological assessment* is, fundamentally, classifying and quantifying the current status of selected behavior classes, selected because of their social significance. This is true of all important classes of behaviors—interests, needs, values, and personality traits, as well as abilities (Lubinski & Thompson, 1986; Meehl, 1986a).

Assessment of abilities is usually done (a) to predict behavior individuals are capable of displaying and (b) to evaluate individuals' readiness to acquire other behavior. Both purposes involve assessing the current status of the behavior repertoire, which includes the cognitive, motor, and perceptual ability domains. The latter distinctions denote different emphases rather than discreteness of category, inasmuch as all molar behavior involves blends of all three.

Regarding abilities, psychologists are interested in normative assessment, or what a person is capable of doing compared with others. Assessment of this kind has been

referred to as *aptitude, ability,* or *skill assessment.* The distinctions implied by these terms are not always clear. As with the categories of ability domains, these categories of assessment more appropriately denote contrasting points of emphasis.

Aptitudes, abilities, and skills all represent categories of behavior classes. Abilities and skills are often considered conceptually similar, but abilities are the broader, more molar category. *Aptitude* is a more elusive term, often defined as the *potential* for acquiring additional or subsequent skills. Thus, the MCAT assesses a premed student's potential for success in medical school, or the LSAT assesses a prelaw student's potential for success in law school. But in both cases, what is being assessed is the current status of a behavioral repertoire. Even the proficiencies that achievement tests test represents behavior classes (although typically they are arbitrary classes, established by instructional curricula).

If these distinctions are useful (i.e., ability/skill vs. aptitude), they are useful for distinguishing different *purposes* for assessment, as opposed to denoting *what it is* that is being assessed. Aptitude assessment is conducted for the purpose of *forecasting* the likelihood of certain behavior. (Given certain test scores and a certain GPA from a particular university, what is the probability that Ms. Jones will graduate from engineering school and how much engineering knowledge will she assimilate over the course of five years of engineering training?) By contrast, ability and skill assessment is typically (but not always) for the purpose of *evaluating the current status* of an individual's behavior repertoire. Although aptitude and ability assessment may stress different purposes, to say that qualitatively different attributes are being indexed (e.g., *potential* vs. *actual*) is simply not accurate or theoretically sound. *Potential* and *actual* are both being indexed by *any* procedure used to assess human capability.

The frequently encountered terms, *latent talent* and *hidden ability,* often confuse the issue because these terms imply that what is being assessed is different from manifest behavior. But the assessment of talent *always* involves behavioral evidence. It may be appropriate, for example, to characterize a gifted athlete from a distant country who has phenomenal quickness, running speed, and strength, but is ignorant of the game of football, as having latent talent for football. But this characterization is based on a lot of behavior, a lot of *manifest* behavior. For it to be scientifically meaningful to say that someone has exceptional talent for anything, *exceptional* behavior must be evinced.

Talent is public and the manifestation of talent is quantifiable. Furthermore, to the extent that the behavior observed shares communality with the (predicted) behavior of interest (which would be true in our gifted athlete example), the likelihood of a valid inference about "latent talent" is increased. This, of course, also pertains to aptitude assessment of all other kinds of human capability.

For example, for over 20 years, the Study of Mathematically Precocious Youth (SMPY) has demonstrated that approximately one to two percent of 7th graders are ready for college courses in mathematics (Benbow, 1988; Stanley, 1983). These students are selected as follows: If students score in the top one to two percent in their grade level on standardized achievement tests, they are given the opportunity to take the SAT-M. For these students, their SAT-M scores reproduce the same distribution found for 12th-grade college-bound students (Benbow, 1988). They have the *aptitude* for college courses. But this diagnosis is based on the *current* level of their quantitative ability (albeit a great deal of exceptional behavior). As we will show below, to be gifted in any given domain means that you have *more* behaviors in the domain in question or that your behaviors are more effective or more efficient. Quite literally, to be intellectually gifted means that you have

more intellectual behaviors in your repertoire than others.

Just before the last *Handbook* appeared, Cleary, Humphreys, Kendrick, and Wesman (1975) analyzed the dimensions typically used to distinguish tests of human capability. They stressed that there are no differences *in kind* between intelligence and achievement, or between aptitude and achievement. There are, instead, four dimensions appropriate to the description of tests and the behavior repertoires they sample:

- *Breadth of material sampled.* Most intelligence and aptitude tests are broad, whereas most achievement tests are more circumscribed, in terms of the range of behaviors sampled.

- *Curriculum represented.* Achievement tests tend to be tied to a particular curriculum or educational program. Aptitude tests, on the other hand, reflect both formal and informal instruction.

- *Recency of learning sampled.* In general, achievement tests sample *new* learning, that is, behaviors recently acquired, whereas aptitude tests sample older learning.

- *Purpose of assessment.* Aptitude tests are used for predictive purposes, but the same items, if used to assess current knowledge, are thought of as constituting an achievement test (see Cronbach & Snow, 1977).

All tests of human capability can be characterized by these dimensions. Tests that purport to measure either aptitude or achievement have much in common. This reality has been stressed in Standard 8.3 of the most recent edition of *Standards for Educational and Psychological Testing* (APA, AERA, & NCME, 1985): "It should not be assumed that, because the words 'aptitude' or 'ability' are used in the title of a test, it measures a construct distinct from what is measured by an achievement test" (p. 52).

Indeed, Cronbach (1990), in his most recent measurement text, defines *aptitude test* as a "measure intended to predict success in a job, educational program, or other practical activity. Usually an ability test" (p. 701). Just as Dunnette and Borman (1979) have argued that the three traditional kinds of validities—content, criterion, and construct—should not be considered wholly distinct, but rather should be combined in common purpose, so do we assert that the three categories of human capabilities—aptitude, achievement, and ability—should be combined into a *generic behavior class* if we are to understand better the nature of our measuring instruments and the proficiencies they measure.

Psychological Meaningfulness and the Criterion of Scientific Significance

The psychological literature on human capability reveals a large number of purportedly distinct abilities, especially within the cognitive domain. Guilford's (1967) model, for example, proposed 120 factors (more recently, 180 factors), which motivated Carroll (1989a) to remark, "I like to say that Guilford fell victim to 'hardening of the categories' about halfway through his project" (p. 45). And, indeed, most people in the field feel that there is quite a bit of redundancy in Guilford's model. But the specific number of abilities still remains unadjudicated. Are there seven, as Thurstone (1938) suggested, or only one dominant dimension, as Spearman (1904) would have us believe? And what classes of abilities are most important to assess?

There is an important concept in the experimental literature that has been neglected in recent years. It was introduced by Spence (1948) as *the criterion of scientific significance.*

The basic idea is this: For a psychological construct to be scientifically significant, measures of the construct must not only display a respectable degree of internal consistency and replicability, but they must also relate to an array of meaningful psychological criteria. That is, they must display relationships with external criteria that we are interested in predicting and understanding. There are many measures of ability that meet the first requisite, but relatively few that meet the second. We believe that consideration of Spence's criterion would result in fewer trivial constructs and more scientifically significant measures within the ability domain.

To be sure, this idea is not new. The importance of linkage to external criteria has been discussed some by factor analysts and other methodologists. Vernon (1961), for example, stressed the need for factors to relate to a "capacity of daily life" (p. 27), although he admitted that what constitutes this criterion is somewhat subjective. Humphreys (1962) has suggested that the construct of general intelligence (*g*) should be splintered only when differential or incremental validity is displayed across meaningful external criteria. Snow (1980) has used the term *worldly significance* in the same vein, whereas Kelley (1939), McNemar (1964), and Stanley (personal communication, 1991) prefer *social utility*. We will employ this criterion to evaluate both the concepts and the measures of familiar, as well as newer, abilities.

Ability measures may appear to index different constructs, if we go by their labels. If, indeed, they measure distinct behavioral functions, they should have distinct correlates and show incremental validity when added to established ability measures. For example, in discussing advances in information processing approaches, Sternberg (1981) noted, "the incremental validity of information processing scores over psychometric scores has yet to be demonstrated for interesting external criteria" (p. 1186). To be scientifically significant and not simply to be rebuilding existing measures, information processing instruments must do something meaningful that goes beyond what conventional psychometric measures currently offer. Achieving high degrees of reliability in experimental laboratory preparations is not enough.

Dunnette (1966) captured the essence and the importance of this idea years ago under the heading "The Delusions We Suffer."

> A common delusion seems to arise out of the early recognition that gathering data from real people emitting real behaviors in the day-to-day world proves often to be difficult, unwieldy, and just plain unrewarding. Thus, many retreat into the relative security of experimental or psychometric laboratories where new laboratory or test behaviors may be concocted to be observed, measured, and subjected to an endless array of internal analyses. These usually lead to elaborate theories and taxonomies, entirely consistent with themselves but lacking the acid test of contact with reality. Last year, McNemar (1964) summarized once more for us the pathetic record of factor analytically derived tests for predicting day-to-day behavior: Psychologists who choose to partake of the advantages of the more rigorous controls possible in the psychometric or experimental laboratories must also accept responsibility for assuring the day-to-day behavioral relevance of the behavioral observations they undertake. (p. 346)

The importance of coupling meaningful external correlates with internally consistent measurement operations has resurfaced in contemporary discussions. In a recent symposium on abilities, motivation and methodology, Jenkins (1989) remarked, "I hope that in 20 years when this group meets again, we will have really important things to say about psychological structures of organism-in-the-

real-world. That will truly be a test of success of this whole endeavor"(p. 490). We recommend the proceedings of this symposium (Kanfer, Ackerman, & Cudeck, 1989), especially Jenkins' chapter.

The Nature and Organization of Cognitive Abilities

Contemporary, well-established measures of cognitive abilities, if we stay with those predictive of criterion behaviors in industrial and organizational settings, had their origins in factor analytic findings dating back to Spearman (1904). Although Thurstone (1938) gave us the term, it was Spearman who first called attention to the *positive manifold* (the positive intercorrelations displayed among all cognitive ability tests), and formulated as its explanation *g*, the underlying factor common to all forms of cognitive functioning and manifested in systematic sources of individual differences across all cognitive ability tests. Spearman theorized that *g* represented *mental energy*. Although the construct is still prominent in contemporary work on cognitive abilities, the surplus meaning of mental energy that Spearman attached to this entity is no longer seriously entertained.

Spearman (1927) thought mental energy was the fuel that ran the content-specific engines for the many different kinds of cognitive tasks. This idea provided the foundation for Spearman's two-factor theory (Spearman, 1914), with which many of Spearman's contemporaries (and subsequent factor theorists as well) took issue. The idea of a single regnant cognitive functioning capacity appeared too simplistic, and many tried to decompose *g* into its constituent components. These more molecular factors were viewed as the *primary abilities*. Early discussions of these primaries appeared reminiscent of faculty psychology. They were viewed as the psychological building blocks of cognitive functioning, akin to atoms in matter. Individuals who pioneered this approach were, most notably, Thurstone (1938), Cattell (1971), and Guilford (1967).

Other more behaviorally oriented theorists approached the problem differently, finding the explanation of the positive manifold in intimately intertwined stimulus-response bonds (e.g., Ferguson, 1954; Thomson, 1951; Thorndike, 1926; Tryon, 1935). These bonds were not thought of as directly linked to separate cognitive components that underlie cognitive functioning. Rather, the underlying structure for cognitive functioning was conceptualized as overlapping neural mechanisms, functioning collectively as a biological system.

Interestingly, this latter group's thinking is compatible with Skinner's (1969) ideas about the nature of intelligence.[1]

> To say that intelligence is inherited is not to say that specific forms of behavior are inherited. Phylogenic contingencies conceivably responsible for "the selection of intelligence"do not specify responses. What has been selected appears to be a susceptibility to ontogenetic contingencies, leading particularly to greater speed of conditioning and the capacity to maintain a large repertoire without confusion. (p. 183)

These, then, were the two traditions that were brought to bear on the problem of explaining the covariation among cognitive ability tests. One was aimed at uncovering the basic components thought to underlie cognitive functioning, whereas the other conceived of cognitive behavior as resulting from multiple mechanisms operating in concert. The former tradition is found in contemporary cognitive psychology (Sternberg, 1984, 1985, in press), whereas the latter tradition is found in more behaviorally based treatments of cognitive abilities (Humphreys, 1979, in press). We will return to these two different ways of conceptualizing cognitive abilities, but for now,

what is central is that both groups were addressing the same phenomenon, the positive manifold, and the question of how best to conceptualize its psychological significance in the most parsimonious way.

The Nature and Structure of the Positive Manifold

The consensus is growing among several contemporary investigators that cognitive abilities can be arranged hierarchically (Ackerman, 1989; Carroll, 1989a, 1989b; Cronbach, 1984; Cronbach & Snow, 1977; Gustafsson, 1984, 1988; Humphreys, 1979, 1982, 1985; Lohman, 1989; Snow, Kyllonen, & Marshalek, 1984). Concurrent with this perspective is the view that cognitive abilities can be arranged, pictorially, in a *radex*. This idea, illustrated in Figure 1, is, we believe, a most useful approach to the problem of how best to depict the domain of cognitive abilities.

Guttman (1954) had originally suggested this way of organizing cognitive abilities and, as it turns out, this framework is highly compatible with hierarchical schemes, starting with Burt (1949) and Vernon (1947, 1950; see also Ackerman, 1987, 1989; Humphreys, 1962, 1979; Lohman, 1989; Marshalek, Lohman, & Snow, 1983). The radex reveals rather clearly that there are at least two ways in which cognitive abilities, and measures thereof, can be psychologically close (or can covary): by sharing either *content* or *complexity*. Content is held constant as complexity varies along dimensions radiating from the centroid of the radex to its periphery, whereas complexity is held constant as content varies around circular bands defined by the radii of differing distances from the centroid of the radex.

To solidify this concept, Figure 2, panel *a*, provides a theoretical skeleton of a "perfect" radex (containing 10 tests); panel *b* contains a four-factor hierarchical solution (to be elaborated on below), depicting hypothetical

FIGURE 1

Radex Organization of Human Abilities

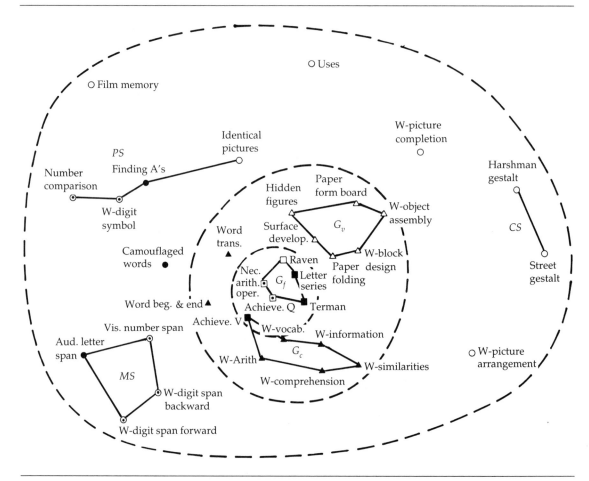

Note: Each point in the diagram represents a test. These tests are organized by content and complexity. Complex, intermediate, and simple tests are indicated by squares, triangles, and circles, respectively. Distinct forms of content are represented as black (verbal), dotted (numerical), and white (figure-spatial). Clusters of abilities that define well-known factors are indicated by a G. G_f = fluid ability, G_c = crystallized ability, G_v = spatial visualization. Tests having the greatest complexity are located near the centroid of the radex.

From "The Complexity Continuum in the Radex and Hierarchical Models of Intelligence" by B. Marshalek, D. F. Lohman, and R. E. Snow, 1983, *Intelligence, 7*, p. 122. Copyright 1983 by Ablex Publishing Corporation. Reprinted with the permission of Ablex Publishing Corporation.

degrees of association between the tests; and finally, panel *c* organizes these tests hierarchically. By studying the geometric distances (panel *a*) and hypothetical values (panel *b*),

the two ways in which psychological tests can be close are clearly revealed. These three schemes are simply different ways chosen by different investigators to organize the

FIGURE 2

Parallelism Between the Radex and the Hierarchical Factor Model

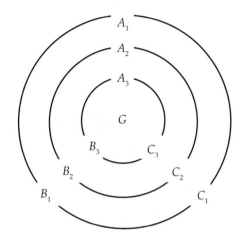

(a) Radex Scaling for 10 Tests

	G	A	B	C
A_1	1	3	0	0
A_2	2	4	0	0
A_3	3	3	1	1
B_1	1	0	3	0
B_2	2	0	4	0
B_3	3	1	3	1
C_1	1	0	0	3
C_2	2	0	0	4
C_3	3	1	1	3
G	4	2	2	2

(b) A Corresponding
Hierarchical Factor Matrix

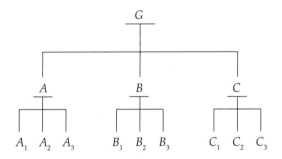

(c) The Associated Hierarchical Factor Diagram

Note: This is a hypothetical example illustrating the degree of overlap between the radex and the hierarchical factor model.

From "The Topography of Ability and Learning Correlations" by R. E. Snow, P. L. Kyllonen, and B. Marchalek in *Advances in the Psychology of Human Intelligence* (Vol. 2, p. 61), R. J. Sterenberg, Ed. (1984), New Jersey: Erlbaum. Copyright 1984 by Erlbaum. Reprinted by permission.

psychometrics of the radex. All are highly compatible.

The radex is composed of an indefinite number of simplexes and circumplexes. Simplexes are revealed by showing that along the complexity dimensions, which extend from the centroid to the periphery, correlations between tests diminish as a function of their distance from one another. Circumplexes, on the other hand, are revealed by traveling along a circular band defined by a constant degree of complexity. As tests diverge from one another within a circular band, they change in content but not complexity, and their correlations diminish. These correlations continue to decrease, reaching their theoretical minimum at a 180° arc, when the tests are exactly opposite one another on the circular band. (A line drawn between two such tests, passing through the centroid, traces the diameter of the circular band.) To the extent that tests covary, they are close to one another within this two-dimensional space. At least two dimensions, then—content and complexity—are necessary to triangulate a test's specific location.

A number of regions in Figure 1 are labeled to denote groupings of abilities of special theoretical importance. For example, Cattell's (1971; Horn & Cattell, 1966) distinction between G_f *(fluid)* and G_c *(crystallized)* abilities are illustrated in Figure 1. As initially proposed, G_f was thought to reflect a physiological parameter of the individual—raw potential, or the capacity to learn. G_c, in contrast, was construed as indexing the acquisitions of learning or the cultural products of experience. Just as g has lost the surplus meaning Spearman originally attached to it (viz., *mental energy*), G_f and G_c are currently thought of more as just differing clusters of abilities and less as biological potential versus stored experience. Cronbach (1977) has noted that "fluid ability is itself an achievement.... [It is] the residue of indirect learning from varied experience" (p. 287; for similar views but for different reasons, see Horn, 1985; Humphreys, 1981; Scarr & Carter-Saltzman, 1980; Snow & Yalow, 1982).

The G_f, G_c, and G_v *(spatial visualization)* clusters of Cattell and Horn correspond to Vernon's (1950, 1961) g *(general intelligence* or the *general factor)*, *v:ed (verbal-numerical-educational)* and *k:m (practical-mechanical-spatial)*, respectively. These are the most common splinterings (into roughly two halves) of the positive manifold or radex. Further parallels between Cattell/Horn and Vernon are given by Gustafsson (1984, 1988) and Lohman (1989). Other investigators, like Thurstone (1938), preferred to subdivide these

broad factors into more circumscribed abilities at uniform levels of abstraction and common content. In doing so, smaller clusters are formed at greater distances from one another as well as from the centroid of the radex. Some of these areas are also labeled on Figure 1.

Much of the early factor analytic work was aimed at mapping the covariation displayed among the cognitive abilities with the fewest dimensions possible. How many continua are necessary to extract psychological significance from the communality shared among these tests has been a matter of much debate: one dominant dimension, as Spearman (1904) proposed? a few dimensions—"seven primaries"— as Thurstone (1938) advocated? or as many as 120 to 180, as Guilford (1985) has hypothesized? The covariation that these theorists wished to explain involved the same space, but the number of dimensions needed to map this space remains the issue. Some comments about factor analysis might help to focus this discussion.

Factor Analysis

The goal of factor analysis is to condense the information in the covariation of n variables to a smaller set of m factors. The amount of covariation among the variables in a matrix defines the common variance. Common variance can be estimated by computing the squared multiple correlation between each variable and all of the other variables and then summing these (n) R^2s. This sum, divided by the number of variables, estimates the common variance proportion of the total variance that the variables share.

In the context of factor analysis, the variance for each variable has three components: common, specific, and error variance. Common and specific variance compose the variable's reliable variance (viz., r_{xx}, with the complement, $1 - r_{xx}$, being error variance); whereas specific and error variance constitute the variable's unique variance (viz., $1 - h^2$, where

h^2 = common variance by conventional factor-analytic notation).

Therefore, the decomposition of the total variance in a correlation matrix into common and unique components can be expressed as:

$$R^2 1 \cdot 2,3,4,...,n \qquad 1 - R^2 1 \cdot 2,3,4,...,n$$
$$R^2 2 \cdot 1,3,4,...,n \qquad 1 - R^2 2 \cdot 1,3,4,...,n$$
$$R^2 3 \cdot 1,2,4,...,n \qquad 1 - R^2 3 \cdot 1,2,4,...,n$$
$$\vdots \qquad\qquad \vdots$$
$$R^2 n \cdot 1,2,3,4,...,n-1 \quad 1 - R^2 n \cdot 1,2,3,4,...,n-1$$

$$\frac{\sum R^2}{n} = \text{common variance}$$

$$\frac{\sum (1 - R^2)}{n} = \text{unique variance}$$

common variance + unique variance = total variance = 1.00

Factor analysis strips away the unique variance in a correlation matrix (the specific and error variance of each variable) and focuses on the common variance or *communality* (h^2) among the variables. The psychometric objective of factor analysis is *not* so much to understand the *nature* of the variables but rather to account for the *covariation* among the variables. What is at issue is how best to map this covariation with the fewest number of dimensions (factors). To the extent that the communality of a matrix is appreciable—as it is for heterogeneous collections of cognitive ability tests—the covariation of the variables can be expressed by fewer dimensions than there are variables in the matrix. This task, with respect to cognitive abilities, has occupied the professional careers of many prominent psychometricians (Carroll, 1989a; Cattell, 1971; Guilford, 1967, 1985; Horn, 1986; Humphreys, 1962; Kelley, 1928; Spearman, 1927; Thurstone, 1938; Thurstone & Thurstone, 1941; Vernon, 1950, 1961).

To the extent that a group of variables covary appreciably with one another, their covariation may collectively be characterized by one dimension or a *general factor*. If the situation is more complex—for example, if certain pockets of variables form distinct covarying subgroups—factor analytic solutions result in multiple factors, one for each subgroup. Through this procedure, a finite set of (m) factors—appreciably smaller than the number of variables under analysis—can characterize most of the common variance. (If desired, factor scores can be generated to estimate individual differences on each factor; Harman, 1976; Rummel, 1970.) This technique is a very useful tool—it can often reduce the number of variables in a matrix to a much smaller subset, thereby dispensing with the redundancy that runs through individual measures. A few factors can replace a long list of variables!

The final product of a factor analysis is a factor matrix, with as many rows as there are variables and as many columns as there are factors (see Radex solution, Figure 2, panel *b*). Factors are simply dimensions or axes "placed" within the multidimensional space that represents a correlation matrix. Factor loadings are correlations between the variables and the factors.

The extent to which factors and variables are correlated can also be expressed geometrically. Variables (or factors) can be represented as geometric vectors, and the cosine of the angle formed at their intersection is numerically equal to their correlation. Variables are independent when their vectors cross at 90° (cosine 90° = .00, hence r_{xy} = .00). Conversely, they correlate at unity when their vectors lie on the same line, in the same or opposite direction (cosine 0° and cosine 180°, hence r_{xy} = 1.00 and –1.00, respectively). Cosines of angles between 0° and 90° take on positive values between 1.00 and 0.00 (positive correlations), whereas those between 90° and 180° take on negative values between 0.00 and –1.00 (negative correlations).[2]

One reason for going through all of this is to demystify the nature of psychometric factors. They are simply *arbitrary* dimensions placed into a space representing correlations. The goal of factor analysis is to characterize

TABLE 1

Table of Intercorrelations Defining Two Factors

	1	2	3	4
1		90	75	75
2			75	75
3				90
4				

Three Factor Solutions

	Orthogonal		Oblique		Hierarchical		
	I	II	I	II	*g*	I	II
1	837	447	949	000	865	390	000
2	837	447	949	000	865	390	000
3	447	837	000	949	865	000	390
4	447	837	000	949	865	000	390

Note: The correlation between the oblique factors is .831.

the covariation between (*empirical*) variables with the smallest possible number of (*theoretical*) factors. And there are different ways of placing factors in a correlation-matrix space to account for the common variance.

Because factor matrices contain correlations between variables and factors, the principles of multiple regression apply. When for each factor, the factor loadings are squared, summed, and the sum divided by the amount of common variance in the matrix (which is the sum of the communalities), the result is the proportion of common variance accounted for by each factor. When all these proportions are summed (for factor solutions yielding independent or uncorrelated factors), the sum is the proportion of common variance accounted for by the factor solution.

Orthogonal (independent factors) and *oblique* (correlated factors) solutions are well-known methods of factoring, but *hierarchical methods* (featuring orthogonal solutions) are rapidly gaining popularity. (We hope they soon will appear in conventional statistical packages.) One of the more attractive hierarchical techniques is the Schmid and Leiman (1957) solution, which transforms an oblique factor solution into a pattern of orthogonal factors arranged in two (or more) tiers. Descriptions of the Schmid-Leiman approach, with computational examples, may be found in Ackerman (1987), Carroll (1985, 1989b), and Humphreys (1962, 1982, 1984).

Table 1 compares the results of these three kinds of factor solutions for a hypothetical correlation matrix. The intercorrelation of four variables is shown. Variables 1 and 2 might be measures of the same ability, say, verbal ability, whereas variables 3 and 4 are measures of, say, mathematical ability. Three kinds of factor solutions are illustrated. The orthogonal solution shows two factors that are hard to interpret. The oblique solution appears to be better than the orthogonal in the Thurstonian sense of simple structure, but the factors are correlated ($r = .831$). The hierarchical factors are uncorrelated and highly interpretable but do require more factors than the other solutions. However, when the correlation matrices being factor analyzed are large, hierarchical solutions can be just as parsimonious as the other solutions.

Hierarchical solutions place the most comprehensive factor (i.e., the general factor) at the vertex. With respect to cognitive abilities, the general factor may be interpreted as the overall level of the cognitive repertoire, or the general factor, or general intelligence, essentially, Spearman's g but without the surplus meaning. Individual differences on this factor reflect complexity or sophistication of the repertoire. The branches and twigs that splinter off this base organize the remaining common variance along circular bands of content in the radex. All of this description is found conceptually in Vernon's (1961) early work on the structure of human abilities (Figures 3, 4, and 5), which parallels the theoretical model given earlier (Figure 2, panels *a*, *b*, and *c*, respectively). Vernon's construction of cognitive abilities clearly is consistent with and overlaps the radex.

There are other advantages to the Schmid-Leiman hierarchical approach. First, independent factors can stand alone as reference dimensions, whereas the correlation of oblique factors requires interpretation. Second, the nature of the loadings in the hierarchical solution can often provide insight into how best to arrange or order tests in terms of their content (the more circumscribed tests tend to be identified more with particular forms of content, e.g., linguistic, numerical, or figural). And finally, major and minor group factors can be evaluated for incremental validity in terms of external correlations over and above the contribution of the general factor to ascertain whether they account for additional psychologically meaningful variance or whether they are merely pieces of common variance having little or no psychological significance.

It should be stressed that whatever the factor solution, this is only half the picture with respect to the criterion of scientific significance. Once a factor solution is obtained, the predictive efficacy of each factor must be assessed in order to address the other half of the criterion of scientific significance. The external correlates of each factor must be evaluated for their psychological meaningfulness. Factor analysis does *not* reveal what proportion of the common variance in a correlation matrix is responsible for useful external correlates. It only tells us what proportion of the reliable variance of each variable is shared with other variables in the matrix and how much of this communality is accounted for by the *m* factors. It does *not* tell us which factors have meaningful correlates.

In our view, it is not essential for the factors in a factor analysis to account for all of the common variance in a correlation matrix. There is no reason to suppose that all of the common variance in a correlation matrix should be represented in the factor matrix. In fact, there is good reason to suppose that this should *not* be the goal of factor analysis. Some of the common variance undoubtedly represents correlated method variance that we should gratefully discard. This idea is not new, although its extension to the problem of determining the number of factors is. Non-attribute but reliable variance is contained in all psychometric measures. These components function as nuisance variables that distort predictor-criterion relationships. These sources of variance have been discussed as *method variance* (Campbell & Fiske, 1959), *construct irrelevancies* (Cook & Campbell, 1976), *systematic bias* (Humphreys, 1976), *constant error* (Loevinger, 1954), systematic *ambient noise* (Lykken, 1968), and *crud* (Meehl, 1990b). It is the type of bias that Cronbach and his colleagues have tried to minimize via their generalizability

FIGURE 3

Vernon's Conceptualization of Human Abilities: A Spatial Representation

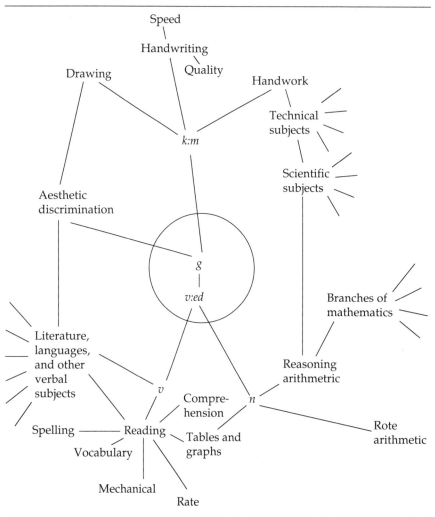

From *The Structure of Human Abilities* (2nd ed., p. 47) by P. E. Vernon, 1961, New York: Routledge, Chapman, & Hall. Copyright 1961 by Routledge, Chapman, & Hall. Adapted by permission.

methodology (Cronbach, Gleser, Nanda, & Rajaratnam, 1972; Cronbach, Rajaratnam, & Gleser, 1963). It is a well-known concern.

It is also important not to be misled by the distinctive content of supposedly contrasting measures. Ostensibly distinct scales might be tapping the same source of individual differences—but in content-unique ways—through converging operations. Spearman was aware of this possibility early in his career, when he formulated the concept of the *indifference of the indicator*—that is,

FIGURE 4

Vernon's Conceptualization of Human Abilities: An Empirical Solution

Tests		Group Factors					
		g	*k:m*	*v:ed*	*v*	*n*	*h²*
0	Progressive Matrices	.79	.17				.65
	Dominoes (nonverbal)	.87					.75
	Group test 70, Pt. 1	.78	.13				.62
4	Squares	.59	.44				.54
8	Assembly	.24	.89				.85
2	Bennett mechanical	.66	.31				.54
25	Verbal	.79		.29	.45		.90
	Dictation	.62		.54	.48		.90
14	A.T.S. spelling	.68		.41	.43		.82
21	Instruction	.87		.23	.09		.82
3A	Arithmetic Pt. I	.72		.49		.39	.91
	Arithmetic Pt. II	.80		.38		.16	.82
23	A.T.S. arithmetic	.77		.36		.32	.82
	Variance percent	52.5	8.7	8.4	6.9		76.5

From *The Structure of Human Abilities* (2nd ed., p. 23) by P. E. Vernon, 1961, New York: Routledge, Chapman, & Hall. Copyright 1961 by Routledge, Chapman, & Hall. Adapted by permission.

that all cognitive ability tests index *g* to varying degrees. Later in his career, he commented on the lack of appreciation of this concept:

What really does manifest a dominant influence upon the conception of the mental processes involved in tests is the suggestion emanating from language. When once a test has received a name, this has generally been accepted as expressing its sole essential character. Few are the analysts who have pushed their examination beyond this merely popular stage. (Spearman & Jones, 1950, p. 143)

FIGURE 5

Vernon's Conceptualization of Human Abilities: A Hierarchical Representation of Factors at Contrasting Levels of Generality

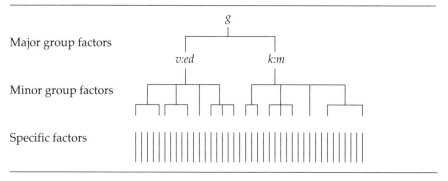

Note: Minor group factors correspond to Thurstone's primaries. Specific factors refer to individual tests.

From *The Structure of Human Abilities* (2nd ed., p. 22) by P. E. Vernon, 1961, New York: Routledge, Chapman, & Hall. Copyright 1961 by Routledge, Chapman, & Hall. Adapted by permission.

Just as there has been a problem in experimental psychology of conflating hypothesis testing with theory testing (Meehl, 1967, 1978), so has there been an equally detrimental problem in correlational psychology of considering tests with different content and different labels to be measuring different abilities (and even different underlying processes). This is, of course, the problem of reification of factors, a problem with a long history in factor analytic research. To be sure, factors can represent real entities and distinct underlying processes *if* internal and external relationships justify it. But the factor analysis of cognitive abilities appears to show, by and large, a structure indicative of continua of complexity and content rather than of discrete breaks. Although robust major group factors can be extracted reliably, from a hierarchical point of view they are better construed as more focused or more concentrated behavioral repertoires developed with differing emphases on distinct symbol systems. As linguistic, numerical, and figural kinds of content merge within the radex along concentric bands of uniform complexity, we find sectors with symbol compositions that tend to reflect blends of linguistic-numerical, numerical-figural, or figural-linguistic hybrids.

To summarize, the products of factor analysis should be required to have meaningful external correlates. This is an important requirement because, although all common variance is reliable variance, not all common variance is scientifically significant variance. Scientific significance is never established via factor analysis alone. Scientific significance requires the establishment of external relationships; it requires going beyond the internally consistent statistical relationships among indicators. Otherwise, we might simply have little more than common variance due to method sources of variance that function systematically to create reliable factors and distort the interpretability of other factors, but contain little substance outside the testing situation. Kelley (1939) had a name for such factors; he called them "mental factors-of-no-importance."

Assessing the Scientific Significance in Factor Structures at Different Levels of Generality

There are several conventional test batteries that assess multiple factors at uniform levels of generality (cf. Carroll, 1989b, pp. 165–166). Many studies are conducted with these instruments each year to uncover the "latent structure" of different predictor-criterion relations. Consider, however, the following.

Suppose that multiple regression equations using moderately correlated group factors as predictors can account for slightly more variance than that achieved by the general factor. It is still possible that the successive R^2-change increments could have been contributed by the common variance of the group factors (i.e., the variance they share not only with each other but also with the general factor), rather than by their specific variances. For example, conventional measures of spatial and mathematical ability share common variance, but not all of their common variance is shared with verbal ability. In a two-predictor regression equation with verbal ability entered first, the incremental validity contributed by mathematical ability might be due to that proportion of its common variance shared with spatial ability. Hence, the R^2 increment is actually due to the fact that the two-predictor variate (verbal plus mathematical) is now a better estimator of the common variance in cognitive tests—that is, the general factor—and not, as one might assume, due to the contribution of the specific variance associated with either group factor. Yet it is to the specific variance of each group factor that we typically attribute the incremental validity shown by multiple predictors.

If it is the general factor cutting across cognitive tests that shares variance with the criterion of interest, then successive R^2 increments might simply mean that the aggregate variate, with the addition of each contributing variable

(e.g., verbal + mathematics + spatial), provides a better estimator of the general factor via successive approximation. This possibility should be considered when multiple predictor equations are being evaluated (see "The Criterion Problem" below).

Furthermore, sample-specific bias compounds the problem. Because multiple predictors enhance the likelihood of capitalizing on sample specific variance, thus inflating R^2s, it is imperative to compare multiple regression equations using major or minor group factors with simple regression equations using the general factor via their comparative cross-validated R^2_{cv}s (see below). It may be that, for the more intellectually demanding professions, the valid variance of multiple predictor batteries (i.e., the predicted variance or R^2 that holds up on cross-validation), is simply g variance that is being better estimated by successive approximation with the use of the multiple predictors. And the reason regression coefficients shrink more on cross-validation when multiple predictors are used, in contrast to the situation for a single predictor that measures the general factor, is that more complex variates are more likely to generate more sample-specific noise.

With a single global measure of general intelligence, however, most of the reliable variance is common with the general factor. The proportion of specific variance in the total variance is minimized. (There may be chunks of specific variance sprinkled throughout the global measure of general intelligence, but the aggregation of common variance attenuates their contribution to the composites' total variance.) In a regression equation that uses a global measure of general intelligence, most of the measure's reliable variance is attribute variance associated with the communality that is found in all cognitive tests. If criterion performance is also g-saturated, then the regression coefficient will not shrink much on cross-validation. If samples are large and representative of the population of applicants, the structural

FIGURE 6

Three-variable Variate

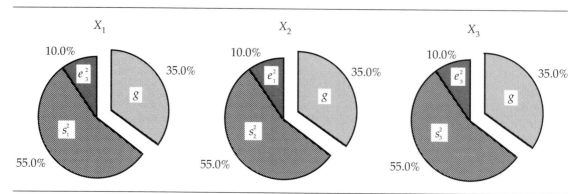

Note: Three hypothetical variables having the same amount of common, specific, and error variance. As individual components of a predictor variate, most of the variance of each component is specific variance.

parameters b or beta will tend to capture most of the predictor-criterion covariation from sample to sample.

This contrasts sharply with the situation for multiple predictors. With multiple predictors, there is more noise attached to each regression coefficient because only a little common variance enters into the valid (cross-validated) predictor-criterion correlation. There is more slippage from sample to sample because several structural parameters are being estimated. This can be illustrated quantitatively, using the following formula and the hypothetical values found in Figure 6.

The basic formula for the correlation of a composite $(X_1 + X_2 + \ldots + X_N)$ with another measure, Y, or a source of variance, is:

$$r_{Y(X_1 + X_2 + \ldots + X_N)} = $$

$$\frac{\Sigma CYX_i}{[\Sigma Var(X_i) + 2 \Sigma \Sigma CX_iX_j]^{1/2}}$$

where:

ΣCYX_i = the sum of all the covariances between Y and the constituents, X_i, of the composite

$\Sigma Var(X_i)$ = the sum of all the X_i variances

and

$\Sigma \Sigma CX_iX_j$ = the sum of all the constituent covariances

Figure 6 shows three hypothetical variables. Each shares 35 percent of its variance with a general factor ($r_{gX_i} = .59$), and each has 55 percent specific variance (so for each, $r_{xx} = .90$). Given these values, each variable is correlated with the other (.59 x .59) or $r_{X_iX_j} = .35$. If we aggregate these variables, their overlap with this general factor increases to (see Figure 7):

$$r_{g(X_1 + X_2 + X_3)} = $$

$$\frac{(.35)^{1/2} + (.35)^{1/2} + (.35)^{1/2}}{[1 + 1 + 1 + 2(.35) + 2(.35) + 2(.35)]^{1/2}}$$

$$= .786$$
$$r^2 = .618$$

Further, the correlation of this composite and an individual component of specific variance (of which there are three), is:

FIGURE 7

Three-variable Composite

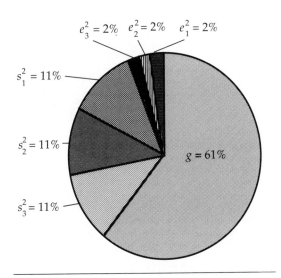

$X_1 + X_2 + X_3$

$e_3^2 = 2\%$ $e_2^2 = 2\%$ $e_1^2 = 2\%$

$s_1^2 = 11\%$

$s_2^2 = 11\%$

$g = 61\%$

$s_3^2 = 11\%$

Note: When the three components found in Figure 6 are aggregated, most of the composite's variance is variance shared with a general factor common to each. Moreover, the influence of any one form of specificity is considerably reduced.

$$r_{s_i(X_1 + X_2 + X_3)} =$$
$$\frac{(.55)^{1/2}}{[1 + 1 + 1 + 2(.35) + 2(.35) + 2(.35)]^{1/2}}$$
$$= .328$$
$$r^2 = .108$$

And finally, the correlation of the composite and an individual component of error variance (of which there are three) is:

$$r_{e_i(X_1 + X_2 + X_3)} =$$
$$\frac{(.10)^{1/2}}{[1 + 1 + 1 + 2(.35) + 2(.35) + 2(.35)]^{1/2}}$$
$$= .14$$
$$r^2 = .0196$$

If we can assume that criterion performance has a large general factor associated with it, then the composite, $(X_1 + X_2 + X_3)$, is much more descriptively apt at characterizing the construct-relevant predictor/criterion covariation than the three variables taken in weighted combination (viz., the three-variable variate). There will be less slippage in the cross-validation of the composite than there will be for the three-variable variate because all of the relevant information is contained in the composite and only one structural parameter is being estimated. Aggregation in the composite attenuates the individual components of specific variance so that each component contributes less to the composite's overall variance. Figure 7 shows how the individual components of specific variance are attenuated in the composite. Because they are independent sources of variation, they do not aggregate (covariation is necessary for aggregation!). To summarize, large components of specific variance not only can mask common variance contributions to predictor/criterion covariation, they may also distort estimation by capitalizing on sample specific noise through the estimation of multiple parameters. Aggregation can be used to minimize these undesirable effects.

If, however, components of specific variance are relevant to the criterion, then using a multiple-variable variate will improve prediction of the criterion over the use of the composite. For example, Humphreys (1985) and Vernon (1961) have shown that, for certain criteria, *v:ed* and *k:m* can improve on prediction from *g* alone, and the improvement holds up on cross-validation. This is because relevant specific variance of *v:ed* and *k:m* adds to the general factor variance that both hold in common. Furthermore, McNemar (1964) has shown that it is profitable to splinter the major group factor, *v:ed*, into verbal (*v*) and quantitative or numerical (*n*) minor group factors for the differential prediction of academic criteria. In such instances, use of the more complex multiple predictor equation is justified.

Criticisms of General Factor

Cronbach (1989) has criticized the dominant dimension approach to defining general intelligence, inasmuch as estimating the centroid of a radex varies as a function of the tests an investigator chooses to employ. How does one know where the desired centroid is or should be? This is a valid criticism. It applies to all sets of tests, and we are unaware of an analytic solution. Furthermore (for reasons he delineates in Cronbach, 1975a, and other writing), the actual centroid for any collection of cognitive ability tests is, to some degree, in a state of flux (and this is true for both interindividual and *intra*individual differences). After all, premiums are placed on different sets of skills, cognitive behaviors develop and change over generations, opportunities vary, and so on, enough to suggest that the patterns of phenotypic traits are dynamic in a manner not unlike that of genetic drift. Finally, if this criticism is valid for the general factor, it is also valid for the major and minor group factors derived factor analytically or built by aggregating minor or specific factors systematically.

However, there are methods with which to assess how conceptually close two measures are. At the least, existing measures can be assessed for their conceptual and empirical interchangeability. Furthermore, because several instruments are available that purport to measure the general factor (and less general factors), these different measures, built by different investigators, provide the opportunity to establish convergent validity and demonstrate constructive replication (Lykken, 1968).

This is an important consideration because measures can correlate in the high .90s and still display different patterns of external correlations (McCornack, 1956). The possible range of correlation that a measure, m_2, can display with a criterion, c, given that we know the correlation of m_2 with an equivalent measure, m_1, and the correlation between m_1 and c, is given by the following formulas for upper and lower limits:

Upper limit of $r_{m_2c} = r_{m_1c} r_{m_1m_2} + [(r_{m_1c})^2$

$$(r_{m_1m_2})^2 - (r_{m_1c})^2 - (r_{m_1m_2})^2 + 1]^{1/2} \qquad (1a)$$

Lower limit of $r_{m_2c} = r_{m_1c} r_{m_1m_2} - [(r_{m_1c})^2$

$$(r_{m_1m_2})^2 - (r_{m_1c})^2 - (r_{m_1m_2})^2 + 1]^{1/2} \qquad (1b)$$

Table 2, taken from Jensen (1980a), reveals the extent to which a (*new*) measure, m_2, having a given correlation with a (*known*) measure, m_1, can vary in its correlation with a criterion variable, c, across different values of $r_{m_1m_2}$. As Table 2 reveals, the possible range of correlation with the criterion is incredible, even for $r_{m_1m_2} = .95$. This shows that two measures ought not to be considered empirically interchangeable, solely on the basis of a high correlation between the two (or their *congruence coefficient*).

A way to evaluate the extent to which two measures are interchangeable is provided by the concept of *extrinsic convergent validation*, an elaboration of the multitrait multimethod matrix method advanced by Fiske (1971).[3] According to Fiske, measures of the same construct should not be considered empirically interchangeable until they display similar patterns in their correlational profiles. That is, two independent measures of the same ability cannot be considered interchangeable unless they display similar correlational patterns of corresponding convergent and discriminant correlations as well as other correlations with external criteria in the intermediate range.

TABLE 2

Upper and Lower Limits of the Possible Range of Criterion Validity
(r_{cm2}) for Test M_2 When Criterion Validity of Test M_1 Is r_{cm1}
and the Correlation Between the Two Tests Is r_{m1m2}

r_{m1m2} (or r_{cm1})	r_{cm1} (or r_{m1m2})								
	.10	.20	.30	.40	.50	.60	.70	.80	.90
.95	.41	.49	.58	.67	.75	.82	.89	.95	.99
	−.21	−.11	−.01	.09	.20	.32	.44	.57	.72
.90	.52	.61	.69	.76	.83	.89	.94	.98	1.00
	−.34	−.25	−.15	−.04	.07	.19	.32	.46	.62
.85	.61	.69	.76	.82	.88	.93	.97	1.00	.99
	−.44	−.35	−.25	−.14	−.03	.09	.22	.36	.53
.80	.68	.75	.81	.87	.92	.96	.99	1.00	.98
	−.52	−.43	−.33	−.23	−.12	.00	.13	.28	.46
.75	.73	.80	.85	.91	.95	.98	1.00	1.00	.96
	−.58	−.50	−.41	−.31	−.20	−.08	.05	.20	.39
.70	.78	.84	.89	.93	.97	.99	1.00	1.00	.94
	−.64	−.56	−.47	−.37	−.27	−.15	−.02	.28	.32
.65	.82	.87	.92	.96	.98	1.00	1.00	.97	.92
	−.69	−.61	−.53	−.44	−.33	−.22	−.09	.06	.25
.60	.85	.90	.94	.97	.99	1.00	.99	.96	.89
	−.73	−.66	−.58	−.49	−.39	−.28	−.15	.00	.19

To illustrate this point, Table 3 contains three extrinsic convergent validation profiles. These data are from the 12th-grade cohort of Project TALENT.[4] The first profile is for an information test of world literature (24 items, including prose and poetry, and several questions that are based on required reading in many high schools); the second is for vocabulary (30 items, designed to assess nontechnical words); the final profile is for a reading comprehension test (48 items, designed to assess comprehension of written material across a wide range of topics). The last two measures are excellent markers of verbal ability as well as general intelligence, whereas the first measure is typically considered farther from the centroid of the radex, but in the same slice of content. (Using conventional nomenclature, it would be considered more of an *achievement* measure.) The profiles consist of

TABLE 3

Extrinsic Convergent Validation Profiles
Across Three Measures Having Verbal Content

	Literature	Vocabulary	Reading Comprehension
Aptitude Tests			
Mechanical reasoning	.43	.52	.54
2–D visualization	.25	.32	.35
3–D visualization	.35	.43	.47
Abstract reasoning	.45	.53	.61
Arithmetic reasoning	.54	.63	.63
High-school math	.57	.59	.57
Advanced math	.42	.43	.39
Information Tests			
Music	.67	.68	.62
Social studies	.74	.74	.71
Mathematics	.62	.63	.57
Physical science	.64	.67	.60
Biological science	.57	.61	.56
Interest			
Physical sciences	.24	.25	.22
Biological sciences	.26	.25	.22
Public service	.16	.12	.12
Literary-linguistic	.37	.32	.32
Social service	.07	.06	.07
Art	.32	.30	.29
Music	.23	.20	.20
Sports	.12	.12	.13
Office work	−.35	−.29	−.27
Labor	−.08	−.06	−.06

Note: These correlations were based only on female subjects (male profiles are parallel). $N = 39,695$. Intercorrelations for the three measures were the following: literature/vocabulary = .74, literature/reading comprehension = .71, and vocabulary/reading comprehension = .77.

correlations with an array of Project TALENT measures, with different locations in the radex as well as outside of it.

Vocabulary and reading comprehension display the highest degree of correlation, $r_{xy} = .77$. Recall from formula 1 that this degree of correlation can result in external correlations that can range over 1.25 correlational value points for r_{m2c} when $r_{m1c} = .30$! However, our analysis reveals that both markers of verbal ability map essentially the same nomothetic span (network of correlates), at least as regards these criteria. These correlational profiles can be different when new variables are used, but in the context of the present variables, vocabulary and reading comprehension can be considered empirically interchangeable. In fact, the information test maps essentially the same space, which illustrates how fundamentally similar "achievement" and "aptitude" tests can be.

Building Measures of Constructs

In the early days of factor analytic research, most American investigators adopted the Thurstonian (1938) approach to guide test construction. Test batteries were constructed to map the "underlying" natural cleavages of the ability domain at uniform levels of molarity. The conviction that there was more to cognitive functioning than one dominant dimension was buttressed by the belief that all meaningful criteria were complex and multidimensional. The agendum was to build a finite set of measures that were relatively independent and specifically designed to account for different sectors of the complex criterion variable. What was needed to account for such criteria as school performance and job performance were multifactor test batteries with components that would map onto unique slices of the criterion pie. But as the evidence accumulated, it became apparent that the communality on both sides of the prediction equation was not fully appreciated.[5]

The Thurstonian approach makes some fairly strong assumptions about the nature and organization of cognitive functioning. It assumes that little is measured in common by the different tests, for example, of verbal, quantitative, spatial, pictorial, perceptual, and problem-solving abilities. Such multifactor batteries are predicated on the *specificity* of the measures rather than on the communality they share. So, if you have a battery of, say, 10 tests whose intercorrelations are all around .10, you have very little of the *general factor*—unless one test is a measure of general intelligence and the others have little to do with cognitive functioning. (Recall that Figures 1 and 2 show how it is possible for ability tests to covary on two dimensions, content *and* complexity.)

An alternative approach assumes that there are no "factor pure" tests—pure, that is, as conventionally conceived: a test that measures one, and only one, dimension. This notion of purity has tended to conflate statistical purity with psychological purity (Hulin & Humphreys, 1980). We maintain that, within the full range of human capability, cognitive functioning covaries with many measures having different content (e.g., verbal, spatial, quantitative, pictorial). Even Guilford (Guilford & Michael, 1948) seemed aware of this. When discussing the measurement of a person's pure factor score, he observed that it was usually necessary to add *suppressor variables* to partial out *g* or other unwanted content. As Vernon (1961) pointed out in response, why not just admit that all cognitive ability tests *do* involve *g*, instead of artificially removing it by rotation (pp. 133–134). If Guilford's suggestion were followed, the use of suppressors might actually result in the *loss* of scientifically significant variance when systematic bias in the measure is maximized.[6]

The following methodology, developed by Humphreys (1952, 1962, 1984), can be used to build measures of human behavior capability, whether cognitive, motor, or perceptual, regardless of level of abstraction. (Later, we will show that this methodology also has important ramifications for criterion development.)

First, it is assumed that the variance of observed scores, X, can be analyzed into three components:

$$X^2 \text{(total variance)} = A^2 \text{(attribute variance)} + B^2 \text{(bias variance)} + E^2 \text{(error variance)}$$

Attribute variance comes from systematic sources of individual differences that constitute the attribute of interest. Ideally, attribute variance should approach unity. Bias variance is also systematic (i.e., reliable), but reflects one or more consistent sources of variation distinct from the attribute of interest (e.g., a systematic response style or one of the several forms of method variance). Collectively, attribute and bias variance constitute true score variance in classical test theory (bias being reliable variance that is not associated with the attribute of interest). Finally, the third component of variance is error variance, random variation, or error in the classical sense.

In the context of factor analysis, it is easy to see that common variance cuts across both attribute and bias components to varying degrees as a function of the nature of the variables. Variance overlap among the several variables will involve both components, hence both will contribute to the communality in the matrix. Thus, factors can arise from either form of reliable variance or, more typically, from both.

The goal of measurement under these circumstances is to maximize attribute variance while minimizing both bias and error variance. To achieve this goal, the item pool has to be made more heterogeneous, the only requirement being that all items index the targeted construct to some degree. Item heterogeneity will serve to offset the relative prominence that any one component of bias can attain on the measure, at the same time that the items are adding, little by little, to the proportion of common attribute variance captured by the measuring instrument. This is the psychometric property of *aggregation* discussed by Green (1978) in his classic paper, "In Defense of Measurement." The idea is to have as many different types of items as possible, with each type possibly carrying with it a different kind of bias, so that, individually, each source of bias will tend to contribute minimally to the overall variance of the aggregate. This methodology is therefore designed to build up the communality of attribute variance running through the several items, while simultaneously minimizing any specific bias associated with any given type of item content or item format. The point is, *aggregation depends on covariation.* Without covariation, the benefits of aggregation will not be realized (see Roznowski, 1987; Roznowski & Hanisch, 1990; Rushton, Brainerd, & Pressley, 1983).

This approach to measurement recognizes that all forms of multi-item assessment will carry components of method variance bias, inextricably combined with the construct-valid variance of the attribute of interest. The objective is to minimize this unwanted bias variance. To use a psychophysical analogy, the goal is to amplify signal (attribute variance) and attenuate noise (bias variance).[7] What we are discussing here at the item level is completely equivalent to our earlier discussion of aggregation at the group factor level illustrated in Figures 6 and 7.

Carroll (1985) has recently developed a similar procedure for building measures of factors:

> How can one develop or select two or more variables to reflect a factor without making them identical? It would be undesirable to make them identical or equivalent because the underlying common factor might then reflect also a specific factor in the variables, and the factor would be overdetermined. The solution is to include task variation, over the several variables, that is expected to be irrelevant to the definition of the ability.... Irrelevant task variation can be introduced by varying required knowledge bases. (p. 30)

For our earlier example (see Table 3), and given these considerations, it follows that a more optimal measure of verbal ability (Vernon's minor group factor *v*) would be obtained by aggregating *reading comprehension* and *vocabulary* than by using either measure alone, and an even more optimal measure would be obtained if the information test *literature* were combined with these two.

If the general factor captures much of the common variance and absorbs the variance due to major or minor group factors (constructed using the foregoing methodology), that should be no cause for concern. If the specific variance of a lower order factor is meaningful (i.e., has external correlates beyond the general factor), incremental validity beyond the general factor will reveal that fact. This methodology brings out the content-specific variance of lower order group factors without attempting to control for complexity.

There is another reason for considering major and minor group factors even when most of the common variance is captured by the general factor in samples with the full range of talent. In more select samples, the range of individual differences due to the general factor decreases and the demand on more concentrated or specialized cognitive abilities increases, thereby increasing the likelihood that measures with more focused content will account for more of the criterion variance. For example, philosophers and engineers may possess comparable levels of the general factor (i.e., their level of complexity on the radex is roughly equivalent), but the density of verbal skills relative to spatial skills will be greater for philosophers, and the reverse would be true for the engineers (i.e., their level of sophistication with contrasting symbolic content differs). If measures of verbal and spatial ability were correlated for a sample combining philosophers and engineers, the correlation will most likely be negative. Job performance for either group would not be predicted too well from a general factor measure because the level of complexity required is about the same for both occupations. Rather, because each occupation requires facility with different content, assessment of the cognitive ability repertoire beyond the general factor will be required for differential prediction. The major group factors *v:ed* and *k:m* are likely to be better predictors than the general factor, and perhaps even the minor group factors (e.g., *v*, *n*, and *s*) would

contribute. These more circumscribed dimensions cannot compete with the general factor in normative samples, but in more select samples they may account for *more* criterion variance than the general factor. Herein may lie the solution to longstanding concerns about the significance of intraindividual differences in conventional multiability profiles. Profile scatter (dispersion) may be highly significant in certain contexts. However, these intra-individual differences, reflecting contrasting degrees of sophistication within different regions of the radex, can only be evaluated with precision after removing the communality these dimensions share, that is, the general factor.

Although the general factor is the most prominent dimension in the radex (absorbing about half the common variance of cognitive ability tests), there are other important lower order factors as well. Just as validity coefficients of minuscule size can be useful when the selection ratio is stringent and the base rate is low (Taylor & Russell, 1939), there are circumstances when lower order factors can be quite useful. Measures that are highly correlated in samples with the full range of talent will often pull apart (*dissociate*) in samples that are more select. In this circumstance, there is opportunity for lower order factors to become effective predictors, hence the scientific significance of such factors can be thought to be conditional, or population specific. In the psychological study of occupations, especially the higher level professions, an important first step might be to ascertain deviant attributes. If restriction of range is observed on any of these deviant attributes, a more focused assessment of lower order factors would be warranted.

The Criterion Problem

Assessing the construct validity of ability measures is inextricably intertwined with assessing the construct validity of relevant criteria (Dunnette & Borman, 1979; James, 1973; Kavanagh, MacKinney, & Wolins, 1971; Smith, 1976; Tenopyr, 1977). Given this, before we can discuss the *prediction problem*—how to optimize prediction from abilities, some discussion of the criterion problem seems necessary. Indeed, few problems are more significant to industrial and organizational psychologists (Dunnette, 1963; Smith, 1976).

Ratings are the most used form of performance evaluation; hence, methods that enhance their quality are of great import. An important theory of ratings has reemerged that shares many elements in common with our previous discussion about aggregation. Landy and Farr (1980, pp. 98–99) called attention to this theory in their *Psychological Bulletin* article. The formulation was introduced by Wherry (1952) when he was working on problems of performance assessment in the military. Until recently, his treatment remained in esoteric technical reports (although Wherry taught this formulation to many students in the 1950s and 1960s at Ohio State University). More recently, Landy and Farr (1983) published a small chapter by Wherry (1983) as an appendix in *The Measurement of Work Performance: Methods, Theory, and Application*. Readers are referred to this source for a more detailed exposition (see also Wherry & Bartlett, 1982).

Wherry (1983) partitions the variance in ratings into systematic and random components, and then further partitions the systematic into *true* and *bias* aspect components. This is done in a way very much in line with our earlier discussion of the decomposition of scale variance (i.e., attribute variance, bias variance, and error):

$$v_{\text{rating}} = v_{\text{true aspect}} + v_{\text{bias aspect}} + v_{\text{random error}}$$

Wherry's (1983) analysis also partitions the components of bias further and includes ways to minimize the influence of distinct forms of bias, the various nuisance variables that attenuate the predictor-criterion correlation.

This analysis underscores the need to be wary about the components of reliability (e.g., during reliability checks on the raters). Rater reliability, like test reliability, can be enhanced by increasing true variance *or* bias variance or both. If it is bias variance that enhances reliability, we have the same problem that is encountered in test construction, namely, that what we are measuring more reliably is actually what we are less interested in. This perspective differs somewhat from that expressed by Schmidt, Hunter, and Pearlman (1981), who maintain that, because correlations between criterion measures typically approach 1.00 when such correlations are corrected for attenuation, such measures are essentially equivalent at the true score level. They go on to say, "These considerations point to the conclusion that the only function of multiple criterion scales is to increase reliability of the composite (overall) criterion measure" (p. 175). But optimal aggregation increases both reliability and validity.

The link between Wherry's theory of ratings and the aggregation of indicators of indifference (on the predictor side) is clear. Wherry (1983) even states that this "parallels Spearman's two-factor theory of intelligence. Obviously, the true expression should probably contain group or common factors as well as a general one, but for convenience we should restrict our discussion to the simpler case" (p. 288). We include this discussion of Wherry's theory because investigators may wish to consider aggregating criterion ratings in this manner so that systematic bias can be minimized. Aggregation is a powerful technique that should be used on both sides of the predictor-criterion equation. (It may be more than coincidence that Wherry, 1959, also developed one of the early hierarchical solutions in factor analysis.)

Systematic bias contaminates the validity of all psychometric measures. It cannot be removed completely in any assessment, but it can be minimized. When constructing *cross-validation profiles* with multiple criteria (see below), some criterion measures may collectively converge more accurately on a criterion dimension when they are aggregated. Furthermore, correlations with aggregated criterion measures as well as with the individual constituents of these composites can be included in cross-validation profiles, providing the investigators with the opportunity to have their cake and eat it, too. Such cross-validation profiles would allow research consumers to decide for themselves which criteria are most important for their purposes, how these criteria should be combined, and what the optimal predictor set is for their chosen criteria (Schmidt & Kaplan, 1971).

Tenopyr (1977) has argued that the process of construct validation involves establishing structural relations between aggregates of heterogeneous predictors and criteria that share common variance:

> We know from elementary factor theory that the correlation between any two variables equals the sum of the crossproducts of their common factor loadings. Putting it more simply, to have high predictive value, a test must essentially involve the same constructs to the same degree as a measure of the job behavior. It would seem, then, that any interpretation of a content-based employment test strictly in terms of tasks is inadequate. A content-based test or any other test used in prediction must share common constructs with job behavior. (p. 50)

To the extent that large communalities are shared by both the predictors and the criteria, or by subgroupings of each, global models of structural relations are likely to serve applied and theoretical purposes best. For example, for a wide range of occupations that demand a lot of information processing, the *overall level* of the cognitive repertoire is what is important. To some degree, different forms of symbolic content can "compensate" for each other. (Perhaps most cognitively demanding occupations are more like this than not.) In psychology, for instance, if GRE-V provides as much information about the likelihood of completing graduate training as GRE-Q does (across most areas of psychology), the two measures can be combined. In this situation, disparate patterns that aggregate to the same level will reflect near-equivalent readiness to acquire the required repertoires of psychological knowledge. However, in other domains, the density of specific kinds of symbolic-manipulation ability may be more central. Under these circumstances, it is important to assess not only the complexity (level) of the cognitive repertoire, but also the content (density) of its particulars. For a number of academic and occupational environments, the same level of the general factor emanating from different forms of symbolic content does not make for the same ability requirements. Thus, in English literature and law, facility with linguistic material is much more important than facility with numerical or figural symbols, whereas the converse is true in architecture, engineering, and the physical sciences generally. The implication here for the criterion problem is that criterion measures should assess one's facility with the actual specific content and products of the domain.

In an article on the *real test bias*, Frederiksen (1984) makes a compelling case that tests *are* biased if they do not assess important facets of criterion behavior necessary for the required performance. This would imply that for figurally or spatially demanding occupations (such as architecture, engineering, and many of the creative arts), the appropriate criteria should include created products. Below, we will suggest that measures of spatial ability (*S*) would undoubtedly contribute incremental validity to measures of *G* (*general factor*), *V*, and *N*. This hypothesis is best tested with criteria in which variance overlaps with the *specificity* of spatial ability measures (good criterion examples include building, drawing, and designing).

Perhaps expert raters could independently assess the products of these more hands-on, less verbal, disciplines. For example, if raters displayed an average interrater correlation of .45, an aggregate based on 5, raters would generate an estimated reliability (via Spearman-Brown) of .80. For ability measures distinct from the general factor to have incremental validity, they must share variance with criteria that are not loaded with the general factor. Such ratings may provide a needed vehicle to pull contruct-valid variance from the paper-and-pencil-loaded general factor. This again reflects Tenopyr's idea of establishing construct validity by linking predictor and criterion communalities, but the communalities in this case must be independent of the general factor. Criterion *attribute variance* that is independent of the general factor is the portion that will give scientific significance to measures of cognitive abilities beyond g. Ackerman (1987) provides examples of how perceptual and motor abilities factor into performance and how these attributes fit into dynamic behavioral changes throughout the skill acquisition process. But these abilities and processes will go undetected if the criterion variables used are not sensitive to systematic sources of individual differences beyond the general factor.

The Prediction Problem and Determining a Predictor Set: Combining Cross-validation With Extrinsic Convergent Validation

The preceding discussion suggests that it might be useful, when comparing competing predictors, to construct *cross-validation profiles* much like the extrinsic convergent validation profiles shown in Table 3. This would allow investigators to examine the comparative validity of contrasting predictor sets across several criteria. It is possible for different predictors to produce different validities for different criteria; therefore, comparison across multiple criteria is of the essence when evaluating competing predictors.

The comparison of several predictor sets in terms of multiple criteria is illustrated in Table 4, which contains a synthetic example. The five predictor sets being compared on n criteria include a measure of g and four combinations of major (*v:ed, k:m*) and minor (*V, N & S*) group factors. The question is whether the multiple predictors are getting at no more than the criterion variance captured by the general factor, or whether there are profitable components of specific variance that warrant the use of group factors in the prediction equation. In the illustration, only the major group factor combination (*v:ed, k:m*) consistently improves on the predictive efficiency of g, although for specific criteria, other combinations may improve on g.

Consider also our earlier synthetic example in Figures 6 and 7. The first equation would be a regression equation with one predictor, the three-variable composite. The fifth equation would involve three predictors, the three variable variate, say, the group factors, verbal (*V*), numerical (*N*), and spatial (*S*) ability. If the valid portion of the predicted variance acounted for by the three predictors is due solely to their communality and not to their specificity, on cross-validation the R^2 would shrink more for the three-predictor variate than for the composite, because having more predictors increases the likelihood of capitalizing on sample-specific noise (which is what cross-validation corrects for).

Consider, on the other hand, the one-predictor equation. Most of the variable's reliable variance is g variance. Therefore, the beta weight will be based mostly on the common variance (the g variance, found in all cognitive ability tests). The shrinkage in R^2 will be much less because only one parameter is being estimated, and it contains all of the relevant attribute variance. Thus, to the extent that criteria are saturated with g, cross-validation coefficients should be essentially equivalent for the single-predictor equation and the

TABLE 4

A Synthetic Example of Five Cross-validation Profiles for Predicting Multiple Criteria With Contrasting Predictor Scales

Criterion Variables	Predictor Sets				
	g R^2_{cv}	$v{:}ed, k{:}m$ R^2_{cv}	$k{:}m, N$ R^2_{cv}	$V, N, k{:}m$ R^2_{cv}	V, N, S R^2_{cv}
C_1	.39	.43	.38	.37	.35
C_2	.34	.36	.34	.33	.31
C_3	.31	.34	.30	.29	.29
C_4	.30	.32	.30	.31	.28
C_5	.26	.35	.27	.30	.38
C_N	.31	.34	.34	.39	.30

Note: For each criterion variable, the beta weights for the predictor variable(s) will vary as a function of the least squares maximization procedure on the screening sample.
g = general intelligence
$v{:}ed$ = verbal/numerical/educational
$k{:}m$ = practical/mechanical/spatial
N = numerical ability
S = spatial ability
V = verbal ability

multiple predictor equation if the latter is composed of the constituents of the former.

This analysis shows why multiple aptitude test batteries should be evaluated not only in terms of their incremental validity (over that achieved by measures of general intelligence) but also in terms of their cross-validation. Predictive validities can be spuriously inflated simply because adding variables can increase the R^2 significantly in large samples. It also distorts the interpretations we place on predictor constructs. (Statistically significant findings should *always* be evaluated for substantive significance.)

However, as we noted earlier, there is good reason to believe that in many applied contexts the construct of general intelligence may be splintered profitably. Vernon's major group

factors, *verbal-numerical-educational (v:ed)* and *practical-mechanical-spatial (k:m)*, collectively provide incremental validity over general intelligence in a number of contexts, as do the minor group factors, verbal, numerical, and spatial ability. The likelihood of such differential validities occurring is moderated by the intellectual level required of the occupation. Range truncation on the general factor will increase the likelihood that the major and minor group factors will be useful for prediction.

We offer a simple methodology for ascertaining when further splintering of general intelligence is warranted. Start with an ordinary univariate regression equation involving general intelligence to serve as the baseline. Then proceed to more complex variates, first, by splintering general intelligence into *v:ed* and *k:m,* and then by splintering these major group factors, following a logical hierarchical descent from larger to more circumscribed factors. For example, *v:ed* may be splintered into verbal (*V*) and numerical (*N*) ability; *k:m* could be evaluated as a third variable, or splintered, and the process can continue.

The criterion for splintering is twofold. First, more complex predictor variates (i.e., multiple variable variates) must display incremental validity over and above that shown by less complex predictor variates (viz., composites). Second, on cross-validation, the more complex variates must account for more criterion variance than the less complex variates.

For cognitively demanding occupations, as in our earlier example of philosophers and engineers, the general factor (general intelligence) is expected to "fall out" of the predictor variate while lower order factors (more content-focused abilities) surface and become more predictively central.

Investigators must also take into account sample statistics that might vary from study to study, such as reliabilities and standard deviations of both predictors and criteria, level of the general factor for screening (development) and calibration (cross-validation) samples, and sample size. With what we now know about the roles such basic statistics play in affecting validity coefficients (see below), *it behooves all investigators to report these statistics routinely.*

The above methodology also speaks to Cronbach's (1971) point that all tests have *multiple* validities. Validity is based on the accuracy of inferences. It is not tests that are validated; inferences are. As cross-validation profiles are developed across different populations and occupational contexts, the construct validity of individual predictors and predictor sets will be better understood.

The importance of cross-validating predictor composites of a few variables selected from a larger pool (such as cognitive abilities) has

recently been restressed in *Standards for Educational and Psychological Measurement* (APA, AERA, & NCME, 1985, Standard 1.25):

> When a small number of predictors is selected from a large pool and weights are simultaneously determined...selecting variables and weights and for estimating validity coefficients should take into account the bias in the weights and validity coefficients; otherwise the weights and validity coefficients should be cross-validated. (p. 18)

It is hoped that the procedure described above will forestall the possibility of ostensibly different measures appearing to show that different constructs are related to performance when, in reality, it is the common variance of more global measures and not the specificity of their constituents that is responsible for the meaningful predictor/criterion covariation that holds up under cross-validation.

Ability Domains: Cognitive, Perceptual, and Psychomotor

Human abilities are typically grouped into three domains: cognitive, perceptual, and psychomotor. But, of course, these are not discrete categories. All three categories provide unique and valuable information for predicting criterion behaviors, and dimensions from all three categories have met the criteria for scientific significance. Recent reviews have summarized the current status of the three domains; see, for example, Fleishman and Quaintance (1984), Hartigan and Wigdor (1989), Gottfredson (1986), Landy (1990), and Wigdor and Garner (1982). An issue of *Personnel Psychology* (Sackett, 1990) is devoted to the Army's Selection and Classification Project (Project A) and includes discussions of predictor and criterion development for both ability and nonability domains.

The above sources provide a broad review of contemporary validation research with the

TABLE 5

Predicting Job Performance

Job Family	Complexity Levels		Regression Equation			Multiple Correlation	Number of Jobs
I	1	Set-up	JP = .40 GVN + .19 SPQ	+ .07 KFM		.59	21
III	2	Synthesize/coordinate	JP = .58 GVN			.58	60
IV	3	Analyze/compile/compute	JP = .45 GVN	+ .16 KFM		.53	205
V	4	Copy/compare	JP = .28 GVN	+ .33 KFM		.50	209
II	5	Feeding/offbearing	JP = .07 GVN	+ .46 KFM		.49	20

Note: These job families were based on the data-people-things classification system; however, numerical order does not reflect complexity.

Family   I: Set-up precision work (e.g., machinist, cabinet maker, metal fabricator)

Family II: Feeding, offbearing (e.g., shrimp picker, corn husking machine operator, cannery worker, spot welder)

Family III: Synthesize, coordinate (e.g., retail food manager, fish and game warden, biologist, city circulation manager)

Family IV: Analyze, compile, compute (e.g., automotive mechanic, radiologic technician, automotive parts counterman, high school teacher)

Family V: Copy, compare (e.g., assembler, insulating machine operator, forklift truck operator)

GVN   =   Cognitive ability

SPQ   =   Perceptual ability

KFM   =   Psychomotor ability

From "Test Validation for 12,000 Jobs: An Application of Job Classification and Validity Generalization Analysis to the GATB" (Test Research Rep. No. 45) by J. E. Hunter, 1983. Washington, DC: U.S. Department of Labor, U.S. Employment Service.

use of ability predictors. Many of the studies discussed draw on existing, well-known multitest batteries such as the *General Aptitude Test Battery* (GATB), the *Differential Aptitude Tests* (DAT), and the *Armed Services Vocational Aptitude Battery* (ASVAB).[8] These are excellent instruments, and the data they provide are useful. We hope that future research will expand coverage to other measures as well as to ways of aggregating existing measures that will enhance the validities of predictor composites and simplify the predictor variates.

Meaningful analyses can also be achieved with existing large-scale data sets. For example, Table 5 contains data from Hunter's (1983b) analysis of GATB data for 12,000 jobs. The GATB has eight scales and one general-factor composite scale. Hunter aggregated these scales to form three composites: cognitive, perceptual, and psychomotor, assembled from the GATB scales as follows: cognitive composite = G (general ability) + V (verbal ability) + N (numerical ability); perceptual composite = S (spatial ability) + P (form perception) + Q (clerical perception); and psychomotor composite = K (motor coordination) + F (finger dexterity) + M (manual dexterity). These composites were then validated as predictors of job performance for five job families (groupings of jobs based on their level of complexity). Table 5 summarizes their findings. Table 5 shows that, as job complexity increases, the regression weights for the cognitive composite increase, whereas those for the psychomotor composite decrease.

Note that the perceptual composite contributed to the prediction in only one equation. Because the perceptual composite could be predicted almost perfectly from the other two composites, some authors have considered using only two composites, cognitive and psychomotor, to predict job performance. This may not be wise in certain circumstances. Our concern is this: There is reason to believe that spatial ability involves more than what the GATB's spatial measure, S, captures. The GATB does not measure all regions of the radex uniformly. Spatial ability also includes mechanical reasoning, which is not assessed by the GATB. There are many tests of spatial ability: Eliot and Smith (1983) have compiled a directory of almost 400 spatial tests. Lohman (1989) has stated that spatial abilities can be organized hierarchically, but so far, results of factor analytic studies focusing exclusively on this domain are less than clearcut. Nevertheless, if these factor analytic results were used to select tests that were then aggregated, we suspect that a spatial ability aggregate would contribute incremental validity in certain prediction contexts (e.g., scholastic prediction in engineering, architecture, physical sciences, and the creative arts). Although Hunter's (1983b) five-family categorization has its uses, narrower groupings might prove even better for prediction purposes.

Other studies have shown that spatial ability is a useful predictor. In Project A, for example, McHenry, Hough, Toquam, Hanson, and Ashworth (1990) found that a spatial test provided more incremental validity than any other cognitive ability beyond the general factor in the prediction of general soldiering proficiency and core technical proficiency. For these occupations, spatial ability added two to three percent to the predicted variance. Humphreys, Lubinski, and Yao (under review), using Project TALENT data, assembled two composites from three group factors: mathematical (M), spatial (S), and verbal (V) abilities. One composite (V-Math) consisted of V +

M (essentially Vernon's $v{:}ed$), whereas the other composite (S-Math) was formed by combining $S + M$ (so M was a component in both composites). Three groups of subjects were then selected using these composites: *high intelligence* (top 20% on both composites), *high spatial* (top 20% on the S-Math only), and *high verbal* (top 20% on V-Math only). Using longitudinal data obtained 11 years after high school graduation, these investigators found that for both genders, twice as many physical scientists were found in the high spatial group as in the high verbal group. A disproportionate number of creative artists came from the high spatial group as well. The authors suggest that a number of students who are academically able with respect to disciplines like architecture, engineering, and many of the physical sciences might not pass conventional screening for academic admission because such screening tends to be limited to the use of verbal and numerical/quantitative (i.e., $v{:}ed$) measures. Other studies have shown that spatial ability contributes incremental validity over a wide range of jobs (Humphreys, 1986; Smith, 1964; Vernon, 1961).

We suggest that investigators pursue spatial ability as a separate construct. We suspect that spatial ability draws on several underlying psychological systems. For instance, based on the correlates of many spatial ability measures, it is reasonable to hypothesize that spatial ability draws on both the cognitive and perceptual systems. This would mean that aggregating GATB spatial (S), form perception (P), and clerical perception (Q) may act to "pull" the construct validity of the spatial ability measure away from its cognitive components. Hunter (1983b) notes that spatial ability is more valid than the perceptual composite (S, P, Q) for artistic and scientific jobs (jobs classified at a more specific level than the five more general job families shown in Table 5), but concludes that this advantage is trivial. We think that this minuscule advantage can become more substantive if more broadly defined spatial measures were used.

Table 5 also depicts a well-established finding: As the information processing demands of jobs decrease, the validity of psychomotor composites increases (Hartigan & Wigdor, 1989; Hunter, 1983a, 1983b; Thorndike, 1985). But nonetheless, psychomotor abilities appear together with cognitive abilities as significant predictors for conceptually demanding jobs. Guion (1965) distinguished between *psychomotor* and *sensorimotor* abilities. The former stresses kinetic movement and control, whereas the latter requires some form of sensory discrimination to structure subsequent muscular movement. This distinction reflects again how abilities and skills resist classification into discrete categories. Readers are referred to Fleishman's work on motor ability dimensions (e.g., Fleishman, 1966; Fleishman & Quaintance, 1984). Dunnette's 1976 chapter in this *Handbook*'s first edition provides brief descriptions of these dimensions as well as dimensions of physical fitness. (See also Hogan's [1991] chapter on physical abilities in volume 2 of this *Handbook*.)

Psychomotor and sensorimotor abilities will continue to receive justifiable attention in future research on human abilities. Thorndike (1985), for example, aggregated the psychomotor abilities of the GATB, examined it as a predictor across a heterogeneous collection of job categories, and concluded that

> the motor dimension appears to be significant for job performance, and since it is relatively independent of the cognitive dimension ... it deserves to be given weight in any prediction.... It is likely that 10 or 15 percent increase in predicted criterion variance can be achieved. (p. 253)

Perhaps "any prediction" might be too sweeping, but these remarks do stress the importance of this class of abilities.

With respect to cognitive abilities, a number of contemporary investigators have commented on the central importance of general intelligence (i.e., the general cognitive factor) in the prediction of important criteria (Brand, 1987; Carroll, 1982; Gottfredson, 1986; Humphreys, 1979; Hunter, 1986; Jensen, 1980a; Schmidt, 1988; Thorndike, 1985). The *Journal of Vocational Behavior* devoted an entire issue to this topic in 1986 (Gottfredson, vol. 29, pp. 293–450). To be sure, the primacy of general intelligence in the prediction of academic and vocational criteria has always had its proponents (Berdie, Layton, Hagenah, & Swanson, 1962; Humphreys, 1962; Jenkins & Paterson, 1961; McNemar, 1964; Vernon, 1947, 1950). However, it is also well documented that in predicting these criteria it is possible to account for more criterion variance by using components (major and minor factors) of general intelligence instead of the usual full-scale score. In addition, perceptual and motor abilities can contribute to the prediction as well.

Given these studies of long standing, the current stress on the importance of the general factor would appear to be retrogressive. Why did Ackerman (1988b) remark, in his review of Gottfredson's (1986) "The *g* Factor in Employment Testing," that the special issue might have well been labeled, "Found: Our Intelligence. Why?"

The return of interest to general intelligence (or more precisely, the general factor in cognitive abilities) appears to be due to how well the construct has done by itself, so as to warrant a special status among predictors of criteria in the academic world and the world of work. Carroll (1982), for example, has noted that "a large part of whatever predictive validity the DAT and other multiple aptitude batteries have is attributable to an underlying general factor that enters into the various subtests" (pp. 83–84). Although incremental validity can be achieved by fractionating general intelligence, the amount of increase (even if valid and worthwhile) is minuscule compared with what general intelligence does by itself (Gottfredson, 1986, vol. 29, no. 3, whole issue) *for the criterion variables it has been used to predict.* Table 6 gives recent data from Project A that show once again how significant a predictor the general cognitive factor is. Table 6 also shows the incremental validities for other predictors, some of these being nonability variables. However, the general factor accounts for the lion's share of criterion variance of all kinds. Other research programs have observed similar results.

Reviewing 20 years of research on aptitude-treatment interaction (ATI), Cronbach and Snow (1977) concluded:

> While we see merit in a hierarchical conception of abilities, with abilities differentiated at coarse and fine levels, we have not found Guilford's subdivision a powerful hypothesis.... Instead of finding general abilities irrelevant to school learning, we found nearly ubiquitous evidence that general measures predict amount learned or rate of learning or both. And, whereas we had expected specialized abilities rather than general abilities to account for interactions, the abilities that most frequently enter into interactions are general. Even in those programs of research that started with specialized ability measures and found interactions with treatment, the data seem to warrant attributing most effects to general ability. (pp. 496–497)

More recently, Snow (1989) made even stronger statements:

> In contrast to earlier predictions of Cronbach and Gleser, measures of general ability (G) enter interactions more frequently than other indices of aptitude, despite the fact that measures of G also typically show strong aptitude main effects. Many different measures have been used to reach this conclusion....

Given new evidence and reconsideration of old evidence, G can indeed be interpreted as 'ability to learn' as long as it is clear that these terms refer to complex processes and skills and that a somewhat different mix of these constituents may be required in different learning tasks and settings. The old view that mental tests and learning tasks measure distinctly different abilities should be discarded, even though we still lack a theory for integrating the two. (p. 22)

General ability, the general cognitive factor (or the complexity dimension of the radex), is indeed one of psychology's most powerful variables. The significance of this psychological parameter may stem in part from many of its correlates observed outside of academic or vocational settings, correlates that clearly contribute to instrumental effectiveness in these settings. Brand (1987) and Jensen (1980a, chap. 8) provide one with a good feel for these correlates. The nomothetic span of general intelligence is indeed among the broadest and deepest of any of psychology's constructs. The importance of this network for industrial and organizational psychologists extends beyond performance and training criteria. Many of the positive correlates have implications (corollary as well as direct) for academic or workplace behaviors—for example, breadth and depth of interests, physical health, responsiveness to psychotherapy, moral reasoning capacity, sense of humor, social skills, achievement motivation, and practical knowledge. Many of the negative correlates also have implications—accident-proneness, alcoholism, crime and delinquency, racial prejudice, smoking, and obesity, for example. (For additional correlates, the interested reader is referred to the table assembled by Brand, 1987, pp. 254–255.)[9] It would appear that a large number of socially valued attributes are "pulled along" by the general factor to such an extent that when we

TABLE 6

Mean Validity and Incremental Validity for Multiple Sets of Predictors and Criteria

	Predictor Domain					
Job Performance Factor	General Cognitive Ability (K = 4)	General Cognitive Ability Plus Spatial Ability (K = 5)	General Cognitive Ability Plus Perceptual Psychomotor Ability (K = 10)	General Cognitive Ability Plus Temperament/ Personality (K = 8)	General Cognitive Ability Plus Vocational Interest (K = 10)	General Cognitive Ability Plus Job Reward Preference (K = 7)
Core technical proficiency	.63	.65	.64	.63	.64	.63
General soldiering	.65	.68	.67	.66	.66	.66
Effort and leadership	.31	.32	.32	.42	.35	.33
Personal discipline	.16	.17	.17	.35	.19	.19
Physical fitness and military bearing	.20	.22	.22	.41	.24	.22

Notes: Validity coefficients were corrected for range restriction and adjusted for shrinkage. Incremental validity refers to the increase in R afforded by the new predictors above and beyond the R for the Army's current predictor battery, the ASVAB.
K is the number of predictor scores.

From "Project A Validation Results: The Relationship Between Predictor and Criterion Domains" by J. J. McHenry, L. M. Hough, J. L. Toquam, M. A. Hanson, and S. A. Ashworth, 1990, *Personnel Psychology*, 43, p. 346. Copyright 1990 by *Personnel Psychology*. Reprinted by permission.

analyze the determinants of, say, supervisor or peer ratings or work performance in general, we have to be quite aware of the scope of this network.[10]

Validity Generalization

Validity generalization is an important concept, not only for industrial and organizational psychology (where it was developed), but for psychology in general. Even sympathetic observers have remarked that psychology as a science lacks the systematic cumulation of knowledge so characteristic of the physical sciences (Meehl, 1978). Validity generalization (VG) is an exception. VG studies employ meta-analytic techniques to ascertain the generalizability and stability of forecasting equations based on individual differences in abilities (e.g., those found in Table 5). These meta-analytic reviews have shown that validities are transportable across job situations and within job families.

Annual Review chapters on personnel selection routinely include a section on this topic (Dunnette & Borman, 1979; Guion & Gibson, 1988; Hakel, 1986; Schmitt & Robertson, 1990; Tenopyr & Oeltjen, 1982; Zedeck & Cascio, 1984). Validity generalization is receiving as much attention as any topic in contemporary industrial and organizational psychology. A panel debate, "Forty Questions About Validity Generalization and Meta-analysis" (Schmidt, Pearlman, Hunter, & Hirsh, 1985) and "Commentary" (Sackett, Tenopyr, Schmitt, & Kahn, 1985, vol. 38), covered over 100 pages in *Personnel Psychology,* an exchange characterized by Cronbach (1988, p. 12) as "exhaustive." A more recent review is given in Hartigan and Wigdor (1989, especially chap. 7).

The general finding was that although the magnitude of the validity coefficients did vary across jobs that differed in complexity, cognitive abilities have shown at least some validity for all jobs. Monotonic increases in job complexity accompany increases in validity coefficients for broad groups of cognitive abilities and, conversely, decreases in validity coefficients for psychomotor abilities. Validity coefficients were often appropriately transportable across broad groupings of jobs and different organizational situations.[11] We know this now—these conclusions can be found in major textbooks in industrial and organizational psychology (e.g., Cascio, 1991; Landy, 1989; Muchinsky, 1989)—but we did not always know it (cf. Albright, Glennon, & Smith, 1963, p.18; Ghiselli, 1966, p. 28).

One of the most misleading myths in the history of industrial psychology was that validity coefficients and prediction equations for job performance were situation specific. This sentiment was captured by Guion (1965):

The first and most persuasive generalization that can be made is that jobs within...various organizational groupings, as well as the organizational climates in which they may be found, will demonstrate extensive variability. A test or procedure that may be found highly predictive in one situation may, therefore, prove to be of no value at all in another apparently similar one. (p. 415)

Contrast the above with the following recommendations from the latest edition of *Standards for Educational and Psychological Measurement* (APA, AERA, & NCME, 1985):

When adequate local validation evidence is not available, criterion-related. evidence of validity for a specified test use may be based on validity generalization from a set of prior studies, provided that the specified test-use situation can be considered to have been drawn from the same population of situations on which validity generalization was conducted. (Primary)...Comment: Several methods of validity generalization and simultaneous estimation have proven useful. In all methods, the integrity of the inference depends on the degree of similarity between the local situation and the prior set of situations. Present and prior situations can be judged to be similar, for example, according to factors such as the characteristics of the people and job functions involved. (Standard 1.16, pp. 16–17)

and later:

Employers should not be precluded from using a test if it can be demonstrated that the test has generated a significant record of validity in similar job settings and for highly similar people or that it is otherwise appropriate to generalize from other applications. (p. 59)

Finally, a recent publication by the National Academy of Sciences includes an entire chapter on validity generalization and supports its assumptions and methods (Hartigan & Wigdor, 1989).

Quite a change! Why?

A number of factors may have contributed to the myth of *situational specificity,* among them, small sample sizes characteristic of most validation studies, range restriction in the applicant and employee samples, and unreliability in the predictors and criteria. As Pearlman et al. (1980) insightfully observe: "The visions of complexity entertained by many psychologists in the field may stem largely from a tendency to interpret variance created by statistical artifacts as real"(p. 400).

Validity generalization research involves the estimation of two parameters: *true validity* and the *standard deviation of true validity.* Search for the best statistical estimation procedures has resulted in an extensive literature. Linn and Dunbar (1986) provide an excellent review of these procedures, finding that all of them produce estimates that are very close. If anything, the procedures tend to overestimate the true standard deviation. Schmidt and Hunter (1981, p. 1132) have listed a number of factors that contribute to variability in validity coefficients across situations:

- Sampling error
- Criterion unreliability
- Test (predictor) unreliability
- Range restriction
- Criterion contamination or deficiency (Brogden & Taylor, 1950)
- Computational and typographical errors (Wolins, 1962)
- Variation in the equivalence of measures employed

According to Schmidt and Hunter (1981), approximately 72 percent of the variance in observed validity coefficients is traceable to the first four sources of disturbance, and 85 percent of this 72 percent is due to the first source, sampling error.

To be sure, that validity generalization occurs across jobs and organizations does not preclude situational specificity under certain circumstances. Also, that validities are comparable does not imply that tests are unbiased in the sense of generating equally accurate inferences for different demographic groups. Systematic trends of over- or underprediction can occur. For example, underprediction for women in academia (Linn, 1973) and in the military (Linn, 1984) is discussed by Linn and Dunbar (1986).

Actually, validity generalization is only one manifestation of construct validity (Hunter, 1980). As Loevinger (1957) has perceptively noted some time ago: "Since predictive, concurrent, and content validities are all essentially ad hoc, construct validity is the whole of validity from a scientific point of view" (p. 636). That is, construct validity is what enables scientists to extrapolate or infer from an organized body of data—knowledge—in a manner that increases the likelihood their inferences will be confirmed. Construct validity also embraces the concept of generalizability that Cronbach and his colleagues (Cronbach, Gleser, Nanda, & Rajaratnam, 1972; Cronbach, Rajaratnam, & Gleser, 1963) have studied extensively. As comparable results accrue with the use of different predictor or criterion measures targeted at the same constructs, the generalizability of measures and boundary conditions of constructs become more clearly defined. To know how a construct operates (which is the goal of construct validation research), we must first know the domains in which it operates.

This discussion may also be linked to Lykken's (1968) three-tiered concept of replication—constructive, operational, and literal (in order of greater to lesser degree of risk and scientific soundness). The many replications of the general factor and the finding of similar predictor-criterion structural relations with the use of different measures constitute examples of constructive replication. This also captures the spirit of synthetic validity.

The concept of validity generalization continues to undergo refinement of the "normal science" kind (Kuhn, 1970). Both theoretical and applied psychologists will profit from assimilating the findings of validity generalization. The distributions of validity coefficients assembled in the validity generalization studies are rather impressive and may cause some to wonder if the fluctuations in the phenomena they are trying to understand (in other contexts) are not simply due to sampling error. For the applied areas, validity generalization may soon acquire the ascendancy that actuarial prediction has over clinical prediction (Meehl, 1954). Perhaps validity generalization will be assimilated by the field more quickly (Meehl, 1986b).

Predictor-Criterion Structural Relations

In applied psychology, the linear model is ubiquitous (Dawes, 1979). The preceding discussion was based entirely on linear relationships between predictor and criterion. People have tried repeatedly to transform existing predictors or look for systematic trait × trait (Ghiselli, 1972; Zedeck, 1971) or trait × treatment (Cronbach, 1957) interactions, but these more complex second-order relationships tended to fail to replicate (Cronbach, 1975a), even in fields outside of industrial and organizational psychology (Tellegen, 1988; Tellegen, Kamp, & Watson, 1982; Wiggins, 1973). In a special issue on moderator variables in the *Journal of Applied Psychology*, published more than 15 years after Saunders' (1956) "citation classic" on this concept, Ghiselli (1972) wrote,

"It is possible that moderators are as fragile and elusive as that other will-o-the-wisp, the suppressor variable" (p. 270). The status of moderator variables has not changed, but they continue to be discussed at length in classrooms and seminars without any convincing examples. We continue to tell our students, "Keep looking. It's an attractive concept."

Perhaps it is not outrageous to suggest that to the extent that ability predictor-criterion variables covary, they "simply" do so linearly. At the level of analysis of conventional psychometric abilities, it may be that monotonic transformations (e.g., X^2 or $X^{1/2}$) as well as predictor-predictor interactions ($X_1 X_2$) do not covary with meaningful criteria more precisely than linear trends (particularly in ways that replicate and cross-validate). This was essentially the conclusion that was reached about configural scoring at the item level (Lykken, 1956; Meehl, 1950), namely, it was an intriguing idea that unfortunately did not pan out empirically.

We are not suggesting that programs designed to uncover higher order trends and interactions be discontinued, but it is a reasonable hypothesis that linear relationships will continue to dominate forecasting equations (i.e., those that cross-validate). Some of the most solid work in psychological prediction is confined to the linear model (Dawes, 1979; Dawes & Corrigan, 1974; Dawes, Faust, & Meehl, 1989). Although there is much work yet to be done in validity generalization (including predictor and criterion development) given its current success using the linear model, substantial advances are unlikely to emanate from deviating too much from this framework. The amount of variance accounted for with the five equations in Table 5 is impressively high, high enough to make one wonder how much additional variance is left to account for, *using only ability dimensions as predictors, however transformed* (see below).

Prediction: The $r_{xy} = .50$ Barrier

How high should validity coefficients be? The applied psychological literature is full of examples of criterion-prediction validities that cluster around .20 to .30, with almost none of them exceeding .50. The notion that there is a *validity ceiling* at $r = .50$ (also known as the *.50 barrier*) can be traced back to Hull. Hull (1928, p. 193) believed that abilities contribute about 50 percent to criterion performance (other sources of influence include "industry or willingness," 35%, and "chance or accident," 15%), so his utopian expectation for this domain's predictive potential was about $r_{xy} = 0.71$. However, because of measurement error and the nature of psychological phenomena, he seriously doubted that validities above .50 would ever be obtained.

In recent articles, Meehl (1990a, 1990b) suggests that theoretical predictions in psychology, and indeed in all sciences, should be accompanied by ranges of tolerance. When faced with an estimation or prediction problem, such as accounting for the variance in work performance, psychologists should at least have *some feel* for how much to expect from their predictors. Given that all psychologically significant criterion behaviors are multiply determined and that many of these determining factors are unknown, estimates will always be much less than 1.0. But how much less than unity is tolerable? What fraction of the total criterion variance can we reasonably expect to account for with ability? This analysis is important because it adjusts our expectations and suggests when we should look beyond ability to other predictors.

Because we have had difficulty accounting for more than 25 percent of the criterion variance, several writers have expressed disenchantment with conventional ability tests as predictors and have argued that perhaps a different conceptualization of the problem is called for, stressing *process* factors, for example, as opposed to *products* (such as ability). Consider the following nonability factors that undoubtedly account for variance in work performance:

- *Sheer energy level.* This attribute might profitably be fractionated into cognitive versus psychomotor energy.

- *Interests and needs.* How satisfying does the individual find the occupation in general, and the job and work setting in particular?

- *Personality style.* To what extent does the individual's personality style correspond to the temporal characteristics of the job, such as the pace and cycles of the work (Dawis & Lofquist, 1984)? Style can be defined to include a variety of expressive and response tempo attributes, even such characteristics as speech (slow vs. rapid), certain mannerisms (some endearing, others aversive), and certain types of interpersonal presence (e.g., some extreme forms would be the animalistic presence of the socially poised psychopath or the debilitating preoccupation of the manic manifested in irritated impatience: "Why does everyone have to move *so* slowly?")

- *Nonbehavioral personal attributes.* These would include such attributes as body build, gender, height, race, weight, physical attractiveness, and health (which, of course, is relevant to behavior).

- *The short half-life of generalizations in the social sciences.* As pointed out by Cronbach (1975a), this is due to a multitude of factors including economic and political influences that moderate the significance of other personal attributes.

- *Chance or simply luck.* Chance is one of the most underestimated of factors. In psychology, for example, the demonstration that chance plays a critical role in close interpersonal relationships (Berscheid & Walster, 1969) would suggest that psychologists should lower their expectations about criterion prediction.

The long-standing discussion of the .50 barrier always seems to see the glass half empty and then seeks to remedy the deficit by adding more abilities (or by improving the assessment of existing abilities), as opposed to trying other classes of attributes such as those enumerated above. This barrier may be merely the asymptotic limit of what the ability domain has to offer, and accounting for 25 percent of the variance in any socially important area with *one* class of attributes is impressive (contemporary findings are approaching 50%; see Tables 5 and 6). It is curious why some psychologists keep demanding more incremental validity from *this* domain instead of trying other classes of attributes.

Much contemporary discussion in cognitive experimental psychology expresses dissatisfaction with traditional psychometrics, arguing that no new knowledge is coming from this area. But then it proceeds to reconceptualize abilities as if the remaining unpredicted variance had to be accounted for by ability factors. Most of this variance is probably accounted for by other factors. If those with contrary views would assign percentages to these other factors, such as the variables listed above (we are sure there are others we have missed), we can then see what is left.

The extent to which these factors add incremental validity to ability variables will better enable us to determine the ceiling for psychological variables. Furthermore, there is good reason to suspect that these valued nonability factors have more differential validity for the less intellectually demanding occupations. Nonability attributes can be compensated for by other personal qualities. Someone who is physically attractive can "get away with" being a little aloof, whereas someone not

as attractive can nevertheless be equally as effective with a charming personality. Other nonability attributes can be treated in similar fashion, but not ability. No matter how attractive or charming, a person requires a certain degree of intellectual ability to run a large corporation or to teach in law school. Given an intellectually demanding occupation such as lawyer, physician, military officer, business executive, or engineer, and assuming we can already account for 50 percent of the criterion variance (which seems a lot to us), how much more should we expect to glean from ability *if* our knowledge of this domain were comprehensive?

Other nonability attributes: Full explication of the following idea is beyond the compass of this chapter, but it might be useful to reflect more comprehensively on the concept of *response capability,* if only briefly. Throughout our treatment, we have focused on conventional abilities assessed psychometrically using T-data (i.e., tests having right and wrong answers). One can, however, think of abilities more broadly, say, as *response capabilities.* Wallace (1965) made this point years ago in a thought-provoking paper entitled, "An Abilities Conception of Personality: Some Implications for Personality Assessment," published in the *American Psychologist.* (Unfortunately, the article culminated with an unnecessary extreme environmentalistic position that undoubtedly put off otherwise sympathetic readers.) The idea is that the concept of *response capability* goes beyond conventional ability concepts.

Consider one of Wallace's examples, *social skill,* "the efficiency with which a person can elicit positive statements from others" (p. 132). Such skills clearly have implications for one's "net" interpersonal, and hence organizational, effectiveness. Should high levels of gregariousness be thought of as an ability? Perhaps, if one's occupation involves intense levels of social contact. But for a research scientist, this tendency might be construed in negative terms, say, *inability to withstand social isolation* (Wallace, 1965, p. 133). Several *nonability* attributes surely have implications for performance in industrial settings in both debilitating and facilitating ways. Extreme levels of *anxiety* or *negative affect* (Watson & Clark, 1984) and *anhedonia* (Meehl, 1975) are most likely detrimental across most contexts, whereas exceptional levels of *hedonic capacity* (Meehl, 1975) or *positive affect* (Tellegen, 1985) and *low anxiety* (Lykken, 1968) probably function more often than not in performance-enhancing ways.

In one of her early books on counseling psychology, Tyler (1953) noted:

> Many educators, counselors included, act as though they assumed that while ability is a fixed quantity not subject to change, effort and motivation can be manipulated at will. Nothing could be farther from the truth. One of the most difficult things to cope with in counseling is a state of chronic underachievement. The student with an IQ of 160 who has just slid by in high school and is making marginal grades in college is operating under a crippling set of habits which are probably as deep-seated as anything in his personality. (p. 120)

Perhaps the inverse of such debilitating attributes would be useful to assess in conjunction with conventional abilities to paint a more comprehensive picture of individuals' actual assets, capabilities, and tendencies. Some of this is currently being done by a Project A team (McHenry et al., 1990), and the results have been combined with ability assessment to enhance prediction. Perhaps underachievers (both academic and occupational) have particularly low status on some of these more central attributes (e.g., intellectual efficiency). This status could mark low levels of dimensions of great catalytic significance when measured in reverse.

The Prediction Problem: Is There a Threshold?

It is often remarked that having ability is all well and good, but there is a point of diminishing returns beyond which more ability has little to add (Wallach, 1976). People (psychologists as well as laypersons) have been heard to say this, and there are many reasons for this belief—not the least of which is selective recall of exceptions (Dawes, 1979). When based on data, this statement almost always involves a highly skewed distribution within a highly select range of ability (Linn, 1982b). Sometimes correlations are computed using dichotomous or trichotomous criterion variables. For example, the correlation of GRE scores with graduate GPAs (a criterion variable typically having only two or three values, with disparate frequencies) is usually in the .20 to .30 range (Linn, 1982b). The comment is often made that because GRE only accounts for less than 10 percent of the variance in graduate school grades, the test cannot be worth much.

The problem with this conclusion is that it is based on a severely restricted range of ability—students who have been admitted to graduate programs. This was the burden of McNemar's (1964) criticism of some early research on creativity. Several investigators had commented on the minuscule relationship between indices of creativity and general intelligence when, in fact, the samples only comprised individuals in the top five to six percent in ability. When ability distributions are restricted (e.g., a first-year graduate class, or a department's faculty), most individuals fall within a very small ability range. The people performing at exceptional levels (such as straight-A students or highly rated faculty) are so few that their bivariate points contribute little to the overall predictor-criterion correlation. The confounding that compensatory attributes create, discussed earlier, further confuses the picture.

The following example gives a more even-handed treatment to ability parameters within the upper ranges of talent. The data were collected on eighth-grade students who were identified by the Study of Mathematically Precocious Youth (SMPY) as being in the top 1 percent of ability. These students were initially given the *Scholastic Aptitude Test* (SAT) and subsequently tracked longitudinally. Predictive validities were obtained by correlating students' eighth-grade SAT-M with their scores on the *College Board Achievement Tests* (Math 1, Math 2, Biology, Chemistry, and Physics). The latter tests were given just before the students entered college (i.e., after a four-year interval). The predictive validities ranged from .16 to .57, with a mean of .40 for the females ($N = 95$), and from .39 to .52, with a mean of .45 for the males ($N = 223$). (Sample sizes given are average, inasmuch as not all students took all five tests.) On two Advanced Placement calculus tests, the females had validities of .42 and .44, and the males, .38 for both (these are raw correlations; they are not corrected for attenuation!). These correlations demonstrate that individual differences assessed among the top 1 percent of ability in the population can have meaningful predictive validities across a four-year temporal gap.

Furthermore, in a subsequent analysis using *nontest* criteria, Benbow (1992) compared the achievement profiles of the highest and lowest fourths of a larger group of gifted students defined as before (that included the previously mentioned group). Sample sizes averaged 100 females and 367 males for the top 25 percent, and 282 females and 248 males for the bottom 25 percent. Data on a variety of criteria—earning a college degree, intellectual level of college attended, honors won, college GPA, attending graduate school, and intensity of involvement with math and science—all favored the top fourth significantly and substantively, regardless of gender. Individual differences even in the top 1 percent of ability *do* have important psychological implications. However, it takes out-of-level testing to detect these

differences (Keating & Stanley, 1972; APA, AERA, & NCME, 1985). We do not generally observe such differences because it is so seldom that we encounter a large enough sample of subjects at this level who span a substantial range of ability. But when representative samples within these ranges are assessed and criteria with sufficiently high ceilings are used, profound psychological differences emerge. This should not be surprising because this "tip" of the distribution does include about one-third of the ability range. Galton (1869) discussed this phenomenon in some detail, and the work of Julian Stanley (1983) is spiced with several fascinating examples documenting the particulars of such differences.

The most important attribute for successful performance in any highly select domain often has the least variation among the factors that contribute to achievement in that domain. This applies to all types of abilities: cognitive, perceptual, psychomotor, and even nonability attributes. (This would extend, for example, to running speed among National Football League [NFL] wide receivers, as well as height among players in the National Basketball Association [NBA]; Lubinski & Humphreys, 1990b, p. 390.) For further confirmation of this perspective, see convergent data bearing on this issue from an older age group in the latest volume of Lindzey's (1989) *A History of Psychology in Autobiography* (Vol. 8). The question to be answered is, What behavioral attributes distinguish this elite group of psychologists from psychologists in general?

Test Bias and Group Differences

Since the publication of the last *Handbook*, a voluminous literature has emerged on *test bias*. The scope of the scientific concern with this topic is reflected in the attention attracted by Jensen's book (1980a), *Bias in Mental Testing* (e.g., receiving "target article" treatment in *Behavioral and Brain Sciences;* Jensen, 1980b). Several scientific panels, both within psychology (Cleary et al., 1975) and in the larger scientific community (Hartigan & Wigdor, 1989; Wigdor & Garner, 1982), have been convened to examine the differential accuracy of statistical predictions of behavior made on the basis of test scores for different demographic groups. The *Journal of Vocational Behavior* (Gottfredson, 1988, vol. 33, no. 3) devoted a whole issue to "Fairness in Employment Testing" (edited by L. Gottfredson). Ackerman and Humphreys (1991) provide an excellent discussion of this topic in the first volume of this *Handbook*. Because we wholly concur with their treatment of the many issues they address, we will refer readers to their chapter and focus our discussion on extensions, implications, and new methodologies within this topic area. In addition to the Ackerman and Humphreys chapter, Cronbach (1975b), Humphreys (1988a, in press), and Linn (1982a, 1982b) will provide readers with other excellent reviews of the central issues and empirical findings that this literature has to offer. Also, a number of test validity issues are treated in more than just their psychometric aspects by Linn (1989) and Wainer and Braun (1988).

To add to this literature, we offer a recently developed methodology for the analysis of group differences in performance. Lubinski and Humphreys (manuscript under review) have shown that cross-validation coefficients, obtained with conventional predictor and criterion variables, can approach unity if the correlations are computed from the means for segmented intervals of the predictor and criterion variables (instead of using individual scores). This methodology is particularly noteworthy because when analyzing *group* differences in behavior, the appropriate unit of analysis should be an aggregate. This may seem obvious after the fact, but it has not been discussed in any great detail in the aforementioned literature. Typical test bias studies have employed conventional regression techniques applied to individual scores when comparing the accuracy of prediction for two or more groups, as discussed in detail in the references mentioned above.

Consider an alternative approach: Divide the predictor variable into approximately equal class intervals, say, by .20 standard deviations. Then compute bivariate means for individuals within each segment on both the predictor and the criterion variable. Then correlate these values. It is not atypical to observe correlations in the high .90s for conventional individual differences measures using this procedure. With the correlation this high, a regression equation can predict the mean level of performance in subsequent groups with great precision. Even group performance at different ages and different stages of development can be predicted with near certainty. Figure 8 presents data from Lubinski and Humphreys (manuscript under review). These data are from Project TALENT (Flanagan et al., 1962), and are based on male subjects from each of four classes, grades 9 through 12—over 180,000 high school students (about 45,000 from each class). The predictor variable for this analysis was Project TALENT's Intelligence composite and the criterion variable was a (nonacademic) General Information composite (consisting of 143 information items about, e.g., fishing, food, esoteric colors, architecture, law, the Bible, photography, games, ballet, accounting, business, and sales).

Figure 8 shows a regression equation based on a randomly selected screening sample of half of the male 12th-grade students (about 19,000 subjects). First, the Intelligence composite scale was divided into intervals of approximately .20 standard deviations. Means for the predictor and criterion variables were then computed for individuals within each predictor segment. These segment means were then standardized, based on the respective (predictor and criterion) means and standard deviations of the entire sample. A regression equation was then computed, based on 20 standardized data points (the predictor-criterion bivariate means; see Figure 8).

FIGURE 8

Cross-validation Analysis of the Regression of Group Means of General Information on Group Means of General Intelligence

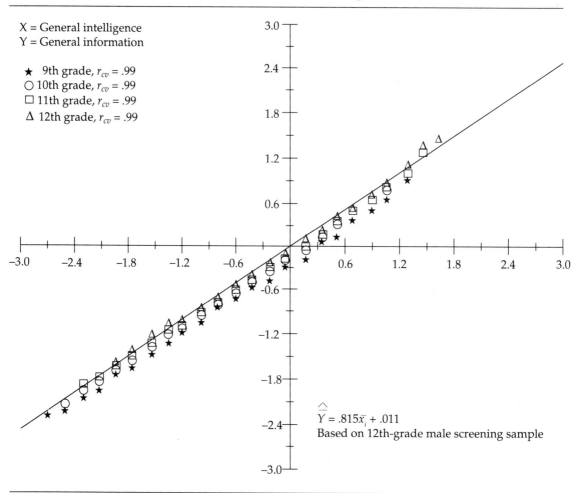

X = General intelligence
Y = General information

★   9th grade, r_{cv} = .99
○ 10th grade, r_{cv} = .99
□ 11th grade, r_{cv} = .99
△ 12th grade, r_{cv} = .99

$$\widehat{Y} = .815\bar{x}_i + .011$$
Based on 12th-grade male screening sample

Note: Data points represent bivariate means for General Information and TALENT's Intelligence composite.

Following this, the screening sample's raw-score interval values and statistics were used to divide and standardize the predictor scales for the remaining four groups: the other half of 12th-grade males (about 19,000 subjects) and the other three grade cohorts, grades 9 through 11 (about 45,000 subjects each). These groups served as the cross-validation *calibration* samples. The observed criterion values were then plotted (see Figure 8), along with the regression line based on the grade 12 screening sample. The cross-validated coefficients, computed by correlating these observed values with the predicted values, are also given in Figure 8. As Figure 8 reveals, the cross-validation coefficients all approached unity, and as grade level decreased (from 12th to 9th), systematic trends of *over*prediction were observed.

The overprediction trends reported here have also been observed in conventional regression analyses of contrasted groups (viz., groups having the lower mean on the predictor tend to be systematically overpredicted; Cleary et al., 1975; Linn, 1982b; Stanley, 1971). However, the present analysis offers a degree of precision heretofore unattainable. It would be informative to employ the foregoing methodology to other applied problems in industrial psychology as well as in psychology generally. For example, a pressing problem currently facing this country is the critical need for more engineers and physical scientists. Much research has focused on the black-white mean difference in cognitive abilities, but both these groups tend to be excelled by Asians in quantitative ability. Moreover, more than any other group, Asians tend to be limited by a GPA ceiling effect, inasmuch as Asians produce a disproportionate number of 4.0 (straight A) GPAs (Humphreys, 1988b). Hence, systematic trends of *under*prediction might be expected for this demographic group. The present methodology can be used to highlight the magnitude of such trends in a standard-score metric. (Interestingly, Asians are over-represented in the National Academy of Sciences by a ratio of 10 to 1; Havender, 1980; Vernon, 1982. Does this group differ from other groups on important work-related nonability attributes?)[12]

The foregoing methodology assumes a homoscedastic predictor-criterion relation. The precision offered by this analysis applies to *predicting group behavior, not the behavior of individuals*. Basic sample statistics should be reported so that the prediction error for individuals can be estimated. The same precision illustrated in Figure 5 may be shown by using conventional regression techniques and entering a group mean for X (in contrast to the raw score for an individual) to predict the average group performance (in contrast to an

individual's criterion performance). The enhanced precision can be seen in the modification of the individual standard error of estimate (SEE) for group estimation:

Individual SEE = $S_y(1 - r^2_{xy})^{1/2}$

Group SEE = $S_y(1 - r^2_{xy})^{1/2} / (n)^{1/2}$

For the group SEE, because we are predicting a mean with a mean, the SEE is reduced by the conventional standard error of the mean: the square root of the sample size, n.

In our present example, the Information and Intelligence composites correlated .78. Using the standard deviation of the grade 12 males, which, for the Information composite was 20.41, the SEE for an individual would be 12.77. For a group of, say, 100 individuals, the group SEE would be (individual SEE/$100^{1/2}$) or 12.77/10 = 1.28. This amount of prediction error is quite small, considering that the standard deviation of the Information composite is over 15 times this value. Thus, we can achieve great precision in the prediction of group performance by using this relatively simple methodology. (For further treatment of this methodology, see Lubinski & Humphreys, manuscript under review.)

Gender Differences in Cognitive Abilities: Implications for Meta-analytic Reviews

Several writers discussing gender differences in cognitive abilities have concluded that females have excelled in the verbal domains and males in mathematics and spatial visualization (Maccoby & Jacklin, 1974; Tyler, 1965). To a degree, this generalization still holds today. But gender differences in means on these attributes appear to be decreasing. Several meta-analytic reviews (Hyde, Fennema, & Lamon, 1990; Hyde & Linn, 1988; Linn & Hyde, 1989) and cross-sectional studies (Feingold, 1988) indicate that females and males are slowly converging toward a common mean.[13] However, these reviews and studies of gender differences only discuss differences of the first moment, that is, differences in means. There are other moments about the mean on which differences between groups may be observed. The second, third, and fourth moments quantitatively characterize variance, skewness, and kurtosis, and there are data suggesting that these statistics deserve more attention (Lubinski & Humphreys, 1990a).

A long history of individual differences research finds that males are more variable than females on many abilities, even on abilities for which females have the higher mean (Lubinski & Benbow, 1992; Lubinski & Humphreys, 1990a). Perhaps one reason that the hypothesis of greater male variability has not received the attention it deserves is to be found in the unenlightened attitudes that developed about the subject, exemplified in these forgettable remarks made by E. L. Thorndike (1906):

> The restriction of women to the mediocre grades of ability and achievement should be reckoned with by our educational systems. The education of women for such professions as administration, statesmanship, philosophy, or scientific research...is far less needed than education for such professions...where the average is essential. (p. 213)

Fortunately, but rather belatedly, we have put such attitudes behind us (for the most part). Contemporary discussions of gender differences almost always contain the caveat that the overlap in distributions is far greater and much more significant than the difference between means.

The importance of the hypothesis of greater male variability (and its implications) has been revisited recently in *Behavioral and Brain Sciences* by Benbow (1988) and several commentators (Becker & Hedges, 1988; Humphreys, 1988b; Jensen, 1988). Benbow's work focused on mathematical talent, but, as several of the

commentators pointed out, greater male variability has been observed on other cognitive abilities as well.

Discussing the hypothesis, Jensen (1980a) has placed the most stock on evidence based on "the largest, most representative sample ever tested in a single study on a group IQ test" (p. 628). This sample, although drawn back in 1932, consisted of all the children in Scotland between the ages of 10.5 and 11.5, except for the deaf and blind (N of about 87,000). The mean difference between the genders was trivial, but the male standard deviation was significantly larger than the female standard deviation (by one IQ point). Given a difference of this size, the overrepresentation of males at the extreme tails of the distribution (say, 3 or 4 standard deviations out) was striking. Gottfredson (1988) shows how, for groups manifesting a mean difference, group proportions change in different segments of the upper and lower tails of the distribution. The same phenomenon occurs for a variability difference.

Table 7 shows some Project TALENT data for over 360,000 students. Three ability composites were aggregated to measure English language, mathematical, and spatial abilities (see Lubinski & Humphreys, 1990a, for the psychometric details). For these three composites, plus the Intelligence composite previously discussed (Figure 8), males displayed greater variability, even for the English Language composite, on which the females consistently scored the higher mean.

Greater male variability was also observed in data for other nationally representative samples, collected for the National Growth Study of the Educational Testing Service (Hilton, Beaton, & Bower, 1971). This study ran from 1961 to 1967, with data collection every two years, to assess (among other things) representative statistics on the *Sequential Tests of Educational Progress* (STEP) and the *School and College Ability Test* (SCAT). These tests cover a range of academic topics including mathematics, science, social studies, reading, writing, and

TABLE 7

**Means and Standard Deviations for Four Ability Composites
From Project TALENT for Grades 9 Through 12 by Gender**

	English Language		Mathematics		Spatial		Intelligence	
	M_x	S_x	M_x	S_x	M_x	S_x	M_x	S_x
Grade 9								
Females	87.65	17.29	15.35	6.43	60.15	20.07	145.36	52.58
Males	79.51	18.11	16.01	6.98	69.18	22.54	142.48	54.22
Grade 10								
Females	92.29	17.43	16.65	7.08	63.42	20.80	157.35	52.69
Males	84.37	18.12	18.05	7.65	74.45	22.77	156.40	54.27
Grade 11								
Females	96.63	16.91	17.77	8.02	66.22	20.94	169.97	52.13
Males	89.28	17.89	20.69	8.90	79.01	22.96	173.56	53.95
Grade 12								
Females	100.27	16.55	18.60	8.15	68.49	21.31	180.08	51.56
Males	92.73	17.56	22.46	9.32	82.35	23.31	184.98	53.82

Note: Sample sizes for each cohort by gender follow: grade 9, females = 49,393, males = 49,968; grade 10, females = 47,119, males = 48,543; grade 11, females = 45,428, males = 43,851; grade 12, females = 40,116, males = 38,392. Detailed descriptions of these ability composites may be found in Lubinski and Humphreys (1990a).

verbal and quantitative abilities. With few exceptions, males were found to display more variability on these measures than females. Stanley et al. (1992) recently analyzed female-versus-male effect sizes for 86 nationally standardized tests. This analysis included data collected in the 1980s. Tests studied included the *Advanced Placement* (AP) examinations, the advanced (subject) tests of the *Graduate Record Examinations* (GRE), and the *Differential Aptitude Tests* (DAT). Repeatedly, males displayed greater variability on these measures, even on scales for which the effect sizes favored the females.

The implication of greater male variability for gender representation when stringent selection criteria are employed is obvious.

Furthermore, to the extent that these findings are valid and robust, an overrepresentation of males at the *lower* end of ability distributions should be anticipated as well. Because equal representation is a cherished value in our society, the facts about differences—in variability and not just in mean—should be scrupulously compiled. As a minimum, reporting descriptive statistics should be made a requirement for all published studies—to reverse a trend in research publication that has seen simple descriptive statistics sacrificed to accommodate the elliptical elaboration of abstruse analyses of the data. The development of methodologies for meta-analytic reviews has been fortuitous: We now appreciate the significance of standard deviations as well as means.

Whatever the causes of greater male variability may be, it is first important to establish the facts of the matter. The same principle applies to group differences in general.

Conclusion

We began our discussion with an important concept imported from experimental psychology: the criterion of scientific significance. We will close as well with another concept from experimental psychology: achievement versus topographical accounts of behavior.

A major emphasis throughout this chapter has been aggregation across diverse content, both within and between predictor and criterion domains. Psychologists have tended to label things *components* on the basis of surface features of the variables on both sides of our forecasting equations. These components typically share variance, and we have tended to underestimate their overlap. Just because entities or events share features that allow classification in a group, this does not constitute even a rudimentary basis for a scientific taxonomy. Cattell (1946) called such groupings without covariation *semantic traits*—classes found in the dictionary but having no scientific viability.

In contrast, the groupings we have recommended are predicated on parsimony emanating from covariation. At both item and scale level for predictors and criteria, indicators that have diverse content can be aggregated to converge collectively on the dominant dimensions defined by their communality. Aggregation also minimizes the bias inherent in all psychological measurement operations. The resulting structures will reflect broad dimensions that have meaningful correlates. Important systematic sources of individual differences tend to be associated with multiple indicators that have diverse content (Cattell's *source traits*, but not his *surface traits*). Indeed, given our discussion

on how construct validity is maximized by aggregating content-heterogeneous items and scales, it is questionable whether *any* surface trait *could* possess scientific significance.

This discussion is linked to the distinction between an *achievement* versus a *topographical* account of behavior (MacCorquodale & Meehl, 1954). Topographical accounts focus on the surface features of behavior, its form and content, whereas achievement accounts focus on what the behaviors actually accomplish or achieve, regardless of their response topography (Lubinski & Thompson, 1986). In modern learning theory, achievement accounts are almost always preferred. Different behavior patterns (often *perceived* as distinct abilities or skills) can function equivalently in achieving the same goals. The question is, To what extent are these ostensibly different behaviors interchangeable? To what degree do different topographies reflect only a subtle psychological difference that does not prevent them from being psychologically equivalent? Part of being a good psychologist is knowing which classes of behavior are important (i.e., scientifically significant) and which are equivalent to others. Behavior topography is deceptive. We tend to perceive components in topography, components like those reified in faculty psychology or "vectors of mind." We tend to seek recurring features in recurring events. But to assess whether our perceptions are scientifically meaningful, we have to show covariation and forecasting efficiency. Disparate behavior topographies can be grouped if they share communality. Furthermore, to the extent this communality is shared with other broad classes of behavior (not only other classes of response capability but also criterion behavior classes of interest), it becomes possible to forecast the likelihood of developing subsequent behaviors. It is in this sense that the more behaviors one has, the greater the readiness one has for developing other behaviors.

Normal Science

If one thing is apparent from the foregoing treatment of human abilities, it is that we have stayed almost exclusively with well-known sources of individual differences and traditional methods of prediction (i.e., the linear model). This decision was intentional. These variables and methods have much to offer, and the scientific significance of contemporary and future innovations will have to be measured against their achievements. If reformulations framed as paradigmatic shifts are to achieve scientific significance, they must surpass what existing techniques offer. Too often, new paradigms are advanced as replacements for existing methods without any empirical basis to support their superiority.

For example, Pavlovian and instrumental conditioning procedures have been used, with remarkable results, in studies about the behavioral consequences of drugs. Commenting on the orderliness engendered by Pavlovian and instrumental conditioning procedures in the drug evaluation field, at a time when basic principles of learning theory were considered passé, MacCorquodale (1971) wrote:

> I suppose, however, that research workers in any specialized area would really prefer to get very durable, highly reproducible but wholly innovative and hopefully disconfirming outcomes. When this happens, one can get lots of extra mileage out of his results by brandishing a new paradigm at everyone else, or at least hinting at one, and proclaiming a scientific revolution. I have heard none of that sort here. We are all still in business so far as I can see, but we have a lot of new information about a new class of discriminative, reinforcing, and eliciting stimuli. That is news; it is useful and it is constructive. But it is not revolutionary, and I am delighted. (p. 217)

Today, some 20 years after those remarks, the animal model of abuse liability of drugs is arguably the most scientifically significant animal model in all of psychology

These remarks are offered to stress that like longstanding principles from learning theory, the available methodologies for assessing human abilities can generate new knowledge that will not have a "short half-life" (Cronbach, 1975a) so characteristic of the many fads and fashions in psychology's history (Dunnette, 1966). The field of human abilities in industrial and organizational psychology has much going for it. All indications are that more useful and enduring knowledge will be generated by existing techniques, if used appropriately. Many times, investigators all too lightly dismiss well-established principles and do not assimilate existing knowledge and techniques for acquiring further knowledge, in the hope of hitting on something wholly innovative and totally creative. In fact, it is our view that creative achievements typically involve the rearrangement of existing well-established facts in novel ways.

In this chapter, we have tried to indicate throughout which articles we think are essential reading to enhance the likelihood of instrumentally effective rearrangements of existing knowledge. To this list, we add the methodological treatments by Lykken (1968, 1991) and Meehl (1990a, 1990b). These contributions also discuss some sociological influences that impede the conduct of meaningful research.

These closing remarks are offered not with the intent of deterring novel approaches, but rather because we perceive the need for researchers on human abilities to have more of a common methodological and substantive knowledge base. *There isn't all that much to assimilate,* but what we do know ought to be known by all. So that readers are aware that others have expressed similar concerns, it might be useful to quote a recent exchange by two senior investigators who have built their reputations on sound logic and normal science:

> The paradigm shift has been used to justify doing anything and everything except science.
> (Lloyd G. Humphreys, 1990, p. 153).

> I, too, think Kuhn's impact on the soft areas of psychology is unhealthy. That Humphreys arrives at views similar to mine…is reassuring to me.
> (Paul E. Meehl, 1990b, p. 173)

After all this, we leave you with not a few facts and ideas, and a not-so-short list of recommended readings.

We have profited from correspondence and discussions with a number of colleagues and friends whose talents are conspicuously public to all who know them: Camilla P. Benbow, Kathy A. Hanisch, Lloyd G. Humphreys, Paul E. Meehl, and Julian C. Stanley.

Notes

1   Although it is true that many behaviorists reject the idea of a general factor (Schmidt, 1988), upon closer analysis, concepts and findings from behavior-analytic perspectives are not incompatible with findings from individual differences research (Hull, 1945; Lubinski & Thompson, 1986; Meehl, 1986a).

2   Cattell (1950, pp. 23–27) provides an excellent introduction to the geometric interpretation of factors.

3   This idea is actually an extension of the multitrait-multimethod matrix (Campbell & Fiske, 1959). The complementary of the two ideas is especially featured by organizing the matrix around traits, as opposed to methods, and placing the correlation profiles of different measures of the same trait directly beneath the resulting monotrait triangles (see Lubinski, Tellegen, & Butcher, 1983).

4   Throughout this chapter, data from Project TALENT (Flanagan et al., 1962) will be presented to illustrate principles as well as to shed light on some unresolved empirical issues. These data were obtained from a stratified random sample of the nation's high schools. The sample contains four cohorts, grades 9 through 12, with approximately 100,000 subjects per cohort. The information collected by Project TALENT includes scores for several dozen conventional ability, interest, and personality measures, as well as biographical information, with many of the same measures used across all four cohorts. These subjects were also followed up longitudinally at three time points: 1, 5, and 13 years after high school graduation. For more detail on this huge data set, readers are referred to Wise, McLaughlin, and Steel (1979).

5   Humphreys (1962) described his experience of attempting, for seven years during the 1950s, to assemble unique predictor equations for military assignments, using Thurstone's primaries. He was able to achieve differential validity only with two large composites corresponding to Vernon's two major group factors, *v:ed* and *k:m*. Vernon (1947, 1961) has reported on a similar experience. See also Thorndike 1985, 1986.

6   Guilford has been inconsistent in his discussions of the general factor, sometimes even in the same article. In discussing optimal conditions for investigating his SI model, Guilford (1961) noted that "the selection of the population of individuals is important. In the study of intellectual abilities, there should be relative homogeneity in age, education, sex, and *general intellectual level*" (p. 8, italics added). And later, "These and other factorial learning studies should nail in its coffin for all time the notion that there is a single, general learning ability" (p. 15).

7   Both applied and theoretical psychologists might employ this procedure profitably in other contexts. For example, construct-irrelevant specific variance, rather than construct-relevant variance, is a problem with many paradigms in experimental cognitive psychology. We have concluded that the concepts of true and error scores are meaningful only in the context of reliability. As soon as we move to validity, the reliable variance of a predictor variable invariably splits into common and specific components. These two components, in turn, always split into construct-relevant and construct-irrelevant (bias) variance components.

8   Detailed descriptions of these instruments are provided by Dunnette (1976) and in *Personnel Psychology* (1990, *43*, whole issue).

9   For a discussion of the influence of socioeconomic status versus intelligence on socially valued criteria, see Lubinski and Humphreys (1992).

10   In a recent development, Ackerman (1987) has augmented the conceptual scheme of the radex to include perceptual and psychomotor abilities. The resulting conceptual structure, represented as a cylinder, is useful in conceptualizing the acquisition of skill and the role of different abilities in skill acquisition. Detailed development of this model, including its relation to information processing accounts of cognitive functioning and learning, are given in Ackerman (1987, 1988a).

11   Vernon (1961), while commenting on his work in the military, actually formulated the hypothesis for validity generalization with respect to the general factor:

> It often happened that recruits who failed in one Service job had to be reallocated, and it was usually found necessary to move them to a job requiring lower general ability and application. If they were transferred to another job at the same level, in which they claimed some interest or experience, only too often they failed again. The layman's notion that there exists a niche or special type of work ideally suited to the specialized aptitudes of each individual appeared to be much less true than the view that all types of work and all employees fall along a single high-grade to low-grade continuum. The success of women workers at skilled engineering jobs during the war further supports this view. (p. 122)

However, Vernon (1961) also appreciated the differential validity offered by more detailed ability assessment.

> Psychologists giving guidance are justified in making the fullest possible use of *g*, *v:ed*, and *k:m* tests, but thereafter their success is likely to depend chiefly on the extent to which they can gauge each candidate's previous relevant experience, ... motivation, ...[and] specific attitudes. (p. 128)

12   For a fascinating discussion of how a "minority" population, having slightly more talent than a "majority" population (as a group), may be overrepresented when extreme cutting scores are employed, see Page (1976, pp: 305–306).

13   Stanley et al. (1992) has suggested that these trends should be interpreted with caution. He writes:

> Are girls catching up with boys, and boys with girls, in cognitive respects where they once differed considerably? Feingold (1988) thought they were, based largely on his analysis of scores from two test batteries over a long period. This is hard to determine, partly because for the last 20 years or longer many test publishers have tried to minimize what some call gender "bias" by studying each test item carefully. Inevitably, a number of the "worst offenders" tend to be discarded from one revision of the test or test battery to the next. Some idea of how extensive and intensive this screening is could be obtained by studying the research and operational resources that Educational Testing Service and the College Board now devote to remedying item bias of many sorts, to what might be called "equity in testing." Their PSAT, SAT, GRE, high school achievement tests, Advanced Placement Program examinations, and others are combed over for gender, ethnic, and racial differences in various items, item types, subtests, and tests. It seems reasonable to conjecture that gender differences for its tests may decline, even without any alteration in the cognitive behavior of the examinees. (p. 43)

References

Ackerman, P. L. (1987). Individual differences in skill learning: An integration of psychometric and information processing perspectives. *Psychological Bulletin, 102,* 3–27.

Ackerman, P. L. (1988a). Determinants of individual differences during skill acquisition: Cognitive processes and information processing. *Journal of Experimental Psychology: General, 117,* 299–329.

Ackerman, P. L. (1988b). A review of Linda S. Gottfredson (Ed.), The *g* factor in employment. *Journal of Vocational Behavior* [Special issue]. *Educational and Psychological Measurement, 48,* 553–558.

Ackerman, P. L. (1989). Individual differences and skill acquisition. In P. L. Ackerman, R. J. Sternberg, & G. Glaser (Eds.), *Learning and individual differences: Advances in theory and research* (pp. 164–217). New York: Freedman.

Ackerman, P. L., & Humphreys, L. G. (1991). Individual differences theory in industrial and organizational psychology. In M. D. Dunnette & L. M. Hough (Eds.), *Handbook of industrial and organizational psychology* (2nd ed., vol. 1). Palo Alto, CA: Consulting Psychologists Press.

Albright, L. E., Glennon, J. R., & Smith, W. J. (1963). *The use of psychological tests in industry.* Cleveland, OH: Howard Allen.

American Psychological Association, American Educational Research Association, & National Counsel on Measurement in Education. (1985). *Standards for educational and psychological testing.* Washington, DC: American Psychological Association.

Becker, B. J., & Hedges, L. H. (1988). The effects of selection and variability in studies of gender differences. *Behavioral and Brain Sciences, 11,* 183–184.

Benbow, C. P. (1988). Sex differences in mathematical reasoning ability in intellectually talented preadolescents: Their nature, effects, and possible causes. *Behavioral and Brain Sciences, 11,* 169–183, 217–232.

Benbow, C. P. (1992). Academic achievement in mathematics and science of students between ages 13 and 23: Are there differences among students in the top one percent of mathematical ability? *Journal of Educational Psychology, 84,* 51–61.

Berdie, R. F., Layton, W. L., Hagenah, T., & Swanson, E. O. (1962). *Who goes where to college?* Minneapolis: University of Minnesota Press.

Berscheid, E., & Walster, E. (1969). *Interpersonal attraction.* New York: Addison-Wesley.

Brand, C. (1987). The importance of general intelligence. In S. Magil & C. Magil (Eds.), *Arthur Jensen: Consensus and controversy* (pp. 251–265). New York: Falmer Press.

Brogden, H. E., & Taylor, E. K. (1950). A theory and classification of criterion bias. *Educational and Psychological Measurement, 10,* 159–186.

Brunswik, E. (1956). *Perception and the representative design of experiments.* Berkeley: University of California Press.

Burt, C. (1949). The structure of the mind: A review of the results of factor analysis. *British Journal of Educational Psychology, 19,* 100–114.

Campbell, D. T., & Fiske, D. W. (1959). Convergent and discriminant validation by the multitrait-multimethod matrix. *Psychological Bulletin, 93,* 81–105.

Carroll, J. B. (1982). The measurement of intelligence. In R. G. Sternberg (Ed.), *Handbook of human intelligence* (pp. 29–120). Cambridge: Cambridge University Press.

Carroll, J. B. (1985). Exploratory factor analysis: A tutorial. In D. K. Detterman (Ed.), *Current topics in human intelligence: Vol. 1. Research methodology* (pp. 25–58). Norwood, NJ: Ablex.

Carroll, J. B. (1989a). Factor analysis since Spearman: Where do we stand? What do we know? In R. Kanfer, P. L. Ackerman, & R. Cudeck (Eds.), *Abilities, motivation, and methodology* (pp. 43–67). Hillsdale, NJ: Erlbaum.

Carroll, J. B. (1989b). Intellectual abilities and aptitudes. In A. Lesgold & R. Glaser (Eds.), *Foundations for a psychology of education* (pp. 137–197). Hillsdale, NJ: Erlbaum.

Cascio, W. F. (1991). Applied psychology in personnel management (4th ed.). Englewood Cliffs, NJ: Prentice-Hall

Cattell, R. B. (1946). *Description and measurement of personality.* Yonkers-on-Hudson: World Book Company.

Cattell, R. B. (1950). *Personality: A systematic theoretical and factual study.* New York: McGraw-Hill.

Cattell, R. B. (1971). *Abilities: Their structure, growth, and action.* Boston: Houghton Mifflin.

Cleary, T. A., Humphreys, L. G., Kendrick, S. A., & Wesman, A. (1975). Educational uses of tests with disadvantaged students. *American Psychologist, 30,* 15–41.

Cook, T. D., & Campbell, D. T. (1976). The design and conduct of quasi-experiments and true experiments in field settings. In M. D. Dunnette (Ed.), *Handbook of industrial and organizational psychology* (1st ed., pp. 223–326). Chicago: Rand McNally.

Cronbach, L. J. (1957). Two disciplines of scientific psychology. *American Psychologist, 12,* 671–684.

Cronbach, L. J. (1971). Test validity. In R. L. Thorndike (Ed.), *Educational measurement* (pp. 443–507). Washington, DC: American Council of Education.

Cronbach, L. J. (1975a). Beyond the two disciplines of scientific psychology revisited. *American Psychologist, 30,* 116–127.

Cronbach, L. J. (1975b). Five decades of public controversy over mental testing. *American Psychologist, 30,* 1–14

Cronbach, L. J. (1977). *Educational psychology* (3rd ed.). New York: Harcourt Brace Jovanovich.

Cronbach, L. J. (1984). *Essentials of psychological testing* (4th ed.) New York: Harper & Row

Cronbach, L. J. (1988). Five perspectives on the validity argument. In H. Wainer & H. I. Braun (Eds.), *Test validity* (pp. 3–18). Hillsdale, NJ: Erlbaum.

Cronbach, L. J. (1989). Construct validity after thrity years. In R. L. Linn (Ed.), *Intelligence: Measurement, theory, and public policy* (pp. 147–171). Urbana: University of Illinois Press.

Cronbach, L. J. (1990). *Essentials of psychological testing* (5th ed.). New York: Harper & Row.

Cronbach, L. J., Gleser, G. C., Nanda, H., & Rajaratnam, N. (1972). *The dependability of behavioral measurements: Theory of generalizability of scores and profiles.* New York: Wiley.

Cronbach, L. J., Rajaratnam, N., & Gleser, G. C. (1963). Theory of generalizability: A liberalization of reliability theory. *British Journal of Statistical Psychology, 16,* 137–163.

Cronbach, L. J., & Snow, R. E. (1977). *Aptitudes and instructional methods: A handbook for research on interactions.* New York: Irvington.

Dawes, R. M. (1979). The robust beauty of improper linear models in decision making. *American Psychologist, 34,* 571–582.

Dawes, R. M., & Corrigan, B. (1974). Linear models in decision making. *Psychological Bulletin, 81,* 95–106.

Dawes, R. M., Faust, D., & Meehl, P. E. (1989). Clinical versus actuarial judgment. *Science, 243,* 1668–1674.

Dawis, R. V., & Lofquist, L. H. (1984). *A psychological theory of work adjustment: An individual differences model and its applications.* Minneapolis: University of Minnesota Press.

Dunnette, M. D. (1963). A note on the criterion. *Journal of Applied Psychology, 47,* 251–254.

Dunnette, M. D. (1966). Fads, fashions, and folderol in psychology. *American Psychologist, 21,* 343–352.

Dunnette, M. D. (1976). Aptitudes, abilities, and skills. In M. D. Dunnette (Ed.), *Handbook of industrial and organizational psychology* (1st ed., pp. 473–520). Chicago: Rand McNally.

Dunnette, M. D., & Borman, W. C. (1979). Personnel selection and classification systems. In M. R. Rosenzweg & L. W. Porter (Eds.), *Annual Review of Psychology* (Vol. 30, pp. 477–525). Palo Alto, CA: Annual Reviews.

Eliot, J. C. , & Smith, I. M. (1983). *An international dictionary of spatial tests.* Windsor, England: NFER-Nelson.

Feingold, A. (1988). Cognitive gender differences are disappearing. *American Psychologist, 43,* 95–103.

Ferguson, G. A. (1954). On learning and human ability. *Canadian Journal of Psychology, 8,* 95–112.

Fiske, D. T. (1971). *Measuring the concepts of personality.* Chicago: Aldine-Atherton.

Flanagan, J. C., Dailey, J. T., Shaycoft, M. F., Gorham, W. A., Orr, D. B., & Goldberg, I. (1962). *Design for a study for American youth.* Boston: Houghton Miffin.

Fleishman, E. A. (1966). Human abilities and the acquisition of skill. In E. A. Bilodeau (Ed.), *Acquisition of skill.* New York: Academic Press.

Fleishman, E. A., & Quaintance, M. K. (1984). *Taxonomies of human performance: The description of human tasks.* Orlando, FL: Academic Press.

Frederiksen, N. R. (1984). The real test bias: Influences of testing on teaching and learning. *American Psychologist, 39,* 193–202.

Galton, F. (1869). *Hereditary genius: An inquiry into its laws and consequences.* London: Collins.

Ghiselli, E. E. (1966). *The validity of occupational tests.* New York: Wiley.

Ghiselli, E. E. (1972). Comment on the use of moderator variables. *Journal of Applied Psychology, 56,* 270.

Gottfredson, L. S. (Ed.). (1986). The *g* factor in employment [Special issue]. *Journal of Vocational Behavior, 29, 3,* 293–450.

Gottfredson, L. S. (Ed.). (1988). *Journal of Vocational Behavior, 32.*

Gottfredson, L. S. (Ed.). (1988). Reconsidering fairness: A matter of social and ethical priorities. *Journal of Vocational Behavior, 33*(3), 293–319.

Green, B. F. (1978). In defense of measurement. *American Psychologist, 33,* 664–670.

Guilford, J. P. (1961). Factorial angles to psychology. *Psychological Review, 68,* 1–20.

Guilford, J. P. (1967). *The nature of human intelligence.* New York: McGraw-Hill.

Guilford, J. P. (1985). The structure-of-intellect model. In B. B. Wolman (Ed.), *Handbook of intelligence theories, measurement, and applications* (pp. 225–266). New York: Wiley.

Guilford, J. P., & Michael, W. B. (1948). Approaches to univocal factor scores. *Psychometricka, 13,* 1–22.

Guion, R. M. (1965). *Personnel testing.* New York: McGraw-Hill.

Guion, R. M., & Gibson, W. M. (1988). Personnel selection and placement. *Annual Review of Psychology, 39,* 349–374.

Gustafsson, J. E. (1984). A unifying model for structure of intellectual abilities. *Intelligence, 8,* 179–203.

Gustafsson, J. E. (1988). Hierarchical models of individual differences in cognitive abilities. In R. J. Sternberg (Ed.), *Advances in the psychology of human intelligence* (Vol. 5, pp. 35–71). Hillsdale, NJ: Erlbaum.

Guttman, L. (1954). A new approach to factor analysis: The radex. In P. Lazarsfeld (Ed.), *Mathematical thinking in the social sciences* (pp. 258–348). Glencoe, IL: Free Press.

Hakel, M. D. (1986). Personnel selection and placment. *Annual Review of Psychology, 37,* 351–380.

Harman, H. H. (1976). *Modern factor analysis* (rev. 3rd ed.). Chicago: University of Chicago Press.

Hartigan, J. A., & Wigdor, A. K. (1989). *Fairness in employment testing: Validity generalization, minority issues, and the General Aptitude Test Battery.* Washington, DC: National Academy Press.

Havender, W. R. (1980). Individual versus collective social justice. *Behavioral and Brain Sciences, 3,* 345–346.

Hilton, T. L., Beaton, A. E., & Bower, C. P. (1971). *Stability and instability in academic growth: A compilation of longitudinal data.* Princeton, NJ: Educational Testing Service.

Hogan, J. C. (1991). Physical abilities. In M. D. Dunnette & L. M. Hough (Eds.), *Handbook of industrial and organizational psychology* (2nd ed., vol. 2, pp. 753–831). Palo Alto, CA: Consulting Psychologists Press.

Horn, J. L. (1985). Remodeling old models of intelligence. In B. B. Wolman (Ed.), *Handbook of intelligence: Theories, measurement and application* (pp. 267–300). New York: Wiley.

Horn, J. (1986). Intellectual ability concepts. In R. J. Sternberg (Ed.), *Advances in the psychology of human intelligence* (Vol. 3, pp. 35–78). Hillsdale, NJ: Erlbaum.

Horn, J. L., & Cattell, R. B. (1966). Refinement and test of the theory of fluid and crystallized intelligence. *Journal of Educational Psychology, 57,* 253–270.

Hulin, C. L., & Humphreys, L. G. (1980). Foundations of test theory. In A. P. Maslow, R. H. McKillip, & M. Thatcher (Eds.), *Construct validity in psychological measurement* (pp. 5–12). Princeton, NJ: Educational Testing Service.

Hull, C. L. (1928). *Aptitude testing.* Yonkers, NY: World Book Co.

Hull, C. L. (1945). The place of innate individual differences in a natural science theory of behavior. *Psychological Review, 52,* 133–142.

Humphreys, L. G. (1952). Human abilities. *Annual Review of Psychology, 3,* 5–15.

Humphreys, L. G. (1962). The organization of human abilities. *American Psychologist, 17,* 475–483.

Humphreys, L. G. (1976). A factor model for research on intelligence and problem solving. In L. B. Resnick (Eds.), *The nature of intelligence* (pp. 329–339). Hillsdale, NJ: Erlbaum.

Humphreys, L. G. (1979). The construct of general intelligence. *Intelligence, 3,* 105–120.

Humphreys, L. G. (1981). The primary mental ability. In M. P. Friedman, J. P. Das, & N. O'Connor (Eds.), *Intelligence and learning* (pp. 87–120). Plenum Press.

Humphreys, L. G. (1982). The hierarchical factor model and general intelligence. In N. Hirschberg & L. G. Humphreys (Eds.), *Multivariate applications in the social sciences* (pp. 223–240). Hillsdale, NJ: Erlbaum.

Humphreys, L. G. (1984). General intelligence. In C. R. Reynolds & R. T. Brown (Eds.), *Perspectives in mental testing* (pp. 221–248). New York: Plenum.

Humphreys, L. G. (1985). General intelligence: An integration of factor, test, and simplex theory. In B. B. Wolman (Ed.), *Handbook of intelligence: Theories, measurement and application* (pp. 201–224). New York: Wiley

Humphreys, L. G. (1988a). Trends in levels of blacks and other minorities. *Intelligence, 12,* 231–260.

Humphreys, L. G. (1988b). Sex differences in variability may be more important than sex differences in means. *Behavioral and Brain Sciences, 11,* 195–196.

Humphreys, L. G. (1990). View of a supportive empiricist. *Psychological Inquiry, 1,* 153–155.

Humphreys, L. G. (in press). Intelligence from the standpoint of a (pragmatic) behaviorist. In D. K. Detterman (Ed.), Current topics in human intelligence: Series of intelligence (Vol. 4). Norwood, NJ: Ablex.

Humphreys, L. G., Lubinski, D., & Yao, G. (manuscript under review). *Engineering schools can profitably broaden the base from which they recruit students.*

Hunter, J. E. (1980). Construct validity and validity generalization. In *Proceedings of a Conference on Construct Validity in Psychological Measurement* (pp. 199–129). Princeton, NJ: U.S. Office of Personnel Management and Educational Testing Service.

Hunter, J. E. (1983a). *The dimensionality of the General Aptitude Test Battery and the dominance of the general factor over specific factors in the prediction of job performance for USES* (Test Res. Rep. No. 44). Washington, DC: U.S. Department of Labor, U.S. Employment Services.

Hunter, J. E. (1983b). *Test validation for 12,000 jobs: An application of job classification and validity generalization analysis to the General Aptitude Test Battery* (Test Res. Rep. No. 45). Washington, DC: U.S. Department of Labor, U.S. Employment Services.

Hunter, J. (1986). Cognitive ability, cognitive aptitudes, job knowledge, and job performance. *Journal of Vocational Behavior, 29,* 340–362.

Hyde, J. S., & Linn, M. G. (1988). Gender differences in verbal ability: A meta analysis. *Psychological Bulletin, 104,* 139–155.

Hyde, J. S., Fennema, E., & Lamon, S. J. (1990). Gender differences in mathematical performance: A meta-analysis. *Psychological Bulletin, 107,* 139–155.

James, L. R. (1973). Criterion models and construct validity for criteria. *Psychological Bulletin, 80,* 75–83.

Jenkins, J. J. (1989). The more things change, the more they stay the same: Comments from an historical perspective. In R. Kanfer, P. L. Ackerman, & R. Cudeck (Eds.), *Abilities, motivations, and methodology: The Minnesota symposium on learning and individual differences* (pp. 475–491). Hillsdale, NJ: Erlbaum.

Jenkins, J. J., & Paterson, D. G. (1961). *Studies in individual difference: The search for intelligence.* New York: Appleton-Century-Crofts.

Jensen, A. R. (1980a). *Bias in mental testing.* New York: Free Press.

Jensen, A. R. (1980b). Précis of bias in mental testing. *Behavioral and Brain Sciences, 3,* 325–371.

Jensen, A. R. (1988). Sex differences in arithmetic computation and reasoning in prepubertal boys and girls. *Behavioral and Brain Science, 11,* 198–199.

Kanfer, R., Ackerman, P., & Cudeck, R. R. (1989). *Abilities, motivation and methodology: The Minnesota symposium on learning and individual differences.* Hillsdale, NJ: Erlbaum.

Kavanagh, M. J., MacKinney, A. C., & Wolins, L. (1971). Issues in managerial performance: Multitrait-multimethod analysis. *Psychological Bulletin, 75,* 34–49.

Keating, D. P., & Stanley, J. C. (1972). Extreme measures for the exceptionally gifted in mathematics and science. *Educational Researcher, 1,* 3–7.

Kelley, T. L. (1928). *Crossroads in the mind of man: A study of differential mental abilities.* Stanford, CA: Stanford University Press.

Kelley, T. L. (1939). Psychological factors of no importance. *Journal of Educational Psychology, 30,* 139–143.

Kuhn, T. S. (1970). *The structure of scientific revolutions* (2nd ed.). Chicago: University of Chicago Press.

Landy, F. J. (1990). *Psychology and work behavior* (4th ed.). Pacific Grove, CA: Brooks/Cole.

Landy, F. J., & Farr, J. L. (1980). Performance rating. *Psychological Bulletin, 87,* 72–107.

Landy, F. J., & Farr, J. L. (1983). *The measurement of work performance: Methods, theory, and applications.* New York: Academic Press.

Lindzey, G. (1989). *A history of psychology in autobiography: Volume 8.* Stanford, CA: Stanford University Press.

Linn, M. C., & Hyde, J. S. (1989). Gender, mathematics, and science. *Educational Researcher, 18,* 17–19, 22–27.

Linn, R. L. (1973). Fair test use in selection. *Review of Educational Research, 43,* 139–164.

Linn, R. L. (1982a). Admissions testing on trial. *American Psychologist, 37,* 279–291.

Linn, R. L. (1982b). Ability testing: Individual differences, prediction, and differential prediction. In A. K. Wigdor & W. R. Garner (Eds.), *Ability testing: Uses, consequences, and controversies* (pp. 335–388). Washington, DC: National Academy Press.

Linn, R. L. (1984). Selection bias: Multiple meanings. *Journal of Educational Measurement, 21,* 33–47.

Linn, R. L. (1989). *Educational measurement* (3rd ed.). New York: Collier Macmillan.

Linn, R. L., & Dunbar, S. B. (1986). Validity generalization and predictive bias. In R. A. Berk (Ed.), *Performance assessment methods and applications* (pp. 203–236). Baltimore, MD: Johns Hopkins Press.

Loevinger, J. (1954). Effect of distortion on item selection. *Educational and Psychological Measurement, 14,* 441–448.

Loevinger, J. (1957). Objective tests as instruments of psychological theory [Monograph No. 9]. *Psychological Reports, 3,* 635–694.

Lohman, D. F. (1989). Human intelligence: An introduction to advances in theory and research. *Review of Educational Research, 59,* 333–373.

Lubinski, D., & Benbow, C. P. (1992). Gender differences in abilities and preferences: Implications for the math/science pipeline. *Current Directions in Psychological Science, 1,* 61–66.

Lubinski, D., & Humphreys, L. G. (1990a). A broadly based analysis of mathematical giftedness. *Intelligence, 14,* 327–355.

Lubinski, D., & Humphreys, L. G. (1990b). Assessing spurious "moderator effects": Illustrated substantively with the hypothesized ("synergistic") relation between spatial and mathematical ability. *Psychological Bulletin, 107,* 385–393.

Lubinski, D., & Humphreys, L. G. (1992). Some bodily and medical correlates of mathematical giftedness and commensurate levels of socioeconomic status. *Intelligence, 16,* 99–115.

Lubinski, D., & Humphreys, L. G. (manuscript under review). *Seeing the forest from the trees: When predicting the behavior or status of groups, correlate means.*

Lubinski, D., Tellegen, A., & Butcher, J. N. (1983). Masculinity, femininity, and androgyny: Viewed and assessed as distinct concepts. *Journal of Personality and Social Psychology, 44,* 428–439.

Lubinski, D., & Thompson, T. (1986). Functional units of human behavior: A dispositional analysis. In T. Thompson & M. Zeiler (Eds.), *Analysis and integration of behavioral units* (pp. 315–334). Hillsdale, NJ: Erlbaum.

Lykken, D. T. (1956). Method of actuarial pattern analysis. *Psychological Bulletin, 53,* 102–107.

Lykken, D. T. (1968). Statistical significance in psychological research. *Psychological Bulletin, 70,* 151–159.

Lykken, D. T. (1991). What's wrong with psychology anyway? In D. Chiccetti & W. Grove (Eds.), *Thinking clearly about psychology.* Minneapolis: University of Minnesota Press.

Maccoby, E. E., & Jacklin, C. N. (1974). *The psychology of sex differences.* Stanford, CA: Stanford University Press.

MacCorquodale, K. (1971). Reinforcing stimulus functions of drugs: Interpretations II. In T. Thompson & R. Pickens (Eds.), *Stimulus properties of drugs* (pp. 215–217). New York: Appleton-Century-Crofts.

MacCorquodale, K., & Meehl, P. E. (1954). Edward C. Tolman. In W. K. Estes et al., *Modern learning theory* (pp. 177–266). New York: Appleton-Century-Crofts.

Marshalek, B., Lohman, D. F., & Snow, R. E. (1983). The complexity continuum in the radex and hierarchical models of intelligence. *Intelligence, 7,* 107–127.

McCornack, R. L. (1956). A criticism of studies comparing item-weighting methods. *Journal of Applied Psychology, 40,* 343–344.

McHenry, J. J., Hough, L. M., Toquam, J. L., Hanson, M. A., & Ashworth, S. A. (1990). Project A validation results: The relationship between predictor and criterion domains. *Personnel Psychology, 43,* 335–353.

McNemar, Q. (1964). Lost: Our intelligence? Why? *American Psychologist, 19,* 871–882.

Meehl, P. E. (1950). Configural scoring. *Journal of Consulting Psychology, 14,* 165–171.

Meehl, P. E. (1954). *Clinical vs. statistical prediction: A theoretical analysis and review of the evidence.* Minneapolis: University of Minnesota Press.

Meehl, P. E. (1967). Theory testing in psychology and physics: A methodological paradox. *Philosophy of Science, 34,* 103–115.

Meehl, P. E. (1975). Hedonic capacity: Some conjectures. *Bulletin of the Menninger Clinic, 39,* 295–307.

Meehl, P. E. (1978). Theoretical risks and tabular asterisks: Sir Karl, Sir Ronald, and the slow progress of soft psychology. *Journal of Consulting and Clinical Psychology, 46,* 806–834.

Meehl, P. E. (1986a). Trait language and behaviorese. In T. Thompson & M. Zeiler (Eds.), *Analysis and integration of behavioral units* (pp. 335–354). Hillsdale, NJ: Erlbaum.

Meehl, P. E. (1986b). Causes and effects of my disturbing little book. *Journal of Personality Assessment, 50,* 370–375.

Meehl, P. E. (1990a). Why summaries in psychological research on psychological theories are often uninterpretable. *Psychological Reports, 66,* 195–244.

Meehl, P. E. (1990b). Appraising and amending theories: The strategy of Lakatosian defense and two principles that warrant it. *Psychological Inquiry, 1,* 108–141, 173–180.

Muchinsky, P. M. (1990). *Psychology applied to work: An introduction to industrial and organizational psychology* (3rd ed.). Pacific Grove, CA: Brooks/Cole.

Page, E. B. (1976). A historical step beyond Terman. In D. P. Keating (Ed.), *Intellectual talent: Research and development* (pp. 295–307). Baltimore, MD: Johns Hopkins University Press.

Pearlman, K. (1980). Job families: A review and discussion of their implications for personnel selection. *Psychological Bulletin, 87,* 1–28.

Pearlman, K., Schmidt, F. L., & Hunter, J. E. (1980). Validity generalization results for tests used to predict job proficiency and training success in clerical occupations. *Journal of Applied Psychology, 65,* 373–406.

Roznowski, M. (1987). Use of tests manifesting sex differences as measures of intelligence: Implications for measurement bias. *Journal of Applied Psychology, 72,* 480–483.

Roznowski, M., & Hanisch, K. A. (1990). Building systematic heterogeneity into work attitudes and behavior measures. *Journal of Vocational Behavior, 36,* 361–375.

Rummel, J. R. (1970). *Applied factor analysis* (2nd ed.). Evanston, IL: Northwestern University Press.

Rushton, J. P., Brainerd, C. J., & Pressley, M. (1983). Behavioral development and construct validity: The principle of aggregation. *Psychological Bulletin, 94,* 18–38.

Sackett, P. R. (Ed.). (1990). *Personnel Psychology, 43.*

Sackett, P. R., Tenopyr, M. L., Schmitt, N., & Kahn, J. (1985). Commentary on forty questions about validity generalization and meta-analysis. *Personnel Psychology, 38,* 697–798.

Saunders, D. R. (1956). Moderator variables in prediction. *Educational and Psychological Measurement, 16,* 209–222.

Scarr, S., & Carter-Saltzman, L. (1980). Twin method: Defense of a critical assumption. *Behavior Genetics, 9,* 527–542.

Schmid, J., & Leiman, J. (1957). The development of hierarchical factor solutions. *Psychometricka, 22,* 53–61.

Schmidt, F. L. (1988). The problem of group differences in ability scores in employment selection. *Journal of Vocational Behavior, 33,* 272–292.

Schmidt, F. L., & Hunter, J. E. (1981). Employment testing: Old theories and new research findings. *American Psychologist, 36,* 1128–1137.

Schmidt, F. L., Hunter, J. E., & Pearlman, K. (1981). Task difference and the validity of aptitude tests in selection: A red herring. *Journal of Applied Psychology, 66,* 166–185.

Schmidt, F. L., & Kaplan, L. B. (1971). Composite vs. multiple criteria: A review and resolution to the controversy. *Personnel Psychology, 24,* 419–434.

Schmidt, F. L., Pearlman, K., Hunter, J. E., & Hirsh, H. R. (1985). Forty questions about validity generalization and meta-analysis. *Personnel Psychology, 38,* 697–789.

Schmitt, N., & Robertson, I. (1990). Personnel selection. *Annual Review of Psychology, 41,* 289–319.

Skinner, B. F. (1969). *Contingencies of reinforcement: A theoretical analysis.* New York: Appleton-Century-Crofts.

Smith, I. M. (1964). *Spatial ability: Its educational and social significance.* San Diego, CA: Knapp.

Smith, P. C. (1976). Behaviors, results, and organizational effectiveness: The problem of criteria. In M. D. Dunnette (Ed.), *Handbook of industrial and organizational psychology* (1st ed., pp. 745–775). Chicago: Rand McNally.

Snow, R. E. (1980). Aptitude processes. In R.E. Snow, P. A. Federico, & W. E. Montague (Eds.), *Aptitude, learning, and instruction: Vol.1. Cognitive analyses of aptitude.* Hillsdale, NJ: Erlbaum.

Snow, R. E. (1989). Aptitude-treatment interaction as a framework for research on individual differences in learning. In P. L. Ackerman, R. J. Sternberg, & R. G. Glasser, *Learning and individual differences: Advances in theory and research* (pp. 13–59). New York: Freedman.

Snow, R. E., Kyllonen, P. C., & Marshalek, B. (1984). The topgraphy of ability and learning correlations. In R. J. Sternberg (Ed.), *Advances in the psychology of human intelligence* (Vol. 2, pp. 47–104). Hillsdale, NJ: Erlbaum.

Snow, R. E., & Lohman, D. F. (1989). Implications of cognitive psychology for educational measurement. In R. L. Linn (Eds.), *Educational measurement* (3rd ed., pp. 263–331). New York: Collier Macmillan.

Snow, R. E., & Yalow, E. (1982). Education and intelligence. In R. J. Sternberg (Ed.), *Handbook of intelligence* (pp. 493–585). Cambridge, England: Cambridge University Press.

Spearman, C. (1904). "General intelligence": Objectively determined and measured. *American Journal of Psychology, 15,* 201–292.

Spearman, C. (1914). Theory of two factors. *Psychological Review, 21,* 101–115.

Spearman, C. (1927). *Abilities of man: Their nature and measurement.* New York: Macmillan.

Spearman, C., & Jones, L. L. (1950). *Human ability.* London: Macmillan.

Spence, K. W. (1948). The postulates and methods of "behaviorism." *Psychological Review, 55,* 67–78.

Stanley, J. C. (1971). Predicting college success of the educationally disadvantaged. *Science, 171,* 640–647.

Stanley, J. C. (1983). Introduction. In C. P. Benbow & J. C. Stanley (Eds.), *Academic precocity: Aspects of its development* (pp. 1–8). Baltimore, MD: Johns Hopkins University Press.

Stanley, J. C. (1991). Personal communication from a panel discussion. In *The Henry B. and Jocelyn Wallace National Research Symposium on Talent Development.* Iowa City, IA.

Stanley, J. C., Benbow, C. P., Brody, L. E., Dauber, S., & Lupkowski, A. (1992). Gender differences on eighty-six nationally standardized achievement and aptitude tests. In N. Colangelo, S. G. Assouline, and D. L. Ambroson (Eds.), *Talent development: Proceedings from the 1991 Henry B. and Jocelyn Wallace national research symposium on talent development* (pp. 42–65). New York: Trillium Press.

Sternberg, R. J. (1981). Testing and cognitive psychology. *American Psychology, 36,* 1181–1189.

Sternberg, R. J. (1984). Toward a triarchic theory of human intelligence. *Behavioral and Brain Sciences, 7,* 269–287.

Sternberg, R. J. (1985). *Beyond IQ: A triarchic theory of human intelligence.* New York: Cambridge University Press.

Sternberg, R. J. (in press). Theory-based testing of intellectual abilities: Rationale for the Sternberg triarchic abilities test. In H. Rowe (Ed.), *Intelligence: Reconceptualization and measurement.* Hillsdale, NJ: Erlbaum.

Taylor, R. C., & Russell, J. T. (1939). The relationship of validity coefficients to the practical effectiveness of tests in selection. *Journal of Applied Psychology, 23,* 565–578.

Tellegen, A. (1985). Structure of mood and personality and their relevance to assessing anxiety, with an emphasis on self-report. In A. H. Tuma & J. D. Maser (Eds.), *Anxiety and the anxiety disorders* (pp. 681–706). Hillsdale: NJ: Erlbaum.

Tellegen, A. (1988). The analysis of consistency in personality assessment. *Journal of Personality Assessment, 56,* 621–663.

Tellegen, A., Kamp, J., & Watson, D. (1982). Recognizing individual differences in predictive structure. *Psychological Review, 89,* 95–105.

Tenopyr, M. L. (1977). Content-construct confusion. *Personnel Psychology, 30,* 47–54.

Tenopyr, M. L., & Oeltjen, P. D. (1982). Personnel selection and classification. *Annual Review of Psychology, 33,* 581–618.

Thomson, G. (1951). *The factor analysis of human abilities* (5th ed.). New York: Houghton Mifflin.

Thorndike, E. L. (1906). Sex in education. *The Bookman*, 23, 211–214.

Thorndike, E. L. (1926). *The measurement of intelligence*. New York: Bureau of Publications, Teachers College, Columbia University.

Thorndike, R. L. (1985). The central role of general ability in prediction. *Multivariate Behavioral Research*, 20, 241–254.

Thorndike, R. L. (1986). The role of general ability in prediction. *Journal of Vocational Behavior*, 29, 332–339.

Thurstone, L. L. (1938). Primary mental abilities. *Psychometric Monographs* (No. 1).

Thurstone, L. L., & Thurstone, T. G. (1941). Factorial studies of intelligence. *Psychometric Monographs* (No. 2).

Tryon, R. C. (1935). A theory of psychological components—an alternative to "mathematical factors." *Psychological Review*, 42, 425–454.

Tyler, L. E. (1953). *The work of the counselor*. New York: Appleton-Century-Crofts.

Tyler, L. E. (1965). *The psychology of human differences* (3rd ed.). New York: Appleton-Century Crofts.

Vernon, P. E. (1947). Research on personnel selection in the Royal Navy and British Army. *American Psychologist*, 2, 35–51.

Vernon, P. E. (1950). *The structure of human abilities*. Andover Hants, England: International Thompson Publishing Services.

Vernon, P. E. (1961). *The structure of human abilities* (2nd ed.). London: Methuen London Ltd.

Vernon, P. E. (1982). *The abilities and achievements of Orientals in North America*. New York: Academic Press.

Wainer, H., & Braun, H. I. (1988). *Test validity*. Hillsdale, NJ: Erlbaum.

Wallace, J. (1965). An abilities conception of personality: Some implications for personality measurement. *American Psychologist*, 20, 132–138.

Wallace, S. R. (1965). Criteria for what? *American Psychologist*, 20, 411–417.

Wallach, M. A. (1976). Tests tell us little about talent. *American Scientist*, 64, 57–63.

Watson, D., & Clark, L. A. (1984). Negative affectivity: The disposition to experience negative emotional states. *Psychological Bulletin*, 96, 465–490.

Wherry, R. J. (1952). *The control of bias in ratings: A theory of rating* (Personnel Research Board Rep. No. 922). Washington, DC: Department of the Army, Personnel Research Section.

Wherry, R. J. (1959). Hierarchical factor solutions without rotations. *Psychometrika*, 24, 45–51.

Wherry, R. J. (1983). Wherry's theory of ratings. In F. J. Landy & F. L. Farr (Eds.), *The measurement of work performance: Methods, theory and applications* (pp. 283–303). New York: Academic Press.

Wherry, R. J., & Bartlett, C. J. (1982). The control of bias in ratings: A theory of rating. *Personnel Psychology*, 35, 521–551.

Wigdor, A. K., & Garner, W. R. (1982). *Ability testing: Uses, consequences, and controversies*. Washington, DC: National Academy Press.

Wiggins, J. S. (1973). *Personality and prediction: Principles of personality assessment*. Reading, MA: Addison-Wesley.

Wise, L. L., McLaughlin, D. H., & Steel, L. (1979). *The Project Talent Data Handbook*. American Institutes for Research, Palo Alto, CA.

Wolins, L. (1962). Responsibility for raw data. *American Psychologist*, 17, 657–658.

Zedeck, S. (1971). Problems with the use of moderator variables. *Psychological Bulletin*, 76, 295–310.

Zedeck, S., & Cascio, W. F. (1984). Psychological issues in personnel decisions. *Annual Review of Psychology*, 35, 461–518.

CHAPTER 2

Developmental Determinants of Individual Action: Theory and Practice in Applying Background Measures

Michael D. Mumford
George Mason University

Garnett S. Stokes
University of Georgia

The cry "shotgun empiricism" has represented the most common criticism of background data measures. However, recent advances in our understanding of the processes of continuity and change across the lifespan have helped stimulate new conceptions of the role of background data in psychology. After presenting an early history of background data, this discussion will focus on the nature of biodata inventories, comparing them with other descriptors of individuality. The argument is presented that the effective application of background data measures in predicting performance requires a quantitative definition of a developmental pattern. The meaningfulness of a developmental pattern is best established using a construct validation framework. A theoretical model for defining and explaining developmental patterns is described, and evidence supporting the model is presented. Item specification procedures are considered crucial for establishing validity; consequently, strategies for item development are outlined in detail. Next, scaling procedures are reviewed and evaluated in terms of their development, reliability, validity, and generality. Rational, empirical, and factorial scales are discussed in detail, and subgrouping is offered as an alternative to more traditional scaling procedures. Applications of background data in classification, individual differences, organizational development, and theoretical efforts are discussed. By applying the systematic construct validation procedures outlined in this chapter, the nature and scope of background data research will likely offer more to the field of industrial and organizational psychology.

HUMAN INDIVIDUALITY CAN be defined in many ways. One commonly accepted definition holds that people are the sum total of their behavior and experience (Allport, 1937). Recognizing that people's past behavior and experiences play a crucial role in determining the course of their lives, psychologists have displayed an abiding interest in the potential applications of life history information (C. A. Dailey, 1960; Galton, 1902). Life history data can be cast in many forms. Information concerning an individual's life history can be obtained from diaries and narrative biographies, while clinicians often obtain it through a series of interviews. Developmental psychologists, on the other hand, construct life history descriptions by tracking observational records over time.

Over the years, however, applied psychologists have come to rely on a particular form of life history information referred to as scored autobiographical data or background data. Even a cursory review of the literature is sufficient to indicate that our faith in this assessment technique is not misplaced. For instance, reviews by Ghiselli (1973), Asher (1972), Davis (1984), Owens (1976), and Reilly and Chao (1982) indicate that scales derived from this descriptive information are among our best available predictors of criteria ranging from theft to leadership performance. Studies by Lunneborg (1968), Turnage and Muchinsky (1984), and McClelland and Rhodes (1969) further indicate that this relatively straightforward assessment technique often yields better prediction than far more elaborate assessment procedures.

In this chapter, we address a number of issues pertinent to the development and application of background data measures. We then focus on general psychological principles underlying the application of background data measures in performance prediction. Following this theoretical effort, we consider certain practical issues arising in item development and scale construction as they impinge on the known psychometric characteristics of background data scales. Finally, we examine some promising new avenues for the application of life history information outside of the selection arena. We hope this effort serves not only to underscore the progress that has been made in a century of research, but also to set a sound foundation for a new wave of more sophisticated and extensive application by both theorists and practitioners.

Background Data

Early History

As recently as 1944 Guthrie enunciated what could well serve as an article of faith for bio-data researchers when he said,

> An individual's...past affiliations, political and religious, offer better and more specific predictions of his future than any of the traits that we usually think of as personality traits. When we know how men adjust themselves through learning to their situation, and also know the situations to which they have been exposed...we know the men themselves and there is no need to speculate concerning the deeper reaches of the soul until we

can explore these with similar knowledge. (Guthrie, 1944, p. 66)

Research utilizing biographical data has extended in a thin, sometimes interrupted line since the turn of the century, and psychologists cannot lay claim to initiating it. Thus, at the 1894 Chicago Underwriters' meeting (see Ferguson, 1961), Colonel Thomas L. Peters of the Washington Life Insurance Company of Atlanta, Georgia, proposed that one way to improve the selection of life insurance agents would be for managers to require all applicants to answer a list of standardized questions, such as the following:

- Present residence?

- Residences during the previous ten years?

- Birth place and date?

- Marital status?

- Dependent or not dependent for support on own daily exertions?

- Amount of unencumbered real estate?

- Occupation during previous ten years?

- Previous experience in life insurance selling? For what companies? For what general agents? When and where?

- Claims, if any, for unsettled accounts?

- References?

Such a list had been developed and used by Peters and his associates in the Georgia Association of Life Insurers. So it was not a group of psychologists, as many have believed, but a group of individuals in business who created what is truly the granddaddy of standardized personal history and application blanks.

Only a few years later Galton (1902) made his now famous statement to the effect that

the future of each man is mainly a direct consequence of the past—of his own biological history, and of those of his ancestors. It is, therefore, of high importance when planning for the future to keep the past under frequent review, all in its just proportion. (p. 2)

For over a decade after Galton, little was apparently written on biographical data or research utilizing it. However, in 1915 Woods (see Ferguson, 1961, 1962) attempted an empirical analysis of the responses of good and poor salespeople to the individual items of an application blank, and in 1917 Scott, following Woods' lead, included an application blank or personal history record among his "Aids in the Selection of Salesmen." By 1922 Goldsmith had published an article on "The Use of the Personal History Blank as a Salesmanship Test" in which the procedures of empirical item analysis and weighting were made quite explicit. Only three years later Manson (1925) reported on combining items for sales selection via multiple regression, Kenagy and Yoakum (1925) examined background factors and personal data in relation to general sales success, and Cope (see Anonymous, 1925) suggested their potential value in selecting public employees. Viteles (1932) completed a study during 1926 in which he established that an objective scoring scheme for an application blank could be used in the selection of taxicab drivers. Indeed, cross-validated on 188 new hires, a given critical score would have rejected 60 percent of poorest earners, 18 percent of average earners, and 22 percent of best earners.

In 1942, Allport reviewed the use of personal documents in psychological science. He listed them as including autobiographies, questionnaires, verbatim recordings, diaries, letters, and expressive and projective productions. He also noted that biographical data had been used in studies of attitudes and that there was apparent concern with criteria for the life history. All in all, Allport characterized the use of personal documents prior to 1920 as "uncritical," but noted that when properly handled, they do conform to the requirements of science.

Just when the notion of casting item options of an application blank into multiple-choice form first emerged is not clear. What is clear is that the military establishment of World War II enjoyed considerable success in their use of a scored biodata form. Guilford and Lacey (1947) reported average validities of 0.35 to 0.40 in predicting success of Air Force student pilots in training and comparable *r*s for navigators of 0.25 and 0.30. Similarly, Parish and Drucker (1957) reported on a 16-year research program by the Adjutant General's Office (AGO), U.S. Army, and noted that the biodata blank had been the most consistently successful device for predicting peer and tactical officer ratings of leadership in Officer Candidate School (OCS; $r = 0.45$). They also noted that a specially constructed inventory key predicted a pass versus resign criterion to the extent of an r of 0.50. Along closely related lines, Roy, Brueckel, and Drucker (1954) found the biodata blank more valid ($r = 0.26$) than any combination of ten tests of aptitude, attitude, and physical proficiency in predicting ROTC leadership ratings of officers and cadet peers at six schools ($N = 2,003$). Findings in the massive Officer Integration Program were essentially similar.

The Personnel Research Branch, AGO, U.S. Army, held a central place in activities involving wartime and early postwar uses of scored biographical data. Within this group, no one was a more outspoken champion and exponent of the biodata approach than Henry (1966), around whom much productive activity took place. He repeatedly pointed out that the consulting firm of Richardson, Bellows, and Henry found background data to be the best single predictor of a broad spectrum of industrial criteria, and he documented this finding through some 25 studies done at the New Jersey–based Standard Oil Company and its affiliates (Owens, 1976). In addition, he stimulated both conferences and research (e.g., see Owens & Henry, 1966) in a fashion that clearly made him a focal point for later developments.

Nature of Background Data

This brief historical review indicates that the basic principles used in constructing background data measures have been available for some time and underscores the point that application of this technique is based on a relatively straightforward assumption common to all life history measures: People's past behavior and experiences condition their future behavior and experiences. This is not to say that people necessarily behave in the future precisely as they have in the past, or that background data items are sensitive solely to issues of nurture. Instead this statement implies that prior learning and heredity, along with the environmental circumstances in which they express themselves, make some forms of behavior more likely than others in new situations. As a result, assessment of earlier behaviors and experiences permits some accuracy in predicting future behaviors and experiences given a knowledge of environmental demands.

Background data measures can be distinguished from other life history measures by considering the particular strategy used to capture this predictive information. Background data measures generate a description of the individual's life history through a retrospective, quasi-longitudinal, self-report format (Mikesell & Tesser, 1971). This format entails presenting individuals with a common set of questions about their behavior and experiences in particular situations likely to have occurred earlier in their lives. Thus, an item might ask, "During high school, how many times a month did you go out on dates?" In responding to these questions, people are asked to recall what they typically did or did not do or how they typically reacted to the situation presented, and then to choose the response option(s) best describing their prior behavior and experiences. Background data items can thus be regarded as tapping that part of people's developmental histories reflected in their characteristic ways of interacting with the environment.

As a vehicle for describing people's life histories, background data items have a number of advantages. First, because items can be presented through computers or paper-and-pencil questionnaires, much descriptive information can be collected at relatively low cost. Second, by presenting people with a standardized set of questions and response options, quantifiable descriptions of life histories are obtained. Third, because items provide an operationally well-defined description of life history influences, they can be structured to yield information having substantively meaningful developmental implications.

Other advantages of these items are relevant to their formats for collecting life history data. Although background data items may examine material similar to that covered by demographic questionnaires, they permit a wider range of past behavior and experiences to be examined in a fashion that facilitates substantive interpretation of pertinent developmental influences (Mumford & Owens, 1982). Objectivity certainly argues for direct observations. Background data items, however, allow this broader range of past behavior and experiences to be assessed at a substantially lower cost. Finally, Mosel and Wade (1951) have shown that interviews can capture descriptive information similar to that provided by background data items. Unlike interviews, however, background data items are not affected by observer attributions and do not involve the same expense. Background data items commonly provide a more valid and economical assessment of life history events than interview data.

Recent discussions have noted the similarity between background data measures and standard, self-report personality inventories (Hough, 1989; Mitchell, 1989). Earlier research by Rawls and Rawls (1968) indicates that background data items will predict status on personality scales, and Hough (1989) has demonstrated that factors obtained from background data are similar to factors obtained with personality, interest, cognitive, and physical ability data. Although it appears that there is some overlap in the descriptive information provided by personality and background data inventories, the two are not equivalent. Unlike items on most personality inventories, background data items focus on prior behavior and experiences occurring in specified life situations. They provide assessment within the interactionist framework that is the best available vehicle for understanding the development of many differential characteristics, including not only personality attributes, but also interests, values, skills, and certain aptitudes and abilities (Magnusson, 1988; Magnusson & Endler, 1977; Schooler, 1984).

Because background data items examine reactions to various situations, it is not surprising that they share many characteristics with interest inventories. Typically, interest inventories ask individuals to describe their liking for, or willingness to enter into, certain situations. By asking people to recall their reactions to past situational exposures, background data measures capture a likely determinant of interests, and so the kind of overlap noted by Eberhardt and Muchinsky (1984) and Hough (1989) might be expected. This observation underscores the fact that one way background data and personality measures differ is the focus of background data items on behavioral choices and situational preferences. It furthermore suggests that some overlap with value and attitude measures might be expected.

The similarity between background data measures and indices of cognitive abilities has received less attention. Aptitude, ability, and achievement measures present people with an immediate, somewhat artificial problem-solving situation intended to elicit maximum performance. The individual's success in solving these problems then serves to predict performance potential on related tasks. With background data measures, a description of typical behavior and experience in real-life situations is called forth from memory and used to predict performance. As a result, background data measures cannot provide upper bound descriptions of performance potential, although they may prove useful in predicting observed performance levels. This distinction suggests that background data measures may have more in common with measures of practical intelligence (Wagner & Sternberg, 1985) than traditional cognitive measures. To the extent, however, that the expression of traditional cognitive capacities is influenced by prior developmental events, or these abilities influence the conditions and outcomes of various situational exposures, some degree of relationship would be expected between background data measures and ability inventories (Schoenfeldt & Lissitz, 1974; Terman, 1959).

Taken as a whole, it appears that background data items share much in common with personality and interest inventories. Background data measures, however, are broader because they capture prior behavior and experiences that condition both selection of situations and behavioral reactions to these situations. Yet, as illustrated in our comparison of background data and ability inventories, one can expect background data measures to be related to measures of any differential characteristic that develops at least in part as a function of prior life experiences. This suggests that some caution must be used in equating background data measures with any particular kind of differential characteristic. Of course, it is the ability of background data items to capture the developmental events impinging on many forms of later behavior and experiences

that makes them particularly useful in performance prediction.

Prediction and Validation

Developmental Patterns and Prediction

Background data items capture prior behavior and experiences in discrete situations that occurred earlier in people's lives. One implication of this is that whenever a background data item predicts performance, it must represent an antecedent or sign for later performance. This observation led Owens (1976) to argue that performance prediction using background data items is based on a developmental strategy. In other words, to predict performance through background data items one must acquire a set of background data items capable of capturing prior behaviors and experiences impinging on the later expression of criterion performance.

Most criterion performances are held to be conditioned by the operation of multiple causal influences. Thus, leadership performance might be conditioned by intelligence, dominance, power, subordinate skills, and economic resources, among other variables (Fiedler & Garcia, 1987; Lord, DeVader, & Alliger, 1986; Yukl, 1973). In the case of background data measures, we are necessarily interested only in those influences that are a property of the individual, such that dominance and intelligence would be of concern rather than economic resources or subordinate skills. We also wish to predict performance based on properties of the individual. The developmental orientation of background data measures implies that this might be accomplished in one of two ways. First, one might seek items reflecting behaviors and experiences contributing to the development of these individual differences. Second, an attempt might be made to identify items reflecting the prior operation of these differences as manifest in behavior and experiences elicited by situations occurring earlier in people's lives. Mumford and Owens (1987) have referred to these two strategies for item specification as the *indirect* and *direct* approaches, respectively.

Of course, no single item will provide a fully adequate marker for the prior operation or development of individual differences variables. Moreover, items will vary considerably in differential representation of relevant variables. Further, these variables will not be of equal importance in determining performance, and so items must be weighted to capture differential importance or influence. Effective prediction requires that behavioral and experiential antecedents of these variables be identified and weighted based on their relationship or contribution to criterion performance. Thus, Mumford and Owens (1987) argued that the effective application of background data measures in performance prediction requires a quantitative definition of a developmental pattern.

A variety of techniques might be used to define developmental patterns. Traditionally, however, these patterns of differential developmental influences have been defined through an empirical keying strategy. When empirical keys are used, the item responses of members of a criterion group, such as good performers, are contrasted with the item responses of the members of a reference group, such as the current pool of job applicants, from which criterion group members are to be drawn. Items or item response options are then weighted on the basis of their ability to discriminate group members, and the validity of the pattern is assessed in terms of its ability to predict criterion performance and the stability of prediction in a cross-validation sample (Schwab & Oliver, 1974). Hence, the meaningfulness of the pattern is established through demonstrated stability of prediction without any necessary reference to broader theory or item content.

Certainly, this empirical keying strategy is consistent with the multivariate nature of background data and establishes the meaningfulness of a developmental pattern with regard to specific inferences to be drawn concerning later performance. Nonetheless, a purely empirical approach to pattern definition has been criticized (Korman, 1968). Dunnette (1962) has argued that such unadulterated empiricism may stymie development of theory, and Henry (1966) has pointed out that the resulting lack of understanding may, in the long run, set undue bounds on the predictive power of background data measures. Other work by Dunnette, Kirchner, Erickson, and Banas (1960), Wernimont (1962), and Schwab and Oliver (1974) indicates that this approach may also yield unstable measures of limited general value due to capitalization on idiosyncratic differentiating influences operating in a particular sample.

In a somewhat different vein, Thayer (1977) has noted that any empirical keying strategy assumes that the criterion in use provides a fully adequate representation of the performance of ultimate interest. Hence, the utility inferences drawn from these validity coefficients will diminish along with the quality of the criterion measure used to represent the performance of ultimate interest. Thus, an ostensibly impressive validity coefficient of .60 may result in grossly misleading inferences about outcomes that are of ultimate interest.

Pace and Schoenfeldt (1977) and O'Leary (1973) have questioned the rote application of a purely empirical approach to pattern definition on somewhat different grounds. They argue that rote empiricism may yield misleading inferences in the individual case due to the operation of non–job-relevant variables. For instance, an item asking "How far do you live from work?" might predict turnover but be an indirect measure of social class if the job were located in a "high rent" district. Hence, a potentially stable worker who does not live near the job might be unduly excluded.

This argument has since been extended by Mumford and Owens (1987), who note that the utility of a strict empirical strategy will be influenced by the quality of the item pool in use. They suggest that an empirical key will yield poor prediction and misleading inferences concerning individual performance, regardless of overall predictive power, when the item pool is (a) deficient due to a failure to capture the antecedents influencing the causal variables that significantly affect later performance for some or all individuals; (b) contaminated by the inclusion of antecedent behavior and experiences reflecting irrelevant, extraneous, or confounding influences with respect to the determinants of later performance; or (c) biased by a failure to capture shifts across age, race, sex, and other groups in the antecedent behaviors or causal influences conditioning performance. Without some evidence indicating that these item problems are not present, drawing firm conclusions concerning the predictive efficiency of background data measures may prove difficult because poor prediction might be attributed either to inadequate items or an intrinsic failure of background data items to predict. Schwab and Oliver's (1974) study provides one illustration of the principle. Information about the item pool was not provided for the clerical, unskilled labor, and machinists' jobs under consideration; thus, the failure of the empirical keys to cross-validate could just as easily be attributed to poor items as to the inappropriateness of background data measures.

Construct Validity

Our foregoing observations suggest that a single cross-validated coefficient may not provide a sufficient basis for appraising the meaningfulness of the developmental pattern defined by a background data measure. Given the extant literature, the question arises as to how one might go about appraising meaningfulness of these developmental patterns.

Any background data measure represents an attempt to organize people's prior behavior and experiences in such a way as to allow general lawlike statements concerning their likely behavior and experiences in future situations. Of course, there are many ways of organizing people's prior behavior and experiences, only some of which may be meaningful. As with any other psychological test, our ultimate concern in validation is to establish the substantive meaningfulness of the organization we have imposed on people's past behavior and experiences (Messick, 1975, 1980).

Exactly what constitutes an empirical demonstration of meaningfulness has long been debated (Mulaik, 1986). Although points of view differ concerning exactly how one should go about establishing the meaningfulness of an interpretive, organizing structure (Cook & Campbell, 1979), Cronbach and Meehl (1955) and Simon (1953, 1977), among others, have argued that meaning arises from the definition of functional relationships, allowing inferences to be drawn concerning the likely status of an object given certain known conditions. In essence, then, meaning is established using a set of propositional relational statements, derived from underlying theoretical conceptions that can be shown to hold in reality.

Similar thoughts concerning the nature of construct validity have been put forth by James, Mulaik, and Brett (1982), Landy (1986), and Guion (1974, 1980). These observations, moreover, lead to three important conclusions. First, many inferences might be drawn concerning the future implications of a developmental pattern; thus, the construct validation of any background data measure will never really be complete. Instead, inferences of meaningfulness must be based on the overall pattern of evidence. Second, as the number and diversity of the confirmed inferences increase, there is a stronger basis for an inference of meaningfulness. Third, there is no one absolute strategy for specifying and establishing the existence of interpretable, functional relationships. Rather, a variety of different strategies might be used, including those falling under the traditional rubrics of content and criterion-related validity (Cook & Campbell, 1979; Guion, 1980).

These statements should not be taken to imply that criterion-related validity is of no importance. Because criterion-related validation strategies focus directly on establishing whether the constructs representing the developmental pattern will predict performance in the target situation, they provide a critical source of validation evidence given the purpose of assessment. Thus, it is hardly surprising that the meaningfulness of background data scales is commonly assessed on the basis of this evidence (Ghiselli, 1973; Kirchner & Dunnette, 1957; Mosel, 1952; Owens, 1976; Owens, Schumacher, & Clark, 1957; Reilly & Chao, 1982). Although the value of criterion-related evidence is undoubted, a construct validation framework points to a number of strategies that might be used to improve the quality of criterion-related validation evidence.

For instance, any operational criterion only approximates, to some degree, the ultimate criterion of concern. Thus, to the extent that a background data measure can be shown to predict multiple alternative operationalizations of the criterion construct, a stronger basis for inferring meaningfulness is provided. This point is nicely illustrated in a study by Buel, Albright, and Glennon (1966) in which a 33-item key developed to predict scientific innovation in a petroleum company correlated .52, .29, and .32, respectively, with ranking, patent, and publication rate criteria. This pattern of results provides greater confidence in the value of the key as a predictor.

A stronger inference of meaningfulness is also justified when a measure's predictive power can be shown to generalize to other jobs or job situations where performance is conditioned by similar causal constructs.

Illustrations of this principle may be found in Richardson, Bellows, Henry, & Co.'s (1984a, 1984b, 1984c) attempts to generalize their background data keys across entry-level managerial positions in a number of organizations and in the work of C. W. Taylor and his colleagues on the generality of creativity keys (Ellison, James, & Carron, 1970; Ellison & Taylor, 1962; James, Ellison, Fox, & Taylor, 1972, 1974; C. W. Taylor & Ellison, 1967).

More recent work by Rothstein, Schmidt, Erwin, Owens, and Sparks (1990) has shown how meta-analysis procedures can be used to accrue additional evidence for the generality and meaningfulness of background data scales. This work is intriguing because it suggests that background data measures of constructs, such as self-esteem and work ethic values, promoting skill development in a variety of new situations may prove especially likely to evidence generalized predictive power (Fleishman & Mumford, 1989; Mumford, Reiter-Palmon, & Snell, in press; Mumford, Uhlman, & Kilkullen, in review; Murphy, 1989).

An additional lesson that can be drawn from this construct validation framework concerns the use of multiple kinds of criterion measures. When multiple, well-founded criteria can be obtained, alternative hypotheses drawn with regard to these criteria may provide a stronger basis for inferences of meaningfulness. Hough (1984) has, in fact, applied this strategy in developing a behavioral consistency background data measure intended to capture job relevant skills, arguing that these skills should increase with experience as well as predict performance. Thus, her finding that correlations on the order of .30 were obtained for job experience criteria (years of experience) permitted a stronger inference of validity than would have been possible considering only the relationship with job performance.

As multiple relational inferences are drawn, one moves into the domain of pure construct validity arguments. Broadly speaking, relational inferences of this sort might follow one of two forms, either focusing on the relationships among certain aspects of the background data items in use or focusing on relationships with external measures. The latter strategy has been employed in studies by Owens (1976) and Klimoski (1973). In the Owens (1976) investigation, the meaningfulness of a set of factorially derived background data scales was supported, based on the correlations obtained with a set of personality and values measures. For instance, a women's cultural/literary scale was found to yield a positive relationship with measures of cognitive values ($r = .32$) and integrative complexity ($r = .29$), but yielded negative relationships with indices of authoritarianism ($r = -.18$) and economic values ($r = -.19$). Similarly, Klimoski (1973) factored the engineering background data items developed by Chaney and Owens (1964) and Kulberg and Owens (1960), then determined how these factors were related to occupational positions of 960 engineering students more than five years after graduation. Because the research interest factor was found to be related to movement into research positions while the athletic participation and self-perception factors were found to be related to movement into managerial positions, some evidence indicative of meaningfulness was obtained for these background data scales.

Although a few studies have used internal relationships as part of an attempt to assess meaningfulness (DuBois, Loevinger, & Gleser, 1952; Matteson, 1978; Owens, 1976), the most sophisticated effort along these lines may be found in a recent study by Schoenfeldt and Mendoza (1988). In this investigation, a model of managerial work behavior was used to specify managerial activity dimensions having a priori, explicitly defined relationships with each other. Subsequently, background data items were constructed to capture prior behavior and experiences indicative of the hypothesized managerial competencies, role preferences, and style preferences. Items were administered to 1,500 college students, and structural equation models were used to determine whether item responses could be accounted for by the dimensions they were intended to tap and their interrelationships. It was found that the hypothesized model accounted for much of the variance in item responses, thereby providing evidence of the measure's meaningfulness.

The Schoenfeldt and Mendoza (1988) investigation also underscores the importance of underlying theory in validating background measures. Without hypotheses concerning the determinants of performance and the developmental events influencing them, items of testable content cannot be developed, and without such items strong tests of construct validity cannot be conducted. Thus, hypotheses concerning the developmental determinants of performance play a role in all validation efforts.

Content Validity

In recent years, investigators have become more sensitive to the fact that the procedures used in item specification can provide a basis for inferring meaningfulness (Guion, 1977, 1980; Lawshe, 1985). This content validity argument can also be applied to background data measures based on the procedures used in item development. Because the construction of a content-valid measure requires an adequate sampling of behaviors from some predefined domain, an argument for content validity can be made when evidence is provided that (a) the variables influencing behavior in the target situations have been accurately specified through a careful and thorough job analysis (Fine & Wiley, 1971; D. C. Myers & Fine, 1980); (b) prior behaviors and experiences that would act to signal the earlier expression of these variables or contribute to their development have been identified (Chaney & Owens, 1964; Pannone, 1984); and (c) items have been carefully developed to accurately assess the developmental hypotheses (Owens & Henry, 1966).

In considering this strategy for generating content validity evidence, the emphasis is placed on content validity vis-à-vis generative psychological processes rather than face validity. Content-valid background data items need not look like criterion performance, however desirable this may be for user acceptance. Rather, they must capture developmental influences relevant to the variables that are conditioning behavior. This point is of some importance since in many situations where direct job-relevant experience is lacking, content-valid items can still be developed despite limited face validity. Further, this process orientation underscores the fact that content validity arguments must consider potential differences in the meaning of different subpopulation patterns in important influences, as well as the developmental events influencing the emergence and expression of the variable. Thus, content-valid items need not be the same for men and women or across cultures. Finally, it is important that a sufficient sample of events be generated to provide for a reliable assessment of each variable across subpopulations.

The predictive utility of systematic item development procedures has been illustrated in studies by Quaintance (1981) and Williams (1961). In these investigations, items were classified on the basis of whether hypotheses concerning how they influenced or reflected the development of criterion performance could or could not be formulated. It was found that items for which such hypotheses could be formulated were significantly more likely to yield sizable predictive validity coefficients. In a related investigation, Redmond and Nickels (1989) attempted to identify hypotheses as to why items would predict academic performance and social effectiveness using the direct and indirect approaches. When 20-item empirical keys were constructed using items selected at random as well as items selected based on direct and indirect hypotheses, it was found that keys constructed using items based on hypotheses produced larger cross-validities than keys constructed using items selected at random. However, the direct approach keys performed better than the indirect keys when small numbers of items were in use, perhaps due to the large number of developmental events conditioning the ontogeny of various variables.

Despite the support these studies provide for the predictive utility of item pools derived from causal hypotheses, many investigators denigrate the value of this sort of validity evidence because substantively meaningful items often fail to yield significant criterion-related validity coefficients in empirical keying efforts. On the other hand, it should be recognized that such effects can also be attributed to (a) the lack of well-founded hypotheses (Case & Stewart, 1957; Siegel, 1956a), (b) a poorly articulated framework for hypothesis development (McGinnies & Vaughan, 1957), and (c) the use of small restricted incumbent samples in many empirical keying efforts (Morrison & Sebald, 1974; J. H. Myers & Errett, 1959).

Recent studies using content validation strategies have shown that systematic item development procedures may prove of substantial value in drawing inferences concerning the meaningfulness of background data measures. For instance, D. C. Myers and Fine (1980) and Pannone (1984) generated background data items intended to assess prior experience with job relevant tasks, and the resulting scales were found to yield interpretable patterns of relationships with other relevant measures, while proving of some value as an applicant screening tool. Using the behavioral consistency approach (Wernimont & Campbell, 1968), Hough (1984) found that life history essays intended to capture relevant constructs evidenced validity as potential predictors of performance while yielding substantively interpretable descriptions of performance potential.

In addition to the desirable characteristics demonstrated in these studies, the construction of content-valid measures may serve investigators in a number of other ways. First, by orienting item generation around an underlying causal system, new kinds of item screening efforts become possible because items failing to correlate with other indices of the construct can be eliminated. Second, the generation of items in relation to underlying constructs makes it possible to develop parallel forms, and this is advantageous whenever retesting is required or test security is of concern. Third, by focusing item development on performance-relevant dimensions, transient applicant pool characteristics are unlikely to exert as much influence on the validity of background data scales, thereby enhancing stability. Fourth, these procedures should tend to minimize the problems associated with deficiency, contamination, and bias by targeting item development on the determinants of performance while freeing background data measures from absolute dependence on a single, fallible criterion measure. Fifth, by focusing item development on well-specified dimensions, validity generalization efforts become more plausible, and it becomes possible to formulate general item pools for use in multiple studies. Finally, because background data items seek to capture antecedents of performance, examination of the results obtained in multiple studies employing this approach might prove useful in attaining some understanding of criterion performance, thereby facilitating intervention design and theory development (Barron & Harrington, 1981).

Taken as a whole, these observations suggest that application of content and construct validation principles will prove of substantial value. Not only will the availability of this evidence permit stronger inferences of meaningfulness, it will also serve to eliminate many of the more common criticisms of background data measures. Given the substantial utility of content and construct validation efforts in this regard, one must wonder why these validation strategies have been so slow to take root in the background data literature. One plausible answer lies in the nature of empirical keys. The specificity of empirical keys to a particular sample and criterion measure may not be a disadvantage in performance prediction (Mitchell & Klimoski, 1982). This very same specificity does, however, make it difficult to attain a general understanding of patterns of differential development and, therefore, the kind of constructs or relational networks we should be using in our validation efforts. Given the importance of well-defined constructive networks in drawing inferences concerning a measure's content and construct validity, it is not surprising that it has proven difficult to extend our validation efforts to incorporate these notions.

The Nature of Developmental Patterns

Defining General Patterns

Recognizing that the criterion specificity of empirical keys limits our ability to attain a general understanding of patterns of differential development and thus the constructs conditioning the predictive power of background data measures, Owens (1968, 1971, 1976) suggested a potential solution to this problem. He argued that it might be possible to identify general patterns of differential development without reference to particular criterion measures. Subsequent studies designed to elucidate the factors giving rise to these general patterns of differential development might be used to obtain a general understanding of the ontogeny of these patterns and suggest the kind of constructs we might use in efforts to examine a specific kind of criterion performance.

In an initial attempt to determine whether these general patterns of differential development could be identified, Owens and

Schoenfeldt (1979) administered 389 background data items (*Biographical Questionnaire; BQ*) focusing on behavior and experiences occurring during childhood and adolescence to 1,037 men and 897 women entering the University of Georgia. After men's and women's item responses had been subjected to separate principal component analyses, their component scores were used to form a set of profiles, and the similarity of these profiles was assessed using a d^2 index (Cronbach & Gleser, 1953). A modified Ward and Hook (1963) clustering procedure was then used to group individuals together in such a way as to minimize within-group variation while retaining the smallest number of subgroups possible. This analysis yielded 23 male and 15 female subgroups.

Subsequent examination of the characteristics of these subgroups indicated that (a) most individuals (73%) could be adequately described by virtue of assignment to a single subgroup; (b) these subgroups were sufficiently stable that they could be applied in new samples with no more than a 10 percent loss in the number of individuals assigned to a single subgroup; (c) subgroup members' differential characteristics on the background data items and component scores were sufficiently cohesive that a brief consensual label could be devised which appeared to summarize the crucial characteristics of their pattern of differential development; and (d) these patterns were sufficiently stable that they could be used to account for the differences subgroup members manifested on a battery of standard psychological inventories, including measures such as the *Scholastic Aptitude Test* (SAT), the *Strong Interest Inventory*, the *California F Scale*, and the *Eysenck Personality Inventory*. Table 1 presents a brief description of some of these subgroups for the male subjects.

To determine whether these developmental patterns did indeed provide a general description of differential development, their ability to account for a variety of criterion performances was assessed. To accomplish this, a series of 50 field studies was conducted. In these investigations select subgroups were identified, and hypotheses were formulated about how they should perform on tasks drawn from different domains. Subgroup status was found to predict a remarkably wide range of criterion performances, such as academic over- and underachievement (Klein, 1972), Rorschach responses (Frazier, 1971), vocational interests (Jones, 1970; L. L. Thomas, 1982), and drug use (Strimbu & Schoenfeldt, 1973). Table 2 presents a summary of the results obtained in these studies broken down by content area. Overall, it was found that subgroup status was an effective predictor of performance in approximately 80 percent of the studies and that the observed differences were consistent with the subgroups' characteristic developmental pattern. Especially salient, however, was the finding that these subgroups were particularly likely to capture differences in motivationally and dispositionally loaded criteria.

Having provided some evidence that it was possible to identify patterns of development manifesting general cross-criteria predictive implications, a series of later investigations attempted to elucidate the predictive characteristics of these subgroups. In an initial effort along these lines, Feild and Schoenfeldt (1975a) administered a 58-item background data inventory (*College Experience Inventory;* CEI) examining significant behaviors and experiences occurring during the college years to members of the initial Owens and Schoenfeldt (1979) subgroups as they graduated from the university. The CEI items were then factored and a canonical discriminant analysis was used to determine how well membership in the Owens and Schoenfeldt (1979) subgroups would predict collegiate behavior and experiences. This analysis revealed that membership in the adolescent subgroups could account for 33 percent of the variance in the first canonical variate in collegiate behaviors and experiences. In a related investigation, Davis (1984) administered a 116-item background data

TABLE 1

Description of Male Biographical Subgroups in Terms of Distinctive Stands on Selected Biographical Factors, Reference Measures, and Feedback Data

Group	Subgroup	Description
Indifferent low-achieving artists	Biodata	(H) SES; (L) pseudointellectualism, scientific and athletic interest
	Reference	(H) music teacher (Strong); (L) long-term goals, cognitive values
	Feedback	(H) music majors, drug users; CGPA = 2.73
Traditional, science-oriented achieving leaders	Biodata	(H) academic achievement; (L) social introversion
	Reference	(H) social-religious conformity, HS grade point, Reverse F; (L) inhibition
	Feedback	(H) biological science, physical science majors, campus leaders; CGPA = 3.08
Cognitively simple, nonachieving business major	Biodata	(H) pseudointellectualism; (L) agressiveness-independence
	Reference	(H) negative emotionality, conceptual simplicity; (L) SAT
	Feedback	(H) business, law, health, and physical education majors, careless in completion of BQ; CGPA = 2.55
Unconventional, overachieving, self-directed leaders	Biodata	(H) academic achievement; (L) religious activity
	Reference	(H) radicalism, advertising, psychiatrist, librarian (Strong); (L) tender-minded, F scale, externalization, social-religious conformity, negative emotionality, conceptual simplicity, neuroticism
	Feedback	(H) law majors, campus leaders, drug users, over-achievers, homosexuals; CGPA = 3.07
Analytical independents	Biodata	(H) scientific interest; (L) parental control
	Reference	(H) emotional exposure, cognitive complexity, long-term goals
	Feedback	(H) speech pathology and education, biological science majors, probations, drug users; CGPA = 2.81

T A B L E 1

Description of Male Biographical Subgroups in Terms of Distinctive Stands on Selected Biographical Factors, Reference Measures, and Feedback Data (continued)

Group	Subgroup	Description
Cognitively complex religious converters	Biodata	(H) agressiveness-independence, academic attitude, religious activity; (L) social introversion, scientific interest
	Reference	(H) F scale, social-religious conformity, long-term goals, emotional exposure, cognitive complexity, extraversion, neuroticism, occupational level (Strong); (L) computer programmer and osteopath (Strong)
	Feedback	(H) music, speech and journalism, social science majors, careful in completing BQ; CGPA = 3.04
"Eggheaded" leaders	Biodata	(H) social introversion, positive adjustment response bias; (L) parental control, athletic interest
	Reference	(H) HS grade point, SAT, printer (Strong); (L) physical goals, positive emotionality and emotional exposure, extraversion, life insurance salesman and chamber of commerce executive (Strong)
	Feedback	(H) language, physical science, agriculture, dramatic arts, pharmacy majors, leaders; CGPA = 3.16
Business-oriented "Fraternity Joe"	Biodata	(H) academic attitude, SES
	Reference	(H) economic values, physical goals, extraversion; community recreation director, chamber of commerce executive, credit manager (Strong); (L) physicist, dentist, artist (Strong)
	Feedback	(H) business, humanities majors; CGPA = 2.79

Note: Only a limited number of the male subgroups are represented here for the purpose of illustration. More detailed information may be obtained by consulting Owens and Schoenfeldt (1979).

H = high; L = low; HS = high school; CGPA = college grade point average; SAT = *Scholastic Aptitude Test*; Biodata refers to factor scores on Owens' *Biographical Questionnaire*; Reference refers to scores obtained on various measures of personality, interests, values, and cognitive abilities; Feedback refers to results obtained from field studies on a number of different subgroups.

TABLE 2

Summary of Feedback Study Results

Domain[a]	Study Results[b]		
	Number of Studies	Number Positive	Percent Positive
Personality	8	8	100
Interests, attitudes, values, and motives	12	10	83
Cognition, creativity, and decision making	8	7	88
Social processes	7	5	71
Learning and memory	4	3	75
Perception	2	1	50
Physical and physiological phenomena	3	1	33
Methodology	4	3	75

[a] Domain is by major distinction in literature and studies were classified into mutually exclusive domains despite some cross-domain implications.
[b] Study results differ from Owens and Schoenfeldt (1979) due to the inclusion of some new studies and the use of only studies having subgroup implications herein.

questionnaire (*Post-College Experience Inventory;* PCEI) examining behaviors and experiences in developmentally significant situations likely to occur during the first 10 years following graduation. After factoring the PCEI items and examining the ability of Owens and Schoenfeldt's (1979) subgroups to account for variance in these factor scores using Feild and Schoenfeldt's (1975a) canonical discriminant techniques, he found that these patterns would account for 17 percent of the variance in postcollege behaviors and experiences. Thus, it appears that these general developmental patterns in some way condition a variety of later behavior and experiences, although the strength of this predictive power diminishes over time.

In an extension of these initial efforts, Jackson (1982) used the procedures proposed by Owens and Schoenfeldt (1979) to formulate a set of male and female subgroups based on the collegiate and postcollegiate background data.

Examination of the resulting subgroups indicated that effective solutions, in terms of the number of individuals fitted to a single subgroup and the interpretability of the subgroups' item characteristics, could be obtained in these later developmental periods. While this generality data is of some interest in its own right, of greater interest are the results obtained when movement across the subgroups identified in these three developmental periods was examined. In this study, Stokes, Mumford, Jackson, and Owens (1990) examined how individuals moved from the adolescent subgroups to the collegiate subgroups to the postcollegiate subgroups. The results obtained in a series of chi-square analyses indicated that the members of an initial adolescent subgroup tended to enter only 2 or 3 of some 13 collegiate subgroups, while the members of a given collegiate subgroup tended to enter 2 or 3 of the 11 postcollege subgroups.

Figure 1 presents the movement from adolescence subgroups to college and postcollege subgroups for members of one male and one female subgroup. The patterns of behavior people manifested in later years tended to be consistent with those they displayed earlier in their lives, thereby suggesting that earlier developmental patterns tended to condition later developmental patterns.

The existence of these systematic relationships suggested to Mumford and Owens (1984) that it might be possible to formulate general developmental patterns extending across these three developmental periods. To accomplish this, 417 men and 358 women who had responded to the adolescent, collegiate, and postcollegiate background data items were identified. Responses to the items contained in all three inventories were then factored separately by gender, and men and women were subgrouped using the procedures used by Owens and Schoenfeldt (1979). It was found that 84 percent of the men and 87 percent of the women could be fitted to a single one of the 15 male and 17 female subgroups. Examination of mean differences characterizing members of each subgroup on the background data and reference measures indicated that (a) these subgroups captured interpretable developmental patterns associated with substantively interpretable differences on both the background data items and reference measures, (b) across periods there might be changes in the nature of subgroup members' characteristic behavior and experiences, and (c) these changes tended to be consistent with their earlier pattern of behavior experiences that would affect their ability to cope with the environmental demands confronting them in new development periods imposing different task requirements.

Explaining Developmental Patterns: The Ecology Model

Having shown that general patterns of differential development could be identified,

patterns which to some extent were maintained over time, the next question to arise concerned how one might account for the nature and ontogeny of these patterns. To address this issue, Mumford, Stokes, and Owens (1990) and Stokes, Mumford, and Owens (1989) have proposed a general theoretical framework they have referred to as the *ecology model*. Essentially, this model views the individual as an active, purposeful entity, who through learning, cognition, and action seeks to maximize personal adaptation in a world of shifting environmental opportunities (Bandura, 1986; Caspi, 1987; Endler, 1982; Lerner, 1978; Magnusson, 1988; Riegel, 1975; Tobach, 1981). Although the channeled nature of early development tends to minimize differences in children's early adaptive efforts, hereditary differences, variation in early experiences, and resulting mental structures for construing the world provide the child with an initial differential structure (Kagan, Sontag, Baker, & Nelson, 1958; A. Thomas & Chess, 1977, 1981; Vailliant & McArthur, 1972). As the child matures, however, near the time of adolescence he or she confronts a problem endemic to human life (Buhler, 1968; Erikson, 1963)—that is, the world presents a variety of situations and potential activities in these situations that might, in some way, satisfy the individual's needs. Because individuals have only limited time and energy available, however, they must choose among those alternatives in a way that maximizes long-term adaptation.

Broadly speaking, it is assumed that people select situations based on the perceived reinforcement value of the outcomes associated with potential courses of action. Any situation and the feasible activities in it provide a limited set of potentially reinforcing outcomes, and these goal states have different values based on the individual's unique pattern of needs and values. To react to the goal-attainment payoffs available in a situation, however, the individual must perceive the availability of these rewards and the feasibility of reward attainment through a given course of action. Thus, in choosing

FIGURE 1

Male Pathway

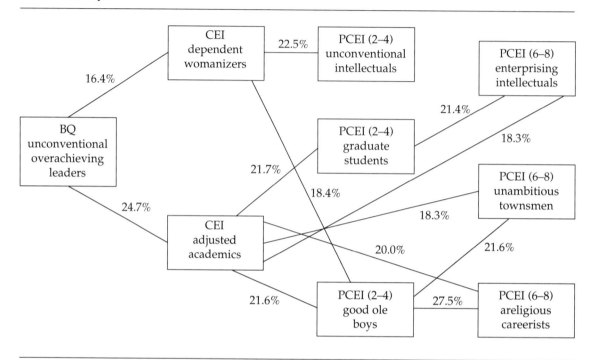

situations individuals express a key part of themselves vis-à-vis operative needs and values, as well as beliefs about themselves, the situation, and the requirements for reinforcement.

Once an individual enters a situation and initiates actions intended to bring about certain kinds of reinforcers, however, a new process begins. As this person engages in activities intended to bring about reinforcement, he or she begins to develop those attributes which condition effective goal attainment, while becoming more knowledgeable about and sensitive to the reinforcement value of activities in a certain class of situations. Because individuals tend to seek situations providing valued outcomes while rejecting situations where goal attainment fails to satisfy their needs and values, a repetitive pattern of choice behavior

results. Over time this process of choice, development, and choice leads to the emergence of highly refined sets of characteristics for the identification of situations providing valued outcomes, along with well-developed capacities for engaging in the activities leading to goal attainment.

Because the rewards provided by any single class of situations are unlikely to satisfy all of a person's needs and values, people seek out different kinds of situations. Overall long-term adaptation is maximized only to the extent that the individual's selection of situations and the capacities developed in all these situations are complementary and compensatory rather than competing. Thus, the individual comes to choose a cohesive set of situations while developing and expressing a cohesive pattern of differential characteristics. Some patterns of

FIGURE 1

Female Pathway (continued)

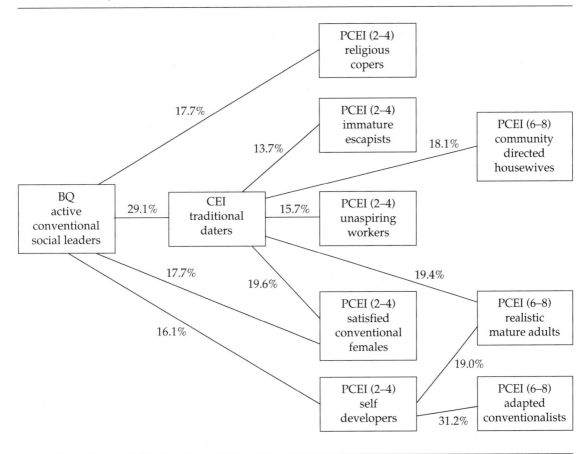

situational selection and activities should come to occur far more frequently than others because of the structured nature of human differences, the broader social environment, and the powerful structuring influences induced by entry into certain crucial social roles, such as a profession.

Investigating Developmental Patterns: Model Support

The postulates of this model provide a plausible explanation for the results obtained in earlier investigations concerning the general developmental patterns defined through the use of subgrouping techniques. As alluded to in the preceding paragraph, this model can account for the emergence of shared patterns of differential development and, by virtue of the self-propagating nature of choice behavior, the tendency of these patterns to maintain themselves over time. Further, the expectation that these patterns entail an integrated set of differential capacities and goal preferences extending across multiple situations explains why they would predict a variety of criterion performances. While these observations argue for the potential explanatory power of the model, additional support for its utility has been provided in an extended series of theoretical tests described below.

One implication of the model is that change in a developmental pattern should be associated with changes in the ability of a pattern of situational selections to satisfy a person's needs and values. In the Stokes, Mumford, Jackson, and Owens (1990) study cited earlier, subgroups that did and did not follow predictable patterns of movement from one developmental period to the next were identified. Subsequently, scores on the background data factors and personality measures were used as predictors of consistent or inconsistent movement in a series of discriminant analyses. Inspection of the variables yielding significant loadings on these discriminant functions suggested that unpredictable patterns of movement were associated with maladjustment in the preceding developmental period. Similarly, Mumford, Wesley, and Shaffer (1987) argued that the degree of certainty with which an individual could be assigned to a developmental pattern should be conditioned by congruence between environmental opportunities and the individual's needs and values. In a series of discriminant analyses contrasting individuals who could and could not be assigned to a developmental pattern at the time of college entry, the background data factors and personality measures indicated that individuals who expressed a preference for the traditional social roles permeating the adolescent environment were more likely than others to be capable of being unambiguously assigned to a single developmental pattern.

Following up on this observation, Wesley (1989) hypothesized that individuals who unambiguously manifested a coherent developmental pattern in their earlier lives would be more affected by both good and poor environmental fit than individuals who, due to continuing exploration, were less embedded in a developmental pattern. To investigate this hypothesis, Wesley (1989) used the adolescent and collegiate items to form a set of background data subgroups. After the meaningfulness of these patterns was established, in a test where 80 percent of 485 hypotheses concerning expected subgroup differences on the personality measures were confirmed, the a posteriori probabilities derived in assigning individuals to subgroups were used to classify an individual as clearly expressing a cohesive developmental pattern ($p \leq .80$) or not expressing a cohesive developmental pattern ($p < .80$). The postcollegiate data were then used to construct job satisfaction, life satisfaction, job involvement, job level, and job search activity criteria, and an individual's probability of membership in a given job family was determined. The job families were specified as congruent or incongruent with the earlier developmental pattern. In a series of analysis of variance tests, it was found that the fit of the developmental pattern with job family demands influenced women's job satisfaction ($\eta = .13$; $p < .05$), job involvement ($\eta = .26$; $p < .01$), and job level ($\eta = .54$; $p < .001$), and men's job satisfaction ($\eta = .20$; $p < .05$), job involvement ($\eta = .23$; $p < .05$), and job level ($\eta = .49$; $p < .001$). Further, individual fit with a developmental pattern interacted with a person's job congruence in determining men's but not women's life satisfaction ($\eta = .13$; $p < .05$) and job involvement ($\eta = .13$; $p < .05$) such that men more congruent with a developmental pattern experienced higher and lower levels of life satisfaction and job involvement as a result of good and poor job matches than men less committed to a pattern. This interaction was not obtained for women, and although this sex difference might be explained based on the relative salience of men's and women's career concerns within this sample, the existence of the main effects and interactions is consistent with the ecology model and its implications.

In another rather different investigation, Hein and Mumford (1988) argued that different patterns of causal variables would operate for individuals seeking qualitatively different kinds of reinforcers in a common situation. A set of background data subgroups was obtained to investigate this possibility. For each subgroup, the personality variables related to high and low levels of religious involvement, as measured by background data items, were established in a series of two-way chi-square tests. After the phi coefficients had been signed for directionality without respect to level, they were used to form profiles for each subgroup, and these subgroups were grouped together using a Ward and Hook (1963) procedure to identify clusters of subgroups for whom religious involvement had similar meaning. This analysis yielded two clusters of subgroups—one labeled Expressives, who apparently accepted or rejected religion based on its utility as a vehicle for evaluative, emotional expression, and one labeled Instrumentals, who apparently accepted or rejected religion based on its ability to provide personal services. When moderated simplex models were constructed to describe continuity and change within the Instrumental and Expressive clusters, it was found that very different models were required to describe the ontogeny of religious involvement. These models are presented in Figure 2. As can be seen, background data variables such as collegiate Bohemianism ($\varphi = -.12$) and literary pursuits ($\varphi = -.21$) contributed to the rejection of religious involvement only in the Expressive cluster, whereas variables such as adolescent social effectiveness ($\varphi = .20$) and family relationships in young adulthood ($\varphi = .17$) contributed to religious involvement in the Instrumental cluster.

Implications of Developmental Patterns

Certainly, the nature and implications of the ecology model are not unique nor were they intended to be. Nonetheless, if it is granted that this model provides at least one plausible system for explaining the nature and ontogeny of general patterns of differential development,

then one might ask what it implies about the kind of constructs we should search for in attempts to identify developmental patterns that not only predict a particular kind of criterion performance, but also possess some construct and content validity.

The ecology model emphasizes the crucial role of situational choice in determining the emergence of developmental patterns. Moreover, these choices are held to be driven by the reward value of certain kinds of activities permitted by the situation. This, in turn, suggests that motivational constructs will be an important determinant of the predictive power of developmental patterns. Thus, life history events might be identified to indicate an attraction to or a willingness to devote energy to activities in situations offering rewards similar to those provided in the job situation. Alternatively, one might seek negative events or the explicit rejection of situations and activities offering relevant rewards (Harrell, 1960). Prediction also might be obtained from life events contributing to development of those needs and values making job-relevant rewards attractive.

The ecology model suggests that a developmental pattern involves a set of differential attributes that develop to facilitate the attainment of desired outcomes while conditioning future situational choice by increasing the likelihood of reward in certain kinds of situations. In job settings, the activities required for goal attainment are commonly held to demand certain knowledges, skills, abilities, and other personal characteristics (KSAOs; Dunnette, 1966; Fleishman & Quaintance, 1984; N. G. Peterson & Bownas, 1982). This suggests that the identification of life events indicating successful engagement in activities requiring the application of KSAOs similar to those required on the job might prove to be useful predictors. Life history events contributing to the development of these KSAOs and/or encouraging effective application in relevant situations might also contribute to prediction.

FIGURE 2

Continuity and Change in Religious Involvement

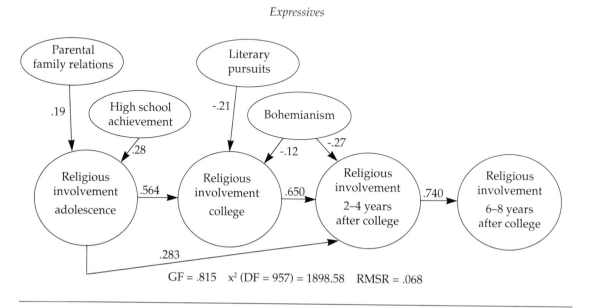

Expressives

GF = .815   x² (DF = 957) = 1898.58   RMSR = .068

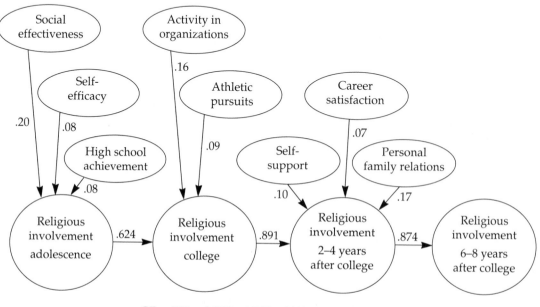

Instrumentals

GF = .782   x² (DF = 1859) = 3932.04   RMSR = .089

FIGURE 2

Continuity and Change in Religious Involvement (continued)

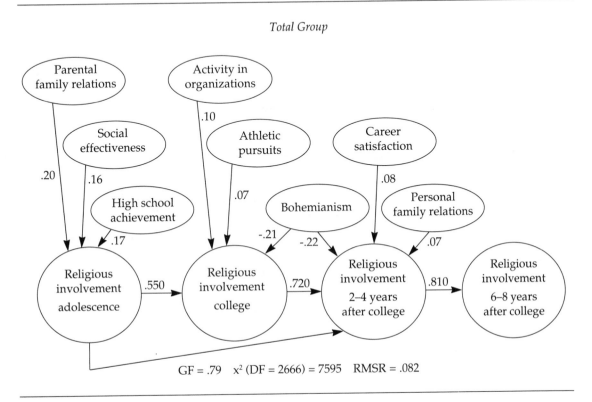

Total Group

GF = .79   x² (DF = 2666) = 7595   RMSR = .082

In a recent study, Nickels (1989) employed these principles in an attempt to delimit the kind of constructs likely to condition the ontogeny of predictive developmental patterns. Three basic categories of differential capacities, or personal resources, capable of contributing to the performance of various activities were identified: *intellectual, personality,* and *social.* Additionally, two categories of motivational variables were identified that might affect situational selection and resource application: *choice processes* (incorporating variables influencing the desirability of certain rewards) and *filter processes* (incorporating moderator variables capable of influencing perceptions of rewards or reward attainability). Figure 3 presents a schematic overview of these categories, along with some illustrations of the kind of constructs in each.

Having defined these general categories of constructs, Nickels (1989) then conducted a systematic review of the human differences literature to identify those variables, or dimensions of human differences, within each category likely to have a marked impact on the emergence of coherent development patterns. After definitions of the resulting 44 dimensions had been formulated, a sample of 10 to 15 individuals was asked to rate the extent to which each of Owens and Schoenfeldt's (1979)

FIGURE 3

Construct Categories Drawn From Ecology Model

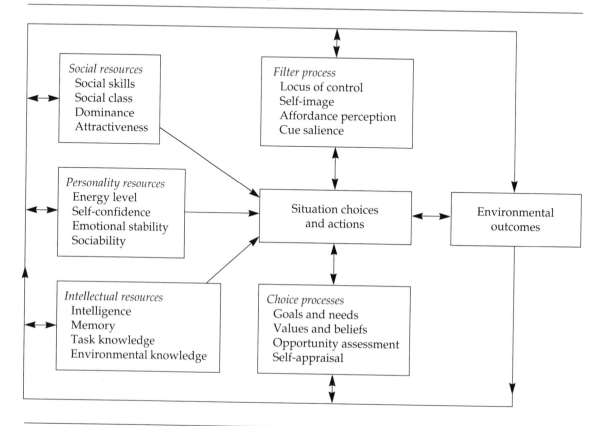

389 items captured prior behavior and experiences that would involve expression of the dimension. To determine whether an item's ability to discriminate general patterns of differential development was contingent on its dimensional status, a policy-capturing study was conducted. Here, discrimination scores were generated for each of the 389 items based on their ability to differentiate men or women expressing the general patterns of differential development identified by Owens and Schoenfeldt (1979). These male and female item discrimination scores were then regressed on item dimensional ratings.

The 22 best dimensions identified in these regression analyses and their associated regression weights are presented in Table 3. Also presented are the associated multiple Rs and cross-validated Rs as generated using holdout samples of items and subjects. As may be seen, dimensions drawn from all five categories predicted discrimination of developmental patterns, yielding cross-validities of .30 and .37 for the male and female subgroups. More centrally, the kind of dimensions found to condition the emergence of developmental patterns such as self-esteem, verbal ability, dominance, organization, social adroitness, and interest

TABLE 3

**Regression Weights of Dimensions
Predicting Discrimination of Development Patterns**

Dimensions	*Standardized Beta Weights*[a]	
	Men	Women
Terminal values	.02	-.08
Introversion	-.08	.06
Verbal skills	.03	.06
Persistence	.06	-.02
Coping skills	.02	-.09
Visualization	-.27	-.17
Practicality	-.24	-.28
Sociability	.01	-.07
Morality	.15	.18
Attention span	.06	.04
Social adroitness	.11	-.15
Self-actualization	-.01	.17
Self-esteem	.24	.27
Interest expression	.17	.03
Fluency	-.25	-.22
Organization	.07	.19
Empathy	.19	.05
Emotional stability	-.18	-.01
Agreeableness	-.12	-.07
Originality	.04	.20
Dominance	.23	.22
Performance standards	-.04	.05
Multiple *R*	.46	.51
Cross-validated *R* (People)[b]	.30	.37
Cross-validated *R* (Items)[b]	.32	.41

Note: Developmental patterns were defined using subgroups described in Owens and Schoenfeldt (1979).

[a] Betas have a mean of 0.
[b] Holdout samples of both individuals and items were obtained and used for cross-validation.

expression were consistent with both the ecology model and the broader literature. In a follow-up series of analyses where item scores on these dimensions were used to specify item pools to be used in constructing empirical keys to predict academic achievement, academic withdrawal, general adjustment, job involvement, job satisfaction, and life satisfaction criteria, it was found that items specified on the basis of this dimensional structure predicted performance about as well as item pools specified on the basis of item content validity evaluations and predicted performance better than item pools specified at random. The first finding was not surprising because item pools defined using the dimensional structure showed substantial overlap with those defined on the basis of content validity evaluations.

The Nickels (1989) study is of interest because it suggests the kinds of constructs we might look at in defining meaningful developmental patterns while suggesting that items intended to capture these constructs may display some content validity. It is true, however, that dimensional relevance was defined here with reference to general patterns of differential development in a collegiate population, and therefore may prove of limited value in attempts to discriminate the developmental patterns applying to a particular kind of criterion performance in a given organizational setting. On the other hand, by documenting the utility of these general kinds of constructs, this study suggests how one might go about defining relevant dimensions in organizational settings. The typical standard job analysis technique for defining KSAOs relevant to differential performance is one way industrial and organizational psychologists define relevant dimensions in organizational settings (Fleishman & Quaintance, 1984; N. G. Peterson & Bownas, 1982). Similarly, occupational reinforcer analysis (Borgen, 1988; Dawis & Lofquist, 1984; Dawis, Lofquist, & Weiss, 1968) might be used to identify crucial choice and filter process dimensions. Items intended to capture the prior expression of these constructs in behavior and experiences contributing to the development of these constructs can then be written.

In generating these items, however, the nature of differential development suggests a number of other considerations that should be considered. One of these pertains to the need for adequate sampling. The ecology model indicates that a number of reinforcers might be offered by any situation and that individuals may differ with respect to the situations in which they seek these rewards. Thus, an accurate appraisal of the rewards sought by an individual requires an examination of multiple prior situations. The importance of situational sampling is further underscored by the potential operation of multiple rewards in a situation and thus the need to aggregate over multiple situations to obtain an accurate appraisal of any given reinforcer. Similarly, in attempts to appraise relevant resources or KSAOs, it should be recognized that KSAO expression might be conditioned by a number of developmental influences and might contribute to reward attainment in a number of different situations. Thus, items that sample a range of significant developmental influences or successful application of these KSAOs in a number of situations should be used to appraise relevant KSAOs.

In sampling situations and activities, it is important to attend to three facts. First, any attempt to employ this strategy is contingent on the individual's prior exposure to these situations. Thus, situation and activity sampling must focus on events that might have occurred in the lives of most individuals. Second, the potential for at least some developmental change in preferred rewards and KSAOs implies that this sampling should focus on relatively recent events or events that have relatively stable long-term implications (VonDralek, Lerner, & Schulenberg, 1986). Third, in specifying item content, it is important to identify situations where the individual had some degree of discretion in exactly when, where, and how an activity occurred, since situations inducing powerful common effects are unlikely to reveal the unique character of an individual's developmental pattern (Kendrick & Funder, 1988).

The need to consider the feasibility of situational exposure and behavioral variability in developmentally significant situations points to another important predictive implication of the model. As individuals move through the life span, there are normative age-related shifts in the situations individuals are exposed to and expected behavior in these situations (Caspi, 1987; Havighurst, 1952; Levinson, 1986). Thus, reward preferences may be expressed in different kinds of situations as individuals move through their lives. Moreover, the activities required in these situations and their associated KSAO requirements may also change. This point has also been underscored in the work of Ferguson (1967), who notes that the predictive implications of insurance purchases for salesmen changes systematically with age. This indicates that it may sometimes be necessary to tailor items to the particular age groups under consideration.

Several studies have examined potential shifts in the predictive power of background data measures for different racial, gender, and socioeconomic groups (Reilly & Chao, 1982). Most studies have indicated that race and socioeconomic status are not associated with differences in causal systems (Dunnette et al., 1982; Jensen, 1980; Richardson, Bellows, Henry, & Co., 1984a, 1984b, 1984c), provided that all group members have had some exposure to the relevant predictive situations (Pace & Schoenfeldt, 1977). However, work by Reilly and Chao (1982) and Nevo (1976) indicates that different causal systems or item indicators of common causes may operate to determine the performance of men and women in at least some job settings. This suggests the need for separate item pools or within-group keying when situations having common reinforcer or KSAO implications cannot be identified.

Our foregoing observations indicate that the formulation of background data measures intended to manifest substantial construct and content validity will require some attention to both the principles of differential development and the practical implications of the systems giving rise to general patterns of differential development. Although these observations also imply a need to approach background data

from a broader conceptual framework, the principles implied by the framework are consistent with standard operating procedures in other areas of personnel selection and psychological measurement. When this fact is considered in light of the stronger validity inferences permitted by application of content and construct validation principles, along with their ability to address many of the more common criticisms leveled against background data measures, it would seem that application of these principles could do much to enhance the utility of background data measures. Many of these objectives can be reached simply through the systematic specification of causal influences and developmental markers. Systematic item development procedures are, however, necessary to gain an understanding of the nomothetic network giving rise to general patterns of differential development.

Item Construction

Item development procedures represent a crucial concern in the development of construct-, content-, and criterion-valid background data measures. The following discussion considers certain issues bearing on the definition of a meaningful and potentially valid pool of background data items. We begin by examining issues likely to arise in formulating the conceptual framework guiding item specification. We then turn to issues bearing on item content and the conditions of item administration.

Situation Analysis

Our previous discussion of developmental patterns indicates that past behavior and experiences predict performance because they reflect the prior development of KSAOs and motivational influences conditioning entry into, and performance in, certain sets of situations. This observation suggests that item development must begin with a careful specification of the jobs or job families that constitute the targeted situations for performance prediction. It is noted that in defining these targeted situations, an attempt should be made to ensure that the jobs or job families are sufficiently homogeneous so that a similar set of dispositional and motivational influences can be assumed to operate.

Once the targeted situations have been specified, the next step in item development will be definition of the behaviors required for adequate performance (Levine & Zachert, 1951). Typically, this will be accomplished through standard job analysis procedures intended to specify the behaviors required to perform the specified job or subset of job activities (Hough, 1984; Pannone, 1984; Russell, Mattson, & Devlin, 1988). Some attention should be given, however, to the environmental conditions under which those behaviors are elicited and the processes likely to underlie effective performance (Fine & Wiley, 1971; Fleishman & Quaintance, 1984). Information concerning those environmental factors conditioning the availability of certain reinforcers or leading to shifts in the KSAOs required to obtain these reinforcers should also be obtained. A case in point might be found in changes in employment policy, work conditions, or equipment availability over time or organizational units, all of which might influence available rewards and work requirements and thus the KSAOs and motivational constructs conditioning performance.

Variable Specification

After one has formulated an adequate understanding of the situations and the nature of performance, definition of the developmental domain may begin. Because the ecology model holds that behavior and experiences are conditioned by the KSAOs and motivational influences arising from people's earlier environmental transactions, it follows that domain definition should begin by specifying (a) the

KSAOs contributing to effective performance and (b) the motivational variables leading individuals to apply these differential capacities in the pursuit of job-relevant reinforcers. A variety of issues pertaining to the definition of performance must be addressed to provide a basis for specification of the pertinent causal influences (Mitchell, 1986).

Any attempt to define the domain of relevant causal influences should begin with a precise definition of exactly what kind of criterion behaviors are to be predicted. This definition of the behaviors to be elicited by the situation (e.g., sales volume, low absenteeism, patent awards, or high performance ratings) should be phrased in such a way that each kind of distinct performance is treated as a separate entity. In specifying criterion behaviors, all behaviors relevant to performance may be specified or only those behaviors likely to differentiate good and poor performers may be specified. Although both strategies have some relative strengths and weaknesses, the first approach is likely to be employed when a stable, limited domain of behaviors underlies performance due to its greater comprehensiveness and feasibility of application. A focus on critical differentiating behaviors is likely to prove more attractive in complex domains involving a range of potential behaviors.

Having defined the behaviors of interest in these situations, the nature of the KSAOs and the motivational variables conditioning their expression must be determined. Extant theory provides one vehicle for specifying the causal influences conditioning behavioral expression. For instance, Schoenfeldt and Mendoza (1988) used extant research concerning the nature of effective leadership to define the differential attributes conditioning leadership performance. Similarly, Anastasi and Schaefer (1969) and Schaefer and Anastasi (1968) used available literature concerning the correlates of creativity to specify the differential characteristics likely to condition creative production among adolescents.

Theoretically based strategies of this sort offer substantial advantages with respect to construct validity and item generation. In a specific job setting, however, they may prove of limited value due to the lack of prior research. Under these conditions, investigators tend to use more empirically oriented job analysis techniques, such as observations by job analysts and structured incumbent evaluations, to identify the KSAOs and motivational variables conditioning performance.

When the job analyst strategy is used, direct observation of job activities is used to specify relevant KSAOs and motivational variables. Here, a review of documentary materials, interviews with subject matter experts, or observations of incumbent performance are used to generate hypotheses concerning relevant KSAOs and motivational variables. In conducting these observational analyses, some attention should be given to the appropriateness of the sampling procedures used to generate these observations and the causal inferences drawn from them. Further, the resulting inferences concerning relevant KSAOs and motivational variables should be presented to panels of subject matter experts to determine whether the critical elements determining performance have been specified. One illustration of this approach in the generation of background data measures has been provided by Hough (1984). She used critical incident techniques to identify the KSAOs influencing the performance of federal attorneys and found that the resulting scales yielded effective performance prediction. In another study, Russell et al. (1988) used dimensions formulated for the Navy's Officer Fitness Report to specify KSAOs, such as leadership and goal setting, that influence performance at the Naval Academy.

Other studies have used other types of job analysis procedures, such as task and KSAO analysis, to obtain job descriptive information. For instance, studies by Levine and Zachert (1951) and Pannone (1984) attempted to define the domain of relevant variables through an examination of job tasks. Although task data may prove especially useful when a direct sampling approach is applied in item specification, its value may be limited when there is a need to explicitly delineate underlying constructs in item development. Under these conditions, the KSAOs influencing task performance might be identified using worker-oriented job analysis systems, such as Fleishman's (1972, 1975) ability requirement scales, which were used to identify the resources conditioning performance among Federal Bureau of Investigation special agents (Mumford, Cooper, & Schemmer, 1983).

All of these strategies clearly have some value as vehicles for specifying relevant item pools or constructs. Although research is not available contrasting their relative merits as they pertain to the validity of background data measures, it seems likely that comprehensive definition of KSAOs and motivational variables may require different techniques in different predictive situations. Further, multiple techniques might be used to ensure a comprehensive definition of relevant causal influences.

It should also be recognized that investigators may sometimes wish to focus construct definition on certain aspects of the overall domain of relevant developmental influences. In many situations, it may be preferable to focus on KSAOs rather than motivational variables. Similarly, it may prove desirable to focus only on KSAOs likely to be best measured with biographical information rather than other KSAOs, such as intelligence, that might be measured more appropriately using an alternative format. It should be demonstrated that the retained variables are important determinants of differential performance and can be appropriately assessed through indices of prior behavior and experience.

Item Specification

Specification Strategies.   Once the structure of the developmental domain is defined by KSAOs and motivational variables conditioning performance in the target situations (Mumford & Owens, 1987), the next step is item specification. This step involves generation of hypotheses that a given form of prior behavior or experience (a) contributes to the development of the relevant KSAOs and motivators or (b) is a sign of prior development of the relevant constructs. The first approach, the indirect approach, uses extant literature to guide hypothesis generation about developmental determinants of target KSAOs. The second approach, the direct approach, focuses on generating hypotheses about prior situations where performance on the variable was exhibited.

The indirect approach relies on underlying developmental theory and situations that might lead to the development of the target characteristics. The direct approach identifies situations that call forth behavior manifestly similar to or required on the job. The two strategies differ in their concern with content validity, face validity, or manifest job relevance.

Illustrations of the indirect approach can be found in La Gaipa (1969), Morrison and Sebald (1974), Anastasi and Schaefer (1969), Malloy (1955), and Owens and Schoenfeldt (1979). This approach tends to be applied in areas where the developmental underpinnings of performance-relevant constructs are reasonably well understood. Illustrations of the direct approach can be found in Hough (1984), Keinan, Friedland, Yitzhacky, and Moran (1981), Pannone (1984), Schmidt, Caplan, Bemis, Decuir, Dunn, and Antone (1979), Russell (1988), and Schoenfeldt and Mendoza (1988). Pannone, for example, hypothesized that prior experience should contribute to job knowledge and thus to better performance. This led to the generation of a series of background data items asking individuals if they had performed related or similar tasks in other situations. Similarly,

Schmidt et al.'s (1979) behavioral consistency approach required applicants to write essays illustrating prior activities that would fall under specified behavioral performance dimensions. In essence, this technique allows subjects to generate items in relation to the dimensions of job performance.

Typically, the behavior consistency or direct strategies have sought past activities in situations where successful performance is likely to require application of the same KSAOs due to similarity in performance demands. For instance, if writing skills were found to be an important KSAO, one might formulate the hypothesis that grades on college term papers would provide an index of writing skills. In the case of the indirect approach, however, the hypothesis that parental linguistic training leads to the development of writing skills might lead to an item specification asking, "How many books were in the home when you were growing up?" As shown in studies by Walther (1961, 1962), Siegel (1956a, 1956b), Owens and Schoenfeldt (1979), and Kulberg and Owens (1960), the indirect approach has also proved useful in item generation.

By using job content as a framework for item specification, investigators can, to some extent, free themselves from the need to specify discrete causal variables and generate specific hypotheses concerning how prior behavior and experiences would contribute to or reflect the prior development of relevant KSAOs and motivational variables. Further, manifest similarity in behavioral content may contribute to applicant acceptance. One should recognize, however, that application of the direct strategy is based on two assumptions. First, it assumes that applicants will have been exposed to situations permitting the expression of relevant behaviors. Second, it assumes that the KSAOs and motivational variables conditioning behavior and experiences in these situations are similar to those found on the job. Thus, in generating item specifications, an attempt should be made to ensure that experiential opportunities did, indeed, exist for most applicants, and expert judgments or the available literature should be used to ensure that similar variables could be expected to operate in conditioning differential performance in the targeted situations.

Thus, one should not assume that behavioral consistency, or the direct strategy, a priori implies adequate item specification. When the assumptions specified above are met, a behavioral consistency strategy does provide a highly effective vehicle for item specification because multiple influences can be captured in a given item specification and because prior expression of KSAOs or motivational variables often provides a sound basis for anticipating their expression in similar job situations.

Although both the direct and indirect approaches have value in item specification, they do display certain unique strengths and weaknesses. The direct approach allows hypotheses to be formulated with reference to the known content of the predictive situation, therefore providing investigators with relatively clearcut guidelines for item specification. Moreover, this technique does not require a well-developed theory concerning the developmental determinants of performance and is likely to yield item specifications directly relevant to job content. On the other hand, items formulated using the direct approach may be sensitive to faking through occupational stereotypes (Brumback, 1969; Klein & Owens, 1965; Lautenschlager, 1985b; Mumford & Owens, 1987). Additionally, the direct approach assumes prior exposure to situations calling forth similar behavior and experiences, and this assumption may not hold in many selection situations. The indirect approach avoids these problems to some extent by focusing on underlying developmental influences. It is, however, a technique best used in situations where there is a well-founded understanding of the developmental determinants of performance.

Direct and indirect strategies may use similar information gathering strategies. For example, Siegel (1956a) obtained life history essays and used the events described therein as a basis for constructing indirect items. Russell et al. (1988) proposed an extension of this essay approach. They identified five KSAOs critical to the performance of naval officers and asked students to write essays indicative of past performance on these dimensions. A content analysis of the developmental events mentioned in the essays was used to generate indirect items. In a subsequent empirical keying effort, cross-validated *r*s in the .20 to .30 range were obtained for leadership, academic, and military performance criteria. On the other hand, Schmidt et al. (1979) and Hough (1984) used an essay technique in a direct way to elicit information about the prior demonstration of relevant constructs.

The utility of essay techniques also indicates some other potential sources of life record information that might be used in generating item specifications. One such source may be found in career document materials such as biographies or termination interviews (Howe, 1982). Another source of item specifications may be found in interviews conducted with more successful and less successful incumbents, especially when the content of interview protocols is contrasted across these groups (D. C. Myers & Fine, 1980). Finally, item specifications might be generated on the basis of impressions obtained from co-workers or supervisors concerning the prior behavior and experiences characterizing good and poor performers on various dimensions.

Two other sources of information have also been used in item specification. First, many investigators have used the known predictive characteristics and factor loadings of background data items to form hypotheses about their ability to capture certain KSAOs and motivational variables (Brown, 1978; D. A. Peterson & Wallace, 1966; Tanofsky, Shepps, & O'Neill, 1969). Second, as Siegel (1956a) has so eloquently pointed out, the investigator's own experiences and knowledge of the general psychological literature often provide a crucial, if somewhat subjective, basis for item specification. Siegel's (1956a) efforts have also served to underscore one further point—that in many situations, investigators will find it useful, and perhaps necessary, to use multiple item specification techniques.

Operational Considerations.   Certain operational requirements dictated by the nature of background data items need to be addressed. First, an adequate item specification should describe the situation or situations where the pertinent KSAOs or motivational variables might operate to condition differential behavior and experiences. Second, the specification should describe the kind of behavior and experiences occurring in this situation that would contribute to the development of, or reflect the prior development of, the relevant KSAO or motivational constructs. Third, item specification should describe the kinds of behaviors and experiences reflecting differential expression of the relevant construct so that the information can be used in constructing response options. Thus, an item specification for writing skills (the construct) might ask, "In your high school English classes (the situation), how well did you do on essay exams (the experience)?" with response options being defined to reflect typical grades, such as, "I usually got an A."

Items may be lost in prescreening, and reliability is enhanced when multiple items are available; thus, it is prudent for investigators to formulate 10 to 15 items or item specifications for each of the KSAOs and motivational variables defining the structure of the developmental domain. This rule of thumb might be modified, depending on the nature of the constructs under consideration. For instance, the number of requisite item specifications might decrease somewhat if prior studies give reason to expect that these specifications provide effective markers of the relevant variables. A larger number of item specifications should be generated, however, when it is important to minimize deficiency and contamination through aggregation over multiple situations. For example, a larger number of specifications might be generated when there is a need to cover the expression of these KSAOs and motivational variables across a range of eliciting situations to minimize potential deficiencies arising from the selective expression of these attributes in different situations. Finally, based on the findings obtained in the Redmond and Nickels (1989) study cited earlier, the indirect approach may require a larger number of item specifications than the direct approach.

In generating item specifications, at least four other considerations should be kept in mind. First, an attempt should be made to identify situations most individuals would have been exposed to in their earlier lives. Second, behaviors and experiences should be sought that will yield adequate variation in the sample at hand. Third, prior behaviors or experiences should be examined in situational contexts that would not be subject to the operation of a variety of contaminating influences. Fourth, if items are to be employed across age, race, and sex groups, an attempt should be made to identify situations to which members of all groups would have been exposed and behaviors or experiences that reflect operation of the same KSAO and motivational constructs in these situations. This last operation will, of course, serve to minimize the impact of potential bias and reduce the need for within-group scaling.

Item Formats and Content

Item Formats.   The hypotheses formulated in item specification indicate that certain behaviors or experiences occurring in a given set of situations are likely to condition performance. By formulating questions asking individuals to describe the nature or extent to which they have manifested these behaviors in earlier life situations, item specification hypotheses provide a basis for casting items in a multiple-choice format. Owens (1976) identified seven formats commonly used in translating these specifications into formal background data items: binary (yes–no); continuum, single choice; noncontinuum, single choice; noncontinuum, multiple choice; noncontinuum plus escape option; continuum plus escape option; and common stem, multiple continua. Table 4 provides an illustration of each of these item formats. For the most part, the information presented in Table 4 is self-explanatory. However, two further comments are in order. First, when noncontinuum formats are in use, each response option effectively constitutes an item unto itself with respect to scaling and control for chance differences. Second, the nature of the item format selected and the number of response options specified should be guided by the item specification hypothesis and the nature of the behavior or experiences at hand as they are manifest in people's lives.

Owens, Glennon, and Albright (1962) attempted to assess the characteristics of these alternative item formats as they would affect the accuracy of assessment. To accomplish this, 200 items were administered to 25 research scientists and 18 engineering students at the beginning and end of a two-month period. Comparison of the more and less stable items indicated that consistency was enhanced by (a) keeping questions as simple and brief as possible, (b) graduating the response options on a numerical continuum, (c) providing an escape clause when all possible alternatives have not been covered by the response options, and (d) wording response options and questions in such a way as to provide a pleasant or neutral connotation. Taken as a whole, these findings argue for the use of the continuum-type item format modified to include escape clauses.

This conclusion finds some support in a study by Lecznar and Dailey (1950). In their study, each background data item was either scored on an underlying continuum or each response was scored as a noncontinuous item.

They found that both techniques yielded comparable initial validities but that continuum item scoring showed less shrinkage upon cross-validation. When this observation is considered in light of the greater interpretability and reliability of continuum-type items, it suggests that the continuum format should be used whenever possible.

A recent study by Reiter-Palmon, Uhlman, and DeFilippo (1990) also suggests that some attention should be given to the origination of item response continuums. In this study, response continuums to 389 background data items were classified based on their departmental implications. Response continuums were classified as negative (personal loss), limiting (restricting future options), positive (personal gain), and enhancing (opening up future options). Subsequently, empirical keys were constructed to predict various criteria using different types of items. It was found that some criteria, such as adjustment, were better predicted by negative items, whereas academic achievement was better predicted by positive or enhancing items. Given these findings, it appears that item response continuums should be specified with respect to the nature of the performance attribute at hand and its implications for differential development.

Item Content.   Another way of examining the characteristics of background data items focuses on phrasing of the questions flowing from initial item specifications. For instance, Asher (1972) has suggested that the phrasing of background data items may differ in the degree to which the behavior and experiences to be recalled reflect information that is (a) verifiable versus unverifiable, (b) specific versus general, (c) internal versus external, (d) factual versus interpretive, (e) calling for discrete behaviors versus behavioral inferences, (f) seeking long-term historic versus relatively recent historic events, and (g) calling for memory versus conjecture concerning past behavior and experiences.

T A B L E 4

Item Formats

1. *Binary items*

   Have you found your life to date to be pleasant and satisfying?
   a. Yes
   b. No

2. *Continuum, single choice*

   What is your weight?
   a. 132 or under
   b. 133–155
   c. 156–175
   d. 176–195
   e. over 195

3. *Noncontinuum, single choice*

   What was your marital status at college graduation?
   a. Single
   b. Married, no children
   c. Married, one or more children
   d. Widowed
   e. Separated or divorced

4. *Noncontinuum, multiple choice*

   Circle each of the following from which you have ever suffered:
   a. Allergies
   b. Asthma
   c. High blood pressure
   d. Ulcers
   e. Headaches
   f. Gastrointestinal upsets
   g. Arthritis

5. *Noncontinuum plus escape option*

   When have you been most likely to have a headache?
   a. When I've strained my eyes
   b. When I haven't eaten on schedule
   c. When I've been under tension
   d. January 1st
   e. Never have headaches

TABLE 4

Item Formats (continued)

6. *Continuum plus escape option*

What was your length of service in your most recent full-time job?
a. Less than 6 months
b. 6 months to 1 year
c. 1 to 2 years
d. 2 to 5 years
e. More than 5 years
f. No previous full-time job

7. *Common stem, multiple continua*

Over the past five years, how much have you enjoyed each of the following?
(Use continuum 1 to 4 at right below.)
a. Loafing or watching TV   1. Very much
b. Reading   2. Some
c. Constructive hobbies   3. Very little
d. Home improvement   4. Not at all
e. Outdoor recreation
f. Music, art, or dramatics, etc.

Based on a review of the extant literature, Asher (1972) concluded that the reliability and validity of background data items might be improved by (a) focusing item content on verifiable behavior and experiences whenever possible and (b) making item content and response options sufficiently specific in terms of the events to be recalled to avoid ambiguity in interpretation and memory distortion. Some support for the second postulate was obtained in a recent study by Barge (1988), who had psychologists and graduate students rate item content for (a) heterogeneity, or the breadth and complexity of the behaviors and experiences covered by the item; (b) behavioral discreteness, or the extent to which items address actual discrete behaviors and experiences rather than general evaluations of behavioral dispositions, traits, or impressions of events; and (c) behavioral consistency, or the extent to which item content parallels or samples the activities involved in performance. In a sample of four Army occupational specialities, it was found that the items likely to predict core technical and general task proficiency criteria were likely to be low on heterogeneity and high on behavioral discreteness and consistency.

The verifiability issue suggested by Asher (1972) has been examined in a study by Shaffer, Saunders, and Owens (1986). In this investigation, a background data questionnaire was readministered five years later to 237 college students, and at the same time, their parents were asked to complete selected portions of the questionnaire as they believed their child would have at age 18, the time of initial administration. Items were then classified as objective indicators focusing on externally observable behaviors, or as subjective indicators focusing on internal or covert behaviors and experiences. When the reliability of these items was examined, it was found that the more objective verifiable items yielded a median retest reliability of .64 for males and .66 for females, and the more subjective items yielded a median retest reliability of .41 for males and .44 for females. However, in both cases, it was found that an individual's descriptions yielded sizable positive correlations with parent's descriptions of their child's behavior and experiences, thereby suggesting that lack of verifiability does not necessarily imply falsification.

Although these findings indicate that objective, verifiable items should be preferred, this should not be at the expense of adequate assessment of more complex KSAO and motivational constructs calling for subjective appraisals. First, given the limited reliability of item data, the retest coefficients Shaffer et al. (1986) obtained for more subjective items were reasonable. Second, as noted by Asher (1972) and demonstrated in studies by Walther (1961, 1962), more subjective items may prove to be especially effective predictors when performance-relevant KSAOs and motivational variables are reflected in covert situational reactions. This point has been underscored in a study by Buel (personal communication, 1971), who found that background data items intended to capture values, attitudes, and beliefs related to performance tend to predict complex criterion performances involving these elements more effectively than demographic items, despite the latter's apparent objectivity and greater reliability.

Item Prescreening

Content Screening. Following initial translation of specification into a set of formal items, prescreening to ensure the substantive and psychometric adequacy of the items should be conducted. A study by Majesty (1967) indicates that rational item screening can be used to minimize bias and objectionable content. In this study, 1,036 students completed 205 background data items, and it was found that gender, race, and religion could be predicted by both rational and empirical scales. A later study by Mumford et al. (1983) used a rational screening technique where two panels of subject matter experts were asked to review item content for objectionability in content and potential bias against subpopulations, such as women and minority group members. After elimination of items held to be biased or to represent an invasion of privacy by two or more of the subject matter experts, the resulting background data measure was found to be unbiased in a differential regression line analysis. When these results are considered in light of B. D. Smart's (1968) observations indicating that expert judges appear to employ a consistent set of rules in evaluating potential bias and objectionable content in background data items, it appears that such rational screening efforts may do much to enhance the quality of our operational item pools. This seems especially true since these panel review techniques might also be used to screen items for clarity and the appropriateness of available response options (Mumford, Cooper, & Schemmer, 1983).

It is also possible to extend these prescreening efforts to the appraisal of item content. Although initial work along these lines was not promising (Schmitt & Ostroff, 1986), later studies by Carrier, Dalessio, and Brown (1990), Barge (1988), and Nickels (1989) have provided evidence indicating that expert judges can determine the relevance of items to job content and underlying constructs. The Nickels (1989) study is of particular interest in this regard because judges were asked not only to evaluate the items' relevance to specific causal variables, but also to evaluate their content validity with regard to six criterion performances. Nickels' findings indicated that 10 to 15 raters were sufficient to generate interrater agreement coefficients of .70 with regard to item dimensional status. He also found that evaluations of item relevance to a criterion yielded a median agreement coefficient of .73 with 10 raters as well as relevance scores which were consistent with the nature of the criterion. These relevance scores were also found to yield correlations of .40 with a measure of the item's status on dimensions held to condition criterion performance.

Our preceding observations suggest that item prescreening efforts might legitimately be extended to evaluations of item content. These evaluations could be obtained by having panels of subject matter experts review item content in relation to the targeted categories of KSAOs and motivational constructs. Items that subject matter experts did not believe tapped the hypothesized constructs or failed to display sufficient overall job relevance might then be considered for elimination or revision. Not only should this technique help ensure the validity of the final scale, it also provides useful content and construct validation evidence.

Statistical Screening.   Once the initial pool of background data items has been formulated and reviewed, item tryout may begin. The revised items would be administered to a tryout sample of 100 to 200 individuals drawn from the target population. An excellent paradigm for using tryout information in item screening may be found in Owens and Schoenfeldt (1979). First, the variability of item responses is examined, and items failing to yield sufficient variation to prove useful in marking patterns of differential development are eliminated. Second, items yielding response distributions inconsistent with the item generating hypotheses are identified, and marked departures from expectation provide a basis for item elimination. Third, the remaining items are correlated, and an item is considered for elimination if it fails to yield the expected correlations with other items tapping the same or other substantively relevant aspects of the developmental domain. By breaking these analyses down by subpopulation, marked shifts in item response distributions or correlational patterns may be used to determine whether there is a need for within-group scaling procedures.

Item Characteristics

The available literature suggests that well-developed background data items display a number of useful characteristics. For instance, item retest reliabilities tend to be sizable given the limitations of item data, seldom yielding retest coefficients below .40 over relatively long intervals (Shaffer et al., 1986). When more objective, verifiable items are examined over shorter intervals, retest coefficients in the high .80s or low .90s are common (Owens, 1976). In addition, Plag and Goffman (1967) have presented evidence indicating that many background data items display relatively low intercorrelations, and this observation has been confirmed in a number of other studies (Kavanagh & York, 1972; Owens, 1976; Siegel, 1956a). As Owens (1976) notes, this relative independence permits a relatively small set of background data items to capture a great deal of descriptive information and recommends their application to classification problems.

Because most complex criterion performances are influenced by a variety of factors, any single item is unlikely to yield a fully adequate assessment of performance potential. Despite this fact, a variety of studies has shown that background data items capturing salient antecedents of performance can yield sizable predictive validity coefficients (Mosel, 1952; D. A. Peterson & Wallace, 1966; Plag & Goffman, 1967; Zachert & Levine, 1952). Although few would debate the potential predictive power of well-developed background data items, a number of authors have voiced some concern about the stability of the predictive statements generated by these items.

In a series of studies, Wernimont (1962), Roach (1971), and Dunnette et al. (1960) reexamined the predictive power of the items included in background data keys initially developed by Kirchner and Dunnette (1957) and Minor (1958). It was found that items yielding significant prediction in these initial efforts were not likely to display substantial predictive power in later years. Attempts have been made to explain these effects on the basis of initial capitalization on chance (Schwab & Oliver, 1974) and failure to maintain item security (Hughes, Dunn, & Baxter, 1956), as well as changes in labor market conditions, personnel policies, and the requirements for adequate performance (Roach, 1971; Thayer, 1977). In certain local instances, it is true that all of these factors may limit the predictive stability of background data items. A study by Brown (1978) highlights the importance of some of the factors, specifically highlighting the need for understanding the predictor and criterion construct.

In Brown's (1978) study, the background data items administered in 1933 that had been found to predict sales performance in the insurance industry and had survived intermittent rescalings were identified. The predictive power of these items was again assessed using individuals hired in 1969 and 1971, and these items were found to predict survival and productivity more than 30 years later. In examining the nature of these items, such as organizational membership, offices held in organizations, amount of life insurance owned, and number of dependents, it is clear that these items captured KSAOs and motivational variables likely to represent key determinants of performance in sales positions. Thus, if (a) item development procedures allow effective assessment of the more important KSAOs and motivational influences determining performance, (b) test security is maintained, and (c) policy or equipment changes have not led to changes in the fundamental nature of performance, it appears that background data items may yield stable prediction whenever broader cultural changes have not invalidated the utility of these items for assessing relevant KSAOs and motivational variables.

Item Application

Response Distortion. Research on recall, faking, and memory distortion provides some further guidelines for item development and application. Sources influencing the accuracy of responses to most self-report instruments

include memory errors and carelessness (van Rijn, 1980) as well as the degree of respondent self-insight, misinterpretation, and motivational biases (Guilford, 1959). Motivational bias includes both the operation of more subtle response sets that bias responding and willful misrepresentation. *Faking* is the term frequently used to represent the inaccuracies due to both response bias and dissimulation.

Several studies have demonstrated the near perfect correspondence between application blank information and verified work history information (Cascio, 1975; Keating, Paterson, & Stone, 1950; Mosel & Cozan, 1952), though Goldstein's (1971) results did not lend support for such accuracy. Doll (1971) demonstrated that certain item characteristics (objectivity and continuum type) influence fakability as a function of induced response set. Schrader and Osburn (1977) showed that college students improved their scores substantially when instructed to "fake good." Haymaker and Erwin (1980) constructed a faking key that could be used to adjust biodata scores without detracting from the scale's validity.

Lautenschlager (1985b) examined the influence of various warnings on biodata responses in a sample of recent military enlistees and found that with the particular form examined, the empirical key was not transparent—that is, it was not easy to determine how one should fake good. Klein and Owens (1965) found that a form keyed to predict a subjective criterion in a college student sample was more fakable than one keyed to predict an objective criterion. Taken together, these findings suggest that faking is less likely to be successful when applicants lack a clear-cut stereotype to fake due to the nature of the criterion or the use of subtle nontransparent items.

Other research has examined the kind of items most likely to result in faking. Larson, Swarthout, and Wickert (1967) found that faking is most likely to occur on self-evaluation items and least likely to occur when items focus on the description of past behavior in well-defined situations. In a related vein, Shaffer et al. (1986) found that parents were more likely to agree with their children's responses to more objective items as opposed to items calling for more subjective self-evaluations. Thus, it appears that item objectivity may limit distortion.

An issue closely related to response distortion is the susceptibility of item responses to response sets such as social desirability. French, Lewis, and Long (1976) examined the influence of social desirability on item responses collected in a research setting. They found that social desirability had little impact on factor scores, but was moderately correlated with mean item responses. Shaffer and Ames (1983) investigated social desirability in a larger pool of items, again collected in a research setting. Eighty-five of 389 items significantly correlated with scores on a social desirability measure, but the correlations were relatively small, on the order of .10 to .20, and mostly occurred with self-evaluation items rather than objective, verifiable items. Although these findings indicate that social desirability is not of great concern in a research context when there is no strong self-presentation incentive, there is still uncertainty as to how job applicants might respond.

This issue has been examined in a recent investigation by Hogan and Stokes (1989), who contrasted social desirability effects in applicant and incumbent groups of sales personnel. Social desirability was found to operate in both applicant and incumbent samples, but it contributed to, rather than detracted from, criterion-related validity coefficients for predicting turnover. These findings not only underscore the importance of incentive, but also indicate that social desirability influences may lead to differential effects in applicant and incumbent samples, resulting in the development of biodata keys

in incumbent and applicant groups which are not equivalent.

Although it is difficult to draw firm conclusions from the available studies, the studies do suggest certain techniques that might be used to reduce distortion. For instance, the use of criteria and items intended to mask occupational stereotypes might prove useful. Items focusing on discrete behaviors are likely to be answered more honestly, particularly if they are verifiable, and this recommends their application. Since many important biodata items are not of the verifiable, objective type, however, placement of the objective items throughout the biodata questionnaire might be used to reduce distortion on all items. Because Cohen and Lefkowitz (1974) have demonstrated some predictability in faking, a faking key similar to that developed by Haymaker and Erwin (1980) could be constructed to adjust biodata scores. Alternatively, Norman's (1963) technique for imposing faking keys on standard empirical keys might be employed. It should be noted, however, that the assumption that an accurate life history form is more valid than one that is less accurate has not yet been demonstrated. Furthermore, empirical keying, by virtue of its ability to reduce transparency and specify weights under conditions where applicant faking is implicitly taken into account, may itself serve to minimize the potential impact of applicant faking on performance prediction.

Group Differences. Because it is possible that the developmental patterns underlying performance may vary with subpopulation status, some attention has been given to the need to formulate separate questions, response options, and item weights within different subpopulations. In this regard, studies by Laurent (1962) and Ferguson (1967) have indicated that the reliability and validity of background data items may vary with age. Effects of this sort, however, may not be observed when items have been carefully designed to apply to all members of the age groups at hand. Similarly, studies by Mumford, Shaffer, Jackson, Neiner, Denning, and Owens (1983), Nevo (1976), Russell et al. (1988), Webster, Booth, Graham, and Alf (1978), Ritchie and Boehm (1977), and Federico, Federico, and Lundquist (1976) indicate that the predictive characteristics of background data items are likely to differ for men and women. These findings suggest that, when there is reason to expect that normative age and sex-role expectations have led to shifts in relevant developmental patterns and the meaning of item responses, adjustments in item content or within-groups scaling should be considered.

On the other hand, although one study by Toole, Gavin, Murdy, and Sells (1972) reported differences in the predictive characteristics of background data items for blacks and whites, significant ethnic group differences have not been obtained in most studies (Baehr, 1976; Cascio, 1976; Cherry, 1969; Lefkowitz, 1972; Malone, 1978; Murray, Ellison, & Fox, 1973; Richardson et al., 1984a, 1984b, 1984c; Ritchie & Boehm, 1977; Sharf, 1980). Thus, it appears that there is sufficient similarity in the developmental patterns underlying performance across ethnic groups to permit application of a common item pool, provided that appropriate item specification procedures have been used.

Administration Conditions.   Little research is available examining the conditions under which background data items should be administered. With regard to questionnaire design, however, a few points of conventional wisdom should be mentioned. In administering items to applicants, it is generally desirable to scatter items tapping a common construct throughout the questionnaire. It is also desirable to place a number of more concrete, verifiable items up front. These operations, like the use of distractor items, may serve to minimize faking.

Background data items can be completed rather rapidly. Typically, applicants can answer three or four questions a minute. Thus, a large number of items can be administered in a short time period. Given this observation and the fact that there is no conceivable reason for speeding item responses, time limits should be generous and imposed, if at all, only for reasons of administrative convenience. Because these items make few cognitive demands, investigators may find it desirable to administer them at the end of more demanding cognitive test sessions.

As noted earlier, there is no reason why background data items cannot be presented through on-line computer systems. When this proves possible, it may be desirable to do so because a number of advantages accrue to the maintenance of item response files. The availability of such files will, for instance, facilitate periodic rescaling and provide a mechanism for monitoring shifts in the applicant pool. Furthermore, the availability of such data will facilitate extension of initial concurrent validation studies to predictive efforts.

In applying background data measures, three other administrative concerns are noteworthy. First, like any other test, the security of scoring procedures should be maintained (Hughes, Dunn, & Baxter, 1956). Second, sound professional practice and the need for honest responses indicate that applicants should be provided with some assurance of confidentiality. Third, significant changes in job demands or applicant pool characteristics should be monitored and new item pools should be generated as necessary.

Scaling Procedures

Systematic item development procedures of the sort we have just discussed may do much to justify inferences of meaningfulness by ensuring adequate content and construct validity. Moreover, by focusing item development on expression of those KSAOs likely to condition performance, these procedures should provide a sound foundation for criterion-related validation studies. Nonetheless, no single item, however well specified, is likely to yield adequate prediction of complex real-world criterion performances due to the limited reliability of item data and the multivariate nature of differential development. Thus, techniques are required for scaling these items in a manner that maximizes joint predictive power.

Empirical keying continues to be the preferred technique for scaling background data items (Mumford & Owens, 1987). However, a number of alternatives to the empirical keying approach have been proposed in the literature, including rational scales (Pannone, 1984), factorial scales (Owens, 1976), and subgrouping (Owens & Schoenfeldt, 1979). Of these alternatives, rational scaling has received the least attention in the biodata literature, perhaps because it represents the scaling technique most dependent on a well-founded understanding of performance antecedents and systematic item development procedures. With the emergence of more comprehensive theoretical systems and item specification strategies, however, rational scaling has become more feasible. The following pages present information separately for each of the three scaling strategies: rational scales, empirically keyed scales, and factorial scales.

Rational Scales

A variety of techniques has been used to develop rational scales (Hough, 1984; Pannone, 1984; Schrader, 1975; Siegel, 1956a, 1956b). Although the particular techniques used in hypothesis generation differ, all rational scaling procedures involve the specification of a priori hypotheses indicating that certain items should be grouped together into a scale. Thus, rational techniques tend to emphasize the content and construct validity of the resulting scaling system. As Ash (1983) points out, there is still a need to establish the criterion-related validity of rational scales to determine whether the

theoretically specified categories of antecedent events do predict later performance.

Three critical steps are involved in rational scaling efforts consistent with the ecology model. First, investigators must have a well-defined set of target situations where there is little ambiguity as to whether individuals will be exposed to comparable situational contingencies. In the industrial setting, most rational scaling efforts begin with an exhaustive job analysis describing the nature of the predictive situation and the behaviors required for adequate performance (Hough, 1984; D. C. Myers & Fine, 1980; Pannone, 1984; Schmidt et al. 1979).

Second, once the nature of adequate performance has been defined, the KSAOs conditioning performance in the targeted situations must be specified. In the direct approach, overt behavioral requirements for performance are specified using either empirically derived job analysis data (Pannone, 1984) or available theoretical data concerning the characteristics of performance (Keinan et al., 1981). The indirect approach used by Mumford, Cooper, and Schemmer (1983) identifies antecedent events conditioning the development of underlying KSAOs using worker-oriented job analysis techniques, such as Fleishman's (1975) KSAO taxonomy. Because this construct specification step constitutes a critical foundation for rational scaling, some attempt should be made to document the relevance of the proposed constructs through (a) analysis of the extant literature (Keinan et al., 1981) or (b) by having panels of subject matter experts review the relevance and comprehensiveness of the proposed behavioral dimensions or underlying determinants giving rise to the constructs of interest (Hough, 1984; Mumford, Cooper, & Schemmer, 1983; Myers & Fine, 1980).

The third necessary step in rational scale construction entails item generation and assignment of items to a particular scale using the structure specified in the course of construct definition. This can be accomplished by asking individuals how frequently and successfully they have engaged in behaviors or activities similar to those required on the job (Pannone, 1984). As indicated in the work of J. T. Dailey (1948), DuBois et al. (1952), and Hough (1984), information regarding success may be especially important for predicting performance. However, items examining behavioral expression in analogous situations, entry into situations calling for these activities, and indications of interest in such endeavors may prove useful in capturing motivationally loaded aspects of job behavior. Thus, items can also be formulated on the basis of underlying developmental theory or available empirical data with reference to the constructs held to determine performance.

Scaling and Screening. Once a set of constructs and items subsumed under these constructs have been specified, one has in essence generated a rational scale. In fact, one can formulate a scale simply by summing the item scores intended to tap some construct. However, this method assumes that all the items effectively index the construct at hand. This is not likely to be the case unless an unusually well-developed theoretical framework is available indicating the antecedents of each construct. As a result, most rational scaling efforts include, as a critical component, some form of item screening. These item screening efforts might take two forms: (a) rational screening of item content and (b) statistical screening.

Traditionally, the statistical screening of items for rational scales has been accomplished through internal consistency analysis. This strategy is illustrated in the work of DuBois et al. (1952) in which background data items were grouped into clusters based on judged content similarity, and the three items yielding the highest within-cluster correlations were then used to define the cluster. The remaining items were added to the initial clusters on the basis

of their correlations with the core items. This procedure was repeated in an iterative sequence until all items had been added to a cluster or dropped for failure to yield a sizable correlation with the items included in any one cluster. A variation on this procedure proposed by Matteson and Osburn (1970) and Matteson, Osburn, and Sparks (1969) employed a computer algorithm to assign items to clusters so as to maximize cluster independence as well as within-cluster homogeneity. Of course, a simplified version of this scaling strategy would simply involve eliminating all items yielding item-total correlations below some specified minimum, say .30 (Mumford & Owens, 1987).

Screening items on the basis of internal consistency is, however, only one possible quantitative approach. For instance, in constructing rational background data scales, Mumford and Owens (1982) examined not only the intercorrelations among items but also the pattern of relationships with a set of external measures. Application of this strategy was justified on the grounds that items belonging in a common scale not only should be highly correlated, but should display roughly the same pattern of relationships with external measures. Alternatively, one might consider developing scales by excluding items that fail to yield differences between known groups, such as good and poor performers, thereby linking rational and empirical scaling strategies through item selection. Finally, it is possible to eliminate items from a scale for reasons such as insufficient variation or failure to coincide with some a priori expected response distribution.

In contrast to the purely quantitative strategies, a more substantively based judgmental approach can be used. Essentially, this strategy involves eliminating items that, in the opinion of subject matter experts, fail to display adequate relevance to performance requirements. An initial test of this strategy may be found in Schmitt and Ostroff (1986), who examined 17 background data items embedded in an interview protocol and asked eight judges to evaluate the overall utility of this information for appraising performance. Subsequent calculations of Lawshe's (1975) content validity ratio (CVR) indicated only limited agreement. A later study by Carrier et al. (1988), however, indicates that in larger samples, stronger CVR coefficients may be obtained and that these CVR judgments yield significant correlations with observed item validities.

Taken as a whole, these studies indicate that subject matter experts can identify past behavior and experiences likely to be relevant to performance. Moreover, work by Nickels (1989) using an indirect item specification approach suggests, in accordance with the recommendations of Fleishman and Quaintance (1984), that adequate interjudge agreement is more likely to be obtained when (a) judges are provided with a common evaluative framework through explicit behavioral definitions of the particular kinds of performance under consideration and (b) the background data items are phrased in an unambiguous fashion where behavior and experiences in the situation are clearly specified. In fact, when these conditions are met, Nickels' findings indicate that interrater agreement coefficients on the order of .75 may be obtained in samples of 10 to 15 judges. Because reasonably accurate and valid judgments of item content can be obtained given an adequate descriptive base, it seems operationally feasible to screen out items yielding low judged relevance values in rational scale construction.

Of course, the judgmental and statistical approaches are not incompatible, since one maximizes internal consistency and reliability and the other maximizes relevance. Thus, investigators might profitably use both approaches in scale construction. Further, it is possible that judgments of item relevance or internal consistency coefficients might be used to generate item weights. Although prior empirical keying research leads to the expectation that these differential weighting schemes will not prove of great value (Mumford & Owens, 1987; Owens, 1976), research is not available explicitly examining this issue as it applies to rational scales.

Reliability and Validity. One of the earliest studies examining the predictive power of a rationally developed biodata scale is the risk-taking scale developed by Torrance and Ziller (1957). This scale consisted of past behavior and experiences indicative of an engagement in risk-seeking activities, such as playing poker and cutting class. Arguing that risk-taking is an essential requirement for combat leaders, Himelstein and Blaskovics (1960) administered the scale to a sample of combat officers and obtained a .41 correlation with peer evaluations of combat leadership. The scale was also found to yield correlations ranging from .28 to .52 against six performance ratings and two measures of combat effectiveness and had a split-half reliability of .98. In a related study, DuBois et al. (1952) used their procedure for rational scale construction and found that the resulting scales were relatively independent. Moreover, these scales were found to be capable of predicting Air Force training criteria at the .30 level across a number of occupational fields.

In a related set of investigations, Siegel (1956a, 1956b) obtained a set of background data items intended to describe significant aspects of student life and had expert judges define an initial set of item clusters intended to capture significant aspects of this domain. Subsequently, item-total correlations were generated within and across clusters, and the clusters were reconstituted based on this information and manifest item content. The 11 scales formulated from the items assigned to each cluster yielded a median retest reliability coefficient of .86. Due to the relative independence of background data items, however, somewhat lower internal consistency coefficients were obtained, yielding a median value of .65. In later follow-up analyses, it was found that the scales were capable of predicting indices of academic performance at the .30 level. Further, the items yielded an interpretable pattern of relationships with a set of personality and interpersonal value indices.

Matteson (1978) has also examined the predictive power of the rational approach where items were grouped into homogeneous clusters. In a sample of production workers, he found that the 11 scales generated using this technique yielded multiple Rs of .41, .43, and .37 for predicting training performance, supervisory evaluations of initial job performance, and supervisory evaluations of later job performance. Similarly, Mumford, Cooper, and Schemmer (1983) found that a set of homogeneous background data scales would yield multiple Rs of .30 for predicting the performance of FBI special agents. Taken as a whole, these studies indicate that indirect rational scaling of background data items can yield reliable measures capable of predicting various kinds of performance indices.

The second line of investigation into the construction of rational background data scales stems from the behavioral consistency approach of Schmidt et al. (1979). Essentially, this approach specifies the major behavioral dimensions of job performance, and behaviorally anchored rating scales are developed for appraising the quality of past activities falling under these dimensions. In operation, individuals are asked to write brief statements describing past activities relevant to each behavioral dimension. Judges then read the activity statements and evaluate the quality of the activities using the behaviorally anchored scales.

Using a somewhat similar approach, Hough (1984) studied a sample of 329 attorneys. She identified nine performance dimensions, such as planning and organizing, oral communication, and assertive advocacy. Subsequent ratings of attorney accomplishment indicated interrater reliabilities between .70 and .80. Moreover, the scales yielded criterion-

related validity coefficients in the mid-.20s against job performance rankings, job performance ratings, and task evaluations and yielded the expected moderate positive relationships with indices of job experience. In a related study, Russell (1988) used structured interview techniques to obtain similar background data information on nine dimensions, such as strategic planning, staffing, and customer relations. Judges' evaluations of these interview protocols for 66 senior managers were obtained, and the ratings were found to yield median correlations of .21 and .14, respectively, when *discrete* dimensional scores were correlated with job performance ratings and an index of yearly bonuses.

Another strategy for implementing the rational approach has been suggested by D. C. Myers and Fine (1980) and Pannone (1984). This strategy begins by defining the tasks or activities performed on the job. Subsequently, people are asked about the frequency or success with which they have engaged in similar activities in the past. In an initial study employing this strategy in a sample of 221 electrical workers, Pannone (1984) used task analysis techniques to identify common job activities. Applicants were then asked whether they had performed this activity in the past. After summing the ratings, the scale was found to yield a correlation of .44 with scores on a job knowledge test. This scale also yielded correlations of .13 and .35 with years of experience in electrical work and years of work experience. Finally, using a nonexistent task item to mark faking, it was found that the correlation of scale scores with job knowledge rose to .55 in the group of nonfakers and dropped to .26 in the group of fakers. In a somewhat different vein, Keinan et al. (1981) identified life events where motion sickness might occur and subsequently developed items asking about the occurrence of symptoms under these conditions. When this inventory was administered to a sample of 190 Israeli sailors, the resulting scale was found to correlate .46 with sickness induced on sea duty and to contribute to performance prediction at sea.

Comparative Findings. One study has contrasted the predictive efficiency of rational biodata scales with empirical biodata scales. Items for both types of scales came from the same item pool. In this study, Berkeley (1953) found that (a) empirical keys yielded larger criterion-related validity coefficients in the initial scale construction sample; (b) empirical keys displayed greater shrinkage in their validity coefficients upon cross-validation; (c) homogeneous rational scales and empirical keys yielded similar results upon cross-validation; and (d) homogeneous rational scales produced interpretable patterns of criterion relationships, but the empirical keys did not. Hornick, James, and Jones (1977) obtained similar results in a study contrasting the utility of empirical and rational scales in the appraisal of climate perceptions. Taking a somewhat different tack, Schrader (1975) contrasted the predictive efficiency of background data scales consisting of items grouped rationally versus statistically to maximize homogeneity. In a sample of some 1,600 employees drawn from a large petrochemical company, it was found that scales formed on the basis of expert judgment performed about as well as scales derived using the factor analytic strategy of maximizing shared variance.

Two recent studies by Schoenfeldt (1989) and Mumford, Uhlman, and Kilkullen (in press) have also examined the predictive characteristics of rational scales. Broadly speaking, the findings obtained in these studies suggest that rational scales targeted on performance-relevant constructs yield prediction similar to that obtained from empirical keys and factorial scales. A recent extension of this work by Uhlman, Reiter-Palmon, and Connelly (1990) also examined the relative predictive power of rational scales and empirical keys. Here, however, the number of variables entered into the regression equation was fixed

such that 22 construct scores or scores on the 22 best items were used as predictors. When the number of predictor variables was controlled in contrasting rational scales and empirical keys, it was found, upon cross-validation, that the rational scales yielded better prediction than the empirical keys. Thus, it appears that rational scales represent an attractive alternative to more traditional scaling procedures, such as empirical keying.

Empirically Keyed Scales

Historically, biodata forms have been constructed to maximize prediction rather than enhance conceptual understanding. Items that discriminate between high and low groups on the criterion variable of interest are retained in a final scale, and items that fail to discriminate are discarded. The blind empirical approach has been criticized for its lack of contribution to scientific understanding. Moreover, the ecology model suggests that the traditional empirical approach fails to maximize prediction because it may not take into account varying developmental patterns among both good and poor performers.

A variety of strategies for empirically keying biodata items exists. One important difference in the strategies is whether each option is examined as a binary variable or all the options of an item are scored as points along a continuum. Regardless of the strategy, in most investigations items or options failing to yield a statistically significant difference in a *t* test, correlation, or chi-square analysis are eliminated. When sample sizes are large, however, statistical significance is less relevant and effect sizes become important in final item selection.

According to Guilford (1954), differential weighting of items beyond simple unit weights has been found to be most profitable when the intercorrelations among background data items are low and relatively few items are in use. Since most background data measures contain a number of items and item reliabilities limit the stability of scoring weights, little is usually gained from the application of more complex weighting schemes (Owens, 1976).

The procedure most frequently used to construct background data keys has been the weighted application blank. According to England (1971), the *vertical percent method* involves determining the percentage of individuals in the criterion and reference groups choosing an alternative and then arriving at the difference between these two percentages. Strong's (1941) tables are then used to assign weights to each response option on the basis of these differences. The *horizontal percent method* is similar to the vertical percent method, but requires less calculation. Both weighting strategies have been credited to Stead and Shartle (1940). In the correlational or *pattern scoring method* (Lecznar & Dailey, 1950), weights are assigned to items based on the magnitude of the relationship observed between each item and the criterion. Another method is the *deviant response scoring technique* (Malloy, 1955; Webb, 1960), which employs a correlational or weighted application blank strategy to construct item weights for criterion groups consisting of individuals above or below the regression line after partialing out the variance attributable to an initial predictor set. Finally, Telenson, Alexander, and Barrett (1983) have proposed a *rare response scoring technique* in which items' responses are weighted on the basis of how few individuals select a given response option.

Studies comparing these weighting techniques have yielded some important findings (Mumford & Owens, 1987). For instance, England (1971) has suggested that the percent scoring methods will generally yield more stable weights than the available alternatives. However, research by Lecznar and Dailey (1950) and Malone (1978) indicates that, although the method of treating response options as binary variables and scoring the options according to the extent they discriminate between criterion groups may initially yield

higher validities, the correlational and regression procedures yield equal or somewhat better cross-validated coefficients and show less shrinkage in cross-validation. A linear discriminant function was found to be superior to the horizontal percentage method in terms of descriptive power in a study by Smith and George (1987), and Aamody and Pierce (1987) demonstrated the superiority of traditional item-criterion keying over Telenson et al's (1983) rare response method. According to Campbell (1974), both validity and sample size affect the outcome of such comparisons. He used a Monte Carlo approach to investigate three weighting strategies: multiple regression, zero-order validity, and unit weights. He concluded that multivariate prediction should not be attempted when the sample size is less than 150, that unit weights are best if the sample size is less than 150, but even then, unit weighting is risky if too many nonvalid predictors or items are added. He also concluded that unless sample validity is greater than .50 and the sample size is greater than 250, multiple regression weights should not be used. Instead, zero-order validity coefficients should be used as weights.

Webb (1960) and Malloy (1955) contrasted variants of the weighted application blank approach with the deviant response procedure when adding a biodata form to an existing test. The deviate scores are equal to the difference between actual criterion values and predicted criterion values using all existing predictors (Stead & Shartle, 1940). It was found that in the initial keying sample the deviant response procedure added more to prediction than a standard empirical key. However, the Webb (1960) study suggests that the predictive power of deviant response keys may not hold up under cross-validation due to the poor reliability of residual scores. Finally, Telenson et al. (1983) have found that based on predictive efficiency, the rare weighting technique was clearly superior to the vertical and horizontal percent approaches.

Thayer (1977) has argued that more attention should be given to the criterion in the development of empirical keys. Unfortunately, few studies in the background data literature have devoted substantial effort to criterion development, in part because they have tended to employ relatively simple criteria such as turnover. However, the ambiguities arising in the Telenson et al. (1983) study, as a result of the contaminating influence of geographic area, suggest the importance of this issue. Studies by Malloy (1955), Laurent (1962), and Klein and Owens (1965) point to the enhanced efficiency of empirical keys formulated on the basis of well-constructed criterion measures.

Selecting the criterion that the biodata form will predict is clearly a critical step. The effectiveness of the biodata form depends on the criterion used in its development. Successful performance is an operationalization of effective adaptation to the organizational environment. If the criterion selected to measure effective adaptation is deficient, contaminated, or biased, the effectiveness and utility of the biodata form is greatly hampered.

The predictive power of an empirical key depends not only on a well-developed criterion, but also on the definition of the validation sample or reference group. Because selection studies have focused primarily on job applicants, the issue of reference group definition has not received much attention (Mumford & Owens, 1987). However, the generality of the reference group in part determines the generality of an empirical key, just as shifts in the composition of a reference group lead to changes in an empirical key's predictive power. Different kinds of reference groups may produce substantial differences in the nature of the resulting keys such that different keys may be obtained when the reference group consists of job incumbents rather than job applicants. In one study, Hogan and Stokes (1989) demonstrated the nonequivalence of predictive and concurrent designs for the empirical development and validation of biodata for applicant

selection. Within the same company and predicting a turnover criterion among sales representatives, a cross-validated key developed on a very large sample of applicants differed almost completely in content from that developed on a very large sample of incumbents. The cross-validated key developed on the incumbent sample failed to predict turnover in the applicant sample. Thus, both reference group composition and a well-developed criterion are important items to consider.

Another consideration in identifying criterion groups and establishing criterion cutoffs is the number of employees available. Cascio (1982) has recommended that there should be at least 125 individuals within each criterion group. Sample size becomes even more critical with the development of empirical keys because of the need for cross-validation. Although estimates of the best group division for cross-validation vary, England (1971) recommended that one-third more individuals be included in the validation group compared to the cross-validation group. However, other researchers have argued that empirical cross-validation is inferior to formula estimates of shrinkage because of computational and logistical costs as well as questions regarding the accuracy of the estimates provided through traditional cross-validation (Murphy, 1984; Schmitt, 1982). Although formula estimates of shrinkage have become very popular, Mitchell and Klimoski (1986) found their use questionable because they overestimated shrinkage for rationally developed, empirically keyed biodata scales and underestimated shrinkage for more empirically oriented methods. Clearly, further research is needed on this issue.

Reliability.   Relatively little information is available concerning the reliability of empirically keyed background data scales. The majority of studies investigating the reliability of biodata keys have used the test-retest method, and the reliability coefficients obtained have been found to be very high. Chaney and Owens

(1964) administered an 82-item form to 49 male college students and again 19 months later and obtained a retest coefficient of .85. Erwin and Herring (1977) reported that correlations between the biodata scores of Army recruits obtained during enlistment processing and several weeks after entering the Army were .91 and .85, using biographical information blanks (BIBs) of 67 and 36 items, respectively. The Life Insurance Marketing and Research Association (LIMRA) reported a test-retest reliability of .90 based on samples of 5,000 job applicants with an interval of up to five days (LIMRA, 1979). The Institute for Behavioral Research in Creativity (IBRIC, 1968) reported retest reliabilities ranging from .82 to .88 for ninth-grade students in North Carolina. Finally, Shaffer et al. (1986) evaluated item reliabilities of Owens' 118-item *Biographical Questionnaire* (BQ) over a five-year period and found average reliability estimates of .56 for males and .58 for females. However, reliability estimates obtained for objective items were significantly higher than those obtained for subjective items. Due to the heterogeneity of most empirical keys, internal consistency estimates of reliability have tended to be considerably lower.

Validation Studies. Of most interest to many researchers with respect to empirical keys is their validity in predicting various criteria. One of the first large scale reviews of biodata validity was conducted by Ghiselli (1966). A number of additional reviews have also appeared in the literature, including those by Asher (1972), Barge and Hough (1986), Dunnette (1962), England (1971), Henry (1966), Hunter and Hunter (1984), Mumford and Owens (1987), Owens (1976), Reilly and Chao (1982), Schuh (1967), and Vineberg and Joyner (1982). Most of the reviews have indicated that, in general, biodata predictors are among the best predictors of a wide range of criteria and sometimes rival cognitive ability tests in the validity coefficients obtained in criterion-related studies.

Hunter and Hunter (1984) provided summaries and interpretations of the data reported in the reviews conducted by Dunnette (1972), Reilly and Chao (1982), and Vineberg and Joyner (1982). Average biodata validities in their reviews were .34 (based on 115 correlations), .38 (based on 44 correlations), and .25 (based on 16 correlations), respectively. Table 5 presents average validity coefficients for biodata produced in Hunter and Hunter's meta-analysis conducted with four different criterion variables. Their meta-analysis only analyzed cross-validated biodata keys and showed validities ranging from .26 for tenure and promotion criteria to .37 for prediction of supervisory ratings.

Barge and Hough (1986) reviewed over 100 studies conducted since 1960 using biodata. Eighteen correlational studies investigating performance in training yielded a median validity coefficient of .25. In predicting job proficiency, 36 studies were summarized. The overall median validity coefficient was .32. However, coefficients were notably higher for concurrent studies than they were for predictive studies. The same pattern was obtained among the 33 studies examining prediction of job involvement, such as job satisfaction, absenteeism, turnover, and tenure. The overall median coefficient was .30, but concurrent studies yielded higher validities than did predictive studies. Barge and Hough (1986) also summarized findings in a fourth criterion category: adjustment. The six studies identified were all conducted in the military and involved substance abuse, delinquency, and unfavorable discharge. The median correlation was .26.

In light of the findings of numerous reviews of the criterion-related validity of biodata, it is clear that empirically keyed background data measures are among our best available predictors of training and job performance, with most coefficients lying between .25 and .37. The results available in the broader

TABLE 5

Average Validity Coefficients for Background Data

Criterion	Average Validity	SD of Validity	Number of Correlations	Total Sample Size
Supervisory ratings	.37	.10	12	4,429
Promotion	.26	.10	17	9,024
Training success	.30	.11	11	6,139
Tenure	.26	.15	23	10,800

Note: Only cross-validated coefficients are included in this table.

From "Validity and Utility of Alternative Predictors of Job Performance" by J. E. Hunter and R. F. Hunter, 1984, *Psychological Bulletin, 96*, p. 86. Copyright 1984 by the American Psychological Association. Reprinted by permission.

literature suggest that empirical biodata keys may be valid predictors of a variety of criteria in addition to proficiency, training, and turnover—such as occupational choice (Albright & Glennon, 1961; Mumford & Owens, 1982), criminality (Frazier, 1971), personality attributes (Laughlin, 1984; Rawls & Rawls, 1968; Schuh, 1967), honesty (Haymaker, 1986), and the effects and use of clinical treatments (Carter & Fasullo, 1982; Porch, Collins, Wertz, & Friden, 1980). Thus, it appears that empirically keyed biodata scales may have substantial value in addressing a variety of problems outside the areas of industrial and organizational selection and placement.

Stability and Generality. The validity of biodata keys has been criticized for lacking both stability across time and generality across organizations and cultures. Hughes et al. (1956) first noted a problem with the erosion of validity across time, observing over a three-year period a steady decline in the validity of a weighted application blank. Others have noted similar difficulties (Dunnette et al., 1960;

Schuh, 1967; Wernimont, 1962). However, Brown's (1978) study contradicted earlier investigations when he noted virtually no loss in the validity of 10 biodata items in a form originally validated in 1933 and used for hiring life insurance agents in 1939 and between 1969 and 1971. Brown did, however, note that the item validities had changed over the time period investigated, with some items losing their predictiveness and others increasing their predictive validity. Hunter and Hunter (1984) have criticized Brown's study because he evaluated his data on the basis of statistical significance rather than on the basis of validity, and they argued that an examination of the validity coefficients demonstrates the same decay in validity across time as that found in previous studies. More recently, Rothstein, Schmidt, Erwin, Owens, and Sparks (1990) provided indirect evidence supporting the stability of biodata validities up to 11 years later in a meta-analysis of approximately 11,000 first-line supervisors in 79 organizations.

Explanations for declining validity across time include the confidentiality of the scoring key, the range restriction that results from use of the key, capitalization on chance in the original group, the low base rates for some item responses, and the size of the sample used for development of the key. Periodic reweighting and rescaling of items is clearly a concern.

A few studies have examined the generality of empirically keyed biodata measures across organizations. Schmidt, Hunter, and Caplan (1981) found that a background data measure did not generalize across two petroleum industry jobs. In contrast, Brown (1981) examined the situation specificity of a biodata inventory in a sample of life insurance salespersons. Data from more than 12,000 agents contracted by 12 companies were examined. Although the keys were generalizable, Brown concluded that as much as 38 percent of the variability in validity coefficients could be due to differences in the twelve companies. Similar results were obtained by Levine and Zachert (1951). In contrast, Rothstein et al. (1990) found substantial generalizability of the empirically keyed biodata form constructed by Richardson, Bellows, Henry, and Co. (1981) for selection of first-line supervisors. However, their results may have overestimated the amount of generalizability because they performed their meta-analysis on biodata keys which were developed on large samples in multiple organizations, and items had been included in the keys based, in part, on their generalizability across organizations.

Cross-cultural studies of biodata key validity have provided some evidence of the generalizability of biodata forms across different cultures. A composite criterion of management success was predicted from a biodata form originally developed for managers in the United States (Laurent, 1970). Samples from Denmark, the Netherlands, and Norway were used for comparison. The reported validities were similar in all samples, ranging from .44 in the United States to .61 in Denmark. However, several items had been changed or deleted to fit local cultural conditions. Hinrichs, Haanpera, and Sonkin (1976) found a moderate degree of consistency on a biodata key developed in Finland for predicting sales success. Coefficients ranged from .38 to .72 in samples obtained from the United States, Sweden, Portugal, Norway, and France. These results suggest that empirically keyed background data display some generality in the same occupation in Western cultures. Although they found some evidence for generalizability, they also found that the more different the population was from the original one, the more difficult it was to generalize accurately. To the extent that the required KSAOs are similar in the occupations across different cultures, generalizability would be expected. Future research should investigate the generalizability of empirical keys in non–European countries. Cassens' (1966) finding that factors were similar between biodata forms completed by individuals in the United States and Latin America suggest that empirical keys should generalize even to non–European countries.

Sex and Race Differences.   With respect to race, there has been very little evidence for differential validity of biodata keys. Cascio (1976) found coefficients of .58 for minorities and .56 for nonminorities with the same ten items predicting turnover for both groups. In addition, the work of LIMRA (1979), Frank and Erwin (1978), and Rothstein et al. (1990) have demonstrated comparable validity for majority and minority groups. Reilly and Chao's (1982) review concluded that the validity and fairness of biodata can be expected to hold across racial groups. However, the process of the "blind empirical" approach makes it possible that items highly correlated with race (or gender) might be selected for a final key. For example, Pace and Schoenfeldt (1977) mention a study in which having a Detroit address was negatively correlated with the criterion. Since more blacks than whites live in the city, this item would probably have adverse impact. Rational screening of items could prevent this problem (Owens, 1976).

Conclusions regarding gender differences in biodata keys indicate that different keys may be needed for men and women (Barge & Hough, 1986; Reilly & Chao, 1982). Although Rothstein et al. (1990) found that biodata validities were not moderated by sex, Ritchie and Boehm's (1977) study of management potential found higher validity coefficients for women than men. A study of Navy Hospital Corps trainees (Webster et al., 1978) found that men scored significantly higher on 5 of 11 key items, and women scored higher on 2 items. Research conducted by LIMRA (1979) reported very little difference in the validity coefficients obtained for men and women, but their predictor had been rescaled within subgroups. Nevo's (1976) study found that different items were valid for men and women. Validity coefficients reported for the 13-item key were .36 for men and .18 for women. However, differential range restriction within subgroups may have been the cause (Barge & Hough, 1986). Sex differences found at the factor level (Eberhardt & Muchinsky, 1982; Owens & Schoenfeldt, 1979) and subgroup level (Brush & Owens, 1979; Owens & Schoenfeldt, 1979) corroborate the evidence just cited that different keys may be necessary to achieve comparable validities for men and women. However, the issue needs further research.

Factorial Scales

As an alternative to empirical keys and rationally developed keys, there has been some interest in the use of factor analytic techniques to identify psychologically meaningful summary dimensions to predict criteria of interest. Typically, exploratory factor analytic or principal components procedures are used to identify potential solutions that will yield the smallest number of dimensions accounting for the largest proportion of item variance. Two or three potential solutions are often identified, and each is typically rotated to an orthogonal criterion. The rotated solutions are evaluated with respect to simple structure and psychological meaningfulness, and the solution that optimizes both criteria is generally retained for scaling (Mumford & Owens, 1987).

For developing dimensional scales, items yielding loadings below .30 on any given dimension are often eliminated. Subsequently, dimensional scales are formulated either by using the scoring coefficient matrix to provide item weights or by assigning unit weights in accordance with the direction of the loading.

Because of the relative independence of background data items and the heterogeneity of most item pools, it is unusual to find factor analytic solutions that account for a large proportion of the total item variance. Typically, component analyses account for somewhere between 20 to 50 percent of the total item variance (Baehr & Williams, 1967; Morrison, Owens, Glennon, & Albright, 1962; Mumford & Owens, 1987; Owens, 1976). However, 70 to 90 percent of the items commonly yield loadings above .30 on one or more dimensions (Mumford & Owens, 1987). It has generally been found that dimensions are defined by items of homogeneous content (Owens, 1976). For example, items reflecting parental warmth will typically produce high loadings on one dimension, and items reflecting social involvement will fall together under another dimension. As might be expected given the independence of homogeneous clusters, Baehr and Williams (1967) found that orthogonal and oblique solutions yielded roughly equivalent results.

Reliability. Reliability estimates obtained for factors derived from biodata inventories are relatively high. Mumford and Owens (1982) found retest reliabilities for factors ranging from .91 to .97 for men and from .77 to .97 for women. Bryson (1969) obtained average one-week retest estimates of factorial scales approximating .90. Shaffer et al. (1986) found factor stability estimates over a 5-year period of .49 to .91 for men and .50 to .88 for women. The average factor reliability was .78 for men and .76 for women. Factors assessing more objective past experiences were more reliable than those assessing less objective experiences.

Internal consistency estimates of factorially developed scales have been lower than retest coefficients. Baehr and Williams (1967) reported KR-20 estimates of reliability ranging from .43 to .76 with a vocationally heterogeneous sample of 680 men. Hinrichs, Haanpera, and Sonkin (1976) reported reliabilities ranging from .65 to .78 on a 104-item form administered to five samples.

Validity.   The content and construct validity of factorial scales has not received attention in the literature. This is unfortunate, since the application of confirmatory factor analytic techniques would provide a vehicle for establishing the content and construct validity of these factorial scales. Evidence for the criterion-related validity of factorial scales is also somewhat lacking. Denning (1983) reported on research conducted at Dupont demonstrating that a number of biodata factors successfully differentiated individuals who had industrial accidents from those who did not during a two-year period. Injured employees were found to be significantly higher in socioeconomic status, sensation seeking, manual labor experience, sociability, competitiveness, responsibility, and initiative and lower in emotionality. Although some of these results seemed counterintuitive, a cluster analysis of the injured group revealed the presence of two distinct subgroups of injured employees, with one fitting the traditional profile of the accident-prone individual. In the same study, a group of biodata factors predicted 24 percent of the variance in self-ratings of safety performance and 6 percent of the variance in supervisory ratings of safety performance. Five factor scales were found to predict supervisory ratings of creativity and performance as well as patent disclosure in a study conducted by Morrison et al. (1962) in a sample of 418 petroleum scientists.

In a related study, Morrison (1977) used 8 background data factors to predict performance in a sample of 250 processing and heavy equipment operators. Cross-validated multiple Rs of .35 and .53, respectively, were obtained from a weighted combination of scores on these scales. Childs and Klimoski (1986) factor analyzed a 72-item biodata inventory and derived five biodata factors: social orientation, economic stability, work ethic orientation, educational achievement, and interpersonal confidence. These factors differentially predicted three composite measures of success, including job success ($R = .31$), personal success ($R = .25$), and career success ($R = .49$). Their results were comparable to those reported by Davis (1984). Vandenventer, Taylor, Collins, and Boone (1983) found that scores on background data factors predicted success in an air traffic controller's school, and Engdahl (1980) found that they would predict occupational values. Studies by Lucchesi (1984), Neiner and Owens (1982), and Mumford and Owens (1984) examined background data factors derived in earlier developmental periods for predicting individuals' scores on background data factors derived in later developmental periods, and each study found substantial relationships among the factors. Neiner and Owens (1985) used biodata factors to predict vocational choice among college graduates and found that approximately 20 percent of the variance in occupational choice was accounted for by the biodata factors. Small (1980) used biodata factors to differentiate accounting majors from other college business majors. She found that academic achievement and social introversion factors significantly discriminated between the groups. Cooper and Shaffer (1987) investigated the differentiation of traditional versus nontraditional career choices for women using biodata factors. They found that women who chose traditional careers were lower in cultural-literary interests, scientific-artistic interests, and academic achievement and higher in popularity with the opposite sex and social maturity. Cooper and Shaffer's model accounted for 10 percent of the variance in career choice. Stokes, Mecham, Block, and Hogan (1989) investigated the relationship between biodata factors obtained from two biographical inventories measuring adolescent and postcollege life experiences, respectively, and the 32 job dimensions derived from the *Position Analysis Questionnaire* (PAQ; McCormick, Jeanneret, & Mecham, 1972). The PAQ job dimensions provided descriptions of the jobs held by individuals in the sample, such as sources of information used on the job, job context, and mental and physical demands. Their study demonstrated that for predicting job dimensions, factors from both time periods were related, but those obtained postcollege were more predictive than those obtained from adolescent life experiences. Further research is needed examining the predictive power of factorial background data scales.

Stability and Generality.   A number of studies have attempted to examine the stability or generality of the dimensional structures obtained in factor or component analysis of background data items. Mumford, Shaffer, Jackson, Neiner, Denning, and Owens (1983) contrasted the dimensional structure obtained in three item pools when male and female item responses were factored separately and when they were factored together. It was found that a joint factoring of male and female item responses reduced the percentage of total variance accounted for and yielded dimensions that proved more difficult to interpret than those obtained in separate male and female analyses. Moreover, it was found that there were differences in the content and nature of the dimensions emerging in the various male and female analyses. These results suggested that it may not be appropriate to apply a common dimensional structure to summarize the life history of men and women. However, a study conducted by Stokes, Lautenschlager, and Blakley (1987) examining sex differences in the factor

structure of the 118-item version of Owens' *Biographical Questionnaire* found that, although mean differences were likely to appear in factor scores, the components obtained for both sexes were very similar. Other researchers have reached a similar conclusion. Before definite conclusions can be drawn regarding sex differences in factor structures, more research is clearly required.

On the other hand, Gonter (1979) obtained similar dimensional structures for blacks and whites within a sex group. These results suggest that within a given culture, a common dimensional structure and set of scales may be applied to the members of different ethnic groups. Although the results of this investigation should not arbitrarily be extended across cultural lines, one study does argue for the stability of dimensional structures obtained across Western cultural groups. Cassens (1966) factor analyzed a 62-item background data scale directed at the early identification of management potential. The sample consisted of 105 U.S. managers, 74 U.S. managers working in Latin America, and 382 Latin American managers working in five countries. Of the 10 factors identified, 9 emerged in all three samples.

A few studies have also examined the stability of dimensional structures over time and samples. For instance, the results reported by Owens and Schoenfeldt (1979) found that the predictive characteristics of principal components derived from samples of approximately 2,000 men and women were stable in independent samples, with no more than a 10 percent loss in predictive power. Further, Mumford and Owens (1984) did not observe any cohort effects on the components derived in the analysis of three background data questionnaires administered to seven cohorts over a 10-year interval. Finally, Ames (1983) found that even with the addition of a substantial number of new items to the pool used by Owens and Schoenfeldt (1979), roughly the same number of male and female dimensions emerged in an orthogonal principal components analysis.

Two studies have examined the stability of the dimensional structures obtained from background data items over substantial time periods. In one, Eberhardt and Muchinsky (1982) readministered the original Owens and Schoenfeldt (1979) background data form to a sample of midwestern freshmen approximately 10 years later. Because they obtained virtually the same dimensional structure in the male sample but found marked differences in the dimensional structure for the female sample, they concluded that changes in the nature of women's roles during this period had induced some instability in the dimensional structure. Although this seemed to be a reasonable interpretation, particularly since the changes they found indicated greater similarity between men and women, a study by Lautenschlager and Shaffer (1987) reexamined the component stability of Owens's *Biographical Questionnaire* (BQ) in light of a reanalysis of the original data used to develop the 118-item form of the BQ. Results demonstrated that the components were stable across time and geographic location for both men and women. Methodological differences between the two studies, rather than changing life experiences, led to the apparent instability found for women in the Eberhardt and Muchinsky (1982) study.

In a somewhat different study of factor stability across time, Neiner and Owens (1982) examined the relationship between factors obtained from a biodata form measuring adolescent life experiences and one measuring early postcollege life experiences obtained seven years later. Canonical correlations were used to determine whether life experience factors were similar across the two inventories. The correlations obtained for the same set of subjects between the underlying dimensions ranged from .56 to .64. Thus, the biodata dimensions appeared reasonably stable across a seven-year period, even though the two biodata forms were developed to represent different periods in the life of an individual.

Another set of studies has examined age effects on the dimensional structures obtained in factorings of background data items. Schmuckler (1966) examined age differences in factor structures and found similar principal components across three age groups in a sample of 439 middle management executives. Rock and Freeberg (1969) administered a biodata form to seventh, ninth, and eleventh graders and found that of 11 factors extracted, all but 3 showed reasonably good stability across age groups. One study by Mumford, Shaffer, Ames, and Owens (1983) examined the stability of the male and female dimensional structure produced by a common item pool in two age groups known to be facing different developmental tasks. Different dimensional structures were obtained in these two age groups. Thus, when the age grading of behavior and experiences has resulted in marked shifts in the nature of individuals' lives, there may be a need to apply different dimensional structures in different age groups.

Comparative Findings. Mitchell and Klimoski (1982) contrasted the predictive power of empirical keys and factorial scales, and they found that the empirical key predicted licensure of real estate salespersons better than a weighted combination of six factorial scales in both the validation and cross-validation samples. However, the factorial scales showed less shrinkage in cross-validation. Though factorial scales may not predict as well as empirical keys in a particular situation, factorial scales may display somewhat greater generality and stability. Some support for this conclusion may be found in a comparison of the results obtained in the Morrison et al. (1962) factorial study of innovation among petroleum scientists with the results obtained in the Smith, Albright, Glennon, and Owens (1961) study of empirical keys in predicting the same criterion among petroleum scientists. In addition to their greater stability and generality, the development of factorial scales can yield psychologically meaningful dimensions. Hough (1989) recently demonstrated that biodata are manifestations of individual differences variables. Some factors commonly obtained in background data studies are provided in Mumford and Owens (1987). Among the most common were adjustment, academic achievement, intellectual/cultural pursuits, introversion versus extroversion, social leadership, maturity, and career development. Given the nature and content of common factorial scales and with increased concern for construct validity, one should expect factor scales to exhibit greater generality and stability when compared to a purely empirical scaling strategy. Such factorial scales should have substantial value as a vehicle for obtaining some understanding of the basic dimensions of life history and of performance determinants.

Summary of Scaling Techniques

In the preceding sections, we have examined the characteristics of rational, empirical, and factorial scales for summarizing background data items. Broadly speaking, it appears that all three methods show adequate reliability. It also appears that when constructed with some attention to the psychometric requirements for scale construction using a well-developed and appropriate item pool, all three of these techniques can be used to predict a number of complex criterion performances.

Future studies should consider not only the relative merits of these scaling techniques with respect to the predictive situation at hand, but also the relative merits of alternative scaling procedures that have not received a great deal of attention in the literature. Among available techniques, latent trait modeling, nonlinear regression, and confirmatory modeling appear promising. It is also possible that multidimensional scaling strategies might prove useful. However, it is important to recognize that the multifaceted nature of individual development implies that some vehicle

must be found for combining the resulting scales to obtain an overall index of predictive power (Frank, 1980).

Prediction Strategies: Subgrouping

When investigators wish to predict performance on a number of criteria and in a variety of job situations and employee populations, constructing numerous empirical scales may be burdensome. In addition, the specificity of empirical keys prohibits the cross-situational and cross-sample comparisons that often play an important role in theory construction (Mumford, Weeks, Harding, & Fleishman, 1988).

Recognition of these problems led Owens (1976) to argue that more general procedures for the definition of performance-relevant developmental patterns were required. Although the processes giving rise to cohesive patterns of differential development are complex, the ecology model holds that some individuals should come to display substantial similarities in the pattern of environmental transactions manifest in their behavior and experiences over time. Owens (1968, 1971, 1976, 1978) reasoned that if this were true, then the specification of generalized patterns of environmental transactions might provide the basis for the construction of more general developmental patterns capable of predicting a range of criterion performances. Such a subgrouping approach takes advantage of cluster analysis rather than linear, multivariate analysis in measuring individual differences.

Techniques for Subgroup Definition

Owens (1968, 1971, 1976, 1978) suggested a three-step solution to the problem of grouping people. First, background data items must be developed which are capable of appraising behavior in or reactions to a variety of situations likely to have occurred earlier in people's lives. Second, some technique must be found to appraise the relative similarity of individuals in their expression of these behaviors and experiences. Third, a set of decision rules must be formulated for determining when two or more individuals display sufficient similarity to permit assignment to a common category.

Owens and Schoenfeldt (1979) proposed a general paradigm for addressing each of these issues. They argued that subgrouping would require a relatively extensive item pool capable of capturing a number of developmentally significant behaviors and experiences. In their initial investigation, this was accomplished by formulating some 2,000 item specifications that were eventually reduced to 389 operational items using various screening strategies. Although subsequent studies (Gustafson, 1987; Jackson, 1982; Schoenfeldt, 1974; Shaffer, 1987) have shown that meaningful subgroups can be developed using smaller pools of 50 to 100 items, it appears that the success of such efforts is highly dependent on the appropriate specification of critical developmental events.

Because these items are to be used to describe or define modal patterns of environmental transactions, three other issues are likely to arise in generating the descriptive base required for subgrouping. First, it is possible that certain modal or prototypic patterns of environmental interchange may occur relatively infrequently in the population under consideration (Mumford & Owens, 1984). Thus, a comprehensive definition of the relevant transactional patterns will require a fairly large sample, typically one including more than 400 individuals (Owens & Schoenfeldt, 1979). However, if the investigator is interested in identifying only the more common or frequently expressed patterns, smaller samples of 100 or more individuals might be used, although loss in the accuracy of classification assignments is likely (Block, 1971; A. Thomas & Chess, 1981). Second, these transactional patterns will be most clearly expressed when a variety of situations occurring at a number of points in the

course of people's lives are examined. As the descriptive base is narrowed to capture behavior and experiences occurring in a limited time frame, some loss in generality and accuracy can be expected (Block, 1971; Mumford & Owens, 1984). Third, and finally, this descriptive base should focus on behavior and experiences in situations to which most individuals are likely to have been exposed if meaningful comparative statements are to be made. When this condition cannot be met, separate subgroupings should be conducted (Mumford, Shaffer, Jackson, Neiner, Denning, & Owens, 1983).

Having specified a reasonably general descriptive base and sample, the next issue in subgrouping is the assessment of individuals using these measures. Owens and Schoenfeldt (1979) note that analytic limitations and the need for a reliable description of KSAOs leads most investigators to use item aggregates such as principal components techniques in defining similarity (Owens & Schoenfeldt, 1979). Rationally based scaling systems might also be profitably employed in a reasonably well-defined set of situations where the potential developmental determinants can be specified with some certainty.

As Owens and Schoenfeldt (1979) note, regardless of the particular strategy used to appraise individuals, the next necessary step in subgrouping entails the assessment of relative similarity. Although a number of indices are available for appraising the similarity of individuals in terms of their scores on a profile of discrete measures (Fleishman & Quaintance, 1984), with a few exceptions (e.g., Baer, 1970), most subgrouping studies have followed Owens and Schoenfeldt's (1979) recommendation that Cronbach and Gleser's (1953) d^2 index be used. Initially, application of this index was based on its sensitivity to all three elements of profile similarity as jointly manifest in the pattern, elevation, and scatter of people's item or item aggregate scores. Recent work by Rounds, Dawis, and Lofquist (1979) contrasting nine alternative similarity indices indicates that this index may also provide a particularly accurate appraisal of profile similarity.

Given this overall definition of relative similarity, some vehicle must be found for grouping individuals together in such a way as to maximize within-group similarity and between-group differentiation. Because the Ward and Hook (1963) clustering algorithm explicitly seeks to maximize within-group similarity and between-group differentiation, Owens and Schoenfeldt (1979) recommended its application. Essentially, this technique begins by treating each individual as a subgroup, then combining the two most similar individuals into a new subgroup. The relevant d^2 values are then recalculated based on the average profile of this new subgroup, and the procedure is repeated in an iterative sequence until all individuals have been combined into a single subgroup. At each step in this sequence, the within-group sums of squares are calculated. This information is used to determine the number of subgroups to be retained by determining the point at which there is a sharp increase in within-group variation as a result of combining individuals who do not really belong together.

Although a variety of other clustering algorithms are available that might also be used to define background data subgroups (Anderberg, 1973), Monte Carlo studies by Blashfield (1976) and Blashfield and Morey (1980) indicate that the Ward and Hook algorithm is effective in classifying people into groups. However, other studies by Feild and Schoenfeldt (1975b) and Zimmerman, Jacobs, and Farr (1982) indicate that to control for the drift of early assignees in this hierarchical procedure, the group centroids should be used as seed points in a subsequent nonhierarchical analysis where individuals are reallocated to subgroups. This process must be repeated several times until the group centroids stabilize (Feild & Schoenfeldt, 1975b). Once this has been accomplished, the resulting

subgroups may be viewed as reflecting a modal pattern of past environmental transactions likely to be shared by a number of individuals. New individuals may be assessed in terms of the known characteristics of extant subgroup members following the construction of discriminant functions for assigning individuals to these subgroups.

Solution Characteristics. In the first implementation of this paradigm, Owens (1976) and Owens and Schoenfeldt (1979) administered 389 background data items concerned with behavior and experiences in developmentally significant situations likely to occur during childhood and adolescence to 1,037 men and 897 women. Men's and women's item responses were then factored and subgrouped in accordance with the procedures previously outlined. This analysis yielded 23 male and 15 female subgroups. An extensive series of follow-up investigations was then carried out to define the characteristics of these subgroups.

In this initial investigation it was found that most individuals could be described by these patterns; only 7 percent of the sample constituted isolates who could not be assigned to any subgroup, and the majority, 73 percent, could be assigned to a single subgroup. The remaining 20 percent of the sample constituted overlapping cases who could be described within the classification structure by two or more subgroups. Other investigators have obtained similar classification rates in industrial samples (Brush & Owens, 1979) and in older samples intended to identify prototypic patterns of differential development during college and young adulthood (Jackson, 1982). Mumford and Owens (1984) obtained somewhat higher fit statistics when a more extensive item pool covering multiple developmental periods was in use. Taken as a whole, these observations suggest that given an adequate descriptive base, the procedures proposed by Owens and Schoenfeldt (1979) can be used to identify patterns of prior behavior and experiences capable of describing most individuals by permitting relatively unambiguous subgroup assignments.

Typically, the number of subgroups retained in these studies has hovered around 15, although some investigators have retained as few as 3 or 4 subgroups (Baer, 1970; Gavin, 1975; Tanofsky et al., 1969) and others have retained as many as 23 (Jackson, 1982; Owens & Schoenfeldt, 1979). The somewhat subjective nature of the scree test procedures employed in subgroup definition, and differences in the desired level of generality, may, in part, account for these results. Comparison of the Jackson (1982) and Owens and Schoenfeldt (1979) investigations with the Baer (1970), Gavin (1975), and Tanofsky et al. (1969) studies does suggest, however, that a larger number of subgroups tends to emerge with increases in sample size, the heterogeneity of the population, and the number of descriptors in use.

Also typical of subgrouping studies is the substantial cross-group differences in the number of individuals assigned to each subgroup. For instance, Mumford and Owens (1984) identified male subgroups containing as many as 50 and as few as 9 individuals. These results might be expected, given that the structured, nonrandom nature of differential development indicates that some patterns of environmental transactions should occur more frequently than others. In practical predictive studies, relatively small groups are often eliminated. This elimination may lead to some loss in overall predictive power when Bayesian techniques are being used to generate individualized predictive statements (Lissitz & Schoenfeldt, 1974; Novick, 1974; Schoenfeldt & Lissitz, 1971, 1974).

Stability and Generality.   One approach to the assessment of stability has been used by Schoenfeldt (1974) and Owens and Schoenfeldt (1979). Here a cross-validation strategy was used in which the initial background data form was administered to six freshman classes

entering the University of Georgia between 1968 and 1977. Subsequently, the discriminant functions derived in the initial 1968 cohort were applied in the later cohorts. It was found that the new samples could be fitted to the initial Owens and Schoenfeldt (1979) subgroups with no more than a 10 percent loss in the number of individuals assigned to a single subgroup. Further, Schoenfeldt (1974) noted that the relative number of individuals assigned to the later cohorts was maintained in later years. Thus, it appears that the Owens and Schoenfeldt (1979) subgroups provided a reasonably stable description of patterns of differential development over time, at least within samples drawn from the same university.

The generality of subgroup solutions to other geographical locations or cultures has also been addressed. Anderson (1972) readministered the Owens and Schoenfeldt (1979) questionnaire at two southeastern universities and one midwestern university. She found that the same subgroup structure could be applied in all three samples, although the proportion of individuals assigned to each subgroup varied somewhat. In a related study, however, Johnson (1972) readministered this questionnaire in a small Mississippi state junior college and found that the initial Owens and Schoenfeldt (1979) structure could not be generalized due to marked differences in people's life histories. Thus, marked differences in the nature of significant life events in different populations may require the formulation of new subgrouping structures.

This point has been underscored in a study by Mumford, Shaffer, Jackson, Neiner, Denning, and Owens (1983). In this study, three distinct background data questionnaires were used to construct separate subgroups for men and women, as well as a set of subgroups applying to both men and women. They found that attempts to combine the male and female samples in subgrouping resulted in a 20 percent loss in the number of individuals who could be unambiguously assigned to a single subgroup. Although these results are in accordance with various empirical keying studies (Reilly & Chao, 1982), they also suggest that there are sufficient differences in men's and women's life experiences to prohibit the definition of a common set of developmental pathways unless items are explicitly selected so as to be applicable to both men and women (Brush & Owens, 1979). Although further research is needed, particularly studies focusing on cross-cultural differences, these results indicate that the developmental patterns identified in subgrouping should not be arbitrarily assumed to generalize to different subpopulations.

Validity. Only a limited number of studies have examined the ability of subgrouping techniques to predict real-world criteria. Broadly speaking, these studies have examined the predictive power of background data subgroups with respect to (a) educational performance and preference criteria, (b) job choice and job performance criteria, and (c) general social adjustment criteria.

Initially, studies examining the predictive power of background data subgroups focused on the prediction of educational criteria. In one set of investigations, Schoenfeldt (1970, 1974) found that members of the initial Owens and Schoenfeldt subgroups displayed marked differences in their declared college majors and on academic performance criteria such as college GPA, the dean's list, academic probations and dismissals, and number of course withdrawals. Other investigations by H. A. Klein (1972), Mumford (1983), Mappus (1979), and Nutt (1975) have shown that subgroup membership predicts academic over- and underachievement, college attrition, and movement into graduate school.

In a separate investigation, Ames (1983) administered a set of background data items to veterinarians and subsequently used the procedures formulated by Owens and Schoenfeldt (1979) to formulate a set of background data

subgroups. It was found that the resulting subgroups differentiated those individuals who did and did not remain in veterinary medicine. These subgroups were also found to discriminate between veterinarians focusing on research as opposed to practice. In another investigation, Brush and Owens (1979) administered 263 background data items to 1,987 nonexempt employees of a petrochemical company. The kinds of items selected were chosen to reflect experiences commonly reported by employees in industrial settings. A principal components analysis of the items resulted in identifying nine factors, including trade skills, family relationships, achievement motivation/self-confidence, academic success, athletic and extracurricular interests, socioeconomic level, personal work-related values, introversion, and organized institutional affiliation. A subsequent subgrouping using the procedures outlined by Owens and Schoenfeldt (1979) resulted in the identification of 18 subgroups. Subsequent analyses examining the job assignments of these individuals indicated that the members of these subgroups displayed a differential affinity for various job categories, as well as differing in turnover rates and performance.

In a related set of investigations, L. R. Taylor (1968) and Pinto (1970) administered background data forms to two independent samples of salesmen and formulated a set of subgroups. In the Taylor study, it was found that 83 percent of the more successful salesmen were drawn from three of the nine subgroups identified. In the Pinto (1970) study, it was found that the subgroups displayed differential termination rates and that subgroup status predicted attrition at the .60 level in both a model development and cross-validation sample. Similar results have been obtained in a study by Tanofsky et al. (1969), who found that four background data subgroups defined in a sample of 1,525 insurance salesmen exhibited significant differences in dollar volume of insurance sold. Finally, Gavin (1975) administered a 38-item background data form to 162 bank managers and obtained three subgroups. Subsequent analyses indicated that subgroup members differed not only in job level, but also in their job perceptions.

Similar findings have been obtained in studies of the relationship between subgroup membership and more general forms of social behavior. For instance, Boardman, Calhoun, and Schiel (1972) found that 5 of the initial Owens and Schoenfeldt subgroups, comprising 22 percent of the total sample, contained 55 percent of the individuals holding one or more leadership positions in 235 campus organizations. In a somewhat more wide-ranging study, Feild and Schoenfeldt (1975a) identified 12 dimensions summarizing behavior and experiences during the college years. In a series of discriminant analyses, it was found that 74 percent and 89 percent of the variance in the male and female factor scores, respectively, was related to subgroup membership in Owens and Schoenfeldt's (1979) adolescent subgroups. Other studies conducted by Baer (1970), Lewis (1973), and Strimbu and Schoenfeldt (1973) have shown that background data subgroups also differ on somewhat more discrete criteria such as delinquency rate, homosexuality, and drug use. Moreover, studies by Ruda (1970) and Small (1982) indicate that subgroup membership may be related to interpersonal perception and attraction both in school and in the workplace.

Taken as a whole, the results obtained in these studies indicate that background data subgroups differ in terms of later behavior and experiences in both occupational and educational settings. As Owens and Schoenfeldt (1979) point out, the nature of these relationships has generally proved to be consistent with the initial inferences concerning the implications of subgroup membership.

These studies point to an important characteristic of subgroups. More specifically, they appear to be especially effective predictors of situational choice, fit assessment, and

motivationally or dispositionally loaded criteria. Some support for this notion has been obtained in a study by Mumford, Connelly, and Clifton (1990). This study compared the ability of subgroups and rational scales to predict performance and affective or evaluative criteria. It was found that subgroups were better predictors of affective criteria, such as job and life satisfaction, while rational scales were better predictors of performance criteria, such as college grades. These two types of scales, however, evidenced complex relationships suggesting, in accordance with the ecology model, that the background data predictors of affect and performance may be related to each other in a complex manner contingent on the long-term implications of a developmental pattern (Mumford, Snell, & Reiter-Palmon, in press; Mumford, Uhlman, & Kilkullen, in review).

Comparative Findings.   Few studies are currently available contrasting subgroups with other methods of prediction using biodata. Nonetheless, it seems reasonable to expect that empirical keys will be more effective predictors of the specific criteria for which the keys are developed. However, background data subgroups may prove to be more efficient predictors of a wider range of criteria because subgroups may more easily be developed to predict multiple criteria.

At least two studies have examined the predictive power of subgroups and linearly derived factorial and rational scales. In one of these investigations, Feild, Lissitz, and Schoenfeldt (1975) contrasted the predictive power of adolescent background data factor scores and adolescent subgroups with respect to measures of collegiate behavior and experiences. In a series of canonical analyses, it was found that the adolescent background data factors and the adolescent subgroups each predicted collegiate behavior and experiences equally well. However, it was also found that by combining both factor score information and subgroup membership information, some improvement in prediction was obtained, thereby indicating that the subgroups captured unique predictive variance. A similar conclusion was reached in a study examining safety criteria by Harland, Peck, and McBride (1975). Another study conducted by Frank (1980) found that subgroups and linear scales used in subgroup construction proved to be equally effective predictors of tenure and performance criteria. Although these studies argue for the comparability of information obtained from linear scales and subgroups, in accordance with the comments of Owens (1978), Hein and Mumford (1988), Tesser and Lissitz (1973), and Mumford, Stokes, and Owens (1990), their comparability would only be expected when criterion performance is determined primarily by main effects rather than by the complex interactions that can be captured with subgroups. Thus, subgrouping may offer an alternative to traditional biodata keying methods.

General Applications

Classification. Schoenfeldt (1974) proposed a general assessment classification model that includes subgroups of homogeneous people, in terms of their prior transactional patterns, and subgroups of homogeneous jobs. The performance of subgroups in each job family is specified, and individuals are placed in job families where their subgroup has performed well. Schoenfeldt (1974) and Brush and Owens (1979) conducted initial tests of this system in academic and industrial settings. Results from both studies demonstrated the utility of forming subgroups of persons and subgroups of jobs (i.e., job families) for job description and classification. Rather than using the traditional approach of selecting the right person for the right job, the focus of the Schoenfeldt and Brush and Owens models is on classifying individuals to the job family for which they have the necessary characteristics. At present, Stokes

and Mecham have been pursuing the utility of biodata subgroups formed in late adolescence for predicting job family assignment 10 to 12 years later. Preliminary results have been promising (Stokes et al., 1989).

Although the results obtained in these initial investigations were promising, a major roadblock to routine application of the assessment-classification model has been a lack of techniques indicating how subgroup-level descriptive information should be translated into the individualized assessments required for differential job assignments. A potential solution to this problem has been suggested by Schoenfeldt and Lissitz (1971, 1974), Lissitz and Schoenfeldt (1974), and Mumford, Stokes, and Owens (1990), who have argued for the application of a modified Bayesian approach. Here, individualized predictions are generated by obtaining the individual's probability of membership in each alternative subgroup, using discriminant function techniques (Owens & Schoenfeldt, 1979), and then establishing the probability of known subgroup members displaying adequate performance on the criterion of interest. Subsequently, the probability of a new individual displaying adequate performance on these criteria may be obtained using the formulas outlined in detail in Mumford, Stokes, and Owens (1990).

Of importance in using these formulas is, first, that predictions can be generated for all individuals, even those who are not good fits within a single subgroup, because the implications of their probability of membership in each group are considered. Second, this system incorporates the fact that the same criterion might not be applicable in all job families. Third, because probabilities stabilize rapidly and information concerning the performance of subgroup members can be accumulated over time, this system can be applied even in generating predictions for relatively small job families. When the sample size required for initial subgroup specification prohibits application of subgrouping techniques, or under conditions where only a few jobs and one or two criteria are of concern, investigators might prefer to use an alternative strategy, such as Lunneborg's (1968) multiple differential prediction approach or Morrison's (1977) factorial strategy.

Individual Organizational Actions.   Organizational personnel have found it difficult to implement individualized programs for training, job redesign, motivational enhancement, or performance appraisal that take into account individual differences in responses to them, largely because such individualized systems are costly. Background data provide the information necessary for adjusting organizational actions to the needs of the individual. Subgroups of individuals who respond differentially to various forms of training or rewards for performance could be identified, and the subgroup information could provide a vehicle for tailoring organizational actions to the needs of the individual.

With regard to rewards for performance, managers could be encouraged to provide an individual with those rewards preferred by the members of the subgroup that he or she occupies, resulting in more powerful reinforcement for performance at the individual level and higher performance and productivity at the aggregate level than would be obtained by using the same rewards for all individuals. This information might also be employed in conjunction with personnel needs to guide recruiting efforts in attracting the types of individuals needed for openings.

Subgrouping also provides a vehicle for formulating systematic career development programs. By establishing the typical criterion performance for subgroups at different positions in an organizational hierarchy, along with the number of subgroup members entering each position, each subgroup's likely career paths in the organization can be tracked. Moreover, studies of high- and low-performing members of subgroups could be conducted to identify experiences needed to increase

performance. The information obtained could be used to construct the career development program. These are only a few examples of the use of the subgrouping technique in an organization.

Organizational Development.   One advantage of background data in general, and the subgrouping strategy in particular, is that it allows complex person-by-situation interactions to be captured (Magnusson, 1988; Owens, 1978). Moreover, the ecology model suggests that the selection of, perception of, and choice of activities in a given environment allow the individual to create a personally adaptive job environment. Recently, Schneider (1987a, 1987b) has proposed a model that specifies how individual actions lead to the creation and maintenance of a particular kind of organizational environment. This theory, referred to as the *attraction, selection, attrition* (ASA) *model*, begins with the notion that individuals will be attracted to organizations and jobs providing positively valued reinforcers and, in turn, that organizations will select and promote individuals whose KSAOs are consistent with the organizational environment. People whose transactions with the organizational environment are ineffective in the sense that desired reinforcers are not provided for requisite activities are likely over time to leave the organization. This self-propagating process is adaptive for both the individual and the organization, provided it represents a structure conjoint with demands for goal attainment.

There are a number of parallels between Schneider's (1987a, 1987b) ASA model and the ecology model we have proposed in order to account for the emergence of coherent patterns of environmental transactions. Both models suggest that individuals perceive and are attracted to situations providing the opportunity for and possibility of attaining desired reinforcers or goals using available resources. Moreover, both models suggest that individuals will make decisions and choose courses of action consistent with their niche and style as it is manifest in their selective application of resources in the cause of goal attainment. Finally, both models indicate the self-perpetuating nature of these transactional patterns, albeit on an individual and an aggregate level, respectively.

These parallels between the ASA and ecology models suggest that background data information might prove of substantial value in both attaining an understanding of organizational behavior and designing interventions intended to enhance long-term organizational adaptation. For instance, one way to define the unique properties and characteristics of an organization is by defining the subgroup composition of the organization at different levels of the organizational hierarchy and in different functional areas. By comparing this information to aggregate population data reflecting the frequency of subgroup membership, one might determine the kinds of people attracted to the organization, those individuals' likely roles in the organization, and the nature of the individuals whose transactional patterns are sufficiently consistent with organizational culture to result in movement into leadership and cultural-maintenance roles. The known characteristics of subgroup members and their preferred transactional patterns might then be used to define the unique characteristics of the organization and draw inferences concerning the likely actions an organization should choose in addressing various environmental opportunities.

Information pertaining to the characteristic subgroup composition of an organization might also prove of substantial value in organizational development efforts. One potential application is the selective identification and promotion of individuals to cope with organizational change. For instance, Schneider (1987a, 1987b) has argued that the self-propagating nature of the ASA process should over time lead to a narrowing of the kinds of individuals found in the organization, particularly

the organizational elite. This narrowing of focus may, in turn, result in a lack of adaptation. However, if subgroup composition were used to document this effect, it could be used to suggest the kinds of individuals who must be added to the mix to preserve diversity and flexibility. Similarly, when changes in the nature of the organizational operating environment are expected, the new demands likely to be made on organizational members could be specified. The characteristic pattern of subgroup members' responses to relevant KSAOs might then be used to identify for recruitment or promotion those individuals who would be especially likely to respond adaptively to this anticipated event. Thus, background measures, by guiding the introduction of new types of individuals into the organizational environment, could be used to offset the classic criticism that standardized testing only serves to maintain the status quo.

Resource availability and social interactional problems are somewhat difficult to address and continue to represent historical roadblocks to effective organizational change efforts. Nonetheless, when the implications of the ecology model are considered in light of Schneider's (1987a, 1987b) ASA model, a few potential strategies come to mind. For instance, an organization might use the ecology model to create a sheltered, separate suborganization to address some new opportunity, as has been the case in the computer industry and some research laboratories. Another strategy might involve the selective transfer of nonadaptive individuals in key change areas and their subsequent replacement by more adaptive types. Regardless of whether these or other potential change strategies are used, it is important to recognize that changes in personnel should be accompanied by the requisite changes in the social and physical aspects of the job setting through systematic redesign programs that facilitate or make possible resource application and provide personally valued reinforcers for use of these resources.

Theory Development. In linking background data and the ecology model to Schneider's (1987a, 1987b) ASA theory of organizational behavior, the preceding discussion points to an important role of background data measures. By seeking to capture individuals' behavior and experiences in relatively discrete situations likely to have occurred earlier in their lives, background data measures provide recall indices of potential antecedent events. Although antecedent status does not fully establish causality, it is true that antecedent status is commonly held to constitute a minimum condition for causal inferences. Cognizance of this principle led Sontag (1971), Fiske (1979), and Howe (1982), among others, to argue that the systematic definition of antecedent-consequent relationships might be used as a basis for theory development. Thus, by virtue of their ability to capture the life history events related to various kinds of later behavior and experiences, background data measures might also be expected to provide a useful tool in initial theory development.

At least two areas of research have emphasized the role of background data measures in theory development. Beginning with the work of Roe (1956), a number of investigators interested in creativity have used background data measures in attempts both to predict creative potential and to attain an understanding of the developmental influences providing a basis for later innovation (Albright & Glennon, 1961; Barron & Harrington, 1981; Buel et al., 1966; James et al., 1972, 1974; Smith, Albright, Glennon, & Owens, 1961; C. W. Taylor & Ellison, 1968). In one study Morrison et al. (1962) factored a set of life history items that were effective predictors of research creativity. The factors they identified displayed substantial overlap with the core characteristics Barron and Harrington (1981) found to be consistently related to

innovative achievement across occupational fields.

One obvious implication of these observations is that background data measures might provide a useful vehicle for identifying antecedent motivational and noncognitive determinants of innovation. Studies by Schaefer and Anastasi (1968) and Anastasi and Schaefer (1969) have served to confirm and extend this conclusion. Examining early antecedents of creativity in adolescent boys and girls, they found that strong continuing interests, unusual experiences, and an intellectually stimulating family background provided a consistent early background leading to the later emergence of creativity. In a later theory-based review of the literature focusing on more developmentally oriented studies, Gustafson and Mumford (1988) found that these same early influences provided a basis for the development of creativity by facilitating the availability and application of multiple knowledge structures.

Not only is evidence available for the utility of background data measures as a tool for theory development in the creativity literature, a number of studies concerned with vocational interests and career choice have also underscored the potential utility of background data measures. Kuhnert and Russell (1990) have argued that research relating biodata to leadership theory would benefit both researchers and practitioners in understanding leadership behavior and managerial selection. Related to vocational interests, studies by Chaney and Owens (1964) and Kulberg and Owens (1960) examined background data items related to the expression of sales, research, and general engineering interests. In these initial investigations, research engineers were found to display a more independent intellectual orientation in their earlier lives, and sales interests were associated with a more gregarious social orientation accompanied by an early family environment which was likely to encourage social interaction. In a later study, Mumford and Owens (1982) examined the background data items related to a variety of vocational interests. Following a rational clustering of the items correlated with each of the 22 basic interest scales of the *Strong Interest Inventory*, it was concluded that social learning theory might provide an adequate framework for explaining interest development.

Studies by Neiner and Owens (1985) and Eberhardt and Muchinsky (1984) have also underscored the relationship between vocational interests and prior life history events using a factorial approach. Other work by Eberly (1980), Engdahl (1980), and Rounds, Dawis, and Lofquist (1979) have indicated that background data measures are related to occupational reinforcer patterns. Smart (1989) has recently demonstrated the relative importance of life history in influencing the development of Holland's (1973) vocational types. Finally, Graef, Wells, Hyland, and Muchinsky (1985) have examined the background data factors related to vocational indecision and obtained an interpretable pattern of correlates consistent both with Tyler's (1965) earlier observations and with social learning theory.

Taken as a whole, these studies indicate that background data measures might provide a useful tool in theory development efforts. The nature of the more successful studies along these lines, however, points to four important conclusions concerning the theoretical application of background data measures. First, as underscored in the Anastasi and Schaefer (1969) study and the Morrison et al. (1962) investigation, background data measures appear most likely to prove useful in theory construction efforts when the item pool in use has been formulated on the basis of well-defined developmental hypotheses where multiple items have been developed to tap each of these hypotheses. Second, it appears that such efforts are more likely to prove effective when a relatively broadly defined item pool is used that explicitly seeks to cover a number of alternative developmental hypotheses. Third, these efforts consistently appear to be more successful when some attention is given to potential underlying causal constructs in item development and when these results are considered in light of broader theory. Finally, the success of these efforts to some extent appears to depend on the use of carefully specified criterion measures.

Conclusions

Implicit in our observations concerning the theoretical applications of background data measures is one of the more important conclusions to be drawn from this review. The cry "shotgun empiricism" has historically been the most common criticism of background data measures. Given the early work of Siegel (1956a), Torrance and Ziller (1957), and Chaney and Owens (1964), one might wonder whether this hue and cry has ever been completely justified. Even to the extent that this criticism was justified, however, one can still ask whether our predecessors had any real choice in the matter, given a field where there was little or no consensus concerning the existence of consistent or coherent patterns of behavior and experience over time and given that studies of differential development in adulthood were few and far between.

Nonetheless, this empirical research told us that there was something about individuals' past behavior and experiences that conditioned their future potentialities. When this solid empirical observation was considered in light of the recent theoretical advances in our understanding of the processes giving rise to continuity and change in differential behavior and the maturation of various longitudinal studies examining the operation of these processes in adults' lives, it became possible to formulate a viable theoretical framework for attaining an understanding of how coherent patterns of behavior and experiences emerge across the life span. Certainly, this theoretical framework remains in the incipient stages of its development. However, the work conducted to date has laid a sound foundation for this idealized future. More centrally, however, by allowing us to specify the mechanisms by which past behavior and experiences condition people's behavior and experiences in new situations, it is now possible to take a more theoretically oriented approach in the development and application of background data measures.

By applying systematic construct validation principles of the sort recommended in this chapter, we believe that the nature and scope of background data research will offer far more, not only to industrial psychology, but to the field as a whole. In the industrial area, the systematic specification of job situations and specification of the KSAOs conditioning performance in these situations does much to enhance our understanding of job behavior and thereby the systematic definition of antecedent events. Further, by attaining a more sophisticated understanding of how individual development conditions people's behavior in the workplace, we believe, in accordance with Schneider (1987a, 1987b), that a great deal may be revealed about the nature of organizations and career development processes. This will hopefully serve to stimulate the emergence of new concepts about organizational behavior as well as the development of new technologies for solving organizational problems.

The authors gratefully acknowledge the contributions made by William A. Owens and Paul C. Sparks. Without their wisdom, experience, and insightful research, this chapter would not have been possible. We also would like to acknowledge the contributions to the biodata literature made by our other colleagues in the field. Finally, we would like to thank Michele Mobley, Betty Jean Thorpe, Wanda Abbott, Bernie Nickels, Scott Wesley, Michael Hein, Craig Russell, and Ed Fleishman for their support and comments.

References

Aamody, M. G., & Pierce, W. L. (1987). Comparison of the rare response and vertical percent methods for scoring the biographical information blank. *Educational and Psychological Measurement, 47*, 505–511.

Albright, L. E., & Glennon, J. R. (1961). Personal history correlates of physical scientists' career aspirations. *Journal of Applied Psychology, 45*, 281–284.

Allport, G. W. (1937). *Personality: A psychological interpretation*. New York: Holt, Rinehart & Winston.

Allport, G. W. (1942). The use of personal documents in psychological science. *Social Science Research Council Bulletin*, No. 49.

Ames, S. D. (1983). *Prediction of research vs. applied interests in veterinarians*. Unpublished master's thesis, University of Georgia, Athens.

Anastasi, A., & Schaefer, C. E. (1969). Biographical correlates of artistic and literary creativity in adolescent girls. *Journal of Applied Psychology, 54*, 462–469.

Anderberg, M. R. (1973). *Cluster analysis for applications*. New York: Academic Press.

Anderson, B. B. (1972). *An inter-institutional comparison on dimensions of student development: A step toward the goal of a comprehensive developmental-integrative model of human behavior*. Unpublished doctoral dissertation, University of Georgia, Athens.

Anonymous (1925). A method of rating the history and achievements of applicants for positions. *Public Personnel Studies, 3*, 202–209. (Methods and data credited to Gertrude V. Cope)

Ash, R. A. (1983). The behavioral consistency method of training and experience evaluation: Content validity issues and completion rate problems. *Public Personnel Management, 12*, 115–127.

Asher, E. J. (1972). The biographical item: Can it be improved? *Personnel Psychology, 25*, 251–269.

Baehr, M. E. (1976). *National validation of a selection test battery for male transit bus operators*. Washington, DC: U.S. Department of Commerce National Technical Information Service.

Baehr, M. E., & Williams, G. B. (1967). Underlying dimensions of personal background data and their relationship to occupational classification. *Journal of Applied Psychology, 51*, 481–490.

Baer, D. J. (1970). Taxonomic classification of male delinquents from autobiographical data and subsequent recidivism. *Journal of Psychology, 76,* 27–31.

Bandura, A. (1986). *Social foundations of thought and action: A social cognitive theory.* Englewood Cliffs, NJ: Prentice-Hall.

Barge, B. R. (1988). *Characteristics of biodata items and their relationship to validity.* Unpublished doctoral dissertation, University of Minnesota, Minneapolis.

Barge, B. R., & Hough, L. M. (1986). Utility of biographical assessment: A review and integration of the literature. In L. M. Hough (Ed.), *Utility of temperament, biodata, and interest assessment for predicting job performance: A review of the literature* (pp. 91–130) (ARI Research Note No. 88–02). Alexandria, VA: U.S. Army Research Institute.

Barron, F., & Harrington, D. M. (1981). Creativity, intelligence, and personality. *Annual Review of Psychology, 32,* 439–476.

Berkeley, M. H. (1953). A comparison between the empirical and rational approaches for keying a heterogeneous test. (Lackland AFB, TX). *USAF Human Resources Research Bulletin,* No. 53–24.

Blashfield, R. K. (1976). Mixture model tests of cluster analysis: Accuracy of four agglomerative hierarchical methods. *Psychological Bulletin, 83,* 377–388.

Blashfield, R. K., & Morey, J. (1980). A comparison of four clustering methods using MMPI Monte Carlo data. *Applied Psychological Measurement, 4,* 57–64.

Block, J. (1971). *Lives through time.* Berkeley, CA: Bancroft.

Boardman, W. K., Calhoun, L. G., & Schiel, J. H. (1972). Life experience patterns and the development of college leadership roles. *Psychological Reports, 31,* 333–334.

Borgen, F. H. (1988). Occupational reinforcer patterns. In S. Gael (Ed.), *The job analysis handbook for business, government, and industry.* New York: Wiley.

Brown, S. H. (1978). Long-term validity of a personal history item scoring procedure. *Journal of Applied Psychology, 63,* 673–676.

Brown, S. H. (1981). Validity generalization in the life insurance industry. *Journal of Applied Psychology, 66,* 664–670.

Brumback, G. B. (1969). A note on criterion contamination in the validation of biographical data. *Educational and Psychological Measurement, 29,* 439–443.

Brush, D. H., & Owens, W. A. (1979). Implementation and evaluation of an assessment classification model for manpower utilization. *Personnel Psychology, 32,* 369–383.

Bryson, J. B. (1969, April). The dimensions of early human experience. In W. A. Owens (Chair), *Developmental implications of biographical data.* Symposium presented at the meeting of the Southern Society for Philosophy and Psychology, Miami, FL.

Buel, W. D., Albright, L. E., & Glennon, J. R. (1966). A note on the generality and cross-validity of personal history for identifying creative research scientists. *Journal of Applied Psychology, 50,* 217–219.

Buhler, C. (1968). The course of human life as a psychological problem. *Human Development, 11,* 1–16.

Campbell, J. P. (1974). *A Monte Carlo approach to some problems inherent in multivariate prediction: With special reference to multiple regression* (Tech. Rep. No. 2002). Office of Naval Research, Personnel and Training Research Programs.

Carrier, M. R., Dalessio, A. T., & Brown, S. H. (1990). Correspondence between estimates of content and criterion-related validity values. *Personnel Psychology, 43,* 85–100.

Carter, J. A., & Fasullo, B. B. (1982). A study of student utilization behavior at an urban university health center. *College Student Journal, 16,* 343–347.

Cascio, W. F. (1975). Accuracy of verifiable biographical information blank responses. *Journal of Applied Psychology, 60,* 767–769.

Cascio, W. F. (1976). Turnover, biographical data, and fair employment practice. *Journal of Applied Psychology, 61,* 576–580.

Cascio, W. F. (1982). *Applied psychology in personnel management.* Reston, VA: Reston Publishing.

Case, H. W., & Stewart, R. G. (1957). Some personal and social attitudes of habitual traffic violators. *Journal of Applied Psychology, 41,* 46–50.

Caspi, A. (1987). Personality in the life course. *Journal of Personality and Social Psychology, 53,* 1203–1213.

Cassens, F. P. (1966). *Cross-cultural dimensions of executive life history antecedents.* Greensboro, NC:

The Creativity Research Institute, The Richardson Foundation.

Chaney, F. B., & Owens, W. A. (1964). Life history antecedents of sales, research, and general engineering interest. *Journal of Applied Psychology, 48,* 101–105.

Cherry, R. L. (1969). Socioeconomic level and race as biographical moderators. *Dissertation Abstracts International, 30*(4-B), 1937.

Childs, A., & Klimoski, R. J. (1986). Successfully predicting career success: An application of the biographical inventory. *Journal of Applied Psychology, 71,* 3–8.

Cohen, J., & Lefkowitz, J. (1974). Development of a biographical inventory blank to predict faking on personality tests. *Journal of Applied Psychology, 59,* 404–405.

Cook, T. D., & Campbell, D. T. (1979). *Quasi-experimentation: Design and analysis issues for field studies.* Chicago: Rand McNally.

Cooper, L., & Shaffer, G. S. (1987, March). *Biodata used to predict career choice.* Paper presented at the annual meeting of the Southeastern Psychological Association, Atlanta, GA.

Cronbach, L. J., & Gleser, G. C. (1953). Assessing similarity between profiles. *Psychological Bulletin, 50,* 456–473.

Cronbach, L. J., & Meehl, P. E. (1955). Construct validity in psychological tests. *Psychological Bulletin, 52,* 281–302.

Dailey, C. A. (1960). The life history as a criterion of assessment. *Journal of Counseling Psychology, 7,* 20–23.

Dailey, J. T. (1948). *Development of the Airman Classification Test battery.* Banksdale AFB: Air Training Command.

Davis, K. R. (1984). A longitudinal analysis of biographical subgroups using Owens' developmental-integrative model. *Personnel Psychology, 37,* 1–14.

Dawis, R. V., & Lofquist, L. H. (1984). *A psychological theory of work adjustment.* Minneapolis: University of Minnesota Press.

Dawis, R. V., Lofquist, L. H., & Weiss, D. J. (1968). A theory of work adjustment (a revision). *Minnesota Studies in Vocational Rehabilitation, XXIII.*

Denning, D. (1983, March). *Correlates of employee safety performance.* Paper presented at the annual meeting of the Southeastern Industrial and Organizational Psychology Association, Atlanta, GA.

Doll, R. E. (1971). Item susceptibility to attempted faking as related to item characteristic and adopted fake set. *Journal of Psychology, 77,* 9–16.

DuBois, P. H., Loevinger, J., & Gleser, G. C. (1952). *The construction of homogeneous keys for a biographical inventory.* Human Resources Research Bulletin, No. 52-18. Lackland AFB, TX: U.S. Air Force

Dunnette, M. D. (1962). Personnel management. *Annual Review of Psychology, 13,* 285–314.

Dunnette, M. D. (1966). *Personnel selection and placement.* Monterey, CA: Brooks/Cole.

Dunnette, M. D., Kirchner, W. K., Erickson, J., & Banas, P. (1960). Predicting turnover among female office workers. *Personnel Administration, 23,* 45–50.

Dunnette, M. D., Rosse, R. L., Houston, J. S., Hough, G. M., Toquam, J. L., Lammlein, S. E., King, K. W., Bosshardt, M. J., & Keys, M. A. (1982). *Development and validation of an industry-wide electric power plant operator selection system.* Minneapolis: Personnel Decisions Research Institute.

Eberhardt, B. J., & Muchinsky, P. M. (1982). An empirical investigation of the factor stability of Owens' Biographical Questionnaire. *Journal of Applied Psychology, 67,* 138–145.

Eberhardt, B. J., & Muchinsky, P. M. (1984). Structural validation of Holland's hexagonal model: Vocational classification through the use of background data. *Journal of Applied Psychology, 69,* 174–181.

Eberly, R. A. (1980). *Biographical determinants of vocational values.* Unpublished doctoral dissertation, University of Minnesota, Minneapolis.

Ellison, R. L., James, L. R., & Carron, T. J. (1970). Prediction of R&D performance criteria with biographical information. *Journal of Industrial Psychology, 5,* 37–57.

Ellison, R. L., & Taylor, C. W. (1962). The development and cross-validation of a biographical inventory for predicting success in science. *American Psychologist, 17,* 391–392.

Endler, N. S. (1982). Interactionism: A personality model, but not yet a theory. *Nebraska Symposium on Motivation, 30,* 155–200.

Engdahl, B. E. (1980). *The structure of biographical data and its relationship to needs and values.* Unpublished doctoral dissertation, University of Minnesota, Minneapolis.

England, G. W. (1971). *Development and use of weighted application blanks* (Bulletin No. 55). Minneapolis: Industrial Relations Center, University of Minnesota.

Erikson, E. H. (1963). *Childhood and society.* New York: Norton.

Erwin, F. W., & Herring, J. W. (1977, August). *The feasibility of the use of autobiographical information as a predictor of early Army attrition* (TR–77–A6). Alexandria, VA: U.S. Army Research Institute for Behavioral and Social Sciences.

Federico, S. M., Federico, P. A., & Lundquist, G. W. (1976). Predicting women's turnover as a function of met salary expectations and biodemographic data. *Personnel Psychology, 29,* 559–566.

Feild, H. S., Lissitz, R. W., & Schoenfeldt, L. F. (1975). The utility of homogeneous subgroups and individual information in prediction. *Multivariate Behavioral Research, 10,* 449–462.

Feild, H. S., & Schoenfeldt, L. F. (1975a). Development and application of a measure of students' college experiences. *Journal of Applied Psychology, 60,* 491–497.

Feild, H. S., & Schoenfeldt, L. F. (1975b). Ward and Hook revisited: A two part procedure for overcoming a deficiency in the grouping of persons. *Educational and Psychological Measurement, 35,* 171–173.

Ferguson, L. W. (1961). The development of industrial psychology. In B. H. Gilmer (Ed.), *Industrial psychology* (pp. 18–37). New York: McGraw-Hill.

Ferguson, L. W. (1962). *The heritage of industrial psychology.* Hartford, CT: Author.

Ferguson, L. W. (1967). Economic maturity. *Personnel Journal, 46,* 22–26.

Fiedler, F. E., & Garcia, J. E. (1987). *New approaches to effective leadership: Cognitive resources and organizational performance.* New York: Wiley.

Fine, S. A., & Wiley, W. W. (1971). *An introduction to functional job analysis: Methods for manpower analysis* (Monograph No. 4). Kalamazoo, MI: W. E. Upjohn Institute.

Fiske, D. W. (1979). Two worlds of psychological phenomena. *American Psychologist, 34,* 733–739.

Fleishman, E. A. (1972). On the relation between learning, abilities, and human performance. *American Psychologist, 27,* 1017–1032.

Fleishman, E. A. (1975). Toward a taxonomy of human performance. *American Psychologist, 30,* 1127–1149.

Fleishman, E. A., & Mumford, M. D. (1989). Abilities as causes of individual differences in skill acquisition. *Human Peformance, 2,* 225–239.

Fleishman, E. A., & Quaintance, M. K. (1984). *Taxonomies of human performance: The description of human tasks.* Orlando, FL: Academic Press.

Frank, B. A. (1980). A comparison of an actuarial and a linear model for predicting organizational behavior. *Applied Psychological Measurement, 4,* 171–181.

Frank, B. A., & Erwin, F. W. (1978). *The prediction of early Army attrition through use of autobiographical information questionnaires* (Tech. Rep. No. TR–78–A11). Alexandria, VA: U.S. Army Research Institute.

Frazier, R. W. (1971). *Differential perception of individuals subgrouped on the basis of biodata responses.* Unpublished doctoral dissertation, University of Georgia, Athens.

French, N. R., Lewis, M. A., & Long, R. E. (1976, March). *Social desirability responding in a multiple choice biographical questionnaire.* Paper presented at the annual meeting of the Southeastern Psychological Association, New Orleans.

Galton, F. (1902). *Life history album* (2nd ed.). New York: Macmillan.

Gavin, J. F. (1975). Organizational climate as a function of personal and organizational variables. *Journal of Applied Psychology, 60,* 135–139.

Ghiselli, E. E. (1966). *The validity of occupational aptitude tests.* New York: Wiley.

Ghiselli, E. E. (1973). The validity of aptitude tests in personnel selection. *Personnel Psychology, 26,* 461–477.

Goldsmith, D. B. (1922). The use of the personal history blank as a salesmanship test. *Journal of Applied Psychology, 6,* 149–155.

Goldstein, I. L. (1971). The application blank: How honest are the responses? *Journal of Applied Psychology, 55,* 491–492.

Gonter, R. (1979). *Comparison of blacks and whites on background data measures.* Athens, GA: Institute for Behavioral Research.

Graef, M. I., Wells, D. L., Hyland, A. M., & Muchinsky, P. M. (1985). Life history antecedents of vocational indecision. *Journal of Vocational Behavior, 27,* 276–297.

Guilford, J. P. (1954). *Psychometric methods* (2nd ed.). New York: McGraw-Hill.

Guilford, J. P. (1959). *Personality*. New York: McGraw-Hill.

Guilford, J. P., & Lacey, J. I. (1947). Printed classification tests. *AAF Aviation Psychology Research Program Reports*. Washington, DC: U.S. Government Printing Office.

Guion, R. M. (1974). Open a new window: Validities and values in psychological measurement. *American Psychologist, 29,* 287–296.

Guion, R. M. (1977). Content validity—The source of my discontent. *Applied Psychological Measurement, 1,* 1–10.

Guion, R. M. (1980). On trinitarian doctrines of validity. *Professional Psychology, 11,* 385–398.

Gustafson, S. B. (1987). *Person and situation subgroup membership as predictive of job performance and job perceptions*. Unpublished doctoral dissertation, Georgia Institute of Technology, Atlanta.

Gustafson, S. B., & Mumford, M. D. (1988). Creativity syndrome: Integration, application, and innovation. *Psychological Bulletin, 104,* 27–41.

Guthrie, E. R. (1944). Personality in terms of associative learning. In J. McV. Hunt (Ed.), *Personality and the behavior disorders* (Vol. 1, pp. 49–68). New York: Ronald Press.

Harland, R. M., Peck, R. C., & McBride, R. S. (1975). The prediction of accident liability through biographical data and psychometric tests. *Journal of Safety Research, 7,* 16–52.

Harrell, T. W. (1960). The validity of background data items for food company salesmen. *Journal of Applied Psychology, 44,* 31–33.

Havighurst, R. J. (1952). *Developmental tasks and education*. New York: Longmans/Green.

Haymaker, J. C. (1986, August). *Biodata as a predictor of employee integrity and turnover*. Paper presented at the annual meeting of the American Psychological Association, Washington, DC.

Haymaker, J. C., & Erwin, F. W. (1980). *Investigation of applicant responses and falsification detection procedures for the MAP* (Tech. Rep. 1–80). Washington, DC: Richardson, Bellows, and Henry, Inc.

Hein, M. B., & Mumford, M. D. (1988, August). *Continuity and change: An integration of the idiographic and nomothetic perspective*. Paper presented at the annual meeting of the American Psychological Association, Atlanta, GA.

Henry, E. R. (1966). *Research conference on the use of autobiographical data as psychological predictors*. Greensboro, NC: The Creativity Research Institute, The Richardson Foundation.

Himelstein, D., & Blaskovics, T. L. (1960). Prediction of an intermediate criterion of combat effectiveness with a biographical inventory. *Journal of Applied Psychology, 44,* 166–168.

Hinrichs, J. R., Haanpera, S., & Sonkin, L. (1976). Validity of a biographical information blank across national borders. *Personnel Psychology, 29,* 417–421.

Hogan, J. E., & Stokes, G. S. (1989, April). *The influence of socially desirable responding on biographical data of applicant versus incumbent samples: Implications for predictive and concurrent research designs*. Paper presented at the annual meeting of the Society of Industrial and Organizational Psychology, Boston.

Holland, J. C. (1973). *Making vocational choices: A theory of careers*. Englewood Cliffs, NJ: Prentice-Hall.

Hornick, C. W., James, L. R., & Jones, A. P. (1977). Empirical item keying versus a rational approach to analyzing a psychological climate questionnaire. *Applied Psychological Measurement, 1,* 489–500.

Hough, L. M. (1984). Development and evaluation of the "accomplishment record" method of selecting and promoting professionals. *Journal of Applied Psychology, 69,* 135–146.

Hough, L. (1989, April). Biodata and the measurement of individual differences. In T. W. Mitchell (Chair), *Biodata vs. personality: The same or different classes of individual differences?* Symposium presented at the annual meeting of the Society for Industrial and Organizational Psychology, Boston.

Howe, M. J. (1982). Biographical evidence and the development of outstanding individuals. *American Psychologist, 37,* 1071–1081.

Hughes, J. F., Dunn, J. F., & Baxter, B. (1956). The validity of selection instruments under operating conditions. *Personnel Psychology, 9,* 321–324.

Hunter, J. E., & Hunter, R. F. (1984). Validity and utility of alternative predictors of job performance. *Psychological Bulletin, 96,* 72–98.

Institute for Behavioral Research in Creativity (IBRIC). (1968). *Manual for Alpha Biographical Inventory*. Greensboro, NC: Predictions Press.

Jackson, K. E. (1982). *A further look at life history defined subgroup homogeneity across time.* Unpublished doctoral dissertation, University of Georgia, Athens.

James, L. R., Ellison, R. L., Fox, D. G., & Taylor, C. W. (1972). Reliability estimated by scoring key equivalence across samples. *Journal of Applied Psychology, 56,* 500–505.

James, L. R., Ellison, R. L., Fox, D. G., & Taylor, C. W. (1974). Prediction of artistic performance from biographical data. *Journal of Applied Psychology, 59,* 84–86.

James, L. R., Mulaik, S. A., & Brett, J. M. (1982). *Causal analysis: Assumptions, models, and data.* Beverly Hills, CA: Sage.

Jensen, A. (1980). *Bias in mental testing.* New York: Free Press.

Johnson, R. (1972). *Homogeneous subgroups based on biographical data as predictors of educational success in a junior college.* Unpublished doctoral dissertation, University of Georgia, Athens.

Jones, E. L. (1970, May). *The affinity of biodata subgroups for vocational interests.* Paper presented at the annual meeting of the Georgia Psychological Association, Atlanta.

Kagan, J., Sontag, L. W., Baker, C. T., & Nelson, V. L. (1958). Personality and IQ change. *Journal of Abnormal and Social Psychology, 56,* 261–266.

Kavanagh, M. J., & York, D. R. (1972). Biographical correlates of middle managers' performance. *Personnel Psychology, 25,* 319–332.

Keating, E., Paterson, D. G., & Stone, C. H. (1950). Validity of work histories obtained by interview. *Journal of Applied Psychology, 34,* 1–5.

Keinan, G., Friedland, N., Yitzhaky, J., & Moran, A. (1981). Biographical, physiological, and personality variables as predictors of performance under sickness-inducing motion. *Journal of Applied Psychology, 66,* 233–241.

Kenagy, H. G., & Yoakum, C. S. (1925). *The selection and training of salesmen.* New York: McGraw-Hill.

Kendrick, D. T., & Funder, D. C. (1988). Profiting from controversy: Lessons from the person-situation debate. *American Psychologist, 43,* 23–34.

Kirchner, W. K., & Dunnette, M. D. (1957). Applying the weighted application blank technique to a variety of office jobs. *Journal of Applied Psychology, 41,* 206–208.

Klein, H. A. (1972). *Personality characteristics of discrepant academic achievers.* Unpublished doctoral dissertation, University of Georgia, Athens.

Klein, S. P., & Owens, W. A. (1965). Faking of a scored life history blank as a function of criterion objectivity. *Journal of Applied Psychology, 49,* 452–454.

Klimoski, R. J. (1973). A biographical data analysis of career patterns in engineering. *Journal of Vocational Behavior, 3,* 103–113.

Korman, A. K. (1968). The prediction of managerial performance: A review. *Personnel Psychology, 21,* 295–322.

Kuhnert, K. W., & Russell, C. J. (1990). Using constructive developmental theory and biodata to bridge the gap between personnel selection and leadership. *Journal of Management, 16*(3), 1–13.

Kulberg, G. E., & Owens, W. A. (1960). Some life history antecedents of engineering interests. *Journal of Educational Psychology, 51,* 26–31.

La Gaipa, J. J. (1969). Biographical inventories and style of leadership. *Journal of Psychology, 72,* 109–114.

Landy, F. J. (1986). Stamp collecting versus science: Validation as hypothesis testing. *American Psychologist, 41,* 1183–1192.

Larson, R. H., Swarthout, D. M., & Wickert, F. R. (1967, March). *Objectionability and fakability of biographical inventory items.* Paper presented at the annual meeting of the Midwestern Psychological Association, Chicago.

Laughlin, A. (1984). Teacher stress in an Australian setting: The role of biographical mediators. *Educational Studies, 10,* 7–22.

Laurent, H. (1962). Early identification of management talent. *Management Record, 24,* 33–38.

Laurent, H. (1970). Cross-cultural cross-validation of empirically validated tests. *Journal of Applied Psychology, 54,* 417–423.

Lautenschlager, G. J. (1985a). Within subject measures for the assessment of individual differences in faking. *Educational and Psychological Measurement, 46,* 309–316.

Lautenschlager, G. J. (1985b, March). Controlling response distortion of an empirically-keyed biodata questionnaire. In G. S. Shaffer (Chair), *Twenty years of biodata research.* Symposium presented at the annual meeting of the Southeastern Psychological Association, Atlanta.

Lautenschlager, G. J., & Shaffer, G. S. (1987). A reexamination of the component stability of Owens's Biographical Questionnaire. *Journal of Applied Psychology, 72,* 149–152.

Lawshe, C. H. (1975). A quantitative approach to content validity. *Personnel Psychology, 28,* 563–575.

Lawshe, C. H. (1985). Inferences from personnel tests and their validity. *Journal of Applied Psychology, 70,* 237–238.

Lecznar, W. B., & Dailey, J. T. (1950). Keying biographical inventories in classification test batteries. *American Psychologist, 5,* 279.

Lefkowitz, J. (1972). Differential validity: Ethnic group as a moderator in predicting tenure. *Personnel Psychology, 25,* 223–240.

Lerner, R. M. (1978). Dialectics and development. *Human Development, 21,* 1–20.

Levine, A. S., & Zachert, V. (1951). Use of a biographical inventory in the Air Force classification program. *Journal of Applied Psychology, 35,* 241–244.

Levinson, D. J. (1986). A conception of adult development. *American Psychologist, 41,* 3–13.

Lewis, M. A. (1973). *Life experience characteristics of homosexual activists.* Unpublished master's thesis, University of Georgia, Athens.

Life Insurance Marketing and Research Association, (LIMRA). (1979). *Agent selection research questionnaire.* Hartford, CT: LIMRA.

Lissitz, R. W., & Schoenfeldt, L. F. (1974). Moderator subgroups for the estimation of educational performance: A comparison of prediction models. *American Educational Research Journal, 11,* 63–75.

Lord, R. G., DeVader, C. L., & Alliger, G. M. (1986). A meta-analysis of the relationship between personality traits and leadership perceptions: An application of validity generalization procedures. *Journal of Applied Psychology, 71,* 402–410.

Lucchesi, C. Y. (1984). *The prediction of job satisfaction, life satisfaction, and job level from autobiographical dimensions: A longitudinal application of structural equation modeling.* Unpublished doctoral dissertation, University of Georgia, Athens.

Lunneborg, C. E. (1968). Biographical variables in differential vs. absolute prediction. *Journal of Educational Measurement, 5,* 207–210.

Magnusson, D. (1988). Individual development from an interactional perspective. In D. Magnusson (Ed.), *Paths through life* (Vol. 1). Hillsdale, NJ: Erlbaum.

Magnusson, D., & Endler, N. S. (1977). Interactional psychology: Present status and future prospects. In D. Magnusson & N. S. Endler (Eds.), *Personality at the crossroads: Current issues in interactional psychology.* Hillsdale, NJ: Erlbaum.

Majesty, M. S. (1967). *Identification of race, sex, and religion through life history* (AD695–827). Springfield, VA: Clearinghouse for Federal Scientific and Technical Information.

Malloy, J. (1955). The prediction of college achievement with the life experience inventory. *Educational and Psychological Measurement, 15,* 170–180.

Malone, M. P. (1978). *Predictive efficiency and discriminatory impact of verifiable biographical data as a function of data analysis procedure.* Unpublished doctoral dissertation, University of Minnesota, Minneapolis.

Manson, G. E. (1925). What can the application blank tell? *Journal of Personnel Research, 4,* 73–99.

Mappus, L. A. (1979). *Biographical information as an indicator of potential success in postgraduate study.* Unpublished master's thesis, University of Georgia, Athens.

Matteson, M. T. (1978). An alternative approach to using biographical data for predicting job success. *Journal of Occupational Psychology, 51,* 155–162.

Matteson, M. T., & Osburn, H. G. (1970). A Fortran program series for generating relatively independent and homogeneous keys for scoring biographical inventories. *Educational and Psychological Measurement, 30,* 664–671.

Matteson, M. T., Osburn, H. G., & Sparks, C. P. (1969). *A computer based methodology for constructing homogeneous keys with applications to biographical data.* Houston, TX: Personnel Psychology Services Center, University of Houston.

McClelland, J. N., & Rhodes, F. (1969). Prediction of job success for hospital aides and orderlies from MMPI scores and personal history data. *Journal of Applied Psychology, 53,* 49–54.

McCormick, E. J., Jeanneret, P., & Mecham, R. C. (1972). A study of job characteristics of job dimensions as based on the Position Analysis Questionnaire [Monograph]. *Journal of Applied Psychology, 36,* 347–368.

McGinnies, E., & Vaughan, W. (1957). Some biographical determiners of participation in a group discussion. *Journal of Applied Psychology, 41,* 179–185.

Messick, S. (1975). The standard problem: Meaning and values in measurement and evaluation. *American Psychologist, 30,* 955–966.

Messick, S. (1980). Test validity and the ethics of assessment. *American Psychologist, 35,* 1012–1027.

Mikesell, R. H., & Tesser, A. (1971). Life history antecedents of authoritarianism: A quasi-longitudinal approach. *Proceedings of the 74th convention of the American Psychological Association, 6,* 136–137.

Minor, F. J. (1958). Prediction of turnover of clerical employees. *Personnel Psychology, 11,* 393–402.

Mitchell, T. W. (1986, April). *Specialized job analysis for developing rationally-oriented biodata prediction systems.* Paper presented at the annual meeting of the Society for Industrial and Organizational Psychology, Chicago.

Mitchell, T. W. (1989, April). Do biodata measure personality: Different, better, and/or more? In T. W. Mitchell (Chair), *Biodata vs. personality: The same or different classes of individual differences?* Symposium presented at the annual meeting of the Society for Industrial and Organizational Psychology, Boston.

Mitchell, T. W., & Klimoski, R. J. (1982). Is it rational to be empirical? A test of methods for scoring biographical data. *Journal of Applied Psychology, 67,* 411–418.

Mitchell, T. W., & Klimoski, R. J. (1986). Estimating the validity of cross-validity estimation. *Journal of Applied Psychology, 71,* 311–317.

Morrison, R. F. (1977). A multivariate model for the occupational placement decision. *Journal of Applied Psychology, 62,* 271–277.

Morrison, R. F., Owens, W. A., Glennon, J. R., & Albright, L. E. (1962). Factored life history antecedents of industrial research performance. *Journal of Applied Psychology, 46,* 281–284.

Morrison, R. F., & Sebald, M. L. (1974). Personal characteristics differentiating female executives from female non-executive personnel. *Journal of Applied Psychology, 59,* 656–659.

Mosel, J. N. (1952). Prediction of department store sales performance from personal data. *Journal of Applied Psychology, 36,* 8–10.

Mosel, J. L., & Cozan, L. W. (1952). The accuracy of application blank work histories. *Journal of Applied Psychology, 36,* 365–369.

Mosel, J. L., & Wade, R. R. (1951). A weighted application blank for reduction of turnover in department store sales clerks. *Personnel Psychology, 4,* 177–184.

Mulaik, S. A. (1986). Toward a synthesis of deterministic and probabilistic formulation of causal relationships by the functional relations concept. *Philosophy of Science, 53,* 313–337.

Mumford, M. D. (1983). *Life history dimensions and types between ages 18 and 30.* Unpublished doctoral dissertation, University of Georgia, Athens.

Mumford, M. D., Connelly, M. S., & Clifton, T. C. (1990). *The meaning of life history measures: Implications for scaling strategies.* Unpublished report, Center for Behavioral and Cognitive Studies, George Mason University, Fairfax, VA.

Mumford, M. D., Cooper, M., & Schemmer, F. M. (1983). *Development of a content valid set of background data measures.* Bethesda, MD: Advanced Research Resources Organization.

Mumford, M. D., & Owens, W. A. (1982). Life history and vocational interests. *Journal of Vocational Behavior, 21,* 330–348.

Mumford, M. D., & Owens, W. A. (1984). Individuality in a developmental context: Some empirical and theoretical considerations. *Human Development, 27,* 84–108.

Mumford, M. D., & Owens, W. A. (1987). Methodology review: Principles, procedures, and findings in the application of background data measures. *Applied Psychological Measurement, 11,* 1–31.

Mumford, M. D., Reiter-Palmon, R., & Snell, A. F. (in press). Background data and development: Structural issues in the application of life history measures. In G. S. Stokes, M. D. Mumford, & W. A. Owens (Eds.), *The biodata handbook: Theory, research, and applications.* Palo Alto, CA: Consulting Psychologists Press.

Mumford, M. D., Shaffer, G. S., Ames, S. P., & Owens, W. A. (1983). *Analysis of PCEI responses over time.* Athens, GA: Institute for Behavioral Research.

Mumford, M. D., Shaffer, G. S., Jackson, K. E., Neiner, A., Denning, D., & Owens, W. A. (1983). *Male-female differences in the structure of background data measures.* Athens, GA: Institute for Behavioral Research.

Mumford, M. D., Snell, A. F. & Reiter-Palmon, R. (in press). Personality and background data: Life history and self concepts in an ecological system. In G. S. Stokes, M. D. Mumford, & W. A. Owens (Eds.), *The biodata handbook: Theory, research, and applications.* Palo Alto, CA: Consulting Psychologists Press.

Mumford, M. D., Stokes, G. S., & Owens, W. A. (1990). *Patterns of life adaptation: The ecology of human individuality.* Hillsdale, NJ: Erlbaum.

Mumford, M. D., Uhlman, C. E., & Kilkullen, R. J. (in review). The structure of life history: Implications for the construct validity of background data scales. *Human Performance.*

Mumford, M. D., Weeks, J. L., Harding, F. D., & Fleishman, E. A. (1988). Relationships between student characteristics, course content, and training outcome variables: An integrative modeling effort. *Journal of Applied Psychology, 73,* 614–627.

Mumford, M. D., Wesley, S. S., & Shaffer, G. S. (1987). Individuality in a developmental context. II: The crystallization of developmental trajectories. *Human Development, 30,* 291–321.

Murphy, K. R. (1984). Cost-benefit considerations in choosing among cross-validation methods. *Personnel Psychology, 37,* 15–22.

Murphy, K. R. (1989). Is the relationship between cognitive abilities and job performance stable over time? *Human Performance, 2,* 183–200.

Murray, S. L., Ellison, R. L., & Fox, D. G. (1973, August). *Racial fairness of biographical predictors of academic performance.* Paper presented at the meeting of the American Psychological Association, Montreal.

Myers, D. C., & Fine, S. A. (1980). *Development of preemployment experience questionnaires.* Bethesda, MD: Advanced Research Resources Organization.

Myers, J. H., & Errett, W. (1959). The problem of preselection in weighted application blank studies. *Journal of Applied Psychology, 43,* 94–95.

Neiner, A. G., & Owens, W. A. (1982). Relationships between two sets of biodata with seven years separation. *Journal of Applied Psychology, 67,* 146–150.

Neiner, A. G., & Owens, W. A. (1985). Using biodata to predict job choice among college graduates. *Journal of Applied Psychology, 70,* 127–136.

Nevo, B. (1976). Using biographical data to predict the success of men and women in the Army. *Journal of Applied Psychology, 61,* 106–108.

Nickels, B. J. (1989). *The construction of background data measures: Developing procedures to maximize construct, content, and criterion-related validity.* Unpublished doctoral dissertation, Georgia Institute of Technology, Atlanta.

Norman, W. T. (1963). Personality measurement, faking and detection: An assessment of a method for use in personnel selection. *Journal of Applied Psychology, 47,* 317–324.

Novick, M. R. (1974). Moderator subgroups and Bayesian N group regression: Some concluding remarks. *American Educational Research Journal, 11,* 91–92.

Nutt, J. J. (1975). *An examination of student attrition using life experience subgroups.* Unpublished master's thesis, University of Georgia, Athens.

O'Leary, L. R. (1973). Fair employment, sound psychometric practice, and reality. *American Psychologist, 28,* 147–150.

Owens, W. A. (1968). Toward one discipline of scientific psychology. *American Psychologist, 23,* 782–785.

Owens, W. A. (1971). A quasi-actuarial basis for individual assessment. *American Psychology, 26,* 992–999.

Owens, W. A. (1976). Background data. In M. D. Dunnette (Ed.), *Handbook of industrial and organizational psychology.* Chicago: Rand McNally.

Owens, W. A. (1978). Moderators and subgroups. *Personnel Psychology, 31,* 243–247.

Owens, W. A., Glennon, J. R., & Albright, L. E. (1962). Retest consistency and the writing of life history items: A first step. *Journal of Applied Psychology, 46,* 329–332.

Owens, W. A., & Henry, E. R. (1966). *Biographical data in industrial psychology: A review and evaluation.* Greensboro, NC: The Creativity Research Institute, The Richardson Foundation.

Owens, W. A., & Schoenfeldt, L. F. (1979). Toward a classification of persons. *Journal of Applied Psychology, 64,* 569–607.

Owens, W. A., Schumacher, C. F., & Clark, J. B. (1957). The measurement of creativity in machine design. *Journal of Applied Psychology, 41,* 297–302.

Pace, L. A., & Schoenfeldt, L. F. (1977). Legal concerns in the use of weighted application blanks. *Personnel Psychology, 30,* 159–166.

Pannone, R. D. (1984). Predicting test performance: A content valid approach to screening applicants. *Personnel Psychology, 37,* 507–514.

Parish, J. A., & Drucker, A. J. (1957). *Personnel research for officer candidate school* (Tech. Research Rep. No. 117). USA TAGO Personnel Research Branch.

Peterson, D. A., & Wallace, S. R. (1966). Validation and revision of a test in use. *Journal of Applied Psychology, 46,* 416–419.

Peterson, N. G., & Bownas, D. A. (1982). Skill, task structure, and performance acquisition. In E. A. Fleishman & M. D. Dunnette (Eds.), *Human performance and productivity: Human capability assessment.* Hillsdale, NJ: Erlbaum.

Pinto, P. R. (1970). *Subgrouping in prediction: A comparison of moderator and actuarial approaches.* Unpublished doctoral dissertation, University of Georgia, Athens.

Plag, J. A., & Goffman, J. M. (1967). The Armed Forces Qualification Test: Its validity in predicting military effectiveness for naval enlistees. *Personnel Psychology, 20,* 323–340.

Porch, B. E., Collins, M., Wertz, R. T., & Friden, T. P. (1980). Statistical prediction of change in aphasia. *Journal of Speech and Hearing Research, 23,* 317–321.

Quaintance, M. K. (1981). *Development of a weighted application blank to predict managerial assessment center performance.* Unpublished doctoral dissertation, George Washington University, Washington, DC.

Rawls, D., & Rawls, J. R. (1968). Personality characteristics and personal history data of successful and less successful executives. *Psychological Reports, 23,* 1032–1034.

Redmond, M. R., & Nickels, B. J. (1989, April). *Application of direct and indirect item development strategies in the construction of background data measures.* Paper presented at the annual meeting of the Southeastern Psychological Association, Atlanta.

Reilly, R. R., & Chao, G. T. (1982). Validity and fairness of some alternative employee selection procedures. *Personnel Psychology, 35,* 1–62.

Reiter-Palmon, R., Uhlman, C. E., & DeFilippo, B. (1990). *Influence of life event implications on the predictive validity of background data measures.* Paper presented at the meetings of the Southeastern Psychological Association, Atlanta, GA.

Richardson, Bellows, Henry, & Co. (1984a). *Executive summary: The manager profile record.* Washington, DC: Author.

Richardson, Bellows, Henry, & Co. (1984b). *Technical reports: The candidate profile record.* Washington, DC: Author.

Richardson, Bellows, Henry, & Co. (1984c). *Technical reports: The supervisory profile record.* Washington, DC: Author.

Richardson, Bellows, Henry, & Co. (1981). *Supervisory profile record* (Tech. Rep. Vols. 1, 2, & 3). Washington, DC: Author

Riegel, K. F. (1975). Toward a dialectical theory of development. *Human Development, 18,* 50–64.

Ritchie, R. J., & Boehm, V. R. (1977). Biographical data as a predictor of women's and men's management potential. *Journal of Vocational Behavior, 11,* 363–368.

Roach, D. E. (1971). Double cross-validation of a weighted application blank over time. *Journal of Applied Psychology, 55,* 157–160.

Rock, D. A., & Freeberg, N. E. (1969). Factorial invariance of biographical factors. *Multivariate Behavioral Research, 4,* 195–209.

Roe, A. (1956). *The psychology of occupations.* New York: Wiley.

Rothstein, H. R., Schmidt, F. L., Erwin, F. W., Owens, W. A., & Sparks, C. P. (1990). Biographical data in employment selection: Can validities be made generalizable? *Journal of Applied Psychology, 75,* 175–184.

Rounds, J. B., Dawis, R. V., & Lofquist, L. (1979). Life history correlates of vocational needs for a female adult sample. *Journal of Counseling Psychology, 26,* 487–496.

Rounds, J. B., Dawis, R. V., & Lofquist, L. (1987). Measurement of person-environment fit and prediction of satisfaction in the theory of work adjustment. *Journal of Vocational Behavior, 31,* 297–318.

Roy, H., Brueckel, J., & Drucker, A. J. (1954). Selection of Army and Air Force reserve training corps students. *USA Personnel Research Branch Notes, 28.*

Ruda, E. S. (1970). *The effect of interpersonal similarity on management performance.* Unpublished doctoral dissertation, Purdue University, Lafayette, IN.

Russell, C. J. (1988, April). *Biographical information generated from structured interviews for the selection of top level managers.* Paper presented at the annual meeting of the Society for Industrial and Organizational Psychology, Dallas.

Russell, C. J., Mattson, J., & Devlin, S. E. (1988, April). *Predictive validity of biodata items generated from retrospective life experience essays.* Paper presented at the annual meeting of the Society for Industrial and Organizational Psychology, Dallas.

Schaefer, C. E., & Anastasi, A. (1968). A biographical inventory for identifying creativity in adolescent boys. *Journal of Applied Psychology, 52,* 42–48.

Schmidt, F. L., Caplan, J. R., Bemis, S. E., Decuir, R., Dunn, L., & Antone, L. (1979). *The behavioral consistency method for unassembled examining.* Washington, DC: U.S. Office of Personnel Management.

Schmidt, F. L., Hunter, J. E., & Caplan, J. R. (1981). Validity generalization results for jobs in the petroleum industry. *Journal of Applied Psychology, 66,* 261–273.

Schmitt, N. (1982, August). Formula estimation of cross-validated multiple correlation. In D. L. Grant (Chair), *The many faces of cross-validation.* Symposium conducted at the annual meeting of the American Psychological Association, Washington, DC.

Schmitt, N., & Ostroff, C. (1986). Operationalizing the "behavioral consistency" approach: Selection test development based on a content oriented strategy. *Personnel Psychology, 39,* 91–108.

Schmuckler, E. (1966). *Age differences in biographical inventories: A factor analytic study.* Greensboro, NC: The Creativity Research Institute, The Richardson Foundation.

Schneider, B. (1987a). The people make the place. *Personnel Psychology, 40,* 437–453.

Schneider, B. (1987b). E = f (PB): The road to a radical approach to person environment fit. *Journal of Vocational Behavior, 31,* 353–361.

Schoenfeldt, L. F. (1970, March). *Life experience subgroups as moderators in the prediction of educational criteria.* Paper presented at the annual meeting of the American Educational Research Association, Minneapolis.

Schoenfeldt, L. F. (1974). Utilization of manpower: Development and evaluation of an assessment-classification model for matching individuals with jobs. *Journal of Applied Psychology, 59,* 583–595.

Schoenfeldt, L. F. (1989, August). *Biographical data as a new frontier in employee selection.* Paper presented at the meetings of the American Psychlogical Association, New Orleans.

Schoenfeldt, L. F., & Lissitz, R. W. (1971). A Bayesian framework for the application of moderator variables. *JSAS Catalog of Selected Documents in Psychology, 1,* 3–4.

Schoenfeldt, L. F., & Lissitz, R. W. (1974). Moderator subgroups and Bayesian group regression: Some further comments. *American Educational Research Journal, 11,* 87–90.

Schoenfeldt, L. F., & Mendoza, J. (1988, August). *The content and construct validation of a biographical questionnaire.* Paper presented at the annual meeting of the American Psychological Association, Atlanta.

Schooler, C. (1984). Psychological effects of complex environments during the life span: A review and theory. *Intelligence, 8,* 254–281.

Schrader, A. D. (1975). *A comparison of the relative utility of several rational and empirical strategies for forming biodata dimensions.* Unpublished doctoral dissertation, University of Houston, Houston.

Schrader, A. D., & Osburn, H. G. (1977). Biodata faking: Effects of induced subtlety and position specificity. *Personnel Psychology, 30,* 395–404.

Schuh, A. L. (1967). The predictability of employee tenure: A review of the literature. *Personnel Psychology, 20,* 133–152.

Schwab, D. P., & Oliver, R. L. (1974). Predicting tenure with biographical data: Exhuming buried evidence. *Personnel Psychology, 27,* 125–128.

Shaffer, G. S. (1987). Patterns of work and nonwork satisfaction. *Journal of Applied Psychology, 72,* 115–124.

Shaffer, G. S., & Ames, S. P. (1983, March). *The impact of social desirability and acquiescence on personal history measures.* Paper presented at the annual meeting of the Southeastern Psychological Association, Atlanta.

Shaffer, G. S., Saunders, V., & Owens, W. A. (1986). Additional evidence for the accuracy of biographical information: Long-term retest and observer ratings. *Personnel Psychology, 39,* 791–809.

Sharf, J. C. (1980). Validity generalization. In J. Klein (Ed.), *Biodata: An alternative selection tool.* Proceedings of a conference presented by the Personnel Testing Council of Southern California. Los Angeles, CA: Personnel Testing Council of Southern California.

Siegel, L. A. (1956a). A biographical inventory for students: Construction and standardization of the instrument. *Journal of Applied Psychology, 40,* 5–10.

Siegel, L. A. (1956b). A biographical inventory for students: II: Validation of the instrument. *Journal of Applied Psychology, 40,* 122–126.

Simon, H. A. (1953). Causal ordering and identifiability. In W. C. Hood & T. C. Koopmans (Eds.), *Studies in econometric method.* New York: Wiley.

Simon, H. A. (1977). *Models of discovery.* Dordrect, Holland: Reidel.

Small, N. J. (1980). *An examination of the utility of a biographical information questionnaire for early identification of accountants.* Unpublished master's thesis, University of Georgia, Athens.

Small, N. J. (1982). *Subgroup membership as a predictor of interpersonal attraction.* Athens, GA: Institute for Behavioral Research.

Smart, B. D. (1968). Reducing offensiveness of biographical items in personnel selection. *Studies in Higher Education, 95,* 14–21.

Smart, J. C. (1989). Life history influences on Holland vocational type development. *Journal of Vocational Behavior, 34,* 69–87.

Smith, M. C., & George, D. I. (1987). Weighted application forms for personnel selection: A comparison of old and new methodologie. *Australian Psychologist, 22,* 351–375.

Smith, W. J., Albright, L. E., Glennon, J. R., & Owens, W. A. (1961). The prediction of research competence and creativity from personal history. *Journal of Applied Psychology, 45,* 59–62.

Sontag, L. W. (1971). The history of longitudinal research: Implications for the future. *Child Development, 42,* 987–1002.

Standard Oil Co. (NJ). (1962). *Social science research reports: Selection and placement,* Vol. II. New York: Author.

Stead, N. H., & Shartle, C. L. (1940). *Occupational counseling techniques.* New York: American Book Company.

Stokes, G. S., Lautenschlager, G. J., & Blakley, B. (1987). *Sex differences in the component structure of a biographical questionnaire.* Athens, GA: Institute for Behavioral Research.

Stokes, G. S., Mecham, R. C., Block, L. K., & Hogan, J. E. (1989, April). *Classification of persons and jobs.* Poster presented at the annual meeting of the Society for Industrial and Organizational Psychology, Boston.

Stokes, G. S., Mumford, M. D., Jackson, K. E., & Owens, W. A. (1990). Sequential study. In M. D. Mumford, G. S. Stokes, & W. A. Owens, *Patterns of life history: The ecology of human individuality.* Hillsdale, NJ: Erlbaum.

Stokes, G. S., Mumford, M. D., & Owens, W. A. (1989). Life history prototypes in the study of human individuality. *Journal of Personality, 57,* 509–545.

Strimbu, J. L., & Schoenfeldt, L. F. (1973). Life history subgroups in the prediction of drug usage patterns and attitudes. *JSAS Catalog of Selected Documents in Psychology, 3,* 83.

Strong, E. K. (1941). *The vocational interests of men and women.* Stanford, CA: Stanford University Press.

Tanofsky, R., Shepps, R. R., & O'Neill, P. J. (1969). Pattern analysis of biographical predictors of success as insurance salesmen. *Journal of Applied Psychology, 53,* 136–139.

Taylor, C. W., & Ellison, R. L. (1967). Biographical predictors of scientific performance. *Science, 155,* 1075–1080.

Taylor, L. R. (1968). *A quasi-actuarial approach to assessment.* Unpublished doctoral dissertation. Purdue University, Lafayette, IN.

Telenson, P. A., Alexander, R. A., & Barrett, G. V. (1983). Scoring the biographical information blank: A comparison of three weighting techniques. *Applied Psychological Measurement, 7,* 73–80.

Terman, L. M. (1959). *The gifted group at mid-life.* Stanford, CA: Stanford University Press.

Tesser, A., & Lissitz, R. W. (1973). On an assumption underlying the use of homogeneous subgroups in prediction. *JSAS Catalog of Selected Documents in Psychology, 3,* 38.

Thayer, P. W. (1977). Somethings old, somethings new. *Personnel Psychology, 30,* 513–524.

Thomas, A., & Chess, S. (1977). *Temperament and development.* New York: Brunner/Mazel.

Thomas, A., & Chess, S. (1981). The role of temperament in the contributions of individuals to their development. In R. M. Lerner & N. A. Busch-Rossnagel (Eds.), *Individuals as producers of their own development: A life span perspective* (pp. 231–256). New York: Academic Press.

Thomas, L. L. (1982). The biographical antecedents of vocational choice. *Dissertation Abstracts International, 46B,* 2031.

Tobach, E. (1981). Evolutionary aspects of the activity of the organism and its environment. In R. M. Lerner & N. A. Busch-Rossnagel (Eds.), *Individuals as producers of their own development: A life span perspective* (pp. 37–68). New York: Academic Press.

Toole, D. L., Gavin, J. F., Murdy, L. B., & Sells, S. B. (1972). The differential validity of personality, personal history, and aptitude data for minority and non-minority employees. *Personnel Psychology, 25,* 661–672.

Torrance, O. P., & Ziller, R. C. (1957). *Risk and life experience: Developing a scale for measuring risk taking tendencies.* Lackland AFB, TX: USAF Personnel Training Research Center.

Turnage, J. J., & Muchinsky, P. M. (1984). A comparison of the predictive validity of assessment center evaluations versus traditional measures in forecasting supervisory job performance: Interpretative implications of criterion distortion for the assessment paradigm. *Journal of Applied Psychology, 69,* 595–602.

Tyler, L. E. (1965). *The psychology of human differences.* New York: Appleton-Century-Crofts.

Tyler, L. E. (1978). *Individuality.* San Francisco: Jossey-Bass.

Uhlman, C. E., Reiter-Palmon, R., & Connelly, M. S. (1990). *Empirically keyed and rationally scaled background data measures.* Paper presented at the meetings of the Southeastern Psychological Association, Atlanta, GA.

Vaillant, G. L., & McArthur, C. L. (1972). Natural history and male psychological health in the adult life cycle from 18 to 50. *Seminars in Psychiatry, 4,* 415–427.

Vandenventer, A. D., Taylor, D. K., Collins, W. E., & Boone, J. O. (1983). *Three studies of biographical factors associated with success in air traffic control specialist screening/training at the FAA Academy.* Washington, DC: Federal Aviation Administration.

van Rijn, P. (1980). *Biographical questionnaires and scored application blanks in personnel selection.* Washington, DC: U.S. Office of Personnel Management, Personnel Research and Development Center Alternatives Task Force.

Vineberg, R., & Joyner, J. N. (1982). *Prediction of job performance: A review of military studies.* Alexandria, VA: Human Resources Research Organization.

Viteles, M. (1932). *Industrial psychology.* New York: Norton.

VonDralek, F. W., Lerner, R. M., & Schulenberg, J. E. (1986). *Career development: A life span developmental approach.* Hillsdale, NJ: Erlbaum.

Wagner, R. K., & Sternberg, N. J. (1985). Practical intelligence in real world pursuits: The role of tacit knowledge. *Journal of Personality and Social Psychology, 49,* 436–458.

Walther, R. H. (1961). Self description as a predictor of success or failure in foreign service clerical jobs. *Journal of Applied Psychology, 45,* 16–21.

Walther, R. H. (1962). Self description as a predictor of rate of promotion of junior foreign service officers. *Journal of Applied Psychology, 46,* 314–316.

Ward, J. J., & Hook, M. E. (1963). Application of an hierarchical grouping procedure to the problem of grouping profiles. *Educational and Psychological Measurement, 23,* 69–81.

Webb, S. C. (1960). The comparative validity of two biographical inventory keys. *Journal of Applied Psychology, 44,* 177–183.

Webster, E. G., Booth, R. F., Graham, W. K., & Alf, E. F. (1978). A sex comparison of factors related to success in Naval Hospital Corps School. *Personnel Psychology, 31,* 95–106.

Wernimont, P. F. (1962). Reevaluation of a weighted application blank for office personnel. *Journal of Applied Psychology, 46,* 417–419.

Wernimont, P. F., & Campbell, J. P. (1968). Signs, samples, and criteria. *Journal of Applied Psychology, 52,* 372–376.

Wesley, S. S. (1989). *Background data subgroups and career outcomes: Some developmental influences on person-job matching.* Unpublished doctoral dissertation, Georgia Institute of Technology, Atlanta.

Williams, W. E. (1961, April). *Life history antecedents of volunteers versus non-volunteers for an AFROTC program.* Paper presented at the annual meeting of the Midwestern Psychological Association, Chicago, IL.

Yukl, G. A. (1973). *Leadership in Organizations.* Englewood Cliffs, NJ: Prentice-Hall.

Zachert, V., & Levine, A. S. (1952). Education and the prediction of military school success. *Journal of Applied Psychology, 36,* 266–268.

Zimmerman, R., Jacobs, R., & Farr, J. (1982). A comparison of the accuracy of four methods of clustering jobs. *Applied Psychological Measurement, 6,* 353–366.

Organizational Behavior: Individual, Group, and Environmental Influences

The final three chapters of volume 2 of the *Handbook* and the first two chapters in the present volume are addressed to the broad theme of *Attributes of Individuals in Organizations*. These five chapters provide comprehensive overviews of current knowledge and research directions in the measurement of individual differences in physical abilities, vocational interests and values, personality, aptitudes, skills, and proficiencies, and work and nonwork experiences as they are reflected in background or "biodata" questionnaires. Authors of the foregoing five chapters have provided impressive compilations of the array of individual attributes and behavioral potentialities brought to an organizational workplace by members of its work force.

We turn now to a broader level of analysis—one that focuses on individual, group, and organizational influences on the functioning of the total organization as well as the functioning of individuals and work groups comprising any organization.

Accordingly, the next six chapters of this volume include in-depth discussions of organizational leadership (chapter 3), group influences on individuals (chapter 4), intergroup relations and their effects (chapter 5), relations between organizations and their environments (chapter 6), considerations dictated by relations with consumers of the organization's products and services (chapter 7), and, finally, principles that are central in thinking about and developing measures of organizational productivity (chapter 8).

Chapter 3 by G. Yukl and D. Van Fleet [Theory and Research on Leadership in Organizations] reviews and evaluates major leadership theories and summarizes findings from empirical research on the topic over the last half century. Early on, they comment about the difficulty encountered in their effort to understand and integrate an array of diverse theories and often inconsistent research findings. A degree of clarity is brought to the problem by their organization of the chapter according to types of research approach: *trait, behavioral, power and influence, situational,* and *transformational/charismatic*.

In an effort toward integration of the research literature, they comment that much of the research on leadership effectiveness has tried to examine a leader's influence by examining *end-result* variables. After noting that Likert (1967) recognized long ago that a leader's influence on the end result is, in fact, mediated by a plethora of intervening variables, Yukl and Van Fleet argue that future research studies will profit greatly by designs that track causal paths between leader actions, effects of such actions on *intervening* variables, and, in turn, on *end-result* measures. Their discussion of current issues in leadership research leads to an outline for a research agenda that promises significant increases in our understanding of leadership in the years ahead. It is apparent to Yukl and Van Fleet that the trend over the last decade had, in fact, witnessed an increasing number of studies that straddle more than one approach or theory; thus, research on leadership is becoming less pedestrian, broader in perspective, and far more likely to facilitate development of an integrated, general theory of leadership.

The implied direction of causality in efforts to understand leadership is from the individual leader to other individuals or to groups of individuals. In contrast, J. R. Hackman, in chapter 4 [Group Influences on Individuals in Organizations], examines group influences on individuals. His chapter reviews the effects of organizational groups on the beliefs, attitudes, and behaviors of their members. His analysis of group influences is one of the most comprehensive available. Mechanisms of group influence are discussed according to three primary sources: *ambient stimuli* that pervade the group setting and impinge on all members, *discretionary stimuli* that are provided selectively between group members depending on what specific individuals say or do, and the structure of *group norms* and ways in which adherence to the norms are enforced. These three sources are discussed systematically according to their *informational* impact on member beliefs and knowledge, their *affective* impact on member attitudes, values, and emotions, and their *behavioral* impact on members' actions.

Throughout the chapter, Hackman gives particular attention to contextual, structural, and personal variables that govern the strength and constructiveness of group effects on members. Several specific mechanisms (such as reinforcement contingencies, levels of member arousal, shaping of member beliefs, etc.) through which groups wield their influence are elaborated and illustrated with both examples from natural settings and results from studies in laboratory and field settings. Attention is also given to conditions of reciprocal influence wherein individuals succeed in changing the structure and dynamics of their groups.

Hackman has brilliantly documented the effects of groups on the beliefs, attitudes, and behaviors of individuals in organizations. Any analysis of causal elements underlying overall organizational outcomes will be richly enhanced by taking account of the influences mentioned and elaborated on in this chapter.

R. Guzzo and G. Shea, in chapter 5 [Group Performance and Intergroup Relations in Organizations], examine several schools of thought related to issues of group performance in organizations. They comment on trends toward increasing reliance on groups in organizations and the need for better theory and research on the design of high performing work teams. In discussing intergroup relations and task performance, they focus on what has been termed *realistic conflict theory*. Realistic conflict theory refers to the likelihood of intergroup conflict as a product of the types of goal structures under which groups are often required to operate. Guzzo and Shea express concern about a relative lack of research on intergroup cooperation. They call for increased research attention on how intergroup relations influence the performance effectiveness of groups in organizations.

In contrast with what appears to be rather limited research on intergroup cooperation, Guzzo and Shea are optimistic about an increased emphasis on research concerning performance of real groups in organizations. They identify and discuss each of six research themes, namely, *group composition, group development, social interaction processes, the nature of group tasks, motivational issues in groups,* and *contextual influences on group performance.*

In summarizing their chapter, they comment on a need for future research to address (a) the nature of effective leader behavior for managing teams as contrasted with managing individuals, (b) the rapidly emerging use of group problem solving and decision making made increasingly feasible by rapid advances being made in teleconferencing technology and applications of that technology, and (c) the possibility of devising and validating specialized *staffing* methods for building word teams so as to maximize team performance and intergroup cooperation.

In chapter 6, G. Davis and W. Powell provide an impressive and comprehensive review of the state of the art in macro-organizational behavior as it relates to organization-environment relations. They trace research and theory on organizational environments since such research began to assume salience in the 1960s. They comment briefly on the pivotal work by Katz and Kahn (1966), which focused attention on the *open systems* nature of organizations. The open systems perspective stimulated rapid expansion of research and thinking about how factors in an organization's environment should be expected to influence organizational performance and design.

Because lines of research on organization-environment relations over the last three decades has become so extensive and heterogeneous, Davis and Powell did not attempt a synthesis. Instead, they have presented six major contemporary lines of research with the goal of presenting each fairly, understandably, and candidly so that readers may understand the different orientations of each approach in relation to relevant units of analysis, questions remaining unanswered, and the relevant empirical work still to be done. Accordingly, their chapter focuses on thorough discussions and critiques of the six most influential theoretical approaches on organizations and environments during the 1970s and 1980s: *Thompson's contingency theory, transaction cost economics, resource dependence theory, network approaches, organizational ecology,* and *new institutionalism.* They emphasize both points of conflict and convergence among these approaches.

In their final sentence, Davis and Powell state: "We close not with the perennial plea for more research, but with admiration for the accomplishment of the past two decades and anticipation of the work that is to come." The editors join Professors Davis and Powell in their admiration of work done and anticipation of work yet to come. Moreover, we applaud them for their balanced review. We anticipate that their chapter will be instrumental in influencing enhanced activity and scholarship in the areas related to organization-environment relations in the years ahead.

An organization's survival must depend ultimately on the extent to which its goods and services are viewed as desirable and worthy of purchase by a reasonable number of consumers. J. Jacoby, W. Hoyer, and A. Brief make a strong argument in chapter 7 [Consumer Psychology] that principles drawn from consumer psychology are of crucial importance to organizational psychology and to the nature of the design and functioning of organizations and organizational structure.

In fact, their intent in chapter 7 goes beyond what has just been stated. They provide compelling evidence that consumer psychology provides concepts that add substantially to the field of industrial and organizational psychology. Consumer psychology is presented as being *central* instead of ancillary to industrial and organizational psychology. In support of their view, they present conceptual and empirical contributions of consumer psychology in six specific domains: *information processing and decision making, customer satisfaction, motivation, situational influences, communication,* and *innovation.* Coverage in each of the subject areas is in-depth and comprehensive—providing convincing support for arguing that consumer and organizational psychology share similar problems, methodologies, and explanatory concepts.

In closing, the authors elaborate further on how a number of psychological concepts are, in fact, studied under different labels in consumer psychology and organizational psychology. Thus, concepts labeled *brand switching, selling, product design,* and *market segmentation* in consumer psychology have analogues in organizational psychology, respectively, as *job changing, recruitment, human factors design,* and *occupational segmentation.* The authors express a hope that their chapter will stimulate research necessary for establishing the more general applicability of many of the theories and models of social and cognitive psychology. There is every reason to believe that their hope will be fulfilled.

In chapter 8, the final chapter of this section, R. Pritchard [Organizational Productivity] provides a primer on the conceptualization and measurement of organization productivity. After commenting on and illustrating the extent of confusion about productivity that exists in the literature, Pritchard develops a conceptual approach that attempts to integrate a number of specific issues.

His conceptual approach is used to highlight important elements in measuring productivity—including the types of work where measurement is feasible, the importance of complete measurement, issues of reliability and validity, objective versus subjective measures, and the critical importance of measuring elements of work that can be changed by workers. A most important part of chapter 8 is Pritchard's comparison of several productivity measurement systems according to a number of primary purposes—ranging from the desirability of an overall index to the feasibility of allowing for nonlinearities and the possibility of making comparisons across distinct work units. Pritchard's summarizing comments constitute a set of simple but critically important conclusions that should be given close attention by anyone who presumes to measure the productivity of persons, work units, departments, or organizations. Pritchard is upbeat in his concluding comment: "It is clear that the behavioral approach has made major contributions already, and we can make many more. The future looks very bright."

Taken together, the six chapters of this section provide a comprehensive overview of individual, group, and environmental influences and their effects on organizational functioning. Authors of each chapter have provided not only their views of current knowledge but also focused research agendas for generating new knowledge. Current knowledge combined with that generated by ongoing research efforts should help to assure increasingly effective functioning of organizations and of the individuals and groups of which they are comprised in the years ahead.

–Marvin D. Dunnette
–Leaetta M. Hough

CHAPTER 3

Theory and Research on Leadership in Organizations

Gary Yukl
State University of New York at Albany

David D. Van Fleet
Arizona State University West

*This chapter reviews and evaluates major leadership theories and summarizes findings from empirical research on the topic over the last half century. The review considers the traits, skills, activities, and behavior of leaders, as well as power and influence, situational approaches, and charismatic and transformational leadership. We examine methodological issues, competing paradigms, and conceptual problems and discuss directions for future research and theory.**

Introduction

THE STUDY OF leadership has been an important and central part of the social science literature for nearly a century (Mumford, 1906–1907; Van Fleet & Yukl, 1986a). Books, articles, and papers on leadership number in the several thousands, and the publication of new manuscripts continues at a rapid rate. Publications on leadership can be found in a variety of professional and practitioner journals in several disciplines, including management, psychology, sociology, political science, public administration, and educational administration (Van Fleet, 1975). As the number of publications on leadership continues to grow, social scientists have struggled to comprehend and integrate the diverse theories and often inconsistent findings (e.g., Bass, 1990; Fiedler & House, 1988; Hollander & Offermann,

* Portions of this chapter are updates of the 1989 review article by Gary Yukl, with permission of the Editor of the *Journal of Management*.

1990; Van Fleet & Yukl, 1986a; Yukl, 1989a, 1989b).

The purpose of this chapter is to provide an overview of the literature on organizational leadership, with an emphasis on recent trends and developments likely to dominate the field through the turn of the century. The volume and scope of the literature precludes detailed descriptions of individual studies or an exhaustive bibliographic listing of leadership references. Instead, major theories are described briefly, general findings in descriptive and hypothesis-testing research are summarized, and important issues and controversies are identified. We begin by examining the continuing controversy over how to define leadership.

Definitions of Leadership

After a comprehensive review of the leadership literature, Stogdill (1974) concluded that "there are almost as many definitions of leadership as there are persons who have attempted to define the concept" (p. 259). Leadership has been defined in terms of individual traits, leader behavior, interaction patterns, role relationships, follower perceptions, influence over followers, influence on task goals, and influence on organizational culture. Most definitions involve an influence process but appear to have little else in common. Definitions of leadership differ in many respects, including important differences in who exerts influence, the purpose of influence attempts, and the manner in which influence is exerted. The differences reflect deep disagreement about identification of leaders and the nature of leadership processes. Differences between researchers in their conception of leadership affect the choice of phenomena to investigate and interpretation of the results.

One major controversy involves the locus of leadership in organizations. Some theorists believe that leadership is inherent in the social influence processes occurring among members of a group or organization, and leadership is a collective process shared among the members.

The opposing view is that all groups have role specialization, including a specialized leadership role wherein one person has more influence than other members and carries out some leadership functions that cannot be shared without jeopardizing the success of the group's mission. Which assumption is made about the nature of leadership determines whether research will be focused on the attributes and actions of a single, formal leader, or on reciprocal influence processes and the leadership functions performed by a variety of people in the organization, including informal leaders. Both approaches appear to provide unique insights, and both may contribute to a better understanding of leadership in large organizations.

Some theorists would limit the definition of leadership to an exercise of influence resulting in enthusiastic commitment by followers, as opposed to indifferent compliance or reluctant obedience. This definition limits leadership to specified types of influence processes with specified outcomes. Proponents of this view argue that a person who uses authority and control over rewards, punishments, and information to manipulate or coerce followers is not really "leading" them. On the other hand, a narrow, restrictive definition discourages examination of some types of influence processes that may be important for understanding why a manager or administrator is effective or ineffective in a given situation. Many famous political leaders and business leaders throughout recorded history resorted occasionally to the use of coercion or manipulation to accomplish their objectives.

A similar controversy continues over the differences between leadership and management. It is obvious that a person can be a leader without being a manager, and a person can be a manager without leading. Indeed, some managers do not even have subordinates, say, for instance, a "manager" of financial accounts. Nobody has proposed that managing and leading are equivalent, but the degree of overlap is a point of sharp disagreement. Some writers contend that the two are qualitatively different, even mutually exclusive. For example, Bennis and Nanus (1985) proposed that "managers are people who do things right and leaders are people who do the right thing" (p. 21). Zaleznik (1977) proposed that managers are concerned about how things get done, and leaders are concerned with what things mean to people. The essential distinction appears to be that leaders influence commitment, whereas managers merely carry out position responsibilities and exercise authority. A contrary view is taken by writers who see considerable overlap between leadership and management and find no good purpose served by assuming it is impossible to be both a manager and leader at the same time.

Definitions are somewhat arbitrary, and controversies about the best way to define leadership usually cause confusion and animosity rather than providing new insights into the nature of the process. At this point in the development of the field, it is not necessary to resolve the controversy over the appropriate definition of leadership. For the time being, it is better to use the various conceptions of leadership as a source of different perspectives on a complex, multifaceted phenomenon. A definition of leadership should not predetermine the answer to the research question of what makes a leader effective or ineffective. Whenever feasible, leadership research should be designed to provide information relevant to the entire range of definitions, so that over time it will be possible to compare the utility of different conceptualizations and arrive at some consensus on the matter (Yukl, 1989a).

Thus, we define leadership broadly in this chapter. Leadership is viewed as a process that includes influencing the task objectives and strategies of a group or organization, influencing people in the organization to implement the strategies and achieve the objectives, influencing group maintenance and identification, and influencing the culture of the organization.

The terms *manager* and *leader* will be used interchangeably, without any assumption that a particular manager necessarily exhibits the qualities associated with effective leadership. We believe that research should focus on leadership as a process, not on leaders as stereotyped individuals. Attempts to classify people into mutually exclusive stereotypes such as leader versus manager, autocratic versus democratic leader, and transformational versus transactional leader, impede progress in understanding leadership rather than facilitate it.

Overview of Leadership Research and Theory

The field of leadership is presently in a state of ferment and confusion. Most of the theories are beset with conceptual weaknesses and lack strong empirical support. Empirical studies have been conducted on leadership effectiveness, but many of the results are contradictory or inconclusive. The confused state of the field can be attributed in large part to the disparity of approaches, the narrow focus of most researchers, and the absence of broad theories to integrate findings from the different approaches. Most researchers deal only with a narrow aspect of leadership and ignore the other aspects. Likewise, most leadership theories deal only with a limited set of the variables relevant to leadership (Yukl, 1989a).

Leadership has been studied in different ways, depending on the researcher's conception of leadership and methodological preferences. Most of the studies divide naturally into distinct lines of research and can be classified according to whether the primary focus is on leader traits, behavior, power and influence, or situational factors. Transformational and charismatic leadership, a subject that became popular in the 1980s, can be viewed as a hybrid approach that involves elements from each of the other approaches. Major findings from each line of research are reviewed next in separate sections of this chapter. Methodological issues and controversies that involve more than one line of research are discussed later.

The Trait Approach

The trait approach emphasizes the personal attributes of leaders. Early leadership theories attributed success to possession of extraordinary abilities such as tireless energy, penetrating intuition, uncanny foresight, and irresistible persuasive powers. Hundreds of trait studies were conducted during the 1930s and 1940s to discover these elusive qualities. Reviews of this research found the results disappointing (Gibb, 1954; Mann, 1959; Stogdill, 1948). Differences were found between leaders and nonleaders on some traits, but these findings only tell us something about the type of people most likely to occupy leadership positions, not what type of people will be successful as leaders. Results for the relationship between traits and leader success were usually weak and inconsistent. Thus, the early studies failed to support the basic premise of the trait approach that a leader must possess a particular set of universally relevant traits—the "right stuff"—to be successful.

Although attention shifted in the 1950s from leader traits to leader behavior, some trait research continued and progress has been made in discovering how leader traits relate to leadership effectiveness and advancement. Advances in trait research have been due in part to a change of focus from abstract personality traits and general intelligence to specific skills and traits that can be related directly to behaviors required for effective leadership in a particular situation. Progress has been due also to the use of more effective research methods to supplement the traditional approaches. Most early trait studies compared leaders to nonleaders with respect to scores on personality and ability tests, or they examined correlations between test scores and effectiveness criteria. Since the 1950s, trait researchers have relied more on other methods. For example, researchers at AT&T (Bray, Campbell, & Grant, 1974; Howard & Bray, 1988) examined how career advancement of AT&T managers was predicted by a variety of trait measures taken in assessment centers. Boyatzis (1982) used *behavior event interviews*, a variation of the critical incident method, to infer traits and skills from incidents reported by managers. McCall and Lombardo (1983) used interviews to compare individuals who had successful management careers to individuals who advanced into middle or top management but subsequently "derailed."

The continuing search for traits related to effective leadership has revealed a moderately consistent pattern of results, and many of the results are stronger and less ambiguous than those found in the early trait research. The cumulative findings from more than half a century of research indicate that some traits increase the likelihood of success as a leader, even though none of the traits guarantee success (Bass, 1990; Kirkpatrick & Locke, 1991; Lord, DeVader, & Alliger, 1986; Yukl, 1989a). Consistent with a situational view, the relative importance of different traits for leader effectiveness appears to depend in part on the leadership situation. Findings for personality traits will be examined separately from findings for skills.

Traits Related to Leader Effectiveness

Individual traits that appear to be related to managerial effectiveness and advancement include high energy level, stress tolerance, integrity, emotional maturity, and self-confidence (see reviews by Bass, 1990; Kirkpatrick & Locke, 1991; Yukl, 1989a). High energy level and stress tolerance help people cope with the hectic pace and unrelenting demands of most managerial jobs, the frequent role conflicts, and the pressure to make important decisions without adequate information. Leaders with high emotional maturity and integrity are more likely to maintain cooperative relationships with subordinates, peers, and superiors. *Emotional maturity* means that a leader is less self-centered (has concern for other people), has more self-control (less impulsive, able to delay gratification and resist hedonistic temptations), has more stable emotions (not prone to extreme mood swings or outbursts of anger), and is less defensive (more receptive to criticism, more willing to learn from mistakes). *Integrity* means that a person's behavior is consistent with espoused values and that the person is honest and trustworthy. *Self-confidence* makes a leader more persistent in pursuit of difficult objectives, despite initial problems and setbacks. Without strong self-confidence, a person is less likely to make influence attempts, and any influence attempts made are less likely to be successful.

Motivation is another aspect of personality related to managerial effectiveness and advancement. In a program of research conducted by McClelland and his colleagues, leader motives were measured with a projective test (McClelland & Boyatzis, 1982; McClelland & Burnham, 1976). The three motives investigated were need for power, need for achievement, and need for affiliation. Someone with a high need for power enjoys influencing people and events and is more likely to seek positions of authority. Someone with a high need for achievement enjoys attaining a challenging goal or accomplishing a difficult task, prefers moderate risks, and is more ambitious in terms of career success. Someone with a high need for affiliation enjoys social activities and seeks close, supportive relationships with other people. The research found that effective leaders in large, hierarchical organizations tend to have a *socialized power orientation* (i.e., a strong need for power combined with high emotional maturity), a moderately strong need for achievement, and a relatively weak need for affiliation. Although only a few trait studies have included behavior measures, the optimal motive pattern can be understood better by examining the implications for leadership behavior and use of power.

The research by McClelland and his colleagues found that leaders with a socialized power orientation use their influence to build subordinate commitment to organizational goals, and they seek to empower and develop subordinates by using more consultation, delegation, and coaching. In contrast, managers with a personalized power orientation (i.e., strong need for power combined with low emotional maturity) are interested primarily in personal aggrandizement and domination of others. These managers are likely to do things that jeopardize task objectives and interpersonal relations, such as trying to manipulate and coerce people, trying to undermine potential rivals, taking credit for successful activities without acknowledging contributions by others, covering up mistakes and problems, and finding scapegoats to blame when failure occurs. Managers with moderately high achievement motivation seek opportunities involving challenging objectives, and they take the initiative to identify problems and assume responsibility for solving them. However, achievement motivation contributes to leadership effectiveness only if a manager's efforts are directed toward building a successful team rather than toward the manager's own individual achievement. If a manager's achievement motivation is too strong relative to power motivation, the manager will be reluctant to delegate, and subordinates are unlikely to develop a strong sense of shared responsibility and task commitment (McClelland & Burnham, 1976).

Similar results were found in another program of research on managerial motivation conducted by Miner and his colleagues (Berman & Miner, 1985; Miner, 1978). More than 33 studies were conducted over a period of 25 years using a projective test called the *Miner Sentence Completion Scale* to predict managerial advancement. The most relevant components of managerial motivation for advancement in large bureaucratic organizations were desire for power, desire to compete with peers (similar to achievement motivation), and a positive attitude toward authority figures. A positive attitude toward authority figures is important because a manager who resents authority figures is unlikely to maintain effective relations with superiors and develop the upward influence necessary to carry out position responsibilities.

Skills Related to Leader Effectiveness

Skills relevant for carrying out a leader's duties and responsibilities are another predictor of leader effectiveness. It is not enough to have the appropriate personality traits; a person also needs considerable skill to be effective as a leader. Unfortunately, the conceptualization of leadership skills has not received much attention, and little effort has been made to refine and validate the early skill taxonomies proposed by Katz (1955) and Mann (1965). Nevertheless, these relatively simple taxonomies provide a useful scheme for integrating the extensive research on leadership skills. Three basic categories of skills are technical skills, conceptual skills, and interpersonal skills. *Technical skills* include knowledge of products and services, knowledge of work operations, procedures, and equipment, and knowledge of markets, clients, and competitors. *Conceptual skills* include ability to analyze complex events and perceive trends, recognize changes, and identify problems and opportunities; ability to develop creative, practical solutions to problems; and ability to conceptualize complex ideas and use models, theories, and analogies. *Interpersonal skills* include understanding of interpersonal and group processes, ability to understand the motives, feelings, and attitudes of people from what they say and do (empathy, social sensitivity), ability to maintain cooperative relationships with people (tact, diplomacy, conflict resolution skills), and oral communication and persuasive ability. A fourth category—*administrative skills*—refers to the ability to perform relevent managerial functions such as planning, delegating, and supervising. This is an ambiguous skill category because it appears to involve a combination of specific technical, cognitive, and interpersonal skills.

Most trait research has looked for skills that are universally relevant for leadership effectiveness. In general, the research supports the conclusion that technical skills, conceptual skills, interpersonal skills, and administrative skills are necessary in most managerial positions (Bass, 1990; Boyatzis, 1982; Hosking & Morley, 1988; Mann, 1965). Some specific skills within these broad skill categories are probably useful for all leaders, including analytical ability, persuasiveness, speaking ability, memory for details, empathy, and tact. However, the relative importance of most specific skills probably varies greatly depending on the situation. Unfortunately, only a limited amount of research has examined how situational differences moderate the relationship between skills and leader effectiveness.

One aspect of the situation that appears to influence skill requirements is a manager's level of authority (Boyatzis, 1982; Jacobs & Jaques, 1987; Katz & Kahn, 1978; Mann, 1965). For example, executives usually need more conceptual skill than supervisors. Skill requirements are also influenced by the type of organization. The technical expertise needed by a manager varies greatly from one type of organization to another (Boyatzis, 1982; Kotter, 1982; Shetty & Peery, 1976). Even for the same type of organization, the optimal pattern of skills may vary depending on the prevailing business strategy (Gupta & Govindarajan, 1984; Szilagyi & Schweiger, 1984). More theory-based research is needed to link skills to the unique skill requirements of different types of leadership positions and to the social and political context (Hosking & Morely, 1988).

Trait Patterns and Balance

There has been an increasing trend in the trait research to take a more holistic view and examine patterns of leader traits and skills, rather than continuing the earlier approach of focusing on each trait as a separate predictor of leadership effectiveness or advancement. One example of this approach is the research on managerial motivation described earlier. By itself, a trait such as need for power or need for achievement is not strongly correlated with leader effectiveness, and it is difficult to interpret any correlation that is found. However, the overall pattern of managerial motivation is more predictive of managerial effectiveness, and the results are consistent with our knowledge about the types of behavior required for effective leadership. Another example is research showing that leadership emergence depends jointly on the ability to recognize what followers want in different situations and the flexibility to respond appropriately to follower expectations in different situations (Zaccaro, Foti, & Kenny, 1991).

Another key concept coming out of the trait approach is the idea of balance. In some cases, balance means that the optimal amount of some trait is a moderate amount rather than either a very low or very high amount of the trait. For example, leaders need self-confidence to be effective in influencing others to believe in them and their proposals, but excessive self-confidence makes a leader unresponsive to negative information and insensitive to dissenting views. Unfortunately, most trait studies are not guided by theory explaining how traits are related to effectiveness, and they test only for simple, linear relationships. There is a need for more theory-based studies that include analyses to test whether a curvilinear relationship is supported by the data.

Sometimes balance means tempering one trait with another, such as tempering a high need for power with the emotional maturity required to ensure that subordinates are empowered rather than dominated. Leaders often find themselves in situations involving trade-offs between competing values (Quinn & Rohrbaugh, 1983). Concern for the task must be balanced against concern for people (Blake & Mouton, 1982). Concern for a leader's own needs must be balanced against concern for organizational needs. Concern for the needs of subordinates must be balanced against concern for the needs of superiors, lateral peers, and clients. Desire for change and innovation must be balanced against need for continuity and predictability. More research is needed on the way in which effective leaders balance competing values.

The concept of balance can be extended to shared leadership. In some cases, balance involves different leaders in a management team who have complementary attributes that compensate for each other's weaknesses and enhance each other's strengths (Bradford & Cohen, 1984). A better understanding of leadership in an organization may be gained by examining the pattern of traits for the executive team rather than focusing on the traits of a single leader such as the CEO. To date there has been little research on the trait patterns in executive teams.

The trait approach was dominant in the early days of leadership research, then fell out of favor for a long period, and only recently has regained some credibility with leadership theorists. Traits offer the potential to explain why people seek leadership positions and why they act the way they do when they occupy these positions. Much progress has been made in trait research, and it is now evident that some traits and skills increase the likelihood of leadership success, even though they do not guarantee success and their relative importance depends on the situation. Despite this progress, the utility of the trait approach for understanding leadership effectiveness is limited by the abstract nature of traits. The causal chain from traits to effectiveness criteria such as group performance is long and tenuous. Traits interact with situational demands and constraints to influence a leader's behavior, and this behavior interacts with other situational variables to influence group process variables, which in turn affect group performance. The potential contribution of the trait approach continues to be limited by the lack of attention to variables mediating the relationship between leader traits and effectiveness criteria. It is difficult to understand how leader traits can affect subordinate motivation or group performance unless we examine how traits are expressed in the actual behavior of leaders. We turn next to a review of research on leadership behavior.

The Behavioral Approach

The behavioral approach emphasizes what leaders and managers actually do on the job and the relationship of this behavior to leader effectiveness. Major lines of behavior research include description of typical patterns of managerial activities, classification of leadership behaviors into taxonomies of behavior categories, and identification of behaviors related to criteria of leadership effectiveness.

Managerial Activities

Most research on the nature of managerial work has involved descriptive methods such as direct observation, diaries, and anecdotes obtained from interviews. One line of research since the early work by Carlson (1951) seeks to discover what activities are typical of managerial work. Reviews of this research have been published by McCall and Segrist (1980) and Hales (1986). The typical pattern of managerial activity reflects the dilemmas faced by most managers (Kotter, 1982). Relevant information

exists only in the heads of people who are widely scattered within and outside of the organization. Managers need to make decisions based on information that is both incomplete and overwhelming, and they require cooperation from many people over whom they have no formal authority. The descriptive research shows that managerial work is inherently hectic, varied, fragmented, reactive, and disorderly (Kanter, 1983; Kaplan, 1986; Mintzberg, 1973). Many activities involve brief oral interactions that provide an opportunity to obtain relevant, up-to-date information, discover problems, and influence people to implement plans. Many interactions involve people besides subordinates, such as lateral peers, superiors, and outsiders.

Descriptive research on managerial decision making and problem solving provides additional insights into the nature of managerial work (Cohen & March, 1986; Gabarro, 1985; McCall & Kaplan, 1985; Mintzberg & McHugh, 1985; Schweiger, Anderson, & Locke, 1985; Simon, 1987). Decision processes are highly political, and most planning is informal and adaptive to changing conditions. Effective managers develop a mental agenda of short- and long-term objectives and strategies (Kotter, 1982). The network of relationships inside and outside of the manager's unit is used to implement plans and strategies. For plans involving significant innovations or affecting the distribution of power and resources, it is necessary for the manager to forge a coalition of supporters and sponsors, which may involve expanding the network of contacts and allies (Kanter, 1983; Kaplan, 1984). Effective managers are able to recognize relationships among the streams of problems, issues, and opportunities they encounter. By relating problems to each other and to informal objectives, a manager can find opportunities to solve more than one problem at the same time (Isenberg, 1984; McCall & Kaplan, 1985).

We have made considerable progress in understanding managerial work, but there is much yet to be learned (Hales, 1986). More research is needed to integrate description of activity patterns with description of the purpose of the activities, description of the functional behaviors used to accomplish the purpose, and description of the skills needed to do it effectively.

Taxonomies of Behaviors

A major question in behavior research is how to classify leadership behavior in a way that facilitates research and theory on leadership effectiveness. Early research conducted during the 1950s at Ohio State University sought to identify relevant aspects of leadership behavior and measure these behaviors with a questionnaire filled out by subordinates of leaders. Factor analysis of preliminary questionnaires (Fleishman, 1953; Halpin & Winer, 1957) revealed that subordinates perceived the behavior of their leader primarily in terms of two independent categories, one dealing with task-oriented behaviors (*initiating structure*) and the other dealing with people-oriented behaviors (*consideration*). The resulting questionnaires, called the *Leader Behavior Description Questionnaire* (LBDQ) and the *Supervisory Behavior Description* (SBD or SBDQ) dominated survey research on leadership behavior for the next two decades. Even efforts by Stogdill, one of the Ohio State University leadership researchers, to develop a more sophisticated taxonomy of leader behavior was not successful in breaking the fixation of researchers and theorists on the simple, two-factor conceptualization. Stogdill (1963) developed a revised leadership questionnaire (LBDQ XII) with twelve categories of behavior, but most researchers continued to use only the consideration and initiating structure scales from the LBDQ-XII or from one of the earlier Ohio State leadership questionnaires. Even

now after the shortcomings of the two-factor model are widely acknowledged, a few researchers are still using the old questionnaires.

The simple two-factor taxonomy of task-oriented behavior and people-oriented behavior provided a good starting point for conceptualization of leadership behavior, but these broadly defined behaviors are too abstract to provide a basis for understanding how leaders handle the specific role requirements confronting them. Further progress in the behavior research requires a shift in focus to more specific aspects of behavior (Yukl, 1981). Since the effort by Stogdill (1963) to develop a better way to classify leadership behavior, several other researchers and theorists have proposed taxonomies with more specific categories of leadership or managerial behavior. These taxonomies have been based on a variety of different research methods, including use of experts to develop categories to classify observations of managers (Luthans & Lockwood,1984; Mintzberg,1973), factor analysis of leader behavior description questionnaires (Morse & Wagner, 1978; Yukl & Nemeroff, 1979), and factor analysis of managers' ratings of the importance of different job responsibilities (Page & Tornow,1987). Despite differences in the purpose and level of abstraction for the various taxonomies, some commonalities are evident among the behavior categories (Yukl, 1989a).

Yukl proposed an integrating taxonomy with 14 generic categories of behavior applicable to any leader or manager (see Table 1). All of the behavior categories are relevant for leadership effectiveness, but their relative importance varies across situations, and they can be enacted in different ways in different situations. The behaviors are measured with a questionnaire called the *Managerial Practices Survey* (Yukl, Wall, & Lepsinger, 1990), but the categories can be used also to code descriptions of leader behavior from observation, diaries, and critical incidents.

TABLE 1

Definition of Managerial Practices

Planning and organizing: Determining long-term objectives and strategies, allocating resources according to priorities, determining how to use personnel and resources efficiently to accomplish a task or project, and determining how to improve coordination, productivity, and effectiveness

Problem solving: Identifying work-related problems, analyzing problems in a systematic but timely manner to determine causes and find solutions, and acting decisively to implement solutions and resolve crises

Clarifying: Assigning work, providing direction in how to do the work, and communicating a clear understanding of job responsibilities, task objectives, priorities, deadlines, and performance expectations

Informing: Disseminating relevant information about decisions, plans, and activities to people who need the information to do their work

Monitoring: Gathering information about work activities and external conditions affecting the work, checking on the progress and quality of the work, and evaluating the performance of individuals and the effectiveness of the organizational unit

Motivating: Using influence techniques that appeal to logic or emotion to generate enthusiasm for the work, commitment to task objectives, and compliance with requests for cooperation, resources, or assistance; also setting an example of proper behavior

Consulting: Checking with people before making changes that affect them, encouraging participation in decision making, and allowing others to influence decisions

Recognizing: Providing praise and recognition for effective performance, significant achievements, and special contributions

Supporting: Acting friendly and considerate, being patient and helpful, and showing sympathy and support when someone is upset or anxious

Managing conflict and team building: Facilitating the constructive resolution of conflict and encouraging cooperation, teamwork, and identification with the organizational unit

Networking: Socializing informally, developing contacts with people outside of the immediate work unit who are a source of information and support, and maintaining contacts through periodic visits, telephone calls, correspondence, and attendance at meetings and social events

Delegating: Allowing subordinates to have substantial responsibility and discretion in carrying out work activities and giving them authority to make important decisions

Developing and mentoring: Providing coaching and career counseling and doing things to facilitate a subordinate's skill acquisition and career advancement

Rewarding: Providing tangible rewards such as a pay increase or promotion for effective performance and demonstrated competence by a subordinate

The Two-factor Taxonomy and Leader Effectiveness

A primary objective of behavior research has been to identify the consequences of different types of leadership behavior. The typical approach in this research is to examine differences in behavior patterns between effective and ineffective leaders, or to assess the correlation between measures of leader behavior and criteria of leadership effectiveness.

Most of the behavior studies in the 1950s, 1960s, and 1970s relied on the Ohio State leadership scales. Hundreds of studies examined the correlation of leader initiating structure and consideration with subordinate satisfaction and performance. In addition, a few laboratory and field experiments were conducted to determine the effects of leader task and relationship behavior on subordinate satisfaction and performance. Except for the finding that leader consideration is usually correlated positively with subordinate satisfaction, the results from this behavior research have been contradictory and inconclusive in the United States (Yukl, 1989a).

In Japan, 30 years of research on performance-oriented (task) and maintenance-oriented (people) behavior by leaders found more consistent evidence that both types of behavior are necessary for leadership effectiveness (Misumi, 1985; Misumi & Peterson, 1985). The stronger pattern of results in Japan may be due in part to selection of behaviors relevant for the type of work performed by the sample used in each study. Cultural differences may also account for the divergent results found in Japan. Comparative research provides evidence that different types of leader behavior are considered appropriate in different cultures (Smith, Misumi, Tayeb, Peterson, & Bond, 1989).

Overall, the research based on a two-factor conceptualization of leadership behavior has added little to our knowledge about effective leadership. This massive research effort was unsuccessful for a variety of reasons. An underlying assumption in much of the research was that leader behaviors can be classified into separate, mutually exclusive sets of task-oriented and people-oriented behaviors, and extensive use of both sets of behaviors is necessary for a leader to be effective (Larson, Hunt, & Osborn, 1976; Nystrom, 1978). This assumption has been criticized by theorists who view task and people orientation as values rather than as distinct types of leader behaviors (Blake & Mouton, 1982). Any type of leadership behavior has implications both for achieving the task and for maintaining effective relationships with people, and any particular behavior incident can be located in a two-dimensional space in relation to the two underlying value dimensions. For example, when a manager walks around the work facility and talks to subordinates to observe how the work is going, this monitoring behavior may be done in a way that reflects concern for interpersonal relationships as well as concern for the task. In general, effective leaders show substantial concern in their behavior both for task objectives and for the people who must carry out the task (Blake & Mouton, 1982; Sashkin & Fulmer, 1988). However, effective leaders act in ways that are qualitatively different from leaders with high concern only for the task, high concern only for people, or low concern about both the task and people. The types of behavior items that embody both concerns simultaneously are seldom included in the leader behavior questionnaires used to test the proposition that a high-high pattern of leadership behavior is optimal.

A second reason for failure of the two-factor approach was lack of attention to the situational relevance of leader behaviors. Some task-oriented and people-oriented behavior is necessary for any leader, but the relative importance of specific forms of this behavior varies from situation to situation (Yukl, 1989a). It is not enough for a leader to show high concern both for task objectives and relationships with subordinates; the specific behaviors selected by the leader to express these concerns must be relevant for the task, the organizational context, and the subordinates who will perform the task. Effective leaders select behaviors that are appropriate for their situation (Blake & Mouton, 1982; House & Mitchell, 1974; Yukl, 1981). For example, some clarifying of subordinate work roles is necessary by all leaders, but the appropriate amount, form, and timing of the behavior depends on the complexity and uniqueness of the task and the competence and experience of the leader's subordinates. Ineffective leaders may be unable to determine what behaviors are appropriate for the situation, or they may recognize what behavior is appropriate but lack the skills or motivation needed to carry it out. Later in this chapter we will examine situational theories that attempt to explain why some behaviors are more relevant in particular situations.

Participative Leadership and Leader Effectiveness

The decades from 1950 to 1980 also witnessed considerable research in another, more narrowly defined aspect of leadership behavior, namely participative leadership (e.g., consulting with subordinates individually or making joint decisions with them as a group). This aspect of behavior involves power sharing and can be viewed as part of the power-influence approach as well as part of the behavior approach. Since the pioneering studies by Lewin, Lippitt, and White (1939) and Coch and French (1948), social scientists have been interested in studying the consequences of participative leadership. The research has employed a variety of methods, including laboratory experiments, field experiments, correlational field studies, and qualitative case studies involving interviews with effective leaders and their subordinates.

Several recent reviews have attempted to summarize the empirical, quantitative research

(Cotton, Vollrath, Froggatt, Lengnick-Hall, & Jennings, 1988; Miller & Monge, 1986; Schweiger & Leana, 1985; Wagner & Gooding, 1987), but the various reviewers did not agree in their interpretation of the findings (e.g., see Cotton, Vollrath, Lengnick-Hall, & Froggatt, 1990; Leana, Locke, & Schweiger, 1990). Overall, the research evidence from the quantitative studies is not sufficiently strong and consistent to draw any firm conclusions. In contrast, the findings from descriptive case studies of effective managers have been more consistently supportive of the benefits of participative leadership (Bradford & Cohen, 1984; Kanter, 1983; Kouzes & Posner, 1987; Peters & Austin, 1985; Peters & Waterman, 1982). This research found that effective managers used a substantial amount of consultation and delegation to empower subordinates and give them a sense of ownership for activities and decisions. The effectiveness of power sharing and delegation tends to be supported also by research on self-managed groups (Manz & Sims, 1987, 1989).

In summary, after 40 years of research, we are left with no definitive conclusion about the general consequences of participative leadership except that it sometimes results in higher satisfaction and performance, and other times does not. Lack of progress in this research may be due to the fact that most studies focus on the general question of whether participative leadership is better than autocratic leadership, rather than identifying the conditions necessary for participative procedures to be effective (Yukl, 1981). A contingency approach emphasizing limiting conditions for participative leadership is incorporated in the Vroom and Yetton (1973) theory discussed later in the chapter.

Specific Leader Behaviors and Effectiveness

In the past decade, an increasing amount of research has examined how specific types of leadership behavior are related to leader effectiveness. This empirical research suggests that managerial effectiveness is predicted better by specific behaviors (e.g., positive reward behavior, clarifying, monitoring, problem solving) relevant to the leadership situation than by broad measures such as initiating structure and consideration.

A number of studies examined positive reward behavior by the leaders. Podsakoff, Todor, Grover, and Huber (1984) reviewed this literature and found that praise and contingent rewards usually increase subordinate satisfaction and performance. The importance of recognition and appropriate rewards has been noted also in descriptive studies of leadership in effective organizations (Peters & Austin, 1985; Peters & Waterman, 1982).

Clarifying is the primary component of initiating structure, and a number of studies have been conducted on the use of clarifying behavior by leaders (e.g., explaining responsibilities, assigning work, giving instructions, setting priorities, setting deadlines, setting standards). For example, in questionnaire research reported by Yukl, Wall, and Lepsinger (1990), clarifying was related to managerial effectiveness in four out of six samples of leaders. Setting specific, challenging, but realistic goals is an important component of clarifying behavior, and in the motivation literature there is ample evidence from field experiments that goal setting by a manager results in better subordinate performance than no goals or "do your best" instructions (e.g., Locke & Latham, 1990).

Evidence for the importance of other leadership and managerial behaviors is provided by descriptive research and by some questionnaire studies with an independent criterion of managerial effectiveness. Several studies found relationships between planning and managerial effectiveness, although effective planning was usually informal and flexible rather than formal and rigid (Carroll & Gillen, 1987; Kotter, 1982; Yukl, Wall, & Lepsinger,1990).

Problem solving behavior was also related to managerial effectiveness in some of these same studies. In observational research, Komaki (1986) found that monitoring was related to the effectiveness of supervisors, and a similar result was found in some research using questionnaires (Yukl, Wall, & Lepsinger,1990). Motivating behaviors (e.g., emphasizing the importance of the work, inspiring task commitment, role modeling) were related to leadership effectiveness in research using questionnaires (Yukl, Wall, & Lepsinger,1990), in research involving content analysis of biographies for famous military leaders (Van Fleet & Yukl, 1986b), in research with critical incidents about air force officers (Yukl & Van Fleet,1982), and in research on charismatic and transformational leaders (see a later section in this chapter). Evidence that networking behavior is related to advancement comes from an observation study of managers (Luthans, Rosencrantz, & Hennessey, 1985), and networking behavior was found to be important for managerial effectiveness in research involving interviews with managers (Kaplan, 1986; Kotter, 1982). Finally, descriptive research involving effective managers suggests that behaviors such as coaching, mentoring, and team building are important for developing subordinate skills and confidence and strengthening their identification with the organization and its mission (Bennis & Nanus, 1985; Bradford & Cohen, 1984; Peters & Austin, 1985; Tichy & Devanna, 1986).

Evaluation of the Behavioral Approach

The long fixation on consideration and initiating structure appears to have come to an end, and most researchers now realize that it is necessary to examine more specific types of behaviors to understand leadership effectiveness. However, in comparison to the hundreds of studies on task-oriented and people-oriented behavior, the number of studies on specific behaviors (other than participative leadership) is still quite small. More research on specific aspects of behavior is needed to identify the situations where each type of behavior is relevant. Whenever possible, this research should include a careful analysis of the situation to identify in advance the behaviors likely to be the most relevant for the type of leaders in the sample. When analyzing relationships between a large set of behavior variables and criterion variables, it is desirable to make specific hypotheses about expected relationships, rather than conducting a "fishing expedition" that exploits chance results. If possible, intervening variables mediating the effects of leader behavior should be included in the research to allow analysis of causal linkages.

As we found in the trait research, the behavior research suffers from a tendency to look for simple answers to complex questions. Most research on leadership effectiveness has focused on behaviors individually rather than examining how effective leaders use patterns of specific behaviors to accomplish their agendas. It is likely that specific behaviors interact in complex ways and that leadership effectiveness cannot be understood unless these interactions are studied. For example, monitoring is useful for discovering problems, but unless something is done to solve problems when they are discovered it will not contibute to the effectiveness of the leader. Planning is likely to be ineffective unless it is based on timely, accurate information gathered from monitoring, consulting, and networking, and there is little point in developing plans unless the leader also influences people to support and implement them. Delegating is unlikely to be effective unless the leader clarifies the subordinate's new responsibilities, ensures that the subordinate accepts them, monitors progress in an appropriate way, and provides necessary support, resources, and assistance.

Descriptive studies of managerial work suggest that complementary behaviors are woven together into a complex tapestry such that the whole is greater than the sum of the parts (Kaplan, 1986). A leader's skill in selecting and enacting appropriate behaviors is related to the success of the outcome, but different patterns of behavior may be used to accomplish the same outcome—such as in the idea of equifinality. In future research it is essential to pay more attention to the overall pattern of leadership behavior rather than becoming too preoccupied with any particular component of it.

Behavior taxonomies are descriptive aids that may help us analyze complex events and provide better understanding about them. However, it is important to remember that all behavior taxonomies are arbitrary and that they have no validity in any absolute sense. Unfortunately, there has been too much preoccupation with finding and using the correct set of behavior categories. In many of the field studies on managerial behavior, only a few "correct" behaviors were measured, resulting in numerous missed opportunities to collect rich, descriptive information about the behavior of leaders in organizations. In both questionnaire and observational research, it is essential to be flexible about the behavior constructs used in analyzing patterns of leadership behavior, rather than assuming that we already know in advance what constructs will be most useful.

Power and Influence Approach

The power possessed by a leader is important not only for influencing subordinates, but also for influencing peers, superiors, and people outside the organization, such as clients and suppliers. Major questions in research on power include identification of different types of power, an understanding of how leaders gain or lose power, an understanding of how different amounts and types of leader power are related to leadership effectiveness, and an understanding of how influence behavior is related to effective leadership.

Types of Power

Efforts to understand power usually involve distinctions among various forms of power. The power taxonomy proposed by French and Raven (1959) differentiates five types of power: legitimate, reward, coercive, expert, and referent. This taxonomy has dominated the conceptualization of power sources and research on leader power for three decades. However, the French and Raven taxonomy does not include all of the different types of power now recognized by researchers. For example, Yukl and Falbe (1991) found evidence for two additional power sources, namely agent persuasiveness and control over information.

Another conceptualization of power that continues to be widely accepted is the dichotomy between *personal power* stemming from attributes of the person, and *position power* stemming from attributes of the situation (Bass, 1960). Empirical support for this two-factor conceptualization was found in the study by Yukl and Falbe (1991). The research indicated that the two types of power are relatively independent, and each type of power has several distinct but partially overlapping components. Position power includes legitimate authority, reward and coercive power, and control over information. Personal power includes expert power, referent power, and persuasiveness. However, even between position and personal power there are some interconnections. For example, control over information is a source of position power, and expertise is a source of personal power, but control over information may enhance a person's relative expertise in comparison to others who lack this information.

McCall (1978) proposed that power depends on being in the right place at the right time with the right resources. It is not enough for a person to have expertise or information, there must also be the opportunity to use expertise to solve problems for others dependent on the person, or to use exclusive information to influence decisions. An interaction model (i.e., person ×

position) may be more useful than an additive model (i.e., person + position) for explaining why some people have more power than others. More research is needed to identify how position and personal power jointly determine a leader's influence over subordinates, peers, and superiors.

How Leaders Acquire and Lose Power

One major question addressed by power research is the way leaders acquire or lose power during their interaction with subordinates and others in their organization. The study of reciprocal influence processes between leader and followers has been an important line of research for learning about emergent leadership and the acquisition of power by leaders. *Social exchange theory* (Hollander, 1978) describes the process by which greater status and expert power are accorded someone who demonstrates loyalty to the group and competence in solving problems and making decisions. Innovative proposals are a source of increased expert power when successful, but leaders lose power if failure occurs and it is attributed to poor judgment, irresponsibility, or pursuit of self-interest at the expense of the group. Research testing exchange theory is very limited, but generally supportive. Research on charismatic leadership provides additional evidence that leaders gain influence after proposing innovative strategies that prove to be successful (Conger, 1989; Conger & Kanungo, 1990).

The manner in which characteristics of the person and position combine to determine relative power is described by *strategic contingencies theory* (Hickson, Hinings, Lee, Schneck, & Pennings, 1971; House, 1988b; Salancik & Pfeffer, 1977a). How much power is gained by demonstrating competence in solving problems depends on the importance of the problems for the operations of other organizational units and for the overall performance of the organization. The acquisition and maintenance of power also depends on the extent to which the person has unique skills and resources that are difficult to replace. Once power is obtained, leaders often use it in ways designed to protect their dominant position in an organization (Pfeffer, 1981). Strategic contingencies theory explains acquisition of power by organizational subunits and coalitions as well as by individual leaders. Evidence for the theory is limited but mostly supportive (e.g., Brass, 1984, 1985).

Reciprocal Influence in Leader-Subordinate Dyads

One variation of exchange theory, called *leader-member exchange theory* (LMX), describes how leaders develop different exchange relationships over time with different subordinates (Dansereau, Graen, & Haga, 1975; Graen & Cashman, 1975). LMX theory was formerly called *vertical dyad linkage theory* because of its focus on dyads rather than leader-to-group relationships. The theory examines both downward and upward dyadic links formed by a leader, and it considers the implications for leader effectiveness and advancement in the organization.

According to LMX theory, leaders typically establish a special relationship with a small number of subordinates (the in-group) who function as assistants, advisors, and lieutenants. These subordinates are given greater influence, autonomy, and tangible benefits in return for greater loyalty, commitment, and assistance in performing administrative duties. The exchange relationship with the remaining subordinates (the out-group) is substantially different. The leader's influence is based primarily on position power, and there is less mutual influence. To satisfy the terms of the exchange relationship and receive the standard benefits (compensation and continued membership in the organization), out-group subordinates need only comply with formal role requirements and legitimate directions from the leader.

The theory has been extended to include a manager's upward dyadic relationships. A leader who has a favorable exchange relationship with his or her own boss has more potential for establishing a special exchange relationship with subordinates (Cashman, Dansereau, Graen, & Haga, 1976). Moreover, longitudinal research in Japan found that a favorable upward exchange relationship is predictive of a person's advancement rate in the organization (Wakabayashi & Graen, 1984).

In another recent revision of the LMX theory, the development of relationships in a leader-subordinate dyad was described in terms of a *life cycle model* with three possible stages (Graen & Scandura,1987; Graen & Uhl-Bien, in press). The relationship begins with an initial testing phase in which the leader and subordinate evaluate each other's motives, attitudes, and potential resources to be exchanged; changes in the role of the subordinate are negotiated through a series of mutually reinforcing behavior cycles. If the relationship proceeds to the second stage, the exchange arrangement is refined, and mutual trust, loyalty, and respect are developed. Some exchange relationships advance to a third (mature) stage, wherein exchange based on self-interest is transformed into mutual commitment to the mission and objectives of the work unit. According to Graen and Uhl-Bien, this final stage corresponds to Burn's (1978) conception of transformational leadership, and the initial stage corresponds to transactional leadership.

At the present time, LMX theory is more descriptive than prescriptive. It describes a typical process of role making by leaders, but it doesn't specify what pattern of downward exchange relationships with different subordinates is optimal for leadership effectiveness. Some of the more recent studies have found that a special downward exchange relationship with a subordinate results in greater loyalty and performance by the subordinate (Graen, Novak, & Summerkamp,1982; Graen, Scandura & Graen, 1986; Scandura & Graen, 1984; Vecchio

& Gobdel, 1984). However, the theory has never been clear about the desirability of having sharply differentiated in-groups and out-groups. A sharply differentiated in-group is likely to create feelings of resentment and undermine team identification among subordinates who are excluded from the in-group (McClane 1991; Yukl, 1989a). It is likely that effective leaders establish a special exchange relationship with all subordinates, not just with a few favorites. A leader can use some aspects of a special exchange relationship, such as greater delegation of responsibility and sharing of administrative functions with a few subordinates, while also developing a relationship of mutual trust, supportiveness, respect, and loyalty with the other subordinates. It is not necessary to treat all subordinates exactly the same, but each should perceive that he or she is an important and respected member of the team rather than a "second-class citizen."

Even as a descriptive theory, LMX theory has a number of conceptual weaknesses. Some important issues, such as the process of role making, did not receive enough attention in the initial versions of the theory (Dienesh & Liden, 1986; Vecchio, 1983; Vecchio & Gobdel, 1984), although the recent revisions attempt to remedy this deficiency. Actual research on the process of role making is still very limited (Duchon, Green, & Taber, 1986; Kim & Organ, 1982). The measures of LMX need further refinement, and it is important to make a clearer separation between measures of the quality of relationship (e.g., perceptions of mutual trust, loyalty, and respect), measures of specific types of leader behavior (e.g., delegating, consulting, and mentoring), and measures of outcomes (e.g., effort, commitment, and performance).

Power and Leader Effectiveness

Much of the research coming under the power-influence approach attempts to explain leadership effectiveness in terms of the amount and type of power possessed by a leader and the way power is exercised. Most research on the consequences of power for leader effectiveness has relied on questionnaires measuring the target person's perceptions of the agent's power. The questionnaires used in most of the early research on leader power had several deficiencies (see Podsakoff & Schriesheim, 1985), including reliance on single-item scales (prone to low content validity and weak measurement), use of rankings rather than ratings of power (ipsative scoring distorts correlations with criterion variables), and measurement of power in terms of importance as a reason for compliance rather than as potential influence derived from position and person characteristics (importance scores may be more biased). Recent research has made progress in developing better power measures (Hinkin & Schriesheim, 1989; Rahim, 1988; Yukl & Falbe, 1991).

In general, the research with power questionnaires indicates that effective leaders rely primarily on personal power to motivate subordinate commitment to task objectives and leader strategies. However, the results from research with power questionnaires may be biased by attributions and social desirability. For example, subordinates may attribute more personal power to leaders known to be effective than to leaders known to be ineffective. There is evidence from other types of research that position power is relevant for leader effectiveness. Research on legitimate power indicates that it is a major source of daily influence on routine matters for managers in formal organizations (Katz & Kahn, 1978; Thambain & Gemmill, 1974; Yukl & Falbe, 1991). Research on positive reward behavior, which is based on reward power, finds that it has beneficial effects on subordinate satisfaction and performance when rewards are made contingent on subordinate performance and are perceived to be legitimate and equitable (Podsakoff, Todor, & Skov, 1982; Sims & Szilagyi, 1975). Even punishment, which is based on coercive power, can be used to influence behavior by subordinates in some situations (Arvey & Ivancevich, 1980; Podsakoff, Todor, & Skov, 1982). For example, coercive power is essential for dealing with rebels or criminals who jeopardize the mission of the organization or threaten to undermine the leader's legitimate authority. Thus, although position power may be less important than personal power, it is not irrelevant. A more tenable proposition is that effective leaders rely on a combination of power sources (Kotter, 1985; Yukl, 1989a; Yukl & Taber, 1983). Referent and expert power are needed to supplement position power, and they are used to make nonroutine requests and motivate commitment to tasks that require high effort, initiative, and persistence.

Empirical research on how much power is needed for leadership effectiveness is still very limited. The amount of position power needed by a leader probably depends on the nature of the organization, task, and subordinates. In general, a moderate amount of position power is probably optimal. Leaders who lack sufficient position power to make necessary changes, facilitate the work of subordinates, reward competent subordinates, and punish or expel chronic troublemakers will find it difficult to develop a high performing organization. On the other hand, too much position power entails the risk that the leader will be tempted to rely on it exclusively and neglect alternative forms of influence, such as rational persuasion, consultation, and inspirational appeals. It is a common theme in literature that great power can corrupt a leader to misuse it, leading to resentment and possible rebellion (McClelland, 1975; Zaleznik, 1970). Some evidence on this question is provided in laboratory research by Kipnis (1972), who found that leaders with greater reward power used it more to influence subordinates, devalued the worth of subordinates, maintained more social distance from subordinates, and attributed subordinate effort to leader use of power rather than to subordinate motivation. In situations where leaders have substantial position power, it appears to

be desirable to have some organizational constraints on the use of this power. Examples of constraints include regulations prohibiting particular forms of power abuse by managers, appeals procedures and independent review boards to protect subordinates, and formal decision procedures to ensure that power is not centralized too strongly in a few individuals (Yukl, 1981).

Some theorists have proposed that the manner in which power is exercised largely determines whether it results in enthusiastic commitment, passive compliance, or stubborn resistance (McCall, 1978; Sayles, 1979; Yukl, 1981; Yukl & Taber, 1983). Effective leaders exert both position power and personal power in a subtle, easy fashion that minimizes status differentials and avoids threats to the self-esteem of subordinates. In contrast, leaders who exercise power in an arrogant, manipulative, domineering manner are likely to engender resistance. As yet, evidence on the way power is exercised is very limited, and more research on this topic is clearly needed. The exercise of power involves the influence behavior of leaders, and research on influence tactics is discussed next.

Influence Tactics

A new bridge between the power and behavior approaches is research on influence tactics. Research with critical incidents and questionnaires has found that a variety of different tactics are used by managers in influence attempts with subordinates, peers, and superiors (Kipnis, Schmidt, & Wilkinson, 1980; Mowday, 1978; Schilit & Locke, 1982; Schriesheim & Hinkin, 1990; Yukl & Falbe, 1990; Yukl, Falbe, Youn, & Tracey, 1991). The most common tactics are listed and defined in Table 2.

The choice of tactics for a particular influence attempt depends somewhat on the status of the target person and the objective of the influence attempt (Erez & Rim, 1982; Erez, Rim, & Keider, 1986; Kipnis, Schmidt, &

TABLE 2

Definition of Influence Tactics

Legitimating tactics: The person seeks to establish the legitimacy of a request by claiming the authority or right to make it, or by verifying that it is consistent with organizational policies, rules, practices, or traditions.

Rational persuasion: The person uses logical arguments and factual evidence to persuade you that a proposal or request is practical and likely to result in the attainment of task objectives.

Inspirational appeals: The person makes a request or proposal that arouses enthusiasm by appealing to your values, ideas, and aspirations, or by increasing your confidence that you can do it.

Consultation: The person seeks your participation in planning a strategy, activity, or change for which your support is desired or is willing to modify a proposal to deal with your concerns and suggestions.

Exchange: The person offers an exchange of favors, indicates willingness to reciprocate at a later time, or promises you a share of the benefits if you help accomplish a task.

Pressure: The person uses demands, threats, frequent checking, or persistent reminders to influence you to do what he or she wants.

Ingratiation: The person seeks to get you in a good mood or to think favorably of him or her asking you to do something.

Personal appeals: The person appeals to your feelings of loyalty and friendship toward him or her when asking you to do something.

Coalition tactics: The person seeks the aid of others to persuade you to do something or uses the support of others as a reason for you to agree.

Upwards appeals: The person gets assistance from higher management to influence you to do something.

Wilkinson, 1980; Yukl & Falbe, 1990). For example, pressure is used more in downward influence attempts than in lateral or upward influence attempts, consistent with the greater amount of position power leaders have over subordinates than over peers or superiors. Some tactics such as ingratiation, rational persuasion, and personal appeals tend to be used more in initial influence attempts, whereas other tactics such as pressure, exchange, coalitions, and upward appeals (a special form of coalition)

tend to be used more often in follow-up influence attempts after the agent has met initial resistance by the target (Yukl, Falbe, Youn, & Tracey, 1991).

Some tactics are more effective than others in gaining commitment, although the outcome of any influence attempt will likely depend in part on the specific situation, including the direction of influence, the relationship between agent and target, the agent's power over the target, and the perceived legitimacy and relevance of the agent's request. Early research on the consequences of using different influence tactics found only weak and inconsistent results (Mowday, 1978; Schilit & Locke, 1982). Subsequent research by Yukl et al. (1991) with questionnaires and critical incidents found strong, convergent results across research methods. The most effective tactics for obtaining target commitment were rational persuasion, consultation, and inspirational appeals; the least effective tactics were pressure, coalition tactics (including upward appeals), and legitimating tactics. Ingratiation, exchange, and personal appeals were intermediate in effectiveness. However, influence tactics that rarely resulted in target commitment (e.g., pressure, legitimating tactics) were sometimes effective for obtaining compliance.

Influence attempts often involve the use of multiple tactics at the same time. Preliminary research with critical incidents suggests that rational persuasion is the tactic used most often in combination with another tactic (Yukl et al., 1991). The research with critical incidents found that use of tactic combinations sometimes increased the success of the influence attempt. For example, rational persuasion was more effective when combined with consultation, inspirational appeals, or exchange than when used alone as a single tactic.

In addition to overt influence attempts, leaders may use political tactics such as gaining control over organizational processes for making key decisions and using power to fill key executive positions with coalition members (Pfeffer, 1981; Porter, Allen, & Angle, 1981). As yet there has not been enough research to reach any firm conclusions about the consequences of using influence tactics and political tactics, and more research is clearly desirable. However, the initial results appear consistent with the proposition that effective leaders use a variety of tactics and select tactics that are appropriate for the situation (Howell & Higgins, 1990; Kotter, 1985; Yukl, 1989a).

Evaluation of the Power and Influence Approach

Influence is a fundamental concept in leadership, and the power-influence approach appears to provide unique insights about leadership emergence and effective leadership. Nevertheless, this line of research has suffered from a lack of attention. The amount of research on power and influence has been meager in comparison to research on traits and behavior. Theory development has been slow, and not enough effort has been made to refine and test the few promising theories that have been proposed.

However, a recent surge of studies on power and influence over the past few years may signal a growing interest in this important topic. There is much to be done. Conceptualization of power remains fuzzy, and there are many conceptual problems to be resolved. There is much confusion about the best way to define and measure leader power (Yukl, 1989a). Power may be defined as potential influence or as enacted influence. Power may be viewed as influence over the attitudes and behavior of people or as influence over events. Power may be measured in terms of target perceptions or in terms of objective characteristics of an agent and the agent's position. There may be important differences in the meaning of power at dyadic, group, and organizational levels of analysis.

In addition to the research questions mentioned earlier in this section, a number of other issues need more attention. We need to learn more about the way power changes over time as a result of the leader's use, misuse, and disuse of it. We need more longitudinal research on reciprocal influence processes within dyads and groups. We need to develop a better understanding of the relationship between leader power and influence behavior. Finally, more effort is needed to integrate the diverse but related literatures on power, influence tactics, organizational politics, conflict resolution, participation, charisma, and empowerment.

The Situational Approach

The situational approach emphasizes the importance of contextual factors such as the leader's authority and discretion, the nature of the work performed by the leader's unit, the attributes of subordinates, and the nature of the external environment. Situational research and theory falls into two major subcategories. One line of research treats leader behavior as a dependent variable; researchers seek to discover how the situation influences behavior and how much variation occurs in managerial behavior across different types of managerial positions. The other line of research (*contingency theories*) seeks to discover how situational variables moderate the relationship between leader attributes (e.g., traits, behavior) and measures of leader effectiveness. There has been much more research on the latter approach than on the former, perhaps because it is compatible with the common bias to perceive leaders as causal agents who shape events rather than being shaped by them.

Situational Determinants of Leader Behavior

Leaders adapt their behavior to the role requirements, constraints, and demands of the leadership situation. One theory for describing how the situation influences managerial behavior is *role theory* (Kahn, Wolfe, Quinn, & Snoelk, 1964). The role expectations from superiors, peers, subordinates, and outsiders are a major influence on a leader's behavior. Other theories have identified key aspects of the situation that create demands and constraints on a manager.

Stewart (1976, 1982) conducted extensive research using observation, interviews, and diaries to describe managerial jobs and improve our understanding of managerial behavior. Based on this research, she formulated *demands-constraints-choices theory*. According to the theory, a manager's pattern of interactions and the amount of time spent with subordinates, peers, superiors, and outsiders depends on the nature of the work and whether it is self-generating or reactive, repetitive or variable, uncertain or predictable, fragmented or sustained, hurried or unhurried. Stewart concluded that the core demands of managerial jobs have important implications for selection and promotion decisions, since different job situations require somewhat different patterns of traits and skills.

The *multiple influence model* (Hunt & Osborn, 1982; Osborn & Hunt, 1975) emphasizes the influence of macro-level situational determinants on a manager's behavior. These situational variables include level of authority in the organization, size of work unit, function of work unit, technology, centralization of authority, lateral interdependence, and forces in the external environment. A leader's behavior is also influenced by micro-level situational variables such as task complexity, task interdependence among subordinates, subordinate goal orientation, and group cohesiveness.

Most research investigating how leaders are influenced by the situation uses a comparative approach to examine similarities and differences in leader behavior across situations. This research is still very limited, and results are difficult to interpret due to confounding among different aspects of the situation. Nevertheless, it is evident that the behavior of a leader is influenced by the situation. Comparative research on situational determinants of leader activities and behavior is reviewed by Bass (1990) and Yukl (1989a).

Only a few researchers have considered how a leader interprets information about the situation and selects an appropriate response. Attribution theory has been used to explain how leaders interpret information about the performance of individual subordinates, especially evidence of substandard performance. Green and Mitchell (1979) described the reaction of a manager to poor performance by a subordinate as a two-stage process, which includes attribution of causality and selection of a response. First, managers try to determine whether poor performance is due to something internal to the subordinate (e.g., lack of effort, lack of ability) or to external problems beyond the subordinate's control (e.g., obstacles and constraints, inadequate resources or support, insufficient information, bad luck). The theory specifies the types of information considered by managers and the way it is interpreted. The type of attribution made by a manager influences the manager's response. When an external attribution is made, the manager will try to change the situation, for example, by providing more resources, providing assistance in removing obstacles, providing better information, or changing the task to reduce inherent difficulties. For an internal attribution of insufficient ability, the manager's likely response is to provide detailed instruction or coaching, monitor the subordinate more closely, set easier goals and deadlines, or switch the subordinate to an easier task. For an internal attribution of insufficient subordinate effort, the manager's likely response is to give directive or nondirective counseling, monitor the subordinate more closely, find new incentives and inducements, or give a warning, reprimand, or punishment. Several studies have provided evidence supporting the major propositions of the model (e.g., Mitchell, Green, & Wood, 1981).

The theory and research on situational demands is concerned primarily with explaining variations in behavior across situations, not with explaining why a particular type of behavior is more effective in a particular situation. Nevertheless, this research provides some insights into the reasons for managerial effectiveness. Despite the situational demands and pressures, managers have choices in what

aspects of the job to emphasize, how to allocate time, and with whom to interact (Kotter, 1982; Stewart, 1982). Managerial effectiveness depends in part on how well a manager understands demands and constraints, copes with demands, overcomes constraints, and recognizes opportunities. Effective leaders are able to reconcile the role conflicts caused by incompatible role expectations from different role senders, and they take advantage of role ambiguity as an opportunity for discretionary action. They seek to expand their range of choices, exploit opportunities, and shape the impressions formed by others about their competence and expertise (Kieser, 1984; Pfeffer & Salancik, 1975; Stewart, 1982; Tsui, 1984). Over the long run, effective leaders act to modify the situation to make it more favorable (Yukl, 1981). Making a link back to the section on leader traits, cognitive and technical skills determine how well a leader is able to process information about the situation, and a leader's motives and personality determine how the leader will respond to problems and opportunities.

Contingency Theories of Leader Effectiveness

Situational theories are based on the assumption that different behavior patterns (or trait patterns) will be effective in different situations, and that the same behavior pattern is not optimal in all situations. A variety of situational theories describe how aspects of the situation moderate the relationship between leader behavior (or traits) and outcomes. In the remainder of this section, we will briefly describe and evaluate eight situational theories of leader effectiveness. Theories concerned with charismatic and transformational leadership also involve situational elements, but these theories will be reviewed later in the chapter.

Path-Goal Theory. According to *path-goal theory* (Evans, 1970; House, 1971), leaders motivate higher performance in subordinates by acting in ways that influence them to believe valued outcomes can be attained by making a serious effort. Aspects of the situation such as the nature of the task, the work environment, and subordinate attributes determine the optimal amount of each type of leader behavior for improving subordinate satisfaction and performance. Initial propositions involved only supportive and instrumental leadership, which are similar respectively to consideration and initiating structure. A later revision of the theory by House and Mitchell (1974) added two other leader behaviors—participative and achievement-oriented leadership. Reviews of research on path-goal theory (Evans, 1986; Indvik, 1986) found that some studies support some aspects of the theory. However, methodological limitations of the validation research, such as overreliance on questionnaire data from the same respondents and difficulties in measuring intervening motivational processes, suggest that the theory has yet to be adequately tested.

Path-goal theory has a number of conceptual limitations (Schriesheim & Kerr, 1977; Yukl, 1989a). The theory focuses on subordinate motivation as the explanatory process for the effects of leadership, and it ignores other explanatory processes, such as a leader's influence on organization of the work, resource levels, and skill levels. Some of the propositions are based on questionable assumptions, such as the assumption that role ambiguity is always unpleasant, and the assumption that expectancies will be increased by leader clarification of role requirements (Stinson & Johnson, 1975). Finally, like most leader behavior theories developed during the 1970s, the propositions of path-goal theory (House, 1971) were formulated initially in terms of broad behavioral categories. It is likely that stronger support would be found for the theory if some key propositions were restated in terms of more narrowly defined behaviors such as clarifying work roles and giving contingent rewards (Yukl, 1981).

Situational Leadership Theory. Hersey and Blanchard's *situational leadership theory* (1969, 1988) proposes that the optimal amount of task-oriented and relations-oriented behavior by a leader depends on subordinate maturity. The theory prescribes different amounts of the two behaviors depending on a subordinate's confidence and skill in relation to the task. The theory has been popular at management development workshops but not with leadership scholars. Only a few studies have tested the theory (Blank, Weitzel, & Green, 1990; Hambleton & Gumpert, 1982; Vecchio, 1987), and they find only partial, weak support for it. A number of writers have pointed out conceptual weaknesses in the theory, including ambiguous constructs, oversimplification, and lack of intervening explanatory processes (e.g., Blake & Mouton, 1982; Graeff, 1983; Yukl, 1989a). For example, the conceptualization of maturity is ambiguous, many relevant situational variables are ignored, and the theory fails to provide a coherent, explicit rationale for the hypothesized relationship between leader behavior and effectiveness in different situations.

Leadership Substitutes Theory. *Leadership substitutes theory* (Howell, Bowen, Dorfman, Kerr, & Podsakoff, 1990; Kerr & Jermier, 1978) describes aspects of the situation—called *substitutes* and *neutralizers*—that reduce the importance of formal leaders in organizations. According to the theory, supportive and instrumental behavior by a formal leader is redundant or irrelevant in some situations. Various characteristics of the subordinates, task, and organization serve as substitutes for these leadership behaviors. For example, extensive prior experience by subordinates in doing a task serves as a substitute for instrumental leadership behavior (the leader does not need to provide much instruction in how to do the work). Neutralizers are aspects of the situation that prevent a leader from acting in a particular way or negate the effects of a particular type of leader behavior. For example, lack of leader authority over rewards constrains or neutralizes attempts to motivate subordinates by promising to reward them for effective performance. Only a few studies have been conducted to test propositions about specific substitutes and neutralizers (Freeston, 1987; Howell & Dorfman, 1981,1986; Jermier & Berkes, 1979; Kerr & Jermier, 1978; Podsakoff et al., 1984). This research was reviewed by McIntosh (1988). Some support was found for some hypotheses, but it is still too early to assess the validity and utility of the theory.

Yukl (1989a) has pointed out a number of conceptual limitations of the theory. A detailed rationale for each substitute and neutralizer is lacking, and there are no intervening variables to explain underlying causal relationships. A sharper focus on explanatory processes would help to differentiate between substitutes that reduce the importance of a leadership behavior and substitutes that involve the same leadership behavior by persons other than the designated leader. For example, the importance of directing subordinates may be reduced by conditions that make the work simple and repetitive (e.g., automation, formalized standard procedures) or by the existence of alternative sources of necessary guidance (e.g., prior professional training, coaching by experienced co-workers, job aids). Another limitation of the theory is reliance on categories of leader behavior that are defined too broadly to be linked closely to situational conditions. A couple of studies have attempted to address these limitations (Howell & Dorfman, 1986; Jermier & Berkes, 1979), but further refinement of the theory is desirable together with more empirical research.

Normative Decision Theory. *Normative decision theory* (Vroom & Yetton, 1973) specifies the decision procedures most likely to result in effective decisions in a particular situation. The model identifies five decision procedures (e.g., autocratic decision by the leader, autocratic decision after seeking additional information, consultation with individuals, consultation with the group, a group decision). Seven situational variables determine how a particular decision procedure will affect decision outcomes. The situational variables, expressed in dichotomous terms, are as follows: (a) whether decision quality is important, (b) whether the decision problem is structured, (c) whether the leader already has sufficient information to make a good decision, (d) whether subordinate acceptance is important for effective implementation, (e) whether subordinate acceptance is likely with an autocratic decision, (f) whether subordinates share the organizational objectives sought by the leader, and (g) whether conflicts exist among subordinates. The model includes several decision rules based on assumptions about the likely effects of using each decision procedure under a particular set of conditions. For example, one rule states that a group decision should be avoided if subordinates do not share the leader's task objectives, because it is unlikely to result in a high-quality decision.

Normative decision theory deals only with a small part of leadership, but positive features of the model include the use of specific aspects of behavior rather than broad behaviors, inclusion of meaningful intervening variables (i.e., decision quality and acceptance), and identification of important situational variables. Vroom and Jago (1988) reviewed research on the model and concluded that the results are mostly supportive, although some decision rules were supported better than others (Crouch & Yetton, 1987; Ettling & Jago, 1988; Field, 1982; Field & House, 1990; Field, Read, & Louviere, 1990; Heilman, Hornstein, Cage, & Herschlag, 1984; Tjosvold, Wedley, & Field, 1986).

Vroom and Jago (1988) proposed a revised version of the model designed to correct some of the weaknesses in the earlier version. The revised model (a) incorporates additional situational variables (amount of subordinate information, time constraints, proximity of subordinates), (b) includes additional criteria (decision time, subordinate development), (c) allows a manager to determine the relative priority of the various criteria, and (d) reduces the feasible set to a single best procedure based on these priorities. It is too early to evaluate the validity and utility of the revised model. Vroom and Jago (1988) report that it was more effective than the original model in initial tests.

Both the original and revised model share some conceptual weaknesses (Yukl, 1989a). Decision processes are treated as single, discrete episodes, even though many important decisions in organizations involve reciprocal influence processes with multiple parties interacting repeatedly over an extended time period. An implicit assumption is made that managers have the skills to use each decision procedure, which is often not the case (Crouch & Yetton, 1987; Field, 1979). Finally, the model fails to acknowledge the possibility that effective leaders are able to influence the situation and thereby avoid constraints on the range of feasible decision procedures.

LPC Contingency Theory. Fiedler's (1967, 1978) *contingency theory* deals with the moderating influence of three situational variables (position power, task structure, and leader-member relations) on the relationship between a leader trait and leader effectiveness. The leader trait, called the *least preferred co-worker* (LPC) score, is the sum of the leader's ratings (on a set of bipolar adjective scales) of the person with whom the leader could work least well. The interpretation of LPC scores has changed several times over the years, and the meaning is still not clear. Fiedler regards LPC as an indicator of a leader's motive hierarchy, with affiliation needs dominant for high LPC leaders and task achievement needs dominant for low LPC leaders. Rice (1978) proposed that research on LPC favors a value-attitude interpretation such that low LPC leaders value task success whereas high LPC leaders value interpersonal success.

The model specifies that high LPC leaders are more effective in some situations and low LPC leaders are more effective in others. Many studies have been conducted to test the model. Reviews by Strube and Garcia (1981) and Peters, Hartke, and Pohlmann (1985) conclude that the research tends to support the model, although not for every situation and not as strongly in field studies as in laboratory studies. However, several writers have pointed out methodological problems in the validation research such as weak measures, possible confounding of variables, and questionable analyses (see reviews by Vecchio, 1983; Yukl, 1989a). Moreover, the model has serious conceptual deficiencies that limit its utility for explaining leadership effectiveness, such as its narrow focus on a single leader trait, ambiguity about what the LPC scale really measures, and absence of explanatory processes.

Cognitive Resources Theory. The *cognitive theory* examines the conditions under which a leader's cognitive resources, such as intelligence, experience, and technical expertise, are related to group performance (Fiedler, 1986; Fiedler & Garcia, 1987). Situational variables such as interpersonal stress, group support, and task complexity determine whether a leader's intelligence and experience enhance group performance. The theory proposes that a leader's cognitive resources affect group performance only when the leader is directive and the task unstructured. According to the theory, leader intelligence is related to group performance only when stress is low, because high stress interferes with the use of intelligence to solve problems and make decisions. Leader experience will be related to group performance under high stress but not under low stress, presumably because experienced leaders rely mostly on experience for solving problems when under high stress, whereas they rely mostly on intelligence under low stress.

Cognitive resource theory is new, and not much research has been conducted yet to evaluate it. The available evidence is reviewed by Fiedler and Garcia (1987). Most of the validation studies to date have methodological deficiencies, including reliance on surrogate measures of experience such as time in job, which may be contaminated by extraneous variables (see Bettin & Kennedy, 1990), and failure to measure important intervening processes such as leader behavior, decision processes, and decision quality. The theory also has some conceptual weaknesses. For example, the intervening processes used to explain moderated relationships are still very sketchy and incomplete, and likely differences between leaders in their reactions to stress are not recognized.

Multiple Linkage Model. The *multiple linkage model* (Yukl, 1981, 1989a) was developed to guide research on effective managerial behavior in different situations. The current version of the model begins with the assumption that the performance by a work unit depends primarily on six explanatory variables: subordinate effort, subordinate ability, organization of the work, teamwork and cooperation, availability of essential resources, and external coordination of work unit operations with other parts of the organization. Some situational variables directly influence the intervening variables, and other situational variables determine the relative importance of each intervening variable in a particular situation. Leaders can influence these intervening variables in a number of ways, although the effects of leader behavior depend in part on the situation. In the short term, most leader actions are intended to correct deficiencies in the intervening variables, whereas in the longer term, leaders seek to make the situation more favorable by actions such as influencing subordinates to internalize values and beliefs relevant to the unit's mission, developing subordinate skills through improved selection and training,

implementing programs to improve the unit's equipment and facilities, initiating new products or activities, forming coalitions to gain more control over resources, and modifying the formal structure of the unit.

The multiple linkage model was based on findings in prior research, and as yet, little new research has been conducted to directly test and refine the model. The major conceptual weakness of the model is the lack of specific propositions about which leader behaviors influence which intervening variables in which situations. The model is a general framework that identifies relevant variables and some of the likely causal linkages among them, rather than a formal theory with precise propositions.

Leader-Environment-Follower-Interaction Theory. Wofford (1982) proposed a situational leadership theory called *leader-environment-follower-interaction* (LEFI) *theory* that is somewhat similar to the multiple linkage model. According to LEFI Theory, the effects of leader behavior on subordinate performance are mediated by four intervening variables: ability to do the work, task motivation, clear and appropriate role perceptions, and the presence or absence of environmental constraints. A leader can influence subordinate performance by influencing the intervening variables, but leader effectiveness depends on selection of behaviors that are appropriate for the situation. Wofford differentiated between diagnostic behaviors used to assess the intervening variables and corrective behaviors used to deal with any deficiencies that are found. Leader behavior is influenced in turn by leader traits, situational variables, and feedback from the intervening and outcome variables.

The following leadership behaviors may be used when appropriate to achieve optimal levels of subordinate ability: use appropriate selection procedures to identify qualified subordinates, provide necessary training, and redesign the job to match subordinate skills better. The following behaviors may be used when appropriate to achieve optimal levels of subordinate motivation: select subordinates with a high need for achievement, set specific but challenging goals for them, provide feedback and encouragement, use monetary incentives, and use participation, competition, and job redesign to increase intrinsic motivation. The following behaviors may be used when appropriate to achieve role accuracy and clarity: provide instruction and guidance, set specific goals and provide feedback, increase formalization, or redesign the job. The following behaviors may be used when appropriate to deal with constraints in the work environment: reorganize the work, modify technology, provide resources, and remove physical constraints.

The complexity of Wofford's theory makes it difficult to test. Wofford and Srinivasan (1984) report supportive results for some of the hypotheses from laboratory experiments with students in which leader behavior was manipulated. However, more research is needed to test the theory adequately.

Evaluation of the Contingency Theories

The contingency theories provide some insights into the nature of effective leadership, but they share a number of weaknesses that limit their utility. Most of the theories are stated in a very general way, and it is difficult to derive specific testable hypotheses for them. Moreover, the key variables are usually defined so broadly that they are difficult to operationalize and measure. As a consequence, most of the empirical research provides only an indirect or partial test of the theories.

Another limitation of the contingency theories is inadequate development of intervening explanatory processes. Four of the theories—namely, situational leadership theory, leadership substitites, LPC contingency theory, and cognitive resource theory—are especially weak with regard to identification of intervening variables. Path-goal theory has intervening variables for motivational processes but not for other processes affected by leaders. The two theories with an extensive set of intervening variables—multiple linkage theory and LEFI theory—do not specify how the variables interact with each other to affect end result variables such as group performance.

All of the contingency theories contain situational moderator variables, but once again, these are often ambiguous and difficult to operationalize. For example, task structure and task complexity have been defined and measured in many different ways. It is common in the research to use surrogates for situational variables (e.g., job type for task structure), and the surrogates are sometimes of doubtful relevance or are confounded with other variables, making it difficult to interpret any positive findings.

Practicing managers are likely to find the contingency theories difficult to apply to their jobs. The complex theories do not translate readily into specific behavioral guidelines for managers. Moreover, most managers are so busy dealing with immediate problems that they do not have time to stop and analyze the situation with a complicated model (McCall, 1977). Managers faced with dynamic and uncertain situations would need exceptional diagnostic skills in order to apply the contingency theories.

Transformational and Charismatic Leadership

Max Weber theorized about charismatic leadership back in the 1920s, and after his writings were translated into English (Weber, 1947), they stimulated interest in charisma by sociologists and political scientists. However, it was not until the 1980s that researchers in psychology and management showed much interest in charismatic leadership. The transformation and revitalization of organizations became an especially relevant topic in the 1980s, after many executives in the United States finally acknowledged the need to make major changes in the way things are done in order to survive the increasing economic competition from foreign companies. The distinction between charismatic and transformational leadership remains unclear, and we have only begun to identify the similarities and differences (e.g., Avolio & Bass, 1988; Yukl, 1989a).

Transformational leadership refers to the process of influencing major changes in the attitudes and assumptions of organization members (organization culture) and building commitment for major changes in the organization's objectives and strategies. Transformational leadership involves influence by a leader on subordinates, but the effect of the influence is to empower subordinates who become leaders and change agents also in the process of transforming the organization. Thus, transformational leadership is usually viewed as a shared process, involving the actions of leaders at different levels and in different subunits of an organization, not just those of the chief executive (Burns, 1978). Theoretical analyses of transformational leadership can be found in several books (e.g., Bass, 1985; Bennis & Nanus, 1985; Kouzes & Posner, 1987; Schein, 1985; Tichy & Devanna, 1986) and articles (Harrison, 1987; Kuhnert & Lewis, 1987; Sashkin, 1988; Trice & Beyer, 1991).

Charismatic leadership is defined more narrowly and refers to follower perception that a leader possesses a divinely inspired gift and is somehow unique and larger than life (Weber, 1947). Followers not only trust and respect the leader, as they would with a transformational leader, but they also idolize or worship the leader as a superhuman hero or spiritual figure (Bass, 1985). According to House (1977), the indicators of charismatic leadership include a follower's trust in the correctness of the leader's beliefs, unquestioning acceptance of the leader, affection for the leader, and willing obedience. Thus, with charismatic leadership the focus is on an individual leader rather than on a leadership process that may be shared among multiple leaders.

Most of the theories on charismatic and transformational leadership consider leader traits, power, behavior, and situational variables, thereby taking a broader perspective than earlier leadership theories. In addition, the newer theories have some unique aspects that set this line of research apart from the rest of the leadership literature. The best known theories of charismatic and transformational leadership and findings in empirical research are reviewed in the remainder of this section.

House's Theory of Charismatic Leadership

House (1977) proposed a theory that identifies how charismatic leaders behave, how they differ from other people, and the conditions under which they are most likely to flourish. As noted earlier, the theory specifies indicators of charismatic leadership that involve attitudes and perceptions of followers about the leader. The theory also specifies leader traits that increase the likelihood of being perceived as charismatic, including a strong need for power, high self-confidence, and strong convictions. Behaviors typical of charismatic leaders include (a) impression management to maintain follower confidence in the leader, (b) articulation of an appealing vision that defines the task in terms of ideological goals in order to build follower commitment, (c) communication of high expectations for followers to clarify expectations, and (d) expression of confidence in followers' ability to build their self-confidence. In addition, charismatic leaders set an example in their own behavior for followers, called *behavior modeling*, and if necessary they act to arouse follower motives appropriate for the task.

As yet there has not been much empirical research to test the theory. House, Woycke, and Fodor (1988) content analyzed inaugural addresses by U. S. presidents and biographies of cabinet members serving under each president; supporting evidence was found for most of the propositions about the motive pattern and behavior of charismatic leaders. Howell and Frost (1989) conducted a laboratory experiment in which leader behaviors were manipulated and found that charismatic behaviors resulted in higher subordinate satisfaction and performance. Research on the *pygmalion effect*, wherein followers perform better when a leader shows confidence in them, also supports some aspects of the theory (Eden, 1984, 1990; Sutton & Woodman, 1989).

Bass (1985) noted some conceptual limitations and recommended extending the theory to include additional traits, behaviors, indicators of charisma, and facilitating conditions. For example, he proposed that charismatic leaders are more likely to appear where formal authority has failed to deal with a severe crisis and traditional values and beliefs are questioned.

Conger and Kanungo's Theory of Charismatic Leadership

The version of charismatic theory proposed by Conger and Kanungo (1987) is based on the assumption that charisma is an attributional phenomenon. Followers attribute charismatic qualities to a leader based on their observations of the leader's behavior and outcomes associated with it. The behaviors are not assumed to be present in every charismatic leader to the same extent, and the relative importance of each behavior for attribution of charisma varies somewhat with the situation. The behaviors include the following: (a) enthusiastically advocating an appealing vision that is highly discrepant from the status quo, yet still within the lattitude of follower acceptance, (b) making self-sacrifices and risking personal loss of status, money, or membership in the organization in the pursuit of the espoused vision, and (c) acting in unconventional ways to achieve the espoused vision. Traits

enhancing attributions of charisma include: (a) self-confidence, (b) impression management skills, (c) the cognitive ability needed to assess the situation and identify opportunities and constraints for implementing strategies, and (d) the social sensitivity and empathy required to understand the needs and values of followers. With respect to power, attributed charisma is more likely for a leader who relies mostly on expert and referent power to influence followers rather than authority or participation. As for situational variables, charismatic leaders are more likely to emerge when there is a crisis requiring major change or followers are otherwise dissatisfied with the status quo. However, even in the absence of a genuine crisis, a leader may be able to create dissatisfaction in order to demonstrate superior expertise in dealing with the problem in unconventional ways.

The theory was based in part on results from earlier research on charismatic leaders and in part on research by Conger and Kanungo (1987) comparing charismatic to noncharismatic executives. Follow-up research to evaluate the theory is still very limited. In survey research with new scales measuring charismatic behaviors from their theory, Conger and Kanungo (1990) found that the behaviors were related to attributed charisma. Support was found also in research using interviews and observation to study the behavior of managers identified as charismatic (Conger, 1989).

Burns' Theory of Transformational Leadership

This early theory of transformational leadership was developed mostly from descriptive research on political leaders. Burns (1978) described leadership as a process of evolving interrelationships in which leaders influence followers, and leaders are influenced in turn to modify their behavior as they meet responsiveness or resistance. Transformational leadership is viewed as both a micro-level influence process between individuals, and as a macro-level process of mobilizing power to change social systems and reform institutions. According to Burns, transformational leaders seek to raise the consciousness of followers by appealing to higher ideals and moral values such as liberty, justice, equality, peace, and humanitarianism, not to baser emotions such as fear, greed, jealousy, or hatred. Followers are elevated from their "everyday selves" to their "better selves." For Burns, transformational leadership may be exhibited by anyone in the organization in any type of position. It may involve people influencing peers or superiors as well as subordinates. Burns contrasted transformational leadership with transactional leadership, in which followers are motivated by appealing to their self-interest. He also differentiated transformational leadership from influence based on bureaucratic authority, which emphasizes legitimate power and respect for rules and tradition.

Bass' Theory of Transformational Leadership

Building on the earlier theory by Burns, Bass (1985) proposed a more detailed theory to describe transformational processes in organizations and to differentiate between transformational, charismatic, and transactional leadership. Bass defined transformational leadership in terms of the leader's effect on followers. Leaders transform followers by making them more aware of the importance and value of task outcomes, by activating their higher-order needs, and by inducing them to transcend self-interest for the sake of the organization. As a result of this influence, followers feel trust and respect toward the leader, and they are motivated to do more than they originally expected to do.

Bass views transformational leadership as more than just another term for charisma. Charisma is defined as a process wherein a leader influences followers by arousing strong emotions and identification with the leader. Bass considers some charisma to be a

necessary but not sufficient condition for transformational leadership. Two other components of transformational leadership besides charisma are intellectual stimulation and individualized consideration. Intellectual stimulation is a process wherein leaders increase follower awareness of problems and influence followers to view problems from a new perspective. Individualized consideration is a subset of behaviors from the broader category of consideration, and it includes providing support, encouragement, and developmental experiences to followers. Charisma, intellectual stimulation, and individualized consideration interact to influence changes in followers, and the combined effects distinguish between transformational and charismatic leadership. Transformational leaders seek to empower and elevate followers, whereas in charismatic leadership, the opposite sometimes occurs. That is, many charismatic leaders seek to keep followers weak and dependent and to instill personal loyalty rather than commitment to ideals.

Bass defined transactional leadership in broader terms than Burns, and it includes not only the use of incentives to influence effort, but also clarification of the work needed to obtain rewards. Bass views transformational and transactional leadership as distinct but not mutually exclusive processes, and he recognizes that the same leader may use both types of processes at different times in different situations.

Research to test this new theory is still in the early stages. Most of the research to date has involved the *Multifactor Leadership Questionnaire* (Bass, 1985). This research usually finds a correlation between transformational leadership and various criteria of leader effectiveness (Bass, Avolio, & Goodheim, 1987; Hater & Bass, 1988; Seltzer & Bass, 1990; Waldman, Bass, & Einstein, 1987; Waldman, Bass, & Yammarino, 1990). However, the limitations of the questionnaire and the likelihood of attributional errors even in studies with an independent criterion make it difficult to draw any firm conclusions. The early versions of this questionnaire had serious methodological problems. For example, the questionnaire asked respondents if they had greater enthusiasm, effort, and new ways of thinking as a result of something the leader did, but specific, observable behaviors causing these outcomes were not identified. Bass and his colleagues have revised the questionnaire, but it is too early yet to determine whether the deficiencies have been corrected.

Descriptive Research

Much of the research on charismatic and transformational leadership has been descriptive and qualitative. Several researchers used interviews, sometimes supplemented by observation, to describe the actions of leaders previously identified as transformational (Bennis & Nanus, 1985; Conger, 1989; Kouzes & Posner, 1987; Peters & Austin, 1985; Tichy & Devanna, 1986). The descriptions of effective transformational leaders were analyzed to identify characteristic behaviors, traits, and influence processes. Another type of descriptive research on charismatic leaders consists of intensive case studies of individual leaders (e.g., Roberts, 1985; Roberts & Bradley, 1988; Trice & Beyer, 1986). Other researchers content analyzed the behavior of famous leaders described in biographical accounts, or content analyzed the leader's speeches and writings (e.g., Burns, 1978; House, Woycke, & Fodor, 1988; Van Fleet & Yukl, 1986a; Westley & Mintzberg, 1988; Willner, 1984). In still another approach, Yukl and Van Fleet (1982) content analyzed critical incidents describing effective behavior by military officers to identify characteristic examples of inspirational behavior.

The descriptive research tends to be too imprecise for reaching firm conclusions about the nature of transformational and charismatic leadership behavior, but it provides some insights into the types of behavior typical of these leaders. The studies find that it is important for the leader to articulate a clear and appealing vision relevant to the needs and values of followers. Communication of this vision is facilitated by the leader's actions, by what the leader attends to, and by the use of emotional appeals, symbols, metaphors, rituals, and dramatic staged events. The intellectual components of the vision appear important for influencing how followers interpret events and for persuading followers that the leader's strategy for attaining the vision is feasible.

Although charismatic and transformational leaders use many of the same behaviors, the descriptive research suggests that there are also some important differences. Transformational leaders appear more likely to take actions to empower followers and change the organization in ways that will institutionalize new values. The leader behaviors involved in this process are many of the same ones found in earlier behavior research to be important for leadership effectiveness. Transformational leaders delegate significant responsibility and authority, eliminate unnecessary bureaucratic constraints, provide coaching and training in skills followers need to take initiative and solve problems, encourage participation in making important decisions, encourage open sharing of ideas, concerns, and relevant information, promote cooperation and teamwork, and encourage constructive problem solving to resolve conflicts. Transformational leaders also modify the organization's structure and management systems (e.g., budgeting and resource allocation procedures, appraisal and reward systems, selection and promotion criteria, training and socialization programs, design of physical facilities) to emphasize and institutionalize key values and objectives.

Some social scientists have highlighted the negative aspects or "dark side" of charisma (Conger, 1989; Hogan, Raskin, & Fazzini, 1990; Yukl, 1989a). Musser (1987) described the differences between positive and negative charismatics in terms of whether they seek to instill devotion to ideological goals or to themselves. Howell (1988) interpreted the difference in terms of socialized versus personalized power orientation and emphasis on internalization versus identification. Kets de Vries and Miller (1985) described the origins and consequences of charismatic leaders who are extremely narcissistic. The descriptive research suggests the following problems are likely to occur with negative charismatics (Conger, 1989):

- They have difficulty maintaining effective relationships due to their lack of genuine concern for the needs and welfare of other people and their use of persuasive skills to manipulate and exploit people.

- They start grandiose projects to glorify themselves, and the projects are often unrealistic due to the leader's inflated self-assessment and unwillingness to seek and accept advice from others. They tend to ignore or reject evidence that a plan or strategy is encountering serious difficulties, thereby reducing the chance of correcting problems in time to avert a disaster.

- These leaders are willing to spend time in high visibility activities to promote a vision, but are unwilling to spend the time necessary to guide and facilitate the implementation of a vision. They tend to vascillate between extremes of loose delegation when things are going well and overcontrolling behavior when trouble occurs with a project.

- These leaders seek to manage impressions about their unique importance to the organization by taking credit for any successes and failing to acknowledge important contributions made by other people. They are defensive about mistakes, deny responsibility for failure, and seek scapegoats to blame for failures.

- The same type of impulsive, unconventional behavior that helps the leader to be perceived as charismatic by some people is likely to alienate other people, including powerful members of the organization who are needed as supporters rather than enemies.

- They fail to develop competent successors. These leaders try to keep subordinates weak and dependent, and they may seek to undermine or remove people with the leadership qualities of a potential successor. Thus, a leadership crisis is likely to occur when the leader dies or departs.

Evaluation of Transformational and Charismatic Leadership Theories

The theories discussed in this section are still quite new, and there is insufficient evidence to evaluate each individual theory. Nevertheless, collectively they appear to make an important contribution to our understanding about leadership processes. It is interesting to note that some of the "new" wisdom found in the literature on transformational leadership repeats themes of the 1960s, although the prescriptions are often clothed in different jargon. The need to empower subordinates and develop a sense of ownership for what goes on in the organization echoes the emphasis on power sharing, mutual trust, participative decision making, quality of work life, and supportive relationships by writers such as Argyris (1964), McGregor (1960), and Likert (1967). More unique contributions include the following: (a) recognition of the importance of emotional reactions by followers to leaders, (b) recognition that symbolic processes and management of meaning are as important as management of things, (c) recognition of cognitive processes involved in the attribution of charisma to leaders by followers, and (d) recognition that leadership processes are embedded within the culture of the organization, shaping it and being shaped by it.

Although charismatic and transformational theories make an important contribution to our understanding of leadership processes, we still have much to learn about these subjects. The similarities and differences between charismatic and transformational leaders need greater clarification. For example, is it possible to be transformational and highly charismatic at the same time? Bass (1985) proposed that charisma is a necessary component of transformational leadership, but the descriptive research on transformational leaders suggests that many of them are not perceived as charismatic by followers. Perhaps the attribution of charisma is weakened when a leader reduces the dependence of followers on the leader by empowering them, building their commitment to new values and organizational objectives, and institutionalizing changes in the organization. Other interesting questions that require additional research include the following:

- What conditions are necessary for the emergence of charismatic leaders?

- How do leaders develop a vision that will appeal to followers?

- How do leaders obtain the commitment of followers to a new vision, especially in a large organization where there are competing visions?

- How do leaders empower followers, and what aspects of the process are most important?

- How do leaders influence and enhance the self-efficacy and self-image of followers?

- How do leaders change the culture and institutionalize new values and strategies in the organization?

- How is charismatic leadership related to the long-term effectiveness of an organization, and what are the tradeoffs between benefits and costs of charismatic leaders?

- How can we identify and ensure the selection of people who will be positive charismatics or transformational leaders rather than negative charismatics?

- How can we develop the positive attributes of charismatic and transformational leadership in managers, while at the same time avoiding the negative aspects?

Current Issues About Research Methods and Paradigms

Progress in increasing our knowledge about leadership depends on the adequacy and appropriateness of the research methods used to study leadership. There are a number of controversies about research methods used to study leadership (see Bass, 1990; Yukl, 1989a). We will consider the following issues: (a) the choice of relevant criteria of leadership effectiveness, (b) the extent of attributional biases about leadership importance, (c) the choice of appropriate data collection methods, (d) the appropriate level of data analysis, (e) the utility of studying shared leadership processes, and (f) the relevance of training studies for evaluating leadership theories.

Criteria of Leadership Effectiveness

One important methodological issue is the choice of relevant criteria to evaluate leadership effectiveness. Like definitions of leadership, conceptions of leader effectiveness differ from writer to writer. The choice of an effectiveness criterion can bias the findings of research toward a particular conception of effective leadership. The criteria used to evaluate leadership effectiveness have been very diverse, and difficulty in integrating the results from research using widely divergent criteria is yet another obstacle to the development of a general theory of effective leadership.

One commonly used measure of leader effectiveness is the extent to which the leader's group or organization performs its task successfully and attains its goals. In some cases, objective measures of performance or goal attainment are available, such as profit growth, profit margin, sales increase, market share, sales relative to targeted sales, return on investment, productivity, cost per unit of output, costs in relation to budgeted expenditures, and so on. In other cases, subjective ratings of leader effectiveness are obtained from the leader's superiors, peers, or subordinates. The relative advantage of subjective versus objective measures and of a composite criterion versus separate criteria continues to be debated in leadership as it is in personnel psychology.

Much of the research on leadership effectiveness has examined only a leader's influence on end-result variables such as subordinate performance. Long ago Likert (1967) recognized that the influence of leaders on end-result variables is mediated by intervening variables (e.g., subordinate attitudes and behavior, group processes and properties) that reflect the influence of leader actions much sooner than end-result variables. It is easier to assess leader influence on intervening variables than on end-result variables, which are affected by many things besides the actions of a single leader. Few studies have been designed to systematically track the causal paths of leader effects on intervening and end-result variables.

Questionnaire measures of subordinate satisfaction with the leader have been used in many studies to evaluate leadership effectiveness (Bass, 1990). A smaller number of studies have used objective measures that reflect follower dissatisfaction and hostility toward the leader (e.g., subordinate absenteeism, voluntary turnover, grievances, complaints to higher management, requests for transfer, slowdowns, and deliberate sabotage of equipment and facilities). In recent years, researchers have measured other attitudes and behavior relevant to leader effectiveness, such as subordinate commitment to the leader's proposals and strategies, commitment to the organization, self-efficacy, and organizational citizenship behavior. In addition, leadership effectiveness is occasionally measured in terms of leader contribution to the quality and efficiency of group processes, as perceived by followers or outside observers. Examples of these intermediate criteria include the level of cooperation and teamwork, the effectiveness of group problem solving and decision making, the efficiency of role specialization and organization of work activities, and the readiness of the group to deal with change and crisis.

Some of the criteria of leadership effectiveness may be negatively correlated. For example, growth in sales or output is sometimes achieved at the cost of reduced efficiency and lower profits. Likewise, as noted earlier, some charismatic leaders have a very strong influence over the attitudes and behavior of followers, but lead them down a path of eventual disaster for the organization. Tradeoffs can occur even within the same criterion at different points of time. For example, profits may be increased in the short run by neglecting activities that have a delayed effect on profits, such as maintenance of equipment, research and development, investment in new technology, and development of employee skills and loyalty. In the long run, the net effect of cutting these essential activities is likely to be lower profits.

The selection of effectiveness criteria in leadership research is usually very subjective and arbitrary. It is influenced by the objectives and values of the person making the evaluation, as well as by opportunities and difficulties of data collection in a particular research setting. To avoid excessive bias and to cope with the problems of partially incompatible criteria, it is usually best to include a variety of different criteria and to examine the influence of the leader on each criterion and the causal paths among criteria over an extended time period. Multiple conceptions of effectiveness, like multiple conceptions of leadership, serve to broaden our perspective and enlarge the scope of inquiry (Yukl, 1989a).

Research on leadership succession illustrates some of the criterion problems encountered in evaluating the magnitude of leadership influence on the effectiveness of an organization. Succession studies examine changes in performance occurring after changes in leadership. It is assumed that, if leadership is important, changes in top leadership should be associated with changes in the performance of the organization. Results from studies by Salancik and Pfeffer (1977b) and Lieberson and O'Connor (1972) were interpreted by some writers (e.g., Brown, 1982; Pfeffer, 1977) as evidence that organizational effectiveness depends primarily on factors beyond the leader's control, such as the economic conditions, market conditions, governmental policies, and technological change. However, Day and Lord (1989) found that results from the two succession studies were understated due to methodological problems such as failure to correct for the effects of organization size, failure to correct dollar-denominated criteria for effects of inflation, use of criteria not influenced directly by leaders (e.g., stock prices), and failure to allow enough time for new leaders to influence quantitative performance outcomes. Methodological problems in succession research are also discussed by Thomas (1988).

Attributional Biases About Importance of Leadership

A number of writers have argued that the importance of leadership is exaggerated by the need for people to explain events in a way that fits their assumptions and implicit theories (Calder, 1977; Meindl, Ehrlich, & Dukerich, 1985; Pfeffer, 1977). Organizations are complex social systems of patterned interactions among people. In their effort to understand the causes, dynamics, and outcomes of organizational processes, people interpret events in simple, human terms. Stereotypes, implicit theories, and simplified assumptions about causality help people make sense of events that other-wise would be incomprehensible. One especially prevalent explanation of organizational events is to attribute causality to the influence of leaders. Leaders are pictured as heroic figures who are capable of determining the fate of their organizations.

The emphasis on leadership as a cause of organizational events reflects a common cultural bias toward explaining experience primarily in terms of the rational actions of people, as opposed to uncontrollable natural forces, actions by supernatural beings, or random events not susceptible to human comprehension. A related cause is the widespread faith in human organizations as rational, goal-oriented systems that fulfill the needs of members and contribute to the general welfare of society. The people who occupy positions of top leadership in organizations symbolize the promise of organizations in modern civilization (Meindl, Ehrlich, & Dukerich, 1985).

The attributional biases about leaders are exploited and magnified by political leaders and top executives who seek to create the impression that they are in control of events. Symbols and rituals, such as elaborate inaugural ceremonies, reinforce the perceived importance of leaders (Pfeffer, 1977). Successes are announced and celebrated; failures are suppressed or downplayed. Symbolic action is most likely when situational constraints and unpredictable events make it impossible for management to exert much influence over organizational performance. In this situation it is all the more important to maintain the impression that organizational leaders know what they are doing and are making good progress toward attaining organizational objectives (Bettman &

Weitz, 1983; Salancik and Meindl, 1984; Staw, McKechnie, & Puffer,1983).

Research on attributional biases indicates that people tend to exaggerate the importance of leadership as a cause of organizational performance. However, the attribution research does not demonstrate that leaders are unable to influence events and outcomes in their organizations. Taken together, the attribution research, the research on leadership importance (e.g., Day & Lord, 1989; Pfeffer & Davis-Blake, 1986; Smith, Carson, & Alexander,1984; Thomas, 1988; Weiner & Mahoney,1981), and the research on charismatic and transformational leaders supports the conclusion that top executives are able to exert a moderate influence on the performance of their organizations. Thus, an accurate conception of leadership importance appears to lie between the two extremes of heroic leader and impotent figurehead.

Data Collection Methods

A 'major controversy about research methodology concerns the relative advantage of quantitative, hypothesis-testing research and descriptive, qualitative research (Morgan & Smircich, 1980; Strong, 1984). There is disagreement about what research methods (e.g., questionnaires and observation) are appropriate for studying leadership and what type of empirical data are needed to advance our understanding of leadership processes.

As we saw earlier, some critics of quantitative, hypothesis-testing research contend that it has an inherent bias toward exaggerating the importance of individual leaders. Most quantitative research on leadership behavior uses questionnaires filled out by subordinates or peers. The respondents are given the difficult task of retrospectively rating how often or how much a leader exhibited some behavior over a period of several months or years. There is growing evidence that these leader behavior descriptions are biased by attributions and other

cognitive processes. One source of bias is respondent attributions based on information about leader effectiveness and other social cues (Cronshaw & Lord, 1987). For example, subordinates will likely attribute more desirable behaviors to leaders of high-performing groups than to leaders of low-performing groups, even though the actual behavior of the leaders was the same (Lord, Bining, Rush, & Thomas, 1978; Mitchell, Larson, & Green, 1977). It is likely that leader behavior ratings on questionnaires are also influenced by stereotypes and implicit assumptions about the nature of leadership (Phillips & Lord, 1986).

The amount of bias in behavior description questionnaires depends in part on the type of items used. A study by Gioia and Sims (1985) found that ratings of leader behavior were less accurate when the behaviors were ambiguous rather than concrete and easily observable. Bias may be affected also by the response format of the items. Most leader behavior description questionnaires ask how often each behavior is used rather than asking whether it is used in a skillful manner at an appropriate time. A frequency format may reduce the relevance of the measures, especially if a scale has many behaviors that are ineffective when overused or when used at inappropriate times (Shipper, 1991; Yukl, 1981).

Although evidence of rater bias raises doubts about measurement accuracy in behavior research involving questionnaires, the extent of the problem remains to be determined. Most research on the limitations of questionnaires consists of laboratory studies in which subjects had limited opportunity to observe leaders directly. The question of rater bias needs to be examined further with research in field settings.

Critics of questionnaire-correlational research advocate greater use of descriptive methods such as observation, interviews, and intensive case studies (e.g., Bennis & Nanus, 1985; Bryman, Bresnen, Beardworth, & Keil, 1988; Kotter, 1982; Luthans, Rosenkrantz, &

Hennessey, 1985). However, these descriptive research methods also have limitations, regardless of whether the form of data analysis is qualitative or quantitative (House, 1988a; Martinko & Gardner, 1985). Standards for the application and evaluation of qualitative methods are not as explicit as those for traditional quantitative methods, and interpretations based on qualitative methods are sometimes very subjective. The data collection methods in descriptive research are also susceptible to biases and distortions. Information obtained from critical incidents and interviews may be biased by selective memory for aspects of behavior consistent with the respondent's stereotypes and implicit theories about effective leadership. Direct observation is susceptible to selective attention and biased interpretation of events by the observer due to stereotypes and implicit theories. Attribution errors may occur if an observer or interviewer has information about unit performance.

Descriptive research methods do not automatically provide rich, detailed information about leadership processes; they are sometimes used in very superficial ways. For example, in some observation studies the observer merely checks off predetermined categories to classify events rather than writing narrative descriptions to be coded at a later time. This highly structured observation may focus attention away from the most interesting aspects of the events being observed, and unlike narrative description, it precludes other researchers from verifying the coding or reclassifying events in terms of different category systems. It is rare to find observational studies in leadership that include supplementary methods, such as interviews with key figures, to discover the context and meaning of events. Some exceptions are the study by Morris, Crowson, Hurwitz, and Porter-Gehrie (1981) and the study by Brown and Hosking (1986). However, there are risks as well as benefits from supplementary interviews; observers who ask leaders about their behavior increase the

likelihood of becoming involved in the very processes under observation, thereby risking objectivity.

The limitations of each type of methodology make it desirable to use multiple methods in research on leadership (Jick, 1979; Yukl & Van Fleet, 1982). It is important to select methods that are appropriate for the type of knowledge sought rather than merely using whatever methods seem most convenient. The purpose of the research should dictate the methodology and choice of samples, not the other way around. Unfortunately, much of the research literature in leadership appears to be the result of uninspired researchers seeking yet another use for a questionnaire or test laying around on the shelf.

Leadership researchers are not limited to questionnaire-correlational studies and descriptive field studies. Controlled experiments in laboratory and field settings are appropriate for some types of leadership research and should be used more often. Field experiments can be conducted over a fairly long time interval with a combination of descriptive methods (e.g., interviews, observation, diaries) and repeated application of questionniares. Some other research methods that may have promise for studying particular aspects of leadership include protocol analysis (Schweiger, 1983), stimulated recall (Burgoyne & Hodgson,1984) and SYMLOG (Bales, Cohen, & Williamson, 1979), detailed ethnographic analysis (Strong, 1984), and realistic simulations (Kaplan, Lombardo, & Mazique, 1985).

Group Versus Individual Level of Analysis

Issues involving level of analysis have complicated interpretation of research results from questionnaires and raised questions about comparison of findings across studies. One issue is the appropriate level of analysis for research on the relationship of leadership behavior, power, or traits to effectiveness criteria. Analysis of consequences can be made at the individual level (e.g., correlate subordinate perception of leader power or behavior with a criterion of subordinate performance or satisfaction) or at the group level (e.g., aggregate subordinate ratings of each type of leader behavior or power and correlate the mean scale scores with a criterion of leader effectiveness). There are both advantages and disadvantages for each level of analysis. On the negative side, group-level analysis obscures differences in a leader's behavior toward different subordinates (Dansereau & Dumas, 1977). However, on the positive side, averaging ratings from several subordinates tends to reduce the effects of perceptual biases and rating errors (e.g., leniency, attributions, differential opportunity to observe leader) in behavior ratings made by individual subordinates.

There is continuing controversy about the appropriate level of analysis. Some theorists contend that it depends on the level of measurement for the predictor and criterion variables. Other theorists argue for multiple levels of analysis. For example, Dansereau, Alutto, and Yammarino (1984) proposed a method (within and between analysis, or WABA) for analyzing results at both levels simultaneously and separating the effects of average leader behavior from differential behavior toward individual subordinates. The method has been applied in several studies, and the results indicate that different conclusions about leadership effects are likely to be drawn depending on the level of analysis (Avolio & Yammarino, 1990; Yammarino, 1990; Yammarino & Bass, 1990). However, WABA is not appropriate when only a group-level criterion is available.

The WABA method provides some unique insights. However, there is so much ambiguity in data from most leader description questionnaires that interpretation of the results is still difficult even when WABA is used. To reduce the ambiguity of results, researchers should attempt to improve the accuracy of leadership questionnaires, and questionnaire data should be supplemented with information obtained from other methods such as interviews, diaries, and observations.

Interpretation of Leadership Training Experiments

Field experiments in organizations are rare, and training studies are probably the most common form of field experiment on leadership. Most of the training experiments have been used to test leadership theories (see reviews by Bass, 1990; Latham, 1988). The typical approach is to compare the performance of managers trained in a particular leadership theory to the performance of managers in an untrained control group. Performance is usually measured with ratings made by the manager's immediate superior. If the trained managers perform better after training and they perform better than the control group, then the results are interpreted as supporting the theory.

Unfortunately, it is difficult to interpret positive results from this type of study because a number of rival hypotheses exist. For example, performance of the managers may have improved because of criterion contamination (superiors knew which managers were trained and were biased in rating them), differential treatment (superiors knew which managers were trained and provided more encouragement and assistance to facilitate training success), residual learning (trainees gained insights about effective practices from other managers in the training or acted differently after becoming aware of problems previously ignored), and networking during training (managers improved their working relationships with peers who participated in the training, thereby increasing cooperation and mutual problem solving after training). These rival hypotheses are not mutually exclusive, and each may explain higher performance ratings after training, even though trainees did not learn the leadership theory showcased in the training or did not apply it back on the job.

Some special problems occur for tests of contingency theories. A training study should not be interpreted as supporting a contingency theory in which leader behavior is the focal independent variable unless the researcher demonstrates that performance improved only after behavior changed in a way consistent with the leadership theory. Measures of behavior over a period of several months before and after training are necessary to evaluate changes in behavior. A training study cannot be interpreted as supporting only the showcased theory if the behavior change is consistent also with other leadership theories.

In some tests of leadership theories the focal independent variable is a trait or skill rather than leader behavior. An example is an intervention to increase managerial motivation or interpersonal skills. In this type of study, it is not enough to demonstrate that training resulted in an increase in managerial effectiveness. The study should confirm that training increased the focal trait or skill and did not increase other traits or skills that could account for the improvement in effectiveness. Furthermore, it is much easier to interpret the results if measures of intervening processes are included (e.g., leader behavior, influence processes). In summary, more attention needs to be paid to the design of future training studies intended to test theories of leadership.

Individual Versus Shared Leadership

Most research and theory on leadership has favored a definition of leadership that emphasizes the primary importance of unilateral influence by a single, "heroic" leader. As noted earlier, the prevalence of this perspective is due in part to our attributional biases. An alternative perspective is in terms of shared leadership processes and systems dynamics. According to this perspective, leadership in large organizations involves reciprocal influence processes among multiple individuals at different levels, in different subunits, and within executive teams. Leadership processes cannot be understood apart from the dynamics of the social system in which they are embedded (Dachler, 1988). The importance of a systems perspective is supported by research on power struggles and political processes in organizations (Mintzberg, 1983; Pfeffer, 1981).

Bradford and Cohen (1984) contend that the stereotype of the "heroic leader" undermines effective leadership by a chief executive. The heroic leader is expected to be wiser and more courageous than anyone else in the organization and to know everything that is happening in it. However, these expectations are unrealistic, and leaders are seldom able to live up to them. Shared responsibility for leadership functions and empowerment of subordinates is more effective than heroic leadership, but it is unlikely to occur as long as people expect the leader to take full responsibility for the fate of the organization.

The extent to which leadership can be shared, the conditions facilitating success of shared leadership, and the implications for design of organizations are all important and interesting questions that deserve more research. As yet, we have only begun to examine these research questions. A few social scientists have examined shared leadership in executive teams or at different levels in the organization (Barnes & Kriger, 1986; Eisenstat & Cohen, 1990; Krantz, 1990; Vanderslice, 1988). Research on self-managed autonomous work groups has explored the consequences of sharing leadership functions formerly performed by a first-level supervisor (Hackman, 1986, 1990; Kerr, Hill, & Broedling, 1986; Manz & Sims, 1987, 1989). Other researchers have examined leadership as a shared process embedded within social systems (Brown & Hosking, 1986; Crouch & Yetton, 1988; Dachler, 1984; Jacobs & Jaques, 1987). Lawler (1984) examined the implications of a systems approach for understanding the effectiveness of participative leadership. Viewing leadership in terms of reciprocal, recursive influence processes among multiple parties in a systems context is a very different research paradigm from the study of unidirectional effects of a single leader on subordinates. New methods may be needed to describe and analyze the complex nature of leadership processes in social systems.

Conclusion

Our review of different lines of leadership research conducted during the past 50 years clearly shows a prevailing pattern of segmentation and narrow focus in most of the theories and empirical studies. In trait research there has been little concern for direct measurement of leadership behavior or influence, even though it is evident that the effects of leader traits are mediated by leadership behavior and influence. In behavior research, leader traits are seldom considered, even though they influence a leader's behavior; likewise, power is seldom considered, even though some behavior is an attempt to exercise power. In research on power, leadership behavior is rarely examined except in studies that deal explicitly with influence tactics, and there has been little concern for traits except ones that are a source of leader power. The situational theories examine how the situation enhances or nullifies the effects of a few selected leader behaviors or traits, rather than taking a broader view of the way traits, power, behavior, and situation all interact to determine leadership effectiveness. Some theories of transformational and charismatic leadership incorporate a broader variety of variables (e.g., leader traits, behavior, power, and situation), but these theories focus only on particular aspects of leadership and ignore other aspects (Yukl, 1989a).

Despite the prevailing pattern of segmentation in leadership research, the number of studies that straddle more than one approach is slowly increasing, and the different lines of research are gradually converging. When the sets of variables from different approaches are viewed as part of a larger network of interacting variables, they appear to be interrelated in a meaningful way (Yukl, 1989a). We have made considerable progress in unraveling the mysteries surrounding the subject of leadership, and the rate of progress appears to be accelerating (House, 1988a; Yukl, 1989a). A broader perspective on leadership processes in future research would facilitate development of an integrated, general theory of leadership.

The last decade has seen a significant increase in the scope of inquiry and variety of methodology. Some interesting trends are beginning to emerge in leadership theory and research. The pendulum appears to be swinging back from extreme situationalism to a more balanced theoretical perspective that acknowledges the possible coexistence of both universal and situational elements of leadership. For example, the universal proposition that the behavior of effective leaders demonstrates high concern for both the task and people is not inconsistent with the situational proposition that leaders act in different ways depending on the situation. Another trend is increased use of cognitive theories to describe how leaders and followers perceive each other, instead of relying entirely on mechanistic behavior theories to explain leadership processes. Cognitive approaches were found in a number of the theories reviewed in this chapter. Still another emerging trend is the growing interest in examining leadership as a shared process embedded within social systems. Most of the prevailing leadership theories have been simple, unidirectional models of causality that focus on what a leader does to subordinates, but there is growing recognition that new theories and methods are needed to describe interactive leadership processes that unfold over time in social systems.

A final issue that is relevant to further development of knowledge about leadership processes is the growing awareness that leadership concepts and theories are subjective efforts by social scientists to interpret ambiguous events in a meaningful way, not precise descriptions of real events and immutable natural laws (Astley, 1985; Dachler, 1988). Social scientists interpret events for each other and for practitioners, just as leaders interpret events for followers, and this interpretation is itself a reflection of the prevailing culture and values (Calas & Smircich, 1988). Some social scientists, like some leaders, are more skilled at selling their ideas, and once a theory becomes widely known, it takes considerable time and negative evidence to lay it to rest. Perhaps the growing awareness of the extent to which our field is subjective and arbitrary rather than objective and systematic will help to make leadership researchers a little more humble about their theories and measures, and practitioners a little less preoccupied with finding the latest secret remedy for leadership success.

References

Argyris, C. (1964). *Integrating the individual and the organization*. New York: Wiley.

Arvey, R. D., & Ivancevich, J. M. (1980). Punishment in organizations: A review, propositions, and research suggestions. *Academy of Management Review, 5*, 123–132.

Astley, W. G. (1985). Administrative science as socially constructed truth. *Administrative Science Quarterly, 30*, 497–513.

Avolio, B. J., & Bass, B. M. (1988). Transformational leadership, charisma, and beyond. In J. G. Hunt, B. R. Baliga, H. P. Dachler, & C. A. Schriesheim (Eds.), *Emerging leadership vistas* (pp. 29–49). Lexington, MA: Lexington Books.

Avolio, B. J., & Yammarino, F. J. (1990). Operationalizing charismatic leadership using a levels-of-analysis framework. *Leadership Quarterly, 1*, 193–208.

Bales, R. F., Cohen, S. P., & Williamson, S. A. (1979). *SYMLOG: A system for the multiple level observation of groups*. New York: Free Press.

Barnes, L. B., & Kriger, M. P. (1986, Fall). The hidden side of organizational leadership. *Sloan Management Review*, 15–25.

Bass, B. M. (1960). *Leadership, psychology, and organizational behavior*. New York: Harper.

Bass, B. M. (1990). *Bass and Stogdill's handbook of leadership: Theory, research, and managerial applications* (3rd ed.). New York: Free Press.

Bass, B. M. (1985). *Leadership and performance beyond expectations*. New York: Free Press.

Bass, B. M., Avolio, B. J., & Goodheim, L. (1987). Biography and the assessment of transformational leadership at the world class level. *Journal of Management, 13*, 7–20.

Bennis, W. G., & Nanus, B. (1985). *Leaders: The strategies for taking charge*. New York: Harper & Row.

Berman, F. E., & Miner, J. B. (1985). Motivation to manage at the top executive level: A test of the hierarchic role-motivation theory. *Personnel Psychology, 38*, 377–391.

Bettin, P. J., & Kennedy, J. K., Jr. (1990). Leadership experience and leader performance: Some empirical support at last. *Leadership Quarterly, 1*, 219–228.

Bettman, J. R., & Weitz, B. A. (1983). Attributions in the board room: Causal reasoning in corporate annual reports. *Administrative Science Quarterly, 28*, 165–183.

Blake, R. R., & Mouton, J. S. (1982). Management by grid principles or situationalism: Which? *Group and Organization Studies, 7*, 207–210.

Blank, W., Weitzel, J. R., & Green, S. G. (1990). Test of the situational leadership theory. *Personnel Psychology, 43*, 579–597.

Boyatzis, R. E. (1982). *The competent manager*. New York: Wiley.

Bradford, D. L., & Cohen, A. R. (1984). *Managing for excellence: The guide to developing high performance organizations*. New York: Wiley.

Brass, D. J. (1984). Being in the right place: A structural analysis of individual differences in an organization. *Administrative Science Quarterly, 29*, 518–539.

Brass, D. J. (1985). Technology and the structuring of jobs: Employee satisfaction, performance, and influence. *Organizational Behavior and Human Decision Processes, 35*, 216–240.

Bray, D. W., Campbell, R. J., & Grant, D. L. (1974). *Formative years in business: A long term AT&T study of managerial lives.* New York: Wiley.

Brown, M. C. (1982). Administrative succession and organizational performance: The succession effect. *Administrative Science Quarterly, 29,* 245–273.

Brown, M. H., & Hosking, D. M. (1986). Distributed leadership and skilled performance as successful organization in social movements. *Human Relations, 39,* 65–79.

Bryman, A., Bresnen, M., Beardworth, A., & Keil, T. (1988). Qualitative research and the study of leadership. *Human Relations, 4*(1), 13–30.

Burgoyne, J. G., & Hodgson, V. E. (1984). An experiental approach to understanding managerial action. In J. G. Hunt, D. M. Hosking, C. A. Schriesheim, & R. Stewart (Eds.), *Leaders and managers: An international perspective on managerial behavior and leadership.* New York: Pergamon Press.

Burns, J. M. (1978). *Leadership.* New York: Harper & Row.

Calas, M. B., & Smircich, L. (1988). Reading leadership as a form of cultural analysis. In J. G. Hunt, B. R. Baliga, H. P. Dachler, & C. A. Schriesheim (Ed.), *Emerging leadership vistas.* Lexington, MA: D. C. Heath.

Calder, B. J. (1977). An attribution theory of leadership. In B. M. Staw & G. R. Salancik (Eds.), *New direction in organizational behavior.* Chicago: St. Clair.

Carlson, S. (1951). *Executive behavior: A study of the work load and working methods of managing directors.* Stockholm: Strombergs.

Carroll, S. J., Jr., & Gillen, D. J. (1987). Are the classical management functions useful in describing managerial work? *Academy of Management Review, 12,* 38–51.

Cashman, J., Dansereau, F., Jr., Graen, G., & Haga, W. J. (1976). Organizational understructure and leadership: A longitudinal investigation of the managerial role-making process. *Organizational Behavior and Human Performance, 15,* 278–296.

Coch, L., & French, J. R. P., Jr. (1948). Overcoming resistance to change. *Human Relations, 1,* 512–532.

Cohen, M. D., & March, J. G. (1986). *Leadership and ambiguity: The American college president* (2nd ed.). Cambridge, MA: Harvard Business School Press.

Conger, J. A. (1989). *The charismatic leader: Behind the mystique of exceptional leadership.* San Francisco: Jossey-Bass.

Conger, J. A., & Kanungo, R. (1987). Toward a behavioral theory of charismatic leadership in organizational settings. *Academy of Management Review, 12,* 637–647.

Conger, J. A., & Kanungo, R. N. (1990). *A behavioral attribute measure of charismatic leadership in organizations.* Paper presented at the annual meeting of the Academy of Management, San Francisco.

Cotton, J. L., Vollrath, D. A., Froggatt, K. L., Lengneck-Hall, M. L., & Jennings, K. R. (1988). Employee participation: Diverse forms and different outcomes. *Academy of Management Review, 13,* 8–22.

Cotton, J. L., Vollrath, D. A., Lengnick-Hall, M. L., & Froggatt, K. L. (1990). Fact: The form of participation does matter—A rebuttal to Leana, Locke, and Schweiger. *Academy of Management Review, 15,* 147–153.

Cronshaw, S. F., & Lord, R. G. (1987). Effects of categorization, attribution, and encoding processes on leadership perceptions. *Journal of Applied Psychology, 72,* 97–106.

Crouch, A., & Yetton, P. (1987). Manager behavior, leadership style, and subordinate performance: An empirical extension of the Vroom-Yetton conflict rule. *Organizational Behavior and Human Decision Processes, 39,* 384–396.

Crouch, A., & Yetton, P. (1988). The management team: An equilibrium model of management performance and behavior. In J. G. Hunt, B. R. Baliga, H. P. Dachler, & C. A. Schriesheim (Eds.), *Emerging leadership vistas.* Lexington, MA: Heath.

Dachler, H. P. (1984). Commentary on refocusing leadership from a social systems perspective. *Leaders and managers: International perspectives on managerial behavior and leadership.* New York: Pergamon Press.

Dachler, H. P. (1988). Constraints on the emergence of new vistas in leadership and management research: An epistemological overview. In J. G. Hunt, B. R. Baliga, H. P. Dachler, & C. A. Schriesheim (Eds.), *Emerging leadership vistas.* Lexington, MA: Heath.

Dansereau, F., Alutto, J. A., & Yammarino, F. (1984). *Theory testing in organizational behavior: The varient approach.* Englewood Cliffs, NJ: Prentice-Hall.

Dansereau, F., & Dumas, M. (1977). Pratfalls and pitfalls in drawing inferences about leadership behavior in organizations. In J. G. Hunt & L. L. Larson (Eds.), *Leadership: The cutting edge.* Carbondale: Southern Illinois University Press.

Dansereau, F., Jr., Graen, G., & Haga, W. J. (1975). A vertical dyad linkage approach to leadership within formal organizations: A longitudinal investigation of the role making process. *Organizational Behavior and Human Performance, 13,* 46–78.

Day, D. V., & Lord, R. G. (1989). Executive leadership and organizational performance: Suggestions for a new theory and methodology. *Journal of Management, 14,* 453–464.

Dienesh, R. M., & Liden, R. C. (1986). Leader-member exchange model of leadership: A critique and further development. *Academy of Management Review, 11,* 618–634.

Duchon, D., Green, S. G., & Taber, T. D. (1986). Vertical dyad linkage: A longitudinal assessment of antecedents, measures, and consequences. *Journal of Applied Psychology, 71,* 56–60.

Eden, D. (1984). Self-fulfilling prophecy as a management tool: Harnessing pygmalion. *Academy of Management Review, 9,* 64–73.

Eden, D. (1990). *Pygmalion in management: Productivity as a self-fulfilling prophecy.* Lexington, MA: Lexington Books.

Eisenstat, R. A., & Cohen, S. G. (1990). Summary: Top management groups. In J. R. Hackman (Ed.), *Groups that work and those that don't* (pp. 78–86). San Francisco: Jossey-Bass.

Erez, M., & Rim, Y. (1982). The relationship between goals, influence tactics, and personal and organizational variables. *Human Relations, 35,* 877–878.

Erez, M., Rim, Y., & Keider, I. (1986). The two sides of the tactics of influence: Agent vs. target. *Journal of Occupational Psychology, 59,* 25–39.

Ettling, J. T., & Jago, A. G. (1988). Participation under conditions of conflict: More on the validity of the Vroom-Yetton model. *Journal of Management Studies, 25(1),* 73–83.

Evans, M. G. (1970). The effects of supervisory behavior on the path-goal relationship. *Organizational Behavior and Human Performance, 5,* 277–298.

Evans, M. G. (1986). *Path-goal theory of leadership: A meta analysis.* Unpublished manuscript, University of Toronto.

Fiedler, F. E. (1967). *A theory of leadership effectiveness.* New York: McGraw-Hill.

Fiedler, F. E. (1978). The contingency model and the dynamics of the leadership process. In L. Berkowitz (Ed.), *Advances in experimental social psychology.* New York: Academic Press.

Fiedler, F. E. (1986). The contribution of cognitive resources to leadership performance. *Journal of Applied Social Psychology, 16,* 532–548.

Fiedler, F. E., & House, R. J. (1988). Leadership: A report of progress. In C. L. Cooper (Ed.), *International review of industrial and organizational psychology.* Greenwich, CT: JAI Press.

Fiedler, F. E., & Garcia, J. E. (1987). *New approaches to leadership: Cognitive resources and organizational performance.* New York: Wiley.

Field, R. H. G. (1979). A critique of the Vroom-Yetton contingency model of leadership behavior. *Academy of Management Review, 4,* 249–257.

Field, R. H. G. (1982). A test of the Vroom-Yetton normative model of leadership. *Journal of Applied Psychology, 67,* 523–532.

Field, R. H. G., & House, R. J. (1990). A test of the Vroom-Yetton model using manager and subordinate reports. *Journal of Applied Psychology, 75,* 362–366.

Field, R. H. G., Read, P. C., & Louviere, J. J. (1990). The effect of situation attributes on decision making choice in the Vroom-Jago model of participation in decision making. *Leadership Quarterly, 1,* 165–176.

Fleishman, E. A. (1953). The description of supervisory behavior. *Personnel Psychology, 37,* 1–6.

Freeston, K. (1987). Leader substitutes in educational organizations. *Educational Administration Quarterly, 23(2),* 45–59.

French, J., & Raven, B. H. (1959). The bases of social power. In D. Cartwright (Ed.), *Studies of social power.* Ann Arbor, MI: Institute for Social Research.

Gabarro, J. J. (1985, May–June). When a new manager takes charge. *Harvard Business Review,* 110–123.

Gibb, C. A. (1954). Leadership. In G. Lindzey (Ed.), *Handbook of social psychology.* Cambridge, MA: Addison-Wesley.

Gioia, D. A., & Sims, H. P., Jr. (1985). On avoiding the influence of implicit leadership theories in leader behavior descriptions. *Journal of Educational and Psychological Measurement, 45,* 217–237.

Graeff, C. L. (1983). The situational leadership theory: A critical review. *Academy of Management Review, 8,* 285–296.

Graen, G., & Cashman, J. F. (1975). A role making model of leadership in formal organizations: A developmental approach. In J. G. Hunt & L. L. Larson (Eds.), *Leadership frontiers.* Kent, OH: Kent State University Press.

Graen, G., Novak, M., & Sommerkamp, P. (1982). The effects of leader-member exchange and job design on productivity and satisfaction: Testing a dual attachment model. *Organizational Behavior and Human Performance, 30,* 109–131.

Graen, G. B., & Scandura, T. (1987). Toward a psychology of dyadic organizing. *Research in Organizational Behavior, 9,* 175–208.

Graen, G. B., Scandura, T. A., & Graen, M. R. (1986). A field experimental test of the moderating effects of growth need strength on productivity. *Journal of Applied Psychology, 71,* 484–491.

Graen, G. B., & Uhl-Bien, M. (in press). The transformation of work group professionals into self-managing and partially self-designing teams: Toward a theory of leadership-making. *Journal of Management Systems.*

Green, S. G., & Mitchell, T. R. (1979). Attributional processes of leaders in leader-member exchanges. *Organizational Behavior and Human Performance, 23,* 429–458.

Gupta, A. K., & Govindarajan, V. (1984). Business unit strategy, managerial characteristics, and business unit effectiveness at strategy implementation. *Academy of Management Journal, 27,* 25–41.

Hackman, J. R. (1986). The psychology of self-management in organizations. In M. S. Pollack & R. O. Perloff (Eds.), *Psychology and work: Productivity, change, and employment* (pp. 85–136). Washington, DC: American Psychological Association.

Hackman, J. R. (1990). *Groups that work (and those that don't).* San Francisco: Jossey-Bass.

Hales, C. P. (1986). What do managers do? A critical review of the evidence. *Journal of Management Studies, 23,* 88–115.

Halpin, A. W., & Winer, B. J. (1957). A factorial study of the leader behavior descriptions. In R. M. Stogdill & A. E. Coons (Eds.), *Leader behavior: Its description and measurement.* Columbus: Bureau of Business Research, Ohio State University.

Hambleton, R. K., & Gumbert, R. (1982). The validity of Hersey and Blanchard's theory of leader effectiveness. *Group and Organization Studies, 7,* 225–242.

Harrison, R. (1987, Autumn). Harnessing personal energy: How companies can inspire employees. *Organizational Dynamics,* 4–21.

Hater, J. J., & Bass, B. M. (1988). Superiors evaluations and subordinates' perceptions of transformational and transactional leadership. *Journal of Applied Psychology, 73,* 695–702.

Heilman, M. E., Hornstein, H. A., Cage, J. H., & Herschlag, J. K. (1984). Reactions to prescribed leader behavior as a function of role perspective: The case of the Vroom-Yetton model. *Journal of Applied Psychology, 69,* 50–60.

Hersey, P., & Blanchard, K. H. (1969). Life cycle theory of leadership. *Training and Development Journal, 23*(2), 26–4.

Hersey, P., & Blanchard, K. H. (1988). *Management of organizational behavior* (5th ed.). Englewood Cliffs, NJ: Prentice-Hall.

Hickson, D. J., Hinings, C. R., Lee, C. A., Schneck, R. S., & Pennings, J. M. (1971). A strategic contingencies theory of intra-organizational power. *Administrative Science Quarterly, 16,* 216–229.

Hinkin, T. R., & Schriesheim, C. A. (1989). Development and application of new scales to measure the French and Raven bases of social power. *Journal of Applied Psychology, 74,* 561–567.

Hogan, R., Raskin, R., & Fazzini, D. (1990). The dark side of charisma. In K. E. Clark & M. B. Clark (Eds.), *Measures of leadership.* West Orange, NJ: Leadership Library of America.

Hollander, E. P. (1978). *Leadership dynamics: A practical guide to effective relationships.* New York: Free Press.

Hollander, E. P., & Offermann, L. R. (1990). Power and leadership in organizations. *American Psychologist, 45,* 179–189.

Hosking, D., & Morley, I. E. (1988). The skills of leadership. In J. G. Hunt, B. R. Baliga, H. P. Dachler, & C. A. Schriesheim (Eds.), *Emerging leadership vistas* (pp. 89–106). Lexington, MA: Heath.

House, R. J. (1971). A path-goal theory of leader effectiveness. *Administrative Science Quarterly, 16,* 321–339.

House, R. J. (1977). A 1976 theory of charismatic leadership. In J. G. Hunt & L. L. Larson (Eds.),

Leadership: The cutting edge. Carbondale: Southern Illinois University Press.

House, R. J. (1988a). Leadership research: Some forgotten, ignored, or overlooked findings. In J. G. Hunt, B. R. Baliga, H. P. Dachler, & C. A. Schriesheim (Eds.), *Emerging leadership vistas.* Lexington, MA: Heath.

House, R. J. (1988b). Power and personality in organizations. *Research in Organizational Behavior* (Vol. 10, pp. 305–357). Greenwich, CT: JAI Press.

House, R. J., & Mitchell, T. R. (1974, Fall). Path-goal theory of leadership. *Contemporary Business, 3,* 81–98.

House, R. J., Woycke, J., & Fodor, E. M. (1988). Charismatic and noncharismatic leaders: Differences in behavior and effectiveness. In J. A. Conger & R. N. Kanungo (Eds.), *Charismatic leadership: The elusive factor in organizational effectiveness.* San Francisco: Jossey-Bass.

Howard, A., & Bray, D. W. (1988). *Managerial lives in transition: Advancing age and changing times.* New York: Guilford Press.

Howell, J. M. (1988). Two faces of charisma: Socialized and personalized leadership in organizations. In J. A. Conger & R. N. Kanungo (Eds.), *Charismatic leadership: The elusive factor in organizational effectiveness.* San Francisco: Jossey-Bass.

Howell, J. M., & Frost, P. (1989). A laboratory study of charismatic leadership. *Organizational Behavior and Human Decision Processes, 43,* 243–269.

Howell, J. M., & Higgins, C. A. (1990). Leadership behaviors, influence tactics, and career experiences of champions of technological innovation. *Leadership Quarterly, 1,* 249–264.

Howell, J. P., Bowen, D. E., Dorfman, P. W., Kerr, S., & Podsakoff, P. M. (1990). Substitutes for leadership: Effective alternatives to ineffective leadership. *Organizational Dynamics, 19,* 21–38.

Howell, J. P., & Dorfman, P. W. (1981). Substitutes for leadership: Test of a construct. *Academy of Management Journal, 24,* 714–728.

Howell, J. P., & Dorfman, P. W. (1986). Leadership and substitutes for leadership among professional and nonprofessional workers. *Journal of Applied Behavioral Science, 22,* 29–46.

Hunt, J. G., & Osborn, R. N. (1982). Toward a macro-oriented model of leadership: An odyssey. In J. G. Hunt, U. Sekaran, & C. Schriesheim (Eds.), *Leadership: Beyond establishment views* (pp. 196–221). Carbondale: Southern Illinois University Press.

Indvik, J. (1986). Path-goal theory of leadership: A meta-analysis. In *Proceedings of the Academy of Management Meetings,* 189–192.

Isenberg, D. J. (1984, November–December). How senior managers think. *Harvard Business Review,* 81–90.

Jacobs, T. O., & Jaques, E. (1987). Leadership in complex systems. In J. Zeidner (Ed.), *Human productivity enhancement* (pp. 7–65). New York: Praeger.

Jermier, J. M., & Berkes, L. J. (1979). Leader behavior in a police command bureaucracy: A closer look at the quasi-military model. *Administrative Science Quarterly, 24,* 1–23.

Jick, T. D. (1979). Mixing qualitative and quantitative methods: Triangulation in action. *Administrative Science Quarterly, 24,* 602–611.

Kahn, R. L., Wolfe, D. M., Quinn, R. P., & Snoek, J. D. (1964). *Organizational stress: Studies in role conflict and ambiguity.* New York: Wiley.

Kanter, R. M. (1983). *The change masters.* New York: Simon & Schuster.

Kaplan, R. E. (1984, Spring). Trade routes: The manager's network of relationships. *Organizational Dynamics,* 37–52.

Kaplan, R. E. (1986). *The warp and woof of the general manager's job* (Tech. Rep. No. 27, pp. 1–32). Greensboro, NC: Center for Creative Leadership.

Kaplan, R. E., Lombardo, M. M., & Mazique, M. S. (1985). A mirror for managers: Using simulation to develop management teams. *Journal of Applied Behavioral Science, 21,* 241–253.

Katz, D., & Kahn, R. L. (1978). The social psychology of organizations (2nd ed.). New York: Wiley.

Katz, R. L. (1955, January–February). Skills of an effective administrator. *Harvard Business Review,* 33–42.

Kerr, S., Hill, K. D., & Broedling, L. (1986). The first-line supervisor: Phasing out or here to stay? *Academy of Management Review, 11,* 103–117.

Kerr, S., & Jermier, J. M. (1978). Substitutes for leadership: Their meaning and measurement. *Organizational Behavior and Human Performance, 22,* 375–403.

Kets de Vries, M. F. R., & Miller, D. (1985). Narcissism and leadership: An object relations perspective. *Human Relations, 38,* 583–601.

Kieser, A. (1984). How does one become an effective manager? In J. G. Hunt, D. Hosking, C. A. Schriesheim, & R. Stewart (Eds.), *Leaders and managers: International perspectives on managerial behavior and leadership* (pp. 90–94). New York: Pergamon Press.

Kim, K. I., & Organ, D. W. (1982). Determinants of leader-subordinate exchange relationships. *Group and Organization Studies, 7,* 77–89.

Kipnis, D. (1972). Does power corrupt? *Journal of Personality and Social Psychology, 24,* 33–41.

Kipnis, D., Schmidt, S. M., & Wilkinson, I. (1980). Intra-organizational influence tactics: Explorations in getting one's way. *Journal of Applied Psychology, 65,* 440–452.

Kirpatrick, S. A., & Locke, E. A. (1991). Leadership: Do traits matter? *The Academy of Management Executive, 5*(2), 48–60.

Komaki, J. (1986). Toward effective supervision: An operant analysis and comparison of managers at work. *Journal of Applied Psychology, 71,* 270–278.

Kotter, J. P. (1982). *The general managers.* New York: Free Press.

Kotter, J. P. (1985). *Power and influence: Beyond formal authority.* New York: Free Press.

Kouzes, J. M., & Posner, B. Z. (1987). *The leadership challenge: How to get extraordinary things done in organizations.* San Francisco: Jossey-Bass.

Krantz, J. (1990). Lessons from the field: An essay on the crisis of leadership in contemporary organizations. *The Journal of Applied Behavioral Science, 26,* 49–64.

Kuhnert, K. W., & Lewis, P. (1987). Transactional and transformational leadership: A constructive/developmental analysis. *Academy of Management Review, 12,* 648–657.

Latham, G. P. (1988). Human resource training and development. *Annual Review of Psychology, 39,* 545–582.

Larson, L. L., Hunt, J. G., & Osborn, R. N. (1976). The great hi-hi leader behavior myth: A lesson from Occam's razor. *Academy of Management Journal, 19,* 628–641.

Lawler, E. E., III (1984). Leadership in participative organizations. In J. G. Hunt, D. Hosking, C. A. Schriesheim, & R. Stewart, *Leaders and managers: International perspectives on managerial behavior and leadership* (pp. 316–322). New York: Pergamon Press.

Leana, C. R., Locke, E. A., & Schweiger, D. M. (1990). Fact and fiction in analyzing research on participative decision making: A critique of Cotton, Vollrath, Froggatt, Lengnick-Hall, and Jennings. *Academy of Management Review, 15,* 137–146.

Lewin, K., Lippitt, R., & White, R. K. (1939). Patterns of aggressive behavior in experimentally created social climates. *Journal of Social Psychology, 10,* 271–301.

Lieberson, S., & O'Connor, J. F. (1972). Leadership and organizational performance: A study of large corporations. *American Sociological Review, 37,* 117–130.

Likert, R. (1967). *The human organization: Its management and value.* New York: McGraw-Hill.

Locke, E., & Latham, G. P. (1990). *A theory of goal setting and task performance.* Englewood Cliffs, NJ: Prentice-Hall.

Lord, R. G., Bining, J. F., Rush, M. C., & Thomas, J. C. (1978). The effect of performance cues and leader behavior on questionnaire ratings of leader behavior. *Organizational Behavior and Human Performance, 21,* 27–39.

Lord, R. G., DeVader, C. L., & Alliger, G. M. (1986). A meta-analysis of the relation between personality traits and leadership perceptions: An application of validity generalization procedures. *Journal of Applied Psychology, 61,* 402–410.

Luthans, F., & Lockwood, D. L. (1984). Toward an observation system for measuring leader behavior in natural settings. In J. G. Hunt, D. Hosking, C. A. Schriesheim, & R. Stewart (Eds.), *Leaders and managers: International perspectives on managerial behavior and leadership.* New York: Pergamon Press.

Luthans, F., Rosenkrantz, S. A., & Hennessey, H. W. (1985). What do successful managers really do? An observational study of managerial activities. *Journal of Applied Behavioral Science, 21,* 255–270.

Mann, F. C. (1965). Toward an understanding of the leadership role in formal organization. In R. Dubin, G. C. Homans, F. C. Mann, & D. C. Miller (Eds.), *Leadership and productivity.* San Francisco: Chandler.

Mann, R. D. (1959). A review of the relationship between personality and performance in small groups. *Psychological Bulletin, 56,* 241–270.

Manz, C. C., & Sims, H. P., Jr. (1987). Leading workers to lead themselves: The external leadership of self-managing work teams. *Administrative Science Quarterly, 32,* 106–128.

Manz, C., & Sims, H. P. (1989). *Superleadership: Leading others to lead themselves.* Englewood Cliffs, NJ: Prentice-Hall.

Martinko, M. J., & Gardner, W. L. (1985). Beyond structured observation: Methodological issues and new directions. *Academy of Management Review, 10,* 676–695.

McCall, M. W. (1977). Leaders and leadership: Of substance and shadow. In J. Hackman, E. E. Lawler, Jr., & L. W. Porter (Eds.), *Perspectives on behavior in organizations.* New York: McGraw-Hill.

McCall, M. W. (1978). *Power, influence, and authority: The hazards of carrying a sword.* (Tech. Rep. No. 10). Greensboro, NC: Center for Creative Leadership.

McCall, M. W., & Kaplan, R. E. (1985). *Whatever it takes: Decision makers at work.* Englewood Cliffs, NJ: Prentice-Hall.

McCall, M. W., & Lombardo, M. M. (1983). *Off the track: Why and how successful executives get derailed* (Tech. Rep. No. 21). Greensboro, NC: Center for Creative Leadership.

McCall, M. W., & Segrist, C. A. (1980). *In pursuit of the manager's job: Building on Mintzberg* (Tech. Rep. No. 14). Greensboro, NC: Center for Creative Leadership.

McClane, W. E. (1991). Implications of member role differentiation: Analysis of a key concept in the LMX model of leadership. *Group and Organization Studies, 16,* 102–113.

McClelland, D. C. (1975). *Power: The inner experience.* New York: Irvington.

McClelland, D. C., & Boyatzis, R. E. (1982). Leadership motive pattern and long term success in management. *Journal of Applied Psychology, 67,* 737–743.

McClelland, D. C., & Burnham, D. H. (1976, March–April). Power is the great motivator. *Harvard Business Review,* 100–110.

McIntosh, N. J. (1988). *Substitutes for leadership: Review, critique, and suggestion.* Paper presented at the annual meeting of the Academy of Management, Anaheim, CA.

McGregor, D. (1960). *The human side of enterprise.* New York: McGraw-Hill.

Meindl, J. R., Erlich, S. B., & Dukerich, J. M. (1985). The romance of leadership. *Administrative Science Quarterly, 30,* 78–102.

Miller, K. I., & Monge, P. R. (1986). Participation, satisfaction, and productivity: A meta-analytic review. *Academy of Management Journal, 29,* 727–753.

Miner, J. B. (1978). Twenty years of research on role motivation theory of managerial effectiveness. *Personnel Psychology, 31,* 739–760.

Mintzberg, H. (1973). *The nature of managerial work.* New York: Harper & Row.

Mintzberg, H. (1983). *Power in and around organizations.* Englewood Cliffs, NJ: Prentice-Hall.

Mintzberg, H., & McHugh, A. (1985). Strategy formation in an adhocracy. *Administrative Science Quarterly, 30,* 160–197.

Misumi, J. (1985). *The behavioral science of leadership: An interdisciplinary Japanese research program.* Ann Arbor, MI: The University of Michigan Press.

Misumi, J., & Peterson, M. (1985). The performance-maintenance (PM) theory of leadership: Review of a Japanese research program. *Administrative Science Quarterly, 30,* 198–223.

Mitchell, T. R., Green, S. G., & Wood, R. E. (1981). *An attributional model of leadership and the poor performing subordinate: Development and validation.* In L. L. Cummings & B. M. Staw (Eds.), *Research in organizational behavior* (Vol. 3). Greenwich, CT: JAI Press.

Mitchell, T. R., Larson, J. R., Jr., & Green, S. G. (1977). Leader behavior, situational moderators, and group performance: An attributional analysis. *Organizational Behavior and Human Performance, 18,* 254–268.

Morgan, G., & Smircich, L. (1980). The case for qualitative research. *Academy of Management Review, 5,* 491–500.

Morris, V. C., Crowson, R. L., Hurwitz, E., Jr., Porter-Gehrie, C. (1981). *The urban principal.* Washington, DC: National Institute of Education.

Morse, J. J., & Wagner, F. R. (1978). Measuring the process of managerial effectiveness. *Academy of Management Journal, 21,* 23–35.

Mowday, R. (1978). The exercise of upward influence in organizations. *Administrative Science Quarterly, 23,* 137–156.

Mumford, E. (1906-1907). Origins of leadership. *American Journal of Sociology, 12,* 216-240, 367–397, 500–531.

Musser, S. J. (1987). *The determination of positive and negative charismatic leadership.* Unpublished manuscript, Messiah College, Grantham, PA.

Nystrom, P. C. (1978). Managers and the hi-hi leader myth. *Academy of Management Journal, 21,* 325–331.

Osborn, R. N., & Hunt, J. G. (1975). An adaptive-reactive theory of leadership: The role of macro variables in leadership research. In J. G. Hunt & L. L. Larson (Eds.), *Leadership frontiers.* Kent, OH: Kent State University Press.

Page, R., & Tornow, W. W. (1987, April). *Managerial job analysis: Are we farther along?* Paper presented at the annual meeting of the Society for Industrial and Organizational Psychology, Atlanta.

Peters, L. H., Hartke, D. D., & Pohlman, J. T. (1985). Fiedler's contingency theory of leadership: An application of the meta-analysis procedures of Schmidt and Hunter. *Psychological Bulletin, 97,* 274–285.

Peters, T. J., & Austin, N. (1985). *A passion for excellence: The leadership difference.* New York: Random House.

Peters, T. J., & Waterman, R. H., Jr. (1982). *In search of excellence: Lessons from America's best-run companies.* New York: Harper & Row.

Pfeffer, J. (1977). The ambiguity of leadership. *Academy of Management Review, 2,* 104–112.

Pfeffer, J. (1981). *Power in organizations.* Marshfield, MA: Pittman.

Pfeffer, J., & Davis-Blake, A. (1986). Administrative succession and organizational performance: How administrator experience mediates the succession effect. *Academy of Management Journal, 29,* 72–83.

Pfeffer, J., & Salancik, G. R. (1975). Determinants of supervisory behavior: A role set analysis. *Human Relations, 28,* 139–153.

Phillips, J. S., & Lord, R. G. (1986). Notes on the practical and theoretical consequences of implicit leadership theories for the future of leadership measurement. *Journal of Management, 12,* 31–41.

Podsakoff, P. M., & Schriesheim, C. A. (1985). Field studies of French and Raven's bases of power: Critique, reanalysis, and suggestions for future research. *Psychological Bulletin, 97,* 387–411.

Podsakoff, P. M., Todor, W. D., Grover, R. A., & Huber, V. L. (1984). Situational moderators of leader reward and punishment behavior: Fact or fiction? *Organizational Behavior and Human Performance, 34,* 21–63.

Podsakoff, P. M., Todor, W. D., & Skov, R. (1982). Effects of leader contingent and non-contingent reward and punishment behaviors on subordinate performance and satisfaction. *Academy of Management Journal, 25,* 810–821.

Porter, L. W., Allen, R. W., & Angle, H. L. (1981). The politics of upward influence in organizations. In L. L. Cummings & B. M. Staw (Eds.), *Research in organizational behavior* (Vol. 3). Greenwich, CT: JAI Press.

Quinn, R. E., & Rohrbaugh, J. (1983). A spatial model of effectiveness criteria: Towards a competing values approach to organizational analysis. *Management Science, 29,* 363–377.

Rahim, M. A. (1988). The development of a leader power inventory. *Multivariate Behavioral Research, 23,* 491–503.

Rice, R. W. (1978). Construct validity of the least preferred co-worker score. *Psychological Bulletin, 85,* 1199–1237.

Roberts, N. C. (1985). Transforming leadership: A process of collective action. *Human Relations, 38,* 1023–1046.

Roberts, N. C., & Bradley, R. T. (1988). Limits of charisma. In J. A. Conger & R. N. Kanungo (Eds.), *Charismatic leadership: The elusive factor in organizational effectiveness.* San Francisco: Jossey-Bass.

Salancik, G. R., & Meindl, J. R. (1984). Corporate attributions as strategic illusions of management control. *Administrative Science Quarterly, 29,* 238–254.

Salancik, G. R., & Pfeffer, J. (1977a). Who gets power and how they hold on to it: A strategic contingency model of power. *Organizational Dynamics,* 3–21.

Salancik, G. R., & Pfeffer, J. (1977b). Constraints on administrative discretion: The limited influence of mayors on city budgets. *Urban Affairs Quarterly, 12,* 474–498.

Sashkin, M. (1988). The visionary leader. In J. A. Conger & R. N. Kanungo (Eds.), *Charismatic leadership: The elusive factor in organizational effectiveness* (pp. 122–160). San Francisco: Jossey-Bass.

Sashkin, M., & Fulmer, R. M. (1988). Toward an organizational leadership theory. In J. G. Hunt, B. R. Baliga, H. P. Dachler, & C. A. Schriesheim (Ed.), *Emerging leadership vistas.* Lexington, MA: Heath.

Sayles, L. R. (1979). *What effective managers really do and how they do it.* New York: McGraw-Hill.

Scandura, T. A., & Graen, G. B. (1984). Moderating effects of initial leader-member exchange status on the effects of leadership intervention. *Journal of Applied Psychology, 69,* 428-436.

Schein, E. H. (1985). *Organizational culture and leadership.* San Francisco: Jossey-Bass.

Schilit, W. K., & Locke, E. A. (1982). A study of upward influence in organizations. *Administrative Science Quarterly, 27,* 304–316.

Schriesheim, C. A., & Hinkin, T. R. (1990). Influence tactics used by subordinates: A theoretical and empirical analysis and refinement of the Kipnis, Schmidt, and Wilkinson subscales. *Journal of Applied Psychology, 75,* 246–257.

Schriesheim, C. A., & Kerr, S. (1977). Theories and measures of leadership: A critical appraisal. In J. G. Hunt & L. L. Larson (Eds.), *Leadership: The cutting edge.* Carbondale: Southern Illinois University Press.

Schweiger, D. M. (1983). Is the simultaneous verbal protocol a viable method for studying managerial problem solving and decision making? *Academy of Management Journal, 26,* 185–192.

Schweiger, D. M., Anderson, C. R., & Locke, E. A. (1985). Complex decision making: A longitudinal study of process and performance. *Organizational Behavior and Human Decision Processes, 36,* 245–272.

Schweiger, D. M., & Leana, C. R. (1985). Participation in decision making. In E. A. Locke (Ed.), *Generalizing from laboratory to field settings.* Boston: Heath-Lexington.

Seltzer, J., & Bass, B. M. (1990). Transformational leadership: Beyond initiation and consideration. *Journal of Management, 16,* 693–703.

Shetty, Y. K., & Peery, N. S. (1976). Are top executives transferable across companies? *Business Horizons, 19*(3), 23–28.

Shipper, F. (1991). Mastery and frequency of managerial behaviors relative to subunit effectiveness. *Human Relations, 44,* 371–388.

Simon, H. (1987). Making managerial decisions: The role of intuition and emotion. *Academy of Management Executive, 1,* 57–64.

Sims, H. P., Jr., & Szilagyi, A. D. (1975). Leader reward behavior and subordinate satisfaction and performance. *Organizational Behavior and Human Performance, 14,* 426–437.

Smith, J. E., Carson, K. P., & Alexander, R. A. (1984). Leadership: It can make a difference. *Academy of Management Journal, 27,* 765–776.

Smith, P. B., Misumi, J., Tayeb, M., Peterson, M., & Bond, M. (1989). On the generality of leadership style measures across cultures. *Journal of Occupational Psychology, 62,* 97–107.

Staw, B. M., McKechnie, P. I., & Puffer, S. M. (1983). The justification of organizational performance. *Administrative Science Quarterly, 28,* 582–600.

Stewart, R. (1976). *Contrasts in management.* Maidenhead, Berkshire, England: McGraw-Hill UK.

Stewart, R. (1982). *Choices for the manager: A guide to understanding managerial work.* Englewood Cliffs, NJ: Prentice-Hall.

Stinson, J. E., & Johnson, T. W. (1975). The path goal theory of leadership: A partial test and suggested refinement. *Academy of Management Journal, 18,* 242–252.

Stogdill, R. M. (1948). Personal factors associated with leaderhip: A survey of the literature. *Journal of Psychology, 25,* 35–71.

Stogdill, R. M. (1963). *Manual for the leader behavior description questionnaire, Form XII.* Columbus: Ohio State University, Bureau of Business Research.

Stogdill, R. M. (1974). *Handbook of leadership: A survey of the literature.* New York: Free Press.

Strong, P. M. (1984). On qualitative methods and leadership research. In J. G. Hunt, D. M. Hosking, C. A. Schriesheim, & R. Stewart (Eds.), *Leaders and managers: An international perspective on managerial behavior and leadership.* New York: Pergamon Press.

Strube, M. J., & Garcia, J. E. (1981). A meta-analytic investigation of Fiedler's contingency model of leadership effectiveness. *Psychological Bulletin, 90,* 307–321.

Sutton, C., & Woodman, R. (1989). Pygmalion goes to work: The effects of supervisor expectations in a retail setting. *Journal of Applied Psychology, 74,* 943–950.

Szilagyi, A. D., & Schweiger, D. M. (1984). Matching managers to strategies: A review and suggested framework. *Academy of Management Review, 9,* 626–637.

Thambain, H. J., & Gemmill, G. R. (1974). Influence styles of project managers: Some performance correlates. *Academy of Management Journal, 17,* 216–224.

Thomas, A. B. (1988). Does leadership make a difference to organizational performance? *Administrative Science Quarterly, 33,* 388–400.

Tichy, N. M., & Devanna, M. A. (1986). *The transformational leader.* New York: Wiley.

Tjosvold, D., Wedley, W. C., & Field, R. H. G. (1986). Constructive controversy: The Vroom-Yetton model and managerial decision making. *Journal of Occupational Behavior, 7,* 125–138.

Trice, H. M., & Beyer, J. M. (1986). Charisma and its routinization in two social movement organizations. *Research in Organization Behavior* (Vol. 8, pp. 113–164). Greenwich, CT: JAI Press.

Trice, H. M., & Beyer, J. M. (1991). Cultural leadership in organizations. *Organization Science, 2,* 149–169.

Tsui, A. (1984). A role set analysis of managerial reputation. *Organizational Behavior and Human Performance, 34,* 64–96.

Vanderslice, V. J. (1988). Separating leadership from leaders: An assessment of the effect of leader and follower roles in organizations. *Human Relations, 41,* 677–696.

Van Fleet, D. D. (1975). Changing patterns of significant authors on leadership and managerial effectiveness. *Journal of Management, 1,* 39–44.

Van Fleet, D. D., & Yukl, G. (1986a). A century of leadership research. In D. A. Wren (Ed.), *One hundred years of management.* Academy of Management, 12–23.

Van Fleet, D. D., & Yukl, G. (1986b). *Military leadership: An organizational perspective.* Greenwich, CT: JAI Press.

Vecchio, R. P. (1983). Assessing the validity of Fiedler's contingency model of leadership effectiveness: A closer look at Strube and Garcia. *Psychological Bulletin, 93,* 404–408.

Vecchio, R. P. (1987). Situational leadership theory: An examination of a prescriptive theory. *Journal of Applied Psychology, 72,* 444–451.

Vecchio, R. P., & Gobdel, B. C. (1984). The vertical dyad linkage model of leadership: Problems and prospects. *Organizational Behavior and Human Performance, 34,* 5–20.

Vroom, V. H., & Jago, A. G. (1988). *The new leadership: Managing participation in organizations.* Englewood Cliffs, NJ: Prentice-Hall.

Vroom, V. H., & Yetton, P. W. (1973). *Leadership and decision making.* Pittsburgh: University of Pittsburgh Press.

Wagner, J. A., & Gooding, R. Z. (1987). Shared influence and organizational behavior: A meta-analysis of situational variables expected to moderate participation-outcome relationships. *Academy of Management Journal, 30,* 524–541.

Wakabayashi, M., & Graen, G. B. (1984). The Japanese career progress study: A seven-year follow-up. *Journal of Applied Psychology, 69,* 603–614.

Waldman, D. A., Bass, B. M., & Einstein, W. O. (1987). Effort, performance and transformational leadership in industrial and military service. *Journal of Occupational Psychology, 60,* 1–10.

Waldman, D. A., Bass, B. M., & Yammarino, F. J. (1990). Adding to contingent reward behavior: The augmenting effect of charismatic leadership. *Group and Organization Studies, 15,* 4, 381–391.

Weber, M. (1947). *The theory of social and economic organizations* (T. Parsons, Trans.). New York: Free Press.

Weiner, N., & Mahoney, T. A. (1981). A model of corporate performance as a function of environmental, organizational, and leadership influences. *Academy of Management Journal, 24,* 453–470.

Westley, F. R., & Mintzberg, H. (1988). Profiles of strategic vision: Levesque and Iacocca. In J. A. Conger & R. N. Kanungo (Eds.), *Charismatic leadership: The elusive factor in organizational effectiveness.* San Francisco: Jossey-Bass.

Willner, A. R. (1984). *The spellbinders: Charismatic political leadership.* New Haven: Yale University Press.

Wofford, J. C. (1982). An integrative theory of leadership. *Journal of Management, 8,* 27–47.

Wofford, J. C., & Srinivasan, T. N. (1984). Experimental tests of leader-environment-follower interaction theory of leadership. *Organizational Behavior and Human Performance, 32,* 33–54.

Yammarino, F. J. (1990). Individual and group-directed leader behavior descriptions. *Educational and Psychological Measurement, 50,* 739–759.

Yammarino, F. J., & Bass, B. M. (1990). Transformational leadership and multiple levels of analysis. *Human Relations, 43,* 975–995.

Yukl, G. (1971). Toward a behavioral theory of leadership. *Organizational Behavior and Human Performance, 6*, 414–440.

Yukl, G. (1981). *Leadership in organizations.* Englewood Cliffs, NJ: Prentice-Hall.

Yukl, G. (1989a). *Leadership in organizations* (2nd ed.). Englewood Cliffs, NJ: Prentice-Hall.

Yukl, G. (1989b). Managerial leadership: A review of theory and research. *Journal of Management, 15,* 251–289.

Yukl, G., & Falbe, C. M. (1990). Influence tactics and objectives in upward, downward, and lateral influence attempts. *Journal of Applied Psychology, 75,* 132–140.

Yukl, G., & Falbe, C. M. (1991). The importance of different power sources in downward and lateral relations. *Journal of Applied Psychology, 76,* 416–423.

Yukl, G., Falbe, C. M., Youn, J. Y., & Tracey, B. (1991). *Multi-method research on the consequences of using different influence tactics with subordinates, peers, and superiors.* Unpublished manuscript. SUNY, Albany, NY.

Yukl, G., & Lepsinger, R. (1989). An integrating taxonomy of managerial behavior: Implications for improving managerial effectiveness. In J. W. Jones, B. D. Steffy, & D. W. Bray (Eds.), *Applying psychology in business: The manager's handbook.* Lexington, MA: Lexington Press.

Yukl, G., & Nemeroff, W. (1979). Identification and measurement of specific categories of leadership behavior: A progress report. In J. G. Hunt & L. L. Larson (Eds.), *Crosscurrents in leadership.* Carbondale: Southern Illinois University Press.

Yukl, G., & Taber, T. (1983, March–April). The effective use of managerial power. *Personnel,* 37–44.

Yukl, G., & Van Fleet, D. (1982). Cross-situational, multi-method research on military leader effectiveness. *Organizational Behavior and Human Performance, 30,* 87–108.

Yukl, G., Wall, S., & Lepsinger, R. (1990). Preliminary report on validation of the management practices survey. In K. E. Clark & M. B. Clark (Eds.), *Measures of leadership.* West Orange, NJ: Leadership Library of America.

Zaccaro, S. J., Foti, R. J., & Kenny, D. A. (1991). Self-monitoring and trait-based variance in leadership: An investigation of leader flexibility across multiple group situations. *Journal of Applied Psychology, 76,* 179–185.

Zaleznik, A. (1970, May–June). Power and politics in organizational life. *Harvard Business Review,* 47–60.

Zaleznik, A. (1977). Managers and leaders: Are they different? *Harvard Business Review, 55*(5), 67–78.

CHAPTER 4

Group Influences on Individuals in Organizations

J. Richard Hackman
Harvard University

This chapter reviews the effects of organizational groups on the beliefs, attitudes, and behaviors of their members. These effects have three different bases: (a) the ambient stimuli that pervade the group setting and impinge on all members of a given group, (b) discretionary stimuli that members provide to one another selectively, depending on what specific individuals say and do, and (c) the structure of group norms and the ways groups enforce adherence to them. Special attention is given to the conditions under which influence flows in the opposite direction— that is, when individuals succeed in changing the structure and dynamics of the groups of which they are members. The chapter concludes with a discussion of the implications of the material for the health and performance of groups and their members over the long term.

Introduction

GROUP AND INTERPERSONAL relationships powerfully affect how people think, feel, and act at work. This chapter analyzes the dynamics and consequences of group influences and explores ways they can be structured and managed to foster team effectiveness and individual well-being.

Although understanding the dynamics of group-individual relationships in organizations

remains a conceptual and empirical challenge, the potency of such relationships has been recognized for decades. Probably the most widely known study of group effects was performed at the Hawthorne plant of the Western Electric Company in the late 1920s (Roethlisberger & Dickson, 1939, summarized by Homans, 1950). That research program, which was designed to assess the impact of working conditions such as lighting and rest pauses on employee productivity, had a surprising result. Objective working conditions turned out to be much less powerful in affecting worker behavior than were various psychological and social conditions that evolved over the course of the project. Particularly significant was the finding that workers developed a strong group identity as the research progressed, which in turn spawned group norms that powerfully shaped on-the-job behavior.

The Hawthorne studies showed the power of simply having a group where none existed before. Another classic, the Tavistock research on coal mining, showed what can happen when existing groups are broken up (Trist & Bamforth, 1951). Coal miners in the Tavistock study worked together in small, highly interdependent groups of eight or fewer members. A technological change (shifting from a "shortwall" to a "longwall" method of removing coal) required that existing groups be recomposed into large work units of 40 to 50 men. These new groups still had a single supervisor, but the workers often were widely separated from one another within the mines. Even though they were still highly interdependent (indeed, a mistake or poor performance by any individual could affect everyone in the unit), existing interpersonal relationships were severely disrupted. Soon after the changes were introduced, productivity deteriorated and worker indifference and alienation increased. Ultimately, a norm of low productivity developed—apparently as a means of coping with the emotional and technological difficulties that had been created by the change in work methods.

Such difficulties are not, of course, an uncommon outcome of major technological changes. Negative effects were especially strong in the Tavistock study, however, because exactly those social units that could have been most helpful to individuals in making appropriate adjustments (i.e., the existing work groups) were themselves done away with as a part of the change. The individual workers were, in effect,

left without a social anchor—and the eventual consequences were negative for both the company and the people.

Considering both the Hawthorne and Tavistock findings, it is tempting to conclude that groups are good for both people and organizations—that they should be created if they do not already exist, and that existing groups should never be destroyed but instead should be strengthened whenever possible. The world is not so simple. While there is no question that groups are consequential for people and for organizations, the *direction* of their effects is an entirely separate question. In the Hawthorne research, for example, some groups enforced norms about work behavior that were consistent with company policies, but others did the opposite. And a case described by Theodore Newcomb (1954, cited in Golembiewski, 1962, pp. 223–224) shows just how destructive group influences can become. The group Newcomb studied had established a production norm of 50 units a day, but one particular worker wanted to produce more than that. Her attempts to do so were so successfully discouraged by her peers that she became disheartened and her output finally dropped even below the 50-unit norm. Subsequently, the composition of the group was changed and the individual no longer worked with those who had established and enforced the 50-unit norm. Her output soon doubled.

A third classic study, by Coch and French (1948), provides some clues about factors that influence the direction of group norms. These authors studied an organization in which, as was the case in the Tavistock study, management changed work practices. The changes were implemented in three ways: (a) with direct participation by all affected employees, (b) with participation through a representative, and (c) without any participation. In all three conditions, the organizational changes heightened the group identity of members and resulted in the creation of group norms that decreased within-group variation in individual productivity. In the direct-participation condition, group norms supported high productivity. In the no-participation condition, they enforced low productivity. And in the representation condition, there was an initial fall-off of productivity followed by slow movement toward higher production, suggesting that it took longer for individual workers to understand and/or to accept the new procedures when they personally were not involved.

Each of the three classic studies examined organizational changes that altered the strength of the groups in which individuals worked. Individual behavior was powerfully affected in each case—sometimes for the better, sometimes not. By the end of the chapter, we should have a fairly rich understanding of the dynamics and consequences of such effects.

Dynamics of Group Effects on Individuals

Why do groups have such a pervasive and substantial impact on the behavior and attitudes of individuals in organizations? One way of approaching a general response to this question is to note that groups control many of the stimuli to which individuals are exposed in the course of their organizational activities.[1] *Stimuli* are defined simply as those aspects of the environment to which an individual potentially can attend and that potentially can influence his or her behavior. Thus, stimuli include people, verbal and overt behaviors emitted by people, written materials, objects, aspects of the physical environment, money, and so on.

Two Types of Stimuli. One's group memberships largely define one's "social universe." That is, being a member of some groups (and not being a member of others) restricts and specifies the domain of stimuli to which individuals are exposed. Different groups deal with, and provide access to, different classes of stimuli; therefore, what stimuli are available to

a person depends in part on the groups to which he or she belongs.

Stimuli that potentially are available to all group members (i.e., whose availability is contingent only on group membership per se) are called *ambient* stimuli. Ambient stimuli pervade the group and/or its environment, and group members are normally exposed to them as a regular part of their life in the group. Indeed, members have relatively little choice about encountering the ambient stimuli associated with their group. Among the most important types of ambient stimuli are the other people in the group, materials in the task the group is working on, and aspects of the workplace of the group. Different groups trade in different kinds of coin, and how members behave is affected to some degree by what that coin is.

Other stimuli are transmitted or made available to individuals differentially and selectively at the discretion of the other group members. Such stimuli are called *discretionary* stimuli. Discretionary stimuli can include direct messages of approval or disapproval, physical objects, money, instructions about (or models of) appropriate behavior, and so on. The actual contents of ambient and discretionary stimuli can be the same; the difference is that for discretionary stimuli the group has direct and intentional control over their administration.

Internal group dynamics are critical in understanding when discretionary stimuli will be administered to an individual group member by his or her peers and what the impact of those stimuli will be. The particular discretionary stimuli to which an individual is exposed depends jointly on the attributes of the person (including his or her behavior) and the characteristics of the group (including what stimuli are under the group's discretionary control and the views of group members about which behaviors should be encouraged and which should be discouraged). Obviously, the behavior of individual group members can be shaped significantly by the decisions his or her peers make about what discretionary stimuli to provide and withhold under what circumstances.

Three Types of Group Effects.   The stimuli that individuals encounter in a group can influence (a) their informational states, (b) their affective states, and (c) their behaviors. An individual's *informational state* includes both his or her current beliefs (e.g., about the organization or about one's self) and his or her accumulated knowledge (e.g., about one's job duties). A group can influence a member's informational state through direct instruction and feedback, by providing behavioral models that signal how things are in the group or the organization, and by supplying standards against which individuals can assess their own beliefs and actions.

An individual's *affective state* includes his or her attitudes (e.g., likes and dislikes about the organization), his or her current level of arousal, and his or her personal values (e.g., the kinds of personal and organizational outcomes that are desired). The group can influence the affective state of a member by providing (or withholding) direct social satisfactions, by providing access to valued stimuli external to the group, or by altering the beliefs or behaviors with which one's attitudes are entwined.

An individual's *behavior* can be influenced by stimuli encountered in the group setting in two ways: (a) directly, when the stimuli received by the individual serve to reward or punish certain behaviors, or (b) indirectly, by shaping the member's informational and affective states—that is, by altering what the person thinks or believes, or what he or she likes or feels. See Table 1 for a summary of the types of stimuli and their effects.

Since group-supplied stimuli generally are both immediate and highly salient, they can have strong effects on member attitudes, beliefs, and behaviors. Indeed, it can be argued that the groups to which a person belongs, together with the tasks that he or she performs, provide more stimuli that directly affect actual work behavior than do any other aspects of the organizational environment. This suggests that the group and task environment of an individual may be among the primary proximal causes of variation in individual behavior in organizations. Thus, much of the impact of *organizational level* variables (e.g., organization size, number of hierarchical levels in an organization) may be through their effects on the ways that groups are structured and tasks designed. These effects, in turn, determine the kinds of stimuli to which individuals are exposed on a day-to-day basis—and, ultimately, the direction of individual and organizational behavior. For a more detailed exposition of this point of view, see Porter, Lawler, and Hackman (1975); for a related position, see Rousseau (1978).

**Conceptual Framework
for the Chapter**

The first part of this chapter examines the effects of ambient stimuli on member informational, affective, and behavioral states—that is, the top row in Table 1.

In the second section, we move to the bottom row and assess the effects of group-supplied discretionary stimuli, beginning with a discussion of why groups send discretionary stimuli to their members and why individual members often seek out such stimuli. We then turn to the informational and affective effects of discretionary stimuli and to their behavioral consequences.

The third section examines group norms and their effects on member behavior. One of the most efficient and powerful ways for a group to influence member behavior is by creating and enforcing norms. Norms specify the conditions under which discretionary stimuli are used by the group to reinforce desired behavior and to inhibit behavior that is not desired. Considerable attention is given to how norms operate in groups in organizational settings and to the consequences of member deviance from norms—including the

TABLE 1
_____

The Availability and Impact of Group-supplied Stimuli

	Impact of Stimuli		
	Informational (On member beliefs and knowledge)	Affective (On member attitudes, values, and emotions)	Behavioral (Directly on individual or social behavior)
Ambient (Pervade the group setting)			
Discretionary (Provided at the discretion of other group members)			

Availability of Stimuli

From "Group Influence on Individuals" by J. R. Hackman, 1976. In M. D. Dunnette (Ed.), *Handbook of Industrial and Organizational Psychology* (1st ed., p. 1457). Chicago: Rand McNally. Copyright 1976 by M. D. Dunnette. Reprinted by permission.

circumstances under which deviating individuals influence their groups rather than vice versa.[2]

Impact of Ambient Stimuli

The groups to which an individual belongs identify the social universe of that individual and define his or her position within that universe. One's set of group memberships in an organization define a person's organizational location just as one's spatial position defines his or her location in the physical universe. In both cases, location (i.e., group memberships in the former case, physical location in the latter) determines both the quantity and the substantive character of the stimuli to which one is exposed in the course of his or her day-to-day activities.

The analogy is illustrated by a study of married student housing units at M.I.T. conducted many years ago by Festinger, Schachter, and Back (1950). These authors hypothesized that an important basis of friendship formation was the occurrence of *passive contacts*. These are brief encounters made as one goes about one's normal business—in this case, walking about the neighborhood, going to or from one's apartment, and so on. As predicted, both the physical distance among apartments and the *functional distance* among them (e.g., the degree to which it was necessary to pass someone else's door to, say, empty the garbage—regardless of the actual distance involved) did strongly predict observed friendship patterns among residents.

The M.I.T. study shows how a person's location in physical space determines the stimuli (in this case, social stimuli) that he or she encounters and that such contacts can have long-term consequences. Similar findings have been reported for many other kinds of physical settings (see Paulus & Nagar, 1989, for a review). The same processes that occur in the physical universe also operate vis-à-vis one's location in the social universe. That is, simply being a member of some groups and not others will exclude numerous stimuli from an individual's experience—and literally force other stimuli to one's attention. These are what we are referring to as ambient stimuli, and they vary strikingly from group to group.

Some groups, for example, deal more with physical materials than with ideas and plans. Members of some groups exchange stimuli that have high threat value (such as budget data that bear on the viability of members' organizational units), while members of other groups trade in more innocuous materials. Even the attributes of the other people in a group serve as ambient stimuli. All male versus all female versus mixed gender groups, for example, provide members with very different constellations of ambient stimuli. As pointed out by Levine and Moreland (1990, pp. 595–596), gender composition creates a *context* for member behavior (as opposed to a *direct cause* of behavior) that significantly shapes what transpires in a group.

The ambient stimuli present in a group setting can affect members in a variety of ways. They are, after all, stimuli—and, therefore, they potentially can be linked to any response of which a person is capable. In this chapter, however, attention is restricted to those effects likely to be of significance for understanding behavior in organizations.

In the pages that follow, we will first examine the impact of ambient stimuli on the informational states of group members, focusing on how such stimuli influence (a) members' awareness of the positive and negative outcomes that are available in the organizational environment and (b) members' perceptions of the behaviors that lead to the attainment or avoidance of those outcomes. We will then turn to the effects of ambient stimuli on members' affective states. Here we examine how such stimuli influence (a) the motivational states that propel and direct the behavior of individual group members and (b) the overall affective character of the group experience for the individual. The section ends with a discussion of the ways ambient stimuli contribute to social inertia in groups—and how they sometimes can be used as a point of intervention to change group behavior.

Informational Impact

Clearly, behavior in groups is shaped significantly by the information people have about the group and the environment. It is also true, however, that others in a group have a great deal of direct control over the information that is made available to individual members. Thus, the bulk of our discussion of member informational states is reserved for the section on discretionary stimuli. Here we will focus mainly on the cue value of ambient stimuli— that is, how ambient stimuli signal members about what outcomes are available and how they can be obtained.

Cuing Available Outcomes. Because people spend a great deal of time in groups, they generally become quite skilled in identifying, quickly and accurately, the different kinds of satisfactions that can be obtained in different groups. In just a moment or two of observation, for example, it is possible for most people to detect cues that signal whether or not a given group offers the chance to develop strong friendship ties, whether the group is one in which a misstep could lead to psychological emasculation, whether the group is one in which there is the possibility of sexual "action," and so on. The ambient stimuli that pervade a group are key in making such discriminations. Groups that offer the potential for certain kinds of satisfactions are characterized by similar configurations of ambient stimuli— and group members notice and respond to these similarities.

Cuing Behavior-Outcome Expectancies. That ambient stimuli can cue a member's awareness of the opportunity for certain personal satisfactions is only half the story. Once an opportunity has been identified, the member must then decide how to behave to obtain it. This decision depends on his or her perceptions of "what leads to what" in the group setting. These perceptions also are informed by the ambient stimuli that characterize a group.

Merely knowing, for example, that someone believes that social satisfactions can be obtained in a given group will not, by itself, allow prediction of the person's behavior. If, however, we also know that the individual believes that conforming to the attitudes of other members usually increases social acceptance in groups similar to this one, then behavioral prediction becomes possible. In the present case, it would be reasonable to predict that the person would try to obtain social satisfactions by agreeing with and reinforcing the opinions of other members—rather than, for example, by being assertive and confronting.

Through their histories in various kinds of groups, people learn that certain cues (or configurations of cues) are reliable indicators of behavior-outcome linkages. When these cues are present among the ambient stimuli in a new group, the previously learned contingencies between specific behaviors and their outcomes are reactivated (or made cognitively salient). At this point, the individual can be said to have a *behavior-outcome expectancy* for the present group.[3]

Unless there are discernible and reasonably stable associations between the presence (or absence) of certain ambient stimuli and the existence of particular types of behavior-outcome contingencies, the mechanism just posited will not help individuals behave adaptively in new group settings. Fortunately, the work of Barker and his associates (Barker, 1968; Barker & Wright, 1955), as well as observations from everyday life, suggest that groups with similar configurations of ambient stimuli do tend to have similar behavior-outcome contingencies.

Consider, for example, the ambient stimuli that might characterize a traditional elementary school class: chairs lined up in rows and bolted to the floor, an older person standing behind a desk at the front of the room, a large blackboard, communications routinely passing back and forth between the older person and the young people (but not often among the young people), and so on. These stimuli, by themselves, provide a new member with considerable information about the behavior-outcome contingencies that operate in that group. Based on previous experience in groups characterized by similar ambient stimuli, the new member may (correctly) conclude that sitting quietly but attentively in a chair will result in no unpleasant exchanges with the older person, that loud or frequent interaction with other members while the older person is talking will lead to unpleasantries, and so on.

Actual experience in the group is not necessary to derive these behavior-outcome expectancies; the ambient stimuli present in the setting, coupled with the individual's previous experience, are completely sufficient. Consider one other example. A manager known to the author has a job that requires him to visit and work with a diversity of organizational groups—some of which are characterized by free, open, and confronting exchanges of ideas and feelings, and others by rationality, tact, and suppression of emotional expression. The manager reports that he usually is able to tell from a few minutes of observation (and without speaking himself) which type the group is, simply by noting how group members arrange themselves and address one another. In one group previously unfamiliar to him, for example, the manager noted that the group members situated themselves rather formally around a conference table, that all thoughts were expressed in intellectual and sometimes rather abstract terms, and that very little tentativeness or uncertainty was present in their interactions. On the basis of these observations, the manager concluded that a direct and confronting intervention by him about the direction being taken by the group (especially if said with feeling) would be resisted and negatively valued. When the opportunity for such an intervention arose, the manager made it and confirmed his prediction.

The point of the example is that the manager was able to generate predictions about the nature of the behavior-outcome contingencies in the group strictly on the basis of his observations of the ambient stimuli that characterized it, without actually observing these contingencies in operation in that specific group. In other words, the ambient stimuli cued a set of expectancies for the manager about what interpersonal behaviors would lead to what outcomes in the group.

There are, of course, occasions when ambient stimuli prompt behavior-outcome expectancies that turn out to be partially or wholly incorrect. In such cases, the misinformed individual is likely to be reeducated by other members through the selective application of discretionary stimuli. For example, a person may engage in behavior x based on an expectancy that for groups such as the present one, behavior x leads to desirable outcome y. If other group members actually respond with less-desirable outcome z, the person must begin to revise his or her behavior-outcome expectancies for that group. Indeed, it is through such application of discretionary stimuli that group members

develop and enforce behavioral norms—which we will discuss later.

To summarize, the ambient stimuli present in a group setting serve as cues that signal what behaviors are likely to lead to what outcomes. Ambient stimuli are especially useful for this purpose to nonmembers and to new members who have not yet had the opportunity to test for themselves the properties of the behavior-outcome contingencies that operate in the group.

Affective Impact

Arousing Member Motive States.   The motivation of group members to seek out or avoid certain outcomes can be altered by the ambient stimuli present in the group setting. The mechanisms by which this takes place have been described in detail by McClelland (1951; McClelland, Atkinson, Clark, & Lowell, 1953), Atkinson (1954), and others. In brief, McClelland posits that if an individual previously has experienced substantial pleasure (or pain) in the presence of some particular set of stimuli, that affective state will become conditioned (in the Pavlovian sense) to the stimuli that were present at the time of those experiences. In new situations where those stimuli again are present, the prior affective state is fractionally reactivated—the glow that comes as one imagines taking yet another bow after a performance, for example, can be almost palpable. This reactivated affective state serves as an incentive for the individual to engage in behaviors that he or she expects will lead to the previously rewarding state of affairs (or that will avoid previous costs). McClelland and his associates (see Atkinson, 1958; McClelland et al., 1953) have carried out many studies showing how situational cues arouse and depress need states from their normal levels (but for a skeptical review of some of this work and its conceptual underpinnings, see Klinger, 1966).

When most or all group members have similar previous experiences, their need states can be simultaneously and similarly shaped by ambient stimuli present in a given group setting. The result can be immediate and intense group activity oriented toward achievement of some particular satisfaction. This may happen, for example, at parties, at professional conventions, at singles bars, and at board-of-directors meetings. The content of the ambient stimuli will differ greatly across these settings, as will the motive states likely to be aroused by them. But in each case the ambient stimuli serve simultaneously to heighten the motivation of individuals to achieve a particular class of outcomes and to increase the degree to which motivational orientations are shared among members. The result can be a mutually reinforcing pattern of group behavior oriented toward attainment of those outcomes.

Providing Direct Personal Satisfactions. So far, we have seen how the ambient stimuli in a group setting can cue members about satisfactions that are available there and how they can enhance or depress members' motivation to achieve those satisfactions. Ambient stimuli also can be *directly* satisfying (or frustrating). An advertising copywriter who happens to be an airplane buff, for example, probably will experience membership on the agency's airline account team as more satisfying than membership on the aspirin team—simply because of the content of the team's work.

The affective value of the ambient stimuli a person encounters is, of course, a joint function of the stimuli themselves and of the individual's personal needs. Only a masochist, perhaps, would be repelled by a group in which members traded exclusively in love, status, and goodwill. The majority of the stimuli encountered in real-life groups, however, are open to a variety of affective interpretations by different individuals.

Thus, an individual's attraction to a given group depends in part on the fit between that person's needs and the ambient stimuli present in the group setting. This does not deny that the interpersonal dynamics that develop in a group usually are more potent for members than are ambient stimuli. The point is that, other things being equal, ambient stimuli contribute nontrivially to the motivation of individual members to gain and maintain group membership.

When, for example, a status-conscious person perceives the members of a certain group to be highly prestigious, he or she may be highly motivated toward membership merely because of the association with prestigious people. Whether or not interaction with these people actually turns out to be rewarding to the individual (or whether such interaction even takes place) can be irrelevant: Witness the "hangers-on" who surround celebrities despite the fact that they are totally ignored by them. Similarly, when the stimuli associated with the task of the group are positively valued by an individual, that person's motivation to maintain group membership may be high—again, quite independently of whether or not other personal rewards are anticipated from group membership (Back, 1951; Thibaut, 1950).

When most or all of the members of some group find that the ambient stimuli associated with the group are rewarding, group development is facilitated. The reason is that group members share a perception of the group as a site where valued stimulation is received, and, therefore, they have a shared stake in maintaining its existence and viability. This state of affairs may be especially characteristic of voluntary groups formed on the basis of shared special interests (e.g., the Oakwood Art Appreciation Club). In such groups, the stimuli encountered in the group setting (in this case, works of fine art) are both the basis for individual membership and the "glue" that holds the group together. Reliance on shared positive valuation of ambient stimuli for maintaining individual commitment to a group, however, is fraught with danger over the long term. When and if members become less attracted to the ambient stimuli that originally engaged and sustained their interest, they are likely to drift away and the group may eventually dissolve—unless members generate in their interaction new bases for member commitment.

Finally, it should be noted that the ambient stimuli an individual encounters as a group member may be experienced as negative rather than as positive. If an individual experiences these stimuli as generally noxious or unpleasant, he or she would be unlikely to develop a high level of attraction to the group—and, indeed, may elect to withdraw from it unless there are other compensating advantages of group membership.

Recall, for example, the study of married student housing described earlier. Friendships among people who lived close to one another undoubtedly would not have developed if those individuals had experienced one another as highly unpleasant. Indeed, Festinger (1953) describes a different housing project in which passive contact among residents (which occurred because of physical proximity) failed to lead to the development of friendships among them. Many residents of this project had been forced to move there against their wishes because of an acute housing shortage. Because the project was government sponsored, many residents assumed that their neighbors were low-class people with whom it was undesirable to associate. As a consequence (and without checking out their assumptions), a large proportion of the residents did not use the passive contacts they had with their neighbors as occasions for initiating interaction and thereby developing friendships.

The impact of ambient stimuli on individual affective states can spread to the group as a whole and alter its overall affective tone. An example of this process is provided by George (1990). She found that when the personal disposition of most group members is to express positive (or negative) affect, the affective tone of the group as a whole becomes positive (or negative) as well. To explain this phenomenon, George uses Schneider's (1987) attraction-selection-attrition framework, which posits that a given work environment tends to attract, select, and retain people who have similar personal characteristics. When the group setting attracts and retains people who generally are happy, then all group members will be faced with a collection of smiling faces much of the time; when the group attracts gloomy people, frowning faces will predominate. These ambient stimuli, it appears, are sufficient to shape the affectivity of the group as a whole.

Behavioral Impact

Ambient stimuli can either impede or facilitate behavioral change in groups. First, we will see how ambient stimuli contribute to the social inertia that characterizes many intact groups in organizations. Then we will reverse perspective and explore how ambient stimuli can be used as the basis for group-focused organizational interventions.

Ambient Stimuli and Social Inertia. Ambient stimuli help maintain stability in organizational groups—but also tend to inhibit change, even when change may be needed. There are at least three reasons why this is so.

Ambient stimuli rarely are noticed and discussed. By their nature, ambient stimuli are part of the background of group functioning. For this reason, group members usually are unaware of their continuing impact—just as fish in water, if fish could think, would be unaware of the powerful effects of *their* environment. Ambient stimuli are just there, they are always there, and few people realize how powerfully they may be shaping what is going on. It is not a coincidence that Edward Hall (1969) titled his book on the behavioral impact of physical space "The *Hidden* Dimension."

Moreover, the operation of ambient stimuli is largely covert. While discretionary stimuli are administered and reacted to overtly and visibly in the interaction process of a group, ambient stimuli realize their effects by influencing members' private and implicit assumptions about what behaviors are appropriate or desirable. For this reason, their impact on group behavior usually cannot be discerned either by members or by outside observers.[4] Unless the private effects of ambient stimuli are brought to the attention of group members, the behavioral patterns they sustain are likely to persist indefinitely—even if those behaviors are dysfunctional.

The diversity of ambient stimuli impinging on a group becomes narrowed and restricted over time. As a group gains stability and develops a history, members tend to block certain classes of stimuli from collective attention and to focus on certain others. It is not unusual, for example, for a group to find a place and time to meet where "distractions" (i.e., ambient stimuli that members view as irrelevant to the purpose of the meeting) are minimized.

Further, groups often develop norms that decrease the likelihood that members will encounter certain kinds of stimuli. A managerial group, for example, might develop a norm specifying that, say, topics having to do with the pay or promotional status of individual members are not to be mentioned in the group, or emotional exchanges are out of bounds, or the group will focus on issues having to do with day-to-day organizational functioning rather than with long-range planning or with organizational values, and so on. Indeed, Goffman (1963, chap. 11) has described a very pervasive group norm that requires members to ignore extraneous stimuli present in the environment and to act as if they are fully engrossed in the main task of the group—even if they actually are not.

In many cases, such norms develop very gradually, and group members may not even be aware of the restriction or narrowing of focus that has taken place. When this happens,

the group will become a more predictable place and members may come to share a pleasant sense of being comfortable together. But the universe of stimuli to which members are exposed also will be sharply restricted, and stimuli in the environment that are unusual or potentially unsettling may never be explicitly examined. In some cases, this can have unintended and unfortunate implications for the effectiveness of the group (see Gersick & Hackman, 1990, and Janis, 1982).

This discussion is not meant to imply that groups should uncritically welcome all ambient stimuli that impinge from the external environment. Some such stimuli really can be distracting, disruptive, and dysfunctional. What is needed instead is for members to develop and maintain a monitoring stance vis-à-vis the ambient stimuli that pervade the group setting. When members are aware of these stimuli and their possible effects on the group, then they have a basis for making deliberate choices about which of them should be taken seriously and which safely can be ignored.

Group members tend not to test publicly the private inferences they generate from ambient stimuli. It is tempting to suggest that the assumptions and expectancies that derive from ambient stimuli in group settings will have little impact on behavior in well-established groups, since the validity of these assumptions can be checked directly in the group itself. In fact, group members rarely test explicitly the behavioral norms and implicit strategies that guide their behavior (Argyris, 1969; Shure, Rogers, Larsen, & Tassone, 1962; Weick, 1969, pp. 11–12). Therefore, unless a member has direct personal experience that contradicts his or her prior assumptions about what behaviors are appropriate, revision of those assumptions is unlikely.

Such direct confirmation (and disconfirmation) is much more likely to occur for behaviors a group member expects to lead to positive outcomes than for those expected to generate negative outcomes. Few people would test their perception that a pot of water is scalding hot by dipping a hand into it, and the same logic applies to group behaviors that are viewed a priori as likely to generate negative consequences. Thus, it is possible for a behavior that actually would be functional for a group never to be exhibited because each individual group member fears, privately and falsely, that the behavior will lead to negative outcomes. In such cases, the expectancies initially prompted by ambient stimuli in the group setting may never be tested explicitly and may continue to guide the behavior of group members indefinitely.

The general tendency of group members to avoid discussing certain group process issues is a good case in point. In task-oriented organizational groups, process observations often are considered bad form and are negatively valued. As a result, many individuals have developed an expectancy that making such comments will lead to unpleasant or anxiety-arousing consequences. Hackman and Morris (1975) found, for example, that of 100 laboratory groups (each composed of three persons working on a 15-minute task), only 142 comments were made about the performance strategy being used by the group—fewer than two comments per group. Further, the few comments about group strategy that were made almost never reflected a deliberate and planned attack by the group on major strategic issues. Instead, they tended to occur immediately after one member had behaved in a way that violated the implicit norms that had been guiding group behavior. In many groups, this "deviant" act appeared to unfreeze other group members from their previous unwillingness to discuss issues of strategy. Indeed, the process discussions that subsequently occurred in these groups turned out to facilitate group performance: The judged creativity of group products was found to be positively and significantly related to the number of comments about performance strategy that members made.

In summary, the ambient stimuli present in a group setting often prompt fairly strong inferences by group members about the behaviors that are appropriate and inappropriate in that group. The failure of most groups to discuss such inferences explicitly can perpetuate shared and incorrect assumptions about the actual usefulness of various behaviors and inhibit behavioral change.

Ambient Stimuli and Behavioral Change. Ambient stimuli can serve as a point of intervention for helping groups overcome the very inertia that, unmanaged, they can sustain. Two types of intervention merit comment: educating members about the impact of ambient stimuli, and designing situations so that the ambient stimuli present are as consistent as possible with group purposes.

Educating Group Members. At least in the short term, it is difficult for an individual to alter his or her learned responses to situational cues, especially if those responses have been learned over an extensive history of group memberships. Nor can an individual readily stop experiencing certain events as rewarding and others as punishing. It often is possible, however, for a group to change some of the ambient stimuli in the setting and thereby to provide all members with a different set of cues. If members' learned responses to these new stimuli are different from their responses to the old ones, then behavioral change should result.

Even though it may be relatively easy for group members to alter the ambient stimuli they encounter (e.g., by meeting in a different place at a different time), an educational or consultative intervention may be needed to get change under way. An educational program might, for example, help members explore the perceptions, implicit assumptions, and motives that may be affecting group dynamics. Members could be encouraged to examine the ambient stimuli that may have prompted or sustained these motivational and cognitive orientations. And, finally, they could be helped to discuss these new understandings in a way that facilitates shared awareness of the hidden determinants of group behavior.

Existing evidence (as well as a good deal of folklore) suggests that such educational programs might be particularly helpful to groups in adapting to a changing external environment. The work of Steele (1969, 1973) on the physical surroundings of a group is a good case in point. Steele uses the term *pseudo-fixed feature space* to designate physical features that are readily changeable or movable but that are perceived and treated as if they were fixed.[5] He notes that most people take their physical surroundings as immutable givens, even when those surroundings may be easily changeable, and even when their arrangement is inimical to group purposes. Once group members come to perceive the physical environment as under their control—and therefore as changeable—they often are able to devise new arrangements that better facilitate the attainment of group goals.

Task and Situational Design.   Just as members of a group may themselves attempt to change the ambient stimuli that impinge upon them, so also can an external agent attempt to engineer these stimuli to affect group behavior in specified ways. There are three primary sources of ambient stimulation that are potentially manipulable in this regard: (a) the people who compose the group, (b) the situation or environment in which the group functions, and (c) the task of the group.

Although it is true that the stimulus characteristics of the individuals who compose a group are part of the universe of ambient stimuli to which members are exposed, it is doubtful that changes in those characteristics per se would generate much behavioral change in groups. The reason, as suggested by research on group composition (e.g., see the early review by Haythorn, 1968), is that the overt behavior of group members— which is highly variable and discretionary—is enormously more potent in affecting what happens in groups than are members' static

characteristics. The present discussion, therefore, is limited to task- and stimulus-based ambient stimuli.

It often is possible to manipulate the stimulus characteristics of a task or situation to highlight the availability of certain rewards (or punishments) and to make particularly salient the behaviors that generate these outcomes. The literature on work design, for example, explicitly specifies how jobs can be structured so that certain types of rewards (specifically, intrinsic satisfactions) become salient and the paths to obtaining these rewards (specifically, effective work toward organizational goals) are made clear (Hackman & Lawler, 1971; Hackman & Oldham, 1980). These ideas have been applied specifically to the design of work for groups by Cummings (1981), Hackman (1987), and others.

The group task also determines the substantive content of group activities—that is, the nature of the materials worked with and the kinds of stimuli exchanged among group members. As has been shown by studies of task effects on group behavior (Hackman & Morris, 1975; Kent & McGrath, 1969), task content affects both the motivation of individual group members (e.g., how much they want to remain in the group and participate in its activities) and the pattern of interaction that takes place among them (e.g., see the work of Foa, 1971, on the exchange of resources). Because the group task affects behavior on a number of fronts simultaneously, anyone wishing to influence group behavior would be well advised to give careful attention to the design of the work that the group performs.

The potency of the physical environment in which a group performs has been documented in detail by Sundstrom and Altman (1989). It has been known for some time that both group development and interpersonal interaction are significantly shaped by environmental constraints and cues. Sundstrom and Altman go further: They suggest (pp. 196–204) that there is a dialectic of opposing forces in organizational groups, one promoting interaction among members, the other fostering differentiation among them. Different types of groups, they suggest, require a different point of balance on this dialectic, and they show how the configuration of a group's physical space can help achieve an appropriate balance for four different types of work groups.

Summary.   Research suggests that the following three classes of ambient stimuli may have special leverage in interventions aimed at changing behavior in groups:

- Environmental features and work contents that typically are taken as given by group members and whose impact derives in part from the fact that they *are* unnoticed or unacknowledged

- Stimuli that themselves are rewarding or punishing and that therefore affect the attractiveness of the group

- Stimuli in the task or the physical environment that serve as cues, signaling group members about (a) rewards or punishments that potentially are available in the group setting and (b) the conditions under which these outcomes become available

These three statements are, obviously, very general. Unfortunately, present knowledge about the dynamics of ambient influences on group behavior does not permit much more than general statements. Little is known, for example, about the specific characteristics of tasks and situations that have the greatest cue value for group members, and findings are only beginning to become available about the impact of the content of group activities on group processes (Hackman, 1990, pp. 479–493). Further, virtually no data are available to suggest which ambient stimuli are likely to be perceived (and responded to) in similar ways by large numbers of individuals in a given culture, and which are more susceptible to idiosyncratic interpretation by individuals

based on their particular prior experiences in groups and on their personal needs and values.

Before it becomes possible to use ambient stimuli to effect changes in group behavior, much more needs to be known about the operating characteristics of those stimuli. It is relatively easy to identify the potential sources of ambient stimuli in group settings. It is much harder to predict their impact on the motivation and cognitive orientations of individual group members—and, more importantly, to specify how these effects are assembled into group level phenomena.

Conclusion

Although we have focused exclusively on ambient stimuli in the preceding pages, the mechanisms discussed also apply to discretionary stimuli. When, for example, an individual is presented with a discretionary stimulus, such as a friendly smile from another group member, that stimulus can affect his or her motive states and/or cognitive expectancies through exactly the same mechanisms that operate for ambient stimuli. Discretionary stimuli, of course, have many additional effects on individual and social behavior in groups, as will be seen in the next section. But it should be kept in mind throughout that discretionary stimuli can and do affect behavior in groups through the same mechanisms as do ambient stimuli.

Sometimes it is difficult to distinguish the effects of ambient stimuli from those of discretionary stimuli. Consider, for example, a case in which an organization member is promoted from an employee work group to membership in a supervisory group. This change of groups is likely to result in a simultaneous change of both the ambient and the discretionary stimuli that the person encounters in his or her work activities. If the person's attitudes, beliefs, and behaviors are found to be more promanagement after the promotion, which set of stimuli should be viewed as having caused the change?

Organizational psychologists typically have relied almost exclusively on discretionary stimuli to explain such phenomena. In the example just given, it probably would be suggested that the employee ceased to be reinforced for antimanagement statements and behavior (as may have been the case before the promotion), and now is rewarded by his or her new peers for engaging in promanagement activities. While such an explanation obviously should not be overlooked, it may be that the ambient stimuli that pervade the new group setting also are significant determinants of the observed changes.

Many pages have been written on ambient stimuli and their effects on group behavior. The reason is that these pervasive and often unnoticed stimuli generally have taken a backseat to concepts such as norm development and conformity—more glamorous concepts, perhaps, but surely not deserving of all the attention of organizational social psychologists. Ambient stimuli also can be powerful determinants of what happens in groups and, at the same time, are generally easy to manipulate and change, whether by an external agent or by group members themselves. Additional research on ambient stimuli and their effects surely will generate findings that are both conceptually interesting and useful in practice.

Impact of Discretionary Stimuli

So far, we have focused on the impact of ambient stimuli—that is, those stimuli that pervade the group setting and are encountered by all group members. We now turn to discretionary stimuli. They also can provide group members with information, or they can have affective consequences, or both. The difference is that discretionary stimuli are under the direct control of the group and are administered to individual members on a contingent basis, depending on the member's behavior or the opinions he or she expresses.

Exchange of Discretionary Stimuli in Groups

We begin by examining the reasons groups send discretionary stimuli to their members and the reasons individuals in groups seek such stimuli from their peers. We then turn to the effects of discretionary stimuli on member informational states and on member affective states. Direct group influences on member behavior are taken up in the next major section.

Why Groups Initiate Discretionary Stimuli

To Educate and Socialize.   Influencing member attitudes, beliefs, or behaviors is the main purpose of some groups—for example, religious study groups, political education groups, physical fitness clubs, and so on. In such cases, the group serves explicitly as a socializing agent for its members. Sometimes this is at the request of the member ("Educate me") and sometimes it is not ("I'll put up with all this religious talk because it's part of being a member of the Church Youth Fellowship, but that's not the main reason I'm here"). In either case, groups that are oriented primarily toward the education or socialization of their members rely heavily on discretionary stimuli to bring about the desired changes. Such stimuli typically are dispensed quite selectively, contingent upon the progress of each group member, and may provide the members with information, with rewards for "correct" ideas or behavior, or with punishment for being "incorrect."

To Produce Uniformity.   Even when member socialization is not a major group purpose, there still are numerous occasions when groups take the initiative in meting out discretionary stimuli to their members. Group members often believe, for example, that a high level of uniformity among them is needed to attain group goals and use their control of discretionary stimuli to achieve such uniformity. In many cases, it indeed is helpful if a work group has uniform procedures for dealing with frequently encountered tasks. Uniformity allows members' reliably to predict the behavior of their peers and thereby to achieve a reasonable level of coordination and efficiency. Similarly, it may be useful for group members to hold similar beliefs about the external environment, especially if the group must respond as a unit to that environment. Finally, it is critical to the performance of groups such as musical ensembles and athletic teams that all members have a high level of knowledge and skill. In all these cases, discretionary stimuli can be used to achieve the desired uniformity.

Groups also seek uniformity for purely maintenance reasons—that is, to keep the group intact and functioning smoothly, regardless of the consequences for task performance (Cartwright & Zander, 1968, p. 142). The very survival of a group can be threatened by too much individualistic or idiosyncratic behavior on the part of a few members. Unresolved disputes among members about what the group should be doing also can threaten the viability of the group as a social system. These dangers no doubt contribute to members' collective uneasiness when they perceive that their group has great diversity of thought, feeling, or behavior. The response, in many cases, is an insistence on achieving consensus among all members for any matter of consequence—falling back on "majority rule" only as a second-best way of proceeding. (See Davis, 1973, and Stasser & Davis, 1981, for a discussion of the antecedents and consequences of various decision rules used by groups.)

Despite the many benefits of uniformity, and despite the substantial investment of time and energy by group members to achieve it, it is possible to have too much of it. In his discussion of the ill-fated Bay of Pigs invasion undertaken by President John Kennedy and his advisors in 1961, Janis (1982) provides a striking example of how group-initiated pressures toward uniformity can backfire. Janis quotes Arthur Schlesinger explaining why he had not pressed more urgently his objections to the plan:

> In the months after the Bay of Pigs I bitterly reproached myself for having kept so silent during those crucial discussions in the Cabinet Room, though my feelings of guilt were tempered by the knowledge that a course of objection would have accomplished little save to *gain me a name as a nuisance.* I can only explain my failure to do more than raise a few timid questions by reporting that one's impulse to blow the whistle on this nonsense was simply undone by the circumstances of the discussion. (Schlesinger, 1965, p. 255; emphasis added)

Had there been less pressure toward uniformity in the Kennedy group, Janis argues, the strong reservations about the invasion plan held by Schlesinger and others might have been seriously considered and the disaster averted.

Although the task effectiveness of the Kennedy group in the Bay of Pigs case clearly was low, the pressures toward uniformity that pervaded the group may well have served a useful maintenance function for the group—protecting members from having to deal with potentially disruptive or anxiety-arousing interpersonal conflicts. This is not an uncommon pattern: Pressures for uniformity are functional for maintaining the group but at the expense of its task effectiveness. The pressures toward uniformity of production in work groups are a case in point (Roethlisberger & Dickson, 1939; Roy, 1952; W. F. Whyte, 1955). By establishing and enforcing a norm of uniform production among members, a work group may achieve a heightened feeling of togetherness and simultaneously avoid dealing with a number of thorny interpersonal problems that might arise if each group member were allowed to work to the full extent of his or her capability (Mathewson, 1931).

To Produce Diversity. Apparently contrasting to the pressures toward uniformity discussed above is the tendency for groups to use discretionary stimuli to create and maintain diversity among members. This tendency is seen vividly in the role differentiation process that occurs in virtually all groups.[6] Shortly after a group has formed, members begin to differentiate between those who will have leadership responsibility and those who will be followers, and between those who will specialize in task activities and those who will perform maintenance functions (Bales & Slater, 1955; Gibb, 1969, especially pp. 268–271; Slater, 1955; Thibaut & Kelley, 1959, chap. 15).[7] As group members gain experience working together, additional differentiation takes place and a highly elaborated division of labor may emerge, complete with subleaders responsible for different classes of task activity (Biddle & Thomas, 1966, pt. 7; Guetzkow, 1960). Group maintenance functions often become highly differentiated as well. For example, one member (often the group wit) may be expected to reduce the level of interpersonal tension when it gets dangerously high, another may be responsible for providing encouragement and support when the work slows down, a third may provide social reinforcement to members who work especially hard, and so on.

Not all groups need to develop their own role structure. Many groups in organizations have formal roles preassigned, thereby cutting short the process of role differentiation. In a work group with an assigned supervisor or foreman, for example, the leadership role is both defined and occupied a priori. But when someone declines to fulfill his or her role in accord with members' expectations, serious disruption of the group process invariably occurs—and the members' interest in maintaining a differentiated role structure again becomes visible.

For example, Mills (1967, chap. 6) describes members' distress when the assigned leader of a seminar on executive management for military officers chose not to perform the executive functions expected of him and instead asked members to organize their own learning experiences. Similar distress may be experienced initially by the subordinates of a manager who returns home from an off-site management seminar with a new and unexpected way of enacting his or her formal leadership role (Argyris, 1962, chap. 10). Difficulties also are experienced by group members when they and their formal leader agree on the definition of the leader's role, but group members feel that the leader is not performing the role in a satisfactory manner. In such cases, an informal or "shadow" organization may be formed within the group, one that has its own set of differentiated roles and that may either complement the formal role structure or compete with it (Roethlisberger & Dickson, 1939).

In summary, group members create differences among themselves and then regularize and stabilize those differences over time. This phenomenon is so robust that some theorists have argued that all systems exhibit a basic tendency toward disorder and disorganization, a tendency that must somehow be controlled if a system is to survive (Allport, 1955, p. 475). Thus, both uniformity and structured diversity may be essential to maintain the viability of a group as a social system. In this context, the striving of a group for diversity among members parallels its pressures toward uniformity: Both processes, although superficially contradictory, reflect a tendency toward organization, order, and predictability. By judiciously controlling the discretionary stimuli at its command, a group can move simultaneously toward uniformity and toward diversity—for example, by inculcating a common set of work values across all members at the same time as generating a task-appropriate division of labor among them, or by creating a common set of beliefs about the external environment while spawning a number of different functional leadership roles.

Why Individuals Seek Out Discretionary Stimuli. When groups dispense discretionary stimuli to individual members, those members must react in one way or another. But individuals also can take the initiative and actively seek out discretionary stimuli from their peers. Members are proactive as well as reactive: They often know what they want, seek it out in their physical and social environments, and learn by observation and experimentation the best way to get it.

To Obtain Information. Groups are heavily used by individuals as sources of data about reality—especially when the relevant data are not available (or are costly to obtain) in the material world (Festinger, 1950). Although an individual is unlikely to turn to a group to learn which switches control which lights in the group meeting room (he or she can quickly determine that by trial and error), the person may well seek out other members to confirm his or her views about matters that ca-not reliably be determined autonomously, such as the trustworthiness of the group's manager.

Individuals use groups not only for information about external reality but also for data about themselves. Socially obtained information is central to many theories of how the self-concept is developed and maintained. Cooley's (1922) use of the term *looking glass self,* for example, highlights the importance of self-knowledge gained from the actions and reactions of others. And the original use of the term *reference group* had explicitly to do with individuals seeking data from others for use in developing a more complete self-understanding (Berkowitz, 1969). Other research (some of which is reviewed in more detail later) has shown how individuals seek data from others to determine their own level of ability and the validity of their opinions (e.g., Festinger, 1954), to test the appropriateness of their degree of satisfaction with the rewards and costs they

are experiencing (e.g., Merton & Kitt, 1950; Patchen, 1961), and even to label appropriately the emotions they are experiencing (e.g., Schachter, 1964).

Group-controlled information, be it about external reality, about the self, or about specific behaviors and skills, can be sought by the individual for either intrinsic or instrumental reasons. A group member can derive intrinsic satisfaction simply from learning about or coming to know the proximal world. Festinger, for example, posited a drive for people to know about the accuracy of their beliefs and opinions about the world in his theory of social communication (1950), and an analogous drive to know about oneself in his theory of social comparison (1954). R. W. White's (1959) notion of *effectance motivation* also points to the importance of information from one's peers. White suggests that individuals are driven to master their environment—that is, to find out how the environment can be manipulated and what the consequences of such manipulations are. Thus, individuals would be expected for intrinsic reasons alone to seek from other group members information about how they might manipulate the environment and skillfully accomplish their work.

Often there also are instrumental reasons to seek information from one's group. If a person wishes to obtain rewards that exist in the organizational environment, he or she must understand both that environment (specifically, the behavior-outcome contingencies that operate there) and himself or herself (specifically, his or her own ability to execute the behaviors that generate the desired outcomes). The degree to which individuals can obtain such information on their own is limited by their time and place perspectives. Heavy reliance on other group members for assistance in learning about the organizational world is therefore the rule rather than the exception.

To Obtain Group-controlled Rewards. Groups control stimuli that can directly satisfy or frustrate their members. Some such stimuli affect members' psychological well-being—for example, those that enhance (or depress) a member's self-esteem, those that help a member adapt to environmental stress (or that exacerbate experienced stress), and so on. Other stimuli have more to do with physical or material well-being—for example, those that affect safety, comfort, or affluence.

Although many such stimuli are "owned" by the group and therefore can be administered directly, others are located in the environment and are mediated by the group. A group might recommend one of its members for a company's exceptional performance award, for example. Or a work team might be asked to choose the member who will represent the team at a conference on new work techniques, thereby rewarding that individual by giving him or her the opportunity to get some rest and maybe even learn something.

Whether such stimuli are controlled directly or are mediated by the group, individuals who aspire to them must behave in ways that convince their colleagues that they are deserving. As will be seen, groups can use this dependency to exert considerable influence on the beliefs, expressed attitudes, and overt behaviors of their members.

Conclusion and a Caveat to the Reader. Group-individual relationships in organizations typically are discussed in the research literature as a process in which the individual conforms in some degree to group expectations in exchange for social acceptance from his or her peers. In this view, the individual's dilemma is how to maintain his or her autonomy and still obtain sufficient social acceptance.

Group-individual relationships in organizations actually are considerably more complex than that. Groups send discretionary stimuli to their members for many different reasons and have a diversity of resources (not just social acceptance) to offer. Similarly, members use their group memberships to serve a variety of personal needs and are affected by group-supplied discretionary stimuli in many different ways—some of which have nothing at all to do with behavioral conformity.

As we examine the dynamics of these effects, I will talk of things that groups "do" vis-à-vis their members, for example, "the group sanctions a member for exceeding the production quota." Such actions do not mean that groups act as intact units, consciously planning and executing behaviors just as individuals do. To take such a position would be to reify the group in a way that is not congruent with how groups actually operate. Instead, I talk about "group behavior" vis-à-vis an individual member merely as a shorthand way of referring to the behavior of other people with whom that member has meaningful and continuing contact. I could just as well refer to his or her *peers* or *role set* in this regard; the term *group* is used because it is convenient, and because much of the research literature having to do with the effects of peers or role partners on organization members is conceptualized and discussed using group terminology. Or, as put by Moore (1969):

> Groups act through individuals, but it is equally true that individuals act *on behalf of groups,* or in conformity with other socially sanctioned expectations.... Neglect of the first part of the preceding statement can lead to a kind of social anthropomorphism, or the "group mind fallacy."... But neglect of the second part of the statement can lead to a kind of atomistic view of human behavior that is equally fallacious. One position is as inane as the other. (p. 289, emphasis in original)

Effects of Discretionary Stimuli on Member Informational States

This section examines the effects of group-supplied discretionary stimuli on (a) the beliefs members hold about the group and the environment, (b) the beliefs members hold about themselves, and (c) members' work-related knowledge and skills.

Shaping Beliefs About the Group and the Environment. Relying only on their own senses and experiences, organizational members can obtain neither complete nor entirely accurate views of their environment. Therefore, individuals frequently turn to others in their work groups to learn "how things are" in the group and the organization. This gives groups a ready-made opportunity to affect members' beliefs.

Few groups pass up that opportunity because it is in the best interest of the group as a whole for all members to have the same general perceptions of and beliefs about the group and the environment. When there is turbulence in the environment, members value especially strongly the social reassurance that shared beliefs can provide. They also find internal disagreement more anxiety-arousing than usual, and therefore they are strongly motivated to make sure all members see things the same way. This phenomenon is evident in a troubled organization studied by Burns (1955), where two different groups perpetuated two very different sets of belief about organizational reality. One group, composed of older workers, spent a great deal of time reminding each other just how awful things were in the firm. Various organizational features (such as the bonus system, formal communication procedures, and so on) invariably were discussed in deprecating terms. A second group, whose members were younger, had a quite different assessment of reality. While they did not endorse the organizational features deprecated by their older colleagues, they did more frequently view them

as challenges—aspects of the system to be improved upon or to be overcome. In both groups, members actively and continuously provided information about the organization to their peers that served to preserve the protective social reality of their respective groups.

Another time when groups vigorously use discretionary stimuli to shape member beliefs is when new members arrive. Because the perceptions and beliefs of new members are almost certain to differ from those shared by veterans, the newcomers represent a threat to the status quo. Groups often seek to minimize this threat by bringing new members' perceptions and beliefs into line as quickly as possible—even though doing so also minimizes the possibility that the group will learn something from the newcomers' fresh perspectives (Janis, 1982; Maier & Solem, 1952; Moreland & Levine, 1989).

The process groups use to influence the perceptions of new members can be subtle, as is illustrated by a conversation I observed between two longtime members of a work group. The topic of the conversation was the frustrations the veterans recently had experienced at the hands of management. The exchange ran its course without either participant appearing to notice that a new employee was standing nearby and listening to every word. Questioned later, one of the veterans admitted that the entire conversation had been staged, and that its main purpose was to teach the newcomer that it was useless to suggest any changes in how things were done, because management never pays any attention. This interaction surely had a substantial effect on the beliefs of the new member, both because he had so little personal experience in the organization (and therefore was dependent on others for information about it) and because "overhearing" the conversation made what was said more credible than otherwise would have been the case.

Observation as a Source of Beliefs. So far, we have focused on stimuli that are communicated directly from the group to its members. Some-times it works the other way around: Individuals (especially new members) actively seek from their peers information about the group, about the organization, and about the environment (Comer, in press). Since in some circles it is not considered good form to ask explicitly about important matters such as rewards, costs, and behavior-outcome contingencies, members may obtain this information more subtly—namely, by observing their peers in action, noting the consequences, and then making private inferences about how the world works.

The group has some control over such inferences (recall, for example, the conversation that was staged to get a message across to a newcomer). By and large, however, it is much more difficult for group members to fake their actual behavior than it is to communicate verbally a slightly distorted view of reality. This is true especially for information about consequential matters such as rewards and costs, because members who attempt overtly to mislead an observer put their own outcomes at risk.

There also are traps for learners who rely too much on personal observation to make sense of the environment. What works for some group members (such as high-status veterans), for example, may backfire when tried by a new or low-status individual. Because it is risky to base one's behavior mainly on beliefs about reality gleaned from observations of others, most people draw simultaneously on several sources of information to enrich their understanding of the environment. When a person discovers consistency across both data sources and time, he or she should be able to make attributions about reality with considerable confidence (Campbell, 1961; Heider, 1958) and then proceed to base his or her behavior on those attributions with relative safety.

Beliefs and the Behavior of Group Members.
Groups clearly cannot and do not attempt to provide members with information about all

aspects of organizational reality. Beliefs that are mostly irrelevant to actual behavior (and, therefore, that are not likely to disrupt the group), for example, generally are overlooked. Surely a group would not bother to work on new members' beliefs about matters such as the number of employees in the organization, the color of the office walls, and so on. Instead, communication is likely to focus on the following two topics (see the earlier discussion of the informational impact of ambient stimuli):

- What rewards and costs are present in the environment, and who controls them?

- What behaviors by group members can secure the rewards while avoiding the costs?

Both of these aspects of reality are directly relevant to the behavior and outcomes of individual group members. Therefore, they are important both to individuals (because people generally like to maximize their gains and minimize their costs) and to the group (because if individuals go off half-cocked on the basis of faulty information they may spoil things for everybody). Thus, one should observe a great deal of information sharing about the characteristics of the group's manager, since the boss is both a direct source of rewards and costs and someone who controls the contingencies that link behaviors and outcomes. Similarly, pay and promotion systems, the characteristics of the work that members perform, and the work group itself all are topics about which groups are likely to influence the beliefs of their members.

When group members continually reinforce their common views on some matter, as was the case for the group of older workers described by Burns, the resulting belief structures can become quite resistant to change—even if those structures cease to reflect objective reality accurately. It is not uncommon, for example, for members of a work group to persist in believing that management will lower the rate if members produce over the standard in a piecework incentive system (e.g., at the Bank Wiring Room in the Hawthorne studies). Neither assurances from management nor objective guarantees to the contrary are likely to dent the beliefs of individuals in such groups as long as members continue to reinforce their shared views about how the system works. Many management-initiated change programs have foundered on precisely this obstacle.

Untangling Normative and Informational Influences on Beliefs. Although there is an enormous research literature on belief and opinion conformity, most of this work has been conducted in the experimental laboratory and has focused on subjects' beliefs or judgments about physical materials or factual information. There have been relatively few studies of the ways groups in organizations shape the beliefs of their members about rewards, costs, and behavior-outcome contingencies—the beliefs that most directly affect organizational behavior. For this reason, applications of findings from the experimental literature on conformity must be made with caution. The jump from a laboratory study in which group members estimate the magnitude of weights to a natural setting in which they must figure out the likely consequences of contemplated actions is a large jump indeed.

The experimental literature is of considerable help, nonetheless, in differentiating between two major types of social influence: informational versus normative influence. *Informational influence* results in revision of one's private belief states. *Normative influence,* on the other hand, results in changes in what one *says* his or her beliefs are—but not necessarily in what is privately believed. Or, as defined by Deutsch and Gerard (1955), informational social influence is "an influence to accept information obtained from another as *evidence* about reality," whereas normative social influence is "an influence to conform with the positive

expectations of another" (p. 629, emphasis in original; see also Kaplan, 1987, and Kelley, 1952).

The distinction is an important one, because it bears directly on the pervasiveness and permanence of group influences on individuals. If a member is merely acting as if he or she holds a set of beliefs because of normative expectations, his or her behavior may be consistent with those beliefs only when the group is salient. Further, the person may have difficulty adjusting to the group in the long run because of the conflict between the way he or she must act and his or her real beliefs. If, on the other hand, a group does succeed in altering a person's private beliefs, its impact will be both pervasive and enduring (Allen, 1965, pp. 136–144; Kiesler, 1969, chap. 11).

It is difficult to distinguish between the two influence processes, in part because messages exchanged in the real world usually are double-barreled. That is, a group member may ostensibly be given a helpful report of the way things are in the organization as a matter of information—but behind the informational content is the additional message that the member is normatively *expected* to see things the same way and to behave accordingly.

The problems involved in separating normative from informational influence are well illustrated in classic experiments by Asch (1951) and Sherif (1936, 1965). In the Asch research, subjects were asked to match the length of a given line with one of three obviously unequal lines, an objectively easy task. Subjects in groups of eight (seven confederates and one naive subject) were required to state their judgments aloud. On critical trials, the naive subject was faced with a unanimous majority of peers who gave an incorrect answer. About one-third of the responses of the naive subjects on these trials were erroneous and in agreement with the answers of the confederates.[8]

In the Sherif research, subjects were asked to estimate the movement of a spot of light that was shown momentarily in a dark room.

The light did not actually move, but appeared to do so because of the autokinetic effect. When subjects were tested alone, each individual subjectively defined a reference point or standard against which subsequent judgments were made. When subjects were tested in groups, announcing their estimates of the amount of movement publicly, a common standard or reference point developed after a few trials, and the subsequent estimates of all group members converged around that standard. Moreover, when subjects in the group condition subsequently were tested individually, they continued to use the group-defined standard as the reference point for their judgments.

It might appear that the Asch subjects were conforming for strictly normative reasons (i.e., they feared being ridiculed if they did not go along with the group, even though they knew the group was incorrect) and that the Sherif subjects were using the group solely for informational purposes (i.e., in the absence of hard sense data, they used the subjective reports of other members as information). The situation is not, however, that straightforward. Asch (1958, pp. 178–179) reports that interviews with subjects revealed three different explanations for why they conformed, and only one of the three has an unambiguously normative flavor:

- *Distortion of perception.* A few subjects were unaware that their estimates had been distorted by the majority; they believed that they were giving correct estimates throughout.

- *Distortion of judgment.* These subjects reported that while they saw what they saw, their own perception must somehow have been incorrect since everyone else saw it differently. Most subjects were in this category.

- *Distortion of action.* These subjects were aware that they were correct, but deliberately chose to go along with the majority out of an "overmastering need not to

appear different from or inferior to others... [or] an inability to tolerate the appearance of defectiveness in the eyes of the group" (p. 179).

In the Sherif experiment, it is tempting to conclude that only informational influence was operating. Since the light objectively did not move at all, subjects could not have had much confidence in their own estimates—and therefore the data provided by others should have been quite helpful in making sense of an inherently ambiguous situation. It also is possible, however, that subjects changed their initial (and private) estimates after hearing the reports of others because they feared that they would seem foolish if they said aloud what they really thought they saw. There simply is no way to tell for sure.

Following the pioneering work of Asch and Sherif, many researchers sought to experimentally disentangle normative from informational social influences on individual beliefs and opinions (see Tajfel, 1969, for a summary of this work). In general, it was found that substantial social influence remains even when group characteristics are manipulated to minimize normative forces on the individual (e.g., by minimizing group cohesion or by creating conditions in which a real group does not even exist). Further, there is evidence that people are influenced by other group members even when they believe that their own responses are anonymous and when they are unaware that they are being influenced (as was the case for many subjects in the Sherif research). It is reasonable to assume, therefore, that *both* normative and informational influence processes are operating in organizational groups—a conclusion also reached in studies of social influences on individual judgment (Ono & Davis, 1988). As Tajfel (1969) notes, "the experiential substratum of the yielding subject's response is perhaps, in the last analysis, an epistemological issue which can never be fully resolved on a purely empirical level" (p. 348).

Conditions for Accepting Group-supplied Information About Reality. Groups sometimes have enormous influence over the perceptions and beliefs of their members; other times, members seem all but immune to group influence. What accounts for the difference? Once again, there is a vast literature in the conformity tradition regarding the conditions under which individuals accept group influence; and, once again, it is difficult to distinguish in these studies the operation of normative versus informational social influence (O'Reilly & Caldwell, 1985). Reviews of this literature are provided by Allen (1965), Kiesler (1969, chaps. 10 and 11), Levine and Russo (1987), and Tajfel (1969, pp. 347–357).

In general, research shows that member acceptance of group-supplied data about reality is a function of three interrelated factors.

Characteristics of the environment. To the extent that the targets of members' perceptions or beliefs are ambiguous or unclear, members' reliance on the group for information about those targets increases (Asch, 1951; Wiener, 1958). Reality in organizational settings often is quite fuzzy compared to that of the physical world. Thus, groups have considerable influence on member views about consequential features of the organization such as the contingencies that link behaviors and outcomes.

Characteristics of the group. Members tend to accept group-supplied data about reality to the extent they perceive the group to be a credible (i.e., competent, successful, and/or trustworthy) source of information (Kelman, 1950; Rosenberg, 1961). Such perceptions can be either relatively enduring ("This is an awfully competent group; I'd better listen to what they say") or transitory ("They were right yesterday, so I guess I should pay attention to them today"). Although the degree to which a group is seen as attractive by a member has been shown to affect acceptance of normative influence attempts, it is doubtful that attractiveness per se plays an important part in the acceptance of primarily informational materials from the group (Downing, 1958). Unanimity of views within the group, however, does strongly affect acceptance of group-supplied information (Allen & Levine, 1971), perhaps because unanimity increases the perceived credibility of the group.

Characteristics of the perceiver. Members who feel poorly qualified personally to assess the environment tend to rely heavily on the group for information about it (Kelley & Lamb, 1957; League & Jackson, 1964). Low self-confidence can be either a relatively enduring characteristic of a person, or a momentary state induced by recent failures to perceive or assess the environment accurately. The degree of group influence on member beliefs about the environment, then, should vary substantially over time as the situation changes and as members' self-perceptions change.

The joint operation of these three factors is nicely illustrated by a controversy that flared up in the late 1970s about the relative potency of objective versus social reality in influencing organization members' perceptions of, and reactions to, their jobs. Some years earlier, several researchers had proposed that when jobs have certain characteristics (such as skill variety, autonomy, and built-in feedback), job incumbents who value challenge and opportunities for growth will exhibit high satisfaction, internal motivation, and high quality performance (Hackman & Lawler, 1971; Hackman & Oldham, 1976; Turner & Lawrence, 1965). Some commentators, most notably Salancik and Pfeffer (1977), questioned this contention and suggested that a person's perception of his or her job may be affected as much by *social* factors (such as cues from one's co-workers) as by any so-called "objective" characteristics of the work itself (Salancik & Pfeffer, 1978).

Following the influential Salancik and Pfeffer articles, numerous studies were conducted to test the relative potency of job characteristics and social cues in influencing job perceptions. Many of these studies were laboratory experiments using a "horse race" design—that is, both the objective properties of the task and the cues to which subjects were exposed were manipulated to see which class of variables most powerfully affected subjects' perceptions of their jobs. Thomas and Griffin (1983), in a careful review of these studies, show that the findings are just what would be expected—namely, that job perceptions are affected *both* by objective task characteristics and by social cues.

The larger question—that is, how the objective and social environments *interactively* shape job perceptions—simply cannot be answered by horse race studies. To address the larger question requires, first, that the work being done be consequential for the job incumbent over a period of time considerably longer than the duration of a typical session in the experimental laboratory. Also required are real work groups—sets of people with whom the job incumbent is significantly interdependent and with whom he or she anticipates future interaction. And, finally, any robust answer also must take account of individual differences, that is, characteristics of people that potentially can affect how they respond to their tasks and to their co-workers.

Two studies illustrate the payoff from moving in this direction. The first, by Griffin (1983), involved a laboratory pretest followed by a field experiment in which both task characteristics and informational cues (albeit from a supervisor rather than from an intact work group) were manipulated. As predicted, Griffin found that both independent variables affected job perceptions. But he also found interactions among them. For perceptions of performance-related job characteristics (task identity, variety, autonomy, and feedback), the task manipulation accounted for an average of 51 percent of the variation in perceptions, compared to 32 percent for the manipulation of social cues. For perceptions of interpersonal aspects of the job (dealing with others and friendship opportunities), on the other hand, the task manipulation controlled only 2 percent of the variance, compared to 78 percent for the

manipulation of social cues. Clearly, the objective and the social environment are differentially potent for different features of the work environment.

The second study, by Weiss and Shaw (1979), examined task characteristics, social cues (through attitudes expressed by other workers in a training film viewed by subjects), *and* individual differences—specifically, subjects' field dependence and self-esteem. Once again, both the objective properties of the task and the cues provided by other workers influenced subjects' task perceptions. But the social cues shaped perceptions only for field-dependent and low self-esteem subjects; they had almost no effect on the job perceptions of field-independent and high self-esteem subjects.

Taken together, these two studies suggest that to understand (let alone to change) how people perceive their jobs, one must consider all three of the classes of variables listed at the beginning of this section: (a) the objective environment (in this case, the properties of the job), (b) characteristics of the group (especially the credibility of the group and the informational cues it provides), and (c) characteristics of the person (specifically, his or her need for, and readiness to accept, group-provided information).

The lesson from this extended example is not merely that both the objective and the social environment affect organization members' beliefs; anyone who has spent any time in an organization already knows that. The lesson, instead, is that to predict a group member's beliefs about his or her organizational environment, one must attend to the *interactions* among contextual, group, and individual difference variables. To look at only one of these three factors or, worse, to play them off against one another to see which is the most potent, is to badly misconstrue the way social systems really operate.

Shaping Beliefs About the Self. Just as groups can affect members' perceptions of the environment, so can they influence the beliefs people hold about themselves. For example, Burke and Bennis (1961) found that over the course of a three-week group training experience, individual members and their peers tended to converge in their perceptions of each person on three dimensions: (a) friendliness-evaluation, (b) dominance-potency, and (c) participation-activity. The authors document that this phenomenon was due not merely to changes in others' perceptions of individuals (although such changes did take place), but also to changes in the beliefs individuals held about themselves.

How do such changes in beliefs about the self come about? To address this question, we must distinguish between two means by which groups can affect individuals' self-perceptions: comparative appraisal and reflected appraisal (Jones & Gerard, 1967). In *comparative appraisal,* one determines his or her standing on some attribute simply by observing relevant others; no explicit action by the others vis-à-vis the observer is required. Thus, to assess one's relative skill on a task being performed simultaneously by all group members, an individual might simply watch the performance of others as he or she is working and compare his or her own performance to how they seem to be doing.

Although in his original statement of the theory of social comparison Festinger (1954) focused solely on individuals' use of comparative data to learn about their abilities and the validity of their opinions, subsequent research has shown that comparative appraisal provides data relevant to a wide variety of beliefs people hold about themselves—including beliefs about their personality characteristics, their status in a social system, and so on (Singer, 1966).[9] Further, although individuals generally prefer persons similar to themselves for comparative purposes, research has demonstrated that people seek out and use data from discrepant others as well, especially when better or more useful information can be

obtained from someone who is dissimilar (Arrowood & Friend, 1969; Kruglanski & Mayseless, 1987, 1990; Latane, 1966; Suls & Miller, 1977; Taylor & Lobel, 1989; Wheeler et al., 1969).

In *reflected appraisal,* it is others' behaviors toward the target person that provide the basis for self-assessment. Consistent with Cooley's (1922) idea of the "looking glass self," individuals gain self-understanding by inferring what they must be like given the way others behave toward them. As Jones and Gerard (1967, p. 322) note, individuals often stage situations in which it is especially likely that others will exhibit behaviors toward them that can be used to refine their own self-perceptions.

Individuals are cognitively active in both comparative and reflected appraisal, seeking information about the self and using that information to generate self-descriptive inferences and attributions. Sometimes, however, it is the group that takes the initiative to shape a member's self-perceptions—for example, by providing a person with explicit evaluations or characterizations. When a group member is told, for example, to "stay out of the way while we do this task—you're no good at it," little inferential activity is required for that person to conclude that his or her task-relevant abilities are not all that they could be.

Direct communications intended to influence a member's self-perceptions can facilitate a group's efforts to regulate and coordinate member behavior. If all members' beliefs about themselves are congruent with others' views of them—that is, if everyone "knows his or her place"—then everyone is likely to behave in a group-appropriate fashion with a minimum of fuss. For example, if a member genuinely believes that his or her skills are mostly irrelevant to the group task, then he or she is unlikely to argue for a central role in task performance activities.

Sometimes groups attempt to induce members to believe things about themselves that are objectively untrue. One way of dealing with a new member whose great competence poses a threat to current members, for example, is to convince the newcomer that he or she is, in fact, not so very talented. Alternatively, when a group faces an extremely difficult task, members may collude to convince one of their number that he or she can easily surmount the challenge—burying their own uncertainties in a burst of enthusiasm and simultaneously building the confidence and motivation of the individual on whose shoulders the success or failure of the group rests.

We already have seen that a member is more likely to accept group-supplied information about external reality when he or she is uncertain of his or her own ability to assess that reality. Thus, if a group can use its control of discretionary stimuli to manipulate the beliefs of a member about himself or herself so that the person comes to doubt his or her own perceptual or judgmental abilities, the dependence of that member upon the group for information about *other* matters should dramatically increase. Such a strategy can result in extremely strong group influences on a member's beliefs about reality.

Increasing Job-relevant Knowledge and Skill. We turn now to ways that groups use discretionary stimuli to affect a quite different kind of informational state—namely, a member's task-relevant knowledge and skill. The distinction between this section and the preceding one parallels that of Ryle (1949) between "learning that" and "learning how." Ryle argues that acquiring information (learning *that*) can be accomplished directly, as when groups use discretionary stimuli to shape members' beliefs. Learning *how,* on the other hand, can be accomplished only gradually, through ongoing coaching, practice, and example.

Groups play a key role in helping their members learn *how,* for several reasons. Trial and error in learning a new skill or behavior pattern can be quite inefficient, and the help of other group members permits an individual

to cut short the learning process as well as to lessen the personal risks to which he or she is exposed while learning. Moreover, many skills and role behaviors are almost impossible to master without the active involvement of other people—for example, learning how to manage part of an organization, or becoming skilled in operating a sophisticated piece of equipment (Kemper, 1968). In his book *The Making of a Surgeon,* William Nolen describes the many ways in which fledgling surgeons are dependent on other members of their medical teams in developing the capability to execute surgical procedures with even minimum adequacy.

Groups can assist their members in developing job-relevant knowledge and skills in three ways: (a) through direct instruction, (b) by providing feedback to members about their behavior, and (c) by providing models of correct or appropriate behaviors.[10]

Direct Instruction.   By itself, direct instruction is useful only for simple skills and role behaviors. Simply being told how to drive a car or how to perform an appendectomy, for example, is not sufficient to master these skills. The importance of direct instruction in skill and role learning to new group members should not be underestimated, however. If a group elects not to instruct a new member, his or her adaptation can be severely impaired: Not knowing how to do something as simple as placing a long-distance telephone call can be highly stressful in one's early days on the job. Even though direct instruction, by itself, is insufficient for helping members develop a full repertoire of work-related skills, it usually is a necessary part of such learning and represents an important discretionary resource that the group can provide to, or withhold from, its members.

Feedback.   Feedback from other group members serves two major functions for a learner: It provides information about what behaviors are "right" (or appropriate) and "wrong" (or inappropriate) in fulfilling one's duties, and it

provides reinforcement, rewarding right behaviors and punishing wrong ones. Both functions, of course, can help members hone and
refine their job-relevant knowledge and
skills.

It is well established that informational
feedback (in the form of another's responses to
one's task activities) can enhance learning
(Rhine, 1960), memory (Allen & Bragg, 1968a),
and concept identification (Allen & Bragg,
1968b). Feedback that is rewarding or punishing in character also can facilitate the learning
of skills and role behaviors (Bandura, 1977;
Berger & Lambert, 1969; Walters & Parke, 1964).
Of special relevance here is research that
shows how group member roles can be changed
through selective reinforcement of certain of
the incumbent's behaviors (Bavelas, Hastorf,
Gross, & Kite, 1965; Sarbin & Allen, 1968a). In
the Sarbin and Allen study, for example, reinforcing feedback from high-status group members increased the participation of initially
reticent group members, and negative feedback tended to decrease the participation of
members who initially were highly verbal.

Unfortunately, there has been relatively little
research on how feedback from one's fellow
group members affects skill and role learning
in organizational groups. Although there is a
rapidly growing research literature that applies the principles of behavior modification to
behavior in organizational settings (e.g., Davis
& Luthans, 1980; Luthans & Kreitner, 1975), the
bulk of this work deals with the impact of
supervisor-administered reinforcers on the behavior of individual workers. There recently
has been some movement toward application
of the operant model to the behavior of intact
teams (e.g., Komaki, Desselles, & Bowman,
1989); perhaps we soon will see more research
on feedback-based skill development processes
that occur *within* organizational groups.

Modeling. One of the most powerful ways
for a group to help its members learn skills and
role behaviors is by providing for them models
of appropriate behavior. The earliest analyses
of modeling and imitative learning focused on
situations in which the learner simply matched
the behavior of a model (Miller & Dollard,
1941). These studies showed that an observer
who watched a model engage in some behavior
and be rewarded for it would engage in the
same behavior—if the observer also was motivated to obtain the reward. If that behavior
subsequently was reinforced, then it became
established in the person's repertoire.

Although learning through matching is one
way that people use others to develop their
skills, it is not the whole story. As social learning theorists have pointed out, individuals can
acquire robust symbolic representations of new
activities by observing models even in the absence of direct reinforcement (Bandura, 1977;
Manz & Sims, 1986). Thus, learning through
modeling can occur without immediate reinforcement of the new behavior, and such
learning can be stored away by the individual
for later use. Reinforcement is seen by social
learning theorists as a condition that can
facilitate learning from models (because reinforcement—or anticipated reinforcement—
heightens attention to the model and retention
of what the model does), but it is no longer
viewed as a necessary condition for learning
to occur.

There is a large research literature on modeling (Bandura, 1965, 1977; Rosenbaum &
Arenson, 1968; Walters, 1968), and some of
these studies do address leader and group behavior in organizations (e.g., Sims & Manz,
1984; Walter, 1975, 1976). Once again, however,
relatively little research has examined the ways
members of groups in organizations use each
other as models to increase their job-relevant
skills or their ability to enact their roles compe-
tently. Particularly useful would be studies
that illuminate within-group modeling processes—that is, the conditions under which
individual group members use their peers as
models in developing their own knowledge
and skill.

Summary.   Although it is clear that individuals in organizations are substantially dependent on members of their work groups for developing their knowledge and skill, research that examines how this occurs via group-mediated discretionary stimuli remains relatively scarce. The matter deserves attention because of the increasing complexity of many tasks and roles in contemporary organizations. Individuals who must master complex jobs are especially likely to encounter difficulties if left entirely to their own devices. These individuals, then, especially need all three of the aids to learning that a group can provide: direct instruction, feedback, and model provision.

The need for help from one's fellow group members, of course, also renders a person dependent on the group—and does so at a time when he or she is running a risk of personal failure. For this reason, a group's ability to influence a member in other ways (e.g., by obtaining behavioral or attitudinal conformity on matters not immediately relevant to the task at hand) also is likely to be particularly high at times when the person is attempting to develop his or her work-related knowledge and skill.

Effect of Discretionary Stimuli on Member Affective States

We now turn from the informational states of group members to their affective states—what members like and dislike, and how affectively engaged they are at work. First we explore the effects of discretionary stimuli on member preferences, attitudes, and values. Then we turn to member arousal and examine ways that group-induced changes in arousal can enhance or depress individual performance.

Changing Member Preferences, Attitudes, and Values.   Numerous studies have documented that groups can powerfully shape their members' preferences, attitudes, and values.[11]

One of the most informative is Lieberman's (1956) longitudinal study of how the attitudes of unionized manufacturing workers evolved over a period of almost three years. During that time, the group memberships of many of the workers changed dramatically. In the first year of study, 23 workers were promoted to foreman and 35 were elected union stewards. Some time later, 8 of the new foremen returned to the worker role (because of cutbacks associated with an economic recession), as did 14 of the union stewards (because they chose not to run again in union elections, or because they ran and were defeated).

Lieberman assessed the attitudes of the workers before any changes took place, after the initial round of changes, and after some of the workers had returned to their original roles. Thus, the study was a naturally occurring field experiment in which the groups that the workers were members of changed once—and then, for some of them—changed back. Lieberman measured workers' attitudes toward management, toward the union, and toward two different reward systems—one espoused by the union and one by management.

Workers who became foremen became markedly more promanagement (and more critical of the union) soon after they assumed their new role. When some of these individuals subsequently changed back to the worker role, their attitudes eventually reverted to those they previously had held. The attitudes of foremen who remained in management did not change. These role changes also involved changes in the groups with which the individuals were associated—and, therefore, changes in the source and nature of the attitude-relevant stimuli to which they were exposed. If one assumes that groups of supervisory personnel tend to exchange stimuli and encourage views that are more promanagement and antiunion than do groups of workers, then the observed changes in the attitudes of new foremen (and the reversion of these attitudes for those who returned to the worker role) make good sense.

Results for workers who became union stewards were less strong. Following election to the union steward role, there was some change in the prounion, antimanagement direction, but the amount of attitude change was not as large for the workers who became foremen. Also, those who returned later to the worker role tended not to revert to their previously held attitudes. This is not a surprising finding, since becoming a steward involves a much less significant change in group membership than does becoming a foreman: Although union stewards have increased contact with other union stewards and with higher union officers, they maintain their close involvement with the worker group.

The Lieberman study provides solid evidence that one's group memberships influence one's attitudes and values.[12] But attitude change does not always occur when there is a change of group membership. Sometimes members resist group influences even when exposed to them more or less continuously, as Theodore Newcomb demonstrated in a field study of Bennington College students in the 1930s (Newcomb, 1952).

Newcomb found that the political attitudes of most students at Bennington tilted in a liberal direction during their college years. Since a liberal point of view was dominant among students and faculty at Bennington at that time, Newcomb's findings would seem to fit well with those of Lieberman. Yet there were some students for whom the modal changes did not take place. These students, it turned out, were those who did not accept their membership group (i.e., other students and faculty at Bennington) as a positive point of reference for their attitudes. Some of these students actively rejected Bennington as a reference group; others seemed simply to ignore the college. The rejectors tended to adopt attitudes opposite to those of the majority, while those who ignored the college were not much affected one way or the other. These latter students invariably had some *other* group of which they were a member

(often the family) that they continued to use as the main point of reference for their political attitudes.

Data consistent with Newcomb's findings are provided by Siegel and Siegel (1957), also in a college environment. A group of students expressed an interest in living in prestigious "row" houses (former sorority houses). These students tended to score high on the Ethnocentrism–Fascism (E–F) scale, which reflects decidedly conservative values. Only some of these students were actually able to move into row houses, however, because of logistic problems; the remainder were assigned to less prestigious dormitories. After one year, three groups had emerged: (a) row house occupants for whom the row house group was both a membership and a reference group; (b) dormitory occupants who still wanted to move to a row house—that is, for whom the row was a reference group but not a membership group; and (c) dormitory occupants who no longer wanted to move to a row house—that is, for whom the row was neither a membership group nor a reference group. The E–F scale scores of the first group (membership and reference group) remained quite high; scores of the second group (reference but not membership group) showed only a slight drop; and scores of the last group (neither membership nor reference group) dropped substantially.

To understand the mechanisms through which attitude changes such as those just discussed occur, and to identify the factors that determine the magnitude of group effects on attitudes, we must look into the psychological mechanisms through which they occur. There are three of them.

Mechanism One: Changing Behavior With Affective Changes Following.   When a group succeeds in getting a member to change his or her behavior, attitude change often follows. Consider, for example, a work group that subtly convinces one of its members that he should occasionally fudge some production numbers to foil the supervisor's persistent attempts to raise production. Over time, the attitude of the worker toward the supervisor may become increasingly negative as his attitudes gradually come into consistency with his overt behavior.

Two general explanations have been offered for the pervasive tendency of behavior and attitudes to become consistent over time: *dissonance reduction* (Festinger, 1957) and *self-perception* (Bem, 1965). The former explanation, in brief, is that people experience a state of tension or dissonance when they find themselves doing things that are inconsistent with their existing attitudes and beliefs. If a person cannot conveniently reduce this tension by changing or terminating the behavior, then his or her attitudes may change to fit with it—thereby getting rid of the noxious attitude-behavior inconsistency. Self-perception theory generates nearly identical predictions but explains them differently. In essence, people observe themselves engaging in a behavior and, in attempting to make sense of that behavior, attribute to themselves an attitude that would be an appropriate reason for it. A person might notice, for example, that she works very hard and very long hours, and conclude that she must therefore really like her work.

For both dissonance reduction and self-perception, the more a group overtly coerces the individual to engage in a behavior by using very potent rewards or punishments, the less substantial the attitude change. One feels little dissonance from engaging in a slightly aversive behavior for a large reward, nor does one have to look to one's own attitudes to find a reason for that behavior—the extrinsic reward suffices, and attitude change is unlikely. This is one reason why the use of group methods to brainwash prisoners of war often are unsuccessful: The coercion to "confess and repent" can be so strong that prisoners are able to attribute their acquiescence to group-supplied rewards and punishments rather than to any real change of their own values (Schein, 1956). When, on the other hand, a group is able to get

a member to behave differently using subtle influence (e.g., "Come on, everybody else is doing it, don't be a laggard!"), then substantial attitude change may result.

Mechanism Two: Changing Beliefs With Affective Changes Following. Many attitudes are based on the beliefs that a person holds about the attitude object (Fishbein, 1967; Rosenberg, 1956). One way to change an attitude, then, is to change the underlying beliefs. To make an attitude more favorable, beliefs that carry positive affect would be strengthened and beliefs that carry negative affect would be weakened; to make an attitude more negative, the reverse would be done. Consider, for example, a worker who has a positive attitude toward the concept of labor unions. He believes that unions lead to better pay, that they keep management from exploiting workers, and that they generally contribute to a healthy national economy. If, as in the Lieberman research described earlier, that individual were promoted to management, he might be subjected to stimuli that would weaken the strength of his prior beliefs and perhaps introduce others in their place—for example, that unions hinder industrial progress, that some union officials are corrupt, and so on. Attitude change almost certainly would follow such changes in beliefs.

For Mechanism Two to be effective, three conditions must be met. First, there must be at least moderate ambiguity about the attributes of the attitude object. Second, the beliefs of the focal group member must be open to change by group-supplied data. And third, the group must be valued by the individual and/or seen as a source of trustworthy data about the attitude object. Thus, Mechanism Two is likely to be much more potent in influencing the attitudes and values of new, uncertain, and low-status group members than those of relatively self-confident veterans.

Mechanism Three: Direct Change of Affect. Consider the experience of a person who recently attended a concert of contemporary classical music for the first time. She found the performance quite arousing (noticing, for example, that her heart was beating faster than usual), but also mystifying. Initially unsure whether or not she liked the music, she could not help but notice how enthusiastically other members of the audience applauded. On the way home, she found herself reflecting on how much she liked this strange new music.

The experience of the concert-goer is not unusual. When people are physiologically aroused by something but have no ready explanation for their arousal, they tend to seek out and use cues from others to label their aroused state (Nisbett & Valins, 1972; Schachter, 1964). Thus, group-supplied cues in ambiguous and arousing situations can directly determine members' affective reactions. The phenomenon is quite robust: Research has shown that cues from other group members can influence attitudes even when one is *not* especially aroused (Salancik & Pfeffer, 1978; S. White & Mitchell, 1979). On the other hand, most research on this phenomenon has been conducted in contrived and short-term settings; it is not clear how powerful the effect is in organizational settings that are populated by experienced members with confidence in—and sometimes even public commitment to—their personal likes and dislikes. Such individuals, compared to subjects in laboratory experiments and to new organization members who are not yet sure of their affective judgments, are relatively immune to this type of group influence.

There is a second way that groups can directly shape the attitudes of their members—namely, through classical conditioning. Conditioning principles operate for affective responses just as they do for cognitive and behavioral responses (B. E. Lott, 1955; Staats & Staats, 1958). Thus, if a target stimulus is paired with another stimulus that elicits positive affect, the target stimulus gradually will come to elicit positive affect when presented alone. Further, the person's affective reaction will generalize from the target stimulus to new stimuli that are similar to it, following the principle of mediated generalization (Kalish, 1969).

Groups that control reinforcing stimuli, therefore, can directly condition the attitudes of their members. This may be part of what was happening at Bennington College at the time of the Newcomb study discussed earlier. Recall that the most popular students at the college in those days tended to have liberal political attitudes. When in the presence of the popular students, therefore, other students presumably were exposed simultaneously to social reinforcement (i.e., attention from people who were admired) *and* to liberal political viewpoints—exactly the conditions that can condition a person's attitudes.

Newly conditioned attitudes gradually become internalized and thereafter persist even if the eliciting stimulus disappears entirely. Indeed, just being a member of a group that satisfies one's personal needs can be sufficient for an individual to internalize the dominant values of that group (Thelen, 1950, pp. 32–33). A group that satisfies members' needs, then, can have effects on attitudes and values that persist even after the group itself has disbanded (see also Kelman, 1958).

Conclusion.   In general, groups have stronger influences on members' beliefs (see the previous section) than they do on attitudes. In studies of group effects on beliefs, subjects may assume (often correctly) that their peers have more or better knowledge of the state of the world than they do. But attitudes are more personal. Because people "own" their attitudes more than their beliefs about the world, they are less likely to accept uncritically others' views about how much they should like or value something. Thus, affective states are relatively less vulnerable to change via group-supplied discretionary stimuli than are beliefs. Consistent with this reasoning, Crutchfield (1955) found that conformity did not occur for subjects' preferences (among line drawings) as it did for cognitive judgments. He concluded that preferences may be immune from group pressure.

Crutchfield's conclusion is too strong. A member who does not much care about the group or the resources it controls may indeed be relatively immune to group influences on his or her attitudes. The same is true for someone who uses a different group as his or her primary point of reference, or for someone who is deeply and securely committed to a set of personal values. All three of the mechanisms dicussed in this section require that the individual be dependent to some extent on the group for social comparison and/or for need satisfaction.

When a group is important to the individual, on the other hand, group-supplied stimuli can strongly influence his or her likes and dislikes. Often these effects occur naturally, as a by-product of normal group interaction: Neither the individual nor other group members may be cognizant of what is happening or how it is happening. But when a group deliberately and judiciously uses its control over discretionary stimuli to modify the attitudes or values of its members, as is the case for some self-help and evangelical groups (Cushman, 1986), the amount of change realized can be very large indeed.

Altering Member Arousal. There is a second kind of affective state that can be influenced by group-supplied discretionary stimuli—namely, the level of physiological arousal or activation that a member experiences. As will be seen, member arousal is affected simply by the presence of other people in the group setting. These ambient effects, however, are greatly amplified or attenuated by the content of the discretionary stimuli exchanged among group members.

Increasing Arousal. In an insightful untangling of previous research on social facilitation, Zajonc (1965) proposed that the mere

presence of other people increases an individual's level of arousal, with effects on their performance that will be discussed below. Soon after Zajonc's seminal article appeared, researchers began to question whether it is the *mere* presence of others, or the presence of others who are in some specified relationship to the individual, that increases arousal. Few would doubt that it is arousing for the boss to be looking over one's shoulder while one is trying to compose a letter on a computer, for example. But what if there happen to be some strangers across the room talking with one another, apparently oblivious to what one is doing? Would arousal still increase?

To address this question, Cottrell, Wack, Sekerak, and Rittle (1968) had some individuals perform a task in the presence of two blindfolded confederates who presumably were merely waiting in the experimental room to become visually adapted before participating in a color-perception experiment; other subjects worked in the presence of an audience (specifically, confederates who were *not* blindfolded and who were positioned so they could observe the subject). Although arousal level in this study was inferred from differences in performance rather than from direct measures, the results suggest that the *mere* presence of others is not sufficient to raise arousal. Similar findings were obtained by Henchy and Glass (1968), who concluded that the effects predicted by Zajonc occur only when the presence of other people increases a performer's evaluation apprehension.

Other research (and there are now literally hundreds of relevant studies), however, has supported Zajonc's original position that even the mere presence of others is sufficient to modestly elevate a performer's arousal (Bond & Titus, 1983; Geen, 1989; Geen & Gange, 1983; Guerin, 1986; Sanders, 1981; Schmitt, Gilovich, Goore, & Joseph, 1986). Even if a person is doing his or her work privately but in the vicinity of other group members (a common condition for members of groups in organizations), that person's arousal may be a bit higher than it would have been had the person been working entirely alone. And if the other group members provide an actively threatening or intensely encouraging climate, which also happens in organizational groups, then arousal can rise to very high levels indeed.

Decreasing Arousal and Anxiety. There also is a body of research evidence documenting that the presence of other people can *reduce* a person's level of anxiety and arousal. A number of researchers, following Schachter's (1959) pioneering work on the psychology of affiliation, have shown that individuals who are highly aroused (especially when the arousal is due to fear) actively seek out others in the same situation and prefer to spend their time in a group rather than alone. Other people, it appears, provide comfort and support that can reduce experienced arousal.

For example, Gerard and Rabbie (1961) informed subjects that they would receive a painful electric shock and found that they preferred to spend the time waiting for the shock in the company of others rather than alone. In a subsequent study, Rabbie (1963) increased the uncertainty (and, presumably, the arousal) of some subjects by telling them that only one out of each group of four subjects actually would receive the shock; others were told that everyone would receive the shock. Results showed that subjects in the uncertain condition wanted to await the shock in a group more strongly than did those in the certain condition.

Although Schachter (1959) contends that fearful individuals want to be with others even if they cannot actually converse with them, Rabbie (1963) found that they have a stronger desire to be in a group in which they can talk together than in one in which conversation is not possible. There are, unfortunately, no data available to show explicitly how the conversation that takes place among aroused people helps or hinders anxiety reduction. But if it is true that the mere presence of others can reduce anxiety in some circumstances, then supportive or genuinely accepting social interaction should be dramatically helpful.

These findings from experimental studies are consistent with field studies that show how group members under external stress often become closer and more cohesive. When, for example, a natural disaster strikes or threatens a community, individuals frequently exhibit levels of mutual support, reassurance, and cooperation that previously were unknown. Similar phenomena often (but not always) occur when the survival of a group or an organization is threatened by an external agent— including threat from another group or organization (Klein, 1971; Sherif, 1936).

Summary. In some circumstances, being in a group increases one's level of arousal and anxiety, and in other cases, group membership provides comfort. When an individual has reason to believe that other group members will provide negative, explicitly evaluative, or strongly encouraging stimuli, his or her level of arousal increases; when the person expects the stimuli to be comforting or reassuring, arousal decreases.

Existing evidence is based largely on studies in which a person is (or expects to be) in the presence of other people but does not actually interact with them. Presumably these arousal-increasing and arousal-decreasing effects would be considerably magnified if other group members provided discretionary stimuli that unambiguously confirmed the individual's expectations—whether those expectations had to do with the possibility of being socially evaluated or with the possibility of being comforted and reassured.

Implications for Performance. What are the implications of group-enhanced (or group-depressed) arousal for an individual's performance effectiveness? The answer depends, most of all, on the characteristics of the task that is being performed—specifically, whether the task is one for which the person's dominant response is likely to be correct (Zajonc, 1965). Since the production of dominant responses is facilitated when a person is in an aroused state, arousal should foster performance effectiveness on well-learned tasks in which the dominant response needs merely to be executed by the performer (termed *performance* tasks by Zajonc). By the same token, arousal should impair effectiveness for new or unfamiliar tasks for which the dominant response is likely to be incorrect (termed *learning* tasks by Zajonc).

In general, the considerable body of research on social facilitation supports Zajonc's predictions, although it appears that facilitation effects, by themselves, control a relatively small portion of the overall variation in individual performance (Bond & Titus, 1983). Recently, researchers have begun to examine individual differences that may interact with the presence of others in determining performance outcomes—such as performer gender (Robinson-Staveley & Cooper, 1990) and a person's expectations about whether an audience's evaluation will be positive or negative (Sanna & Shotland, 1990). Other researchers are exploring a variety of cognitive mechanisms that may operate in producing facilitation effects (e.g., Seta, Seta, Donaldson, & Wang, 1988). These new research directions should further enrich understanding about the dynamics of facilitation processes.

Our present interest, however, has to do with influences on individual task performance. We know from existing evidence that merely working in the presence of other group members modestly increases arousal. We also know that the impact of a group on an individual's arousal is amplified if other members assume a strong and explicitly evaluative stance toward the performer or if they provide strong encouragement—such as when a basketball player's teammates cheer as he or she prepares to shoot a last-second,

game-determining free throw. For well-learned tasks, these group influences should enhance member performance; for new and unfamiliar tasks, they should have the opposite effect.

What can be said about individual performance when the presence and interaction of other group members serves to *decrease* his or her level of arousal—as, for example, when people under stress coalesce into groups? When the other members of the group are a source of support, comfort, or acceptance to the individual, thereby decreasing his or her arousal level, performance effectiveness should follow a pattern exactly opposite to that just described: The group should impair effectiveness for performance tasks (because arousal helps on these tasks, and arousal is being lowered), and it should facilitate effectiveness for learning tasks (because for these tasks arousal is harmful, and it is being lowered).

The relationships predicted above are summarized in Figure 1. As the group becomes increasingly threatening, evaluative, or strongly encouraging, effectiveness should increase for performance tasks and decrease for learning tasks. When the group is experienced as increasingly supportive, comforting, or unconditionally accepting, effectiveness should decrease for performance tasks and increase for learning tasks. And when the individual does not experience his or her relationship with the group as at all affectively significant, performance should not be noticeably affected.

Consider, for example, situations in which group members provide a person with extremely intense and explicitly evaluative or threatening stimuli. In such cases, arousal level should become exceedingly high. According to traditional wisdom in psychology, performance effectiveness (even on well-learned tasks) deteriorates under these conditions (Cofer & Appley, 1964, pp. 392–398; Scott, 1966). Yet McGrath (1976) has pointed out that the predicted tail-off in effectiveness under high arousal has not been satisfactorily

FIGURE 1

**Individual Performance Effectiveness as a Function
of Type of Task and Experienced Relationship to the Group**

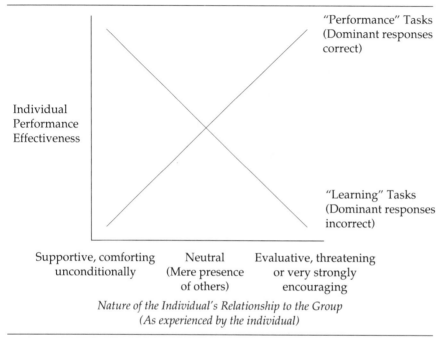

From "Group Influence on Individuals" by J. R. Hackman, 1976. In M. D. Dunnette (Ed.), *Handbook of Industrial and Organizational Psychology* (1st. ed., p. 1510). Chicago: Rand McNally. Copyright 1976 by M. D. Dunnette. Reprinted by permission.

demonstrated. McGrath further argues, and provides field-experimental evidence to support his position, that performance on well-learned tasks may be a positive linear function of arousal even at very high levels of arousal (other factors, such as task difficulty, held constant). That prediction is, of course, consistent with the relationships suggested in Figure 1.

By and large, research on the relationship between group-prompted arousal and individual performance effectiveness has not been designed or conducted in a way that illuminates how the phenomenon operates in actual organizational situations. It is clear, however, that individuals in organizations do use their group memberships as a means of achieving more comfortable levels of arousal. Individuals in high-pressure managerial jobs, for example, often find that they need to gather around themselves a few trusted associates who can provide reassurance and continuing acceptance when the going gets especially tough. Affiliation presumably helps reduce the manager's level of arousal and thereby increases the likelihood that he or she will be able to come up with new or original ways of perceiving and dealing with unfamiliar tasks he or she confronts. If the model depicted in Figure 1 is correct, however, this practice should not boost performance of the more routine, well-learned parts of the job.

It is well known that overly routine jobs can decrease a worker's level of arousal to such an extent that performance effectiveness is impaired (Scott, 1966). It seems quite possible to design the social environment of workers on routine jobs to partially compensate for the deadening effects of the job itself and thereby improve performance on well-learned tasks (such as undemanding monitoring or vigilance tasks). But, once again, there is scant research evidence on whether and how this can happen for people who perform work in ongoing organizational groups.

Impact of Group Norms

Previous sections examined how group-supplied discretionary stimuli influence members' informational and affective states. We have seen that behavior change is a common but indirect consequence of changes in member beliefs and attitudes. It also is true, of course, that a person can be affected *directly* by the discretionary stimuli controlled by his or her fellow group members. Indeed, one of the most general principles of psychology is that an individual's behavior can be shaped by anyone who has control of stimuli that are valued by that person.

Since most groups do control resources that their members value, all that groups need to do to regulate member behavior is to make those resources contingent on individuals' behaviors. When members want one of their peers to engage in some behavior (or to stop engaging in it), they can manage discretionary stimuli so that the person understands that it is in his or her best interest to comply with their wishes. While powerful, this process can consume much time and energy; it is not an efficient way to coordinate or control members' activities, especially if the group is large. Regulation of member behavior more commonly is accomplished using *behavioral norms*. Norms are

powerful, efficient, and so pervasive that one commentator has suggested that "it is only in imagination that we can talk about a human group apart from norms" (Davis, 1950, p. 53).

This section examines the attributes and the effects of group norms—including when people are likely to comply with them and what happens when someone deviates from them. We begin by specifying five attributes of norms that distinguish them from other features of groups in organizations:

Norms are structural characteristics of groups that summarize and simplify group influence processes. Although numerous definitions and conceptualizations of norms have been proposed, there is general agreement that norms are structures rather than processes and that their main function is to regulate and regularize member behavior (Bates & Cloyd, 1956; Festinger, Schachter, & Back, 1950; Golembiewski, 1962, chap. 5; Homans, 1950; Levine & Moreland, 1990, pp. 600–601; Rommetveit, 1955; Thibaut & Kelley, 1959, chap. 8). Thus, norms are an important means of bypassing the need to continuously use discretionary stimuli to control the behavior of individual members.

Norms apply only to behavior—not to private thoughts and feelings. Although some writers discuss the effects of group norms on member beliefs and attitudes, norms are treated here as applying exclusively to the actual behavior of group members. Since this usage includes verbal behavior, what members say they believe or what they say their attitudes are can be under normative control. Note, however, that verbal compliance with group norms does not necessarily reflect a member's private beliefs and attitudes. As pointed out earlier, group-supplied discretionary stimuli can indeed affect one's private attitudes and beliefs—but that process is considerably more complex and subtle than merely coercing someone to verbally agree with the majority view of a group.

Norms usually regulate only those behaviors that are viewed as important by group members.

Groups generally develop norms only for those behaviors that otherwise would have to be controlled by direct and more or less continuous social influence (Thibaut & Kelley, 1959). As Feldman (1984) notes, these tend to be behaviors that "ensure group survival, increase the predictability of group members' behavior, avoid embarrassing interpersonal situations, or give expression to the group's central values" (p. 47).

Just because members view some behavior as important, however, does not mean that it really is. Many groups develop norms about behaviors that members *believe* to be important but whose links to the actual well-being of the group are tenuous at best. This is, perhaps, the case for the detailed dress codes that continue to be enforced in some groups; members may agree that uniformity of dress is important to the group—but be hard-pressed to explain why this is so.

Norms usually develop gradually, but group members can choose to shortcut the norm development process. Norms about behavior typically evolve over time as members use discretionary stimuli to regulate the occurrence of behaviors they believe to be important. Indeed, Machotka (1964, chap. 11) argues that the process of norm formation and enforcement can be so gradual and covert as to be invisible to an observer. Yet that process also is lawful, and a number of organizational scholars have developed models of it (Bettenhausen & Murnighan, 1985; Feldman, 1984; Gersick & Hackman, 1990; Opp, 1982).

It is, of course, possible for a group deliberately to shortcut the norm development process. If for some reason members decide that a particular norm would be desirable or helpful, they may agree to institute it simply by declaring that from now on the norm exists. Someone might say, for example, "We seem to interrupt each other a lot in this group; let's have a norm that nobody talks until the other person is finished." If all group members

were to accept that proposal, then one should observe marked differences in group interaction subsequently.

Not all norms apply to everyone. Many norms do not apply uniformly to all group members. High-status members, for example, often have more freedom to deviate from the letter of the norm than do other people. Also, groups can establish a norm that applies only to one member or to a small subset of members. In such cases, roughly following Thibaut and Kelley (1959, pp. 142–147), we may speak of that norm as representing the role of the person or subset to whom it applies.

A Model of Group Behavioral Norms

An elegant conception of the structure of group norms has been proposed by Jackson (1960, 1965, 1966). This model, which is based on the distribution of members' approval and disapproval for various behaviors that might be exhibited in a given situation, represents norms in two-dimensional space: The abscissa is the amount of the behavior exhibited, and the ordinate is the amount of approval and disapproval felt. What Jackson calls a *return potential curve* can be drawn in this space. This curve shows the pattern and intensity of approval and disapproval associated with various possible behaviors. An example of a return potential curve is shown in Figure 2.

The *return potential model* (RPM) can be used to describe any situation in which a group norm regulates member behavior. To apply the model, one would obtain from group members (or infer from observations of behavior in the group) the amount of approval or disapproval associated with various behaviors and, from these data, plot a return potential curve. The curve in Figure 2, for example, might describe a norm about how much members talk during group meetings.

FIGURE 2

Schematic Representation of the Return Potential Model (RPM) of Normative Structure

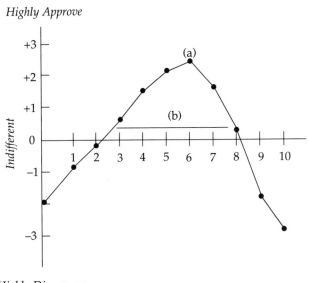

Note: The ordinate is an axis of evaluation; the abscissa is an axis of behavior.

From "Structural Characteristics of Norms" by J. Jackson, 1965. In I. D. Steiner and M. Fishbein (Eds.), *Current Studies in Social Psychology* (p. 303). New York: Holt, Rinehart and Winston. Copyright 1965 by J. Jackson. Reprinted by permission.

It shows that both too little and too much talking are disapproved, but that the intensity of disapproval is stronger for talking too much than for talking too little. (The units of behavior in Figure 2 are arbitrary; in practice, the abscissa would be scaled using units appropriate to the behavior in question.)

A return potential curve theoretically can assume any shape. March (1954), in a formulation similar to that of Jackson, suggests three basic types of norms: (a) the preferred-value norm, (b) the unattainable-ideal norm, and (c) the attainable-ideal norm. A *preferred-value norm* is of the general type shown in Figure 2 and just described: Both too little and

too much of the behavior are disapproved. *Unattainable-ideal* and *attainable-ideal* norms are depicted in Figure 3. An unattainable-ideal norm specifies "the more the better." Thus, among a group of scholars, the more insightful one's contributions the better; or on a football team, the more tackles made the better. March gives the following example of an attainable-ideal norm: A football team is in possession of the ball on the opponents' twenty-yard line. A halfback will earn increasing approval as he carries the ball increasing distances, but only up to twenty yards. After that, he will have made a touchdown and can gain no further approval; twenty-one yards is

FIGURE 3

Unattainable-ideal and Attainable-ideal Norms Shown as Return Potential Curves

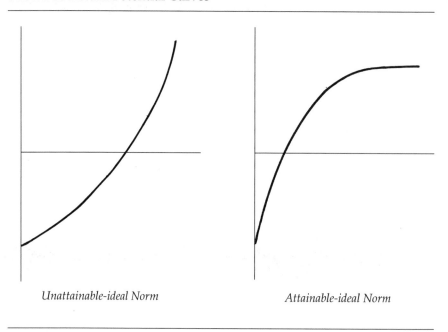

Unattainable-ideal Norm   Attainable-ideal Norm

From "Group Norms and the Active Minority" by J. G. Marsh, 1954. *American Sociological Review, 19*, 733–741.

just as good as twenty-five. There are, of course, many other possible curves that could describe other types of norms.

The RPM can be used to generate quantitative measures of the properties of group norms. Jackson (1965, 1966) identifies five specific characteristics of norms that can be assessed using the model:

- *Point of maximum return*—the point on the behavior dimension that generates the highest level of approval (point *a* in Figure 2)

- *Range of tolerable behavior*—the segment of the behavior dimension that is approved (range *b* in Figure 2)

- *Potential return difference*—the overall amount of approval or disapproval associated with norm-regulated behaviors. This index is computed by taking the algebraic sum of the ordinate values across all behaviors. The potential return difference, then, can be positive, neutral, or negative, depending on the relative emphasis a group places on rewards versus sanctions in regulating member behavior.

- *Intensity*—the overall strength of approval and disapproval associated with norm-regulated behaviors. This index is computed by summing the absolute values of the ordinates across all behaviors. Thus, intensity reflects the overall amount of affect associated with a norm, regardless of whether that affect is predominately positive or negative. This measure is useful in comparing the amount of normative regulation characteristic of different groups and in assessing the relative importance of different norms enforced by the same group.

- *Crystallization*—the degree of consensus among group members about the amount of approval or disapproval associated with each point on the behavior dimension. Crystallization is defined as the amount of variation in members' approval for each behavior, summed across all points on the behavior dimension. Crystallization indexes a group's potential for effective control of member behavior: Unless there is at least moderate agreement among members about the level of approval or disapproval associated with each behavior, it will be difficult for them to take concerted action to enforce the norm.

Jackson and his colleagues have applied the return potential model to a number of group and organizational settings, both for understanding the internal dynamics of social systems and for making comparative studies of them (see Jackson, 1988, for a bibliography of this research). Findings to date suggest that the RPM is well suited for studies of groups in organizations, for four reasons.

First, the RPM offers a means of quantifying norm characteristics that can be applied directly in field situations. Quantitative descriptors of norms rarely have been used in research on the norms of organizational groups. Second, the model permits and encourages explicit comparisons between the norms that characterize a total group (operationalized as the mean return potential curve across all group members) and these same norms as experienced by individual members. Such comparisons can provide significant insight into the dynamics of individual-group relationships. Third, the

model can be used to compare norms that regulate different classes of behaviors within a given group, and even to study how a group may enforce a given norm differently for various group members (depending, for example, on the role or status of a member).

Finally, the RPM provides a tool for use in diagnosing group norms as a first step in an intervention that seeks to improve group functioning. It can help group members see, objectively and simply, what their group norms actually are and how they may be guiding behavior in ways that are surprising or unintended. Raising implicit norms to the level of explicit awareness and discussion in this way can provide a strong impetus for change.

Compliance With Group Norms

When norm-specified behaviors are congruent with the personal attitudes, beliefs, and behavioral dispositions of group members, compliance is a nonissue: Members behave in norm-appropriate ways of their own accord.[13] More interesting are circumstances when members act in ways that are *not* consistent with their personal attitudes or beliefs. What factors lead someone to comply with group norms when he or she is not personally disposed to do so? Research evidence points to three classes of variables—those having to do with properties of the group *norm* itself, of the *person* behaving, and of the person's *role* in the group.

The Norm.   In general, norms that are both well crystallized and highly intense engender greater compliance than those that are not. Because members agree about how much approval or disapproval is associated with each behavior controlled by a well-crystallized norm, the group's response to an action that lies outside the range of tolerable behavior will be clear rather than confused. Thus, a member who deviates is likely to experience the rest of the group as being unanimous, or nearly so, in support of the norm—a condition that has been shown strongly to affect conformity (Asch, 1955; Miller & Tiffany, 1963). Moreover, because other members' feelings of approval or disapproval are strong (true by definition for intense norms), their response to deviant behaviors is likely to be decisive.

A group is said to have *normative power* when its norms are both well crystallized and intense (Jackson, 1975), and member compliance with such norms typically is high. Consider, for example, the cockpit crew of a commercial aircraft. Even though the crews with whom individual pilots fly change frequently, all pilots know that after takeoff the pilot who is actually flying the aircraft instructs the pilot not flying to raise the landing gear—and that the gear is not to be raised until that call is made. Because of the intensity and crystallization of this norm, deviation from it is almost never observed. It would be highly consequential—and negatively so—if the pilot not flying were to raise the gear before being told to do so by the pilot flying.

Now consider a norm that is highly crystallized but low in intensity, a state of affairs that Jackson calls *vacuous consensus*. Less behavioral compliance would be expected for such a norm, simply because group members care less about the behavior in question—even though they are in agreement about what they prefer. To illustrate, let us remain in the cockpit. In certain types of aircraft, crews develop a norm about whose hat is to be hung on which wall hook when crew members enter the cockpit. The norm is well crystallized, in that everyone agrees that each hook belongs to a certain crew member, but its intensity usually is very low. If someone were to hang his or her hat on the wrong hook, the other crew members probably would just go ahead and use the remaining hooks. Perhaps someone would make a joke to signal that the norm had been violated—but the group would be unlikely to make a serious attempt to enforce compliance.

Finally, consider the reverse state of affairs: a norm that is high in intensity but poorly crystallized. According to Jackson, this state of affairs has high *conflict potential*. People *care* about the behavior in question, but they do not *agree* about it. This can be illustrated with a final cockpit crew example. In all airlines, norms about how checklists are to be read and responded to typically are both intense and well crystallized—but these norms differ from company to company. In some airlines, for example, certain items on a checklist are to be read and checked silently by a crew member; other airlines require the same items to be read aloud and responded to affirmatively by another crew member. Now consider a cockpit in which one crew member is a high-tenure veteran and another is an experienced pilot but new to this particular airline. That crew is prone to conflict potential because each member is likely to have strong feelings about checklist discipline but different expectations about exactly who is supposed to do what in running the checklist.

In sum, highly intense and well-crystallized norms are likely to result in both high member compliance and swift correction of any norm violations that do occur. Well-crystallized but low-intensity norms can yield orderly behavior—but members will have little motivation to correct violations. And highly intense but poorly crystallized norms are, in general, more likely to spawn conflict than to foster behavioral uniformity among members.

The Person.   From an observer's perspective, there appears to be great variation in the degree to which different people comply with group norms. Following Ferguson (1944), it is tempting to view these individual differences as manifestations of members' personalities. One can easily think of certain people who seem always to conform, for example. Other people seem always to do the opposite of what the group wants. Others show great variability—sometimes conforming, sometimes not.

And still others seem always to go their own independent way, apparently without regard for group norms or peer influence.[14]

As tempting as dispositional explanations are, they are not entirely satisfactory because an individual's response to any one group may in fact depend on the norms of *another* group (such as when an individual's behavior seems to be independent of one group's norms because he or she actually is conforming to contrary norms of a second group). The individual differences question, then, must be broadened to include *all* groups of which a person is a member. What characteristics of people affect their choices about the groups to which they will conform?

That question requires examination of individuals' needs and wants. A person generally complies with a group's norms when he or she finds the rewards for compliance (or the sanctions for noncompliance) to be sufficiently attractive (or repellent) that his or her best interest is served by going along. When someone is a member of multiple groups with inconsistent norms, he or she tends to comply with the norms of the group that has the greatest control over those resources that he or she most values. Sometimes this will result in an individual *appearing* to be a "conformer" or an "independent person," when in fact, he or she is simply attempting to maximize the return from the broader set of groups of which he or she is a member.[15]

Research findings generally support this proposition: The more an individual is attracted to a group (or the more the person values group-controlled social rewards), the more he or she conforms. Thus, compliance tends to be very high in cohesive groups, where members care a great deal about being together and about continuing their mutually satisfying social interaction. On the other hand, people who do not much need or care about the social rewards that can be provided by their fellows (for example, very high-status members or very low-status members who are not committed to remaining in the group) tend to show relatively low compliance with group norms. Literature relevant to these issues is reviewed in detail by Allen (1965), Hare (1962), Kiesler (1969), and Lott and Lott (1965).

There are a number of caveats to these generalizations. First, we must keep in mind (see the earlier discussion of group influences on members' affective states) that groups in organizations can shape the very needs and wants that subsequently affect members' compliance with group norms. If a group succeeds in increasing the value members place on the rewards it mediates, then a high degree of compliance should be observed—even if members did not much care about the group's rewards when they first joined it. Second, groups may not need to actually *use* the stimuli under their control to obtain compliance. It can be sufficient for a member to know that the group has the *potential* to administer such stimuli: One does not need to be struck down by a bolt of lightning to know the fear of God. It is also true, on the other hand, that when a group is not present in a given situation, or when members' responses are made in private, behavioral compliance decreases—presumably because the group has little opportunity to apply rewarding or punishing stimuli in such circumstances (Allen, 1965, pp. 145–146; Kiesler, 1969).

The relationships discussed above between a member's need for group-controlled rewards and his or her compliance with group norms assumes that other things (such as the size of the group and the person's commitment to the task) are constant. Other things never are.[16] As Graham (1962) notes, if it really mattered to a subject to make a correct judgment in an Asch-type conformity situation, the person surely would make it.

The Role. How faithfully a member complies with group norms depends not only on the properties of the norm itself and on his or her personal needs and wants, but also on the individual's role in the group. Occupants of some roles have far more behavioral latitude than do others. Hollander's (1958, 1964) concept of *idiosyncrasy credit* provides one inviting way to understand this phenomenon.

According to Hollander, idiosyncrasy credits permit a member to exhibit some deviant behaviors without incurring the pressures or sanctions that typically are applied to members who violate a group norm. There are three ways to build one's cache of idiosyncrasy credits. First, they can be imported. A member who has high external status typically brings along a positive credit balance when he or she joins a group. Some years ago, Jodie Foster, already a movie star, was a student at Yale University. She surely enjoyed a positive balance of idiosyncrasy credits in student groups of which she was a member during her time as an undergraduate.

Second, assignment to a high-status role within a group can add to one's balance of idiosyncrasy credits. Even in a group of peers, a member who has been assigned the role of team leader begins with a larger credit balance than that enjoyed by rank-and-file members. Finally, group members can generate idiosyncrasy credits over time by being "good group citizens"—that is, by generally conforming to the expectations of the group and by contributing to the attainment of group goals (Hollander, 1960).

Although research tests of the Hollander model have yielded mixed results (e.g., see Bray, Johnson, & Chilstrom, 1982; Ridgeway, 1981; and a review by Levine, 1989, pp. 213–215) there is considerable evidence that does fit with its predictions. Consider, for example, new rank-and-file members of a group. They should not have a balance of idiosyncrasy credits to draw upon, and therefore should not have much freedom to deviate from group norms early in their tenure. Consistent with this prediction, Hughes (1946) found that new members of a work group were expected by their peers to conform more closely to group

production norms than were other group members.

Also as predicted, there is evidence that higher status members are better able to resist conformity pressures than are their lower status peers (Harvey & Consalvi, 1960). Even individuals with quite high status do not have unlimited freedom, however. The findings of Wiggins, Dill, and Schwartz (1965), for example, suggest that a high-status person may be free to deviate only as long as his or her activities are not severely detrimental to group goal achievement. For moderate to low deviation in the Wiggins et al. study, a high-status member received fewer negative reactions than did a moderate-status member; but when the deviation of the high-status member clearly and seriously impaired task performance, he received much more hostility from his peers than did a lower status member who was equally deviant. Similar findings are reported by Alvarez (1968) and Lortie-Lussier (1987).

These studies suggest that the freedom to deviate is fairly fragile even for a high-status group member who has built up a nest egg of idiosyncrasy credits—particularly when other members view the deviation as intentional and as stemming from one's personal disposition (Giordano, 1983). Low-status members find themselves in even more severe straits: They have few idiosyncrasy credits, so their group-given freedom to deviate without incurring sanctions is limited. Worse, if they do deviate, they run an especially high risk of being rejected, because lower status usually implies lesser value to the group. For those low-status members who feel marginally involved in the group and who care only a little about its activities, there is not much at stake: They can behave pretty much as they wish, and if rejection comes, it does not hurt too much. Low-status members who do value their group membership, however, have a problem: They have neither wide behavioral latitude nor much capability to improve things other than by being "good" for a long period of time.

Dealing With Deviance

Normative control of behavior in groups is, of course, never perfect. Even when a norm is intense and well crystallized, people sometimes engage in behaviors that lie outside the range of tolerable behavior. Regardless of whether the deviant behavior is deliberate or inadvertent, it is by definition disapproved by other members. But then what happens? There are three possibilities. One, the group can take action to *correct* the deviant member's behavior. Two, the group can psychologically or behaviorally *reject* the deviant. And three, the group can *accommodate* to the deviant member by changing its norm so that the behavior previously viewed as unacceptable is now agreeable or even actively endorsed. In this latter case, the deviant member changes the group rather than vice versa. Each of these three alternatives will be examined; for a detailed review of the literature on factors that affect groups' responses to deviance, see Levine (1989, pp. 200–218).

Correcting the Deviant. Perhaps the most common response when a group member violates a norm is the use of discretionary stimuli to bring the offending member back into line. When the violation is inadvertent, which often is the case for deviant behaviors by new group members, the correction usually can be accomplished swiftly and relatively painlessly. This is illustrated in the experience of a colleague in her first weeks as a new member of a consulting firm. When her consulting team returned to the office from a day in the field, the leader suggested that the group take a few minutes to reflect on the day. Because no one else seemed to have anything to say, my colleague offered up her own thoughts about the day's events. When she had finished, others joined in. The same thing happened at the end of the team's second day. At the end of the third day, however, a veteran team member took my colleague aside and explained that, for

this team, the word *reflect* meant that one was supposed to sit quietly, consider privately what had transpired, and perhaps even make some notes to one's self—but certainly not interfere with others' reflections by talking out loud. That was all it took: My colleague never again violated her team's norm about debriefing behavior by speaking up when it was time to reflect on the day.

When a norm violation is deliberate, however, the group's response is likely to be stronger and more pointed. Recall, for example, Arthur Schlesinger's statement that he had tempered expressing his objections to President Kennedy's Bay of Pigs invasion plans because he feared that vigorous protest would only "gain me a name as a nuisance." It is easy to see how Schlesinger might have developed that belief, given the following event:

> At a large birthday party for his wife, Robert Kennedy, the Attorney General, who had been constantly informed about the Cuban invasion plan, took Schlesinger aside and asked him why he was opposed. The President's brother listened coldly and then said, "You may be right or you may be wrong, but the President has his mind made up. Don't push it any further. Now is the time for everyone to help him all they can." (Janis, 1972, pp. 41–42)

In both of the above examples, a representative of the group used discretionary stimuli to correct the behavior of a member who had violated a group norm. What happened is consistent with research findings that members increasingly direct communications toward anyone who expresses an opinion that deviates from the majority view (Berkowitz & Howard, 1959; Emerson, 1954; Festinger & Thibaut, 1951; Schachter, Ellertson, McBride, & Gregory, 1951; Schachter et al., 1954). Although researchers generally have not analyzed the actual *content* of communications directed to the deviant member (Berkowitz, 1971), increased communication with the deviant member typically has been interpreted as reflecting an attempt to bring the member's behavior into line.[17]

Sometimes no interpretation is required to understand the intent of a communication—for example, in the exchange between Kennedy and Schlesinger, or when a group blatantly uses its control over material resources, or even takes physical action, to correct a deviant member. The practice of *binging* (hitting someone forcefully on the upper arm), for example, is an altogether unambiguous act sometimes used by work teams to shape up a member who is violating a norm about production quantity (Homans, 1950).

When group members take concerted action to correct the behavior of a member who is violating an intense, well-crystallized norm, they have a good chance—but no guarantee—of success. What happens when a member persists in going his or her own way? We turn to this question next.

Rejecting the Deviant. The application of discretionary stimuli intended to persuade or pressure a deviant to change persists only so long. If there is no change in the member's behavior, the group may, to use Festinger's (1950) phrase, "change the composition of the psychological group." A number of early studies provided moderate support for the hypothesis that a person who persistently deviates from group norms or from the expectations associated with a particular role may eventually be rejected by his or her peers (Berkowitz & Howard, 1959; Schachter, 1951; Schachter et al., 1954).

When rejection occurs, communication to the deviant from other group members should drop off markedly, but research has not satisfactorily demonstrated that this happens. Schachter (1951) did observe a decline in communications to the deviant late in the group session by members who subsequently indicated (on sociometric measures) that they had rejected the person. This occurred, however, only in groups that were both highly cohesive and dealing with a topic directly relevant to the purpose of the group. And a replication of the Schachter study by Emerson (1954) failed to find a decline in communication to the deviant under any circumstances.

A clue about why there was not a more obvious drop-off in communications to the deviant in these studies is provided by Sampson and Brandon (1964). These authors trained a confederate to respond to group norms in two different ways. In one condition, the confederate either conformed to or deviated from the modal opinion of other members during the course of a group discussion. In the other condition, the confederate presented herself prior to the official start of the group discussion as either a racial bigot (the deviant position) or as a liberal (the conforming position). Results showed that the opinion deviant received more communications than did either the opinion conformant or the bigot. But the opinion deviant was rarely rejected—not even at the end of the experimental session when she still had not changed. The bigot, on the other hand, received relatively few communications but often was rejected. Apparently group members rejected outright (and, therefore, did not communicate at all with) a member whom they viewed as having no hope for change (the bigot), but spent a great deal of communicative effort trying to convert the member who potentially was influenceable (the opinion deviant). These results suggest—and naive observations of groups in organizations affirm—that groups view rejection of a member as a quite serious act, something to be done only when all else has failed or when members view the deviant as completely incorrigible.[18]

That rejection is done rarely and reluctantly may actually contribute to the health and well-being of groups as social systems. According to Dentler and Erikson (1959), groups *need* deviant members and therefore cannot afford to eliminate them entirely. Some norms, especially important ones, become visible only when they are violated. By violating norms with which other members routinely comply, deviants mark for the group the outer bounds of acceptable behavior. In this fashion, deviant members help a group clarify what is distinctive about the group and central to its identity. Moreover, because deviants typically receive negative outcomes from the group, members are reminded of the range of consequences that the group has under its control. The incentive value of conformity may be enhanced as a result.

In a number of ways, then, deviant members contribute positively to the stability of a group and to the maintenance of its identity. As a consequence, Dentler and Erikson argue, the role of the deviant often becomes *institutionalized* within the group, and members subsequently resist any suggestion that the deviant be expelled (1959, p. 102). When a member is assigned the role of institutionalized deviant, energy that previously had been spent contending with that person is freed up for other uses. Moreover, members avoid the need to confront the anxieties and uncertainties that invariably surface when someone actually is rejected. Finally, the group no longer has to take seriously the possibility that there is merit in the views or behavior of the deviant member. In all, to institutionalize a deviant is a comfortable way for a group to deal with an inherently uncomfortable situation. That this comfort may come at a price (which it does, as will be seen presently) is unlikely to be apparent to members at the time.

Accommodating to the Deviant. So far, we have focused on what groups do to bring norm-violating members back into line. Sometimes, however, it is the group, not the deviant, that changes. Beginning with a classic series of studies by Serge Moscovici and his associates, there has emerged, first in Europe and more recently in the United States, a substantial body of knowledge about the conditions under which the majority in a group accommodates to, rather than converts, members whose ideas and behaviors differ from their own. For reviews of this line of research, see Levine (1989), Levine and Russo (1987), Maass and Clark (1984), Maass, West, and Cialdini (1987), Moscovici (1980), and Nemeth (1986).[19]

The prototypic research design in the Moscovici tradition is an almost exact reversal of the classic Asch conformity paradigm. Asch (1951) focused on the response of a single naive subject after several confederates had given preprogrammed incorrect responses. Moscovici, by contrast, focused on the responses of majority members (who were the naive subjects) when one or more confederates gave incorrect responses. In one early study, for example, two deviants consistently identified the color of blue-tinted slides as green. Subsequently, almost one-third of the naive subjects in the majority also made at least one green response (Moscovici, Lage, & Naffrechoux, 1969). Clearly, social influence flows in both directions between majorities and minorities in groups.

The question, then, is what the conditions are under which minority members, even as they are receiving corrective discretionary stimuli from their peers, can turn the tables and bring the group around to their position. Consider, for example, a lone deviant, someone demographically dissimilar to other group members, who at unpredictable times offers up alternative ways of behaving—and does so in a dogmatic style, despite the fact that his alternatives invariably are hard for others to comprehend. The chances that this individual will succeed in influencing the behavior or views of the majority are essentially nil. Most likely, all he will elicit from his peers is behavior aimed at getting him to be quiet, or at getting him out of the group altogether. Now consider two members who consistently behave in ways that clearly are at variance with group norms—but who also listen carefully to others' attempts to influence them and who respond thoughtfully, flexibly, and with conviction. These members have a very good chance of eventually altering the group norms that they have been violating.

Consistent with these examples, research evidence suggests that minority members are influential in groups when they present to the majority a clear, consistent, and credible alternative—something that is easy to comprehend but hard to dismiss. Specifically, minority influence should be greatest when the following five conditions are met:

The minority members offer an alternative to the majority position that is clear and unambiguous. If there are but small shades of difference in the behavior or views of the majority and the minority, then majority members may find it easy to assimilate minority views or behaviors, or to coexist with the differences on grounds that they are not important enough to bother with. The same may be true if majority members cannot understand or make sense of an ambiguous or complicated minority position. For a minority to sway the majority, it must be clear to all that the minority position can neither be ignored nor easily reconciled with the status quo.

Minority members maintain their position consistently over time. A central tenet of Moscovici's theory, and one of the earliest empirical findings in tests of the theory, is that minorities influence majorities in groups only when they hold consistently to their position (Maass & Clark, 1984; Moscovici, 1980; Nemeth, Mayseless, Sherman, & Brown, 1990; Nemeth, Swedlund, & Kanki, 1974). When minorities are erratic or inconsistent in their views or behavior, they have little or no influence. Thus, minority members who seek to sway a group to their position must hold their ground firmly even as they are subjected to influence attempts intended to bring them back into line.

There is, however, one qualification to this generalization: Minority members generally are more influential if they begin by conforming to majority norms and introduce their deviant views or behavior later in the life of the group (Levine, Saxe, & Harris, 1976; Levine, Sroka, &

Snyder, 1977). This strategy, of course, is consistent with the position of Hollander (1958), discussed earlier, that one's latitude to deviate depends on having a positive balance of idiosyncrasy credits. Research that has explicitly compared the Moscovici and Hollander prescriptions affirms that initial conformity does facilitate subsequent influence (but see Bray, Johnson, & Chilstrom, 1982, and Lortie-Lussier, 1987, for qualifications to this generalization).

Minority members stay together and present to the rest of the group a united front. Although majorities often give the appearance of unanimity, this may be because majority members have never needed to scrutinize the basis of their norms. When confronted by a subgroup that is (or that at least seems to be) of one mind, the majority is prompted to more actively consider its position. Such explorations can make visible previously hidden differences among members, introduce perspectives not previously considered, and open possibilities for change (Nemeth, 1986). For this to happen, however, minority members must sustain a common, relatively seamless position (Moscovici & Lage, 1976). Moreover, it takes more than one person to crack a majority: A solo deviant has little hope of converting a group to his or her position, notwithstanding the model provided for generations of students by Henry Fonda in the motion picture *Twelve Angry Men.* The solo deviant needs at least one solid supporter, and they must be strong enough to maintain a united front even as majority members express dislike for them (Nemeth & Wachtler, 1974, 1983) and attempt to identify, highlight, and widen differences among them.

Minority members succeed in avoiding rejection or institutionalization as the "group deviants." Although we have seen that groups are reluctant to overtly reject deviating members, minority members who press their case consistently and with conviction run a real risk of being assigned the *role* of deviant. Thus, those who wish to influence the majority must walk something of a tightrope, neither backing off so much that their views are not taken seriously, nor coming on so strong that they and their views are encapsulated and set aside. Research shows that the latter risk is especially high in two circumstances. One is when the interpersonal style of minority members is rigid or dogmatic. An unacceptable advocacy style makes it easy for majority members to dismiss beliefs, attitudes, or behaviors that they find unpalatable (Mugny, 1982). The second is when those advocating minority positions are *double minorities*—that is, they are dissimilar demographically or in identity group membership as well as in views or behavior (Clark & Maass, 1988; Maass, Clark, & Haberkorn, 1982; Martin, 1988). Both circumstances make it easier for a group to reject or dismiss the minority position than would be the case if the deviant members were "people like us" who behave reasonably and flexibly (but see Volpato, Maass, Mucchi-Faina, & Vitti, 1990, for a more differentiated view).

Group members who also are members of minority identity groups are at special risk. Because of their identity group memberships, these individuals may hold views or behave in ways that differ from the majority position in organizational groups. And because they are "double minorities" they may find that fellow group members do not take their positions seriously. Minority members may be tempted to respond by escalating the extremity of their views (or the intensity with which they express them) in hopes of influencing the majority—or, at least, engaging majority members in discussion about the proper way to think or act. Such escalation, however, may backfire, resulting in the rejection of double-minority members or in their institutionalization as group deviants. For group members who also are members of minority identity groups, the tightrope that must be walked to successfully influence the majority is both high and slippery.

The position advocated by the minority is consistent with dominant cultural values. Minorities generally have greater influence when what they are advocating is consistent with the zeitgeist (Clark, 1988; Clark & Maass, 1988; Maass, Clark, & Haberkorn, 1982; Paicheler, 1979). In these days, for example, it surely would be easier for a prodiversity minority to affect the norms of a demographically homogeneous majority than it would be for an antidiversity minority to succeed in a demographically mixed group. Although research in the Moscovici tradition has shown that minorities have far greater influence in groups than traditionally has been acknowledged in American social science, even minorities who meet all four of the above conditions are unlikely to succeed if they are attempting to swim upstream against a major current of the times.

In sum, the Moscovici tradition has served as a useful corrective to the American tendency to look from the group down, to emphasize majority influence and the social control of individuals. Although majority influence can be extraordinarily powerful in enforcing group norms, it runs the risk that members will maintain private reservations about the rightness of the majority position even as they behaviorally comply with it. Minority influence is more subtle but has more staying power. Indeed, research has shown that minority influence sometimes has no immediate behavioral effects at all, resulting instead in changes in majority members' private thoughts or feelings that only later are manifested in overt behavior (Maass & Clark, 1983; Nemeth & Wachtler, 1974).

Nemeth (1986) has argued that majority and minority influence invoke two different kinds of thought processes—specifically, that majority influence induces convergent thinking and that minority influence induces divergent thinking. That position is controversial, and the controversy is not yet resolved. What *has* been established empirically is that minority influence can expand the number of perspectives considered by a group, induce constructive intermember conflict, and promote originality of thought and action. Moreover, these effects have been shown to occur even when the minority position is substantively incorrect (Nemeth & Kwan, 1985, 1987; Nemeth & Staw, 1989; Nemeth & Wachtler, 1983).

The implication of these findings, as Nemeth notes, is that majority and minority influence should be differentially helpful to groups in different circumstances. When a group has a performance task to accomplish (i.e, one that members already know how to do, that merely requires well-motivated and well-coordinated execution), then majority influence should serve the group well. Minority influence, on the other hand, should be especially helpful for learning tasks when new ideas or perspectives are required for success.

Clearly, majority and minority influence each has its advantages—and its liabilities. The challenge for task-performing groups is to balance the two kinds of influence to achieve energy and efficiency even while remaining open to new ideas and learning. A group that relies too much on majority influence surely will succeed in taking the hill—but it may be the wrong hill. A group that is too open to minority perspectives, however, may well come up with an innovative plan of action to which all members are committed—but one that arrives too late to be of use. The best groups, presumably, have both minority and majority influence flowing simultaneously, with one or the other in ebb depending on the state of the group and its work.

Deviance and Group Effectiveness. The research findings described in the preceding pages depict a fairly primitive group process. Caricatured a bit, it operates as follows: Uniformity, conformity to norms, and adherence to one's role is the rule. When someone deviates, other members provide potent doses of discretionary stimuli intended to persuade or coerce the person to get back into line. This pressure continues until the individual (a) caves in and stops expressing deviant thoughts or exhibiting deviant behavior, (b) is psychologically or bodily rejected by the group or becomes

institutionalized as the group deviant, or (c) finally convinces the other group members—most likely in concert with one or more like-minded peers—of the rightness of his or her views or behavior.

The more the group has control of discretionary stimuli that are valued by group members, the more it can realize the first alternative—that is, it can effectively eliminate most signs of member deviance. In such circumstances, members may faithfully behave in accord with their roles in the group, refrain from violating group norms, and publicly endorse the "right" attitudes and beliefs. From all visible indicators, all may seem well with the group.

This pattern of dealing with deviance is dysfunctional for group well-being, however, for two reasons. First, if members comply primarily because of the application of pressure from their peers or the expected application of that pressure, the group runs the risk that commonly accompanies majority influence: public compliance at the expense of private acceptance (Campbell & Fairey, 1989; Kelman, 1961; Kiesler, 1969, pp. 279–295). And when a group is populated by individuals who are saying and doing one thing but thinking and feeling another, high effectiveness in the long haul is unlikely.

Second, to the extent that a group uses discretionary stimuli to swiftly extinguish any signs of deviance, it loses the opportunity to explore the usefulness and validity of the very norms and roles it is enforcing. For example, if compliance to a given behavioral norm is enforced so effectively that deviance from it never occurs, the group will be unable to discover whether that norm helps or hinders goal achievement. Just as it has been said that an unexamined life is not worth living, so it may also be true that an unexamined norm is not worth enforcing.

Despite these and other risks of excessive majority influence, the research literature documents that groups have a strong tendency to stamp out (or at least sweep under the rug) behaviors that are not congruent with traditional standards of acceptability. Groups rarely attempt to work through issues such as why people deviate from group norms, what the consequences of deviance are for the group, or ways that deviance can best be dealt with for the good of both individual members and the group as a whole. This style of social behavior is consistent with the observation of Argyris (1969) that most groups operate in accord with what he has called Pattern A interpersonal rules. In a Pattern A world, conformity takes precedence over experimentation, intellective and cognitive matters drive out feelings and emotionality, and interpersonal behavior is characterized more by diplomacy, mistrust, and caution than by interpersonal openness, trust, and risk-taking.

Consider, for example, the finding of Dentler and Erikson (1959, discussed earlier) that groups rarely reject deviants explicitly and instead assign them to special roles. It is doubtful that this phenomenon reflects a conscious and deliberate decision by group members that the group would be served best by retaining the deviant and using his or her behavior to help maintain group boundaries and equilibrium. More likely is that group members simply find themselves unable and unwilling to take on the emotional and interpersonal challenge of carrying out an overt rejection. By gradually defining a special role for the deviant member, the behavioral problem can be defused in the short term without having to deal with issues that are not discussable in a Pattern A world. The fact that there may be some functional payoffs for the group as a consequence of the deviant's continued group membership, then, is more a happy coincidence than the outcome of an informed and deliberate collective choice.

Despite some instances (such as that just described) in which Pattern A interpersonal behavior can lead to apparent solutions to problems that would be difficult for members to deal with directly, Argyris argues that Pattern A behavior impairs group effectiveness in the long run. For generating short-term solutions to easy tasks and interpersonal problems (such as, How can we get Richard to shut up so we can get back to work?), a Pattern A solution may be fine. But for more basic and more important problems (such as, How can we more effectively deal with and learn from our individual and collective failures?), groups that operate according to Pattern A rules are highly unlikely to generate lasting solutions based on valid data.

The tendency of groups to persist in handling deviance in accord with Pattern A rules is overdetermined and unlikely to change spontaneously. As noted earlier, it is emotionally stressful as well as challenging for group members to deal openly with questions of conformity, deviation, and interpersonal relationships. Moreover, many groups have a metanorm that inhibits discussion of their strategies for handling anxiety-arousing interpersonal matters such as these—a norm that itself is usually not discussable (Argyris, 1982). Finally, group dynamics having to do with deviance and dissent invariably are driven in part by psychodynamic forces of which members are not even aware (Elmes & Gemmill, 1990). For all these reasons, it is unlikely that members spontaneously will try out alternative strategies for dealing with deviance.

It may be impossible, therefore, for most groups to move beyond traditional patterns of interpersonal behavior without outside professional assistance. Even with assistance, as Bion (1959) points out, it may take a great deal of time and effort before members can overcome the basic assumptions that guide their early behavior and meld themselves into an effective and genuinely interdependent work group. Bion's prediction is borne out by Argyris (1985), who found that it can take literally years of work before managers become sufficiently skilled in alternative interpersonal strategies to be able to use them in real time when the interpersonal stakes are high.

So far, behavioral research is only beginning to provide the insights and tools that will be needed to help groups and their members better manage within-group influence processes. The development of such tools, clearly, will require a considerable investment of time and talent by social scientists. The potential payoff of this work, however, is commensurate with the investment required: If groups can be helped to learn how to deal skillfully with issues of conformity and deviance, then both team effectiveness and the personal well-being of group members should be greatly enhanced.

Conclusion: Social Influence and Group Effectiveness

This chapter has described and analyzed group influences on individuals in organizations. The focus has been on the means by which ambient stimuli, discretionary stimuli, and group norms alter member beliefs, attitudes, and behaviors. Throughout, we have given special attention to those contextual, structural, and personal variables that govern the strength and the constructiveness of group effects on members. To conclude the chapter, let us alter the perspective slightly and review what has been covered in terms of five mechanisms through which groups wield their influence.

Mechanisms of Group Influence

Groups provide the immediate context for individual thought and action. The attributes of the people in a group, the characteristics of its task, and the properties of the place where the group works collectively provide a stimulus-rich context for individual behavior. These ambient stimuli, which are pervasive but typically unnoticed by group members, have multiple effects. They cue members about available outcomes and means of obtaining them, they arouse or depress individuals' motives, and they even provide members with direct satisfactions and frustrations. Although ambient stimuli operate on individuals, they can

substantially influence the group as a whole when individuals' reactions to them are similar and mutually reinforcing.

Groups enhance or depress member arousal. The mere presence of other members in the group setting, as ambient stimuli, can affect an individual's level of arousal and thereby alter his or her behavior and work effectiveness. Performance tasks, it will be recalled, are executed better when arousal is high; learning tasks are better accomplished when arousal is low. A group's influence on member arousal extends far beyond the passive presence of other members, however. Groups can be actively and vigorously threatening or encouraging; alternatively, they can be caringly supportive and reassuring. The impact of such interpersonal interventions on a member's arousal, and therefore on his or her performance, can be profound.

Groups directly and contingently reinforce specific individual behaviors. The selective application of discretionary stimuli by a group shapes member behavior in real time. Although using discretionary stimuli in this way is appropriate for managing behavior in unfamiliar situations and on nonroutine tasks, this mechanism is quite inefficient. It requires, for example, more or less constant monitoring of behavior in the group as well as mindful decision making about what to say or do to individual members under what circumstances. These activities can result in an unacceptably high proportion of the group's energy being spent on "overhead" activities. A second potential problem is the persistence of member behavior. Although individuals may behave closely in accord with the wishes of their fellow members while in their presence, that behavior may not be sustained when the other members are absent. Finally, using discretionary stimuli to control member behavior runs a risk that the person may choose an action opposite to what is desired—even if that action is not in his or her best interest. When people believe that their freedom of choice is being constrained by others, they often reassert control by behaving perversely, a phenomenon that Brehm (1972) calls *psychological reactance*. Ironically, reactance is most likely to occur precisely when the discretionary stimuli used to manage individual behavior are especially strong—and therefore are likely to be experienced by members as controlling.

Groups affect behavior indirectly by shaping members' beliefs and attitudes. Because people generally try to behave in ways that are consistent with their beliefs and attitudes, group-induced changes in members' private thoughts and feelings have indirect effects on behavior. Especially potent are group influences on members' *expectancies* about behavior-outcome relationships (a belief state) and the *valences* they attach to outcomes (an affective state). As noted earlier, the expectancy theory of motivation posits that these particular beliefs and attitudes combine to determine volitional behavior. If, as a result of group influence, a person comes to believe that a certain set of outcomes will be obtained if he or she exhibits a given behavior, and if those outcomes come to be highly valued by the person, then he or she is likely to engage in the behavior spontaneously. This mechanism for group influence, then, is far more subtle than the direct use of discretionary stimuli to manage behavior. It also is more likely to generate a member's commitment to the behavior (the person, after all, has chosen it on his or her own), and there is little risk of psychological reactance. Therefore, the behavior is likely to persist across time, to generalize across situations, and to be exhibited even when other group members are not present. The major drawback of this mechanism is that changes in beliefs and attitudes generally do not occur quickly; indeed, if a member has not accepted the group as a point of reference, its impact on his or her beliefs and attitudes may be nil. It takes both time and acceptance before overt behaviors

that stem from group-induced changes in beliefs and attitudes are publicly exhibited.

Groups create and maintain normative structures that efficiently and powerfully shape and constrain behavior. Because norms are structural features of groups, they do not themselves generate stimuli that impinge on individuals. They are, nonetheless, among the most potent devices groups have for controlling members' behavior. Indeed, an especially strong norm (i.e., one that is both intense and well crystallized) may be invisible to an observer because members never risk violating it. Veteran members may rely on behavioral routines that lie well within the norm-specified range of tolerable behavior, and new members may learn quickly what behaviors are acceptable and adjust their behaviors accordingly.

Group norms are so efficient and powerful in controlling behavior that it is difficult to imagine how a group could sustain well-coordinated collective action without them. The problem, as we saw in the previous section, is that strong norms can result in the suppression of innovative ideas and perspectives. With persistence, two or more dissenting members sometimes can alter majority-enforced norms—or, at least, get the majority to review and reconsider what is being enforced. A deviant individual acting alone, however, is more likely to be converted to the majority position or to become institutionalized as the group deviant than to set in motion processes that help the group harvest the many benefits of minority influence.

The potency of each of the five mechanisms summarized here is greater the more "groupy" a group is. Moreover, several of the mechanisms may operate simultaneously. Even while a group is enforcing a norm that favors high members' productivity, for example, it also may be using discretionary stimuli to alter members' beliefs and attitudes about the consequences of working hard and well. It can be nearly impossible for an individual in a groupy group to maintain his or her own, unique direction when subjected to multiple, redundant group influences that persist over time.

Groupy is not, of course, a term in good currency among social scientists. A term that *is* in good currency, one that means much the same thing, but one that has been assiduously avoided throughout this chapter, is *cohesiveness*. Let us end the chapter by taking a relatively close look at this concept. Laypersons, and not a few scholars, tend to view group cohesiveness as a good thing, as a state that promotes both task effectiveness and member happiness. The following discussion means to dampen just a bit enthusiasm for the concept.

Cohesiveness, Conformity, and Performance

In general, the more cohesive a work group, the more members conform to group norms—for two different but mutually reinforcing reasons. First, it has long been recognized that pressures toward uniformity and conformity are greater in groups that are highly cohesive than in those that are not (Festinger, 1950). Second, group members are likely to value especially strongly the interpersonal rewards that are available in highly cohesive groups, precisely because of the strong positive feelings they have for each other and for the group as a whole. They are unlikely to place these rewards at risk by ignoring or defying pressures to comply with group standards. There is ample research evidence confirming the positive relationship between cohesiveness and conformity (Berkowitz, 1954; Lott & Lott, 1965, pp. 292–296; O'Reilly & Caldwell, 1985; Rutkowski, Gruder, & Romer, 1983; Schachter et al., 1951; Tajfel, 1969, pp. 334–347).

Evidence regarding the relationship between cohesiveness and performance, on the other hand, is problematic. Findings simply do not support the proposition that there is a straightforward positive association between cohesiveness and either individual or team

performance (Mudrack, 1989b; Stogdill, 1972). Rather than abandon the plausible hypothesis that more cohesive groups perform better, many researchers have turned their attention to moderator variables. Perhaps cohesiveness does foster performance, but only for certain types of tasks. Or only for groups composed in a certain way. Or only when the group leader uses a certain style. The search for the critical variables continues, as documented in a brief but pointed review by Levine and Moreland (1990, pp. 603–605). It may be, however, that untangling the cohesiveness-performance relationship will require more than just locating the right moderator variables. There are two additional considerations.

Direction of Norms.   While highly cohesive groups can ensure that most member behavior falls within norm-specified limits, the direction of those norms—that is, whether they support high or low productivity—is not related to how cohesive a group is (Berkowitz, 1954; Darley, Gross, & Martin, 1952; French, 1951; Schachter et al., 1951; Seashore, 1954).[20]

In the research by Schachter and his associates and by Berkowitz, for example, conditions of high versus low cohesiveness and high versus low productivity norms were created by experimental manipulation. The productivity of individual members was closer to the group norm in the highly cohesive groups for both high production and low production norms. Complementary findings are reported by Seashore (1954) using survey techniques. In a study of over 200 work groups in a machinery factory, Seashore found no correlation between cohesiveness and productivity, but, as would be expected, a negative relationship between cohesiveness and the amount of within-group variation in member productivity.

Openness to Dissent.   We saw earlier in the chapter that when majority influence dominates in a group, there is less tolerance for dissenting views and deviant behavior and little likelihood that members will actively explore the validity of the norms they are enforcing. Since majority influence is dominant in highly cohesive groups, such groups are especially vulnerable to this problem.

Research by Janis (1972, 1982) nicely illustrates the phenomenon. Janis suggests that when groups become excessively close-knit and develop a clubby feeling of "we-ness" (precisely the features of highly cohesive groups), they become susceptible to a pattern of behavior he calls *groupthink*. Among the several symptoms of groupthink are a marked decrease in the openness of group members to discrepant or unsettling information and a simultaneous unwillingness to examine seriously and to process such information if it does come to the group's attention. The result, Janis argues, is increased likelihood that the group, in a spirit of goodwill and shared confidence, will develop and implement a grossly inappropriate and ineffective course of action. Janis has shown how this phenomenon may have contributed to a number of historical fiascoes planned and executed by groups of government officials—such as the Bay of Pigs invasion and Britain's appeasement policy toward Hitler prior to World War II.[21]

Should Cohesiveness Be Avoided? Should one conclude from this analysis that it is advisable to discourage group cohesiveness, thereby decreasing the chances that performance-impairing norms or dissent-discouraging processes will develop? Such a position would indeed protect people and organizations from the seamy side of group dynamics, from the risks documented by Buys (1978) in scholarly prose and described by an apparently terrified *Time* magazine writer as follows:

A group has a life of its own that is far more than, and bizarrely different from, the sum of the individuals in it. The group belongs to a different moral order from the individual. It has its appetites and impulses, its voice, its collective will and emotions and personality. It has a mind of its own that can be frightening and inexplicable, like a domesticated animal, a pit bull or rottweiler, that may turn unpredictably vicious, attacking the children, doing wild-animal things no one could foresee. (Morrow, 1991, pp. 16–17)

But to protect against the negative excesses of groups by keeping them weak, or by discouraging them altogether, also would eliminate the very real benefits that tightly knit groups can bring to people and to organizations (Leavitt, 1975).[22] A cohesive group has some features akin to those of an audio amplifier: Whatever one puts in, be it annoying static or beautiful tones, comes out louder and carries farther. What, then, is required to increase the likelihood that what comes out of groups in organizations will be beautiful rather than painfully unpleasant? Is it possible to have, simultaneously, effective normative control of member behavior *and* support for minority influence processes that promote originality of thought and openness to alternative perspectives?

This question, in various forms, has been on the minds of scholars for some time (e.g., see Vroom, 1969, pp. 226–227), but progress in resolving it has been slow. It is clear that there is a relationship between the properties of group norms, including their direction, and the culture and climate of the surrounding organization. What is less clear is the direction of causation in that relationship. Do features of the broader organization somehow trickle down to groups and show up in their norms? Or do reverberations from group norms trickle up and eventually shape organizational culture and climate? And, to the present point, if one were interested in *altering* the direction of group norms, where would one begin—with the group, or with the context?

Although there are no definitive answers to such questions, it may be that the crux of the matter has to do with the *basis* of the cohesiveness that exists in a group—that is, with the reasons why members are attracted to a group and seek to stick together.

Task Versus Social Bases for Cohesiveness. In virtually all the research cited here cohesiveness was based on the interpersonal rewards present or potentially available in the group. The control of a group over its members in such circumstances derives largely from its capability to provide or withhold valued social satisfactions. As we have seen, this highly interpersonal orientation can create problems for a group and its members.

Were the basis for cohesiveness a shared commitment to the group task rather than the maintenance of interpersonal harmony, group dynamics might be quite different. The criterion for when to accept information and influence from others in the group, for example, might change from something like, Will questioning what is being said by the leader risk my being rejected or ridiculed? to Will such questioning help move our collective work forward? Group norms would still be strong in such groups, but they would encourage behaviors that facilitate performance effectiveness (such as actively questioning assumptions and explicitly testing the appropriateness of existing norms) rather than those that serve mainly to promote interpersonal comfort. This change in orientation also should tilt the direction of norms governing individual productivity toward high rather than low performance (Zaccaro & McCoy, 1988).

Findings consistent with this view were obtained many years ago by Back (1951) and by Thibaut and Strickland (1956). Back induced in dyads three different types of cohesiveness based on (a) personal attraction, (b) the prestige of being a group member, and (c) the task itself. The first two bases of cohesiveness are, of course, primarily interpersonal in nature, and

they prompted predictable patterns of social interaction. In the *personal attraction* condition, for example, members tended to make the interaction into a longish, pleasant conversation and to resent any rejection of an influence attempt; in the *prestige* condition they acted cautiously, took few interpersonal risks, and generally focused more on their own behavior and its interpersonal impact than on the work. In the *task* condition, however, group members did not spend much energy on interpersonal issues but instead worked intensely and efficiently on task activities.

An explicit comparison of the effects of task-based and interpersonal cohesion recently has been conducted by Zaccaro and Lowe (1988). These researchers experimentally created high and low levels of both task-based and interpersonal cohesion, and assessed the consequences for group interaction and performance. Only high task cohesion facilitated performance; groups high in interpersonal cohesion did not perform better than those low in interpersonal cohesion. High interpersonal cohesion did, however, generate more communication and higher interpersonal attraction among members. These results are exactly what would be predicted, and lend credence to the position that the *basis* of group cohesiveness may be critical in determining how, and how well, groups function.[23]

The problem in attempting to develop task-based cohesiveness in real-world work groups is twofold. First, many tasks in organizations are not set up in ways that engender the commitment of the people who perform them. The opposite often is true: The task may be so uninvolving that the group opts for a more interesting or satisfying alternative—such as "beating the system" or simply "enjoying one another's company." In such cases, the considerable power that cohesive groups have over their members may be used in ways that impair both the achievement of organizational goals and the personal learning of group members. Second, it is quite difficult, even when a task is objectively important, for group members to move beyond a focus on interpersonal rewards. The Kennedy cabinet during the Bay of Pigs crisis, for example, certainly had an important task. But the heavy investment each person had in remaining a valued member of that high-status, high-prestige group apparently was so strong that, for most of them, "not rocking the interpersonal boat" overwhelmed "raising the difficult questions."

To overcome these problems and create conditions that foster both efficient collective action and openness to dissent and learning requires more than just well-structured work. Existing evidence suggests that four organizational conditions are needed (for details, see Hackman, 1986, 1990; or Hackman & Walton, 1986). First is a clear, engaging direction for the group, a purpose or mission that stretches and tests the talent and imagination of the group and its members. Second is a well-structured performing unit—that is, a team that has the right number and mix of members, whose task is a whole and meaningful piece of work for which the group is responsible and for which it gets direct feedback, and that has real authority to manage its own internal processes. Third is an organizational context that supplies the group with ample informational and material resources, and that recognizes and reinforces the accomplishments of the group and its members. And fourth is hands-on leadership that provides team members with expert coaching and consultation about how to solve the problems and exploit the opportunities they encounter—and does so in a way that strengthens rather than undermines the group's ability to manage itself.

Group leaders, it will be recalled, generally have a positive balance of idiosyncrasy credits and more freedom to deviate from existing group norms than do rank-and-file group members. A leader who uses that latitude to push the limits and test the validity of existing norms, and to support exploration of the views and behaviors of members who hold minority

positions, can do much to help his or her group become a cohesive team that contributes simultaneously to organizational goal attainment, to the health of the group as a performing unit, and to the personal well-being of individual group members.

Work on this chapter was supported in part by Cooperative Agreement NCC 2-457 between NASA and Harvard University. Helpful bibliographic assistance was provided by Mark Cannon, Lynn Hilger, Bill Kahn, and Ruth Wageman.

Notes

1   The stimulus-focused approach taken in this chapter is but one of several possible conceptual strategies for analyzing group influences on individuals in organizations. Viable alternatives, which are not explicitly incorporated into the present treatment, include the social impact theory of Latane (1981), the social influence model of Tanford and Penrod (1984), and the group situation theory of Witte (1987). An attempt at formal integration of these models recently has been offered by Witte (1990). Reviews of the literature on a variety of issues having to do with social influence are found in collections of papers edited by Hendrick (1987) and by Paulus (1989).

2   Although certain issues relevant to the effectiveness of intact work groups are dealt with in the chapter, the focus is explicitly on social influence processes in organizational groups. We do not deal here with the considerable research literature on group problem solving, decision making, and task effectiveness. For reviews on these topics, see Hackman (1987); McGrath (1984); Sundstrom, DeMeuse, and Futrell (1990); and Stasser, Kerr, and Davis (1989).

3   This perspective derives from the expectancy theory of motivation, as originally formulated by Lewin (1938) and Tolman (1932), and applied to organizational settings by Vroom (1964) and others.

4   The likelihood that ambient stimuli will be overlooked as an explanation for group member beliefs, attitudes, and behaviors is further increased by the tendency of observers to base causal explanations either on proximal, salient events or on the

dispositions of individual actors (Jones & Nisbett, 1971). Because the group interaction process and the characteristics of individual group members offer apparently sufficient explanations, observers may never seriously entertain the possibility that what is transpiring has been shaped by the ambient stimuli that pervade the group setting.

5   The term explicitly refers to the *psychological* character of the physical environment. It complements the notions of *fixed feature space* and *semi-fixed feature space* of Hall (1969), which refer, respectively, to the objective permanence versus movability of the physical surround.

6   As used here, the term *role* refers simply to expectations that are shared by group members about who is to carry out what types of activities under what circumstances (Bates, 1956; Levinson, 1959; Thibaut & Kelley, 1959, chap. 8).

7   The distinction between *task* and *maintenance* functions is similar to the distinctions made by Homans (1950) between *internal* and *external* systems and by Bales (1953) between *task* and *socio-emotional* roles. For summary lists of task and maintenance functions that may become part of the roles of group members, see Benne and Sheats (1948, pp. 42–45) and Thibaut and Kelley (1959, p. 276). For a perceptive description of the dynamics and consequences of role differentiation in a boys' street-corner gang, see W. F. Whyte (1943).

8   For a detailed account of the findings of this study, see Friend, Rafferty, and Bramel (1990). These authors show how textbook accounts of the Asch study often distort the actual findings, accentuating subjects' conformity and deemphasizing their considerable independence.

9   Indeed, some writers have postulated that one's affective states (including attitudes, emotions, and motivational orientations) can best be understood when viewed as beliefs about the self (Bem, 1970, chap. 5; Schachter, 1964). Despite the considerable elegance of this view, we will defer consideration of the effects of group-supplied stimuli on member attitudes, values, and the like until the next major section, which focuses explicitly on how discretionary stimuli shape member affective states.

10   These three processes roughly parallel the functions of a coach for an actor learning a dramatic role. For a discussion of the dramaturgic model of complex role learning, see Goffman (1959) and Sarbin and Allen (1968b).

11   As used here, a *preference* refers to a choice by an individual regarding which of a finite number of stimuli or alternatives he or she likes best; an *attitude* is simply the amount of positive or negative affect an individual has for some person, thing, or concept; and a *value* is the amount of positive or negative affect an individual holds regarding some abstract ideal or end state. The three concepts are grouped because they all reflect an individual's affect toward something; they differ mainly in generality and in the level of abstraction of the referent.

12   It must be noted, however, that the properties of the *jobs* of the workers studied by Lieberman changed as well. In this case, it is likely that the changes in job characteristics reinforced the influences of the workers' new groups; this would not necessarily be true in other settings.

13   It should be noted, however, that the reason group members are predisposed toward compliance with the norm in such cases may be that the group previously has inculcated in them attitudes and beliefs that are consistent with it.

14   These four modes of responding (conformity, anticonformity, variability, and independence) were explicated by Willis (1965). More recently, Nail (1986) has provided a systematic review and theoretical integration of the ways individuals can respond to social influence. Reviews of the role of individual differences in conformity more generally are provided by Hare (1962, pp. 32–35), Marlowe and Gergen (1969), and Mehrabian and Ksionzky (1970).

15   Research on member compliance generally has focused on how groups use interpersonal rewards and sanctions to obtain member compliance with group norms. Little attention has been given to the use of material rewards, to the provision of information as a reward, or to the control of access to external rewards. The emphasis on interpersonal rewards and sanctions should not substantially restrict the generality of research findings, however, since interpersonal stimuli are the most commonly used means of obtaining norm compliance and moreover are powerful motivators for most people.

16   In an application of self-attention theory to the prediction of compliance with group standards, for example, Mullen (1983) found that member self-attentiveness increased as subgroup size decreased—resulting in higher conformity. And it has been found that the higher an individual's personal stake in a performance situation (i.e., something else is valued more than the group's behavior-contingent rewards or sanctions), the less the person conforms (Vaughan & Mangan, 1963).

17 Given that a *role* in a group is a set of behavioral norms that apply specifically to the role occupant, similar dynamics should occur when someone fails to fulfill his or her role in the group. Thus, a leader who quits leading, or who violates members' expectations about *how* he or she should lead, is deviating from a group norm—and therefore becomes a possible target of communications aimed at shaping up his or her behavior.

18 All three studies cited here (i.e., those of Schachter, of Emerson, and of Sampson & Brandon) were laboratory investigations that lasted less than an hour. In that time period it is doubtful either that influence attempts addressed to the deviant would have ceased with any finality, or that the sociometric rejection of the deviant would have approached maximum severity. To my knowledge, there has been no longitudinal study of deviation, communication, and rejection that examines what happens to a deviant after group members have made their best effort to get a person to change. In such circumstances, a sharper reduction of communication to the deviant or a more clear-cut rejection might be observed—despite the equivocal findings of short-term laboratory investigations of these same phenomena.

19 Research on minority influence generally addresses majority-minority differences in beliefs or attitudes; few studies deal explicitly with minority influences that involve overt behavioral violations of group norms. Although the generality of existing research findings remains an open question, it is reasonable to assume that they apply to violations of behavioral norms as well as to deviant beliefs and attitudes.

20 Cohesiveness was operationalized in these studies in a variety of ways. The Schachter and the Berkowitz studies employed an induction of congeniality to manipulate cohesiveness; the Seashore study used a questionnaire measure of group-supplied satisfactions; and the French and the Darley studies used a sociometrically based index. These differences illustrate a general and persistent problem with the concept—namely, confusion and disagreement about how it should be conceptualized and measured (Drescher, Burlingame, & Fuhriman, 1985; Evans & Jarvis, 1980; Hogg, 1987; Keyton &

Springston, 1990; Mudrack, 1989a; Stokes, 1983; Zander, 1979).

21 While the groupthink model is both popular and plausible, empirical support for it is mixed (Flowers, 1977; Leana, 1985; McCauley, 1989), and some scholars have proposed alternative theoretical mechanisms to explain the same phenomenon (e.g., see G. Whyte, 1989).

22 Sometimes managers are more than willing to accept this tradeoff. In an analysis of the role of groups in different types of organizations, Walton and Hackman (1986) found that control-oriented organizations tend not to use groups as performing units and, historically, have attempted to weaken even those groups that form spontaneously. In commitment-oriented organizations, on the other hand, groups are a favored design feature and are actively supported. Apparently managers in commitment-oriented organizations are as hopeful about the potential benefits of groups as their counterparts in control-oriented organizations are fearful of their risks.

23 A similar point was made many years ago by Gross and Martin (1952), who distinguished cohesiveness based on interpersonal attraction among members from that based on the group's ability to mediate attainment of otherwise unavailable individual goals (see also Hagstrom & Selvin, 1965). More recently, Tziner (1982) has argued that this distinction could help resolve confusion about the nature and effects of cohesiveness. Although Tziner's argument is plausible, it differs from the one being made here. Both socioemotional and instrumental cohesiveness place a person in a state of dependency on the group for valued *individual* outcomes—social acceptance in the former case and personal instrumental gain in the latter. Therefore, the dysfunctional dynamics often associated with excessively high cohesiveness would be predicted in both cases. When, however, cohesiveness is based on shared commitment to a *collective* task for which members are interdependent, more constructive group dynamics should ensue (Sakurai, 1975).

References

Allen, V. L. (1965). Situational factors in conformity. In L. Berkowitz (Ed.), *Advances in experimental social psychology* (Vol. 2). New York: Academic Press.

Allen, V. L., & Bragg, B. W. (1968a). Effect of group pressure on memory. *The Journal of Psychology, 69,* 19–32.

Allen, V. L., & Bragg, B. W. (1968b). Effect of social pressure on concept identification. *Journal of Educational Psychology, 59,* 302–308.

Allen, V. L., & Levine, J. M. (1971). Social support and conformity: The role of independent assessment of reality. *Journal of Experimental Social Psychology, 7,* 48–58.

Allport, F. H. (1955). *Theories of perception and the concept of structure.* New York: Wiley.

Alvarez, R. (1968). Informal reactions to deviance in simulated work organizations: A laboratory experiment. *American Sociological Review, 33,* 895–912.

Argyris, C. (1962). *Interpersonal competence and organizational effectiveness.* Homewood, IL: Irwin-Dorsey.

Argyris, C. (1969). The incompleteness of social psychological theory: Examples from small group, cognitive consistency, and attribution research. *American Psychologist, 24,* 893–908.

Argyris, C. (1982). *Reasoning, learning, and action.* San Francisco: Jossey-Bass.

Argyris, C. (1985). *Strategy, change and defensive routines.* Boston: Pitman.

Arrowood, A. J., & Friend, R. (1969). Other factors determining the choice of a comparison other. *Journal of Experimental Social Psychology, 5,* 233–239.

Asch, S. E. (1951). Effects of group pressure upon the modification and distortion of judgments. In H. Guetzkow (Ed.), *Groups, leadership, and men.* New Brunswick, NJ: Rutgers University Press.

Asch, S. E. (1955, November). Opinions and social pressure. *Scientific American, 193,* 31–35.

Asch, S. E. (1958). Effects of group pressure upon the modification and distortion of judgments. In E. E. Maccoby, T. M. Newcomb, & E. L. Hartley (Eds.), *Readings in social psychology* (3rd ed., pp. 174–183). New York: Holt, Rinehart and Winston.

Atkinson, J. W. (1954). Explorations using imaginative thought to assess the strength of human motives. In M. R. Jones (Ed.), *Nebraska symposium on motivation: 1954.* Lincoln: University of Nebraska Press.

Atkinson, J. W. (1958). *Motives in fantasy, action, and society.* Princeton: Van Nostrand.

Back, K. W. (1951). Influence through social communication. *Journal of Abnormal and Social Psychology, 46,* 190–207.

Bales, R. F. (1953). The equilibrium problem in small groups. In T. Parsons, R. F. Bales, & E. A. Shils (Eds.), *Working papers in the theory of action.* New York: Free Press.

Bales, R. F., & Slater, P. E. (1955). Role differentiation in small groups. In T. Parsons & R. F. Bales, (Eds.), *Family, socialization, and interaction process.* Glencoe, IL: Free Press.

Bandura, A. (1965). Vicarious processes: A case of no-trial learning. In L. Berkowitz (Ed.), *Advances in experimental social psychology* (Vol. 2). New York: Academic Press.

Bandura, A. (1977). *Social learning theory.* Englewood Cliffs, NJ: Prentice-Hall.

Barker, R. G. (1968). *Ecological psychology.* Stanford, CA: Stanford University Press.

Barker, R. G., & Wright, H. F. (1955). *Midwest and its children.* New York: Harper and Row.

Bates, A. P., & Cloyd, J. S. (1956). Toward the development of operations for defining group norms and member roles. *Sociometry, 19,* 26–39.

Bates, F. L. (1956). Position, role, and status: A reformulation of concepts. *Social Forces, 34,* 313–321.

Bavelas, A., Hastorf, A. H., Gross, A. E., & Kite, W. R. (1965). Experiments on the alteration of group structure. *Journal of Experimental Social Psychology, 1,* 55–70.

Bem, D. J. (1965). An experimental analysis of self-persuasion. *Journal of Experimental Social Psychology, 1,* 199–218.

Bem, D. J. (1970). *Beliefs, attitudes, and human affairs.* Belmont, CA: Brooks/Cole.

Benne, K., & Sheats, P. (1948). Functional roles of group members. *Journal of Social Issues, 4,* 41–49.

Berger, S. M., & Lambert, W. W. (1969). Stimulus-response theory in contemporary social psychology. In G. Lindzey & E. Aronson (Eds.), *The handbook of social psychology* (2nd ed.). Reading, MA: Addison-Wesley.

Berkowitz, L. (1954). Group standards, cohesiveness, and productivity. *Human Relations, 7,* 509–519.

Berkowitz, L. (1969). Social motivation. In G. Lindzey & E. Aronson (Eds.), *The handbook of social psychology* (2nd ed.). Reading, MA: Addison-Wesley.

Berkowitz, L. (1971). Reporting an experiment: A case study in leveling, sharpening, and assimilation. *Journal of Experimental Social Psychology, 7,* 237–243.

Berkowitz, L., & Howard, R. C. (1959). Reactions to opinion deviates as affected by affiliation need (*n*) and group member interdependence. *Sociometry, 22,* 81–91.

Bettenhausen, K., & Murnighan, J. K. (1985). The emergence of norms in competitive decision-making groups. *Administrative Science Quarterly, 30,* 350–372.

Biddle, B. J., & Thomas, E. J. (1966). *Role theory: Concepts and research.* New York: Wiley.

Bion, W. R. (1959). *Experiences in groups.* New York: Basic Books.

Bond, C. F., & Titus, L. J. (1983). Social facilitation: A meta-analysis of 241 studies. *Psychological Bulletin, 94,* 265–292.

Bray, R. M., Johnson, D., & Chilstrom, J. T., Jr. (1982). Social influence by group members with minority opinions: A comparison of Hollander and Moscovici. *Journal of Personality and Social Psychology, 43,* 78–88.

Brehm, J. (1972). *Responses to loss of freedom: A theory of psychological reactance.* Morristown, NJ: General Learning Press.

Burke, R. L., & Bennis, W. G. (1961). Changes in perception of self and others during human relations training. *Human Relations, 14,* 165–182.

Burns, T. (1955). The reference of conduct in small groups: Cliques and cabals in occupational milieux. *Human Relations, 8,* 467–486.

Buys, C. J. (1978). Humans would do better without groups. *Personality and Social Psychology Bulletin, 4,* 123–125.

Campbell, D. T. (1961). Conformity in psychology's theories of acquired behavioral dispositions. In I. A. Berg & B. M. Bass (Eds.), *Conformity and deviation.* New York: Harper and Row.

Campbell, J. D., & Fairey, P. J. (1989). Informational and normative routes to conformity: The effect of faction size as a function of norm extremity and attention to the stimulus. *Journal of Personality and Social Psychology, 57,* 457–468.

Cartwright, D., & Zander, A. (1968). *Group dynamics: Research and theory* (3rd ed.). New York: Harper and Row.

Clark, R. D. (1988). On predicting minority influence. *European Journal of Social Psychology, 18,* 515–526.

Clark, R. D., & Maass, A. (1988). The role of social categorization and perceived source credibility in minority influence. *European Journal of Social Psychology, 18,* 381–394.

Coch, L., & French, J. R. P., Jr. (1948). Overcoming resistance to change. *Human Relations, 1,* 512–532.

Cofer, C. N., & Appley, M. H. (1964). *Motivation: Theory and research.* New York: Wiley.

Comer, D. R. (in press). Organizational newcomers' acquisition of information from peers. *Management Communication Quarterly.*

Cooley, C. H. (1922). *Human nature and the social order.* New York: Scribner's.

Cottrell, N. B., Wack, D. L., Sekerak, F. J., & Rittle, R. H. (1968). Social facilitation of dominant responses by presence of an audience and the mere presence of others. *Journal of Personality and Social Psychology, 9,* 245–250.

Crutchfield, R. S. (1955). Conformity and character. *American Psychologist, 10,* 191–198.

Cummings, T. G. (1981). Designing effective work groups. In P. C. Nystrom & W. H. Starbuck (Eds.), *Handbook of organizational design* (Vol. 2). London: Oxford University Press.

Cushman, P. (1986). The self-besieged: Recruitment-indoctrination processes in restrictive groups. *Journal for the Theory of Social Behaviour, 16,* 1–32.

Darley, J., Gross, N., & Martin, W. (1952). Studies of group behavior: Factors associated with the productivity of groups. *Journal of Applied Psychology, 36,* 396–403.

Davis, J. H. (1973). Group decision and social interaction: A theory of social decision schemes. *Psychological Review, 80,* 97–125.

Davis, K. (1950). *Human society.* New York: Macmillan.

Davis, T., & Luthans, F. (1980). A social learning approach to organizational behavior. *Academy of Management Review, 5,* 281–290.

Dentler, R. A., & Erikson, K. T. (1959). The functions of deviance in groups. *Social Problems, 7,* 98–107.

Deutsch, M., & Gerard, H. B. (1955). A study of normative and informational social influences upon individual judgment. *Journal of Abnormal and Social Psychology, 51,* 629–636.

Downing, J. (1958). Cohesiveness, perception, and values. *Human Relations, 11,* 157–166.

Drescher, S., Burlingame, G., & Fuhriman, A. (1985). Cohesion: An odyssey in empirical understanding. *Small Group Behavior, 16,* 3–30.

Elmes, M. B., & Gemmill, G. (1990). The psychodynamics of mindlessness and dissent in small groups. *Small Group Research, 21,* 28–44.

Emerson, R. M. (1954). Deviation and rejection: An experimental replication. *American Sociological Review, 19,* 688–693.

Evans, N. J., & Jarvis, P. A. (1980). Group cohesion: A review and reevaluation. *Small Group Behavior, 11,* 359–370.

Feldman, D. C. (1984). The development and enforcement of norms. *Academy of Management Review, 9,* 47–53.

Ferguson, L. W. (1944). An analysis of the generality of suggestibility to group opinion. *Character and Personality, 12,* 237–243.

Festinger, L. (1950). Informal social communication. *Psychological Review, 57,* 157–166.

Festinger, L. (1953). Group attraction and membership. In D. Cartwright & A. Zander (Eds.), *Group dynamics: Research and theory.* Evanston, IL: Row, Peterson.

Festinger, L. (1954). A theory of social comparison processes. *Human Relations, 7,* 117–140.

Festinger, L. (1957). *A theory of cognitive dissonance.* Stanford, CA: Stanford University Press.

Festinger, L., Schachter, S., & Back, K. (1950). *Social pressures in informal groups.* Stanford, CA: Stanford University Press.

Festinger, L., & Thibaut, J. (1951). Interpersonal communication in small groups. *Journal of Abnormal and Social Psychology, 46,* 92–99.

Fishbein, M. (1967). A behavior theory approach to the relations between beliefs about an object and the attitude toward the object. In M. Fishbein (Ed.), *Readings in attitude theory and measurement.* New York: Wiley.

Flowers, M. (1977). A laboratory test of some implications of Janis's groupthink hypothesis. *Journal of Personality and Social Psychology, 1,* 288–299.

Foa, U. G. (1971, January 29). Interpersonal and economic sources. *Science, 171,* 345–351.

French, R. L. (1951). Sociometric status and individual adjustment among naval recruits. *Journal of Abnormal and Social Psychology, 46,* 64–71.

Friend, R., Rafferty, Y., & Bramel, D. (1990). A puzzling misinterpretation of the Asch "conformity" study. *European Journal of Social Psychology, 20,* 29–44.

Geen, R. G. (1989). Alternative conceptions of social facilitation. In P. B. Paulus (Ed.), *Psychology of group influence* (2nd ed.). Hillsdale, NJ: Erlbaum.

Geen, R. G., & Gange, J. J. (1983). Social facilitation: Drive theory and beyond. In H. H. Blumberg, A. P. Hare, V. Kent, & M. Davies (Eds.), *Small groups and social interactions* (Vol. 1). Chichester, England: Wiley.

George, J. M. (1990). Personality, affect, and behavior in groups. *Journal of Applied Psychology, 75,* 107–116.

Gerard, H. B., & Rabbie, J. M. (1961). Fear and social comparison. *Journal of Abnormal and Social Psychology, 62,* 586–592.

Gersick, C. J. G., & Hackman, J. R. (1990). Habitual routines in task-performing teams. *Organizational Behavior and Human Decision Processes, 47,* 65–97.

Gibb, C. A. (1969). Leadership. In G. Lindzey & E. Aronson (Eds.), *The handbook of social psychology* (2nd ed.). Reading, MA: Addison-Wesley.

Giordano, P. C. (1983). Sanctioning the high-status deviant: An attributional analysis. *Social Psychology Quarterly, 46,* 329–342.

Goffman, E. (1959). *The presentation of self in everyday life.* Garden City, NY: Doubleday.

Goffman, E. (1963). *Behavior in public places.* New York: Free Press.

Golembiewski, R. T. (1962). *The small group.* Chicago: University of Chicago Press.

Graham, D. (1962). Experimental studies of social influence in simple judgment situations. *Journal of Social Psychology, 56,* 245–269.

Griffin, R. W. (1983). Objective and social sources of information in task redesign: A field experiment. *Administrative Science Quarterly, 28,* 184–200.

Gross, N., & Martin, W. T. (1952). On group cohesiveness. *American Journal of Sociology, 57,* 546–554.

Guerin, B. (1986). Mere presence effects in humans: A review. *Journal of Experimental Social Psychology, 22,* 38–77.

Guetzkow, H. (1960). Differentiation of roles in task-oriented groups. In D. Cartwright & A. Zander (Eds.), *Group dynamics: Research and theory* (2nd ed.). Evanston, IL: Row, Peterson.

Hackman, J. R. (1976). Group influences on individuals. In M. Dunnette (Ed.), *Handbook of industrial and organizational psychology* (1st ed., pp. 1455–1525). Chicago: Rand McNally.

Hackman, J. R. (1986). The psychology of self-management in organizations. In M. S. Pallack & R. O. Perloff (Eds.), *Psychology and work: Productivity, change, and employment.* Washington, DC: American Psychological Association.

Hackman, J. R. (1987). The design of work teams. In J. W. Lorsch (Ed.), *Handbook of organizational behavior.* Englewood Cliffs, NJ: Prentice-Hall.

Hackman, J. R. (Ed.). (1990). *Leading groups in organizations.* San Francisco: Jossey-Bass.

Hackman, J. R., & Lawler, E. E. (1971). Employee reactions to job characteristics. *Journal of Applied Psychology Monograph, 55,* 259–286.

Hackman, J. R., & Morris, C. G. (1975). Group tasks, group interaction process, and group performance effectiveness: A review and proposed integration. In L. Berkowitz (Ed.), *Advances in experimental social psychology* (Vol. 9). New York: Academic Press.

Hackman, J. R., & Oldham, G. R. (1976). Motivation through the design of work: Test of a theory. *Organizational Behavior and Human Performance, 60,* 159–170.

Hackman, J. R., & Oldham, G. R. (1980). *Work redesign.* Reading, MA: Addison-Wesley.

Hackman, J. R., & Walton, R. E. (1986). Leading groups in organizations. In P. S. Goodman (Ed.), *Designing effective work groups.* San Francisco: Jossey-Bass.

Hagstrom, W. O., & Selvin, H. C. (1965). Two dimensions of cohesiveness in small groups. *Sociometry, 28,* 30–43.

Hall, E. T. (1969). *The hidden dimension* (2nd ed.). Garden City, NY: Doubleday.

Hare, A. P. (1962). *Handbook of small group research.* New York: Free Press.

Harvey, O. J., & Consalvi, C. (1960). Status and conformity to pressures in informal groups. *Journal of Abnormal and Social Psychology, 60,* 182–187.

Haythorn, W. W. (1968). The composition of groups: A review of the literature. *Acta Psychologica, 28,* 97–128.

Heider, F. (1958). *The psychology of interpersonal relations.* New York: Wiley.

Henchy, T., & Glass, D. (1968). Evaluation apprehension and the social facilitation of dominant and subordinate responses. *Journal of Abnormal and Social Psychology, 10,* 446–454.

Hendrick, C. (Ed.). (1987). *Group processes.* Newbury Park, CA: Sage.

Hogg, M. A. (1987). Social identity and group cohesiveness. In J. C. Turner, M. A. Hogg, P. J. Oakes, S. D. Reicher, & M. S. Wetherell (Eds.), *Rediscovering the social group: A self-categorization theory.* Oxford, England: Blackwell.

Hollander, E. P. (1958). Conformity, status, and idiosyncrasy credit. *Psychological Review, 65,* 117–127.

Hollander, E. P. (1960). Competence and conformity in the acceptance of influence. *Journal of Abnormal and Social Psychology, 61,* 361–365.

Hollander, E. P. (1964). *Leaders, groups, and influence.* New York: Oxford University Press.

Homans, G. C. (1950). *The human group.* New York: Harcourt, Brace and World.

Hughes, E. C. (1946). The knitting of racial groups in industry. *American Sociological Review, 11,* 512–519.

Jackson, J. (1960). Structural characteristics of norms. In N. B. Henry (Ed.), *Dynamics of instructional groups: The fifty-ninth yearbook of the National Society for the Study of Education.* Chicago: University of Chicago Press.

Jackson, J. (1965). Structural characteristics of norms. In I. D. Steiner & M. Fishbein (Eds.), *Current studies in social psychology.* New York: Holt, Rinehart and Winston.

Jackson, J. (1966). A conceptual and measurement model for norms and roles. *Pacific Sociological Review, 9,* 35–47.

Jackson, J. (1975). Normative power and conflict potential. *Sociological Methods and Research, 4,* 237–263.

Jackson, J. (1988). *The return potential model for norms and roles: A bibliography of published and unpublished writing.* Unpublished manuscript.

Janis, I. L. (1972). *Victims of groupthink.* New York: Houghton Mifflin.

Janis, I. L. (1982). *Groupthink* (2nd ed.). Boston: Houghton Mifflin.

Jones, E. E., & Gerard, H. B. (1967). *Foundations of social psychology.* New York: Wiley.

Jones, E. E., & Nisbett, R. E. (1971). The actor and the observer: Divergent perceptions of the causes of behavior. In E. E. Jones, D. E. Kanouse, H. H. Kelley, R. E. Nisbett, S. Valins, & B. Weiner (Eds.), *Attribution: Perceiving the causes of behavior.* Morristown, NJ: General Learning Press.

Kalish, H. I. (1969). Stimulus generalization: Alternative explanations. In M. H. Marx (Ed.), *Learning: Processes*. New York: Macmillan.

Kaplan, M. F. (1987). The influencing process in group decision making. In C. Hendrick (Ed.), *Group processes*. Newbury Park, CA: Sage.

Kelley, H. H. (1952). Two functions of reference groups. In G. E. Swanson, T. M. Newcomb, & E. L. Hartley (Eds.), *Readings in social psychology*. New York: Holt, Rinehart and Winston.

Kelley, H. H., & Lamb, T. W. (1957). Certainty of judgment and resistance to social influences. *Journal of Abnormal and Social Psychology, 55*, 137–139.

Kelman, H. C. (1950). Effects of success and failure on "suggestibility" in the autokinetic situation. *Journal of Abnormal and Social Psychology, 45*, 267–285.

Kelman, H. C. (1958). Compliance, identification, and internalization: Three processes of attitude change. *Journal of Conflict Resolution, 2*, 50–60.

Kelman, H. C. (1961). Processes of opinion change. *Public Opinion Quarterly, 25*, 57–78.

Kemper, T. D. (1968). Reference groups, socialization, and achievement. *American Sociological Review, 33*, 31–45.

Kent, R. N., & McGrath, J. E. (1969). Task and group characteristics as factors influencing group performance. *Journal of Experimental Social Psychology, 5*, 429–440.

Keyton, J., & Springston, J. (1990). Redefining cohesiveness in groups. *Small Group Research, 21*, 234–254.

Kiesler, C. A. (1969). Group pressure and conformity. In J. Mills (Ed.), *Experimental social psychology*. New York: Macmillan.

Klein, S. M. (1971). *Workers under stress: The impact of work pressure on group cohesion*. Lexington: University Press of Kentucky.

Klinger, E. (1966). Fantasy need achievement as a motivational construct. *Psychological Bulletin, 66*, 291–308.

Komaki, J. L., Desselles, M. I., & Bowman, E. D. (1989). Definitely not a breeze: Extending an operant model of effective supervision to teams. *Journal of Applied Psychology, 74*, 522–529.

Kruglanski, A. W., & Mayseless, O. (1987). Motivational effects in the social comparison of opinions. *Journal of Personality and Social Psychology, 53*, 834–842.

Kruglanski, A. W., & Mayseless, O. (1990). Classic and current social comparison research: Expanding the perspective. *Psychological Bulletin, 108*, 195–208.

Latane, B. (Ed.). (1966). Studies in social comparison. *Journal of Experimental Social Psychology*, (Suppl. 1).

Latane, B. (1981). Psychology of social impact. *American Psychologist, 36*, 343–356.

League, B. J., & Jackson, D. N. (1964). Conformity, veridicality, and self-esteem. *Journal of Abnormal and Social Psychology, 68*, 113–115.

Leana, C. (1985). A partial test of Janis' groupthink model: Effects of group cohesiveness and leader behavior on defective decision making. *Journal of Management, 11*, 5–17.

Leavitt, H. J. (1975). Suppose we took groups seriously... In E. L. Cass & F. G. Zimmer (Eds.), *Man and work in society*. New York: Van Nostrand Reinhold.

Levine, J. M. (1989). Reaction to opinion deviance in small groups. In P. B. Paulus (Ed.), *Psychology of group influence* (2nd ed.). Hillsdale, NJ: Erlbaum.

Levine, J. M., & Moreland, R. L. (1990). Progress in small group research. *Annual Review of Psychology, 41*, 585–634.

Levine, J. M., & Russo, E. M. (1987). Majority and minority influence. In C. Hendrick (Ed.), *Group processes*. Newbury Park, CA: Sage.

Levine, J. M., Saxe, L., & Harris, H. J. (1976). Reaction to attitudinal deviance: Impact of deviate's direction and distance of movement. *Sociometry, 39*, 97–107.

Levine, J. M., Sroka, K. R., & Snyder, H. N. (1977). Group support and reaction to stable and shifting agreement/disagreement. *Sociometry, 40*, 214–224.

Levinson, D. J. (1959). Role, personality, and social structure in the organizational setting. *Journal of Abnormal and Social Psychology, 58*, 170–180.

Lewin, K. (1938). The conceptual representation and the measurement of psychological forces. *Contributions to Psychological Theory, 1*, No. 4.

Lieberman, S. (1956). The effects of change in roles on the attitudes of role occupants. *Human Relations, 9*, 385–402.

Lortie-Lussier, M. (1987). Minority influence and idiosyncrasy credit: A new comparison of the

Moscovici and Hollander theories of innovation. *European Journal of Social Psychology, 17*, 431–446.

Lott, B. E. (1955). Attitude formation: The development of a color-preference response through mediated generalization. *Journal of Abnormal and Social Psychology, 50*, 321–326.

Lott, A. J., & Lott, B. E. (1965). Group cohesiveness as interpersonal attraction: A review of relationships with antecedent and consequent variables. *Psychological Bulletin, 64*, 259–309.

Luthans, F., & Kreitner, R. (1975). *Organizational behavior modification*. Glenview, IL: Scott, Foresman.

Maass, A., & Clark, R. D. (1983). Internalization versus compliance: Differential processes underlying minority influence and conformity. *European Journal of Social Psychology, 13*, 45–55.

Maass, A., & Clark, R. D. (1984). Hidden impact of minorities: Fifteen years of minority influence research. *Psychological Bulletin, 95*, 428–450.

Maass, A., Clark, R. D., & Haberkorn, G. (1982). The effects of differential ascribed category membership and norms on minority influence. *European Journal of Social Psychology, 12*, 89–104.

Maass, A., West, S. G., & Cialdini, R. B. (1987). Minority influence and conversion. In C. Hendrick (Ed.), *Group processes*. Newbury Park, CA: Sage.

Machotka, O. (1964). *The unconscious in social relations*. New York: Philosophical Library.

Maier, N. R. F., & Solem, A. R. (1952). The contribution of a discussion leader to the quality of group thinking. *Human Relations, 5*, 277–288.

Manz, C. C., & Sims, H. P. (1986). Beyond imitation: Complex behavioral and affective linkages resulting from exposure to leadership training models. *Journal of Applied Psychology, 71*, 571–578.

March, J. G. (1954). Group norms and the active minority. *American Sociological Review, 19*, 733–741.

Marlowe, D., & Gergen, K. J. (1969). Personality and social interaction. In G. Lindzey & E. Aronson (Eds.), *The handbook of social psychology* (2nd ed.). Reading, MA: Addison-Wesley.

Martin, R. (1988). Ingroup and outgroup minorities: Differential impact upon public and private response. *European Journal of Social Psychology, 18*, 39–52.

Mathewson, S. B. (1931). *Restriction of output among unorganized workers*. New York: Viking.

McCauley, C. (1989). The nature of social influence in groupthink: Compliance and internalization.

Journal of Personality and Social Psychology, 57, 250–260.

McClelland, D. C. (1951). *Personality*. New York: Sloane.

McClelland, D. C., Atkinson, J. W., Clark, R. A., & Lowell, E. L. (1953). *The achievement motive*. New York: Appleton-Century-Crofts.

McGrath, J. E. (1976). Stress and behavior in organizations. In M. D. Dunnette (Ed.), *Handbook of industrial and organizational psychology*. Chicago: Rand McNally.

McGrath, J. E. (1984). *Groups: Interaction and performance*. Englewood Cliffs, NJ: Prentice-Hall.

Mehrabian, A., & Ksionzky, S. (1970). Models for affiliative and conformity behavior. *Psychological Bulletin, 74*, 110–126.

Merton, R. K., & Kitt, A. S. (1950). Contributions to the theory of reference group behavior. In R. K. Merton & P. F. Lazarsfeld (Eds.), *Continuities in social research: Studies in the scope and method of the American soldier*. Glencoe, IL: Free Press.

Miller, G. R., & Tiffany, W. R. (1963). The effects of group pressure on judgments of speech sounds. *Journal of Speech and Hearing Research, 6*, 149–156.

Miller, N. E., & Dollard, J. (1941). *Social learning and imitation*. New Haven, CT: Yale University Press.

Mills, T. M. (1967). *The sociology of small groups*. Englewood Cliffs, NJ: Prentice-Hall.

Moore, W. E. (1969). Social structure and behavior. In G. Lindzey & E. Aronson (Eds.), *The handbook of social psychology* (2nd ed.). Reading, MA: Addison-Wesley.

Moreland, R. L., & Levine, J. M. (1989). Newcomers and oldtimers in small groups. In P. B. Paulus (Ed.), *Psychology of group influence* (2nd ed.). Hillsdale, NJ: Erlbaum.

Morrow, L. (1991, April). Rough justice. *Time*, pp. 16–17.

Moscovici, S. (1980). Toward a theory of conversion behavior. In L. Berkowitz (Ed.), *Advances in experimental social psychology* (Vol. 13). New York: Academic Press.

Moscovici, S., & Lage, E. (1976). Studies in social influence: III. Majority vs. minority influence in a group. *European Journal of Social Psychology, 6*, 149–174.

Moscovici, S., Lage, E., & Naffrechoux, M. (1969). Influence of a consistent minority on the responses of a majority in a colour perception task. *Sociometry, 32,* 365–379.

Mudrack, P. E. (1989a). Defining group cohesiveness: A legacy of confusion. *Small Group Behavior, 20,* 37–49.

Mudrack, P. E. (1989b). Group cohesiveness and productivity: A closer look. *Human Relations, 42,* 771–785.

Mugny, G. (1982). *The power of minorities.* London: Academic Press.

Mullen, B. (1983). Operationalizing the effect of the group on the individual: A self-attention perspective. *Journal of Experimental Social Psychology, 19,* 295–322.

Nail, P. R. (1986). Toward an integration of some models and theories of social response. *Psychological Bulletin, 100,* 190–206.

Nemeth, C. J. (1986). Differential contributions of majority and minority influence. *Psychological Review, 93,* 1–10.

Nemeth, C. J., & Kwan, J. (1985). Originality of word associations as a function of majority vs. minority influence. *Social Psychology Quarterly, 48,* 277–282.

Nemeth, C. J., & Kwan, J. (1987). Minority influence, divergent thinking, and detection of correct solutions. *Journal of Applied Social Psychology, 17,* 786–797.

Nemeth, C. J., Mayseless, O., Sherman, J., & Brown, Y. (1990). Exposure to dissent and recall of information. *Journal of Personality and Social Psychology, 58,* 429–437.

Nemeth, C. J., & Staw, B. M. (1989). The tradeoffs of social control and innovation in groups and organizations. In L. Berkowitz (Ed.), *Advances in experimental social psychology* (Vol. 22). New York: Academic Press.

Nemeth, C. J., Swedlund, M., & Kanki, B. (1974). Patterning of the minority's response and their influence on the majority. *European Journal of Social Psychology, 4,* 53–64.

Nemeth, C. J., & Wachtler, J. (1974). Creating the perceptions of consistency and competence: A necessary condition for minority influence. *Sociometry, 37,* 529–540.

Nemeth, C. J., & Wachtler, J. (1983). Creative problem solving as a result of majority and minority influence. *European Journal of Social Psychology, 13,* 45–55.

Newcomb, T. M. (1952). Attitude development as a function of reference groups: The Bennington Study. In C. G. Swanson, T. M. Newcomb, & E. L. Hartley (Eds.), *Readings in social psychology* (Rev. ed.). New York: Holt, Rinehart and Winston.

Newcomb, T. M. (1954). *Social psychology.* New York: Dryden.

Nisbett, R. E., & Valins, S. (1972). Perceiving the causes of one's own behavior. In E. E. Jones, D. E. Kanouse, H. H. Kelley, R. E. Nisbett, S. Valins, & B. Weiner (Eds.), *Attribution: Perceiving the causes of behavior.* New York: General Learning Press.

Nolen, W. A. (1970). *The making of a surgeon.* New York: Random House.

Ono, K., & Davis, J. H. (1988). Individual judgment and group interaction: A variable perspective approach. *Organizational Behavior and Human Decision Processes, 41,* 211–232.

Opp, K. D. (1982). The evolutionary emergence of norms. *British Journal of Social Psychology, 21,* 139–149.

O'Reilly, C. A., & Caldwell, D. F. (1985). The impact of normative social influence and cohesiveness on task perceptions and attitudes: A social information processing approach. *Journal of Occupational Psychology, 58,* 193–206.

Paicheler, G. (1979). Polarization of attitudes in homogeneous and heterogeneous groups. *European Journal of Social Psychology, 9,* 85–96.

Patchen, M. (1961). *The choice of wage comparison.* Englewood Cliffs, NJ: Prentice-Hall.

Paulus, P. B. (Ed.). (1989). *Psychology of group influence* (2nd ed.). Hillsdale, NJ: Erlbaum.

Paulus, P. B., & Nagar, D. (1989). Environmental influences on groups. In P. Paulus (Ed.), *Psychology of group influence* (2nd ed.). Hillsdale, NJ: Erlbaum.

Porter, L. W., Lawler, E. E., & Hackman, J. R. (1975). *Behavior in organizations.* New York: McGrawHill.

Rabbie, J. M. (1963). Differential preferences for companionship under threat. *Journal of Abnormal and Social Psychology, 67,* 643–648.

Rhine, J. (1960). The effects of peer group influence upon concept-attitude development and change. *Journal of Social Psychology, 51,* 173–179.

Ridgeway, C. L. (1981). Nonconformity, competence, and influence in groups: A test of two theories. *American Sociological Review, 46,* 333–347.

Robinson-Staveley, K., & Cooper, J. (1990). Mere presence, gender, and reactions to computers: Studying human-computer interaction in the social context. *Journal of Experimental Social Psychology, 26*, 168–183.

Roethlisberger, F. J., & Dickson, W. J. (1939). *Management and the worker.* Cambridge: Harvard University Press.

Rommetveit, R. (1955). *Social norms and roles.* Minneapolis: University of Minnesota Press.

Rosenbaum, M. E., & Arenson, S. J. (1968). Observational learning: Some theory, some variables, some findings. In E. C. Simmel, R. A. Hoppe, & C. A. Milton (Eds.), *Social facilitation and imitative behavior.* Boston: Allyn & Bacon.

Rosenberg, L. A. (1961). Group size, prior experience, and conformity. *Journal of Abnormal and Social Psychology, 63*, 436–437.

Rosenberg, M. J. (1956). Cognitive structure and attitudinal effect. *Journal of Abnormal and Social Psychology, 53*, 367–372.

Rousseau, D. M. (1978). Characteristics of departments, positions, and individuals: Contexts for attitudes and behavior. *Administrative Science Quarterly, 23*, 521–540.

Roy, D. (1952). Quota restriction and gold bricking in a machine shop. *American Journal of Sociology, 57*, 427–442.

Rutkowski, G. K., Gruder, C. L., & Romer, D. (1983). Group cohesiveness, social norms, and bystander intervention. *Journal of Personality and Social Psychology, 44*, 545–552.

Ryle, G. (1949). *The concept of mind.* London: Hutchinson.

Sakurai, M. M. (1975). Small group cohesiveness and detrimental conformity. *Sociometry, 38*, 340–357.

Salancik, G. R., & Pfeffer, J. (1977). An examination of need-satisfaction models of job attitudes. *Administrative Science Quarterly, 22*, 427–456.

Salancik, G. R., & Pfeffer, J. (1978). A social information processing approach to job attitudes and task design. *Administrative Science Quarterly, 23*, 224–253.

Sampson, E. E., & Brandon, A. C. (1964). The effects of role and opinion deviation on small group behavior. *Sociometry, 27*, 261–281.

Sanders, G. S. (1981). Driven by distraction: An integrative review of social facilitation theory and research. *Journal of Experimental Social Psychology, 17*, 227–251.

Sanna, L. J., & Shotland, R. L. (1990). Valence of anticipated evaluation and social facilitation. *Journal of Experimental Social Psychology, 26*, 82–92.

Sarbin, T. R., & Allen, V. L. (1968a). Increasing participation in a natural group setting: A preliminary report. *The Psychological Record, 18*, 1–7.

Sarbin, T. R., & Allen, V. L. (1968b). Role theory. In G. Lindzey & E. Aronson (Eds.), *The handbook of social psychology* (2nd ed.). Reading, MA: Addison-Wesley.

Schachter, S. (1951). Deviation, rejection, and communication. *Journal of Abnormal and Social Psychology, 46*, 190–207.

Schachter, S. (1959). *The psychology of affiliation.* Stanford, CA: Stanford University Press.

Schachter, S. (1964). The interaction of cognitive and physiological determinants of emotional state. In L. Berkowitz (Ed.), *Advances in experimental social psychology* (Vol. 1). New York: Academic Press.

Schachter, S., Ellertson, N., McBride, D., & Gregory, D. (1951). An experimental study of cohesiveness and productivity. *Human Relations, 4*, 229–238.

Schachter, S., Nuttin, J., Demonchaux, C., Maucorps, P. H., Osmer, D., Duijker, H., Rommetveit, R., & Israel, J. (1954). Cross-cultural experiments on threat and rejection. *Human Relations, 7*, 403–439.

Schein, E. H. (1956). The Chinese indoctrination program for prisoners of war. *Psychiatry, 19*, 149–172.

Schlesinger, A. M. (1965). *1000 days.* Boston: Houghton Mifflin.

Schmitt, B. H., Gilovich, T., Goore, N., & Joseph, L. (1986). Mere presence and social facilitation: One more time. *Journal of Experimental Social Psychology, 22*, 242–248.

Schneider, B. (1987). The people make the place. *Personnel Psychology, 40*, 437–453.

Scott, W. E. (1966). Activation theory and task design. *Organizational Behavior and Human Performance, 1*, 3–30.

Seashore, S. (1954). *Group cohesiveness in the industrial work group.* Ann Arbor: Institute for Social Research, University of Michigan.

Seta, C. E., Seta, J. J., Donaldson, S., & Wang, M. A. (1988). The effects of evaluation on organizational processing. *Personality and Social Psychology Bulletin, 14*, 604–609.

Sherif, M. (1936). *The psychology of social norms*. New York: HarperCollins.

Sherif, M. (1965). Formation of social norms: The experimental paradigm. In H. Proshansky & B. Seidenberg (Eds.), *Basic studies in social psychology*. New York: Holt, Rinehart and Winston.

Shure, G. H., Rogers, M. S., Larsen, I. M., & Tassone, J. (1962). Group planning and task effectiveness. *Sociometry, 25*, 263–282.

Siegel, A. E., & Siegel, S. (1957). Reference groups, membership groups, and attitude change. *Journal of Abnormal and Social Psychology, 55*, 360–364.

Sims, H. P., & Manz, C. C. (1984). Observing leader verbal behavior: Toward reciprocal determinism in leadership theory. *Journal of Applied Psychology, 69*, 222–232.

Singer, J. E. (1966). Social comparison—progress and issues. In B. Latane (Ed.), Studies in social comparison. *Journal of Experimental Social Psychology* (Suppl. 1), 103–110.

Slater, P. E. (1955). Role differentiation in small groups. *American Sociological Review, 20*, 300–310.

Staats, A. W., & Staats, C. K. (1958). Attitudes established by classical conditioning. *Journal of Abnormal and Social Psychology, 57*, 37–40.

Stasser, G., & Davis, J. H. (1981). Group decision making and social influence: A social interaction sequence model. *Psychological Review, 88*, 523–551.

Stasser, G., Kerr, N. L., & Davis, J. H. (1989). Influence processes and consensus models in decision-making groups. In P. Paulus (Ed.), *Psychology of group influence* (2nd ed.). Hillsdale, NJ: Erlbaum.

Steele, F. I. (1969). *Problem solving in the spatial environment*. Unpublished manuscript, Department of Administrative Sciences, Yale University.

Steele, F. I. (1973). *Physical settings and organizational development*. Reading, MA: Addison-Wesley.

Stogdill, R. M. (1972). Group productivity, drive, and cohesiveness. *Organizational Behavior and Human Performance, 8*, 26–53.

Stokes, J. P. (1983). Components of group cohesion: Intermember attraction, instrumental value, and risk taking. *Small Group Behavior, 14*, 163–173.

Suls, J. M., & Miller, R. L. (Eds.). (1977). *Social comparison processes: Theoretical and empirical perspectives*. Washington, DC: Hemisphere.

Sundstrom, E., & Altman, I. (1989). Physical environments and work group effectiveness. In L. L. Cummings & B. Staw (Eds.), *Research in organizational behavior* (Vol. 11). Greenwich, CT: JAI Press.

Sundstrom, E., DeMeuse, K., & Futrell, D. (1990). Work teams: Applications and effectiveness. *American Psychologist, 45*, 120–133.

Tajfel, H. (1969). Social and cultural factors in perception. In G. Lindzey & E. Aronson (Eds.), *The handbook of social psychology* (2nd ed.). Reading, MA: Addison-Wesley.

Tanford, S., & Penrod, S. (1984). Social influence models: A formal integration of research on majority and minority influence processes. *Psychological Bulletin, 95*, 189–225.

Taylor, S. E., & Lobel, M. (1989). Social comparison activity under threat: Downward evaluation and upward contacts. *Psychological Review, 96*, 569–575.

Thelen, H. A. (1950). Educational dynamics: Theory and research. *Journal of Social Issues, 6*(2).

Thibaut, J. W. (1950). An experimental study of the cohesiveness of under-privileged groups. *Human Relations, 3*, 251–278.

Thibaut, J. W., & Kelley, H. H. (1959). *The social psychology of groups*. New York: Wiley.

Thibaut, J., & Strickland, L. H. (1956). Psychological set and social conformity. *Journal of Personality, 25*, 115–129.

Thomas, J., & Griffin, R. (1983). The social information processing model of task design: A review of the literature. *Academy of Management Review, 8*, 672–682.

Tolman, E. C. (1932). *Purposive behavior in animals and men*. New York: Century.

Trist, E. L., & Bamforth, K. W. (1951). Some social and psychological consequences of the long-wall method of coal-getting. *Human Relations, 4*, 1–38.

Turner, A. N., & Lawrence, P. R. (1965). *Industrial jobs and the worker*. Boston: Harvard Graduate School of Business Administration.

Tziner, A. (1982). Differential effects of group cohesiveness types: A clarifying overview. *Social Behavior and Personality, 10*, 227–239.

Vaughan, G. M., & Mangan, G. L. (1963). Conformity to group pressure in relation to the value of the task material. *Journal of Abnormal and Social Psychology, 66*, 179–183.

Volpato, C., Maass, A., Mucchi-Faina, A., & Vitti, E. (1990). Minority influence and social categorization. *European Journal of Social Psychology, 20,* 119–132.

Vroom, V. H. (1964). *Work and motivation.* New York: Wiley.

Vroom, V. H. (1969). Industrial social psychology. In G. Lindzey & E. Aronson (Eds.), *The handbook of social psychology* (2nd ed.). Reading, MA: Addison-Wesley.

Walter, G. A. (1975). Effects of videotape feedback and modeling on the behaviors of task group members. *Human Relations, 28,* 121–138.

Walter, G. A. (1976). Changing behavior in task groups through social learning: Modeling alternatives. *Human Relations, 29,* 167–178.

Walters, R. H. (1968). Some conditions facilitative of the occurrence of imitative behavior. In E. C. Simmel, R. A. Hoppe, & C. A. Milton (Eds.), *Social facilitation and imitative behavior.* Boston: Allyn & Bacon.

Walters, R. H., & Parke, R. D. (1964). Social motivation, dependency, and susceptibility to social influence. In L. Berkowitz (Ed.), *Advances in experimental social psychology* (Vol. 1). New York: Academic Press.

Walton, R. E., & Hackman, J. R. (1986). Groups under contrasting management strategies. In P. S. Goodman (Ed.), *Designing effective work groups.* San Francisco: Jossey-Bass.

Weick, K. E. (1969). *The social psychology of organizing.* Reading, MA: Addison-Wesley.

Weiss, H. M., & Shaw, J. B. (1979). Social influences on judgments about tasks. *Organizational Behavior and Human Performance, 24,* 126–140.

Wheeler, L., Shaver, K. G., Jones, R. A., Goethals, F. G., Cooper, J., Robinson, J. E., Gruder, C. L., & Butzine, K. W. (1969). Factors determining choice of a comparison other. *Journal of Experimental Social Psychology, 5,* 219–232.

White, R. W. (1959). Motivation reconsidered: The concept of competence. *Psychological Review, 66,* 297–333.

White, S., & Mitchell, T. (1979). Job enrichment versus social cues: A comparison and competitive test. *Journal of Applied Psychology, 64,* 1–9.

Whyte, G. (1989). Groupthink reconsidered. *Academy of Management Review, 14,* 40–56.

Whyte, W. F. (1943). *Street corner society.* Chicago: University of Chicago Press.

Whyte, W. F. (1955). *Money and motivation.* New York: Harper and Row.

Wiener, M. (1958). Certainty of judgment as a variable in conformity behavior. *Journal of Social Psychology, 48,* 257–263.

Wiggins, J. A., Dill, F., & Schwartz, R. D. (1965). On "status-liability." *Sociometry, 28,* 197–209.

Willis, R. H. (1965). Conformity, independence, and anticonformity. *Human Relations, 18,* 373–388.

Witte, E. H. (1987). Behaviour in group situations: An integrated model. *European Journal of Social Psychology, 17,* 403–429.

Witte, E. H. (1990). Social influence: A discussion and integration of recent models into a general group situation theory. *European Journal of Social Psychology, 20,* 3–27.

Zaccaro, S. J., & Lowe, C. A. (1988). Cohesiveness and performance on an additive task: Evidence for multidimensionality. *The Journal of Social Psychology, 128,* 547–558.

Zaccaro, S. J., & McCoy, C. (1988). The effects of task and interpersonal cohesiveness on performance of a disjunctive group task. *Journal of Applied Social Psychology, 18,* 837–851.

Zander, A. (1979). The psychology of group process. *Annual Review of Psychology, 30,* 417–451.

Zajonc, R. B. (1965). Social facilitation. *Science, 149,* 269–274.

CHAPTER 5

Group Performance and Intergroup Relations in Organizations

Richard A. Guzzo
University of Maryland

Gregory P. Shea
University of Pennsylvania

For well over half a century groups in organizations have been formally studied, resulting in a literature that is quite diverse. Our concern in this chapter is the task performance of groups in organizations. To address this concern, we organize existing literature in terms of schools of thought. That is, the chapter emphasizes conceptual, theoretical paradigms for understanding causes and correlates of group performance. These schools of thought reflect the following: the works of Bion and Homans, sociotechnical theory, interaction process, group development, composition, goals, contextual influences on performance, and intergroup relations and group performance. The chapter also considers the future. We find that the trend toward greater reliance on groups in organizations will continue; that the disciplines of social and organizational psychology will diverge in their study of groups; that organizationally relevant research and theory will empha-size the impact of the organizational context—for example, the systems and practices by which groups are rewarded, supported, provided resources and the like—rather than, say, the nature of group member interaction as a determinant of group effectiveness; and that a mix of clinical and multivariate causal modeling methods will appear with greater frequency.

Introduction

THE IMPORTANCE OF groups to organizations has long been recognized. In an early comprehensive textbook on psychology and organizations, Viteles (1932) discussed "the problem of the group" (p. 619). Viteles argued that "the individual is always acting under group conditions" (p. 619) and that from this arise problems of supervision and management, such as labor-management conflict. The eye-opening Hawthorne studies (Roethlisberger & Dickson, 1939) called attention to the role of informal work groups in organizations and their potential impact on productivity and attitudes of individual workers. The Hawthorne studies were initially simple studies that grew complex as unanticipated social influences became a target of study. Similarly, early studies of pay and individual motivation changed their character as the influences of fellow group members were seen to shape individual responses to various forms of incentive pay plans (Whyte, 1955).

For the most part these studies emphasized the impact of groups on individuals—that is, how an individual responded to pay, a job assignment, a management request, or some other aspect of work was regarded as influenced by the norms, shared beliefs, and orientations of the group in which the individual was a member. From this perspective, the group is a part of the context in which an individual works, and understanding that group context is essential to understanding individual behavior. The chapter by Hackman in this volume examines, in detail, group influences on individuals.

A different line of research, starting later yet alive and well today, views groups as essential performing units in organizations. Here the group is not context but kernel. The emphasis is on collective performance and the factors that determine it.

An example of research emphasizing the group as the essential performing unit is Janis'

(1972, 1982) work on *groupthink*. Groupthink is a term used to signify a syndrome of ineffective decision making by a group. Elements of this syndrome include limited information search, misperceptions of data, and a false sense of a group's righteousness. Note that while Janis' work recognizes the impact of the group on individuals (e.g., group pressures may prevent individuals from voicing an unpopular point of view), the core concern of Janis' work is the decision making performance of a group *as an entity*. Janis' work also conveys the importance of groups to organizations. He studied high-level governmental groups whose decisions had consequences for the lives and well-being of entire societies.

Today more than ever, organizations rely on work groups, as evidenced by the appearance of project teams, focus groups, autonomous work groups, quality circles, multifunction work teams, and team CEOs. Indeed, it has been argued that developments in management practices and organization design in the 1970s and 1980s "undermine [individuals] as basic organizational units" (Davis, 1977, p. 241), that teams rather than individuals now dominate industry (Thurow, 1983), and that the trend of increased prominence of groups will continue far into the future (e.g., Reich, 1983). Leavitt (1975) was among the first to explore the possibilities of groups rather than individuals being truly regarded as the basic building blocks of organizations. Imagine groups being hired, trained, appraised, rewarded, promoted, and fired. Although he thought "groupy" organizations premature in the 1970s, such organizations were seen as consonant with cultural trends that would influence future management practices.

Leavitt's predictions may have come true. As early as 1982 Peters and Waterman (1982) argued that "small groups are, quite simply, the basic organizational building blocks of excellent companies" (p. 126). Many examples exist of organizations now staffing with groups in mind. The hiring process created to staff the start-up Saturn Corporation, for example, explicitly accounted for the group to which an applicant would belong in making hiring decisions. Other organizations reward team performance. The J. C. Penney Company, for example, has paid bonuses to sales associates based on team rather than individual sales receipts. And recently a considerable amount of attention in the popular press has been given to the heightened emphasis on groups as essential units in overall organizational performance (e.g., *Dumaine* 1990). Leavitt's (1975) groupy organizations are not yet the prevailing reality of organizational life, but things are moving in that direction.

Scope and Objectives

There is no dearth of literature about groups. Thousands of studies exist that investigate more than can be imagined about such topics as membership, norms, development, leadership, roles, attraction, dominance, attitudes, abilities, preferences, and conflict in groups. A challenge in the construction of this chapter is determining what is "in" and "out," essential and ancillary to our understanding of effective task performance by groups. In response to this challenge we will try to make clear the scope and objectives that define our approach.

Scope. This chapter draws on a wide range of empirical and theoretical literature relevant to groups in organizational settings. Relevance is a matter of degree, of course, determined by such factors as the setting in which research on groups took place, the type of group studied, and the issues examined. In general, we emphasize research conducted on what McGrath (1984) calls *natural* groups, those that exist independent of a researcher's activities and purposes. These include formal and informal groups in organizations as well as groups found in other settings. Such groups can be short- or long-lived, broad or narrow in their activities. McGrath also speaks of *concocted* groups,

those that have some qualities of natural groups but were modified in some way for the purpose of research (e.g., membership was determined by a researcher) and *quasi* groups, those that are highly constrained by the researcher in their activity and setting . Research and theory based on concocted and quasi groups often have relevance to the understanding of groups in organizations, and literature based on the study of such groups is reviewed in this chapter.

Further, *schools of thought* regarding groups in organizations are emphasized in this chapter. In reviewing existing literature, emphasis is given to theoretical and conceptual paradigms for understanding group performance rather than details of particular studies or offshoots of existing paradigms. Thus, one will not find in the chapter detailed reviews of large numbers of empirical reports with methodological critiques of each report; rather, the chapter tends toward summaries of existing evidence, going into detail about data sparingly. Further, methodological issues of group research are not, per se, a major focus of the chapter. Differences in methods as related to different schools of thought will, however, be addressed, especially as they help illuminate and explain those schools of thought.

The *group as a performing unit* is the primary unit of analysis in this chapter. For the groups of concern here, *work* is the occasion for the group coming into being and *working* is the principle transaction connecting group members to each other and the group to its environment. Thus, research and theory that addresses group dynamics in general, without an explicit connection to task performance by groups, is of secondary relevance to this chapter.

The dynamics of *relations between groups* in organizations, especially in terms of conflict and cooperation, have been studied for several years. The chapter by Thomas in this volume addresses conflict in depth. Issues of conflict are of interest in the present chapter as they relate to task performance by interacting groups. That is, a central concern is how changes in perceptions, feelings, and behavior of group members, so often brought about by intergroup dynamics, relate to the task performance of groups at work. As we shall see, unfortunately, while there are many data on, for example, relationships between intergroup dynamics and the perceptions and feelings of group members, there are few data on the connection between intergroup relations and the effectiveness with which groups perform tasks.

Objectives. This chapter has few but ambitious objectives. One is to review the variety of existing schools of thought on group performance as they relate to understanding groups and teams in the workplace. These schools of thought are summarized, compared, and evaluated. A second objective is to present current theoretical frameworks for understanding group performance in organizations. That perspective is influenced by prior schools of thought but is distinct from them because of what is and is not emphasized as causes of effective group performance. A third objective is to address the implications of various schools of thought for the design, management, and change of work groups in organizations. A final objective is to analyze cogently the future of research, theory, and practice with regard to work groups in organizations.

A Definition and Orientation

Definition of Group. What is a group? McGrath (1984) points out that often we are fuzzy in our specification of what we mean when we use the word *group*. This fuzziness is a consequence of the inherently nondistinct boundary between groups and nongroups. That is, some social aggregates (e.g., audiences, crowds) can display some group features but are really considerably less of a group than, say, a work crew. In this light, "groupness" is a matter of degree. Thus, McGrath's definition

of groups as "those social aggregates that involve mutual awareness and potential mutual interaction" (p. 7) was offered with the proviso that there are differing degrees of groupness. Shaw (1981) reviews a variety of definitions and offers his own: "two or more persons who are interacting with one another in such a manner that each person influences and is influenced by each other person" (p. 8). Brown (1988) states that "a group exists when two or more people define themselves as members of it and when its existence is recognized by at least one other member" (pp. 2–3).

These are minimalist definitions, outgrowths of research on basic social processes in concocted or quasi groups, in McGrath's (1984) terms. For the purpose of this chapter, we define groups as Hackman (1982) defines them, following the work of Alderfer (1977). Specifically, our interest is in the effectiveness of *real* groups with a *task* to perform in an *organization*. A real group is defined by Hackman (1982) as a social system that has the following properties: It is perceived to be an entity by its members and by nonmembers familiar with it; its members have some degree of interdependence; and a differentiation of roles and duties takes place in the group. In McGrath's (1984) terms, natural groups in organizations are of interest. A group task exists when group members are collectively responsible for measurable group-level outputs. The organization, in addition to being the context to which we wish to generalize our conclusions about group performance, is often regarded as the source of some of the most powerful influences on group effectiveness. Additionally, we make no distinction between the terms *group* and *team*. Either label applies to the type of entity just defined.

Minimum group size is a slippery issue, and we avoided the issue of size in the preceding paragraph. Weick (1969) gives a succinct account of some implications of group size. He speaks of *crucial transitions* in size, transitions that permit a greater variety of social processes to occur. Weick's crucial transitions are from two to three (three allows a coalition or a majority to appear); from three to four (thus permitting equal alliances); from four to seven (creating the possibility of alliances among subunits, not just among individuals); and from seven to nine (nine permits coalitions within and between subunits to appear). One might quibble and assert that a transition from four to five is crucial as well, since five is the minimum number required to observe nonisolated minorities (i.e., minorities who do not stand alone), since nonisolated minorities have been shown to exert influence differently than an isolated minority (Levine, 1980). The point we wish to make is that size is indeed a crucial issue in terms of what is possible in groups. However, our knowledge of groups often is not very sensitive to matters of group size. Surely the distinction between dyads and larger social units is important, and there has been research on the relationship between group size and performance on differing types of group tasks. But by and large, size is not a core concern in theories of work group effectiveness.

Orientation. Although inclusive, the definition of groups we advocate buys trouble. Most research is not done with natural groups. McGrath and Altman (1966) estimated that less than 5 percent of the more than 2,000 studies of groups performed up to that time were done in natural settings. It is doubtful the percentage has since changed substantially. Can we, having stated that our concern is with real groups at work in organizations, justifiably make statements about work group performance from research that mostly does not investigate the kinds of groups of interest here?

We can, although with caution. The definition we adopt refers to the object of our inquiry, the target we wish to understand. The sources of our understanding, however, often are data and theory derived from the study of social aggregates that, according to the definition, could not be called natural or real work groups. We agree with McGrath (1984) that the distinction between what is and is not a group is often a matter of ambiguous degree and groups under any definition share elements with other grouplike social aggregates. We thus make use of literature based on groups not completely like those we seek to understand, cognizant that the greater the similarity between target and source groups the more confident we can be when extrapolating from the latter.

One further point about the nature of groups draws on a discussion by Karl Popper (1972) of the differing natures of social systems. Popper distinguishes between systems that are like clocks and those that are like clouds. Clocks operate in an orderly way. The actions of each component are predictable from the other, synchronized, and unified. Other systems are more like clouds. Clouds lack the orderliness of clocks. Clouds change form, grow and shrink, and are strongly affected by environmental conditions. The movements of molecules and particles making up a cloud are nearly impossible to predict precisely.

We believe that groups as social systems in organizations are more like clouds than clocks. Although there are some regularities in group behavior, groups share with clouds an absence of neat orderliness and, like clouds, are highly responsive to contextual influences. Similarly, just as an understanding of some of its molecules and particles does not give us an understanding of the entire cloud, so too do we fail to appreciate the nature of a group when we focus only on its elemental members. The actions and attributes of one group member often do not accurately predict another's. Finally, we believe that the behavior of groups does not unfold like clockwork. Rather, variation is the rule. Much of this variation is due to the impact of the diverse organizational contexts in which groups work. Thinking of groups as clouds gives us a realistic, usable foundation for understanding—and managing—groups at work.

Structure of the Chapter

With this orientation in mind, we can now turn to a review of several schools of thought about work groups. The review starts by examining some early perspectives that regard groups as intact social entities to be thought of holistically. Included here are the theories of Bion and Homans followed by the sociotechnical perspective. Although the review is not strictly ordered chronologically, these schools of thought emerged in the 1940s and 1950s. Then schools of thought that gained prominence in the 1950s and 1960s are addressed, including theories of group process and development and perspectives tied to sociopsychological research on small groups. Current research on group development also is examined. Another line of inquiry that has currency as well as decades of precedent is that concerned with the fit between individuals and groups. Group goals and models of task performance derived from social psychology are reviewed as well. Finally, more recent models of work group effectiveness are examined as are perspectives on intergroup relations at work.

Bion and the Group-as-Whole Perspective

One approach to understanding groups at work centers on the theorizing of W. R. Bion. Bion drew on his wartime experiences with groups, especially small therapy groups, and reformulated existing psychoanalytic concepts to explain the behavior of group members as well as of groups as a whole (Bion, 1961). Admittedly, the contemporary utility of Bion's theory for groups at work is not great. We address it because it constitutes a school of thought that has had a great influence on subsequent theorizing, although the debt of later theorists to Bion's work may not always have been explicitly recognized.

For Bion, the critical unit of analysis is the group viewed as a social system. Within that social system are members who at any time may act in concert as a single integrated system or who may form interdependent subsystems. The forces or motives for members' actions are usually unconscious, according to Bion.

This emphasis on the unconscious in groups can be traced back to Freud and Le Bon (Brown, 1988). Le Bon (1897) spoke of the loss of rationality and personal identity in crowds (and, by implication, groups of any size) and their replacement by an unconscious *group mind.* The operation of a group mind was regarded as the reason why people in collectives could become barbaric, foolish, or uncaring. Similarly, Freud (1921/1961) saw groups as tending toward extreme behavior because of the operation of unconscious forces. For Freud, the forces concerned the emotional identifications group members have with each other and, especially importantly, with the group leader. Unlike Le Bon, Freud thought a group "capable of high intellectual performance, provided it is organized in the correct manner" (Taylor & Moghaddam, 1987, p. 18).

Bion (1961) departed from earlier theorists by explicitly theorizing about the role of unconscious forces in the accomplishment of tasks. Central to any group, according to Bion, is its *primary task.* Every group, however casual, meets to *do* something, to fulfill some function or set of functions, and this primary task provides the reason for the group's existence. The primary task can be almost anything: to produce widgets, maximize return on investments, or cure patients. Primary tasks for groups of employees are usually quite clear in organizations.

Work group activity in service of the primary task is regarded as planned, rational, coordinated, and explicit. However, such activity was infused with, and sometimes replaced by, activity attributable to unconscious forces in every group, according to Bion (1961). Three basic types of unconscious forces are identified by Bion: *dependency, fight-flight,* and *pairing.* Dependency forces concern feelings of insecurity or inadequacy among members. Member behavior that denotes immaturity, know-nothingness, or incompetence may be expressions of dependence. Deifying a group's leader and viewing him or her as omnipotent also can be an expression of dependence. The leader is often a focus of dependency behaviors.

Fight-flight behavior is thought to be an expression of concern for the survival or maintenance of the group. The group can survive (e.g., enhance its identity, strengthen its bonds among members) by fighting with another group, for example, or by fleeing to preserve itself when necessary. Fighting within a group also can be an expression of a concern for the survival of social subsystems within a group.

Pairing is concerned with friendship, love, and intimate relations among group members. Hopeful expectations about unity and pleasant relations among group members can be regarded as products of pairing forces.

Within any group, individual group members are seen as more or less disposed toward acting on these forces, depending on the forces' valence for members. Thus, some individuals may act more due to pairing forces while other act more strongly due to dependence forces. Whatever the valence of these forces for particular members, groups are to be understood, from Bion's perspective, as social systems that are constantly subject to two sets of forces: those reflecting the primary task and those reflecting unconscious forces. According to Rioch (1970), "what one sees in reality is a work group which is suffused by, intruded into, and supported by the basic assumption group" (p. 62). Thus, a work group may not be able to accomplish its primary task if, for example, the leader cannot direct the members (Turquet, 1978), or fighting among group members may divert energy from the accomplishment of primary tasks. In a positive way, pairing

assumptions may provide the cohesion needed by a group to do its work.

In summary, key ideas in Bion's (1961) work that appear in subsequent theorizing by others are the assertions that (a) the group as a whole is an appropriate and powerful level of analysis, (b) a primary task occasions the creation of all groups, and (c) in addition to a primary task, powerful unconscious forces exist within groups and influence behavior as well. Further, the specific character of these unconscious forces addresses fundamental concerns in the behavioral science of groups, such as cohesiveness (pairing), inter- and intragroup conflict and coalitions (fight-flight), and leader-member relations (dependency).

There are several, though sometimes vague, implications of this perspective for the design and management of effective work group performance. These include the requirement that work group performance be understood not only as a product of rationally designed and executed work procedures but also of irrational expressions of basic, unconscious motives shared in varying degrees by group members. Usually we think of the operation of such basic motives as impeding the accomplishment of primary tasks, though Bion's theory allows for the contribution of such forces to effective task accomplishment. Definitive testing of Bion's theory has not taken place and, as previously mentioned, it is little used as a guide to the design or management of work groups. However, the theory does speak to the potential value of altering the composition of a group to attain the "right" mix of motive strengths among members. Additionally, the theory can be evoked when heightening group members' awareness of the potential influence of basic, unconscious forces and how those forces might be expressed in ways that do not interfere with task accomplishment. This could be accomplished through sensitivity training, for example. As a school of thought, then, Bion's work has potential value for organizations and their work groups, though there is little rigorous research to assess its merit and applicability to the workplace.

Homans' Theory

In 1950 George C. Homans published *The Human Group*. In it, he presented data he had reanalyzed from existing studies of groups (e.g., Whyte's [1943] study of neighborhood gangs) and presented a general theory of group behavior. His general theory was based on groups at work in organizations, such as accounts of the work group in the Bank Wiring Observation Room (Roethlisberger & Dickson, 1939), as well as groups in virtually all other settings. His general theory was thus meant to apply to groups at work in organizations.

For Homans (1950), every group has boundaries, and "outside the boundary lies the group's environment" (p. 86). Further, Homans' theory depicts groups as social systems made up of two subsystems—the *external* and the *internal*. The external subsystem is conditioned by the *environment*, which itself has three critical aspects: *physical* (or spatial), *technical*, and *social*. These aspects of the environment condition or influence the operation of a group's external subsystem and thus influence the overall behavior of a group. By way of illustration, the environment of the Bank Wiring Observation Room group was characterized by a particular layout of work stations (spatial), available tools (technical), and relationships with management (social). These environmental characteristics shaped relations among group members and required adaptations of groups in order for the groups to survive in that environment.

Whereas the external subsystem in a group is directly conditioned by the environment, the environment's impact on the internal subsystem of a group, according to Homans, is mediated by its impact on the external subsystem. Thus, the internal subsystem in a group is a result of the operation of the external subsystem, as that external subsystem is influenced by the environment. However, the external subsystem also is postulated to be influenced by the operation of the internal subsystem. Thus, there is mutual causation in Homans' model: The external and internal subsystems influence each other.

To explain the particulars by which external and internal subsystems operate, Homans' theory refers to three *elements* common to both internal and external systems in groups. The elements are *activity*, *interaction*, and *sentiment*. Activities are a basic unit of action carried out by an individual. Activities of the external system of the Bank Wiring Observation Room group included soldering and inspecting; activities of the internal system of the same group included expressions of friendship or hostility by a group member.

Interaction occurs when one member's activity stimulates a response from another group member. Interactions vary on several dimensions (e.g., frequency). In the external system of the Bank Wiring Observation Room group, interactions included episodes of group members trading jobs or helping each other at their work. Examples of interactions in the internal system included group members pooling their money to bet on horses or "binging" each other (playfully punching another on the upper arm).

Sentiments are feelings, motives, attitudes. In short, sentiments are subjective states that give rise to behavior, in Homans' view. Sentiments in the external system of the Bank Wiring Observation Room group included members' preferences for earning high wages or wishing to remain a part of the organization. In the internal system, sentiments included expressions of liking or antagonism toward a fellow group member.

The elements (activity, interaction, sentiment) are regarded as interrelated within and between each of the two subsystems (internal and external) in which they occur. Thus, certain work activities of a group member bring about interactions with a fellow group member. These interactions can, in turn, enhance the favorability of sentiments held by the parties to the interaction. Homans offers several propositions about the effects of changes in sentiment, interaction, and activity, such as the proposition that increases in the favorability of sentiments in the internal system lead to increased interactions in both the internal and external systems of groups.

Homans' theory is insightful in several ways. First, by describing two subsystems, internal and external, the theory accounts for the familiar distinction between task-oriented and socioemotional aspects of group life. This distinction has existed for many years (e.g., see Benne & Sheats, 1948, for an early statement of this distinction in these terms) and, in a loose way, is not unlike Bion's (1961) distinction between activities driven by a group's primary task and those activities that reflect affective and/or irrational motives. The theory also explicitly addresses the existence of a mutual influence between the internal and external subsystems in groups.

Second, Homans' theory explicitly recognizes the importance of a group's environment. His is the earliest sophisticated account we know of that addresses contextual influences on group performance. In this regard, Homans observes that usually more than one scheme of organization within a group is possible in any environment. That is, the structure and process of work groups in the same organization will vary, as they are rarely completely fixed by the physical, technical, and social features of a work environment. This point is illustrated in the work of Shea and Guzzo (1987a), who found that the degree of task interdependence among group members differed considerably among a sample of work groups operating in the same organization and subject to essentially the same physical, technical, and social demands. Thus, in relatively similar environments one should be able to observe quite different patterns of task-oriented and socioemotional behavior in groups at work.

Third, Homans points out that the relationship between a group and its environment is one of action and reaction. That is, groups not only are influenced by their environment but also influence it.

Fourth, Homans' theory is dynamic, recognizing that relationships among determinants of group behavior change over time, though the theory does not articulate the particular patterns or sequences of changes among determinants of group behavior.

Although the theory makes these contributions to our understanding of relationships among elements of groups and between groups and their environments, it has little to say about certain immediate concerns in an organization, such as why some groups are more productive than others. Effective groups, according to the theory, are those that survive, and survival depends on the appearance in a group of sentiments, activities, and interactions adaptive to the group's environment. As a criterion of effectiveness, survival has a rather distant horizon and is of little practical value with regard to the day-to-day performance of work groups. Nonetheless, the theory underlying this definition of effectiveness provides a rare, coherent account of group behavior that allows groups in very different settings (work, family, school) to be understood in comparable terms. Unfortunately, there are few empirical tests of the theory as applied to work groups.

Sociotechnical Theory

Sociotechnical theory began to develop in the early 1950s in conjunction with Tavistock Institute projects in the British coal mining industry. It provided a counterpoint to prevailing "mechanistic" theories of organization and management, such as Weber's theory of bureaucracy and Taylor's theory of scientific management. The core idea in sociotechnical theory is that any group, organization, or other social aggregate contains technical and social systems. Further, the perspective assumes that "attempts to optimize for either...system alone will result in the suboptimization of the sociotechnical whole" (Trist, 1981).

The technological system concerns the transformation of raw material into useful output and the social system is what links the human operators of the technology with the technology itself and with each other (Rousseau, 1977). These two systems are regarded as distinct from each other in the sense that technical systems follow laws of natural science, while social systems follow laws of human sciences (Trist, 1981). Technical and social systems are, nonetheless, intertwined. The technical system shapes the functions and tasks at work and thereby establishes parameters within which a social system can operate. Each system has its own goals.

Sociotechnical theory posits that optimization of both systems in the pursuit of each system's goals leads to high technical performance and a positive social experience at work. Joint optimization, in turn, is accomplished by structuring work appropriately. Principles of the sociotechnical framework for the appropriate structuring of work include (a) regarding the work system as an essential entity, (b) emphasizing the centrality of the work group to that work system, (c) permitting groups to regulate themselves, and (d) encouraging the development of multiple skills in group members (Rousseau, 1977; Trist, 1981). More specifically, sociotechnical theorists hold that individual job holders should have "the opportunity to use a variety of skills, to make decisions, to complete meaningful, whole pieces of work, to learn how well one is performing, to interact with others, and to learn" (Rousseau, 1977). These characteristics reflect the influence of Bion (1961) and Emery (1964, 1976) and resemble those of Herzberg, Mausner, Peterson, and Capwell (1957) and other job design theorists (cf. Hackman & Oldham, 1980). A key difference, however, is

the centrality of the work group in sociotechnical theory and its place in the broader organizational system.

Sociotechnical theory also posits that joint optimization requires autonomous work groups* (Pearce & Ravlin, 1987). Autonomous work groups exercise control over the factors affecting them and are thought to be the key determinant of better results and higher satisfaction (Trist, 1981). At least three conditions enhance such autonomy: *task differentiation, boundary control,* and *task control* (Cummings, 1978, 1981). Task differentiation refers to how distinct and differentiable the group's task is from the work of other organizational units. The greater the differentiation, the better. Boundary control concerns how much group members can affect transactions with their environment. Finally, task control concerns the extent to which employees have control over the actual process of performing the group's work versus doing their work according to the specifications and directives of others.

The appeal of sociotechnical theory probably stems in part from its explicit action orientation and its model of man as striving, growing, learning, and democratic, and as a creator of the future. This orientation stands in clear contradistinction to scientific management with its naive if not misleading assumptions about motivation and its view that organizational objectives and tasks are largely givens and issues of how to organize are largely problems of allocation.

A slowly growing body of literature exists that assesses the impact of autonomous work groups and thus, by implication, the validity of sociotechnical principles. Much of this literature consists of case studies. As regards performance, Pearce and Ravlin (1987) reviewed

*For purposes of our exposition of sociotechnical theory, we will use the term *autonomous work groups* and make no distinctions among the various other labels that have been applied to the type of work group we are considering. These labels include *self-regulating work group, semiautonomous work group, self-managing teams,* and others.

research during the period from 1970 to 1986 and reached favorable conclusions about the positive effect of autonomous work groups on task performance. They caution, though, that few statistical analyses exist to support the various qualitative observations of the impact of autonomous work groups on productivity.

Goodman (1979, 1986) presents a quantitative account of a case in which self-regulating work groups were instituted in a coal mine. Goodman found that, indeed, highly cohesive teams were able to be formed when sociotechnical principles were applied. However, he concluded that the change to self-regulating work groups had only small positive effects on performance. A more optimistic assessment is reported by Trist, Susman, and Brown (1977). Of further interest is Goodman's (1986) conclusion that, in this case, nonhuman factors (physical conditions, equipment) influenced performance more strongly than did human factors. Undoubtedly there are many other instances in which social and technical factors combine unequally to determine work group effectiveness.

Wall, Kemp, Jackson and Clegg (1986) investigated the implementation of sociotechnical principles to create autonomous work groups in a British confectionery firm. They found that the intrinsic job satisfaction of work group members rose in response to the creation of autonomous work groups. However, there were no apparent effects of such arrangements on other variables, such as general work motivation, mental health, or performance. Cordery, Mueller, and Smith (1991) also report that employee attitudes became more favorable following the adoption of autonomous work groups but that the existence of such work groups was associated with increased levels of absenteeism and turnover.

Goodman, Devadas, and Hughson (1988) reviewed the confectionery study, comparing it to two other cases in which sociotechnical principles were applied to the design and management of work groups. The other two cases were the famous Topeka (Walton, 1972) case and the aforementioned coal mine study. Goodman et al. (1988) conclude that the use of work teams according to sociotechnical principles can raise productivity as well as attitudes. Citing meta-analytic work by Macy, Izumi, Hurts, Norton, and Smith (1986), Goodman et al. (1988) state that self-regulating work groups have a general positive impact on productivity but more specific, selective effects on attitudes. Note that positive attitudes toward one's job or organization are regarded as indicators of the optimization of the social, humanistic ends to be met by working.

In summary, sociotechnical theory has several implications for the design and management of work groups. According to this school of thought, effective group performance (defined as the joint optimization of social and task goals) requires that groups regulate themselves. This capacity to self-regulate depends on the extent to which groups are differentiated from others in the organization, control their transactions with the organizational environment in which they exist, and have the capacity to determine how their work is executed. It also depends on group members possessing sufficient skills appropriate to the task.

The emphasis on groups as social systems with an organizational environment is quite pronounced in the sociotechnical framework, an emphasis shared with Homans' (1950) theory. The emphasis in Homans' theory is on groups adapting to environmental demands. In the sociotechnical framework, the emphasis is on the creation of group autonomy and control over its environment. Like Homans' theory, the sociotechnical framework is meant to be applicable to a wide range of organizational settings. And while the research on sociotechnical principles is limited, the pattern of evidence supports the validity of the sociotechnical perspective.

Interaction Process and Group Performance

Without question, the dominant way of thinking about group performance reflects an input–process–output model. This historically has dominated group research and theorizing and it dominates today. In this model, *input* typically refers to the things group members bring to the group, including expertise, status, personality attributes, abilities, experience, and demographic attributes. *Process* refers to the interaction among group members, typically including the social exchange of information, influence attempts, leadership efforts, and expressions of approval or disapproval of fellow group members. *Output*, of course, refers to the products yielded by groups. These might include ideas, decisions, plans, artistic creations, and widgets. The model, then, is explicitly causal: The nature (quantity, originality) of group outputs are a result of the nature of the group interaction process, which itself is a consequence of the members' inputs. Figure 1(A) shows this model in its simplest form.

Figure 1 also depicts some alternative formulations of the dominant model, following Hackman (1987). In the first of these alternative formulations (B), the influence of process on output is retained. The major variation is that input factors are depicted as having a direct effect on group output. That is, the effects of inputs are not all mediated by the group interaction process. The second of the alternative formulations (C) constitutes a more radical departure from dominant thinking. Here any mediating, causal role of the interaction process is eliminated. In this version, inputs directly determine both the nature of group member interaction and group outputs, but the nature of member interaction is not crucial to understanding why some groups yield better outputs than others.

In subsequent sections of this chapter, various elaborations on the three versions of the

FIGURE 1

Possible Roles of Group Process

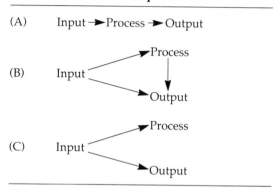

(A)   Input → Process → Output

(B)   Input → Process → Output

(C)   Input → Process → Output

input–process–output framework are addressed. For example, some elaborations address the nature of the inputs, expanding the definition of inputs to include organizational or contextual factors, not just member characteristics. Other elaborations specify the particular features of the interaction process regarded as most important to effective group performance, the meaning of effectiveness, and the role of the nature of the task (is it an input or is it a mediator of the process-output connection?) in group performance. In the present section, we address the causal role of group interaction process in group performance. Research evidence on interventions to change the interaction process to bring about changes in the performance effectiveness of groups also is reviewed.

Process Losses and Group Performance

McGrath (1984) points out that sociopsychological research on groups can be organized according to various general themes, some of which pertain to interaction patterns among group members and the task performance of groups. It is this line of sociopsychological research that is of principal concern here. We regard it as a school of thought concerning group task performance, and its cornerstone is Steiner's (1972) book, *Group Process and Productivity*. While Steiner's work integrated a number of research studies preceding it, it is his formulations that have shaped much subsequent investigation.

The general model of task performance offered by Steiner is:

Actual productivity =
potential productivity – process losses

Potential productivity is the highest level of performance attainable by a group. According to the model, potential productivity is determined by the available resources (e.g., information, strength) within a group. *Actual productivity* fails to match potential productivity, according to the model, due to process losses in groups. *Process losses* are a result of less-than-optimal ways of combining members' resources into a group product.

Sources of Process Losses.   Where do process losses come from? According to Steiner, two principal sources are deficits of *coordination* and *motivation*. For example, large group size or missed communication among members can cause problems of integrating members' contributions. Member motivation can also be affected by group size. Evidence on the phenomenon labeled *social loafing* (i.e., reductions in member effort) indicates that group members often exert less effort as group size increases (Latane, 1986; Latane, Williams, & Harkins, 1979; Steiner, 1972). Social loafing, though, appears to be a function of more than mere group size. Evidence shows social loafing to be greater when (a) group members feel their contributions are dispensable (Weldon & Mustari, 1988), (b) members experience low control over task outcomes (Price, 1987), (c) members are neither identifiable nor subject to evaluation or comparison to others (Harkins & Szymanski, 1987), and

(d) tasks are not intrinsically meaningful (Brickner, Harkins, & Ostrom, 1986).

Individuals Versus Groups.   Another line of research related to Steiner's (1972) work concerns individual versus group performance. Hill (1982) reviewed studies of individual versus group performance on tasks involving learning, concept mastery, and problem solving and concluded that, in general, group performance was superior to that of its average member but often inferior to that of its most competent individual. Explanations of why groups may not do as well as their most competent individual invoke the notion of process losses resulting in suboptimal use of member resources. It should be noted that the bulk of research on individual versus group performance has been done using relatively simple tasks performed as part of laboratory settings; little work has addressed individual versus group performance on complex tasks in organizational settings. Indeed, the issue is moot when the tasks given to groups at work could not reasonably be done by individuals working alone.

One specific area in which the superiority of individual versus group performance has been extensively investigated is brainstorming. Diehl and Stroebe (1987) reviewed the results of 22 studies on this issue and conducted 4 more of their own. As regards the *quantity* of ideas produced, the same number of people working alone (referred to as a *nominal* group) consistently produce more ideas than that number of people working as a group. This difference is termed a *productivity loss* in brainstorming groups. No such clear productivity loss existed with regard to the *quality* of ideas produced. Diehl and Stroebe's own studies tested explanations of why the quantity productivity loss in brainstorming groups exists. Their data show that social loafing is not a powerful source of the productivity loss in brainstorming groups. Rather, *production blocking* is the source. Production blocking occurs because only one member of a group can speak at a time. Consequently, people get distracted from their ideas by those of others, people forget ideas as they are forced to suppress them while listening, or ideas are held back because they seem irrelevant or meager following what somebody else just said. The implications of Diehl and Stroebe's analysis are straightforward: When groups must make decisions, it is better to generate ideas by having members work alone and have members act as a group for the evaluation of and choice among ideas.

Models of Input Conversion.   One line of work that Steiners' (1972) both continued and stimulated more of is the creation of formal models of the processes of converting group member inputs into a group product. Davis' (1973, 1980) work on social decision schemes is an example. It maps the rules used by groups to convert individual preferences (or solutions) into group decisions, such as *majority wins, truth wins* (one member's preferences prevail), or *truth supported wins* (one member's preferences prevail if supported by at least one other member). This approach has been used, for example, to model how mock juries arrive at decisions of guilt or innocence.

Shiflett (1979) also theorized about conversion processes in groups. He presented a model that describes group outputs as a consequence of *resources* (member knowledge, skill, etc.) and *transformers,* which are "variables that have an impact on resources and determine the manner in which they are incorporated into and related to the output variables" (Shiflett, 1979, p. 67). In organizations, transformers might include situational constraints or facilitators (e.g., see Schoorman & Schneider, 1988) and leadership style. Shiflett's (1979) recognition of factors in the organizational context which both shape the nature of resources available to a group and the processes by which resources are converted in outputs is one of the earliest.

Tasks.   The optimal process of converting a group's resources into group products, according to Steiner (1972), depends heavily on the nature of the task a group is performing. Steiner offered what he called a partial typology of group tasks. This partial typology has had a strong influence on subsequent sociopsychological research. Steiner (1972) distinguished between *unitary* and *divisible* tasks. The former (but not the latter) requires a single group output. Several types of unitary tasks are then distinguished, each of which has implications for how individuals ought to combine their resources into a single group output. *Additive* tasks require that group members' resources be summed for maximal productivity (as in groups of farm workers picking produce). *Disjunctive* tasks require that only one member do the task for the group to succeed (as when solving a puzzle). *Conjunctive* tasks require that each group member must individually succeed if the group is to succeed (as when every member of a hockey team must not be "offside" when advancing a puck down the ice). *Discretionary* tasks are those for which resources can be combined in any way seen fit by the group. This typology has been used to study the effects on performance of such variables as group size. (Larger groups should do better on additive and disjunctive tasks but poorer on conjunctive tasks.)

Although intriguing, this typology of tasks has seen virtually no use in organizational settings. That is, the work that groups do in organizations has not been successfully described in terms of these task properties. (For that matter, there is very little analysis of group or team tasks in the manner that jobs for individuals have been described through any of the familiar job analysis techniques.)   Consequently, the research and modeling that relies on Steiner's (1972) typology has not had much relevance to the workplace.

The role of the nature of the task, though, often appears in research and theory on group performance. In causal theories of group performance, tasks tend to be cited in either of two ways. In one, tasks moderate the link between interaction process and group outputs. That is, the relationship of process to performance depends on the nature of the task. This is how Steiner (1972) cited tasks. Alternatively, tasks are cited as stimuli to group performance. From this perspective, the nature of the task motivates (or fails to motivate) performance in groups. Sociotechnical theory, as described earlier, cites tasks in this way, as does work-related job design to group performance (e.g., Hackman & Oldham, 1980). A different approach to the role of task is offered by Driskell, Hogan, and Salas (1987). They adopt Holland's (1966) typology of vocational interests and apply it to describe tasks. Thus, for example, some tasks are imaginative/aesthetic in nature and others are mechanical/technical. Driskell et al. then outline a series of propositions about the optimal fit of personality type to groups.

Summary.   The sociopsychological perspective on process losses as a source of deficiencies in group performance is made up of a number of diverse orientations. These orientations all place *interaction process* in the key, mediating role in the transformation of member inputs into group outputs. The orientations differ, though, in their relative emphasis on matters of effort loss, coordination difficulties, or the role of the task in the transformation of inputs into outputs.

Overall, the task performance school of thought in sociopsychological investigations of groups has strongly emphasized (a) the comparison of group to individual performance, (b) the rules or methods by which the resources of individuals are combined into group products, (c) sources of suboptimal use of individual resources, and (d) the role of the task as a moderator of the process-output relationship. It has not emphasized groups as indivisible performing units, as have other schools of thought (e.g., sociotechnical theory). Further, the task performance school has a *closed system* flavor. That is, available resources mostly are

viewed as inherent qualities of group members (such as knowledge and abilities). How groups transact with and draw resources from their environments and apply them to task performance is not addressed (Shiflett's [1979] work is an exception). Further, the *process loss* school of thought has been criticized because it typically views resources as static (Hill, 1982). Perhaps a more fundamental criticism by Hill (1982) and others (Collins & Guetzkow, 1964; Hackman & Morris, 1975; Michaelson, Watson, & Black, 1989) is that too often *gains* are neglected in this perspective (for data bearing on this, see Michaelson et al., 1989). Further, process loss as a concept has been sharply attacked by McGrath (1991). McGrath finds the term pejorative and sees in it an implication that any group whose action does not conform to an experimenter's or manager's preconceptions of what should be comes to be seen as a deficient, flawed group in need of fixing (usually by importing a researcher's or consultant's favored technique for improving group performance). Instead, McGrath suggests we appreciate *equifinality* in groups (i.e., that multiple paths to the same end exist) and that "real" groups usually have multiple objectives on their agenda that must be considered in the hunt for process losses.

The task performance school of thought, though, does raise several issues relevant to understanding the effectiveness of work groups in organizations, including the nature of the task, the role of motivation and coordination in group performance, and, by implication, the relative merits of groups versus individuals as organizational building blocks. However, general prescriptions for the design and management of work groups are relatively limited. As we have seen, one action recommendation from brainstorming research is to have individuals, not groups, engage in idea production. And from social loafing research one can derive the recommendations that groups should be given intrinsically interesting tasks to perform, that individual members should feel they are important to the fate of the group, and individual contributions should remain identifiable and subject to evaluation and comparison. These recommendations are not unlike many existing principles of enlightened human resource management. We turn now to an examination of a very different orientation toward group process and group performance than the orientation just reviewed, albeit one that views problems of interaction as causes of poor task performance by groups.

What About Cohesiveness?

Group cohesiveness refers to the forces that bind members to each other and to their group. It is a concept of wide appeal. Often, especially in the lay view of group performance, cohesiveness is thought to be a precursor of effective team performance.

The data on the relationship between cohesiveness and performance are not unambiguous. Using a Hunter-Schmidt meta-analytic approach, Evans and Dion (1991) analyzed 18 estimates from 372 groups and found a corrected mean correlation between cohesion and performance of +.42. Evans and Dion are cautious in their interpretation of this figure because of the number of studies not accounted for in their analysis and because of the limited types of groups (e.g., concocted groups, sports teams) in the sample of studies they reviewed. In a tantalizing footnote in their report, Evans and Dion report knowledge of an unpublished set of 26 estimates of the relationship between cohesiveness and performance, citing Stogdill (1972). In that set of studies, the uncorrected mean correlation between cohesion and performance is −.19 and is based on a much larger sample.

Some of the earliest work may still yield the best insights into the cohesiveness-performance relationship (Schachter, Ellerston, McBride, & Gregory, 1951; Seashore, 1954). Seashore (1954) studied factory workers in 228 groups and found that cohesiveness and performance were indeed related. However, the direction of that relationship depended on group norms. When norms existed for high productivity, cohesiveness and productivity were positively related. When group norms called for low productivity, cohesiveness and productivity were negatively related. Seashore studied rather large groups (over 25 workers per group, on average). Schachter et al. (1951) found essentially the same result in an experimental study of three-person groups of college students.

To summarize, it appears that the relationship between group cohesiveness and performance is not simple. Rather, it is contingent on norms. It remains plausible that other contingency factors operate as well.

T-groups and the Process Orientation

Kurt Lewin influenced the study of small groups in several ways. He initiated an era of basic laboratory research on groups (by articulating a vision, by energizing students and colleagues to engage groups as objects of study, and by creating the Center for Group Dynamics). Lewin also played a crucial role in developing the action-oriented training laboratory at the National Training Laboratory (NTL) in Bethel, Maine. NTL yielded the T-group, a form of training in group dynamics designed to increase self-knowledge and the capacity to understand relationships in groups. T-groups themselves usually comprise but a part of a learning laboratory, other parts being skill exercises, theory sessions, and intergroup exercise (Benne, Bradford, & Lippitt, 1964). Premises underlying T-groups include participants' responsibility for their learning and the role of staff as facilitators of members' examination of their own behavior, feelings, and reactions.

It was assumed that the learning gained through T-groups would change behavior in other settings, such as the workplace (Benne et al., 1964). Yet, as we shall see, empirical evidence supporting the assumption behind T-groups is difficult to find (Campbell & Dunnette, 1968; Schwartzman, 1986).

There appear to be many factors that affect learning in T-group settings and the transfer of that learning to other settings. These factors include individual personality and orientation, trainer style, organizational style and structure, and technological constraints in the work-place. The duration of T-group learning and its appropriateness to work life generally and work group performance particularly has been questioned by many (Campbell & Dunnette, 1968), and it appears that the impact of T-group training on individual or group performance is modest at best and conditional on several situational factors.

Applied to work groups, the T-group focus on interpersonal interaction in groups reflects a core assumption that such interaction process influences performance effectiveness. On the surface, it makes sense that more competent and open relations among group members should lead to better group task performance. Process losses are a common theme in discussions of group performance. That is, the level of task accomplishment attained by a group is thought to be inhibited by misunderstandings among group members, less-than-optimal interpersonal communication, aversive feelings experienced as a member of a group, and so on. Consequently, attempting to improve the social interaction among group members is thought to pay off in improved task accomplishments. T-group training is one method of improving social interaction. Other methods exist as well (e.g., process consultation without T-group training). Collectively, these methods are known as *team building* or *team development* (Dyer, 1987).Essential to the value of any of these methods, however, is the premise that improved relations yield improved task performance. How valid is this premise?

Several reviews of literature on interventions to improve the social interaction process exist (Buller & Bell, 1986; Kaplan, 1979; Shea & Guzzo, 1987b; Sundstrom, De Meuse, & Futrell, 1990; Tannenbaum, Beard, & Salas, in press; Woodman & Sherwood, 1980).

Woodman and Sherwood (1980) reviewed team development studies up to 1980, and Sundstrom et al. (1990) and Tannenbaum et al. (in press) reviewed studies reported through the next decade. The conclusions of these three reviews are similar: Such interventions have a reliably positive effect on member attitudes and perceptions but have no reliable impact on task effectiveness. In particular, interventions designed to change the interpersonal processes in groups are least likely to effect any change in group performance. However, those interventions attempting to change the *task* process in groups are more successful, though not consistently so (Sundstrom et al., 1990; Woodman & Sherwood, 1980). Interventions to change task process include such things as helping groups clarify member roles or general group objectives. Work by Herold (1978, 1979) also is relevant. Herold classified interventions as either principally social or technical/task in nature. Herold reported evidence that when interventions did not fit the task demands (e.g., interpersonal skill training for a group working on a task for which satisfying relations among members were not essential), performance decreased. When the intervention fit task demands (e.g., technical assistance on tasks with high technical complexity), performance increased. Tannenbaum et al. (in press) report that more powerful research designs are being used more often to test the effects of team building interventions and that increasing proportions of such studies are examining organizational indicators, not just team-level indicators, of the effects of team-building interventions.

These substantive findings suggest that team building and related process interventions are not universally useful but may succeed in raising group performance in some circumstances. More recent models of work group effectiveness, to be discussed later, tend to move away from emphasizing the importance of the social interaction process within a group as a determinant of its effectiveness and toward emphasizing contextual influences on effectiveness.

Group Development: Differing Views

Interest in T-groups and related process interventions led many researchers to take an interest in group development or maturation. No single school of thought on group development predominates, although considerable literature exists. Some work focuses on how it is that individuals come together as a group in the first place (e.g., Moreland, 1987). The greater portion of the literature, though, focuses on postinception issues and has as a basic tenet that groups are not ready at inception to perform effectively. Rather, the group passes through developmental stages, such as *forming, storming, norming,* and *performing* (Tuckman, 1965). The first three stages, which concern the specification of norms, roles, goals, plans, and the resolution of conflicting viewpoints and interests, are seen as necessary prerequisites to the final stage of performing (Tuckman, 1965).

Data supporting the existence of these stages comes largely from therapy, the ad hoc laboratory, or training groups. The kinds of people in such groups, the circumstances by which they got there, the temporary character of so many of these groups, and the fact that such groups lack an organizational context potentially limit the generalizability to the workplace of theories of stages of work group development. Indeed, Ginnett (1990) provides a conspicuous counterpoint to the idea that groups must pass through stages of development in order to work effectively. Ginnett shows that a cockpit crew of an airliner, within 10 minutes, can move from being three strangers assigned to fly together for the first time to a group capable of successfully performing the complex and demanding job of flying an airplane. Ginnett (1990) argues that

traditional models of group development are derived from studies of groups that "import little from [an] organizational context" (p. 445). In contrast, it is the strong organizational context that provides the rules, task definitions, information, and resources needed for the crew to become immediately effective. Such contextual forces remove the group's need to develop plans, assign roles, determine and allocate resources, set norms, resolve conflicts, or do the other things traditional models of group development describe.

Gersick's (1988, 1989) work also tackles the formidable issue of group development. Her research is not so much concerned with the continuing paradoxes or polarities of group life as it is with the evolution from group inception to task completion. Gersick finds that groups do not progress through stages of development on their way to task accomplishment. Rather, the development observed in groups is characterized as *punctuated equilibrium* tied to the calendar life of groups. Specifically, at about the midpoint between the time groups start their work and the due date for completion, groups undergo a dramatic change in how they think about their work, their approach to it, and the energy they put into it. While groups may be learning and making some minor accomplishments prior to the midpoint, it is not until the midpoint transition that groups make tangible progress toward their goal. Gersick's research is a challenge to traditional views of group development and it has the merit of being empirically demonstrated in different settings.

Another critique of the group development perspective addresses one of its conceptual foundations: that group development results from *resolving* conflicts (Berg & Smith, 1987). Berg and Smith argue instead that opposites are a part of group life and that exploration of them is an ongoing and necessary component of group life. They offer examples of continuing, unresolved paradoxes common to life in groups, such as those of identity (individual vs. group), dependency (independence vs. dependence), intimacy (accepting and initiating personal disclosures), and trust (trust requires trust). Paradoxes are not resolved, in the view of Berg and Smith (1987). Rather, they persist, though different paradoxes will have salience at different times. The balancing of, say, how much an individual's identity rests with a group or the intimacy among group members changes, and the change is less a resolution than it is the beginning of the next change.

This approach resembles somewhat Bales' (1985) recent work depicting three vectors of group space and the movement of groups and individuals along those vectors. The approach also parallels that of Altman et al., which rests on three basic ideas: opposition, relatedness of opposites, and the dynamic character of relationship between opposites (Altman, Vinsel, & Brown, 1981; McGrath, 1984). Altman contends that social relationships contain two basic polarities: openness/closeness and stability/change. The polarities are themselves connected and neither dominates. Altman views any extreme within a polarity as self-limiting, hence the system tends to withdraw from its own limits. Altman sees no ideal state, only temporary balance points and, consequently, treats change as a persistent and fundamental aspect of social interaction, being simultaneously desirable and undesirable, since people seek both stability and change.

McGrath (1991) speaks to matters of group development in his TIP (time, interaction, performance) theory of groups. McGrath asserts that group research historically has failed to account for the physical, temporal, and social (e.g., organizational) contexts in which groups exist, largely because empirical evidence on groups has been collected in what he calls *context-stripped* conditions. Groups we meet in everyday life, according to McGrath (1991), are not much like the ones empirically studied. As a consequence, we possess rather limited theories of group phenomena.

McGrath's (1991) view of the nature of groups is that they are loosely coupled (i.e., members are loosely coupled to each other and the group is loosely coupled to the social context in which it exists) and purposive. At any one time a group can be regarded as engaging in a focal task, but groups typically have multiple, concurrent tasks, according to McGrath. Further, groups contend with generic temporal problems (e.g., ambiguity regarding time, scarcity of time), solving such problems through synchronization of behaviors ("entrainment"). And while McGrath's account of the modes of behavior in groups includes the types of behavior previously described as forming, storming, performing and the like, such behaviors definitely do not occur in fixed sequences or phases.

Some of the most intriguing data on group development concerns not what groups experience on their way to becoming capable of performing a task but rather how the level of group performance relates to the age or longevity of groups. Katz's (1982) study of research and development teams in an organization revealed that team performance declined as groups aged. Further, evidence indicated that the decline was a function of decreased communication among team members and between teams and outsiders. The longer teams existed (beyond a few years), the less they communicated and the poorer they performed. Stein (1982) also reviewed evidence that older, more established groups tend to be lower in creativity when making decisions than newer groups. Ziller's (1965) work on open versus closed groups—the essential difference between them being changes of membership versus stability of membership—showed that open groups were often more creative. Many specific variables are intertwined and bundled together in the study of group performance over time. Consequently, it is not clear exactly what causes declines in performance over time, although Katz's (1982) evidence regarding communication is compelling.

In general, earlier perspectives on group development suggested that groups must move through a sequence of developmental stages or resolve some set of conflicts before the group becomes capable of performing effectively. The specific issues of conflict or labels for the stages have never been completely agreed on, but the general developmental perspective is common among competing theories within this school of thought. More recent theorizing has emphasized the nonappearance of stages (Gersick, 1988, 1989; Ginnett, 1990) and the nonresolution of conflicts (Altman et al., 1981; Bales, 1985; Berg & Smith, 1987) in groups.

Prescriptions for the design and management of work groups that can be drawn from studies of group development literature are relatively few. Ancona's (1987) comment that group development research fails to "adequately address developmental issues in task groups within organizations" (p. 220) echoes this sentiment. However, the work of Katz (1982) and Ziller (1965) speak to the usefulness of disbanding or at least periodically reconstituting teams in the interest of effective task performance, though such tactics might have limited practicality. Gersick's (1988, 1989) work suggests that groups can be effective without steady progress toward a goal. Consequently, it may not always be appropriate to manage groups by establishing benchmarks of progress tied to equal divisions of calendar time. Gersick's work also suggests that skill in managing the midpoint transition may be of benefit to a group at work. Ginnett's (1990) work suggests that investments in team development activities for newly formed groups may sometimes be ill-spent resources, especially for groups with strong organizational contexts. Berg and Smith's (1987) advice on managing groups effectively calls for adopting an attitude of approaching the anxiety associated with the unsettled paradoxes of group life rather than fleeing from them, and having group leaders facilitate exploration of paradoxical tensions, although such recommendations are rather nonspecific.

Group Composition and Fit With Individuals

What is the proper composition of a group? Which types of people best work together? In what ways must group members be compatible in order to work together effectively? Why? These are questions asked in one school of thought on group performance, that which emphasizes the proper "fit" of people into groups. The questions, however, are of concern to virtually all perspectives on group performance. Like mixing colors in a painting, this school of thought is concerned with the effects of different parts on the whole.

As with certain other paradigms for understanding group performance, the composition/individual-group–fit paradigm is not internally coherent. That is, there is no unified view of just which personal factors (personality traits, attitudes, needs) ought to be considered in combination as determinants of group task effectiveness. Nonetheless, the differing views all share the idea that certain combinations of people in a group are more likely to result in more effective group performance than other combinations.

For example, the performance of groups with either similar or dissimilar cultural backgrounds was studied by Fiedler and colleagues (Fiedler, 1966; Fiedler, Meuwese, & Oonk, 1961). Cultural similarity was defined in terms of native language, religious, or regional differences. Performance differences in groups were unrelated to cultural differences among group members. Recent interest in organizational demography would seem to have many implications for work group effectiveness. For example, O'Reilly, Caldwell, and Barnett (1989) also found that turnover among group members is related to work group demography, and Zenger and Lawrence (1989) found that the demography of work unit members predicts the frequency of technical communications. In these studies demography was assessed in terms of age and tenure and no direct measures of work group effectiveness were obtained. Jackson et al. (1991) studied the demographic heterogeneity of top management teams in bank holding companies. Although the study did not assess the relation between group heterogeneity and performance effectiveness, it did find that more demographically heterogeneous teams had higher rates of member turnover than did the less heterogeneous teams. Heterogeneity was assessed in this study through several measures, including age, tenure, experience outside the financial industry, military experience, and various aspects of prior education.

Research on group problem solving and creativity provided an early confirmation of the effects of composition on group performance. For example, groups made up of people with dissimilar personality profiles have been found to perform better than groups made up of people with similar personality profiles (Hoffman, 1959; Hoffman & Maier, 1961) in terms of the quality and innovativeness of solutions produced. Stein (1982) also reviews evidence that groups made up of people with heterogeneous characteristics tend to be more creative when using *synectics*, a creativity-enhancing technique. Synectics is a technique meant to stimulate creative problem solving through the use of metaphors and analogies to depict problems, thus making them "strange" or "unfamiliar" and facilitating their unconventional resolution (Stein, 1975). The value of heterogeneity among members in decision making groups is implied by the work of Janis (1982) and others (e.g., Ziller, 1965), who prescribe diversity among group members as a means of enhancing the quality of group decision making. Hence, it appears that staffing groups in a way that maximizes member differences may contribute to performance in problem solving and decision making (Guzzo, 1986).

Not surprisingly, group performance is positively related to the abilities of its members (Hill, 1982). However, it may be that certain combinations of member ability are more efficacious than others. Some research has formed homogeneous and heterogeneous groups on the basis of members' intellectual abilities and examined the performance of those groups on a subsequent intellectual test (e.g., Goldman, 1965; Laughlin, Branch, & Johnson, 1969). Some results indicated that groups made up of mixed levels of ability tended to do better than groups made up of individuals with similar levels of ability. Other research, though, has shown that placing similarly talented people in a group can indeed be an effective way of staffing groups when group members are high in ability. Tziner and Eden's (1985) study of military crews showed that a high-ability member's contribution to performance was most pronounced when all other crew members also were high in ability. Tziner and Eden state that "talent is used more effectively when concentrated than when spread around" (p. 91). The type of tasks performed may be important in determining the relationship between group effectiveness and individual-group fit with respect to ability (Guzzo, 1988) and may help explain differences between studies such as Laughlin et al. (1969) and Tziner and Eden (1985). The former examined performance on a purely intellectual task while the latter examined performance on a wide variety of military tasks over a two-month period.

One of the more noted theories of individual-group fit has been presented by Schutz (1955, 1958, 1967). Schutz's Fundamental Interpersonal Relations Orientation (FIRO) is a theory not only of *which* personal attributes of members, in combination, affect group performance but also of *why* this is so. Schutz argued that three basic human needs are expressed in group interaction. These are needs for *inclusion* (a desire to accept or be accepted by others), *control* (a desire to influence or be influenced), and *affection* (a desire to like and love others and be liked and loved in return). Schutz asserts that people develop patterned ways of expressing these needs as adults in groups, ways that are a product of childhood experiences.

The basic assumption is that groups composed of people with compatible need expressions will be more effective than groups composed of people with incompatible need expressions. Compatibility exists in multiple dimensions. *Originator* compatibility refers to the fit of people who tend to initiate inclusion, control, and affection in a group with those who tend to receive it. Compatible groups are populated by initiators and receivers. *Interchange* compatibility concerns the agreement among group members about just how much inclusion, control, and affection should be expressed in a group. In an incompatible group, for example, some members may desire more expression of affection than others. Originator and interchange compatibility are regarded in the theory as the two primary determinants of overall compatibility in groups, although a third type also has been specified, *reciprocal* compatibility. Reciprocal compatibility can best be thought of as referring to the extent to which any two people in a group mutually satisfy each other's preferences regarding the expression of inclusion, control, and affection. (A group can be regarded as a set of $n \times (n-1)/2$ pairs of people, where n = number of people in the group). A measure for assessing the three needs and their two forms of expression is the FIRO-B index.

Evidence provided by Schutz (1958) supported the theory's prediction that compatible groups are more effective than incompatible groups. Reddy and Byrnes (1972) found that compatibility on the dimensions of control and affection related to performance (in terms of time to task completion) in groups of managers studied in a laboratory setting. In contrast, results failing to detect relationships between compatibility and group performance also have been reported (e.g., Hill, 1982; Moos & Spiesman, 1962; Shaw & Nickols, 1964). Hill (1982), in fact, found that *in*compatibility was related to the productivity of teams of systems analysts. Thus, evidence concerning relationships between need compatibilities as defined by Schutz and group task effectiveness is quite inconclusive. More recently,

considerable interest has been shown in the degree of compatibility in terms of cognitive styles as assessed by the *Myers-Briggs Type Indicator* ® assessment instrument, although there is little research evidence presently available that substantiates a relationship of such compatibility to group performance.

As Shaw's (1981) literature review attests, the nature of the social interaction in a group (who talks to whom, expressions of attraction among members) are certainly affected by the mix of group member characteristics. Effective task performance, however, is a different issue. The importance of composition, demography, and individual-group fit are not widely investigated for their connection to task performance, and when they are, the evidence often is mixed. Ability is an exception. Greater member ability leads to better group performance (Hill, 1982), and there appears to be a positive interaction effect such that groups composed of all high-ability people perform better than the sum of their abilities would predict (Tziner & Eden, 1985). One domain in which some support exists for the value of heterogeneity is in problem solving tasks, although even here the evidence is not completely consistent. Further, there is little specification of the intervening psychological processes that would mediate the effects of heterogeneity on effective performance. The development of better theory in this regard would be quite useful as a guide to future research and to organizations explicitly seeking to staff for team effectiveness.

Group Goals and Task Performance

The operation and effects of goals on individual task performance has been much investigated in industrial and organizational psychology. Distinct from that literature but in some ways analogous to it is a body of research and theory on goals and group performance. Research on group goals involves two general themes. One is personal versus group goals and the reconciliation or irreconciliation of the sometimes multiple, competing objectives of a group and its various members. The other, more analogous to the individual performance goal literature, addresses the effect of group goals on performance, including reactions to successful and unsuccessful goal attainment. We will deal with these themes in order.

Personal Versus Group Goals

Research on conflicts between personal and group goals has been concerned mostly with inconsistencies between one member's personal interests or goals and another's or between one member and the group as a whole. Task performance by the group has not been a popular dependent variable in such research. Rather, such goal inconsistencies have been more frequently examined as they relate to matters of interpersonal dynamics within groups, as illustrated by the assertion by Mackie and Goethals (1987) that "intragroup life is marked by a seeking of isomorphism between individual and group goals" (pp. 150–151). The processes by which isomorphism, or goal compatibility, is sought include exercising social influence, engaging in cooperative or competitive interaction, or the dynamics of inclusion and exclusion (e.g., leaving or joining a group), according to Mackie and Goethals (1987).

Cartwright and Zander (1968) speak of *person-oriented motives* and *group-oriented motives* held by members of groups. Person-oriented motives concern personal ends or goals that can exist independent of one's group membership and the attainment of which can be facilitated or obstructed by a group. Group-oriented motives concern attainments of the group. These two motives coexist in groups. It is the interdependence among these motives that is thought to determine such things as remaining a member of the group and expending energy in the pursuit of group goals.

In 1977, Zander summarized and extrapolated from research on group motivation and performance and summarized several points, including the following: (a) the stronger the group-oriented motives of members, the better the group performs, (b) the desire for group goal attainment often overwhelms the desire for the attainment of personal goals, and (c) the desire for group success increases as a group experiences prior success. This emphasis on the dynamics of individuals' motivation for group success is rare among schools of thought on the determinants of effective group performance.

Goals and Performance

Early findings on the impact of goals on performance come from the work of Zander (e.g., Zander & Medow, 1963; Zander & Newcomb, 1967). They found, for example, that group goals can bring about high group performance, especially when performance feedback is available (Zander, 1971), regardless of the goal difficulty level. Group goal levels are more likely to rise after a success than fall after a failure, and group members evaluate their groups according to discrepancies between aspired-to goals and actual group goal attainment (Zander, 1971; Zander & Medow, 1963).

A different perspective on understanding how group goals affect performance involves the concept of tension. According to this perspective, the establishment of task-related goals creates a tension within group members, and the tension persists until it is reduced by goal attainment (Horwitz, 1954). Pritchard, Jones, Roth, Stuebing, and Ekeberg, (1988), without invoking the concept of goal-induced tension, provide a further demonstration of the positive impact of goals on group performance in an organization. Whatever the specific mediating mechanisms, research findings show that goals for groups produce performance consequences for groups much as they do for individuals (Shaw, 1981).

Recent Models of
Work Group Effectiveness

To this point, we have reviewed schools of thought that have been in existence a decade or more and, for the most part, have some appreciable body of research associated with them. As we have seen, sometimes only small portions of that existing body of research directly relates to understanding the causes of effective performance in work groups. That is, dependent variables other than performance effectiveness are more frequently studied.

Recently, considerably more attention has been given to performance effectiveness as a dependent variable. In fact, there has been a burgeoning interest in work groups in organizations, leading to the appearance of several theoretical models of work group effectiveness. We turn now to these models. Because these models are recent, relatively little research has accumulated with which to assess their validity. However, as a set the models seem quite testable, at least in many of their essential components, and we expect research on the models to appear over the next few years. These models are quite eclectic, and it will become readily apparent that they owe much to the various schools of thought reviewed thus far.

We believe the appearance of these models marks an important change in the stream of research on group dynamics. More specifically, the nature of inquiry into group effectiveness has changed from, What can be learned from basic social psychological research in group dynamics that is useful for understanding performance effectiveness by groups? to What are the peculiar features of organizations that determine the effectiveness of the groups at work? This new wave in research on group effectiveness is not simply a shift from basic to applied research. The new wave is quite basic in that it is theory driven and it pursues what are believed to be fundamental determinants of group effectiveness. Newer theories tend to regard the group as whole, and place a much greater emphasis on *contextual* influences on group performance rather than just on intragroup factors. Related to the emphasis on contextual factors is the choice of research methods. More recent research tends to be done in the settings to which findings are meant to be generalized: organizations. Traditionally, laboratories have been the most frequent settings for group research (McGrath, 1984; McGrath & Altman, 1966). In fact, McGrath and Altman (1966) reported that only 5 percent of group research to that date was conducted in naturally occurring settings. The theoretical and methodological orientations of recent developments clearly are entwined: Newer theories emphasize contextual influences on performance, the very influences laboratory settings are designed to hold constant or minimize. Relatedly, newer theories are quite multivariate. Thus, research methods are being adopted (e.g., qualitative observation, causal modeling) that permit simultaneous examination of multiple influences.

Indeed, we believe that the popularity of multivariate model-fitting, anthropological-style methods of qualitative research, and action research that mixes qualitative and quantitative data will continue to increase in the study of groups at work. These approaches are consonant with an increased emphasis on studying naturally occurring, "real" groups over time at work. Correspondingly, experimental methods involving concocted and quasi groups will decline in the investigation of group performance effectiveness as a dependent variable. Perhaps work group effectiveness research will become its own domain apart from group dynamics research done in a more traditional, experimental sociopsychological vein. We do not advocate such a breach, we merely predict it. And we are not alone. Two social psychologists, Levine and Moreland (1990), after reviewing sociopsychological research completed during the 1980s, have this to say:

Despite all the excellent research on small groups within social psychology, that discipline has already lost its dominance in this field. The torch has been passed to (or, more accurately, picked up by) colleagues in other disciplines, particularly organizational psychology. They have no doubts about the importance of small groups and are often in the forefront of group research. So, rather than lamenting the decline of interest in groups, we should all be celebrating its resurgence, albeit in a different locale. (p. 620)

What is the shape of these more recent models of work group effectiveness?

Input–Process–Output Foundations

Hackman and Morris (1975) published a widely cited review of evidence concerning the traditional view that group performance effectiveness is best understood in terms of an input–process–output framework, as discussed earlier. Their conclusions, abstracted, were that (a) the group interaction process clearly is affected by the nature of inputs in terms of member skills, status differences, and so on; (b) some evidence, though scarce, confirms the view that differences in the group interaction process are indeed related to differences in group performance effectiveness; however, (c) little evidence exists to confirm the *mediating* role of the interaction process in the relationship between inputs and outputs. That a general, unified input–process–output theory could ever adequately account for group effectiveness was dismissed as impossible by Hackman and Morris (1975). Instead, more focused, targeted models were advocated.

Hackman and Morris (1975) proposed their own framework for understanding group performance effectiveness. This model highlighted three categories of input variables as important determinants of ultimate performance effectiveness. These categories of inputs are *group composition, norms,* and *task design.* The aspects of member interaction identified as important to performance effectiveness were *use of member skill, use of appropriate task performance strategies,* and *member effort* (amount and coordination). The relation of the interaction process, summarized in terms of the three aspects just mentioned, to performance effectiveness was not a simple one, in Hackman and Morris' view. Rather, that relationship depends on *critical task contingencies.* For example, for certain tasks member effort may be very important in determining effectiveness but not for other tasks, depending, say, on the members' expertise. Note that task plays two roles in this model. On one hand, the nature of the task is considered a moderator of the relationship between member interaction and performance effectiveness. On the other hand, the nature of a group's task also is an initiating factor in a causal chain leading to performance effectiveness.

The emphasis on task design as an input factor that influences group effectiveness opened the door to contextual influences on work group effectiveness in theorizing grounded in previous sociopsychological research and provided one of several links to sociotechnical thought. The particulars of how the design of tasks influences work group effectiveness were elaborated in later works (e.g., Hackman, 1987; Hackman & Oldham, 1980). In essence, the design of the task is regarded as having motivational consequences for group members, primarily affecting the level of effort applied toward the group's work. Motivating tasks are those that permit the use of varied skills, are important, are whole rather than fragmented, provide group members autonomy in carrying out their work, and are rich in performance feedback. These characteristics of motivating tasks for groups are like those postulated to be motivating for individuals working alone (Hackman & Oldham, 1980). Hackman and

Oldham (1980) further emphasized the role of the organizational context in group effectiveness. In particular, an organization's *technology, human resource management practices,* and *control practices* were identified as additional contextual factors.

Hackman's (1987) work extends the theme of contextual influences on work group effectiveness. Here reward systems, education and training opportunities, and information management are identified as aspects of an organization that are input factors influencing the level of work group effectiveness. The impact of these input factors on effectiveness is mediated by interaction process in groups. Further, the effect of interaction process on effectiveness is itself moderated by the sufficiency of material resources. Another set of input factors in the Hackman (1987) model are what he terms matters of group design, including the design of the group task, the group's composition, and the performance-related norms of the group. The Hackman (1987) model also discusses the notion of positive and negative synergy. Synergy can be thought of as energy or effort of group members that, if positive, leads to creative and innovative performance, and if negative, inhibits performance. In the Hackman model, synergy arises from the nature of the group interaction process. Data bearing on the model are reported in Hackman (1990). This book is a collection of qualitative accounts that make use of concepts from the Hackman (1987) model to explain and interpret the performance of a wide variety of work groups in organizations.

Gladstein (1984) presented an input–process–output model of group performance that draws heavily on prior research in group dynamics and was tested through multivariate model fitting. There are many specific variables within Gladstein's model, grouped into categories of determinants of effectiveness. Categories of inputs are *group composition* (e.g., distribution of member skills), *group structure* (e.g., group size), *available resources*

(e.g., training availability), and *organizational structure* (e.g., rewards for performance). These input factors are thought to have both direct effects on group effectiveness and indirect effects mediated through group interaction *process.* The link between interaction process and effectiveness is itself regarded as dependent on characteristics of the group's *task,* such as task complexity or interdependence among group members.

Gladstein's (1984) model shares much with Hackman's (1987) and Nieva, Fleishman, and Reick's (1978) work in giving primacy to contextual influences on group effectiveness. However, the models assign different causal roles to the same or similar variables. For example, Gladstein's (1984) model assigns task complexity a moderating role in the group process–group outcome relationship (similar to the Hackman & Morris [1975] work). Such a variable would be an input variable, in Hackman's (1987) view. It thus appears that a shared set of factors are becoming recognized as determinants of group performance effectiveness but that disagreement exists concerning their exact operation.

A modified form of an input–process–output model of work group effectiveness is offered by Sundstrom et al. (1990). Sundstrom et al. cite three types of factors influencing team effectiveness at work: the organizational context, group boundaries, and group development. In the Sundstrom et al. model each of these factors influences and is influenced by team effectiveness. Further, organizational context influences boundary conditions and vice versa, and boundary conditions influence team group development. There is thus reciprocal causation throughout the model.

Elements of the organizational context cited as influencing effectiveness include task design, organizational culture, mission (goal) clarity, autonomy of a team, feedback, reward systems, the physical environment, and training and consultation support. Several of these elements are like certain input factors cited by Hackman (1987) and Gladstein (1984). Boundaries largely concern the nature of the relationship of the group to its organizational context. In particular, effective work groups are seen as those characterized by an appropriate degree of differentiation from the broader organization—a point this model shares with sociotechnical theory—while at the same time being appropriately integrated in the system. The concept of team development, as used by Sundstrom et al., reflects the premise that teams change over time in how they operate and that these changes affect and are affected by the level of team effectiveness. The concept of team development in this model incorporates much of what is contained in the concept of group interaction process as used in previous literature. In the Sundstrom et al. model, such process is a potential but not a necessary cause of effectiveness: Like the Gladstein (1984) model, effectiveness in this model can be regarded as a direct, unmediated consequence of organizational conditions.

Goodman, Ravlin, and Argote (1986) examined recent models of group performance, almost all of which highlight the role of organizational context in determining work group effectiveness. Some of these models more strongly emphasize interaction process than do others. A model formulated by Nieva et al. (1978) is described by Goodman et al. (1986). In this model, *team performance,* the prime dependent variable, is regarded as made up of both individual and collective accomplishments and the interaction necessary to bring about those accomplishments. Antecedents of team performance include *member resources, team characteristics,* and *task characteristics.* These antecedents are themselves thought to be a product of various *external demands,* such as aspects of organizational structure or management practices, although the Nieva et al. model is less explicit than the work of Hackman (1987), Gladstein (1984), or Sundstrom et al. (1990) in articulating

the particular aspects of the organizational context that impinge on effective team performance.

Two other models that emphasize organizational context fall in the sociotechnical school of thought reviewed earlier. Pearce and Ravlin (1987) cite the following as conditions for effective group performance: appropriate *task conditions* (e.g., a challenging assignment), *organizational conditions* (e.g., managerial support), and *personnel* (e.g., employees who value autonomy). These conditions, combined with factors such as a heterogeneous membership and incentives for innovative behavior, can lead to effective team performance, according to Pearce and Ravlin (1987). Kolodny and Kiggundu's (1980) model emphasizes *task and social conditions* as determinants of group effectiveness. The task conditions refer to physical arrangements at work that may be highly situationally specific. The social conditions in the Kolodny and Kiggundu (1980) model are *leadership, organizational arrangements* for the execution of work (e.g., division of labor, personnel policies), and *group characteristics.* The term *group characteristics,* as used by Kolodny and Kiggundu, really refers to issues of member composition, such as the homogeneity or heterogeneity of members' backgrounds, age, and the like. The impact of these task and social factors on how well groups perform their work is mediated by the interplay of leadership, group member interaction, and the technical skills of group members. Like the model of Sundstrom et al. (1990), this model points out dynamic influences among the variables of interest. Of particular interest in both models is the idea that the level of performance effectiveness attained by a group influences the leadership and organizational arrangements it subsequently experiences. A similar point is made by Hackman (1987) and Shea and Guzzo (1987b).

The work of Shea and Guzzo (1987b) proposes that group effectiveness is a consequence of three key factors: *outcome interdependence, task interdependence,* and *potency.*

Outcome interdependence exists when group members share a common fate. The greater the importance and number of consequences that follow from task performance, the greater the outcome interdependence. Thus, the extent to which organizational pay and recognition systems reward groups determines the level of outcome interdependence among members of a group and, according to Shea and Guzzo (1987b), greater outcome interdependence leads to greater effectiveness. Task interdependence refers to the extent to which group members must interact and depend one each other in order for the group to accomplish its work. Task interdependence is not regarded as a direct cause of effective group performance. Rather, it is viewed as moderating the impact of outcome interdependence. Outcomes for effective task performance can be distributed to group members noncompetitively or competitively. Building on the work of Miller and Hamblin (1963), Shea and Guzzo (1987) assert that distributions that foster competition among group members increase group productivity only when task interdependence is low. When task interdependence is high, noncompetitive distributions enhance group performance. Potency refers to a collective belief in a group that it can be effective (Guzzo, Yost, Campbell, & Shea, in press). This is essentially a motivational term, not unlike the concept of self-efficacy (Bandura, 1982) elevated to the group level. The stronger the belief that the group can succeed, the greater its effectiveness, according to Shea and Guzzo (1987a).

Like the Kolodny and Kiggundu (1980) model, the Shea and Guzzo (1987b) model posits dynamic relationships among the determinants of effectiveness. That is, past levels of effectiveness in groups alter the current sense of potency. Also, the manner in which outcomes for performance are distributed to group members can affect, over time, the degree of task interdependence in how the group carries out its work. And like all recent models of work group effectiveness, the Shea and Guzzo

model emphasizes the influence of organizational context. For example, in this model contextual influences such as technology, control systems, and history influence, respectively, task interdependence, outcome interdependence, and the sense of potency. Shea and Guzzo (1987a) report empirical support for some of the model's propositions. Elements of this model have been incorporated in a more recent theoretical account of work group effectiveness offered by Guzzo and Campbell (1990). This latter model emphasizes the role of potency as a determinant of team effectiveness as well as three other factors: (a) the extent to which the organization provides teams with resources, (b) the nature of team goals and their alignment with the broader business unit and organizational goals, and (c) the extent to which organizations reward teams for their accomplishments.

Intergroup Relations and Task Performance

Intergroup relations are studied at many levels of analysis. At a macrosociological level of analysis, colonialism and social movements can be viewed as expressions of intergroup dynamics (Kidder & Stewart, 1975). Race relations can be studied as a product of intergroup dynamics both at a societal (van de Berghe, 1972) and organizational (Alderfer, 1977, 1987; Brett & Rognes, 1986) level. Behavior between two individuals, too, can be understood as a product of intergroup relations (Alderfer, 1987; Tajfel, 1982).

Indeed, much of intergroup theory is predicated on the assumption that group memberships affect the behavior of both groups as collectives and their individual members. Rice (1969) contended that all interactions between individuals contain an intergroup component. That is, how two people act toward each other to some degree reflects their respective group memberships and the relations that exist among those groups. Tajfel (1982), for example, argues that the effects of group memberships can be the overwhelming force in determining interpersonal relations. Sherif (1966) proposed that intergroup behavior occurs "whenever individuals belonging to one group interact, collectively or individually, with another group or its members *in terms of their group identification*" (p.12). Group identification refers to the concept that one's own identity, and thus the perception of others' identity, is defined at least in part by reference to who is "in" or "out" of the various groups existing in an environment. In addition to groups, other social referents could be individuals or institutions, such as a church. This orientation has characterized intergroup writing for 30 years (cf. Tajfel, 1982; Taylor & Moghaddam, 1987; Turner, 1987).

In addition to its concern with the impact of intergroup conflict on individual attitudes and behavior, intergroup research also largely concerns psychological processes that guide group members' behavior and perceptions in an intergroup context. Still other research concerns the amelioration of intergroup conflict.

However, there is relatively little research directly bearing on how relations between groups in organizations influence the effectiveness with which those groups perform their work. There is much, though, that implies that task performance is often impaired by adversarial relations between groups. However, we must remain open to the possibility that discordant relations among groups may at times contribute to enhanced work performance. The following sections review schools of thought on intergroup relations in organizations.

Realistic Conflict

The realistic conflict perspective assumes that conflict exists between groups as a result of incompatible group interests. Put simply, "real" conflicts of interest are the root cause of intergroup friction. Such a perspective has an easy applicability to organizational life in which competition between groups (departments, work crews, etc.) may exist for budget, space, personnel, prestige, and so on. The perspective emphasizes functional relations between groups and views humans as calculative and attempting to maximize their gains.

An early explorer of realistic intergroup conflict was Sherif (e.g., Sherif, 1966), particularly noted for the Robbers Cave experiments. In these studies, groups of boys at a summer camp were put in situations in which there were to be winners and losers (e.g., in contests such as tug-of-war). Such competitions had pervasive effects. In-group solidarity increased, for example, while attitudes toward and regard for the competitor group deteriorated. More aggressive boys emerged as leaders within the groups. Acts of sabotage against the other team were made. And, generally, the boys' perceptions of what was fair or deserved was strongly colored by their group memberships and experiences. Intergroup conflicts were resolved, and attitude and behavior change followed, when the groups were placed in a series of situations in which they had to cooperate in order to achieve a "superordinate goal" that, if attained, would benefit each team (e.g., restoring the water supply to the camp).

Blake, Shepard, and Mouton (1964) extended the basic ideas and principles of realistic conflict theory to intergroup relations in organizations and provided several accounts of instances in which interventions succeeded in reducing dysfunctional intergroup conflict. The interventions included training in awareness of the psychological consequences of intergroup conflict and the identification of superordinate goals. An account of intergroup relations in organizations rooted in the realistic conflict perspective is offered by Brett and Rognes (1986). Ways of resolving such conflicts, according to Brett and Rognes, include (a) designing away the necessity for relations between groups by changing the organizational structure, (b) creating lateral structures to break down barriers between groups (e.g., liaison roles), (c) enhancing the skills of organizational members in personally managing intergroup relations, and (d) using mediators to resolve conflicts. The particular circumstances determine which of these is likely to be most effective.

Intergroup Relations in Organizational Contexts

A more organizationally centered perspective on intergroup relations comes from the work of Alderfer (1977, 1987). This perspective focuses on the group as a whole and emphasizes the importance of understanding groups as embedded in social systems in which other groups exist. This work also takes a clinical approach to research and stresses the value of applying intergroup theory in order to understand not only the relationship among groups in an organization but also the relationship between researchers and the organizational groups with whom they work (Alderfer & Smith, 1982).

Alderfer's (1987) theory holds that both *organizationally* and *nonorganizationally based group memberships* operate in the workplace. Organizationally based groups can mirror *task* and *hierarchical* differences (Alderfer, 1987; Smith, 1982). Nonorganizationally based groups are referred to by Alderfer as *identity* groups. Their essential characteristic is that people join them at birth. Identity groups in organizations often are evident on the basis of gender, ethnicity, family, and generation. Individuals therefore belong to a number of groups at all times. The number and variety of group membership carried by organizational members ensures conflicts. Thus, groups in organizations may find themselves in conflict because of differences in members' basic identities (e.g., racial identities) as well as because of such things as competition for scarce resources or ambiguous jurisdictions.

According to Tajfel (1982), the importance of one's group identifications depends on factors such as awareness of membership, the value one places on membership, and the emotional investment in the awareness and evaluations (Tajfel, 1982). Alderfer (1987; Alderfer & Smith, 1982) extended the list of factors influencing the importance of group identifications to include the organizational context. Part of the context concerns formal management practices. For example, reward systems that stimulate competition between groups for rewards may stimulate heightened task performance but may also have adverse effects, especially when cooperation is required among groups for the work to be done or when competing groups have the opportunity to interfere with each other's work (Tajfel, 1982; Worchel, 1979; Worchel, Andreoli, & Folger, 1977; Worchel, Axsom, Ferris, Samaha, & Schweitzer, 1978). The organizational context also concerns the general patterns of behavior and experiences at work that reflect differences between groups. For example, the experience of being a black supervisor of a work group predominantly made up of whites depends on how the supervisor "carries" his or her racial group membership and how group members carry theirs. According to Alderfer (1987), the influence of intergroup relations on individuals' affect, cognitions, and behavior often is unconscious.

In summary, this perspective recognizes the influences of group membership on the behavior of individuals. Individuals are viewed as carrying multiple group memberships with them, and interaction among individuals can be construed as intergroup interaction carried out by representatives of different groups embedded in a system populated by multiple groups. The abundance of groups and group memberships makes conflict within and between groups inevitable in organizations. Several implications of this perspective exist. One is that the resolution of troublesome interpersonal relations may rest not in effecting some sort of personal change but rather by effecting change in the relations between the groups to which individuals belong. Additionally, a starting point for changing intergroup relations at work is an examination of one's own group, since the influence of group membership is often an unconscious process. And interventions designed to reduce the dysfunctional aspects of intergroup relations—such as interpersonal skill development, joint problem-solving by groups in conflict, and the creation of superordinate goals to unify groups—can indeed be effective, according to this perspective, as long as they are appropriate to the underlying basis (e.g., identity, hierarchy) of intergroup strife.

Cognitive Social Psychology Perspective

Social cognition is a stream of research and theorizing that seeks to understand how people "make sense of other people and themselves" (Fiske & Taylor, 1984, p. 12) by analyzing basic cognitive processes such as perceiving, storing, retrieving, responding to, and evaluating information. Applied to the topic of intergroup relations, the social cognition approach defines groups in terms of perceived social entities (not, for example, in terms of actual interdependencies or role relationships). The self and others are then categorized as members or nonmembers of such entities. Categorization affects the evaluation of and subsequent behavior toward others (Fiske & Taylor, 1984; Stephan, 1985; Turner & Giles, 1981).

Provocative evidence regarding the importance of simple in-group/out-group perceptual categorizations comes from research by Tajfel, Flament, Billig, and Bundy (1971). They found that people can form social categories on the basis of information about trivial differences between themselves and others, even in the absence of social contact or any form of exchange. Once a "we-they" distinction is perceived, evidence suggests that people tend to discriminate against out-group members and in favor of in-group members and to

further perceive out-group members as inferior, adversaries, and competitive (Fiske & Taylor, 1984; Turner, 1981). Thus, the root cause of intergroup conflict is categorical perceptions, according to the social cognition perspective, and perceived social categories can be induced with minimal information and without any history of or current interaction among people.

As Turner (1981) argues, the basis of intergroup behavior is how people see themselves, not what attitudes they hold or how they feel toward others or what social relationships with others might exist. Consequently, Turner asserts that the most effective strategy for overcoming the adverse effects of intergroup conflict and discrimination is to change perceptions and identifications concerning who is in and out of the perceived social categories. Although Turner faults "classical" strategies of increasing contact and creating superordinate goals to reduce intergroup frictions, Fiske and Taylor (1984) argue that such techniques have merit. The most successful attempts to reduce the adverse consequences of intergroup dynamics may well involve a combination of factors designed to alter perceptions, behavior, and the context in which they exist.

Other Perspectives

There are many theoretical perspectives that have been invoked to explain the dynamics of intergroup relations. Taylor and Moghaddam (1987) review several of these, including those tied to Freudian perspectives, equity theory, relative deprivation theory, and other theories focused more on intergroup relations on a societal level (e.g., relations between classes). Equity and relative deprivation theories were formulated initially to deal with individual perceptions and behaviors. They have been extended, by implication, to deal with groups, although neither theory has been applied extensively to intergroup relations in organizations.

Summary

Realistic conflict theory regards intergroup conflict as a product of the goal structures under which groups operate. Research within this tradition has generated an extensive understanding of the consequences of intergroup conflict on members' perceptions, attitudes, and behavior toward the out-group. Alderfer's (1987) work accepts the proposition that goal structures can bring about intergroup conflict in organizations but also emphasizes the importance of other influences on intergroup relations, such as identity group differences. Alderfer also emphasizes unconscious, rather than calculative, influences of intergroup relations. The social cognition perspective emphasizes categorical perceptions as the root of intergroup conflict. The objective context in which groups exist is considerably less important in this perspective than in the others. Research within this framework has demonstrated that intergroup biases can be induced even in quite minimal social contexts.

As has been mentioned, none of these perspectives focuses on the direct impact of relations between groups on group performance effectiveness, concerning themselves instead with dynamics of cooperation and competition between groups for both intragroup and intergroup processes. Stephan (1985) summarizes some of the major findings that have implications for group task performance. These include the finding that cooperation and competition within groups often occur hand in hand with cooperation or competition between groups, intergroup competition can spur effort within competing groups, high intragroup cooperation in combination with intergroup competition usually results is a worsening of relations between groups, and cooperative actions between groups usually improves the relations between those groups, especially when the differing groups succeed in a cooperative task. Some tantalizing evidence on the effects of

cooperative versus competitive relationships on performance within groups is offered by Brown and Abrams (1986, cited by Brown, 1988). In a controlled study they found that group members performed better when they believed their group was in a cooperative rather than competitive relation with another group. Does this finding generalize? Do groups embedded in a cooperative organizational context perform better than groups in other sorts of contexts? Questions such as these need to be addressed by future research to better understand how intergroup relations influence the performance effectiveness of groups in organizations.

A Partial Synthesis and Analysis

Thus far we have reviewed the theoretical cores, empirical status, and practical implications of several schools of thought that bear on group performance in organizations. We find it impossible to reduce the variation in these schools of thought to a few simple statements. However, there are some themes that cut across various schools of thought, and it is these themes that we will use in this section to contrast and consolidate elements of the various schools of thought. The six themes concern (a) group composition, (b) group development, (c) the social interaction process, (d) the nature of group tasks, (e) motivational issues in groups, and (f) contextual influences on group performance. Some of the practical implications associated with each theme also will be discussed in this section. In the final section of the chapter we will return to a brief consideration of the future of research, theory, and practice regarding groups in organizations.

Group Composition

No school of thought is indifferent to matters of group composition in the determination of performance effectiveness. However, there are differences in the specification of which personal attributes are most important and, more generally, the relative importance of composition. Theory and research that emphasize interpersonal fit in terms of needs (Schutz, 1967), personality (Hoffman & Maier, 1961), and abilities (Tziner & Eden, 1985) clearly are theories that explicitly view group composition as an important determinant of effectiveness. Other theorists also emphasize group composition, though giving it a lesser role (e.g., Hackman, 1987). From another perspective (e.g., the work of Steiner, 1972, and others), group composition primarily determines the resources available to a group working on a task, especially an intellective task, and the concern is with the optimal utilization of available resources. From this perspective, the match among members is less important than the sum of resources they carry with them into the group.

The "right" combination of members has been very difficult to specify. Hackman and Oldham (1980) provide the following guidelines for staffing groups: Choose the members with the greatest task-relevant expertise, select or develop group members with at least moderate levels of interpersonal skill, do not overpopulate the group, and strike a balance of homogeneity and heterogeneity among members. Guzzo (1988) discussed some of the same issues in staffing groups and emphasized that fewer rather than more members are to be preferred in the interest of effectiveness and suggested that heterogeneous members can be expected to perform better on cognitive, decision-making tasks, but not necessarily on other kinds of tasks.

Issues of composition other than who or how many should be in a group include (a) who controls group membership and (b) permanence or stability of membership. Sociotechnical theory asserts that groups in organizations must have autonomy to be effective, and one of the primary expressions of autonomy is a group's self-determination of its membership. Little is known about the consequences of self-determination because it is so rarely used in practice and because such a nontraditional approach to staffing has many possible policy complications. For example, if group members select fellow group members on the basis of likeness to themselves, will the result be a too homogeneous organization? Also, on just what grounds will selection decisions be made? Will ability dominate or will "sociometric" considerations, and with what consequences? A study by Colarelli and Boos (in press) using students compared sociometric (e.g., based on personal disclosure and social interaction) and ability bases of group membership. They found little difference in group performance as a function of basis of composition but did find that the sociometric method yielded greater within-group communication, cohesion, and satisfaction.

Group membership usually is thought of as unchanging. The reality of organizations, though, is that group membership frequently changes due to turnover, promotions, and the like. Evidence reviewed earlier suggests that groups lose their effectiveness as they age (e.g., Katz, 1982) and are less creative when membership is stable rather than changing (Ziller, 1965). As regards the composition and staffing of groups in organizations, then, it may often be useful to think of planned changes in group membership to revitalize groups and counter potential ill effects of long-term membership stability.

Group Development

A long-standing line of thinking holds that group development is essential to effective task performance. Accordingly, groups are regarded as needing to pass through stages of development to reach a "maturity" level that enables task performance to be done well. Tuckman's (1965) work, with its catchy summary of developmental stages in terms of forming, storming, norming, and performing, is highly representative of this approach.

An alternative view, shared by many, is that it is inappropriate to think of a fixed sequence of developmental stages in a group which, when completed, enable the group to perform effectively. Work by Gersick (1988, 1989), for example, documents rather sudden lurches from little locomotion toward task completion to rapid movement in that direction. The change is said to come at the midpoint of a group's calendar life. Ginnett (1990) documents an example of a new team that can become effective immediately, largely due to the influence of the organizational context. McGrath (1991), too, dismisses the notion of a sequence of phases. Others, such as Altman et al. (1981), Bales (1985), and Berg and Smith (1987), argue that groups never reach a developmental plateau and instead must constantly struggle with the nonresolution of forces and paradoxes inherent to group life.

Other theoretical perspectives attend to developmental processes in groups, though with varying degrees of explicitness. Hackman (1987) is concerned with the capacity of group members to work together effectively in the future. Effective groups are thus not only good at their present task but also will be good at future tasks. Homans (1950) is concerned with adaptation in groups. From this perspective, group development is a continual process of meeting environmental demands in order for the group to sustain itself. In a sense, the notion of self-regulating work groups as offered by sociotechnical theory (e.g., Cummings, 1978) also is concerned with developmental processes, although no specific phases are cited as benchmarks of developmental processes in groups. Kolodny and Kiggundu (1980) and Shea and Guzzo (1987a) provide models that explicitly address changing relationships among the determinants of work group effectiveness over time. However, neither perspective presents an ideal endpoint or developmental plateau to be attained by groups. While most schools of thought give at least a nod to the idea that groups mature and otherwise change over time, the connections between task effectiveness and such change are rarely clear. However, it does now seem clear that newly formed groups in organizations can be expected to become immediately effective without investing in consultation or training to develop them to a performance-ready plateau.

Social Interaction Process

Interaction process refers to how group members behave and react to each other regarding such things as exchanging information, expressing feelings, forming coalitions, or supporting or rejecting a group leader. Two types of interaction among group members are those concerning *expressive* (affective or socioemotional) concerns and those concerning *instrumental* or task-related concerns. The terms *expressive* and *instrumental* are used by Bales (1953) and are at the root of his interaction process analysis (IPA) method of measuring behavior among group members. Examples of expressive interaction include showing antagonism, affection, dependency, and support toward a fellow group member or one's group. Examples of instrumental interaction include asking for information and giving suggestions in problem-solving groups.

Schools of thought differ in the importance assigned to expressive and instrumental member interactions as precursors of effectiveness. Bion (1961) and Schutz (1967), for example, heavily emphasize expressive interactions as determinants of effectiveness, as does the group process orientation in the T-group tradition. That is, adequate socioemotional expression in groups is seen as a precondition for effective task performance (e.g., Bales, 1955; Likert, 1967; Schutz, 1967). Rarely is the association turned around: Effective task performance is not often cited as a precondition for satisfactory expressive interaction in groups. Definitions of what is adequate social process differ according to different theories. For Schutz (1967) it concerns mutual need fulfillment by group members, while for Likert (1967) it concerns openness among members to each other and an atmosphere of trust.

Nonetheless, the view that expressive interaction is more basic or fundamental to groups than instrumental interaction underlies attempts to increase group performance by changing the style of expressive interaction among members through various team-building interventions or sensitivity training interventions. As noted earlier, the past decade has seen many theorists take issue with the idea that "proper" expressive, socioemotional interaction among group members is essential to effective task performance. The reason is that there is only sparse evidence that interventions designed to alter the expressive interaction among group members reliably enhance task performance (Eden, 1985; Herold, 1978, 1979; Kaplan, 1979; Sundstrom et al., 1990; Woodman & Sherwood, 1980). Such evidence suggests (a) the view that adequate expressive interaction is a precursor to successful task performance in groups is not tenable and, in terms of practice, (b) team-building interventions that focus on changing the manner of interpersonal interaction in groups are not a viable route to improved task performance effectiveness at work. However, the quality of expressive interaction in groups may still be very important in influencing the attitudinal and affective consequences of being in a group (e.g., liking fellow members, feelings of self-worth because of membership in a group).

Other theoretical views that emphasize the role of the interaction process in the determination of task effectiveness stress the importance of instrumental interactions. For example, the models of Hackman (1987) and Shea and Guzzo (1987a) are of this sort. Still other theories of effectiveness, especially those within the sociotechnical school of thought,

explicitly emphasize both aspects of member interaction in explaining effectiveness (as do Homans, 1950; Gladstein, 1984; and Kolodny & Kiggundu, 1980).

The Nature of Group Tasks

Several schools of thought emphasize the nature of tasks groups perform as a factor influencing their effectiveness. Tasks are seen as playing an important role in determining effectiveness in at least three ways: as sources of individual member motivation, as factors moderating the link between member interaction and effectiveness, or as determinants of the instrumental interactions among group members.

Hackman and Oldham (1980) stress the motivating qualities of tasks, asserting that some tasks elicit more effort from group members than others, and that increased effort is likely to result in increased effectiveness. Tasks that elicit high effort are those that require the use of several skills by group members, are meaningful and make a difference to others, provide lots of feedback to group members, and can be performed with autonomy. Thus, the task is seen as a source of motivation for high performance. Sociotechnical perspectives on group performance also point to the design of the task as influencing motivation.

Sociopsychological research in the Steiner (1972) tradition has emphasized task demands as moderators of the payoffs of different methods of combining member input into group products. According to this perspective, for example, a strategy of adding together the inputs of group members working in parallel will be effective for some tasks but not for others, while for still other tasks group success can be attained by any one member acting alone. Simply put, processes of combining inputs must be consonant with task demands for groups to perform effectively.

Tasks as determinants of instrumental interaction within groups is given importance in the theories of Shea and Guzzo (1987a), Nieva et al. (1978), Kolodny and Kiggundu (1980), Pearce and Ravlin (1987), and Goodman, Ravlin, and Schminke (1987), among others. These theories tend to remain rather abstract in their use of task as a determinant of within-group interaction, not specifying critical features of tasks the way Hackman and Oldham (1980) do when specifying how tasks can have motivational influences on group members. As Goodman et al. (1987) point out, though, a common underlying theme among theorists citing tasks is that degree of uncertainty in tasks is an important feature.

We lack useful typologies of tasks for understanding the group at work in organizations. Although typologies of group tasks have been constructed, they have little applicability to organizational settings because of the simplicity with which they depict tasks. While a considerable amount of work has been devoted to the description of tasks and jobs performed by individuals at work, little headway has been made toward describing group tasks apart from the extension by Hackman and Oldham (1980) of principles of individual job design to group job design.

Motivational Issues in Groups

In addition to the task as a source of motivation in groups as addressed by Hackman and Oldham (1980) and the sociotechnical perspective, other schools of thought cite motivational dynamics as important determinants of group effectiveness. Steiner (1972), for example, speaks of motivational deficits that inhibit group productivity. These motivational deficits might arise from too many people in a group or from the lack of individual member accountability. Motivation can be enhanced, according to Steiner, by providing rewards-based group accomplishments. Social loafing as discussed by Latane et al. (1979) also is an example of a motivational deficit that may exist in many groups because

of the problem of identifying individual contributions and holding members accountable for them.

Group goals, especially if clear and difficult, also can be motivating, according to Zander (1980). Group goals are the result of overt agreement among group members concerning what they want the group to accomplish. Incentive values of success and failure that energize the behavior of group members are associated with these goals. Motives for group achievement are regarded as separate from individually oriented motives (e.g., personal glory) that might also influence member behavior.

Homans' (1950) work speaks of motivational dynamics in groups in a more diffuse way than most other perspectives. For Homans, all group members have internal states (i.e., sentiments) that give rise to activity and interaction in groups and are subsequently affected by a group's activity and interaction. These sentiments include feelings, drives, and motives. Similarity of sentiments within a group affects how groups adapt to environments and, by implication, how effective groups can be when performing tasks.

Shea and Guzzo (1987a) use the concept of potency to refer to a shared belief among members that their group can effectively carry out its work. They drew on Sayles' (1958) work showing that industrial work groups behaved consistent with their members' beliefs about the group's power. Factors affecting the sense of potential effectiveness, according to Shea and Guzzo (1987a), are such things as the availability of resources within the group and its environment, performance feedback, and the performance history of a group and its organization.

In sum, models of group performance differ in that they regard the motivation to perform effectively as deriving from several possible sources (e.g., task, rewards, goals, feedback). These models agree, however, in highlighting motivation as a central determinant of effectiveness. The sources of motivation include the design of group tasks, goals, rewards, and a sense of potency shared among group members. It should be recognized that motivation for excellent collective (e.g., group) performance is likely to stem from many sources, some of which are calculative (instrumentality-like) and others which are based on psychological identification with a group and the internalization of group norms (Shamir, 1990).

Contextual Influence on Group Performance

A theme prevalent in recent models of work group effectiveness is that a work group's environment determines its effectiveness. An early expression of this influence is found in Homans (1950), and more recent elaborations of it include Hackman (1987), Nieva et al. (1978), Gladstein (1984), Shea and Guzzo (1987a), Sundstrom et al. (1990), sociotechnical theory (e.g., Cummings, 1978, 1981; Kolodny & Kiggundu, 1980), and intergroup theory (e.g., Alderfer, 1987). For Homans (1950), the survival, and hence effectiveness, of a group is determined by how it adapts its sentiments, activities, and interactions to the demands of its environment. Sociotechnical theorists assert that group effectiveness can be attained when groups are differentiated from their environment and have control over boundary-spanning transactions. The admission of an outsider to the group is an example of a boundary-spanning transaction, as is the acquisition of raw materials. Other models of work group effectiveness assign the environment the role either of conditioning process-output links (e.g., Gladstein, 1984; Hackman, 1987) and/or directly influencing the group and its level of performance (e.g., Nieva et al., 1978; Shea & Guzzo, 1987a).

As noted earlier, newer models of work group effectiveness are far more context-specific than previous models principally derived from sociopsychological investigation. Thus, these models place a heavy emphasis on the nature of the organizational context in depicting the determinants of group effectiveness. Many features of the organization context are cited, such as reward systems (Shea & Guzzo, 1987a), human resource support systems (Hackman, 1987), managerial support (Pearce & Ravlin, 1987), organizational structure (Gladstein, 1984), and leadership (Kolodny & Kiggundu, 1980). Other possible important aspects of organizational environments for groups are discussed by Ancona (1987). Further, some theoretical perspectives (Cummings, 1978; Hackman, 1987; Homans, 1950; Pearce & Ravlin, 1987) attach importance to the degree to which groups can control transactions with their environments as a determinant of effective performance. Thus, organization environments not only impinge on groups, but groups affect their environments.

An interesting analysis of why quality circles, one form of groups in organizations, often disappear after a rather short life in American organizations is that they are not integrated into the organizational system (Ledford, Lawler, & Mohrman, 1988). According to Ledford et al. the average life of quality circles is about 1.5 years. They suggest that quality circles lead a short life and often have low impact because the organizational context does not support them (see also Barrick & Alexander, 1987; Griffin, 1988). For example, reward systems do not recognize quality circle achievement and performance appraisals do not account for quality circle performance. Other types of groups in organizations, such as autonomous work groups, are more thoroughly integrated into and supported by the organizational context, and in such cases a climate for team group effectiveness can be created (Schneider, Brief, & Guzzo, in press).

The emphasis on the environment is a notable departure from earlier theories of group effectiveness and, to some extent, coincides with a deemphasis of expressive interaction among members as a determinant of effectiveness. Further, the practical implications of an emphasis on environmental influences are straightforward: Improvements in group effectiveness can best be obtained by changing the circumstances in which groups work. Thus, organizational reward systems can be changed to recognize team accomplishments, group and organizational goals must be actively managed to ensure that group and organizational goals are aligned, technical and human resource support systems can be adapted to promote the welfare of work groups, and so on. A diagnosis of the contextual factors facilitating or inhibiting group effectiveness should precede implementing changes in order to identify the specific changes to be made to enhance effectiveness.

A Glimpse Ahead

Many people have chronicled the history of small-group research and theory. Steiner (1974) asked what happened to the small group in sociopsychological research. He argued that research resources were devoted to individual, especially cognitive phenomena, at the expense of small groups as objects of inquiry. Goodstein and Dovico (1979) documented the decline during the 1960s and 1970s in the number of articles published in the *Journal of Applied Behavioral Science* that concerned groups. Zander (1979) recounts group dynamics research topics by decades from pre-1940 through the 1970s. He, too, found a drought in group research during the 1960s and early 1970s. He also found great stability in the methods used to investigate groups (the sociopsychology experiment being dominant) and in certain topics of study (group pressures on individuals, interpersonal behavior in mixed-motive situations). Zander also noted that few full-blown theories of group dynamics have appeared and that those that have appeared are "long on logic and short on researchability" (p. 280). Interestingly, Zander cited the causes of productivity in groups and the effects of group environments as topics

that had received too little research attention to date.

Hackman and Morris (1978) examined developments in group research in the 1970s and ventured predictions about the shape of things to come. They predicted that clinical, idiographic, and ethnographic methods of inquiry would become more prevalent, that models of group decision making would advance in sophistication and applicability, and that teams would increasingly be used by organizations to get work done. These predictions seem to be in the process of being fulfilled, judging from prevailing organizational practices and recent journal articles and books. However, we think other changes in research methods are in the works in addition to the move toward clinical methods predicted by Hackman and Morris. As we stated earlier, we think more research on groups will involve the study of groups in naturally occurring contexts and increasingly will make use of multivariate causal modeling techniques to analyze determinants of group effectiveness. Further, we believe that the laboratory experiment will be increasingly less prevalent as a method of studying group effectiveness. Instead, field experiments of the sort by Pritchard, Jones, Roth, Stuebing, and Ekeberg (1988) and Wall et al. (1986) will become more prevalent. These are examples of studies that investigate theories while at the same time attempt to do some good in organizations being researched, such as raising productivity or enhancing the quality of life at work. In short, we believe that many future studies of work group effectiveness will be done in a way that simultaneously serves theory and practice (Lawler, Mohrman, Mohrman, Ledford, & Cummings, 1985).

Researchers on groups in organizations, we feel, are mounting an alternative paradigm to that which governs sociopsychological researchers interested in groups. Earlier we cited Levine and Moreland's (1990) words that social psychology had passed the torch of group research on to organizational psychology. We think this is true with respect to *effectiveness* as a dependent variable, but not necessarily so with respect to other phenomena, such as influence processes in groups or the perceptual biases toward outgroups. However, we do think that there is a danger of an unfortunate schism developing between social and organizational psychology. This schism is due to the divergence of both substantive focus and methodological practices. Nonorganizational group researchers may concede the issue of effective task performance to organizational researchers interested in groups, and organizational researchers may deem other topics the province of social psychology. As for methods, the psychology experiment continues to dominate small group research in social psychology, while other methods are coming to dominate organizational research on groups. The unfortunate quality of the rift is simply the loss of opportunity to meld data and theory from the two disciplines of psychology and the attendant inefficiencies in the knowledge-generation process and incoherence among theories. Perhaps the one topic area that holds the greatest potential for fruitful exchange between social and organizational researchers is intergroup dynamics. Each camp, though, will have to overcome its own in-group biases in order to collaborate effectively with the other.

What new topics will appear as centers of attention in organizational group effectiveness research? In addition to continued research on contextual influences on team effectiveness, we anticipate the appearance of three other topic areas that will be vigorously examined. One is *leadership*. The focus here will be on how leaders manage teams versus individuals. The skills and behaviors needed to manage teams effectively will be investigated. Hackman and Walton (1986) have made initial efforts in this direction. Second, the role of *computerization* and software that permits managers in different locations to act as a group in making decisions will be a topic of major interest in the near future. The focus here will be not so much on managers' reactions to the necessary software or hardware, but rather on how

information is communicated, stored, and combined in the service of effective decision making. Finally, we think issues of *staffing* for effective team performance will be a target of research attention. That is, the identification and selection of individuals best suited for team-based organizations and best suited for membership in particular teams will be increasingly addressed.

References

Alderfer, C. P. (1977). Group and intergroup relations. In J. R. Hackman & J. L. Suttle (Eds.), *Improving the quality of work life* (pp. 227–296). Pallisades, CA: Goodyear.

Alderfer, C. P. (1987). An intergroup perspective on group dynamics. In J. W. Lorsch (Ed.), *Handbook of organizational behavior*. Englewood Cliffs, NJ: Prentice-Hall.

Alderfer, C. P., & Smith, K. K. (1982). Studying intergroup relations embedded in organizations. *Administrative Science Quarterly, 27*, 35–65.

Altman, I., Vinsel, A. M., & Brown, B. B. (1981). Dialectic conceptions in social psychology: An application to social penetration and privacy regulation. In L. Berkowitz (Ed.), *Advances in Experimental Social Psychology* (Vol. 14). New York: Academic Press.

Ancona, D. G. (1987). Groups in organizations: Extending laboratory models. In C. Hendrick (Ed.), *Group processes and intergroup relations* (pp. 207–230). Newbury Park, CA: Sage.

Bales, R. F. (1953). The equilibrium problem in small groups. In T. Parsons, R. F. Bales, & E. A. Shils (Eds.), *Working papers in the theory of action*. New York: Free Press.

Bales, R. F. (1955). How people interact in conferences. *Scientific American, 192*, 31–35.

Bales, R. F. (1985). The new field theory in social psychology. *International Journal of Small Group Research, 1*, 1–18.

Bandura, A. (1982). Self-efficacy mechanism in human agency. *American Psychologist, 37*, 122–147.

Barrick, M., & Alexander, R. A. (1987). A review of quality circle efficacy and the existence of positive-findings bias. *Personnel Psychology, 40*, 579–592.

Benne, K. D., Bradford, L. P., & Lippitt, R. (1964). The laboratory method. In L. P. Bradford, J. R. Gibb, & K. D. Benne (Eds.), *T-group theory and the laboratory method.* New York: Wiley.

Benne, K. D., & Sheats, P. (1948). Functional roles of group members. *Journal of Social Issues, 4,* 41–49.

Berg, D. N., & Smith, K. K. (1987). *Paradoxes of group life.* San Francisco: Jossey-Bass.

Bion, W. R. (1961). *Experiences in groups.* New York: Basic Books.

Blake, R. R., Shepard, H. A., & Mouton, J. S. (1964). *Managing intergroup conflict in industry.* Houston: Gulf.

Brett, J. M., & Rognes, J. K. (1986). Intergroup relations in organizations. In P. S. Goodman (Ed.), *Designing effective work groups.* San Francisco: Jossey-Bass.

Brickner, M., Harkins, S., & Ostrom, T. (1986). Personal involvement: Thought provoking implications for social loafing. *Journal of Personality and Social Psychology, 51,* 763–769.

Brown, R. (1988). *Group processes.* Oxford: Basil Blackwell.

Brown, R. J., & Abrams, D. (1986). The effects of intergroup similarity and goal interdependence on intergroup attitudes and task performance. *Journal of Experimental Social Psychology, 22,* 78–92.

Buller, P. F., & Bell, C. H. (1986). Effects of team building and goal setting on productivity: A field experiment. *Academy of Management Journal, 29,* 305–328.

Campbell, J. P., & Dunnette, M. D. (1968). Effectiveness of T-group experiences in managerial training and development. *Psychological Bulletin, 70,* 73–104.

Cartwright, D., & Zander, A. W. (Eds.). (1968). *Group dynamics research and theory* (3rd ed.). New York: Harper and Row.

Colarelli, S. M., & Boos, A. L. (in press). Sociometric and ability-based assignment to work groups: Some implications for personnel selection. *Journal of Organizational Behavior.*

Collins, E. B., & Guetzkow, H. (1964). *A social psychology of group processes for decision-making.* New York: Wiley.

Cordery, J. L., Mueller, W. S., & Smith, L. M. (1991). Attitudinal and behavioral effects of autonomous group working: A longitudinal field study. *Academy of Management Journal, 34,* 464–476.

Cummings, T. G. (1978). Self-regulating work groups: A sociotechnical synthesis. *Academy of Management Review, 3,* 625–634.

Cummings, T. G. (1981). Designing effective work groups. In P. C. Nystrom & W. Starbuck (Eds.), *Handbook of organizational design* (Vol. 2, pp. 250–271). Oxford: Oxford University Press.

Davis, J. H. (1973). Group decision and social interaction: A theory of social decision schemes. *Psychological Review, 80,* 97–125.

Davis, J. H. (1980). Group decision and procedural justice. In M. Fishbein (Ed.), *Progress in social psychology.* Hillsdale, NJ: Erlbaum.

Davis, L. E. (1977). Job design: Future directions. In L. E. Davis & J. C. Taylor (Eds.), *Design of jobs* (2nd ed.). Santa Monica, CA: Goodyear.

Diehl, M., & Stroebe, W. (1987). Productivity loss in brainstorming groups: Toward the solution of a riddle. *Journal of Personality and Social Psychology, 53,* 497–509.

Driskell, J. E., Hogan., R., & Salas, E. (1987). Personality and group performance. In C. Hendrick (Ed.), *Group process and intergroup relations.* Newbury Park, CA: Sage.

Dumaine, B. (1990, May 7). Who needs a boss? *Fortune.*

Dyer, W. G. (1987). *Team building.* Reading, MA: Addison-Wesley.

Eden, D. (1985). Team development: A true field experiment at three levels of rigor. *Journal of Applied Psychology, 70,* 94–100.

Emery, F. E. (1959). *Characteristics of sociotechnical systems.* London: Tavistock Institute of Human Relations.

Emery, F. E. (1964). *Report on the Hunsfoss Project* (Tavistock Document Series). London: Tavistock Institute of Human Relations.

Emery, F. E. (1976). *The futures we are in.* Leiden, Netherlands: Martinus Nijhoff.

Evans, C. R., & Dion, K. L. (1991). Group cohesion and performance: A meta-analysis. *Small Group Research, 22,* 175–186.

Fiedler, F. E. (1966). The effect of leadership and cultural heterogeneity on group performance: A test of the contingency model. *Journal of Experimental Social Psychology, 2,* 237–264.

Fiedler, F. E., Meuwese, W. A. T., & Oonk, S. (1961). Performance of laboratory tasks requiring group creativity. *Acta Psychologica, 18,* 100–119.

Fiske, S. T., & Taylor, S. E. (1984). *Social cognition.* Reading, MA: Addison-Wesley.

Freud, S. (1961). *Group psychology and the analysis of the ego.* In J. Strachey (Ed. & Trans.), *The standard edition of complete psychological works of Sigmund Freud* (Vol. 18). London: Hogarth Press. (Original work published 1921)

Gersick, C. J. G. (1988). Time and transitions in work teams: Toward a new model of group development. *Academy of Management Journal, 31,* 9–41.

Gersick, C. J. G. (1989). Marking time: Predictable transitions in work groups. *Academy of Management Journal, 32,* 274–309.

Ginnett, R. C. (1990). The airline cockpit crew. In J. R. Hackman (Ed.), *Groups that work (and those that don't): Creating conditions for effective teamwork.* San Francisco: Jossey-Bass.

Gladstein, D. (1984). Groups in context: A model of task group effectiveness. *Administrative Science Quarterly, 29,* 499–517.

Goldman, M. A. (1965). A comparison of individual and group performance for varying combinations of initial ability. *Journal of Personality and Social Psychology, 1,* 210–216.

Goodman, P. S. (1986). The impact of task and technology on group performance. In P. Goodman (Ed.), *Designing effective work groups* (pp. 120–167). San Francisco: Jossey-Bass.

Goodman, P. S. (1979). *Assessing organizational change: The Rushton quality of work experiment.* New York: Wiley.

Goodman, P. S., Devadas, R., & Hughson, T. L. G. (1988). Groups and productivity: Analyzing the effectiveness of self-managing teams. In J. P. Campbell & R. J. Campbell (Eds.), *Productivity in organizations* (pp. 295–327). San Francisco: Jossey-Bass.

Goodman, P. S., Ravlin, E. C., & Argote, L. (1986). Current thinking about groups: Setting the stage. In P. S. Goodman (Ed.), *Designing effective work groups* (pp. 1–33). San Francisco: Jossey-Bass.

Goodman, P. S., Ravlin, E., & Schminke, M. (1987). Understanding groups in organizations. In L. L. Cummings & B. M. Staw (Eds.), *Research in organizational behavior* (Vol. 9, pp. 121–173). Greenwich, CT: JAI Press.

Goodstein, L. D., & Dovico, M. (1979). The decline and fall of the small group. *Journal of Applied Behavioral Science, 15,* 320–328.

Griffin, R. W. (1988). Consequences of quality circles in an industrial setting: A longitudinal assessment. *Academy of Management Journal, 31,* 388–358.

Guzzo, R. A. (1986). Group decision making and group effectiveness in organizations. In P. S. Goodman (Ed.), *Designing effective work groups* (pp. 34–71). San Francisco: Jossey-Bass.

Guzzo, R. A. (1988). Financial incentives and their varying effects on productivity. In P. Whitney & R. B. Ochsman (Eds.), *Psychology and productivity* (pp. 81–92). New York: Plenum.

Guzzo, R. A., & Campbell, R. J. (1990, August). *Conditions for team effectiveness in management.* Paper presented at the annual meeting of the Academy of Management, San Francisco.

Guzzo, R. A., Yost, P. R., Campbell, R. J., & Shea, G.P. (in press). Potency in groups: Articulating a construct. *British Journal of Social Psychology.*

Hackman, J. R. (1982, December). *A set of methods for research on work teams.* (Tech. Rep. No. 1). New Haven, CT: Yale School of Organization and Management, Research Program on Group Effectiveness.

Hackman, J. R. (1987). The design of work teams. In J. W. Lorsch (Ed.), *Handbook of organizational behavior* (pp. 315–342). Englewood Cliffs, NJ: Prentice-Hall.

Hackman, J. R. (Ed.). (1990). *Groups that work (and those that don't): Creating conditions for effective teamwork.* San Francisco: Jossey-Bass.

Hackman, J. R., & Morris, C. G. (1975). Group tasks, group interaction process, and group performance effectiveness: A review and proposed integration. In L. Berkowitz (Ed.), *Advances in experimental social psychology* (Vol. 8). New York: Academic Press.

Hackman, J. R., & Morris, C. G. (1978). Group process and group effectiveness: A reappraisal. In L. Berkowitz (Ed.), *Group processes.* New York: Academic Press.

Hackman, J. R., & Oldham, G. R. (1980), *Work redesign.* Reading, MA: Addison-Wesley.

Hackman, J. R., & Walton, R. E. (1986). Leading groups in organizations. In P. S. Goodman (Ed.), *Designing effective work groups* (pp. 72–119). San Francisco: Jossey-Bass.

Harkins, S. G., & Szymanski, K. (1987). Social loafing and social facilitation: New wine in old bottles. In C. Hendrick (Ed.), *Group process and intergroup relations.* Newbury Park, CA: Sage.

Herold, D. M. (1978). Improving the performance effectiveness of groups through a task-contingent selection of intervention strategies. *Academy of Management Review, 3,* 315–325.

Herold, D. M. (1979). The effectiveness of work groups. In S. Kerr (Ed.), *Organization behavior.* Columbus, OH: Grid Publishing.

Herzberg, F., Mausner, B., Peterson, R. O., & Capwell, D. F. (1957). *Job attitudes: Review of research and opinion.* (Chap. 5, pp. 123–165). Pittsburgh, PA: Psychological Services of Pittsburgh.

Hill, M. (1982). Group versus individual performance. Are N + 1 heads better than one? *Psychological Bulletin, 91,* 517–539,

Hoffman, L. R. (1959). Homogeneity of member personality and its effect on group problem-solving. *Journal of Abnormal and Social Psychology, 58,* 27–32.

Hoffman, L. R., & Maier, N. R. F. (1961). Sex differences, sex composition, and group problem solving. *Journal of Abnormal and Social Psychology, 63,* 453–456.

Holland, J. L. (1966). A psychological classification scheme for vocations and major fields. *Journal of Counseling Psychology, 13,* 278–288.

Homans, G. C. (1950). *The human group.* New York: Harcourt, Brace.

Horwitz, M. (1954). The recall of interrupted group tasks: An experimental study of individual motivation in relation to group goals. *Human Relations, 7,* 3–38.

Jackson, S. E., Brett, J. F., Sessa, V. I., Cooper, D. M., Julin, J. A., & Peyronnin, K. (1991). Some differences make a difference: Individual dissimilarity and group heterogeneity as correlates of recruitment, promotions, and turnover. *Journal of Applied Psychology, 76,* 675–689.

Janis, I. L. (1972). *Groupthink.* Boston: Houghton Mifflin.

Janis, I. L. (1982). *Groupthink: Psychological studies of policy decisions and fiascoes.* Boston: Houghton Mifflin.

Kaplan, R. E. (1979). The conspicuous absence of evidence that process consultation enhances task performance. *Journal of Applied Behavioral Science, 15,* 346–360.

Katz, R. (1982). The effects of group longevity on project communication and performance. *Administrative Science Quarterly, 27,* 81–104.

Kidder, L. H., & Stewart, V. M. (1975). *The psychology of intergroup relations.* New York: McGraw-Hill.

Kolodny, H., & Kiggundu, M. N. (1980). Towards the development of a sociotechnical systems model in woodland mechanical harvesting. *Human Relations, 33,* 623–645.

Latane, B. (1986). Responsibility and effort in organizations. In P. S. Goodman (Ed.), *Designing effective work groups.* San Francisco: Jossey-Bass.

Latane, B., Williams, K., & Harkins, S. (1979). Many hands make light the work: The causes and consequences of social loafing. *Journal of Personality and Social Psychology, 37,* 822–832.

Laughlin, P. R., Branch, L. G., & Johnson, H. H. (1969). Individual versus triadic performance on a unidimensional complementary task as a function of initial ability level. *Journal of Personality and Social Psychology, 12,* 144–150.

Lawler, E. E., Mohrman, A. M., Mohrman, S. A., Ledford, G. E., & Cummings, T. G. (Eds.). (1985). *Doing research that is useful for theory and practice* (pp. 126–149). San Francisco: Jossey-Bass.

Leavitt, H. (1975). Suppose we took groups seriously…. In E. L. Cass & F. G. Zimmer (Eds.), *Man and work in society* (pp. 67–77). New York: Van Nostrand Reinhold.

Le Bon, G. (1897). *The crowd: A study of the popular mind.* London: Unwin.

Ledford, G. E., Lawler, E. E., & Mohrman, S. A. (1988). The quality circle and its variations. In J. P. Campbell & R. J. Campbell (Eds.), *Productivity in organizations* (pp. 255–294). San Francisco: Jossey-Bass.

Levine, J. M. (1980). Reaction to opinion deviance in small groups. In P. B. Paulus (Ed.), *Psychology of group influence.* Hillsdale, NJ: Erlbaum.

Levine, J. M., & Moreland, R. L. (1990). Progress in small group research. In M. R. Rosenzweig & L. W. Porter (Eds.), *Annual review of psychology, 41,* 585–634. Palo Alto, CA: Annual Reviews.

Likert, R. (1967). *The human organization.* New York: McGraw-Hill.

Mackie, D. M., & Goethals, G. R. (1987). Individual and group goals. In C. Hendrick (Ed.), *Group processes.* Newbury Park, CA: Sage.

Macy, B. A., Izumi, H., Hurts, C. M. M., Norton, L., & Smith, R. (1986). *Meta-analysis of United States work improvement and organizational change experiments: Methodology and preliminary results*. Paper presented at the annual meeting of the Academy of Management, Chicago.

McGrath, J. E. (1984). *Groups: Interaction and performance*. Englewood Cliffs, NJ: Prentice-Hall.

McGrath, J. E. (1991). Time, interaction, and performance (TIP): A theory of groups. *Small Group Research, 22*, 147–174.

McGrath, J. E., & Altman, I. (1966). *Small group research: A synthesis and critique of the field*. New York: Holt, Rinehart and Winston.

Michaelson, L. M., Watson, W. E., & Black, R. H. (1989). A realistic test of individual versus group consensus decision making. *Journal of Applied Psychology, 74*, 834–839.

Miller, L. K., & Hamblin, R. L. (1963). Interdependence, differential rewarding, and productivity (Abridged version, pp. 349-358). *American Sociological Review, 28*, 768–777.

Moos, R. H., & Spiesman, J. C. (1962). Group compatibility and productivity. *Journal of Abnormal and Social Psychology, 65*, 190–196.

Moreland, R. L. (1987). The formation of small groups. In C. Hendrick (Ed.), *Group processes*. Newbury Park, CA: Sage.

Nieva, V. F., Fleishman, E. A., & Reick, A. (1978). *Team dimensions: Their identity, their measurement, and their relationships* (Final Tech. Rep. for Contract No. DAHC19-78-C-0001). Washington, DC: Advanced Research Resources Organization.

O'Reilly, C. A., Caldwell, D. F., & Barnett, W. P. (1989). Work group demography, social integration, and turnover. *Administrative Science Quarterly, 34*, 21–37.

Pearce, J. A., & Ravlin, E. C. (1987). The design and activation of self-regulating work groups. *Human Relations, 40*, 751–782.

Peters, T. J., & Waterman, R. H. (1982). *In search of excellence: Lessons from America's best-run companies*. New York: Harper and Row.

Popper, K. R. (1972). *Objective knowledge*. London: Oxford University Press.

Price, K. H. (1987). Decision responsibility, task responsibility, identifiability, and social loafing. *Organizational Behavior and Human Decision Processes, 40*, 330–345.

Pritchard, R. D., Jones, S. D., Roth, P. L., Stuebing, K. K., & Ekeberg, S. E. (1988). Effects of group feedback, goal setting, and incentives on organizational productivity [Monograph]. *Journal of Applied Psychology, 73*, 337–358.

Reddy, W. B., & Byrnes, A. (1972). The effects of interpersonal group composition on the problem solving behavior of middle managers. *Journal of Applied Psychology, 56*, 516–517.

Reich, R. B. (1983). *The next American frontier*. New York: Times Books.

Rice, A. K. (1969). Individual, group, and intergroup processes. *Human Relations, 22*, 565–584.

Rioch, M. J. (1970). The work of Wilfred Bion on groups. *Psychiatry, 35*, 68–66.

Roethlisberger, F. J., & Dickson, W. J. (1939). *Management and the worker*. Cambridge, MA: Harvard University Press.

Rousseau, D. M. (1977). Technological differences in job characteristics, employee satisfaction, and motivation: A synthesis of job design research and sociotechnical systems theory. *Organizational Behavior and Human Performance, 19*, 18–42.

Sayles, L. R. (1958). *The behavior of industrial work groups*. New York: Wiley.

Schachter, S., Ellerston, N., McBride, D., & Gregory, D. (1951). An experimental study of cohesiveness and productivity. *Human Relations, 4*, 229–238.

Schneider, B., Brief, A. P., & Guzzo, R. A. (in press). Establishing a climate for productivity improvement. In W. K. Hodson (Ed.), *Maynard's industrial engineering handbook* (4th ed.). New York: McGraw-Hill.

Schoorman, F. D., & Schneider, B. (Eds.). *Facilitating work effectiveness*. Lexington, MA: Lexington Books.

Schutz, W. C. (1955). What makes groups productive? *Human Relations, 8*, 429–465.

Schutz, W. C. (1958). *FIRO: A three dimensional theory of interpersonal behavior*. New York: Rinehart.

Schutz, W. C. (1967). *JOY: Expanding human awareness*. New York: Grove Press.

Schwartzman, H. B. (1986). Research on work group effectiveness: An anthropological critique. In P. S. Goodman (Ed.), *Designing effective work groups* (pp. 237–276). San Francisco: Jossey-Bass.

Seashore, S. E. (1954). *Group cohesiveness in the industrial work group*. Ann Arbor: University of Michigan Press.

Shamir, B. (1990). Calculations, values, and identities: The sources of collectivistic work motivation. *Human Relations, 43,* 313–332.

Shaw, M. E. (1981). *Group dynamics* (3rd ed.). New York: McGraw-Hill.

Shaw, M. E., & Nickols, S. A. (1964). *Group effectiveness as a function of group member compatibility and cooperation requirements of the task* (Tech. Rep. No. 4, ONR Contract NR 170–266, Nonr–580[11]). Gainesville: University of Florida. Cited in Shaw, M. E. (1981). *Group dynamics* (3rd ed.). New York: McGraw-Hill.

Shea, G. P., & Guzzo, R. A. (1987a). Group effectiveness: What really matters? *Sloan Management Review, 28,* 25–31.

Shea, G. P., & Guzzo, R. A. (1987b). Groups as human resources. In K. M. Rowland & G. R. Ferris (Eds.), *Research in personnel and human resources management* (Vol. 5, pp. 323–356). Greenwich, CT: JAI Press,

Sherif, M. (1966). *Group conflict and cooperation.* London: Routledge and Kegan Paul.

Shiflett, S. (1979). Toward a general model of small group productivity. *Psychological Bulletin, 86,* 67–79.

Smith, K. K. (1982). *Groups in conflict.* Dubuque, IA: Kendall-Hunt.

Stein, M. I. (1975). *Stimulating creativity: Vol. 2. Group procedures.* New York: Academic Press.

Stein, M. I. (1982). Creativity, groups, and management. In R. A. Guzzo (Ed.), *Improving group decision making in organizations.* New York: Academic Press.

Steiner, I. D. (1972). *Group process and productivity.* New York: Academic Press.

Steiner, I. D. (1974). Whatever happened to the group in social psychology? *Journal of Experimental Social Psychology, 10,* 94–108.

Stephan, W. G. (1985). *Intergroup relations.* In G. Lindzey & E. Aronson (Eds.), *Handbook of social psychology* (3rd ed.,vol. 2). New York: Random House.

Stogdill, R. M. (1972). Group productivity, drive, and cohesiveness. *Organizational Behavior and Human Performance, 8,* 26–43.

Sundstrom, E., De Meuse, K. P., & Futrell, D. (1990). Work teams: Applications and effectiveness. *American Psychologist, 45,* 120–133.

Tajfel, H. (Ed.). (1982). *Social identity and intergroup relations.* Cambridge: Cambridge University Press.

Tajfel, H., Flament, C., Billig, M. G., & Bundy, R. F. (1971). Social categorization in intergroup behavior. *Journal of Experimental Social Psychology, 10,* 149–177.

Tannenbaum, S. I., Beard, R. L., & Salas, E. (in press). Team building and its influence on team effectiveness: An examination of conceptual and empirical developments. In K. Kelley (Ed.), *Issues, theory, and research in industrial/organizational psychology.* Amsterdam: Elsevier.

Taylor, D. M., & Moghaddam, F. M. (1987). *Intergroup relations.* New York: Praeger.

Thurow, L. C. (1983). *Dangerous currents.* New York: Random House.

Trist, E. L. (1981). *The evolution of sociotechnical systems: A conceptual framework and an action research program.* Toronto: Ontario Quality of Working Life Centre.

Trist, E. L., Susman, G. I., & Brown, G. R. (1977). An experiment in autonomous working in an underground coal mine. *Human Relations, 30,* 201–236.

Tuckman, B. W. (1965). Developmental sequence in small groups. *Psychological Bulletin, 63,* 384–399.

Turner, J. C. (1981). The experimental social psychology of intergroup behavior. In J. C. Turner & H. Giles (Eds.), *Intergroup behavior.* Chicago: The University of Chicago Press.

Turner, J. C. (1987). *Rediscovering the social group.* Oxford, England: Basil Blackwell.

Turner, J. C., & Giles, H. (Eds.), (1981). *Intergroup behavior.* Chicago: The University of Chicago Press.

Turquet, P. (1978). Leadership: The individual and the group. In G. Gibbard, J. Hartman, & R. Mann (Eds.), *Analysis of the group.* San Francisco: Jossey-Bass.

Tziner, A., & Eden, D. (1985). Effects of crew composition on crew performance: Does the whole equal the sum of its parts? *Journal of Applied Psychology, 70,* 85–93.

van den Berghe, P. (Ed.). (1972). *Intergroup relations.* New York: Basic Books.

Viteles, M. S. (1932). *Industrial psychology.* New York: Norton.

Wall, T. D., Kemp, N. J., Jackson, P. R., & Clegg, C. W. (1986). Outcomes of autonomous work groups: A long-term field experiment. *Academy of Management Journal, 29,* 280–304.

Walton, R. E. (1972, November/December). How to counter alienation in the plant. *Harvard Business Review.*

Weick, K. E. (1969). *The social psychology of organizing.* Reading, MA: Addison-Wesley.

Weldon, E., & Mustari, E. L. (1988). Felt dispensability in groups of coactors: The effects of shared responsibility and explicit anonymity on cognitive effort. *Organizational Behavior and Human Decision Processes, 41,* 330–351.

Whyte, W. F. (1943). *Street corner society.* Chicago: University of Chicago Press.

Whyte, W. F. (1955). *Money and motivation.* New York: Harper.

Woodman, R. W., & Sherwood, J. J. (1980). The role of team development in organizational effectiveness: A critical review. *Psychological Bulletin, 88,* 166–186.

Worchel, S. (1979). Intergroup cooperation. In W. Austin & S. Worchel (Eds.), *The social psychology of intergroup relations.* Monterey, CA: Brooks/Cole.

Worchel, S., Andreoli, V. A., & Folger, R. (1977). Intergroup cooperation and intergroup attraction: The effect of previous interaction and outcome of combined effort. *Journal of Experimental Social Psychology, 13,* 131–140.

Worchel, S., Axsom, D., Ferris, F., Samaha, G., & Schweitzer, S. (1978). Determinants of the effect of intergroup cooperation on intergroup attraction. *Journal of Conflict Resolution, 22,* 429–439.

Zander, A. W. (1971). *Motives and goals in groups.* New York: Academic Press.

Zander, A. W. (1977). *Groups at work.* San Francisco: Jossey-Bass.

Zander, A. W. (1979). The study of group behavior during four decades. *Journal of Applied Behavioral Science, 15,* 272–282.

Zander, A. W. (1980). The origins and consequences of group goals. In L. Festinger (Ed.), *Retrospections on social psychology.* New York: Oxford University Press.

Zander, A. W., & Medow, H. (1963). Individual and group levels of aspiration. *Human Relations, 16,* 89–105.

Zander, A. W., & Newcomb, T. (1967). Group levels of aspiration in United Fund campaigns. *Journal of Personality and Social Psychology, 9,* 157–162.

Zenger, T. R., & Lawrence, B. S. (1989). Organizational demography: The differential effects of age and tenure distributions on technical communications. *Academy of Management Journal, 32,* 353–376.

Ziller, R. C. (1965). Towards a theory of open and closed groups. *Psychological Bulletin, 64,* 164–182.

CHAPTER 6

Organization-Environment Relations

Gerald F. Davis
Northwestern University

Walter W. Powell
University of Arizona

This chapter provides a critical review of the development of theory and research on organizations and environments during the 1970s and 1980s, focusing in particular on the six most influential theoretical approaches during this period: Thompson's contingency theory, transaction cost economics, resource dependence theory, network approaches, organizational ecology, and the new institutionalism. Over this period, researchers have increasingly focused on units of analysis larger than the organization, such as the network, population, or sector, and both empirical work and theory have come to concentrate on patterns of change over time rather than on static relationships among variables. Thus, contingency theory, transaction costs, and resource dependence each characterizes the environment primarily in terms of other organizations and describes how the focal organization deals with its exchange partners; network approaches focus on how the organization's position in a larger network of information and resource exchange affects its activities; and both ecological and institutional approaches shift the figure and ground of organization-environment relations, making changes in the population or field of organizations itself the object of inquiry rather than strictly the cause of particular organizational actions. Points of conflict and convergence among these approaches are emphasized.

Introduction

IN THE FIRST edition of this *Handbook*, Starbuck (1976) began his excellent overview of research on organization-environment relations by noting that the task reminded him of Jonah attempting to swallow the whale. Starbuck lamented that the relevant literature had grown so extensive and heterogeneous that any effort at synthesis would be difficult. After three decades of research in this area, any attempt at synthesis is not only daunting but foolish; hence, we choose a different tack.[1]

We do not present a portrait of a tidy, well-ordered field of inquiry. Purists may prefer a unified "normal science" view to the multiple, and at times conflicting, perspectives that we review and assess. But we think much is to be gained by focusing on significant ongoing streams of research and theory. Each of the perspectives we present—resource dependence, transaction cost economics, networks, institutional analysis, and population ecology—are well represented by groups of scholars doing empirical studies, making theoretical strides, and generally advancing the arguments of their respective "camps." Each of these perspectives is also represented by either important recent theoretical statements (see Hannan & Freeman, 1989; Pfeffer, 1987; Williamson, 1985) and/or edited volumes collecting the most current empirical work and theoretical exegesis (see Carroll, 1988; Mizruchi & Schwartz, 1987; Powell & DiMaggio, 1991; Singh, 1990; Wellman & Berkowitz, 1988; Williamson & Winter, (1989; Zucker, 1988). In our view, these different lines of inquiry represent the most robust current research on organization-environment relations.

We have tried to organize the various literatures in a manner that renders them commensurable and that hopefully offers insight for both newcomers and veterans to the field. Let us stress at the outset that many ostensible points of contention among the various approaches are attributable to either divergent views about the logic of action or to a focus on different levels of analysis. We highlight key concepts and working assumptions, lay out the basic research questions, and present representative works. We emphasize both the strengths and weaknesses of the approaches and conclude with brief discussions of new frontiers and points of convergence with other lines of inquiry. Our goal is to present the major arguments that scholars use to make sense of organization-environment relations.

The Nature of the Environment

Research on organizational environments began to assume salience in the 1960s due to a number of studies that illustrated how factors in an organization's environment influenced organizational performance and design as well as turnover. Katz and Kahn's (1966) pivotal work focused attention on the *open systems* nature of organizations, and this perspective gained wide influence in subsequent research. Early work fell largely into two camps: (a) studies adopting a focal organization or organization set perspective (Dill, 1958; Evan, 1966); and (b) studies that described dimensions by which environments could be analyzed (Emery & Trist, 1965; Terreberry, 1968).

The focal organization approach assumed that the environment consisted of all relevant factors external to an individual organization. Dill (1958) offered the term *task environment* to describe the key elements outside an organization's boundaries. Evan (1966) used the notion of the *organization set* to characterize each of the organizations that a focal organization interacted with to procure inputs and to market outputs. Warren, Rose, and Bergunder (1974) added an important cultural dimension to the environment, pointing to the critical role played by ideologies, political values, and professional norms in shaping the task environment.

Other scholars were persuaded that the environments of organizations were becoming more complex (due to competition, governmental regulation, pressures from private interests, technological change, etc.) and were also changing rapidly (Emery & Trist, 1965; Terreberry, 1968). Consequently, they attempted to develop conceptual schemes for assessing patterns of variation in organizational environments. Were environments stable or turbulent? munificent or scarce? simple or complex?

These early efforts were valuable at directing attention to the role of the environment, but they had limited impact on future research.[2] Subsequent researchers made progress by being clearer about *units of analysis*—is the object of theoretical interest the transaction, the focal organization, the population or sector of organizations?—and *levels of analysis*—does the explanation make primary reference to the actions of individuals, organizations, governments, or broader, more diffuse social forces? Eventually, methodological and theoretical innovations enabled researchers to identify more clearly the totality of actors and attributes that shape organizational behavior.

We turn now to more contemporary lines of research, organizing divergent approaches under three general rubrics: (a) dyadic models of organization-environment relations, (b) perspectives that stress the embeddedness of organizations in interorganizational networks or domains, and (c) approaches that focus on the organization of environments. We believe this partition is pedagogically useful. It reflects important differences in levels of analysis or, if you prefer, divergent lenses with which to view organizational behavior. In moving from a dyadic portrait to a more complex picture of an interorganizational network to a more macro focus on the organization of the environment, we shift levels and focus on larger units of analysis. And as we go from attention to the actions of individual organizations to a focus on organizational fields, sectors, or populations, the importance of individual action recedes. Obviously, when we

look at a focal organization, management strategy looms large, but when our level of analysis is an industry or sector, the actions of individuals and single organizations assume much less salience. In the research reviewed, this change in focus involves an inevitable tradeoff of more extensive characterizations of particular environments for a "big picture" approach in which fine-grained particularities are often lost.

Dyadic Models of the Environment: The Adaptive Organization

Work in the late 1960s and 1970s began to treat an organization's environment as an important determinant of organizational structure and to focus explicit attention on how variations in exchange relationships led to different patterns of organizational action. The three most important approaches to come out of this line of research and theory are (a) Thompson's contingency theory, (b) Pfeffer and Salancik's resource dependence theory, and (c) Williamson's transaction costs economics.

Common to these three approaches is the centrality of the focal organization: The environment must be taken into account in order to explain the behavior of organizations, but it is still variation at the level of an individual organization that is being explained. Uncertainty is one of the most critical features of the environment in each of these approaches, and a good deal of organizational behavior consists of adaptive responses to environmental uncertainty. Resource exchange relations are taken as the primary source of uncertainty in all of these approaches. This implies that the most important elements of the environment from the focal organization's perspective (and therefore from the perspective of the researcher who wants to explain its behavior) are those organizations that provide it with inputs or that make exchanges for its outputs. Finally, the importance of technology in affecting organizational outcomes is down-played in these approaches (as compared with previous work such as Woodward, 1965), and all organizations are assumed to be more or less similar—that is, acquiring resources in an un-certain world and staffed by boundedly ratio-nal managers who seek to optimize both their own and the organization's interests.

Each of these perspectives is also distin-guished by its ability to inform empirical work. Whereas much of the initial writings of the 1960s on the environment tended to be long on metaphor and short on testable implications, a large number of empirical propositions can be derived from each of these three theories.

Thompson's Contingency Theory

James Thompson (1967) in his classic *Organi-zations in Action* portrayed the basic problem of the organization as achieving rationality in an uncertain world. Organizations are created to pursue some desired outcomes, yet they are faced with technologies and environments of varying levels of uncertainty that limit their ability to plan and execute actions to achieve desired ends. Thus, much organizational be-havior can be understood as efforts to achieve a resolution of the tension between uncertainty and organizational rationality.

Thompson viewed organizations as *open systems*, fundamentally interdependent with environments over which they had only limited control, yet subject to criteria of ratio-nality. Organizations can be thought of as tak-ing on three levels of responsibility and control (Parsons, 1960): (a) a *technical level*, concerned with achieving the processing tasks of the organization; (b) a *managerial level*, charged with controlling and servicing the technical unit; and (c) an *institutional level*, which articu-lates the organization with the community and its institutions. These three levels correspond to different sources and levels of uncertainty. Thompson's most basic hypothesis is that in order to achieve rationality and self-control,

the organization seeks to seal off its technical core from environmental uncertainty by set-ting apart both the resource-acquisition and output-disposal functions from this technical core. Thus, we see greater uncertainty at the managerial and institutional levels; in particu-lar, the institutional level is oriented to an en-vironment over which it has little control, subjecting it to the highest levels of uncer-tainty. The managerial level is left to mediate between the technical core and the outside environment.

Conception of the Environment.   Thompson conceives of the environment in terms of sev-eral key dimensions: (a) the organization's *do-main*, or the claims it stakes out for itself; (b) its *task environment*, that is, the elements of its en-vironment with which it is most interdepen-dent; and (c) the *power and dependence relations* implied by the nature of its domain and task environment. The organization's domain is defined by the claims that the organi-zation makes in terms of its range of products, the customers it serves, and the types of services it renders (Levine & White, 1961). When there exists *domain consensus*, that is, recognition of the organization's claims by those within the organization and others with whom the orga-nization interacts, the organization has a rela-tively well-defined role in a larger system. This provides a basis for expectations about what the organization will and will not do, hence providing the organization with a guide for future action.

The most relevant parts of this larger sys-tem from the organization's point of view compose its task environment (Dill, 1958): (a) customers or clients; (b) suppliers of ma-terials, labor, capital, equipment, and work space; (c) competitors for markets and re-sources; and (d) regulatory groups, including government agencies, unions, and interfirm associations (Thompson, 1967, pp. 27–28). These are the individuals and organizations that make a difference to the focal organization by helping or hindering it in setting and attaining its goals. The task environment is pluralistic, composed primarily of other organizations with their own domains and task environments. But the dependence of the organization on this pluralistic environment introduces threats to its rationality—in dealing with their own networks of interdependence, organizations in the task environment may not be counted on for continuing support indefinitely. Thus, dependency on the task environment creates contingencies or potential sources of uncertainty for the organization. In addition, elements of the task environment may pose constraints on organizational action. These contingencies and constraints imposed by the task environment limit the organization's ability to act.

Following Emerson (1962), Thompson (1967) posits that the organization's dependence on an element of its task environment increases "(1) in proportion to the organization's need for resources or performances which that element can provide and (2) in inverse proportion to the ability of others to provide the same resource or performance" (p. 30). Dependence is thus related to the concentration or dispersion of elements in the task environment that provide some form of support. For instance, an organization that faces a monopolistic supplier for a critical resource is highly dependent on that supplier, and, similarly, an organization that has only one buyer for its outputs (e.g., a defense contractor that sells only to the government) is also extremely dependent.

Power is simply the obverse of dependence. In our example, the government would have a great deal of power over the defense contractor. By this definition, power and dependence are not a zero-sum game: Organizations can and do become increasingly interdependent. Organizations may gain increasing power over each other or they may become increasingly dependent on each other. As we have seen, however, dependence implies a greater potential for constraint and contingencies imposed by the task environment, creating greater

uncertainty for the organization. Thus, one of the key tasks for the organization seeking to achieve rationality is the management of its interdependence.

Strategies for Achieving Organizational Rationality. The organization seeks to manage the uncertainty imposed by its interdependence with the environment in two ways: (a) through *internal* strategies of adaptation and adjustment, or organizational design, and (b) through *external strategies*, or modes of interaction. As we have noted, the primary method the organization uses for achieving rationality is to buffer or seal off its core technologies. This can be achieved in several ways that require only minimal changes in organizational design. Organizations can stockpile both inputs and outputs, shifting the environmental uncertainty from the technical core to the resource procurement and output disposal components of the organization. This is typically costly, however, and so the organization in an unsteady environment will seek to smooth out or level inputs and outputs; for example, utilities offer lower rates during off-peak times in an attempt to level out demand over the course of the day. These two devices, stockpiling and leveling, are rarely sufficient to fully eliminate environmental fluctuations and uncertainty from the organization's technical core. Consequently, organizations turn to more complex ways of structuring themselves to deal with environmental uncertainty.

According to Thompson, the basic issue of where to place the organization's boundary is in large measure determined by the loci of critical contingencies in the environment. This issue of where the line between an organization and its environment is drawn is also critical to resource dependence theory and the transaction costs approach, the other two theories considered in this section. For Thompson, a costly but effective way to cope with a part of the environment that creates uncertainty for the organization is to internalize it—to place the organization's boundary around that element of the environment. Thus, the expansion of organizational boundaries is not a random process of growth; rather, growth will tend to be in the direction of the crucial contingencies facing the organization, that is, those aspects of the technology or task environment that are the source of the greatest uncertainty for the organization. Vertical integration is to be expected of organizations employing *long-linked* technologies (such as large-scale manufacturers), while those employing *mediating* technologies (such as banks or other services that link together clients) will tend to grow by increasing the populations served, as this is the source of the greatest environmental uncertainty. The basic point, then, is that uncertainty generates pressures for the organization to grow in order to absorb the uncertainty. This process may be limited, however, by such obstacles as government intervention (e.g., antitrust laws limiting vertical integration) or limited resources on the organization's part.

A final aspect of organizational structure determined by environmental uncertainty is the complexity of the boundary-spanning element. The general proposition is that the complexity of the environment is reflected in the complexity of the organization's structure, or the number and variety of units. A heterogeneous task environment presents the organization with a great number of constraints, and a dynamic task environment presents the organization with a great number of contingencies. The organization responds to this kind of uncertainty by setting up units designed to cope with specific contingencies. Thus, "the more constraints and contingencies the organization faces, the more its boundary-spanning component will be segmented" (Thompson, 1967, p. 73). This argument is extended in later theoretical work by institutional theorists (see Powell, 1988; Scott & Meyer, 1991).

In addition to these internal structural adaptations, the organization uses strategies for interaction with the task environment in order to manage its interdependence and shield the internal workings of the organization from uncertainty. Where the basic injunction for internal adaptation was to internalize the uncertainty, the basic strategy for external adaptation is to minimize dependence and to seek power. Because dependence implies constraints or contingencies, the organization will seek to minimize them first by maintaining alternatives (e.g., securing contracts with more than one supplier of a critical resource) and second by seeking power relative to those on whom the organization is dependent. One way to acquire power is to acquire prestige—establishing a positive image of the organization with relevant constituencies helps to control the organization's dependence on these groups by making support of the organization more attractive. In more highly institutionalized sectors where organizational outputs are difficult to evaluate, these types of processes may become critically important. DiMaggio and Powell (1983) cite the case of a public television station that adopted a multidivisional organizational structure, not because of any pressing technical need, but more to enhance the organization's credibility with corporate sponsors. Such legitimacy-driven strategies become a major theme in the institutional approach to organizations.

Power may also be acquired through the use of *cooperative strategies,* such as contracting, coopting, or coalescing with elements of the task environment that are potential sources of uncertainty. The organization, in effect, seeks to create a *negotiated environment* (Cyert & March, 1963) where the future is more predictable. Organizations may achieve power over each other through the exchange of commitments which, while reducing environmental uncertainty, also constrain the organization's action in the future. Three types of commitments (Thompson, 1967, pp. 35–36), in increasing order of the constraint they impose, are (a) *contracting,* or "the negotiation of an agreement for the exchange of performances in the future";

(b) *coopting*, "the process of absorbing new elements into the leadership or policy-determining structure of an organization as a means of averting threats to its stability or existence"; and (c) *coalescing*, "a combination or joint venture with another organization or organizations in the environment." These different strategies for managing dependence by gaining power correspond to differing levels of concentration/dispersion in the task environment.

Critique. Thompson's theory is an extremely powerful and suggestive synthesis of theoretical work on organizations originating from several fields—sociology, psychology, and economics, among others. Its direct impact on later work, such as its emphasis on interorganizational power and dependence and on strategies for linkage and interaction at the organizational level, can be seen in resource dependence theory, the next theoretical approach reviewed. Although it informed a decade of empirical work, perhaps its greatest influence has been on later theory-building: Resource dependence theory, transaction cost analysis, and institutional theory all draw heavily on Thompson's insights into the nature of organizations and their dealings with the environment.

One difficulty with Thompson's approach is that concepts are presented at a very abstract level. Uncertainty, the central concept of the theory, is vague and is not dimensionalized and made into a tractable, measurable concept. The relation of uncertainty to other concepts is also not as direct as Thompson would seem to imply. For example, the mere fact that elements in the environment are concentrated is not sufficient to introduce uncertainty; most organizations get all their supply of electricity, a crucial input, from a single supplier, yet this is hardly a source of great uncertainty, as this theory would tend to imply. This suggests that the uncertainty construct deserves to be unpacked and elaborated, rather than being treated as a unidimensional threat to organizational rationality.

Moreover, Thompson's theory is generic—assumed to apply to all organizations. No mention is made of sectors or industries, which can impose systematic variations in the types of constraints on member organizations and the repertoire of available responses. Nor are any patterns of historical or societal variation in environmental conditions mentioned. Particularly notable in its absence as a serious force in this theory is the government. In our example of the utility in the previous paragraph, the reason that no uncertainty arises from this relationship is because regulations guard against the utility's potential for caprice. Yet because the government's effect on this relationship is indirect (i.e., not through direct exchange), it falls outside the scope of the theory. This is a serious shortcoming that is unfortunately common to all three of the approaches reviewed in this section. Despite these limitations, however, *Organizations in Action* is rightly regarded as an influential and foundational work.

Pfeffer and Salancik's Resource Dependence Theory

Resource dependence theory (Pfeffer & Salancik, 1978) builds on the insights of Thompson (1967) and work on the political economy of organizations (Zald, 1970) while extending the notion of environmental determinism even further than previous approaches. The basic premise of resource dependence theory is that organizational behavior can be explained by looking at the organization's context. If organizations are presumed to be adaptive, then given a small set of assumptions about the organization, it is sufficient to characterize the environment faced to explain the actions and outcomes of the organization. The logic is similar to the doctrine of situationism in social psychology (Bowers, 1973). Resource dependence theory argues that the organization's patterns of dependence on resources from the environment leads the organization to be externally constrained and controlled. Thus, the theory seeks to account for patterns of organizational behavior by reference to patterns of environmental dependence.

The image of organizational action evoked is that of the manager as "finagler"—an adroit broker of varying commitments and constraints. Organizations in this view are characterized as coalitions, or "markets for influence and control" (Pfeffer & Salancik, 1978): Participants trade off their contributions for inducements provided by the organization. These inducements sometimes take the form of policy commitments and control over the organization's activities (Cyert & March, 1963). Organizational goals, then, are not given but are negotiated at least in part through the process of maintaining a coalition of participants sufficient for organizational survival. Regardless of specific policies pursued, however, the most fundamental goal of the organization is survival. Because the organization is an open system, survival requires importing resources from the environment. As noted by Thompson (1967), this dependence on the environment implies some uncertainty that any "rational" organization will seek to manage. In resource dependence theory, however, the organization also seeks to maintain autonomy: As environments become more certain due to the organization's efforts, the organization becomes more constrained in its future actions and limited in its ability to adapt to future contingencies. Certainty gained at the expense of future adaptability can be just as threatening to organizational survival as environmental instability. Thus, organizations face the existential dilemma: certainty or autonomy. Organizational action involves maintaining the tenuous balance between these two partially conflicting motivations.

Conception of the Environment. The environment in resource dependence theory

parallels that described by Thompson (1967): Organizations are dependent on a resource environment that can impose constraints and create uncertainty, both of which are noxious to the focal organization. According to Pfeffer and Salancik (1978),

> the three most elemental structural characteristics of environments are concentration, the extent to which power and authority in the environment is widely dispersed; munificence, or the availability or scarcity of critical resources; and interconnectedness, the number and pattern of linkages, or connections, among organizations. These three structural characteristics, in turn, determine the relationships among social actors—specifically, the degree of conflict and interdependence present in the social system. Conflict and interdependence, in turn, determine the uncertainty the organization confronts. (p. 68)

The most problematic relation from the organization's perspective is that of dependence on external social actors. Dependence is determined by three factors: (a) the importance of the resource, which depends on the relative magnitude of the exchange (the proportion of inputs or outputs accounted for by the exchange) and the criticality of the resource (the ability of the organization to function without this resource or without a market for this output); (b) the degree of discretion that the external actor has over the allocation and use of the resource, which is affected by ownership or possession of the resource, control of access, and the ability to make rules regulating the resource; and (c) the concentration of the resource, or the degree to which the external actor has few potential competitors for supplying the resource or a substitute (cf. Emerson, 1962). When this type of dyadic dependence is asymmetric, that is, when the organization is dependent on the external actor more than the actor is dependent on the focal organization, then the organization is potentially subject to external control by that actor. In addition, dependence creates uncertainty—exchange partners cannot be counted on indefinitely. Thus, much organizational activity can be understood as tactics to manage external control attempts and the uncertainty created by interdependence.

Managing Dependence. Organizations that have power based on their control of critical resources can make demands on the focal organization that threatens its long-term survival by imposing constraints on future actions. The focal organization can respond to its *demand environment* in two ways: (a) by compliance or adaptation, or (b) by avoiding or managing influence attempts. Pfeffer and Salancik (1978, p. 44) cite ten conditions facilitating compliance. Pfeffer (1985) summarizes as follows:

> When power is asymmetric, and when the external organization has the legitimate right to use that power, and further, when the behavior of the focal organization is under its own control and is observable, external control efforts will be more likely to be attempted and to be successful. (p. 418)

Although there is some evidence supporting the notion that resource dependence facilitates interorganizational influence (Pfeffer, 1972a; Salancik, 1979), empirical work in this area has been somewhat limited (Pfeffer, 1985).

Compliance is not the organization's only possible response to environmental demands, however. In fact, compliance may carry threats to the focal organization: It may be costly in the short term, and it may constrain future adaptation. Even if compliance does not carry these direct threats, it may have costs by marking the focal organization as one that can be influenced in the future. Thus, organizations try to cope with environmental demands, and the interdependence that can give rise to these demands,

by managing the conditions of social control and by managing and avoiding dependence on particular exchanges. Resource dependence has made its most significant contribution by examining the use of various types of environmental linkages as strategies of managing interdependence.

As Thompson (1967) pointed out, one response to uncertainty caused by environmental interdependence is to absorb it through merger. Three types of mergers are considered in resource dependence theory: (a) vertical, (b) horizontal, and (c) conglomerate or diversification. Pfeffer and Salancik (1978) argue that each of these is undertaken by organizations in order to stabilize critical exchanges. *Vertical mergers,* or mergers with suppliers or buyers, are hypothesized to be responses to problematic *symbiotic* interdependence (i.e., situations where one actor uses the by-products of the other). From the definition of dependence above, this implies that firms should be more likely to merge with those firms with whom they have important exchange relationships—organizations that provide a large proportion of the resources the focal organization uses or those that absorb a large proportion of the focal organization's output. In the case of buyer-seller interdependence, large exchanges are most likely to be problematic when the focal organization operates in a more concentrated industry, giving the supplier greater power. Pfeffer (1972b) found results consistent with these predictions: Mergers were more frequent between industries that had significant buyer-seller relationships, and the relation between purchase interdependence and merger activity tended to be stronger in more concentrated industries.

Horizontal merger, or merger with competitors, is hypothesized to be a response to *commensalistic* interdependence, that is, interdependence with others who compete for the same resources. Pfeffer and Salancik (1978) argue that the uncertainty caused by competitors bears a curvilinear relationship to industry concentration: At low levels of concentration, the actions of any single competitor have negligible influence on the focal organization's outcomes, while at the highest levels of concentration the actions of a competitor have a great deal of impact on the focal organization, but these actions can be predicted with a fair bit of confidence based on previous behavior. In addition, tacit understandings among competitors are most feasible at the highest levels of concentration. Therefore, competitive uncertainty is highest at intermediate levels of concentration: The actions of individual competitors have a significant impact, but there are too many to allow stable expectations to arise or to create shared anticompetitive agreements. Thus, organizations face the greatest uncertainty and have the greatest interest in managing competitive interdependence in industries of intermediate concentration. Pfeffer and Salancik (1978, p. 125) present industry-level results consistent with this prediction.

Diversification, the final type of growth strategy considered, is posited to be a response to high levels of dependence that cannot be managed in other ways. Organizations facing suppliers or buyers who account for a large portion of the organization's exchanges and for whom the organization has few potential substitutes are particularly vulnerable to influence attempts and uncertainty. Resource dependence theory predicts that organizations under these conditions will seek to reduce their dependence by expanding into other domains, thereby reducing their reliance on any single exchange partner. For example, firms that do a large proportion of their business with the government, a type of dependence that cannot be managed by vertical integration, should be more likely to diversify in order to manage this dependence. Pfeffer and Salancik (1978) report results consistent with this hypothesis. In general, then, resource dependence theory argues that growth through merger will tend in the direction of the organization's most problematic dependencies. Independent of its

effects on profit, size tends to increase stability and reduce uncertainty; thus, growth often represents a viable strategy for coping with organizational interdependence.

In addition to merger, organizations may use less extreme strategies for managing their interdependence by establishing a negotiated environment (Cyert & March, 1963) through the use of *interfirm linkages*. Such linkages allow organizations to coordinate their actions to mutual benefit, creating a collective interorganizational structure that reduces uncertainty and increases access to resources. Interfirm linkages provide access to information as well as a channel for communication and may be a first step in getting ongoing support from the linked party.

> Organizations coordinate in many ways—cooptation, trade associations, cartels, reciprocal trade agreements, coordinating councils, advisory boards, boards of directors, joint ventures, and social norms. Each represents a way of sharing power and a social agreement which stabilizes and coordinates mutual interdependence. (Pfeffer & Salancik, 1978, p. 144)

Such linkages do not offer the absolute control that merger affords, but they are much less costly and more flexible.

The most prolific line of research in the resource dependence tradition has focused on patterns of interlocks among boards of directors. An *interlock* occurs when the same individual sits on the boards of two corporations. Interlocks represent a form of cooptation—bringing a representative of some element of the environment into policy-making bodies of the organization. Following previous arguments, intraindustry interlocks should be most prevalent when uncertainty is greatest, that is, when industry concentration is intermediate. Consistent with this prediction, Pfeffer and Salancik find the number of interlocks within an industry to follow an inverse U-curve relationship with industry concentration. Pfeffer (1972c) also found the size and composition of the board to be predicted by the organization's need for linkage to the environment. This line of research has been pursued vigorously by Burt (1983), who has developed and formalized many of the notions of resource dependence theory and built upon better sources of data and methodological advances to produce compelling analyses of inter- and intraindustry directorate linkages across the U.S. economy. Burt's (1983) results suggest that three types of interorganizational linkage—direct interlocks among boards of directors, ownership ties, and indirect interlock ties between firms via financial institutions—tended to be overlapping or *multiplex,* mapping onto the same patterns of interindustry constraint. This is consistent with the results reported in Pfeffer and Salancik (1978), who found that patterns of resource dependencies predict similar patterns of organizational linkage regardless of the form of link. Burt's theoretical orientation differs from that of Pfeffer and Salancik (1978) primarily in that he places greater emphasis on the structure of relations among organizations and industries and the constraints these impose on the organization's autonomy, rather than on the strength of these relations, as did Pfeffer and Salancik (see Burt, 1980b). This conception proves to be empirically superior at predicting directorate ties (Burt, 1983, chap. 7). Additionally, Burt's research on the effects of autonomy on profitability put him in more direct contact with the concerns of economics than did previous work on resource dependence.

Critique. Resource dependence theory can be criticized on both empirical and theoretical grounds. The primary difficulty with much of the empirical work, including virtually all the research cited in Pfeffer and Salancik (1978), is that it is performed at an inappropriate level of analysis. The theory concerns the actions of individual organizations, yet most of the studies cited above were conducted at the aggregate industry level. The use of zero-order correlations for most analyses is also unfortunate, as statistical control was not available to rule out competing hypotheses. Further, in most cases the theory was not tested using all variables relevant for measuring interdependence (i.e., resource importance, concentration, and discretion). Thus, for example, the fact that the baking industry gets most of its inputs from the farming industry does not imply dependence in the absence of the other two conditions; yet such a result would be implied by the types of correlational analyses reported in Pfeffer and Salancik (1978). Finally, Pfeffer (1987) notes that the results of the original studies have not always been replicated by other investigators, bringing into question the robustness of the theory.

Despite these difficulties, resource dependence theory has proven to be one of the most fruitful frameworks for the analysis of organization-environment relations. Galaskiewicz (1985a) points out that the theory has many powerful hypotheses that have not been fully explored. For example, hypotheses concerning when organizations are likely to engage in collective action, or when the state will be invoked to deal with organizational interdependence, have thus far received little attention[3] (but see the work of Mizruchi, cited in the section on networks). Thus, much unrealized potential still exists for this perspective. On the other hand, the theory contains unresolved difficulties stemming from some fundamental ambiguities in its formulation. Perhaps the most prominent of these is the question of whether managerial action seeks primarily to pursue greater environmental certainty, as suggested by Thompson (1967), or greater autonomy and profitability, per Burt (1983). Pfeffer and Salancik (1978) take no clear stand on this, stating at some points that organizations "are willing to bear the costs of restricted discretion for the benefits of predictable and certain exchanges" (p. 183), yet at other points implying that the maintenance of discretion and power drives managerial action. This autonomy versus certainty dilemma is noted but not resolved in a theoretically satisfying way. As a result, it is not clear whether resource dependence theory is falsifiable: Analytically, it is no doubt true that virtually any significant organizational action increases either autonomy or certainty; thus, if actions that achieve either of these managerial goals are considered to be consistent with the theory, it is difficult to imagine a state of affairs that would contradict the theory. This problem is highlighted in Burt's (1983) work, where considerations of profitability achieved via structural autonomy are paramount, making the revised theory consistent with the spirit of microeconomics.

Williamson's Transaction Costs Economics

The transaction costs economics (TCE) approach to organizations (Williamson, 1975, 1981, 1985) begins with an even more fundamental question than, What do organizations do? From an economic perspective, a more puzzling question is, Why are there organizations at all? In traditional microeconomic theory, firms are merely production functions, vectors of inputs and outputs. The organizational properties of these black boxes are assumed to be essentially irrelevant to the economic functions they serve. The key question, initially posed by Coase (1937), is why these functions could not be carried out by an individual entrepreneur buying and selling her inputs and outputs in markets. Why, Coase asked, should tasks that are not inherently tied together by technology be performed in the context of a single, hierarchically organized governance structure?

The short answer to this question is because markets fail. Under some conditions, exchanges are not efficiently organized through markets. Thus, drawing on literature in economics, contract law, and organization theory, the theoretical agenda for TCE has been to trace the conditions of market failure and to relate them to the existence of organizations (or hierarchies) and the forms they take.

Several assumptions are critical for this approach. The behavioral assumptions are two: First, individuals are *boundedly rational* (Simon, 1957); that is, people are assumed to be intentional or goal-directed, but limited in their cognitive capacities. Second, at least some individuals are inclined to be opportunistic, or "self-interest seeking with guile" (Williamson, 1975, p. 26). This is not a general assumption about human behavior—it is only necessary that some people are prone to act opportunistically and that it is not easy to tell these people from the rest. An additional assumption is that any exchange relation can be analyzed as a contracting problem. The transaction costs framework treats contracting—implicit, explicit, simple, complex—as pervasive in economic life. This focus on the contractual aspects of organizations is one of the distinctive features of the transaction costs approach. Finally, the transaction or exchange is taken as the basic unit of analysis. According to Williamson (1981), a transaction occurs "when a good or service is transferred across a technologically separable interface" (p. 552).

Williamson's notion is that the primary purpose served by organizations is the reduction of *transaction costs*, the "frictions" that accompany exchange relations. It is important to distinguish transaction costs from production costs, that is, those of capital, materials, land, and labor. *Transaction costs* are the costs of planning, adapting, and monitoring task completion. Initially, this central concept was defined only denotatively—as the economic equivalent of friction in physical systems, or costs that arise when parties to an exchange don't operate harmoniously. In more recent statements, Williamson (1985) gives a relatively more fine-grained characterization of transaction costs. Transaction costs can arise during the negotiation or execution of a contract. The first type of costs includes drafting, negotiating, and safeguarding the agreement, while the second includes *maladaption costs,* the costs of haggling if the contract must be altered, the setup and running costs of governance structures that resolve disputes (including the courts and other arbitrative bodies), and bonding costs (Williamson, 1985, pp. 20–21).

Transactions can be described in terms of three dimensions, each of which affects the costs of contracting for the transaction. First, transactions differ in the amount of uncertainty they entail. Some are simple exchanges that are accomplished effortlessly (e.g., buying a dozen half-inch nuts), while others are subject to more or less uncontrollable events in the future (e.g., hiring a lab to research an exotic new weapons system using untried technology). Second, transactions differ in their frequency (e.g., a large one-time buy vs. a monthly purchase). Third, transactions differ in the degree to which the individuals or organizations involved need to invest in assets peculiar to that exchange, that is, that cannot be used in other exchanges as effectively. For example, a steel manufacturer that locates a plant next to an auto manufacturer that is its main buyer or a clerk who learns a company's unique filing system, both have made investments that would be lost to some extent if the exchange were to stop. It is this dimension of *asset specificity* that is critical in understanding the existence of hierarchical organizations and the forms they take. As Williamson (1985) puts it, asset specificity is "the big locomotive to which transaction cost economics owes much of its predictive content" (p. 56).[4]

Asset specificity is critical because it transforms the nature of exchange relations, rendering them both valuable and vulnerable. To use the example of our steel producer who locates a plant next door to its major buyer, we can see that both the buyer and supplier have a special interest in keeping this relationship vital. The steelmaker can sell to the auto manufacturer at a reduced rate because of its lower transportation costs, saving the manufacturer money. But this relation benefits both parties: The car manufacturer saves money, and the steel producer, knowing this, can count on the manufacturer as a steady customer. Because this relation may allow the auto manufacturer to sell products for lower prices than competitors who do not have such a relationship, the relation is also an economically advantageous one. In effect, asset specificity creates a situation of small numbers, in this case *bilateral supply* (Williamson, 1985), where each partner becomes dependent on the other. Thus, asset specificity creates a special relation that both partners to a transaction have an incentive to protect.

The variation of transactions on the three dimensions of uncertainty, frequency, and asset specificity determines the costs of contracting and, by implication, the types of governance structures that surround exchanges, that is, market, organization, or some intermediate or hybrid form. Williamson (1985, pp. 59–60) argues that contrary to what one might expect based on Thompson (1967) or resource dependence theory, the effects of uncertainty and frequency on whether or not a transaction will be brought within an organization are contingent upon the prior existence of asset specificity. Uncertainty per se is not a sufficient condition, because without some degree of asset specificity to vest exchange partners in a particular relationship, new trading relations could be arranged relatively easily on the open market. When asset specificity is present, however, uncertainty (i.e., unpredictable events that affect contract execution) increases the number of occasions that arise to renegotiate and therefore increases the transaction costs due to haggling, misunderstandings, opportunistic behavior, or the relation being discontinued. Similarly, if transactions are infrequent, the cost of bringing the activity inside the organization would not be justified. It is only when one or both of the transacting parties has committed resources to the relationship that cannot be redeployed within the context of another exchange relation that it becomes more efficient to arrange transactions within an organization rather than through the market.

It is worth noting here that such problems would not arise were it not for bounded rationality and opportunism. If both parties were omniscient, it would be possible to map out all future contingencies relevant to the contract in advance and write the contract with explicit arrangements for such possible eventualities. Due to bounded rationality, however, uncertainty often outstrips our cognitive capacities to write such contingent claims contracts. Similarly, even uncertainty and bounded rationality would not be a problem if both sides could be counted on to act honorably when unanticipated events come up that affect contract execution. The possibility that one side will try to take advantage of the other on these occasions, however, creates a risk that neither may be willing to take. Note that it is not necessary that one or both always act opportunistically but only that there is no easy way for each to be sure of the other's trustworthiness. Thus, it is the simultaneous occurrence of bounded rationality, opportunism (or its potential), uncertainty, and small numbers (due primarily to asset specificity) that creates the conditions for hierarchical organizations to exist as adaptive solutions to problems of market failure.

How do organizations solve these problems that cause markets to fail? According to Williamson (1981),

> the advantages of firms over markets in harmonizing bilateral exchange are three. First, common ownership reduces the incentives to suboptimize. Second, and related, internal organization is able to invoke fiat to resolve differences, whereas costly adjudication is needed when an impasse develops between autonomous traders. Third, internal organization has easier and more complete access to the relevant information when dispute settling is needed. The incentive to shift

> bilateral transactions from markets to firms increases as uncertainty is greater, since the costs of harmonizing the interface vary directly with the need to adjust to changing circumstances. (p. 559)

Organizations may not solve these problems perfectly; indeed, TCE recognizes that running an organization is costly. The cost of constructing an organization to govern transactions will only be justified if these costs are outweighed by benefits gained by not leaving problematic exchanges to the hazards of the market.

Conception of the Environment. The environment in the transaction costs approach is conceived in a manner very similar to Thompson's framework and to resource dependence theory. Much of the focus is on the organization set, that is, those actors in the environment with whom the focal organization engages in significant exchange relations. Both suppliers and customers transact with the organization, and therefore relations with both these actors can be analyzed in contracting terms.

TCE differs from the other approaches in focusing more explicit attention on the employment relation. Whereas Thompson and Pfeffer and Salancik tend to follow the inducement-contribution notion of organizational membership outlined by March and Simon (1958) and to proceed from there, TCE treats the employment relation as problematic and takes variation in the types of employment contracts used by organizations as a matter worth explanation (see Williamson, Wachter, & Harris, 1975).[5] On the other hand, TCE gives relatively less attention to the role of interorganizational competition. This stems in part from the *efficiency* orientation of the transaction costs approach, which tends to assume that the invisible hand of the market drives competition. In contrast, Pfeffer and Salancik (1978) pay more explicit attention to the role of other firms as competitors.

Other key features of the environment are treated as implicit assumptions in TCE. A crucial notion is that organizations are subject to strong selection pressures. It is assumed that the environment operates to favor organizations that are more efficient at managing transactions over those who are less so through exerting a sort of natural selection over the long run (suggested by Williamson, 1985, pp. 22–23, to typically entail a period of five to ten years). Thus, whereas the previous approaches focused primarily on the organization's adaptive strategies, TCE maintains a much stronger role for environmental selection to operate in favor of those organizations that have effectively reduced transaction costs and against those that have not. To paraphrase Thompson, organizations adapt to efficiency pressures—or else!

Finally, the larger culture plays a subtle role in some of the work in the TCE tradition. Williamson and Ouchi (1981) note that some governance structures depend on the culture in which they are embedded. For example, *soft contracting* is more likely to be successful in cultures such as Japan, where dishonesty and other opportunistic behavior are subject to social sanctions. In a culture where organizations are dominated by graduates of MBA programs, on the other hand, *hard* contracts that take for granted the possibility of opportunism are likely to prevail. This will be reflected in the management styles observed in these different cultures.

Key Areas of Research. A large number of studies have investigated variants of the basic hypothesis that transactions are assigned to organizational forms (or *governance structures*) so as to reduce transaction costs. We categorize this work into two key areas: (a) research dealing with where to place an organization's boundary (the *efficient boundaries* or *make-or-buy* problem), which has recently included consideration of intermediate forms of governance such as long-term contracts; and

(b) work concerned with the internal structure of organizations, including the structure of the employment relation and the use of the multidivisional form or M-form.

The question of whether an organization should buy a component on the market or make it internally was one of the first to be examined in transaction costs terms. Organizations contain one or more units that are *irreducible* due to the technology involved, that is, units that cannot be further broken down into smaller units. The efficient boundaries problem asks which of these basic units should be grouped together inside a single organizational boundary. Not surprisingly, the answer turns on the level of transaction costs incurred by the alternative modes of organizing exchanges between these units, which in turn depends on the uncertainty, frequency, and asset specificity involved in the transaction. According to Williamson (1981), recurrent transactions with an intermediate level of uncertainty will be arranged as follows:

> Classical market contracting will be efficacious whenever assets are nonspecific to the trading parties; bilateral or obligational market contracting will appear as assets become semispecific; and internal organization will displace markets as assets take on a highly specific character. (pp. 558–559)

Stuckey's (1983) detailed analysis of backward vertical integration strategies in the aluminum industry is easily the best industry-level study of the boundary problem. Williamson and Ouchi (1981, pp. 356–359) have analyzed the movement of manufacturers toward forward integration into distribution in the late nineteenth century, suggesting that variation in the degree of integration can be explained in transaction cost terms, and Monteverde and Teece (1982) show that an estimate of the engineering cost for developing a component (a type of asset specificity) significantly predicted the degree of vertical integration of its production by General Motors and Ford. Walker and Weber (1984) also examined 60 make-or-buy decisions in a division of a large automobile manufacturer. They found that, although their measures of asset specificity and uncertainty of future demand were significantly related to vertical integration, "in general, the effect of transaction costs on make-or-buy decisions was substantially overshadowed by comparative production costs" (p. 387). Unfortunately, asset specificity was proxied with level of market competition for suppliers, a measure consistent with several alternate explanations, indicating that this study provides at best weak evidence for the importance of transaction costs in make-or-buy decisions.[6]

Much recent work in TCE has focused on the choice among governance structures to *make* or *buy* in particular long-term contracts. Wiggins (1990) has analyzed the efficiency tradeoffs between long-term contracts and internal organization; Joskow (1985) has done extensive studies of long-term contracts for the supply of coal for coal-burning electric utilities; and Paley (1985) has detailed how informal contracts allow transportation companies to avoid regulatory constraints. These studies highlight how transaction cost economizing leads to the choice of alternative ways by which to govern exchange relations.

In addition to vertical integration, two other issues of organizational structure have received considerable attention: the structure of the employment relation and the use of the multidivisional form or M-form. Williamson (1981) argues that human assets can be described by their degree of firm specificity and by the extent to which productivity can be measured or monitored, and that variation on these dimensions will determine the type of employment contract observed. Human asset specificity comes from on-the-job training and "earning by doing," skills not highly useful to other employers. When skills are acquired that

are unique to a particular employer, as with knowing an idiosyncratic and complex payroll system, the organization and the employee both have an incentive to protect the employment relation, because if it were to be severed the firm would lose an already-trained employee and have to invest in training another, and the employee would lose the additional pay that comes from already being trained. When human assets are nonspecific and it is easy to monitor individual productivity, an internal spot market will prevail; that is, organizations and employees have little investment in the relation and, therefore, the organization will not take elaborate steps to protect it. This describes the situation facing migrant farm workers, where the "contract" is in essence renegotiated each day. When human assets are nonspecific but it is difficult to meter productivity, employees will be organized as *primitive teams*. When human assets are somewhat firm-specific but metering tasks is easy, an *obligational market* will be observed, such as the use of internal labor markets, seniority, and other devices to bind the worker to the firm.[7] Finally, when human assets are specific to the firm and it is difficult to monitor productivity, *relational teams* will prevail. This implies the use of socialization by the organization and a high degree of job security, as in the *clan* type organization described by Ouchi (1980).

The multidivisional structure, or M-form organization, has been widely adopted by large American firms (see Chandler, 1962). Williamson (1975) argues that this structure came to dominate corporate life because it economized on transaction costs: Central management was relieved of the burden of making daily operating decisions, allowing it to concentrate on "the big picture" and alleviating the loss of control that comes from an overextended functional structure. Additionally, the introduction of a quasi market into the internal structure through the creation of competition between operating divisions mutes the ability of managers to behave opportunistically. The efficiency of this innovation has been argued for and tested by Armour and Teece (1978), who found that large firms in the petroleum industry that adopted the M-form prior to 1968 earned a significantly higher return on stockholder's equity (about two percentage points higher on average) than competitors with a functional form. Fligstein (1985) argued, following Williamson's (1975) discussion, that larger organizations and organizations experiencing greater growth should be more likely to adopt the M-form, as they stand to lose the most from retaining a functional form stretched beyond its capacity. But in his analysis, which controlled for other possible explanations, Fligstein found almost no empirical support for this hypothesis in a sample of America's largest corporations between 1919 and 1979. Taken together, these two studies suggest that the reduction of transaction costs may be a consequence of adopting the M-form, but not its cause, a topic we will touch on below.

Critique. In a relatively short time, TCE has had a major influence on research in organization theory. Recognizing that all kinds of governance structures have inherent flaws, TCE is thus a comparative exercise: One form of governance must always be compared with another. Williamson has focused the attention of organizational researchers on the question of what the critical attributes are with respect to which transactions differ. To be sure, a good deal of additional work remains to be done to operationalize the notion of transaction costs. Nevertheless, the general argument—that the comparative efficiency of alternative modes of economic organization varies systematically with the attributes of transactions—is an enduring and original contribution to the analysis of organization-environment relations.

There is no shortage of detractors from this approach, however, particularly among organizational sociologists. Perrow (1981, 1986) argues that the willful neglect of power in this approach blinds it to issues of control and domination. He also contends that the failure to define adequately the nature of transaction costs biases TCE in favor of the choice of hierarchy. More concretely, parties in contracting situations are treated as free agents voluntarily entering into agreements, yet the migrant worker in our example is hardly in the same situation at the bargaining table as his potential employer. Such processes are common in the workplace yet, thus far, have received little attention in the transaction costs approach. A second general criticism of TCE is that many of the costs that Williamson associates with market transactions are reproduced and even exacerbated by bringing transactions inside an organizational boundary (Dow, 1987). Hierarchies may provide mechanisms to resolve disputes, but organizational life can also promote more extensive and costly strife (e.g., between individuals or departments); hierarchies allow routine performance monitoring, but large-scale fraud or embezzlement against an organization requires an insider (Granovetter, 1985). To be sure, Williamson's claim is a comparative one—that hierarchy is superior in these respects to market relations. But clearly as Dow (1987), Putterman (1986), Powell (1990), and others have pointed out, he neglects the myriad alternative forms of organization, for example, networks, nonprofits, cooperatives, small firm consortia, relational contracts, and so forth, that are alternatives to hierarchical control under a wide range of conditions. Moreover, Dow (1987) makes the telling point that no attention is given to the possibility that hierarchical authority might be abused by superiors in an opportunistic fashion, rather than always serving as a device for curbing opportunism among lower level employees.

Granovetter (1985) argues that the characters who populate TCE are *undersocialized,* that is, their actions lack the sort of social context within which human action is in fact embedded. Exchange partners vested in a relationship due to asset specificity are described as if they were playing a Prisoner's Dilemma game, each coolly calculating and distrustful of the other, their actions unconstrained by any sense of obligation and determined by potential pay-offs rather than by membership or social affiliations or by a history of past associations. More broadly, Zald (1987) points out that macro political processes are outside the scope of this theory; thus, the application of this approach to every economic institution will both oversimplify and depoliticize the historical record.[8]

To these criticisms we will add an observation about the scope of TCE. A key assumption is that competition and market forces exert strong selection pressures on governance structures, winnowing out unfit forms. But selection pressures are not uniformly distributed across the economy. In some sectors—such as industries dominated by oligopolies—and in some branches of the public sector and perhaps in the nonprofit sector, selection pressures operate with modest force, and thus there is no driving environmental force shaping the choice of governance structure. The assumption of efficiency is not a substitute for a well-thought-out consideration of the organization's environment. Granovetter (1985) makes the case rather pointedly that "the operation of alleged selection pressures is here neither an object of study nor even a falsifiable proposition but rather an article of faith" (p. 503). One place to start rectifying this is to consider pressures for efficiency as variable, not fixed. Additionally, it should be noted that selection pressures are not causes of organizational behavior, strictly speaking; rather, their effects shape the consequences of behavior. To the extent that selection and efficiency pressures are muted or operate only over prolonged periods, the degree to which they shape organizational behavior in the short run is problematic indeed, and as the apocalyptic line from John Maynard Keynes goes, in the long run we are all dead.

Limits to the Organization-centered Paradigm

The three approaches described above—Thompson's contingency theory, Pfeffer and Salancik's resource dependence theory, and Williamson's transaction costs economics—greatly extended the power and scope of organization theory by bringing the organization's environment into clearer focus. Fundamental issues, such as how an organization decides where to place its boundaries, received fresh insights. In addition, new issues, such as what factors determine the types of relations the organization maintains with external actors, were raised and probed. Yet each of these approaches is limited by the basic assumptions they invoke. Each assumes that organizations are rather proactive and flexible in their ability to adapt. Each focuses primary attention on dyadic exchange with members of the organization set to explain an organization's actions and structure. And each assumes a fairly high degree of rationality (albeit bounded) in the choices that organizations or their leaders make. We briefly scrutinize each of these assumptions.

Organizations are constrained in their ability to adapt by a number of factors, both external and internal. Stinchcombe (1965) long ago noted the seemingly peculiar tendency of organizational structures to be "imprinted" at the organization's birth. He argued that organizations are created using the social technology of the day, leading to cohorts of organizations sharing much in common but differing from other cohorts. Organizations are founded in "spurts," with particular structures tending to dominate waves of foundings. Stinchcombe (1965) argues that structures are preserved for three reasons: (a) because the form is (still) the most efficient; (b) because structures tend to become *institutionalized*, infused with value beyond any technical or economic efficiency; and (c) because organizations with particular structures may operate in sectors with little competition from alternative, ostensibly better forms. Stinchcombe's second and third points argue against the generality of adaptive models of organizations, which presume a fair bit of fluidity and discretion on the part of organizations and their managers with respect to the organization's structure.

Hannan and Freeman (1984) build on Stinchcombe's insights with their arguments for *structural inertia* in organizations. Structural inertia exists "when the speed of reorganization is much lower than the rate at which environmental conditions change" (Hannan & Freeman, 1984, p. 151). Organizations in general succeed at what they do and survive into the future because they are able to produce outcomes with high reliability and because they accede to environmental demands for accountability. Maintaining reliability and accountability may be necessary for an organization to survive, but they are also constraining forces, generating pressures for inertia. Age and size both increase this tendency toward structural inertia. As a consequence, many organizations become trapped by their own competency.

Change efforts typically threaten vested interests within the organization. Change rarely can be implemented without the consent of those outside top management, yet this consent may not be forthcoming when it threatens the distribution of power in the organization. Those who stand to lose under a new regime typically will fight harder than those who stand to gain, and powerful vested interests may have more effective resources for stalling change compared to those who favor a new set of arrangements.

Even if organizations do manage to alter themselves, their continuing success is by no means guaranteed. Attempts at reorganization lower the organization's reliability, increasing the probability of organizational death, and this risk increases with the time it takes to accomplish reorganization. Furthermore, if a new structure is put into place successfully, the organization will lose much of its accumulated wisdom stored in the old structure, thus becoming subject to the "liability of newness" all over again (Hannan & Freeman, 1984). In a sense, organizations seeking to make significant changes in order to adapt to environmental pressures are damned if they do and damned if they don't: Failure to adapt to threatening environments may be fatal, while adaptation also carries its own risks. Yet these facts of organizational life receive scant attention from the adaptive approaches to organization-environment relations. This is an important limitation on the scope of these theories.

According to the various adaptive perspectives, exchanges with other actors in the environment are the primary means by which the environment effects organizations. But the environment is not bounded by the organization set, and exchange is not the only relation of relevance for explaining organizational outcomes. Organizations are subject to legal and regulatory sanctions at the local and national levels. Professional and trade associations, as well as political advocacy groups, can place tremendous normative pressures on organizations. Organizational strategies for coping with the uncertainty that surrounds exchange relations can be limited or facilitated by governments. Thus, analysts who focus on dyadic exchange relations of a focal organization to the exclusion of the larger political economy in which it operates (Zald, 1970) will be limited in their ability to explain organizational behavior.

Organizations are also situated in more or less elaborated networks, linked by information as well as resource exchanges, friendship ties among elites, and directorate interlocks with common partners, among others. Ties may be dense, weak, or absent; they may extend from the local to the transnational level, interacting with political processes at each step.

The dynamics of these networks have profound implications for the constituent elements, yet network effects are lost by exclusive attention to dyadic exchange relations. Thus, the models of organization-environment relations that give theoretical primacy to exchange lose some of their explanatory power by downplaying or ignoring the political economy and interorganizational networks in which organizations are embedded.

Organizations are assumed to be essentially *rational actors* in each of the approaches described above. But many organizational theorists contend that such an assumption is rather problematic: Organizations are limited in their ability to know and learn from their environment, and actions are often symbolic or habitual rather than prospectively and technically rational. March and Olsen (1 976) argue compellingly for the limitations of rational actor models of organizational decision making. Ambiguity is pervasive in organizations: Objectives are inconsistent and ill-defined; cause-effect relationships are poorly understood, particularly linkages between organizational actions and environmental outcomes; history is difficult to recollect and interpret; and patterns of attention and participation in decision processes are extremely fluid. Decisions, rather than being the outcome of rational processes of bureaucratic procedure or political bargaining, may be the result of a "garbage can process," where problems, solutions, and participants are linked together at a particular point in time by a choice opportunity. Decisions and goals may be emergent, not the direct intention of any of the parties at the outset. And choices may be based on intuition or tradition and faith, rather than on a rational calculus linking consequences to objectives.

Organizational deviations from rational choice may be rooted in basic facts of human cognition and information processing and in the very structure and operation of organizations. Kiesler and Sproull (1982) argue that managers charged with noticing change in the environment and interpreting such change so

that decisions are possible are subject to a raft of perceptual, information processing, and motivational biases. Representations of the environment tend to be causally simplistic, outdated, consistent with preexisting beliefs, and resistant to change; thus, the rationality of organizational decision processes is limited by the reigning definition of the situation. Moreover, Starbuck (1983) argues that most of the time organizational action, because of the construction of organizations out of standard operating procedures, is unreflective and nonadaptive. Most actions are not the result of conscious decision processes, but rather flow from *action generators,* automatic programs of behavior independent of specific stimuli. Societal standards of rationality require that actions be justified, however, and these justifications become solidified and rationalized over time. Organizations need explicit disconfirmation of the rationality of action-justification pairings before they are able to "unlearn." Thus, previous justifications constrain the ability of organizations to engage in thoughtful decision making, and this pathology worsens over time, dooming most organizations to short lives (Starbuck, 1983).

It would seem, then, that prospective rationality does not underlie many actions of individuals in organizations or of organizations themselves. This poses a serious challenge to theories of organization-environment relations that presume adaptive, boundedly rational action on the part of organizations. It is in large measure due to these weaknesses that alternative approaches to the analysis of organizations and their environments have been developed.

Beyond Dyadic Models: Network Approaches to Interorganizational Relations

Over the past decade, new approaches combining traditional sociological concerns with methodological advances in the analysis of networks have emerged and flourished as viable alternatives to dyadic exchange-based models. This work takes a fundamentally sociological approach to the study of organizations by viewing organizations as embedded in networks of social ties that both empower and constrain action. This line of inquiry is motivated less by a concern with organizational design and managerial practice and much more by substantive concerns with the sources of stability and change in social systems.

Network (or *structural*) approaches are premised on the assumption that structures of interorganizational relations are consequential for understanding the actions of organizations.[9] This contrasts with the *atomistic* imagery of much of contemporary social science, in which behavior is viewed as adaptive responses to sets of incentives, and social relations are largely irrelevant, at most a drag on efficiency (see Granovetter, 1985, for an extended critique). Although network approaches build on the insights of resource dependence theory, where the most significant aspects of the organization's environment are other organizations and where resource exchanges confer power and dependence, structural analysis places much greater weight on the means by which an organization's position in a wider network of relations shapes its actions. Moreover, it is not simply direct relations among organizations that are significant: Both direct and indirect linkages can have an impact on individual and corporate action. Thus, for example, you are more likely to find out about a job opening through a weak tie (someone with whom you are somewhat acquainted but who travels in different circles, such as an old classmate from high school) than from a strong tie (a close friend who associates with most of the same people you do): Close friends are likely to have access to the same contacts and information that you already have and thus provide redundant information, whereas acquaintances are a bridge to contacts you would not have had otherwise (Granovetter, 1973).

Indeed, in some recent work the interorganizational network itself is no longer simply "the environment" of its constituent organizations but an object of study in its own right (Mizruchi & Schwartz, 1987). This reversal of figure and ground is accompanied by a focus on emergent properties of networks. Network systems can be centralized and hierarchical like a bureaucracy, with a dominant organization at the peak (cf. Mintz & Schwartz, 1985), they can be balkanized into multiple more-or-less hierarchical clusters (cf. Roy & Bonacich, 1988), they can be disorganized and even fractious, like a highly competitive industry. Such different structures are significant both for the life chances of constituent organizations and for the explanation of organizational behavior. The implication for organizational theory is clear: Much as an individual caught in a traffic jam knows only the immediate cause of her distress, while someone surveying the scene from a helicopter above has a more comprehensive picture, a view of the organization's interorganizational environment that extends beyond the immediate context is crucial to this approach.

Conception of the Environment

The general rubric of network analysis embraces a diversity of perspectives on organizational behavior; this work is united more by method than by theory. There is sufficient commonality among the approaches, however, to portray common elements in broad strokes.[10] By definition, a network is composed of a set of relations or *ties* among actors (in this case, organizations). A tie between actors has both content (the type of relation) and form (the strength of the relation). The content of ties can include information or resource flows, advice or friendship ties, and shared personnel or members of the board of directors; indeed any type of social relation can be mapped as a tie. Thus, organizations are typically embedded in multiple, often overlapping, networks—

resource exchange networks, information or advice networks, board of director interlock networks, and so on.

To the extent that they take a focal organization perspective, network researchers focus either on the set of relations an organization has with those to which it is tied (its *ego network*) or on its position in the larger network system, often described in terms of its degree of *centrality* or *prestige*. Centrality describes the extent to which an actor is tied to many others in the system and (in some versions) the extent to which these others are in turn tied to many others themselves (see Bonacich, 1987). Another way to characterize network position is in terms of *autonomy* and *constraint*. Structural autonomy is the ability to pursue actions without constraint from others; firms have high structural autonomy to the extent that they operate in concentrated industries (with limited intraindustry competition) while their buyers and suppliers are competitive among themselves, thus ensuring only limited constraint from external actors (Burt, 1980a). Finally, two actors are *structurally equivalent* to the extent that they share similar patterns of ties to other actors in the system (e.g., firms in the same industry who have similar sets of buyers and suppliers—see White, Boorman, & Breiger, 1976).

For a variety of reasons, including historical public policy concerns and the wide availability of data, one type of network has received the lion's share of attention from interorganizational researchers: the *interlocking directorate network* that is formed by having the same individuals sit on multiple boards of directors. An individual who sits on the boards of two organizations is said to create an *interlock* tie between those firms. A vast literature can be traced back as far as the turn of the century, when public concerns with trusts and cartels ultimately led to a section of the Clayton Act barring interlocks among competitors in 1914. Because of the position of boards of directors at the very top of the decision-making hierarchy

of most organizations, the fact that the same individuals often sit on two, three, or even more boards affords a potential for common control that many have found unsettling. Interlocks among competitors, for example, could be used for collusion, and some have argued that banks control large segments of the economy by placing representatives on the boards of their subject firms (e.g., see Kotz, 1978). Interlocks among direct competitors are rather rare now (Zajac, 1988), and more recent interlock researchers have focused more on overall network position rather than specific ties (Mariolis & Jones, 1982).[11]

Two points are worth noting regarding network research: First, as a relatively new field there remains a good deal of controversy around the merits of various methods and measures and how best to interpret them (e.g., see Burt, 1987 and Galaskiewicz & Burt, 1987, on comparisons of structural equivalence and cohesion as competing explanations for diffusion effects in networks). Second, it is crucial when evaluating this research to keep in mind the content of the network ties being considered. Although many network ties are *multiplex* (i.e., the ties have multiple contents), this is not necessarily so, and an organization that is central in an information exchange network may be peripheral in a resource exchange network (e.g., a trade association). Thus, network position (such as degree of centrality) is only meaningful in terms of the ties that compose the network. Our trade association has little exchange-based power over its members, which limits its ability to compel actions, but as an information broker it can be crucial for mobilizing collective action: It may be able to persuade, but it cannot force.

Key Areas of Research

Most research on interorganizational networks has proceeded from two perspectives that use similar methods to pursue somewhat different agendas. In the interorganizational perspective, organizations are the primary actors, and individuals act as agents of these organizations, whereas in the intraclass perspective individuals are the primary actors and organizations are their tools (see Palmer, 1983, and Pfeffer, 1987, for discussions of these contrasting approaches). Common to both these approaches is an overwhelming predominance of empirical research on the interlock network.

Research from the interorganizational perspective has tended to follow the logic of resource dependence theory: Networks of interorganizational resource exchanges confer power and dependence, which in turn motivate organizations to establish ties to other organizations (such as interlocks) to reduce uncertainty. In the aggregate, these ties form a network, albeit a messy and impermanent one, that changes in response to shifts in resource exchange patterns. Interorganizational networks formed through the actions of individual organizations subsequently can be used as mechanisms of diffusion and cohesion, but they are rarely used as devices for the exercise of power, and no enduring power structure emerges to allow ongoing collective political coordination (Glasberg & Schwartz, 1983). Research in this stream tends to focus on the organizational purposes served by interlocks, such as decreased uncertainty and cooptation.

The intraclass approach has focused largely on the role of intercorporate networks in facilitating cohesion among the corporate elite. Interlocks provide a foundation for such order by linking virtually all large corporations into a single dense network, with banks in central (heavily interlocked) positions that correspond to their economically important function of directing the flows of capital (Mintz & Schwartz, 1985). Moreover, the individuals who create the interlocks (*multiple directors*) are argued to form an *inner circle* of the corporate elite that is able to act in the interest of this elite in its political dealings, thereby facilitating

interorganizational political cohesion (Useem, 1984). Thus, much research in this stream focuses on the creation and maintenance of social order among corporations and the ability of network ties to facilitate collective action.

Although the motivations behind these two lines of research are somewhat different, in practice there is a great deal of commonality in both their methods and findings, and thus we treat them as a single body of work, which we cluster into three areas: (a) research on the formation, maintenance, and aggregate properties of interorganizational networks; (b) effects of networks on organizational structure, ideology, and action; and (c) consequences of networks for organizational effectiveness.

Formation, Maintenance, and Aggregate Properties of Interorganizational Networks. Researchers from both interorganizational and intraclass perspectives have focused much attention on the conditions under which organizations form and maintain interlocks. The transformation of the American economy from entrepreneurial to corporate at the end of the 19th century was accompanied by the elaboration of an interindustry interlock network, with the railroad, coal, and telegraph industries forming an early and enduring core among industrials; ties across industries became increasingly dense but maintained a spoked wheel pattern, with core industries tightly interlinked and peripheral industries tied to the core but not to each other (Roy, 1983). Roy found that ties across industries seemed to facilitate both resource exchange and ownership relations. In a longitudinal study, Mizruchi and Stearns (1988) found that firms were more likely to appoint representatives of financial institutions to their board when solvency and profitability were declining and when the demand for capital corresponded with macroeconomic conditions such as declining interest rates or a contraction stage of the business cycle, suggesting an interplay between the formation of intercorporate networks and larger economic forces. Burt (1983) found that both direct interlocks and indirect financial interlocks (i.e., where members of two boards are both members of a financial institution's board) as well as common ownership of establishments trace market-based constraints on profitability. And Lang and Lockhart (1990) found that after the onset of deregulation in the airline industry, which increased competitive uncertainty, airlines focused their indirect interlocking more on direct competitors than they did before deregulation.

A second set of studies is premised on the argument that particular interlocks may be created for various reasons that have little to do with organizational purposes, such as social ties between the CEO and the board member, but that those which serve organizational purposes are likely to be reestablished when they are accidentally severed (e.g., the multiple director dies or retires; Palmer, 1983). Thus, studying the factors associated with the reconstitution of interlock should shed light on the purposes they serve. By and large, firms do not rush to reconstitute accidentally broken ties: Only about one out of six were repaired among Fortune 500 firms in the mid-1960s, suggesting that these ties are rarely used as vehicles of formal coordination between firms (Palmer, 1983). Interlocks among large American corporations in the 1960s were more likely to be reconstituted when the firms involved were linked by some mechanism of formal coordination and were headquartered in the same city, and where at least one of the firms' interlocks involved an executive of one of the firms (Palmer, Friedland, & Singh, 1986). Using a broader time frame for reconstitution and a sample that included all disrupted ties (rather than only accidentally broken ties), Ornstein (1984) found a much higher rate of reconstitution among Canadian firms; reconstitution was more likely when the two firms had multiple shared directors, when at least one tie

was created by an executive of one of the firms, and when the firms were partly owned either by a third party or by each other. Finally, management-controlled firms were more likely to reconstitute ties, and ties to financial institutions were much more likely to be reconstituted, whereas long-lived ties (which are more likely to have outlived their usefulness) were actually less likely to be reconstituted, according to a long-term study of interlock reconstitution (Stearns & Mizruchi, 1986). Stearns and Mizruchi introduce the notion of *functional reconstitution*, where a firm replaces a broken tie with a tie to a different firm in the same industry. These authors found the factors that affected direct reconstitution of a broken tie to a financial institution differed from those affecting functional reconstitution; they argue this difference implies that direct reconstitution is more likely to reflect interorganizational power relations.

The centrality of particular firms in the overall network has also received attention. Thompson (1967) argued that organizations match the elaborateness of their boundary-spanning element to the complexity of their environment. Thus, New York banks tend to be the most well-connected business organizations, as the direction of the economy as a whole is implicated in their investment decisions (Mintz & Schwartz, 1985). Large industrial firms such as AT&T, General Electric, and IBM also cast their interlock nets broadly and are therefore better able to gather information about their environments (Davis, in press). Moreover, while particularities may come and go, as the reconstitution research indicates, overall centrality is remarkably stable (Mariolis & Jones, 1982), implying that there is an order to the intercorporate network.

At the level of the network as a whole, researchers have uncovered several regularities that characterize the network of interlocks among the largest American corporations. In a sweeping study of the power structure of business in the 1960s, Mintz and Schwartz (1985) observed that a handful of major New York banks and insurance companies formed a stable core at the top of the interlock network. They argue that financial institutions do not use their network centrality to control other corporations directly, as previous commentators have suggested, but primarily to gather economy-wide information that guides their investment decision making. Corporations are subject to a unique dependence on capital, and thus the flow of capital both creates opportunities and places constraints on what is possible for large corporations. By directing capital flows to some areas and withholding it from others, banks bring a hegemonic order to economic life, and the interorganizational "war of all against all" that economic theories lead us to expect does not appear.

Apparently, however, the current interlock network structure did not arise fully formed: Clusters of interlocks among railroads, which were the largest and most powerful nonfinancial corporations at the turn of the century, mapped onto several balkanized communities of interest linked by common ownership rather than forming a single hierarchical network. This finding argues that interest groups based on common ownership (e.g., by the Morgan or Rockefeller families), apparently uncommon today, formed a basis for the earliest interlock networks (Roy & Bonacich, 1988).

Finally, Burt (1988) analyzed input-output tables for 77 broad industry categories to find that the boundaries and degree of structural autonomy of markets (defined by patterns of exchanges among industries) were highly stable throughout the 1960s and 1970s and accounted for enduring inequalities in profit margins in these industries.[12]

Effects of Networks on Organizational Structure, Ideology, and Action. In contrast to the large body of work describing the factors influencing the construction and maintenance of network ties, relatively little work has been done on the effects of interorganizational ties. More recent studies have sought to remedy this gap by examining the effects of network ties on the diffusion of organizational structures and actions and the political behavior of large corporations.

In perhaps the only study documenting network effects on changes in major aspects of organizational structure, Palmer, Jennings, and Zhou (1989) found that firms were more likely to adopt the multidivisional form (described above in the section on transaction cost economics) when they had ties to other firms that had already adopted one. Nonfamily-owned firms in the Twin Cities contributed more to local charities when the CEOs had network ties to the philanthropic elite (Atkinson & Galaskiewicz, 1988), and these organizations seemed to emulate the contributions of firms whose executives had ties to the organization's boundary spanners (Galaskiewicz & Wasserman, 1989). And Davis (1991) found that large corporations were quicker to adopt a poison pill takeover defense to the extent that they were interlocked with firms that had already adopted one. Thus, network centrality appeared to be self-reproducing: More central firms were able to gain early access to information about protective strategies that flowed across nework ties, thus maintaining their centrality in the face of the threat of takeover.

The effect of network ties on corporate political ideology and behavior has received substantial study since Useem's (1984) explication of the *inner circle* thesis. Political sociologists have debated for decades whether corporations are able to form a united front in the pursuit of government policy or whether they are generally fractious and competitive and therefore unable to form an enduring coalition. Useem (1984) argued that directors who sit on multiple boards are uniquely placed to overcome the differences dividing corporations so that these corporations are able to pursue common political goals. Thus, more central firms made more PAC contributions to incumbents and less to conservatives in the 1980 elections, but they were more likely to be involved with conservative policy organizations, suggesting that PAC contributions are used to further corporate interests but that policy organizations are used to pursue collective interests (Clawson & Neustadtl, 1989). Mizruchi and Koenig (1986; Mizruchi, 1989) found that interindustry constraint increased the degree of similarity of PAC contributions made by firms in those industries, and indirect interlocking through financial institutions as well as common ownership by financials increased the similarity of PAC contributions, which argues that interorganizational ties facilitate political cohesion. Political cohesion among organizations does not necessarily mean that these organizations are more effective at getting what they want, however: Earlier in this century, industries with more extensive network ties to economic, political, or social organizations were no more effective than other industries at having their interests taken into account by the State Department (Roy, 1981). This finding, however, is likely to reflect its time setting (cf. Laumann & Knoke, 1987).

Consequences of Networks for Organizational Effectiveness. Interorganizational ties bear a complicated relation to different aspects of organizational effectiveness. According to Burt (1983), an industry's profitability is strongly related to the degree of exchange-based constraint it faces but has very little relation to the interlock ties it maintains with other industries. Thus, organizations seemed to direct their interlock ties toward their most severe constraints on profitability, but these ties did not provide any obvious profit advantage. Similarly, in a more recent study of Canadian firms in the mid-1960s, Richardson (1987) found that the total number of ties between financials and nonfinancials had no effect on profitability. However, having ties that had been broken and replaced was positively related to profitability

when the broken tie and the replacement were created by executives of the nonfinancial but somewhat negatively related when both ties were created by executives of the financial. Richardson also found evidence that profitability leads to replaced ties and not the other way around, which is consistent with the idea that more profitable firms are better able to maintain representation on financials' boards, whereas less profitable firms may have to submit to having financial representatives on their boards.

Wiewel and Hunter (1985) discovered that the liability of newness (i.e., the higher failure rates faced by new organizations) was partially ameliorated by network ties to previously existing similar organizations, which can provide experienced insider personnel, access to credit, external legitimacy, and so on.

Finally, in what is undoubtedly the most comprehensive study of interorganizational networks to date, Laumann and Knoke (1987) examine the network structures of two national policy domains, energy and health, during the Carter years. They proceed from the premises that organizations are the most important actors in governmental policy formation and that the network of ties among these actors is crucial for explaining their participation and influence in policy events. This pathbreaking study introduces such a large battery of new concepts and theory that no short summary would suffice. Its most distinctive contribution, however, is its conceptualization of both actors and events (in this case, events in the process of national policy decision making) having both individual properties and relational properties that aggregate in ways that are consequential for policy outcomes. Organizations are linked to other organizations by ties of information transmission, resource transactions, and boundary penetration; events are linked by their ordering in time and their institutional setting as well as by their similarity to each other; and organizations are linked to events in an action system, which has systemic properties that arise from the properties and relations of the constituent organizations and events. Laumann and Knoke combine this framework with exotic statistical techniques to analyze the individual and network factors determining organizational participation and effectiveness in national policy making. This study sets a new standard of theoretical and methodological sophistication for organizational research.

Critique. Network approaches to interorganizational relations have provided an excellent ground for combining research on organizations with more traditional sociological concerns, such as problems of social order and the role of societal elites. Research in this area has made the most of methodological advances; indeed, network methods have far outstripped network theory (cf. Burt, 1980a), which is the greatest weakness of the research reviewed here. The formation, maintenance, and mapping of network ties has received a great deal of attention, but comparatively little work has focused on whether an organization's position in various networks in fact has any significance for understanding its behavior. Much of the focus of network researchers on interlocks among boards of directors can be attributed to the extreme data demands that network methods make, coupled with the ready public availability of data on boards of directors. But increasingly sophisticated statistical techniques continue to uncover rather modest findings.

A curious irony of network research is that despite its imperative to focus on the causal importance of structures of relations among actors rather than simply the properties of those actors, the research itself tends to treat network positions as properties themselves. Thus, studies often treat interlock network centrality as if it were a feature of an organization like size. But as we mentioned early in this section, centrality only has significance in

terms of the ties from which it is derived. Given that only a small minority of interlock ties seem to trace enduring social relations among firms, it is not always clear what content these ties have and, therefore, what an organization's position in the interlock network signifies.

The obvious remedy for the apparent primacy of method over substance in network research is to bring the content of the ties, rather than merely the structure formed by these ties, back in. Social ties among organizations can be consequential, but not all of them need be. Stinchcombe (1990) suggests that the dynamic and causal theory of a structure has to be built into the analysis of the links.

> We need to know what flows across
> the links, who decides on those flows
> in the light of what interests, and what
> collective or corporate action flows from
> the organization of links, in order to
> make sense of inter-corporate relations.
> (p. 381)

More recent network research, including much of the work reviewed here, has taken steps to remedy this weakness. The notion that board interlocks are used by competitors for collusion, which dates back to the earlier part of this century, has little evidence to support it today (cf. Zajac, 1988), and few researchers cling to the belief that interlocks are used by corporations such as banks to exercise direct control over their hapless corporate stooges (see Glasberg & Schwartz, 1983, for a critique). Instead, the most sophisticated work today sees the interlock network as a mechanism for the diffusion of information rather than for the exercise of explicit control (Davis, 1991; Mintz & Schwartz, 1985; Useem, 1984). The future of network approaches seems to lie with combining the methodological sophistication they have brought to the study of interorganizational relations with the substantive concerns of other areas of organizational sociology.

The Organization of the Environment: Ecological and Institutional Perspectives

In contrast to dyadic or network models of organization and environment relations, ecologists and institutionalists pay much less attention to the efforts of organizations to manage and control their environments. The central thrust of ecological and institutional thinking is on the structure and composition of the environment. Most ecological and institutional research maintains that organizational change is largely shaped by changes in the environment (through population-level demographic processes of organizational foundings and death or through broad social changes promulgated by the state or sovereign professions). Consequently, these approaches suggest that change in individual organizations contribute considerably less to large-scale social transformations.

Not surprisingly, then, a common criticism of ecological and institutional research is their respective inattention to organizational change and adaptation. In large part, these criticisms are fair. Both ecologists and institutionalists emphasize the structural inertia that besets established organizations, the manner by which organizational structures and practices become valued for their own sake and organizational policies become locked in. To the extent that ecologists and institutionalists emphasize external environmental conditions and constraints, they downplay organizational innovation and adaptation. Similarly, organizational politics are not primary concerns of ecologists and institutionalists.

Initially, ecological and institutional approaches were seen as competing theories, but as the common criticisms noted above suggest, there has been a marked convergence of these two perspectives (see the discussions in Hannan & Freeman, 1989, and Powell & DiMaggio, 1991; also see empirical studies by Barnett &

Carroll, 1990; Carroll & Huo, 1986; Hannan, 1986; Singh, Tucker, & Meinhard, 1991).[13] In several key respects the two approaches are more alike than different. Both share an appreciation for the fact that history matters a great deal and both attempt to connect organizational theory with topics in general sociology. Both are increasingly animated by related questions: How do changes in institutional environments influence the survival of organizations? How do ecological processes contribute to fundamental changes in the institutional order? Still, as the reader will soon note, there are considerable points of divergence in key concepts and methods: Organizational ecologists borrow freely from population biology and have made important contributions to mathematical sociology, while institutionalists are closely linked to research on the professions and the state and have expanded the horizons of sociologists of culture.

Ecological Perspectives

The animating question for ecological research was stated by Hannan and Freeman (1977, paraphrasing the ecologist Evelyn Hutchinson). "Why are there so many kinds of organizations?" The core of the ecological approach is an effort to explain the diversity of organizational forms across the social landscape and to account for changes in the mixture of forms. This *population ecology of organizations* (Hannan & Freeman, 1977) starts with the observation that the variety and mix of organizational forms in society is fundamentally a property of aggregates of organizations. *Mix* has no analogue at the level of the individual organization (Hannan & Freeman, 1986); thus, any explanation of organizational diversity must be posed at a higher level of analysis. Moreover, whereas adaptive approaches would explain the mix of organizational forms as the result of choices by previously existing organizations, ecologists point out that diversity may also result from deaths of old forms and births of new ones.

Thus, building on Hawley's (1950, 1968) theory of human ecology, researchers began to study dynamic processes at the population level of analysis. The fruitfulness of this approach is evidenced by burgeoning empirical studies adopting this perspective. Organizational ecology can take three levels (Carroll, 1984a): (a) an *organizational* level, which focuses on the demography and development of individual organizations; (b) a *population* level, which focuses primarily on selection processes; and (c) a *community* level, which emphasizes macro-evolutionary processes. While the developmental approach has spawned some extremely interesting work (we would place Langton, 1984, and Nelson & Winter, 1982, under this rubric), the ecological literature has been dominated by studies adopting the population level of analysis and, to a much lesser extent, the community level.

The Language of Organizational Ecology. Organizational ecology has introduced an entire battery of new concepts and language for describing organizations and their environments. Perhaps the most basic notion is that of a population of organizations. Intuitively, a population is simply a class of organizations facing similar environmental vulnerabilities (Hannan & Freeman, 1977), usually organizations sharing the same form. Form can be defined by internal attributes of organizations, such as the organization's *blueprint for action* (indicated by the formal structure or patterns of activity), or by the set of (external) relations and dependencies the organization has with its environment (Hannan & Freeman, 1989). Organizations sharing a common form constitute a population when they are bounded within a common system, usually defined by geography, political boundaries, or markets.[14]

The shift to a population level of analysis is accompanied by a shift in the locus of causality, from the rational and adaptive organization to the environment. The economic theory of the firm sees organizational decision makers as optimizing, but "from a population ecology perspective, it is the environment which optimizes. Whether or not individual organizations are consciously adapting, the environment selects out optimal combinations of organizations" (Hannan & Freeman, 1977, p. 939–940). Because resources such as people and money are limited, societies have a limited carrying capacity for organizations, and thus under many conditions organizations are engaged in a struggle for existence against others in their niche (i. e., those drawing on the same pool of resources, such as members of the same industry). In equilibrium, the population that survives in a niche will be the one that is "isomorphic" to the environment, whereas "that population with the characteristic less fit to environmental contingencies will tend to be eliminated" (Hannan & Freeman, 1977, p. 943). Over time, ecologists have softened their emphasis on optimization and fit in favor of more diffuse selection models (e.g., Hannan & Freeman, 1989).

The use of organizational models based on selection processes has triggered controversy.[15] Much of this controversy stems from a misunderstanding of the uses of evolutionary theory in the social sciences. Some readers assume that evolutionary models imply either progress or superior fitness. But ecologists do not claim that selection logic implies that the organizations that have survived are more efficient or more deserving of their success. Indeed, selection models are always built on the assumption of the importance of randomness of success.

Framework of Assumptions. Ecological models of organizations obviously owe a great intellectual debt to models of biotic evolution. The traffic in intellectual technology between population biology and organizational ecology has required a rethinking of many of the assumptions previously held by organizational scholars. The basic task is to justify the implicit and sometimes explicit analogy between (populations of) organizations and (populations of) organisms. Points of weak fit are apparent: Organizations can change their structure, organisms cannot; information is carried through nongenetic means within and among organizations; and individual organizations can expand virtually without limit, whereas a mouse cannot grow into an elephant (Hannan & Freeman, 1977).[16] Ecologists have mustered intriguing arguments in favor of their approach, however, and these arguments have led to a revitalized debate over some of the basic assumptions of organizational analysis. The critical theoretical issues have concerned the degree of *plasticity* of organizations, or just how malleable organizations are, the extent to which a population is an appropriate level of analysis, and how organizational forms can be defined.

Hannan and Freeman (1977, 1984) argue for the proposition that organizations in the modern world experience strong pressures to retain their form over time rather than engage in structural change. Internal constraints on adaptation include investment in plant and equipment, informational limits, intraorganizational politics, and the institutionalization of organizational routines, while external constraints include barriers to entry and exit and legitimacy concerns. In addition, organizations are selected by the environment in the first place based on their ability to perform reliably and to account rationally for their actions. But this reliability and accountability demand that the organization's structure be reproducible from day to day, which in turn generates strong inertial pressures. Thus, structural inertia is a consequence of generalized selection pressures in society that favor reliable and accountable organizations over other types of collective actors. Structural inertia increases with the organization's age and size, while in most instances death rates decrease with both (Hannan & Freeman, 1984). Consequently, ecologists argue that the variation in observed

organizational forms is attributable to the deaths of relatively stable, inert organizations and the births of new organizational forms, rather than to wholesale adaptation by existing populations. If we accept this argument, then ecological models have fairly general applicability to organizational life in the modern world.[17]

A second issue concerns the theoretical usefulness of the population concept. The notion of a group of organizations sharing common form and similar environmental vulnerabilities is intuitively appealing, yet it has proved difficult to operationalize in a satisfying way. Baron and Bielby (1980) point out that organizations may differ greatly in structure even when they are of similar size and age and operate within the same industry and locality. This raises the question of how organizations should be classified, a crucial concern for taking a population perspective. McKelvey (1978, 1982) has approached this issue by drawing on taxonomic and specie concepts from biology. Organisms pass down specie characteristics through the gene pool. The organizational equivalent of the gene pool is the *tech pool*, composed of the characteristic operational technologies and managerial technologies shared by members of a group of organizations. An organizational specie is then defined as a group that shares *dominant competencies*, but that is sufficiently isolated from other populations by the fact that these competencies are not easily learned or transmitted across groups (McKelvey, 1982, p. 192).[18] This isolation may be due to geographic or cultural factors. For example, the geographical isolation of firms operating in the same industry in Silicon Valley promotes personnel movement among Valley firms but isolation from firms in other industries, thereby maintaining the integrity of the population.

More recently, Hannan and Freeman (1986) have argued that rather than classifying organizations into populations based on shared formal characteristics or common patterns of environmental dependency, a more fruitful approach may be to focus on the processes that create, sustain, and erode boundaries around populations. This would provide a first step in identifying the structure of a niche as well as the forms that occupy it. "Instead of beginning with problems of classification, this approach begins with the question: Where do organizational forms come from?" (Hannan & Freeman, 1986, p. 60). They suggest that segregating processes tend to create the conditions for greater similarity of forms within a population, while blending processes tend to blur the distinctions between forms in different populations.

Most current *macro* researchers are reluctant to develop an all-purpose definition of a population or an organizational field. Instead, they argue that the definition of an organizational population should be determined by the theoretical or substantive problem.[19] Hence, concerns with classification should be secondary to identifying the boundaries around forms (Hannan & Freeman, 1986).

Key Areas of Research. *Organizational Birth.* Stinchcombe's (1965) treatment of several issues associated with organizational foundings has critically informed ecological research on organizational births. We consider two questions informed by Stinchcombe's classic paper. First, how do prevailing social conditions affect the characteristics of organizations founded during a particular historical time period? Second, how do variations in the social environment affect the rate of organizational foundings?

Organizational characteristics at founding. Stinchcombe explained the peculiar fact that organizations founded at roughly the same time tend to be structurally similar to each other and dissimilar to those founded at other times by arguing that organizations are *imprinted* at the time of their birth and reflect the prevailing social technology of the day. One of the crucial assumptions of the ecological school is that these imprinted structures, once in place, are relatively inert. Aldrich and Mueller (1982) trace the origins of different types of organizational forms that appeared in the U.S. economy to broad-scale historical changes in the environment. They identify epochal transitions in the forms of organization that dominate the social landscape— the movement from prefactory to factory production in the early to mid-19th century, from competitive to monopoly capitalism in the late 19th and early 20th century, and from early to mature monopoly capitalism after World War I—and relate these to variations in the availability of capital, materials, labor, and infrastructure as well in the role of the state.

Tushman and Anderson (1986) show how the evolutionary logic of technological change affects the environments of organizations and the structure of industries. They argue that, within particular product classes, technological innovations that build on pre-existing competences will consolidate the positions of organizations that already dominate an industry and increase the barriers to new entrants, whereas in the rarer case of radically new technologies, such as biotechnology or superconductivity, space will be open to new organizations that are not trapped by sunk costs and skills tied to older technologies and that therefore can exploit innovations (see also Abernathy & Clark, 1985; Powell & Brantley, 1991). They found that in the airline, cement, and minicomputer industries, new entrants were more likely to initiate radical technological breakthroughs than existing firms, suggesting that a new technological regime provides both the opportunity and the means for new organizational forms to be founded based around that technology. Finally, Boeker (1988) found that the initial strategy chosen by new organizations in the semiconductor industry reflected both the functional background of the entrepreneur who founded the organization and the period in which it was founded, consistent with the imprinting hypothesis.

Rates of founding. Stinchcombe (1965) argued that certain social conditions, such as revolutions, quicken the pace at which new organizations are brought into existence by shifting social alignments and freeing resources that can be used by entrepreneurs. Of course, more pedestrian variations in the environment also affect founding rates. Ecological researchers have studied how both environments and characteristics of the population itself alter the incidence of new organizations. Pennings (1982) studied the environmental conditions that stimulate organizational births in three different industries across 70 American urban communities, finding that the factors fostering organizational fecundity differed substantially between manufacturers of plastic products, electronic components, and telecommunications equipment. McCarthy, Wolfson, Baker, and Mosakowski (1988) discovered that local citizens' organizations opposing drunk driving, such as Mothers Against Drunk Driving, appeared earlier in counties with higher education levels, greater population density, more government resources, and a higher level of grievances—thus supporting the view that social movement organizations depend primarily on the existence of human resources that can be mobilized for social action. On the other hand, in their study of trade associations, Aldrich and Staber (1988) contend that the pattern of growth of this population does not seem tied to environmental characteristics, such as a fluctuating demand for their services due to changing levels of government regulation, but rather to the diffusion of the trade association form across industries. Together these studies suggest that the existence of a social infrastructure may be a necessary but not sufficient condition for organizational founding and that processes at the level of the organizational population could play a part.

Indeed, Delacroix and Carroll (1983) show that the cycles of newspaper foundings in Argentina (1800–1900) and Ireland (1800–1925) reflect both political turbulence and population dynamics. They posit that the death of existing organizations frees resources with which to found new organizations so that the number of newspaper deaths in the recent past should increase rates of founding up to a point; high levels of death, however, signal entrepreneurs that the environment is inhospitable and thus depress birth rates, implying a curvilinear relationship between prior deaths and births. Prior foundings should also have a curvilinear effect: Up to a point, an increasing birth rate signals a munificent environment, encouraging entrepreneurial imitation and increasing the subsequent rate of foundings, but very high levels of founding will use up the resources needed for starting new organizations and will thus decrease subsequent foundings. Data from both nations supported this model. In addition, years of political turbulence were marked by an increase in the number of newspapers founded in both Argentina and Ireland. In a similar analysis of the newspaper industry in the San Francisco Bay area throughout its history, Carroll and Huo (1986) found only weak support for the hypothesized relationship between prior and subsequent foundings, but again found that in years of political turmoil the founding rate was higher than in calmer years, a finding consistent with Stinchcombe's (1965) argument that turmoil creates or frees resources for organizational founding.[20]

Much research has also been done on demographic effects on organizational populations. Hannan and Freeman (1987) argue that a population's density (i.e., the mere count of organizations currently in a population) can have two effects on subsequent founding rates. Positive density dependence occurs when the number of subsequent foundings increases with the size of the population. Density increases founding rates by (a) increasing the number of organizations of a particular form, who can then use their experience to create similar organizations, and (b) increasing the legitimacy of an organizational form, as the form comes to be taken for granted simply through its prevalence. Negative density dependence occurs because a larger population will experience increased competition for limited resources, thus depressing founding rates. Positive density dependence is argued to dominate when the population is smaller, while negative density dependence dominates in larger populations (Hannan & Freeman, 1988a). The combination of these two effects yields an inverted U-curve relation between density and founding rates. Using the population of national labor unions founded between 1836 and 1985, Hannan and Freeman (1987) tested their model of density dependence as well as Delacroix and Carroll's (1983) hypothesis of entrepreneurial imitation, finding significant results for all the hypothesized effects. They argue that density dependence implies that the population faces a carrying capacity, that is, that there is a rough empirical limit to the population size that the environment will support. A similar analysis for founding rates in the semiconductor industry (Hannan & Freeman, 1988a) found support only for positive density dependence rather than the curvilinear effects found for unions, which the authors attribute to this industry's relative growth and its expanding markets (which imply an environment with an expanding carrying capacity).

Organizational Death. The bulk of ecological research thus far has examined rates of mortality among organizations. Organizational death is pervasive: There were over 70,000 business bankruptcies and almost 400,000 business deaths in 1985 (Aldrich & Marsden, 1988). Death is an unequivocal indicator of organizational performance, and it is also the means by which environmental selection operates. Thus, relating mortality rates to characteristics of organizations, populations, and their environments is central to organizational ecology.

Four broad areas of research on organizational mortality can be distinguished: liabilities of age and size, specialism and generalism, internal crisis and transformation, and environmental and population characteristics. All have been studied in the context of organizational death rates. We will consider each in turn.

Liabilities of age and size. One of the truisms of organizational research is that an organization's likelihood of failure is considerably higher during its early years than later in its life cycle. Stinchcombe (1965) attributed this liability of newness to both internal and external features of younger organizations. Members of newly founded organizations, especially those possessing a new type of structure, must learn new roles and relationships as the organization's operations get established. This process takes time away from the organization's "real" business and leaves it more vulnerable to failure. To compound this vulnerability, new organizations lack the external legitimacy of older organizations as well as the stable relationships with environmental constituencies that older ones have, making it more difficult to attract members and sources of support. Both these internal and external features lead to a higher death rate during the initial years.

The liability of newness hypothesis, that organizational mortality declines with age, has rapidly become perhaps the best-documented regularity in ecology. In an ambitious effort, Carroll (1983) compared three different statistical models of death rates across 52 archival datasets covering populations of retail stores, manufacturing firms, and craft, service, and wholesale organizations, finding that death rates decline with age in quite diverse organizational populations.[21] The liability of newness hypothesis has also found support in populations of newspapers in Argentina and Ireland (Carroll & Delacroix, 1982), national labor unions and semiconductor manufacturers (Freeman, Carroll, & Hannan, 1983), newspaper organizations in seven American metropolitan areas (Carroll, 1984b), voluntary social service organizations in metropolitan Toronto (Singh, Tucker, & House, 1986), and telephone companies in early 20th century Iowa (Barnett & Carroll, 1987). Caution is called for in interpreting these findings, however—as Freeman, Carroll, and Hannan (1983) point out, apparent age dependence could be a statistical artifact if the researcher has not been careful to control for heterogeneity in the population. If some types of organizations within a population are born feebler than others but this is not measured and controlled, it will appear as if mortality rates decline with age when what is actually happening is the early death of feeble organizations and the survival of their more robust counterparts.[22]

One liability that is likely to be confounded with age is smallness. Aldrich and Auster (1986) argue that compared to larger organizations, small organizations have more difficulty and pay greater costs in raising capital, face tax laws that favor selling out through merger, experience a proportionally greater load of paperwork from government regulation, and face tough competition from larger firms in securing labor, all of which increase the likelihood of death through dissolution or merger. Newer organizations tend to be smaller, and thus the liability of newness could merely reflect the liability of smallness.[23]

Despite the considerable evidence supporting the liability of newness hypothesis, relatively little effort has been made to unpack the ingredients of age to determine which factors are effective in warding off organizational death.[24] An exception is the work of Singh, Tucker, and House (1986), which asks to what extent external factors such as lower legitimacy and weak exchange relations are responsible for the liability of newness in a population of voluntary social service organizations. They found that organizations with a high degree of support and legitimacy experienced lower death rates that declined over time, while rates for organizations with less external legitimacy

did not decline. Hence, in the social service sector in Toronto, aging alone is not sufficient to overcome the liabilities of newness. This supports the notion that it is not newness per se that poses such a hazard for young organizations but rather other features, such as size, that are correlated with age.

Specialism and generalism. What kinds of environmental conditions favor specialist organizations, and when are generalists more likely to prosper? Ecologists argue that the answers to these questions can be used to explain the relative prevalence of specialist and generalist organizations, as selection pressures move populations over time in the direction of structural isomorphism. Freeman and Hannan (1983) adapted Levins' (1968) *fitness-set theory* to these questions, arguing that the issue of form can be reframed as one of niche width. A population's *niche width* is defined by its

> tolerance for changing levels of resources, its ability to resist competitors, and its response to other factors that inhibit growth. A population which has wide tolerance, meaning it can reproduce in diverse circumstances, is said to have a broad niche. Populations with more limited ranges of tolerance are called specialists... Specialist populations follow the strategy of betting all of their fitness chips on specific outcomes; generalists hedge their bets. (Freeman & Hannan, 1983, pp. 1118–1119)

A generalist must have some slack so that it can adapt to changes in the environment, while specialists tend to be leaner. Whereas adaptive theories generally argue that variable environments will favor generalists, according to niche width theory this is only true when changes are relatively infrequent, allowing generalists time to readjust; specialists are in a better position when fluctuations are both large and frequent. However, an analysis of death rates of specialist and generalist restaurants in 18 California cities over a three-year period failed to support this particular hypothesis (Freeman & Hannan, 1983).

An alternative approach to modeling the dynamics of specialist and generalist populations is proposed by Carroll (1985, 1987) in his model of *resource partitioning*. He argues that generalism and specialism are fundamentally interrelated: The success of generalist organizations creates the conditions for the success of specialists. Specifically, when a population of generalist newspapers becomes dominated by a handful of firms, there will be more resources available for specialist papers that target specific audiences (e.g., ethnic or professional groups) who cannot be catered to as effectively by a large dominant daily paper. Whereas early in the history of the newspaper industry a city may have had several competing general interest dailies that appealed to different groups, the trend toward greater concentration over time shifted the dominant strategy for generalists to one of playing to the middle, leaving groups with more specific concerns to the specialists. Data on newspapers in seven American metropolitan areas supported this model: When resources were more concentrated among general interest newspapers, specialists enjoyed a lower mortality rate than specialists operating in less concentrated markets, suggesting that the internal dynamics of the population of generalists leads over time to concentration in this population, opening niche space for specialists.[25]

Internal crisis and transformation. Reorganization can be traumatic for organizations, and crises—whether anticipated or not—can be fatal. Hannan and Freeman (1977, 1984) argue that organizations that attempt to adapt to their environments by reorganizing their activities or restructuring themselves face two sorts of difficulties: First, planned change can be difficult to accomplish because of various sunk costs, political considerations, and the

institutionalization of structures and procedures; and second, organizations that manage to change dramatically may recreate the liability of newness, as the procedures and role structures painstakingly worked out through trial and error are swept aside. While an organization may retain its external legitimacy in the wake of reorganization, its internal structure will no longer reflect its accumulated history and thus will be robbed of its previous survival value, increasing the chances of the organization's failure.

This model of the effects of organizational change was compared with an adaptive model, which predicts that change will increase the organization's viability, and a model of random organizational action, which suggests that planned change will not have a consistent effect either way (Singh, House, & Tucker, 1986). This study found that different types of changes had different effects in a population of voluntary social service organizations: Changes in structure and goals, which Hannan and Freeman (1984) posit as particularly disruptive, had no effect; changes in service area made early in life were associated with an increased risk of death; and early changes in chief executive and physical location were both linked to decreased death rates, consistent with an adaptive interpretation. On the other hand, Carroll (1984b), in a test of the succession-crisis hypothesis, found that managerial succession (in this case, the departure of the first publisher) was followed by a jump in the death rate of newspapers founded between 1800 and 1975 in seven American cities. This event was particularly precarious when the publisher who left was also the editor. These contrary findings on the effects of executive succession may be due to the different roles played by these different leaders: Founding publishers of newspapers are likely to be highly committed, intimately tied to the everyday activities of the newspaper, and personally tied to external sources of support, whereas executives who depart early in the career of a voluntary organization may have experienced a poor fit with the organization, making their replacement an adaptive change. A revised position suggested by Scott (1987a, pp. 200–203) that could reconcile the seemingly inconsistent results on the effects of change would view changes in core features of the organization (such as the fundamental mission and values of the organization) as more problematic, consistent with the ecological or selection view, while changes in peripheral aspects of the organization (such as short-run strategies) are best described by an adaptive perspective.

Environmental and population characteristics. Surprisingly, relatively little work has been done concerning the effects of environmental variations on the death rates in populations of organizations. Carroll and Delacroix (1982) found that increased national economic development at the time of the organization's founding enhanced the expected life-span of newspapers in Argentina and Ireland, although apparently at a decreasing rate. They also found that Argentine newspapers born during years of political turmoil had lower life expectancies than those organized during calmer years. They speculated that such organizations are likely to be opportunists who thrive on the resources that are freed in periods following social disruption but are then out-competed in more stable resource regimes. Carroll and Huo (1986) analyzed how task and institutional environments exerted different selection pressures on the population of newspaper organizations in the San Francisco-Oakland-San Jose area. This study again found that newspapers born during political turbulence were shorter lived; the costs of raw materials and the rate of illiteracy in the populace were associated with an increased hazard of death, while population size and the density of industrial establishments in the area apparently promoted longevity. They concluded that the institutional environment is more important in explaining the birth and death rates of newspapers, whereas the effects

of the task environment are more strongly felt on organizational performance.

Population-level processes as well as external environmental processes affect the mortality rates of organizational populations. The effects of density on death rates mirror those described above for birth rates: According to Hannan and Freeman (1988b), a greater population size increases a population's legitimacy and capacity for political and legal action, thereby decreasing death rates, but at higher densities competition for limited resources is more acute, thus increasing death rates. The combination of these two opposing effects is again a curvilinear relation between density and mortality: The disbanding rate for organizations falls with increasing density to a point corresponding roughly to the population's carrying capacity, then rises with density after that as competitive effects prevail. Analyses of populations of American national labor unions and semiconductor manufacturers supported this hypothesis (Hannan & Freeman, 1988a, 1988b). Similar effects of density dependence have been found by Barnett and Carroll (1987) for Iowa telephone companies. Singh, House, and Tucker (1986) found density to be negatively associated with the hazard of death, although apparently this is not a U-curve relation, perhaps indicating that the carrying capacity for this population has not been reached. As the only set of empirical regularities uniquely attributable to ecological research, the effects of density on organizational birth and death rates are certain to receive continued attention from ecologists (cf. Barnett, 1990; Carroll & Hannan, 1989a, 1989b; Delacroix, Swaminathan, & Solt, 1989).

Community Dynamics.   The discovery of complex and significant relations among population density and founding and death rates, discussed above, argues for the importance of taking the emergent properties of populations into account. That characteristics of one population have been found to have patterned impacts on those of another argues for taking the next step to the community level of analysis (Astley, 1985). The analysis of community dynamics has attracted growing attention. Brittain and Freeman (1980) describe the semiconductor industry in terms of the uncertainty, grain, and compatibility of resource states that characterize various niches within it, as well as the density of populations occupying them. They argue that r-strategists, who apply a *first mover* strategy by moving into new niches as they open, thrive under conditions of resource uncertainty and frequent innovation, while as the number of organizations occupying a niche increases toward its total carrying capacity, K-strategists, who thrive on efficiency, will tend to out-compete their opportunistic predecessors. Carroll (1985) found the degree of concentration of resources among generalist organizations to be related to increased life expectancies for specialists operating in the same environment. Hannan and Freeman (1987) studied the cross-effects of craft unions and industrial unions, finding that craft union founding rates decline with the density of industrial unions, but that surges in the number of industrial union foundings increase the rate of birth among craft unions. Characteristics of the craft union population had no discernible effect on the much smaller population of industrial unions.

In a study of Iowa telephone companies, Barnett and Carroll (1987) found that two subpopulations—(a) commercial, usually urban companies and (b) mutual (cooperative), usually rural companies—had complex effects on each other's growth and death rates both within their own county and on their nonlocal counterparts. They concluded that their findings "are consistent with a hypothesis of community-level competition: Networks of mutual and commercial companies, united as interdependent communities, may have competed with other such networks" (pp. 411–412). Furthermore, these populations had symbiotic effects on each other: The probability of a mutual company's offering long-distance service was positively related to the density of commercial companies, and the density of mutuals had a similar effect on commercials. Barnett (1990) found that the density of organizations using a complementary technology significantly decreased the hazard of death experienced by early telephone companies in Pennsylvania, indicating mutually beneficial relations among these organizations. Together, these findings support a view of communities of organizational populations variously linked by competitive and mutualistic relationships; these interdependencies must be understood to have a complete view of any single population's natural history.

Critique. Organizational ecology differs substantially from previous adaptive approaches to organization-environment relations and as a result has faced both theoretical stumbling blocks and criticisms not encountered by other work. Defining organizational form and population in a theoretically satisfying way, specifying the role and nature of environmental selection, and delineating forms of change that shape the structure of organizational populations have all been contentious topics. We will discuss each of these issues and some potential resolutions in turn.

Defining Form and Population. Basic to defining a population is the task of determining what an organizational form is: Populations are defined as bounded sets of organizations sharing a common form. Early work on ecology defined organizational form as "a blueprint for organizational action" that can be inferred from an organization's formal structure, patterns of activity, or normative order (Hannan & Freeman, 1977, p. 935). Yet almost without exception, empirical research within the ecological school has defined populations by their purposes or outputs, at best making rough distinctions between specialists and generalists. Semiconductor manufacturers, newspapers, labor unions, and telephone companies are all presumed to share a common form among themselves, yet little if any inquiry is made into their formal or informal structures.

Various alternatives to defining form by internal characteristics of organizations have been suggested. Astley (1985) argues for a community ecology approach that conceptualizes "population forms in terms of their functional roles vis à vis other populations within technologically interdependent communities" (p. 225). Hannan and Freeman (1986) see two complementary techniques for discerning form: (a) by applying network models to data on resource flows among organizations, one can identify sets of organizations that share structurally equivalent positions and external dependencies and infer a common form, and (b) by locating boundaries that separate populations and determining the processes that sustain or erode them, one can begin to identify niche structures and the forms that they define. These approaches are not in conflict: Organizations that share a functional role within a community and are bounded within a common system are likely to have similar patterns of dependencies. But as critics have been quick to point out, trying to identify populations in terms of the niches they occupy involves a certain amount of circular reasoning (Young, 1988).

The Role and Nature of Environmental Selection. Selection pressures pervade the theoretical structure of organizational ecology. They are usually assumed to operate on members of populations with an even hand, selecting out those whose forms are not compatible with their environment. Yet this imagery tends to overemphasize the distinction between organization and environment and to downplay the active strategies by which organizations construct their own environment. Research on interorganizational networks points out how network position can distort the selection pressures faced by organizations. Moreover, ecologists have been rather cavalier about

defining the exact nature of a competitive regime: Is it production efficiency, accountability, reliability, legitimacy, or some combination of these factors?[26]

Even though ecologists are not inattentive to matters of politics, we think their work would be enhanced if they were to develop arguments testing models of selection on political or network grounds. The technologically interdependent communities described by Astley (1985) are themselves embedded in a legal and political framework. State and national governments are influenced by political action committees, chambers of commerce, trade associations, and other forms of organizational collective action; in turn, governments provide the institutional structure in which organizations live and die. With the increasing mobility of business investment, competition takes place at even higher levels. State governments and local business communities vie with each other over the locations of plants and other investments, and national governments engage in a diffuse competition for business investment through their attitudes toward unions, tax laws, social welfare policies, and trade policies (Burawoy, 1985; Lindblom, 1977). Thus, competition and its effects occur simultaneously at the level of the organization and the community of organizations as well as at the state and national level, suggesting that a much broader view of selection processes is appropriate.

Forms of Change.   Theorists of biological evolution have debated the nature of evolutionary change in populations for some time, and this debate has been reproduced in organizational ecology. At issue is whether the character of populations is determined gradually through selective retention or whether change occurs primarily through abrupt bursts in which old populations die and new ones are born, followed by periods of stasis (the doctrine of *punctuated equilibrium*). While population ecology theory is not inconsistent with a punctuationalist view, in practice most ecological research is implicitly gradualist, taking populations as given and looking at the forces that shape them over time (Astley, 1985; see also Isaac & Griffin, 1989, for a critique of the ahistorical approach to labor history taken by ecologists). Research on the effects of technological innovation on industries (e.g., Tushman & Anderson, 1986) suggest that there is considerable merit in attempting to model punctuated equilibrium more explicitly.

A more radical problem for the ecological program is posed by current events that highlight the distinctive nature of capitalist firms within the world of organizations. Ecological researchers often proceed as if there were sufficient commonality among organizations to model the same organizational processes (such as density dependence in birth and death rates) across very different populations. It is assumed that American labor unions, semiconductor firms, early telephone companies, newspapers, and breweries in various areas of the world, and voluntary social service organizations in Toronto all share timeless causal regularities by dint of the fact that we can refer to them as organizations. Thus, one can explain changes in the mix of organizational forms over time through the births and deaths of inert forms.

We suggest that the facts of recent American corporate history pose a serious challenge to the viability of this project. Of the Fortune 500 firms in 1980, over one-quarter were subjected to a takeover or buyout attempt during the subsequent decade, most hostile, and most successful (Davis & Stout, 1990). A common post-buyout practice was to sell off units (deconglomeration) in order to pay off the financing of the buyout, leaving the organization that remained a radically restructured one. Those organizations that avoided being taken over typically underwent massive defensive restructurings, as did a large proportion of the firms that did not experience a takeover attempt (Hirsch, 1987). The financial conception of the corporation that now dominates American

business (Fligstein, 1990) allowed parts of organizations to be traded like baseball cards. Conversely, the firms in this population that failed through bankruptcy during the 1980s can be counted on one hand. Thus, what was perhaps the most radical remix of consequential organizations in American history occurred through processes that (a) are unique to capitalist firms that are publicly owned and (b) bear no resemblance to the births and deaths of biotic forms. Ecologists might respond that there is nothing special about the Fortune 500 (after all, there are more than 500 shoeshine stand organizations in Manhattan alone) or that we should consider such takeovers and restructurings to be the deaths of old (presumably inert) organizations and the births of new ones (cf. Hannan & Freeman, 1977); readers can decide for themselves on the merits of this position.

Future Directions. Ecological research has in many ways grown beyond the initial theoretical statements of population ecology. The jettisoning of a strict biological metaphor, which seems to have had a persistent appeal for students of organizations since the advent of open systems theories, has brought organizational ecology more in line with many of the classic concerns of organizational studies: technology and interdependence (Barnett & Carroll, 1987; Tushman & Anderson, 1986), relations of organizations with their institutional environments (Carroll & Huo, 1986), resource mobilization and social movements (McCarthy et al., 1988), and organizational demography and recruitment processes (McPherson, 1983). These developments suggest that organizational ecology may be well served by consolidating its strengths and integrating the concerns and intellectual technology of other approaches, in particular the institutional and network perspectives. But ecology's distinctiveness—its methodological rigor and dynamic approach to modeling and the explicit attention to a population perspective (Wholey

& Brittain, 1986)—must be highlighted. These tools have allowed the discovery of unexpected regularities: Curvilinear density dependence in founding and death rates and the findings of population and community dynamics are features of organizational life that would have remained unknown without taking a dynamic, population-level approach.

Ecologists have made headway on some of the thornier problems (e.g., adequate specification of organizational forms, the appropriate units and levels of analysis, the nature of organizational and population boundaries) that their perspective raises. We suspect that ecological research will remain controversial for some time precisely because its main intellectual goal—to develop theory at the population level—recognizes that initial assumptions must be made that (a) greatly simplify such key processes as competition and legitimation and (b) abstract much of the organizational detail and complexity that characterize what goes on in organizations. Ecologists clearly think this tradeoff is worth making; others may be less persuaded.

Institutional Perspectives

The label *institutionalist* has a long but ambiguous pedigree. Such diverse "masters" of social science as the sociologists Durkheim and Parsons and the economists Commons and Veblen were comfortable under the institutionalist flag. In contemporary social science there are, perhaps, as many new institutionalisms as there are disciplines.[27] In this section we attend to the family of writings, often tagged as the new institutionalism, that have had the most impact on organization theory.[28] Yet even within organizational studies, institutionally oriented research exhibits little of the coherence or the formalism associated with, say, population ecology or transaction cost economics. In this respect, the new institutionalism has an affinity with network research: "It is often easier to gain

agreement about what it is not than about what it is" (DiMaggio & Powell, 1991).

Perhaps the most novel tenet of the institutional approach is the insistence that organizational environments must be viewed in cultural as well as technical and economic terms (Scott, 1983). Organizations and their members are embedded in cultural systems composed of rules, norms, and taken-for-granted assumptions that define the way their worlds operate. Two of the most powerful sources of cultural blueprints are the modern professions and the modern state. Consequently, the institutional approach directs attention both toward the macro level of state structures, legal systems, and the sovereign modern professions and to the micro level of everyday interactions. It is in large part at this level of individual interaction and cognition that institutional practices and beliefs are translated into both constraints on action and "tool kits" that can be used to construct and legitimate new courses of action.

Although ecological and institutional approaches differ markedly in the relative weight they assign to human volition and organizational adaptability, there is growing recognition that these two perspectives share a number of insights. Both focus on the collective organization of the environment, insisting that the environment of organizations is made up of other organizations and that the demographic and structural properties of the environment shape organizational behavior. But ecologists attend primarily to demographic processes—organizational foundings, transformations, and deaths. Institutionalists contend that key features at the environmental level influence not only demographic processes but the internal structure of organizations within a given field as well.

A number of new insights are suggested by the institutional approach. Environments are viewed as comprised not only of technical requirements, bundles of resources, and patterns of communication, but also of cultural elements—symbols of legitimacy, belief systems, and professional claims (Scott, 1983). DiMaggio and Powell (1983) contend that "organizations compete not just for resources and customers, but for political power and institutional legitimacy, for social as well as economic fitness" (p. 150). Demonstrating social fitness often entails conforming to *rational myths* (Meyer & Rowan, 1977)—beliefs that specify what activities need to be carried out and what types of actors must be used to achieve specific social purposes. Because of their specificity and goal-directedness, such beliefs are rational. At the same time, however, these beliefs are like myths in the sense that their efficiency is presumed on the basis of their wide adoption, or their championing by groups who have been granted the right to determine such matters. Meyer and Rowan (1977) point out that there are multiple and diverse sources of rational myths: public opinion, educational systems, laws, courts, professions, ideologies, regulatory structures, certification and accreditation bodies, and governmental requirements.

Moreover, they tell us that in modern nation states, the forms and sources of widely held beliefs have themselves become more rationalized: Folkways and traditions and customs give way to laws, rules, and regulations; forms of traditional authority are replaced by the nation state, the professions, and systems of law. Thus, through its focus on processes that confer legitimacy on particular activities, the institutional approach directs attention away from material factors such as the location of physical resources or customers and toward the state and the professions, which shape organizational life both directly by imposing constraints and requirements and indirectly by creating and promulgating new rational myths.

Institutional theory combines a rejection of the assumptions of *rational actor* models popular in economics with an interest in institutions as independent variables, a turn toward cognitive and cultural explanations, and a concern with properties of supraindividual units of analysis that cannot be reduced to simple aggregations of the characteristics and actions of individuals. The constant and repetitive quality of much of organizational life results not from the calculated actions of self-interested individuals but from the fact that practices come to be taken for granted as "the way we do things." The model of behavior is one in which "actors associate certain actions with certain situations by rules of appropriateness" (March & Olsen, 1984, p. 741); these patterned responses are absorbed through socialization, education, on-the-job learning, or through acquiescence to convention. Individuals in organizations face choices all the time, but in making decisions they seek guidance from the experiences of others in comparable situations and by reference to standards of obligation.[29]

The Language of Institutional Theory. As with each of the perspectives we have reviewed, practitioners tend to develop their own distinctive language in the form of a battery of widely used concepts and arguments. Three topics are highlighted in this approach: institutionalization as both a cognitive outcome and an exogenous process, organizational fields as key units of analysis, and processes of institutionalization that promote conformity within fields.

Institutionalization. What does it mean to say that something has become institutionalized? Curiously, institutional theorists seem to be of two minds on this key issue (see Jepperson, 1991, for a commendable effort to clarify the conceptual variety that characterizes this approach). A cognitively oriented line of argument stresses that practices that are institutionalized are the product of ongoing repetitive interactions that gradually acquire a rulelike, social fact quality. That is, a pattern of activity is *institutionalized* when it comes to be taken for granted and therefore persists without serious questioning or efforts to make it continue (cf. Abelson, 1981, on the concepts of script and schema in psychology).

A second line of argument locates institutionalization within formal aspects of organizations, rather than as by-products of the interactions of individuals. This work associates institutional processes with the actions of the state, the professions, and other central organizations to establish a collective normative order. Research in this vein focuses on the causes and consequences of conformity to demands by such central organizations and on the ways in which the environment "interpenetrates the organization" (Meyer & Rowan, 1977).

In practice, institutionalists often invoke both meanings, thus, it is not easy to assign scholars to either label. At this point, the result is some conceptual ambiguity and methodological confusion. The ultimate goal is fairly clear, however: to understand how organizational practices and forms are developed and legitimated, come to be taken for granted, and eventually fall into disfavor. Clearly, this cycle has both micro (cognitive) and macro features to it.

Organizational Fields.   The appropriate unit of analysis in the study of institutionalization is the organizational field or societal sector.[30] The basic assumption is that organizations exist in socially constructed fields, composed of similar organizations that are responsible for a definable area of institutional life. An organizational field includes key suppliers, resource and product consumers, regulatory agencies, and professional associations, as well as other organizations that produce a similar service or product. The virtue of this approach is that it focuses attention not simply on competing units or on networks of organizations that directly interact with each other, but on the totality of relevant actors.

The structure of an organizational field is not easily determined a priori but must be defined on the basis of empirical investigation.

Two examples might be useful here. The organizational field in the study of health-care provision might include hospitals, HMOs, insurance companies, federal and state regulatory bodies, medical and nursing schools and professional associations, and pharmaceutical and hospital-supply companies. The key boundary issue is the extent to which these varied groups take each other's behavior into account in formulating their actions. The organizational field in research on the high arts could span museums, symphony orchestras, theaters, public agencies concerned with the arts, private collectors and commercial galleries, foundations and granting agencies, as well as university departments and schools and trade and professional associations. The critical issue is the degree to which members of fields are structured into a common community.

DiMaggio and Powell (1983) argue that the process by which an organizational field comes to be structurally defined consists of four parts: (a) an increase in the extent of interaction among organizations within a field, (b) the emergence of sharply defined interorganizational structures of domination and patterns of coalition, (c) an increase in the information load with which organizations in a field must contend, and (d) the development of a mutual awareness among participants in a set of organizations that they are involved in a common enterprise.

Processes of Institutionalization.   Assuming that organizations view themselves as members of a field or sector, what factors shape their orientation toward one another? In particular, how do organizational practices become institutionalized within a field? There are several mechanisms conducive to *organizational isomorphism,* for example, structural similarities among organizations within a field. Some of these processes encourage homogenization within a field directly by leading to structural and behavioral changes in organizations themselves. Others work indirectly by shaping the assumptions and experiences of the individuals who staff organizations. DiMaggio and Powell (1983) posit three general types of institutional pressures: (a) coercive forces that stem from political influence and problems of legitimacy, (b) mimetic changes that are responses to uncertainty, and (c) normative influences resulting from professionalization. These three mechanisms are, of course, likely to intermingle in specific empirical settings, but they tend to derive from different conditions and may lead to different outcomes. Indeed, institutional pressures may be cross-cutting and lead to conflict (Powell, 1988; Scott, 1987b).

Coercive influence results from both formal and informal pressures exerted on organizations by other organizations upon which they are dependent, as well as by strongly held cultural expectations in the society at large. In some circumstances, organizational change is a direct response to government mandate: Manufacturers adopt new pollution control technologies to conform to environmental regulations, nonprofits maintain accounts and hire accountants to meet the requirements of the tax laws, restaurants maintain minimum health standards, and organizations hire affirmative action officers to fend off allegations of discrimination.

Uncertainty is a powerful force that encourages mimetic or imitative behavior among the members of an organizational field. When organizational technologies are poorly understood, that is, when managers are unclear about the relationship between means and ends, when there is ambiguity regarding goals, or when the environment is highly uncertain, organizations often model themselves after other organizations. The modeled organization may be unaware of the modeling or may have no desire to be copied; it merely serves as a convenient source of organizational practices that the borrowing organization may use. Models may be diffused unintentionally, indirectly through employee transfer

or turnover, or explicitly by organizations such as consulting firms or industry trade associations. In this view, the ubiquity of certain kinds of modern management practices is credited more to the universality of mimetic processes than to any concrete evidence that the adopted models enhance efficiency.

A third source of organizational change is normative and stems, to a considerable degree, from the culture of professionalism. Two aspects of professionalism are particularly relevant. One of these is the growth of professional communities based on knowledge produced by university specialists and legitimated through academic credentials; the second is the growth and elaboration of formal and informal professional networks that span organizations and across which innovations may diffuse rapidly. Universities and professional training institutions are important centers for the development of organizational norms among professionalized managers and staff. Professional and trade associations are another vehicle for the development and spread of normative rules about organizational and professional behavior.

Key Areas of Research. Much of the early empirical work focused on the diffusion of governmental policies (Tolbert & Zucker, 1983) and on public and nonprofit organizations in such areas as education, health care, mental health, and the arts (e.g., see the studies in Meyer & Scott, 1983, or the bulk of the illustrative examples in DiMaggio & Powell, 1983). Education is the sector that has undoubtedly received the greatest scrutiny by institutionalists (Kamens, 1977; Meyer, 1977, 1983a, 1983b, 1988; Meyer & Rowan, 1978; Meyer, Scott, & Strang, 1987; Rowan, 1982; Scott & Meyer, 1988; Tolbert, 1985). We briefly summarize this extensive literature, drawing freely from the aforementioned sources.

The 20th century has seen a wholesale expansion of the roles of the states and the federal government in American education (Meyer, Scott, & Strang, 1987). State control has expanded in most domains of schooling (e.g., accreditation, curriculum guidelines, personnel certification, etc.). This process of state expansion is uneven across the states and is subject to conflict and debate, but the general trend is clear. Moreover, since the 1960s, the federal role has grown as well. But instead of a national educational policy, federal programs take the form of categorical or special purpose programs. This heightened complexity in the larger environment has several consequences for schools. The more highly structured policy-making becomes, the more schools focus on conforming to the official categories provided by the larger environment. But this conformity may involve only an organization's formal structure (i.e., its organizational chart of reporting relationships, its rules and procedures, etc.), which is readily visible to the outside world. In order to be perceived as legitimate by the wider environment, educational organizations adapt their formal structure to conform to institutional norms.

In numerous studies, John Meyer, W. Richard Scott, and their colleagues found wide consensus among superintendents, principals, and teachers on formal policies—grades, curricular materials, and so forth—but very little agreement, even within schools, about teaching methodologies or substantive measures of educational effectiveness. In other words, educational organizations evince loose coupling between their formal structures and their everyday activities. For example, understanding about using grades on a scale from A to F and an annual progression from K through 12 is largely taken for granted, yet understanding about what is effective in the classroom is not. The advantages of adherence to fieldwide norms and requirements on readily visible attributes are many: increased support, legitimacy, stability, internal and external commitment, eligibility for funding, enhanced attractiveness to personnel, and protection against charges of malfeasance or negligence. Moreover, by conforming to institutionalized

expectations, schools avoid close scrutiny of or control over their instructional activities.

Much of the initial theorizing about institutional environments was grounded in these studies of educational organizations (see Meyer & Rowan, 1977; Meyer, Scott, & Deal, 1981). In this research, the distinction between technical and institutional environments looms large. The former involves organizations whose success is dependent on solving technical problems, that is, achieving high standards of production, while the latter consists of organizations, such as schools, whose survival requires conformity to the normative demands of the larger environment. In technical environments, organizations are evaluated by their outputs. These firms closely monitor production and buffer their technical cores from environmental influences according to Thompson (1967). Institutional environments are composed of organizations judged more by the appropriateness of their form than by their outputs. The distinction between technical and institutional environments suggested that organizations in technical environments were rewarded for efficient production, while organizations in institutional environments were compensated for conformity and legitimacy.

Drawing on research on the arts and culture industries (DiMaggio, 1983; Powell & Friedkin, 1986), DiMaggio and Powell (1983) made a similar contrast between competitive and institutional isomorphism (see also Fennell, 1980). The concept of *isomorphism* is borrowed from Hawley (1968); it refers to a constraining process that forces one unit in a population to resemble other units that face the same set of circumstances. In the ecological approach, competitive isomorphism is driven by selection processes that weed out unfit organizations. The institutional approach initially emphasized accommodation, rather than competition, with environmental forces that promote sectorwide conformity. Such a view seemed apt for cultural activities, especially those in the nonprofit arena. The production of culture relies on a weak technical base (i.e., it is hard to draw up a blueprint for a successful artistic project, just as it is difficult to articulate a widely generalizable program for rehabilitating criminals). Arts organizations typically have ambiguous or conflicting goals (e.g., publish great books and make money); and market tests for *fitness* are sometimes softened by public and philanthropic support. In this field, as in education, formal conformity to fieldwide expectations often insure continued survival.

But dichotomies between the technical and institutional or competitive and institutional environments proved primitive. Both approaches ceded too much terrain to competitive market forces (Powell, 1985, 1991) and failed to recognize that some organizations confront multiple, conflicting demands (Scott, 1987b). In particular, Scott has highlighted the health care sector as one in which organizations must contend with vigorous technical and competitive pressures as well as stringent regulatory and institutional demands.

Health care sectors—both medical and mental health—have proven to be another fertile ground for institutional analysis (see Alexander & Scott, 1984; Fennell, 1980; Meyer, 1986; Scott, 1985; Scott & Black, 1986; Zucker, 1987). Like education, health care has experienced an expansion in state controls and regulatory pressures and the growth of multiple layers of oversight and coordination. But the institutional environment of health care is characterized by conflict among competing jurisdictions. The state, Scott (1987b) suggests, prefers more centralized forms of control and coordination, while the medical professions opt for more decentralized systems of procedures and rules; at the same time, health care organizations compete vigorously for patients and race to adopt the latest technologies.

The research on health care, along with a burgeoning strand of research on institutional processes in the professions and in proprietary sectors, made it clear that technical and institutional pressures are not mutually exclusive; rather, they are best regarded as dimensions along which organizational environments vary.[31] Sectors can face environments characterized by high technical pressures, high institutional pressures, neither, or both. Some sectors, such as banking or transportation, face both strong competitive and technical demands as well as pressures from various regulatory bodies and consumer groups to conform to procedural requirements. As a result, we find that the administrative structures of organizations in these fields are larger and more complex than those of organizations facing less complex environments (Powell, 1988; Scott & Meyer, 1991). In general, organizations of this type carry out tasks that combine complex technical requirements with a strong "public good" component. Schools, arts organizations, churches, and many professional service firms face strong institutional environments but relatively weak technical demands. In contrast, firms in manufacturing may experience some institutional pressures with respect to employment policies, safety standards, or pollution controls, but their main concern is production efficiency. Finally, one can imagine classes of organizations with both weak technical bases and fairly minimal institutional pressures. Exercise clubs or video stores would fit in this category.

In tandem with a broader view of the comingling of technical and institutional demands in some fields, there has been much more research on for-profit firms that falls under the general rubric of institutional theory. We should note, however, that one of the striking features of the new institutionalism is its broad diffusion into many areas of organization theory and general sociology. This popularity comes at a cost, however, because much of the work under an institutional banner employs divergent concepts, different and at times even contradictory hypotheses, and dissimilar boundary conditions. Indeed, it is not always clear what an institutional account is opposed to: Is institutionalism an alternative to rational actor accounts or arguments that depict the collective as primarily an additive outcome of micro-level interactions? an alternative to causal models that highlight single-level explanations? an approach that is complementary with other extant perspectives but adds a needed element of context? or a residual category that purportedly soaks up unexplained variance? In practice, so-called institutional arguments have been all of these; hence, caution flags are warranted.

We selectively review some of this contemporary work, with an eye toward highlighting research on the role of the professions, patterns of diffusion or adoption of particular policies or legal agendas, and structural change in organizations. We think that despite some lack of clarity about what an institutional argument amounts to, these lines of research have proved valuable.

One of the key tenets of the institutional approach is that the professions play a key role in shaping the institutional environment. Consequently, researchers have focused their attention on both the organization of the professions, notably law and accounting, as well as on patterns of change in professional standards. There are studies of the training and promotion procedures in law firms (Tolbert, 1988; Tolbert & Stern, 1989), the uses of management-by-objectives policies in accounting firms (Covaleski, Dirsmith, & Heian, 1990), and the organization of the legal departments of multinational corporations (Miyazawa, 1986). These internal organizational studies are complemented by research on professional practice, which analyzes the championing and adoption of policies promulgated by professional bodies.[32] Covaleski and Dirsmith (1988) examined how the use of specific budgetary rules took on symbolic value and shaped the political relations between the University of Wisconsin and state government. Their story is both fascinating and suggestive: The university had long been an advocate of more rational, professional

government, only they did not expect this advocacy to reshape their own budgetary process. This is one of the few studies that examines how organizations strategically respond to institutional pressures by trying to pacify and bargain with institutional stakeholders (see also Edelman, 1990b).

Mezias (1990) has studied a much broader diffusion process, the adoption of the investment tax credit among Fortune 200 corporations. His study has a 22-year time frame and makes a persuasive case that this change in accounting methods is best explained by an examination of the actions of the accounting profession, federal regulatory bodies, and the early adopting firms, not by the self-interested motives or characteristics of the adopting corporations. This research does two things notably well: It pushes our understanding of how the institutional environment is collectively organized (no simple dominance account would explain the interactions of the Big 8 accounting firms, the accounting standards boards, and the multiple regulatory authorities), and it incorporates the actions of large firms into the macro environment.

The diffusion of standards, laws, and even structural changes, such as the multidivisional form and matrix management, are all being studied by scholars using an institutional lens. We attend to key aspects of this line of research below, but first we note that there is considerable ambiguity about two issues in this work: the boundaries of the institutionalization process and the motives of the actors involved. Despite the use of the field or sector concept in much of the theoretical writing, the empirical studies seem to focus on important processes of institutionalization that cross fields. Sometimes the fields are bounded by region or industry, but in other studies the scope is as broad as the 100 or 200 largest U.S. corporations, or even the formation of personnel departments throughout U.S. industry. This inconsistent operationalization robs institutional explanations of some of their explanatory power. Similarly, scholars vary widely in terms of their accounts of motives.

In one of the earliest empirical studies, Tolbert and Zucker (1983) examined the introduction of civil service procedures during the period 1880 to 1935. In the early years, adoption of civil service reforms is associated with demographic characteristics of the cities (i.e., number of immigrants, city size, and working class population). In these cases, cities appeared to be adopting governmental reforms that would improve the authority of city officials and exclude immigrants and working class people from power. These are rational or self-interested motives for those in power. But after 1915, these characteristics no longer predict adoption. Tolbert and Zucker suggest that later adopters were trying to appear up to date: Civil service reforms had come to signal modern, rational city government, and thus adoption was widespread. Such an account is not fully persuasive; conditions change, power holders come and go, perhaps later incumbents were responding rationally to a new set of circumstances. Moreover, by leaving institutionalization as a residual category (i.e., failing to find that measured characteristics predict adoption is taken as evidence that adoption had become institutionalized), this research may be argued to stack the deck in favor of finding evidence for institutionalization.

In other research, motives are exempted entirely from analysis. Edelman (1990a) suggests that "it would be very difficult to distinguish empirically between such disparate motives for the formalization of due process rights as efficiency, control, and legitimacy" (p. 1403). We are bothered by both the loose boundary issue and by the limited attention to motives because they render the scope of institutional theory problematic. Nevertheless, these are initial studies of a new line of theorizing and it behooves us to examine the results.

Galaskiewicz (1985b, 1985c; Galaskiewicz & Wasserman, 1989) has done fascinating work on the development of corporate philanthropy in Minneapolis and St. Paul. The Twin Cities are noted for their vigorous program of corporate support for the nonprofit sector. He has shown how a general consensus on the role of philanthropy has become institutionalized among large corporations housed there and how this philanthropic mind-set is championed by corporate public affairs officers and rewarded by the social elite of the Twin Cities. This research stresses the role of interorganizational networks: When actors are faced with uncertainty, they turn to others whom they know, trust, and admire for guidance. The boundary or field in this work is defined geographically by membership in the Twin Cities corporate philanthropy community, either as a donor or recipient.

In other studies, however, researchers have adopted much broader and more diffuse boundaries and have not attended to the actual process of information transmission. Baron, Dobbins, and Devereaux Jennings (1986) underscore the role of the federal government and the newly emerging field of personnel administration in their analysis of the proliferation of so-called modern personnel practices throughout the core of the American economy during the middle of this century. Their sample covers nearly every major manufacturing industry. Similarly, Dobbin, Edelman, Meyer, Scott, and Swidler (1988) and Edelman (1990a, 1990b) employ broad samples in their studies of the adoption of due process procedures in corporations. Edelman's (1990a, 1990b) work is a nice combination of event history methods, commonly used by ecologists, and clear development of a theory of the legal environment. In her 1990a study, she looks at the changes in personnel practices of 52 organizations following the legislative reforms of the civil rights era. She maps these changes with measures of the intermediary role of personnel professionals as well as the corporation's proximity to the *public sphere,* for example, significant regulatory or contractual linkages to government. The expansion of due process rights was rapid, going significantly beyond direct legislative mandate. Of course, the governance of employee rights is ripe for symbolic manipulation. She does not investigate whether formal rules are closely tied to actual practices. But in a subsequent paper (Edelman, 1990b), with a much larger sample of business, educational, and government organizations, she examines equal employment opportunity laws with an eye toward how organizations mediate the adoption of these reforms. EEO is especially vulnerable to mediation, she notes, because the meaning of compliance is vague, the legal strictures focus more on procedures than outcomes, and enforcement mechanisms are weak. At the individual level, compliance with EEO is a function of internal organizational politics, balanced with considerations of industry norms and professional standards. At the collective level, organizational responses to the law shape societal and legal expectations about what constitutes good faith compliance. This is an important line of work because it shows not just the impact of the legal environment and the diffusion of new legal norms, but how the response of organizations to these new standards shapes the broader definition of what actions are legitimate and acceptable.

Another noteworthy line of inquiry addresses fundamental structural changes in organizations. Here the focus is on decisions to restructure an organization—clearly not a task undertaken for purely symbolic reasons. Thus, to the extent institutional theory is useful in explaining these reorganizations, this approach clearly speaks to core issues involving private sector firms. Still, we note again that this research also employs dissimilar notions about the boundaries of a field. Fligstein (1985) focuses on the largest 100 U.S. corporations over a 60-year period from 1919 to 1979. The critical issue is the decision to adopt a multidivisional structure. He finds that, contrary to what one would predict based on transaction cost economics, this choice is only partly driven by a firm's size or its competitive position. A more complete understanding is gained by examining a firm's responses to changes in federal antitrust law, as well as the tipping points at which a critical number of other firms in the industry have shifted from a functional to a multidivisional structure. He does not argue that economic calculations do not matter, but they are tempered by a corporation's assessment of the likelihood of government regulatory action and the collective choices made by other firms that are regarded as role models. A similar line of analysis is employed in very different arenas by Burns and Wholey (1990) in their study of the adoption of matrix management by hospitals, and by Amburgey and Lippert (1989) in their research on the diffusion of management buyouts.

These diverse areas of research do not as yet have a clean cumulative payoff. Institutional theory and research has proceeded in fits and starts, and in some cases the research bears only a vague family resemblance to the purported theory. Nevertheless, there are several critical points that have been well developed theoretically and have received substantial empirical support. In particular, we know a good deal about the forms and patterns of institutionalization. Rather than simply saying that the environment matters, scholars in this area can now point to both specific collective properties of the environment (e.g., number of levels of controls and types of control systems) and to key agents (the professions and federal and state regulatory bodies) who influence the process by which organizational forms and policies become institutionalized. Moreover, we have an enhanced understanding of the relationship between environmental complexity and internal organizational structure. When environments contain multiple centers of authority and legitimacy (what Scott & Meyer, 1983, term fragmented authority structures) we find greater diversity in organizational forms, greater differentiation among individual organizations, and more levels of administration within organizations (see the summary of this research in Meyer, Scott, & Strang, 1987; also see Powell, 1988; Scott & Meyer, 1991). In contrast, when environments are more homogeneous we find less elaborate internal structures. For example, Tolbert (1988) found that law firms that selected new associates from the same schools as those of their older partners found little need for intensive socialization programs or detailed performance reviews.

Critique. The thrust of institutionally oriented work in organizational theory has been to locate the sources of various organizational practices and structural arrangements within a broader context. Rather than viewing organizational actions as efforts to manage dependencies or reduce transaction costs, institutionalists see organizational actions as legitimacy-enhancing responses to the structure of relationships within organizational environments. In this sense, institutional theory is both more micro and more macro than other approaches. Implicit in the institutional approach is an essentially cognitive or ethnomethodological view of human action as shaped by conventions, built up from the ground level by participants in the course of interactions to the point that much behavior takes on a taken-for-granted quality (DiMaggio & Powell, 1991; Zucker, 1977). At the same time, the institutional perspective employs a more structural focus that emphasizes the incentives created by larger vertical authority structures external to the organization and the role of professional networks in aiding in the diffusion of organizational beliefs and practices.

In some respects this approach is a novel one. It orients organizational research in cultural and normative directions that have been largely ignored. On the other hand, institutional views share a great deal with what we might term general sociology. Not surprisingly, then, one of the key shortcomings is an oversocialized and rather passive view of human agency. Where does action come from and

who benefits from organizational change? Thus far, institutionalists have been rather silent on these issues, but the latest work begins to suggest the outline of a response.

Power and interests have been slighted topics in institutional analysis (DiMaggio, 1988; Perrow, 1986; Powell, 1985). Little attention has been directed toward explaining how organizational incumbents maintain their dominant positions or respond to threats during periods of crisis or instability. Nor has much work been done on how skilled institution-builders put multiple institutional logics to use to fashion strategic change. Efforts to incorporate power into institutional arguments should start with two simple observations: (a) Actors in key institutions realize considerable gains from the maintenance of those institutions, and (b) when organizational fields are unstable and established practices ill-formed, successful collective action often depends on defining and elaborating widely accepted rules of the game. Consequently, the acquisition and maintenance of power within organizational fields requires that dominant organizations continually enact strategies of control, most notably through either the socialization of newcomers into a shared world view or via the support of the state and its judicial arm.

Fligstein (1990) makes this point nicely in arguing that certain corporate strategies were favored by CEOs with marketing and finance backgrounds because they fit their interests and competencies. Successful executives developed conceptions of control that came to dominate their industries and defined appropriate standards of behavior. DiMaggio (1991) shows how early 20th century museum professionals sought radical changes in museum missions and policies, changes that also enhanced their own positions relative to those of their trustees.

Institutional theorists need to move beyond earlier statements that stressed how rules and routines created order and minimized uncertainty and examine how institutional arrangements are also replete with conflict and contradiction (Scott, 1987a). Thus, several fundamental questions remain to be addressed: How persistent are institutions—how mutable are institutionalized practices? When do different institutional logics challenge one another? What is the role of organizational elites in maintaining existing institutions? Under what conditions are challengers and entrepreneurs able to refashion existing rules, buffer themselves from institutional demands, or create new institutional orders? And, finally, what are the tensions between arguments that emphasize the "stickiness" of institutions and approaches that assume an optimization logic, depicting institutions as the results of intentional actions or adaptive solutions to conflicting interests?

We began this section with mention of the growing rapprochement between institutionalism and ecology. Institutionalists are now much more willing to acknowledge the importance of competition and organizational selection than they once were (see Powell, 1991). Ecologists, for their part, now emphasize the importance of institutional factors and explicitly criticize Panglossian models of organizational evolution (Hannan & Freeman, 1989). Singh, Tucker, and Meinhard (1991) provide an apt example of this convergence: Using population models, they demonstrate the effects of institutional change on population dynamics and the salutary effects of institutional legitimacy on the survival rates of voluntary social service agencies in Toronto. They suggest that competition for social fitness has a decided payoff. Rather than deny the importance of competition, institutional theorists now emphasize how competition varies across historical periods and societies and stress the role of institutions in constituting these different regimes, while ecologists use institutional insights to understand how selection criteria vary in different organizational populations (e.g., Barnett & Carroll, 1990).

Conclusion

We began this chapter with a warning that we would not present an integrated body of thought on the topic of organization-environment relations. We chose instead to present various contemporary lines of research, and we have tried to do so candidly and fairly. We stressed that it is critical to understand the different orientations of these approaches to the issues of the relevant unit of analysis and questions of the motives that undergird organizational actions. We think many criticisms of and ostensible points of disagreement among these perspectives are often based on a misunderstanding of what these theories are actually trying to explain.

We have presented a "warts and all" view of the various theoretical camps, trying to be as critical of lines of work that we are associated with as those with which we have personal points of disagreement. But our goal has not been to provoke controversy or appear as curmudgeons. Instead we want to highlight that these are vital avenues of research with questions unanswered and relevant empirical work waiting to be done. We hope that we might encourage a few readers to join in this task.

We also have noted points of convergence among these perspectives and possible topics of affinity. We do not believe that there is a correct, all-encompassing theory of organization-environment relations. In the early stages of theory development, a school of thought may find it expedient (and professionally rewarding) to view its approach as a total causal explanation of organizational phenomena. But as tensions mature, it obviously makes more sense to reorient them in a way that allows for competing theories to contribute to our understanding of organizational behavior. Moreover, we have stressed potential points of synthesis: opportunities to employ network theory to define relevant populations for ecological analysis, possible points of contact between transaction costs economics and networks in analyzing the durability of relationships, and potential collaboration between ecological and institutional theories on issues of how the institutional environment shapes selection processes and how ecological dynamics might result in institutional change. We close not with the perennial plea for more research, but with admiration for the accomplishments of the past two decades and anticipation of the work that is to come.

We thank Paul DiMaggio for his comments on our initial outline of this chapter, Peter Brantley, James Ranger-Moore, and Charles Perrow for comments on an earlier draft, and Marv Dunnette for his patience.

Notes

1 There are a number of recent surveys of the state of the art in macro-organizational behavior (e.g., Aldrich & Marsden, 1988; Pfeffer, 1985) as well as several useful textbooks (Hall, 1987; Perrow, 1986; Scott, 1987a), and we recommend them to interested readers.

2 Scott (1987a, chap. 6) provides a much more detailed guide to these various conceptions of the environment.

3 Many strands of more recent research draw freely on resource dependence arguments. Much of the work on directorate interlocks done from a network perspective incorporates insights from resource dependence theory, and the notion of *coercive isomorphism* in institutional theory (DiMaggio & Powell, 1983) builds directly on Pfeffer's work.

4 For efforts to operationalize transaction costs empirically, see Joskow (1985), Masten (1984), and Stuckey (1983).

5 See Rosen (1988) for a thoughtful review of research on internal labor markets from a transaction costs perspective.

6 Walker and Weber's (1984) results are, in fact, potentially damaging to the transaction costs explanation for vertical integration: They found that volume uncertainty (projected level of fluctuations in

the buyer's future demand for a component) significantly decreased the likelihood of buying a component rather than making it, even though it should be relatively easy to write contingent claims contracts for such situations. Technological uncertainty (frequency of expected changes in specifications and probability of technological improvement in the future), on the other hand, had no effect on make-or-buy decisions. Walker and Weber suggest that this may be due in part to the fact that retooling was paid for by the buyer. But this implies that contracts may be written such that asset specificity (in this case, the costs of retooling) can be rendered unproblematic, obviating the need to bring in an internal supply.

7 See Williamson, Wachter, and Harris (1975) for a full elaboration of this argument and a discussion of the various types of employment contracts that could potentially be constructed.

8 Williamson (1985) agrees with many of these criticisms, admitting that at present "transaction cost economics is crude, it is given to instrumentalist excesses, and it is incomplete" (pp. 390–393). Presumably these are considered to be theoretical problems to be addressed, not fatal shortcomings that doom the theory.

9 In addition to interorganizational relations, network researchers have focused on intraorganizational networks (e.g., Barley, 1990; Burkhardt & Brass, 1990; Nelson, 1989) and network forms of organization (e.g., Eccles & Crane, 1988; Miles & Snow, 1986; Powell, 1987). See Lincoln (1982) for a review relating organizational structures to network structures.

10 Burt (1980a) provides an extensive overview of network models, and we rely on his insights in the discussion of them.

11 Richardson (1987) notes that there have been over 100 studies of directorate interlocks, and the number is still growing. Space limitations require that this review will be rather selective, focusing primarily on the most recent work in this area. See Galaskiewicz (1985a) for a review of earlier research on interorganizational networks.

12 Using marginal rather than proportional measures of exchanges yielded broadly similar results with respect to the stability of market boundaries (Burt & Carlton, 1989).

13 But see also Zucker's (1989) strictures about the dangers of premature or surface convergence.

14 The definition of a population is a matter of some contention among ecologists, with one group allowing populations to be defined by the substantive theoretical issue at hand (Hannan & Freeman, 1977) and the other branch attributing more im-portance to empirically accurate taxonomies of organizational forms and populations (McKelvey & Aldrich, 1983). See Carroll (1984a) for a comparison of these two perspectives on defining organizational populations.

15 See, for example, the critiques of ecology by Perrow, 1986, and Young, 1988.

16 James Ranger-Moore (personal communication, 1991) points out that this is less true of plant ecology (where trees keep growing until they die) than animal ecology, on which most population ecologists draw.

17 Structural inertia, like most ecological constructs, is a relative concept: An organization suffers high inertia when the rate of environmental change exceeds the rate at which the organization can change its structure to survive. Even relatively flexible organizations may be subject to high mortality in uncertain and rapidly changing environments; for example, electronics manufacturers in Silicon Valley may seem agile relative to the Post Office, yet they may barely keep pace with the dynamic computer industry.

18 "Dominant competence is defined as the combined workplace (technological) and organizational knowledge and skills...that together are most salient in determining the ability of an organization to survive" (McKelvey & Aldrich, 1983, p. 112).

19 Carroll (1984a) argues that McKelvey and Aldrich (1983) take an overly rigid view of organizational reality by assuming that such a rigorous and empirically accurate classification scheme is possible given the almost limitless diversity and change inherent in the social world. This issue is not yet settled within the ecological school, although research has tended de facto to side with the latter perspective, which defines population by the theoretical problem at hand.

20 Surprisingly, most of the other measured aspects of the environment of this industry, such as the business cycle and the physical and social infrastructure, did not affect the rates of founding.

21 Carroll argues that, given adequate data that cover a relatively long time period, Makeham's Law is the best-fitting model of organizational mortality and should serve as a baseline for future research.

Makeham's Law describes mathematically a process where rates decline over time to an asymptotic level, at which point rates remain essentially constant. See Tuma and Hannan, 1984 , for a description of this and other dynamic models commonly used in ecological research.

22 In fact, the liability of newness hypothesis does not concern newness per se so much as liabilities of inexperience, low legitimacy, and other characteristics for which age serves as a proxy.

23 This possibility has been taken into account in some studies, however. Freeman, Carroll, and Hannan (1983) report that there is indeed a significant liability of smallness in addition to a liability of newness for American labor unions. Barnett and Carroll (1987) also separated these two variables, finding that increased age and size (number of telephone subscribers) were both associated with longer expected life-spans for early Iowa telephone companies.

24 This problem is due to data limitations, not to any lack of interest by ecologists. The best data sets cover very long periods of time, but the amount of organizational detail tends to decrease in proportion to the time span that is covered.

25 Similar arguments have been made for the book publishing (Powell, 1985) and beer (Porter, 1986) industries.

26 In their most recent work, Hannan and Freeman (1989, pp. 33–38) de-emphasize production efficiency and argue that selection pressures are multidimensional. In many circumstances, they suggest, political ties are paramount.

27 DiMaggio and Powell (1991) provide an overview of these various lines of research, noting their points of divergence and convergence.

28 The intellectual antecedents of the new institutionalism are found in the writings of Selznick (1949, 1957) and Berger and Luckmann (1967). Selznick's studies of the TVA and the Communist Party were based on notions of commitment and cooptation. For him, organizational practices became institutionalized when they were "infused with value beyond the task at hand" (Selznick, 1957, p. 16). The new institutionalism lacks Selznick's moral tone and his focus on informal organizational relations; instead the emphasis is on the more macro cultural understandings and socially accepted "accounts" of action. Berger and Luckman's (1967) work stressed that humans share cognitive

understandings, which emerge through daily inter-action, but these cognitive categories and belief systems come to be perceived as objective, exterior structures that define social reality. Among current institutionalists, Zucker (1977, 1983, 1987) has pursued these phenomenological insights most compellingly.

29 In this respect, institutionalists owe a consider-able debt to scholars working in the Carnegie tradi-tion (Cyert & March, 1963; March & Simon, 1958; Simon, 1945), who taught us that much of organiza-tional behavior, particularly decision making, in-volves rule-following more than calculation of con-sequences.

30 This section and the subsequent one on pro-cesses of institutionalization borrow freely from DiMaggio and Powell (1983).

31 See Scott, 1987b, pp. 125–134, for a fuller discus-sion of this point.

32 There is also a growing literature on the sym-bolic nature of accounting practices (see Carpenter & Dirsmith, 1990; Covaleski & Dirsmith, 1990; Meyer, 1986).

References

Abelson, R. P. (1981). Psychological status of the script concept. *American Psychologist, 36,* 715–729.

Abernathy, W. J., & Clark, K. B. (1985). Innovation: Mapping the winds of creative destruction. *Research Policy, 14*(1), 3–22.

Aldrich, H. E., & Auster, E. (1986). Even dwarfs started small: Liabilities of age and size and their strategic implications. In B. M. Staw & L.L. Cummings (Eds.), *Research in organizational behavior* (Vol. 8, pp. 165–198). Greenwich, CT: JAI Press.

Aldrich, H. E., & Marsden, P. V. (1988). Environ-ments and organizations. In N. J. Smelser (Ed.), *Handbook of sociology*. Beverly Hills, CA: Sage.

Aldrich, H. E., & Mueller, S. (1982). The evolution of organizational forms: Technology, coordina-tion, and control. In B. M. Staw & L.L. Cummings (Eds.), *Research in organizational behavior* (Vol. 4, pp. 33–87). Greenwich, CT: JAI Press.

Aldrich, H. E., & Staber, U. (1988). Organizing busi-ness interests: Patterns of trade association foundings, transformations, and deaths. In G. R.

Carroll (Ed.), *Ecological models of organizations* (pp. 111–126). Cambridge, MA: Ballinger.

Alexander, J., & Scott, W. R. (1984). The impact of regulation on the administrative structure of hospitals: Toward an analytic framework. *Hospital and Health Services Administration, 29,* 71–85.

Amburgey, T. L., & Lippert, P. G. (1989). *Institutional determinants of strategy: The legitimation and diffu-sion of management buyouts.* Unpublished manu-script, University of Wisconsin, Madison.

Armour, H. O., & Teece, D. J. (1978). Organizational structure and economic performance: A test of the multidivisional hypothesis. *Bell Journal of Economics, 9,* 106–122.

Astley, W. G. (1985). The two ecologies: Population and community perspectives on organizational evolution. *Administrative Science Quarterly, 30,* 224–241.

Atkinson, L., & Galaskiewicz, J. (1988). Stock ownership and company contributions to charity. *Administrative Science Quarterly, 33,* 82–100.

Barley, S. R. (1990). The alignment of technology and structure through roles and networks. *Adminis-trative Science Quarterly, 35,* 62–203.

Barnett, W. P. (1990). The organizational ecology of a technological system. *Administrative Science Quarterly, 35,* 31–60.

Barnett, W. P., & Carroll, G. R. (1987). Competition and mutualism among early telephone com-panies. *Administrative Science Quarterly, 32,* 400–421.

Barnett, W. P., & Carroll, G. R. (1990). *How institu-tional constraints shaped and changed competition in the early American telephone industry: An ecological analysis.* Unpublished manuscript, University of Wisconsin, Madison.

Baron, J. N., & Bielby, W. T. (1980). Bringing the firms back in: Stratification, segmentation, and the organization of work. *American Sociological Re-view, 45,* 737–765.

Baron, J. N., Dobbin, F. R., & Jennings, P. D. (1986). War and peace: The evolution of modern per-sonnel administration in U.S. industry. *American Journal of Sociology, 92,* 350–383.

Berger, P. L., & Luckmann, T. (1967). *The social con-struction of reality.* Garden City, NY: Anchor.

Boeker, W. P. (1988). Organizational origins: Entre-preneurial and environmental imprinting at the time of founding. In G. R. Carroll (Ed.), *Ecological models of organizations* (pp. 33–51). Cambridge, MA: Ballinger.

Bonacich, P. (1987). Power and centrality: A family of measures. *American Journal of Sociology, 92,* 1170–1182

Bowers, K. S. (1973). Situationism in psychology: An analysis and a critique. *Psychological Review, 80,* 307–336.

Brittain, J. W., & Freeman, J. H. (1980). Organizational proliferation and density dependent selection. In J. R. Kimberly, R. H. Miles, & Associates, *The organizational life cycle* (pp. 291–338). San Francisco: Jossey-Bass.

Burawoy, M. (1985). *The politics of production.* London: Verso.

Burkhardt, M. E., & Brass, D. J. (1990). Changing patterns or patterns of change: The effects of a change in technology on social network structure and power. *Administrative Science Quarterly, 35,* 104–127.

Burns, L. R., & Wholey, D. R. (1990). *The diffusion of matrix management: Effects of task diversity and interorganizational networks.* Unpublished manuscript, University of Arizona, Tucson.

Burt, R. S. (1980a). Models of network structure. *Annual Review of Sociology, 6,* 79–141.

Burt, R. S. (1980b). Autonomy in a social topology. *American Journal of Sociology, 85,* 307–336.

Burt, R. S. (1983). *Corporate profits and cooptation: Networks of market constraints and directorate ties in the American economy.* New York: Academic Press.

Burt, R. S. (1987). Social contagion and innovation: Cohesion versus structural equivalence. *American Journal of Sociology, 92,* 1287–1335.

Burt, R. S. (1988). The stability of American markets. *American Journal of Sociology, 94,* 356–395.

Burt, R. S., & Carlton, D. S. (1989). Another look at the network boundaries of American markets. *American Journal of Sociology, 95,* 723–753.

Carpenter, B., & Dirsmith, M. (1990). *Sampling and the abstraction of knowledge in the auditing profession: An extended institutional theory perspective.* Unpublished manuscript, University of Scranton, Scranton, PA.

Carroll, G. R. (1983). A stochastic model of organizational mortality: Review and reanalysis. *Social Science Research, 12,* 303–329.

Carroll, G. R. (1984a). Organizational ecology. *Annual Review of Sociology, 10,* 71–93.

Carroll, G. R. (1984b). Dynamics of publisher succession in newspaper organizations. *Administrative Science Quarterly, 29,* 93–113.

Carroll, G. R. (1985). Concentration and specialization: Dynamics of niche width in populations of organizations. *American Journal of Sociology, 90,* 1262–1283.

Carroll, G. R. (1987). *Publish and perish: The organizational ecology of newspaper industries.* Greenwich, CT: JAI Press.

Carroll, G. R. (Ed.). (1988). *Ecological models of organizations.* Cambridge, MA: Ballinger.

Carroll, G. R., & Delacroix, J. (1982). Organizational mortality in the newspaper industries of Argentina and Ireland: An ecological perspective. *Administrative Science Quarterly, 27,* 169–198.

Carroll, G. R., & Hannan, M. T. (1989a). Density delay in the evolution of organizational populations: A model and five empirical tests. *Administrative Science Quarterly, 34,* 411–430.

Carroll, G. R., & Hannan, M. T. (1989b). Density dependence in the evolution of populations of newspaper organizations. *American Sociological Review, 54,* 524–541.

Carroll, G. R., & Huo, Y. P. (1986). Organizational task and institutional environments in ecological perspective: Findings from the local newspaper industry. *American Journal of Sociology, 91,* 838–873.

Chandler, A. D., Jr. (1962). *Strategy and structure.* New York: Doubleday.

Clawson, D., & Neustadtl, A. (1989). Interlocks, PACs, and corporate conservatism. *American Journal of Sociology, 94,* 749–773 .

Coase, R. H. (1937). The nature of the firm. *Economica N.S., 4,* 386–405.

Covaleski, M. A., & Dirsmith, M. W. (1988). An institutional perspective on the rise, social transformation, and fall of a university budget category. *Administrative Science Quarterly, 33,* 562–588.

Covaleski, M. A., Dirsmith, M. W., & Heian, J. B. (1990). *Formal and informal management control in professional bureaucracies: An extended institutional theory perspective.* Unpublished manuscript, University of Wisconsin, Madison.

Cyert, R. M., & March, J. G. (1963). *A behavioral theory of the firm.* Englewood Cliffs, NJ: Prentice-Hall.

Davis, G. F. (in press). Agents without principles? The spread of the poison pill through the intercorporate network. *Administrative Science Quarterly*.

Davis, G. F., & Stout, S. K. (1990). *The rise and fall of the market for corporate control: A dynamic analysis of the characteristics of large takeover targets, 1980–1989.* Unpublished manuscript, Kellogg Graduate School of Management, Northwestern University.

Delacroix, J., & Carroll, G. R. (1983). Organizational foundings: An ecological study of the newspaper industries of Argentina and Ireland. *Administrative Science Quarterly, 28,* 274–291.

Delacroix, J., Swaminathan, A., & Solt, M, E. (1989). Density dependence versus population dynamics: An ecological study of failings in the California wine industry. *American Sociological Review, 54,* 245–262.

Dill, W. R., (1958). Environment as an influence on managerial autonomy. *Administrative Science Quarterly, 2,* 409–443.

DiMaggio, P. J. (1983). State expansion and organizational fields: A blockmodel approach. In R.H. Hall & R. E. Quinn (Eds.), *Organizational theory and public policy* (pp. 147–161). Beverly Hills, CA: Sage.

DiMaggio, P. J. (1988). Interest and agency in institutional theory. In L. G. Zucker (Ed.), *Institutional patterns and organizations.* Cambridge, MA: Ballinger.

DiMaggio, P. J., & Powell, W. W. (1983). The iron cage revisited: Institutional isomorphism and collective rationality in organizational fields. *American Sociological Review, 48,* 147–160.

DiMaggio, P. J., & Powell, W. W. (1991). Introduction to the new institutionalism. In W. W. Powell & P. DiMaggio (Eds.), *The new institutionalism in organizational analysis.* Chicago: University of Chicago Press.

Dobbin, F., Edelman, L., Meyer, J. W., Scott, W. R., & Swidler, A. (1988). The expansion of due process in organizations. In L. G. Zucker (Ed.), *Institutional patterns and organizations* (pp. 71–98). Cambridge, MA: Ballinger.

Dow, G. K. (1987). The function of authority in transaction cost economics. *Journal of Economic Behavior and Organization, 8,* 13–38.

Eccles, R. G., & Crane, D. B. (1988). *Doing deals: Investment banks at work.* Boston: Harvard Business School Press.

Edelman, L. B. (1990a). Legal environments and organizational governance: The expansion of due process in the American workplace. *American Journal of Sociology, 95,* 1401–1414.

Edelman, L. (1990b). *Legal ambiguity and symbolic structures: Organizational mediation of civil rights law.* Unpublished manuscript, University of Wisconsin, Madison.

Emerson, R. M. (1962). Power-dependence relations. *American Sociological Review, 27,* 31–40.

Emery, F. E., & Trist, E. L. (1965). The causal texture of organizational environments. *Human Relations, 18,* 21–32.

Evan, W. (1966). The organization set: Toward a theory of interorganizational relations. In D. Thompson (Ed.), *Approaches to organizational design.* Pittsburgh: University of Pittsburgh Press.

Fennell, M. L. (1980). The effects of environmental characteristics on the structure of hospital clusters. *Administrative Science Quarterly, 25,* 484–510.

Fligstein, N. (1985). The spread of the multidivisional form among large firms, 1919-1979. *American Sociological Review, 50,* 377–391.

Fligstein, N. (1990). *The transformation of corporate control.* Cambridge, MA: Harvard University Press.

Freeman, J., & Hannan, M. T. (1983). Niche width and the dynamics of organizational populations. *American Journal of Sociology, 88,* 1116–1214.

Freeman, J., Carroll, G. R., & Hannan, M. T. (1983). The liability of newness: Age dependence in organizational death rates. *American Sociological Review, 48,* 692–710.

Galaskiewicz, J. (1985a). Interorganizational relations. *Annual Review of Sociology, 11,* 281–304.

Galaskiewicz, J. (1985b). *Social organization of an urban grants economy: A study of business philanthropy and nonprofit organizations.* Orlando, FL: Academic Press.

Galaskiewicz, J. (1985c). Professional networks and the institutionalization of the single mind set. *American Sociological Review, 50,* 639–658.

Galaskiewicz, J., & Burt, R. S. (1991). Interorganization contagion in corporate philanthropy. *Administrative Science Quarterly, 36,* 88–105.

Galaskiewicz, J., & Wasserman, S. (1989). Mimetic and normative processes within an interorganizational field: An empirical test. *Administrative Science Quarterly, 34,* 454–479.

Glasberg, D. S., & Schwartz, M. (1983). Corporate ownership and control. *Annual Review of Sociology, 9,* 311–332.

Granovetter, M. (1973). The strength of weak ties. *American Journal of Sociology, 78,* 1360–1380.

Granovetter, M. (1985). Economic action and social structure: The problem of embeddedness. *American Journal of Sociology, 91,* 481–510.

Hall, P. (1987). A historical overview of the private nonprofit sector. In W. W. Powell (Ed.), *The nonprofit sector* (pp. 3–28). New Haven, CT: Yale University Press.

Hannan, M. T. (1986). *A model of competitive and institutional processes in organizational ecology* (Tech. Rep. 86–13). Ithaca, NY: Cornell University, Department of Sociology.

Hannan, M. T., & Freeman, J. (1977). The population ecology of organizations. *American Journal of Sociology, 82,* 929–964.

Hannan, M. T., & Freeman, J. (1984). Structural inertia and organizational change. *American Sociological Review, 49,* 149–164.

Hannan, M. T., & Freeman, J. (1986). Where do organizational forms come from? *Sociological Forum, 1,* 50–72.

Hannan, M. T., & Freeman, J. (1987). The ecology of organizational founding: American labor unions, 1836–1985. *American Journal of Sociology, 92,* 910–943.

Hannan, M. T., & Freeman, J. (1988a). Density dependence in the growth of organizational populations. In G. R. Carroll (Ed.), *Ecological models of organizations.* Cambridge, MA: Ballinger.

Hannan, M. T., & Freeman, J. (1988b). The ecology of organizational mortality: American labor unions, 1836–1985. *American Journal of Sociology, 94,* 25–52.

Hannan, M. T., & Freeman, J. (1989). *Organizational ecology.* Cambridge, MA: Harvard University Press.

Hawley, A. H. (1968). Human ecology. In D. L. Sills (Ed.), *International encyclopedia of the social sciences* (pp. 328–337). New York: Macmillan

Hawley, A. (1950). *Human ecology.* New York: Ronald Press.

Hirsch, P. (1987). *Pack your own parachute: How to survive mergers, takeovers, and other corporate disasters.* Reading, MA: Addison-Wesley.

Isaac, L. W., & Griffin, L. J. (1989). Ahistoricism in time-series analyses of historical process: Critique, redirection, and illustrations from U.S. labor history. *American Sociological Review, 54,* 873–890.

Jepperson, R. L. (1991). Institutions, institutional effects, and institutionalism. In W. W. Powell & P. J. DiMaggio (Eds.). *The new institutionalism in organizational analysis* (pp. 143–163). Chicago: University of Chicago Press.

Joskow, P. (1985). Vertical integration and long-term contracts. *Journal of Law, Economics, and Organization, 1,* 33–80.

Kamens, D. H. (1977). Legitimating myths and educational organizations: The relationship between organizational ideology and formal structure. *American Sociological Review, 42,* 208–221.

Katz, D., & Kahn, R. L. (1966). *The social psychology of organizations.* New York: Wiley.

Kiesler, S., & Sproull, L. (1982). Managerial responses to changing environments: Perspectives on problem sensing from social cognition. *Administrative Science Quarterly, 27,* 548-570.

Kotz, D. (1978). *Bank control of large corporations in the United States.* Berkeley: University of California Press.

Lang, J. R., & Lockhart, D. E. (1990). Increased environmental uncertainty and changes in board linkage patterns. *Academy of Management Journal, 33,* 106–128.

Langton, J. (1984). The ecological theory of bureaucracy: The case of Josiah Wedgewood and the British pottery industry. *Administrative Science Quarterly, 29,* 330–354.

Laumann, E. O., & Knoke., D. (1987). *The organizational state: Social choice in national policy domains.* Madison, WI: University of Wisconsin Press.

Levine, S., & White, P. E. (1961). Exchange as a conceptual framework for the study of interorganizational relationships. *Administrative Science Quarterly, 5,* 583–601.

Levins, R. (1968). *Evolution in changing environments.* Princeton, NJ: Princeton University Press.

Lincoln, J. R. (1982). Intra- (and inter-organizational networks. *Research in the Sociology of Organizations, 1*, 1–38.

Lindblom, C. E. (1977). *Politics and markets: The world's political-economic systems.* New York: Basic Books.

March, J. G., & Olsen, J. P. (1976). *Ambiguity and choice in organizations.* Bergen, Norway: Universitetsforlaget.

March, J. G., & Olsen, J. P. (1984). The new institutionalism: Organizational factors in political life. *American Political Science Review, 78*, 734–747.

March, J. G., & Simon, H. A. (1958). *Organizations.* New York: Wiley.

Mariolis, P., & Jones, M. H. (1982). Centrality in corporate interlock networks: Reliability and stability. *Administrative Science Quarterly, 27*, 571–584.

Masten, S. (1984). The organization of production: Evidence from the aerospace industry. *Journal of Law and Economics, 27*, 403–418.

McCarthy, J. D., Wolfson, M., Baker, D. P., & Mosakowski, E. (1988). The founding of social movement organizations: Local citizen's groups opposing drunk driving. In G. R. Carroll (Ed.), *Ecological models of organizations.* Cambridge, MA: Ballinger.

McKelvey, B. (1978). Organizational systematics: Taxonomic lessons from biology. *Management Science, 24*, 1428–1440.

McKelvey, B. (1982). *Organizational systematics.* Berkeley: University of California Press.

McKelvey, B., & Aldrich, H. (1983). Populations, natural selection, and applied organizational science. *Administrative Science Quarterly, 28*, 101–128.

McPherson, M. (1983). An ecology of affiliation. *American Sociological Review, 48*, 519–532.

Meyer, J. W. (1977). The effects of education as an institution. *American Journal of Sociology, 83*, 55–77.

Meyer, J. W. (1983a). Centralization of funding and control in educational governance. In J. W. Meyer & W. R. Scott (Eds.), *Organizational environments: Ritual and rationality* (pp. 179–198). Beverly Hills, CA: Sage.

Meyer, J. W. (1983b). Innovation and knowledge use in American public education. In J. W. Meyer & W. R. Scott (Eds), *Organizational environments: Ritual and rationality* (pp. 233–260). Beverly Hills, CA: Sage.

Meyer, J. W. (1986). Institutional and organizational rationalization in the mental health system. In W. R. Scott & B. L. Black (Eds.), *The organization of mental health services* (pp. 15–29). Beverly Hills, CA: Sage.

Meyer, J. W. (1986). Social environments and organizational accounting. *Accounting, Organizations, and Society, 11*, 345–356.

Meyer, J. W., & Rowan, B. (1977). Institutionalized organizations: Formal structure as myth and ceremony. *American Journal of Sociology, 83*, 340–363.

Meyer, J. W., & Rowan, B. (1978). The structure of educational organizations. In M. W. Meyer et al. (Eds.), *Environments and organizations* (pp. 78–109). San Francisco: Jossey-Bass.

Meyer, J. & Scott, W. R. (1983). *Organizational environment: Ritual and rationality.* Beverly Hills, CA: Sage.

Meyer, J. W., Scott, W. R., & Deal, T. E. (1981). Institutional and technical sources of organizational structure. In H. D. Stein (Ed.), *Organization and the human services.* Philadelphia: Temple University Press.

Meyer, J. W., Scott, W. R., & Strang, D. (1987). Centralization, fragmentation, and school district complexity. *Administrative Science Quarterly, 32*, 186–201.

Meyer, J. W., Scott, W. R., Strang, D., & Creighton, A. (1988). Bureaucratization without centralization: Changes in the organizational system of American public education, 1940–1980. In L. G. Zucker (Ed.), *Institutional patterns and organizations* (pp. 139–167). Cambridge, MA: Ballinger.

Mezias, S. (1990). An institutional model of organizational practice: Financial reporting at the Fortune 200. *Administrative Science Quarterly, 35*, 431–457.

Miles, R. E., & Snow, C. C. (1986). Organizations: New concepts for new forms. *California Management Review, 28*(3), 62–73.

Mintz, B., & Schwartz, M. (1985). *The power structure of American business.* Chicago: University of Chicago Press.

Miyazawa, S. (1986). Legal departments of Japanese corporations in the U.S.: A study of organizational adaptation to multiple environments. *Kobe University Law Review, 20*, 99–162.

Mizruchi, M. S. (1989). Similarity of political behavior among large American corporations. *American Journal of Sociology, 95*, 401–424.

Mizruchi, M. S., & Koenig, T. (1986). Economic sources of corporate political consensus: An examination of interindustry relations. *American Sociological Review, 51*, 482–491.

Mizruchi, M. S., & Schwartz, M. (1987). The structural analysis of business: An emerging field. In M. S. Mizruchi & Michael Schwartz, *Intercorporate relations: The structural analysis of business.* New York: Cambridge University Press.

Mizruchi, M. S., & Schwartz, M. (Eds.). (1987). *Intercorporate relations: The structural analysis of business.* New York: Cambridge University Press.

Mizruchi, M. S., & Stearns, L. B. (1988). A longitudinal study of the formation of interlocking directorates. *Administrative Science Quarterly, 33*, 194–210.

Monteverde, K., & Teece, D. J. (1982.). Supplier switching costs and vertical integration in the automobile industry. *Bell Journal of Economics, 13*, 206–213.

Nelson, R. E. (1989). The strength of strong ties: Social networks and intergroup conflicts in organizations. *Academy of Management Journal, 32*, 377–401.

Nelson, R. R., & Winter, S. G. (1982) *An evolutionary theory of the firm.* Boston: Belknap.

Ornstein, M. (1984). Interlocking directorates in Canada: Intercorporate or class alliance? *Administrative Science Quarterly, 29*, 210-231.

Ouchi, W. G. (1980). Markets, bureaucracies, and clans. *Administrative Science Quarterly, 25*, 129–142.

Paley, T. (1985). The avoidance of regulatory constraints: The use of informal contracts. *Journal of Law, Economics, and Organization, 1*, 155–175.

Palmer, D. (1983). Broken ties: Interlocking directorates and intercorporate coordination. *Administrative Science Quarterly, 28*, 40–55.

Palmer, D., Jennings, P. D., & Zhou, X. (1989). *Growth strategies and institutional prescriptions: Adoption of the multidivisional form by large U.S. corporations, 1963–1968.* Paper presented at the annual meeting of the American Sociological Association, San Francisco.

Palmer, D., Friedland, R., & Singh, J. V. (1986). The ties that bind: Organizational and class

bases of stability in a corporate interlock network. *American Sociological Review, 51*, 781–796.

Parsons, T. (1960). *Structure and process in modern societies.* New York: Free Press.

Pennings, J. M. (1982). Organizational birth frequencies: An empirical investigation. *Administrative Science Quarterly, 27*, 120–144.

Perrow, C. (1981). Markets, hierarchies and hegemony: A critique of Chandler and Williamson. In A. Van de Ven & W. F. Joyce, *Organizational design.* New York: Wiley.

Perrow, C. (1986). *Complex organizations: A critical essay* (3rd ed.). New York: Random House.

Pfeffer, J. (1972a). Interorganizational influence and managerial attitudes. *Academy of Management Journal, 15*, 317–330.

Pfeffer, J. (1972b). Merger as a response to organizational interdependence. *Administrative Science Quarterly, 17*, 382–394.

Pfeffer, J. (1972c). Size and composition of corporate boards of directors: The organization and its environment. *Administrative Science Quarterly, 17*, 218–228.

Pfeffer, J. (1985) Organizations and organization theory. In G. Lindzey & E. Aronson (Eds.), *The handbook of social psychology* (3rd ed.). New York: Random House.

Pfeffer, J. (1987). A resource dependence perspective on interorganizational relations. In M. S. Mizruchi & M. Schwartz (Eds.), *Intercorporate relations: The structural analysis of business.* Cambridge: Cambridge University Press.

Pfeffer, J., & Salancik, G. R. (1978). *The external control of organizations: A resource dependence perspective.* New York: Harper & Row.

Porter, M. (Ed.). (1986). *Competition in global industries.* Boston: Harvard Business School Press.

Powell, W. W. (1985). *Getting into print: The decision-making process in scholarly publishing.* Chicago: University of Chicago Press.

Powell, W. W. (1987). Hybrid organizational arrangements: New form or transitional development? *California Management Review, 30*(1), 67–87.

Powell, W. W. (1988). Institutional effects on organizational structure and performance. In L. G. Zucker (Ed.), *Institutional patterns and organizations: Culture and environment.* Cambridge, MA: Ballinger.

Powell, W. W. (1990). Neither market nor hierarchy: Network forms of organization. In B. M. Staw & L. L. Cummings (Eds.), *Research in Organizational Behavior, 12,* 295–336.

Powell, W. W. (1991). Expanding the scope of institutional analysis. In W. W. Powell & P. J. DiMaggio (Eds.), *The new institutionalism in organizational analysis.* Chicago: University of Chicago Press.

Powell, W. W., & Brantley, P. (1991). Competitive cooperation in biotechnology: Learning through networks. In N. Nohria & R. Eccles (Eds.), *Networks and organizations.* Boston: Harvard Business School Press.

Powell, W. W., & DiMaggio, P. J. (Eds.). (1991). *The new institutionalism in organizational analysis.* Chicago: University of Chicago Press.

Powell, W. W., & Friedkin, R. (1986). Politics and programs: Organizational factors in public television decision making. In P. J. DiMaggio (Ed.), *Nonprofit enterprises in the arts* (pp. 245–269). New York: Oxford University Press.

Putterman, L. (Ed.). (1986). *The economic nature of the firm.* New York: Cambridge University Press.

Richardson, R. J. (1987). Directorship interlocks and corporate profitability. *Administrative Science Quarterly, 32,* 367–386.

Rosen, S. (1988). Transactions costs and internal labor markets. *Journal of Law, Economics, and Organization, 4,* 49–64.

Rowan, B. (1982). Organizational structure and the institutional environment: The case of public schools. *Administrative Science Quarterly, 27,* 259–279.

Roy, W. G. (1981). The vesting of interests and the determinants of political power: Size, network structure, and mobilization of American industries, 1886–1905. *American Journal of Sociology, 86,* 1287–1310.

Roy, W. G. (1983). The unfolding of the interlocking directorate structure of the United States. *American Sociological Review, 48,* 248–257.

Roy, W. G., & Bonacich, P. (1988). Interlocking directorates and communities of interest among American railroad companies. *American Sociological Review, 53,* 368–379.

Salancik, G. R. (1979). Interorganizational dependence and responsiveness to affirmative action: The case of women and defense contractors. *Academy of Management Journal, 22,* 375–394.

Scott, W. R. (1983). The organization of environments: Network, cultural, and historical elements. In J. W. Meyer & W. R. Scott, *Organizational environments: Ritual and rationality.* Beverly Hills, CA: Sage.

Scott, W. R. (1985). Conflicting levels of rationality: Regulators, managers and professionals in the medical care sector. *Journal of Health Administration Education, 3*(2), 113–131.

Scott, W. R. (1987a). *Organizations: Rational, natural, and open systems* (2nd ed.). Englewood Cliffs, NJ: Prentice-Hall.

Scott, W. R. (1987b). The adolescence of institutional theory. *Administrative Science Quarterly, 32,* 493–511.

Scott, W. R., & Black, B. L. (Eds.). (1986). *The organization of mental health services: Societal and community systems.* Beverly Hills, CA: Sage.

Scott, W. R., & Meyer, J. W. (1983). The organization of societal sectors. In W. R. Scott & J. W. Meyer (Eds.), *Organizational environments: Ritual and rationality* (pp. 129–153). Beverly Hills, CA: Sage.

Scott, W. R., & Meyer, J. W. (1988). Environmental linkages and organizational complexity: Public and private schools. In H. M. Levin & T. James (Eds.), *Comparing public and private schools* (pp. 128–160). New York: Falmer Press.

Scott, W. R., & Meyer, J. W. (1991). The organization of societal sectors. In W. W. Powell & P. J. DiMaggio (Eds.), *The new institutionalism in organizational analysis.* Chicago: University of Chicago Press.

Selznick, P. (1949). *TVA and the grass roots.* Berkeley: University of California Press.

Selznick, P. (1957). *Leadership in administration.* New York: Harper & Row.

Simon, H. A. (1945). *Administrative behavior.* New York: Macmillan.

Simon, H. A. (1957). *Models of man.* New York: Wiley.

Singh, J. V. (Ed.). (1990). *Organizational evolution: New directions.* Newbury Park, CA: Sage.

Singh, J. V., House, R. J., & Tucker, D. J. (1986). Organizational change and organizational mortality. *Administrative Science Quarterly, 31,* 587–611.

Singh, J. V., & Lumsden, C. J. (1990). Theory and research in organizational ecology. *Annual Review of Sociology.*

Singh, J. V., Tucker, D. J., & House., R. J. (1986). Organizational legitimacy and the liability of newness. *Administrative Science Quarterly, 31,* 171–193.

Singh, J. V., Tucker, D. J., & Meinhard, A. G. (1991). Institutional change and ecological dynamics. In W. W. Powell & P. J. DiMaggio (Eds.), *The new institutionalism in organizational analysis* (pp. 390–422). Chicago: University of Chicago Press.

Starbuck, W. H. (1976). Organizations and their environments. In M. D. Dunnette (Ed.), *Handbook of industrial and organizational psychology.* New York: Rand McNally.

Starbuck, W. H. (1983). Organizations as action generators. *American Sociological Review, 48,* 91–102.

Stearns, L. B., & Mizruchi, M. S. (1986). Broken tie reconstitution and the functions of interorganizational interlocks: A reexamination. *Administrative Science Quarterly, 31,* 522–538.

Stinchcombe, A. L. (1965). Social structure and organizations. In J. G. March (Ed.), *Handbook of organizations.* Chicago: Rand McNally.

Stinchcombe, A. L. (1990). Weak structural data (review of Mizruchi and Schwartz). *Contemporary Sociology, 19,* 380–382.

Stuckey, J. (1983). *Vertical integration and joint ventures in the aluminum industry.* Cambridge, MA: Harvard University Press.

Terreberry, S. (1968). The evolution of organizational environments. *Administrative Science Quarterly, 12,* 590–613.

Thompson, J. D. (1967). *Organizations in action.* New York: McGraw-Hill.

Tolbert, P. (1985). Resource dependence and institutional environments: Sources of administrative structure in institutions of higher education. *Administrative Science Quarterly, 30,* 1–13.

Tolbert, P. (1988). Institutional sources of organizational culture in major law firms. In L. G. Zucker (Ed.), *Institutional patterns and organizations* (pp. 101–113). Cambridge, MA: Ballinger.

Tolbert, P., & Stern, R. (1989). *Organizations and professions: Governance structures in large law firms.* Unpublished manuscript, School of Industrial and Labor Relations, Cornell University, Ithaca, NY.

Tolbert, P. S., & Zucker, L. G. (1983). Institutional sources of change in the formal structure of organizations: The diffusion of civil service reform, 1880–1935. *Administrative Science Quarterly, 28,* 22–39.

Tuma, N. B., & Hannan, M. T. (1984). *Social dynamics: Models and methods.* New York: Academic Press.

Tushman, M. L., & Anderson. P. (1986). Technological discontinuities and organizational environments. *Administrative Science Quarterly, 31,* 439–465.

Useem, M. (1984). *The inner circle: Large corporations and the rise of business political activity in the U.S. and U.K.* New York: Oxford University Press.

Walker, G., & Weber, D. (1984). A transaction cost approach to make-or-buy decisions. *Administrative Science Quarterly, 29,* 373–391.

Warren, R., Rose, S., & Bergunder, A. (1974). *The structure of urban reform.* Lexington, MA: D.C. Heath.

Wellman, B., & Berkowitz, S. D. (Eds.). (1988). *Social structures: A network approach.* New York: Cambridge University Press.

White, H. C., Boorman, S. A., & Breiger, R. L. (1976). Social structure from multiple networks: Pt. 1. Blockmodels of roles and positions. *American Journal of Sociology, 81,* 730–780.

Wholey, D. R., & Brittain, J. W. (1986). Organizational ecology: Findings and implications. *Academy of Management Review, 11,* 513–533.

Wiewel, W., & Hunter, A. (1985). The interorganizational network as a resource: A comparative case study on organizational genesis. *Administrative Science Quarterly, 30,* 482–496.

Wiggins, S. N. (1990). The comparative advantage of long-term contracts and firms. *Journal of Law, Economics, and Organization, 6,* 155–170.

Williamson, O. E. (1975). *Markets and hierarchies: Analysis and antitrust implications.* New York: Free Press.

Williamson, O. E. (1981). The economics of organization: The transaction cost approach. *American Journal of Sociology, 87,* 548–577.

Williamson, O. E. (1985). *The economic institutions of capitalism: Firms markets, relational contracting.* New York: Free Press.

Williamson, O. E., & Ouchi, W. G. (1981). The markets and hierarchies program of research:

Origins, implications, prospects. In A. H. Van de Ven &W. F. Joyce, *Organizational design*. New York: Wiley.

Williamson, O. E., Wachter, M. L., & Harris, J. E. (1975). Understanding the employment relation: The analysis of idiosyncratic exchange. *Bell Journal of Economics, 6,* 250–278.

Williamson, O. E., & Winter, S. (1989). *Journal of Law, Economics, and Organization* [Special issue], 4(1).

Woodward, J. (1965). *Industrial organization*. New York: Oxford University Press.

Young, R. C. (1988). Is population ecology a useful paradigm for the study of organizations? *American Journal of Sociology, 94,* 1–24.

Zajac, E. J. (1988). Interlocking directorates as an interorganizational strategy: A test of critical assumptions. *Academy of Management Journal, 31,* 428–438.

Zald, M. N. (1970). Political economy: A framework for comparative analysis. In M. N. Zald, *Power in organizations*. Nashville, TN: Vanderbilt University Press.

Zald, M. N. (1987). The new institutional economics. *American Journal of Sociology, 93,* 701–708.

Zucker, L. G. (1977). The role of institutionalization in cultural persistence. *American Sociological Review, 42,* 726–743.

Zucker, L. G. (1983). Organizations as institutions. In S. B. Bacharach (Ed.), *Research in the Sociology of Organizations, 2,* 1–47. Greenwich, CT: JAI Press.

Zucker, L. G. (1987). Normal change or risky business: Institutional effects on the hazard of change in hospital organizations. *Journal of Management Studies, 24,* 671–700.

Zucker, L. G. (Ed.). (1988). *Institutional patterns and organizations*. Cambridge, MA: Ballinger.

Zucker, L. G. (1989). Combining institutional theory and population ecology: No legitimacy, no history. *American Journal of Sociology, 54,* 542–545.

CHAPTER 7

Consumer Psychology

Jacob Jacoby
New York University

Wayne Hoyer
University of Texas, Austin

Arthur Brief
Tulane University

*Consumer and industrial psychology are viewed as different and independent
domains of psychology, with both tracing much of their conceptual underpinnings
back to social psychology. The thesis of this chapter is that it would be of mutual
benefit for both organizational and consumer psychology to examine the manner
in which equivalent concepts and issues are addressed by the other. Given the
focus of this volume, primary emphasis was placed on considering how consumer
psychological concepts and research might prove useful to organizational psychology. Specific concepts examined include information processing and decision
making, customer satisfaction, situational influences, motivation, communication,
and innovation.*

Introduction

THE TRADITIONAL VIEW that was held for
the first six decades of consumer and industrial psychology was that the former—along
with personnel, organizational, and human
engineering psychologies—was subsumed
under the latter (e.g., American Psychological
Association, 1965; Guion, 1965; Katzell, 1958).
Industrial psychology was considered a subdiscipline of psychology, and consumer
psychology was considered a specialty of
the subdiscipline (although some definitions
of industrial psychology had to be stretched
to make this point; cf. Guion, 1965, p. 817).
Perhaps this view was justified when (a) the

consumer psychologist and the industrial psychologist were one and the same person, (b) this person was the only psychologist in the organization, and (c) this person was primarily management-oriented and interested in the consumer qua purchaser, that is, in adding to the profits of the firm. However, there are some fundamental distinctions between the other specialties of industrial psychology, taken as a whole, and consumer psychology, which give reason to doubt the traditional view.

As early as 1958, Katzell (1958), in his review of the field of industrial psychology, noted that consumer psychology "has a different set of dependent and independent variables" (p. 237). At its most basic level, industrial psychology is concerned with the behavior of people inside organizations as workers and producers of goods and services, while consumer psychology is concerned with the behavior of people outside of organizations as purchasers and users of these goods and services. Industrial psychologists are primarily interested in how to make employees happier, more productive, or both, the objective being to develop more efficient and effective organizations. Thus, it tends to be a management-oriented discipline.

Consumer psychology, while historically management-oriented, is largely no longer so. Consumer behavior includes both purchase and consumption components, and for at least two decades, many consumer psychologists have been more interested in the consumer qua consumer than in the consumer qua purchaser. Thus, while consumer psychology is obviously an applied form of psychology, it is not so obviously a specialty of industrial psychology. From the perspective of many, industrial and consumer psychology are siblings in the household of applied psychology, sharing a common parentage in the more fundamental areas of psychology. As such, the relationship is more closely one of lateral peership than anything hierarchical.

Consumer psychology, which studies the dynamics underlying decisions and behavior regarding the acquisition, use, and disposition of products, services, time, and ideas (Jacoby, 1975a, 1976a), is potentially a broader field than industrial psychology. Probably the greatest point of similarity between the two lies in its relation to organizational psychology. In the process of trying to understand human behavior in their respective contexts, both consumer and organizational psychology can trace a major portion of their conceptual and methodological heritage back to social psychology and, more recently, cognitive psychology. Consumer psychology has drawn heavily from the social psychological literature on attitudes, communication, and persuasion and from cognitive psychology in such areas as memory, information processing, and decision making; organizational psychology has traditionally focused on the social psychological studies of leadership, group behavior, and motivation and only more recently has turned to the cognitive areas.

The direction of information flow between these fields is not all one way. Both organizational and consumer psychology provide excellent testing grounds for general social and cognitive psychological propositions. While both social and cognitive psychology are essentially broad-gauged, basic disciplines, the validity of their propositions must be examined in specific applied contexts. Together, the working-producing and buying-using contexts account for the majority of the contemporary person's waking hours, and it is only natural that these psychological concepts be incorporated and tested in these domains (cf. Jacoby, 1975a). While the basic psychologist's laboratory provides a superb setting for rigorously testing explicit hypotheses, the field provides an excellent setting in which to establish construct validity or generality of these findings (Campbell & Stanley, 1963; Cook & Campbell, 1976).

If consumer and industrial and organizational psychology are siblings spawned from the same psychological parents, what can be said of their relationship to each other? Our objective in this chapter is to suggest some answers to this question. This will be done primarily by examining how social and cognitive psychological concepts have been borrowed, sometimes relabeled, and used in consumer and industrial and organizational psychology.

It is important to note that while both consumer and industrial psychology have existed as disciplines of empirical inquiry for comparable time periods (and both may trace their births to Scott, 1903, 1908a, 1908b, 1911a, 1911b, as documented by Ferguson, 1962), the amount of published literature generated in industrial and organizational psychology is somewhat larger than that in consumer psychology. Perhaps one reason is that business firms seem quite willing to share knowledge about the management of people, but considerably less willing to share information on consumer reactions to product development and promotional efforts. It is likely, therefore, that industrial and organizational psychology has a greater number of well-developed, comprehensively examined constructs and well-documented findings. Logically, it would seem to have more to offer the developing field of consumer psychology than vice versa. Given the orientation of the *Handbook*, however, this chapter will focus on how consumer psychology might add to the development of industrial and organizational psychology. Finally, some of the findings of consumer psychology may appear old hat to industrial psychologists. This probably should be viewed as desirable and encouraging in that it reflects a certain degree of construct (qua convergent) validity for both domains. As Vroom (1969) pointed out, ultimately "statements about the determinants of behavior in organizations should be derivable from general theories capable of explaining behavior in other situations" (p. 197). Howard and Sheth (1969) argue in similar fashion that "buying behavior in most cases is merely a part of the interrelated total ongoing pattern, and not a unique kind of behavior independent of other daily activities" (p. 295).

Vroom and Maier (1961) note that

research in industrial social psychology has been based on two general types of models. The first treats the individual as the unit of analysis...[while the] second kind of conceptual model treats the social system as the unit of analysis. (p. 143)

Inasmuch as a consideration of all actual and potential points of contact between consumer and organizational psychology is beyond the scope of this chapter, attention has been limited to representative issues from each of these research traditions. The individual level of analysis is represented by various approaches to human information processing, while the social system approach is represented by the interrelated processes of formal and informal communication. It is important to state that the literature review presented is not intended to be exhaustive but rather to serve as a starting point for research and further investigation into these issues.

Information Processing and Decision Making

The predominant stream of research in consumer behavior from the late 1970s through the 1980s has focused on consumer information processing. Researchers have been vitally interested in examining the processes by which consumers acquire information, process it, and arrive at an evaluation or decision. This emphasis is not surprising, given that most consumer behavior has some form of decision-making activity at its root.

In attempting to understand these processes, many models and frameworks have been posited (e.g., Bettman, 1979; Engel, Blackwell, & Miniard, 1986; Howard & Sheth, 1968). Though specific formulations vary, the general process may be envisioned in terms of six sequential steps: problem recognition, internal information search, external information search, integration of information (or alternative evaluation), decision making, and postdecision outcomes and consumer satisfaction. Motivation and external environmental influences are thought to impact each of these stages.

Each stage is relevant to any organizational context, though some topics are more appropriate and applicable to industrial and organizational psychology than others. Nevertheless, a brief review of these areas may provide unique insights and suggest further research hypotheses in the organizational context. The next section briefly reviews consumer research on each of these major stages and then suggests potential applications to industrial and organizational behavior.

Problem Recognition

The first stage in the consumer's decision process, problem recognition, is defined as "the perception of a difference between the ideal state of affairs and the actual situation sufficient to arouse and activate the decision process" (Engel, Blackwell, & Miniard, 1986, p. 43). That is, individuals consciously (or sometimes unconsciously) assess the extent to which the present situation is satisfactory relative to a reasonable idealized standard. To the extent it is not, the consumer is said to perceive a problem, the individual's system is energized, and goal-oriented behavior begins (Engel et al., 1986).

It is important to note that many models of human behavior depict motives or needs as the primary mechanism for instigating behavior. Problem recognition, however, is a broader concept that encompasses motives as

well as a variety of other causal factors. According to Engel et al. (1986), these include reference groups, family influence, situational influence, and marketing efforts.

Reference group influence occurs because individuals in a social or work context set standards or expectations that are guides or even rules for others to follow. To the extent that social acceptance is important to an individual, these norms can be a powerful determinant of behavior.

Family influence refers to the fact that a decision is often made by more than one individual. In these cases, the ideal state may be defined in terms of what makes others happy (Engel et al., 1986). Although organizations are not officially classified as families, similar motivations may occur in situations where group decision making is required.

Situational influence can result from a variety of factors. For example, the household refrigerator suddenly breaking down is likely to result in the purchase of a new refrigerator within 48 hours. Thus, change in behavior results from a change in environment. In an organizational context, influences could include a change in the marketplace, the introduction of new members into the organization, or a redefinition of work responsibilities.

Finally, *marketing efforts* are directed toward making consumers feel that they are unhappy with their actual state. This is achieved primarily through advertising. The basic notion is to motivate consumers by convincing them that their actual state is unsatisfactory. Similar effects can be obtained through organizational communications.

Internal Information Search

Once problem recognition occurs, the consumer moves to the next stage in the decision process. Often, consumers will want some kind of reason or information on which to base the purchase decision. Most models of the consumer decision process hold that internal information search precedes external information search. This involves a scan of knowledge already stored in memory in order to identify relevant information. Internal search can range from the simple acquisition of one piece of information (e.g., "I'm out of my toothpaste, so I'll go buy my regular brand") to an extensive probing of one's memory for detailed information.

According to Jacoby, Chestnut, Weigl, and Fischer (1976), Bettman (1979), and others, many consumer decisions are based solely on stored knowledge in memory. That is, when reaching a purchase decision, the consumer typically relies exclusively on a vast storehouse of product-related information. Even when this stored information is inadequate and additional information is acquired from the external environment, it is obvious that prior knowledge plays an extremely important role in any decision-making effort.

It is therefore not surprising to find that consumer researchers have become increasingly interested in the role of human memory in the decision-making process. The theoretical base guiding these efforts has been drawn largely from cognitive psychology, and the predominant framework has been the *multiple store theory* of memory.

Although numerous areas of memory research are relevant to both consumer and organizational psychology, two topics are of particular interest. These concern (a) the content and organization of knowledge in memory and (b) memory structures called *schema*. Researchers have focused on what types of product-relevant information are stored in memory and why.

One issue is the extent to which consumers retain information acquired from advertisements. Research indicates that, at the exact moment of purchase, consumers remember very little specific product information obtained from advertisements (Cobb & Hoyer, 1985). This occurs because the cues present in the decision environment do not help in the

retrieval of ad-related information stored in memory, or because ads for competing brands cause interference, or because the ad-related information is not consistent with processing goals (Keller, 1987). Researchers have noted, however, that advertising cues presented at the point of purchase might help and may influence brand decisions (Hutchinson & Moore, 1984; Keller, 1987; Lynch & Srull, 1982). Other types of brand information, especially that resulting from past experience, are stored in memory as well. Examination of stored information is considered important because this information would be a key determinant upon which the purchase decision is based.

Also of interest has been an examination of the structure of the information. For example, researchers have been particularly interested in whether information is organized by brand names or product attributes (Biehal & Chakravarti, 1982a; Johnson & Russo, 1978; Srull, 1983). A general finding is that memory organization can have an influence on how product choices are made (Beattie, 1982; Biehal & Chakravarti, 1982b). If information is organized in memory by brand, then consumers will also process and make the decision by brand. If organized by attribute, consumers are more likely to make a comparative choice. Research has indicated that sequential comparison processing (i.e., when choice options are compared one attribute at a time) is less complex and more efficient than brand processing (Bettman 1979; Jacoby, Jaccard, Kuss, Troutman, & Mazursky, 1987).

In addition, Biehal and Chakravarti (1983) and Lynch, Marmorstein, and Wergold (1988) found that the accessibility of information can play a role in how a choice is made. If information for a particular alternative is difficult to retrieve, the alternative may be ignored in the decision process in favor of brands for which information can be easily retrieved. Also, accessible information may be perceived as more diagnostic (Lynch et al., 1988). Biehal and Chakravarti (1982b) further state that this phenomenon could lead to the choice of a suboptimal brand. In a similar vein, Alba and Chattopadhyay (1986) found that making a particular brand more salient can significantly impair unaided recall of other brands.

Several studies (e.g., Johnson & Russo, 1978; Rip, 1979; Russo & Johnson, 1980) have attempted to examine the nature of information stored in memory regarding familiar consumer products. These studies focused mainly on the inferential level of knowledge stored in memory. The lowest level consists of specific product knowledge and requires no inference at all, while the highest level is a problem solution that must be inferred from lower levels of knowledge. For example, Russo and Johnson (1980) used a categorization system ranging from lower inferential single evaluation brand-attribute levels (e.g., Brand A costs $.79) to higher inferential levels such as best brand statements (Brand A is the best brand). Higher inferential level beliefs are based on complex interrelationships among lower level beliefs. A major finding of this study was that single evaluation brand-attribute values accounted for a majority of statements (62%). No other inference level accounted for more than 11 percent of the statements. It is important to note, however, that higher level global judgments can have a stronger impact on the choice process than lower level factual knowledge (Kardes, 1986).

A major question for organizational psychologists concerns the nature of memory related to organizational decision making. That is, one might ask whether decisions are made on the basis of option-specific (i.e., attribute) information or whether broader level evaluations are used.

Thus, although the nature of the different elements in memory can be varied and complex, it appears that much of what is contained in memory can be reduced to simple attribute statements about the choice alternatives. In other words, one way in which memory for

consumer choice options can be conceptualized is a series of interrelated beliefs. A belief may be defined as "the subjective probability of a relation between the object of the belief and some other object, value, concept, or attribute" (Fishbein & Ajzen, 1975, p. 131). These beliefs can be formed on the basis of (a) direct observation (descriptive beliefs), (b) acceptance of information from some outside source (informational belief), or (c) as the result of an inference process (inferential belief). Although all three types of beliefs can play a significant role in the choice process, Ford and Smith (1987) found that information about a partially described brand (i.e., one that requires the formation of an inference) has a greater impact on choice than fully described brands.

In organizational contexts, beliefs can be formed on the basis of actual work experience, by organizational communications or word-of-mouth communications from co-workers, or from an inference process. Interesting topics for research might be a determination of exactly how beliefs are formed in an organizational context and an assessment of the relative influence of each type of belief in the decision process.

A second major domain of memory focuses on structures called *schema* or *scripts*. According to Taylor and Crocker (1981), a schema is a

> cognitive structure which consists, in part, of a representation of some defined stimulus domain. The schema contains general knowledge about the domain, including the specification of the relationships among its attributes, as well as specific examples of instances of the stimulus domain. (p. 3)

For example, a consumer would possess a schema for automobiles. The schema would contain knowledge about its features (e.g., four wheels, engine, seats), what it does (provide transportation), how much it costs (e.g., expensive) and specific examples (e.g.,

Mercedes, Porsche, Mazda). Schema are central to information processing because they are frequently drawn upon to interpret or understand incoming information. For example, interpreting information from an ad for an automobile would require use of a previously stored automobile schema. In the absence of such schema, miscomprehension is likely to result (Jacoby & Hoyer, 1987).

Scripts are considered a specialized type of schema. According to Schank and Abelson (1977), a script is "a structure that describes an appropriate sequence of events in a particular context" (p. 41). For example, consumers would possess a script for the act of grocery shopping, which would include a specification for a starting point, the order in which aisles would be visited, the speed of shopping, and so on. Thus, scripts can be distinguished in terms of their causal and temporal nature.

Both general schema and scripts are thought to play a key role in the internal search process and in information processing in general. As a result, an increasing number of studies have started to address this topic (Leigh & Rethans, 1983; Smith, Houston, & Childers 1984; Whitney & John, 1983). The basic thrust of this research has been to examine processing differences between individuals who do and do not possess relevant schema. Results generally indicate that the presence of schema can facilitate consumer information processing.

The rise of the consumer psychologist's interest in memory parallels that of the industrial and organizational psychologist's interest in this topic (e.g., Giola & Poole, 1984; Landy & Farr, 1983; Lord, 1985). Industrial and organizational psychologists, however, seem to have attended less to how choice behaviors are affected by the structure of memory or by the presence or absence of schema and focused their attention more on relationships among cognitions, for example, on how scripts may serve as organizational sense-making devices

(e.g., Giola, 1986). Nevertheless, the issues addressed in consumer research represent potentially interesting areas of inquiry in organizational settings. The distinction between the attribute versus brand organization of information in memory might be relevant to how managers organize attribute information about their supervisees—an organizational parallel to brands. Conventionally, it is presumed that information about supervisees is organized by person, being analogous to brand organization; but, it is plausible that some managers organize this information by attributes such as effort, performance, particular knowledge, skills, abilities, or some other characteristic of individuals. If this is the case, then consistent with the consumer literature, one might find that human resource decisions of managers (e.g., compensation and promotion decisions) systematically vary as functions of memory organization with an attribute structure associated with comparative choice processes. Organizational researchers interested in schema appear to assume their presence (e.g., Gioia & Manz, 1985). It seems important to learn if schema are formed in reference to certain kinds of organizational phenomena and not others, and if formation is attributable to the organizational setting in which people find themselves. Not only might this information enhance our understanding of organizational decision making, it might also unmask how organizations, as social aggregates, meaningfully differ from one another. Conceivably, what may be found important in distinguishing between organizations is not, for example, an organization's strategy or structure but rather the schema shared among its elites.

External Information Search

Though internal informational search is central to information processing and decision making, many times the information stored in memory is insufficient to make a decision. As a result, consumers may be motivated to search for additional information from the external environment.

According to Engel et al. (1986), "the extent of search is based on an individual's perception of the *value* to be gained in comparison with the *cost* of acquiring and using that information" (p. 68). The perceived value of the decision would be determined by the importance of the decision (e.g., high price, length of commitment, conspicuousness), perceived risk, availability of information, confidence in one's decision-making ability, time pressure, and attitudes toward shopping. (For a review of this large body of literature, see Beatty & Smith, 1987.) The potential costs of search, however, would be decision delay, opportunity costs of time and money, information overload, and psychological costs (e.g., frustration or tension).

Early research focused on the amount and type of information consumers acquire before making a decision. These efforts (e.g., see Bennett & Mandell, 1969; Claxton, Fry, & Portis, 1974; Newman & Staelin, 1972) attempted to' acquire this data using retrospective questioning. This technique involved nothing more than obtaining postpurchase recall of information-seeking behavior. The deficiencies of this approach were pointed out in Jacoby (1975). In short, consumers have limited ability and/or motivation to recall their search activities. Further, retrospective questioning treats decision-making behavior as a static event rather than the dynamic process it really is. In response to these shortcomings, alternative process methodologies were developed to describe the dynamic aspects of information-seeking behavior. The major characteristic of these approaches is the focus on information seeking as it occurs, as opposed to the attempted recall of such information-seeking after it has occurred. The three most prevalent methodologies are termed (a) verbal protocols (Bettman, 1970, 1971; Payne, 1976), (b) eye movement fixation analysis (Russo, 1978; Russo & Rosen, 1975), and (c) the behavioral process

approach (Jacoby, 1975, 1977; Jacoby, Chestnut, Wiegl, & Fisher, 1976; Payne, 1976).

Verbal protocols consist of asking consumers to "think aloud" while engaging in the decision process. A written record of these verbalizations is termed a *protocol* (Bettman, 1970). Inferences regarding search and decision processes are then based on these data. The main advantage of this approach is that a great deal of detailed information is obtained. Theoretically, these protocols reflect both internal and external information search. The major disadvantage is that the protocols may not accurately reflect relevant decision-making thought processes. Consumers may not have the motivation or the ability to accurately verbalize their internal processes (Nisbett & Wilson, 1977; Wright, 1974c, 1974d). Also, these protocols have the potential to be reactive and therefore alter the nature of cognitive processing (Biehal & Chakravarti, 1989).

Further, it is particularly difficult to obtain verbalizations of thought processes when consumers have prior experience and knowledge regarding the choice options (Bettman, 1977). Thus, it would be difficult to assess the influence of memory and cognitive structure on choice processes. Finally, data collection tends to be quite time consuming, often resulting in very small samples.

The second methodology, *eye movement fixation analysis* (e.g., see Russo & Rosen, 1975), uses some form of sensing device to record the movements of an individual's eyes while examining a stimulus display. These eye movements are then examined for patterns in the sequence of fixations. An advantage of this technique is that a very detailed trace of the information examination process is provided without relying on verbal reports. However, a disadvantage is that eye movements do not reveal information on internal processes so that little information on cognitive processing is provided. Further, the data collection procedure is time consuming, thereby necessitating small sample sizes.

A third methodology, the *behavioral process approach,* usually involves generating and making available an options-by-properties matrix of information. Consumers are then permitted to use as much information from the matrix as they wish before reaching a purchase decision. Early studies (e.g., Jacoby, 1975b, pp. 210–213; Jacoby, Chestnut, & Silberman, 1977; Jacoby, Chestnut, Weigl, & Fisher, 1976; Payne, 1976) made use of an information display board (IDB) containing rows and columns corresponding to the options and properties. Each cell (corresponding to an option-by-property crossing) contained a set of cards on which were printed the specific values of information. Personal computers were used to present information in more recent studies. In early computer studies (e.g., Chestnut, 1977; Hoyer, 1979, 1980), subjects were presented with news of options and properties and asked to call out the corresponding code numbers of the desired information. The researcher then displayed this information on a television monitor, and the search process was recorded by the computer. More recent computer-oriented behavioral process research has dispensed with the need for a computer operator, so that the subject and machine form a self-contained simulation (see Jacoby, Jaccard, Kuss, Troutman, & Mazursky, 1987; Jacoby, Kuss, Mazursky, & Troutman, 1985; Jacoby, Mazursky, Troutman, & Kuss, 1984; Rosen & Olshavsky, 1987).

In all behavioral process research, four major aspects of the search process are of interest: (a) *extent* of search, or how much information is acquired, (b) *content* of search, or just what information is acquired, (c) *sequence* of search, or order in which the information is acquired, and (d) the *source* of information, or where the information is acquired from (Hoyer & Jacoby, 1983; Rosen & Olshavsky, 1987).

A major advantage of this approach is that attention is focused on what information is *actually* acquired during the simulation (i.e., behavior), rather than on what people *say* they

acquire. In addition, this procedure is relatively straightforward and permits the use of large sample sizes. A disadvantage concerns the artificiality of information presentation. Evidence suggests that search strategies are influenced by the format in which information is presented (Bettman & Kakkar, 1977). Since most real-world information displays do not appear in a matrix, external validity may be threatened.

Each of these methodologies has its advantages and disadvantages. Regardless of the specific methodology used, several key findings concerning information acquisition have emerged. First, it is clear that consumers base their decisions on only a small portion of the available information, typically less than 3 percent (Bettman & Kakkar, 1977; Bettman & Park, 1980; Furse, Punj, & Stewart ,1984; Jacoby, Chestnut, & Silberman, 1977; Jacoby et al., 1976; Olshavsky & Granbois, 1979; Payne & Ragsdale, 1978). However, this percentage varies, depending on the nature of the decision. As one example, Midgley (1983) found that approximately 50 percent of buyers of men's clothing seek information extensively. Just which information is used depends on its perceived relevance, perceived novelty, and perceived credibility (Wilton & Myers, 1986).

Second, there are individual differences in the sequence of information accessing. The two most common strategies are processing by brand and processing by attribute (Bettman & Kakkar, 1977; Jacoby et al., 1976; Russo & Rosen, 1975). A common example of this type of processing would be comparison shopping by price. Experts tend to use remarkably different and more efficient sequence strategies than do nonexperts (see Jacoby et al., 1987).

Third, individual difference variables may be related to the type of search strategy employed. For example, Jacoby et al. (1976) found that high consumption frequency of a product was related to processing by options, while low consumption frequency was related to processing by attributes.

Building on the work of Hammond, McClelland, and Mumpower (1980), Ilgen, Fisher, and Taylor (1979), and others, Jacoby et al. (1984) showed how behavioral process research can be used to generate new insights on feedback. Their findings suggest that certain types of feedback ("outcome only" feedback) can actually lead to poorer decision maker performance, yet this is precisely the kind of feedback generally provided in organizational settings. Behavioral process research has also been used to shed light on the development of corporate images (see Mazursky & Jacoby, 1986). In terms of future research, the behavioral process methodology may be useful in the development of "expert systems." According to Penzias (1982), "before we can even try to design an expert system, we must discover what it is that experts do" (p. 28). A behavioral process methodology may be useful in modeling expert behavior.

A related topic relevant to organizational psychology is information overload. As mentioned earlier, consumers have limited processing capacity. If the information load exceeds this capacity, they might become confused and make poorer choices. Research by Jacoby, Speller, and Berning (1974) and Jacoby, Speller, and Kohn (1974) revealed that increasing information load tends to produce (a) dysfunctional consequences in terms of the consumer's ability to select the best brand, and (b) beneficial effects in terms of the consumer's degree of satisfaction, certainty, and lower perceived confusion regarding selection. In other words, subjects felt better with more information, but actually made poorer purchase decisions.

This finding generated considerable controversy in the consumer literature (Jacoby, 1977, 1984; Malhotra, 1984; Russo, 1974; Summers, 1974; Wilkie, 1974). The major argument centered on the analysis and interpretation of the data. The current view can be summarized as follows: Consumers can be overloaded with too much product information, but generally avoid doing so. They are highly selective in how much and just what information they access and tend to stop well short of overloading themselves (Jacoby, 1984). Further, Keller and Staelin (1987) found that quality of information increases decision effectiveness, while quantity of information decreases effectiveness.

Both methodologically and substantively, the consumer literature on external search appears relevant to a number of research programs in industrial and organizational psychology. Methodologically, the behavioral process approach, which facilitates collection of data on the extent, content, and sequence of information search, might be interestingly used in studies of feedback-seeking behaviors (e.g., Ashford & Cummings, 1983; DeNisi, Cafferty, & Meglino, 1984). In particular, this could allow for highly controlled investigation of the sequence in which individuals seek to acquire information about their task performances. Based on results generated by consumer psychologists, one might expect to discover sequence to exert a considerable effect on the quality of judgments people make about their performances. A more substantive example is offered by the conclusion that while consumers are susceptible to information overload, they generally do *not* experience it because they are selective in how much information they access. This implies that the extent of information overload experienced by decision makers within organizations is less problematic than often thought and that understanding of organizational decision making may be enhanced by trying to identify for particular sorts of decisions the extent of information actually accessed and the content of information systematically ignored.

Integration of Information

Much of the literature has focused on the cognitive processes by which consumers combine or integrate various types of information to select one alternative from a set of alternatives. Every choice object can be said to possess specific attributes, and it is the individual's perception of these attributes that guides choice behavior. A number of cognitive choice models have been developed (e.g., Bass & Talarzyk, 1972; Fishbein, 1963; Fishbein & Ajzen, 1975; Wright, 1975), all of which presume that individuals compare various choice alternatives and eventually select one alternative from the set on the basis of one or more attributes. The principal difference between these formulations is in the specification of the processes by which the perceived attributes are combined to form an overall evaluation toward the choice object.

In general, two basic types of models can be identified: simultaneous linear compensatory models and sequential noncompensatory models. *Simultaneous linear compensatory models* are those in which perceived values of the attributes are combined in a linear fashion. The nature of this combinatorial process allows a low score on one particular attribute to be compensated for by high scores on other attributes. *Sequential noncompensatory models* involve sequential processing of alternatives. The choice objects are evaluated on one attribute at a time, and failure to meet adequate standards on a particular attribute eliminates that option from the choice set; an inadequacy on one attribute is not compensated for by high scores on other attributes.

Simultaneous Linear Compensatory Models.

Most of the research on consumer choice has been done in the context of simultaneous linear compensatory models. These approaches are based on the notion that an individual's evaluation of a particular choice object is a function of two major components: (a) his or her beliefs about each of the attributes and (b) an evaluation of these beliefs. As discussed earlier, a belief is defined as a perceived subjective probability of a relationship between an object and some other object, value, idea, or attribute (Fishbein, 1963). The formulation initially applied to consumer choice behavior was first developed by Fishbein (1963). This model is represented by the following equation:

$$A_o = \Sigma B_i \times a_i$$

where:

B_i = belief related to attribute i

a_i = the evaluation (good or bad) of attribute i

Several similar models (e.g., Bass & Talarzyk, 1972; Bettman, Capon, & Lutz, 1975; Cohen, Miniard, & Dickson, 1980; Sheth & Talarzyk, 1972; Troutman & Shanteau, 1976) have subsequently appeared.

Numerous studies have used these models to predict consumer choice, with the resulting correlations typically ranging from .2 to .6 (Lutz & Bettman, 1977; Wilkie & Pessemier, 1973). In addition, Sheluga, Jaccard, and Jacoby (1979) showed that predictions of the model can be improved significantly by including only information that has been acquired from external search (as opposed to all available information). Hoyer (1980) takes this a step further by showing that increased predictability can be achieved by including only searched information recalled from memory (i.e., information can be acquired but forgotten and therefore have no impact on the decision).

The modest predictive performance of these attitude models led Fishbein (1967) to propose that a behavioral intentions model might be a better predictor of behavior. This model differed from the previous attitude model in two respects: *attitude specificity* and the inclusion of normative factors. Fishbein hypothesized that to predict behavior, an attitude should be as specific to the behavior as possible. Thus, if one wanted to predict the purchase of an automobile, the attitude toward *purchasing* this automobile should be assessed rather than the attitude toward the automobile itself (as was done in the earlier model). Fishbein also recognized that other important individuals in one's life can play an important role in the decision. In other words, a decision may not be made entirely by one person.

Based on these factors he proposed the following model of intentions:

$$B \sim BI = \Sigma(Bi\ ai)w + \Sigma(NBj\ Mcj)w$$

where:

B	=	behavior
BI	=	behavioral intention
Bi	=	belief toward performing an act
ai	=	evaluation of belief
NBj	=	normative belief (the person's belief that the referent j thinks she or he should or should not perform the behavior)
Mcj	=	the motivation to comply with referent j
w	=	empirically derived weight representing the component's relative influence

Research using this model has been extensive, and a meta-analysis of a large number of studies has generally supported the usefulness of this formulation (Sheppard, Hartwick, & Warshaw, 1988). This model has been used to predict intentions for female occupations (Greenstein, Miller, & Weldon, 1979), applications for financial loans (Ryan & Bonfield, 1980), alcohol consumption (Schlegel, Crawford, & Sanborn, 1977), family planning (Davidson & Jaccard, 1975), and a variety of consumer products (see Ryan & Bonfield, 1975). In addition, a number of studies have addressed measurement issues related to the model (e.g., Miniard, 1981; Miniard & Cohen, 1979, 1981). On a general level, this newer model can increase the explained percentage of variance in choice by as much as 20 to 30 percent (Ryan & Bonfield, 1975).

Sequential Noncompensatory Models. An area of increasing interest in consumer research is the use of noncompensatory models to understand choice behavior. Three defining characteristics of these models are (a) a

product's undesirable aspects cannot be compensated for by its desirable aspects, (b) the integration of information is nonlinear, and (c) individuals use a sequential decision process in considering the attributes.

The overall nature of these models can be stated as follows: Individuals are hypothesized to employ a hierarchy of attributes in their choice process. It is postulated that there is an acceptable range for a particular attribute such that any attribute whose value was not in this range would be judged unacceptable. The cutoffs used are generally determined by their utility in maximally discriminating between alternatives (Klein & Bither, 1987). The individual proceeds step-by-step through his or her hierarchical ranking of the attributes, eliminating them in a sequential manner. Each individual can have different hierarchies and different tolerance ranges associated with particular attributes. The major noncompensatory models include conjunctive, lexicographic, and disjunctive models.

Several studies (e.g., Park & Schaninger, 1976; Sheluga, 1979; Wright, 1975; Wright & Barbour, 1977) have generally supported the usefulness of these formulations. Evidence suggests (e.g., Wright, 1975) that noncompensatory models serve as a means of simplifying a complex choice task (i.e., products are processed by attribute instead of by brand). However, in many choice tasks, a certain degree of brand-organized information is available, and this information would serve to simplify the choice task and thereby make the use of an optimizing strategy (such as a compensatory model) more feasible. Support for this view comes from several studies (Payne, 1976; Wright, 1975; Wright & Barbour, 1977) where it was found that consumers employ a phased strategy. Initially, a noncompensatory model is used to reduce the complexity of the task. This simplification is then followed by a compensatory strategy. The extent to which the choices are comparable (i.e., can be described using the same nonprice attributes) can play a major role in determining the type of processing (Johnson, 1988).

In summary, a variety of different models have been used to explain consumer choice. Each has its own unique merit and may be useful in explaining the choice process in different contexts. Compensatory models appear to be more appropriate in situations involving extensive deliberation and cognitive effort, while noncompensatory models are more descriptive when less time and effort is spent on the decision.

Low Involvement Decision Models

Many of the models described thus far have been borrowed from such disciplines as social psychology, economics, and cognitive psychology. The problem is that these models were developed to understand processes that elicit considerable commitment on the part of the consumer. However, some authors have suggested that many product decisions may not be that important or "involving" to consumers (e.g., Hupfer & Gardner, 1971; Kassarjian, 1978). Indeed, Wright (1975) notes that these decision models require a degree of cognitive effort that the consumer may be unwilling to spend. Thus, one must question whether these models are accurate representations of how decisions are made for a variety of consumer choice contexts.

Second, most of the previously mentioned models focus on cognitive processing that occurs immediately prior to the act of purchase (or selection). Many decisions, however, are made repeatedly or frequently over time and thus involve continuous—as opposed to discrete—processing (Hogarth, 1981). In these instances, consumers may rely not only on previously acquired product information stored in memory but also on judgments of brand satisfaction or dissatisfaction that occur during postpurchase evaluation (or use).

In light of these issues, Deshpande, Hoyer, and Jeffries (1982) proposed a framework to describe consumer decision making in situations that involve repeated purchases over time and that typically can be considered as low in importance or involvement. The major thrust of this view is that when purchase behavior is preceded by a choice process, it is likely to be very limited (Olshavsky & Granbois, 1979, p. 99). As an example, Hoyer (1984) found that the median amount of time taken to make a laundry detergent purchase was 8.5 seconds. Also, when queried regarding their decision process, over 90 percent of the consumers stated one simple reason for the choice. Thus, the hypothesis is that consumers tend to develop decision rules called *choice tactics*, which are rules of thumb allowing consumers to make quick effortless decisions. Examples would include price tactics (e.g., "Buy the cheapest brand"), performance tactics (e.g., "Buy the brand that best meets my needs"), or normative tactics (e.g., "Buy what my mother buys").

The notion of decision heuristics is not new to the consumer area. However, a choice tactic approach differs from traditional views in its focus on the development of a heuristic over time. That is, if a decision is made fairly often, a focus on the events immediately prior to choice will not provide an accurate picture of the process by which the decision was made. The amount of decision making taking place immediately prior to purchase will be very limited.

An important focus of this type of research is the process of tactic development over repeated purchases. This phenomenon is hypothesized to be a learning process. Initial choices may be either: (a) haphazard, (b) based on modeling the behavior of others, or (c) constructed at the time of choice (Bettman & Zins, 1977). Over time, however, consumers refine their tactics on the basis of feedback either from a previous decision, as in postpurchase evaluation, or from the environment, as in reading an advertisement or magazine article, talking to friends, and so forth.

Thus, through a series of trials that involve either positive, negative, or neutral experience, the postpurchase evaluation will stabilize, and consumers will come to possess a set of very simple decision heuristics. These tactics make it unnecessary for the consumer to engage in extended processing each time a decision is made.

This type of formulation is likely relevant in organizational contexts as well. In many situations, decisions are made repeatedly over time; therefore, the decision makers might also develop efficient decision rules, allowing them to make satisfactory choices with minimal cognitive effort.

Research on how consumers integrate information seems relevant to a number of issues of concern to industrial and organizational psychologists. Research on various combinatory models of overall job satisfaction, relatively speaking, is limited (e.g., Aldag & Brief, 1978; Brief & Roberson, in press; Scarpello & Campbell, 1983). Recall that consumer psychologists closely attend to models of how individuals cognitively integrate information, in part because these models allow one to identify the product attributes that, if changed, would most likely lead to a shift in attitudes. Thus, if one is interested in formulating job attitude change strategies, a greater emphasis needs to be placed on studying combinatory models of overall job satisfaction to isolate those facets (attributes) of jobs that contribute most to overall judgments about job satisfaction. Moreover, the support for sequential noncompensatory models found in studies of consumers suggests that future research results on combinatory models of job satisfaction may imply that undesirable aspects of jobs cannot be compensated for by desirable ones. Such an implication seems relevant to the study of job performance, protest, withdrawal, and other possible consequences of job dissatisfaction (Henne & Locke, 1985).

Moving to the consumer research on low-involvement decision models raises questions about the extent to which industrial and organizational psychologists have recognized that different decision models may hold across different kinds of organizational decisions. With few exceptions (e.g., Beach & Mitchell, 1978), it appears that industrial and organizational psychologists have failed to recognize such potential variability. This lack of recognition and the germane consumer research on low-involvement decisions suggests attempts be made to articulate what constitutes a low-involvement decision in organizations and to investigate these sorts of decisions as such. If, in some contexts, hiring decisions or decisions about effort levels, for instance, are identified as the low-involvement kind, then it would seem of interest to ascertain the choice tactics people use and the process by which these heuristics develop. It may be the case that decisions regarding hiring, effort, and the like have been overintellectualized by investigators, being viewed as highly deliberative and effortfully cognitive, and that viewing them as simple decisions would better help one discover how and why they are made.

Postdecision Outcomes and Consumer Satisfaction

On a common sense level, satisfaction is an important concept in consumer behavior. If satisfied, a consumer is likely to have positive feelings toward the product or company and to repurchase the product in the future. On the other hand, dissatisfaction is more likely to lead to complaints, negative word-of-mouth communication, and future refusal to buy. It is not surprising to find, therefore, that a number of consumer studies have addressed this topic. While several useful findings can be cited, it is also true that inconsistencies and contradictions abound that leave the door open for further theory and research (Doran, 1986).

Evidence of this fact can be found immediately at the definitional stage. According to Day (1980), everyone seems to have an idea of what satisfaction means, but when it comes to a precise definition and operationalization, it doesn't mean the same to everyone. Westbrook (1986) listed a number of definitions, then reduced them to four common basic components:

- Satisfaction is a *subjective feeling state* based on a direct consumption experience with a product or service.

- It is an *evaluative response* that compares the outcome of the consumption experience with prior expectations.

- It is an evaluation that the consumption experience was *worth the value* that the consumer exchanged for it.

- It is an evaluation that the utility of the product or service met the need for which it was acquired.

Probably the most representative definition is that satisfaction is the "summary psychological state resulting when the emotion surrounding disconfirmed expectations is coupled with the consumers prior feelings about the consumption experience" (Oliver, 1981, p. 27). In other words, satisfaction results from a relationship between a consumer's perceived expectations of a product and the favorable experience when first using it.

Central to this definition is the concept of disconfirmation. Nearly all consumer satisfaction/dissatisfaction (CS/D) studies have used some version of this construct. Researchers have differed, however, on how they have operationalized disconfirmation and placed it in a nomological network. Some, for example, merely subtracted expectation scores from performance ratings and called the difference "disconfirmation." Others (e.g., Oliver, 1980; Tse & Wilton, 1988) suggested alternative operationalizations, such as asking for subjective evaluations of whether the product's performance was worse than, about as good as, or better than expectations. Tse and Wilton (1988) demonstrated that this operationalization

explains a greater proportion of variance in satisfaction than the subtraction measure.

It also bears noting that Oliver (1980) conceptualized satisfaction as an *additive combination* of expectations and disconfirmation. That is, satisfaction can result when expectations are high and disconfirmation is slightly negative. Thus, while disconfirmation is almost universally noted as important, it is by no means the sole determinant of satisfaction. Expectations appear to play a major role through an apparent consistency effect.

Another important study (Westbrook, 1987) showed that disconfirmation does not totally mediate the impact of affective responses on satisfaction and other postconsumption responses (i.e., complaining and word-of-mouth communication). After controlling for disconfirmation, positive and negative affective responses to the product still explained significant amounts of variance in the outcome variables. He also found that affect is a two-dimensional construct and that positive and negative affect can be experienced simultaneously with respect to different attributes of the product.

Further controversy has surfaced in relating satisfaction to dissatisfaction. For most researchers, these two constructs are thought to be extreme points on a continuum. Czepiel and Rosenberg (1976, 1977) and Aiello, Czepiel, and Rosenberg (1977) argue, however, that the two constructs are independent and parallel. The basic notion is that one could be theoretically satisfied and dissatisfied at the same time.

Another point of debate has focused on whether satisfaction is an attitude or an emotional evaluation. While many of the early studies on satisfaction/dissatisfaction often describe satisfaction as a type of attitude, recent studies treat the concept more as a temporary feeling (Day, 1984). Since attitude is more a stable phenomenon over time, it seems inappropriate to define satisfaction as an attitude. In line with this view, current research tends to view satisfaction as an emotional response following confirmation experiences.

In regard to the evaluation issue, early work in this area assumed that satisfaction must be the result of a conscious cognitive process. In contrast, Swan and Trawich (1978) present results to indicate that consumers do not necessarily evaluate their consumption experiences consciously and that the degree of conscious evaluation varies by type of product or service.

Theoretical Approaches. Several major approaches have guided theory development in the consumer satisfaction/dissatisfaction area. Among these are economic theory, content theory, cognitive process theory, the disconfirmation paradigm, the comparison level paradigm, and attribution theory.

Economic Theory. Economic theory attempts to explain consumer satisfaction/dissatisfaction in terms of consumer surplus. It is assumed that consumer surplus of goods or value of a specific good would lead to satisfaction and consumer shortage would lead to dissatisfaction (Doran, 1985).

Content Theory. Content theories, on the other hand, specify the particular needs that must be satisfied or the values that must be attained for an individual to be satisfied (Locke, 1976). In the consumer satisfaction literature, the two dominant theories are Maslow's (1954) hierarchy of needs and Herzberg's motivator-hygiene theory (Herzberg, Mausner, & Snyderman, 1959). According to Doran (1985), "the problem of both of these theories in CS/D research is that operationalization and testing has either been absent or limited. Furthermore, when they have been subject to empirical study, results have been generally unsupportive" (p. 11).

Cognitive Process Theory. A number of cognitive process theories have been applied in an attempt to understand consumer satisfaction/dissatisfaction. These include adaptation level theory (Helson, 1964), the theory of cognitive dissonance (Festinger, 1957), exchange theory (Thibaut & Kelly, 1959), Weiner's attribution theory (Weiner & Kukla, 1970), equity theory (Adams, 1963), field theory (Lewin, 1951), and expectancy theory (Vroom, 1964). In particular, two of these theories—equity theory and expectancy theory—have provided conceptual groundwork for the two major paradigms in the CS/D area.

Equity theory (Adams, 1963) examines relationships in terms of inputs and outcomes. The basic propositions are that (a) individuals seek to maximize outcomes relative to inputs and (b) outcomes can be maximized by behaving equitably. In relation to consumer behavior, consumers are said to compare the costs (inputs) of the product to the benefits received (outputs), and if this comparison is equitable, satisfaction occurs.

The basic premises of expectancy theory are that (a) individuals assign values to expected outcomes of various actions and (b) their motivation to act is determined by a perception of their own ability to contribute to the preferred outcomes. Research in the consumer area has indicated that satisfaction is related to fulfillment of expectations (Swan, 1977). In particular, when performance exceeded desired expectations, very high satisfaction occurred (Swan & Trawick, 1979; Swan, Trawick, & Carroll, 1980). Also, if a marketer sets expectations too high, dissatisfaction is likely to result.

Other theoretical perspectives that have been taken include cognitive dissonance (Cardozo, 1965) and cognitive consistency (Olshavsky & Miller, 1972). Cardozo (1965) manipulated expectations and involvement and found that when subjects were not involved with the product (i.e., they did not expend any effort to receive it), they evaluated it very negatively when it did not perform to expectations. But, when they had invested considerable effort to receive the product, they evaluated it less negatively. He attributed this effect to cognitive dissonance, attributing to subjects such reasoning as, "If I went to such pains to receive this ball-point pen, then it must be worth something." Olshavsky and Miller (1972) found that high expectation subjects evaluated a tape recorder more positively in both good and bad performance conditions. They attributed this result to cognitive consistency—subjects wanting to confirm their expectations to appear consistent.

Disconfirmation Paradigm. First posited by Oliver (1981), the disconfirmation paradigm holds that satisfaction is related to the size and direction of the disconfirmation experience, where disconfirmation is related to the consumer's initial expectations (Churchill & Suprenant, 1982). Oliver (1981) defines disconfirmation as

> a mental comparison of an actual state
> of nature with its anticipated probability.
> In common usage, these states of nature
> may be perceived as worse than expected
> (a negative disconfirmation) better than
> expected (a positive disconfirmation)
> or just as expected (a zero confirmation,
> or simply a confirmation). (p. 35)

While a detailed description of this paradigm is beyond the scope of this chapter (see Oliver, 1977a, 1977b, 1981), it is important to note that four constructs comprise the basic paradigm. *Expectations,* as mentioned previously, refer to desired outcomes. *Performance* determines whether or not these outcomes have been achieved. *Disconfirmation* occurs if there is a discrepancy between prior expectations and actual performance. *Satisfaction* results from the consumer's comparison of the reward versus costs in relationship to anticipated consequences.

Oliver and DeSarbo (1988) found strong main effects for all of the constructs in

determining satisfaction. However, much of the research has found that satisfaction is influenced mainly by disconfirmation and, to a lesser extent, prior expectation levels. Further, several studies (Churchill & Suprenant, 1982; Tse & Wilton, 1988) found the impact of these variables held for nondurables but not for durables.

Finally, Anderson (1973) tested six different theoretical explanations of satisfaction by creating a number of different expectation levels and found that the principle of assimilation and contrast provided the most plausible explanation. The results showed that within a reasonable range, performance better or worse than expectations were assimilated to the level of expectations (i.e., no disconfirmation occurred). But outside that range, superior or inferior performance had a contrast effect (i.e., disconfirmation was magnified).

Comparison Level Paradigm. The comparison level paradigm developed by LaTour and Peat (1979a, 1979b, 1980) is an extension of the comparison level theory of Thibaut and Kelley (1959). It was proposed as an alternative to the disconfirmation paradigm, although it incorporates many of its ideas. The basic notion of comparison theory is that individuals possess beliefs about ideal levels of performance on a set of attributes for a particular product or service. The consumer moves toward satisfaction to the extent that performance is above the expected level on attributes, while those below the ideal level move consumers toward dissatisfaction. Overall satisfaction is then an overall additive function of the performance on each individual attribute.

The comparison levels are formed on the basis of three sources: (a) *past experience*—what the individual expects to get based on his or her own usage of contract with the product, (b) the *experience of others*—what levels the consumer believes others have received, and (c) the *present situation*—expectations acquired from formal communications of marketers or based on the unique characteristics of the purchase situation.

While this paradigm can provide some interesting insights, there has been little research to verify its propositions. In one study, LaTour and Peat (1980) found that past experience was the main determinant of satisfaction, but that when this experience is ambiguous, the experience of others can play an important role. Swan and Martin (1981) compared LaTour and Peat's framework to the disconfirmation paradigm and found only modest support for the comparison level paradigm. One aspect of the LaTour and Peat view—that satisfaction is sensitive to perceived product performance minus past performance on similar products—was strongly supported. However, disconfirmation of past-performance expectations was the strongest predictor of satisfaction.

Attribution Theory. Finally, Folkes (1984) presented an attribution theory approach for explaining when dissatisfaction will occur. This theory posits that there are three ways individuals can explain why a product does not fulfill their needs. These are (a) *stability*—are the causes temporary or permanent? (b) *focus*—are they consumer or marketer related? and (c) *controllability*—are these causes under volitional control, or are they factors that cannot be controlled? Dissatisfaction is most likely to be perceived if the causes are permanent and marketer related (Folkes, 1984).

Research Examining Other Causal Factors Related to Satisfaction. Independent of the paradigm employed, many studies have examined exogenous factors, such as situational, temporal, and demographic factors, that may be related to satisfaction. In these studies, satisfaction serves as the dependent variable, and an attempt is made to predict satisfaction in light of these factors.

Although situational factors can be a key determinant of behavior at any point in time,

only a handful of studies have addressed this topic in the CS/D area. For example, Hunt (1977) found that individuals may postpone judgments of dissatisfaction of the circumstances one perceived to be temporary in nature. Granzin and Schelderup (1982) found that only aspects related to a specific situation determined satisfaction for a car repair decision. According to the authors, situational influence appears to operate in anticipated satisfaction through variables like self-confidence, perceived risk, anxiety, and expected benefits.

Much of the recent work has focused on identifying demographic and socioeconomic factors that may affect satisfaction or dissatisfaction (e.g., Ash, 1978; Liefield, 1979; Liefield, Edgecombe, & Wolfe, 1975; Mason & Hines, 1973). Variables examined have included age, socioeconomic status, marital status, family composition, and race. Unfortunately, these studies have often produced mixed and conflicting results. For example, two studies (Ash, 1978; Ash, Gardiner, & Quelch, 1980) found a negative relationship between age and satisfaction, while several others (Hughes, 1977; Mason & Hines, 1973; Miller, 1977; Pickle & Bruce, 1972; Westbrook, 1977) found a positive relationship. Other studies (e.g., Liefield, Edgecombe, & Wolfe, 1975; Miller, 1977; Warland, Hermann, & Willits, 1975) indicated that consumers who voice dissatisfaction with a purchase tend to be well-educated, young, above average in social class, and have relatively high income. Westbrook (1977) and Day and Bodur (1977), on the other hand, found that the relationship between sociodemographic factors and satisfaction tends to be weak. Similar conflicting findings exist for sex differences.

On a general level, however, it appears that general satisfaction does change over an individual's life cycle. Andrews and Withey (1976) and Withey (1977) suggest that satisfaction improves slightly and relatively as people age. This occurs primarily because while both satisfaction and dissatisfaction levels decline toward neutral as individuals age, dissatisfaction declines at a faster rate than satisfaction. This finding was also supported by Ash, Gardiner, and Quelch (1980) and Mason, Beardon, and Crockett (1980).

Customer Service Satisfaction. The service sector of the economy is growing rapidly and presently accounts for nearly 70 percent of the gross national product. Although service is a critical aspect of the CS/D process, a surprisingly small amount of literature has addressed the topic. Most of the work that has been done has dealt with dissatisfaction with automobile repair services (e.g., Beardon, Crockett, & Graham, 1979; Darden & Rao, 1977; Day & Ash, 1978).

Day and Boder (1977) examined 73 service categories, and their most significant finding was that the major reason for dissatisfaction was the quality of supplier performance. Fraudulent marketing practices were mentioned less frequently as causes. When dissatisfaction did occur, most of the respondents (approximately 80%) engaged in mainly negative word-of-mouth communication or supplier boycotts to resolve their dissatisfaction.

In the retail area, results have been less clear. Swan (1977) found that satisfaction with a newly opened department store was related to consumer expectations prior to entering the store and the degree to which these expectations were fulfilled. Rodgers and Sweeny (1979) reported that 20 percent of consumers perceived a deterioration of retail service trends, especially among department stores and general merchandise stores.

More recently, studies have began to examine the human factor in customer service. Westbrook (1981) found that the most crucial component of retail satisfaction was satisfaction with salespeople.

Implications for Industrial and Organizational Psychology. Probably in no other realm than in the study of satisfaction are consumer and industrial and organizational psychologists

closer together in their interests. At the conceptual level, this is evidenced by the similarity of the theoretical orientations employed by both groups. For instance, both consumer and organizational interests in opponent process approaches to satisfaction (Landy, 1978) build on the theoretical work of Solomon (e.g., Solomon & Corbit, 1973). Substantively, the areas merge in their common concern with customer satisfaction as a criterion variable, as exhibited in Schneider's impressive program of research (e.g., Schneider, Parkington, & Buxton, 1980). Schneider and Bowen (1985) have shown that customer perceptions, attitudes, and future consumption intentions were significantly related to the employees' experiences and perception of the organization. A dissatisfied employee results in a dissatisfied customer. Thus, one key to achieving customer satisfaction might be to achieve employee satisfaction.

There are a number of issues and ideas addressed in the consumer satisfaction literature that might profitably be transferred to the study of job satisfaction. For example, while some consumer researchers emphasize the independence of satisfaction and dissatisfaction, not since Herzberg's motivation-hygiene theory was roundly criticized have organizational researchers addressed this independence. Yet recent evidence in other areas of psychology (e.g., Watson & Tellegen, 1985) clearly indicates that positive and negative affect are independent, suggesting that the affective component of such job attitudes as job satisfaction is comprised of two distinct factors. Thus, it would seem worthwhile for organizational researchers, like some consumer psychologists, to once again consider the independence of satisfaction and dissatisfaction. Consumer and organizational researchers are very similar in their interest in satisfaction, and advances in consumer psychology can contribute to organizational psychology. As Schneider and Bowen (1985) state, "many of the principles that have been derived theoretically from a focus on the external customer may also provide insight for researchers who study the internal dynamics of organizations" (p. 425).

Motivation

The subject of motivation is of central concern to almost all branches of psychology, and this is no less true of both consumer and industrial and organizational psychology. Campbell, Dunnette, Lawler, and Weick (1970) classified the various theoretic orientations to motivation into *content* and *process* approaches. The former are primarily concerned with identifying specifically *"what* it is within an individual or his environment that energizes and sustains behavior" (p. 341), while the latter are concerned with identifying the major classes of variables and mechanics that underlie *how* motives operate to determine behavior.

Another way to conceptualize this distinction is in terms of arousal versus direction. While the content approaches attempt to answer the question of what arouses the individual to begin with, the process approaches are concerned with answering the question of why an individual engages in one particular activity at a specified point in time out of the wide variety of possible activities; that is, why did behavior take the specific direction that it did? This implies that the process theories are inextricably related to choice behavior and decision making in that the individual, either consciously or unconsciously, is always selecting one direction (or behavioral alternative) and rejecting others.

To a certain extent, the content versus process distinction postulated by these industrial and organizational psychologists parallels the distinction made between *primary* and *selective* buying motives made by Nicosia (1966). Primary motives are defined as those that lead to the purchase or use of a broad class of products or services (e.g., a car), while selective motives are those that influence the selection of a particular type or brand of the product (e.g.,

Chevrolet). In a sense, primary motives arouse behavior, while selective motives direct it. Again, the development of such parallel structures and concepts in separate areas of inquiry, if occurring independently, does provide an encouraging amount of consensual and construct validity.

A Process Approach: Expectancy Theory

The process approaches probably offer the greatest possibilities for mutual contribution in the areas of information processing and decision making. Campbell et al. (1970) described three basic process approaches: stimulus-response (drive x habit) theory, expectancy theory, and equity theory. Since expectancy theory is thought to have the greatest potential for contribution to industrial and organizational psychology, our emphasis will be on this approach.

The wellsprings of expectancy theory are to be found in the works of Tolman (1932) and Lewin (1938), with subsequent development coming primarily from the personality and social psychologists (Atkinson, 1958; Edwards, 1954; Fishbein, 1967; Peak, 1955; Rosenberg, 1956, 1960; Rotter, 1955). This work also has close parallels to the work by Fishbein (1963) discussed earlier. In essence, expectancy theory maintains that the motivational force to engage in any given behavior out of a set of alternative behaviors is a composite of the perceived likelihood that a given behavior will result in attaining certain outcomes, weighted by the desirability (value or importance) the individual attaches to each of these outcomes.*

Thus, four primary variables are to be considered for each individual: (a) a set of possible behavior alternatives, (b) a set of outcomes, (c) the desirability to the individual of each of

---

* Use of the phrase *outcome desirability* in contrast to the more generally accepted term *value importance* is intentional. The word *outcome* plays a significant role in the conceptual elaboration of the expectancy model as described below, while the word *desirability* reflects the fact that an outcome need only be considered desirable or undesirable, not necessarily important, in order to have motivation properties.

these outcomes, and (d) the individual's perception of the likelihood that engaging in each of the alternative behaviors will lead to each of the outcomes. For any individual at a given point in time, a motivational force is calculated by applying the following basic formula:

$$MF\ Aa\ =\ E(DOk \times EAaOk)$$

where:

$MF\ Aa$	=	the motivational force of alternative a
DOk	=	the desirability of outcome k
$EAaOk$	=	the expectancy that selecting alternatives will result in obtaining outcome k

Expectancy theory thus reflects its Lewinian heritage in that it is a phenomenological field theory. It is the alternatives, outcomes, desirabilities, and expectancies as perceived by the individual and as they exist for him or her at that point in time (i.e., within his or her immediate psychological field) that determine the direction of behavior (i.e., which behavior alternative the individual selects), not necessarily objective reality. Consequently, the dynamic nature of motivated behavior is placed into a static, cross-sectional mold.

Expectancy theory was formally introduced into the industrial psychological literature via Vroom's (1964) expectancy theory of worker motivation. It was subsequently extended and made more explicit by Porter and Lawler (1968), Campbell et al. (1970), and others. A simplified composite version suggested by these formulations is presented in Figure 1. Under the "Behavioral Alternatives" column is included the set of behavioral acts considered possible by the individual under the circumstances (i.e., the "evoked set"; cf. March & Simon, 1958).

Assume that a manager is confronted with a supervisee who recently started arriving late for work every day. The manager's task is to decide on the best course of action at that particular point in time (e.g., personally reprimand the employee, continue to ignore it, ask the employee to see a personnel counselor, fire the employee, ask the boss what to do, etc.). The "Level I Outcome" column lists the possible direct consequences that might result (e.g., the employee will start to arrive on time, the employee's work output will decrease, others in the office will start to come in late, the boss will be disturbed, etc.). "Level II Outcomes" are those consequences one step removed (e.g., if, as a result of counseling, the employee starts to come in on time and his or her productivity does not suffer, then it could lead to praise from the boss, a raise, greater respect from the manager's other supervisees, etc.). Eventually, we come to Level N Outcomes, which describe the basic needs of individuals much as contained in the traditional content formulations (e.g., need for love, respect, or power). Finally, the Ds and Es in Figure 1 represent the desirability of each of the specific outcomes to the individual and the expectancy—essentially a subjective probability estimate—that engaging in the specific behavior (or attainment of a previous level outcome) will lead to the specific outcome under consideration.

While the second through nth level outcomes are heuristic and interesting to consider, it is difficult to specify which outcomes are at which particular level. It is very likely that many outcomes will be at different levels for different people and will vary within one person over time. Probably because of such operational difficulties, very little empirical work bearing on this aspect of the expectancy model exists.

The expectancy formulation raises two important questions: What is the relative contribution of expectancies and desirabilities to the motivation of individuals, and how do expectancies come about and how are they influenced? Applications of the expectancy formulation to consumer behavior provide some tentative answers to these questions.

FIGURE 1

Composite Industrial Psychology Expectancy Model of Motivation

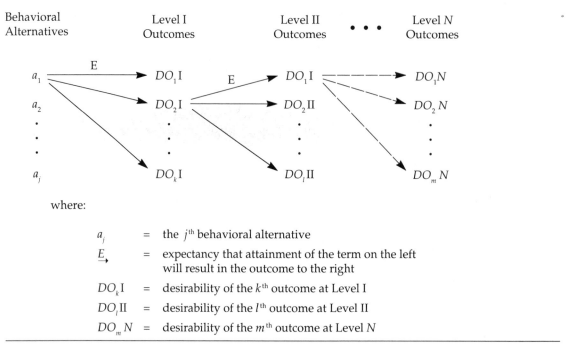

where:

a_j	=	the jth behavioral alternative
$E_{\rightarrow}$	=	expectancy that attainment of the term on the left will result in the outcome to the right
$DO_k I$	=	desirability of the kth outcome at Level I
$DO_l II$	=	desirability of the lth outcome at Level II
$DO_m N$	=	desirability of the mth outcome at Level N

Note: To avoid cluttering, only a few of the expectancies are inserted to illustrate the general notion. Each term to the left should actually have an expectancy arrow connecting it with each and every outcome in the column to its immediate right.

From "Consumer and Industrial Psychology: Prospects for Theory Corroboration and Mutual Contribution" by J. Jacoby, 1976. In M. D. Dunnette (Ed.), *Handbook of Industrial and Organizational Psychology* (p.1047). Chicago: Rand McNally. Copyright 1976 by M. D. Dunnette. Reprinted by permission.

It is easy to apply the basic expectancy model to consumer behavior by representing the alternative courses of action that the individual can take as specific brands or products that he or she can buy. Consider the individual who intends to purchase a single brand from among 15 different brands of toothpaste. Assume further that all brands in the consumer's "evoked set," that is, those brands the consumer considers viable alternatives in the decision process (cf. Howard & Sheth, 1969; March & Simon, 1958), are contained in this display. The set of alternatives is thus clearly defined. Moreover, the first level outcomes are generally well known in regard to most commonly

purchased consumer products. For example, most consumers want a toothpaste to freshen breath, clean teeth, taste good, and prevent decay. Consequently, it is possible, using common purchasing situations, to set up realistic, less ambiguous tests of the model than may be possible in an organizational framework.

Results from such investigations are illuminating. Hansen (1969), in a series of six experiments, found that outcome desirability and perceived expectancy are predictive of both preference statements and choice behavior in simulated purchasing situations, but neither, taken separately, was as good a predictor as total score. Moreover, the number of salient outcomes (i.e., used by the individual to a significant degree in making a choice) are few. Subjects, given anywhere from three to ten appropriate outcomes across the six experiments, tended to reduce the number of outcomes considered by assigning desirability ratings of zero to several outcomes. When the three most desirable outcomes were taken for each subject, predictions were as good as those based on the total number of outcomes. Finally, Hansen found that the expectancies and outcome desirabilities were "highly independent."

Somewhat at variance with these findings is the work of Sheth and Talarzyk (1970). These investigators used a sample of 1,272 respondents from a national sample of female heads of households and six different product categories (frozen orange juice, mouthwash, toothpaste, toilet tissue, lipstick, and brassieres). Each product category contained five brands and five appropriate outcomes. These authors found that, without a single exception in the 30 tests they conducted, the expectancies demonstrated greater predictive power of overall purchase attitudes than did the outcome desirabilities. Moreover, combining the perceived expectancies and outcome desirabilities, as specified by the general formula, resulted in a considerable *lowering* of the predictive power, as opposed to using the expectancies alone. This finding is analogous to the effect that adding a cue with weak predictive power will have on decision-making performance (Dudycha & Naylor, 1966; see also Cox, 1962). Two possible explanations were offered for these results. First, in the process of expressing expectancies on a scale anchored to specific outcomes, outcome desirabilities "are probably already incorporated by the subject." Second, outcome desirabilities "are not specific to a brand but rather general for a product class. Why should they, therefore, be predictive of variances in the attitudes toward specific brands?" (Sheth & Talarzyk, 1970, p. 13).

As one considers the manner in which the expectancy model has been applied to the consumer behavior context, it is possible to see the nature of the outcomes in a different perspective, one that has implications for understanding the genesis of the expectancies. What follows represents a speculative attempt by Jacoby (1976b) to extend the basic expectancy model to encompass more of the elements and mechanisms involved in consumer behavior motivation. It is believed that the resultant formulation more accurately describes the relationships that actually exist and is more capable of capturing the dynamic flow of motivations. In the spirit of this chapter, perhaps this modification, developed to suit a consumer context, will provide insights for ways in which the model might be applied to phenomena in both social and industrial and organizational psychology.

Expectancy Models. The expectancy models adopt what is essentially a "pull" perspective of motivation. In other words, a combination of desired outcomes weighted by their respective expectancies *attract* the individual to one (or perhaps a select few) of the behavioral alternatives. Yet there are other motivational factors that can and do determine the behavioral response. Consider the outcomes notion as applied to the purchase of toothpaste. The salient outcomes, as noted earlier, are usually decay prevention, fresh breath, good taste, and cleaner teeth. Yet what one's dentist recommends, what one sees and hears from advertising, whether one likes the advertisements for one brand and dislikes the advertisements for another, whether one is price conscious and motivated to get the best deal for the money, one's past experiences with the various brands, and so forth, also exert a motivational influence and affect the direction of behavior. These are not desired outcomes in the sense that this concept has been utilized; rather, they are motivational inputs. Stated somewhat differently, *outcomes* are consequences (e.g., obtaining fewer cavities or whiter teeth) perceived as ensuing or likely to ensue from having taken a specific action, while *inputs* are the antecedent factors that push the individual to take specific courses of action. Inputs lead to a given action, while outcomes are perceived as likely to result from having taken that action.

The term *values* (Rosenberg, 1956) can thus be partitioned into *antecedent* (input) and *consequent* (outcome) values. Antecedent and consequent are not meant to imply that these occur at temporally distinct periods in the mind of the individual. They simply take cognizance of the fact that some motivational forces lead to or push an individual to take a certain course of action, while other motivational forces arise from considering the consequences likely to arise from each of the alternatives being considered and serve to attract or pull the individual toward some alternative(s) and away from others.

The notion of functional consequences is critical. *Outcomes* refer to the primary *functional* aspects of the alternatives in the product set; they are the basic purpose for buying and/or using the product to begin with. *Inputs*, on the other hand, are those motivational factors other than perceived functional consequences that influence the selection of one specific behavioral alternative over the other available alternatives. For example, one might like the advertising or packaging for Brand A over Brand B and might, if these are the only two motivational factors operating, be motivated to buy Brand A. Yet such motivational factors can in no way be considered outcomes in the same sense that preventing cavities or cleaning teeth are.

At this point the model would appear as in Figure 2, and the formula for obtaining the motivational force of each alternative is as follows:

$$MF\ Aa\ =\ fE(SIi$$
$$x\quad LIiAa) + E(DOk$$
$$x\quad EAaOk)$$

where:

MF Aa	=	the motivational force of alternative *a*
SIi	=	the significance of input *i*
LIiAa	=	the likelihood that input *i* will lead to selecting alternative *a*
DOk	=	the desirability of outcome *k*
EAaOk	=	the expectancy that selecting alternative *a* will result in obtaining outcome *k*

The term *significance* is used to represent the importance of the input to the individual and can be assessed through questions such as, "How important are your dentist's recommendations when it comes to buying toothpaste?" The likelihoods tie the inputs to specific alternatives and are assessed through questions such as, "How likely is it that what your dentist recommends will lead you to buy Brand X?"

Money is the factor most difficult to classify. For example, while we would consider price of the brand to be an input factor, it may appear to be an outcome when phrased in more general terms like "saving money." However, reference to the primary functional criterion provides the solution. One does not buy toothpaste in order to save money, but to whiten teeth, prevent cavities, and so forth. Consequently, price would be treated as an input factor.

This suggests an interesting question. If first-order outcomes are related to higher-order outcomes, is it not possible for immediately relevant inputs to be related to higher-order inputs? For example, the importance of price (an immediately relevant, first-order input) might be a function of the individual's need to save money and be thrifty (a second-order input), and in turn be a function of the individual's need for self-esteem (or some other higher-level need). In other words, perhaps there is a parallel structure on the input side that reflects the structure on the outcome side,

FIGURE 2

A Basic Input-Output Expectancy Model

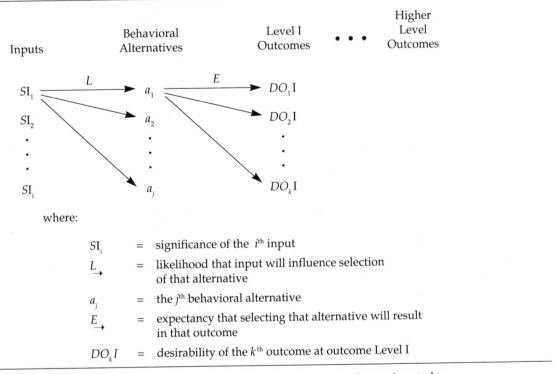

where:

SI_i	=	significance of the ith input
$L_{\rightarrow}$	=	likelihood that input will influence selection of that alternative
a_j	=	the jth behavioral alternative
$E_{\rightarrow}$	=	expectancy that selecting that alternative will result in that outcome
$DO_k I$	=	desirability of the kth outcome at outcome Level I

Note: To avoid cluttering, only a few of the likelihoods and expectancies are inserted to illustrate the general notion.

with both structures eventually terminating in a common pool of basic human needs à la the context taxonomies.

Moreover, separating inputs from outcomes and placing the variables in this format suggest an answer to the question regarding the genesis of outcome expectancies. More specifically, it is conceivable that the expectancies about the purchase of Brand X leading to outcome k are simply a function of selected inputs. In other words, the expectancy that buying Crest will prevent tooth decay is probably a function of what one's dentist recommends, knowledge that this is one of the few brands to have received the American Dental Association's Council on Dental Therapeutics' seal of approval, and one's past experience with the brand ("I switched to Crest ten years ago and haven't had a cavity since"). Furthermore, not only do inputs determine the expectancies, they are also capable of determining the number and importance of the first-level outcomes. For example, advertising has been instrumental in establishing whiter teeth and "need to smell good" (an outcome appropriate for products such as deodorants and colognes) as first-level outcomes possessing high desirability in contemporary American society by tying them to higher-level outcomes (e.g., "If my teeth are white and I smell good, I will probably get promoted, be liked by everyone, and get the girl in the ad." In this way, inputs can affect outcomes without having to go through the brand alternatives.

Thus, with the emergence of feedback loops, what was initially a static cross-sectional model of motivation begins to take on certain dynamic properties. Inasmuch as motivation operates as a dynamic process, this is an advantage over the completely static models.

The resultant model is shown in Figure 3. The various components are situated along an abstract-to-concrete continuum. The most basic human needs representing the most abstract level and the alternatives (in this case, objectively observable and denotable brands) available to the individual at that point in time and defining his or her psychological field constitute the most concrete level.

The dashed lines from the second to the nth order level suggest two things. First, the number of intermediate levels and position of specific values in the structure probably vary across individuals and possibly within each individual from Time 1 to Time 2. Second, not all basic human needs funnel down to affect behavior. Some are relevant and others irrelevant to the choice situation. The latter may be disregarded from further consideration, while the former are further partitioned into outcomes that are *functionally* relevant (i.e., perceived outcomes) and those that are *nonfunctionally* relevant (i.e., perceived inputs).

While the inclusion of basic human needs and higher-order inputs and outcomes serves to place the model into broader perspective, it is probably true that empirical tests of the model's ability to predict specific behaviors need only be confined to the first-order inputs, outcomes, and alternatives. Fortunately, it is at these levels that operationalization is easiest (Jacoby & Olson, 1974). However, to adequately

understand the motivational process, one must trace the first-order inputs and outcomes to their root source.

The model is not truly dynamic in the sense of representing a continuous motivational flow. Rather, it suggests a sequence of discrete points which, given adequate measurement, collectively serve to outline the motivational flow. It is analogous to the frames of a motion picture film and may be termed a *frame model* of the motivational process.

Each frame, as illustrated in Figure 3, represents the individual's motivational state at a given point in time. Note also that Figure 3 reflects the fact that inputs, which can determine the selection of a particular alternative, can affect outcomes directly. Note also that the influence of the outcomes on the inputs is not explicitly outlined. This is because each frame, which represents the individual's phenomenological field at a specific point in time, always reflects *anticipated* rather than actual consequences. The effects of actual consequences have already been incorporated into the psychological field (under past experiences and in the reevaluation of the inputs) and are now ready to influence the next behavioral decision. Each frame represents the here and now. It is theoretically possible to "shoot" as many frames both before and after a behavioral act and over as many behavioral acts (i.e., trials) as one wants, but each frame represents the motivational state of the individual at the point in time at which it is taken. Shifts in perceived significance and desirability values for given inputs and outcomes, respectively, are noted by comparing the appropriate values across frames, not through intraframe analysis.

Finally, the model is capable of, and indeed ideal for, coping with intraindividual conflict situations. Obviously, as it now stands, there is built-in conflict between the competing brands in the alternative set, and there can be conflict within the set of first-order inputs (e.g., "I like the ad for Brand X, but my dentist says

FIGURE 3

The Structure of a Motivational State for Person P at Time T: The Complete Expectancy-frame Model

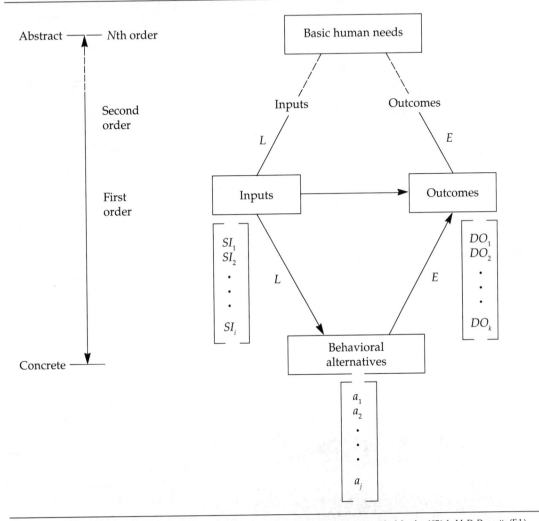

From "Consumer and Industrial Psychology: Prospects for Theory Corroboration and Mutual Contribution" by J. Jacoby, 1976. In M. D. Dunnette (Ed.), *Handbook of Industrial and Organizational Psychology* (p.1051). Chicago: Rand McNally. Copyright 1976 by M. D. Dunnette. Reprinted by permission.

it's bad for my teeth") and within the set of first-order outcomes (e.g., the toothpaste formulas yielding greatest whitening ability generally contain a high number of abrasives harmful to tooth enamel). However, the frame concept also suggests that we apply the model to different strata of conflict as they occur over time. For example, the alternatives in the individual's phenomenological field at Frame 1 may be to buy a Christmas present for a spouse, wash and wax the car, or watch a football game. Given that the individual opts to buy the present, Frame 2 might include an electric toaster, electric knife, and small portable TV. Subsequent to deciding on one of these, Frame 3 would include the various brands perceived as being viable purchase alternatives. Assuming that one can "shoot" frames as easily as they can be conceptualized, the frame concept enables us to follow the psychodynamic flow and processes underlying motivated behavior.

Attention to expectancy theory by industrial and organizational psychologists appears to be waning even though recent research has yielded some conceptual and methodological advances (e.g., Arnold, 1981; Stahl & Harrell, 1981, 1983). However, the cumulative evidence on expectancy theory in industrial and organizational psychology (Schwab, Olian-Gottlieb, & Heneman, 1979) suggests the theory needs to be recast. The model of consumer behavior motivation developed for the earlier *Handbook* (Jacoby, 1976b) and presented here contains certain notions that could be appealing elements of a "new" expectancy theory of interest to industrial and organizational psychologists. The following two examples demonstrate this potential attractiveness.

First, the idea that individuals are pushed (as well as pulled) to a course of action is germane to research on organizational agenda setting (e.g., Dutton, 1986; Dutton & Duncan, 1987). Agenda-setting research is concerned with how organizational members come to decide what issues they will make decisions about. In large part, the motivation to choose between alternative agenda items has not been attended to; rather, attention has focused on contextual factors. The push notion suggests that inputs exist that lead individuals to a given agenda. Identification of such inputs would seem to be one way agenda-setting researchers have to deal with the motivational forces acting on the organizational member they study.

Second, the frames-of-the-motion-picture-film analogy is relevant to the study of the escalation of resource commitment (e.g., Brockner & Rubin, 1984; Staw, 1981). Motivational explanations of escalating commitment have come under fire (e.g., Whyte, 1986). Rather than abandoning a motivational perspective on the problem, we suggest the escalation process be more microscopically and dynamically investigated, incorporating the frames-of-the-motion-picture-film idea. In this way, sequential "shots" of an escalation could be compared in terms of the decision maker's perceived significance and desirability values for given inputs and outcomes. In so doing, we might gain a better understanding of the motivational process underlying the escalation of resource commitment than is afforded by current, rather static views of the process.

The two examples offered suggest another point. In industrial and organizational psychology, expectancy theory generally has been applied to questions of job performance and job choice. The applicability of the Jacoby frame model of expectancy theory to organizational phenomenon is very likely broader than job performance and job choice.

Situational Influences

Much of the work described in this chapter has attempted to provide general models or explanations to describe consumer behavior phenomena. An implicit assumption of many efforts is that individuals tend to behave consistently. However, recent research in human information processing has clearly indicated that individuals are highly responsive to the situation or task at hand (Bettman, 1979; Newell & Simon, 1972; Payne, 1982; Simon, 1981). For example, a consumer who has unlimited time and is relaxed may evaluate brands very carefully and systematically in one situation, while in a pressured situation, the consumer may use a quick and possibly less than optimal decision heuristic. In light of this, a movement toward a more complete theory of consumer behavior must incorporate situational influences into its framework.

According to Belk (1975), a situational influence can be defined as "all those factors particular to a time and place of observation which do not follow from a knowledge of personal (intraindividual) and stimulus (choice alternative) attributes and which have a demonstrable and systematic effect as current behavior" (p. 158). Obviously, a number of factors could fall into this category, but research has tended to focus only on those factors that have a noticeable impact on consumer behavior. Belk (1975) has identified five major classes to which these factors can be categorized: (a) task definition, (b) social surroundings, (c) temporal characteristics, (d) physical surroundings, and (e) antecedent states.

Task Definition

Most research on situational influences has focused on aspects of task definition. While a description of this large body of work is beyond the purpose of this chapter (for an excellent review, see Punj & Stewart, 1983), it is important to mention the type of factors that have been studied. According to Punj and Stewart (1983), two types of task variables have generated interest: solution characteristics and information characteristics. Each of these factors alters the nature of the decision process that ensues.

Solution factors studied are outlined below:

- *The number of alternatives available*
  Multistage decision strategies tend to be used as the number of alternatives increase (e.g., Bettman & Park, 1980; Wright & Barbour, 1977).

- *Decision uncertainty*
  Uncertainty increases the amount of information search (e.g., Hawkins & Lanzetta, 1965).

- *The number of decisions*
  Information acquisition tends to decrease with the number of decisions made (e.g., Chestnut & Jacoby, 1977; Lehmann & Moore, 1980).

- *Decision importance*
  As product importance increases, information search and evaluation also tend to increase (e.g., Gardner, Mitchell, & Russo, 1978; Jacoby, Chestnut, & Fisher, 1978).

- *Task experience*
  Some studies have found that more knowledgeable consumers tend to process by brand versus attribute (e.g., Bettman & Park, 1980; Jacoby, Chestnut, & Fisher, 1978; Lehmann & Moore, 1980). However, in a study of stock market analysts, Jacoby et al. (1985) found that the more accurate analysts processed by at-tribute. Thus, the influence of task exper-ience appears to be moderated by task difficulty. Also, at-tributes associated with greater uncertainty and less favorability tend to be acquired earlier in the search process (Simonson, Huber, & Payne, 1988).

- *Frequency knowledge*
  Frequency knowledge about the mere number of positive and negative at-tributes possessed by a brand can completely dominate other more significant attributes when the decision maker lacks the motivation, opportunity, or ability to process attribute information (Alba & Marmorstein, 1987).

Information characteristics include the following:

- *The number of attributes per alternative*
  Consumers differentially weight information as the number of attributes per alternative increases (e.g., Green, Mitchell, & Staelin, 1977; Lussier & Olshavsky, 1979).

- *Attribute commonality*
  Common dimensions are given greater weight (e.g., van Raaij, 1977).

- *Information format*
  Consumers tend to process and store information in a manner consistent with the information format (e.g., Russo, 1978; Johnson & Russo, 1978). Research has also found that the framing of attributes can have significant impact on how this information is evaluated (Levin & Gaeth, 1988). For example, consumers rate the phrase "75% lean" more favorably than the phrase "25% fat."

- *Information source*
  Personal sources (friends, experts) tend to be more valued than information from salespeople or advertisements (e.g., Staelin & Payne, 1976).

- *Information form*
  Relative (or comparative) formats lead to less time and better accuracy than absolute formats (e.g., Russo, Krieser, & Miyashutz, 1975).

- *Noise level*
  As distraction increases, fewer attributes are used (e.g., Wright, 1974b, 1975).

Social Surroundings

The second type of situational factor, social surroundings, deals with the impact of the presence of other individuals on consumer behavior. Many times our actions are determined or influenced by those who are around us (Krishnamurthi, 1983; Wind, 1976). Although this topic has been studied very little, it is clear that the very visible nature of shopping activity may be altered by those present. For example, the presence of friends or children might alter the nature of the individual decision process (e.g., we buy things we would ordinarily not buy, or vice versa). Also, interactions with salespeople can have an important

effect on the purchase decision. Olshavsky (1973) found that salespeople can play a role at three stages of the sales interaction process, the orientation phase, the evaluation phase, and the consummation phase, but the point of greatest influence is the evaluation phase. Many times consumers gave up their own power of choice and simply followed the salesperson's recommendation. Finally, Tauber (1972) discovered one of the major reasons for visiting retail outlets: to participate in social experiences and interact with others.

Temporal Characteristics

Temporal characteristics deal with the effect of time on consumer behavior. A review of these factors is provided in Jacoby, Szybillo, and Berning (1976). Time as a situational factor can influence the decision process in a number of ways. For instance, the time that has elapsed since the last meal was eaten can determine the amount purchased in a shopping trip (Nisbett & Kanouse, 1968). Due to all the visual food cues, people on an empty stomach are tempted to buy a greater number of items.

More importantly, time has a direct influence on information processing. According to Wright (1974b), information search will be relatively quick and use of information will be minimal when little time is available for decision making. This can also lead to fewer alternatives being considered and greater weight being placed on negative information about alternatives.

Physical Surroundings

Physical surroundings are the most readily apparent features in a given situation and include geographical and institution location, decor, sounds, aromas, lighting, weather, and visible configurations of merchandise or other material surrounding the stimulus object (Belk, 1975). These factors can have a powerful effect on consumer behavior even though the individual is often not consciously aware of their effects.

These factors work largely on a sensory or perceptual level. The physical surroundings affect our sensory modes, which in turn create a set of perceptions that can partially determine the overall perception a consumer has of the purchase situation (Grossbart, Amedeo, & Chinchan, 1979). For example, warm colors such as yellow and red are more likely to attract customers into a retail store than cool colors such as blue and green (Bellizi, Crowley, & Hasty, 1983). Once inside, however, cool colors are preferable because they create a more relaxed and less threatening environment.

Similarly, each of the other physical features can influence the overall affect surrounding the situation. Some are under the control of marketers (e.g., location, decor, sounds), while others are beyond control (e.g., weather); but the important point is that they play a key role in determining the overall nature of the decision process. As one example, Milliman (1986) found that fast music played in a restaurant reduced the service time and customer time at the table. Slow music significantly increased the amount of bar purchases.

Antecedent States

The final category, antecedent states, are aspects specific to each individual that are not permanent. Rather, they are temporary mood states or conditions. In spite of their momentary nature, mood states can play an important role in the decision process.

Mood states represent an important affective factor and can influence consumer behavior in a variety of contexts, including brand selection and advertisement exposure. Most important, however, is that these states can be altered or influenced by very small changes in the physical environment (e.g., the program context in which an ad is presented, a

salesperson's smile, the attractiveness of a model, and the music in a store).

Research indicates that mood states can have an impact on behavior, judgment, and recall. According to Gardner (1985b), "some positive moods appear to increase the likelihood of performance of behaviors with expected positive associations and to decrease the likelihood of performance of behaviors that lead to negative outcomes" (p. 283). The effect of negative moods, however, is more complex and can lead to a variety of different behaviors. (For an excellent review of this research, see Gardner, 1985b.)

Research also indicates that mood states can influence a variety of judgments in mood congruent directions, including evaluations of novel stimuli (e.g., Isen & Shalker, 1982; Veitch & Griffit, 1976), evaluations of familiar stimuli (e.g., Isen, Shalker, Clark, & Karp, 1978; Schwarz & Clore, 1983), and evaluations of the likelihood of mood argument events (e.g., Johnson & Tversky, 1983). Goldberg and Gorn (1987) found that relative to a sad television program, a happy program produced a happier mood as viewers watched both the program and commercials, which, in turn, led to greater perceived commercial effectiveness and more affectively positive cognitive responses.

Mood can further have a major effect on recall of information from memory (Goldberg & Gorn, 1987). According to Gardner (1985b), "recall may be affected by the consumer's mood at the time of exposure of retrieval, or by a match between exposure and retrieval moods" (p. 288; Isen, 1984, provides an extensive review of the effects of mood on cognition). For example, Bartlett and Santrock (1979) and Bower, Manteiro, and Gilligan (1978) indicate that unaided recall is enhanced when mood at the time of retrieval matches mood at the time of encoding (assuming the encoding mood cue can serve as a retrieval cue).

It is important to note that moods can be created or influenced systematically by a variety of different stimuli. According to Gardner

(1985b), the most important and most often studied are service encounters, point-of-purchase stimuli, and communications stimuli.

Mood can influence *service encounters* in many ways. Customers in a good mood are easier to please, evaluate the encounter more positively, and recall positive aspects that relate to the encounter more easily (Gardner, 1985b). "Positive mood states at point-of-purchase may increase shoppers' willingness to perform behavior with negative expected outcomes" (Gardner, 1985b, p. 292). Marketing communications such as advertising can influence consumers' responses outside the store as a result of either the message itself or the context in which it appears. These mood states in turn can affect the processing and evaluation of the message, which is stored for later use.

From its beginnings, industrial and organizational psychology has shown an intense interest in situational influences characterized by a concern with workers' affective and behavioral reactions to various facets of work environments. This long-term interest might be enriched by consideration of what is known about consumer reactions to situational factors. For instance, it may be informative to explore, as suggested by consumer research, whether experienced human resource managers making many personnel decisions tend to acquire less information and to process information differently (by person or by attribute) than those managers who are less experienced in human resource matters and who confront fewer personnel decisions. If such variance across managers is detected, then examination of alternative formats to reduce processing and storage tend to be consistent with information formats.

Another example is the work of consumer researchers on mood states. Industrial and organizational researchers might benefit from the study of how mood may contaminate measures of evaluative reactions to jobs. That is, researchers may inadvertently affect the mood of their subjects through the procedures they use to obtain measures, for example, of job satisfaction. Consumer research indicates this temporarily constructed mood could adversely affect obtained satisfaction scores. Additional links between consumer and organizational research on situational factors could be noted; however, the point of the two examples provided was merely to demonstrate the potential usefulness of such ties.

Research on Communication

Closely related to the decision process is another major focus of consumer research—the communication process. Both organizational and consumer psychology are interested in influencing behavior and in the factors that affect and determine such influence. Organizations will sometimes rely primarily or entirely on persuasive communications to generate compliance with organizationally determined needs and desires. Situations such as these usually occur either when the direct application of authority would be illegitimate or would violate the "psychological contract" (Schein, 1965); or when it is believed that more rapid acceptance would ensue, morale would not suffer, and so forth, if persuasive techniques were used in preference to the direct execution of formal, legitimate authority.

Marketer-advertisers rarely possess the power of direct authority over consumers that is available to management when dealing on an internal matter with members of the firm. Consequently, consumer psychologists direct much attention to the study of persuasive communications. Communication has been defined as a process whereby a source transmits a message through a particular medium to a receiver. Persuasion is that variety of communication in which a source exerts an influence upon the response tendencies, mental states on attitudes, and/or actual behavior of the receiver.

As one considers the manner in which persuasive communication has been examined in industrial and consumer contexts, certain basic similarities in conceptualization, if not in terminology, become apparent. More specifically, the topic of "formal communication" in the organizational context reflects essentially the same characteristics as does the subject of "advertising" in the consumer context. In similar fashion, informal communication is roughly comparable to and may be equated with word-of-mouth advertising, informal leaders in organizations with opinion leaders in the marketplace, organizational change agents with consumer innovators, and the acceptance of organizational change with the acceptance of innovations (i.e., new products or brands). The next sections will examine results of investigations regarding first formal communications such as advertising, followed by a section on informal communications involving the domain of word-of-mouth communications, opinion leaders, and innovators.

Research on Formal Communication

A natural research interest in consumer behavior and advertising has centered on the effect that persuasive messages have on individuals. This is a critical concern in marketing because unless we understand how individuals react to different types of communications, we cannot expect to be able to influence consumers through marketing efforts. Using the vast literature on persuasion from social psychology as both a theoretical and methodological guide, a large number of studies have attempted to determine how the information from these messages is processed and how it may or may not have an impact on the ultimate decision. Although detailed review of this work is beyond the scope of this chapter, there have been key theoretical advances that may have important implications for the industrial and organizational area.

Traditional Model. Much of this work has been based on traditional models of persuasion such as the Yale research paradigm (e.g., Hovland, Janis, & Kelly, 1953), the learning hierarchy model of Colley (1961), the attitude change model of Fishbein and Ajzen (1975), and McGuire's (1978) information processing model (for an excellent review of this vast literature, see McGuire, 1985). The basic premise of these models is that attitudes are influenced only after the message has passed through a series of sequential stages. At the risk of simplifying, these models postulate that the message must first be comprehended and accepted if it is to change attitude. This will lead to a change in beliefs, followed by a change in attitude. Assuming the proper intention is formed, the consumer will be motivated to act. Much research has focused on the types of arguments and messages most likely to lead to belief and attitude change. A smaller proportion of research has focused on the comprehension stage.

Note that the learning hierarchy approach assumes a motivated and active information processor. For situations or topics relatively important to the individual, this appears to be a reasonable assumption, and studies conducted in such contexts have generally produced promising results.

Elaboration Likelihood Model. In many advertising and consumer contexts, however, the product or message is not considered very important (Hupfer & Gardner, 1971). In these low-involvement situations, it may be inappropriate to assume that the viewer will be actively processing the message of interest (Krugman, 1965). In fact, research indicates that for the typical television ad, consumers do not have many thoughts about the advocated brand and its attributes. In response to this conflict, Chaiken (1980) and Petty, Caccioppo, and Schumann (1983) suggested that there are two routes to attitude change: a central route and a peripheral route. The *central route* corresponds to the traditional model of attitude change, consists of largely cognitive information processing, and is more likely to be representative of the attitude change process in high-involvement situations. In low-involvement situations, the *peripheral route* is more likely. Here there is limited elaboration of message arguments, and persuasive effects are more likely to result from execution cues such as source credibility, source likability, the number of arguments in the message, humor, music, and so forth. Further, this process appears to be largely affective in nature.

In support of this notion, Mitchell and Olson (1981) and Gorn (1982) discovered that attitude toward the advertising execution itself did lead to attitude change, in addition to those caused directly by the message arguments. Park and Young (1986) found that music had a facilitative effect on brand attitude for subjects in a low-involvement condition and a distraction effect for those in a cognitive-involvement condition. Also, studies have clearly supported the interaction between involvement level and attitude change route (Batra & Ray, 1984; Chaiken 1980; Gorn, 1982; Lutz, Makenzie, & Belch, 1983; Petty, Caccioppo, & Goldman, 1981; Sanbonmatsu & Kardes, 1988). Specifically, messages that use superior attribute arguments appear to be more successful in high-involvement situations, while source cues (e.g., attractiveness or similiarity) are more effective in low-involvement situations.

Thus, the two-route model emphasizes the importance of carefully analyzing the situation before engaging in a persuasion attempt. In some situations, cognitively based message arguments are likely to be more effective, while in others affectively based execution cues may be more appropriate.

Another area of research makes a similar distinction between cognitive and affective processing. Fiske (1982) extended the categorization research of Rosch (1977) to examine how cognitive and affective processing might occur. A distinction is made between *piecemeal*

processing, where pieces of product information are recalled from memory and combined to form an evaluation (analogous to the central route in the ELM model), and *categorical processing*, which involves the recall of schema-triggered affect (similar to the peripheral route in the ELM model). The latter process occurs in two stages. First, the individual is said to attempt a match between the stimulus and existing schema at a nonanalytic, summary configuration level. If there is a match, then the category level affect (positive or negative) is transferred immediately to the stimulus. If a match cannot be found, the individual must switch to piecemeal processing. Support for this conceptualization in a consumer behavior context is provided by Sujan (1985). She found that self-described "experts" tended to use category-based processing when the product's attributes were consistent with existing schema expectations, but used piecemeal processing when the attributes were experimentally mismatched.

In industrial and organizational psychology, issues regarding source and content (affective versus cognitive) of messages and their interactions with involvement have not been emphasized. More generally, study of organizational communications per se is not well developed. Yet questions regarding how managers can communicate effectively to their employees seem important. For instance, take the case of the need of a chief executive officer to communicate to his or her organizational members a major shift in corporate strategy. It would seem important to know from whom this message should come. Should its content be cognitively or affectively loaded? Should these features vary by levels of employee involvement in strategic issues? Again, answers to these sorts of questions of practical importance are rare.

Much of the work in consumer behavior and social psychology has focused on processes related to the central route of persuasion. Again, a detailed review of this literature is beyond the scope of this chapter. However, there are three recent areas of research that may have particular relevance to industrial and organizational psychology: (a) cognitive responses to communications (central route processing), (b) affective processes (peripheral route processing), and (c) the comprehension and miscomprehension of advertising communications.

Cognitive Responses: Central Route Processing. The high involvement, or cognitive route, to persuasion holds that consumers engage in active processing of a message. According to Wright (1973, 1974a, 1974c, 1975, 1981), the individual will actively analyze an incoming message, relate it to his or her existing memory structure, and form some kind of cognitive response to that message. In essence, these cognitive responses are elaborations of the ideas in the message or evaluative reactions to it (Bettman, 1979). These responses are considered important because they are said to mediate or underlie the effects of the persuasive message.

Although a number of specific cognitive responses can be identified, Wright (1973) classifies these into three major categories: (a) *counterarguments*, which are refutations of claims made in the message; (b) *source derogations*, which are negative thoughts about the source of the message; and (c) *support arguments*, which are agreements with the claims. Counterarguments and source derogations tend to decrease the effectiveness of a message, while support arguments enhance it. The major technique employed in this area is a thought monitoring approach where subjects are asked to list all of their thoughts immediately after receiving a message. These responses are then coded into the various categories for analysis.

A number of studies in both marketing and social psychology have examined these thought verbalizations and their role in the attitude change process (for an excellent review, see Wright, 1980). A major goal has been to establish the validity of the mediation role of the message-evolved thought. Major findings of this research have been that "variations in people's verbalized thoughts often correlate significantly with their post-message attitude statements, especially when the thought-sampling is time-limited, the thought coding reliable, and the subjects are involved in the message processing" (Wright, 1980, p. 166; see also Chattopadhyay & Alba, 1988). Also, parallel effects on thoughts and attitude measures have been reported (e.g., Eagly, 1974; Osterhouse & Brock, 1970). Further, covariance analysis has eliminated a significant treatment effect on this attitude measure (Cook, 1969). Finally, thoughts have been found to be related to various physiological states (Cacioppo, 1977; Cacioppo, Sandman, & Waller, 1978; Lacey & Lacey, 1974).

Other interesting findings have been that (a) distraction can lower counterargument or support argument production (Keating & Brock, 1974; Petty, Wells, & Brock 1976); (b) adding assertions to the message can increase support arguments but has mixed effects on counterarguments (Calder, Insko, & Yardell, 1974; Olson, Toy, & Dover, 1978); (c) involvement may have an effect on increasing thought (particularly counterarguments; see Petty & Cacioppo, 1979; Wright, 1974a, 1974c); and (d) logical assertions discourage counterarguments, while absurd assertions encourage them (Wright, 1980).

The important point, however, is that thought verbalizations may provide useful insights into the reasons why attitude change did or did not occur. This would be particularly true in organizational contexts where employee attitudes are of major concern.

Affective Processes: Peripheral Route. As mentioned previously, a number of models have been developed to gain an understanding of the nature of consumer choice strategies. On a general level, an underlying assumption of most of these models (in particular, multiattribute models) is that consumers evaluate the features of the products under consideration and attach importance weights to these features. These feature-importance combinations, or component utilities, are then combined to arrive at an overall evaluation or preference.

Most importantly, the processes involved are assumed to be cognitive. That is, consumers are thought to engage in cognitive processing to evaluate product attribute information when making a decision. Empirical evidence from studies in social psychology, however, challenges the notion that cognitive processing must precede the formation of a preference (Zajonc, 1980). These studies have suggested that another phenomenon, noncognitive-based affect, plays an important role in the formation of preferences. According to this view, individuals may develop a basic feeling of like or dislike toward an object (Zajonc, 1980). Further, since affect may develop prior to any form of cognitive processing, it may influence or alter the nature of any subsequent processing. In fact, "for many purchases a (cognitive) decision process never occurs, not even on the first purchase" (Olshavsky & Granbois, 1979, p. 100).

Traditional cognitive theories (e.g., Fishbein & Ajzen, 1975; McGuire, 1978) have not provided a full explanation of advertising effects (Ray et al., 1973). Studies of consumer recall reveal that a large proportion of individuals exposed to ads cannot remember the sponsor or the product being advertised (Engel, Blackwell, & Miniard, 1986). Further, several studies (Batra & Ray, 1983; Wright, 1975, 1981) have indicated that, in processing advertisements, consumers tend to have few thoughts about the brand and its attributes. Krugman (1965) also indicated that advertisements may have limited ability to generate change in consumer beliefs. Taken together, these findings suggest that little cognitive processing is occurring in response to advertising messages.

Yet if one turns to data that examines the relationship between advertising and sales, a positive relationship emerges. As a representative example, one study found that $23.24 spent on media advertising produced $55.37 of added sales for manufacturers of five advertised brands (*Project Payout*, 1980). Although one cannot assume a direct relationship between advertising and sales, it appears that advertising does at least influence consumer choice. Therefore, evidence suggests that advertising may sometimes have an effect on purchase behavior that may not be fully explained in terms of cognitive processing. In support, Mitchell and Olson (1981) concluded that product beliefs do not totally mediate brand attitudes. They showed that attitudes toward the ad also influenced brand attitudes. Also, MacKenzie, Lutz, and Belch (1986) evaluated different models with a structural equation methodology and concluded that a model in which attitude toward the ad (Aad) mediates the effects of cognitive responses to the ad on *both* cognitions about the brand and attitude toward the brand seems most accurate.

Given that the influence of advertising may not occur on an entirely cognitive level, a major question concerns the nature of the alternative affective processing. One explanation for this phenomenon has been termed the *mere exposure effect* by Zajonc and others. This view is in contrast to traditional work on the affect concept, which assumes that liking or disliking is a postcognitive event. Zajonc and Markus (1982) have expressed this traditional belief as, "Before you can like something, you must know what it is" (p. 125). Studies of the mere exposure effect, however, have established that positive affect toward an object can be generated simply as a result of repeated exposures to the stimulus object (Zajonc, 1980; Zajonc & Markus, 1982). The explanation for these results is that repeated exposures to a stimulus builds familiarity. Then, since individuals exhibit a tendency to prefer familiar objects to unfamiliar objects, familiarity builds liking.

The mere exposure effect has been demonstrated in a variety of contexts and underscores the importance of familiarity as a source of basic affect. The experimental paradigm used in initial studies of this phenomenon was to expose subjects to stimuli in the initial phase and follow this with tests for liking. Researchers generally found liking or affect to be correlated with frequency of exposure to a stimulus (Kunst-Wilson & Zajonc, 1980; Matlin, 1971; Moreland & Zajonc, 1977, 1979; Wilson, 1979).

These findings can be linked to consumer behavior by noting, as Zajonc and Markus have, that the advertising industry appears to have an intuitive understanding of the importance of affect. Brand names are ingrained in our memories as we are repeatedly exposed to ads, and brand images are created as products are coupled with scenes of good times and beautiful surroundings. Research has supported the notion that repeated exposures to a stimulus leads to the creation of a *conditioned affect* toward the stimulus if certain conditions are present (Harrison, 1977; Sawyer, 1977, 1981). Also, a number of studies have focused on the ability of advertising to increase brand familiarity and to generate feelings of liking (Batra & Ray, 1983; McMahan, 1980; Vadehra, 1980; Wright, 1981) and on the effects of repetition (Batra & Ray, 1986b; Burke & Edell, 1986; Obermiller, 1985; Rethans, Swazy, & Marks, 1986; Sawyer, 1981). In addition, Ray and Batra (1983) have discussed the possible effects of affective ad executions and linked such effects to theoretical phenomenon such as the mere exposure effect and hemispheral lateralization (i.e., left-brain and right-brain processing).

It is important to note that the mere exposure hypothesis has created controversy and has not received universal support (Obermiller, 1985; Rethans, Swazy, & Marks, 1986; Tsal, 1985). However, our main point is that researchers are now recognizing that affect plays a key role in consumer behavior (Batra & Ray, 1986a).

Affect is a complex construct that includes emotions and feelings as well as evaluative impressions (Holbrook & Batra, 1987). While it may be the result of a cognitive process, it may also develop independently of cognition. Theoretically, affect can play a variety of roles in the decision process. These can range from influencing how information is processed (e.g., Petty, Cacioppo, & Goldman, 1981) or stored in memory (Moore & Hutchinson, 1983; Srull, 1983) to determining a product or brand choice (e.g., Gorn, 1982; Zajonc & Markus, 1982). Further, affect can be generated from a variety of sources, whether it be familiarity (Zajonc, 1980), source likability, music (Gorn, 1982), humor, or other stimuli. The extent to which affective reactions will have an impact is a function of audience involvement with the ad (Greenwald & Leavitt, 1984). Higher levels of involvement tend to produce higher levels of cognitive processing. Finally, the act of consumption can be an affective experience in itself. A number of products are consumed in pursuit of fun, amusement, fantasy, arousal, sensory stimulation, and enjoyment (Holbrook & Hirschman, 1982).

A majority of the recent research on affective processes has focused on affective responses to advertising. Holbrook and Batra (1987) outline a general communication model which can be supported by a number of studies (for reviews, see Gardner, 1985a; Holbrook & Batra, 1987). Affect or emotional response is seen as a major determinant of attitudes toward an advertisement which, in turn, is an intervening variable influencing attitude toward the brand. This model is outlined in Figure 4. The importance of emotional responses in influencing attitude toward the ad is emphasized by Edell and Burke (1987). They found that cognitive evaluations of an ad's characteristics (i.e, was it humorous, interesting, etc.) did not account for all of the variance in Aad.

In light of the important mediation role of affective responses, a number of studies have investigated the nature of emotional responses to advertising. Holbrook and Batra (1987) found that feelings of pleasure, domination (i.e., conflict, guilt, helplessness, fear), and arousal clearly mediated the effects of ad content on Aad

FIGURE 4

The Affect-oriented Communication Model

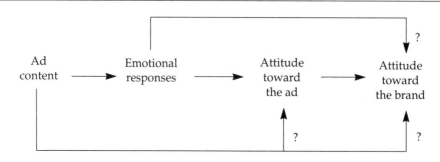

and partially mediated the effects of ad content on attitude toward the brand. Aaker, Stayman, and Hagerty (1986) identified warmth (i.e., "a positive, mild, volatile emotion involving physiological arousal," p. 377) to be strongly related to both Aad and purchase likelihood. Also, responses tended to decrease with repeated exposure. Burke and Edell (1989) identified three dimensions of feelings—upbeat, warmth, and negative—and found that these feelings can influence Aad and A brand over multiple viewings of an ad, different measurement delay periods, and different ad executions.

Edell and Burke (1989) indicate further that both positive and negative feelings can co-occur and be important predictors of ad effectiveness, Aad, and A brand. Allen, Madden, and Twible (1988) replicated this finding and noted that the "processing set" (i.e., an interaction of the nature of the individual's motivation to process information and the context in which the processing takes place) influences the proportion of cognitive to feeling responses.

Industrial and organizational psychologists, like their counterparts interested in consumer behavior, have begun to place a greater emphasis on the role of affect (e.g., Park, Sims, & Motowidlo, 1986). Yet study of the effects of affect on organizational behavior still appears

embryonic. Extrapolating from the consumer literature, fruitful areas of inquiry might involve the study of how phenomenon such as mere familiarity may produce affect in the work setting. Later, in addressing the affective component of job attitudes (Organ & Near, 1985), we will have more to say on the study of affect in industrial and organizational psychology.

Comprehension and Miscomprehension of Advertising Communication

Most major models of persuasion explicitly recognize *comprehension* as a major step in the process (e.g., Engel, Blackwell, & Miniard, 1986; McGuire, 1985). Until recently, theories and research on the persuasion process simply assumed that satisfactory comprehension generally preceded and facilitated attitude and behavior change (Eagly & Chaiken, 1984; McGuire, 1985; Mitchell, 1983). Few studies empirically examined this assumption.

The miscomprehension of communications has recently become an important subject of research in a variety of fields. This is evidenced by an increasing number of studies in marketing, communication, broadcasting, and journalism. In the marketing arena, the two most comprehensive and broad-scale investigations focused on the miscomprehension of televised (Jacoby, Hoyer, & Sheluga, 1980) and magazine (Jacoby & Hoyer, 1987) communications. The 60 stimuli used in the television study included 30-second advertisements, brief program segments, and public affairs announcements that had actually aired over network television. The test was conducted using a nationwide sample of 2,700 television viewers. Miscomprehension was assessed using a six-item true/false quiz administered immediately after viewing. The major finding of this study was that, on average, 29.6 percent of the material was miscomprehended. This rate was higher than expected and illustrated the need for research in this area. Other key findings were that miscomprehension occurred for all types of televised communications to a significant degree, both younger and older viewers had a slightly greater tendency to miscomprehend, and miscomprehension appears to be inversely related to education to a slight degree.

The results of this study generated some debate about how to best measure comprehension and about what goals are appropriate for miscomprehension research (see Ford & Yalch, 1982; Jacob & Hoyer, 1982; and Mizerski, 1982b). The initial study was also responsible for spawning further research. Using a set of communications from Jacoby and Hoyer (1982a), Jacoby, Hoyer, and Zimmer (1983) examined the levels of miscomprehension across three different types of mass media (TV, audio only, and print). Results indicated that printed messages were least miscomprehended and audio-only messages led to the greatest degree of miscomprehension. An identical modality effect was evidenced by Chaiken and Eagly (1976) in the context of examining the persuasive impact of complex legal information.

Other studies supplied converging support for the miscomprehension rates observed in Jacoby and Hoyer (1982a). Lipstein (1980) found 32 percent of advertising and program content of the CBS show "Sixty Minutes" was miscomprehended. Jacoby, Nelson, and Hoyer (1982) obtained miscomprehension rates as high as 50 percent in the case of corrective advertising claims, while Hoyer and Jacoby (1985) obtained in average miscomprehension rate of 33.7 percent for public affairs programming. Jacoby, Troutman, and Whittler (1986) examined factors associated with the miscomprehension of the 1980 preelection debate between incumbent President Jimmy Carter and Ronald Reagan and found a median miscomprehension rate of 23 percent.

Other studies have dealt with some related measurement issues. Schmittlein and Morrison (1983) reanalyzed the estimates obtained from the original study to account for the effects of guessing and yea-saying with true/false items. If these biases are included as part of miscomprehension, their major conclusion was that a more accurate estimate of miscomprehension would be 54 percent (as opposed to 29.6%). If these are not included, they estimate misinformation to average 19 percent. Alpert, Golden, and Hoyer (1983) examined the effect of repetition on miscomprehension and found miscomprehension to remain fairly high across five exposure levels. Gates and Hoyer (1986) and Gates (1986) compared different question formats along with the effects of other question and stimulus characteristics. This research indicates that multiple choice questions may be slightly easier to answer correctly (although the difference is very small) and that performance on a question interacts with whether the question concerned fact or an inference and whether the primary appeal of the ad was cognitive or affective in nature.

The newer work on print communications (Jacoby & Hoyer, 1987) differs from the original in several key respects. Based on the critiques of the earlier work, major improvements in methodology and measurement were incorporated. In particular, greater attention was devoted to sampling and obtaining a target audience, the true/false format was expanded to include a "don't know" response, equal numbers of true and false items were included, and a nonexposed control group was added as a comparison.

The principal findings of this study were that (a) a single reading of a magazine communication results in approximately 60 percent comprehension of the meanings in the communication, (b) virtually all magazines and magazine communications can be expected to be miscomprehended to some degree, (c) approximately 21.4 percent of meanings were miscomprehended, (d) the average "don't know" response is an additional 15.5 percent, (e) editorial communications tend to be associated with slightly higher rates of miscomprehension (23.4%) than are advertising communication (21.4%), and (f) a magazine communication's asserted meanings (i.e., what is factually stated) seem to be less miscomprehended than the inferences (i.e., either intended or unintended meanings that are not explicitly stated) that may be drawn from this literal context.

Other studies have attempted to examine additional factors related to miscomprehension. Hoyer, Srivastava, and Jacoby (1984) found that the presence of printed copy in a television ad is associated with an increase in miscomprehension and, surprisingly, the presence of music seems to lower the rate of miscomprehension slightly. Kuss (1985) and Haedrich and Kuss (1986) examined the miscomprehension of advertisements for German children and discovered that miscomprehension drops off dramatically as one moves from 7-year-olds through 14-year-olds. Harris, Dubitsky, and Bruno (1983) examined the influence process in response to simulated radio commercials. The basic finding from this research is that respondents hearing an ad tend to make inferences regarding the advertised product, which they then believe to be true and to have been explicitly stated by the ad, even though such meanings were neither expressly contained in the communication nor could be logically derived from it. Finally, Celsi and Olson (1988) found that involvement (in the

form of personal relevance of the stimulus) plays a key role in the comprehension process.

The important point of all this work is that even very simple communications such as advertisements can be subject to substantial miscomprehension, and if one desires to accurately communicate a message, miscomprehension should be a major concern. Implications of miscomprehension research to industrial and organizational psychology seem clear. There appears to be a need to investigate the level at which all sorts of organizational communications are comprehended. Goal-setting researchers (e.g., Locke, Shaw, Saari, & Lathman, 1981) may benefit from knowing the degree to which assigned goals are comprehended, particularly for highly complex tasks. Those interested in performance feedback (e.g., Kopelman, 1986) may benefit from investigating how well performance information feedback by supervisors to supervisees is comprehended. As a final example, researchers concerned with compensation systems (e.g., Lawler, 1981) might gain a greater understanding of the efficacy of various pay plans if the degree to which employees comprehended the compensation system is known. It may be the case that, in these and other areas of organizational research, information thought to be satisfactorally understood is miscomprehended by 20 percent or more, as suggested by consumer research. If so, miscomprehension would stand as a rival plausible hypothesis to findings evident in several industrial and organizational literatures and could serve as a vehicle for reconciling seemingly contradictory results in those literatures.

Research on Informal Communication: Word-of-Mouth Processes and Opinion Leaders

In early reviews of the topic, Arndt (1967a, 1967b, 1967c) defined word-of-mouth (WOM) communication as "oral, person-to-person communication between a perceived noncommercial communicator and a receiver concerning a brand, a product, or a service offered for sale" (1967a, p. 190). Arndt's definition says nothing about interpersonal influence or persuasive communications, but simply focuses on the exchange of information between individuals (cf. King & Summers, 1970, p. 44). That the source may or may not have any intent to persuade or that the receiver may be persuaded even if the source had no such intentions (cf. Miller, 1966; Nilsen, 1957) is irrelevant. The distinguishing characteristic of WOM, and that which differentiates it from personal selling (another form of communication directly controlled by the marketer), is that the source is perceived by the receiver to be independent of the manufacturer, advertiser, and/or seller. In the context of organizational behavior, these are not informal job-related conversations such as those that take place between a supervisor and subordinate or conversations generated in lieu of official, written memoranda (cf. Melcher & Beller, 1967).

The vast majority of studies conducted in the consumer behavior context indicate that word-of-mouth information plays a significant role in making the consumer aware of the product and in affecting the decision to buy or not to buy that product, brand, or service and can cause significant shifts in public opinion. In general, "word of mouth emerges as one of the most important, possibly the most important source of information for the consumer" (Arndt, 1967a, p. 238).

Word-of-mouth communication can serve either as a facilitating or retarding force on product acceptance, though word-of-mouth transmitters appear more likely to transmit favorable than unfavorable information (Arndt, 1967a; Engel, Kegerreis, & Blackwell, 1969; Holmes & Lett, 1977). To the extent that one can translate these findings to organizational contexts, there is reason to believe that informal organizational communication operates to the firm's advantage rather than disadvantage. It is not something to be feared and

discouraged by management but to be understood and, if possible, used to further organizational goals.

From the receiver's perspective, however, negative word of mouth has greater impact than favorable word of mouth, and the occurrence of negative word of mouth can be substantial (Diener & Greyser, 1978; Richins, 1983). Weinberger, Allen, and Dillan (1981) further demonstrated that the impact of negative word of mouth persists even when refuted. According to Mizerski (1982a), this power results from the rareness or unexpectedness of negative information leading to greater attention and weighting of the information.

Another important aspect of word-of-mouth information concerns the point in the decision process at which it exerts its significant influence. The mass media seem to be best equipped to create awareness, while word of mouth is the most important source of information in the later stages, particularly in the evaluation stage. This suggests that in those instances where the organization relies on persuasion rather than authority to influence member behavior, formal communications are the best means of indicating what actions are deemed desirable. Informal communication sources will, however, determine how this information is evaluated and whether there will be compliance. Moreover, Sheth's (1968) finding, that word of mouth leads to more rapid adoption than when mass media are the source of the information, suggests that informal communication sources will be more likely to produce rapid compliance than will formal communication sources.

Cunningham (1967) found that word of mouth is engaged in more often and has greater impact on purchases for new products than for established products, thereby suggesting the increased importance of informal communication when attempting to introduce organizational change. Other studies indicate the information exchange usually takes place horizontally rather than vertically, that is, between individuals of similar age and status (Feldman & Spencer, 1965; Katz, 1957; King & Summers, 1967) and that, within these strata, individuals will tend to search for others perceived to be more competent than themselves (Feldman, 1966; King & Summers, 1967). Brown and Reingen (1987) make a further distinction between strong and weak social ties. Weak ties serve a bridging function, which allows information to travel from one subgroup to another, while strong ties are more influential than weak ties and are more likely to be sources of information.

A major issue concerns the processes by which word-of-mouth influence occurs. The most basic conceptualization is the two-step flow-of-communication model, which states that information and influence flow "from [the formal mass media sources] to opinion leaders and *from them* to the less active sections of the population" (Lazersfeld, Berelson, & Gaudet, 1948, p. 151). In a significant extension of the two-step model, in which the information flow is viewed as being unidirectional (i.e., from the media to the opinion leaders and from the opinion leaders to the masses), Bauer (1963) and Cox (1963) contended that consumers have "information needs" that prompt them to take a more active information-seeking role in the communication process. Cox (1963) cited evidence to indicate that such information seeking, where nonopinion leaders initiate conversations with opinion leaders and where opinion leaders seek out information from the mass media, may take place at least as often as does information receiving. Similarly, Cunningham (1967) found that about half the word-of-mouth activity is of the traditional information-receiving variety, while about half was of the information-seeking variety. Moreover, consumers pay more attention to information that they sought than to information volunteered to them (Arndt, 1967c). Finally, the most recent study on this topic (Reingen, 1987) used a graph-theoretic network analysis to examine word-of-mouth behavior and found that, typically,

receivers relied on only one source, even though many had access to several sources.

Note, however, that some research questions the existence of opinion leaders. The thesis is that product-related discussions are a function of the situation rather than a leader-follower role. For example, Belk (1971) found that 80 percent of all word of mouth about coffee took place in a context relevant to the product. Further, Summers (1971, p. 430) found that word-of-mouth communication tended to occur between two individuals and to be "a casual passing of product information" rather than "lecturing" by transmitters.

Regardless of which view is correct, the important point is that individuals are not passive recipients of information. Likewise, organizational members are in all likelihood not passive recipients of formal communications. They, too, must have information needs regarding their various relationships with and within the organization. Hence, they are likely to initiate conversations and seek out information pursuant to the satisfaction of these needs, and it would be in an organization's best interest if it could learn to use all channels of information to which it had access, including word of mouth, to satisfy these needs.

Several possible explanations have been offered to account for the apparently greater persuasive impact of word-of-mouth processes relative to that of the formal mass media. Some of these are based on two particularly important characteristics of word-of-mouth communication, namely, (a) that negative as well as positive information may be exchanged (Leonard-Barton, 1985) and (b) that word of mouth is a two-way form of communication. The first factor suggests that information from a word-of-mouth source is more likely to represent a balanced rather than a one-sided view, as is the case with the mass media, which suggests that word-of-mouth sources are perceived to be less biased and more trustworthy (Arndt, 1967a, 1967b, 1967c; Cox, 1963). Considerable evidence in the social psychological literature indicates that more trustworthy sources have greater persuasive impact.

The flexibility provided by two-way communication permits the occurrence of several other factors that also serve to enhance the effectiveness of word-of-mouth influence. First, "interpersonally communicated information can often be tailored to meet an individual's particular information needs" (Cox, 1963, p. 64). Moreover, "a consumer may be able to develop a great deal more information about a product through consumer channels—particularly information concerning product performance and the social or psychological consequence of a purchase decision" than may be possible to obtain from the more formal sources of product information (Cox, 1963, p. 64). Finally, the feedback aspect of two-way communication would tend, even by itself, to increase the accuracy with which the information is transmitted, because the source can clarify difficult points and answer receiver questions.

Another set of factors that explains the greater persuasive impact of word of mouth relates to the social aspects of the process. "In contrast to the mass media, personal contacts [can] offer social support" (Arndt, 1967a, p. 205). Moreover, word-of-mouth communication is often backed up by subtle social pressures and surveillance. It may also serve a "legitimizing" function by giving the stamp of approval for intended or actual purchase behavior (Engel, Kegerreis, & Blackwell, 1969).

In sum, the evidence indicates word of mouth to be a potent force affecting consumer decision processes and purchasing behavior. The findings in the consumer behavior sphere suggest that informal organizational communication processes are probably of similar importance and deserve considerable more attention and study than they have heretofore received.

Opinion Leaders and Informal Leaders. According to the two-step flow model, some people—termed *opinion leaders*—play a more significant role in the word-of-mouth communication–influence process than do others. The function served by opinion leaders suggests a basic equivalence with the notion of communication *relay points* of *message centers* (Cyert & March, 1955; Shannon & Weaver, 1949) and with the notion of organizational *linking pins* (Likert, 1961). In other words, while the head of a formal organizational unit serves as a linking pin of relay point for information exchange between his or her supervisor and peers at one level and supervisees at another, the evidence noted below suggests that the organization's informal leaders probably serve the identical linking pin function in the firm's informal organization. Consequently, the informal opinion leader provides the logical starting point for those wishing to exert an impact on the organizational system via word-of-mouth processes. The more we know about the characteristics and motives of the opinion leader, the easier it should be to identify them and utilize their unique and valuable talents.

Research thus far has identified several characteristics of the opinion leader. Perhaps most important is that "no matter what their sphere of influence, opinion leaders do actually exceed non-opinion leaders in mass media exposure in general" (Katz & Lazarsfield, 1955, p. 311) and in exposure to mass media relevant to their particular spheres of influence in particular (Summers, 1970). Also, opinion leaders tend to have higher expertise on the topic or product than followers (Jacoby & Hoyer, 1981). Further, leaders receive more information from personal information sources and are more influenced by what others have to say than by information supplied by the formal sources (Katz & Lazarsfeld, 1955; Sheth, 1968). These findings suggest a multistep rather than the traditional two-step flow described above.

Other characteristics of opinion leaders are that they (a) seem to conform more closely to the norms of the social system than does the average group member (Rogers & Cartano,

1962), (b) tend to participate in more social activities than do followers (Rogers, 1983), (c) are generally of the same social class as those they influence (Rogers, 1983), (d) tend to have slightly higher status and be more cosmopolitan in the sense of being oriented beyond the local community (Rogers, 1983), (e) are considered to be more competent than their followers (Katz & Lazarsfeld, 1955), and (f) are more self-confident in their appraisal of the product category (Lampert, 1974; Reynolds & Darden, 1971). Sheer physical mobility and proximity are also factors. Opinion leaders must be accessible and in contact with people to be able to exert any influence (Howard & Sheth, 1969, p. 313; King & Summers, 1967). Finally, evidence indicates that opinion leadership is most likely to occur between individuals who are similar in beliefs, education, values, and social status, than between individuals who are dissimilar in these attributes.

Dichter (1966) suggested that there are four primary bases for opinion leadership motivation. First, product involvement may serve to stimulate word-of-mouth communication, particularly to the extent that the opinion leader's experience with the product produces either moderately pleasurable or moderately unpleasurable experiences. Richins and Root-Shaffer (1988) and Venkatraman (1988) extend this notion in making a distinction between *enduring involvement,* a long-term state, and *situational involvement,* which is transitory. Results of their studies indicated that only enduring involvement was related to opinion leadership. Second, self-involvement will sometimes play a major role in motivating opinion leaders to talk about the product. Such conversations can serve such purposes as gaining attention, showing connoisseurship, suggesting status, giving the impression that the opinion leader has inside information, seeking confirmation of his or her judgment, and/or asserting superiority. Third, the opinion leader may be motivated simply by an altruistic concern for others. Thus, appealing to

such altruism may be sufficient to activate word-of-mouth communication. Finally, advertising for the product may be entertaining in and of itself and, therefore, provide the stimulus for product-related conversations. This suggests that the content of formal communications will be talked about to the extent that they are made interesting.

There are at least two different strategies that could be adopted in trying to identify the organizational counterparts of opinion leaders. First, consistent with the older "trait" approach applied to formal leaders, investigators might attempt to locate individuals within an organization who manifest the characteristics cited above as being possessed by opinion leaders. A second, more dynamic approach would be to start with the basic communication network notion from which the concepts of opinion leadership evolved. Given that opinion leaders are much more active participants in the communication process than their followers, both as receivers and transmitters of formal and informal communications, one could attempt to identify those individuals in the organization who process (i.e., receive and transmit) more organizationally relevant information than do others.

It is our understanding that it has been decades since word-of-mouth communications, as construed in the consumer literature, have been systematically studied in organizations (e.g., Davis, 1959). Given the potency of word of mouth on consumer behavior, it seems the word-of-mouth process represents particularly fertile ground for investigation in organizations. A potential starting point for such study could be the identification of opinion (or informal) leaders in organizations, and the research on networks in organizations (e.g., Tushman & Nadler, 1980) might be usefully applied to this problem. That is, research on word-of-mouth communications in organizations requires the isolation of informal leaders, which could be accomplished by analyzing the positions organizational members hold in intraorganizational networks. Once informal organization leaders are identified, characteristics, motivations, and influence roles could be studied. Based upon the consumer literature, informal organizational leaders are likely to be characterized, for example, as (a) more influenced by information supplied from formal sources, (b) more conforming to organizational norms, and (c) more competent at performing their organizational tasks. Collectively, these proposed characteristics suggest informal leaders represent organizationally functional channels through which information could be transmitted. By "organizationally" functional, we mean channels that formal leaders could use to transmit information. In regard to the informal leader's motivations, the communications literature suggests organizationally functional transmissions might be enhanced to the extent that informal leaders experience their jobs as satisfying (pleasurable) and that they, though performing their role as transmitters, are afforded opportunities to gain attention, to demonstrate status/superiority, to give the impression they have inside information, or to act altruistically. In sum, word-of-mouth communications in organizations are worthy of study and the consumer literature is suggestive of how such research could proceed.

Innovators and the Stimulus Characteristics of Innovations. Related to the issue of word-of-mouth communication and opinion leadership is the acceptance of innovations, that is, change, in the marketplace. Innovations are most frequently defined as any form of a product that has recently become available in a market (Engel, Blackwell, & Miniard, 1986; Rogers, 1983), while innovators are those individuals among the first to incorporate or adopt the innovation into their regular purchasing and usage behavior. Over time, the way a given product is adopted by all those who eventually do adopt it follows a normal distribution. Innovators are typically designated as those who are among the first 2.5 to 10 percent to adopt; later groups are designated in turn as early adopters, early majority, late majority, and laggards (cf. Rogers, 1983; Rogers & Shoemaker, 1971).

Considerable evidence indicates that innovators and early adopters play a significant role, basically through word-of-mouth communication, in the subsequent diffusion of an innovation through the population at large (Arndt, 1967c; Frank, Massy, & Morrison, 1964; Hirschman & Adcock, 1978; King, 1963; Lazer & Bell, 1966; Robertson, 1968; Rogers, 1983; Smith, Olshavsky, & Smith, 1979). Thus, even though they are not responsible for the introduction of change, they may be considered change agents in the sense that they provide the initial toehold and act as instigators to facilitate the acceptance of change by others. Given that the vast majority, perhaps as high as 90 percent (Rogers & Stanfield, 1968), of the new products introduced annually are rejected by consumers, identification of the innovation-prone individual has assumed tremendous practical importance (Cooper, 1981). Generalizations from investigations just cited indicate that, with respect to sociodemographic characteristics, innovators tend to be younger, more mobile, educated, literate, privileged (i.e., have more discretionary income relative to their peers), and to have somewhat higher income and status. Personality characteristics most often cited in connection with innovators are venturesomeness (i.e., possessing favorable attitudes toward trying new ideas and products), the tendency to take greater risks than noninnovators, open-mindedness (Coney, 1973; Jacoby, 1971), and other directedness (Donnelly & Ivancevich, 1974).

With respect to information processing behavior, innovators appear to be more exposed to all forms of communication. This includes marketer-dominated (e.g., advertising), consumer-dominated (e.g., word of mouth), and neutral (e.g., Consumer Reports) sources (Arndt, 1967a; Bohlen, Coughenour,

Lionberger, Moe, & Rogers, 1968). They are more prone to relate unsolicited experiences to others (Engel, Kegerreis, & Blackwell, 1969). They also tend to hear about innovations much earlier than do the noninnovators, engage in an extensive and systematic search for relevant information regarding the innovation (Berning & Jacoby, 1974; Engel, Kegerreis, & Blackwell, 1969) and tend to be heavier users of the product (Taylor, 1977).

Several studies indicate that there is some overlap between being an opinion leader and being an innovator (Baumgarten, 1971; Czepiel, 1974; Hirschman & Adcock, 1978; Robertson, 1971). In fact, Rogers, Daley, and Wu (1982) found that the level of communication from innovators to later adopters for home computers was quite extensive. Conceivably, innovators may simply be that class of opinion leaders most likely to respond favorably to new products. Venkatraman (1987) found that enduring involvement with the product class was a strong predictor of both opinion leadership and innovative behavior.

Certain characteristics of products and conditions under which they are introduced have been found to affect the acceptance of innovations (Hart & Jacoby, 1973; Ostlund, 1974). Considerable research (e.g., Cox, 1967) indicates that the greater the perceived risk associated with a given product, the less likely it is to achieve acceptance. Marketers introducing new products will frequently use money-back guarantees, "cents-off" coupons, and other similar devices to lessen the perceived risk. Hirschman (1982) proposes that product innovations arise from two sources: symbolism (intangible attributes) and technology (tangible attributes). Further, she argues that symbolic innovations will diffuse primarily due to their association with a particular reference group, while technological innovations diffuse because of a need for superior performance.

Based on his review of the literature, Rogers (1983) proposed the following factors as affecting the rate of adoption: relative advantage, compatibility, communicability, complexity, and divisibility. *Relative advantage* refers to the consumer's perception that the new product offering is superior, at least in some important respects, to the products it supersedes. *Compatibility* refers to the goodness of fit between the new product and the values and past experiences of the individual. The poorer the fit, the less likely it is to be accepted. *Communicability* refers to how easy it is for individuals to discuss the new product. The more difficult it is to communicate about a product, the slower its rate of acceptance. Products that are highly visible are usually those easiest to communicate about. *Complexity* refers to the degree to which a new product is difficult to understand or use. Complex products are unlikely to be diffused rapidly. Finally, *divisibility* refers to whether a product can be broken down into smaller "pieces" (e.g., can one buy a single bottle, or must one buy a six-pack?). Consumers forced to buy large units or quantities of a new product are less likely to do so, probably because of the perceived risk involved.

In addition, marketers have identified three major types of innovations. The difference between the three is dependent upon how much change in established behavior the innovation generates (Robertson, 1967). A *continuous innovation* is merely an alteration of an existing product and has the least disruption of established behavior. A *dynamically continuous innovation* has some disrupting effects, but does not generally alter established buying and usage patterns. Examples would include compact disc players and microwave ovens. A *discontinuous innovation* significantly alters behavior patterns. Examples have included the automobile (when first introduced) and computers. The important point is that when an innovation is more discontinuous, resistance to the adoption of the innovation will be greater.

Other factors have been found to result in resistance to innovations as well. These can include cultural barriers, social barriers, personal barriers, and barriers brought about by marketers (Zaltman & Wallendorf, 1983), as well as a number of perceived innovation characteristics (e.g., relative disadvantage, low compatibility, high perceived risk, etc.), and consumer characteristics (e.g., self-confidence or dogmatism; Ram, 1987).

Cultural barriers result from basic belief and value systems. The greater the conflict of a product or view with existing cultural values, the less likely it will be adopted (Zaltman & Wallendorf, 1983). *Social barriers* refer to incompatibilities with group values or norms. Each individual is a member of many groups, and each group exerts varying influences on his or her behavior. To the extent that a new product conflicts with the norms of important groups, the product will be rejected.

Habit and perceived risk form the basis of *personal barriers* to innovation and adoption. To the extent that perceived risk is high and habit is strong, substantial resistance will occur. Finally, the less clear marketers are in communicating information about the product or idea, the greater will be the resistance.

The study of innovation in organizations (e.g., Nord & Tucker, 1987) and of innovative organizations (e.g., Dutton & Freedman, 1985) appears to be of considerable interest to organizational scientists; yet there seems to have been relatively few attempts to couple the germane consumer and organizational literatures (e.g., Brief, Delbecq, Filley, & Huber, 1976; Zaltman, Duncan, & Holbeck, 1973). The following questions may be of interest to organizational psychologists.

- *Can those people who innovate in organizations and who lead innovative organizations be characterized as relatively more youthful, mobile, educated, venturesome, and open-minded than their less innovative counterparts?*

If so, these characteristics may provide clues for identifying opportunities for or a means of facilitating organizational innovations.

- *Can devices like money-back guarantees or "cents-off" coupons be discovered and attached to organizational innovations to lessen perceived risk, thereby facilitating adoption?*

For instance, this question suggests that innovations posed as mere experiments with a finite life might be more acceptable to organizational members than those innovations with no guarantee for return to the status quo.

- *Can some innovations be broken down to smaller pieces and, in this way, more readily sold within organizations?*

This question implies that to enhance adoption it may be advisable to advocate piecemeal rather than wholesale changes in such organizational practice areas as human resources management.

Again, the questions posed and the implications drawn are merely suggestive of the way organizational scientists might build on what consumer behaviorists have learned about innovators and the stimulus characteristics of innovations. Our point is that the adoption of at least some organizational innovations can be construed as voluntary rather than a sole function of hierarchical edict, and, therefore, the consumer literature can likely be employed in ways of thinking about facilitating organizational innovation.

Conclusion

Given that both consumer and organizational psychology have borrowed extensively from social and cognitive psychology, the basic objective of this chapter has been to suggest that each might have something to gain by examining the manner in which various psychological concepts have been considered by the other. The approach has been intentionally speculative, devoted primarily to conjecturing how the variables and findings of consumer psychology might prove useful for those primarily interested in organizational behavior.

Only a few topics that appear to have relevance in both fields were discussed. Many more could have been examined in similar fashion. For example, one could start by selecting specific social and cognitive psychological concepts and note how these might be reflected in both the organizational and consumer contexts. Another possible approach would be to start with a concept indigenous to one domain and consider how it could possibly be applied to the other. As examples, brand switching could be equated with job switching (cf. March & Simon, 1958, pp. 106–108; Nicosia, 1966, pp. 108–112), selling with recruiting (selling a job), product design with person-machine (human factors) applications, and market segmentation with work group segmentation (e.g., managers versus foremen, line versus staff, etc.). Finally, additional possibilities for mutual contribution exist with respect to considering the common methodologies and techniques used in organizational and consumer psychology (e.g., surveys, interviews, questionnaires, attitude scales, and other attitude measuring devices. It should be kept in mind that the possibilities cited are meant to be suggestive, not exhaustive, and numerous others certainly exist.

However, the utility that one domain has for the other goes beyond serving as a rich source of hypotheses. For example, the consumer context, because it contains a large number of variables that are more amenable to control and easier to bring into the laboratory, provides some unique opportunities for testing certain organizational hypotheses. The reverse may also be true; the organizational context, under some conditions, may be able to provide opportunities for cleaner tests of hypotheses regarding consumer behavior.

Finally, investigators cannot help but be encouraged when propositions regarding behavior derived and applied in one domain can also be demonstrated to explain behavior in other domains. Perhaps this chapter will stimulate some of the research necessary for establishing the more general applicability of many of the theories and models of social and cognitive psychology.

References

Aaker, D. A., Stayman, D. M., & Hagerty, M. R. (1986). Warmth in advertising: Measurement, impact, and sequence effects. *Journal of Consumer Research, 12*(4), 365–381.

Adams, J. S. (1963). Towards an understanding of inequity. *Journal of Abnormal and Social Psychology, 67,* 422–436.

Aiello, A, Czepiel, J. A., & Rosenberg, L. J. (1977). Scaling the heights of consumer satisfaction: An evaluation of alternative measures. In R. L. Day (Ed.), *Consumer satisfaction/dissatisfaction and complaining behavior* (pp. 43–50). Bloomington, IN: Indiana University.

Alba, J. W., & Chattopadhyay, A. (1986). Salience effects in brand recall. *Journal of Marketing Research, 23,* 363–369.

Alba, J. W., & Marmorstein, H. (1987). The effects of frequency knowledge on consumer decision making. *Journal of Consumer Research, 14*(1), 14–25.

Aldag, R. J., & Brief, A. P. (1978). Examinations of alternative models of job satisfaction. *Human Relations, 31,* 91–98.

Alpert, M., Golden, L. L., & Hoyer, W. D. (1983). The impact of repetition on advertising miscomprehension and effectiveness. In R. P. Bagozzi & A. Tybout (Eds.), *Advances in Consumer Research, 10* (pp. 130–135). Ann Arbor, MI: Association for Consumer Research.

American Psychological Association. (1965). Guidelines for doctoral education in industrial psychology. *American Psychologist, 20,* 822–831.

Anderson, R. E. (1973, February). Consuler dissatisfaction: The effect of disconcerned expectancy on perceived product performance. *Journal of Marketing Research, 10,* 38–44.

Andrews, F. M., & Whithey, S. B. (1976). *Social indicators of well-being.* New York: Plenum Press.

Arndt, J. (1967a). Perceived risk, sociometric integration, and word of mouth in the adoption of a new product. In D. F. Cox (Ed.), *Risk taking and information handling in consumer behavior* (pp. 289–316). Cambridge, MA: Harvard University Press.

Arndt, J. (1967b). *Word of mouth advertising.* New York: Advertising Research Foundation.

Arndt, J. (1967c). Word of mouth advertising and informal communication. In D. F. Cox (Ed.), *Risk taking and information handling in consumer behavior* (pp. 188–239). Cambridge, MA: Harvard University Press.

Arnold, H. J. (1981). A test of the validity of the multiplicative hypothesis of expectancy-valence theories of work motivation. *Academy of Management Journal, 24,* 128–141.

Ash, S. B. (1978). *Consumer satisfaction/dissatisfaction and complaining behavior with durable products.* Unpublished doctoral dissertation, Indiana University, Bloomington.

Ash, S. B., Gardiner, D. F., & Quelch, J. A. (1980). Consumer satisfaction and dissatisfaction in the elderly market. In R. L. Day & H. K. Hunt (Eds.), *New findings on consumer satisfaction and complaining* (pp. 86–96). Bloomington, IN: Indiana University.

Ashford, S. J., & Cummings, L. L. (1983). Feedback as an individual resource: Personal strategies of creating information. *Organizational Behavior and Human Performances, 32,* 370–398.

Atkinson, J. W. (Ed.). (1958). *Motives in fantasy, action, and society.* Princeton, NJ: Van Nostrand.

Bartlett, J., & Santrock, J. (1979). Affect-dependent episodic memory in young children. *Child Development, 50*(2), 513–518.

Bass, F. M., & Talarzyk, W. W. (1972). An attitude model for the study of brand preference. *Journal of Marketing Research, 9,* 93–96.

Batra, R., & Ray, M. L. (1983). Advertising situations: The implications of differential involvment and accompanying affect responses. In R. J. Harris (Ed.), *Information processing research in advertising* (pp. 127–151). Hillsdale, NJ: Erlbaum.

Batra, R., & Ray, M. L. (1984). How advertising works at contact. In L. Alwitt & A. A. Mitchell (Eds.), *Psychological processes and advertising effects: Theory, research, and application* (pp. 13–43). Hillsdale, NJ: Erlbaum.

Batra, R., & Ray, M. L. (1986a). Affective responses mediating acceptance of advertising. *Journal of Consumer Research, 13*(2), 234–249.

Batra, R., & Ray, M. L. (1986b). Situational effects of advertising repetition: The moderating influence of motivation, ability, and opportunity to respond. *Journal of Consumer Research, 12*(4), 432–35.

Bauer, R. A. (1963). The initiative of the audience. *Journal of Advertising Research, 3,* 2–7.

Baumgarten, S. A. (1971). *The male fashion change agent on the college campus.* Unpublished doctoral dissertation, Purdue University, West Lafayette, IN.

Beach, L., & Mitchell, T. R. (1978). A contingency model for the selection of decision strategies. *Academy of Management Review, 3,* 439–449.

Beardon, W. O., Crockett, M., & Graham, S. (1979). Consumers' propensity to complain and dissatisfaction with automobile repairs. In H. K. Hunt & R. L. Day (Eds.), *Refining concepts and measures of consumer satisfaction and complaining behavior* (pp. 35–43). Bloomington, IN: Indiana University.

Beattie, A. E. (1982). Effects of product knowledge on comparison, memory, evaluation, and choice: A model of expertise in consumer decision making. In A. Mitchell (Ed.), *Advances in Consumer Research, 9* (pp. 336–341). Ann Arbor, MI: Association for Consumer Research.

Beatty, S. E., & Smith, S. M. (1987). External search effort: An investigation across several product categories. *Journal of Consumer Research, 14*(1), 83–95.

Belk, R. W. (1971). Occurence of word-of-mouth buyer behavior as a function of situation and advertising stimuli. In F. C. Allvine (Ed.), *Combined proceedings of the American Marketing Association,* 419–422.

Belk, R. W. (1975). Situational variables and consumer behavior. *Journal of Consumer Research, 2*(3), 157–164.

Bell, W. E. (1963). Consumer innovators: A unique market for newness. In S. A. Greyser (Ed.), *Toward scientific marketing. Proceedings of the winter conference of the American Marketing Association* (pp. 85–95). Chicago: American Marketing Association.

Bellizi, J. A., Crowley, A. E., & Hasty, R. W. (1983, Spring). The effects of color in store design. *Journal of Retailing, 59,* 21–45.

Bennett, P. D., & Mandell, R. M. (1969, November). Prepurchase information seeking behavior of new car purchasers—The learning hypothesis. *Journal of Marketing Research, 6,* 430–433.

Berning, C. A. K., & Jacoby, J. (1974). Patterns of information acquisition in new product purchases. *Journal of Consumer Research, 1*(2), 18–22.

Bettman, J. R. (1970). Information processing models of consumer behavior. *Journal of Marketing Research, 7,* 370–376.

Bettman, J. R. (1977). Data collection and analysis approaches for studying consumer information processing. In W. D. Perrault (Ed.), *Advances in Consumer Research, 4* (pp. 241–247). Atlanta: Association for Consumer Research.

Bettman, J. R. (1979). *An information processing theory of consumer choice.* Reading, MA: Addison-Wesley.

Bettman, J. R. (1979). Memory factors in consumer choice. *Journal of Marketing, 43*(2), 37–53.

Bettman, J. R., Capon, N., & Lutz, R. J. (1975). Cognitive algebra in multi-attribute models. *Journal of Marketing Research, 12,* 151–164.

Bettman, J. R., & Kakkar, P. (1977). Effects of information presentation format on consumer information acquisition strategies. *Journal of Consumer Research, 3,* 233–240.

Bettman, J. R., & Park, C. W. (1980). Effects of prior knowledge and experience and phase of the choice process on consumer decision processes: A protocol analysis. *Journal of Consumer Research, 7*(3), 234–248.

Bettman, J. R., & Zins, M. A. (1977). Constructive choice processes in consumer choice. *Journal of Consumer Research, 4,* 75–85.

Bennett, P. D., & Mandell, R. M. (1969). Prepurchase information-seeking behavior and new car purchases: The learning hypothesis. *Journal of Marketing Research, 6,* 430–433.

Biehal, G., & Chakravarti, D. (1982a). Consumers' use of memory and external information in choice: Macro and micro perspectives. *Journal of Consumer Research, 12*(4), 382–405.

Biehal, G., & Chakravarti, D. (1982b, March). Information presentation format and learning goals as determinants of consumers' memory-retrieval and choice processes. *Journal of Consumer Research, 8,* 431–441.

Biehal, G., & Chakravarti, D. (1983, June). Information accessibility as a moderator of consumer choice. *Journal of Consumer Research, 10,* 1–14.

Biehal, G., & Chakravarti, D. (1989). The effects of concurrent verbalization on choice processing. *Journal of Marketing Research, 26,* 84–96.

Bohlen, J. M., Coughenour, C. M., Lionberger, H. F., Moe, E. O., & Rogers, E. M. (1968). Adopters of new farm ideas. In H. H. Kassarjian & T. S. Robertson (Eds.), *Perpectives in consumer behavior* (pp. 351–361). Glenview, IL: Scott, Foresman.

Bower, G., Monteiro, K. P., & Gilligan, S. (1978). Emotional mood as a context for learning and recall. *Journal of Learning and Verbal Behavior, 17,* 573–585.

Brief, A. P., Delbecq, A. L., Filley, A. C., & Huber, G. P. (1976). Elite structure and values: An empirical analysis of adaptation behavior. *Administration and Society, 8,* 227–248.

Brief, A. P., & Roberson, L. (in press). Job attitude organization: An exploratory study. *Journal of Applied Social Psychology.*

Brockner, J., & Rubin, J. Z. (1985). *Entrapment in escalating conflicts.* New York: Springer-Verlag.

Brown, J., & Reinger, P. H. (1987). Social ties and word-of-mouth referral behavior. *Journal of Consumer Research, 14*(3), 350–362.

Burke, M. C., & Edell, J. A. (1986). Reactions over time: Capturing changes in the real world. *Journal of Consumer Research, 13,* 56–65.

Burke, M. C., & Edell, J. A. (1989). The impact of feelings on ad-based affect and cognition. *Journal of Marketing Research, 26,* 69–83.

Cacioppo, J. T. (1977). *Heart rate, cognitive response, and persuasion.* Unpublished doctoral dissertation, Ohio State University, Columbus.

Cacioppo, J. T., Sandman, C. A., & Walker, B. B. (1978). The effect of operant heart rate conditioning on cognitive elaboration and attitude change. *Psychophysiology, 15,* 330–338.

Calder, B. J., Insko, C. A., & Yandell, B. (1974). The relation of cognitive and memorial processes to persuasion in a simulated jury trial. *Journal of Applied Social Psychology, 4,* 62–93.

Campbell, D. T., & Stanley, J. C. (1963). *Experimental and quasi-experimental designs for research.* Chicago: Rand McNally.

Campbell, J. P., Dunnette, M. D., Lawler, E. E., III, & Weick, K. E., Jr. (1970). *Managerial behavior and human performance.* New York: McGraw-Hill.

Cardozo, R. N. (1965). An experimental study of consumer effort, expectation, and satisfaction. *Journal of Marketing Research, 2,* 244–249.

Celsi, R. L., & Olson, J. C. (1988). The role of involvement in attention and comprehension processes. *Journal of Consumer Research, 15* (2), 210–224.

Chaiken, S. (1980). Heuristic versus systematic information processing and the use of source versus message cues in persuasion. *Journal of Personality and Social Psychology, 39*, 752–766.

Chaiken, S., & Eagly, A. (1976). Communication modality as a determinant of message persuasiveness and message comprehensibility. *Journal of Personality and Social Psychology, 34*(4), 605–614.

Chattopadhyay, A., & Alba, J. W. (1988). The situational importance of recall and inference in consumer decision making. *Journal of Consumer Research, 15*(1), 1–12.

Chestnut, R. W. (1977). *Life insurance policy selection: Monitoring the impact of product beliefs, affect toward agent, and external memory.* Unpublished doctoral dissertation, Purdue University, West Lafayette, IN.

Chestnut, R. W., & Jacoby, J. (1977). Consumer information processing: Emerging theory and findings. In A. G. Woodside, J. N. Sheth, & P. D. Bennett (Eds.), *Consumer and industrial buying behavior* (pp. 119–133). New York: Elsevier North-Holland.

Churchill, G. A., Jr., & Surprenant, C. (1982). An investigation into the determinants of customer satisfaction. *Journal of Marketing Research, 19*, 491–504.

Claxton, J. D., Fry, J. N., & Portis, B. (1974). A taxonomy of prepurchase information-gathering patterns. *Journal of Consumer Research, 1*(3), 35–42.

Cobb, C. J., & Hoyer, W. D. (1985). The influence of advertising at moment of brand choice. *Journal of Advertising, 14*(4), 5–27.

Cohen, J. B., Miniard, P. W., & Dickson, P. R. (1980). Information integration: An information processing perspective. In J. C. Olson (Ed.), *Advances in Consumer Research, 7* (pp. 161–170). Ann Arbor, MI: Association for Consumer Research.

Colley, R. (1961). *Defining advertising goals for measured advertising results.* New York: Association of National Advertisers.

Coney, K. A. (1973). Dogmatism and innovation: A replication. *Journal of Marketing Research, 9*, 453–455.

Cook, T. D. (1969). Competence, counterarguing, and attitude change. *Journal of Personality, 37*, 342–358.

Cook, T. D., & Campbell, D. T. (1976). The design and conduct of quasi-experiments and true experiments in field settings. In M. D. Dunnette (Ed.), *Handbook of industrial and organizational psychology* (1st ed., pp. 223–326). Chicago: Rand McNally.

Cooper, R. G. (1981, Spring). The myth of a better mousetrap: What makes a new product a sucess? *Business Quarterly, 69*–81.

Cox, D. F. (1962). The measurement of information value: A study in consumer decision making. In W. S. Decker (Ed.), *Emerging concepts in marketing. Proceedings of the Winter Conference of the American Marketing Association* (pp. 413–421). Chicago: American Marketing Association.

Cox, D. F. (1963). The audience as communicators. In S. A. Greyser (Ed.), *Toward scientific marketing* (pp. 58-72). Chicago: American Marketing Association.

Cox, D. F. (1967). Risk taking and information handling in consumer behavior. In D. F. Cox (Ed.), *Risk taking and information handling in consumer behavior* (pp. 604–639). Cambridge, MA: Harvard University Press.

Cunningham, S. M. (1967). Perceived risk as a factor in informal communications. In D. F. Cox (Ed.), *Risk taking and information handling in consumer behavior* (pp. 265–288). Cambridge, MA: Harvard University Press.

Cyert, R. M., & March, J. G. (1955, March). Organizational structure and pricing behavior in an oligopolistic market. *American Economic Review,* 129–139.

Czepiel, J. A. (1974). Word-of-mouth processes in the diffusion of a major technological innovation. *Journal of Marketing Research, 11*, 172–180.

Czepiel, J. A., & Rosenberg, L. (1976). Consumer satisfaction: Toward an integrative framework. *Proceedings of the Southern Marketing Association,* 169–171.

Czepiel, J. A., & Rosenberg, L. (1977). The study of consumer satisfaction: Addressing the "so what" question. In H. K. Hunt (Ed.), *Conceptualization and measurement of consumer satisfaction and dissatisfaction* (pp. 92–119). Cambridge, MA: Marketing Science Institute.

Darden, W. R., & Rao, C. P. (1977). Satisfaction with repairs under warranty and perceived importance of warranties for appliances. In R. L. Day (Ed.), *Consumer satisfaction/dissatisfaction and complaining behavior* (pp. 167–170). Bloomington, IN: Indiana University.

Davidson, A. R., & Jaccard, J. J. (1975). Population psychology: A new look at an old problem. *Journal of Personality and Social Psychology, 31*(6), 1073–1082.

Davis, K. (1959). Making constructive use of the office grapevine. In K. Davis & W. G. Scott (Eds.), *Readings in human relations*. New York: McGraw-Hill.

Day, R. L. (1980). How satisfactory is research on consumer satisfaction? In J. C. Olson (Ed.), *Advances in Consumer Research , 7* (pp. 593–597). Ann Arbor, MI: Association for Consumer Research.

Day, R. L. (1984). Modelling choices among alternative responses to dissatisfaction. In T. C. Kinnear (Ed.), *Advances in consumer research* (pp. 496–499). Provo, UT: Association for Consumer Research.

Day, R. L., & Bodur, M. (1977). A comprehensive study of satisfaction with consumer services. In R. L. Day (Ed.), *Consumer satisfaction/dissatisfaction and complaining behavior* (pp. 64–74). Bloomington, IN: Indiana University.

Day, R. L., & Ash, S. (1978). Comparison of patterns of satisfaction/dissatisfaction and complaining behavior for durables, non-durables, and services. In R. L. Day & H. K. Hunt (Eds.), *New dimensions of consumer satisfaction and complaining behavior* (pp. 190–195). Bloomington, IN: Indiana University.

Deshpande, R., Hoyer, W. D., & Jeffries, S. (1982). Low involvement decision processes: The importance of choice tactics. In R. F. Bush & S. D. Hunt (Eds.), *Marketing theory: Philosophy of science perspectives* (pp.155–158). Chicago: American Marketing Association.

DeNisi, A. S., Cafferty, T. P., & Meglino, B. M. (1984). A cognitive view of the performance appraisal process: A model and research proposition. *Organizational Behavior and Human Performance, 33,* 360–396.

Dichter, E. (1966). How word of mouth advertising works. *Harvard Business Review, 44,* 147–166.

Diener, B. J., & Greyser, S. A. (1978). Consumer views of redress needs. *Journal of Marketing, 42,* 21–27.

Dipboye, R. L., Stramler, C. S., & Fontonell, G. A. (1984). The effects of the application on recall of information from the interview. *Academy of Management Journal, 27,* 561–575.

Donnelly, J. H., Jr., & Ivancevich, J. M. (1974). A methodology for identifying innovator characteristics of new brand purchasers. *Journal of Marketing Research, 3,* 331–334.

Doran, L. (1986). *Consumer satisfaction: Comparative overview and review.* Unpublished manuscript, New York University.

Dudycha, L. W., & Naylor, J. C. (1966). Characteristics of the human inference process in complex choice behavior situations. *Organizational Behavior and Human Performance, 1,* 110–128.

Dutton, J. E. (1986). Understanding strategic agenda building in organizations and its implications for managing change. *Scandinavian Journal of Management Studies, 3,* 3–24.

Dutton, J. E., & Duncan, R. (1987). The influence of strategic planning on strategic change. *Strategic Management Journal, 8,* 103–116.

Dutton, J. M., & Freedman, R. D. (1985). External environment and internal strategies: Calculating, experimenting and imitating in organizations. In R. Lamb & P. Shrivastava (Eds.), *Advances in strategic management* (Vol. III). New York: JAI Press.

Eagly, A., & Chaiken, S. (1984). Cognitive theories of persuasion. In *Advances in Experimental Social Psychology, 17* (pp. 267–359). New York: Academic Press.

Eagly, A. H., & Chaiken, S. (1984). Cognitive theories of persuasion. In *Advances in Experimental Social Psychology, 17* (pp. 267–359). New York: Academic Press.

Edell, J. A., & Burke, M. C. (1987). The power of feelings in understanding advertising effects. *Journal of Consumer Research, 14*(3), 421–433.

Edwards, W. (1954). The theory of decision making. *Psychological Bulletin, 51,* 380–417.

Engel, J. F., Blackwell, R. D., & Miniard, P. (1986). *Consumer behavior* (5th ed.). Hinsdale, IL: Dryden Press.

Engel, J. F., Kegerreis, R. J., & Blackwell, R. D. (1969). Word of mouth communication by the innovator. *Journal of Marketing, 33,* 15–19.

Feldman, S., & Spencer, M. (1965). The effect of personal influence in the selection of consumer services. In P. D. Bennett (Ed.), *Proceedings of the Fall conference of the American Marketing Association* (pp. 440–452). Chicago: American Marketing Association.

Feldman, S. P. (1966). Some dyadic relationships associated with consumer choice. In R. M. Haas (Ed.), *Science technology and marketing* (758–776). Chicago: American Marketing Association.

Ferguson, L. W. (1962). *The heritage of industrial psychology.* Hartford, CT: Finlay Press.

Festinger, L. (1957). *A theory of cognitive dissonance.* Stanford, CA: Stanford University Press.

Fishbein, M. (1963). An investigation of the relationships between belief about an object and the attitude toward the object. *Human Relations, 16,* 233–240.

Fishbein, M. (1967). Attitude and prediction of behavior. In M. Fishbein (Ed.), *Readings in attitude theory and measurement.* New York: Wiley.

Fishbein, M., & Ajzen, I. (1975). *Belief, attitude, intention, and behavior: An introduction to theory and research.* Reading, MA: Wesley.

Fiske, S. T. (1982). Schema-triggered affect: Applications to social perception. In M. S. Clark & S. T. Fiske (Eds.), *Affect and cognition: The 17th annual Carnegie symposium on cognition* (pp. 55–78). Hillsdale, NJ: Erlbaum.

Folkes, V. S. (1984). Consumer reactions to product failure: An attributional approach. *Journal of Consumer Research, 10,* 398–409.

Ford, G. T., & Yalch, R. (1982). Viewer miscomprehension of televised communication: A comment. *Journal of Marketing, 46*(4), 27–31.

Ford, G. T., & Smith, R. A. (1987). Inferential beliefs in consumer evaluations: An assessment of alternative processing strategies. *Journal of Consumer Research, 14*(3), 363–371.

Frank, R. E., Massy, W. F., & Morrison, D. G. (1964). The determinants of innovative behavior with respect to a branded, frequently purchased food product. In *Proceedings of the American Marketing Association* (pp. 312–323). Chicago: American Marketing Association.

Furse, D. H., Punj, G. N., & Stewart, D. W. (1984). A typology of individual search strategies among purchasers of new automobiles. *Journal of Consumer Research, 10*(4), 417–431.

Gardner, M. P. (1985a). Does attitude toward the ad affect brand attitude under a brand evaluation set? *Journal of Marketing Research, 22,* 192–198.

Gardner, M. P. (1985b). Mood states and consumer research: A critical review. *Journal of Consumer Research, 12*(3), 281–300.

Gardner, M. P., Mitchell, A. A., & Russo, J. E. (1978). Chronometric analysis: An introduction and an application to low involvement perception of advertisements. In H. K. Hunt (Ed.), *Advances in Consumer Research, 5* (pp. 581–589). Chicago: Association for Consumer Research.

Gates, F. R. (1986, January). Further comment on the miscomprehension of televised advertisements. *Journal of Advertising, 15,* 4–9.

Gates, F. R., & Hoyer, W. D. (1986). Measuring miscomprehension: A comparison of alternative formats. In R. Lutz (Ed.), *Advances in Consumer Research, 13,* 143–146. Provo, UT: Association for Consumer Research.

Gioia, D. A. (1986). Symbols, scripts, and sensemaking: Creating meaning in organizational experience. In H. P. Sims, Jr., D. A. Gioia, & Associates (Eds.), *The thinking organization.* San Francisco: Jossey-Bass.

Gioia, D. A., & Manz, C. C. (1985). Linking cognition and behavior: A script-processing interpretation of vicarious learning. *Academy of Management Review, 10,* 527–539.

Gioia, D. A., & Poole, P. P. (1984). Scripts in organizational behavior. *Academy of Management Review, 9,* 449–459.

Goldberg, M. E., & Gorn, G. J. (1987, December). Happy and sad TV programs: How they affect reactions to commercials. *Journal of Consumer Research, 14,* 387–403.

Gorn, G. J. (1982). The effects of music in advertising on choice behavior: A classical conditioning approach. *Journal of Marketing, 46,* 94–101.

Graen, G. (1969). Instrumentality theory of work motivation: Some experimental results and suggested modifications [Monograph]. *Journal of Applied Psychology, 53,* (2, Pt. 2).

Granzin, K. L., & Schelderup, K. H. (1982). Situation as an influence on anticipated satisfaction. In

A. Mitchell (Ed.), *Advances in consumer research*, 9 (pp. 234–238). Ann Arbor, MI: Association for Consumer Research.

Green, R., Mitchell, A. A., & Staelin, R. (1977). Longitudinal decision studies using a process approach: Some results from a preliminary experiment. In B. A. Greenberg & D. N. Bellenger (Eds.), *Contemporary marketing thought* (pp. 461–466). Chicago: American Marketing Assocation.

Greenstein, M., Miller, R. H., & Weldon, D. E. (1979). Attitudinal and normative beliefs as antecedents of female occupational choice. *Personality and Social Psychology Bulletin, 5,* 356–362.

Greenwald, A. G., & Leavitt, C. (1984). Audience involvement in advertising: Four levels. *Journal of Consumer Research, 11*(1), 581–592.

Grossbart, S., Amedeo, D., & Chinchan, D. (1979). The influence of retail environments on consumer cognitions and feelings. In N. Beckwith et al. (Eds.), *1979 Educators' Conference Proceedings* (pp. 268–273). Chicago: American Marketing Association.

Guion, R. M. (1965). Industrial psychology as an academic discipline. *American Psychologist, 20,* 815–821.

Haedrich, G., & Kuss, A. (1986). Messung des missverstandnisses von werbebotschaften bei kindern underwachsenen. In H. Haase & K. Koeppler (Eds.), *Fortschrifte der Marktpsychologie, 4*. Frankfurt, West Germany.

Hammond, K. R., McClelland, G. H., & Mumpower, J. (1980). *Human judgment and decision making: Theories, methods, & procedures.* New York: Praeger.

Hansen, F. (1969). Consumer choice behavior: An experimental approach. *Journal of Marketing Research, 6,* 436–443.

Harris, R. J., Dubitsky, T. M., & Bruno, K. J. (1983). Psycholinguistic studies of misleading advertising. In R. J. Harris (Ed.), *Information processing research in advertising.* Hillsdale, NJ: Erlbaum.

Harrison, A. A. (1977). Mere exposure. In L. Berkowitz (Ed.), *Advances in experimental social psychology, 10* (pp. 39–83). New York: Academic Press.

Hart, E. W., & Jacoby, J. (1973). The relationship of perceived newness to novelty, recency, and scarcity. *Proceedings of the 81st annual convention of the American Psychological Association, 8*(2), 839–840.

Hawkins, C. K., & Lanzetta, J. T. (1965, December). Uncertainty, importance and arousal as determinants of predecisional imformation search. *Psychological Reports, 17,* 791–800.

Helson, H. (1964). *Adaption level theory.* New York: Harper & Row.

Henne, D., & Locke, E. A. (1985). Job dissatisfaction: What are the consequences. *International Journal of Psychology, 20,* 221–240.

Herzberg, F., Mausner, B., & Snyderman, B. (1959). *The motivation to work.* New York: Wiley.

Hirschman, E. C. (1982). Symbolism and technology as sources for the generation of innovations. In A. Mitchell (Ed.), *Advances in Consumer Research, 9* (pp. 537–541). Ann Arbor, MI: Association for Consumer Research.

Hirschman, E. C., & Adcock, W. O. (1978). An examination of innovative communications, opinion leaders, and innovators for men's fashion apparel. In H. K. Hunt (Ed.), *Advances in Consumer Research* (pp. 308–314). Ann Arbor, MI: Association for Consumer Research.

Hirschman, E. C., & Holbrook, M. B. (1982). Hedonic consumption: Emerging concepts, methods, and propositions. *Journal of Marketing, 46,* 92–101.

Hogarth, R. M. (1981). Beyond discrete biases: Functional and dysfunctioal aspects of judgmental heuristics. *Psychological Bulletin, 90*(2), 197–217.

Holbrook, M. B., & Batra, R. (1987). Assessing the role of emotions as mediators of consumer responses to advertising. *Journal of Consumer Research, 14*(3), 404–420.

Holmes, J. D., & Lett, J. D. (1977). Product sampling and word-of-mouth. *Journal of Advertising Research, 17,* 35–39.

Hovland, C. I., Janis, I. L., & Kelley, H. H. (1953). *Communications and persuasion.* New Haven, CT: Yale University Press.

Howard, J. A., & Sheth, J. N. (1969). *The theory of buyer behavior.* New York: Wiley.

Hoyer, W. D. (1979). *Contraceptive usage decision making: An information processing approach.* Unpublished masters thesis, Purdue University, West Lafayette, IN.

Hoyer, W. D. (1980). *The influence of memory factors on contraceptive information acquisition and choice.* Unpublished doctoral dissertation, Purdue University, West Lafayette, IN.

Hoyer, W. D. (1984, December). An examination of consumer decision making for a common repeat purchase product. *Journal of Consumer Research,* 11, 822–829.

Hoyer, W. D., & Jacoby, J. (1983). Three dimensional information acquisition: An application to contraceptive decision making. In R. P. Bagozzi & A. M. Tybout (Eds.), *Advances in consumer research,* 10 (pp. 618–623). Ann Arbor, MI: Association for Consumer Research.

Hoyer, W. D., & Jacoby, J. (1985).The public's miscomprehension of public affairs programming. *Journal of Broadcasting and Electronic Media,* 29(4), 437–443.

Hoyer, W. D., Srivastava, R. K., & Jacoby, J. (1984). Examining the sources of advertising miscomprehension. *Journal of Advertising,* 13(2), 17–26.

Hughes, D. A. (1977). An investigation of the relation of selected factors to consumer socialization. In H. K. Hunt (Ed.), *Conceptualization and measurement of consumer satisfaction and dissatisfaction* (pp. 300–332). Cambridge, MA: Marketing Science Institute.

Hunt, H. K. (Ed.). (1977). *Conceptualization and measurement of consumer satisfaction and dissatisfaction.* Cambridge, MA: Marketing Science Institute.

Hupfer, N. T., & Gardner, D. M. (1971). Differential involvement with products and issues: An exploratory study. In D. M. Gardner (Ed.), *Proceedings of the 2nd annual conference of the Association for Consumer Research* (pp. 83–92). College Park, MD: Association for Consumer Research.

Hutchinson, J. W., & Moore, D. L. (1984). Issues surrounding the examination of delay effects of advertising. In T. C. Kinnear (Ed.), *Advances in consumer research,* 11 (pp. 650–655). Provo, UT: Association for Consumer Research.

Ilgen, D. R., Fisher, C. D., & Taylor, M. S. (1979). Consequences of individual feedback on behavior in organizations. *Journal of Applied Psychology,* 64, 349–371.

Isen, A. (1984). Toward understanding the role of affect in cognition. In R. J. Wyer, Jr., & T. Srull (Eds.), *Handbook of social cognition* (pp. 179–236). Hillsdale, NJ: Erlbaum.

Isen, A., & Shalker, T. (1982). The effect of feeling state on evaluation of positive, neutral, and negative stimuli: When you "accentuate the positive" do you "eliminate the negative"? *Social Psychology Quarterly,* 45(1), 58–63.

Isen, A., Shalker, T., Clark, M., & Karp, L. (1978, January). Affect, accessibility of material in memory, and behavior: A cognitive loop? *Journal of Personality and Social Psychology,* 36, 1–12.

Jacoby, J. (1971). Innovation proneness as a function of personality. *Journal of Marketing Research,* 8, 244–247.

Jacoby, J. (1975a). Consumer psychology as a social psychological sphere of action. *American Psychologist,* 30(10), 977–987.

Jacoby, J. (1975b). Perspectives on a consumer information processing research program. *Communication Research,* 2, 203–215.

Jacoby, J. (1976a). Consumer psychology: An octennium. In P. Mussen & M. Rosenzweig (Eds.), *Annual Review of Psychology,* 27, 331–358.

Jacoby, J. (1976b). Consumer and industrial psychology: Prospects for theory corroboration and mutual contribution. In M. D. Dunnette (Ed.), *Handbook of industrial and organizational psychology* (1st ed., pp. 1031–1061). Chicago: Rand McNally.

Jacoby, J. (1977). The emerging behavioral decision process technology in consumer decision making research. In W. D. Perrault (Ed.), *Advances in Consumer Research,* 4 (pp. 263–265). Atlanta: Association for Consumer Research.

Jacoby, J. (1984). Perspectives on information overload. *Journal of Consumer Research,* 10(4), 432–435.

Jacoby, J., Chestnut, R. W., & Fisher, W. A. (1978). A behavioral process approach to information acquisition in nondurable purchasing. *Journal of Marketing Research,* 15, 532–544.

Jacoby, J., Chestnut, R. W., & Silberman, W. (1977). Consumer use and comprehension of nutrition information. *Journal of Consumer Research,* 4(2), 119–128.

Jacoby, J., Chestnut, R. W., Weigl, K., & Fisher, W. A. (1976). Prepurchase information acquisition: Description of a process methodology, research paradigm, and pilot investigation. In B. B. Anderson (Ed.), *Advances in consumer research* (pp. 306–314). Cincinnati: Association for Consumer Research.

Jacoby, J., & Hoyer, W. D. (1981). What if opinion leaders didn't know more? A question of nomological validity. In K. B. Monroe (Ed.), *Advances in Consumer Research,* 8 (pp. 299–303).

Ann Arbor, MI: Association for Consumer Research.

Jacoby, J., & Hoyer, W. D. (1982a). Viewer miscomprehension of televised communication: Selected findings. *Journal of Marketing, 46*(4), 12–26.

Jacoby, J., & Hoyer, W. D. (1982b). On miscomprehending televised communication: A rejoinder. *Journal of Marketing, 46*(4), 35–43.

Jacoby, J., & Hoyer, W. D. (1987). *The comprehension and miscomprehension of print communication.* Hillsdale, NJ: Erlbaum.

Jacoby, J., Hoyer, W. D., & Sheluga, D. A. (1980). *Miscomprehension of televised communications.* New York: American Association of Advertising Agencies.

Jacoby, J., Hoyer, W. D., & Zimmer, M. R. (1983). To read, view or listen? A cross-media comparison of comprehension. In J. H. Leigh & C. R. Martin, Jr. (Eds.), *Current issues and research in advertising* (pp. 201–218). Ann Arbor, MI: The University of Michigan.

Jacoby, J., Jaccard, J. J., Kuss, A., Troutman, T., & Mazursky, D. (1987). New directions in behavioral process research: Implications for social psychology. *Journal of Experimental Social Psychology, 23*(2), 146–174.

Jacoby, J., Kuss, A., Mazursky, D., & Troutman, T. (1985). Effectiveness of security analyst information accessing strategies: A computer interactive assessment. *Computers in Human Behavior, 1,* 95–113.

Jacoby, J., Mazursky, D., Troutman, T., & Kuss, A. (1984). When feedback is ignored: The disutility of outcome feedback. *Journal of Applied Psychology, 69,* 531–545.

Jacoby, J., Nelson, M. C., & Hoyer, W. D. (1982). Corrective advertising and affirmative disclosure statements: Their potential for confusing and misleading the consumer. *Journal of Marketing, 46*(1), 61–72.

Jacoby, J., & Olson, J. C. (1974). An extended expectancy model of consumer comparison processes. In S. Ward & P. Wright (Eds.), *Advances in Consumer Research* (Vol. 1, pp. 319–333). Urbana, IL: Association for Consumer Research

Jacoby, J., Speller, D. A., & Kohn, C. A. (1974). Brand choice behavior as a function of information load. *Journal of Marketing Research, 11*(1), 63–69.

Jacoby, J., Speller, D. A., & Berning, C. A. K. (1974). Brand choice and behavior as a function of information load: Replication and extension. *Journal of Consumer Research, 1*(1), 33–42.

Jacoby, J., Szybillo, G. J., & Berning, C. A. K. (1976). Time and consumer behavior: An interdisciplinary overview. *Journal of Consumer Research, 2*(3), 320–339.

Jacoby, J., Troutman, T., & Whittler, T. (1986). Viewer miscomprehension of the 1980 Presidential Debate. *Political Psychology, 7*(2), 297–308.

Johnson, E. J., & Russo, J. E. (1978). The organization of product information in memory identified by recall times. In H. K. Hunt (Ed.), *Advances in Consumer Research, 5* (pp. 79–86). Chicago: Association for Consumer Research.

Johnson, E. J., & Tversky, A. (1983). Affect generalization and the perception of risk. *Journal of Personality and Social Psychology, 45*(1), 20–31.

Johnson, M. D. (1988). Comparability and hierarchical processing in multi-alternative choice. *Journal of Consumer Research, 15*(3), 303–314.

Kardes, F. R. (1986). Effects of initial product judgments on subsequent memory-based judgments. *Journal of Consumer Research, 13*(1), 1–11.

Kassarjian, H. H. (1978). Presidential address 1977: Anthropomorphism and parsimony. In H. K. Hunt (Ed.), *Advances in Consumer Research, 5* (pp. xiii–xiv). Ann Arbor, MI: Association for Consumer Research.

Katz, E. (1957). The two-step flow of communication: An up-to-date report on an operating hypothesis. *Public Opinion Quarterly, 20,* 61–78.

Katz, E., & Lazarsfeld, P. F. (1955). *Personal influence: The part played by people in the flow of mass communications.* Glencoe, IL: Free Press.

Katz, R., Adoni, H., & Parness, P. (1977). Remembering the news: What the picture adds to recall. *Journalism Quarterly, 54,* 231–239.

Katzell, R. A. (1958). Industrial psychology. *Annual Review of Psychology, 9,* 237–268.

Keating, J. P., & Brock, T. C. (1974). Acceptance of persuasion and inhibition of counterargumentation under various distraction tasks. *Journal of Experimental Social Psychology, 10,* 301–309.

Keller, K. L. (1987). Memory factors in advertising: The effect of advertising retrieval cues in brand evaluations. *Journal of Consumer Research, 14*(3), 316–333.

Keller, K. L., & Staelin, R. (1987). Effects of quality and quantity of information on decision effectiveness. *Journal of Consumer Research, 14*(2), 200–213.

King, C. W. (1963). Fashion adoption: A rebuttal to the "trickle down" theory. In S. Greyser (Ed.), *Proceedings of the winter conference of the American Marketing Association* (pp. 108–128). Chicago: American Marketing Association.

King, C. W., & Summers, J. O. (1967). Dynamics of interpersonal communication: The interaction dyad. In D. F. Cox (Ed.), *Risk taking and information handling in consumer behavior* (pp. 240–264). Cambridge: Harvard University Press.

King, C. W., & Summers, J. O. (1970). Overlap of opinion leadership across consumer product categories. *Journal of Marketing Research, 7*, 43–50.

Klein, N. M., & Bither, S. W. (1987). An investigation of utility-directed cut-off selection. *Journal of Consumer Research, 14*(2), 240–256.

Kopelman, R. E. (1986). *Managing productivity in organizations.* New York: McGraw-Hill.

Krishnamurthi, L. (1983). The salience of relevant others and its effect on individual and joint preference: An experimental investigation. *Journal of Consumer Research, 10*(1), 62–72.

Krugman, H. E. (1965). The impact of TV advertising: Learning without involvement. *Public Opinion Quarterly, 29*, 349–356.

Kunst-Wilson, W. R., & Zajonc, R. B. (1980). Affective discrimination of stimuli that cannot be recognized. *Science, 207*, 557–558.

Kuss, A. (1985). Missverstaendnis von Fernsehwerbung. *Werbeforschung und Praxis, 6.*

Lacey, B. C., & Lacey, J. I. (1974). Studies in heart rate and other bodily processes in sensorimotor behavior. In P. A. Obrist, A. H. Block, J. Brener, & L. V. Dicara (Eds.), *Cardiovascular psychophysiology.* Chicago: Aldine Publishing.

Lampert, S. I. (1974). Word-of-mouth activity during the introduction of a new food product. In J. V. Farley, J. A. Howard, & L. W. Ring (Eds.), *Consumer behavior: Theory and application* (pp. 67–88). Boston: Allyn & Bacon.

Landy, F. J. (1978). An opponent process theory of job satisfaction. *Journal of Applied Psychology, 63*, 533–547.

Landy, F. J., & Farr, J. L. (1983). *The measurement of work performance: Methods, theory and applications.* New York: Academic Press.

LaTour, S. A., & Peat, N. C. (1979a). Conceptual and methodological issues in consumer satisfaction research. In W. L. Wilkie (Ed.), *Advances in Consumer Research, 6*, 431–440.

LaTour, S. A., & Peat, N. C. (1979b). Determinants of consumer satisfaction: A field experiment. In *Proceedings of the annual convention of the American Psychological Association, Division 23 Program.*

LaTour, S. A., & Peat, N. C. (1980). The role of situationally-produced expectations, others' experiences, and prior experience in determining consumer satisfaction. In J. C. Olson (Ed.), *Advances in Consumer Research, 7*, 588–592.

Lawler, E. E. (1981). *Pay and organization development.* Reading, MA: Addison-Wesley.

Lazer, W., & Bell, W. E. (1966). The communication process and innovation. *Journal of Advertising Research, 6*, 2–8.

Lazarsfeld, P. F., Berelson, B., & Gaudet, H. (1948). *The people's choice.* (2nd ed.). New York: Columbia University Press.

Lehmann, D. R., & Moore, W. L. (1980). Validity of information display boards: An assessment using longitudinal data. *Journal of Marketing Research, 17*, 450–459.

Leigh, T. W., & Rethans, A. J. (1983). Experiences with script elicitation within consumer decision making contexts. In R. P. Bagozzi & A. M. Tybout (Eds.), *Advances in Consumer Research* (Vol. 10, pp. 667–672). Ann Arbor, MI: Association for Consumer Research.

Leonard-Barton, D. (1985). Experts as negative opinion leaders in the diffusion of a technological innovation. *Journal of Consumer Research, 11*(4), 914–926.

Levin, I. P., & Gaeth, G. J. (1988). How consumers are affected by the framing of attribute information before and after consuming the product. *Journal of Consumer Research, 15*(3), 374–378.

Lewin, K. (1938). *The conceptual representation and the measurement of psychological forces.* Durham, NC: Duke University Press.

Lewin, K. (1951). *Field theory in social science.* New York: Harper & Row.

Liefeld, J. (1979). Urban/rural consumer expectations and evaluations of their consumer realities. In H. K. Hunt & R. L. Day (Eds.), *Refining concepts and measures of consumer satisfaction and complaining behavior* (pp. 95–101). Bloomington, IN: Indiana University.

Liefeld, J., Edgecombe, F. C. H., & Wolfe, L. (1975). Demographic characteristics of Canadian consumer complaints. *Journal of Consumer Affairs, 9,* 73–80.

Likert, R. (1961). *New patterns of management.* New York: McGraw-Hill.

Lipstein, B. (1980). Theories of advertising and measurement systems. *Attitude research enters the 80's.* Chicago: American Marketing Association.

Locke, E. A. (1976). The nature and causes of job satisfaction. In M. D. Dunnette (Ed.), *Handbook of industrial and organizational psychology* (pp. 1297–1349). Chicago: Rand McNally.

Locke, E. A., Shaw, K. N., Saari, L. M., & Latham, G. P. (1981). Goal setting and task performance: 1969–1980. *Psychological Bulletin, 90,* 125–152.

Lord, R. E. (1985). An information processing approach to social perceptions, leadership, and behavioral measurement in organizations. In L. L. Cummings & B. M. Staw (Eds.), *Research in organizational behavior.* Greenwich, CT: JAI Press.

Lussier, D. A., & Olshavsky, R. W. (1979). Task complexity and contingent processing in brands choice. *Journal of Consumer Research, 6*(2), 154–165.

Lutz, R. J., & Bettman, J. R. (1977). Multi-attribute models in marketing: A bicentennial review. In A. G. Woodside, J. N. Sheth, & P. D. Bennett (Eds.), *Consumer and industrial buying behavior* (pp. 137–149). New York: North-Holland.

Lutz, R. J., MacKenzie, S. B., & Belch, G. E. (1983). Attitude toward the ad as a mediator of advertising effectiveness: Determinants and consequences. In R. P. Bagozzi & A. M. Tybout (Eds.), *Advances in Consumer Research , 10* (pp. 532–539). Ann Arbor, MI: Association for Consumer Research.

Lynch, J. G., Marmorstein, H., & Wergold, M. F. (1988). Choices from sets including remembered brands: Use of recalled attributes and prior overall evaluations. *Journal of Consumer Research, 15*(2), 169–184.

Lynch, J. G., & Srull, T. K. (1982). Memory and attentional factors in consumer choice: Concepts and research methods. *Journal of Consumer Research, 9* (1), 18–36.

MacKenzie, S. B., Lutz, R. J., & Belch, G. E. (1986). The role of attitude toward the ad as a mediator of advertising effectiveness: A test of competing explanations. *Journal of Marketing Research, 23,* 130–143.

Madden, T. J., Allen, C. T., & Twible, J. L. (1988). Attitude toward the ad: An assessment of diverse measurement indices under different processing "sets." *Journal of Marketing Research, 25,* 242–252.

Malhotra, N. K. (1984). Reflections on the information overload paradigm in consumer decision making. *Journal of Consumer Research, 10*(4), 436–441.

March, J. G., & Simon, H. A. (1958). *Organizations.* New York: Wiley.

Maslow, A. H. (1954). *Motivation and personality.* New York: Harper & Row.

Mason, J. B., Beardon, W. O., & Crockett, M. (1980). A comparative study of elderly marketplace satisfaction. In R. L. Day & H. K. Hunt (Eds.), *New findings on consumer satisfaction and complaining* (pp. 103–110). Bloomington, IN: Indiana University.

Mason, J. B., & Hines, S. H., Jr. (1973, Winter). An exploratory behavioral and socioeconomic profile of consumer action about dissatisfaction with selected household appliances. *Journal of Consumer Affairs,* 121–127.

Matlin, M. W. (1971). Response competition, recognition, and affect. *Journal of Personality and Social Psychology, 19,* 295–300.

Mazursky, D., & Jacoby, J. (1986). Exploring the development of store image. *Journal of Retailing, 62*(2), 145–165.

McGuire, W. J. (1978). An information processing model of advertising effectiveness. In H. L. Davis & A. J. Silk (Eds.), *Behavioral and management science in marketing* (pp. 156–180). New York: Wiley.

McGuire, W. J. (1985). Attitudes and attitude change. In G. Lindzey & E. Aronson (Eds.), *Handbook of social psychology* (3rd ed.). Reading, MA: Addison-Wesley.

McMahon, H.W. (1980, December). TV loses the "name game" but wins big in personality. *Advertising Age, 54.*

Melcher, A. J., & Beller, R. (1967). Toward a theory of organization communication: Consideration in channel selection. *Academy of Management Journal, 10,* 39–52.

Midgley, D. F. (1983, February). Patterns of interpersonal information seeking for the purchase of a symbolic product. *Journal of Marketing Research, 20,* 74–83.

Miller, G. R. (1966). On defining communication: Another stab. *Journal of Communication, 26,* 88–99.

Miller, J. A. (1977). Data reduction techniques and the exploration of satisfaction segments. In R. L. Day (Ed.), *Consumer satisfaction/dissatisfaction and complaining behavior* (pp. 103–114). Bloomington, IN: Indiana University.

Milliman, R. E. (1986). The influence of background music on the behavior of restaurant patrons. *Journal of Consumer Research, 13*(2), 286–289.

Miniard, P. W. (1981). Examining the diagnostic utility of the Fishbein behavioral intentions model. In K. B. Monroe (Ed.), *Advances in Consumer Research, 8* (pp. 42–47). Ann Arbor, MI: Association for Consumer Research.

Miniard, P. W., & Cohen, J. B. (1979). Isolating attitudinal and normative influences in behavioral intentions models. *Journal of Marketing Research, 16,* 102–110.

Miniard, P. W., & Cohen, J. B. (1981). An examination of the Fishbein-Azjen behavioral intention model's concepts and measures. *Journal of Experimental Social Psychology, 17,* 309–339.

Mitchell, A. A. (1983). Cognitive processes initiated by exposure to advertising. In R. J. Harris (Ed.), *Information processing research in advertising* (pp. 13–42). Hillsdale, NJ: Erlbaum.

Mitchell, A. A. (1986). The effect of verbal and visual components of advertisements on brand attitudes and attitude toward the advertisement. *Journal of Consumer Research, 13*(1), 12–24.

Mitchell, A. A., & Olson, J. C. (1981). Are product attribute beliefs the only mediator of advertising effects on brand attitude? *Journal of Marketing Research, 18,* 318–322.

Mizerski, R. W. (1982a). An attribution exploration of the disproportionate influence of unfavorable information. *Journal of Consumer Research, 9,* 301–310.

Mizerski, R. W. (1982b). Viewer miscomprehension findings are measurement bound. *Journal of Marketing, 46*(4), 32–34.

Moore, D. L., & Hutchinson, J. W. (1983). The effects of ad affect on advertising effectiveness. In R. P.

Bagozzi & A. M. Tybout (Eds.), *Advances in consumer research* (pp. 526–531). Ann Arbor, MI: Association for Consumer Research.

Moreland, R. L., & Zajonc, R. B. (1977). Is stimulus recognition a necessary condition for the occurrence of exposure effects? *Journal of Personality and Social Psychology, 35,* 191–199.

Moreland, R. L., & Zajonc, R. B. (1979). Exposure effects may not depend on stimulus recognition. *Journal of Personality and Social Psychology, 37,* 1085–1089.

Newell, A., & Simon, H. A. (1972). *Human problem solving.* Englewood Cliffs, NJ: Prentice-Hall.

Newman, J. W., & Staelin, R. (1972). Prepurchase information searching for new cars and major household appliances. *Journal of Marketing Research, 9,* 249–257.

Nicosia, F. M. (1966). *Consumer decision processes.* Englewood Cliffs, NJ: Prentice-Hall.

Nilsen, T. R. (1957). On defining commmunication. *The Speech Teacher, 6,* 10–18.

Nisbett, R. E., & Kanouse, D. E. (1968). Obesity, hunger, and supermarket shopping behavior. *Proceedings of the 76th annual convention of the American Psychological Association,* 683–684.

Nisbett, R. E., & Kanouse, D. E. (1969, August). Obesity, food deprivation, and supermarket shopping behavior. *Journal of Personality and Social Psychology, 12,* 289–294.

Nisbett, R. E., & Wilson, T. D. (1977). Telling more than we can know: Verbal reports of mental processes. *Psychological Review, 64,* 231–259.

Nord, W. R., & Tucker, S. (1987). *Implementing routine and radical innovations.* Lexington, MA: Lexington Books.

Obermiller, C. (1985). Varieties of mere exposure: The effects of processing style and repetition in affective response. *Journal of Consumer Research, 12*(1), 17–30.

Oliver, R. L. (1977a). Effect of expectation and disconfirmation on post exposure product evaluations: An alternative interpretation. *Journal of Applied Psychology, 62,* 480–486.

Oliver, R. L. (1977b). A theoretical reinterpretation of expectation and disconfirmation effects on posterior product evaluation experiences in the field. In R. L. Day (Ed.), *Consumer satisfaction/dissatisfaction and complaining behavior* (pp. 2–9). Bloomington, IN: Indiana University.

Oliver, R. L. (1980). A cognitive model of the antecedents and consequences of satisfaction. *Journal of Marketing Research, 17,* 460–469.

Oliver, R. L (1981). Measurement and evaluation of satisfaction processes in retail settings. *Journal of Retailing, 57,* 25–48.

Oliver, R. L., & DeSarbo, W. S. (1988). Response determinants in satisfaction judgments. *Journal of Consumer Research, 14*(4), 495–507.

Olshavsky, R. W. (1973). Customer-salesman interaction in appliance retailing. *Journal of Marketing Research, 10,* 208–212.

Olshavsky, R. W., & Granbois, D. H. (1979). Consumer decision making—fact or fiction? *Journal of Consumer Research, 6,* 93–100.

Olshavsky, R. W. & Miller, J.A. (1972). Consumer expectations, product performance, and perceived product quality. *Journal of Marketing Research, 9,* 19–21.

Olson, J. C., Toy, D. R., & Dover, P. A. (1978). Mediating effects of cognitive responses to advertising on cognitive structure. In K. Hunt (Ed.), *Advances in Consumer Research, 5* (pp. 72–78). Ann Arbor, MI: Association for Consumer Research.

Organ, D. W., & Near, J. P. (1985). Cognition vs. affect in measures of job satisfaction. *International Journal of Psychology, 20,* 241–253.

Osterhouse, R. A., & Brock, T. C. (1970). Distraction increases yielding to propaganda by inhibiting counterarguing. *Journal of Personality and Social Psychology, 15,* 344–358.

Ostlund, L. E. (1974). Perceived innovation attributes as predictors of innovations. *Journal of Consumer Research, 1*(1), 23–29.

Park, C. W., & Schaninger, C. M. (1976). The identification of consumer judgmental rules: Statistical predictions vs. structured protocol. In B. B. Anderson (Ed.), *Advances in Consumer Research, 3* (pp. 184–190). Cincinnati, OH: Association for Consumer Research.

Park, C. W., & Young, S. M. (1986). Consumer responses to television commercials: The impact of involvement and background music on brand attitude formation. *Journal of Marketing Research, 23,* 11–24.

Park, O. S., Sims, H. P., & Motowidlo, S. J. (1988). Affect in organizations: How feelings and emotions influence managerial judgment. In H. P. Sims, Jr., & D. A. Gioia (Eds.), *The thinking organization.* San Francisco: Jossey-Bass.

Payne, J. W. (1976). Heuristic search process in decision making. In B. B. Anderson (Ed.), *Advances in Consumer Research, 3* (pp. 321–327). Cincinnati, OH: Association for Consumer Research.

Payne, J. W. (1982). Contingent decision behavior. *Psychological Bulletin, 92,* 382–402.

Payne, J. W., & Ragsdale, E. K. (1978). Verbal protocols and direct observation of supermarket shopping behavior: Some findings and a discussion of methods. In H. K. Hunt (Ed.), *Advances in Consumer Research, 5* (pp. 571–577). Ann Arbor, MI: Association for Consumer Research.

Peak, H. (1955). Attitude and motivation. In M. R. Jones (Ed.), *Nebraska symposium on motivation* (pp. 149–188). Lincoln: University of Nebraska Press.

Penzias, A. (1982). Psychology tomorrow: The Nobel view. *Psychology Today, 16,* 28.

Petty, R. E., & Cacioppo, J. T. (1979). Issue involvement can increase or decrease persuasion by enhancing message-relevant cognitive responses. *Journal of Personality and Social Psychology, 37,* 1915–1926.

Petty, R. E., Cacioppo, J. T., & Goldman, J. R. (1981). Personal involvement as a determinant of argument-based persuasion. *Journal of Personality and Social Psychology, 40,* 847–855.

Petty, R. E., Cacioppo, J. T., & Schumann, D. (1983). Central and peripheral routes to advertising effectiveness: The moderating role of involvement. *Journal of Consumer Research, 10,* 135–146.

Petty, R. E., Wells, G., & Brock, T. (1976). Distraction can enhance or reduce yielding to propaganda: Thought disruption versus effort justification. *Journal of Personality and Social Psychology, 34,* 874–884.

Pickle, H. B., & Bruce, R. (1972, November). Consumerism and product satisfaction-dissatisfaction: An empirical investigation. *The Southern Journal of Business,* 87–100.

Porter, L. W., & Lawler, E. E. (1968). *Managerial attitudes and performance.* Homewood, IL: Dorsey-Irwin.

Porter, L. W., & Roberts, K. H. (1976). Communication in organizations. In M. D. Dunnette (Ed.), *Handbook of industrial and organizational psychology.* Chicago: Rand McNally.

Project Payout. A review and appraisal of the pilot study in Milgram's Store #40 (1980). New York: The Payout Council, Advertising Research Foundation.

Punj, G., & Stewart, D. W. (1983, September). An interaction framework of consumer decision making. *Journal of Consumer Research, 20,* 181–196.

Ram, S. (1987). A model of innovation resistance. In M. Wallendorf & P. Anderson (Eds.), *Advances in Consumer Research, 14* (pp. 208–12). Provo, UT: Association for Consumer Research.

Ray, M. L., & Batra, R. (1983). Emotion and persuasion in advertising: What we do and don't know about affect. In R. Baggozi & A. Tybout (Eds.), *Advances in Consumer Research, 10* (pp. 543–548). Ann Arbor, MI: Association for Consumer Research.

Ray, M. L., Sawyer, A. G., Rothschild, M. L., Heeler, R. M., Strong, E. C., & Reed, J. R. (1973). Marketing communication and the hierarchy of effects. In R. Clarke (Ed.), *New models for communication research, 10* (pp. 147–176). Beverly Hills, CA: Sage.

Reingen, P. H. (1987). A word-of-mouth network. In M. Wallendorf & P. Anderson (Eds.), *Advances in Consumer Research, 14* (pp. 213–17). Provo, UT: Association for Consumer Research.

Rethans, A. J., Swazy, J. L., & Marks, L. J. (1986, February). Effects of television commercial repetition, receiver knowledge, and commercial length: A test of the two factor model. *Journal of Marketing Research, 23,* 50–61.

Reynolds, F. D., & Darden, W. R. (1971, November). Mutually adaptive effects of interpersonal communication. *Journal of Marketing Research, 8,* 449–454.

Richins, M. L. (1983). Negative word-of-mouth by dissatisfied consumers: A pilot study. *Journal of Marketing, 47,* 68–78.

Richins, M. L., & Root-Shaffer, T. (1988). The role of involvement and opinion leadership in consumer word-of-mouth: An implicit model made explicit. In M. J. Houston (Ed.), *Advances in Consumer Research, 15* (pp. 32–37). Provo, UT: Association for Consumer Research.

Rip, P. D. (1979). *The extent and basis of insight in decision making: A study in consumer behavior.* Unpublished doctoral dissertation, Stanford University, Stanford, CA.

Robertson, T. S. (1967). Determinants of innovative behavior. In R. Moyer (Ed.), *Proceedings of the American Marketing Association* (pp. 32–332). Chicago: American Marketing Association.

Robertson, T. S. (1968). Social factors in innovative behavior. In H. H. Kassarjian & T. S. Robertson (Eds.), *Perspectives in consumer behavior* (pp. 361–370). Glenview, IL: Scott, Foresman.

Robertson, T. S. (1971). *New product diffusion.* New York: Holt, Rinehart, & Winston.

Rodgers, A. L., & Sweeney, D. J. (1979). Satisfaction with retail stores as reflected in consumers' opinions. In H. K. Hunt & R. L. Day (Eds.), *Refining concepts and measures of consumer satisfaction and complaining behavior* (pp. 153–158). Bloomington, IN: Indiana University.

Rogers, E. M. (1983). *Diffusion of innovations.* New York: Free Press.

Rogers, E. M., & Cartano, D. G. (1962). Methods of measuring opinion leadership. *Public Opinion Quarterly, 26,* 435–441.

Rogers, E. M., Daley, H. M., & Wu, T. D. (1982). *The diffusion of home computers: An exploratory study.* Institute for Communication Research, Stanford University, Stanford, CA.

Rogers, E. M., & Shoemaker, F. F. (1971). *Communication of innovations: A cross-cultural approach.* New York: Free Press.

Rogers, E. M., & Stanfield, J. D. (1968). Adoption and diffusion of new products: Emerging generalizations and hypotheses. In F. M. Bass, C. W. King, & E. Pessemeier (Eds.), *Applications of thes sciences in marketing management.* New York: Wiley.

Rosch, E. (1977). Human categorization. In N. Warren (Ed.), *Studies in cross-cultural psychology* (1–49). New York: Academic Press.

Rosen, D. L., & Olshavsky, R. W. (1987). A protocol analysis of brand choice strategies involving recommendations. *Journal of Consumer Research, 14*(3), 440–444.

Rosenberg, M. J. (1956). Cognitive structure and attitudinal affect. *Journal of Abnormal and Social Psychology, 53,* 367–372.

Rosenberg, M. J. (1960). An analysis of affective-cognitive consistency. In C. I. Hovland & M. J. Rosenberg (Eds.), *Attitude, organization and change* (pp. 15–64). New Haven: Yale University Press.

Rotter, J. B. (1955). The role of the psychological situation in determining the direction of human behavior. In M. R. Jones (Ed.), *Nebraska symposium on motivation.* Lincoln: University of Nebraska Press.

Russo, J. E. (1974, December). More information is better: A re-evaluation of Jacoby, Speller, and Kohn. *Journal of Consumer Research, 1,* 68–72.

Russo, J. E. (1978). Eye fixations can rule the world: A critical evaluation and a comparison between eye fixations and other information processing methodologies. In H. K. Hunt (Ed.), *Advances in Consumer Research, 5* (pp. 561–570). Ann Arbor, MI: Association for Consumer Research.

Russo, J. E., & Johnson, E. J. (1980). What do consumers know about familiar products? In J. C. Olson (Ed.), *Advances in Consumer Research, 7* (pp. 417–423). Ann Arbor, MI: Association for Consumer Research.

Russo, J. E., Krieser, G., & Miyashita, S. (1975, April). An effective display of unit price information. *Journal of Marketing, 39,* 11–19.

Russo, J. E., & Rosen, L. D. (1975). An eye fixation analysis of multialternative choice. *Memory and Cognition, 3,* 267–276.

Ryan, M. J. (1982). Behavioral intention formation: A structural equation analysis of attitudinal and social influence interdependency. *Journal of Consumer Research, 9*(3), 263–278.

Ryan, M. J., & Bonfield, E. H. (1975, September). The Fishbein extended model and consumer behavior. *Journal of Consumer Research, 2*(2), 118–136.

Ryan, M. J., & Bonfield, E. H. (1980). Fishbein's intentions model: A test of external and pragmatic validity. *Journal of Marketing, 44,* 82–95.

Sanbonmatsu, D. M., & Kardes, F. M. (1988). The effects of physiological arousal on information processing and persuasion. *Journal of Consumer Research, 15*(3), 379–385.

Sawyer, A. G. (1977). Repetition and affect: Recent empirical and theoretical developments. In A. G. Woodside, J. N. Sheth, & P. D. Bennett (Eds.), *Consumer and industrial buying behavior* (pp. 229–242). New York: North-Holland.

Sawyer, A. G. (1981). Repetition, cognitive responses, and persuasion. In R. E. Petty, T. M. Ostrum, & T. C. Brock (Eds.), *Cognitive response to persuasion.* Hilldale, NJ: Erlbaum.

Scarpello, V., & Campbell, J. P. (1983). Job satisfaction: Are all the parts there? *Personnel Psychology, 36,* 577–600.

Schank, R. C., & Abelson, R. P. (1977). *Scripts, plans, goals, and understanding: An inquiry into human knowledge structures.* Hillsdale, NJ: Erlbaum.

Schein, E. H. (1965). *Organizational psychology.* New York: Prentice-Hall.

Schlegel, R. P., Crawford, C. A., & Sanborn, M. D. (1977). Correspondence and mediational properties of the Fishbein model: An application to adolescent alcohol use. *Journal of Experimental Social Psychology, 13,* 421–430.

Schmittlein, D. C., & Morrison, D. G. (1983). Measuring miscomprehension for televised communication using true-false questions. *Journal of Consumer Research, 10*(2), 147–156.

Schneider, B., & Bowen, D. W. (1985). Employee and customer perceptions of service in banks: Replication and extension. *Journal of Applied Psychology, 70,* 423–433.

Schneider, B., Parkington, J. J., & Buxton, V. M. (1980). Employee and customer perceptions of service in banks. *Administrative Science Quarterly, 25,* 252–267.

Schwab, D., Olian-Gottlieb, J., & Heneman, H., III (1979). Between subjects expectancy theory research: A statistical review of studies predicting effort and performance. *Psychological Bulletin, 86,* 139–147.

Schwarz, N., & Clore, G. (1983). Mood, misattribution, and judgments of well-being: Informative and directive functions of affective states. *Journal of Personality and Social Psychology, 45*(3), 513–523.

Scott, W. D. (1903). *The theory of advertising*. Boston: Small, Maynard.

Scott, W. D. (1908a). *The psychology of advertising*. Boston: Small, Maynard.

Scott, W. D. (1908b). *The psychology of advertising in theory and practice*. Boston: Small, Maynard.

Scott, W. D. (1911a). *Increasing human efficiency in business*. New York: Macmillan.

Scott, W. D. (1911b). *Influencing men in business*. New York: Ronald Press.

Shannon, C. E., & Weaver, W. (1949). *The mathematical theory of communication*. Urbana: University of Illinois Press.

Sheluga, D. A. (1979). *Inferring the internal decision making process by observing information seeking responses*. Unpublished doctoral dissertation, Purdue University, West Lafayette, IN.

Sheluga, D. A., Jaccard, J. J., & Jacoby, J. (1979). Preference, search and choice: An integrative approach. *Journal of Consumer Research, 6*(2), 166–176.

Sheppard, B. H., Hartwick, J., & Warshaw, P. R. (1988). The theory of reasoned action: A meta-analysis of past research with recommendations for modifications and future research. *Journal of Consumer Research, 15*(3), 325–343.

Sheth, J. N. (1968). Perceived risk and the diffusion of innovations. In J. Arndt (Ed.), *Insights into consumer behavior* (pp. 173–188). Boston: Allyn & Bacon.

Sheth, J. N., & Talarzyk (1970). *Relative contribution of perceived instrumentality and value importance components in determining attitudes*. Paper presented at the 1970 Fall conference of the American Marketing Association. [Abstracted in D. L. Sparks (Ed.), *Broadening the concept of marketing*. Chicago: American Marketing Association, 35.]

Sheth, J. N., & Talarzyk, W. W. (1972). Perceived instrumentality and value importance as determinants of attitudes. *Journal of Marketing Research, 9*, 6–9.

Simonson, I., Huber, J., & Payne, J. (1988). The relationship between prior brand knowledge and information acquisition order. *Journal of Consumer Research, 14*(4), 566–578.

Simon, H. A. (1981). *The sciences of the artificial*. Cambridge, MA: MIT Press.

Smith, R. A., Houston, M. J., & Childers, T. L. (1984). Verbal versus visual processing modes: An empirical test of the cyclical processing hypothesis. In T. C. Kinnear (Ed.), *Advances in Consumer Research, 11* (pp. 75–80). Provo, UT: Association for Consumer Research.

Smith, T. F., Olshavsky, R. W., & Smith, M. F. (1979). Smoking behaviors as a diffusion process within age cohort groups: An application of the societal marketing concept. In W. L. Wilkie (Ed.), *Advances in Consumer Research, 6* (pp. 392-395). Ann Arbor, MI: Association for Consumer Research.

Solomon, R. L., & Corbit, J. D. (1973). An opponent process theory of motivation: II. Cigarette addiction. *Journal of Abnormal Psychology, 81*, 158–171.

Srull, T. K. (1983). Affect and memory: The impact of affective reactions in advertising on the representation of product information in memory. In R. P. Bagozzi & A. M. Tybout (Eds.), *Advances in consumer research* (pp. 520–525). Ann Arbor, MI: Association for Consumer Research.

Staelin, R., & Payne, J. W. (1976). Studies of the information seeking behavior of consumers. In J. Carroll & J. W. Payne (Eds.), *Cognition and social behavior* (pp. 185–202). Hillsdale, NJ: Erlbaum.

Stahl, M. J., & Harrell, A. M. (1981). Modeling effort decisions with behavioral decision theory: Toward an individual differences model of expectancy theory. *Organizational Behavior and Human Performance, 27*, 303–325.

Staw, B. (1981). The escalation of commitment to a course of action. *Academy of Management Review, 6*, 577–587.

Sujan, M. (1985, June). Consumer knowledge: Effects on evaluation strategies mediating consumer judgments. *Journal of Consumer Research, 12*, 31–46.

Summers, J. O. (1970). The identity of women's clothing fashion opinion leaders. *Journal of Marketing Research, 7*, 178–185.

Summers, J. O. (1971). New product interpersonal communications. In F. C. Allvine (Ed.), *Combined proceedings of the American Marketing Association, 33*, 428–433.

Summers, J.O. (1974, November). Less information is better. *Journal of Marketing Research, 11*, 467–468.

Swan, J. E. (1977). Consumer satisfaction with a retail store related to the fulfillment of expectations on an initial shopping trip. In R. L. Day

(Ed.), *Consumer satisfaction/dissatisfaction and complaining behavior* (pp. 10–17). Bloomington, IN: Indiana University

Swan, J. E., & Martin, W. S. (1981). Testing comparison-level and predictive expectations models of satisfaction. In K. B. Monroe (Ed.), *Advances in Consumer Research, 8* (pp. 77–82). Ann Arbor, MI: Association for Consumer Research.

Swan, J. E., & Trawick, I. F. (1978). Testing an extended concept of consumer satisfaction. In R. L. Day & H. K. Hunt (Eds.), *New dimensions of consumer satisfaction and complaining behavior* (pp. 56–61). Bloomington, IN: Indiana University.

Swan, J. E., & Trawick, I. F. (1979). Satisfaction related to predictive vs. desired expectations. In H. K. Hunt & R. L. Day (Eds.), *Refining concepts and measures of consumer satisfaction and complaining behavior* (pp. 7–12). Bloomington, IN: Indiana University.

Swan, J. E., Trawick, I. F., & Carroll, M. G. (1980). Satisfaction related to predictive and desired expectations: A field study. In R. L. Day & H. K. Hunt (Eds.), *New dimensions of consumer satisfaction and complaining behavior* (pp. 15–22). Bloomington, IN: Indiana University.

Tauber, E. M. (1972, October). Why do people shop? *Journal of Marketing, 47.*

Taylor, J. W. (1977). A striking characteristic of innovators. *Journal of Marketing Research, 14,* 104–107.

Taylor, S. E., & Crocker, J. (1981). Schematic bases of social information processing. In E. T. Higgins, P. Hermann, & M. P. Zanna (Eds.), *The Ontario symposium on personality and social psychology* (Vol. 1). Hillsdale, NJ: Erlbaum.

Thibaut, J. W., & Kelly, H. H. (1959). *The social psychology of groups.* New York: Wiley.

Tolman, E. C. (1932). *Purposive behavior in animals and men.* New York: Appleton-Century-Crofts.

Troutman, M. C., & Shanteau, J. C. (1976). Do consumers evaluate products by adding or averaging information? *Journal of Consumer Research, 3,* 101–106.

Tsal, Y. (1985). On the relationship between cognitive and affective processes: A critique of Zajonc and Markus. *Journal of Consumer Research, 12*(3), 358–362.

Tse, D. K., & Wilton, P. C. (1988, May). Models of customer satisfaction formation: An extension. *Journal of Marketing Research, 25,* 204–213.

Tushman, M. L., & Nadler, D. (1980). Communication and technical roles in R&D laboratories: An information processing approach. In B. Dean & J. Goldhar (Eds.), *Management of research and innovation.* New York: North-Holland.

Vadehra, D. (1980, May 26). Coke, McDonald's lead outstanding TV commercials. *Advertising Age,* 37–38.

van Raaij, W. F. (1977). Consumer information processing for different information structures and formats. In W. D. Perrault, Jr. (Ed.), *Advances in Consumer Research, 4* (pp. 176–184). Chicago: Association for Consumer Research.

Veitch, R., & Griffit, W. (1976). Good news–bad news: Affective and interpersonal effects. *Journal of Applied Psychology, 6*(1), 69–75.

Venkatraman, M. P. (1988). Investigating the differences in the roles of enduring and instrumentally involved consumers in the diffusion process. In M. J. Houston (Ed.), *Advances in Consumer Research, 15* (pp. 299–303). Provo, UT: Association for Consumer Research.

Vroom, V. H. (1964). *Work and motivation.* New York: Wiley.

Vroom, V. H. (1969). Industrial social psychology. In G. Lindzey & E. Aronson (Eds.), *The handbook of social psychology* (Vol. 5, pp. 196–268). Reading, MA: Addison-Wesley.

Vroom, V. H., & Maier, N. R. F. (1961). Industrial social psychology. *Annual Review of Psychology, 12,* 413–446.

Warland, R. H., Hermann, R. O., & Willits, J. (1975, Winter). Dissatisfied consumers: Who gets upset and who takes what action. *Journal of Consumer Affairs,* 148–163.

Watson, D., & Tellegen, A. (1985). Toward a consensual structure of mood. *Psychological Bulletin, 98,* 219–235.

Weinberger, M. G., Allen, C. T., & Dillon, W. R. (1981). The impact of negative marketing communications: The consumers Union/Chrysler controversy. *Journal of Advertising, 10*(4), 20–28.

Weiner, B., & Kukla, A. (1970). An attributional analysis of achievement motivation. *Journal of Personality and Social Psychology, 15,* 1–20.

Westbrook, R. A. (1977). Correlates of postpurchase satisfaction with major household appliances. In R. L. Day (Ed.), *Consumer satisfaction/dissatisfaction and complaining behavior* (pp. 85–90). Bloomington, IN: Indiana University.

Westbrook, R. A. (1981). Sources of consumer satisfaction with retail outlets. *Journal of Retailing, 57,* 68–85.

Westbrook, R. A. (1986). *Conceptualizing and measuring consumer satisfaction: A review.* Unpublished manuscript, University of Arizona, Department of Marketing, Tucson.

Westbrook, R. A. (1987). Product/consumption/based affective responses and post-purchase processes. *Journal of Marketing Research, 25,* 258–270.

Whitney, J. C., & John, G. (1983). An experimental investigation of intrusion errors in memory for script narratives. In R. P. Bagozzi & A. M. Tybout (Eds), *Advances in Consumer Research , 10* (pp. 661–666). Ann Arbor, MI: Association for Consumer Research.

Whyte, G. (1986). Escalating commitment to a course of action: A reinterpretation. *Academy of Management Review, 11,* 311–321.

Wilkie, W. L. (1974, November). Analysis of effects of information load. *Journal of Marketing Research, 11,* 462–466.

Wilkie, W. L., & Pessemier, E. A. (1973). Issues in marketing's use of multi-attribute attitude models. *Journal of Marketing Research, 10,* 428–444.

Wilson, W. R. (1979). Feeling more than we can know: Exposure effects without learning. *Journal of Personality and Social Psychology, 37,* 811–821.

Wilton, P. C., & Myers, J. G. (1986). Task, expectancy, and information assessment effects in information utilization processes. *Journal of Consumer Research, 12*(4), 469–486.

Wilton, P. C., & Pessemier, E. A. (1981). Forecasting the ultimate acceptance of an innovation: The effects of information. *Journal of Consumer Research, 8* (2), 162–171.

Wind, Y. (1976, June). Preference of relevant others and individual choice models. *Journal of Consumer Research, 4,* 50–57.

Withey, S. B. (1977). Integrating some models about consumer satisfaction. In H. K. Hunt (Ed.), *Conceptualization and measurement of consumer satisfaction and dissatisfaction* (pp. 120–131). Cambridge, MA: Marketing Science Institute.

Wood, Y. (1976). Preference of relevant others and individual choice models. *Journal of Consumer Research, 3*(2), 50–57.

Wright, P. L. (1973). The cognitive processes mediating acceptance of advertising. *Journal of Marketing Research, 10,* 53–67.

Wright, P. L. (1974a). Analyzing media effects on advertising responses. *Public Opinion Quarterly, 38,* 192–205.

Wright, P. L. (1974b). The harassed decision maker: Time pressures, distractions, and the use of evidence. *Journal of Applied Psychology, 59,* 555–561.

Wright, P. L. (1974c). On the direct monitoring of cognitive responses to advertising. In G. D. Hughes & M. L. Ray (Eds.), *Buyer/consumer information processing.* Chapel Hill: University of North Carolina Press.

Wright, P. L. (1974d). Research orientations for analyzing consumer judgment processes. In S. Ward & P. L. Wright (Eds.), *Advances in Consumer Research, 1* (pp. 268–279). Chicago: Association for Consumer Research.

Wright, P. L. (1975). Factors affecting cognitive resistance to advertising. *Journal of Consumer Research, 2*(1), 1–9.

Wright, P. L. (1980, September). Message-evoked thoughts: Persuasion research using thought verbalization. *Journal of Consumer Research, 7,* 151–175.

Wright, P. L. (1981). Cognitive responses to mass media advocacy. In R. E. Petty, T. M. Ostrum, & T. C. Brock (Eds.), *Cognitive responses to persuasion.* Hillsdale, NJ: Erlbaum.

Wright, P. L., & Barbour, F. (1977). Phased decision strategies: Sequels to an initial screening. In M. K. Starr & M. Zeleny (Eds.), *North-Holland/TIMS studies in management science, Vol. 6: Multiple criteria decision making* (pp. 91–109). Amsterdam: North-Holland.

Zaltman, G., Duncan, R., & Holbeck (1973). *Processes and phenomenon of social change.* New York: Wiley.

Zaltman, G., & Wallendorf, M. (1983). *Consumer behavior: Basic findings and management implications.* New York: Wiley.

Zajonc, R. B. (1980). Feeling and thinking: Preferences need no inferences. *American Psychologist, 35,* 151–175.

Zajonc, R. B., & Markus, H. (1982). Affective and cognitive factors in preferences. *Journal of Consumer Research, 9*(2), 123–131.

CHAPTER 8

Organizational Productivity

Robert D. Pritchard
Texas A & M University

This chapter explores a number of issues about organizational productivity. Reasons why productivity has become so important are first discussed, with special emphasis on the importance of productivity growth. Next, the conceptualization of productivity is considered and the confusion in the literature is noted. A number of specific conceptual issues are discussed, such as disciplinary perspectives, efficiency versus effectiveness, the organizational model used, and the unit of analysis used. A conceptual approach is presented that attempts to integrate these issues. To do this, the major question that must be addressed is the purpose for measuring productivity. Issues associated with measuring productivity are then presented, including the importance of complete measurement, reliability and validity issues, the use of objective and subjective measures, measuring things people have control over, and the types of work where measurement is feasible. A list of important characteristics for a good productivity measurement system is then presented, including having both an overall index of productivity and subindices, maintaining differing importance and nonlinearities in the measures, allowing for aggregation across organizational units and for direct comparison of different units, and being able to use both efficiency and effectiveness measures. Specific approaches to productivity measurement are then summarized and compared. In a final section, conclusions about the field are offered.

Introduction

IN THE LAST 10 years, productivity has received so much attention that it is now a household word. We talk with our spouse about how productive our day was. Computer software is advertised as being an aid to productivity. Companies search for programs to improve productivity. The national news contrasts the productivity of the United States with Japan. We write justifications of our work as behavioral scientists by invoking ties to productivity.

Productivity has become so important that it has been formally identified as a national priority. In 1984, a White House conference on productivity was held. Tuttle and Weaver (1986a) cite a 1985 message from President Reagan asking Congress for support of a government-wide program to improve productivity in the federal government and to pass a joint resolution that would make the improvement of productivity a national goal. When a concept in behavioral science gets this sort of national attention, it has indeed become an important societal issue.

The purpose of this chapter is to explore the concept of productivity. First, the reasons for the importance of productivity will be examined, along with the effects of productivity growth. Next, definitions of productivity will be explored, as will the confusion that exists about the conceptualization of organizational productivity and the major conceptual issues involved. An integrated conceptualization will then be presented. Next, measurement issues associated with the concept will be identified and design features of measurement systems noted. Specific approaches to measuring productivity will then be summarized. Finally, conclusions about the field will be offered.

Importance of Productivity

The importance of productivity needs some historical context to be understood. Data on labor productivity have been collected since 1909 (Riggs & Felix, 1983). For many decades, these data were largely within the purview of labor economists and were not particularly of concern to many others. In the 1950s and 1960s, the United States was the most productive country in the world, and there was little doubt that this state of affairs would continue.

However, by the early 1970s, it was clear that this superiority was threatened, especially by Japan and some western European countries. While the United States was still the most productive country, its rate of productivity growth was declining, and a number of other countries were improving their national productivity at a faster rate than the United States (Kendrick, 1984; Mahoney, 1988; Sink, 1985; Taira, 1988; Tuttle, 1983). This led the American Productivity Center (1979) to state that if the trends occurring at that time continued, the productivity of the United States would actually fall behind Japan, West Germany, Canada, and France by the end of the 1980s.

During the 1970s, the reality of this problem became clear to more than just the economists. The effects of these productivity changes started to be felt nationally. The success of the Japanese in U.S. automobile and steel markets led to plant closings and lost jobs. Major U.S. companies were in severe financial difficulties. Unemployment was rising. What had historically been a trade surplus became a trade deficit, and the deficit was increasing. While many causes were responsible for these problems (e.g., Kopelman, 1986), loss of clear U.S. superiority in productivity was seen as one of the major causes.

The productivity issue was picked up by many segments of our society, from the media to labor unions, and was presented as a serious issue. In a special report on productivity, NBC concluded that "unless we solve the problem of productivity, our children will be the first generation in the history of the United States to live worse than their parents" (National Broadcasting Company, 1980). Productivity had become a national issue.

Effects of Productivity Growth

There are very good reasons why this concern for productivity is appropriate. Productivity has a major impact on our lives. Its effects can be seen at three major levels: (a) national, (b) industry and firm, and (c) individual.

Effects at the National Level. There are clear ties between productivity and important economic outcomes. Productivity growth is an important factor in controlling inflation (Kendrick, 1984; Mahoney, 1988; Riggs & Felix, 1983; Tuttle, 1983). In a market economy, the prices paid for goods are determined largely by the costs of the inputs used to produce the goods and the profit margin of the producer. There is a constant upward pressure on the cost of these inputs. For example, the price of labor is continually increasing as we receive pay raises each year. If profit margins are assumed to be roughly constant over time, then increases in the cost of the inputs must be offset by increases in productivity if costs are to be kept constant. More output must be produced with the same, more expensive input. If the increases in the costs of inputs are not offset, the prices of the same goods must go up and inflation occurs.

This description is an oversimplification, since inflation is also influenced by other factors, such as fiscal policy, political decisions at home and abroad, and spending attitudes (Riggs & Felix, 1983). However, productivity growth is an important factor in determining inflation levels.

Another way to look at this same set of relationships is to focus on wages. We all want higher wages. If higher wages are achieved without increased productivity, the cost of the goods goes up, increasing inflation (Kendrick, 1984; Kopelman, 1986). If wages increase with a corresponding increase in productivity, no inflationary pressure is created. This logic is confirmed empirically when economists study growth in real income, that is, change in income relative to change in inflation. Studied over time, productivity growth appears to be responsible for the increase in real income per capita (Kendrick, 1984).

The real cost of goods is also influenced by productivity (Kendrick, 1984; Mali, 1978). Productivity growth results in producing the same goods for lower costs. Again assuming a roughly constant profit margin, the real cost of goods decreases as productivity increases (Fleishman, 1982; Mahoney, 1988).

There are also some important noneconomic factors that are influenced by productivity growth (Fleishman, 1982; Kendrick, 1984; Kopelman, 1986; Mali, 1978; Riggs & Felix, 1983). Increased productivity means generating the same goods and services with less inputs. Thus, it is a way of conserving societal resources ranging from trees to human labor. Looked at another way, increased productivity allows for more available outputs for the same inputs. Thus, we can be closer to a society of plenty while using less of our societal resources.

Productivity growth can also increase the quality of our lives. Kopelman (1986) puts it well by saying that without productivity growth, the economic pie that is divided is of a fixed size. This means that one demand cannot be met without sacrificing another. For example, the cost of social security or medicaid must be contained or taxes increased. A pie of a fixed size results in battles between factions fighting over the resources—for example, environmentalists versus manufacturers, workers versus retirees, majority versus minorities, and so forth. Productivity growth creates the money to continue to increase the size of the pie. Thus, the size of each slice can increase without taking resources from someone else.

Effects at the Industry and Firm Level. Productivity and productivity growth are also important at the level of the industry and the individual firm. If productivity growth of an industry or a firm is higher than its competitors, that industry or firm survives better (Craig & Harris, 1973; Kendrick, 1984; Tuttle, 1983).

If the productivity growth of an industry or firm is higher than the average of its competitors, this leads to lower costs and prices, thus making those products and services more competitive. This leads to higher sales, higher profits, and more job opportunities. The reverse is true for below-average productivity growth. Another way to look at the relationships is from the cost of inputs. When increases in wages or the costs of other inputs exceed gains in production efficiencies, the goods produced from labor and capital become more expensive. Competitiveness is decreased in the world or national marketplace (Riggs & Felix, 1983).

Effects at the Individual Level. Finally, productivity and productivity growth are important to individuals. Aside from the quality of life issues raised above, increasing productivity leads to better use of our time and more leisure time and is a key to advancement in organizations (Kendrick, 1984). Equally important, people like to be productive. It is a central aspect of self-fulfillment and self-respect.

Problems With Defining Productivity

There is agreement that productivity is important and why it is important. In sharp contrast, there is very little agreement on what the term *productivity* means (e.g., Bullock & Batten, 1983; Campbell & Campbell, 1988a; Craig & Harris, 1973; Kopelman, 1986; Tuttle, 1983). It is used as a measure of the efficiency or effectiveness of individuals, groups, organizational units, entire organizations, industries, and nations. It is used as a synonym for output, motivation, individual performance, organizational effectiveness, production, profitability, cost effectiveness, competitiveness, work quality, and what a new product will enable you to increase if you buy it. Productivity measurement is used interchangeably with performance appraisal, management information systems, production capability assessment, quality control measurement, and the engineering throughput of a system.

At least there is general agreement that the use of the term productivity is imprecise (e.g., Campbell & Campbell, 1988b; Craig & Harris, 1973; Muckler, 1982; Tuttle, 1983). Dunnette (1982) put it well when he said, "Productivity indices currently used are diverse, somewhat primitive, and often unclear" (p. 9).

To understand why the term productivity has become so confused, it is necessary to consider the history of the concept. Most of our behavioral concepts are of our own making and attain a more or less agreed upon definition. Productivity is different. It started with the economists and did not become a widespread issue until it became clear that the United States was in danger of losing the industrial superiority that Americans had come to expect. When the effects of the loss of this superiority became apparent, productivity suddenly became a hot issue.

When this happened, a number of disciplines realized that they had something to contribute to solving the problem. Academics such as economists, accountants, industrial engineers, sociologists, psychologists, and management specialists all believed that the content of their disciplines had something to offer to the problem. Practitioners such as managers and management consultants of every description applied their knowledge to this problem.

These people looked at the problem and its potential solutions from their own perspectives, and these perspectives were very different. The economist's definition of productivity and the methods he or she uses for measurement and improvement are very different from those of an industrial engineer (Brief, 1984; Tuttle, 1981).

The confusion in the literature is the effect of this process. Given all the types of people who have been working on productivity, it is not surprising that the exact meaning of the term is unclear. In fact, one response to this literature is to conclude that it is a confusing, unorganized conceptual morass wherein the unwary can venture and never be heard from again. However, this is too pessimistic. A better view is that here is an area where scholars and practitioners from many different disciplines have made contributions, and this is a wonderful opportunity to see and integrate what has been done in areas where psychologists do not often venture. It is a challenge, but much can be learned from the process.

Conceptual Issues

What Productivity Is *Not*

One way to start understanding productivity is to deal with what technical writers agree that productivity is *not*. Productivity is not the same thing as individual performance (Ilgen & Klein, 1988; Mali, 1978; Pritchard, Jones, Roth, Stuebing, & Ekeberg, 1988, 1989; Tuttle, 1983). Individual performance is a measure of how well the individual fulfills his or her role. It is usually an index of the outputs of the individual (e.g., dollars of sales) or, more commonly, an evaluation of how the individual's behavior compares to organizational expectations (e.g., performance appraisals). Such measures are used to evaluate the contribution of a single individual to the functioning of the organization, typically for the purpose of making decisions about how that individual should be treated in areas such as raises, promotions, or training.

In contrast, productivity is an index of output relative to goals (*effectiveness*) or output relative to inputs (*efficiency*). In addition, productivity more explicitly acknowledges that the functioning of a unit or organization requires interdependence between individuals to achieve the organization's objectives. Because of this interdependence, the productivity of the unit or organization is not the simple sum of the performances of the individuals involved. Productivity also includes factors such as how well they cooperate with each other, how

well the personnel are coordinated and managed, the availability of needed resources, and how well priorities are set so that organizational objectives are reached.

There are also some other things that productivity is not. Productivity is not output (Kendrick, 1984; Mali, 1978). Output is the amount of products or services generated by a system. While outputs are part of productivity, productivity also includes inputs or a measure of outputs relative to objectives or goals. Productivity is not profitability (Kendrick, 1984; Kopelman, 1986; Mali, 1978). Profitability includes measurement of the degree of cost recovery; productivity does not (Kendrick, 1984; Mali, 1978). Finally, productivity is not a measure of capability. Concepts like *production capacity* or *output capability* are measures of the potential outputs of a system. Productivity deals with actual output.

Key Issues Across Disciplines

Trying to develop a good conceptualization of productivity from reading the literature is not an easy task. One way to help organize this material and develop a framework for integration is to identify key conceptual issues that cut across this literature. A number of such issues will be discussed in turn. After that, an attempt will be made to integrate and synthesize the issues.

Disciplinary Perspectives. The first of these core issues involves the various disciplinary perspectives from which productivity can be viewed. Many disciplines have made contributions in the area of productivity, each from a very different perspective. For example, in a book of essays on productivity edited by Brief (1984), chapters are included that are written from the perspective of accounting (Denison, 1984; Kaplan, 1982; Mahoney, 1984), sociology (Berg, 1984; Hage, 1984; Pennings, 1984), psychology (Hackman, 1984; Schneider, 1984; Weiss, 1984), and management (Guth, 1984; House, 1984; Kerr, 1984). Tuttle (1981, 1983) formally identifies five distinct perspectives: the economist, the accountant, the industrial engineer, the psychologist, and the manager.

The Economist. The economist sees productivity as the ratio of outputs over their associated inputs, where both outputs and inputs are expressed in real physical volume units (Kendrick, 1977, 1984; Kopelman, 1986; Mahoney, 1988; Silver, 1984). Put another way, productivity is the efficiency of the transformation of inputs into outputs. Outputs are the products created by the process—the cars, the coal, the potatoes. Inputs include all the things needed to produce the outputs— labor, energy, intermediate products purchased as raw materials or supplies, and capital. These outputs and inputs should be expressed in *real physical volume units*. In other words, measures of the amount used or produced should be objectively quantifiable and represent physical entities.

Unfortunately, it is not possible to combine physical measures of inputs and outputs to form such ratios. One cannot take the sum of 1,000 refrigerators, 500 dishwashers, and 2,000 toasters and divide that by the sum of 10,000 hours of labor, 10 tons of sheet metal, and 50,000 kilowatts of electricity. To overcome this problem, each input and output is converted to a common metric—dollars. One can divide the *value* of the refrigerators, dishwashers, and toasters by the *cost* of the labor, materials, and energy.

When all the input and output factors are included in the ratio, the resulting measure is termed *total factor* productivity. When selected measures are used, the result is termed *partial* factor productivity. The most common type of partial factor productivity measure is labor productivity, where outputs are divided by some measure of the amount of labor used to produce them.

The Accountant. Approaches to productivity based on an accounting perspective (e.g.,

Denison, 1984; Hurst, 1980) attempt to describe and improve the financial performance of the organization. This is done through the construction of a series of financial ratios, such as dollars of sales divided by the cost of labor or dollars of profit divided by the capital employed to produce it. Most of these measures have an output/input format and are thus a type of efficiency measure, but they are focused primarily on financial efficiency. Typically, multiple measures are constructed to get an overall picture of organizational functioning.

The Industrial Engineer. The industrial engineer (e.g., Norman & Bahiri, 1972; Rosow, 1981) views productivity as the efficiency of throughput as measured by output to input ratios. It is based on the model of a machine, where productivity is the ratio of useful work (the output) divided by the energy used to produce the work (the input). As such, it has a maximum value of 1.0. Measurement is typically focused on the operational units within the organization rather than the total organization and usually attempts to assess the functioning of a "man-machine" system.

The Psychologist. What Tuttle refers to as the *industrial and organizational psychologist approach* (more properly termed the *behavioral approach* to include our organizational behavior colleagues) focuses primarily on the aspects of productivity that the individual can control, that is, behavior (e.g., Campbell & Campbell, 1988c; Guzzo, 1988; Guzzo, Jette, & Katzell, 1985; Ilgen & Klein, 1988; Schneider, 1984). The assumption is that by changing individuals' behavior, productivity will be changed. Some behavioral researchers inaccurately equate individual behavior/performance with productivity, while some argue that behavior and performance are a component of productivity. It is also assumed that all our interventions, such as selection, training, feedback, and gainsharing, can influence productivity.

The Manager. The broadest but least precisely identifiable perspective is that of the manager (Tuttle (1981, 1983). In this perspective (e.g., Preziosi, 1985; Shetty & Buehler, 1985), productivity includes all aspects of the organization seen as important to effective organizational functioning. It includes efficiency and effectiveness, but also includes quality of output, work disruptions, absenteeism, turnover, and customer satisfaction. No one specific definition of what productivity is nor how it should be measured are specified. Anything that should make the organization function better ipso facto deals with productivity.

Efficiency Versus Effectiveness. Another core conceptual issue is whether an efficiency or an effectiveness approach should be used in measuring productivity. *Efficiency* is a ratio of outputs to inputs. Number of tons of steel produced divided by number of personnel hours used to produce that output would be an efficiency measure. *Effectiveness* is defined as the outputs relative to some standard or expectation. Tons of steel expressed as a percentage of the goal for that month would be an effectiveness measure.

Productivity scholars agree that efficiency is part of the concept of productivity. They disagree on whether effectiveness is also part of productivity. Many see productivity as just efficiency (e.g., Campbell & Campbell, 1988c; Craig & Harris, 1973; Kendrick, 1984; Muckler, 1982; Werther, Ruch, & McClure, 1986). The majority, however, believe that productivity should include both efficiency and effectiveness (e.g., Balk, 1975; Bullock & Batten, 1983; Coulter, 1979; Deprez, 1986; Elkin & Molitor, 1985–1986; Engle, 1979; Guzzo, 1988; Hayes, 1977; Hurst, 1980; Joint Financial Management Improvement Program, 1976; Letzkus, 1973; Mali, 1978; National Center for Productivity and Quality of Working Life, 1977; Neugarten, 1985; Peeples, 1978; Pritchard et al., 1988, 1989; Riggs & Felix, 1983; Tuttle, 1981, 1982, 1983; U.S. Air Force, 1982).

Both efficiency and effectiveness have their advantages and disadvantages (cf. Deprez, 1986; Kendrick, 1984; Kopelman, 1986; Norman & Bahiri, 1972; Tuttle, 1981). Efficiency is widely known and much easier to standardize across organizations, industries, and nations. When we hear that productivity growth in the United States has declined over the last 20 years (e.g., American Productivity Center, 1981), it is an efficiency ratio that is being quoted (i.e., price-deflated gross national product divided by worker hours).

Efficiency is easy to calculate, easy to understand, and is accepted by organizational personnel. Another major advantage is that productivity, when defined as dollar value of physical outputs divided by dollar value of physical inputs, is directly reconcilable with profitability, since productivity (by this definition) multiplied by price recovery equals profitability (Kendrick, 1984; Kopelman, 1986). This feature of the efficiency conceptualization makes it especially attractive to managers.

There are also a number of disadvantages to efficiency measures. An important one is that being highly efficient may be very dysfunctional in the long run. Getting high output with minimal inputs may be done by not expending resources on important long-term needs. For example, lowering quality, failing to cultivate customers, letting equipment deteriorate, and failing to expend resources on training may result in a short-term increase in efficiency, but to the long-term detriment to the organization.

The efficiency conceptualization of productivity also ignores the demand for the product or service. Efficiently generating large amounts of products for which there is no need or market is not helpful to the organization.

Another important disadvantage is that it is very difficult to develop efficiency measures for all the units of the organization. The dollar value of the output/input approach is usable if the unit has outputs that can be converted to dollars. It is not easily usable for units such as a personnel department or for a research and development function.

One common solution to this problem is to measure the organizational outputs that can be valued in terms of dollars and use all costs as inputs, including the costs of units like the personnel department and research and development. However, this solution has the problem that separate units must be combined to calculate the efficiency measure. Thus, the productivity measures coming from such a system are quite macro in nature. This tends to make them insensitive to small changes in productivity, of little benefit to the unit personnel as a guide to operating more productively, and of little value in evaluating the effects of organizational changes on productivity. Another solution to the problem is to express the outputs of the unit in whatever units can be quantified and divide these by inputs. This produces an efficiency measure, but cannot be compared to other units nor aggregated across units.

Another disadvantage of an efficiency approach is that the ratio of the dollar value of outputs to dollar value of inputs is too simple to give an accurate index of efficiency. The costs of some of the inputs are partially a function of costs the organization pays for the parts, supplies, consultants, and other purchased items used to produce the outputs. There are also differences across outputs in selling expenses and markups. In addition, inflation makes comparisons of costs over time difficult. In order to deal with all these complicating factors, efficiency approaches must become substantially more complex than the simple dollar output/dollar input notion. This decreases their initial advantages in the areas of ease of calculation, understandability, and personnel acceptance.

Efficiency measures have other disadvantages as well. They may fluctuate due to factors beyond the control of the organization. An example is the price of raw materials the organization buys. If this price variation is significant, interpreting an efficiency measure is difficult. Part of the variance in the measure is caused by factors outside the control of the organization, thus its meaning as a descriptor of the organization's functioning is decreased. Another disadvantage is that it is difficult to include quality in an efficiency measure. For an input or output to be included in a traditional efficiency ratio, it must be convertible to dollars. Scaling variations in quality in terms of dollars is difficult, and because of this, measures of quality are frequently omitted from efficiency ratios.

Effectiveness is a much broader concept because it includes other factors such as standards, objectives of the organization, expectations of interested parties (e.g., shareholders, regulatory agencies, and customers), and the viability of the organization relative to its competition. Effectiveness is also understandable and easily accepted by personnel. In principle, it can be applied to any unit, from the smallest work group to the entire organization. As such it can be sensitive to small changes in productivity and useful to the operational manager and can serve as a way to evaluate organizational changes. Quality can readily be included, and it does not have the problem of getting accurate and meaningful inflation-adjusted prices for all inputs and outputs of the unit.

Effectiveness measures also have their disadvantages. To use effectiveness, it must be possible to identify meaningful organizational goals and develop measures that are consistent with these goals. Another problem with effectiveness is that meeting organizational goals without consideration of the resources used to do so may not be in the best interests of the organization. An organization could meet its goals very well but use far too many resources in doing so. Thus, effectiveness used alone can be just as dysfunctional as efficiency used alone.

Organizational Models.   A third issue that cuts across the productivity literature has to do with the model of organizations used as the basis for conceptualization and measurement. This is really an issue that comes from the organizational effectiveness literature (e.g., Steers, 1975), but also applies to productivity. While a variety of organizational models have been identified (e.g., Cameron & Whetten, 1983; Quinn & Cameron, 1983; Quinn & Rohrbaugh, 1983), I will focus on three: (a) the natural systems model (Campbell, 1977), (b) the multiple constituency model (e.g., Connolly, Conlon, & Deutsch, 1980; Keeley, 1978; Pennings & Goodman, 1977), and (c) the goal-oriented model (Campbell, 1977).

The Natural Systems Model. This model (e.g., see Georgopoulos & Tannenbaum, 1957; Katz & Kahn, 1978; Yuchtman & Seashore, 1967) assumes that the demands on an organization are so complex and changing that it is not possible to identify a finite set of organizational goals that are definable in any meaningful way. Instead, the natural systems approach assumes that the overall goal of the organization is survival. To maximize survival, different natural systems models propose or assume that specific organizational characteristics must be maximized. Examples of such characteristics include openness of communication, participation in decision making, and organizational trust. In this view, organizational effectiveness is thought of as the degree to which the organization is high on these critical variables.

The Multiple Constituency Model. This model considers the organization as being influenced by groups of individuals (*constituencies*) internal and external to the organization, such as managers, employees, customers, and so forth. These different constituencies have different goals based on their own self-interests. This model of organizations implies that there is no single set of goals or objectives for the organization and organizational effectiveness

must be considered and measured from the perspectives of the different constituencies.

The Goal-oriented Model. This model (e.g., see Barnard, 1938; Etzioni, 1964; Perrow, 1970) assumes that the organization is run by a set of rational decision makers who have a manageable set of goals for the organization that can be defined well enough to be understood and that it is possible to develop a strategy to achieve these goals. Organizational effectiveness can be thought of as the degree to which these goals are met.

Issues of Which Models to Use. The issue of which organizational model to use is more than just a theoretical concern. It is the basis from which the productivity measurement proceeds. If the natural systems or multiple constituency models are accepted, it is not meaningful to assume that a single set of usable goals exists and then try to identify them from the organizational members. Thus, the effectiveness approach to productivity is not really possible using these models, because no single set of goals or objectives can be identified upon which to base the measures. Efficiency measures have a similar problem, since they tacitly assume a fixed and useable goal of producing the most of what the organization already produces with the least amount of organizational resources. In contrast, the natural systems model would require identification of the crucial variables such as openness of communication, and productivity would be measured as the degree to which these variables are maximized. Multiple constituency models would require identification of multiple sets of goals and some integration of them into an overall measurement system.

Compared to most of the conceptual issues, there is considerable agreement about which organizational model to use in conceptualizing productivity. The majority of the literature on productivity assumes the goal-oriented approach to organizations (American

Productivity Center, 1981; Joint Financial Management Improvement Program, 1976; Kendrick, 1984; Kim, 1980; Kopelman, 1986; Mali, 1978; Muckler, 1982; Peeples, 1978; Riggs & Felix, 1983; Tuttle & Weaver, 1986a, 1986b; Tuttle, Wilkinson, & Matthews, 1985).

Units of Analysis.   Another core issue in the conceptualization of organizational productivity is what unit of analysis to use. In popular literature, the term productivity is used to refer to a unit of analysis ranging from the individual to entire countries. In technical literature, however, the units of analysis typically used range from the work group, which is the smallest (Norman & Bahiri, 1972; Tuttle, 1983; Tuttle, Wilkinson, & Matthews, 1985) to the level of national economies.

Some authors (e.g., Campbell & Campbell, 1988c; Gabris, Mitchell, & McLemore, 1985) go so far as to say that productivity should not be used at the individual level of analysis. One argument for this position is that the vast majority of work is done interdependently and thus it is difficult if not impossible to identify the contributions of individuals to the joint process. The contrasting position (e.g., Kopelman, 1986) would be that it is just as conceptually meaningful to discuss the efficiency or effectiveness of an individual as an organization or country.

An Integrated Conceptualization of Productivity

Identifying these broad issues that cut across the productivity literature should serve as a framework for understanding where any given approach to productivity fits into the larger picture. However, it is very tempting to go further and ask what the optimal conceptualization of productivity is. However, this is as dangerous as it is naive. It is dangerous because assuming that the question is worthy of an answer leads to a conceptual dead end. Productivity is an evaluative concept. It is an index of how well some organizational entity is operating. No matter how you conceptualize it, higher productivity is better than lower productivity. However, the organization has many different functions. This suggests that we must identify and agree on what functions we are interested in before we can agree on how to measure them.

The issue becomes clearer if the idea is applied to individuals. If one asks how good an individual is, the obvious answer is: How good *at what?* We may be interested in the person's scholastic performance, mechanical aptitude, or ability at Ping-Pong, but it makes little sense to deal with the *overall* goodness of an individual. Thus, it is inappropriate to try to answer the question of how good an individual is.

Yet we have a history of doing exactly that in other areas. The best example is in the area of organizational effectiveness. Here researchers took the position that organizational effectiveness was a reasonable construct and, with enough work, agreement could be reached on what it meant. Once that was accomplished, the determinants of organizational effectiveness could be examined and this would be a major theoretical and practical contribution. In retrospect, it is not surprising that the area reached a conceptual dead end, most strikingly articulated by Goodman (1979) when he requested "a moratorium on all studies on organizational effectiveness, books on organizational effectiveness and chapters on organizational effectiveness" (p. 4). The problem was that researchers assumed that it made sense to ask how good (effective) the organization is overall, and not how good the organization is *at some function.*

I like to call this approach the "Holy Grail" model. It is the assumption that there is one true conceptualization and measurement approach that can be found if enough scholarly knights overcome enough definitional dragons. The productivity literature abounds with the Holy Grail model. It is subtle but distinctly present. It is most clearly seen when an author implies that there is one best way to conceptualize or measure productivity.

Rather than fall into the trap of the Holy Grail model, my position and that of others (Belcher, 1982; Campbell & Campbell, 1988c; Mahoney, 1988) is that one must first identify the purpose for measuring productivity. There are different purposes, and the different purposes suggest different approaches—no one approach is best.

Identifying Purposes for Measuring Productivity. An exhaustive list of all the possible purposes for measuring productivity would be a long one. However, these multiple purposes fall rather nicely into five major categories, which serve as a useful taxonomic structure:

- *Comparing large aggregations of organizations.* Comparing national economies such as the United States with Japan or comparing the electronics industry to the health care industry are examples. The goal is to see, for example, which nation is more productive.

- *Evaluating the overall productivity of individual organizations for comparison with each other or with some standard.* Assessing the productivity of individual organizations in order to decide whether a particular firm would be a good financial investment would be an example of this application. Comparing organizations to other similar organizations in order to assess their competitive position is another example.

- *Gaining management information.* Here the focus is on a single organization, and productivity deals with the functioning of the human/technological system. Such measurement is used by top management for strategic planning and policy making. The main question is how well the entire organization or major parts of it are functioning and whether this functioning

is improving or declining. Decisions that will be made have to do with allocation of resources to the various organizational functions and with the growth or reduction of these functions.

- *Controlling parts of the organization.* This purpose is often overlooked, especially by psychologists (Weiss, 1989). However, controlling the movement and timing of both material resources and output products is quite important to the efficiency of the throughput process. Under this heading are included such activities as production engineering, quality control, production scheduling, physical distribution, materials management, logistics, and inventory control. Also included would be controlling the functioning in other areas such as the profitability of the organization's capital investment strategy.

The intent of such a productivity measurement system is to assess the quality of functioning of a part of the organization by monitoring that functioning. The goal is to identify whether problems are developing or to assess the effect of changes made in the operations. The major distinction between the management information system and control function is that the management information system is done on a larger part of the organization and typically deals with more macro measures. The control function is typically done on a single, identifiable function using very specific measures unique to that function.

- *Use as a motivational tool* (Algera, 1989). The objective is to improve productivity, and the assumption is that if individuals change their behavior appropriately, productivity will increase. One example of this approach is measuring productivity and feeding the productivity data back to unit personnel, with the assumption that this will produce the appropriate behavior change that will lead to the increase in productivity.

The assumption in measurement for motivational impact is that the personnel in the organization have a great impact on the productivity of the organization. While the technical subsystem is also important, the focus is not on that part of the system directly, but rather on how the technical subsystem is used by the personnel. Therefore, to increase productivity one needs to increase the productivity of the personnel in the organization.

This productivity increase would occur through changes in motivation, where motivation is broadly defined to include amplitude, persistence, and direction of behavior (e.g., Campbell & Pritchard, 1976). Personnel would exert more effort and be more persistent in their efforts. They would work more efficiently; their efforts would be more directly related to organizational objectives. They would also improve their work strategies and would use their own and others' time and efforts with less waste.

Implications of the Various Purposes.   Each of these purposes requires a productivity measurement system that is quite different from and largely incompatible with the others. For example, if one wants to compare national economies, the economic approach is the only really practical method. This means using an efficiency approach with its advantages and disadvantages, because measuring the effectiveness of large numbers of organizations is not feasible. In addition, because of the practical constraints, only very macro measures of inputs and outputs can be used. Because such measures are so broad, they are not useful for management information systems or for day-to-day management. In addition, these macro measures will not be useful for guiding

resource allocation within an organizational unit or for providing information useful for motivational purposes. To be comparable across organizations doing very different things, the only measures that can be used are those that are common across all organizations and for which data are available. This typically limits measures to partial productivity measures, typically focusing on labor productivity. Such measures will not give a complete picture of organizational functioning since they measure only some of the inputs and outputs. Finally, to compare national economies, the goal-oriented model of organizations must be used since the economic approach assumes that all organizations have the goal of generating maximum outputs with the least inputs.

If the purpose is to compare specific organizations to each other, then an economic or accounting approach is most appropriate. With these approaches, indices of productivity could be generated reflecting the functioning of the entire organization, and these indices could be used for comparison purposes. If the comparison is on the financial health of the organizations, then the accounting approach is more appropriate; if the comparison is on more general functioning, the economic approach would probably be chosen.

One main difference between measuring productivity for use as a motivational tool and the other purposes relates to the issue of separating out the effects of factors that personnel can control from those that personnel cannot control. In the other four applications, it is desirable to assess the combined effects of the personnel and the technology (management information system, organizational control) or the combined effects of the personnel, the technology, and the environment (organizational comparison or aggregated organizational comparison). Measuring productivity for motivational purposes implies measuring those aspects of the organization's productivity that the personnel can control. The principle is that to be maximally effective, feedback should be limited to aspects of the work that personnel can control.

There are a number of other differences between the motivational purpose and the other purposes. One difference is that all aspects of the work should be measured. For example, both quantity and quality should be measured if they are both important. The other approaches must frequently be satisfied with incomplete measures of productivity, since measuring all important functions is not feasible. Another difference in the motivational purpose is that the productivity measurement system should be applicable to all units of the organization, not just production or areas where outputs are easily measured. Both effectiveness and efficiency are typically important in the motivational approach, since using just efficiency can produce the significant disadvantages discussed above.

Thus, it is clear that to ask what is the optimal conceptualization of productivity is the wrong question. The proper conceptualization depends on the purpose of measurement. Once the purpose is identified, decisions about which approach to take (e.g., economic vs. behavioral or efficiency vs. effectiveness) or which unit of analysis to use become much easier.

A Definition of Productivity

With all this discussion of the conceptual issues surrounding productivity as background, a definition of productivity can now be presented. *Productivity is how well a system uses its resources to achieve its goals.*

Embedded in this simple definition are a number of important points. First, productivity is a systems concept that can apply to various entities ranging from an individual or a machine to a company, industry, or national economy. The term *productivity* is and can be applied to any of these.

The definition also implies that productivity is a description of how well the system does

something. As such, it is an evaluative concept. A productivity measurement system can evaluate how well the system does a variety of different things. A given measurement system can answer a number of questions about a system, but since different systems with different functions are present in an organization, one measurement system cannot evaluate all the systems and all the functions.

Thus, the developer or user of the productivity measurement system must ask what system and what functions of that system are to be evaluated. One could evaluate how efficiently national economies translate inputs into outputs, how efficiently the supply function works, or how effectively human efforts are translated into meeting organizational goals. These are very different systems and very different characteristics that are being evaluated.

This definition of productivity also includes both efficiency and effectiveness as part of productivity, in that both efficient use of inputs to produce outputs and producing outputs that meet organizational goals are included. As described earlier, some define productivity as simply an efficiency concept, expressed as outputs/inputs. However, this definition has severe limitations, especially in that efficiency alone ignores what the organization needs to produce and what the market is and implicitly devalues the need for allocating inputs to functions that do not have immediate effects on outputs. Another argument in favor of using both efficiency and effectiveness is that a definition of productivity broader than just efficiency has clearly been accepted by scholars and more popular sources. Ilgen and Klein (1988) make a good point when they state that "the definition used by society is much less restrictive (than just efficiency). As a result, this restricted definition is likely to confuse rather than enlighten" (p. 144).

While both efficiency and effectiveness are included in the definition, productivity is different from the concepts of output, production, profitability, production capability, and performance. Output and production refer to the raw amount of output produced without regard to inputs or goals. Production capability is the organization's potential maximum output without regard to inputs or goals. Profitability refers to the difference between revenues and costs. Performance is a fairly nebulous term that typically refers to simple output or an evaluation of behavior.

This definition of productivity also accepts a goal-oriented model of organizations, with some revisions from the natural systems and the multiple constituency models. Like the natural systems model, the definition assumes that all systems in organizations have survival as their primary goal. However, beyond this overriding goal, they also have goals that are identifiable and describable and that are stable enough to guide action. This definition also agrees with the natural systems and multiple constituency approaches that it is inappropriate to think that these goals are totally the product of rational decision making and are the sole determinants of organizational actions. These goals and objectives are frequently determined after considerable activity has taken place rather than before (Simon, 1964; Starbuck, 1965; Weick, 1969). In addition, the determination of objectives is a developmental, evolutionary, and highly political process that is less than totally rational, and objectives sometimes must be set for an unknowable future (Pennings & Goodman, 1977; Pfeffer, 1977; Pfeffer & Salancik, 1977, 1978). Finally, objectives are indeed the result of a process of negotiation of different constituencies with different needs and varying influence (Pennings & Goodman, 1977). However, with all these complexities, the position I have taken is that for the practical purpose of measuring productivity, goals can be identified for the vast majority of organizations that are accurate and relatively stable indicators of the system's objectives.

The specific goals that the productivity measurement system will be based on depends on the objectives of those developing the system. The developers determine the system that will be measured and then identify the goals of that system. If the measurement is for a work group, the ultimate source of the system's goals is typically the management of the organization. However, one could just as easily talk about the productivity of that unit from the perspective of customers or the labor union represented in the work group. If such a group were developing the productivity measurement system, they would identify somewhat different goals for the system (the work unit), and the measurement would assess how well those goals were being met given the resources available.

This definitional approach has definite advantages. It avoids the conceptual bind of needing to specify what unit of analysis is productivity and what is not. For example, a question in the productivity literature is whether it is meaningful to speak of individual productivity. In my approach, an individual is a system with inputs, processing, and outputs just like a group, unit, organization, industry, or national economy. Since we can talk of the productivity of any system, an arbitrary specification of what unit of analysis is appropriate for inclusion in the concept of productivity becomes meaningless. It will typically be impractical to actually measure the productivity of individuals because of the difficulty of such measurement and the interdependencies of individuals in organizations, but in principle, individual productivity is an appropriate concept.

This definition also allows for any disciplinary perspective. The assumption is that all perspectives are valuable for evaluating certain aspects of certain systems. Once the system is identified and the functions or goals to be assessed are determined, whatever disciplinary perspective offers the best tools for the job should be used.

Measurement Issues
Relevant to Productivity

Issues of Measurement

With these conceptual issues in mind, we can now turn to some measurement topics that must be considered in dealing with productivity. Some of these issues are unique to productivity measurement, while others are traditional issues that take on new twists when applied to productivity.

For the remainder of this chapter, I shall assume the behavioral perspective. That is, the purpose for measuring productivity is to improve it through the behavior of individuals in the organization. However, many of the issues raised will also apply to the other purposes.

Scope. A clear message that comes from both the feedback and the productivity literature can be stated simply as *What you measure is what you get*. The idea is that what is measured and especially what is fed back will produce behavior changes that will produce improvements in those things measured (Duerr, 1974; Peeples, 1978; Pritchard et al., 1988, 1989; Tuttle & Weaver, 1986b). This is a powerful phenomenon and has important implications.

One implication is that it is crucial that the system include measurement of all the important functions of the organizational unit, whether that unit be an individual, a group, a department, or an organization. Many authors have argued this point (Algera , 1989; Alluisi & Megis, 1983; Mahoney, 1988; Mali, 1978; Pritchard et al., 1988, 1989; Shetty & Buehler, 1985; Stein, 1986). The point is that because of the power of measurement and feedback, those functions measured take on particular importance in the operation of the unit. Functions not measured are implicitly given a lower priority. It is thus very risky to measure only a subset of the important functions and then expect personnel to focus equal attention on unmeasured functions. For example, measuring quantity and not quality and then expecting unit personnel to carefully attend to both would be a risky expectation. It is very common for this partial measurement to occur, usually because only those organizational functions that are easily measured are used, while those functions that are difficult to measure are ignored.

A second implication of the phenomenon that you get what you measure is that great care must be taken in what is measured so as not to result in unintentional negative consequences. What seems like a perfectly reasonable measure of a function may have negative consequences if unit personnel improve on that measure. Consider a unit that repairs equipment used by other parts of the organization. If a piece of equipment malfunctions, this unit must repair it as quickly as possible to get it back into operation. As a measure of the repair unit's functioning, one could divide the number of pieces of equipment repaired by the number of personnel in the unit. This would be a typical labor efficiency index and would seem to be a reasonable measure. However, to improve on the measure the unit should (a) do each repair faster, (b) make sure it has plenty of work to do so that there will be no idle personnel time, and (c) reduce the number of personnel.

The problem is that if the goal of the unit is to get equipment repaired quickly so that production can continue, labor efficiency is probably not very important. What is important is that the repairs be done rapidly so that down time is minimized. Consequently, reducing the number of personnel or developing a backlog of work so that there will be no idle personnel will in fact be the exact opposite of what should be done to improve the contribution of the repair unit. Both results would increase the time it takes the unit to complete the repairs. Thus, the labor efficiency measure has unintended negative consequences if the unit improves on it.

Reliability and Validity. Reliability and validity are the old standby criteria for good measures. Clearly, these concepts apply to productivity measurement as well. However, applying them to productivity is not a straightforward process.

Reliability estimates of productivity measures are complicated by the fact that productivity is a *state* rather than a *trait* concept. Variation in productivity over time would be expected due to changing work demands, number of personnel, availability of raw materials, and effort levels of personnel. Thus, any sort of test-retest or odd-even reliability measures would be inappropriate. Using these forms of reliability for productivity would be analogous to measuring the temperature each day and concluding that variation was an indication of the unreliability of the thermometer.

Internal consistency estimates of reliability would also be inappropriate. The internal consistency logic would dictate that the various measures of overall productivity should be considered items on an instrument and the intercorrelations between the measures should be the basis of the internal consitency estimate. This approach is inappropriate since there is no reason to expect that the ability of the unit personnel to attend to paperwork should be correlated with the amount of output they produce. One might even expect a negative relationship between indicators of productivity, since increasing the resources applied to one aspect of the work would typically mean removing resources from another.

Validity information is also a more complex issue in productivity measurement. The main problem is that there is no criterion against which to compare the productivity measure. If the unit has a good criterion for productivity, it would be pointless to develop another. Even if this were done, which of the two should be the ultimate criterion is not clear. If the new system does not correlate with the old one, is it because the new system has considerable error or because the old one does? Another explanation for the difference is that one system might include important functions of the unit that the other does not.

Part of the problem is that productivity measurement is an operational definition of organizational policy. Thus, a key validity issue is how well the measurement system captures the policy for that unit. Assessing this is not an easy task.

Objective Versus Subjective Measures. An unfortunate development in our field has been the artificial dichotomy between objective and subjective measures. We make a clear distinction between the two and argue or at least strongly imply that objective measures are better than subjective measures. There is actually much less difference between the two types of measures than this distinction implies (Campbell, 1977; Guion, 1965; Muckler, 1982; Seashore, 1972).

The term *subjective* connotes error, bias, and generally low-quality data. Subjective actually means that judgment is involved in the measurement process. But subjective judgment is involved in any measurement process. As Muckler (1982) noted, "it is not possible to measure anything without the intervention of the human at some point in the measurement process.... Human intervention is rampant in all...steps" (p. 25).

The subjective nature of measurement is particularly an issue in productivity measurement. What measures are chosen is a subjective process: It is based on judgment. The measures represent judgments made by organizational personnel regarding what the unit should be doing. If labor efficiency is measured and fed back to an organizational unit, a judgment has been made that high labor efficiency is an important thing for the unit to have. This is a subjective judgment, making the resulting measurement at least partially subjective in nature.

In addition, most productivity measurement systems attempt to combine the individual measures into an overall index reflecting productivity. To combine measures requires that they be expressed on a common metric and be aggregated. Choice of the common metric is by definition a value judgment. Economists use money, converting each input and output to its value in dollars. This sounds quite objective, but it is actually a subjective decision. It assumes that the financial status of the organization is the only thing of importance and that all functions of the organization can be converted to a dollar equivalent. Neither of these assumptions is completely true, but the decision has been made that they are true enough to make conversion to dollars a useful approach. The choice of an aggregation strategy is also subjective. For example, if different measures are combined according to their importance, judgment is required to decide the relative importance.

The real issue here is that any measurement system is a reflection of organizational policy. The measures reflect (a) what the unit should and should not be doing, (b) how important these functions are relative to each other, and (c) how the functions are combined to produce the overall contribution of the unit. Productivity measures are operational definitions of organizational policy, and policy is by nature subjective. No matter how objective the actual data are, the decisions that were made to select those measures and how they would be combined are subjective judgments. Consequently, the final measurement system must by definition have a strong subjective component.

Thus, whether a measure is subjective or objective is really an irrelevant point. Since all measurement systems are in part subjective, attempting to develop a totally objective system is futile.

What is important is the quality of the data, not its objectivity or subjectivity. Subjective data is seen as suspect because of its potential for bias. In the productivity area, the subjectivity of the measures is a special concern because of the possibility of intentional bias. If the subjective nature of the data can allow unit personnel to fake the data, or if individuals who make the subjective judgments can bias the measurement to inflate or deflate the contribution of a unit, the measurement system will be weakened. The solution is to conduct the measurement so that the data will be unbiased. The issue is not subjectivity—it is data quality.

Controllability. If the purpose of measuring productivity is to increase it through behavior, it is important that the measures be under the control of the personnel. The measures should be such that if personnel change their behavior, the measures change in predictable ways. Giving a unit feedback using measures over which they have little control weakens the power of the feedback system to motivate. In expectancy theory terms (e.g., Campbell & Pritchard, 1976), the relationship between effort and performance is reduced if the unit does not have control over the measures, thus weakening motivation.

Range of Application. Another issue in measurement is the types of work that are applicable for productivity measurement. Such measurement can be seen by many behavioral types as largely applicable to production-oriented settings, where objective measures of output are readily available. This perception is natural since most applications of productivity measurement have historically been made in such settings, and most descriptions of systems use production settings as examples. However, productivity measurement is applicable to almost any type of work. It can be done with professional, administrative, or scientific personnel doing cognitive, creative, or service activities. Measures such as units of scholarly work completed, success in meeting deadlines, number of corrections needed to the work later in the process, degree of customer satisfaction, number of return customers, success in meeting budgets, and number of requests for corrections to paperwork are all perfectly appropriate output measures.

Such measures can be successfully used for productivity measurement in many types of work. For example, the approach to measuring productivity developed by my students and me (Pritchard, 1990; Pritchard et al., 1989) has been successfully developed for production-oriented work but has also been successful for measuring productivity of maintenance personnel, managers of insurance agents, bank personnel at several organizational levels, college professors, and air traffic controllers, as well as for measuring the productivity of an in-house library research unit, and a bar in a restaurant.

When measurement is proposed to personnel in these nonproduction jobs, their first response is typically, "You can't measure what we do." However, if you ask such people if they have any idea how well the unit is doing its job and whether they are doing better or worse than they used to do, they can usually answer. If they can, they are indeed measuring the productivity of the unit. The task of the measurement specialist is to get the information that is in their heads into a quantifiable measurement system.

Design Criteria for a Productivity Measurement System

Productivity measurement presents some unique issues not always present for other measurement problems. Many issues about specific productivity measures are raised in two excellent discussions by Mahoney (1988) and Tuttle (1981). I will deal here with more general issues. Ideally, a productivity measurement system should meet a number of design criteria to be maximally useful in changing productivity through behavior change.

Overall Index of Productivity. A productivity measurement system should produce an overall index of productivity. One reason a single index is important is its motivational value. A single index provides personnel with a sense of improvement or decrement. This allows them to see the results of their efforts and strengthens the ties between behavior and outcomes. A single index is also beneficial for its information value. A large number of pieces of information about organizational functioning can be very difficult to assimilate and use for making decisions.

A single index is also useful for attempts at organizational change. It is valuable for designing interventions such as goal setting and incentives because the single index can readily be used for setting the goal and as the basis for awarding the incentives. Multiple measures require multiple goals and make awarding incentives difficult. Having a single index also makes it fairly easy to evaluate the effects of behavioral, structural, or technological change efforts. Many approaches to measuring productivity use a single index (e.g., Joint Financial Management Improvement Program, 1976; Kim, 1980; Peeples, 1978; Pritchard et al., 1989; Riggs & Felix, 1983; Rowe, 1981; Tuttle & Weaver, 1986a, 1986b; Tuttle, Wilkinson, & Matthews, 1985).

Subindices of Productivity. Related to the use of an overall index of productivity is the use of subindices. Since the vast majority of organizational units do multiple activities, it is important to use multiple indices of productivity that provide information on the separate functions of the unit. Personnel can then see how they are doing on the different functions and change their behavior accordingly. Information on subindices is also useful for identifying problem areas and determining strategies to increase productivity.

Importance Weighting. The various things an organizational unit does are not of equal importance, and this differing importance must be preserved in the measurement system. Measures of quantity, quality, extent to which preventative maintenance is done on schedule, and timeliness of paperwork may all be aspects of the work, but these activities would vary considerably in importance. Thus, some method of importance weighting must be used so differing importance is communicated and so that the measures can be aggregated into the single index in such a way that the differing importance is maintained.

Maintaining Nonlinearities. Another issue in productivity measurement has to do with the fact that there is frequently not a linear relationship between how much an organizational unit does of a given activity and the amount of contribution that level of the activity makes to the overall functioning of the unit. One situation in which this frequently occurs is where the value of the unit's output gets higher and higher until it reaches a point of diminishing returns. For example, a point of diminishing returns is frequently met once a large number of units are being produced and further increases in quantity are not as valuable. Another example occurs in the area of training. Training may be a crucial function in the organization, but training more people than needed to do the work becomes counterproductive.

Pritchard et al. (1989) refer to this as the nonlinearity issue because the function relating amount of output to value or effectiveness of that output is not linear. This means that attempting to get overall importance weights for combining measures is not the most valid approach, since the importance of a measure changes as a function of the existing level of the output. For example, suppose a unit manufactures a product and must also maintain its equipment. Overall, the amount of output is more important than doing preventative maintenance on the equipment. However, if number of units produced is already high and many pieces of equipment are overdue for maintenance, maintenance may become more important than further improvements to the number of units produced.

This problem has been recognized before. Campbell (1977), Kahn (1977), Seashore (1972), and Campbell and Campbell (1988c) have made similar arguments that more is not always better. A solution to the problem has been offered by Pritchard et al. (1989), who have developed a method of accounting for nonlinearities in measures of performance and productivity. Pritchard and Roth (in press) compared a productivity composite that accounted for nonlinearities with one based on a linear system and found that the nonlinear system produced information leading to very different decisions on how to improve productivity than did the linear system. Sawyer, Pritchard, and Hedley-Goode (1990) found similar results when they compared linear and nonlinear composites in performance appraisal measures.

Aggregation Across Units. Another desirable feature of a productivity measurement system is the ability to aggregate the measurement systems of different units into a single broader measurement system. For example, suppose one department of a community mental health organization has six sections. It would be desirable to develop a measurement system for each section and then aggregate those systems upward to produce, first, a single measure for the department, and then a single measure for the multiple departments.

Such aggregation requires that the separate functions of the smallest units be measured and that the measurement for the separate units be expressed in a common metric. Next, since not all units are equal in their contribution to the broader organizational unit, a determination of the relative importance or contribution of each of the units must be made in doing the aggregation.

Comparison of Units. It would also be desirable to be able to directly compare the productivity of units doing quite different things. For example, it would be very informative to be able to compare a maintenance unit with a production unit in the same part of the organization. Such a comparison would be useful for allocating resources, producing competition between units, and awarding outcomes such as incentives and recognition to the units.

What is needed is some way of determining how well the unit is functioning given its resources, compared to other units given their resources. Such a comparison would indicate how good a job each of the units was doing.

Combining Efficiency and Effectiveness Measures. An ideal productivity measurement system should also be able to accommodate both efficiency and effectiveness measures, since both have advantages. A system that could only accommodate one or the other would not be as useful. It is also possible to combine efficiency and effectiveness measures in an attempt to get the advantages of both. One way to do this is to express output on a measure relative to goals or expectations (effectiveness) and then divide that index by the inputs required to produce the output. For example, suppose number of clients served was an important index of the quantity of output for a unit and that the expectation was serving 50 clients per day. If the unit averaged 55 clients per day, an effectiveness index might be $55/50 \times 100 = 110\%$. This could then be divided by an index of labor hours expended to get a measure combining effectiveness and efficiency.

Approaches to Measuring Organizational Productivity

A number of specific approaches to measuring organizational productivity have been suggested (e.g., Craig & Harris, 1973; Deming, 1986; Joint Financial Management Improvement Program, 1976; Kendrick, 1984; Kopelman, 1986; Mali, 1978; National Center for

Productivity and Quality of Working Life, 1978; Peeples, 1978; Pritchard et al., 1989; Riggs & Felix, 1983; Rowe, 1981; Sink, 1985; Tuttle & Weaver, 1986a, 1986b; Tuttle, Wilkinson, & Matthews, 1985). In this section, a sample of these approaches is discussed and compared to the desirable productivity measurement characteristics described above.

Kendrick. Kendrick (1984) discusses several types of measurement systems for single organizations, comparing different firms, and for industry and economy comparisons. Here the focus is on his discussion of a system for measuring the productivity of a single firm. He refers to this system as the American Productivity Center performance measurement system.

This productivity measurement system applies a combination of the economic and the accounting perspectives to the single organization. It is an attempt to develop productivity measures that are reconcilable with profitability measures. Kendrick (1984) makes the assumption that "any form of measure other than profitability risks being sidetracked if it is not reconcilable directly with profitability planning data" (p. 57).

The system starts with the following equation:

Profitability = productivity x price recovery

Profitability is the relationship between the value of the output and the value of the inputs used to produce those outputs. *Productivity* is the relationship between the amount of inputs used and the amount of outputs sold. *Price recovery* is the relationship between unit price and unit cost. It is an index of the ability or desire of an organization to pass on its unit cost changes through price changes.

To conduct the measurement, data are needed on the value, quantity, and price for each time period for each output and input of the unit being analyzed. Using this data, a series of ratios are formed and compared over time. Kendrick notes that there are a number of complexities in using the approach and that sophisticated accounting techniques are required to use it.

The productivity part of the measurement system is an example of the economic/accounting approach, considering productivity to be the efficiency of the translation of inputs into outputs. It has all the advantages and disadvantages of such an approach that were discussed above. Another major advantage of this approach is the reconciliation with profitability. Such approaches also have a significant number of problems when applied to a single firm analysis. Kendrick discusses some of these as does Tuttle (1981) and Mahoney (1988). Essentially, a number of major assumptions have to be made for such approaches to provide valid measurement. For example, when the mix of products changes over time, comparisons of the output/input ratios are difficult to interpret. This would occur when new products or new models of existing products are introduced. One has to assume that such factors will have negligible effects or develop very complex correction factors to account for them.

Deming. One could argue that the Deming (1986) approach, known as *statistical process control,* is not really a productivity measurement system, but rather a method to improve quality. However, because it has considerable application in industry and is a very different approach than most others, it is worth discussion here.

The Deming approach is the outgrowth of his experience since 1950 helping Japanese organizations improve quality. It is based on the assumptions that (a) every goods- or service-producing operation can be viewed as a system with inputs, process, and outputs; (b) quality is what customers want; (c) quality and productivity are related because higher quality leads to decreasing scrap, rework, duplication, and wasted effort; (d) only management can

change the system; and (e) people want to do a good job—that is, the desire to have pride in one's work is a powerful motivator.

Improving quality is the focus of this system. *Statistical process control* (SPC) is the primary means of accomplishing this improvement. The basic technique is to plot multiple measures of quality over time and compare this performance with expected variation in the measures. When the quality measures exceed the expected/acceptable range, personnel are expected to bring the measures back to the acceptable range. This is done by examining rejected units and determining the reason for the rejection. Causes are then prioritized and changes made to correct them. Identification of the causes are based on a series of problem-solving and evaluation techniques.

The measurement part of this approach is essentially the industrial engineering approach of control by measuring system output. What is unique is the focus on quality, the clear specifications of acceptable quality ranges, and the formal problem-solving techniques that take place when variation outside the limits occurs.

Rowe. Rowe (1981) developed a productivity measurement system for white collar workers at Westinghouse. The unit of analysis is the department, and the basic process is to use nominal group techniques to brainstorm ideas for ways of measuring productivity. Departmental management then selects the measures that best meet the departmental objectives. A composite departmental index is generated by weighting the measures by their importance and summing them into an overall index. An overall index aggregating all the different departments into a division-wide index is generated by weighting each department according to its importance.

Peeples. Peeples (1978) describes a productivity measurement system developed for data processing units at GTE. First, the overall objectives of the units were established. In doing this, it became clear that both efficiency and effectiveness measures were needed. Next, measures of each of the objectives were developed. A point system was developed for each measure and points were awarded for different levels of performance on each measure: The higher the performance, the more points awarded. The more important indicators were given more points. The overall index was the sum of the points earned during a given period.

Tuttle. The *methodology for generating efficiency and effectiveness measures* (MGEEM) was developed by Tuttle and his associates (Tuttle & Weaver, 1986a, 1986b; Tuttle, Wilkinson, & Matthews, 1985). This approach is based on a well-developed conceptual foundation with a strong systems orientation. The methodology calls for using a formal measurement coordinator, someone external to the organization who is skilled at group process activities such as running meetings, facilitating group discussions, interviewing, and listening. MGEEM is a top-down approach where the objectives of the unit—termed *key results areas*—are first identified by management. Some of these top managers and their subordinates meet to develop indices that would measure how well the objectives are met. Group discussion and nominal group techniques are used to accomplish this.

Once the specific efficiency and effectiveness measures have been developed, they are combined using the approach suggested by Riggs and Felix (1983). The Riggs and Felix approach is a sophisticated productivity measurement system in its own right. In this approach, the current level of functioning on each indicator is given a value of 3 and the goal for that indicator is given a value of 10. Subgoals are established in between, with point values from 4 to 9. Levels of performance below the current level are given values from 0 to 2. Overall importance weights are established for

each indicator. Productivity for each indicator is the obtained point value multiplied by the importance weight. Overall productivity is the sum of these products. To aggregate across units, the overall productivity score of each unit is weighted by the importance of each unit, typically determined by the number of personnel in each unit.

Pritchard. The last productivity measurement system to be discussed was developed by Pritchard et al. (1989) and is referred to as the *productivity measurement and enhancement system* (ProMES). The most complete description of the system can be found in Pritchard (1990). This system is based on the conceptualization of motivation and roles developed by Naylor, Pritchard, and Ilgen (1980). The first step in the development of this system is for a group of first- and second-line supervisors and representative incumbents to develop the objectives of the unit through group discussion. Next, measures of how well the unit is accomplishing each of the objectives are identified. When consensus is reached by the group, the objectives, termed *products,* and the measures, termed *indicators,* are presented to higher management for approval.

After measures are approved, they are combined into a single index by developing what are termed *contingencies.* A contingency is a graphic function representing the relationship between the amount of an indicator and the contribution that amount of the indicator makes to overall productivity. In essence, the possible values of the indicator are scaled as to how much contribution each value would make to the overall effectiveness of the unit. A series of steps are used in developing contingencies, but the basic process is for the group of supervisors and representative incumbents to go through a set of discussions that result in a step-by-step building of the contingencies and getting them approved by upper management.

The contingencies have two noteworthy features. First, the overall slope of the function expresses the relative importance of the indicator. A steep slope implies that variations in the indicator result in large variations in productivity; a less steep slope implies that variations in the indicator result in smaller variations in productivity. A second noteworthy aspect of the contingencies is that they can be nonlinear. A contingency allows for a constant amount of change in the indicator to result in a differential change in productivity.

Actual applications of the system have indicated that nonlinearities are the rule rather than the exception. For example, Pritchard et al. (1988, 1989) found that none of the 45 indicators in their study of five organizational units were linear.

Once the contingencies are completed and approved by higher management, the overall index of productivity is generated. First, the indicator data for a given time period is collected. Then the corresponding effectiveness score for each indicator is determined from the contingency. For example, if 23 units were produced, there would be a corresponding effectiveness value for that level of output. An analogous effectiveness value for each of the indicators would be calculated from the corresponding contingency. These values are then summed to obtain an overall measure of productivity.

From this basic information, feedback reports are generated and fed back to unit personnel and management on a regular basis. Meetings between incumbents and supervisors are then held to evaluate the reports and identify strategies to improve productivity.

This system also has other features. It will accommodate both efficiency and effectiveness measures. It will allow for aggregation of the measurement system from individual units into larger organizational units and for direct comparison across units doing different things. It also has a mechanism for identifying in quantitative terms what the priorities should be for improving productivity.

Comparison of the Systems

These representative productivity measurement systems vary considerably in the purpose of measurement, the sophistication of the measurement process, and the features the systems include. The similarities and differences are summarized in Table 1. The table starts with the primary purpose of the system from among the five primary purposes described earlier in the chapter. While the primary purpose of each is indicated, a number of the systems are capable of being used for the other purposes as well.

In addition, the desirable characteristics of productivity measurement systems reviewed above are used as the factors against which to compare the different systems. If a system provides an *overall index* of productivity for the unit measured, this is indicated. The next comparison factor is whether the *subindices* measured by the system are *on a common metric*. All the systems described use subindices. The issue here is whether the system can express each of the subindices or multiple measures on a common efficiency or effectiveness metric. *Important weights* and *nonlinearities* refer to whether the system has a formal way of dealing with the varying importance of measures and their nonlinear characteristics. *Aggregation across units* is an indication of whether the system has a described methodology for combining units into broader organizational units. *Direct unit comparison* refers to whether a method of comparing the productivity of units doing different things is presented. The last comparison factor is whether a system accommodates both *efficiency and effectiveness* measures.

In making the comparisons, if a system formally includes a feature such as direct comparison across units, it is so indicated by a "Yes" in that cell. If a feature is not formally discussed by a given system, it gets a "No" in the table. However, it should be noted that it is possible to modify some systems from their original formulation using procedures

TABLE 1

Comparison of Measurement Systems to the Design Criteria

	Kendrick	Deming	Rowe	Peeples	MGEEM	ProMES
Primary purpose	Management Information	Control	Motivation	Motivation	Motivation	Motivation
Overall index	Yes	No	Yes	Yes	Yes	Yes
Subindices on a common metric	Partial	Partial	Yes	Yes	Yes	Yes
Importance weights	No	No	Yes	Yes	Yes	Yes
Nonlinearities	No	No	No	No	No	Yes
Aggregation across units	Partial	No	Yes	No	Yes	Yes
Direct unit comparison	Yes	No	No	No	No	Yes
Efficiency and effectiveness	No	No	Yes	Yes	Yes	Yes

suggested by other approaches to achieve a given feature. A system is given a "Partial" if it has the feature in some methods of its application, but not in all.

Conclusions

A number of conclusions can be drawn from the productivity literature.

- *Without productivity growth, our nation will ultimately have severe problems.* It is clear that productivity growth is vitally important to our economy, our organizations, and our overall quality of life. Thus, the importance that has been placed on productivity and productivity growth is most appropriate.

- *Perspectives on productivity vary widely.* Many different disciplines have made contributions to productivity. These disciplines have very different perspectives on what productivity is, what questions should be addressed in productivity research, and how productivity measurement should be conducted. It is thus important to know the other person's perspective when talking about productivity. Furthermore, it is not uncommon for some individuals to assume that their perspective and approach is the correct one and that others are interlopers in their productivity domain. One should be sensitive to this attitude when dealing with others about productivity.

- *Do not confuse performance with productivity.* Performance and productivity are different things. While definitions of both vary, there is a clear consensus in the productivity literature that they are different. Performance is simply output or, in the case of performance appraisal, an evaluation of behavior. Productivity is output relative to inputs or relative to goals. Psychologists are frequent abusers of this distinction. The terms should not be used interchangeably.

- *Changing performance may or may not change productivity.* With the heavy emphasis on behavior in productivity, it is easy to assume that changing something about individuals will change productivity. For example, one might speak of how selection will improve productivity. However, the link between the individual and productivity is not that simple. For example, suppose we focus on the productivity of a work group. Here individual knowledge, skills, and abilities are translated into individual behavior through a process of training and motivation. The individual behavior is then combined through role perceptions, cooperation, leadership, group level motivational factors, and various constraints such as availability of materials and equipment functioning to result in group output. When this output is reflected against goals or inputs or both, productivity results. Thus, changes in knowledge, skills, and abilities or changes in training or individual motivation have their effects on productivity only indirectly. Consequently, it is a bit simplistic to assume that simply changing individuals will have a strong and direct effect on productivity.

- *Productivity requires unique conceptualization and measurement.* Many of the lessons learned from areas such as criterion development, personnel selection, and organizational effectiveness are quite appropriate for the conceptualization and measurement of organizational productivity. However, there are a number of issues that are unique to productivity. One should not simply assume that a good knowledge of our more traditional content areas will automatically lead to a complete grasp of the productivity area. It is too easy to assume that productivity is really a slight variant on performance appraisal or criterion development. It is not that simple.

- *Good methods of productivity measurement are available.* There are a number of distinct methodologies for measuring productivity, some of which are quite sound.

- *We can have a major impact on productivity.* Powerful methods of productivity measurement have been developed that are especially geared to providing feedback to increase productivity. In addition, while we have not focused on interventions in this chapter, many powerful interventions, such as goal setting, incentives, quality circles, and gainsharing, are available. If used with a good productivity measure, such interventions can result in major increases in productivity.

While we can have a powerful impact on productivity, we must be aware of our limitations. The impact we can have with the behavioral approach is limited by the amount of variance in total organizational productivity attributable to behavior, as opposed to factors such as technology and factors external to the organization. Where variations in behavior do not have much impact on productivity, our contribution will be limited.

Productivity is an area that is important, where we have much more to contribute, and where these contributions are welcomed. It is clear that the behavioral approach has made major contributions already, and we can make many more. The future looks very bright.

I would like to thank Philip Roth, Patricia Galgay Roth, and Margaret Watson for their help in the preparation of this chapter. I would also like to thank them as well as Lawrence Weiss and Amie Hedley for their comments on earlier drafts.

References

Algera, J.A. (in press). Feedback systems in organizations. In C.L. Cooper & I. Robertson (Eds.), *International review of industrial and organizational psychology: 1990.* Chichester, England: Wiley.

Alluisi, E. A., & Megis, D. K. (1983). Potentials for productivity enhancement from psychological research and development. *American Psychologist, 38*(4), 487–493.

American Productivity Center. (1979). *Productivity payoff* [Videotape]. Houston, TX: Author.

American Productivity Center. (1981). *Productivity perspectives.* Houston, TX: Author.

Balk, W. L. (1975, March–April). Technological trends in productivity measurement. *Public Personnel Management,* pp. 128–133.

Barnard, C. (1938). *The function of the executive.* Cambridge, MA: Harvard University Press.

Belcher, J. G., Jr. (1982). *The productivity management process.* Oxford: Planning Executives Institute.

Berg, I. (1984). Unemployment, productivity, and inflation: Misgivings about the sapient orthodoxy. In A. P. Brief (Ed.), *Productivity research in the behavioral and social sciences* (pp. 71–89). New York: Praeger.

Brief, A. P. (Ed.), (1984). *Productivity research in the behavioral and social sciences.* New York: Praeger.

Bullock, R. J., & Batten, D. B. (1983). *Organizational productivity: A measurement review.* Paper presented at the meeting of the Southwest Division of the Academy of Management, Houston, TX.

Cameron, K. S., & Whetten, D. A. (1983). *Organizational effectiveness: A comparison of multiple models.* New York: Academic Press.

Campbell, J. P. (1977). On the nature of organizational effectiveness. In P. S. Goodman, J. M. Pennings, & Associates (Eds.), *New perspectives on organizational effectiveness* (pp. 13–55). San Francisco: Jossey-Bass.

Campbell, J. P., & Campbell, R. J. (Eds.). (1988a). *Productivity in organizations.* San Francisco: Jossey-Bass.

Campbell, J. P., & Campbell, R. J. (1988b). What industrial-organizational psychology has to say about productivity. In J. P. Campbell & R. J. Campbell (Eds.), *Productivity in organizations* (pp. 1–10). San Francisco: Jossey-Bass.

Campbell, J. P., & Campbell, R. J. (1988c). Industrial-organizational psychology and productivity: The goodness of fit. In J. P. Campbell & R. J. Campbell (Eds.), *Productivity in organizations* (pp. 82–94). San Francisco: Jossey-Bass.

Campbell, J. P., & Pritchard, R. D. (1976). Motivation theory in industrial and organizational psychology. In M. D. Dunnette (Ed.), *Handbook of industrial and organizational psychology* (pp. 63–130). Chicago: Rand-McNally.

Connolly, T., Conlon, E. J., & Deutsch, S. J. (1980). Organizational effectiveness: A multiple-constituency approach. *Academy of Management Review, 5,* 211–217.

Coulter, P. B. (1979). Organizational effectiveness in the public sector: The example of municipal fire protection. *Administrative Science Quarterly, 24*(1), 65–81.

Craig, C. E., & Harris, R. C. (1973). Total productivity measurement at the firm level. *Sloan Management Review, 14*(3), 13–28.

Deming, W. E. (1986). *Out of the crisis.* Cambridge, MA: Massachusetts Institute of Technology.

Denison, E. F. (1984). Productivity analysis through growth accounting. In A. P. Brief (Ed.), *Productivity research in the behavioral and social sciences* (pp. 7–55). New York: Praeger.

Deprez, F. L. (1986). Office productivity. *Information Services and Use, 6,* 83–102.

Duerr, E. C. (1974). The effect of misdirected incentives on employee behavior. *Personnel Journal, 53*(12), 890–893.

Dunnette, M. D. (1982). Critical concepts in the assessment of human capabilities. In M. D.

Dunnette & E. A. Fleishman (Eds.), *Human performance and productivity: Vol. 1. Human capability assessment* (pp. 1–11). Hillsdale, NJ: Erlbaum.

Elkin, R., & Molitor, M. (1985-1986). A conceptual framework for selecting management indicators in nonprofit organizations. *Administration in Social Work, 9*(4), 13–23.

Engle, J. E. (1979). *Perspectives on productivity and organizational effectiveness.* Unpublished research report, National Defense University, Washington, DC.

Etzioni, A. (1964). *Modern organizations.* Englewood Cliffs, NJ: Prentice-Hall.

Fleishman, E. A. (1982). Introduction. In M. D. Dunnette & E. A. Fleishman (Eds.), *Human performance and productivity: Vol. 1. Human capability assessment* (pp. xv-xix). Hillsdale, NJ: Erlbaum.

Gabris, G. T., Mitchell, K., & McLemore, R. (1985). Rewarding individual and team productivity: The Biloxi merit bonus plan. *Public Personnel Management, 14*(3), 231–244.

Georgopoulos, B. S., & Tannenbaum, A. S. (1957). A study of organizational effectiveness. *American Sociological Review, 22,* 534–540.

Goodman, P. S. (1979). *Organizational effectiveness as a decision making process.* Paper presented at the 39th annual meeting of the Academy of Management, Atlanta, GA.

Guion, R. M. (1965). *Personnel testing.* New York: McGraw-Hill.

Guth, W. D. (1984). Productivity and corporate strategy. In A. P. Brief (Ed.), *Productivity research in the behavioral and social sciences* (pp. 252–267). New York: Praeger.

Guzzo, R. A. (1988). Productivity research: Reviewing psychological and economic perspectives. In J. P. Campbell & R. J. Campbell (Eds.), *Productivity in organizations* (pp. 63–81). San Francisco: Jossey-Bass.

Guzzo, R. A., Jette, R. D., & Katzell, R. A. (1985). The effects of psychologically based intervention programs on worker productivity: A meta-analysis. *Personnel Psychology, 38,* 275–291.

Hackman, J. R. (1984). Psychological contributions to organizational productivity: A commentary. In A. P. Brief (Ed.), *Productivity research in the behavioral and social sciences* (pp. 207–226). New York: Praeger.

Hage, J. (1984). Organizational theory and the concept of productivity. In A. P. Brief (Ed.), *Productivity research in the behavioral and social sciences* (pp. 91–126). New York: Praeger.

Hayes, F. O. (1977). *Productivity in local government.* Lexington, MA: Lexington Books.

House, R. J. (1984). Commentary on management research. In A. P. Brief (Ed.), *Productivity research in the behavioral and social sciences* (pp. 268–282). New York: Praeger.

Hurst, E. G. (1980). Attributes of performance measures. *Public Productivity Review, 4*(1), 43–50.

Ilgen, D. R., & Klein, H. J. (1988). Individual motivation and performance: Cognitive influences on effort and choice. In J. P. Campbell & R. J. Campbell (Eds.), *Productivity in organizations* (pp. 143–176). San Francisco: Jossey-Bass.

Joint Financial Management Improvement Program. (1976). *Productivity programs in the Federal government: Vol. 1. Productivity trends and current efforts.* Washington, DC: Author.

Kahn, R. L. (1977). Organizational effectiveness: An overview. In P. S. Goodman & J. M. Pennings (Eds.), *New perspectives in organizational effectiveness* (pp. 235–248). San Francisco: Jossey-Bass.

Kaplan, R. S. (1982). *Advanced management accounting.* Englewood Cliffs, NJ: Prentice-Hall.

Katz, D., & Kahn, R. L. (1978). *The social psychology of organizations* (2nd ed.). New York: Wiley.

Keeley, M. (1978). A social-justice approach to organizational evaluation. *Administrative Sciences Quarterly, 23,* 272–292.

Kendrick, J. W. (1977). *Understanding productivity.* Baltimore: Johns Hopkins University Press.

Kendrick, J. W. (1984). *Improving company productivity.* Baltimore: Johns Hopkins University Press.

Kerr, S. (1984). Leadership and participation. In A. P. Brief (Ed.), *Productivity research in the behavioral and social sciences* (pp. 229–251). New York: Praeger.

Kim, J. E. (1980). Cost-effectiveness/benefit analysis of post-secondary occupational programs: A conceptual framework. *Planning and Changing, 11*(3), 150–165.

Kopelman, R. E. (1986). *Managing productivity in organizations: A practical, people-oriented perspective.* New York: McGraw-Hill.

Letzkus, W. (1973). *An analysis of the impact of planning—programming—budgeting on the Air Force Operating Manager* (AFIT–TR–73-2).

Wright-Patterson AFB, OH: Air Force Institute of Technology.

Mahoney, T. A. (1984). Growth accounting and productivity: Comments. In A. P. Brief (Ed.), *Productivity research in the behavioral and social sciences* (pp. 56–67). New York: Praeger.

Mahoney, T. A. (1988). Productivity defined: The relativity of efficiency, effectiveness and change. In J. P. Campbell & R. J. Campbell (Eds.), *Productivity in organizations* (pp. 13–38). San Francisco: Jossey-Bass.

Mali, P. (1978). *Improving total productivity*. New York: Wiley.

Muckler, F. A. (1982). Evaluating productivity. In M. D. Dunnette & E. A. Fleishman (Eds.), *Human performance and productivity: Vol. 1. Human capability assessment* (pp. 13–47). Hillsdale, NJ: Erlbaum.

National Broadcasting Company. (1980). *If Japan can, why can't we?* NBC White Paper. New York: Author.

National Center for Productivity and Quality of Working Life. (1977). *The future of productivity*. Washington, DC: Author.

National Center for Productivity and Quality of Working Life. (1978). *Total performance management: Some pointers for action* (NTIS No. PB300249). Washington, DC: Author.

Naylor, J. C., Pritchard, R. D., & Ilgen, D. R. (1980). *A theory of behavior in organizations*. New York: Academic Press.

Neugarten, D. A. (1985). Strategies and tactics for productivity improvement: Implications for public personnel managers. *Public Personnel Management, 14*(4), 417–428.

Norman, R. G., & Bahiri, S. (1972). *Productivity measurement and incentives*. London: Butterworths.

Peeples, D. E. (1978). Measure for productivity. *Datamation, 24*(5), 222–230.

Pennings, J. M. (1984). Productivity: Some old and new issues. In A. P. Brief (Ed.), *Productivity research in the behavioral and social sciences* (pp. 127–140). New York: Praeger.

Pennings, J. M., & Goodman, P. S. (1977). Toward a workable framework. In P. S. Goodman, J. M. Pennings, & Associates (Eds.), *New perspectives on organizational effectiveness* (pp. 146–184). San Francisco: Jossey-Bass.

Perrow, C. (1970). *Organizational analysis: A sociological review*. Belmont, CA: Wadsworth.

Pfeffer, J. (1977). Power and resource allocation in organizations. In B. M. Staw & G. R. Salancik (Eds.), *New directions in organizational behavior* (pp. 235–266). Chicago: St. Clair Press.

Pfeffer, J., & Salancik, G. R. (1977, Autumn). Organizational design: The case for a coalitional model of organizations. *Organizational Dynamics,* pp. 15-29.

Pfeffer, J., & Salancik, G. R. (1978). *The external control of organizations: A resource dependence perspective*. New York: Harper and Row.

Preziosi, R. C. (1985). Productivity improvement training takes preparation. *Training and Development Journal, 39*(2), 101–102.

Pritchard, R. D. (1990). *Measuring and improving organizational productivity: A practical guide*. New York: Praeger.

Pritchard, R. D., Jones, S. D., Roth, P. L., Stuebing, K. K., & Ekeberg, S. E. (1988). The effects of feedback, goal setting, and incentives on organizational productivity. *Journal of Applied Psychology Monograph Series, 73*(2), 337–358.

Pritchard, R. D., Jones, S. D., Roth, P. L., Stuebing, K. K., & Ekeberg, S. E. (1989). The evaluation of an integrated approach to measuring organizational productivity. *Personnel Psychology, 42*(1), 69–115.

Pritchard, R. D., & Roth, P. J. (in press). Accounting for non-linear utility functions in composite measures of productivity and performance. *Organizational Behavior and Human Decision Processes.*

Quinn, R. E., & Cameron, K. S. (1983). Organizational life cycles and shifting criteria of effectiveness: Some preliminary evidence. *Management Science, 29*(1), 33–51.

Quinn, R. E., & Rohrbaugh, J. (1983). A spatial model of effectiveness criteria: Towards a competing values approach to organizational analysis. *Management Science, 29*(3), 363–377.

Riggs, J. L., & Felix, G. H. (1983). *Productivity by objectives*. Englewood Cliffs, NJ: Prentice-Hall.

Rosow, J. M. (Ed.). (1981). *Productivity: Prospects for growth*. New York: Van Nostrand, Reinhold.

Rowe, D. L. (1981, November). How Westinghouse measures white collar productivity. *Management Review,* pp. 42–47.

Sawyer, J.E., Pritchard, R. D., & Hedley-Goode, A. (1990). *Comparison of non-linear ProMES versus linear procedures for obtaining composite measures in performance appraisal.* Unpublished manuscript, Texas A&M University, Department of Psychology, College Station.

Schneider, B. (1984). Industrial and organizational psychology perspective. In A. P. Brief (Ed.), *Productivity research in the behavioral and social sciences* (pp. 174–206). New York: Praeger.

Seashore, S. E. (1972). *The measurement of organizational effectiveness.* Paper presented at the University of Minnesota, Minneapolis.

Shetty, Y. K., & Buehler, V. M. (1985). *Productivity through people: Practices of well-managed companies.* Westport, CT: Quorom Books.

Silver, M. S. (1984). *Productivity indices: Methods and applications.* Aldershot, England: Gower Publishing.

Simon, H. A. (1964). On the concept of organizational goal. *Administrative Sciences Quarterly, 9,* 1–22.

Sink, D. S. (1985). *Productivity management: Planning, measurement and evaluation, control and improvement.* New York: Wiley.

Starbuck, W. H. (1965). Organizational growth and development. In J. G. March (Ed.), *Handbook of organizations* (pp. 451–533). Chicago: Rand McNally.

Steers, R. M. (1975). Problems in the measurement of organizational effectiveness. *Administrative Science Quarterly, 20,* 546–557.

Stein, J. M. (1986). Public employee productivity: Can outcomes be validly measured at the jurisdictional level? *Public Personnel Management, 15*(2), 111–117.

Taira, K. (1988). Productivity assessment: Japanese perceptions and practices. In J. P. Campbell & R. J. Campbell (Eds.), *Productivity in organizations* (pp. 40–62). San Francisco: Jossey-Bass.

Tuttle, T. C. (1981). *Productivity measurement methods: Classification, critique, and implications for the Air Force* (AFHRL–TR–81–9). Brooks AFB, TX: Manpower and Personnel Division, Air Force Human Resources Laboratory.

Tuttle, T. C. (1982). Measuring productivity and quality of working life. *National Forum, 62*(2), 5–7.

Tuttle, T. C. (1983). Organizational productivity: A challenge for psychologists. *American Psychologist, 38,* 479–486.

Tuttle, T. C., & Weaver, C. N. (1986a). *Methodology for generating efficiency and effectiveness measures (MGEEM): A guide for commanders, managers, and supervisors* (AFHRL Technical Paper, pp. 86–26). Brooks AFB, TX: Manpower and Personnel Division, Air Force Human Resources Laboratory.

Tuttle, T. C., & Weaver, C. N. (1986b). *Methodology for generating efficiency and effectiveness measures (MGEEM): A guide for Air Force measurement facilitators* (AFHRL–TP–86–36, AD–A174 547). Brooks AFB, TX: Manpower and Personnel Division, Air Force Human Resources Laboratory.

Tuttle, T. C., Wilkinson, R. E., & Matthews, M. D. (1985). *Field test of the methodology for generating efficiency and effectiveness measures* (AFHRL–TR–84–54, AD–A158 183). Brooks AFB, TX: Manpower and Personnel Division, Air Force Human Resources Laboratory.

U.S. Air Force Regulation 25-3. (1982). *Air Force Productivity Enhancement Program* (PEP). Washington, DC: Department of the Air Force.

Weick, K. E. (1969). *The social psychology of organizing.* Reading, MA: Addison-Wesley.

Weiss, H. M. (1984). Contributions of social psychology to productivity. In A. P. Brief (Ed.), *Productivity research in the behavioral and social sciences* (pp. 143-173). New York: Praeger.

Weiss, L. G. (1989). *Productivity measurement issues.* Unpublished manuscript, Texas A&M University, Department of Psychology, College Station.

Werther, W. B., Ruch, W. A., & McClure, L. (1986). *Productivity through people.* New York: West.

White House Conference on Productivity. (1984). *Productivity growth: A better life for America* (NTIS #PB 84–159136). Washington, DC: Author.

Yuchtman, E., & Seashore, S. E. (1967). A system resource approach to organizational effectiveness. *American Sociological Review, 32,* 891–903.

Individual and Group Responses and Behavior Change in Organizations

The following five chapters of this volume of the *Handbook* consider patterns of individual and group behavioral responses to variations in organizational policies, practices, and cultures. Some of these individual or group behaviors may be judged as less than optimal or perhaps even detrimental to the level of functioning of individuals or groups as they pursue their organizational roles. If so, actions may be indicated that are designed to change patterns of behavior of individuals, groups, or both.

Accordingly, chapters in this section provide in-depth treatment of the design and implementation of effective employee compensation systems (chapter 9), issues surrounding organizational stress and its possible effects (chapter 10), conflict and negotiation processes (chapter 11), methods of and circumstances related to organizational development interventions (chapter 12), and, finally, models and methods directed toward bringing about individual behavior change in organizations (chapter 13).

B. Gerhart and G. Milkovich, in chapter 9 [Employee Compensation: Research and Practice], provide an unusually comprehensive overview of organizational practices and areas of needed research in the area of employee compensation. They observe that many disciplines (psychology, economics, sociology, finance, and administration) have each given singular attention to issues of employee compensation. Gerhart and Milkovich have resisted the insularity of such an approach and have, in contrast, dealt with compensation as an important interdisciplinary applied field and have evaluated theories and practices according to their usefulness in extending our understanding of the role of compensation in the overall employment exchange.

Their discussion covers five basic aspects of employee compensation: *pay level, pay structure, individual differences in pay, benefits,* and, within each of these areas, issues related to *program administration.* Their thorough discussion of each of the foregoing topics is followed with detailed statements of suggested research directions. The chapter concludes with discussions of special issues: *executive pay levels, equal employment opportunity considerations, international comparisons and effects of globalization,* and *nonmonetary rewards.*

The content of chapter 9 is both substantively and theoretically enriching. Practitioners and scholars alike will find much to guide and challenge them in what Gerhart and Milkovich have covered here.

Chapter 10 [Stress in Organizations], by R. Kahn and P. Byosiere, outlines links in the causal chain extending from organizational antecedents to stress, the nature of stressors generated and the short-term responses evoked by them, and the effects of long-term exposure. In the first few pages, the authors provide a conceptual history of the stress concept and discuss many of the problems, gaps, and disagreements over definitions. Among several models of stress, reflecting a mix of disciplines (psychology, sociology, biology, medicine), Kahn and Byosiere briefly discuss seven that have been historically and conceptually important, before turning to consider at greater length a modification and extension of the model that was the stimulus for a program of research at Michigan's Institute of Social Research (ISR) beginning in 1962 (French & Kahn, 1962).

The authors then devote the bulk of chapter 10 to a comprehensive review of empirical research results according to the primary elements of the modified ISR model: *organizational antecedents to stress, stressors in organizational life, perception and cognition: the appraisal process, responses to stress, ramifying consequences of stress, properties of the person as stress moderators,* and *properties of the situation as stress moderators.*

In summarizing conclusions derived from their review of research results, Kahn and Byosiere discuss results of efforts to evaluate intervention programs that may be offered as methods for preventing or ramifying the undesirable effects of stress. Their conclusion is guardedly optimistic: "Research on stresses of work, in spite of deficiencies we have cited, is not only growing but improving. As for the future, the lines of improvement still needed are clear; models and methods good enough to enable improvement are available; and some excellent examples are already before us."

Kahn and Byosiere have provided an impressive, comprehensive, and current overview of this important area of organizational psychology. Their optimism for improved research and increased knowledge about the nature of stress and the possible prevention of its undesirable effects should be aided by broader attention to what has been presented here.

Chapter 11 [Conflict and Negotiation Processes in Organizations] by K. Thomas develops an integrated overview of the complex fabric of variables involved in conflict and negotiation practices in organizations. Thomas defines conflict as *the process that begins when one party perceives that the other has negatively affected, or is about to negatively affect, something that he or she cares about.*

Beginning with this disarmingly straightforward definition, Thomas confronts the reader with the actual complexity of conflict and negotiation by presenting and discussing the elements of a general process model of conflict episodes according to *awareness, thought and emotions, intentions, behavior, other's reactions,* and *outcomes.*

An important personal belief driving Thomas' discussion throughout this chapter is his concern about the serious shortcomings of the rational-economic assumptions that pervade the conflict literature. The growing body of research on themes involving normative phenomena and emotions have, according to Thomas, been treated merely as "something else worth knowing," instead of being incorporated as an integral part of issues central to the field such as bargaining strategy, third party tactics, and the like.

In our opinion, Thomas, in chapter 11, has recognized the reality of problems actually faced by persons who must be concerned in organizations with issues related to conflict and conflict management. He has developed and presented a foundation for a revised behavioral paradigm that incorporates normative reasoning and emotions along with rational/instrumental reasoning into an integrated model that encompasses the major elements of issues revolving around conflict and conflict management.

J. Porras and P. Robertson, in chapter 12 [Organizational Development: Theory, Practice, and Research], provide a most comprehensive and cogent review of theory, practice, and research in the field of organizational development. *Organizational development* (OD) is described by the authors as the use of planned, behavioral science–based interventions in work settings for the purpose of improving organizational functioning and individual development. The history of OD is quite short, extending over only slightly more than three decades. In that short time, OD has made a number of important contributions. These contributions have been made in spite of the enormous complexity of processes that need to be understood by OD scholars and the unsettled nature of OD's theoretical base.

Porras and Robertson describe all facets of organizational development, its vitality, and its complexity. Their stated purpose is to present the field's theory, practice, and research so that readers may comprehend fully the essence of OD, where it is now and where it is headed. Toward this purpose, an organizing theoretical framework is presented and analyzed according to *change process theory* and *implementation theory*. A wide range of organizational development interventions organized according to four categories of the theoretical framework are described. Fifty published evaluation studies are presented and organized according to how predictions have fared when they have been examined according to categories defined by the authors' theoretical taxonomy.

Porras and Robertson conclude their chapter with a tightly reasoned series of statements about the current status and suggest next steps for OD theory, OD practice, and OD research. In reflecting on the future of organizational development, the authors recall that an early rationale for justifying OD's value to organizations was the need to help organizations cope with turbulent environments. Events during the last dozen years have seen increasing and intensified levels of environmental turbulence.

Porras and Robertson argue convincingly that a primary element of OD's charter is to help organizations adapt to environmental turbulence. Thus, they suggest that OD is, in fact, at a new threshold of opportunity wherein it will be called upon to play a renewed role in developing pertinent theory, implementing systemic change, and engaging in research that can be translated into new methods that are directly useful to organizations. They conclude that these tasks provide a challenging and exciting agenda for the field of OD in the years to come.

The last chapter of this section, chapter 13 [Behavior Change: Models, Methods, and a Review of Evidence], by L. Hellervik, J. Hazucha, and R. Schneider, addresses the topic of adult behavior change. According to Goldstein (1991), citing a report by the Carnegie Foundation (Eurich, 1985), industrial corporations spend more than 40 billion dollars annually on education and training programs. This fact is testimony to what must be widespread belief that most employees need to develop new knowledge, skills, or proficiencies in order to perform their jobs properly. It is also noteworthy that results of a survey among training professionals (Clement, Walker, & Pinto, 1979) show that over 60 percent believe that employees are most in need of improved human relations and communication skills. Thus, one may reasonably assume that a substantial amount of money is spent annually in programs undertaken for the purpose of helping employees to become more effective communicators and, in particular, to enhance their levels of interpersonal competence.

Yet, Hellervik, Hazucha, and Schneider state that many industrial and organizational psychologists and organizational decision makers believe that adults really *do not* change. Early in chapter 13, the authors set the scene as follows:

> Do people change? [This question implies that] people *don't really* change. This implies that change efforts are doomed to *ultimate* failure—that any observed change is merely cosmetic, that it will disappear overnight, or that the change is somehow being faked by modifying external behavior without changing more fundamental internal qualities.

We agree with the authors that pessimism about the likelihood of behavior change among adults is widespread. Fortunately, such pessimism, though widely stated, seems *not* to have affected equally widespread recognition that employees *need* to change—especially in areas involving human relations skills. Moreover, as we have mentioned, programs designed to bring about such changes through training and development are widespread and costly.

In the remaining pages of chapter 13, Hellervik, Hazucha, and Schneider provide convincing evidence that persons do, in fact, respond successfully and permanently to carefully designed developmental opportunities. In so doing, the authors have provided a thorough and scholarly review of relevant evidence, detailing both difficulties encountered and success achieved. A notable contribution is their *proposed framework for behavior change*, a framework that serves to bring diverse literatures together and to classify and document the nature of threats that may stand in the way of otherwise successful behavior intervention programs.

In describing the nature of one major continuing intervention program directed toward behavior change in the workplace, the authors provide a backdrop for summarizing the chapter according to important remaining questions and recommendations for needed research on change. These questions are discussed according to such issues as *malleability versus stability of personal characteristics, external factors most likely to influence behavior change, volition and self-regulation as they affect behavior change, contextual factors and the effectiveness of intervention, pain versus gain in choices to attempt change*, and, finally, *methodological difficulties in doing research about behavior change*.

This chapter about the means, methods, and results of efforts directed toward implementing individual behavior change in organizations is challenging and exciting. Attention to the issues, problems, methods, and solutions proposed here should yield important advances in both theory and technology of behavior change in organizations in the years ahead.

–MARVIN D. DUNNETTE
–LEAETTA M. HOUGH

References

Clement, R. W., Walker, J. W., & Pinto, P. R. (1979, March). Changing demands on the training professional. *Training and Development Journal, 29*, 3–7.

Eurich, N. P. (1985). *Corporate classrooms*. Princeton, NJ: Carnegie Foundation.

French, J. R. P., Jr., & Kahn, R. L. (1962). A programmatic approach to studying the industrial environment and mental health. *Journal of Social Issues, 18*, 1–47.

Goldstein, I. I. (1991). Training in work organizations. In M. D. Dunnette & L. M. Hough (Eds.), *Handbook of industrial and organizational psychology* (2nd ed., vol. 2, pp. 507–619). Palo Alto, CA: Consulting Psychologists Press.

CHAPTER 9

Employee Compensation: Research and Practice

Barry Gerhart
George T. Milkovich
Cornell University

Compensation is at the core of the employment exchange between organizations and individuals. Our chapter reviews research, theory, and practice in five basic aspects of employee compensation: level, structure, individual differences, benefits, and administration. We organize our discussion in each area around definition and properties, determinants, and consequences and suggest directions for research. In addition, four special topics—executive pay, equal employment opportunity, international comparisons, and nonmonetary rewards are discussed. Overall, we conclude that organizations have considerable discretion in decisions regarding the design and administration of compensation policies and that such decisions have important consequences for individual attitudes and behaviors, costs, and therefore, organizational success.

    Employee compensation has received attention from multiple disciplines, including psychology, economics, sociology, finance, and administration. As such, there is the challenge and opportunity to develop and evaluate models based on an interdisciplinary approach. We note, however, that much compensation research has taken a single-discipline perspective, typically using employee compensation as a convenient means to achieve the end of testing a particular theory (e.g., behavioral theories of motivation), rather than viewing it as a field of interest (or end) itself. In the present chapter, we turn this view on its head. Our focus is on compensation as an important interdisciplinary applied field, and we evaluate theories in terms of their usefulness in understanding and managing employee compensation in the employment exchange.

A major goal is to influence future research, including rekindling interest in areas (e.g., structures and benefits) that we believe have not received sufficient attention. We offers several general suggestions. First, the multidimensional nature of employee compensation needs to be clearly recognized. Research will be more valuable to the extent multiple dimensions are studied. Second, employee compensation is one of several employment policy decisions that influence the achievement of individual, group, and organizational objectives. The success of activities in areas such as staffing and training may be helped or hindered by compensation decisions. Similarly, policy and practice in other human resource areas may help or hinder the success of compensation programs. Therefore, research should attempt to examine multiple human resource activities simultaneously where possible. Third, and related, further development and testing of contingency models is needed. Contingency factors may include not only other human resource activities but also employee, job, organization, and external factors. The effectiveness of compensation policies may vary significantly across settings that differ on these contingency factors. It is critical for both theory and practice that such factors be identified and understood more completely. Fourth, human resource activities in areas such as staffing and training can be viewed as alternative investment opportunities. Therefore, it is useful to think in terms of whether an investment in compensation is likely to be more or less effective than an investment in another area or an investment distributed across multiple areas. Fifth, where feasible, multiple measures of effectiveness should be used, including psychological (e.g., attitudes, perceptions), behavioral, and objective (e.g., productivity, profits). Sixth, to adequately test contingency models of employee compensation, designs should, to the degree possible, use multiple employing units to ensure variance in practices, perceptions, and contingency factors, as well as longitudinal data to permit the study of consequences of change in these factors. Such studies will require strong partnerships between academia and industry to successfully define a set of mutually interesting research problems and feasible designs.

Introduction

An organization has the potential to remain viable only so long as its members choose to participate and engage in necessary role behaviors (Katz & Kahn 1966; March & Simon, 1958). To elicit these contributions, an organization must provide inducements of value to its members. This exchange or transaction process is at the core of the employment relationship and can be viewed as a type of contract, explicit or implicit, that imposes reciprocal obligations on the parties (Barnard, 1936; Rousseau, 1990; Simon, 1951; Williamson,

1975). At the heart of that exchange are decisions by employers and employees regarding compensation.

From the organization's perspective, perhaps no other set of decisions are as visible or as consequential for the success or failure of an organization. From a cost perspective alone, effective management of employee compensation is critical, given that it often represents the single largest cost incurred by an organization, typically accounting for 10 to 50 percent of total operating costs and as much as 90 percent of such costs in some labor-intensive (e.g., service) organizations.

Of course, cost is only one part of the picture. It is also necessary to evaluate the employee contributions the organization receives in exchange. Thus, a second reason for studying compensation from the organization's perspective is to assess its impact on a wide range of employee attitudes and behaviors and, ultimately, the effectiveness of the organization and its units. Compensation may directly influence key outcomes like job satisfaction, attraction, retention, performance, flexibility, cooperation, skill acquisition, and so forth. However, its influence may also be indirect—facilitating or constraining the effectiveness of other human resource activities, such as recruitment, selection, training, and development. In either case, its significant costs and its potential for important effects on attitudes, behaviors, and, ultimately, organizational effectiveness suggest that compensation is an area of strategic importance.[1]

For the employee, compensation decisions also have important consequences. Salaries and wages represent the main sources of income for most people and may also be taken as key indicators of a person's social standing or success in life. Benefits, such as health care and pensions, are also important determinants of well-being and financial security among employees and their dependents. Not surprisingly then, employees have sought to influence compensation decisions in a variety of ways—through unions, by supporting government regulation of compensation decisions, and through the courts, for example. Therefore, it is important to understand how individuals are affected by (and react to) different compensation decisions.

Focus of the Chapter

In this chapter, our goals are to define and describe the major decisions that organizations make in managing employee compensation and, based on theory, research, and practice, to evaluate what the outcomes of such decisions

are likely to be under different conditions. We have made several specific decisions in focusing the review.

First, although both parties to the employment exchange are of interest, we focus most of our attention on employer decisions. Compensation, like staffing, recruitment, and training, is an applied area of study where issues tend to be defined in terms of understanding the effectiveness and equity of actual decisions in organizations. Our discussion of employee decisions is mostly limited to cases where a better understanding carries potential implications for organizational practice—for example, understanding what determines individuals' pay satisfaction may help improve the design of compensation programs.

Second, our focus is on compensation itself rather than on compensation as a means of testing particular psychological theories of motivation (see Dyer & Schwab, 1982, on this point). In this sense, our chapter differs from the work of motivation chapters in the first (Campbell & Pritchard, 1976) and second (Kanfer, 1990) editions of this *Handbook* and is similar to the reward systems part of Lawler's (1976) chapter on control systems in the first edition. Although much of our orientation is, of course, psychological, compensation is an area of great interest to other disciplines. Thus, we also draw freely on the economics, sociology, and finance literatures at various points.

Third, our focus on managerial implications has led us to devote relatively little attention in this chapter to what may be termed more tactical questions. For example, such questions might involve the choice between job evaluation or performance appraisal instruments (see Gomez-Mejia & Welbourne, 1988; Milkovich, 1988) or the determinants of compensation (see Gerhart & Milkovich, 1990, for a review). Our main focus in discussing determinants is the relative importance of organizational differences in compensation decisions.

Fourth, we have largely chosen to limit our attention to the monetary aspects of employee compensation. Obviously, there is good reason to believe that many other attributes of jobs—challenge, significance, prestige, supervision, working conditions, co-workers—can also have important effects on employee attitudes and behaviors. But reviewing this literature would greatly expand an already large task. We do not believe that our conclusions regarding pay decisions will be invalidated by this omission, at least not to any greater extent than other obvious omissions (e.g., examining compensation in relative isolation from other intertwined issues like staffing or training). We do, however, discuss the role of pay vis-à-vis other rewards and other employment activities later in the chapter.

Structure of the Chapter

As Figure 1 indicates, we have classified compensation (or pay) decisions into four broad categories that the compensation literature (e.g., Belcher & Atchison, 1987; Heneman, 1985; Heneman & Schwab, 1985; Milkovich & Newman, 1990) suggests are most important: pay level, pay structures, individual differences in pay, and benefits. A potential fifth category, administration, is addressed within each of the four decision areas. In addition to these categories, we have included some special topics under pay decisions—executive pay, equal employment opportunity, international comparisons, and nonmonetary rewards. We suggest that decisions in these areas influence individual and group outcomes that in turn influence unit (e.g., plant, business unit) outcomes and, ultimately, organizational outcomes. Contingency factors are also included in the model in recognition of the fact that the relation between pay decisions and outcome variables may depend on a host of organizational, job, individual, and external factors.

The chapter is organized around the compensation decision areas shown in Figure 1. Within each of the four main decision areas, we structure our discussion around the following:

definition and properties, determinants, consequences, summary, and suggested research directions. Our discussion of contingency factors also takes place within each of the four compensation decision area sections, although in a less structured manner. Finally, our review includes discussion of the four special topics mentioned above.

Pay Level

Definition and Properties

Compensation includes any direct or indirect payments to employees, such as wages, bonuses, stock, and benefits. Ehrenberg and Milkovich (1987) have defined *pay level* as the "average compensation paid by a firm relative to that paid by its competitors" (p. 89). This definition suggests several implications. First, pay level refers to a characteristic of the organization (e.g., Heneman & Schwab, 1979; Mahoney, 1979a). Second, pay level is an attribute defined *relative* to product and labor market competitors. Therefore, pay level research will ordinarily require data on multiple organizations. Third, conclusions regarding relative pay level will depend heavily on how these competing organizations are defined and chosen. Although perhaps not as explicit in the definition, we would add a fourth point, namely, that measuring total compensation goes beyond a consideration of wages and salaries.

Direct pay now represents approximately 72 percent of total compensation costs, with benefits accounting for the remaining 28 percent (Nathan, 1987; U.S. Chamber of Commerce, 1991). Thus, it is less and less correct to equate direct pay with total monetary compensation. Yet there is no single correct way to assess the relative contributions of pay and benefits to total compensation—a particularly relevant issue, given what appears to be the increasingly significant differences in benefits packages offered by different organizations.

FIGURE 1

Compensation Decisions and Consequences

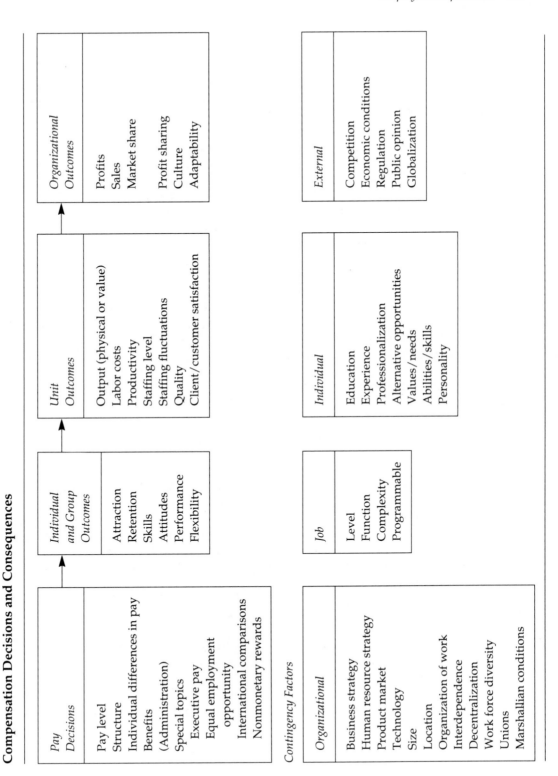

Pay Decisions

Pay level
Structure
Individual differences in pay
Benefits (Administration)
Special topics
Executive pay
Equal employment opportunity
International comparisons
Nonmonetary rewards

Individual and Group Outcomes

Attraction
Retention
Skills
Attitudes
Performance
Flexibility

Unit Outcomes

Output (physical or value)
Labor costs
Productivity
Staffing level
Staffing fluctuations
Quality
Client/customer satisfaction

Organizational Outcomes

Profits
Sales
Market share

Profit sharing
Culture
Adaptability

Contingency Factors

Organizational

Business strategy
Human resource strategy
Product market
Technology
Size
Location
Organization of work
Interdependence
Decentralization
Work force diversity
Unions
Marshallian conditions

Job

Level
Function
Complexity
Programmable

Individual

Education
Experience
Professionalization
Alternative opportunities
Values/needs
Abilities/skills
Personality

External

Competition
Economic conditions
Regulation
Public opinion
Globalization

One way to define relative contribution is in terms of cost to the employer. However, it would be a mistake to equate employer cost with value to the employee, which might be quite different. For example, the type of health coverage that employees select under flexible benefit plans varies more with demographics (e.g., age, sex) than with the dollar cost to employees, suggesting that employees differ in the value attached to different coverage options (Barringer, Milkovich, & Mitchell, 1991). Similarly, the fact that some organizations (e.g., Bank of America) have eliminated retiree health care coverage for all new hires suggests that organizations believe that different groups of employees (in this example, new hires) may differ in the value attached to particular aspects of compensation.

Yet there is little or no research to answer the question of how much value different employee groups attach to different aspects of pay.

The fact that *value to employee* may differ from *cost to employer* suggests that, in some cases, less costly total compensation packages may actually provide total inducements that are of greater value to employees than those associated with more costly packages. For example, although a package including many costly benefit options might be the most expensive, its value to employees might fall short of the value attached to a less costly package of benefits that is better tailored to employee needs or values. Therefore, measurement of one's own and of competitors' pay levels would ideally include the value to employees of different elements of total compensation.

Even limiting the focus to direct pay does not eliminate measurement difficulties. For example, the use of variable pay causes further measurement complexities because pay level can be assessed accurately only in retrospect. To illustrate, although total compensation cost can be reasonably estimated if there is an average wage of $10 per hour, with average annual increases projected (or specified in a contract)

at 6 percent for each of the following two years, this is not the case if the average hourly wage is $9.50, with a chance to make anywhere from $0 to $5 per hour per year more, depending on profits or stock performance. In the past, this issue arose mostly in the context of executive stock options. However, stock options and other types of variable pay are now being expanded to other employee groups.

Unfortunately, most pay level research has focused solely on base salary. Yet surveys suggest that base pay is coming to represent a smaller portion of direct pay (Bureau of National Affairs, 1988; O'Dell, 1987). Only a few studies, often in the area of executive compensation, have also included other components of direct pay, such as bonuses, but mostly in the context of studying determinants of compensation. Virtually no research has examined the role of total compensation in comparisons of organizational success in achieving cost and behavioral objectives.

In setting pay levels, an organization is largely interested in productivity or unit labor cost—the cost to produce a given unit of output. Thus, two organizations with identical pay and benefits may have very different total or unit labor costs because staffing levels are higher in one than the other. Further, even if overall staffing levels were equal, the mix of skills or jobs could differ significantly, thereby providing another source of cost differences. Yet unit labor cost is rarely used when comparing or benchmarking against the competition and setting one's own pay level.

Determinants

Product Market.   Pay levels of labor market and product market competitors play an important role in determining pay level. Mahoney (1979a; see also Dunlop, 1957) argues that product market (industry) competition places an upper boundary on pay level because organizations in a particular industry "encounter similar constraints of technology, raw materials, product demand, and pricing" (p. 122). Thus, an organization will find itself at a competitive disadvantage in the product market if its labor costs exceed those of its competitors because such costs will ordinarily be reflected to some extent in higher prices for its products. For example, if Ford has higher labor costs than Toyota, Ford will have difficulty providing the same quality of automobile at a competitive price. Consequently, product market pressures may act as an upper boundary on employee compensation. (See Krueger & Summers, 1986, 1988, for a review of product market effects on pay.)

Labor Markets.   However, organizations do not compete solely in the product market. They also compete in the market for labor. Ford, for example, competes for engineers, lawyers, and human resource managers not only with other automotive companies but also with companies in the computer, aerospace, electronics, and other industries. A pay level that is too low relative to these competitors could lead to difficulties in attracting and retaining sufficient numbers of quality employees. As such, labor market competition can be seen as placing a lower boundary or floor on pay level (Milkovich & Newman, 1990). The classical economics literature suggests that, taken together, product market and labor market competition may provide relatively little discretion on the part of employers in choosing a pay level (Gerhart & Milkovich, 1990).

Pay Surveys.   Organizations attempt to gather information about pay practices of competitors through the use of pay surveys (see Fay, 1989). However, finding the "going rate" of pay may be easier in theory than in practice. As Rynes and Milkovich (1986) point out, administrative decisions are required about a range of issues, including the following:

- Which employers are included?

- Which jobs are included?

- Which jobs are considered similar enough to use in bench-marking?

- If multiple surveys are used (fairly typical), how are the multiple rates of pay weighted and combined?

Practice in these areas seems to vary across, and probably within, employers.

The choice of employers is probably one of the most important decisions in conducting pay surveys. It goes to the heart of the organization's competitive business strategy and its likely success in attracting and retaining employees who may or may not define their alternative employment opportunities in the same manner. The organization must decide (a) which employers are its key competitors in both its labor and product markets and (b) whether to give more weight to either the product or labor market.

In considering the latter decision, there are probably several factors that argue in favor of emphasizing one or the other. For example, product market comparisons (i.e., a focus on labor costs) are likely to deserve greater weight when (a) labor costs represent a large share of total costs, (b) product demand is elastic (i.e., product demand changes in response to product price changes),[2] (c) the supply of labor is inelastic, and (d) employee skills are specific to the product market (and will remain so).[3] In contrast, labor market comparisons may be more important to the extent that (a) attracting and retaining qualified employees is difficult and (b) the costs of recruiting replacements are high.

As the importance of a particular comparison increases, so too should the resources devoted to information and measurement. For example, if product market comparisons are critical, more resources need to be devoted to measuring compensation (or better, unit labor costs) paid by such organizations. In contrast, if labor market comparisons are important, it is necessary to devote resources to find out to which organizations applicants and employees are being lost.

To what extent do employers actually engage in these information collecting and monitoring activities? We do not have any direct evidence, but data on a related issue (recruiting) seems to indicate that organizations in the Fortune 1000 devote few resources to evaluating recruiting activities (Rynes & Boudreau, 1986). Considering that compensation and recruitment often fall in different administrative parts of the human resource function, it is perhaps even less likely that organizations devote much attention to monitoring the influence of compensation decisions (e.g., emphasizing product market vs. labor market comparisons) on recruiting success outcomes such as applicant attraction.

Although the validity of conclusions reached through the survey process may depend critically on how the competition is defined (i.e., what organizations are chosen for inclusion), little evidence exists on how such choices are made or their implications. Rather, most attention has been focused on potential problems in the job evaluation process, especially in the context of pay equity or comparable worth discussions. Nevertheless, as Schwab (1980) has pointed out, job evaluation is usually "validated" against some measure of the market rate, meaning that the measure of the latter is critical. As Rynes and Milkovich (1986) note, although paying the going rate has been an effective employer defense in pay equity cases where female-dominated jobs are underpaid relative to their job evaluation points, the courts have not really scrutinized whether the measure of the going rate is itself obtained in a valid fashion.

Preliminary evidence of the validity of employer estimates of going rates from the Gerhart and Milkovich (1990) study is not encouraging. One question in the survey asked, "How do you define your target pay level—below the median, at the median, between the median and the 75th percentile,

at the 75th percentile, or above the 75th percentile?" The correlation between these responses and actual relative pay level (adjusted for differences in employee, job, and organizational factors) was .50, suggesting some convergent validity but also a fair amount of unexplained variance in the self-reports. An additional analysis (not reported in the 1990 study) further indicated that none of the 124 organizations reported that they were below the median. Aside from Lake Woebegon (of central Minnesota fame), we know of no population where the laws of statistics permit everyone to be at or above the median. Therefore, this finding again raises the question of how valid assessments of going market rates are likely to be.

Are Pay Level Differences Among Employers Significant?

Before examining the consequences of organizational differences in pay level, it is perhaps necessary to first establish that significant organizational effects on pay exist. There is not a consensus on this issue.

Much of the theory and evidence on this point comes from the economics literature. Standard economic theories of competitive markets (e.g., *human capital theory*, Becker, 1975; *compensating wage differentials theory*, Smith, 1937) tend to view employers as *price takers*, meaning that they must pay the "going rate" if they are to be competitive. If they pay less, they will not be able to attract a sufficient number of qualified employees. If they pay more, their higher costs will drive them out of business. Adam Smith (1937) suggested that the net utility of all jobs was equal when compensating factors such as working conditions, training required, and so forth were factored in. Thus, for example, apparently similar jobs in different organizations may be paid differently because noncompensation job attributes differ between the two jobs. To attract and retain people in jobs having more unfavorable noncompensation attributes, a compensating differential (i.e., higher pay) is required. This view suggests that after accounting for differences in product and labor market competition, the mix of jobs, nonpecuniary job attributes, and the nature of the work force, organizational pay levels will not differ to any significant degree. There is a lively debate regarding the validity of this model, partly because it is so difficult to test (see Brown, 1980; Ehrenberg & Smith, 1988). Specifically, a strong test requires the control of all job attributes and worker ability, which is obviously a difficult task, akin to the problems encountered in the pay discrimination literature.

Empirical evidence on the importance of organizational effects on pay level is mixed. Based on data from one industry (California electronics firms), Leonard (1988) concluded that "firms that deviate from the average (market) wage tend to return towards the market wage" (p. 28). In other words, organizational differences in pay level were found to be insignificant. In contrast, building on the work of Dunlop (1957) and others, Groshen (1988) found that organizational differences in pay level were of a significant magnitude and highly stable over time, suggesting that competitive markets do not completely determine pay and leaving open the possibility that employers may engage in different pay level strategies.

Both the Leonard (1988) and Groshen (1988) studies, however, have limitations. First, neither study controlled for employee characteristics, leaving open the possibility that organizational pay level differences (e.g., in the Groshen study) were a result of different levels of human capital. Second, both studies focused largely on lower-level occupations, mostly blue collar and nonsupervisory white collar jobs. Third, Leonard's (1988) results were obtained on a single industry, which was composed mainly of small employers operating in intensely competitive product and labor markets. This level of competition may exceed that found in much of the rest of the economy, perhaps

helping explain the lack of stable employer differences in his study.

Other studies, not subject to these limitations, suggest that there are stable organizational differences in pay over time. For example, Gerhart and Milkovich (1990) used the Cornell Center for Advanced Human Resource Studies (CAHRS) compensation data base to examine this issue. The sample was composed of roughly 16,000 middle- and top-level managers from 200 organizations followed over a period of up to five years. Extensive controls for organizational differences in human capital, job level, and organizational characteristics were included. They found, consistent with Groshen (1988), that there were significant and stable employer differences in pay level over the five-year period.

Similarly, Weber and Rynes (1991) found significant pay level strategy differences between organizations. Significant employer differences in pay strategy may indeed exist.

Consequences

Why Do Similar Employers Make Different Pay Level Decisions? The research by Groshen (1988) and Gerhart and Milkovich (1990) suggests that similar employers make different pay level decisions. Why is this the case? The answer is important because it serves as a starting point for our examination of the possible cost and behavioral consequences of different pay level strategies. Although the psychological literature, especially expectancy and equity theories, suggests ways in which pay level may influence individual em-ployees or applicants, it does not directly address the question of why organizations engage in different compensation practices. Thus, we look to the economics (efficiency wage models) and strategy literatures.

Efficiency Wage Models. The basic idea behind efficiency wage models is that organizations setting pay higher than their competitors can realize increased efficiency. Three different variants of the model focus on different mechanisms by which this can happen (see Groshen, 1988).

Sorting by ability (or adverse selection). Some employers may pay higher rates of pay as a means of hiring and retaining higher ability employees. (Empirical evidence on pay level and recruiting is reviewed below.) Even if one accepts the implied assumption of valid selection systems, the following question arises: What advantage is there to having higher ability employees if their higher pay offsets their higher productivity? One answer is that some organizations have a technology or work design that is more sensitive to ability than that of their competitors, and they therefore receive a greater productivity return from higher employee ability levels. As one example, Japanese automobile plants in the United States tend to engage in much more intensive screening of job applicants than do U.S. employers. One reason may be that the Japanese companies are more likely to have to live with hiring mistakes because of their emphasis on employment security. However, an additional reason may be that their greater use of self-directed work teams requires more able employees.

Shirking/monitoring and turnover. These two formally identical variants (Yellen, 1984) suggest that worker productivity is often difficult to measure, permitting workers (in the now popular parlance of economists) to *shirk* (i.e., screw around). These models suggest that one way to discourage shirking is to set the pay level above that the worker can obtain elsewhere. The expected effect is that the worker will be less likely to shirk because she or he does not wish to risk losing this premium wage (Shapiro & Stiglitz, 1984). The alternative, by definition, is a lower-paying job (i.e., with a nonefficiency wage employer) or, if all firms raise wages, unemployment (Yellen, 1984). In this sense, "unemployment plays a socially valuable role in creating work incentives" (Yellen, 1984).[4]

Gift exchange/sociological morale. In contrast to the other efficiency wage models, this variant has less of a neoclassical economics orientation, focusing more on social conventions (Yellen, 1984). Akerlof (1984), in describing his *partial gift exchange* model, suggests that "some firms willingly pay workers in excess of the market-clearing wage; in return they expect workers to supply more effort" (p. 79). Or, as Yellen describes it, firms pay "workers a gift of wages in excess of the minimum required, in return for their gift of effort above the minimum required" (p. 204). Akerlof cites Adams' (1965) work on overreward inequity as empirical support. He also notes, however, that "not all studies reproduce the result that 'overpaid' workers will produce more" (p. 82).

These efficiency wage models are open to a number of criticisms. For example, there is the following paradox: If higher pay is used to discourage shirking where monitoring is most difficult, how is it possible to monitor well enough to determine when a worker is shirking enough to warrant termination? The gift exchange variant assumes that overreward equity is a compelling force for increasing worker effort and productivity, yet research shows that overreward equity is very difficult to obtain and maintain, especially outside of the laboratory. (See Campbell & Pritchard, 1976, and Kanfer, 1990, for reviews.)

The Strategy Perspective. A common theme in the compensation management literature is that organizations have considerable discretion in the design of pay policies (Broderick, 1986; Carroll, 1987; Foulkes, 1980; Gomez-Mejia & Welbourne, 1988; Lawler, 1981; Milkovich, 1988). As such, even similar organizations may follow different compensation practices. In this sense, the strategy perspective differs from efficiency wage models, which sometimes seem to assume that whatever compensation system an employer uses must be efficient and is the one best system, given its particular characteristics. It also differs from institutional (and population ecology) approaches, which lean toward environmental determinism (i.e., practices are dictated by the organization's environment). In contrast, the strategy perspective suggests that even similar organizations may follow different strategies, some of which may be more efficient than others.

Strategy can be measured using intentions, actions, or both. A focus on actions (actual compensation policy decisions) may be advisable, given that the correspondence between intentions and actions is not necessarily high (Mintzberg, 1978, 1987; Snow & Hambrick, 1980). In compensation, actions, rather than intentions or plans, are likely to have the greater consequences for costs and employee behaviors. Thus, consistent with business strategy measurement approaches that focus on the content outcome of the strategy process (e.g., Chrisman, Hofer, & Boulton, 1988; Hofer & Schendel, 1978), "realized" pay strategies describe cases where "a sequence of decisions in some area exhibits consistency over time" (Mintzberg, 1978, p. 935; see also Miles & Snow, 1978). In other words, for organizational effects to have strategic properties, they should be stable over time.

The Gerhart and Milkovich (1990) study provides an example of the use of realized compensation strategies. As noted earlier, they did find evidence of significant differences among organizations in pay level decisions. Therefore, the emphasis on organization differences in compensation decisions found in the efficiency wage and strategy literatures has some empirical support. This, in turn, suggests a need to examine the consequences of these organization differences.

What Are the Significant Effects of Pay Decisions? In terms of behavioral outcomes of pay decisions, relative pay level has been typically viewed as having its main impact on attraction and retention, whereas individual differences in pay are often seen as more relevant to performance within the organization. However, these distinctions are becoming less accepted. For example, some of the efficiency wage models reviewed above clearly view pay level as a determinant of effort. In addition, the way individuals are paid may have consequences for the types of individuals attracted and retained. In our discussion, we will focus on empirical evidence regarding pay level effects.[5]

Attraction.   There is ample evidence that pay level can increase the size of the applicant pool, likelihood of job acceptance, and the quality of job applicants. For example, Krueger (1988) found that both the application rate and applicant quality increased for government jobs as the ratio of government to private sector wages increased. Similarly, Holzer (1990) found that higher wages reduced vacancy rates, increased the perceived ease of hiring, and resulted in less time spent on informal training (see also Barron, Bishop, & Dunkelberg, 1985). Other studies reviewed by Rynes and Barber (1990), including studies of military recruitment, point to similar conclusions.[6] See Williams and Dreher (1990, Academy Meeting) for an exception. In addition to recruiting effects, there is also evidence that organizations paying high wages have better quality in their employees in general (Brown & Medoff, 1989).

A very closely related question, How does pay level influence job choice decisions in attracting new employees? has also been examined. As Rynes, Schwab, and Heneman (1983) pointed out, institutionally oriented economists like Reynolds (1951) argued many years ago that pay entered into decisions in a noncompensatory fashion. That is, applicants were believed to have a reservation wage below which they would not accept a job offer, regardless of how attractive it was on other dimensions. Rynes et al. provided empirical support that this hypothesis is indeed accurate under certain conditions, further supporting the idea that pay level is often critical in attraction. The key limiting condition was the degree of variance in pay across organizations competing for the applicants. Applicant decisions became less compensatory as the market variance in pay increased. Simply stated, the greater the variability in pay offers, the more important the pay level.

Similarly, the importance of pay level is also emphasized in Barber's (1990) work on pay as a signal of other attributes. Building on Spence's (1973) work, she found that in the absence of complete and accurate information, applicants may make inferences about nonpecuniary job attributes based on what they know about its relative pay level. These types of inferences increase in importance if one accepts the description of job seekers as typically knowing little about potential jobs (prior to actually being employed) other than the rate of pay and the general type of work (e.g., Reynolds, 1951). This lack of information is likely to be a matter of degree, of course, with applicants for exempt positions often having the opportunity to gather information on other job attributes through plant visits and other means. Nevertheless, pay is always one of the more visible and probably one of the more important attributes in such decisions. Even in cases where pay appears less important, the explanation may be that there is simply little variation among employers in pay level, thus taking it out as a factor in decisions (Rynes et al., 1983). This however, may simply attest to the fact that pay level is so important that organizations monitor it closely so as not to get out of line one way or another (Gerhart & Milkovich, 1990).

In summary, although it is true that pay level is only one attribute among many that determine whether an organization is viewed by applicants as being an "employer of choice" (Milkovich & Newman, 1990, p. 198), evidence suggests that it may be a critical attribute in many cases. Considerable research remains to be done on the signals that pay level sends to applicants (and perhaps current employees).

Satisfaction With Pay. Psychological theories typically specify that pay influences behaviors

through its effect on perceptions and attitudes. One key attitude hypothesized to be related to behaviors such as turnover, absenteeism, and union activity (Heneman, 1985) is pay satisfaction. It is hypothesized to be a function of the discrepancy between perceived pay level and what an employee believes the pay level should be (Heneman, 1985; Lawler, 1971; Locke, 1976). Empirical evidence supports this discrepancy model (Dyer & Theriault, 1976; Rice, Phillips, & McFarlin, 1990). Frame of reference (Smith, Kendall, & Hulin, 1969) and social comparison approaches (e.g., equity theory; Adams, 1963) fit well with the discrepancy model,[7] offering explanations for how the "should be" component of pay satisfaction is determined.[8]

Heneman (1985) has suggested two modifications to the discrepancy model. First, rather than treating pay as unidimensional, pay can be classified into level, structure, system, and form categories (Heneman & Schwab, 1979; these categories parallel our level, structures, individual differences in pay, and benefits decision areas in Figure 1). Second, building upon Dyer and Theriault's (1976) work, Heneman suggested that the model include an additional variable, employee feelings about pay policies and administration.

Dyer and Theriault's (1976) research provided an early indication of the potential importance of procedural justice, in addition to distributive justice, in compensation. Subsequent work by Greenberg (1986) supports the independence of procedural justice. Further, Folger and Konovsky (1989) found that procedural justice explained variance in pay raise satisfaction beyond that accounted for by the actual pay raise and distributive justice perceptions. Although this particular increment was not large, procedural justice perceptions also explained variance in organizational commitment and trust in supervisor, suggesting that its influence on broader organizational attitudes may be greater.

Given a multidimensional definition, the *Pay Satisfaction Questionnaire* (PSQ; Heneman

& Schwab, 1983) was developed to measure satisfaction with four facets of pay satisfaction: level, benefits, raises (referred to earlier as *system*), and structure/administration. Although, as discussed above, structure and administration were viewed as conceptually distinct dimensions, the items designed to measure the two facets clustered together empirically. Heneman and Schwab (1985) provide support for the construct validity of the PSQ. They also note that existing unidimensional pay satisfaction measures (e.g., the pay subscales of the *Job Descriptive Index*, Smith, Kendall, & Hulin, 1969, and the *Minnesota Satisfaction Questionnaire*, Weiss, Davis, England, & Lofquist, 1967) are largely measures of pay level (see also Scarpello, Huber, & Vandenberg, 1988).

Subsequent research has also been generally supportive of the PSQ's construct validity but suggests that its dimensionality may vary by job type and human resource policies (Scarpello et al., 1988). Scarpello and her colleagues found that a three-factor solution fit better than a four-factor solution in most nonexempt employee samples. The level and benefits factors received strong support, as did the structure/administration factor, for the most part. However, the raise items loaded on both the level and structure/administration factors. They speculated that the greater use of merit in pay increase decisions among exempt employees versus more reliance on seniority or across-the-board increases for nonexempt employees may help explain the four-factor solutions for the former and the three-factor solutions for the latter group.

How does this research inform managerial decisions aimed at influencing pay satisfaction? Largely consistent with Figure 1, the obvious levers to pull have to do with level, structures, individual differences in pay, and benefits. However, the fact that administration also arises as an important consideration suggests compensation policy design is only part of the picture—effective implementation and communication of the policy is also likely to be

very important. For example, in addition to the actual pay policy (and how it is perceived), the comparison standard employees use to evaluate their pay also has a tremendous potential impact (Adams, 1963; Berger, Olson, & Boudreau, 1983; Rice et al., 1990). It is entirely possible that well-designed communication programs that contain information about pay levels in other companies could influence the "should be" component and thus pay satisfaction in a much more cost effective way than modifying actual pay. Perhaps the marketing and communications literatures can provide some relevant insights. Managers and researchers, however, will need to consider some ethical issues if this line of inquiry (or practice) is pursued. In any case, research does not as of yet tell us how stable or manipulable employee pay perceptions are. All we can say at this point is that organizations devote significant resources in the form of booklets, videotapes, meetings, and so on to influencing employee pay perceptions, suggesting that they believe such influence is possible.

Withdrawal.   Ehrenberg and Smith's (1988, p. 368) analysis of the evidence led them to conclude that the relation between pay levels and quit rates is strong. Heneman (1985) cites research by Weiner (1980) showing pay satisfaction predicting absenteeism and turnover. Motowidlo (1983) also found that pay satisfaction predicted turnover and further that pay influenced turnover only through its impact on pay satisfaction.

In general, however, Heneman (1985) noted that the amount of research on consequences of pay satisfaction was underwhelming. He suggested that the impact of pay satisfaction may differ across dependent variables. Similarly, the strength of pay satisfaction consequences might vary according to the pay satisfaction dimension. Additional research comparing the relative consequences of pay and other satisfaction facets (e.g., work, supervision, etc.) would also be useful, as would more work that considers the role of contingency factors in determining how satisfaction is translated into individual and group outcomes. As one example, surprisingly little is known about the factors governing applicant and employee choices among the various comparison standards (e.g., organizations in the same product market, organizations in the same labor market) that could be used in evaluating their pay and what the consequences of choosing different standards are.

Staffing Levels.   Pay level also has implications for staffing levels. The economics literature indicates that if an organization's labor costs exceed those of its competitors, its product price will also tend to exceed that of its competitors, reducing demand for its product. Because labor is a derived demand, the reduced product demand would also be expected to reduce employment levels.[9] Reductions in market share and employment levels in U.S. industries (e.g., automobiles, consumer electronics) exposed to foreign competition are a case in point (Kochan & Capelli, 1984).[10] As another (but related) example, although unions raise wages for their members (Lewis, 1983), a consequence may be lower profits for unionized companies (Hirsch, 1991), which may help explain the decline in unions' relative employment levels (Lineneman, Wachter, & Carter, 1990).[11]

These findings are interesting in a couple of respects. First, they reinforce the notion that total compensation cost is also about staffing level, not just compensation level per employee. Second, it also reinforces the importance of relative pay and the argument that product market competition may leave little room for discretion in setting pay level. (Of course, the evidence does not tell us whether contingency factors mentioned earlier, such as the ratio of labor cost to total cost, gives some organizations more flexibility than others.) Third, for individual employees, the downside of achieving high compensation levels is the potential risk of job loss to themselves or their peers.

Return on Investment.   A general problem with almost all compensation research is the lack of a return on investment focus. In broad terms, a goal should be to understand the return on any type of investment in employees or conditions of employment. Resources can be invested in a variety of compensation programs (e.g., raising pay levels, introducing individual pay programs like profit-sharing, redesigning benefits or the pay structure). But which has the greatest expected return in terms of the outcomes discussed? More broadly, at the margin, is it investment in compensation or in some other human resource program, such as staffing, development, or work redesign, that will have the greatest return? We are a long way off from answering such questions, although there has, of course, been some work done in this respect, mostly in the staffing area (see Boudreau in volume 2 of this *Handbook*). Two studies by economists are also relevant in this respect.

Raff and Summers (1987) examined the impact of a pay increase at the Ford Motor Company in 1914. The introduction of assembly-line production and scientific management greatly increased productivity, but turnover rates reached 370 percent and absenteeism averaged 10 percent per day. Although the wage rate of $2.50 per day provided plenty of replacement workers (apparently there were long queues of applicants), Ford decided to double wages to $5.00 per day, partly to alleviate these problems (and also perhaps because of his paternalistic management style). The pay increase reduced quits by 87 percent and absenteeism by 75 percent. It is not terribly surprising that a doubling of wages would have a large impact. The real question, as discussed above, is whether the benefits met or exceeded the costs. Summers, of course, was not able to provide a definitive answer, but suggested that the benefits probably did not completely offset the higher wage costs.

The study by Holzer (1990) cited earlier estimated that approximately 50 percent of higher wage costs were offset by benefits (e.g., in recruiting and training needs) in his sample. Cost/benefit comparisons of this sort require a number of assumptions. Thus, his estimates may not have been very precise for a variety of reasons (Gerhart, 1989). However, this is the direction in which research must move. Many compensation strategies will have an impact, but this is only part of the question—the investment required to generate the impact also matters.

Organizational Performance. Another way to examine the return on investment of compensation and other human resource programs is to study their effects on organizational outcomes. In the only direct study, Gerhart and Milkovich (1990) found no evidence of an effect of compensation level on return on assets. (Although, as will be discussed later, they found that use of variable pay was linked to return on assets.) Nevertheless, care should obviously be taken not to infer that pay level is unimportant. Pay level may very well be extremely important in that an organization cannot afford to differ much from competing organizations. Therefore, although an organization may have difficulty gaining a competitive advantage by distinguishing itself on the pay level dimension, the wrong pay level may put an organization at a serious competitive disadvantage.

Summary

Pay level is a key attribute of compensation design and strategy because of its consequences for cost, attitudinal and behavioral objectives, and, ultimately, organizational performance. Although labor market and product market competition place important constraints on the choice of a pay level, research suggests that even after statistically controlling for differences in individual, job, and organization factors, organizations exhibit differences in pay level that are stable over time.

The literature also suggests, however, that pay level is only one of several important dimensions of pay. For example, employee attitudes toward pay also depend on decisions regarding structure, individual differences in pay allocation, benefits, and administration. Other evidence indicates that organizational differences on these latter dimensions (e.g., individual differences in pay) may be large relative to pay level differences.

Even limiting the focus to pay level, our impression is that benchmarking against competitors often places too little weight on comparisons of total labor costs, or better yet, unit labor costs. Toward this end, factors such as nonsalary payments and staffing levels require closer attention to facilitate better evaluations of the return on investment from different pay level strategies.

Suggested Research Directions

We suggest that future research focus on the following pay level issues.

- *Pay level comparisons.* Organizations choose pay levels based on comparisons with other "relevant" organizations. It would be useful to know more about why particular organizations are chosen for comparison and whether the choices make sense, given that organization's particular strategy. Choices can be evaluated in a number of ways. Examples include the degree of success in controlling labor costs and achieving behavioral objectives such as attraction and retention of valued employees. A return on investment perspective would perhaps be useful.

- *Employee pay level perceptions.* Employee pay satisfaction is hypothesized to be a function of the discrepancy between perceptions of actual pay received and the pay the employee believes she or he should receive. Thus, pay satisfaction and related behaviors, such as attraction or retention, can be influenced by changing either (a) actual (and perceived) pay level or (b) em-ployee perceptions of what their pay level should be. Some evidence suggests relatively limited discretion on the part of most organizations in choosing a pay level. An alternative means of influencing pay satisfaction is to influence employee perceptions of the "should be" component. To what extent can such perceptions be manipulated?

- *Choice of pay comparison standards by employees.* Presumably, an important part of any such influence attempt would be influencing the choice of comparison others. Employees use multiple comparison standards (Goodman, 1974; Scholl, Cooper, & McKenna, 1987), including what employees in other organizations are paid. With what types of organizations do different types of employees make comparisons? Do they think in terms of labor market, product market, or geographic comparisons? How much convergence is there in employee comparisons? Do employees and (their) managers make similar comparisons? Can effective management and communication of information regarding pay in other organizations influence employee comparisons, attitudes, and behaviors?

- *Specific functional relationships between pay level and product market and labor market competitiveness.* Although it has been established that pay level can have substantial effects on product market

and labor market competitiveness, more precise estimates of the specific functional relationships between these elements are needed. For example, exactly how far below the pay level of key labor market competitors can an organization go before it loses key employees and applicants increasingly reject job offers? Is the functional form of such relationships linear or nonlinear? At what point are the direct labor cost savings of lower pay offset by the indirect costs that arise from difficulties in attraction and retention?

- *Pay structures, individual pay, and benefits.* Finally, although there appear to be significant differences in organizations' pay levels, it may be that organizational differences regarding other types of compensation decisions (e.g., individual pay) are greater yet (Gerhart & Milkovich, 1990). Therefore, although much research is needed on pay level decisions, the need for research on decisions regarding structures, individual pay, and benefits may be even greater.

Pay Structures

As indicated by Figure 1, a second set of important pay decisions pertains to structures. Here we consider formal pay structures that are embedded in the formal organization. The pay structure for assistant, associate, and full professors within a university is a familiar example. Several distinct formal structures often exist within a single organization, typically designed along functional/occupational (e.g., executive, clerical, technical) or divisional (e.g., product market) boundaries, and more recently, along knowledge-based progressions.

From a research perspective, the variations in pay structures observed among different organizations (and over time within the same organizations) raise several questions. First, how are structures defined and what are their essential properties? Next, what explains the observed differences across organizations in the properties of pay structures—in the number of distinct structures used by employers, the number of levels, and the differentials among levels, rates of progress, and the procedures and criteria used to design and rationalize them? Finally, what are the consequences of variations in these properties for employee attitudes and behaviors and organizational performance? Are more egalitarian structures, for example, related to employee commitment and willingness to cooperate in work teams? Are employees more motivated to undertake training or to acquire additional knowledge under structures based on knowledge or skill, compared to structures based on jobs? Or, are factors other than structures, such as employee characteristics, more important in determining motivation for advancement and training? The following sections examine the relevant literature and suggest research directions.

Definition and Properties

Pay structures are essentially hierarchies. Milkovich and Newman (1990) define them as "the array of rates paid for different work within a single organization. [They] focus attention on the levels, differentials, and criteria used to determine those pay rates" (p. 31). Much of the focus of empirical research has been on the relational properties (i.e., differentials) of structures. Examples of measures have included the ratio of a position's pay to adjacent positions in the hierarchy (Jaques, 1961; Mahoney, 1979b) or to the average pay of all positions in the structure (Pfeffer & Davis-Blake, 1987). The dispersion (variance) of pay within organizations (and its stability over time) has also been studied (Rabin, 1987; Schaeffer, 1975). Gender and race-based pay equity is also typically measured in terms of ratios. (See

Cain, 1986, for a review; see also the "Equal Employment Opportunity" section in this chapter.)

In addition to ratios, recent studies have used a relatively novel measure, the Lorenz curve, to examine relative pay within organizations (Rabin, 1987; Schaeffer, 1975). Although commonly used to analyze the degree of concentration in nations' income distributions, the Lorenz curve can also be used to measure how evenly pay is distributed among employees within any structure. As shown in Figure 2, the curve depicts the percentage of pay received by a given percentage of employees who are arrayed hierarchically. Pay equality, represented by the diagonal, occurs when each employee receives the same pay—a curve of absolute equality. The degree to which the actual curve deviates from the diagonal represents the degree of concentration of pay in the structure. In this example, because employees are arrayed hierarchically according to their position in the organization, the lowest 10 percent of employees receive 5 percent of the pay distributed in the structure, while the highest 10 percent receive almost 70 percent of the pay. The greater the deviation from the diagonal, the greater the inequality or concentration in the distribution of pay in the structure.

A single quantitative index of the degree of concentration in the pay distribution, the *Gini coefficient*, is used in conjunction with the Lorenz curve. Smaller Gini coefficients indicate less concentration (i.e., less inequality). Other measures of concentration or inequality, such as simple ratios of the pay among adjacent levels or of the pay at a particular level to the average pay of the entire structure, do not yield information on the relative distribution of employees at each pay level within the structure. However, Lorenz curves do, and the Gini coefficient quantifies the degree of concentration in the entire structure, as represented by the shaded area in Figure 2.

FIGURE 2

Example of Lorenz Curve for Measuring Inequality

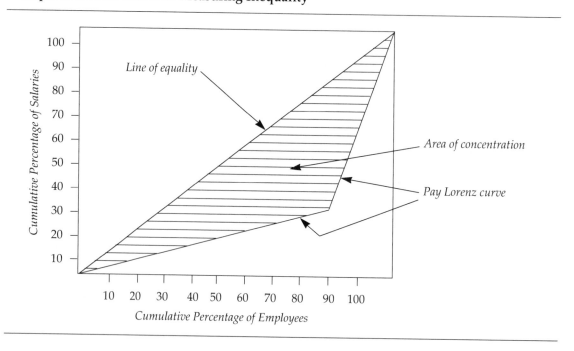

Egalitarian Versus Hierarchical. Consistent with the preceding emphasis on relative pay and degree of inequality, structures can be classified on a continuum anchored by egalitarian on one end and hierarchical on the other. Figure 3 indicates that a structure's place on the continuum depends on characteristics such as the number of distinct structures (or substructures), the number of levels in each, the size of the differentials between levels, and the rate of employee progression through levels. An egalitarian structure (greater equality and a smaller Gini coefficient) would be characterized by fewer differences—fewer distinct structures, fewer levels within each, narrower differentials, and a slower rate of progress.

However, some caution is required when drawing these distinctions because the properties are not independent. Consider two

pay structures of a given range having a maximum–minimum difference of $100,000, a rate for the entry-level position of $50,000, and a rate for the top-level position of $150,000. Defined in terms of levels, an egalitarian structure has a smaller number of levels than a hierarchical structure. But fewer levels result in greater differentials between levels, which is usually taken to be an indicator of a more hierarchial structure. The inconsistency would disappear if the structure with fewer levels also had a smaller (less than $100,000) maximum–minimum difference.

The issue of egalitarian versus hierarchical pay structures arises in various forms. For example, the business press currently focuses on the size of the differentials between chief executive officers (CEOs) and other employees. *Industry Week* (Nelson-Horchler, 1990) recently reported that the differentials

FIGURE 3

Egalitarian Versus Hierarchical Structures

| | Continiuum | |
Properties	Egalitarian	Hierarchical
Distinct structures	Fewer	More
Levels	Fewer	More
Differential	Narrower	Wider
Rate of progression	Slower	Faster

between CEOs and operatives in the United States (35 to 1) was the highest among industrialized countries (e.g., Japan was 15 to 1). *Fortune* (Farnham, 1989) labeled U.S. differentials as excessive, raised concerns about fairness, and coined the term *trust gap*. Similarly, at the opposite end of the spectrum, pay compression, the narrowing of differentials between entry level (or recent hires) and employees at the next higher level (or those hired earlier) has also received attention (Gomez-Mejia & Balkin, 1987).

Administrative Views. Although sharing an interest with researchers in the differential and hierarchical nature of structures, practitioners also focus on additional properties of pay structures, such as:

- Number of distinct hierarchies (e.g., separate ones for executives, office staff, managers and engineers, or dual ladders that combine the latter two)

- Number of levels in each (i.e., salary grades, classes, etc.)

- Pay differentials between adjacent levels (e.g., at least 15% being a rule of thumb)

- Differentials between the maximum and minimum paid within a grade (e.g., 50% for office/clerical and at least 120% for professional and managerial)

- Time it takes an employee to progress through the hierarchy

Administrators also distinguish pay structures based on the procedures used to establish and rationalize them. The American Compensation Association periodically surveys its members to determine the proportions using various job evaluation methods (point factor 55%), knowledge-based plans (15%), and/or market pricing (25%). Procedures used to design and administer also vary in terms of the extent of employee participation, the presence of dispute resolution processes, and the like. Practitioners seem to hold strong beliefs that these properties affect employee attitudes and behaviors and organizational performance. A contemporary example is the belief that fewer distinct structures (break down the barriers), smaller differentials (more equal treatment), fewer levels (delayering), and using knowledge-based factors lead to increased employee commitment, trust, and performance. Some compensation administrators also express the belief that more rapid progress through a given structure has important consequences for behaviors and costs. In other words, they focus on promotion as a motivational device.

From both research and administrative perspectives, these properties of pay structures are of interest insofar as they affect employee behaviors and subsequently organizational effectiveness. It seems obvious that those who determine and administer employee compensation believe that structures matter. Similarly, academics typically devote at least one-third of the space in compensation textbooks to describing the procedures related to pay structures, such as job analysis, job evaluation, knowledge-based pay, market surveys, and pay ranges. Finally, the belief that pay structures matter is reflected in the fads promulgated by pay pundits (e.g., delayering, etc.—see above).

Systematic data on the other properties of interest to administrators (e.g., number of distinct structures, number of levels, rates of progress, ratio of maximum to minimum) are rarely reported in the research literature. However, they are commonly reported in consultant and association surveys. The difference in interest in the properties of pay structures on the part of researchers and practitioners is difficult to rationalize. Those who design and manage employee compensation seem to find the properties of pay structures more relevant than those who conduct research on employee and organization behaviors. It may be that managers' beliefs about the importance of pay structure are misguided, but the related theory and research offers little insight or guidance. In fact, as the next section makes clear, researchers have devoted the bulk of their attention to the measurement properties of administrative procedures like job evaluation.

Administrative Procedures: Job Evaluation and Related Tools. As already discussed, pay structures are often distinguished by the procedures used to establish and rationalize them (Barrett, & Doverspike, 1989; Lawler & Ledford, 1985; Ledford, 1991). Job evaluation, skill-based pay, and market pricing are examples (Berger & Rock, 1991; Milkovich & Newman, 1990). A basic premise underlying these procedures is that they influence employee behaviors directly by signaling what is valued and indirectly through the resulting pay structures. Different procedures may induce different behaviors. Hence, structures based on skills, yet identical in other respects (e.g., pay differentials, number of levels, and rate of progress), are believed to be instrumental in skill-acquisition behaviors. In contrast, job evaluation–based structures are believed to induce job- or promotion-seeking behaviors. Finally, market pricing procedures may be instrumental in encouraging market-enhancing behaviors. Among academics, for example, market-enhancing behaviors might include focusing on publishing and giving presentations at other schools (sometimes to generate outside offers), rather than investing effort in committee service or even teaching. Unfortunately, research into the effects of alternative designs is virtually nonexistent, so decisions about which to use seem to be based on belief rather than evidence (Lawler, 1989).

Measurement and Administrative Perspectives. There is general agreement that the objective of job evaluation is to help achieve an acceptable pay structure (Livernash, 1957; Schwab, 1985). There are two perspectives on achieving acceptability: measurement and administrative (Kerr & Fisher, 1950; Schwab, 1985). The essential difference between the two is that job evaluation is seen as an objective instrument in the measurement perspective, as compared to a flexible set of rules in the administrative view. These different views translate into very different research issues.

Measurement, the dominant view of industrial and organizational psychologists, emphasizes instrumentation, objectivity, and minimalization of errors (Arvey, 1986; Ash, 1948; Lawshe & Satter, 1944). Acceptability from this perspective depends on psychometric properties of the job-evaluation instrument and the quality of the scores obtained. Consequently, the research issues include reliability of evaluation results (Doverspike, Carlis, Barret, & Alexander, 1983; Fraser, 1984), predictability of criteria (Chesler, 1948; Fox, 1962; Schwab & Heneman, 1986), multicolinearity among factors (Fox, 1962; Davis & Sausser, 1991; Lawshe & Satter, 1944), similarity of results obtained from different job evaluation methods (Davis & Sausser, 1991; Gomez-Mejia, Page, & Tornow, 1982; Madigan & Hoover, 1986) and bias of rater and job incumbent characteristics (Arvey, Passino, & Loundsbury, 1977; Doverspike et al.,1983; Huber, 1991; Lawshe & Farbo, 1949; Rynes, Weber, & Milkovich, 1989; Schwab & Grams, 1985).

The flexible rules, or *administrative view,* which emerged primarily from industrial relations research, sees job evaluation as a flexible tool that is used to work out disputes that inevitably arise over pay differentials and rates of progress through the structure. Over 40 years ago, Kerr and Fisher (1950) observed that "the technical core of a plan (instrumentation), on which so much attention is lavished, has generally less bearing on the ultimate results than either the environment into which it is injected or the policies by which it is administered" (p. 87). Research from this perspective has emphasized the importance of workplace norms and customs (Kerr & Fisher, 1950; Livernash, 1980), whether the diversity of the work to be evaluated required single or multiple plans within a single organization (Beal, 1963; Burns, 1978; Remick, 1984; Treiman & Hartmann, 1981), the change in plans over time in response to changes in business conditions and the nature of the work (Milkovich & Broderick, 1991), and the effects of employee participation in the design of pay plans (Carey, 1977; Folger & Konovsky, 1989; Greenberg, 1987; Jenkins & Lawler, 1981; Livernash, 1957, 1980).

To date, however, the majority of research on job evaluation and other administrative procedures has focused on measurement issues such as the choice and weighting of compensable factors, reliability issues, systematic sources of error (e.g., gender effects), and the predictive validity of job evaluation plans. More recently, there has been an increased interest in skill- and knowledge-based plans. We now turn to an examination of these topics.

Mapping Relative Content: Compensable Factors, Multicollinearity, and Weighting. Point job evaluation systems often include seven or more compensable factors. These factors are designed to map the domain of relative work content of the jobs to be evaluated and become the dimensions on which relative contribution (value) of the jobs is estimated. The conventional measurement approach is to extract the factors underlying the work performed through job analysis and some form of factor (or cluster) analysis. However, this approach suffers several limitations: (a) It is not forward looking and presumes the factors in today's work are stable over time; (b) it ignores the organization's strategic purposes as an added source of factors; (c) it often serves to confuse work content with its relative contribution (value) to the enterprise's objectives; and (d) it may become too methodologically cumbersome and costly for the value it adds to pay decisions. As a result, current practice all but omits systematic development of compensable factors. Rather, the typical practice, evidenced by consulting firms and employers' behaviors, is to start with a generic set of factors that are "tuned" via managers' judgment to fit the unique organizational context. More systematic attention is devoted to determining the appropriate criterion and to estimating the factor weights.

Researchers repeatedly report that relatively few factors, 3 to 5, account for the majority of total job evaluation score variations (e.g., Edwards, 1948; Fox, 1962; Lawshe & Farbo, 1949). Those who have observed job evaluation in use speculate that the redundant factors may be required to insure face validity or acceptance among the parties. However, this notion has never been studied. For example, the Hay Guide Chart Profile, a widely used factor comparison plan, is made up of only three factors, and one of these (problem solving) is defined as a percentage of another (know how).

Weighting factors has also received a lot of research journal space. Davis and Sausser (1991), in perhaps the most ambitious study published to date, examined five alternative factor weighting schemes using two job evaluation plans (Federal Evaluation Plan [FEP] and Broad Span Evaluation Techniques [BSET]) on 72 managerial and service jobs in a university setting. The five weighting schemes included natural, unit, rational, partial correlational, and regression. Among their many findings, they reported that the two job evaluation plans differed (a) in the degree of multicollinearity among factors, (b) in the degree of *validity concentration* (i.e., the degree of heterogeneity in the factor covariance structure), and, therefore, (c) in the subsequent effects that the five different weighting schemes had on the plans' ability to predict market wage rates. The greater the multicollinearity of the compensable factors and the more homogeneous their covariance structure, the smaller were the differences in prediction power obtained under different weighting schemes. At their university, using that specific sample of jobs, the predictive power of the FEP factors was less affected by the alternative weighting approaches because they were more highly collinear. The adjusted R^2 obtained from regressing market wages for benchmark jobs on scores using FES and the five weighting models ranged from .78 using natural weights to .82 with regression derived weights. The BSET plan factors were less collinear. Therefore, the weighting had greater effects on the adjusted R^2, ranging from .54 for natural to .81 for the regression approach. Simply stated, weighting matters most when the compensable factors are independent (see Fox, 1962).

Reliability of Job Evaluation. Findings from work on the reliability of job evaluation inform us about the degree to which using point job evaluation systems are subject to error attributable to individuals and groups performing the evaluation. In general, the reliability coefficients for total scores tend to be relatively high (.94–.99), whether using individuals (Lawshe & Wilson, 1947) or groups of evaluators (Schwab & Heneman, 1986). But the average correlations for individual compensable factors vary widely—.39 to .95 on the 10 factors in the Schwab and Heneman (1986) study, and .69 to .96 on the two job evaluation plans used in the Davis and Sausser (1991) study. (See Schwab, 1980, 1985, for a review.)

Systematic Bias in Job Evaluation: Gender Effects. In addition to investigations of random error, considerable recent research has focused directly on the judgments of the evaluators for evidence of systematic cognitive biases that might lead to undervaluation of female-dominated work (Arvey, 1986; Treiman & Hartmann, 1981). Findings from this work are mixed. Several studies report little evidence that gender composition of the evaluators or the job incumbents directly affects job evaluation scores (Arvey, Passino, & Lounsbury, 1977; Grams & Schwab, 1985; Rynes et al., 1989). A review of this evidence (and their own empirical work) led Grams and Schwab to conclude that there is little evidence of direct gender bias in job evaluation. However, Grams and Schwab pointed out that market data, used to estimate the factor weights in the job evaluation plan, may be an indirect source of bias.

Rynes et al. (1989) investigated the effects of job and evaluator gender while accounting for current pay, market survey data, and job evaluation points. A total of 406 compensation administrators assigned pay rates to nine jobs in one of two matched sets, either all predominantly female or all predominantly male. They concluded that no matter how the data were analyzed, job gender does not appear to systematically affect pay decisions. Nevertheless, Rynes et al. also noted that the possibility of indirect discrimination still remains since market survey data and current job rates did affect pay decisions. To the extent that either the market or current job pay rates reflect previous discrimination or cognitive bias (or both), the evaluator's decisions are likely to incorporate these biases. Rynes et al. went on to observe that any study that attempts to determine the influence of job gender on job pay is likely to be confounded since men and women do hold different jobs in society.

Predictive of What? The Criterion Problem. In addition to being reliable and free of bias, job evaluation plans need to demonstrate predictive validity. Almost 45 years of research confirms that statistically derived job evaluation plans can predict pay distributions (Davis & Sauser, 1991; Fox, 1962; Gomez-Mejia et al., 1982; Lawshe & Farbo, 1949; Schwab, 1985; Schwab & Heneman, 1986; Tornow & Pinto, 1976). To illustrate this type of work, Tornow and Pinto (1976) developed a job evaluation plan by regressing current wages of 433 managers on 13 factors derived from the *Management Position Description Questionnaire* (MPDQ; Torrow & Pinto, 1976). The estimated model was then used to predict pay of 56 managers not included in the developmental sample. The model accounted for 81 percent of the variance. Specific results vary in all studies of this type, but typically the adjusted R^2 ranges from the low 80s to mid 90s.

Recall, however, that an objective of job evaluation is to help design and rationalize an acceptable pay structure. Pay structures, as noted, are typically made up of levels, often called grades or classes, and pay differentials. Managerial work structures may include anywhere from 5 to 20 classes or levels (Belcher, 1962; Milkovich & Newman, 1990). Under a point job evaluation plan, these classes are defined in terms of a range of points. How these classes and subsequent pay differences among them get determined is at best an art form. It has not been the subject of any research. Yet we know from experience and press reports that these classes are administratively important. Kanter (1987), for example, argues that they become valued for the status they reflect in the organization. In addition, delayering in organizations (Weber, Driscoll, & Brandt, 1990) focuses explicitly on reducing the number of pay classes.

In the past few years, researchers have begun to recognize that the predictive validity of job evaluation is also a classification problem, not just a continuous distribution problem.

A recurring finding is that the ability of statistically derived job evaluation models to correctly classify jobs into the correct pay class is low. The Control Data study (Gomez-Mejia et al., 1982) reported that 49 to 73 percent of the jobs were within ±1 class of the correct class, and the State of Michigan study (Madigan & Hoover, 1986) reported hit rates ranging from 27 to 73 percent, depending on the weighting method used. Overgeneralizing a tad to make a point, this is equivalent to saying that 73 percent of a University's associate professors would be correctly classified if they were slotted into either assistant, associate, or full professor ranks. In the case of Michigan, an employee could have received up to $427 per month more (or less), depending on the factor weighting scheme used.

Until recently, questions about the appropriate criteria to validate job evaluation have not been considered. Conventional practice has been to validate job evaluation against a criterion pay structure. The criterion used in prevailing practice is either external market rates paid for benchmark jobs, or an agreed upon hierarchy of current pay within the organization, or some combination of the two. Acceptability of the results of job evaluation depends on their correspondence to this criterion structure. Concerns of the type expressed in the selection literature about "the criterion problem" (Smith, 1976) have been largely missing.

Recent questions about the appropriate criterion have sprung from two sources. First, increased sensitivity to discrimination and interest in comparable worth have focused attention on market-based pay differentials for jobs held predominantly by women compared to those held by men (see above). If these pay differentials are biased, then they indirectly bias job evaluation results. Rynes and Milkovich (1986) have also argued that defining the so-called going rates in the marketplace brings into play an administrative procedure that may be susceptible to the same errors and biases as studied in the job evaluation literature. These concerns have led to a search to find a bias-free pay structure to serve as the criterion. Options include using only the market wage differentials for male-dominated jobs (Remick, 1984), partialing out the effects of percentage female (Treiman & Hartmann, 1981), or using a structure negotiated by the relevant parties (e.g., using job evaluation).

Questions about the appropriateness of market or current rates as the criterion also come from work in organizational strategy (Gomez-Mejia & Balkin, 1989; Gomez-Mejia & Welbourne, 1990; Milkovich, 1988; Milkovich & Broderick, 1991). The belief emerging from this literature is that an organization's competitive advantage is affected by the extent to which pay decisions are contingent upon the organization's business strategy and the resulting organizational design. Implied in this line of argument is that mimicking the pay structure reported by competitors in the marketplace may not be optimal for every organization.

Criterion development research is called for here. Virtually no research has been done on the effects of using alternative criteria for validating job evaluation plans and establishing pay structures. Policy capturing could be employed once factors were determined. Perhaps some combination of judgments about organizational strategies and design factors, constrained by market-based data, is required.

All the research discussed so far stops short of examining how pay structures are determined and how pay is assigned to jobs that make up that structure. They only examine one of its key inputs, job evaluation. The bulk of this research has scrutinized job evaluation as a measurement process, investigating various points at which cognitive biases might enter into judgment (e.g., differential perceptions in the analysis and evaluation of job descriptions) and how the instrumentation should be changed or improved to reduce such errors and biases

(e.g., choices of evaluators, compensable factors, and factor scaling, anchors, and weighting). Valuable as this work is, to gain a more complete understanding of pay decision making and pay structures, research models need to be expanded beyond focusing on the psychometric properties of job evaluation.

More completely specified models of what determines the differential pay assigned to jobs and the behavioral consequences of the associated administrative process are required. The research and theories we examined earlier serve as a source of ideas. By way of illustration, research on strategy suggests that it influences the organization and work design, which in turn influence pay structures (i.e., the number of classes, differentials, and so on). Institutional models predict that structures exhibited by other organizations need to be considered. This may be equivalent to using market wage rates. Economic conditions and administrative judgments involved in market surveys may also influence the results obtained through job evaluation. Beyond this work, a review of basic compensation literature reveals that pay structures are based on combination of past pay relationships, individual and intra-organizational negotiations, collective bargaining, and compensation strategies. Anecdotal evidence and personal experience also suggest the importance of other contextual factors, including the presence of outside third parties, such as arbitrators in the public sector, unions, and government regulators (e.g., under Ontario and Minnesota comparable worth laws).

Even more compelling evidence of the need to include contextual factors in job evaluation research comes from recent studies suggesting that information about current pay rates, job grades/classes, and market data influence job evaluation outcomes. As noted earlier, it appears that current pay has both a direct (via market surveys) and indirect (via job evaluation process) effect on the pay assigned to jobs Grams & Schwab, 1985; Mount & Ellis, 1987;

Rynes, Weber, & Milkovich, 1989; Schwab & Grams, 1985). Doverspike, Racicot, and Hauenstein (1987) reported that job grade had a greater effect than market data, although insufficient information was presented about grades and market rates to be confident about generalizability of this finding. Rynes et al. (1989) found that market rates and current pay are stronger determinants than job evaluation scores, thus reinforcing the need to broaden research models beyond job evaluation. In fact, even in-depth case studies of pay determination in single organizations would shed some light, given the undoubted importance of other organizational practices (e.g., decentralization, teams, and delayering; see Gomez-Mejia & Balkin, 1992; Kanter, 1984).

Skill-based Pay Structures. Although job evaluation is a common practice, other administrative procedures are used to help design and manage acceptable pay structures (American Compensation Association, 1988; Bureau of National Affairs, 1991; Mahoney, Rynes, & Rosen, 1984). In fact, skill-based plans are widely touted as a superior alternative to job evaluation (Gupta, Jenkins, & Curington, 1986; Lawler, 1989; Lawler & Ledford, 1985; Luthans & Fox, 1989), although contrarians and skeptics are beginning to be heard from as well (Barrett & Doverspike, 1989).

As Table 1 indicates, skill-based structures pay employees for the skills they possess, demonstrate, and/or apply, in contrast to job-based structures, in which employees are paid for the job they perform (Milkovich & Newman, 1990). Although terms and definitions remain murky, generally these plans are grouped into two types (Luthans & Fox, 1989): (a) knowledge plans, which link pay differentials to the depth of knowledge related to one occupation (e.g., scientists, teachers) and (b) multiskill plans, which link pay differentials to the number of different sets of tasks (breadth) an employee is certified to perform (e.g., all sets of tasks assigned to a production team).

Studies of skill- and knowledge-based plans are virtually nonexistent, although case studies are beginning to appear (e.g., Ledford, 1991) that offer valuable insights into their operations. Again, this topic is fertile research ground. At the risk of pointing out the obvious, all the issues examined, and yet to be examined, concerning job evaluation apply to skill-based plans. By way of illustration, the acceptability of the results of skill-based plans can be scrutinized from measurement and administrative perspectives, the various points in the procedure at which errors and cognitive biases might enter into judgment (e.g., differential perception in competency definitions, analysis, and testing) and how the process can be improved to reduce potential errors and biases (e.g., through choices of competency evaluators, weighting, etc.) studied.

Similarly, criterion problems do not disappear in skill-based plans. If anything, skill-based plans highlight the importance of internal organizational factors in determining the criterion because market-based comparison for benchmark skills are rare. Also, as noted earlier, skill-based structures are believed to induce skill-acquisition behaviors, whereas job evaluation rewards promotion-seeking behaviors. Some have argued that job evaluation plans do, in fact, include skill-based factors, thereby also motivating skill acquisition and promotion-seeking behavior (Dufetel, 1991). An interesting piece of work would be to contrast the historical evolution of craft and teachers' pay schedules, both of which are partially based on skills and knowledge, with contemporary approaches. Finally, there are questions about the effects of contextual conditions (e.g., organizational design, employee attitudes, presence of unions and arbitrators, and comparable worth regulations) on the outcomes of skill-based plans. These also include examining tradeoffs between skill- and job-based pay structures. A cynic might observe that one reason skill-based plans seem attractive to some is that they have yet to take on all

TABLE 1

Knowledge-based Versus Job-based Structures

	Knowledge-based Structures	*Job-based Structures*
Definition	Skills/knowledge	Work performed
Manager's focus	Employee carries wage regardless of tasks	Job carries wage regardless of employee
Employee's focus	Pay increases linked to skill acquisition	Pay increases linked to promotions
Procedures	Assess skills Value skills	Assess jobs Value jobs
Advantages	Flexibility Reduced work force	Pay linked to value of work performed
Limitations	Potential personnel bureaucracy (holding rates, making out) Cost controls	Potential personnel bureaucracy Inflexibilities

the measurement, administrative, and regulatory baggage of job evaluation.

Determinants

Most of the research on pay structure determinants has focused on identifying the factors that account for pay differentials. This work lies primarily in the theoretical domain of labor economics and organizational sociology. Economic models depict industry, human capital, transaction costs, and specific institutional factors such as the presence of unions and gender as the explanation for the variations in differentials and dispersion of wages within an organization (Doeringer & Piore, 1971; Kerr, 1954; Williamson, 1975). For example, the existence of unions results in more egalitarian, narrower differentials for similar work (Freeman, 1982; Freeman & Medoff, 1984). Internal

labor markets may come about as a response to the need for generating firm-specific skills or to control transaction costs. Greater differences in work-related educational attainment within the work force are related to less egalitarian, wider differentials, and some industries (e.g., pharmaceuticals) appear to have greater differentials than others (e.g., insurance), at least within the executive ranks (Rabin, 1987). However, beyond their focus on differentials, economic models exhibit little interest in the other properties of structures.

Several organizational theory models in sociology can be extended to explain variations in internal pay structure. For example, the resource dependency model predicts that the relative power of positions within an organization depends on their relative ability to control resources on which the organization depends to achieve its objectives. Pfeffer and

Davis-Blake (1987) examined the resource dependency model by comparing the relative pay of five mid-level administrative positions in public versus private universities. They hypothesized that positions most critical to dealing with key external constituencies in the external environment (e.g., obtaining resources) would be valued more highly than other positions. Moreover, they argued that the key positions in public and private universities would be different. Consistent with their hypothesis, jobs critical to the objectives of each type of university did receive higher relative pay. For example, the chief development (fundraising) officer and the directors of admissions and alumni affairs received higher relative pay in private university structures, but not in public university structures. In contrast, in the public universities, relative pay was higher for directors of community services, student placement, and athletic directors.

Neoinstitutional models, on the other hand, depict organizations as following patterns exhibited by others in their "organizational fields" (DiMaggio & Powell, 1984) and "orbits of comparison" (Ross, 1957; Wazeter, 1991). By extension, the pay structures adopted by these organizations would conform to accepted practices within an industry, geographic region, or occupational domain. Such organizational mimicry, according to this perspective, is the result of a constraining process that forces one unit in a population to resemble other units that face the same set of environmental conditions. These organizational fields begin to sound very similar to the comparison others used in social comparison models such as equity theory. From the theoretical perspectives of economics and sociology, there is little room for differences in structural properties among similar organizations. Yet, as noted elsewhere in this paper, recent evidence strongly suggests that organizations that are similar in terms of types of employee and jobs, product market, size, and so on do have considerable discretion in the design and administration of both how they pay (see the "Individual Differences in Pay" section) and, to a lesser extent, how much they pay. There is no evidence to suggest the same would not hold for structures as well, especially if decision makers believe they are important.

Although research into the determinants of structures remains largely the domain of economists and sociologists, the logic underlying their models often relies on presumptions about human behavior, and these presumptions represent fertile research ground. The logic underlying institutional theory, that organizations pattern their human resource procedures after others (e.g., Zucker, 1987), relies on the social comparison processes of individuals and groups. Presumably, if similar organizations failed to match the contemporary practices of others in their organization field, then employee expectations would not be met and some dysfunctional outcomes would follow. However, more than two decades of social comparisons research suggests that employees use a more complex, multiple comparison process. Evidence suggests that individuals base their expectations on many referents (Goodman, 1974; Heneman et al., 1978). Scholl et al. (1987), for example, described finding differential equity based on seven referents: job, company, occupation, education, age, system, and self. If institutionalists are correct that organizations simply copy pay structures from other similar organizations, but employee expectations depend on a wider set of referents, then we either need to better understand how employees adapt to the organization or to challenge the logic of institutional models.

Consequences

In the administration literature, pay structures are said to influence many things, including employee turnover (Livernash 1957), strikes (Slichter, Healy, & Livernash, 1960), willingness to accept additional responsibilities (Belcher & Atchinson, 1987; Wallace & Fay,

1988), investment in additional training and skill acquisition (Lawler & Ledford, 1985), and employee trust (Lodge & Walton, 1989). The differentials between levels in the formal structure are seen as incentives that affect employee behaviors and equity perceptions. However, as discussed below, there may be tradeoffs between the incentive and equity effects. Unfortunately, behavioral theory and research offer little guidance regarding the optimal structures for motivating desired behaviors while maintaining a perception of equitable treatment. We now turn to an examination of what the literature does tell us regarding the effects of structures on incentives and equity perceptions.

What Are the Incentive Effects? Two models, *expectancy theory* (Vroom, 1964) and *tournament theory* (Lazear & Rosen, 1981), focus on the possible incentive effects of different structures. For example, expectancy theory focuses on the implications for motivation of both the valence of an outcome (e.g., a pay increase) and the perceived probability (instrumentality) of receiving the outcome as a consequence of a behavioral choice. Thus, for example, an organization could enhance performance through its structure by closely linking promotions to performance and by making sure that the associated pay increase is sufficiently large. The latter implication has spawned research that has examined how large the magnitude of pay increases must be to be meaningful to employees (Krefting, 1980; Krefting & Mahoney, 1977). Extending this work to internal pay structures suggests that optimal differentials may depend on employee characteristics such as income and age and on the type of behavior to be motivated. If current practices serve as a guide, then a 3 to 5 percent pay increase may serve to reinforce previous performance, but a 10 to 15 percent increase may be necessary to induce employees to invest in training or take on added responsibility.[12] However, no research has examined the validity of these rules

of thumb. Thus, a great deal remains to be learned about the incentive effects of different structures on outcomes such as skill acquisition and the desire to advance in the hierarchy of the organization.

Another way of thinking about the incentive effects of structures is to conceptualize them as tournaments. The large differentials between CEOs and other employees (Lazear & Rosen, 1981) and the evidence of organizational career systems for managers (Rosenbaum, 1984) provide some impetus for this approach. Generally, the tournament process determines which employees advance, how fast they advance, and the pay increases they receive for advancing at each level.

Whether it is organizations or more obvious types of tournaments (e.g., golf; see Ehrenberg & Bognanno, 1990), three key features are emphasized. First, payoffs (differentials) are fixed in advance and are based on *relative*, not absolute, performance. Next, the magnitude of the differentials between levels affects effort exerted by all participants, not only those who "win and lose." The motivational presumption in a tournament model is that if the CEO earns significantly more than his or her immediate subordinates, and so on throughout the hierarchy, then each individual will exert more effort. Note this implies that the magnitude of the differentials, at least at the higher levels in the hierarchy, must be sufficiently large to keep everyone motivated to pursue the top prize. Third, optimal magnitudes of these differentials between levels are assumed to exist. Although larger differentials increase effort and create added output, there are associated costs for both individuals and organizations. Therefore, at some point the value of the costs associated with incremental effort exceeds the value of the output. Thus, there is a limit to the incentive effects of increasingly larger differentials within the structure. Consequently, the optimal size of the differential for a new job or for learning a new skill depends on the value of its motivational effects and associated costs.

There is some evidence supporting tournament models. Ehrenberg and Bognanno (1990) studied professional golfers and reported that the greater the dispersion (variance) in the tournament prize structure, the better the scores per hole. However, the different nature of the employment relationship (e.g., interdependencies, its relatively long-term nature, payments typically becoming part of base pay) may limit the generalizability of these findings.[13]

What About Equity and Fairness? Although differentials must be sufficiently large to provide incentives, what about differentials perceived as too large? As discussed earlier, the popular press has devoted considerable attention to the ratio of CEO pay to that of the lowest paid employee in the organization. This ratio is larger in the United States than in other countries such as Japan and Germany. Farnham (1989), for example, asserts that this differential is seen by employees as unfair, resulting in a "trust gap." This focus is, of course, much different than that of the tournament model, which suggests that such differentials are necessary to provide incentives for expending effort and taking on added responsibilities and risks.

However, even confining attention to the equity criterion does not eliminate conflicting views of the appropriateness of particular differentials. Consider again the issue of pay compression (e.g., Gomez-Mejia & Balkin, 1987) to illustrate that although there may be agreement that formal pay structures matter, there is little theoretical or research agreement over why (or how) they matter. Deans (and other managers) often try to explain away compression by saying, "The market made me do it." Deans often argue that compression is the unavoidable and undesired result of salaries for entry-level jobs increasing at faster rates, due to market pressures, than salaries for other positions. Hence, deans need to respond to be able to compete in the labor market for new talent. Rather than unavoidable and undesirable,

another view is that this narrowing of differentials (compression) is simply more egalitarian pay. As already noted, some advocates (e.g., Lawler, 1986; Lodge & Walton, 1989) argue that more egalitarian pay encourages cooperation, higher commitment, and greater teamwork. So, is the narrowing of differentials best described as a negative outcome (compression) or as a positive outcome (egalitarian)? What is the optimal differential, and what understanding does behavioral research and theory offer? We believe that the answer lies in better understanding how contextual factors affect the relationships between pay and employee behaviors. For example, narrow differentials may be related to greater satisfaction and performance when the technology and nature of the work requires cooperation and teamwork compared to more independent and autonmous situations. On the other hand, it is not difficult to think of examples where large pay differentials exist within highly successful (championship) teams (e.g., Michael Jordan and the Chicago Bulls basketball team; Mario Lemieux and the Pittsburgh Penguins hockey team).

Perceived inequity in pay structures is believed to result in detrimental effects such as turnover, grievances, and decreased motivation to perform (Livernash, 1957). Note that the focus is not on the satisfaction with the level of pay (see previous section), but rather on attitudes about relative pay (differentials) in the structure. Frank (1985) goes further, arguing that employees attribute value to the structure itself and to their relative position in it. He argues that employees value the status attached to their relative position in a pay structure. Consequently, they make tradeoffs between the value of their status in their current pay structure and the rate of pay for a new job in another unit and its status in the new pay structure. Using the analogy of a big fish in a little pond, he believes that pay structures influence employees in "choosing the right pond." Employees, like fish and frogs, may forego changing ponds (organizations with new structures) if their status (relative position) in the current pay structure has greater value than the increased pay for the new job and its status. Kanter (1990) even goes so far as to urge employers to cease paying for status and start paying for performance. Others argue that if differentials among jobs (or skills) are not perceived as equitable, individuals will harbor ill will toward employers, resist technological innovations, change employment, and "lack the zest and enthusiasm which makes for high efficiency and personal satisfaction in work" (Jaques, 1961, p. 123).

How Does One Resolve Potential Conflicts of Internal Consistency and External Competitiveness? Organizations also sometimes face a conflict between the goals of internal consistency and external competitiveness in designing their structures. Consistent with our earlier discussion, equity depends on your perspective. For example, although an internal measure of worth may assign equal value to the jobs of marketing manager and information systems manager, a relative undersupply of the latter may result in the external market placing a higher value on information systems managers. As another example, the pharmaceuticals division of an organization may be doing much better than the automobile parts division. Should the marketing manager in pharmaceuticals be paid more than the marketing manager in the automobile parts division? Even if base salaries and benefits were the same, pay differences could easily arise if bonuses were linked to division profits, growth, and so forth.

Lawler (1986) has argued that organizations need to focus greater attention on external competitiveness. He believes that an internal focus encourages employees to compare themselves with others within the organization, rather than focusing on the real competition—other organizations. He also suggests that an internal focus results in employees focusing on promotions rather than on performing well on their current job. Moreover, there is some belief that conflicts between external and

internal equity may be resolved by increasing the pay of all jobs, not just those where competing in the labor market requires higher pay. If true, such organizations would seem to be at a serious labor cost disadvantage in the product market. In a symposium of compensation professionals, the argument was stated even more forcefully:

> We've seen a clear shift in the last ten years...to market pricing as the ultimate survival....To stay in business with the competition out there, your choice is to get down to the market or go out of business. (Levine, 1987, p. 34)

Unfortunately, empirical evidence on the implications of an external versus an internal focus is lacking.

There are also arguments for an internal focus (Carroll, 1987), particularly where employees move across divisions or where teamwork is commonly required (e.g., in project teams). Weber and Rynes (1991) have provided evidence that organizations do differ in their degree of internal versus external orientation and that this is reflected in their pay decisions. For example, their results suggest that externally focused organizations may have lower overall labor costs, as suggested above. However, we know little about the consequences for organizational effectiveness of these various strategies under different contingency conditions.

Summary

There is an extensive research literature on the measurement properties of administrative tools such as job evaluation. However, there is considerably less evidence on the broader questions of determinants and consequences of structures. There is an abundance of anecdotal and qualitative evidence to support the proposition that internal pay structures have consequences for work behaviors. Managers and union officials devote considerable resources to developing and administering pay structures and behave as if the number of distinct structures, number of levels, size of the differentials, and rate of progress matter. Yet little attention has been devoted to understanding the structure-outcome relationship in industrial and organizational psychology. The possible exception is the work on social comparison models, but even this does not offer much guidance to decision makers or much understanding of the effects of the changing properties of pay structures observed in organizations today.

Suggested Research Directions

The industrial and organizational psychology literature is virtually silent about the nature, determinants, and consequences of internal pay structures. We suggest the following topics for future research and theory building.

- *Impact of structural properties on attitudes, behaviors, and organizational effectiveness.* Based on practitioners' behaviors, as well as the administrative and research literatures, structures can be defined in terms of multiple properties. However, little is known about the relative salience of these various properties to employees (and managers) and their relative impact on attitudes, behaviors, and organizational effectiveness.

- *Variation in internal pay structures across organizations.* At an even more basic level, little is known about the degree and type of variation in internal pay structures across organizations. In other words, basic descriptive evidence is lacking. Do similar organizations make use of similar structures? Is structure design systematically related to employee, job, and organizational characteristics? It is clear from the business press that structures are undergoing significant changes in many organizations (e.g., delayering, fewer distinct job classifications, interest in

skill-based pay). These changes offer an opportunity for field research of both a descriptive and substantive nature.

- *Internal consistency versus external competitiveness in pay structures.* Little is known about the degree to which organizations focus on this issue. Descriptive evidence would be useful, as would insight into the consequences of the two strategies for organizational effectiveness. In addition, specification and testing of contingency factors would be useful.

- *Pay structure theories of other disciplines.* Other disciplines, notably economics and sociology, offer theories (e.g., tournament models, resource dependency, institutional models, internal labor markets) that identify important determinants and consequences of pay structures. These formulations often rely on implicit assumptions regarding employee behavior. It would be useful to examine such assumptions in greater depth in light of the state of knowledge in the industrial and organizational psychology literature.

- *Return on investment.* A recurring research theme in this chapter is the need to study decisions from a return on investment perspective. The design and administration of internal pay structures is typically accompanied by a substantial bureaucracy for evaluating (and reevaluating) jobs (or skill blocks). Are the attendant costs of such bureaucracies justified?

- *Consequences of skill- and knowledge-based pay structures.* Although there is some descriptive evidence, there is virtually no research on the consequences of skill-based and knowledge-based pay structures relative to more traditional job-based structures. What are their relative influences on attitudes and behaviors? Are skill-based plans more or less expensive to design and administer? Are they more or less susceptible to systematic biases such as discrimination? What unique problems arise in market pricing of skills and knowledge?

- *Currently marketed products offering quantitative approaches to job evaluation.* Several consulting firms are marketing quantitative approaches to job evaluation. Hay Expert, TPFC's WJQ, and Wyatt's Multicomp are leading examples. These are largely conventional point job evaluation plans that are statistically tailored to the pay structure selected by their clients. All of them use various policy-capturing approaches. Some simply weight compensable factors; others tailor each factor's scale through data-fitting methods, thereby deriving the factor weights and scales that best fit the pay criterion. These products have received little scrutiny by the measurement community. Parallel developments in selection and cognitive tests are often subject to publicly available research. Considering the increasingly important role these commercial plans are playing in establishing pay structures within large organizations, they deserve similar scrutiny.

- *Shift of focus to broad issues.* Although measurement evidence on job evaluation and related procedures is important, it may be time to shift resources to focus more on some of the broader issues mentioned above, such as the effects of different types of structures on attitudes, behaviors, and organizational effectiveness.

- *Political and environmental considerations in job evaluation systems.* One exception

to the preceding statement is the need for empirical evidence on the effects of political and environmental considerations (Kerr & Fisher, 1950) on the successful implementation of job evaluation systems. Even job evaluation systems that are highly successful in the sense of predicting grade levels for jobs can be deemed failures because of a lack of acceptance for nontechnical reasons.

Individual Differences in Pay

The preceding discussion of pay level and pay structures focused on (average) pay differences between organizations where job evaluation and pay surveys were typically used to develop and price pay structures for jobs. So far, we have given little attention to how organizations pay individual employees within such structures. For example, one organization may have a strong link between pay and performance for its middle managers but less so for its production employees, whereas a similar organization may have a weak link between pay and performance among middle managers and other employee groups.

There is good reason to believe that such organizational differences in how individuals are compensated may have some of the most important implications for individual attitudes and behaviors, as well as for organizational performance. Moreover, as Haire, Ghiselli, and Gordon (1967) pointed out over 20 years ago, features of the compensation system other than pay level often "can be varied by a company without increasing the total salary expense" (p. 10). In a study described earlier, Gerhart and Milkovich (1990) echoed this point, suggesting that the largest organizational differences were likely to be in individual pay determination rather than in pay level because there are greater product and labor market restraints on the latter (see earlier discussion). Their empirical evidence bore out this suggestion, indicating that organizations may be most strategic with respect to individual pay determination.

Consistent with the two previous sections, we proceed as follows. First, we describe a simple system for classifying pay programs. Second, we turn to the question of how individual differences in pay are determined. Special emphasis is given to the link between pay and performance. Next, we discuss the potential consequences of different pay plans. Finally, we conclude with a summary and suggested future research directions.

Definition and Properties

In describing individual pay determination, it is convenient to classify the various compensation plans using two dimensions (Milkovich & Wigdor, 1991), based on the following questions. First, are changes in compensation added into base pay (e.g., conventional merit systems) or are they given as one-time payments (i.e., bonuses, lump sums)? Second, are changes in compensation based on individual or group (i.e., work team, plan, business unit, organization) objectives? The resulting grid and classification of plans is shown in Figure 4.

The first dimension, whether the increase is added to the base, can also be viewed as indicating the extent to which pay is a fixed versus variable cost to the organization. For example, a merit increase, as the term is typically used, refers to an increase that is rolled into the base salary. As such, employees are always, to an extent, paid on the basis of past performance, because such increases carry over to future years. In contrast, a lump sum increase (or merit bonus) is ordinarily paid out on a one-time basis. It does not become part of base pay. Therefore, the pay at any given time may be more likely to reflect recent performance than an accumulation of past performance increases. One implication is that rewards can be more directly tied to recent performance using lump sum types of payments. In addition, as pay becomes a more variable cost, organizations

FIGURE 4

Level of Performance Measurement

	Individual	Group
Added in	Merit pay	
Not added in	Merit bonus Piece rate Commission	Gain sharing Profit sharing Ownership

Effect on Base Compensation

may be better able to align compensation costs with ability to pay (e.g., through profit-sharing bonuses or lump sums). Thus, plans that differ on the fixed versus variable pay dimension may differ in terms of both behavioral and cost consequences.

Differences on the second dimension, individual versus group performance criteria, are also likely to have consequences for costs and behaviors. Expectancy theory suggests that motivation (specifically, instrumentality perceptions) will be greater under plans that tie pay to individual (versus group) performance, and empirical evidence supports this hypothesis (Schwab, 1973). However, linking pay to individual performance means that employees can earn large amounts of money, even in years when the company is losing money, and thus is not an effective way of aligning labor costs with ability to pay.

Determinants

At the outset, it is important to distinguish between two related but different questions. First, one can ask what factors account for individual differences in pay within organizations. An extensive literature suggests that education, experience, performance, and other individual differences play some role (Gerhart

& Milkovich, 1989; Medoff & Abraham, 1981; Milkovich & Newman, 1990; Mincer, 1974), depending on the organization.

Second, however, one can ask what factors account for the fact that different organizations use different pay programs (e.g., merit pay, gainsharing, etc.). The empirical evidence on this question is much more sparse, although the section on contingency models later in this chapter provides some conceptual models for thinking about such issues. Again, the two questions are related, and we focus here on the nature of the relation between pay and performance.

Is There Pay for Performance? A recurring question concerns the strength of the relation between pay and performance. In the case of incentive plans, which typically use physical measures of output, this relationship is clear and, barring rate-setting issues, is usually not an issue. But, with the subjective ratings required under a merit pay system, the link between pay and performance may fail to exist or may not always be obvious to employees. Because merit pay is so widely used, especially among white collar employees (Bretz, Milkovich, & Read, 1989; Personick, 1984), we will focus a good deal of our general discussion of pay-for-performance issues on merit pay per se. However, a number of the issues also apply to other pay-for-performance plans.

Several pieces of evidence suggest that the relation between merit and pay is small (e.g., Lawler, 1981, 1989; Milkovich & Newman, 1990; Milkovich & Wigdor, 1991; Teel, 1986; see Heneman, 1990, for a review).[14] For example, Lawler (1989) comments that "all too often only a few percentage points separate the raises given good performers from those given poor performers" (p. 151). For instance, he mentions the problem of *topping out*, which refers to the fact that many organizations use merit increase guidelines (see Table 2 for an example) that reduce the size of the merit increase percentage for employees higher in the salary range or

grade as a means of controlling costs (Milkovich & Newman, 1990). Similarly, some merit increase guidelines also reduce the frequency of within-grade pay increases for employees near the top of the range (Milkovich & Newman).

In fact, merit increase grids in actual usage often appear designed more to meet budgetary goals than to reward merit. Administratively, the process typically begins by first determining the budget for pay increases (based on market movement and ability to pay). Next, the distributions of employees across performance categories and range of positions (e.g., pay quartiles) is assessed because these distributions will have a major impact on the cost of the increase program. Finally, the percentage increases in each cell are decided upon. One might argue that if merit pay or motivation was the primary goal, one would begin instead by establishing increases sufficiently large to motivate employees and then calculate the necessary budget.

In any case, the preceding types of factors may contribute to a weakening of the link between pay and performance. In addition, although the subjective nature of performance assessment under merit pay systems has potential advantages (e.g., factoring in extenuating circumstances), it has the drawback of being open to perceptions of favoritism or other perceptions of unfairness. These factors may all contribute to the perception of a weak relation between pay and performance. A survey by the Hay Group (1986), for example, found that less than one-half of middle managers and professionals thought that "better performers" received "higher pay increases than average or poor performers" (p. 14). Where the perception is of a weak pay-performance link, pay satisfaction among high performers may be low. Dyer and Theriault (1976) did, in fact, report lower pay satisfaction among high performers, although they did not report information on the nature of the reward system in their study.

Evidence of this sort suggests that the pay-performance link may not always be as

TABLE 2

Merit Increase Grid Example

Performance Rating	Position in Salary Range				
	Quintile				
	1	2	3	4	5
Outstanding	9%	8%	7%	6.5%	5%
Exceeds expectations	7%	6%	5.5%	5%	4%
Fully satisfactory	5%	4.5%	4%	3.5%	3%
Needs some improvement	1%	1%	1%	1%	No increase
Unsatisfactory	No increase	No increase	No increase	No increase	No increase

Note: Entries are recommended percentage increases.

Reprinted with permission from *Pay for Performance: Evaluating Performance Appraisal and Merit Pay,* Copyright © 1991 by the National Academy of Sciences. Published by National Academy Press, Washington, DC.

strong as one might wish, and that within some organizations, the link may be particularly weak. Further, even where pay is strongly related to performance, pay for performance perceptions can still be weak (Dreher, 1981). On the other hand, one needs to keep in mind that organizations probably differ significantly in this respect, and in some, both the actual and perceived link may be fairly strong. We now focus on two reasons why the magnitude of the pay-performance link is often underestimated.

Cross-sectional Versus Longitudinal Data. First, and perhaps most important, research often looks at the link between the most recent performance rating and the subsequent pay increase (or worse, the current pay level of an individual) at a single point in time, thus ignoring the fact that performance differences over time often result in an accumulation (and compounding) of pay differences in favor of higher performers. Some of the limitations of using cross-sectional data in studying pay-for-performance can be illustrated by considering Bishop's (1984) useful discussion of the factors that constrain the observed pay-for-performance link. Most relevant are three factors: (a) Performance is typically measured with error (King, Hunter, & Schmidt, 1980); (b) true performance may vary over time; and (c) the present value of an increase is greater than the first year effect. Using longitudinal data would potentially eliminate each problem. Averaging performance over time would help control measurement errors and variations over time in true performance (see Gerhart & Milkovich, 1989)[15] and would also allow an examination of the present value (or similarly, the effects of compounding and accumulation) of pay increases (see Schwab & Olson, 1990).

Greater use of longitudinal data is likely to lead to other conclusions that may come as a surprise to some. For example, Lawler (1989) has spoken of merit bonuses (not rolled into base salary) as a way of avoiding what he refers to as the *annuity feature* of traditional merit increases—a situation where current pay reflects past performance increases rather than current performance. He suggests that merit bonuses can be used to more strongly link pay to performance. However, Schwab and Olson (1990), in a simulation of multiple time periods, did not find that a merit bonus system was superior to a conventional merit system in linking pay and performance in either the current time period or over multiple time periods. Moreover, they did not find *capped* merit systems (i.e., where percentage increases are smaller at higher points within the pay grade) to have any significant influence on the pay-performance relationship.

Role of Promotions.   Second, and related, merit pay increases (i.e., *within-grade* pay increases) are only one factor contributing to salary growth over time. Promotions (i.e., *between-grade* increases) are another major determinant (Gerhart & Milkovich, 1989). In fact, promotions often have a two-fold effect. First, there is typically a pay increase that goes along with the promotion. In 1990, the average promotional increase was about 12 percent, compared with approximately 4.5 percent for merit increases (Hay Group, 1991). Second, in addition, a promotion usually moves the employee to a new pay grade where she or he will most likely be in a low relative position (in the grade), thus having the opportunity to earn larger and perhaps more frequent within-grade increases. Thus, the impact of promotions on performance can have significant consequences for the strength of the pay-performance relation but will show up only with longitudinal data.

Studies that ignore the importance of promotions, not surprisingly, are less likely to find a strong pay-for-performance link. For example, Medoff and Abraham (1981), in a study of professional and managerial employees,

focused exclusively on within-grade analyses and found relatively modest effects of performance on pay. Similarly, Konrad and Pfeffer (1990, p. 270), in a study of college and university faculty, concluded that the effect of productivity on pay was small. However, they focused entirely on the relation between productivity and pay within rank (grade; i.e., assistant, associate, and full professor). This, of course, ignores the possibility that performance may have a large impact on rank or grade. We reanalyzed their data and found the following results. First, a bivariate regression shows, across ranks, that professors with 1 *SD* higher productivity earned $2,234 (18.9%) more. Within rank, 1 *SD* higher productivity resulted in only $1,080 (9.2%) more (based on 4 predictors—productivity and dummy variables for assistant professor, associate professor, and full professor [$R^2 = .504$ vs. adjusted R^2 of .570 in their full model using 25 predictors]). Consequently, ignoring the impact of performance on rank or grade results in a lower estimated link between pay and performance.[16]

Gerhart and Milkovich (1989), in a study of a large, private, diversified organization that provided evidence on the pay-for-performance link, also used longitudinal data but recognized the role of promotions. Among 5,550 exempt male employees,[17] they found an average salary growth (due both to promotions and merit increases) over a 5-year interval of 54 percent. Men, however, *averaging* (over the 5-year period) 1 rating point above the mean experienced 10 percent greater salary growth $(54\% + (.10 \times 54\%) = 59\%)$. This works out to be 9.8 percent per year versus 9.0 percent per year. Projecting the pay of two hypothetical employees over a 20-year period, with both starting at $40,000 per year, results in a cumulative earnings advantage of $220,000 for the higher performing employee (present value = $57,000 using a 9% discount rate or $75,000 using a 7% discount rate). This difference is substantial but would be overlooked if promotions were ignored or if longitudinal data were not used.

The role of promotion in generating pay for performance will be even larger in situations where within-grade performance-based increases are small (e.g., in some public sector employers) or nonexistent (e.g., in some unionized jobs). Although these situations are often thought of as good examples of a lack of pay for performance, the preceding discussion suggests that this is probably not true when one considers the role of promotion.

On the other hand, there has been much recent discussion regarding the possible decline in promotional opportunities in many U.S. organizations (e.g., Kanter, 1989; Kirkpatrick, 1990; Weber, Driscoll, & Brandt, (1990). The concern stems from the extensive retrenchment that many organizations have gone through in the past five years in the form of employment reductions and delayering (eliminating job levels). As one example, General Electric (chemicals division) recently reduced the number of pay grades from 22 to 5. As part of this reduction, 10 layers of management were compressed into 4 levels (Fisher, 1991). The implication of these changes for the role of promotion as a reward remains to be seen. It is conceivable that some organizations will need to place more emphasis on the annual pay increase to achieve pay for performance if promotions become less frequent. However, any such trend among established organizations is likely to be offset by continuing growth of promotional opportunities in smaller organizations, which account for a substantial share of both employment level and growth.

In summary, research has probably underestimated the magnitude of the link between pay and performance because promotion effects and the accumulation (and compounding) of merit increases over time have often been ignored. Despite these limitations, the bulk of the research shows that there is at least some relation between pay and performance. (The link was statistically significant in 23 out of 30 studies in R. Heneman's, 1990, meta-analysis.)

Employee Perceptions of Pay for Performance. Of course, a key question remains unanswered. Even if pay for performance exists in the longer run, are employees aware of this relationship and does it affect their behavior? Do employees respond to pay for performance in a similar fashion, regardless of whether it is largely achieved through annual increases or through promotions? Do employees think in terms of cumulative earnings? Some evidence suggests that they may. For example, Wazeter (1991) argues that new teachers focus more on the top rate on the pay scale rather than the entry point. Of course, this situation may be somewhat unusual in that the pay schedule is public information, and the means of achieving the top of the scale may be based on objective factors such as degrees obtained and years of service. If employees do not always think in terms of cumulative earnings, to what extent can companies communicate this information in such a way that employees will see the long-term advantage of higher performance levels?

Consequences

Some objectives discussed earlier under pay level apply equally to individual differences in pay. For example, although pay satisfaction is related to overall pay level, it will also vary across individuals according to their own pay, frame of reference (Smith et al., 1969), perceived inputs and outputs (i.e., distributive justice or equity; see Adams, 1963, 1965), and perhaps perceived procedural justice (Folger & Konovsky, 1989; Greenberg, 1986). Similarly, although pay level may influence the overall quality of the work force, it is also hypothesized that such factors as individual performance and cooperation of the current work force are likely to depend on the way the organization determines individual pay. Further, the organization's approach to individual pay may also signal prospective applicants, thereby influencing the eventual composition of the work force in another way.

What Impact Do Pay Plans Have on Current Employees? The general assumption underlying many pay plans, especially the "new" variable pay plans, is that there is a significant amount of "untapped energy" (Hammer, 1988; Lawler, 1989) in the work force that can be elicited with the right compensation system. Here we briefly discuss three theoretical explanations for the effects of pay plans on modification and behaviors: reinforcement theory, expectancy theory, and agency theory. The last theory is discussed at greater length because of its relative unfamiliarity to some readers.

Reinforcement Theory. Thorndike's law of effect states that a response followed by a reward is more likely to recur in the future. Applied to employee compensation, this implies that the receipt of a monetary reward following high employee performance will make high performance more likely in the future. The emphasis is on the importance of actually experiencing the reward. This contrasts, for example, with expectancy theory's forward-looking emphasis on expectations (or incentive effects). All three of the theories discussed here, however, stress the importance of behavior-reward contingencies.

Expectancy Theory. In the psychological literature, expectancy theory has been widely used over the past three decades in attempting to understand and predict the motivational and behavioral consequences of different individual pay plans.[18] Behaviors (e.g., performance) are believed to be a function of ability and motivation. The motivational component represents the force to choose one particular behavioral alternative instead of another. This motivational force is hypothesized to be a function of three factors (Vroom, 1964): *expectancy* (the perceived link between effort and behaviors), *instrumentality* (the perceived link between behaviors and valued outcomes like pay),

and *valence* (the value the person expects to derive from outcomes like pay). Thus, for example, employees may choose to work toward different levels of performance, depending on the way different compensation systems influence the three components. Typically, most attention is given to the consequences of compensation programs for instrumentality (e.g., pay for performance) perceptions, although compensation may influence the other two components as well (e.g., skill-based pay to influence expectancy perceptions).[19]

Locke (1968) has argued that pay affects behavior through its influence on gaining acceptance of challenging, specific work goals and maintaining commitment to them. Recent models of goal setting (e.g., Hollenbeck & Klein, 1987) and control theory (Klein, 1989) similarly focus on the subjective expected utility of goal choice and commitment. In other words, a common theme is that goals are a mediating variable between pay and outcomes like performance, although the empirical evidence is not conclusive (Locke, Shaw, Saari, & Latham, 1981; Tolchinsky & King, 1980; Wright, 1989).

Agency Theory. In the economics and finance literatures, agency theory has been widely used to study compensation, particularly executive compensation. Agency theory suggests that an important advantage of the present day corporation is the separation of ownership and control. This separation permits owners (principals) to freely transfer ownership (stock ownership) without disrupting the operations of the firm because their agents (e.g., managers) have taken over the control function (Fama & Jensen, 1983; Hoskisson, Hitt, Turk, & Tyler, 1989). The ability to transfer ownership allows shareholders to diversify their portfolios and thus their risk. This is an important advantage because it allows people to specialize and work to their relative advantage (e.g., managing, being an entrepreneur) and it also helps meet the large capital requirements of modern corporations (Hoskisson et al., 1989; Jensen & Meckling, 1976).

However, the separation of ownership and control creates a situation where the preferences of principals and agents are not ordinarily the same. What is best for the agent may not be best for the owner, giving rise to what are referred to as *agency costs*. As a rather extreme example, the agent might benefit in a narrow economic sense from stealing from the till or embezzling money. Obviously, the owner would not benefit from such behavior. Less extreme, agents may simply not push as hard to make the company a success as an owner might. Another source of divergent preferences stems from the fact that principals can diversify their ownership, but an agent (e.g., a manager) works for just one organization, thus having all of his or her "eggs in one basket." The fact that the agent cannot diversify risk suggests that she or he will be more risk averse than the principal.

Thus, much like expectancy theory, agency theory's focus is on the question of how to motivate someone like an agent to choose to pursue certain behavioral objectives. Also similar is the central role that compensation plays. Agency theory says that the principal must choose a contracting scheme that helps align the interests of the agent with his or her own. These contracts can be classified as either *behavior-oriented* (e.g., merit pay) or *outcome-oriented* (e.g., stock options, commission; (Eisenhardt, 1988).

On the face of it, the most obvious means of aligning the interests of agents with those of the principal(s) would be to use more outcome-oriented contracts. The drawback of such contracts, however, is the increased risk borne by the agent who, as noted above, is less able to diversify his or her risk and is thus more risk averse than the principal. Therefore, to accept this higher risk contract, the agent may require a compensating pay differential (Eisenhardt, 1988; Hoskisson et al., 1989).

Thus, as Eisenhardt (1988) has noted, a key question is, "When is it more efficient to have a contract based on behavior versus a contract at least partially based on outcomes?" (p. 490). Where the principal can easily monitor what the agent has done, a behavior-based contract is more efficient because no risk needs to be transferred to the agent, and thus no compensating differential needs to be paid. In contrast, Eisenhardt states, where monitoring of the agent's behaviors is difficult, the principal must either invest in monitoring/information or structure the contract such that pay is linked at least partly to outcomes.

Several contingency factors have been noted (Eisenhardt, 1988, 1989). First, risk aversion among principals makes outcome-oriented contracts more likely, whereas risk aversion among agents makes them less likely. Second, because of the increased costs of shifting risks to agents, outcome uncertainty makes outcome-oriented contracts less likely because agents are less able to diversify risk. Third, as jobs become less programmable (and more difficult to monitor), outcome-oriented contracts become more likely. Fourth, when outcomes are more measurable, outcome-oriented contracts are more likely. Fifth, outcome-oriented contracts contribute to higher compensation costs because of the risk premium (Conlon & Parks, 1990). Sixth, a tradition or custom of using (or not using) outcome-oriented contracts will make such contracts more (or less) likely.

Studies using retail clerks (Eisenhardt, 1989) and students (Conlon & Parks, 1990) have found support for these predictions. Moreover, in studies of managerial compensation, firms with dominant stockholders as opposed to "management-controlled firms" seem to exhibit stronger links between compensation and financial returns (Gomez-Mejia, Tosi, & Hinkin, 1987; Tosi & Gomez Mejia, 1989), providing support for the idea that managers and owners prefer different compensation systems. Also, a comparison of research and development

(R & D) intensive organizations with others revealed that the R & D intensive group relied more heavily on outcome-oriented compensation arrangements, consistent with the idea that monitoring of behaviors would be more difficult when highly technical and complex work is involved (Milkovich, Gerhart, & Hannon, 1991). Also consistent with the agency theory prediction of a risk premium, pay level was higher in the R & D intensive organizations.

How do agency theory and expectancy theory compare? They are similar in the sense that both focus on (a) explanation of choices, (b) separation of the concepts of behaviors and outcomes (contrary to Eisenhardt's, 1988, suggestion), and (c) motivation and control of performance by tying outcomes to behaviors. They differ in that agency theory focuses more on (a) the specific choice of which governance (often compensation) system will be most efficient to use and (b) the risk-reward tradeoff (Eisenhardt, 1988). The latter is particularly relevant, given the increased attention being paid to variable pay plans, which are often intended to put some pay at risk.[20] Finally, unlike expectancy theory, agency theory explicitly recognizes the importance of an exchange process between two parties.

What Impact Do Pay Plans Have on Composition of the Work Force?   At a general level, pay can influence employee performance in two ways. First, as discussed above, it can influence the performance of the current work force. This is the focus of most of the empirical research on specific pay programs. Second, however, and perhaps less obvious, pay programs can also affect the *composition* of the current work force through self-selection.

For example, Rynes (1987) suggests that "compensation systems are capable of attracting (or repelling) the right kinds of people because they communicate so much about an organization's philosophy, values, and practices" (p. 190). This idea again goes back to the signalling model of Spence (1973). To illustrate,

she discusses the case of sales jobs. If there is not a large incentive component in which individual effort is important, she argues that over time, one or more of the following three consequences is likely: (a) the right people will not be attracted; (b) they are attracted but leave when they discover that their efforts are under-rewarded; (c) they are attracted and retained, but because they are not rewarded for high performance, their performance declines.

In a similar vein, Brown (1990) has suggested that workers know their own productivity and choose to work in organizations where they can maximize their earnings. For example, he argues that highly productive blue collar workers are more likely to choose organizations that pay piece rates versus those that pay straight salaries. Although the notion that there is self-selection by individuals and selection by organizations to find people that fit the pay system (Rynes & Gerhart, 1990), empirical research has only recently begun to appear.

For example, on the retention side, Gerhart (1990b) examined the relation between average performance ratings and salary growth over several years among recent managerial and professional hires. He found that the relation between pay and performance was nonlinear. Salary growth among average performers was substantially greater than that among poor performers. However, salary growth among the highest performers was not much greater than that among average performers. He also found that turnover decisions of high performers were the most sensitive to salary growth. The consequence of these two facts appeared to be relatively high turnover among the highest performers. In other words, the pay system seemed to result in high performers self-selecting out of the organization.

Two other studies are also consistent with the idea that pay systems influence work force composition through self-selection. A study of nonclerical, white collar workers in U.S. Navy laboratories found that turnover among high performers was lower in laboratories using merit pay plans (U.S. Office of Personnel Management, 1988, cited in Milkovich & Wigdor, 1991, p. 91). Gomez-Mejia and Balkin (1989) found that employees who were more willing to take risks were more likely to intend to remain employed with organizations that relied more heavily on variable compensation systems, consistent with Rynes' (1987) arguments.

Still lacking is evidence on the effect that pay systems might have on the attraction of new hires to an organization. In addition to the question raised by Rynes (1987) and Brown (1990) about high performers being attracted to pay for performance, more general questions about fit and self-selection need to be addressed. For example, do variable pay systems having downside risk attract risk takers and discourage risk averse people as found by Gomez-Mejia and Balkin (1989) on the retention side? If a pay system attracts only certain types of people (still an open question; see Bretz, Ash, & Dreher, 1989), what consequences might the resulting employee homogeneity have for future organizational success (Schneider, 1983)?

Is Individual Emphasis a Good Idea? The focus of the preceding theories and mechanisms has been on explaining individual decisions within organizations. In parallel fashion, many of the specific programs discussed below—that is, merit pay, merit bonuses, and individual incentives—typically focus on distinctions between individuals. Yet in many cases, interdependence and the need for teamwork may argue against such differentiation (Lawler, 1989; Lodge & Walton, 1989). This point has been raised in the economics literature (Frank, 1985; Lazear, 1989) and by W. Edwards Deming (1986), who has received much credit for his role in Japan's success. According to Gabor (1990), Deming believes that focusing on the contributions of individual employees is "usually destructive" because "individuals are unfairly penalized...for deficiencies that are linked to the system they work in—which is created by management—rather than behavior over which they have control" (see Tuttle, 1991, p. 99). Deming also has argued that the relative contributions of the system and the individual on observed behavior are "unknowable." He raises the following question: "If the manager cannot accurately determine the contribution of individuals, how can their performance be validly rated?" (see Tuttle, 1991, p. 100).

However, one can also carry the argument in a different direction and raise the possible drawbacks of deemphasizing individual contributions too much. Organizations and work groups are composed of individual employees. As such, they are limited by the nature of these individuals. If, as suggested above, high performance employees are more likely to seek out and remain with organizations that provide rewards for high performance, a problem may arise for organizations that do not recognize top performers with top rewards. They may simply choose to work elsewhere, leaving the organization with members of low and average ability levels. Teamwork and cooperation, without ability, is not a formula for success either.

As examples, consider the consequences to the L.A. Kings of paying hockey player Wayne Gretzsky near the average or (returning to an earlier example) the Chicago Bulls paying Michael Jordan the same as his teammates. To be sure, hockey and basketball are team sports that require teamwork and cooperation, but the Kings and the Bulls would be very different teams without their star performers. Failing to recognize their individual contributions could be a serious mistake because another team would recognize them. It is possible that the Kings and Bulls might have better teamwork and cooperation without Gretzsky and Jordan, but they would most assuredly also have many fewer victories.

Obviously, such examples are no substitute for systematic empirical study. However, they illustrate some of the potential tradeoffs involved in designing reward systems. Deming's criticisms point to the potential drawbacks of individual-oriented plans. (See also Bartol & Martin, 1989; Bretz, Milkovich, & Read, 1989; Longnecker, Sims, & Gioia, 1987; and Markham, 1988, for related information.) These potential drawbacks, together with the goal of making human resources more of a variable cost, have contributed to greater recent attention to gainsharing and profit-sharing plans, which are group-oriented and do not add pay increases into the base (see Figure 1).

What Influence Do Pay Plans Have on Employee Attitudes and Behaviors? As discussed, there is limited evidence of the impact of pay programs on work force composition. Therefore, the bulk of evidence reviewed below pertains to the influence of specific pay plans on current employee attitudes and behaviors. Much of the readily available information and effectiveness evidence on pay plans comes from professional organizations like the Conference Board, the American Compensation Association, and various consulting organizations. Most such evidence is limited to reporting on the frequency with which organizations are using particular pay plans. Even this evidence can be misleading because organizations are often asked to report whether the plan is being used anywhere in their organization. Thus, even an organization having only a pilot program could be counted as using a pay plan.

Evidence of the effectiveness of particular plans is less available and also of questionable value. For example, Table 3 summarizes evidence from a 1990 Conference Board study. As indicated by the table, each pay plan seems to come out as being somewhere between partially successful and highly successful. Virtually no organizations appear to have adopted plans that did not work, which is more than a little suspicious. However, perhaps the most interesting aspect of this pattern of data is that the column headings (compensation plans) can be interchanged without having any effect at all on the interpretation! Obviously, these sorts of

data are of little help in determining which compensation plans tend to work best under different sets of circumstances. The alternative interpretation (to which we do not subscribe) is that contingency factors simply do not matter—the plans work equally well regardless of the conditions.

In a sense, such "research" recalls past criticisms of the nature of research in the compensation field (Dunnette & Bass, 1963; Haire, 1965; Opsahl & Dunnette, 1966). Haire (cited in Opsahl & Dunnette, 1966) suggested that despite the large amount of money spent and the obvious relevance of motivational theory, there was less research and theory in the field of compensation than in any other. Dunnette and Bass suggested that "personnel men [*sic*] had relied on faddish and assumptive practices in administering pay which lack empirical support" (as paraphrased by Opsahl & Dunnette, 1966; see Mahoney, 1979a, p. 84). Finally, Opsahl and Dunnette expressed hope that "the firm of the future will be able to establish compensation policies and practices based on empirical evidence about the behavioral effects of money as an incentive rather than on the untested hunches, and time worn 'rules of thumb' so common in industry today" (see Mahoney, p. 86).

Fortunately, there has been at least some progress in developing a research base to inform practice. For example, Gerhart and Milkovich's (1990) longitudinal study of multiple organizations found evidence that linking pay to organizational performance contributed to higher subsequent organizational performance (as measured by return on assets). However, their study had limited information on the nature of specific pay plans in those organizations.

We now turn to a discussion of specific pay plans and what the available research evidence has to say about their effectiveness under various conditions. It may be useful to keep in mind the grid shown in Figure 4 as we proceed.

Individual Incentives. As Figure 4 indicates, the focus here is on individuals and payments that

TABLE 3

Degree of Success in Achieving Most Important Objectives

	Type of Program			
Degree of Success	*Profit Sharing*	*Individual Gainsharing*	*Individual Incentive*	*Small Group Incentive*
Very successful	33%	29%	29%	30%
Successful	42%	46%	49%	48%
Partially successful	17%	25%	23%	20%
No success	8%	———	———	3%
Totals	100%	100%	100%	100%

Source: "International Trends in Productivity and Unit Labor Costs in Manufacturing" by A. Neef, December, 1986, *Monthly Labor Review*, 12–17.

are not rolled into base compensation. One of the most famous proponents of individual incentives was Frederick Taylor. A favorite story of his had to do with a German laborer named Schmidt (Taylor, 1967). Taylor and his associates observed that most laborers at the steelyard they were studying moved about 12.5 long tons of pig iron per day and earned an average of $1.15 per day in return. Taylor, however, decided that a laborer could move 47 to 48 long tons per day with some modification to the work motions and with the appropriate incentive payment. To prove this contention, he offered Schmidt the opportunity to earn $1.85 per day if he moved 47 to 48 long tons. According to Taylor, Schmidt did subsequently move an average of 47.5 long tons per day (about a 300% increase) in response to the monetary incentive (about a 60% increase in pay). Obviously, this was a very good return on investment, and not surprisingly, there has since been a good deal of research on the productivity-enhancing effects of incentives. For example, a fairly recent study found a good deal of evidence to support the claim that individual incentives *can* have a substantial positive impact on

productivity (Locke, Feren, McCaleb, Shaw, & Denny, 1980).

The key word, however, is *can*. Despite their potential for large productivity payoffs, relatively few employees work under individual incentive plans in the United States for two general reasons. First, they are not applicable to many jobs, such as those with no physical output measure of performance or those where individual contributions are difficult to isolate (or should not be isolated because of, for example, a team approach). Both are typically characteristics of white collar jobs and many blue collar jobs as well.

Second, individual incentives can cause a wide range of what might be called *administrative problems*. These include (a) the cost of time study to set and keep current production standards for multiple jobs (and perhaps machines), (b) the cost of tracking output in these multiple jobs and calculating payments, and (c) the difficulty in setting production standards that are accepted as appropriate by both management and workers. This last problem has received a good deal of attention in discussions of "gaming" by workers (to fool the time study person into setting the standard lower so they can make more money; see Whyte, 1955). Workers may also have serious concerns about working themselves out of a job if their productivity increases substantially. In addition, they may anticipate that once they begin to exceed a standard regularly (and thus make more money), management may decide the standard is too low, yielding excessive labor costs, and raise it.

All of this suggests that individual incentives are most likely to work when there is trust in management and where production standards do not undergo regular change. One much cited example, Lincoln Electric, has an incentive system that works, in part, because it (a) has an employment security practice and (b) changes standards infrequently (partly because technology has been relatively stable in their product market). Another potential problem, sacrificing of quality for quantity, is controlled at Lincoln Electric by paying workers only for output that meets the quality standard.

Merit Pay.   As Figure 4 indicates, the term is used to refer to cases where payments go to individuals and are added in to base compensation. "It is not difficult to view merit pay plan design as a means of overcoming some of the unintended consequences of individual incentive plans" (Milkovich & Wigdor, 1991, p. 78). Nevertheless, other problems may arise in using merit pay plans. As discussed earlier, the strength of the link between performance and pay may be more difficult to establish. Moreover, even where a strong link exists, employees may not necessarily perceive such a link.

Although we suggested earlier that pay is often based to a significant extent on performance, there is much less interpretable evidence on the crucial question of whether pay for performance contributes to increased future performance and other organizational objectives. Although a fair amount of research on this question has now accumulated, methodological problems make it difficult to interpret much of this literature. For example,

R. Heneman (1990) reported that only 4 of the 22 studies he reviewed on this topic used any type of control group. Another 4 studies used a time series design. The remaining 14 used neither. Only 6 studies looked at performance levels subsequent to the implementation or removal of a merit pay plan. Of these, 4 reported a positive effect of merit pay on performance.

To illustrate some of the problems in interpreting these studies, it may be useful to consider a study by Pearce, Stevenson, and Perry (1985) of the implementation of a merit pay system for Social Security Administration managers. They concluded that the "merit pay program had no effect on organizational performance, suggesting that merit pay may be an inappropriate method of improving organizational performance" (p. 261). Several aspects of the study, however, suggest caution in accepting their interpretation. First, no control group was used. Second, to study the impact of a pay-for-performance system, one must first establish that there is indeed pay for performance (much like doing a manipulation check in an experiment to see whether the treatment "takes"). However, in the Pearce et al. study, only one-half of the annual pay increase was based on merit. The other one-half was an across-the-board increase. (Prior to the new pay system, increases had been completely of the across-the-board type). Moreover, in the first year, the merit pool was 4.5 percent. In the second year, it was 2.4 percent. Therefore, it is not clear that major distinctions could be made in rewarding different performance levels. Pearce et al. also reported that the performance measures they included in their study accounted for only 40 percent of the merit increase portion (which, recall, in turn determines 50% of the annual increase). In other words, it appears that Pearce et al. focused on performance measures that accounted for only about 20 percent of managers' annual increases. The timing of the measurements may also be an issue. The majority of Pearce et al.'s study took place before the actual distribution of pay increases under the new plan. Yet reinforcement theory would suggest that behavioral responses (e.g., higher performance) would not occur until after people actually received the reward. Similarly, from an expectancy theory perspective, instrumentality perceptions may not have strengthened until after it was demonstrated that pay and performance were being more strongly linked. In sum, these facts suggest that Pearce et al. may not have really been studying a pay-for-performance system.

The dependent variables in the Pearce et al. (1985) study included factors such as the number of days to process a claim, accuracy of claims processing, and so forth. However, no information was provided on changes in either staffing levels or number of claims filed during the period. In other words, their study did not provide information regarding productivity ratios (e.g., claims per person). Also, their results suggest a strong possibility of floor or ceiling effects in several instances. For example, in the two years immediately preceding the change in the compensation system, performance had already improved by an average of 45 percent across their measures. The days needed to process a retirement or survivor's claim had already dropped from about 60 days to 38 days. The implication is that significant changes in the managerial system (or staffing levels) may have already been made, perhaps leaving relatively little room for further improvement. However, it may be that such improvements were more likely to last under a pay-for-performance compensation system.

A recent study by Kahn and Sherer (1990) examined within-organization variations in the link between pay and performance among managers and the consequences for subsequent performance. They found that bonuses (but not merit pay) were linked to performance. Further, those managers who in the past had bonuses most strongly linked to performance had the highest subsequent performance levels, even controlling for previous performance. In other words, pay for performance seemed to work in

the organization they studied. More work of this kind would be useful. In particular, research that examines the conditions most conducive to the success of pay for performance (i.e., a contingency analysis) would be of value.

Profit Sharing. Profit sharing is a group- or organization-based plan that does not typically roll changes in pay into the base salary (see Figure 4). The logic behind profit sharing seems to be twofold. First, it is seen as a way to encourage employees to think more like owners (see the agency theory discussion) or at least be concerned with the success of the organization as a whole. Individual-oriented plans often place little emphasis on these broader goals. Second, it permits labor costs to vary with the organization's ability to pay. As an example, Union Carbide's plan for its 14,000 U.S. chemical and plastics division employees has frozen base salaries, but if return on capital exceeds 8 percent, employees can get lump sum payments of up to 15.4 percent of base. Larry Doyle, vice president of human resources, points out that Union Carbide secretaries are now "not bashful about nudging managers to stay at a Holiday Inn instead of a more expensive Hyatt" (Jacob, 1990). Profit sharing is in use at several well-known companies, including Hewlett Packard, USX, Ford, General Motors, ALCOA, Caterpillar, Monsanto, and AT&T (Schroeder, 1988; Feldman, 1991). Like Union Carbide, a number of these companies (e.g., AT&T, Monsanto) have replaced some portion of base salary with the potential to earn shares of the profits. In other words, there is not only an upside potential but a downside risk as well. General Motors' new division, Saturn, is also using profit sharing, linking "up to 20 percent of workers' salaries...to the company's profitability" (Levin, 1991).[21]

A comprehensive and useful review of the empirical evidence on profit sharing has been provided by Weitzman and Kruse (1990), who examined two basic types of evidence: attitudes toward profit sharing among both employees and employers, and productivity, usually defined as value added. They concluded that employers believed that profit sharing had a positive effect on productivity and company performance. As illustrated above, however, the validity of employer self-reports are open to question. On the employee side, they also found positive views, but they noted that this was "tempered on the employee side by the risk of fluctuating income" (p. 123). This note of caution was based largely on a Bureau of National Affairs (1988) survey of 1,000 people who were asked which type of pay system they preferred. Most preferred was straight wage salary (63%), followed by individual incentives (22%), and, finally, companywide incentives (12%).

These preferences may raise some questions about Weitzman and Kruse's (1990) overall conclusion about employee views of profit sharing. Examining their summary of attitudinal data more closely, one finds that only one study reported on employee attitudes before and after the implementation of profit sharing. Moreover, this study was based on only 66 blue collar workers and, in fact, involved a Scanlon plan (gainsharing), not profit sharing. Finally, the data from this study, as summarized by Weitzman and Kruse, pertained to cooperation, communication, and participation (on which gainsharing was superior). However, no data on beliefs concerning productivity were provided.

One other study from the Weitzman and Kruse (1990) review compared responses of employees under profit-sharing plans versus those who were not. The employees covered by profit sharing agreed more strongly with the following statements: Employees get their share of company growth, employees get credit for company progress, and employees gain from cost cutting. Note again, however, that there are no direct questions regarding productivity.

The final type of evidence examined by Weitzman and Kruse (1990) concerned the effect of profit sharing on productivity. They found 16 studies that used econometric methods to control for the effects of other factors on productivity. They found that the t value for the profit-sharing coefficient was positive in all 16 studies, greater than 2 in 12 of the 16 studies, and had a mean of 2.46 across studies. They also emphasized that 226 profit sharing coefficients had been estimated across these 16 studies, with 60 percent having positive t values greater than 2. They concluded that "evidence on the connection between profit sharing and productivity is not definitive. Yet it is also not neutral—many sources point toward a positive link; the only quarrel seems to be over magnitudes" (p. 139). Weitzman and Kruse estimate that the mean effect of profit sharing on productivity is 7.4 percent (median = 4.4%).

A skeptic, however, might question some of this evidence. The most important concern has to do with the typical measure of productivity value added. It is not a measure of physical productivity in terms of units produced and so forth. Rather, it is a measure of the extent to which the price or value of a product exceeds or adds to the cost of the factor inputs like labor and capital. Obviously, the price of a product can be influenced by many factors besides productivity. Thus, finding a relation between profits distributed per worker (profit sharing) and value added (productivity), the most typical model used in the studies reviewed, may not provide compelling evidence that profit sharing really affects productivity.

For example, recent contracts between the United Auto Workers (UAW) and the automobile companies have included profit-sharing plans. However, the profit-sharing bonuses have been significantly larger for UAW members at Ford compared with UAW members at General Motors (GM) because profit targets have been met more successfully at Ford. This comparison would generate the type of result found by Weitzman and Kruse in their review—higher profits (productivity) where profit sharing is more heavily emphasized in terms of bonuses per worker—but would not warrant the causal inference that greater profit sharing leads to higher productivity. They seem to sense this problem because they note that a "limitation of the econometric studies is that they shed little light on the mechanisms through which profit sharing may affect productivity" (p. 139).

Given the above, there is still some doubt about the efficacy of profit sharing for improving organizational performance. Based on expectancy theory, in fact, one would expect instrumentality perceptions, and thus individual motivation, to be significantly lower under profit sharing than under individual incentives, merit pay, or gainsharing because the link between an individual's performance and organizational performance (profits) is necessarily constrained by the fact that many other people have as much or more impact. This is sometimes referred to as the *line-of-sight* issue.

For example, returning to the example of the automobile industry, both Ford and GM have had profit-sharing plans in their contract with the UAW since 1984. The average profit-sharing payment at Ford has been $13,225 per worker versus an average of $1,837 per worker at GM (Bureau of National Affairs, 1990). What accounts for the fact that the average payment at Ford has been over seven times greater? It is probably not because Ford UAW members have worked seven times as hard as their counterparts at GM. Rather, workers are likely to view top management decisions regarding products, engineering, pricing, and marketing as more important. Therefore, although profit sharing may, in this case, be useful in achieving the objective of making labor costs variable, the motivational impact is open to question.

Moreover, even the idea of using profit sharing to make labor costs more variable often seems to go out the window exactly when labor costs begin to vary (downward). For example, the much publicized plan for the Dupont Fibers division (e.g., McNutt, 1990) was eliminated when division profits were down and

employees were about to actually experience what downside compensation risk is all about (Santora, 1991). It is likely that management will need to build a persuasive case for why employees should be willing to incur this type of risk, particularly employees at the lower pay levels.

It is not difficult to understand why employees, especially those not in higher paying jobs, would react unfavorably to downside risk in pay. As discussed earlier in the context of agency theory, the fact that employees are tied to a single organization means that they cannot diversify what might be termed their "investment in employment" to avoid employment or pay-related risk. In a similar vein, John Zalusky of the AFL-CIO points out that banks that hold mortgages and utilities that provide services do not adjust monthly bills to fit changes in worker income. Until they do, he suggests that it is unlikely workers will ask their unions to change their approach to variable pay packages.

Another constraint on motivation relates to the fact that the great majority of profit sharing plans are of the *deferred* type. The Bureau of Labor Statistics (Coates, 1991) reports that in 1989, 16 percent of full-time employees in medium and large private establishments participated in a profit-sharing plan, but only 1 percent of employees overall (i.e., 6.3% of those in profit sharing plans) were in cash plans where profits are paid directly to employees as soon as profits are known.

As a final note, profit sharing has been argued to have beneficial effects on employment stability (Weitzman, 1984, 1985). The basic logic is that organizations resort to layoffs of employees because there is no other way to reduce labor costs during difficult economic times. But profit sharing automatically decreases labor costs during such periods, making layoffs less necessary. Research does seem to support this hypothesis (Chelius & Smith, 1990; Gerhart, 1991; Kruse, 1991). Perhaps for this reason and others (e.g., encouraging greater employee involvement), public policy in some countries, including India and much of Latin America, actually mandates profit sharing (Florkowski, 1991). For example, some major Venezuelan industries must disburse 10 percent of each year's profits, capped at an equivalent of 2 months pay for each employee. In India, domestic firms must share 60 percent of net profits. Although the United States does not have any exact counterpart to such mandates, there are tax advantages in the United States (and other countries like France) for using deferred profit sharing and employee stock ownership plans (see below).

Gainsharing.   Gainsharing differs from profit sharing in at least three ways (Hammer, 1988; Schuster, 1990). First, under gainsharing, rewards are based on a productivity measure rather than profits. The goal is to link pay to performance outcomes that employees can control, thus enhancing the line of sight or instrumentality perceptions (as do the following two differences). Second, gainsharing plans usually distribute any bonus payments with greater frequency (e.g., monthly or quarterly versus annually). Third, gainsharing plans distribute payments during the current period rather than deferring them as profit-sharing plans often do. Thus, Milkovich and Wigdor (1991) suggested that

> the adoption of group incentive plans may provide a way to accommodate the complexity and interdependence of jobs, the need for work group cooperation, and the existence of work group performance norms and still offer the motivational potential of clear goals, clear pay-to-performance links, and relatively large pay increases. (p. 86)

Evidence on gainsharing has been favorable. For example, Schuster's (1984a) empirical work, a 5-year study of 28 sites, found positive effects

of a variety of gainsharing plans on productivity. A recent study by Hatcher and Ross (1991) found that changing from individual incentives to gainsharing resulted in a decrease in grievances and a fairly dramatic increase in product quality. (Defects per 1,000 products shipped declined from 20.93 to 2.31.)

Nevertheless, some questions remain about the motivational potential of gainsharing. Milkovich and Wigdor (1991), argue that "such a prediction requires a sizable inferential leap from the expectancy and goal-setting literature"(p. 86) and go on to suggest that "many beneficial effects attributed to gain sharing—including productivity effects—may be as much due to the contextual conditions as to the introduction of gain sharing" (p. 87). The important role of these conditions, which may accompany gainsharing, has also been suggested by Hammer (1988) and might include enhanced work group cooperation, better management-labor relations, increased acceptance of new technologies, and more worker participation (Mitchell, Lewin, & Lawler, 1990).

Although such conditions may be important, it would probably be incorrect (and an overinterpretation) to suggest that the monetary component of gainsharing plans is not important. Quite to the contrary, Schuster (1990) has argued that gainsharing plans have also worked well in cases where the primary focus was on the monetary aspect, unaccompanied by employee involvement or participation. Consistent with this argument, a recent study of several Improshare plans (see Fein, 1981), which emphasize pay but not employee involvement, found positive effects on performance (Kaufman, 1990).

In addition, a study by Wagner, Rubin, and Callahan (1988) examined the effects on productivity of a nonmanagement group incentive payment plan that appears to have most closely resembled an Improshare gainsharing plan, and apparently not accompanied by changes in worker participation. Work tasks were assigned a standard number of hours. If the task was completed in a shorter amount of time, employees shared in the savings. Wagner et al. found a substantial increase in productivity under the plan (103.7%). They also found statistically significant declines in labor costs and grievances. They made some interesting observations about the context of the plan implementation and the effects of the plan on specific behaviors. For example, the company had experience with incentive plans in other plants, which may have reduced employee concerns about rate-cutting. So trust in management may have facilitated success. They also observed greater employee concern for cooperative behaviors (e.g., helping out co-workers with temporary work overloads), as well as co-worker "policing" of quantity and quality to assure equitable contributions.

Pritchard, Jones, Roth, Stuebing, and Ekeberg (1988) found that relatively little work had been done on the impact of incentives where there is employee interdependence (but see Schuster, 1984a, and subsequently, Wagner et al., 1988, for exceptions). They undertook an ambitious 23-month study of the effect of incentives, goal setting, and feedback in 5 separate organizational units (maintenance, receiving, storage and issue, pickup and delivery, and inspection) at an air force base in the southwestern United States. Pritchard et al. (1988) used a baseline period of 8 months, followed by 5 months of feedback only, 5 months of feedback plus goal-setting, and finally, 5 months of feedback plus goal setting plus incentives. They observed large increases in productivity due to feedback alone (50% over baseline), feedback plus goal setting (75% over baseline), but little *additional* effect of incentives. However, Pritchard et al. noted that there may have been a ceiling effect, given the dramatic productivity improvement that had already been obtained. They also suggested that the incentives might have been necessary to sustain the substantial feedback and goal-setting effects over the longer run. In any case, the

results also serve as a reminder that pay programs are only one means of influencing employee behaviors. Goal setting and feedback can also be very powerful (see Kanfer, 1990; Locke et al., 1980).

Perhaps even more interesting than the results were the reactions of decision makers in the Pritchard et al. (1988) study. Despite the dramatic productivity improvements, in 4 of the 5 sections (the 4 were under the same manager) the programs were discontinued. Pritchard et al. (1988) explained that a new manager was "opposed to the use of incentives, especially when used for some units under his command and not for others" (p. 353). The authors also described resistance from people who believed that "personnel should not get something for doing what they were already supposed to do" (p. 354). Finally, Pritchard et al. also found that "some supervisors felt such an incentive system would undermine their power and prerogatives to reward individuals and units informally" (p. 354).

In summary, the evidence on gainsharing seems to tells us at least two things. First, group compensation interventions *can,* like individual incentives, result in significantly higher productivity. Second, however, as with individual incentives, administrative or contextual factors can nevertheless result in such programs being unacceptable to one or more of the affected parties. Schuster (1984b, cited in Hammer, 1988) drew similar conclusions, noting that management adjustment of payout formulas without worker input caused problems. He also reported (Schuster, 1984b) evidence to suggest that plantwide plans may be better than group-specific plans because perceived inequities may arise when groups receive different levels of bonus payments. A different type of perceived inequality, namely, that high performers may feel underrewarded, is something that will need to be examined. A study by Weiss (1987) at AT&T, for example, found that extreme performers (at both the top and bottom) left under a gainsharing plan. This goes back to our earlier discussion about the effect of pay programs on the composition of the work force and, more specifically, the potential effects of group-oriented programs on individual performers.

Employee Ownership.   Stock options.   Stock options are similar in many ways to profit-sharing plans. The basis for payouts is organizational performance in the stock market, and the payouts do not typically go into the base salary (see Figure 4). Important goals of the plan are (a) to motivate employees to act in the best interest of the organization as a whole, (b) similarly, to enhance employee identification with the organization, and (c) to have labor costs vary with organizational performance. Stock options may offer somewhat more potential to encourage employees to think like owners because they actually do achieve some ownership stake if they are able to exercise their options. Briefly, stock options allow the purchase of stock at a fixed price, regardless of the current price. So, for example, if in 1992 an employee receives options to purchase stock at $50 per share and the stock price goes to $60 per share in 1994, she or he can purchase stock (i.e., exercise the options) at $50 per share in 1994, making a profit if the shares are then sold. However, if the stock price goes down to $40 in 1994, the options are worthless ("under water"), at least for the time being.

Stock options have long been a common program for executives, but some organizations, like Pepsi-Cola and Hewlett-Packard, grant them to all employees. There is evidence that this approach is becoming more widespread (Crystal, 1990), but there is also some skepticism about the reasons for this. For example, in the *Personnel* article, Crystal says that "a lot of fog is generated" by such plans, by which he means that it may be used as a way to increase pay without it being noticed as much because the cost is less visible—no direct

payments are made. We return to this issue below. To our knowledge, little evidence exists on the impact of stock options among nonexecutives. One partial exception is the Gerhart and Milkovich (1990) study, which found that organizational performance was higher in organizations that made a greater percentage of employees eligible for long-term incentives like stock options (see the "Executive Pay" section for other evidence).

ESOPS.   Employee stock ownership plans in the United States are defined in the Internal Revenue Code and the Employee Retirement Income Security Act and are generally treated as benefit plans in these and other federal laws (Conte & Svejnar, 1990). However, congressional intent suggests that ESOPs were intended to provide an opportunity for more U.S. citizens to become owners of capital, to provide another source of equity financing for corporations, and to enhance employee motivation and performance (Conte & Svejnar). ESOPs are unique in several respects, including the requirement that plan participants (i.e., employees) be permitted to vote their securities if they are registered on a national exchange (Conte & Svejnar). Although there are other forms of employee ownership, ESOPs are by far the most common (see Hammer, 1988, for more information) and have grown rapidly over the past decade for a variety of reasons, not the least of which are their tax/financing and takeover defense advantages.[22]

Do ESOPs have a positive impact on organizational performance beyond that accounted for by such advantages? Like profit sharing, stock ownership would not be expected to lead to high instrumentality perceptions. Nevertheless, some evidence suggests that ownership does have performance benefits. For example, Hammer (1988) concluded that the "research presents an encouraging picture of employee stock ownership" (p. 356). However, she cautions that we are not yet at the point where causal inferences can be drawn, partly because the mechanism by which ESOPs influence individuals has not been adequately demonstrated. Without knowing why ESOPs are related to organizational performance, it is difficult to rule out alternative explanations. For example, it may be that organizational performance is the cause and ESOPs are the outcome. Both Hammer (1988) and Conte and Svejnar (1990) conclude, however, that the evidence points to greater beneficial effects of ownership in cases where employees participate in decision making. Similarly, Pierce, Rubenfeld, and Morgan (1991) suggest that employee ownership is most likely to influence motivation, attitudes, and behaviors when the "employee-owner comes to psychologically experience his/her ownership in the organization" (p. 139). Klein (1987) reports that employee satisfaction under ESOPs is related both to the monetary and participation components.

There are several concerns with ESOPs. First, participation and voting rights are not always commensurate with the ownership stake. Second, and particularly troublesome, because an ESOP must invest at least 51 percent of its assets in its company's stock (Conte & Svejnar, 1990), diversification of risk is more difficult to achieve, and in many cases, there is no diversification. Thus, employee buyouts of troubled companies or ESOPs used as pension plans carry great risks to employees (Fisher, 1991).

A final note concerns the cost of stock options and ESOPs. At times, there seems to be some tendency to underestimate the cost of plans that are funded through issuing new shares of stock. A recent study at the London School of Economics of 55 top British firms found that the average annual dilution rate of other shares was 0.25 percent, equal to about $445 million in these 55 firms in 1988, which in turn represented about 2.2 percent of pretax profits ("Unseen," 1991). Obviously, such information is highly relevant for evaluating the return on investment of such a plan.

What Contextual Factors Influence Effectiveness of Pay Plans?   No pay program (or set of pay programs) is likely to be equally effective under all sets of conditions. Therefore, looking only at the average effect of a pay program across diverse settings overlooks the possibility that there is a statistical interaction between pay programs and contextual (i.e., contingency) factors of the type contained in Figure 1. This can also be described as a question of *fit*. Some pay programs (or perhaps pay strategies) and organizational strategies are likely to be more congruent than others.[23] As one example of the importance of this question, consider the Gerhart and Milkovich (1990) finding that an increase in the bonus/base pay ratio (i.e., variable pay emphasis) from, for example, .20 to .30 was associated with an increase in return on assets of between .21 and .95 percentage points (e.g., from 6% to 6.21 or 6.95%). Obviously, any such effect represents an average. In some organizations, the payoff might be two or three times as great. In other organizations, perhaps variable pay would actually diminish performance. It would certainly be helpful to know how to distinguish between the two types.

Therefore, as with pay level and structure decisions, it is important that organizations avoid making decisions about individual pay programs based on what others are doing (i.e., playing "follow the leader"). Rather, the contingency approach suggests the need for organizations to decide what pay programs fit best with their overall strategy. Moreover, because contextual factors often change over time, so too, perhaps, will the types of pay programs that fit. Wallace's (1990) empirical study, for example, focused on reasons for changes in pay programs. He reported that many organizations had what he described as well-defined reasons for changing their pay programs. Many of the organizations were driven by changes or threats in their business environments, such as increased multinational competition (manufacturing), deregulation (communications and financial services), increased consumer expectations associated with the emergence of a more service-oriented economy (health care, financial services), and innovation (financial services, computer systems and services firms, software firms, pharmaceutical). According to Wallace, "in all cases, these firms could not have survived or maintained a competitive advantage without changing their modes of operation" (p. 10). This is an interesting statement because there were presumably other organizations facing similar threats in the business environment that did not undertake significant changes, but still survived. Empirical evidence on survival and comparisons of long-term success between organizations that changed and those that did not are greatly needed.

Although knowing which programs are most effective under particular circumstances is a key concern, relatively little work has been done on this question, despite the recognition that context is important (e.g., Lawler, 1971; Milkovich & Wigdor, 1991). On the conceptual side, the situation is changing somewhat with papers by Balkin and Gomez-Mejia (1987), Broderick (1986), Gomez-Mejia and Welbourne (1988), Lawler (1989), and Milkovich (1988). However, empirical work continues to be sparse. The research that does exist tends to use compensation as a dependent variable, focusing on whether organizations use the compensation programs predicted by contingency frameworks (e.g., Balkin & Gomez-Mejia, 1984; Kerr, 1985; Milkovich, Gerhart, & Hannon, 1991). The consequences for performance of compensation programs that are consistent with contingency theory predictions, however, have received only limited empirical attention. Major reasons include the difficulty in (a) generating sufficient numbers of observations on different combinations of pay programs and contingency factors when the organization is the unit of observation and (b) defining and measuring the concept of fit. In addition, it may be that more theoretical

work needs to be done in developing specific, testable contingency framework propositions.

One of the better known contingency frameworks treats stage in the product or organization's life cycle as the key contingency factor in designing compensation systems (Cook, 1976; Ellig, 1981). The argument is that organizations in start-up and growth stages of their product life cycles face strong cash demands to finance capital expansion. They also have an external resource focus based on the need to attract key employees. Thus, start-up and growth firms were advised to emphasize stock options and variable short-term pay increases in lieu of higher base pay as a means of conserving cash for investment and growth. These pay programs, especially stock options, would also encourage the long-term perspective needed to facilitate growth. In contrast, organizations in the maintenance stage of their life cycles would not have the same cash flow problems and need (or potential) for growth. As such, they were advised to place more emphasis on base salary and less on stock options. Although there is some evidence to suggest that life cycle is related to pay system design (e.g., Balkin & Gomez-Mejia, 1987), evidence on consequences for performance is lacking. There are also some conceptual problems with this approach (see Milkovich, 1988).

Another contingency perspective focuses on the need for a match between diversification and compensation strategies (Balkin & Gomez-Mejia, 1990; Berg, 1969; Kerr, 1985; Lorsch & Allen, 1973). Moreover, recent work by Gomez-Mejia (in press) provides evidence on the consequences of such matches for organizational performance. They categorized organizations into four diversification strategy groups: single product, conglomerates, dominant product, and related product. Compensation strategy was classified as either *algorithmic*, which emphasizes internal equity, bureaucratic procedures such as job evaluation, low risk sharing in pay, and seniority, or *experiential*, emphasizing market rates, flexible and decentralized pay policies, personal skills rather than job or hierarchical position, higher risk sharing, and less role for seniority. Gomez-Mejia hypothesized that the algorithmic strategy would be more effective in dominant product and related product organizations because its emphasis on formalized rules and procedures would facilitate coordination and the management of interdependence. Such issues, however, are less important in conglomerates and single product organizations, permitting more flexibility, decentralization, and risk sharing in compensation. Using a combination of profit and stock market performance measures, these hypotheses were generally supported.

Summary

Organizations have a relatively large degree of latitude in choosing how (versus how much) they pay their employees. In our view, the literature indicates that many organizations choose to make rewards contingent on some type of performance criterion, although there appear to be substantial organizational differences in this respect.

Taken as a whole, the literature also leaves little doubt about the fact that how employees are paid has important consequences for individual, group, and organizational performance. On the other hand, an examination of the evidence on any particular pay plan often does not lead to firm conclusions about its consequences. Our sense is that there is relatively strong evidence that individual incentives, merit pay and bonsues, and gainsharing can contribute to higher performance under the right circumstances, especially when one also factors in the possible effects these programs have on work force composition. Although there is also favorable evidence on the performance effects of profit sharing and stock ownership, this evidence tends to be less conclusive because of the added difficulties in ruling out threats to causal

inference (e.g., reciprocal causation, omitted variables).

Suggested Research Directions

Some topics for further research on individual differences in pay follow.

- *Role of context or contingency factors in compensation.* Table 4 provides a suggested design for comparing the effectiveness of different compensation strategies under different conditions (contingency factors). In this particular example, one contingency factor, stage of the organization in its life cycle (Ellig, 1981), is used to illustrate the kind of design needed. The design that emerges when Table 4 and Figure 1 are considered together has three features. First, data on multiple units and multiple organizations are required. Second, longitudinal data are necessary. Third, outcomes ("success") are measured at multiple levels. Thus, if a link is found, say, between compensation and the organization's profitability, possible mediating mechanisms can be examined to help establish why the link exists and whether (or which) causal interpretation is warranted.

- *Relative effectiveness of different pay programs.* As Milkovich and Wigdor (1991) emphasized, there is virtually no evidence that compares the effectiveness of different pay programs. For example, we do not know the relative effects of merit pay versus merit bonuses or of individual versus group incentives. Obviously, a contingency approach would also be applicable here as well.

- *Return on investment of particular programs.* Knowing the effects of programs is only part of the story. The

TABLE 4

Individual Pay Program Research Design Example

Organization 1	Pay Program	Success	Contingency Factors
Unit 1	Merit pay (strong)	Quality, performance, etc.	Growth strategy
Unit 2	Merit pay (weak)	Quality, performance, etc.	Growth strategy
Unit 3	Merit bonuses	Quality, performance, etc.	Growth strategy
Unit 4	Gain sharing	Quality, performance, etc.	Growth strategy
Unit 5	Profit sharing	Quality, performance, etc.	Growth strategy
Unit i	Pay plan i	Quality, performance, etc.	Growth strategy
Organization 2	Pay Program	Success	Contingency Factors
Unit 1	Merit pay (strong)	Quality, performance, etc.	Maintenance strategy
Unit 2	Merit pay (weak)	Quality, performance, etc.	Maintenance strategy
Unit 3	Merit bonuses	Quality, performance, etc.	Maintenance strategy
Unit 4	Gain sharing	Quality, performance, etc.	Maintenance strategy
Unit 5	Profit sharing	Quality, performance, etc.	Maintenance strategy
Unit i	Pay plan i	Quality, performance, etc.	Maintenance strategy
Organization 3	Pay Program	Success	Contingency Factors
.			
.			
.			
Organization i	Pay Program	Success	Contingency Factors

goal should be to know the return on investment of particular programs. Thus, for example, even if individual incentives have large positive effects on productivity, the costs of developing and maintaining standards and monitoring production need to be considered.

■ *Possible influence of pay programs on the composition of the work force.* We do not yet have a good grasp of the extent to which different individual pay programs attract different types of employees. Yet anything that affects the flow of incoming and exiting employees may have important consequences for the nature of the work force (Boudreau & Berger, 1985). One possible avenue of study would be to obtain data on different units within an organization that have different degrees of pay for performance.

Do the units with strong linkages attract the best performers? Do such units outperform the other units?

- *Measuring outcomes at multiple levels.* Consequently, when links are found between these pay programs and unit or organizational performance, it is not clear why. Without this information, it is difficult to have much confidence in the causal relation. In addition, it makes development of contingency models more difficult when there is no evidence on how or through what mechanism the program had an effect. Therefore, we would like to see more attention given to measuring outcomes of pay programs at multiple (i.e., individual, unit, and organizational) levels.

- *Multiple plans.* It would be unfortunate if we have given the impression that the design of compensation systems simply entails a choice between one or the other pay program. To the contrary, in many organizations, employees are covered by multiple plans. So, for example, an employee could work under merit pay, gainsharing, and profit sharing simultaneously. In fact, if each plan is better at achieving some objectives than others, a mix of plans may make a good deal of sense. This again points to a fertile area for future research. Thus, the question may not be what plan is best, but rather what mix of plans would work best.

- *Influence of situational versus dispositional factors.* Thus far, our discussion has implied that employee attitudes and behaviors are malleable and responsive to changes in situational factors such as pay programs. For better or worse, there has been a renewed debate about this assumption (Staw & Ross, 1985; Staw, Bell, & Clausen, 1986; Gerhart, 1987, 1990c; see Judge, 1992, for a review)

that probably requires further empirical evidence.

Benefits

Employee benefits have become an important inducement in the exchange between employers and employees, adding an average cost of $.38 on top of every $1.00 of payroll (U.S. Chamber of Commerce, 1991), thus accounting for about 28 percent of total compensation costs. Beyond costs, the importance of benefits in the employment relationship can be seen in the substantial amount of public policy attention devoted to the benefits area, including the Social Security Act of 1935 and the Employee Retirement Income Security Act (ERISA) of 1974, among many others. These statutes, as well as the tax code's continued treatment of many benefits as tax free, have contributed significantly to benefits growth (Beam & McFadden, 1988; Rosenbloom & Hallman, 1981). Also, wage and price controls during the 1940s and 1950s encouraged employers and unions to negotiate higher benefits levels as a means of circumventing the controls. Interest among public policy makers continues to be strong, as evidenced by the recent introduction of federal legislative bills in areas such as parental (and family) leave and health care. Employees and their dependents rely on benefits such as health care and pensions for economic and personal well-being, and employers are believed to use benefits as a means of achieving important objectives like attraction, retention, and, by implication, organizational effectiveness. Thus, there are a great many stakeholders to consider in studying benefits.

We have organized our discussion of benefits decisions in the following manner. First, we will cover definitional and measurement issues, identifying basic attributes along which benefits decisions can vary. Second, we will very briefly discuss general classes of benefits determinants. Third, we will review the consequences of different benefits decisions. As was the case with pay structures, this discussion of consequences (and that of determinants) is necessarily brief due to the relative lack of attention given to benefits by the research community.

Definition and Properties

We will discuss three attributes of benefits: costs, forms (or types), and level of coverage.

Costs.   Both the level and growth of benefits costs are worth noting. In 1935, benefits accounted for less than 1 percent of total compensation costs. By 1953, their share had risen to 16 percent, and by 1980, to 27 percent. In other words, benefits costs have grown at a much faster rate than wage and salary costs. Thus, as discussed in the "Pay Level" section of this chapter, it is now difficult to study compensation without studying benefits. Yet they have become too important to continue to suffer from the benign neglect of the past.

Although there is evidence of a recent slow-down (during the late 1980s) in overall benefits growth relative to wages and salaries, a notable exception to this overall trend is the continued dramatic growth in the cost of health care benefits. The costs of health care benefits increased 21.6 percent (to $2,313 per employee) in 1990, following increases of 20.4 percent and 17 percent in 1989 and 1988, respectively (Foster- Higgins, 1991). As of 1989, the United States was spending 11.4 percent of its gross domestic product on health care (up from 8.6% in 1979), the largest percentage among developed countries.[24] According to Fisher (1991), total spending on health care amounted to $604 billion in 1989 (private spending of $351 billion, plus government spending of $253 billion).

Despite this large expenditure of resources, there are 37 million U.S. citizens (14.8% of the population) who do not have public or private health insurance. One half of the uninsured are employed adults, one-third are children, and one-sixth are nonemployed adults (Piacentini & Cerino, 1990). Moreover, conventional quality indices such as infant mortality (U.S. ranks highest), life expectancy (U.S. ranks 6th out of 6 countries for men, 4th for women) and office waiting time per visit (14 minutes) raise questions about the return on the nation's investment in health care. Finally, according to public opinion polls, United States citizens are less satisfied with their health care system and more likely to say it needs fundamental change than citizens in other countries. Consequently, as discussed below, there has been a great deal of recent work aimed at containing health care costs by employers and in the public policy arena.

Although the preceding discussion makes it clear that benefits now represent an increasingly significant percentage of total employee compensation costs, the statistics cited may imply more precision in measuring such costs than there really is. One of the central problems is the lack of comparability in the definitions of benefits used by different surveys (and commentators). For example, our experience is that various consultants and government agencies include different forms of benefits in their surveys and often define payroll differently. The Chamber of Commerce surveys are probably the most inclusive, including such benefits as cafeteria subsidies and parking lot costs. Individual employers, such as IBM and AT&T, often report health care cost increases that are one-half as large as the national figures. Although benefits managers in such companies usually attribute such differences to successful management on their part (e.g., cost containment and cost shifting to employees and providers), these differences probably also signal the need for caution in interpreting the statistics. As another example, Lee Iacocca has asserted that health insurance costs for Chrysler employees add $700 to the cost of each car produced in the U.S. Not reported, however, is that the most significant portion of these costs stems from the health care program covering Chrysler's large retiree population.

Forms. At a general level, *forms* of benefits include those benefits that are legally mandated, such as social security, as well as those that are nonmandated, such as pensions, insurance, pay for time not worked, and so on. Our discussion focuses on these nonmandated forms, over which employers and employee exercise the most control and discretion in making choices. By way of illustration, an organization can choose between two basic forms of pensions: defined benefit (i.e., actual pensions payouts are specified) or defined contribution (i.e., levels of investment to pension fund are specified). Further, within each of these, various options exist. For example, employee stock ownership and 401K plans are two widely used forms of defined contribution plans. Similarly, employers must choose which of the various forms of health care insurance to offer. One decision concerns the choice between fee-for-service plans like Blue Cross/Blue Shield, under which providers' charges depend on actual employee use of services, and prepaid plans like HMOs, in which case an initial (fixed) fee is paid.

Level of Coverage. This is another area where organizations face a wide array of choices. In medical care, the levels of coverage may vary across and within health care plans. Prepaid HMOs may include fewer cost-sharing provisions (e.g., deductibles and copayments) but be more limited in coverage (e.g., they tend to limit mental health treatment). Fee-for-service plans typically offer a range of deductibles (e.g., employee must pay $100 before insurance begins to pay) and copayments (e.g., so-called 80/20 features, under which 80% of costs are paid by the insurance plan after an initial deductible is paid).

Determinants

As with other dimensions of employee compensation, we can map out benefits determinants using the general classes of factors—employee, job, organization, and external factors—depicted in Figure 1. However, the volume of research on determinants is probably smaller in benefits than in other areas. Thus, our knowledge of why different organizations have different benefits plans and outcomes is relatively limited. Part of the explanation may stem from the fact that, on average, legally required benefits account for 31 percent of total benefits costs (Nathan, 1987), reducing the amount of employer discretion in the benefits area. Nevertheless, this still leaves a large, nonmandated component that can differ significantly across employers.

Some specific determinants have received empirical attention. For example, benefits tend to be higher in the presence of unions (Freeman & Medoff, 1984) and less competitive product markets (Long & Link, 1983). A consideration of some of the factors discussed below (e.g., demographics, the need to attract and retain valued employees) points to other benefits determinants.

Consequences

The complex array of benefits forms and decisions can make even the most avid reader's eyes glaze over. Yet we have illustrated only a few of the issues and types of benefits with which professionals and employees must deal. Given the complexity of the area, any discussion of the consequences of benefits decisions for employee attitudes and behaviors must, more so than any other area of compensation, pay close attention to employees' understanding and perceptions of their benefits. For example, as pointed out earlier in the "Pay Level" section of this chapter, it would be a mistake to equate the cost of benefits to the value perceived by the employee. Because this point has implications for several important consequences (e.g., benefits satisfaction, attraction), we turn to it first.

What Is the Effect of Employee Perceptions of Benefits?

Consistent with the distinction between benefit costs and perceived value, evidence suggests that employees may be unaware of the financial value of their benefits (Wilson, Northcraft, & Neale, 1985) or even the existence of many benefits. For example, Milkovich and Newman (1990) cite a study where employees were asked to recall which benefits they received. The typical employee was able to list only about 15 percent of the total number.

The Wilson et al. (1985) study focused on employees' perceptions of their health care insurance benefits. Employees were knowledgeable about their own contributions, but not about those made by the employer. Over 90 percent of the employees underestimated both (a) the cost to the employer and (b) what it would cost them to provide the benefits on their own.[25] For example, for one health plan, employees estimated the employer cost to be $22 (the actual cost was $64) biweekly and the market value to be $48 (versus an actual value of $169). In fact, some employees believed that the employer made no contribution at all to their health insurance coverage.

One interpretation of such findings is that employers may, to put it bluntly, be throwing away money on benefits. If employees do not know the benefits exist or fail to attach value to them, the benefits cannot influence their attitudes or behaviors in any positive fashion. As Lawler (1981) has suggested, any action that would enhance employee knowledge would help strengthen the impact of benefits. He advocated increasing employee choice through use of cafeteria or flexible benefits plans as one approach. Organizations have, in fact, moved in this direction, with 61 percent now offering such plans according to a Hewitt Associates survey of 944 large organizations (Bureau of

National Affairs, 1991). Preliminary evidence suggests that flexible benefits do positively influence benefits satisfaction (Barber, Dunham, & Formisano, 1990). Other actions aimed at enhancing employee knowledge include greater use of copayments and deductibles. The success of such approaches awaits evaluation.

What Is the Impact of Individual Differences in Preferences for Benefits?

There is long-standing evidence of significant individual differences in benefit preferences (Davis, Giles, & Field, 1985, 1988; Huseman, Hatfield, & Robinson, 1978; Mahoney, 1964; Nealey, 1963; Nealey & Goodale, 1967; Stonebraker, 1985). Although interpreting these results is often complicated because of a lack of adequate controls (e.g., differences in the experience or use of different forms, employer differences in benefits packages and communication approaches), some findings seem robust (and perhaps even obvious to some): Older workers tend to place more value on pensions; women tend to prefer more time off; and the number of dependents is related to the desire for health insurance.

Such individual differences, of course, lend greater weight to the need for offering employees a choice in the design of their benefits package. The increasing diversity of the work force further reinforces this suggestion. Employers hope that flexible benefits plans will help control costs and enhance employee satisfaction by increasing employee knowledge and improving the fit between employee preferences and benefits.

Survey and anecdotal evidence suggest that employee reactions to flexible plans are positive and that medical care costs are lower under such plans. However, little empirical research has taken advantage of the field opportunities offered by employers' shift to flexible plans (see Barber et al., 1990, for an exception). Little is known about why some employers shift and others do not. Even less is known about how employees make the choices that are so fundamental to such plans, or whether different choices are made (Barringer, Milkovich, & Mitchell, 1991).

Barringer et al. (1991) studied the actual decisions made by employees ($N = 1,500$) among six health care options under a flexible benefit plan offered by a large manufacturing company. Employee choices were modeled as a function of employee and plan characteristics. Results indicated that employee decisions among multiple health plans were significantly influenced by employees' age, income, marital status, and gender. As age and salary increased, the probability of selecting a reduced (less expensive) level of health care coverage decreased. The probability of selecting a lower cost alternative was greater among married employees and female employees.

Perhaps most important, Barringer et al. (1991) found that the cost charged to employees did not have a significant effect on their decisions, suggesting that individuals may be highly risk averse when it comes to health care and only major price increases will induce individuals to change (Friedman, 1974; Holmer, 1984). They raised the alternative possibility, however, that the small effect of cost might have been more a function of the organization's program design than the risk aversion of employees. Specifically, employees were given enough benefit credits to purchase the high coverage options, so out-of-pocket costs were not really a factor. The main cost was foregoing the opportunity to purchase greater amounts of other benefits (e.g., vacation time). Moreover, tax laws required the unused credits to be forfeited. Thus, the authors concluded that employees were given purchasing power and an incentive to use it.

Another study, conducted by IBM, reported that not only did the selection of high coverage options not drop when employee costs were raised, but they found employee satisfaction with their health care benefits actually increased. Simultaneously, the organization had launched a massive communication effort (including

take-home videos). These findings suggest that employee expectations about their benefits are adaptive and communication efforts may have an influence.

What Is the Impact on Employee Satisfaction With Benefits? Initially, Heneman and Schwab (1979) believed that a relationship between benefits and pay satisfaction was not likely. They reasoned that (a) employees were not very knowledgeable about their benefits, (b) external comparisons were unlikely to generate differences because similar patterns of benefits were common within a labor market, and (c) internal comparisons were unlikely to cause differences because many benefits were uniform across employees. Subsequently, however, based on their development of the PSQ (see earlier discussion) and related empirical work (Heneman & Schwab, 1985), they concluded that benefits satisfaction was a separate and independent dimension of pay satisfaction (see also Scarpello et al., 1988).

Other findings suggest that satisfaction with benefits increases with improved coverage and decreases with greater costs to employees (Dreher, Ash, & Bretz, 1988). Further, the relation between benefits satisfaction and coverage levels was stronger among employees possessing accurate information about coverage levels. An advantage of the Dreher et al. (1988) study is that it controlled for the actual benefits level paid to employees. Variation in actual benefits was achieved by studying eight different highway patrol agencies. As the authors noted, "it is not possible to study linkages between benefits and satisfaction without controlling for the direct costs borne by employees and the relationships among all components of the compensation system" (p. 251). Finally, they found that employees' satisfaction with benefits was especially closely linked to health insurance costs.

Generalizing the Dreher et al. (1988) results to current conditions, we would expect increased cost shifting (increased deductibles and copayments, reduced first-dollar coverage, maximum coverage limits) to result in decreases in pay satisfaction. On the other hand, employee expectations may have also shifted in response to publicity about rising costs and to increased communication efforts by employers. In other words, benefits expectations may be adaptive (Helson, 1964), as in "we're lucky to have only a $150 deductible for surgical."

Clearly, one inference that can be drawn from employers' increased communications efforts is that they believe expectations are adaptive. Employers are using a wide variety of media, including brochures, take home videos, computer spreadsheets, and expert systems to communicate and presumably manage employee expectations. We suggest that these are examples of research opportunities, the results of which could inform practice and advance our knowledge.

What Is the Relation of Benefits to Attraction and Retention?   Several forms of benefits are designed to be directly contingent on employee service. Retirement and vacation benefits are two examples. Others, such as the level of participation in employee savings plans and life insurance, are linked to salary levels, and thus, indirectly tied to experience. By linking these benefits to seniority, it is assumed that employees will be more reluctant to change employers. However, the effects of vesting and portability features need to be considered. The effects of service-contingent benefits may be most evident around vesting and portability dates.

There is increasing evidence from labor economics research that pensions and health care reduce voluntary turnover (Mitchell, 1982, 1983; Schiller & Weiss, 1979). Schiller and Weiss also reported that decisions to quit were not only influenced by the existence of pensions, but also by the time of vesting and whether employees contributed. Mitchell (1982) reported gender effects such that pensions were less likely to influence women's turnover

decisions. However, a problem (encountered throughout the chapter) is that the optimal level of mobility is not known. Therefore, some have expressed concern that benefits, like pensions, will restrict mobility too much (Ross, 1958) and not place enough emphasis on encouraging high performance (Allen & Clark, 1987).

Benefits are also believed to influence job-choice decisions. The typical study involves asking graduating students to rank order the importance attached to various factors influencing their job choice (e.g., Huseman, Hatfield, & Driver 1975). Benefits, however, typically rank last, apparently due in part to the fact that students tend to underestimate the value of benefits (Huseman, Hatfield, & Robinson, 1978; Mahoney, 1964; Pergande, 1988). This again raises the question of what organizations receive in return for their large investments in benefits. Lacking effective communication from organizations, applicants may assume that benefits are essentially the same across organizations.

In a recent Gallop poll, respondents claimed they would require $5,000 more in extra pay to choose a job without pension or health and life insurance. These results are consistent with a tradeoff (compensatory model) of the effects of benefits. Tax advantages, lower transaction costs, and group discounts encourage employee interest in giving up some portion of their direct pay in return for more benefit forms, wider coverage, and higher levels of benefits. Dreher, Ash, and Bretz (1988), in fact, found benefits level to be negatively correlated (−.32) with direct pay level. But much remains to be learned about the optimal mix for different employees.

Summary

Benefits represent a large share of total compensation and, therefore, have a great potential to influence the employee, unit, and organizational outcome variables depicted in

Figure 1. The empirical literature indicates that benefits do indeed have effects on employee attitudes, retention, and perhaps job choice. Further, it appears that individual preferences may play a particularly important role in determining employee reactions to benefits. Consequently, many organizations have implemented benefits plans that permit some degree of employee choice in the hope that a better match between preferences and benefits will be obtained, perhaps at a lower total cost to the employer. Finally, some research indicates that employee knowledge of their benefits provisions (and associated spending by the employer) is limited. The implication is that effective communication is another critical factor in determining the influence of benefits provisions on employee reactions.

Suggested Research Directions

As noted, we believe the benefits issues are fertile research grounds that have been largely overlooked by researchers.

- *Factors affecting employee choices.* Employees are increasingly faced with the need to make choices among benefit alternatives. This offers an opportunity to study decision-making models and the effects of individual differences and benefit plan characteristics on the choices made by employees.

- *Subscales for measuring dimensions of benefits satisfaction.* Although the development of the PSQ has provided an instrument for measuring specific facets of pay satisfaction, there may be a need for further subscales to measure dimensions of benefits satisfaction. This would permit research on the relative importance of the various benefits dimensions (e.g., pensions, medical benefits) in determining overall benefits satisfaction.

- *Influence of benefits on employee attitudes and behaviors.* Despite the rapid growth in benefits costs, the state of knowledge about the influence of benefits on employee attitudes and behaviors is dismal. Beyond a handful of studies, employee benefits have been ignored by researchers. Studies examining the links between the forms and levels of coverage with valued outcomes offer potential contributions. At this point, benefits decisions are being primarily made based on beliefs and experience—behavioral research simply does not exist to help inform such decisions. Yet organizations are increasing their communications efforts, changing benefit programs, increasing cost-sharing, and attempting to influence employees' perceptions. These changes provide abundant research opportunities.

- *Methods of effective communication to employees.* Although organizations spend large amounts of money on benefits, it is not clear that such investments have much of an influence on applicants or employees. The complexity of benefits and the fact that employees tend to think about them only when needed contribute to this situation. The implication for practice is that effective communication is of paramount importance in maximizing the "bang for the buck."

Special Topics

Executive Pay

Not surprisingly, top executives receive special attention in the compensation literature because of their potential influence on organizational success (Gomez-Mejia & Welbourne, 1989; Milkovich, 1988; Newman, 1989). The business press (e.g., *Fortune*, *Business Week*) also pays close attention to executive pay, particularly its magnitude and its relation to organizational performance. Much of this attention has been negative, focusing on whether pay levels are (a) too high and (b) sufficiently linked to organizational performance (e.g., shareholder value).

In terms of pay level, Towers, Perrin, Forster, and Crosby (TPF&C) reported that average 1989 total remuneration (base, bonus, value of long-term incentives, benefits, perquisites) of CEOs and CFOs in companies with at least $250 million in annual sales was $543,000 in the United States. According to international comparisons, this level is higher than the $352,000 average in Japan, $287,000 in the former West Germany, $288,000 in the United Kingdom, and $130,000 in Korea (*CompFlash*, 1990). Spending power differences can be even greater. For example, spending power among U.S. executives was found to more than 3 times greater than that of their Japanese counterparts. Another type of comparison has focused on the ratio of CEO pay to that of hourly production workers. TPF&C reports that the average ratio is 35 to 1 in the United States, compared to 15 to 1 in Japan and 20 to 1 in Europe (Nelson-Horchler, 1990). As noted earlier, this ratio has been spoken of as contributing to "the trust gap" in the United States—a trend among employees to acquire a "frame of mind that mistrusts senior management's intentions, doubts its competence, and resents its self-congratulatory pay" (Farnham, 1989).

On the other hand, a case has been made that these executive pay levels are necessary and indeed may not be high enough. First, the pool of people capable of being effective top executives is very small. Thus, an organization competing for this scarce but critical commodity will have to pay the going rate. The supply of talented people becomes even more scarce if many of these people choose different careers, such as investment banking and law, where top performers can make more money than in corporate management (Jensen & Murphy, 1990b; Murphy, 1986). Second, high pay levels relative to lower-level positions can have desirable

motivational effects (see the earlier discussion of tournament models).

There may be somewhat greater consensus that the link between pay and performance is not sufficiently strong. Questions arise from, among other things, examples of what appear to be organizations paying executives relatively large sums of money despite relatively poor organizational performance. It is now a tradition for *Business Week* to present lists in its annual May issue on executive compensation of executives who did the most and executives who did the least for shareholders compared to the pay they received. More systematic evidence has been provided by Jensen and Murphy (1990a) who found that CEO wealth changes by $3.25 for every $1,000 change in shareholder wealth. In a related article, they interpreted this sort of relationship as indicating that "the compensation of top executives is virtually independent of corporate performance" (1990b, p. 138), a conclusion consistent with findings of Kerr and Bettis (1987).

What explains the lack of a stronger pay for performance relation? Jensen and Murphy (1990a) find the situation puzzling (p. 262). They suggest that political forces inside and outside the organization may be responsible for limiting the pay of top performers. More specifically, they refer to "political figures, union leaders, and consumer activists [who] issue now familiar denunciations of executive salaries and urge that directors curb top-level pay in the interests of social equity and statesmanship" (1990b, p. 138). Discussions of the "trust gap" might be an example of what Jensen and Murphy mean.

Others focus on different explanations. Nelson-Horchler (1990), in an *Industry Week* article entitled "The Pay Revolt Brews," raises questions about the process by which executive compensation is set (see also Fierman, 1990a). Nelson-Horchler's article cites research that finds "two-thirds of all directors have registered personal or professional relationships with the CEOs on whose boards they serve" (p. 36). Fierman states that the compensation committee is "always conflicted, usually co-opted... [and it] is an apt time to look at why they so often do a terrible job" (p. 58). Fierman explains that executives set each other's pay on such committees so it is in their own best interest to set high pay for others (as a means of raising their own). Research does, in fact, find that CEO pay is related to the pay level of the board of directors (O'Reilly et al., 1988). Fierman interpreted O'Reilly et al.'s findings as follows: "Instead of laboring to serve the shareholders, a CEO looking to enrich himself could do just as well selecting a compensation committee whose members earn more than he does" (p. 58). To receive a raise of $55,000, the article suggests that the "CEO can either double return on shareholders' equity to 30% or or appoint a new compensation committe member who earns $100,000 more than he does" (p. 58).

Another explanation relies on agency theory, which explicitly recognizes the potential conflict between managers and owners (see earlier discussion). Three types of conflicts are most relevant in discussing executive pay (Lambert & Larcker, 1989, pp. 100–101). First, the primary interest of shareholders is in maximizing their financial returns, but management may allocate resources to expenditures that may not increase shareholder value, such as perquisites (e.g., "superfluous" corporate jets) or empire building through acquisitions that do not add value. Second, managers and shareholders may differ in their attitudes toward risk. As discussed earlier, shareholders can diversify more easily than managers, suggesting that the latter will typically be more risk averse. As a consequence, managers may be more inclined to turn down high potential return projects that are perceived as risky. Third, the time horizons for decision making may differ. For example, if a compensation committee evaluates a manager based on short-term profits, he or she may be less likely to evaluate projects based on the present value of long-term profits expected over the life of the project.

Although there is some disagreement about the factors most responsible for the nature of the pay for performance relation, recommended actions tend to have a common focus. For example, Jensen and Murphy suggest three solutions: (a) requiring that executives become major stockholders, (b) structuring salaries, bonuses, and stock options to provide large rewards for high performance and penalties for poor performance, and (c) making real the threat of dismissal for poor performance.

Jensen and Murphy (1990b) suggested that "it's not how much you pay, but how" (p. 138; see Gerhart & Milkovich, 1990, for a similar conclusion). Given the nonzero (average) link between pay and performance in the literature, at least some organizations must obviously follow recommendations 1 and 2. Recent research suggests that organizations that tie bonuses and long-term incentives, such as stock options, to organizational performance tend to perform better than those that do less of this (Abowd, 1990; Gerhart & Milkovich, 1990; Leonard, 1990). Another recent study, although not examining implications for subsequent organizational performance, found that CEO turnover was higher in organizations that did not meet earnings forecasts (Puffer & Weintrop, 1991).

In discussions of how organizations pay executives, there has also been much attention paid to the time horizon issue referred to by Lambert and Larcker (1989). Typically, U.S. executives (relative to executives in countries like Japan) are described as having a short-term orientation, which may have negative implications for organizational effectiveness (Hayes & Abernathy, 1980). A key culprit is believed to be the structure of managerial compensation and its incentives for short-term (e.g., quarterly) performance (Gomez-Mejia & Welbourne, 1989; Rappaport, 1978; Salter, 1973; Stonich, 1981).[26] Investments in areas such as research and development and employee development that may generate improved future performance may be bypassed in favor of generating higher quarterly or annual earnings. Plans that focus on long-term objectives offer a potential means of getting managers to think like owners. The announcement of such plans seems to elicit positive reactions from the stock market (Brickley, Bhagat, & Lease, 1985). Although this reaction could be because the market assumes that executives are more likely to accept stock options when they expect high corporate performance, there do appear to be other factors associated with the use of long-term incentives. For example, long-term incentives have been found to be positively associated with high research and development intensity (Milkovich, Gerhart, & Hannon, 1991), greater employment stability (Gerhart, 1991), and increased capital investment (Larcker, 1983). All of these suggest that long-term incentives do succeed in extending the time horizon of executives. These advantages may help explain the increase in the use of long-term incentives for senior management, now 28 percent of their total compensation, up from 16 percent in 1982 ("Long-term," 1989).

Equal Employment Opportunity

Race and sex differences in employment outcomes such as compensation are prohibited under the Civil Rights Act of 1964, unless justified by business necessity. Labor market and demographic realities also dictate that organizations pay close attention to equal employment opportunity issues and "managing diversity" (see Broderick, 1991, for a review). Consider two trends. First, the labor force participation rate of women has risen from 37.7 percent in 1960 to 57.7 percent in 1989. During the same period, the rate for men fell from 83.3 percent to 78.1 percent. Second, U.S. Census data show that the white population grew by 6.0 percent between 1980 and 1990. During the same period, population growth among nonwhites was 25.3 percent. The implication is that the share of white males will continue to decline in organizations, meaning that attention to equal

employment opportunity issues in compensation is likely to continue to be important.

Typically, the popular press focuses on raw earnings ratios, which show substantial differentials based on both race and sex. For example, in 1988, among year-round, full-time workers, the ratio of female to male average earnings was .65, and the ratio of black to white earnings was .75 (Ryscavage & Henle, 1990). These ratios have generally risen over the last two to three decades (Blau & Beller, 1988; Carlson & Swartz, 1988; Horrigan & Markey, 1990), but obviously still fall well short of unity. However, the raw ratios ignore the fact that part of the earnings differentials are due to race or gender differences in earnings determinants such as education, labor market experience, and occupation. Although these factors may themselves be tainted by discrimination (employer or societal), it is useful to examine earnings ratios adjusted for such factors. Even though these adjusted ratios are, of course, higher, providing somewhat less of a case for discrimination, it is also clear that they too fall well short of unity. In almost no case do such adjustments account for any more than 50 percent of the earnings differential (Cain, 1986). Thus, defining the latter as 1 minus the earnings ratio, a ratio of, say, .60 would rise to no more than .80 (i.e., differential goes from .40 to .20). Exceptions to this general finding tend to occur only when differences due to employers and narrow job title are eliminated. However, controlling for these latter two factors rests on the tenuous assumption that they are not tainted by discrimination. Moreover, even with controls for these and an extensive array of other variables (e.g., performance rating, college major, degree level, etc.), adjusted ratios fall short of unity (Gerhart, 1990a).

Given evidence that earnings differentials are robust to a range of samples and model specifications, perhaps the best strategy is to attempt to identify the employment activities most responsible in order to know where to target antidiscrimination efforts. Most attention lately has focused on sex-based earnings differentials. In particular, there has been a focus on the pay implications of the sex segregation found within and between occupations (Bielby & Baron, 1984). Some believe that those occupations dominated by women tend to be systematically paid less than their worth (Treiman & Hartmann, 1981).

At the organizational level, job evaluation has been scrutinized as a possible source of underevaluation of women's work. However, as discussed in the "Structures" section of this chapter, the empirical evidence does not support any direct effect of either evaluator gender or the gender composition of the job incumbents. On the other hand, the evidence suggests that market rates influence job evaluation results. Thus, if market rates are discriminatory, job evaluation may indirectly help perpetuate discrimination in pay.

Comparable worth, or pay equity, has been advocated as a public policy that would remedy the undervaluation of women's jobs. The idea is to obtain equal pay for jobs not just of equal content (already mandated by the Equal Pay Act of 1963), but also for jobs of equal value or worth. Typically, job evaluation is used to measure worth. There are, however, a number of potential problems with using job evaluation to implement the comparable worth approach. Fundamentally, values differ, and reaching agreement on the worth of jobs is not straightforward. In addition, proponents have often proposed job evaluation–like procedures to establish worth as an alternative to the market mechanism because the latter is viewed as discriminatory. However, as Schwab (1980) has argued, job evaluation is not well-suited to this purpose for a variety of reasons, including the fact that it is often used as a way of capturing market pay policies, rather than being used independently of the market.

As with any regulation, there are also concerns about obstructing market forces that economic theory suggests provide the most efficient means of pricing and allocating people to jobs. Without market forces in control, some jobs would be paid too much, others too little, resulting in an oversupply of workers for the former, an undersupply for the latter. In addition, some empirical evidence suggests that some proposed pay equity regulatory policies may not have much impact on the relative earnings of women in the private sector (Gerhart & El Cheikh, 1990; Smith, 1988). Further questions about its impact arise when one considers that such policies are targeted at single employers, ignoring sex-based pay differences that arise from men and women working for different employers (see Bielby & Baron, 1986). In other words, to the extent that sex-based pay differences are due to men and women working in different organizations having different pay levels, such policies will have little impact. Perhaps most important, despite the possible sources of invalidity in market rates discussed earlier (Rynes & Milkovich, 1986), the courts have consistently ruled that using going market rates of pay is an acceptable defense in comparable worth litigation suits. Thus, there is no comparable worth legal mandate in the U.S. private sector.

Nevertheless, there has been a great deal of activity in the U.S. public sector at the state level and in both the private and public sector in Ontario, Canada. For example, as of 1989, 20 states in the United States had begun or completed comparable worth adjustments to public sector employees' pay (Milkovich & Newman, 1990). Evidence suggests that such policies can significantly raise women's relative pay where states are willing to invest the money (Orazem & Matilla, 1989). Evidence from Ontario has yet to come in, but should be even more interesting because of the application of the policy to the public sector. Finally, despite the potential drawbacks discussed above, job evaluation is widely mandated as the means of determining the worth of jobs under pay equity laws and agreements.

Another line of inquiry has focused on the role of pay structures (e.g., promotions) in generating pay differences. On the one hand, Gerhart and Milkovich (1989) found in their literature review and in their own empirical study that although women were paid less than men, it was not unusual for women to receive more promotions and larger percentage pay increases than men. Gerhart (1990a) found that virtually all of the earnings differential between men and women in one organization was a result of a one-time pay shortfall at the time of hire that persisted for many years, despite the equal (or better) treatment of women in pay increase and promotion decisions reported by Gerhart and Milkovich (1989). These findings may indicate that when actual job performance (versus general qualifications) can be used in decisions, women may be less likely to encounter unequal treatment. If so, more attention needs to be devoted to what happens at the time of hire to generate pay differences.[27]

On the other hand, evidence from other organizations points to the possibility that the promotion system is indeed a key determinant of pay differences between men and women. A recent study by Cannings and Montmarquette (1991) reported that women received fewer promotions than men, partly because of women's poorer access to informal networks (see also Brass, 1985; Rosen, Templeton, & Kirchline, 1981). One suggested means of improving such access is the use of mentoring programs (Noe, 1988). Empirical evidence is sparse; however, one recent study found that although mentoring had substantial positive effects on the pay of both men and women, it did not explain differences in pay between the two groups because men and women reported receiving equal amounts of mentoring. One possibility is that lower career advancement expectations among women (e.g., Major & Konar, 1984) contributed to women perceiving the same degree of mentoring as being more extensive.

The Department of Labor "glass ceiling" initiative focuses on the specific possibility that women may have equal access to promotional opportunities until they reach the upper echelons of organizations. At that point, they have the top executive positions in sight but are impeded by the glass ceiling. (See Broderick, 1991, for a review.) Evidence provided by Spillerman and Petersen (1990) is consistent with this idea. They found that women's chances of promotion were greater than those of men at lower levels, but smaller at higher levels. In addition, Fierman (1990b) reported on the presence of women and men among the highest paid officers and directors in 799 of the 1,000 largest industrial and service companies in the United States. In 1979, 0.16 percent (10/6400) of this group were women. By 1989, 0.47 percent (19/4012) were women. Although most attention seems to be focused on sex differences, some evidence suggests a similar pattern for blacks. For example, a Korn-Ferry survey of the 1985 Fortune 1000 found that of 1,362 senior executives, 4 (0.3%) were black (Jones, 1986). These statistics suggest the need for further research on identifying the specific employment and compensation practices that are responsible.

International Comparisons

International Competitiveness. When discussing international competitiveness, one focus often seems to be on labor costs. However, there are at least four major problems with such comparisons.

First, as Table 5 suggests, they are very unstable, even over short time periods. The main problem is that the relative standing of the various countries is greatly influenced by changes in the currency exchange rate. For example, between 1985 and 1987, the value of the Japanese yen relative to the U.S. dollar rose 65 percent (Capdevielle, 1989), accounting for more than 80 percent of the rather dramatic narrowing of the cost difference between the two countries. (In local currency [yen], hourly compensation rose a much smaller 6 percent in Japan between 1985 and 1987.) As a consequence, one cannot, in a straightforward

TABLE 5

Hourly Compensation Costs*
Expressed in U.S. Dollars

	1985	1987	1989
United States	100%	100%	100%
Japan	50%	83%	95%
Germany	74%	125%	130%
Sweden	75%	112%	121%
United Kingdom	48%	67%	76%
Mexico	16%	12%	12%**
Singapore	19%	17%	19%
Taiwan	11%	16%	19%

*Includes "pay for time worked, other direct pay, employer expenditures for legally required insurance programs and contractual and private benefit plans, and for some countries, other labor taxes" (Capdevielle, 1989, p. 10).

**1987 data

Source: "International Comparison of Hourly Compensation Costs" by P. Capdevielle, June, 1989, *Monthly Labor Review*, 10–12.

manner, simply factor in relative labor costs in making decisions about where to locate production. Rather, a projection (guess) must also be made about future exchange rates, which appear to be at least as important.

A second major limitation goes back to our earlier point that costs are only one part of the picture—productivity is equally important. Combining information on both productivity and labor per costs yields what is perhaps the most important indicator, unit labor costs, defined as labor costs per output. Unfortunately, the Bureau of Labor Statistics (BLS) does not provide information on international comparisons of productivity or unit labor cost levels because sufficiently reliable data have not yet been developed. Mitchell (1989), however, provides data on gross national product (GNP) per employee, which he refers to as a "very crude" measure of productivity level differences. In

1986, for example, he reports that GNP per employee in Northern Europe and Japan was between 75 percent and 95 percent of that in the United States, British and Italian levels were about 60 percent of the United States, and South Korea about 17 percent. Although these are crude measures, they suggest that the level of U.S. productivity may still be among the highest (if not the highest) in the world.

More precise data on productivity in some specific industries can also be found. For example, Proskech (1991) reports the following data, based on research at the Massachusetts Institute of Technology (Womack, Jones, & Roos, 1990) and other sources. The average number of hours needed to build an automobile is 36 in Europe, 25 for U.S. domestic manufacturers, 22 for Japanese companies operating in the United States, and 17 for Japanese companies operating in Japan. Within countries, the variance can also be large. For example, 3 different Volvo plants in Sweden average 37, 40, and 50 hours, respectively, to build an automobile.

More extensive reliable comparative data are available on productivity and unit labor cost growth. Much attention has been focused on the relatively slower productivity growth in the United States. As Table 6 shows, the United States lagged behind other countries during the period from 1960 to 1985. In particular, Japan's rate of productivity growth was 3 times greater than that in the United States. On the other hand, the United States has held down unit labor cost growth as well or better than the other countries included here. Unfortunately, however, this has been achieved through slower increases in wages (and thus, in standard of living), rather than through growth in productivity. More recent data (see Table 7) show similar trends, but with one hopeful exception—growth in productivity appears to have picked up substantially, helping hold unit labor costs down in a more desirable manner.

Third, Drucker (1988) has argued that "wage levels for blue collar workers are becoming increasingly irrelevant in world competition"

TABLE 6

**Annual Percent Changes in Productivity,
Hourly Compensation, and Unit Labor Costs, 1960–1985**

	*Manufacturing Productivity**	*Hourly Compensation*	*Unit Labor Costs (U.S. $)*	*Unit Labor Costs (Local currency)*
United States	2.7	6.5	3.7	3.7
Japan	8.0	11.9	3.6	5.3
Germany	4.8	9.1	4.1	5.5
Sweden	4.7	11.2	6.2	4.0
United Kingdom	3.5	12.1	8.3	5.0

Note: Rates of change based on the compound rate method.

* Output per hour

Source: "International Trends in Productivity and Unit Labor Costs in Manufacturing" by A. Neef, December, 1986, *Monthly Labor Review*, 12–17.

(p. 32). Consistent with our earlier discussion, he argues that productivity is important, as are quality, design, service, innovation, and marketing. He suggests a rule of thumb whereby offshore production "must be at least 5%, and probably 7% cheaper than production nearby to compensate for the considerable costs of distance: transportation, communications, travel, insurance, finance" (p. 32). As he points out, if wages fall below 15 percent of total cost, then a 50 percent wage differential is needed to offset the costs of offshore production.

This brings us to a fourth problem with focusing only on comparative labor costs in assessing competitiveness. Such comparisons ignore the fact that certain employee skills are simply not available in sufficient quality and quantity in all countries, meaning that certain types of production, let alone the innovation and product quality emphasized by Drucker, are difficult to achieve in many countries. For example, as of 1986, the percentage of the

relevant age group enrolled in high school in Organization for Economic Cooperation and Development (OECD) countries (United States, Western Europe, Japan, Canada, Australia) was 93 percent, compared to 40 percent in the developing countries (Johnston, 1991). Similarly, for college enrollment, the figures in 1986 were 39 percent enrollment in the OECD countries versus 7 percent in developing countries. These data suggest that the lower labor cost found in developing countries may simply reflect the lower level of skills and training available.

Compensation in Japan. The dramatic productivity growth of the Japanese economy and the significant Japanese productivity advantages in highly visible industries (e.g., automobiles; see above) has focused attention on that country's employment system, including compensation. What can be learned from the Japanese approach? Typically, the system is described as resting upon three pillars. The first

TABLE 7

Annual Percent Changes in Productivity,
Hourly Compensation, and Unit Labor Costs, 1985–1989

	*Manufacturing Productivity**	*Hourly Compensation*	*Unit Labor Costs (U.S. $)*	*Unit Labor Costs (Local currency)*
United States	4.7	3.5	−1.1	−1.1
Japan	5.0	4.0	−1.0	13.5
Germany	1.0	4.2	3.2	15.4
Sweden	1.1	7.7	6.5	14.5
United Kingdom	5.0	7.3	2.2	8.3

Notes: Rates of change are based on the compound rate method.

* Output per hour

Source: Calculated from *Monthly Labor Review* tables, June 1991.

pillar is lifetime employment (for about 30% of the labor force). The second pillar is the bonus system. According to Hashimoto (1990, p. 257), as of 1985, production workers in manufacturing in Japan received, on average, 26 percent of their direct annual pay in the form of bonuses. In contrast, U.S. production workers received an average of 0.5 percent of their pay in the form of bonuses. The third pillar is the dominance of enterprise unions, which, as the term suggests, are less tied to industrywide bargaining, and oriented more toward dealing with a particular employer, thus presumably allowing more flexibility in the agreements reached between particular employers and unions. In addition, contracts are typically for a length of one year, which is shorter than the typical duration (three years) in the United States. Both factors are thought to contribute to greater flexibility in base wages among Japanese (versus U.S.) employers. Empirical evidence supports the overall hypothesis that direct compensation is significantly more flexible

in Japan than in the United States (Gordon, 1982).

Although there may be significant value in studying compensation and human resource practices in other countries, some caution is also necessary, because practices, especially when lifted piecemeal out of a larger industrial relations system, may not readily transfer. Two recent studies on the impact of information sharing on the wage negotiation process, one in Japan (Morishima, 1991), the other in the United States (Kleiner & Bouillon, 1988), may help illustrate this point. In Japan, information sharing decreased the (a) length of negotiations, (b) union's initial percentage wage increase demand, and (c) final percentage wage increase settlement. Morishima suggested that findings (a) and (b) support an asymmetric information framework—information sharing reduces the union need to guess or infer what type of settlement management can provide. Finding (c) supports the goal alignment model. He concluded:

if information provided by management can convince the union and the employees that it is to their benefit to have a well-performing firm, the union and employees will be less likely to demand a share of the firm's profits that may hurt firm performance....Unions may perceive that other important goals, such as employment security, also depend on the viability of firm operation and will be jeopardized by setting wages well above the competitive level. (p. 472)

In contrast to Morishima's (1991) results for Japan, findings using a U.S. sample (Kleiner & Bouillon, 1988) found that information sharing led to higher wages and benefits for production employees in both union and nonunion business lines. Moroshima suggests that "the comprehensive labor relations strategy used by Japanese management in order to induce goal alignment is generally lacking in the United States" and that "a piece-meal application of Japanese industrial relations techniques" is not likely to win union cooperation in the United States (p. 482).

Thus, for example, although proponents of variable pay systems might look to Japan as proof of their effectiveness, such comparisons require caution and should perhaps be conducted as a way of generating ideas and stimulating reevaluation of one's own practices. Having production workers receive 26 percent of their annual pay in the form of bonuses, combined with lifetime employment security, as in Japan, is quite different from the same or a lower level of variable pay without employment security as is similar to some U.S. managerial notions.

The Global Market and Compensation. Mirroring what is happening with the organization of production (e.g., Reich, 1990), the world's labor market is undergoing dramatic changes. Johnston (1991) projects that the world labor force will grow by 36 percent between the

years 1985 and 2000. Of the 600 million net new workers, 570 million (95%) will be from developing countries. He predicts that nations having slow growth in their labor forces but expanding service sectors (e.g., Japan, Germany, and the United States) will attract immigrants, while countries producing more educated workers than can be used will export workers (e.g., Argentina, Poland, the Philippines). Johnston points out that the labor market for a number of occupations (e.g., physicists, nursing, software engineers) is already international to varying degrees and is likely to move further in that direction given shifts in the distribution of education across countries. For example, between 1970 and 1985, the share of the world's college students accounted for by the United States, Canada, Europe, the Soviet Union, and Japan dropped from 77 percent to 51 percent (Johnston, 1991). Moreover, Johnston predicts that by the year 2000, their share will fall to about 40 percent.

Johnston (1991) predicts that there will be a movement toward work force standardization across borders. (See the European Community's 1992 initiatives for a current example). He argues that "for a global corporation, the notion of a single set of workplace standards will eventually become as irresistible as the idea of a single language for conducting business" (p. 126), an idea reminiscent of the Kerr, Dunlop, Harbison, and Myers (1960) convergence of industrial relations systems hypothesis. If true, significant changes in compensation are to be expected. Familiarity with other countries' approaches to employee relations and compensation will become more important, as corporations and governments are faced with choosing the most appropriate international standard.

Foreign Service Employees.   These trends suggest that decisions regarding the compensation of foreign service employees will increase in importance. There are several unique challenges that arise due to the different legal systems and customs that prevail in different cultures (Milkovich & Newman, 1990). Thus, for example, in Western Europe, many compensation decisions (e.g., vacations) are mandated by law, eliminating employer discretion. As another example, the relative importance of pay in influencing employees may vary significantly across cultures (Ruiz Quintanilla, 1990).

Newman (1989) suggests that a major decision concerns the choice of an appropriate equity standard in pay setting. For example, should an expatriate's pay be compared to what the same assignment would pay in the home country or in the local country? If based on the home country, two people (e.g., an expatriate and a local country national or expatriates having different home countries) performing the same assignment will often receive very different pay. On the other hand, pay based on local standards (e.g., in a low wage country) may make it virtually impossible to find someone willing to accept the position.

The demise of centrally planned economies in Eastern Europe and the Soviet Union raises other important questions. After decades of working under a system that did not reward individual initiative, risk taking, and achievement, how will people respond to compensation systems that focus on such behaviors? Such changes should present tremendous opportunities for studying the effects of Western compensation systems on attitudes, behaviors, and effectiveness, as well as provide some guidelines concerning their introduction to new settings.

Nonmonetary Rewards

Our focus, of course, has been on monetary rewards. According to Lawler (1971), pay is a reward of unique importance because it is instrumental in obtaining a range of other rewards. However, the work of Maslow (1943), Herzberg, (1966), and others suggests that jobs have many other attributes that can serve as rewards.

Moreover, an exchange perspective implies that pay can be viewed as a return for services rendered—in essence, as an *obligation* rather than a *reward*.

Although we will not attempt a comprehensive review, a few such issues warrant attention because organizations have a limited pool of resources to devote to managing human resources. In structuring monetary compensation, decisions concerning the mix between direct pay and benefits are important. But, at an even more general level, organizations face a choice between allocating resources to pay versus other potential rewards/returns, such as improved supervision, participation, working conditions, advancement opportunities, job design, training, and so forth. Therefore, it is useful to have some insight into both the relative importance of various job attributes to employees, as well as the relative motivational effects on employees (or "bang for the buck") of expenditures in each area.

Expectancy theory, in particular, emphasizes that outcomes (e.g., pay, recognition) of behaviors (e.g., performance) will enhance motivation only if they are valent to employees. Thus, the work by Hertzberg and Maslow inspired a line of research devoted to identifying the outcomes that were most important or valent to employees or applicants on average. Briefly, the importance of pay in such studies appears to depend somewhat on the method used. For example, self-reports of importance suggest that pay is not one of the more important job attributes, although people seem to believe that it is important to others (Jurgensen, 1978). Indirect assessments of importance (e.g., by observing hypothetical job choices using policy-capturing), however, tend to find that pay is a very important attribute (e.g., Zedeck, 1977).[28]

Although expectancy theory treats outcome valences as additive, there has been some suggestion that extrinsic (e.g., monetary) rewards contingent on performance may be nonadditive, actually detracting from intrinsic motivation (deCharms, 1968; Deci, 1972).

This is because the key aspect of intrinsic motivation is a feeling of personal causation (DeCharms). Extrinsic rewards may shift the locus of causation to external sources. In other words, the net effect of spending additional dollars on compensation could be a reduction in overall motivation. Methodological problems with Deci's research have been raised by Calder and Staw (1975). Dyer and Schwab's (1982) review concluded that no clear-cut pattern of results had emerged to either confirm or disconfirm the original hypothesis of nonadditivity. Subsequently, however, a review and empirical study (Ryan, Mims, & Koestner, 1983) concluded that task and performance contingent rewards do decrease intrinsic motivation because of the controlling nature of the feedback inherent in such rewards. However, Ryan et al. also argued that such effects were likely to be found only when the task is interesting and is one "that a person does not typically do to get rewards" (p. 738).

Since then, more empirical research has appeared, but the picture has probably not become much clearer. There has been both supporting (e.g., Jordan, 1986) and nonsupporting evidence (e.g., Scott, Farh, & Podsakoff, 1988) for the nonadditivity hypothesis. Research by Phillips and Freedman (1985) suggests that work values may be a moderating variable. For example, they found, consistent with expectancy theory, that rewards had additive effects for persons with high intrinsic work values, but had nonadditive effects among persons with high extrinsic work values.

Future research on this topic would benefit from attention to the following issues. First, overall motivation and performance need to be measured. Even if contingent monetary rewards are not completely additive, the amount of nonadditivity may not be practically significant. Second, the nature and duration of the tasks used in these studies needs to be reconsidered. For example, coding, proofreading, simple assembly tasks, and the like may not be ideally suited to eliciting high levels of intrinsic motivation. The fact that such tasks last for only 15 to 60 minutes in several of the studies may limit the research in the same way. A test of the hypothesis among, for example, scientists and engineers would be very interesting. Third, more agreement on what constitutes intrinsic (versus extrinsic) rewards would be useful (Dyer & Parker, 1975).

Another way of examining the role of pay vis-à-vis other rewards is to look at their relative motivational effects. The Locke et al. (1980) review mentioned earlier examined the motivational impact of four motivational techniques: monetary incentives, goal setting, participation, and job enrichment. They included only studies that were conducted in the field, used either control groups or before-after designs, and used hard performance criteria (e.g., physical output). Locke et al. found that monetary incentives resulted in the largest median performance improvement (30%), followed by goal setting (16%), job enrichment (8.75 to 17%), and participation (0.5%). They concluded that money was the most effective motivator. The reason lies in the fact that money "as a medium of exchange...is the most instrumental" (p. 379), a conclusion similar to that of Lawler (1971).

A meta-analysis by Guzzo, Jette, and Katzell (1985) examined the average effects of several types of human resource interventions, including compensation, work redesign, and others. They included studies based on criteria similar to those of Locke et al. (1980) but also looked at two additional productivity criteria (besides physical output): withdrawal (turnover and absenteeism) and disruption (accidents and strikes). They found that although financial incentives had a substantial mean effect on the three productivity criteria, the variance of the effect was very large and thus was not statistically different from zero. However, limiting the analysis to only the physical output criterion, they found that financial incentives had, by far, the largest (and statistically significant) mean positive effect. As such, these results are very similar to those of Locke et al.

Suggested Research Directions

Below are listed some suggested topics for research in some of the areas we have discussed in this section.

- *Executive compensation.* Executive compensation research needs to continue its focus on the consequences of different executive pay packages. However, it might be useful to supplement the commonly used financial measures of performance with measures of specific behaviors, as well as psychological outcomes such as goals, values, and philosophies.

- *Equal employment opportunity research.* We believe that equal employment opportunity research should inform public and private policy regarding the main sources of pay differentials based on race and gender. This suggests the need to assess the relative influences of hiring, promotion, and development practices in generating inequality. In addition, "new" benefit programs such as family and parental leave, childcare assistance, and flexible working hours need to be examined for their impact on women's (and men's) ability to balance work and family and advance past the so-called glass ceiling.

  Another suggestion is to study the implications of establishing a reputation as an organization that provides equal opportunities for all employees in its pay-setting process. This has two parts. First, how closely linked is actual organizational success in equal employment opportunity and affirmative action with applicant and employee perceptions of

success? Second, does actual practice—or perceptions—have an influence on attraction and retention and other important outcomes?

- *International dimensions of compensation.* This is largely uncharted territory. We suggest that further descriptive research on national differences in practices would be useful. Further, equity theory should have many applications in studying the various approaches to compensating foreign service employees.

- *Interaction of pay with nonmonetary rewards.* This work would help establish the conditions under which monetary rewards are most likely to have a high return on investment.

Concluding Comments

We began this chapter by saying that decisions regarding compensation are among the most important that an organization must make. Figure 1 provided a general framework for describing specific types of pay decisions and the relevant research evidence. The central focus has been on establishing the consequences for organizations of different compensation decisions or strategies. Although there has been much progress in the compensation literature, more, of course, remains to be done. Figure 1 helps summarize some of the key factors to incorporate in future research. We close with a few notes on compensation's place in the larger picture and some general suggestions for the design of future research.

Pay is only one of many decision areas that determine the nature of the employment exchange. Similarly, from a managerial perspective, there are likely to be multiple paths to the same goal. Thus, decisions regarding organizational and job design, external staffing, internal staffing, and development can influence many of the same outcomes depicted in Figure 1. These human resource decisions can be viewed as contingency factors that either constrain or enhance the effectiveness of pay decisions. Alternatively, pay decisions can be viewed as the contingency factor. In any case, the main point is that pay decisions are made in a complex world where many other influences are at work. The more recognition of this fact given by research, the more valuable its contribution is likely to be.

The different human resource decision areas can also be thought of as alternative levers that can be pulled to achieve a particular objective. This fits well with the return on investment approach that we have suggested at various points in the chapter. The main question to be answered is, Which investment in human resources is most likely to yield the highest return? If the effectiveness of the current work force is not adequate, should the major investment go toward better screening of applicants, development of training programs, or designing pay programs that will enhance individual motivation, cooperation, and so on?

This suggests the need for further conceptual development of contingency models. Such work should focus on generating specific, testable propositions. On the empirical side, we suggest that such research include as many of the following characteristics as possible. First and foremost, the goal should be to capture variation in actual pay practices. This can be accomplished by using multiple employing units (organizations or units within them) or by following changes over time in the same unit(s). Second, research should be longitudinal, not only allowing the study of changes, but also providing the opportunity to track the long-term consequences of pay decisions. Third, research should examine multiple pay decisions simultaneously, rather than looking only at individual pay or only at benefits, for example. Based on our review, the benefits and structure decisions have been especially neglected in the

empirical research (if not the practitioner) literature. It would be useful to compare the relative effects and costs of investments in the different pay decision areas. Finally, future studies should strive to examine the structural process by which compensation decisions and outcomes are linked. To do so, outcome measures will need to be obtained at multiple levels of the organization, including individual, group, unit, and organizational levels where possible.

We should emphasize that these features are put forth simply as goals. Obviously, there are often stumbling blocks on the road to designing and conducting such studies. We suggest that one way of enhancing the probability of attaining these goals is to demonstrate to organizations the practical implications of being able to address the types of issues raised in this chapter. This, of course, goes a long way toward building the partnerships needed between industry and academia that are necessary to conduct much such research (see Dunnette, 1990).

We thank our colleagues and students for helping us focus our ideas over the years. We are expecially indebted to Eric Cousineau for his assistance. Finally, we thank Renae Broderick, Luis Gomez-Mejia, Robert Madigan, Jerry Newman, Donald Schwab, and the editors of this volume for their valuable comments on an earlier draft of this chapter.

Notes

1   Pearce and Robinson (1982) describe strategic decisions as those that (a) require top management involvement, (b) entail allocation of large amounts of company resources, (c) have major consequences for multiple businesses or functions, (d) are future-oriented, (e) require consideration of external factors, and (f) have an impact on the long-term performance of the organization. Many compensation decisions meet these criteria, consistent with the important role attached to compensation in recent books on organization strategy (e.g., Kanter, 1989; Peters, 1987; Porter, 1990).

2 These first two factors are the same as two of Alfred Marshall's (Marshallian) conditions affecting the elasticity of the demand for labor.

3 For example, if products change over time, so too will the relevant product market comparisons. If general skills and abilities are considered important and products change, product market comparisons become less important.

4 This, of course, fits nicely with Marxist discussions of the role of the *reserve army*. Further, Weisskopf, Bowles, and Gordon (1984, cited in Yellen, 1984) have argued that such things as unemployment benefits have contributed to the slowdown in U.S. productivity growth because of the consequent "loss of employer control due to a reduction in the cost of job loss" (Yellen, p. 202).

5 Notable by its absence will be any direct empirical research on efficiency wage models (because there is little).

6 See Williams and Dreher (1990) for an exception.

7 This, of course, does not mean that the equity theory and discrepancy model approaches are identical. For example, under the discrepancy model, preceived actual pay that exceeds perceptions of the "should be" component leads to increased satisfaction. In contrast, equity theory predicts guilt (perceived overreward inequity).

8 Two examples illustrate the importance of the "should be" component. Capelli and Sherer's (1990) study of a two-tier wage plan found that lower tier workers (those paid significantly less for doing the same job) were more satisfied with their pay than the more highly paid first-tier workers because the former group had lower comparison standards (e.g., unemployment, lower paying jobs). A second example is the common finding that despite lower pay levels among women, their pay satisfaction does not usually differ from that of men (Dreher & Ash, 1990).

9 Employment may also be reduced as organizations seek to substitute less expensive production inputs (e.g., new technology) for the costly labor input. Although such substitution may be an efficient response to high labor cost, economic models suggest that efficiency would be higher if labor cost was determined by market forces (and less substitution occurred).

10 Note that the detrimental effects of higher wages depend on the existence of a competitive market.

One violation of this assumption may occur when a union has organized the entire product market, thereby taking wages out of competition. The U.S. automobile industry (before the advent of international competition) provides such an example (Kochan & Capelli, 1984).

11 On their face, these findings do not seem to fit well with the basic premise of efficiency wage models that above-market pay levels can lead to higher overall efficiency. On the other hand, one could perhaps argue that unions may sometimes "artificially" constrain the expected efficiency advantages of higher pay.

12 In real (versus nominal) dollars.

13 Note that an independent line of work on tournaments has been concerned with the possibility that employees promoted earlier in their careers signal that they are of high ability. Whether this early career success comes about as a result of ability or sponsorship, there is evidence that it has a lasting impact, influencing much later career attainment (Rosenbaum, 1979, 1984; Sheridan, Slocum, Buda, & Thompson, 1990), although a study by Forbes (1987) was less supportive. Forbes suggests that significant differences between organizations probably exist. In any case, where early elimination tournaments exist, incentive problems may arise among employees who are passed over early on if they believe they have lost what amounts to the first round of the tournament and are, to a significant extent, overlooked in future promotion decisions.

14 This section draws on Gerhart (1990b).

15 The effectiveness of averaging over time depends on the source of errors (and their independence over time). If the errors tend to be independent, they may average out (see Gerhart & Milkovich, 1989). However, if an employee is rated by the same supervisor year after year, the errors will not be independent and will not average out. However, the use of *relative* ratings (e.g., Guilford, 1954, p. 285) can remove this type of error. As an example of the effect of between-rater differences, Heneman (1986) found that the correlation between objective performance measures and absolute ratings was .27, with relative (e.g., forced distribution—in effect, adjusted for rater differences in rating levels) ratings of .66.

16 Note also that Konrad and Pfeffer (1990) defined productivity as the number of publications.

Quality (e.g., based on the journal) and relative contribution (e.g., based on author order) were not considered. Also, teaching performance, an understandably difficult construct to measure, was defined in terms of number of hours. These omissions may have constrained the observed pay-performance relationship.

17 The pattern of results for women was similar.

18 See the Kanfer chapter in volume 1 of the *Handbook* for a review of expectancy theory.

19 Valances are often taken as a given in compensation, being seen as more strongly influenced by selection decisions. However, compensation (e.g., communication programs) may also have an impact.

20 Not every variable pay plan carries downside risk. In some cases, employees have the opportunity to earn more if objectives are met, but will not have pay deducted if they do not meet the objectives.

21 More information on usage of profit sharing is available in surveys by the American Compensation Association (O'Dell, 1987), Conference Board (1990), and Bureau of National Affairs (1988).

22 The number of employees participating in ESOPs has grown from 4 million in 1980 to 10 million in 1989 (McCormick, 1989). Some of the organizations that have recently set up ESOPs include Avis, Bell Atlantic, Procter & Gamble, Ameritech, ITT, J. C. Penney, 3M, and Anheuser Busch. Some organizations with more established plans, like Sears and Mobile, have recently expanded them. As one example of the tax and financing advantages, dividends on ESOP-owned stock are deductible if paid out in the current year. Their use as a takeover defense is illustrated by considering Delaware, where about one-half of all public companies are incorporated (McCormick, 1989). State law mandates that a takeover bid must acquire 85 percent of stock to gain true control. Thus, an employee ownership stake of 25 percent or even 15 percent that votes with the company's management can be difficult to overcome.

23 Conceptually, fit can be viewed as the correspondence or match between pay program and organization context profiles.

24 As of 1989, for example, the corresponding percentages were less than 7% in Japan, and just over 8% in Canada and Germany (Fisher, 1991).

25 These typically differ because of group discounts for employers.

26 The growth of institutional ownership and the pressures on their investment managers for short-term results is argued to be another important culprit (Graves & Waddock, 1990).

27 One possibility, that women simply negotiate less over starting salaries, did not receive support in one study of graduating MBAs (Gerhart & Rynes, 1991).

28 However, as discussed earlier, importance assessment can vary significantly with the size of market variability of the attribute in question (Rynes et al., 1983). For example, if all job opportunities offer the exact same pay, pay will essentially have zero statistical importance in predicting job choice. The implication is that the importance of pay and other attributes may differ across labor markets.

References

Abowd, J. M. (1990). Does performance-based managerial compensation affect corporate performance? *Industrial and Labor Relations Review, 43*, 52S–73S.

Adams, J. S. (1963). Toward an understanding of inequity. *Journal of Abnormal Psychology, 67*, 422–436.

Adams, J. S. (1965). Inequity in social exchange. In L. Berkowitz (Ed.), *Advances in experimental social psychology*. New York: Academic Press.

Akerlof, G. A. (1984). Gift exchange and efficiency-wage theory: Four views. *American Economic Review, 74*, 79–83.

Allen, S. G., & Clark, R. L. (1987). Pensions and firm performance. In M. M. Kleiner et al. (Eds.), *Human resources and the performance of the firm*. Madison, WI: Industrial Relations Research Association.

American Compensation Association. (1988). *Report on the 1987 Survey of Salary Management Practices*. Scottsdale, AZ: American Compensation Association.

Arvey, R. D. (1986). Sex bias in job evaluation procedures. *Personnel Psychology, 39*, 315–335.

Arvey, R. D., Passino, E. M., & Loundsbury, J. W. (1977). Job analysis as influenced by sex of incumbent and sex of analyst. *Journal of Applied Psychology, 62*, 411–416.

Ash, P. (1948). The reliability of job evaluation rankings. *Journal of Applied Psychology, 32*, 313–320.

Balkin, D. B., & Gomez-Mejia, L. R. (1984). Determinants of R & D compensation strategies in the high tech industry. *Personnel Psychology, 37,* 635–650.

Balkin, D. B., & Gomez-Mejia, L. R. (1987). Toward a contingent theory of compensation strategy. *Strategic Management Journal, 8,* 169–182.

Balkin, D. B., & Gomez-Mejia, L. R. (1990). Matching compensation and organizational strategies. *Strategic Management Journal, 11,* 153–169.

Barber, A. E. (1990). *Pay as a signal in job choice.* Unpublished manuscript, Graduate School of Business Administration, Michigan State University, East Lansing.

Barber, A. E., Dunham, R. B., & Formisano, R. A. (1990). *The impact of flexible benefits on employee benefit satisfaction.* Unpublished manuscript, University of Wisconsin–Madison.

Barnard, C. I. (1936). *The functions of the executive.* Cambridge, MA: Harvard University Press.

Barrett, G. V., & Doverspike, D. (1989, March). Another defense of point factor job evaluation. *Personnel, 33–36.*

Barringer, M., Milkovich, G. T., & Mitchell, O. (1991). *Predicting employee health insurance selections in a flexible benefit environment* (Working Paper No. 91–21). Center for Advanced Human Resource Studies, Cornell University, Ithaca, NY.

Barron, J. M., Bishop, J., & Dunkelberg, W. C. (1985). Employer search: The interviewing and hiring of new employees. *Review of Economics and Statistics, 67,* 43–52.

Bartol, K. M., & Martin, D. C. (1989). Effects of dependence, dependency threats, and pay secrecy on managerial pay allocations. *Journal of Applied Psychology, 74,* 105–113.

Beal, E. F. (1963). In praise of job evaluation. *California Management Review, 5,* 9–16.

Beam, B., & McFadden, J. (1988). *Employee benefits.* Homewood, IL: Irwin.

Becker, G. (1975). *Human capital: A theoretical and empirical analysis, with special reference to education* (2nd ed.). Chicago: University of Chicago Press.

Belcher, D. W. (1962). *Wage and salary administration.* Englewood Cliffs, NJ: Prentice-Hall.

Belcher, D. W., & Atchinson, T. (1987). *Compensation administration.* Englewood Cliffs, NJ: Prentice-Hall.

Berg, N. A. (1969). What's different about conglomerate management? *Harvard Business Review, 47*(6), 112–120.

Berger, C. J., Olson, C. A., & Boudreau, J. W. (1983). The effect of unionism on job satisfaction: The role of work related values and perceived rewards. *Organizational Behavior and Human Performance, 32,* 284–324.

Berger, L., & Rock, M. (1991). *The compensation handbook.* New York: McGraw-Hill.

Bielby, W. T., & Baron, J. N. (1984). A woman's place is with other women: Sex segregation within organizations. In B. F. Reskin (Ed.), *Sex segregation in the workplace.* Washington, DC: National Academy Press.

Bielby, W. T., & Baron, J. N. (1986). Men and women at work: Sex segregation and statistical discrimination. *American Journal of Sociology, 91,* 759–799.

Bishop, J. (1984). The recognition and reward of employee performance. *Journal of Labor Economics, 5,* 36S–56S.

Blau, F. D., & Beller, M. A. (1988). Trends in earnings differentials by gender, 1971–1981. *Industrial and Labor Relations Review, 41,* 513–529.

Boudreau, J. W. (1991). Utility analysis for decisions in human resource management. In M. D. Dunnette & L. M. Hough (Eds.), *Handbook of industrial and organizational psychology* (2nd ed., vol. 2, pp. 621–745). Palo Alto, CA: Consulting Psychologists Press.

Boudreau, J. W., & Berger, C. J. (1985). Decision-theoretic utility analysis applied to employee separations and acquisitions [Monograph]. *Journal of Applied Psychology, 73,* 467–481.

Brass, D. J. (1985). Men's and women's networks: A study of interaction patterns and influence in an organization. *Academy of Management Journal, 28,* 327–343.

Bretz, R. D., Ash, R. A., & Dreher, G. F. (1989). Do people make the place? An examination of the attraction-selection-attrition hypothesis. *Personnel Psychology, 42,* 561–581.

Bretz, R. D., Jr., Milkovich, G. T., & Read, W. (1989). *The current state of performance appraisal research and practice: Concerns, directions, and implications* (Working Paper No. 89-17). Center for Advanced Human Resource Studies, Cornell University, Ithaca, NY.

Brickley, J. A., Bhagat, S., & Lease, R. C. (1985). The impact of long-range managerial compensation plans on shareholder wealth. *Journal of Accounting and Economics, 7,* 115–129.

Broderick, R. F. (1986). *Pay policy and business strategy—toward a measure of fit.* Unpublished doctoral dissertation, Cornell University, Ithaca, NY.

Broderick, R. F. (1991). *The glass ceiling.* Unpublished manuscript, Center for Advanced Human Resource Studies, Cornell University, Ithaca, NY.

Brown, C. (1980). Equalizing differences in the labor market. *Quarterly Journal of Economics, 94,* 113–134.

Brown, C. (1990). Firms' choice of method of pay. *Industrial and Labor Relations Review, 40,* 165S–182S.

Brown, C., & Medoff, J. (1989). The employer size-wage effect. *Journal of Political Economy, 97,* 1027–1053.

Bureau of National Affairs. (1988). *Changing pay practices: New developments in employee compensation.* Washington, DC: Author.

Bureau of National Affairs. (1990, November 5). *Employee Relations Weekly, 8,* 1358.

Bureau of National Affairs. (1991). *Non-traditional incentive pay programs* (Personnel Policies Forum Survey No. 148). Washington, DC: Author.

Burns, M. (1978). *Understanding job evaluation.* London: Institute of Personnel Management.

Cain, G. G. (1986). The economic analysis of labor market discrimination: A survey. In O. Ashenfelter & R. Layard (Eds.), *Handbook of labor economics* (pp. 694–785).

Calder, B. J., & Staw, B. M. (1975). Interaction of intrinsic and extrinsic motivation: Some methodological notes. *Journal of Personality and Social Psychology, 31,* 76–80.

Campbell, J. P., & Pritchard, R. D. (1976). Motivation theory in industrial and organizational psychology. In M. D. Dunnette (Ed.), *Handbook of industrial and organizational psychology* (1st ed., pp. 63–130). Chicago: Rand McNally.

Cannings, K., & Montmarquette, C. (1991). Managerial momentum: A simultaneous model of the career progress of male and female managers. *Industrial and Labor Relations Review, 44,* 212–228.

Capdevielle, P. (1989, June). International comparisons of hourly compensation costs. *Monthly Labor Review, 112,* 10–12.

Capelli, P., & Sherer, P. D. (1990). Assessing worker attitudes under a two-tier wage plan. *Industrial and Labor Relations Review, 43,* 225–244.

Carey, J. F. (1977). Participative job evaluation. *Compensation Review, 4,* 29–38.

Carlson, L. A., & Swartz, C. (1988). The earnings of women and ethnic minorities, 1959–1979. *Industrial and Labor Relations Review, 41,* 530–546.

Carroll, S. J. (1987). Business strategies and compensation systems. In D. B. Balkin & L. R. Gomez-Mejia, (Eds.), *New perspectives on compensation.* Englewood Cliffs, NJ: Prentice-Hall.

Chelius, J., & Smith, R. S. (1990). Profit sharing and employment stability. *Industrial and Labor Relations Review, 43,* 256S–273S.

Chesler, D. J. (1948). Reliability and comparability of different job evaluation systems. *Journal of Applied Psychology, 32,* 465–475.

Chrisman, J. J., Hofer, C. W., & Boulton, W. R. (1988). Toward a system of classifying business strategies. *Academy of Management Review, 13,* 413–428.

Coates, E. M., III. (1991, April). Profit sharing today: Plans and provisions. *Monthly Labor Review,* pp. 19–25.

Compflash. (1990, March). U.S. executives outearn counterparts in other countries by a large margin, 7.

Conference Board. (1990). *Variable pay: New performance rewards* (Research Bulletin No. 246). New York: Author.

Conlon, E. J., & Parks, J. M. (1990). Effects of monitoring and tradition on compensation arrangements: An experiment with principal-agent dyads. *Academy of Management Journal, 33,* 603–622.

Conte, M. A., & Svejnar, J. (1990). The performance effects of employee ownership plans. In A. S. Blinder (Ed.), *Paying for productivity* (pp. 245–294). Washington, DC: The Brookings Institution.

Cook, F. W. (1976). *Strategic compensation.* Princeton, NJ: Cook.

Crystal, G. (1990, December). Executive compensation: Taking stock. *Personnel, 67*(12), 7–8.

Davis, K. R., Giles, W. F., & Field, H. S. (1985, January). Compensation and fringe benefits: How recruiters view new college graduate preferences. *Personnel Administrator,* 43–50.

Davis, K. R., Giles, W. F., & Field, H. S. (1988). *Benefits preferences of recent college graduates* (Report No. 88–2). Brookfield, WI: International Foundation of Employee Benefits Plans.

Davis, K. R., & Sauser, W. I., Jr. (1991). Effects of alternative weighting methods in a policy-capturing approach to job evaluation: A review and empirical investigation. *Personnel Psychology, 44*, 85–127.

deCharms, R. (1968). *Personal causation: The internal affective determinants of behavior.* New York: Academic Press.

Deci, E. L. (1972). The effects of contingent and noncontingent rewards and controls on intrinsic motivation. *Organizational Behavior and Human Performance, 8*, 217–229.

Deming, W. E., (1986). *Out of the crisis.* Cambridge, MA: MIT, Center for Advanced Engineering Study.

DiMaggio, P., & Powel, W. (1984). The iron cage revisited: Institutional isomorphism and collective rationality in organizational fields. *American Sociological Review, 48*, 147–160.

Doeringer, P. B., & Piore, M. J. (1971). *Labor markets and manpower analysis.* Lexington, MA: Heath.

Doverspike, D., Carlis, A. M., Barrett, G. V., & Alexander, R. A. (1983). Generalizability analysis of a point-method job evaluation instrument. *Journal of Applied Psychology, 68,* 476–483.

Doverspike, D., Racicot, B., & Hauenstein, N. (1987). *Job evaluation and labor market effects on simulated compensation decisions.* Paper presented at the annual meeting of the Society of Industrial and Organizational Psychology, Atlanta, GA.

Dreher, G. F. (1981). Predicting the salary satisfaction of exempt employees. *Personnel Psychology, 34,* 579–589.

Dreher, G. F., & Ash, R. A. (1990). A comparative study of mentoring among men and women in managerial, professional, and technical positions. *Journal of Applied Psychology, 75,* 539–546.

Dreher, G. F., Ash, R. A., & Bretz, R. D. (1988). Benefit coverage and employee cost: Critical factors in explaining compensation satisfaction. *Personnel Psychology, 41*, 237–254.

Drucker, P. F. (1988, March 16). Low wages no longer give competitive edge. *Wall Street Journal,* p. 32.

Dufetel, L. (1991, July–August). Job evaluation: Stillat the frontier. *Compensation and Benefit Review,* 53–67.

Dunlop, J. T. (1979). Suggestions toward a reformation of wage theory. In T. A. Mahoney (Ed.), *Compensation and reward perspectives.* Homewood, IL: Irwin.

Dunnette, M. D. (1990). Blending the science and practice of industrial and organizational psychology: Where are we and where are we going? In M. D. Dunnete & L. M. Hough (Eds.), *Handbook of industrial and organizational psychology* (2nd ed., vol. 1, pp. 1–27). Palo Alto, CA: Consulting Psychologists Press.

Dunnette, M. D., & Bass, B. M. (1963). Behavioral scientists and personnel management. *Industrial Relations, 2*, 115–130.

Dyer, L., & Parker, D. F. (1975). Classifying outcomes in work motivation research: An examination of the intrinsic-extrinsic dichotomy. *Journal of Applied Psychology, 60*, 455–478.

Dyer, L., & Schwab, D. P. (1982). Personnel/human resource management research. In T. A. Kochan, D. J. B. Mitchell, & L. Dyer (Eds.), *Industrial relations research in the 1970s: Review and appraisal.* Madison, WI: Industrial Relations Research Association.

Dyer, L., Schwab, D. P., & Theriault, R. D. (1976). Managerial perceptions regarding salary increase criteria. *Personnel Psychology, 29,* 233–242.

Dyer, L., & Theriault, R. (1976). The determinants of pay satisfaction. *Journal of Applied Psychology, 61,* 596–604.

Edwards, P. (1948). Statistical methods in job evaluation. *Advanced Management,* 158–163.

Ehrenberg, R. G., & Bognanno, M. L. (1990). The incentive effects of tournaments revisited: Evidence from the PGA tour. *Industrial and Labor Relations Review, 43*, 74–88.

Ehrenberg, R. G., & Milkovich, G. T. (1987). Compensation and firm performance. In M. Kleiner et al. (Eds.). Madison, WI: Industrial Relations Research Association.

Ehrenberg, R. G., & Smith, R. S. (1988). *Modern labor economics.* Homewood, IL: Irwin.

Eisenhardt, K. M. (1988). Agency- and institutional-theory explanations: The case of retail sales compensation. *Academy of Management Journal, 31,* 488–511.

Eisenhardt, K. M. (1989). Agency theory: An assessment and review. *Academy of Management Review, 14,* 57–74.

Ellig, B. R. (1981, Third Quarter). Compensation elements: Market phase determines the mix. *Compensation Review,* 30–38.

Fama, E. F., & Jensen, M. C. (1983). Separation of ownership and control. *Journal of Law and Economics, 26,* 301–325.

Farnham, A. (1989, December 4). The trust gap. *Fortune,* 56–78.

Fay, C. H. (1989). External pay relationships. In L. R. Gomez-Mejia (Ed.), *Compensation and benefits.* Washington, DC: Bureau of National Affairs.

Fein, M. (1981). *Improshare: An alternative to traditional managing.* Norcross, GA: Institute of Industrial Engineers.

Feldman, S. (1991, January). Another day, another dollar needs another look. *Personnel, 68,* 9–13.

Fierman, J. (1990a, March 12). The people who set the CEO's pay. *Fortune,* 58–66.

Fierman, J. (1990b, July 30). Why women still don't hit the top. *Fortune,* 40–62.

Fisher, A. (1991, May 20). Employees left holding the bag. *Fortune,* 83–93.

Florkowski, G. W. (1991). Profit sharing and public policy: Insights for the United States. *Industrial Relations, 30,* 96–115.

Folger, R., & Konovsky, M. A. (1989). Effects of procedural and distributive justice on reactions to pay raise decisions. *Academy of Management Journal, 32,* 115–130.

Forbes, J. B. (1987). Early interorganizational mobility: Patterns and influences. *Academy of Management Journal, 30,* 110–125.

Foster-Higgins Consulting. (1991). *1990 Survey of Employee Medical Benefits.* New York: Author.

Foulkes, F. K. (1980). *Personnel policies in large nonunion companies.* Englewood Cliffs, NJ: Prentice-Hall.

Fox, W. M. (1962). Purpose and validity in job evaluation. *Personnel Journal, 41,* 482–437.

Frank, R. H. (1985). *Choosing the right pond: Human behavior and the quest for status.* New York: Oxford University Press.

Fraser, S. (1984). Generalizability analysis of a point method job evaluation instrument: A field study. *Journal of Applied Psychology, 69*(4), 643–647.

Freeman, R. B. (1982). Union wage practices and wage dispersion within establishments. *Industrial and Labor Relations Review, 36,* 3–21.

Freeman, R. B., & Medoff, J. (1984). *What do unions do?* New York: Basic Books.

Friedman, B. (1974). Risk aversion and consumer choice of health insurance option. *Review of Economics and Statistics, 56,* 209–214.

Gabor, A. (1990). *The man who discovered quality: How W. Edwards Deming brought the quality revolution to America–The stories of Ford, Xerox, and GM.* New York: Random House.

Gerhart, B. (1987). How important are dispositional factors as determinants of job satisfaction? Implications for job design and other personnel programs. *Journal of Applied Psychology, 73,* 154–162.

Gerhart, B. (1989, May). "Do compensation policies matter?" Discussant comments from the ILR Research Conference, Ithaca, NY.

Gerhart, B. (1990a). Gender differences in current and starting salaries: The role of performance, college major, and job title. *Industrial and Labor Relations Review, 43,* 418–433.

Gerhart, B. (1990b). *Voluntary turnover, job performance, salary growth, and labor market conditions* (Working Paper, No. 90–12). Center for Advanced Human Resource Studies, Cornell University, Ithaca, NY.

Gerhart, B. (1990c). *What is the practical relevance of dispositional effects on job satisfaction?* (Working Paper No. 90–06). Center for Advanced Human Resource Studies, Cornell University, Ithaca, NY.

Gerhart, B. (1991). *Employment stability under different managerial compensation systems* (Working Paper No. 91–02). Center for Advanced Human Resource Studies, Cornell University, Ithaca, NY.

Gerhart, B., & El Cheikh, N. (1991). Earnings and percentage female: A longitudinal study. *Industrial Relations, 30,* 62–78.

Gerhart, B., & Milkovich, G. T. (1989). Salaries, salary growth, and promotions of men and women in a large, private firm. In R. Michael, H. Hartmann, & B. O'Farrell (Eds.), *Pay equity: Empirical inquiries.* Washington, DC: National Academy Press.

Gerhart, B., & Milkovich, G. T. (1990). Organizational differences in managerial compensation and financial performance. *Academy of Management Journal, 33,* 663–691.

Gerhart, B., & Rynes, S. (1991). Determinants and consequences of salary negotiations by graduating male and female MBAs. *Journal of Applied Psychology, 76*(2), 256–262.

Gomez-Mejia, L. R. (in press). Effect of compensation-diversification strategy match on firm performance. *Strategic Management Journal.*

Gomez-Mejia, L. R., & Balkin, D. B. (1987). Pay compression in business schools: Causes and consequences. *Compensation and Benefits Review, 19*(5), 43–55.

Gomez-Mejia, L. R., & Balkin, D. B. (1989). Effectiveness of individual and aggregate compensation strategies. *Industrial Relations, 28,* 431–445.

Gomez-Mejia, L. R., & Balkin, D. B. (1992). *Compensation, organizational strategy, and firm performance.* Cincinnati, OH: Southwestern Publishing.

Gomez-Mejia, L. R., Page, R. C., & Tornow, W. W. (1982). A comparison of the practical utility of traditional, statistical, and hybrid job evaluation approaches. *Academy of Management Journal, 25,* 790–809.

Gomez-Mejia, L. R., Tosi, H., & Hinkin, T. (1987). Managerial control, performance, and executive compensation. *Academy of Management Journal, 30,* 51–70.

Gomez-Mejia, L. R., & Welbourne, T. M. (1988). Compensation strategy: An overview and future steps. *Human Resource Planning, 11,* 173–189.

Gomez-Mejia, L. R., & Welbourne, T. M. (1989). Strategic design of executive compensation programs. In L. R. Gomez-Mejia (Ed.), *Compensation and benefits.* Washington, DC: Bureau of National Affairs.

Gomez-Meija, L. R., & Wellbourne, T. M. (1990). Compensation strategy: An overview and future steps. *Human Resources Planning,* 173–189.

Goodman, P. S. (1974). An examination of referents used in the evaluation of pay. *Organizational Behavior and Human Performance, 12,* 170–195.

Gordon, R. J. (1982). Why U.S. wage and employment behaviour differs from that in Britain and Japan. *The Economic Journal, 92,* 13–44.

Grams, R., & Schwab, D. P. (1985). An investigation of systematic gender related error in job evaluation. *Academy of Management Journal, 28,* 279–290.

Graves, S., & Waddock, S. (1990). Instional ownership and control: Implications for long-term corporate strategy. *Academy of Management Executive 4*(1), 75–83.

Greenberg, J. (1986). Determinants of perceived fairness of performance evaluations. *Journal of Applied Psychology, 71,* 340–342.

Greenberg, J. (1987). Reaction to procedural injustices in payment distributions: Do the means justify the ends? *Journal of Applied Psychology, 72,* 55–61.

Groshen, E. L. (1988). Why do wages vary among employers? *Economic Review, 24,* 19–38.

Guilford, J. P. (1954). *Psychometric methods.* New York: McGraw-Hill.

Gupta, N., Jenkins, G. D., & Curington, W. P. (1986, Spring). Paying for knowledge: Myths and realities. *National Productivity Review,* 107–123.

Guzzo, R. A., Jette, R. D., & Katzell, R. A. (1985). The effects of psychologically based intervention programs on worker productivity: A meta-analysis. *Personnel Psychology, 38,* 275–291.

Haire, M. (1965). The incentive character of pay. In R. Andrews (Ed.), *Managerial compensation.* Ann Arbor, MI: Foundation for Research on Human Behavior.

Haire, M., Ghiselli, E. E., & Gordon, M. E. (1967). A psychological study of pay [Monograph]. *Journal of Applied Psychology, 51,* 1–24.

Hammer, T. H. (1988). New developments in profit sharing, gainsharing, and employee ownership. In J. P. Campbell, R. J. Campbell, & Associates (Eds.), *Productivity in organizations.* San Francisco: Jossey-Bass.

Hashimoto, M. (1990). Employment and wage systems in Japan and their implications for productivity. In A. S. Blinder (Ed.), *Paying for productivity* (pp. 245–294). Washington, DC: The Brookings Institution.

Hatcher, L., & Ross, T. L. (1991). From individual incentives to an organization-wide gainsharing plan: Effects on teamwork and product quality. *Journal of Organizational Behavior, 12,* 169–183.

Hay Group. (1986, October). Compensation trends. *Compensation Quarterly, 3.*

Hay Group. (1991). Annual Survey of Employee Benefits. Philadelphia, PA: Hay Consulting Group.

Hayes, R., & Abernathy, W. (1980). Managing our way to economic decline. *Harvard Business Review, 58*(4), 67–77.

Helson, H. (1964). *Adaptation-level theory.* New York: Harper & Row.

Heneman, H. G., III. (1985). Pay satisfaction. *Research in Personnel and Human Resource Management, 3,* 115–139.

Heneman, H. G., III, & Schwab, D. P. (1979). Work and rewards theory. In D. Yoder & H. G. Heneman, Jr. (Eds.), *ASPA handbook of personnel and industrial relations.* Washington, DC: Bureau of National Affairs.

Heneman, H. G., III, & Schwab, D. P. (1983). Pay satisfaction: Its multidimensional nature and measurement. *International Journal of Psychology, 20,* 129–141.

Heneman, H. G., III, & Schwab, D. P. (1985). Pay satisfaction: Its multidimensional nature and measurement. *International Journal of Psychology, 20,* 129–141.

Heneman, H. G., III, Schwab, D. P., Standal, J. T., & Peterson, R. B. (1978). *Pay comparisons: Dimensionality and predictability.* Proceedings of the annual meeting of the Academy of Management.

Heneman, R. L. (1986). The relationship between supervisory ratings and results-oriented measures of performance: A meta-analysis. *Personnel Psychology, 39,* 811–826.

Heneman, R. L. (1990). Merit pay research. *Research in Personnel and Human Resource Management, 8,* 203–263

Herzberg, F. (1966). *Work and the nature of man.* Cleveland, OH: World Publishing.

Hirsch, B. T. (1991). Union coverage and profitability among U.S. firms. *Review of Economics and Statistics, 69*–77.

Hofer, C. W., & Schendel, D. E. (1978). *Strategy formulation: Analytical concepts.* St. Paul, MN: West.

Hollenbeck, J. R., & Klein, H. J. (1987). Goal commitment and the goal setting process: Problems, prospects, and proposals for future research. *Journal of Applied Psychology, 72,* 212–220.

Holmer, M. (1984). Tax policy and the demand for health insurance. *Journal of Health Economics, 3,* 203–221.

Holzer, H. J. (1990). Wages, employer costs, and employee performance in the firm. *Industrial and Labor Relations Review, 43,* 147S–164S.

Horrigan, M. W., & Markey, J. P. (1990, July). Recent gains in women's earnings: Better pay or longer hours? *Monthly Labor Review, 113*(7), 11–17.

Hoskisson, R. E., Hitt, M. A., Turk, T. A., & Tyler, B. B. (1989). Balancing corporate strategy and executive compensation: Agency theory and corporate governance. *Research in Personnel and Human Resources, 7,* 25–57.

Huber, V. L. (1991). Comparison of supervisor-incumbent and female-male multidimensional jobs evaluation ratings. *Journal of Applied Psychology, 76,* 115–121.

Huseman, R. C., Hatfield, J. D., & Driver, W. (1975). Getting your benefits program understood and appreciated. *Personnel Journal, 57*(10), 560–566.

Huseman, R., Hatfield, J., & Robinson, R. (1978). The MBA and fringe benefits. *Personnel Administrator, 23*(7), 57–60.

Jacob, R. (1990, April). How you'll be paid in the 1990s. *Fortune,* 11.

Jain, R. S. (1988). Employer sponsored benefits. *Monthly Labor Review,* 19–23.

Jaques, E. (1961). *Equitable payment.* New York: Wiley.

Jenkins, G. J., & Lawler, E. E. (1981). Impact of employee participation in pay plan development. *Organization Behavior and Human Performance, 28,* 111–128.

Jensen, M. C., & Meckling, W. H. (1976). Theory of the firm: Managerial behavior, agency costs, and ownership structure. *Journal of Financial Economics, 3,* 305–360.

Jensen, M. C., & Murphy, K. J. (1990a). Performance pay and top-management incentives. *Journal of Political Economy, 98,* 225–264.

Jensen, M. C., & Murphy, K. J. (1990b, May–June). CEO incentives—It's not how much you pay, but how. *Harvard Business Review, 68,* 138–153.

Johnston, W. B. (1991, March–April). Global work force 2000: The new world labor market. *Harvard Business Review, 69,* 115–127.

Jones, E. W. (1986). Black managers: The dream deferred. *Harvard Business Review, 64*(3), 84–93.

Jordan, P. C. (1986). Effects of an extrinsic reward on intrinsic motivation: A field experiment. *Academy of Management Journal, 29,* 405–412.

Judge, T. A. (1992). The dispositional perspective in human resources research. *Research in Personnel and Human Resource Management, 10.*

Jurgensen, C. E. (1978). Job preferences (What makes a job good or bad?). *Journal of Applied Psychology, 63,* 267–276.

Kahn, L. M., & Sherer, P. D. (1990). Contingent pay and managerial performance. *Industrial and Labor Relations Review, 43,* 107S–120S.

Kanfer, R. (1990). Motivation theory and industrial and organizational psychology. In M. D. Dunnette & L. M. Hough (Eds.), *Handbook of industrial and organizational psychology* (2nd ed., vol. 1, pp. 75–170). Palo Alto, CA: Consulting Psychologists Press.

Kanter, R. M. (1984). *The change masters.* New York: Simon & Schuster.

Kanter, R. M. (1989). *When giants learn to dance.* New York: Simon and Schuster.

Kanter, R. M. (1987, March–April). The attack on pay. *Harvard Business Review,* 60–67.

Katz, D., & Kahn, R. L. (1966). *The social psychology of organizations.* New York: Wiley.

Kaufman, R. T. (1990). The effects of Improshare on productivity. *Proceedings of the 43rd annual meeting of the Industrial Relations Research Association.*

Kerr, C. (1954). The balkanization of labor markets. In E. W. Bakke et al. (Eds.), *Labor mobility and economic opportunity,* 99–106.

Kerr, C., Dunlop, J. T., Harbison, F. H., & Myers, C.A. (1960). *Industrialism and industrial man.* Cambridge, MA: Harvard University Press.

Kerr, C., & Fisher, L. H. (1950). Effect of environment and administration on job evaluation. *Harvard Business Review, 28,* 77–96.

Kerr, J. L. (1985). Diversification strategies and managerial rewards. *Academy of Management Journal, 28,* 155–179.

Kerr, J., & Bettis, R. A. (1987). Board of directors, top management compensation, and shareholder returns. *Academy of Management Journal, 30,* 645–665.

Kerr, J., & Slocum, J. W., Jr. (1987). Managing corporate culture through reward systems. *Academy of Management Executive, 1*(2), 99–108.

King, L. M., Hunter, J. E., & Schmidt, F. L. (1980). Halo in multidimensional forced choice performance scale. *Journal of Applied Psychology, 65,* 507–516.

Kirkpatrick, D. (1990, July 2). Is your career on track? *Fortune,* 38–48.

Klein, H. J. (1989). An integrated control theory of work motivation. *Academy of Management Review, 14,* 150–172.

Klein, K. J. (1987). Employee stock ownership and employee attitudes: A test of three models [Monograph]. *Journal of Applied Psychology, 72,* 319–332.

Kleiner, M. M., & Bouillon, M. L. (1988). Providing business information to production workers: Correlates of compensation and profitability. *Industrial and Labor Relations Review, 41,* 605–617.

Kochan, T. A., & Capelli, P. (1984). The transformation of the industrial relations and personnel function. In P. Osterman (Ed.), *Internal labor markets.* Cambridge, MA: MIT Press.

Konrad, A. M., & Pfeffer, J. (1990). Do you get what you deserve? Factors affecting the relationship between productivity and pay. *Administrative Science Quarterly, 35,* 258–285.

Krefting, L. A. (1980). Differences in orientations toward pay increases. *Industrial Relations, 19,* 81–87.

Krefting, L. A., & Mahoney, T. A. (1977). Determining the size of a meaningful pay increase. *Industrial Relations, 11,* 83–93.

Krueger, A. B. (1988). The determinants of queues for federal jobs. *Industrial and Labor Relations Review, 41,* 567–581.

Krueger, A. B., & Summers, L. H. (1986). Reflections on the inter-industry wage structure. In K. Lang & J. Leonard (Eds.), *Unemployment and the structure of labor markets.* London: Basil Blackwell.

Krueger, A. B., & Summers, L. H. (1988). Efficiency wages and the inter-industry wage structure. *Econometrica, 56,* 259–293.

Kruse, D. L. (1991). Profit-sharing and employment variability: Microeconomic evidence on the Weitzman theory. *Industrial and Labor Relations Review, 44,* 437–453.

Lambert, R. A., & Larcker, D. F. (1989). Executive compensation, corporate decision-making, and shareholder wealth. In F. Foulkes (Ed.), *Executive compensation* (pp. 287–309). Boston: Harvard Business School Press.

Larcker, D. (1983). The association between performance plan adoption and corporate capital investment. *Journal of Accounting and Economics, 5*, 3–30.

Lawler, E. E., III. (1971). *Pay and organizational effectiveness.* New York: McGraw-Hill.

Lawler, E. E., III. (1976). Control systems in organizations. In M.D. Dunnette (Ed.), *Handbook of industrial and organizational psychology* (1st ed.). Chicago: Rand McNally.

Lawler, E. E., III. (1981). *Pay and organizational development.* Reading, MA: Addison-Wesley.

Lawler, E. E., III. (1986). What's wrong with point-factor job evaluation. *Compensation and Benefits Review*, 20–28.

Lawler, E. E., III. (1989). Pay for performance: A strategic analysis. In L. R. Gomez-Mejia (Ed.), *Compensation and benefits.* Washington, DC: Bureau of National Affairs.

Lawler, E. E., III, & Ledford, G. E., Jr. (1985). Skill-based pay. *Personnel, 62*(9), 30–37.

Lawshe, C. H., & Farbo, P. L. (1949). Studies in job evaluation 8: The reliability of an abbreviated job evaluation system. *Journal of Applied Psychology, 33*, 158–166.

Lawshe, C. H., & Satter, G. H. (1944). Studies in job evaluation 1: Factor analysis of point ratings for hourly paid jobs in three industrial plants. *Journal of Applied Psychology, 28*, 189–198.

Lawshe, C. H., & Wilson, R. F. (1947). Studies of job evaluation 6: The reliability of two point rating systems. *Journal of Applied Psychology,* 355–365.

Lazear, E. (1989). Pay equality and industrial politics. *Journal of Political Economy, 97,* 561–581.

Lazear, E., & Rosen, S. (1981). Rank order tournaments as an optimum labor contract. *Journal of Political Economy, 89,* 841–864.

Ledford, G. (1991, March–April). Three cases on skill based pay: An overview. *Compensation and Benefits Review*, 11–23.

Leonard, J. S. (1988). Wage structure and dynamics in the electronics industry. *Industrial Relations, 28,* 251–275.

Leonard, J. S. (1990). Executive pay and firm performance. *Industrial and Labor Relations Review, 43,* 13S–29S.

Levin, D. P. (1991, March 17). An outport of change in G.M's steadfast universe. *New York Times.*

Levine, H. Z. (1987). Compensation and benefits today: Board members speak out (Pt. 1). *Compensation and Benefits Review*, 23–40.

Lewis, R. (1983). Union relative wage effects: A survey of macro estimates. *Journal of Human Resources, 1,* 1–27.

Lineneman, P. D., Wachter, M. L., & Carter, W. H. (1990). Evaluating the evidence on union employment and wages. *Industrial and Labor Relations Review, 44,* 34–53.

Livernash, E. R. (1957). The internal wage structure. In G. W. Taylor & F. C. Pierson (Eds.), *New concepts in wage determination.* New York: McGraw-Hill.

Livernash, E. R. (1980). *Comparable worth: Issues and alternatives.* Washington, DC: Equal Employment Advisory Council.

Locke, E. A. (1968). Toward a theory of task motivation and incentives. *Organizational Behavior and Human Performance, 3,* 157–189.

Locke, E. A. (1976). The nature and causes of job satisfaction. In M. D. Dunnette (Ed.), *Handbook of industrial and organizational psychology* (1st ed., pp. 1297–1349). Chicago: Rand McNally.

Locke, E. A., Feren, D. B., McCaleb, V. M., Shaw, K. N., & Denny, A. T. (1980). The relative effectiveness of four methods of motivating employee performance. In K. D. Duncan, M. M. Gruenberg, & D. Wallis (Eds.), *Changes in working life* (pp. 363–388). New York: Wiley.

Locke, E. A., Shaw, K. N., Saari, L. M., & Latham, G. P. (1981). Goal setting and task performance: 1969–1980. *Psychological Bulletin, 90,* 125–152.

Lodge, G., & Walton, R. (1989, Spring). The American corporation and its new relationships. *California Management Review*, 9–24.

Long, J. E., & Link, A. N. (1983). The impact of market structure on wages, fringe benefits, and turnover. *Industrial and Labor Relations Review, 36,* 239–250.

Longnecker, C. O., Sims, H. P., & Gioia, D. A. (1987). Behind the mask: The politics of employee appraisal. *Academy of Management Executive, 1*(3), 183–193.

Long-term incentives: A larger piece of the executive pie. (1989, June). *Compflash.*

Lorsch, J. W., & Allen, S. A. (1973). *Managing diversity and interdependence.* Boston: Harvard Business School.

Lust, J. A., & Danchower, C. (1990). Models of satisfaction with benefits: Research implications based on the nature of the construct. *Journal of Business and Psychology, 5,* 213–221.

Luthans, F., & Fox, M. L. (1989, March). Update on skill-based pay. *Personnel,* 26–31.

MacPherson, D. A., & Stewart, J. B. (1990). The effect of international competition on union and nonunion wages. *Industrial and Labor Relations Review, 43,* 434–446.

Madigan, R. M., & Hoover, D. J. (1986). Effects of alternative job evaluation methods on decisions involving pay equity. *Academy of Management Journal, 29,* 84–100.

Mahoney, T. A. (1964). Compensation preferences of managers. *Industrial Relations,* 135–144.

Mahoney, T. A. (1979a). *Compensation and reward perspectives.* Homewood, IL: Irwin.

Mahoney, T. A. (1979b). Organizational hierarchy and position worth. *Adademy of Management Journal, 22,* 726–737.

Mahoney, T. A., Rynes, S., & Rosen, B. (1984). Where do compensation specialists stand on comparable worth? *Compensation Review, 16*(4), 27–30.

Major, B., & Konar, E. (1984). An investigation of sex differences in pay expectations and their possible causes. *Academy of Management Journal, 27,* 777–792.

March, J. G., & Simon, H. A. (1958). *Organizations.* New York: Wiley.

Markham, S. E. (1988). Pay-for-performance dilemma revisited: Empirical example of the importance of group effects. *Journal of Applied Psychology, 73,* 172–180.

Maslow, A. H. (1943). A theory of human motivation. *Psychological Review, 50,* 370–396.

McCormick, J. (1989, May 30). Taking stock of employee ownerships plans. *USA Today.*

McNutt, R. P. (1990, June). Achievement pays off at Du Pont. *Personnel,* 5–10

Medoff, J. L., & Abraham, K. G. (1981). Are those paid more really more productive? The case of experience. *Journal of Human Resources, 16,* 186–216.

Miles, R. E., & Snow, C. C. (1978). *Organizational strategy, structure, and process.* New York: McGraw-Hill.

Milkovich, G. T. (1988). A strategic perspective on compensation management. *Research in Personnel and Human Resources Management, 6,* 263–288.

Milkovich, G. T., & Broderick, R. F. (1991). Developing a compensation strategy. In L. Berger & M. Rock (Eds.), *Handbook of compensation.* New York: McGraw-Hill.

Milkovich, G. T., Gerhart, B., & Hannon, J. (1991). The effects of research and development intensity on managerial compensation in large organizations. *Journal of High Technology Management Research.*

Milkovich, G. T., & Newman, J. (1990). *Compensation.* Homewood, IL: BPI/Irwin.

Milkovich, G. T., & Wigdor, A. K. (1991). *Pay for performance.* Washington, DC: National Academy Press.

Mincer, J. (1974). *Schooling, experience, and earnings.* New York: National Bureau of Economic Research.

Mintzberg, H. (1978). Patterns in strategy formation. *Management Science, 24,* 934–948.

Mintzberg, H. (1987, July–August). Crafting strategy. *Harvard Business Review, 65,* 66–75.

Mitchell, D. J. B. (1989). *Human resource management: An economic approach.* Boston: PWS-Kent.

Mitchell, D. J. B., Lewin, D., & Lawler, E. E., III. (1990). Alternative pay systems, firm performance, and productivity. In A. S. Blinder (Ed.), *Paying for productivity.* Washington, DC: Brookings Institution.

Mitchell, O. S. (1982). Fringe benefits and labor mobility. *Journal of Human Resources, 17,* 286–298.

Mitchell, O. S. (1983). Fringe benefits and the cost of changing jobs. *Industrial and Labor Relations Review, 37,* 70–78.

Mitchell, O. S. (1988). Worker knowledge of pension provisions. *Journal of Labor Economics, 6,* 21–37.

Moroshima, M. (1991). Information sharing and collective bargaining in Japan: Effects on wage negotiation. *Industrial and Labor Relations Review, 44,* 469–485.

Motowidlo, S. J. (1983). Predicting sales turnover from pay satisfaction and expectation. *Journal of Applied Psychology, 68,* 484–489.

Mount, M. K., & Ellis, R. A. (1987). Investigation of bias in job evaluation ratings of comparable worth participants. *Personnel Psychology, 40,* 85–96.

Murphy, K. (1986, March–April). Top executives are worth every nickel they get. *Harvard Business Review, 64,* 125–132.

Nathan, F. (1987). Analyzing employers' costs for wages, salaries, and benefits. *Monthly Labor Review, 110*(10), 3–11.

Nealey, S. T. (1963, October). Pay and benefits preferences. *Industrial Relations,* 17–28.

Nealey, S. T., & Goodale, J. (1967). Worker preferences among time of benefits and pay. *Journal of Applied Psychology, 51,* 357–361.

Neef, A., & Thomas, J. (1988). International comparisons of labor productivity in manufacturing. *Monthly Labor Review, 111*(12), 27–33.

Nelson-Horchler, J. (1990, June 18). The pay revolt brews. *Industry Week,* 28–36.

Newman, J. M. (1989). Compensation programs for special employee groups. In L. R. Gomez-Mejia (Ed.), *Compensation and benefits.* Washington, DC: Bureau of National Affairs.

Noe, R. A. (1988). Women and mentoring: A review and research agenda. *Academy of Management Review, 13,* 65–78.

O'Dell, C. (1987). *People, performance, and pay.* American Productivity Center, Houston, TX.

Opshal, R. L., & Dunnette, M. D. (1966). The role of financial incentives in industrial motivation. *Psychological Bulletin, 66,* 95–116.

Orazem, P. F., & Matilla, J. P. (1989). A study of structural change in public sector earnings under comparable worth: The Iowa case. In R. Michael et al. (Eds.), *Pay equity: Empirical inquiries.* Washington, DC: National Academy Press.

O'Reilly, C., Main, B., & Crystal, G. (1988). CEO compensation as tournaments and social comparisons: A tale of two theories. *Administrative Science Quarterly, 33,* 257–274.

Pearce, J. A., II, & Robinson, R. B., Jr. (1982). *Formulation and implementation of competitive strategy.* Homewood, IL: Irwin.

Pearce, J. L., Stevenson, W. B., & Perry, J. L. (1985). Managerial compensation based on organizational performance: A time series analysis of the effects of merit pay. *Academy of Management Journal, 28,* 261–278.

Pergande, J. M. (1988). *Organization choice: The role of job characteristics* (Report No. 88–2). Brookfield, WI: International Foundation of Employee Benefit Plans.

Personick, M. E. (1984). White-collar pay determination under range-of-rate systems. *Monthly Labor Review, 107*(12), 25–30.

Peters, T. (1987). *Thriving on chaos.* New York: Knopf.

Pfeffer, J., & Davis-Blake, A. (1987). Understanding organizational wage structures: A resource dependence approach. *Academy of Management Journal, 30,* 437–455.

Phillips, J. S., & Freedman, S. M. (1985). Contingent pay and instrinsic task interest: Moderating effects of work values. *Journal of Applied Psychology, 70,* 306–313.

Piacentini, J. S., & Cerino, T. J. (1990). *EBRI data-book on employee benefits.* Washington, DC: Employee Benefits Research Institute.

Pierce, J. L., Rubenfeld, S., & Morgan, S. (1991). Employee ownership: A conceptual model of process and effects. *Academy of Management Review, 16,* 121–144.

Porter, M. E. (1990). *The competitive advantage of nations.* New York: Free Press.

Pritchard, R. D., Jones, S. D., Roth, P. L., Stuebing, K. K., & Ekeberg, S. E. (1988). Effects of group feedback, goal setting, and incentives on organizational productivity [Monograph]. *Journal of Applied Psychology, 73,* 337–358.

Proskech, S. (1991, July 7). Edges fray on Volvo's brave new humanists. *New York Times,* p. 5.

Puffer, S. M., & Weintrop, J. B. (1991). Corporate performance and CEO turnover: The role of performance expectations. *Administrative Science Quarterly, 36,* 1–19.

Rabin, B. R. (1987). *Executive compensation and firm performance: An empirical analysis.* Unpublished doctoral dissertation, Cornell University, Ithaca, NY.

Raff, D. M. G., & Summers, L. H. (1987). Did Henry Ford pay efficiency wages? *Journal of Labor Economics, 5,* S57–S86.

Rappaport, A. (1978). Executive incentives vs. corporate growth. *Harvard Business Review, 56*(4), 81–88.

Reich, R. B. (1983). *The next American frontier.* New York: Penguin.

Reich, R. B. (1990, January–February). Who is us? *Harvard Business Review, 68,* 53–64.

Remick, H. (1984). *Comparable worth and wage discrimination.* Philadelphia: Temple University Press.

Reynolds, L. G. (1951). *The structure of labor markets: Wages and labor mobility in theory and practice*. New York: Harper & Brothers.

Rice, R. W., Phillips, S. M., & McFarlin, D. B. (1990). Multiple discrepancies and pay satisfaction. *Journal of Applied Psychology, 75,* 386–393.

Rosen, B., Templeton, M. E., & Kirchline, K. (1981). First few years on the job: Women in management. *Business Horizons, 24*(12), 26–29.

Rosenbaum, J. E. (1979). Tournament mobility: Career patterns in a corporation. *Administrative Science Quarterly, 24,* 220–241.

Rosenbaum, J. E. (1984). *Career mobility in a corporate hierarchy*. San Diego: Academic Press.

Rosenbloom, J., & Hallman, G.V. (1981). *Employee benefits planning*. Englewood Cliffs, NJ: Prentice Hall.

Ross, A. M. (1957). The external wage structure. In G. W. Taylor & F. C. Pierson (Eds.), *New concepts in wage determination*. New York: McGraw-Hill.

Ross, A. M. (1958). Do we have a new industrial feudalism? *American Economic Review, 48,* 903–920.

Rousseau, D. M. (1990). New hire perceptions of their own and their employer's obligations: A study of psychological contracts. *Journal of Organizational Behavior, 11,* 389–400.

Ruiz Quintanilla, S. A. (1990). Major work meaning patterns: Toward a holistic picture. In U. Kleinbeck et al. (Eds.), *Work motivation*. Hillsdale, NJ: Elbaum.

Ryan, R. M., Mims, V., & Koestner, R. (1983). Relation of reward contingency and interpersonal context to intrinsic motivation: A review and test using cognitive evaluation theory. *Journal of Personality and Social Psychology, 45,* 736–750.

Rynes, S. L. (1987). Compensation strategies for recruiting. *Topics in Total Compensation, 2,* 185–196.

Rynes, S. L., & Barber, A. E. (1990). Applicant attraction strategies: An organizational perspective. *Academy of Management Review 15*(2), 286–310.

Rynes, S. L., & Boudreau, J. W. (1986). College recruiting in large organizations: Practice, evaluation, and research implications. *Personnel Psychology, 39,* 729–757.

Rynes, S. L., & Gerhart, B. (1990). Interviewer assessments of applicant "fit": An exploratory investigation. *Personnel Psychology, 43,* 178–196.

Rynes, S. L., & Milkovich, G. T. (1986). Wage surveys: Dispelling some myths about the "market wage." *Personnel Psychology, 39,* 71–90.

Rynes, S. L., Schwab, D. P., & Heneman, H. G., III. (1983). The role of pay and market variability in job application decisions. *Organizational Behavior and Human Performance, 31,* 353–364.

Rynes, S. L., Weber, C., & Milkovich, G. T. (1989). Effects of market survey rates, job evaluation and job gender on job pay. *Journal of Applied Psychology, 74,* 114–123.

Ryscavage, P., & Henle, P. (1990). Earnings inequality in the 1980s. *Monthly Labor Review, 113*(12), 3–16.

Salter, M. S. (1973). Tailor incentive compensation to strategy. *Harvard Business Review, 51*(2), 94–102.

Santora, J. E. (1991, February). Du Pont returns to the drawing board. *Personnel Journal, 34–36.*

Scarpello, V., Huber, V., & Vandenberg, R. J. (1988). Compensation satisfaction: Its measurement and dimensionality. *Journal of Applied Psychology, 73,* 163–171.

Schaeffer, R. (1975). *Comparison of organization staffing patterns*. New York: Conference Board.

Schiller, B. R., & Weiss, R. D. (1979). The impact of private pensions on firm attachment. *Review of Economics and Statistics, 61,* 369–380.

Schneider, B. (1983). An interactionist perspective on organizational effectiveness. In K. S. Cameron & D. A. Whetten (Eds.), *Organizational effectiveness: A comparison of multiple models*. Orlando, FL: Academic Press.

Scholl, R. W., Cooper, E. A., & McKenna, J. F. (1987). Referent selection in determining equity perceptions: Differential effects on behavioral and attitudinal outcomes. *Personnel Psychology, 40,* 113–124.

Schroeder, M. (1988, November 7). Watching the bottom line instead of the clock. *Business Week,* 134–136.

Schuster, M. H. (1984a). The Scanlon plan: A longitudinal analysis. *Journal of Applied Behavioral Science, 20,* 23–28.

Schuster, M. H. (1984b). *Union-management cooperation: Structure, process, and impact*. Kalamazoo, MI: Upjohn Institute.

Schuster, M. (1986, Summer). Gainsharing: The state of the art. *Compensation and Benefits Management,* 285–290.

Schuster, M. H. (1990, March). *Gainsharing: Current issues and research needs* (Workshop). Cornell University, School of Industrial and Labor Relations, Ithaca, NY.

Schwab, D. P. (1973). Impact of alternative compensation systems on pay valence and instrumentality perceptions. *Journal of Applied Psychology, 58*, 308–312.

Schwab, D. P. (1980). Job evaluation and pay-setting: Concepts and practices. In E. R. Livernash (Ed.), *Comparable worth: Issues and alternatives.* Washington, DC: Equal Employment Advisory Council.

Schwab, D. P. (1985). Job evaluation research and research needs. In H. Hartmann (Ed.), *Comparable worth: New directions for research.* Washington, DC: National Academy Press.

Schwab, D. P., & Dyer, L. D. (1973). The motivational impact of a compensation system on employee performance. *Organizational Behavior and Human Performance, 9*, 215–225.

Schwab, D. P., & Grams, R. (1985). Sex-related errors in job evaluation: A "real-world" test. *Journal of Applied Psychology, 70*, 533–539.

Schwab, D. P., & Heneman, H. G., III. (1986). Assessment of a consensus-based multiple information source job evaluation system. *Journal of Applied Psychology, 71*, 354–356.

Schwab, D. P., & Olson, C. A. (1990). Merit pay practices: Implications for pay-performance relationships. *Industrial and Labor Relations Review, 43*, 237S–255S.

Scott, W. E., Jr., Farh, J., & Podsakoff, P. M. (1988). The effects of "intrinsic" and "extrinsic" reinforcement contingencies on task behavior. *Organizational Behavior and Human Decision Processes, 41*, 405–425.

Shapiro, C., & Stiglitz, J. E. (1984). Equilibrium unemployment as a worker discipline device. *American Economic Review, 74*, 433–444.

Sheridan, J. E., Slocum, J. W., Jr., Buda, R., & Thompson, R. C. (1990). Effects of corporate sponsorship and departmental power on career tournaments. *Academy of Management Journal, 33*, 578–602.

Simon, H. A. (1951). A formal theory of the employment relationship. *Econometrica, 19*, 293–305.

Slichter, S., Healy, J., & Livernash, E. R. (1960). *The impact of collective bargaining on management.* Washington, DC: Brookings Institution.

Smith, A. (1937). *An inquiry into the nature and causes of the wealth of nations.* New York: Random House.

Smith, P. C. (1976). Behavior, results, and organizational effectiveness: The problem of criteria. In M. D. Dunnette (Ed.), *Handbook of industrial and organizational psychology* (1st ed., pp. 745–775). Chicago: Rand McNally.

Smith, P. C., Kendall, L. M., & Hulin, C. L. (1969). *The measurement of satisfaction in work and retirement.* Chicago: Rand McNally.

Smith, R. S. (1988). Comparable worth: Limited coverage and the exacerbation of inequality. *Industrial and Labor Relations Review, 61*, 227–239.

Snow, C. C., & Hambrick, D. C. (1980). Measuring organizational strategies: Some theoretical and methodological problems. *Academy of Management Review, 5*, 527–538.

Spence, M. A. (1973). Job market signalling. *Quarterly Journal of Economics, 87*, 355–374.

Spillerman, S., & Petersen, T. (1990). *Organizational structure, determinants of promotion, and gender differences in attainment.* Unpublished manuscript, Columbia University, New York.

Staw, B. M., Bell, N. E., & Clausen, J. A. (1986). The dispositional approach to job attitudes: A lifetime longitudinal test. *Administrative Science Quarterly, 31*, 56–77.

Staw, B. M., & Ross, J. (1985). Stability in the midst of change: A dispositional approach to job attitudes. *Journal of Applied Psychology, 70*, 469–480.

Stonebraker, P. W. (1985). Flexibility and incentive benefits: A guide to program development. *Compensation Review, 17*(2), 40–53.

Stonich, P. J. (1981). Using rewards in implementing strategy. *Strategic Management Journal, 2*, 345–352.

Taylor, F. W. (1967). *Principles of scientific management.* New York: Norton.

Teel, K. S. (1986). Are merit raises really based on merit? *Personnel Journal, 65*(3), 88–95.

Tolchinsky, P. D., & King, D. C. (1980). Do goals mediate the effects of incentives on performance? *Academy of Management Review, 5*, 455–467.

Tornow, W. W., & Pinto, P. R. (1976). The development of a managerial job taxonomy: A system for describing, classifying, and evaluating executive positions. *Journal of Applied Psychology, 61*, 410–418.

Tosi, H. L., Jr., & Gomez-Mejia, L. R. (1989). The decoupling of CEO pay and performance: An agency theory perspective. *Administrative Science Quarterly, 34,* 169–189.

Treiman, D. J., & Hartmann, H. I. (1981). *Women, work, and wages: Equal pay for jobs of equal value.* Washington, DC: National Academy Press.

Tuttle, T. C. (1991). Book review of "The men who discovered quality." *Academy of Management Executive, 5*(2), 98–100.

Unseen apples and small carrots. (1991, April 13). *Economist,* 75.

U.S. Chamber of Commerce. (1991). *Employee Benefits 1990.* Washington, DC: U.S. Chamber of Commerce.

Vroom, V. H. (1964). *Work and motivation* (pp. 8–19). New York: Wiley.

Wagner, J. A., III, Rubin, P., & Callahan, T. J. (1988). Incentive payment and nonmanagerial productivity: An interrupted time series analysis of magnitude and trend. *Organizational Behavior and Human Decision Processes, 42,* 47–74.

Wallace, M. J., Jr. (1990). *Rewards and renewal: America's search for competitive advantage through alternative pay strategies.* Scottsdale, AZ: American Compensation Association.

Wallace, M. J., Jr., & Fay, C. H. (1988). *Compensation theory and practice.* Boston: PWS-Kent.

Wazeter, D. L. (1991). *The determinants and consequences of teacher salary schedules.* Unpublished doctoral dissertation, Cornell University, Ithaca, NY.

Weber, J., Driscoll, L., & Brandt, R. (1990, December). Farewell fast track. *Business Week,* 192–200.

Weber, C., & Rynes, S. (1991). Effects of compensation strategy on job pay decisions. *Academy of Management Journal, 34*(1), 86–109.

Weiner, N. (1980). Determinants and behavioral consequences of pay satisfaction: A comparison of two models. *Personnel Psychology, 33,* 741–757.

Weiss, A. (1987). Incentives and worker behavior: Some evidence. In H. R. Nalbantian (Ed.), *Incentives, cooperation and risk taking.* Lanham, MD: Rowman & Littlefield.

Weiss, D. J., Davis, R. V., England, G. W., & Lofquist, L. N. (1967). *Manual for the Minnesota Satisfaction Questionnaire: Minnesota Studies in Vocational Rehabilitation,* Bulletin 22. Industrial Relations Center, University of Minnesota, Minneapolis.

Weitzman, M. L. (1984). *The share economy.* Cambridge, MA: Harvard University Press.

Weitzman, M. L. (1985). The simple macro economics of profit sharing. *American Economic Review, 75,* 937–953.

Weitzman, M. L., & Kruse, D. L. (1990). Profit sharing and productivity. In A. S. Blinder (Ed.), *Paying for productivity.* Wasington, DC: The Brookings Institute.

Whyte, W. F. (1955). *Money and motivation.* New York: Harper & Row.

Williams, M. L., & Dreher, G. F. (1990). *Compensation system attributes and applicant pool characterisstics.* San Francisco: National Academy of Management.

Williamson, O. (1975). *Markets and hierarchies: Analysis and antitrust implications.* New York: Free Press.

Wilson, M., Northcraft, G. B., & Neale, M. A. (1985). The perceived value of fringe benefits. *Personnel Psychology, 38,* 309–320.

Womack, J. P., Jones, D. T., & Roos, D. (1990). *The machine that changed the world.* New York: Macmillan.

Wright, P. M. (1989). Test of the mediating role of goals in the incentive-performance relationship. *Journal of Applied Psychology, 74,* 699–705.

Yellen, J. L. (1984). Efficiency wage models of unemployment. *American Economic Review, 74,* 200–205.

Zedeck, S. (1977). An information processing model and approach to the study of motivation. *Organizational Behavior and Human Performance, 18,* 47–77.

Ziskin, I. (1986). Knowledge-based pay: A strategic analysis. *ILR Report,* 16–22.

Zucker, L. G. (1987). Institutional theories of organization. *American Review of Sociology, 13,* 443–464.

CHAPTER 10

Stress in Organizations

Robert L. Kahn
Philippe Byosiere
University of Michigan

In this chapter, organizational stress is defined as a rapidly expanding field, characterized by disagreements about terminology and definitions but underlying agreement on the variables of interest and their causal relationships. These relationships constitute a hypothetical sequence that begins with organizational antecedents to stress and then identifies the stressors they generate, the perception and appraisal of those stressors by individuals, the short-term responses evoked, and the effects of long-term exposure. At each step in this causal chain, the moderating effects of individual differences and interpersonal relationships are acknowledged.

Eight models that incorporate this sequence and that have been influential in stress research are compared, and empirical findings since 1976 are discussed in terms of an elaboration of the ISR model proposed by the authors. The chapter ends with a critical evaluation of current approaches to stress management and a set of proposals for further improvement in the field seen as already increasing in quality as well as quantity.

Introduction

THE CURRENT STATE of research on stress in organizational settings can be described in terms of eight assertions:

- It is rapidly expanding; during the past decade the accessible bibliography of research on organizational stress has grown from perhaps a hundred to several thousand references.

- Some of this growth reflects the recognition of organizational stress as a research domain defined by the intersection of two previously separate lines of work—organizational research concerned with the effects of organizational demands on individual well-being, and stress research concerned with the source or context in which the stressors arise and the responses occur.

- Like the field of stress research as a whole, the field of organizational stress is marked by vigorous disagreements about models and theories, beginning with the definition of stress itself.

- On close examination, however, these disagreements appear to be more involved with terminology and research priorities than with major substance. Beneath this level of dispute, substantial agreement exists on the major categories of variables relevant for understanding stress and its effects in organizational settings.

- Research on organizational stress shows a considerable divergence between methodological precept and example, that is, between preaching and practice. For example, the importance of obtaining both objective and subjective measures of organizational stresses and responses to them is often asserted but seldom enacted.

- Research on organizational stress has concentrated on the consequences of stressful situations and has neglected the causes of those situations. In other words, stress has been treated overwhelmingly as a dependent variable rather than an intervening or independent variable. As a result, we know too little about the organizational and extraorganizational factors that generate stressful stimuli.

- Organizational theory and research have been too little concerned with organizational and interpersonal factors that might serve as moderators, buffers, or even as antidotes to stresses and their effects. Except for some suggestive work on the stress-buffering effects of social support in the work setting, empirical research in this promising area is almost nonexistent.

- Finally, concomitant with the surge of research activity in the field of organizational stress has come a flood of practitioner activity in the field of stress reduction and stress management. This activity, however, has been little informed by current research, and it has contributed little in the way of tested results. Practitioners who offer advice and service for dealing with organizational stress emphasize methods intended to increase host resistance rather than to decrease the imposition of stress on individuals. Moreover, the methods used are seldom tested, and the methods used by a given practitioner seldom vary. When the remedy is thus constant regardless of the illness, one must consider the possibility that it reflects the enthusiasm of the practitioner rather than the needs of the patient. In short, the mutual enhancement of research and practice is more a potentiality than a fact in the field of organizational stressors.

This chapter reflects our judgments, interpretations, and biases. The exposition of research on organizational stress that follows, however, should enable readers to accept or reject our interpretations and to draw conclusions of their own. We hope for agreement, of course, but we are more concerned that the chapter contribute to understanding the nature, sources, and effects of organizational stress. Its contributions to that goal will be made, if at all, through the research formulations, designs, and findings of research workers in this important territory. It is primarily for them that the chapter is written.

Our exposition of research on stress in organizational settings is built around three main topics—(a) concepts and theories, (b) a review of empirical research, and (c) priorities for future research on organizational stress. These topics and their major components are presented in this chapter.

Stress: Concepts and Theories

Conceptual History

Conceptual disagreements often motivate excursions into etymology and scientific history, and so it has been with the concept of stress. As a result, the history of the stress concept and its various uses has been told often enough to make detailed recapitulation unnecessary here. Readers who want a more thorough review should turn to Lazarus (1966), Hinkle (1974), Mason (1975), or Selye (1982).

The term *stress* has been in the English language for a long time and has still earlier origins in Latin as a verb meaning to injure, molest, or constrain. During the 18th and 19th centuries, the major uses of the term identified it as a force or pressure exerted upon a material object or person, a usage that is close to the more precise definition that developed in science and engineering. In physics, the concept of stress was used in mechanics, the study of solid bodies, where investigators were concerned with the effects of external forces on the size and shape of the objects to which they were applied. Load, measured in units of force per area (e.g., pounds per square inch), was the term used to describe such external forces. Stress referred to the internal resisting force, presumably equal and measured in the same way. Strain or distortion was the resulting change in the object under

study, the ratio of the change in size or shape to its original size or shape.

This precision of definition was not carried into medicine and biology when the concept of stress was borrowed by Osler (1910), Cannon (1935), and others earlier in the 20th century. Osler (1910) referred to some of his patients (or rather, their systems) as being subjected to stress and strain, which he considered to be a factor in many cases of angina pectoris. And Cannon (1935) spoke of his experimental subjects as being "under stress" when they were exposed to such conditions as cold, lack of oxygen, low blood sugar, loss of blood, and "excitement." Neither usage is precise, and the work of both these pioneers leaves us uncertain as to whether they meant the term stress to denote the external condition or force imposed on an organism, or some presumably universalistic response of organisms to such external demands. Selye (1936, 1982), whose influential writings on stress span almost half a century, is more explicit but not always consistent. He wrote in 1936 (p. 3) and reiterated in 1982 (p. 7) that *"stress is the nonspecific (that is, common) result of any demand upon the body,* be the effect mental or somatic."

Since his days as a medical student, Selye had been intrigued by the fact that "diverse noxious agents" seemed to generate the same physiological responses, which he described as involving enlargement and discoloration of the adrenal glands, intense shrinkage of the thymus and lymph nodes, and concomitant development of bloody stomach ulcers. Selye 1936 first observed these responses in laboratory rats that had been injected with extracts of cattle ovaries as part of an experimental series on ovarian hormones. In subsequent work (1960, 1971, 1973, 1975), he described more fully the complex biochemical sequence that he called the *general adaptation syndrome* (GAS) or *stress response.* He clearly intended stress to refer to these altered internal states, and he proposed *stressor* as the term designating the variety of stimuli capable of evoking this common response (GAS). But his usage contin-ued to vary; even the 1982 chapter, in describing physiological changes (enlarged adrenals, shrunken thymus and lymph nodes, and bleeding stomach ulcers) in "alarmed" rats, states that these experimental changes were evoked by the frustrating psychological stress of being immobilized. In this statement, the stress term seems again to have moved outside the organism and is used to describe the external condition (physical restraint) to which the physiological changes were a cumulative response.

Stress research by psychologists and psychiatrists became visible in the scientific literature only after World War II, and much of it stemmed from the experiences of that war. Prominent examples include Grinker and Spiegel's (1945) *Men Under Stress*, Kardiner and Spiegel's (1947) *War Stress and Neurotic Illness*, and Janis' (1951) *Air War and Emotional Stress*. Lazarus' experimental work on the effects of psychological stress on task performance dates from almost the same period (Lazarus, Deese, & Osler, 1952). By 1958, when Janis published his research on surgery as psychological stress, he made an observation that has been repeated often in the decades since and that remains all too true: "Although the term 'psychological stress' is frequently used by psychologists and psychiatrists, there is at present no generally agreed upon definition" (p. 11).

The research contributions of organizational psychologists, which began about this time, did not resolve these conceptual differences. Organizational researchers have tended to study situational variables hypothesized to be stressors, that is, to create anxiety, emotional tension, sleep disorders, gastric disturbances, and other such symptoms. Kahn, Wolfe, Quinn, and Snoek (1964), in one of the earliest of such studies, investigated the hypothesized effects (correlates) of two situational variables, role conflict and role ambiguity, which they referred to as organizational stresses.

In subsequent years, other researchers have studied a wide range of stimuli in work settings, some of them characteristics of the physical work environment, some social or sociotechnical, and some temporal. All these investigators would agree that they were working in the domain of organizational or occupational stress, but they would by no means agree on whether the stress term should be used to designate either the objective stimuli in the work setting, the subjective perception and appraisal of those stimuli by the individual, or some subsequent psychological response. In short, the old arguments of conceptual definition and technology persist; organizational researchers have enlarged the arena without resolving the conflicts. It is appropriate, therefore, to put such conceptual disagreements first in the list of problems and gaps in stress research.

Conceptual Problems and Gaps

Disagreements Over Definitions. These disagreements, as we have seen, are perhaps the most conspicuous of unresolved differences among stress researchers, both those who work in the laboratory and those who work directly in organizational settings. We do not believe, however, that these definitional matters are in themselves a major hindrance to theoretical progress, nor that they can be best resolved by direct efforts to adopt a standard terminology. As we shall see when we consider the commonalities among stress researchers, especially those concerned with work settings and their psychological effects, there is far more agreement about what is important in such research than about definitions. Researchers agree, for example, that it is important to identify the objective sources of stress-indicative responses, the immediate cognitive or affective response to them, and the long-term effect on psychological, physiological, or behavioral functions. In short, the terminological differences mask a substrate of substantial agreement. As for the terminological differ-, ences themselves, so long as investigators are explicit about their own working definitions, readers can translate into the terminology of their choice, and except for the nuisance of doing so, little damage is done. In the long run, we are all likely to adopt the concepts and definitions of a genuinely comprehensive and satisfactory theory of organizational stress. Until our theories and empirical work approach that ideal more nearly, the recurring discussions about conceptual definitions are more valuable for mutual education than for firm conclusions.

Stressors and Stimuli. Stress researchers, except for those content to work wholly within the skin of their subjects, are concerned with identifying and measuring external conditions or events (stimuli) that evoke responses indicative of stress—adverse physiological changes, physical symptoms, psychological tensions, and the like. We will call such stimuli *stressors.* But the range of individual differences is so great that almost any stimulus may evoke stress symptoms in someone. What then? Must we adopt a wholly subjective, or at least individual-specific, definition of stressors? Must we concede that the same stimulus— a final examination or a production quota, or the imposition of a piece rate—is either a stressor or not, depending on the individual?

Basowitz, Persky, Korchin, and Grinker (1955) wrestled with this problem in their research on stress and anxiety, and their conclusions can be appropriately generalized as follows: Any stimulus may in principle arouse a stress response in a particular *individual.* Stress researchers and theorists, however, are interested in that subset of stimuli that produce such responses in most individuals; these stimuli can properly be called *stressors* (or *stresses*, for those who prefer that terminology). This does not condemn us to case-by-case post facto determinations of whether or not a stimulus is stressful. A stimulus is

defined as stressful (i.e., a stressor) because its effect is assumed, hypothesized, and (cumulatively) demonstrated to have certain undesirable effects—adverse physiological changes of the kind described by Selye (1975), decrements in role performance, emotional tensions, onset of physical symptoms such as sleep disorders and gastric disturbances, and so forth—in the population about which we propose to generalize.

When we encounter an individual case in which such a stressor condition generates none of these characteristic stress responses (i.e., strains), we are not led to assert that the stimulus was not a stressor; rather, we become interested in discovering the genetic endowment, previous experience, or coping style that accounts for the person's ability to function without strain under conditions of stress (i.e., the imposition of one or more stressors). In a sense, this is a response-based definition of what constitutes a stressor, but it is not the response of the particular subject under study that sets the definition. Rather, the definition of a stressor, or the level at which any given stimulus can be so designated, is based on the responses of a normal representative population. Those responses may be determined with known probability by means of representative samples; more often they are inferred from the cumulative evidence of previous research.

Individual Differences. To argue that the definition of external stimuli as stressors should be independent of the responses of the individual under study is not to deny the importance of individual differences in stress research. This point becomes obvious in the domain of organizational practice, where the extensive use of tests for selection and placement can be seen as a strategy for locating individuals in jobs that will not exceed their ability to function without undue strain.

The implication for stress research, perhaps especially in organizations, is that main effects are not enough; in addition to learning, for example, that the level of role conflict at work is associated with emotional tensions, we need to know the extent to which that response varies among individuals and what individual characteristics explain the variations. These interaction effects may occur at any of the links in the causal sequence from external stressor to long-term effect on health—that is, between the stressor and the subjects' immediate perception of it, between that perception and the cognitive appraisal of its meaning and potential threat, between those cognitions and short-term responses of emotional and behavioral (and physiological) change, and between such short-term responses and the longer term well-being (health, illness, role performance, quality of life) of the individual.

Most stress research does not include such interaction effects, and there is little agreement about what individual descriptors are most relevant for their assessment: genetic endowment (physical and mental), personality characteristics, child-rearing and early experience, and so on. The aim of including such variables in stress research is to measure and understand those attributes that epidemiologists call *host resistance*, the ability of an individual to function in the presence of a stressor without negative effect. To what extent there are individual characteristics that serve this purpose in a generalized way, enhancing resistance to the whole range of organizational stressors, and to what extent different stressors interact with different individual characteristics, remains to be learned.

Eustress and Distress.   To regard every organizational demand on the person as a stressor, and somehow therefore undesirable, would be naive and unsatisfactory. It would imply that the preferred state of the human being is inactivity, which we know to be untrue. People seek activity, including the kinds of activities that use abilities they value and, not infrequently, activities that challenge those abilities and require the acquisition of new ones.

In his later years, Selye (1982) became increasingly interested in this issue and put increasing emphasis on the distinction between good stress and bad stress or, as he called them, *eustress* and *distress*. He refers to eustress also as the stress of fulfillment. These definitions, which are less than precise, are part of a Selye script about human nature that is part demonstrated fact, part assumption, and perhaps part faith. The key elements begin with the assertion that human beings are by nature intended to work—that is, to set tasks and attempt to complete them successfully. Doing so involves demands on the mind and body, and exposure to these demands evokes that sequence of physiological changes that Selye called the general adaptation syndrome. To that extent, distressing and eustressing stressors (stimuli) would seem to be similar in their effects. The difference seems to lie in the prospects for fulfillment or achievement. Without such challenges and opportunities to use existing capacities successfully, muscles atrophy and mental abilities diminish. With them, the inevitable processes of wear and tear continue, but they cannot be avoided in any case. The idea is not to avoid the stress of life, but to maximize the eustress component.

This is an area of importance and controversy and is therefore in need of investigation. Mason (1975) and Monat and Lazarus (1985) argue that Selye overstates the generality or nonspecificity of the physiological reaction to external stressors. They assert that laboratory and field studies of physical stressors (heat, fasting, exercise) have confounded the effects of the physical stressors themselves and the typically accompanying psychological (cognitive, emotional) factors. Mason (1975) reports heat studies with human beings and monkeys in which heat per se was shown not to increase adrenal cortical hormone levels when measures were taken to avoid "such factors as novelty or extremely sudden or severe temperature changes" (p. 24).

Lazarus (1974) concludes that the nature and severity of the stress disorder depends on at least three factors: (a) the formal characteristics of the environmental demands, (b) the quality of the emotional response generated by the demands, or in particular individuals facing these demands, and (c) the process of coping mobilized by the stressful combination.

Deprivation and Excess. Many variables become stressors not only when present in excess but also when at lower than optimal levels. Examples in organizational life come easily to mind—too much work or too little, supervision too detailed or too general, required interaction with colleagues too frequent or infrequent. Levi (1972) represented this phenomenon schematically in Figure 1, which suggests that stimulus deprivation and excess (understimulation and overstimulation) are equally and symmetrically stressful.

It is a research task, however, to determine the extent to which that idealized curve conforms to the empirical facts, and the facts are almost certain to be different for different variables. For example, it is plausible to hypothesize that both excessive variety and severe lack of variety in work content will be stressful, but we do not know whether the curve thus generated in relation to a specific criterion of stress will be symmetrical or asymmetrical. Moreover, the complete lack of some stimulus conditions may not be stressful; for example, is the absence or near absence of interpersonal conflict stressful?

Few research investigators have dealt with this problem. The common practice in stress research, laboratory and field, is to deal with only half of the Levi schema. Thus, investigators who have studied lack of variety at work (monotony) have not at the same time looked at the effects of excess variety. An exception is the work of French, Caplan, and Harrison (1982) in testing their hypotheses about goodness of fit at work. They found that strain (an index of overall psychological strain) was likely to occur when the job was either too complex or too simple for the individual's preference. The pattern was similar for role ambiguity, responsibility for persons, work load, and overtime; too much and too little of these variables led to increased strain scores. The relationships were neither uniform nor symmetrical, however, and for most variables, excess was more stressful than insufficiency. Moreover, the definition of excess and insufficiency in terms of individually reported preferences was less instructive than definition in more objective terms. The examples remind us of the need for studying hypothesized stressors in their full variable range.

Combinations and Interactions. The logic of experiments, which is often erroneously interpreted to mean manipulating or observing the effects of only one variable at a time, requires adaptation to deal with the multivariate stressors of organizational life. The limited number of laboratory studies that have dealt with the comparative effects of stressors imposed singly and in combination suggest a pattern that is more nearly exponential than additive. For example, Dean (1966) subjected rats to three stimuli—heat, altitude (barometric pressure), and random vibration—separately and in combination. The animal death rate ranged from 0 to 7.5 percent when these stressor conditions were imposed separately, but heat and vibration in combination caused a death rate of 65 percent, and the heat and altitude combination produced similar effects. The experimenter did not assess the effect of all three stressor conditions simultaneously.

For stress research to have the external validity to which we aspire, it must deal increasingly with combinations of stressors and distinguish between their effects as single stressors and in combinations—at least in those

FIGURE 1

Theoretical Model of the Relation Between Physical Stress as Defined by Selye and Various Levels of Stimulation

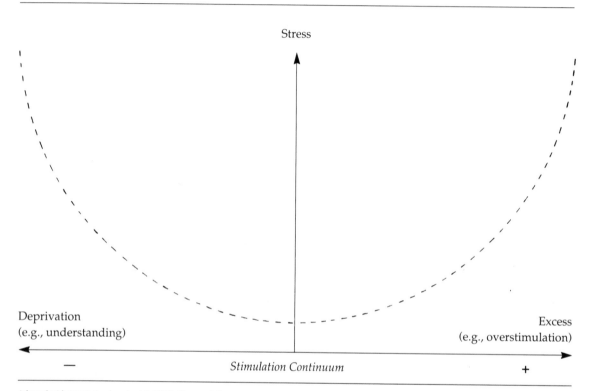

Adapted with permission from Levi, L. (1972). Stress and distress in response to psychosocial stimuli. Laboratory and real life studies on sympathoadreno-medullary and related reactions. *Acta Media Scandinavica, 191* (Supplement No. 528), p. 14. Stockholm, Sweden. Reprinted with permission from L. Levi (1972). *Stress and distress in response to psychosocial stimuli: Laboratory and real life studies on sympathoadrenomedullary and related reactions.* New York: Pergamon Press.

combinations commonly encountered in the world of work.

Short-term Versus Long-term Effects. Toxicologists have learned that the effects of occupational hazards and pollutants are often long deferred. It is plausible that psychosocial stressors at work have long-term effects that are different from those manifested more quickly. There may be threshold effects; the folklore of organizations includes many stories of employees who erupted after long periods of seeming docility. And there may

well be training or adaptation effects, so that a stimulus condition that was initially stressful (i.e., created measurable strains) became less so as tolerance increased or gains in ability were attained. Moreover, these patterns may differ for different indicators of strain; employees who report that they have become habituated to certain noise levels may nevertheless be suffering cumulative hearing loss.

We know little about the short-term versus long-term effects of stressors at work. Laboratory experiments are almost always brief; cross-sectional field studies almost never attempt to determine the time of onset or the duration of exposure to reported stressful stimuli. Field experiments in the reduction of stress through organizational changes or job design are also characteristically brief, and they are unfortunately rare (Orpen, 1982; Payne, Jick, & Burke, 1982). We need to expand the time frame within which to investigate the effects of stress at work. This is best done by means of longitudinal studies, but it can be begun in cross-sectional studies by obtaining information about the time of onset for the conditions of interest.

Markers and Surrogates.   Perhaps the single largest aggregation of research findings that link work and health is the differential incidence of strain indicators (disease, disability, days of work lost) among workers in different industries and occupations. Occupation and industry are markers for stress in these studies, and the findings are of obvious pragmatic value. They become scientifically useful, however, only to the extent that they lead to identification of the variables (stressors) that explain these gross differences among job categories. As organizational psychologists, we want to know the psychological, social, and sociotechnical variables that explain such occupational differences.

Holland (1976) provided a thorough review and critique of the occupational literature, which emphasized its atheoretical character and the consequent difficulties, both in interpreting observed differences and in extending the classification system to include the flood of new jobs. He concluded that a new system of occupational classification was needed. The issue for stress research is more limited: If occupational data are to be directly useful, we need to know the pattern of role demands and opportunities—in short, the pattern of stressors—that characterizes different occupations. In addition to urging occupational researchers to include major stressor measures in their work, stress researchers can routinely

identify occupational categories in their own field studies.

The literature of stressful life events provides a more controversial example of the use of surrogate or marker measures. Critics of the life-events approach point out that most research in this tradition includes no attempt to specify the underlying variables, that is, the properties that make "stressful life events" stressful. The counterargument is that such events—serious illness, bereavement, job loss, and the like—are the real stuff of life and that the stress of life can best be understood in these terms. It can be further argued that some life-event researchers, especially the Dohrenwends and their colleagues, have stipulated very clearly the variables in terms of which they chose specific life events. Nevertheless, most stress research that uses life-event scores as independent variables (stressors) simply reports a summed (or summed and weighted) score as a total measure of stress.

For example, Holmes and Rahe (1967), whose list of 43 life events published as the *Social Readjustment Rating Scale* has been perhaps the most widely used single instrument in stress research, chose those events because the medical charts of patients indicated that such events tended to cluster at the time of disease onset (Holmes & Masuda, 1974). That list and the method of its construction have been criticized on the grounds that identifying the time of disease onset is difficult and uncertain (Dohrenwend, Krasnoff, Askenasy, & Dohrenwend, 1982), that events which "cluster" at that time plausibly include concomitants and effects of the disease as well as causes (Hudgens, 1974), and that the event categories themselves are ambiguous with respect to the nature and magnitude of the imposed stress. For example, "change in responsibilities at work," which is one of the Holmes and Rahe items, mingles gains and losses, changes sought, and changes imposed.

The Dohrenwends and their colleagues have provided stress researchers with a more comprehensive list of events, an explicit description of the sophisticated methods by which it was developed, and some indication of the underlying descriptor variables for each event. These descriptors include breadth of setting, desirability, central actor (respondent or other), and inclusion or exclusion of the event in the hypothesized *pathogenic triad*— events likely to involve physical exhaustion, loss of social support, or *fateful negative* consequences (Dohrenwend et al., 1982).

These variables were used by the authors as modes of stratification in constructing the PERI *Life Events List,* an extremely useful instrument for stress researchers. We believe that the field of stress research can be further advanced by better linking of the life-events and continuous-variable approaches. This requires increased stipulation of the variables that underlie specific event categories.

Stress as a Dependent Variable. For many stress researchers, the topic of investigation begins with a stressor, either induced experimentally or occurring naturally. Organizational psychologists, however, must be concerned with the organizational and extraorganizational properties that are antecedent to the stressors in work settings. In other words, we should think in terms of models in which stressors are intervening variables; we are interested not only in their effects but in their organizational causes.

The reasons are both theoretical and pragmatic. To be an organizational psychologist implies a concern with organizational theory, that is, with the explanation of organizational phenomena. If demotion is stressful, we want to understand why—for example, because it leads to reduced esteem by significant others who communicate that fact in various ways, which leads to reduced self-esteem, and so forth. But we want also to understand the organizational properties, for example, size, managerial philosophy, growth, or shrinkage,

that make demotions more or less frequent, and we want to know the extraorganizational factors, such as industry competitiveness, technological change, or merger, that are likely to affect characteristics at the organizational level. For the present, systematic inquiry into the origins of stressors must be counted among the gaps in organizational stress research.

Some Theoretical Models of Stress

Many models of stress have been proposed by research scholars. The models reflect the mix of disciplines—psychology, sociology, biology, and medicine—that is typical of the field. Most of the models are not explicit about organizational variables, but several are specifically intended to guide organizational research. For purposes of exposition, we have chosen seven, beginning with the most general and ending with the model we use as a basis for reviewing empirical research on stress in organizations. In combination, these models provide a summary of what stress researchers do and aspire to do.

Elliott and Eisdorfer's Framework for Interactions Between the Individual and the Environment

Elliott and Eisdorfer (1982) describe the stress research model that is the most general and perhaps the least explicit regarding organizational variables, two facts that reflect its interdisciplinary origins. It was developed in the course of a study by the Institute of Medicine/National Academy of Sciences by a steering committee of some 24 research workers. Among them were psychologists, sociologists, and research physicians of several specialties—psychiatry, geriatrics, internal medicine, and neuroendocrinology. The framework presented in Figure 2 was developed by the group to review the literature of stress

FIGURE 2

A Framework for Interactions Between the Individual and the Environment

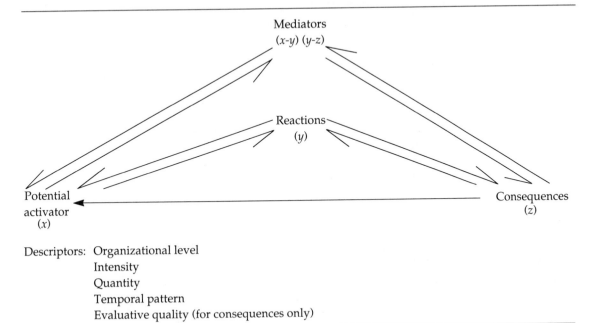

Descriptors: Organizational level
Intensity
Quantity
Temporal pattern
Evaluative quality (for consequences only)

From *Stress and Human Health: Analysis and Implications of Research* (p. 19) by G. R. Elliott and C. Eisdorfer (Eds.), 1982, New York: Springer-Verlag. Copyright 1982 by Springer-Verlag. Reprinted by permission.

research and identify areas of strength and weakness.

The schema involves three primary elements: (a) something in the environment that becomes an activator (stimulus, stressor), (b) individual reactions to that activator, and (c) consequences of those responses. This x-y-z sequence applies in principle to all stress research, although many investigators are concerned with only part of the sequence. As an example of the full x-y-z sequence, Elliott and Eisdorfer (1982) describe the injection of an antigenic substance (activator) under the skin of a healthy individual, which produces an immediate immunologic response (reaction) that neutralizes the antigen and in turn causes local swelling, redness, and tenderness (consequences).

The secondary relationships represented in this model involve mediators and their relationships to each element in the x-y-z sequence. These are included to take account of the fact that reactions to environmental events and conditions (activators) are not uniform across settings or across individuals. Such mediators may be biological, psychological, or social; they are the variables necessary to explain individual and situational differences in reactions to the same activator (stressor) and differences in consequences of the same initial reaction.

For the organizational psychologist interested in stress, this model can be useful, but only as a beginning. It remains to specify the concepts and variables of interest in each of the broad categories (activators, reactions,

FIGURE 3

A Paradigm for Analysis of the Stress Cycle

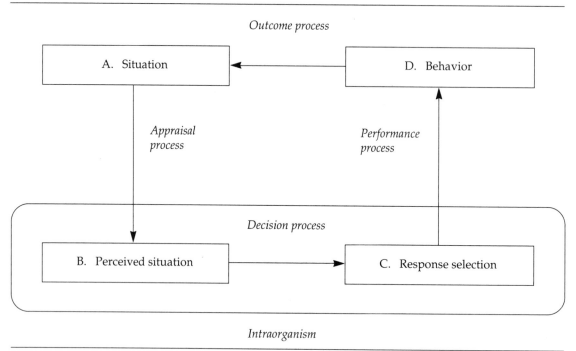

Outcome process

A. Situation ← D. Behavior

Appraisal process

Performance process

Decision process

B. Perceived situation → C. Response selection

Intraorganism

consequences, and mediators) and to specify the relationships (hypotheses and empirical findings) by which they are linked.

McGrath's Paradigm for Analysis of the Stress Cycle

The McGrath (1976) model shown in Figure 3 is similar in simplicity and generality to that of Elliott and Eisdorfer, at least as it initially presented. In the course of his review chapter on stress, McGrath offers a number of elaborations of the model to deal with specific stress situations and outcomes; the basic elements, however, remain the same.

They involve a four-step sequence leading from an external situation to the observable behavior of individuals, which in turn affects the situation. Four processes link these conceptual categories: appraisal, decision making, performance, and outcome. The model adds to that of Elliott and Eisdorfer by stipulating these processes; they are not the only possible processual links, but they emphasize the psychological character of the model. Both the appraisal process that links the objective situation to the situation as perceived by an individual and the decision-making process that links the perceived situation to the selection of responses from the individual's repertoire are essentially psychological.

The McGrath model also includes explicitly the feedback process (i.e., the link labeled "outcome") that connects an individual's behavioral response to the situation that evoked it. This dynamic closing of the loop is an important and neglected aspect of stress research and theory.

Lazarus' Theoretical Schematization of the Stress Process

The work by Lazarus and his colleagues (Lazarus, 1981; Lazarus, De Longis, Folkman, & Gruen, 1985; Lazarus & Folkman, 1984) has been extremely influential in the field of stress research, and although it has been little concerned with causal factors that could be considered organizational, it is in many respects instructive for organizational psychologists. His emphasis on chronic external conditions, or *daily hassles,* as stressors and on the cognitive factors that intervene between such external events and their short-term physiological, emotional, and behavioral consequences are especially important.

The Lazarus model is shown in Figure 4. Lazarus calls his theory of stress cognitive-phenomenological and, consistent with this emphasis, he defines (psychological) stress as a troubled relationship between the person and the environment in which an environmental demand, constraint, or opportunity is judged to tax or exceed the person's resources (Folkman & Lazarus, 1980; Lazarus & Folkman, 1984). The person-environment relationship is mediated by three types of cognitive appraisal, which Lazarus labels primary, secondary, and reappraisal. *Primary appraisal* is the process by which individuals evaluate an encounter with respect to its significance for their own well-being; it attempts to answer the question, "Am I okay or in trouble?" *Secondary appraisal* raises the question of coping—"What can I do about this stressful encounter?" *Reappraisal,* as the term implies, is really another cycle, activated by new information—for example, information about whether one's initial attempt at coping seems to be having the intended effects.

Organizational psychologists can utilize the Lazarus model readily, whether or not they agree with his subjective or at least individualized definition of stress. Organizational researchers will propose their own specific concepts—quantitative overload, or postural constraint, or lack of variety, for example—to fit under the broader environmental descriptors of the Lazarus model, but the basic stress sequence is well suited to their needs. It is consistent with the models of Elliott-Eisdorfer and McGrath, but it makes the cognitive processes more specific. Lazarus's emphasis on the stress process as dynamic is clear in his research, although it is implied in the model only by the references to consecutive times (in the category labeled "mediating processes") and by the three-part temporal sequence of cognitive appraisal.

Dohrenwend's General Paradigm of the Stress Process Extended to Include Antecedents of Stressful Life Events

The central concept in the Dohrenwend, Pearlin, Clayton, Hanburg, Riley, and Rose (1982) model, as shown in Figure 5, is the stressful life event. Such events—death of a loved one, birth of a first child, loss of a job, divorce, and the like—have been found to be consistently associated with increased risk of physical and mental illness (Dohrenwend & Dohrenwend, 1974; Dohrenwend, Krasnoff, Askenasy, & Dohrenwend, 1982; Gunderson & Rahe, 1974; Rabkin & Struening, 1976; Rahe & Arthur, 1978). Stressful life events are seen as jointly determined by circumstances in the environment and by characteristics of individuals: Some environments generate more of such events than others, and some people are more event-prone than others. The events in turn are the immediate causes of the individual's state of stress. That state of stress, finally, may be reflected in undesirable changes in functioning or health, or in no change, or in psychosocial growth. This last

FIGURE 4

A Theoretical Schematization of the Stress Process

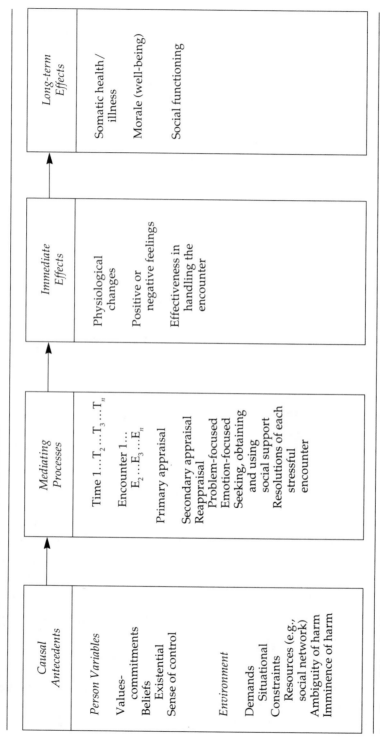

Causal Antecedents	Mediating Processes	Immediate Effects	Long-term Effects

Person Variables
 	
Values-
  commitments
Beliefs
  Existential
  Sense of control
 	
Environment
 	
Demands
Situational
  Constraints
Resources (e.g.,
  social network)
Ambiguity of harm
Imminence of harm
	Time 1...T_2...T_3...T_n
	
	Encounter 1...
	  E_2...E_3...E_n
	
	Primary appraisal
	
	Secondary appraisal
	Reappraisal
	Problem-focused
	Emotion-focused
	Seeking, obtaining
	  and using
	  social support
	Resolutions of each
	  stressful
	  encounter
		Physiological
		  changes
		
		Positive or
		  negative feelings
		
		Effectiveness in
		  handling the
		  encounter
			Somatic health/
			  illness
			
			Morale (well-being)
			
			Social functioning

From "Stress and Adaptational Outcomes: The Problem of Confounded Measures" by R. S. Lazarus, A. Delongis, S. Folkman, and R. Gruen, 1985, *American Psychologist, 40(7)*, pp. 770–779. Copyright 1985 by the American Psychological Association. Reprinted by permission.

FIGURE 5

General Paradigm of the Stress Process Extended to Include Antecedents of Stressful Life Events

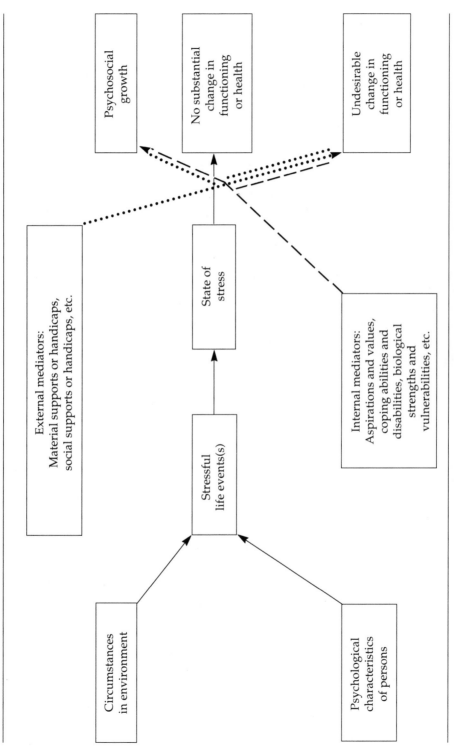

Adapted with permission from Dohrenwend, B. S. (1978). Social stress in the community. *American Journal of Community Psychology, 6*(1), pp. 1–14. Reprinted with permission from Dohrenwend, B. P., Pearlin, L., Clayton, P., Hanburg, B., Riley, R., and Rose, R. M. (1982). Report on stress and life events. In G. R. Elliott & C. Eisendorfer (Eds.), *Stress and human health*, p. 59. New York: Springer Publishing Company.

link in the hypothesized causal sequence, unlike those that precede it, is mediated both by external factors like support, for example, and by internal factors like aspirations and values, coping abilities, and biological characteristics.

The Dohrenwend model shares a number of characteristics with those discussed earlier: the conceptualization of a person's internal state of stress as determined jointly by environmental and personal properties, for example, and the emphasis on internal and external factors as mediating the effect of stress on health and performance. The model is distinctive in its explicit inclusion of psychosocial growth as a possible consequence of stressful experiences, although other theorists do not exclude such outcomes. The main distinguishing feature of the Dohrenwend model, however, is its conceptualization of environmental stressors in terms of discrete events rather than in terms of variable descriptors of environmental properties. The variable measure of external stressors is generated by summing such events; whether they should be weighted or unweighted is a persisting controversy among life-events researchers.

The life-events approach has been very influential in stress research for a period usually described as beginning with the publication of an event-based measurement scale by Holmes and Rahe (1969). Organizational psychologists, however, are likely to be reminded of much earlier work in their own field, the critical-incident approach to measuring employee performance and satisfaction developed by Flanagan (1949, 1954). The criticisms and defenses that have developed around the life-events approach are also reminiscent of the conceptual and methodological arguments about the critical-incident approach. They have been well summarized by Perkins (1982).

Proponents of the life-events approach point to the availability of an instrument and a large substantiating empirical literature. They emphasize the accessibility of life events to memory and self-report, as well as to independent validation. They argue that the life events

approach is rooted in the fundamental notion of homeostasis and of an external stress (stressor) as a source of disequilibrium. Life-events researchers have not concentrated on the work role, but the approach could be adapted to the intensive measurement of that role and its stressors.

Critics have emphasized the mingling of positive and negative events in the measurement process, the limited amount of outcome variance typically explained by the events scores, and the apparent failure of the event scales to tap persisting conditions and daily hassles (Lazarus, 1983). Almost any measure of an external stressor can be cast in terms of events, of course, but to do so trivializes a conceptual issue of importance and reduces it to a matter of methodological preference.

We believe much of the stress experience in work settings can be better conceptualized in terms of persisting conditions and daily hassles than as life events. Certain work-related events and transitions, however, are best studied in ways that reflect their discontinuity. For example, entry and reentry into the labor market, job loss, promotion and demotion, retirement, and job transfer are discrete events, and their event character may be essential to understanding their impact on stressors.

The four stress models just reviewed are not specific to organizational settings and job-related stressors. Even the McGrath model, which was the basis for his 1976 review chapter in the first edition of this *Handbook* (Dunnette, 1976), represents the stress cycle irrespective of the situation in which it arises or the nature of the stressor. A number of stress models have been developed by scholars working primarily on organizational issues, however. Many of these have been published within the past ten years, either in review articles or as proposed guides for future research (Beehr & Franz, 1987; Frankenhaeuser et al., 1989; Ivancevich & Matteson, 1980; Jick & Payne, 1980; Levi, 1981; Payne, Jick, & Burke, 1982; Schuler, 1981), and there is a considerable convergence among them. A few organizational stress models are much older; for example, the original ISR model (French & Kahn, 1962) was developed decades ago, but has continued to evolve as it was utilized in successive research projects. In the following exposition of these models, we have clustered together those that show closest resemblance.

The Ivancevich and Matteson Model for Organizational Stress Research and the Schuler, Jick, and Payne and Beehr and Franz Models

Ivancevich and Matteson (Figure 6; 1980) developed their model in the course of summarizing the empirical findings on organizational stress. It is an excellent model that incorporates many of the strengths of the models already described. It deals with the stress process in full, that is, from the intraorganizational and extraorganizational stressors or antecedents to the specific stresses (or immediate stressors) at work, to the short-term physiological and behavioral outcomes (responses), and to the longer term diseases of adaptation. Within each of these categories, specific variables are identified as especially important. Enduring individual characteristics—demographic, behavioral, cognitive, and affective— are introduced as moderators in the stress sequence. Finally, distinctive among the models we have considered, Ivancevich and Matteson's distinguishes stressors according to level of analysis—individual, group, and organizational. The only significant omission in the model is the role of situational factors (e.g., social support) as potential moderators in the stress sequence. Interpersonal relations are included among the antecedent variables, but not as potential moderators.

Schuler's (1981) model is similar in its specification of organizational (environmental) stressors, its differentiation of responses over time (short, intermediate, and long-term), and in its introduction of individual characteristics as moderators in the stress sequence. Payne, Jick, and Burke (1982, adapted from Jick &

Payne, 1980) add extraorganizational stressors (e.g., family crises) as stressors that interact with those encountered on the job. The figure that depicts their conceptual framework seems to treat properties of the person as consequences of these stressors, but the text makes clear that they are regarded as moderating or exacerbating the effects of the stressors on short-term and long-term outcomes relevant to health. The discussion of stress by Beehr and Franz (1987) is consistent with those by the authors cited above.

Levi's Preventing Work Stress and Frankenhaeuser's Stress, Health, and Job Satisfaction Models

Two of the most important sources of research on organizational stress are located in the Karolinska Institute of the University of Stockholm. They are the Department of Stress Research, directed by Lennart Levi, and the Department of Psychology, where the work on stress is directed by Marianne Frankenhaeuser. The research of both groups (Levi, 1981; Frankenhaeuser, 1989) has been consistently interdisciplinary; bio-psychosocial is an appropriate descriptor. Both groups emphasize self-report as well as independent assessment of major variables, and both groups conduct stress research in field settings as well as in the laboratory. Marshall and Cooper (1979) present a framework that includes many of the stressors and stress sequences with which both groups have been concerned (Figure 7).

This model emphasizes stressors that are generated at work; of the six categories of stressors included in the model (under the heading "Environment-related"), five arise from the job itself and the organizational context of the job. Stress itself appears in the model as a hypothetical construct; it is inferred from its manifestations—physical, behavioral, mental, and organizational. The model is explicit with respect to the stressors to be studied, as it is with respect to outcomes. Outcomes are to be assessed at both the individual (physical

FIGURE 6

A Model for Organizational Stress Research

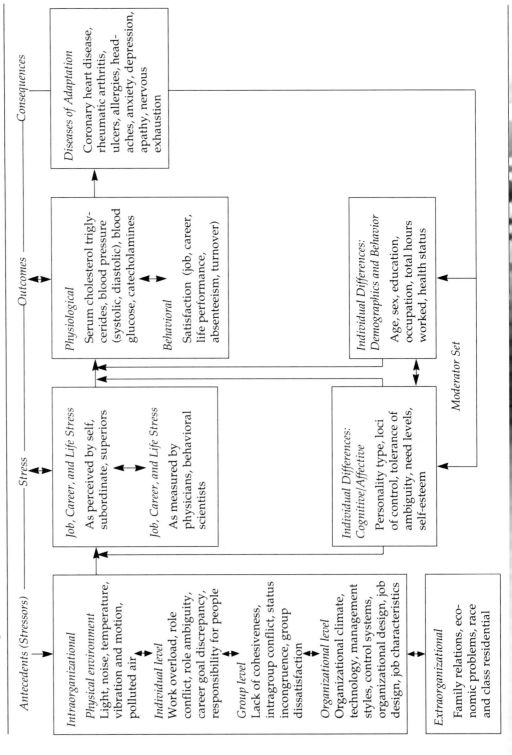

FIGURE 7

Stressors at Work

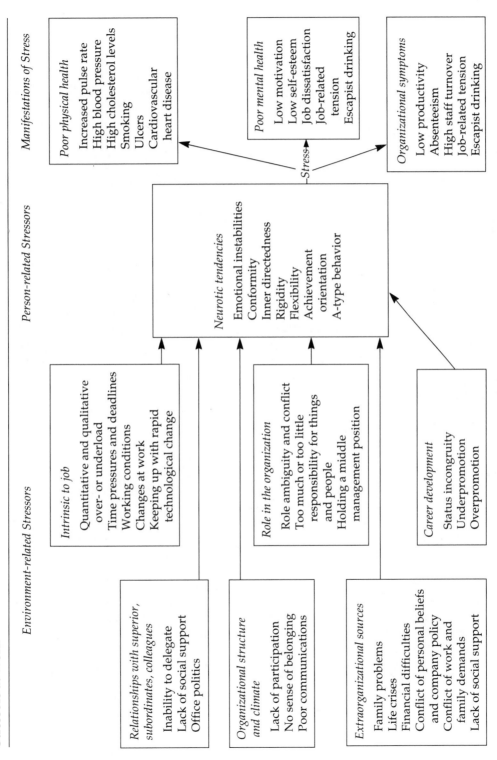

Environment-related Stressors

Person-related Stressors

Manifestations of Stress

Intrinsic to job

Quantitative and qualitative
over- or underload
Time pressures and deadlines
Working conditions
Changes at work
Keeping up with rapid
technological change

*Relationships with superior,
subordinates, colleagues*

Inability to delegate
Lack of social support
Office politics

*Organizational structure
and climate*

Lack of participation
No sense of belonging
Poor communications

Extraorganizational sources

Family problems
Life crises
Financial difficulties
Conflict of personal beliefs
and company policy
Conflict of work and
family demands
Lack of social support

Role in the organization

Role ambiguity and conflict
Too much or too little
responsibility for things
and people
Holding a middle
management position

Career development

Status incongruity
Underpromotion
Overpromotion

Neurotic tendencies

Emotional instabilities
Conformity
Inner directedness
Rigidity
Flexibility
Achievement
orientation
A-type behavior

—Stress→

Poor physical health

Increased pulse rate
High blood pressure
High cholesterol levels
Smoking
Ulcers
Cardiovascular
heart disease

Poor mental health

Low motivation
Low self-esteem
Job dissatisfaction
Job-related
tension
Escapist drinking

Organizational symptoms

Low productivity
Absenteeism
High staff turnover
Job-related tension
Escapist drinking

From "Work Experiences of Middle and Senior Managers: The Pressure and Satisfaction" by J. Marshall and C. Cooper, 1979, *International Management Review, 19,* pp. 81–96. Wiesbaden, W. Germany: Gabler Verlag. Copyright 1979 by *International Management Review.* Reprinted by permission.

and mental health) and organizational levels (productivity, absence, turnover).

As illustrated in Figure 7, the moderating effects of personality are not explicit, nor are the moderating effects of such contextual factors as social support. These relationships are specified, however, in the Frankenhaeuser model (Frankenhaeuser et al., 1989), and they are apparent in the research work of both groups.

The ISR Models

In 1962, French and Kahn published the prototype of these models as a general schema to guide a program of research then getting under way at the Institute for Social Research (ISR) of the University of Michigan—hence, the designation ISR or Michigan model. The model (shown in Figure 8) continues to serve that programmatic function, although it is very general and requires additional specification for each line of investigation. For this reason, there has been a series of derivative models that have in common this meta-theoretical ancestor.

The first of that series was proposed by Kahn, Wolfe, Quinn, and Snoek (1964) to study the effects of role conflict and ambiguity at work. A more recent example is the model developed by French, Caplan, and Harrison (1982) to test hypotheses regarding the effects of goodness of fit (between individual and job) on risk factors for coronary heart disease.

Even in its initial form (French & Kahn, 1962), the ISR model emphasized several principles that have become agreed upon doctrine, if not practice, in research on organizational stress. These include the measurement of the work environment (hypothetical stressors) both objectively and subjectively—that is, both as perceived by the individual under study (psychological environment) and as assessed independently of that person's perceptions (objective environment). The model

also differentiates short-term from long-term consequences of stress, labeling the former as responses and the latter as criteria of health and disease. Moreover, the short-term responses of interest include affective, behavioral, and physiological categories. The omission of cognitive processes, including the sequential appraisal functions central to the Lazarus model, is a deficiency in the original ISR model.

Finally, the 1962 ISR model emphasized two sets of mediator variables that subsequent research has shown to be important—(a) enduring properties of the person and (b) contextual properties (especially interpersonal) of the work situation. Both these sets of mediators have the potentiality of altering the three hypothesized main effects—(a) the effect of objective organizational and job characteristics on the individual's perceptions (psychological environment), (b) the effect of those perceptions on the individual's responses, and (c) the effect of those responses on his or her subsequent state of health or illness. The limitations of the model are mainly three—(a) its level of abstraction, which leaves the task of specification almost entirely in the hands of users; (b) its neglect of the cognitive processes that are important in the stress process, especially as they intervene between immediate perceptions and subsequent responses; and (c) its restriction of outcomes to health and disease. As organizational psychologists, we are interested also in such outcomes as role performance at work and elsewhere and, in the aggregate, the performance and viability of the organization itself. We have attempted to address these limitations in the model shown in Figure 9 and which we will utilize for the remainder of this chapter.

This schema belongs to the ISR family of models, but we have attempted to incorporate in it elements of other models when they have been supported by empirical research. It builds on the original ISR model by specifying many of the variables of interest as well as the conceptual categories to which

FIGURE 8

ISR Model of Social Environment and Mental Health

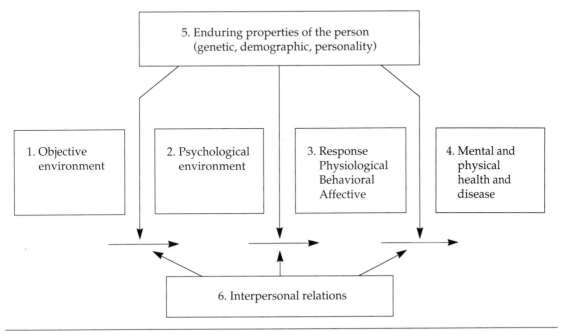

From "A Programmatic Approach to Studying the Industrial Environment and Mental Health" by J. R. P. French, Jr., and R. L. Kahn, 1962, *Journal of Social Issues, 18*(3), p. 2. Copyright 1962 by the Society for the Psychological Study of Social Issues. Reprinted by permission.

they belong, by including organizational antecedents or characteristics that generate specific stressors, by introducing cognition or appraisal as a process that intervenes between stressors and the responses to them, and by specifying organizational as well as individual criteria as affected by the stress sequence.

Five elements are thus identified as comprising a causal sequence that leads from organizational characteristics to specific stressors, from stressors to the perceptual and cognitive processes that constitute appraisal of threat, and then to the immediate responses generated by threat appraisal—physiological, psychological, and behavioral; these lead, finally, to the ramifying or long-term consequences of stress for the individual and for the organization. The solid arrows indicate causal

relationships, either hypothesized or demonstrated, depending on the specific variables in question.

This model includes the moderating relationships characteristic of the ISR models generally; enduring properties of the person (demographic and personality) and of the situation have the potentiality of mediating the causal sequence described above, at each step from organizational antecedents to long-term consequences of stress. Finally, the model acknowledges the possibility that stressors may have effects without involving the processes of perception and cognition that usually intervene. Toxicologists and epidemiologists are perhaps more concerned with such effects than are psychologists, but we should recognize the fact that all

FIGURE 9

Theoretical Framework for the Study of Stress in Organizations

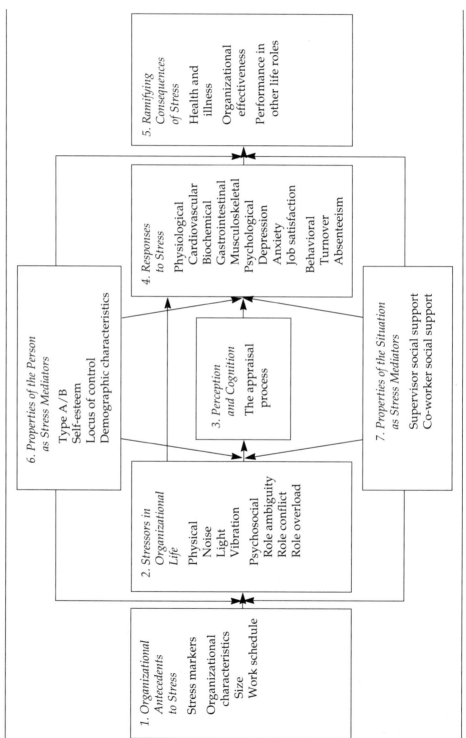

experiences that are ultimately damaging are not so perceived at the time of exposure.

Convergences and Complementarities

None of the models we have reviewed, nor the one we have proposed, include all of the concepts and relationships that interest organizational psychologists as a whole, or even that subset of psychologists who wish to understand the origins, nature, and consequences of stresses generated in organizational life. Some are more specific than others and identify variables rather than more abstract conceptual categories. Some begin with the perception of stress by the individual and thus ignore its more objective antecedents. Some omit the process of cognitive appraisal that is the central concept for others.

Despite these differences, the points of convergence among the various models are notable. To begin with, all of them reflect the conceptualization of stress as involving a process that includes the same basic sequence: (a) the imposition of a damaging or taxing stimulus, (b) a set of psychological responses triggered by that stimulus, and (c) a more or less complex array of consequences in which the well-being of the individual is involved. The models are also in partial agreement about the ways in which the stress sequence is moderated, broadly speaking—that is, with contextual factors that have to do mainly with the adequacy of resources, both material and psychological, and individual characteristics that add up to what epidemiologists call host resistance.

The differences among the models, some of which we regard as complementarities rather than alternatives, are not trivial, however. There is the obvious difference in terminology—stress as external stimulus versus stress as response versus stress as person-situation relationship. There is the related issue of how the stressful stimuli themselves can best be conceptualized—as stressful life events, as daily hassles, or in the more familiar terms of variable language.

The models differ also in the length of the causal sequence that they attempt to describe, both in terms of antecedents and consequences. For organizational psychologists, the inclusion of organizational variables, structural and processual, that affect the likelihood of particular stressors is of obvious importance. At the other end of the stress sequence, a similar issue arises: What is the temporal span and what are the levels of consequences with which stress researchers should concern themselves? The organizational psychologist's answers should include criteria of individual performance as well as satisfaction and health, and criteria of organizational effectiveness as well as individual performance. All these criterion variables, moreover, should be included in their full range so that positive as well as negative outcomes of stress can be made visible.

There is no implication that all these variables can or should be built into any single experiment or field study. They do, however, define the organizational psychologist's domain of aspirations. Let us now consider the extent to which those aspirations are attained in our empirical research.

Empirical Findings

Our review of empirical research on stress will concentrate on studies that have explicit relevance to organizational theory and practice, either because they were conducted in organizational settings or because they attempted to deal with organizational problems, broadly defined. We will concentrate also on research done since 1976, when the preceding edition of the *Handbook* was published. Research from earlier periods and research not explicitly organizational will be included only when it seems important for interpretation and coherence.

The discussion of research findings to follow is organized around eight main topics, the first seven of which correspond to the categories in Figure 9:

- Organizational antecedents to stress

- Stressors in organizational life

- Perception and cognition: the appraisal process

- Responses to stress: physiological, psychological, and behavioral

- Ramifying consequences of stress: health and illness; organizational effectiveness; performance in other life roles

- Properties of the person as stress mediators

- Properties of the situation as stress mediators

- Prevention and intervention

Like any other, this mode of presentation has advantages and disadvantages. Its primary advantage is that the topics themselves correspond to the main components of the theoretical models in current use by those stress researchers who focus on psychosocial factors in organizational settings. The main disadvantage of this topical mode of exposition is the disaggregation of individual studies, so that no one study emerges in its entirety. We have tried to reduce the resulting sense of fragmentation by indicating within each topic the pattern of relationships in which each variable is embedded.

Organizational Antecedents to Stress

Most stress research involves a causal sequence, inferred or implied, that begins with some stressing factor. Thus, laboratory experiments on stress may require subjects to perform some task while listening to recorded noise or may require arithmetic computation under severe time constraints. Field studies may measure such job characteristics as overload, isolation, or postural constraint. These are specific stressors, that is, external stimuli that evoke from most people those psychological

or physiological responses that researchers designate as stress or strain, according to their terminological preferences.

Stressors, in other words, appear in the research literature as independent variables. Both for theoretical and pragmatic reasons, however, it is important to regard these specific stressors also as dependent variables, that is, to ask what antecedent properties of organizational environment technology, structure, or policy have the consequence of creating stressors at the level of specific jobs. Few researchers have investigated this link explicitly. Somewhat more numerous are research projects that demonstrate an association between some antecedent factor, such as organizational size, and some indicator of strain, such as self-reported tension. If such relationships are to be believed, there is necessarily some intervening stressor or stress sequence through which the organizational factor affects individual jobs and work settings, but in this example (from Kahn et al., 1964), these intervening processes are not specified.

Our summary of research on antecedent factors includes research of both kinds—that is, research in which the link is made explicit and research in which some antecedent condition or characteristic is used as a surrogate for a more specific stressor. We will discuss the research on antecedents to job stress in a sequence that begins with the more abstract and remote factors and moves toward those that are more specific and job-connected. This ordering takes us from indicators at the national level to properties of organizations themselves, to their subsystems and role sets, and finally to characteristics of work roles themselves. In addition, there are a few clusters of research that, while they do not fit neatly on this continuum, deal with antecedents to job stressors. These include research in which occupation is used as a surrogate for unspecified stressors, in which change per se is similarly utilized, and in which summed scores of external events are taken as measures of total exposure to stressors.

Social Indicators as Stress Markers. This is a research strategy associated almost exclusively with Harvey Brenner and his colleagues. They have demonstrated repeatedly that for many large populations, regional and national, there are substantial and plausibly lagged correlations between economic conditions and health. The social indicators used in these analyses include economic growth, economic instability, and unemployment levels. These in turn are associated with such criterion variables as institutionalization rates, suicides, and various health indicators. For a review of these studies, see Brenner and Mooney (1983).

Brenner's more recent work (Brenner, 1987a, 1987b) extends this research in several ways. He replicates and extends the basic findings relating economic change and mortality in nine industrialized countries—Australia, Canada, England and Wales, Denmark, Federal Republic of Germany, Finland, France, Sweden, and the United States. Unemployment and business failures predict mortality from heart disease, with a one-year to four-year lag and with controls on such variables as alcohol consumption and cigarette smoking. In eight of the nine countries, the expected inverse relationship was also demonstrated; economic growth was inversely related to mortality from heart disease. A more intensive analysis of the Swedish data (Brenner, 1987b) showed similar relationships to mortality at all ages and from many causes—total cardiovascular disease, cerebrovascular disease, total and ischemic heart disease, total malignancies, disorders of infancy, and even motor vehicle accidents. We believe that the Brenner data are important and deserve to be accepted; the task of specifying the causal mechanisms through which these gross economic changes affect health and mortality remains to be completed, however.

Organizations as Stress-generators: Systems and Subsystems. Organizational size has been hypothesized as a source of stress, although the link has not been specified. Moreover, the evidence is thin and inconsistent. Kahn et al. (1964), in a national survey in which workers estimated the size of their employing firms, found a significant relationship between size and reported job tension, the connection presumed to involve increased formalization and bureaucratization in larger organizations. A Dutch investigation into the relationship of company size to stress and strain found that reported incidence of stressors was greatest in medium-sized as opposed to large companies (Reiche & Van Dijkhuizen, 1979). Research that has investigated the effects of formalization on work stressors, however, has produced few significant findings (Pearce, 1981). Ironically, the most consistent of them is a negative relationship between formalization and role ambiguity (House and Rizzo, 1972; Morris, Steers, & Koch, 1978; Rizzo, House, & Listzman, 1970; Rogers & Molnar, 1976).

Nevertheless, although specific causal connections remain to be demonstrated, evidence continues to accumulate slowly that links phenomena at the organizational level to experienced stress at the individual level. For example, a comparative study of employees in eight organizations of comparable technology tested the hypothesis that illness was actually an organizational phenomenon (Schmitt, Colligan, & Fitzgerald, 1980). Between-company variance was significant, and company means on such variables as work pressure and dissatisfaction with personnel policies were associated with frequency of reported physical symptoms. A more rigorous longitudinal study compared private and semipublic savings banks in Belgium with respect to the incidence of coronary heart disease among male bank clerks, matched by age and sex and free of the disease at the beginning of the 10-year study. Incidence of sudden deaths and nonfatal myocardial infarctions was significantly higher in the private banks than in the semipublic by a margin of 50 percent after major individual coronary risk functions were controlled by multiple logistic analysis. The causal factors remain unidentified, and the possibility that they are entirely reflective of self-selection cannot be ruled out; the hypothesis of organizational determinants remains plausible, however.

Differences of this kind between organizations lead one to wonder to what extent similar differences can be demonstrated between subunits of single organizations. One such study (Parasuraman & Alutto, 1981) found that the five subsystems of a food-processing firm (production, production-supportive, maintenance, adaptive, and managerial) differed significantly in type and magnitude of reported stressors. All seven of the measured stressors are significantly related to felt stress and (negatively) to job satisfaction.

Other studies have found differences in the frequency of stressful events in functionally different subunits, even when occupation and hierarchical level are held constant. For example, Motowidlo, Packard, and Manning (1986) report the frequency of such events in medical and surgical units to be greater than in all other clinical units combined. Numerof and Abrams (1984) report similar differences between nurses in intensive care units, emergency rooms, and hospital nurseries (high stress) as compared to those in pediatrics and obstetrics-gynecology (low stress).

Recent research on the stresses associated with reductions in organizational size (Sutton & D'Aunno, 1989) raises the possibility that change at the organizational level may be an important generator of stressors, even when size itself is not. Most of the research on organizational downsizing has been qualitative, however, and does not include health indicators as outcome variables.

Role Sets as Stress Sources. Although role conflict and role ambiguity are probably the two most frequently studied stressors in organizational life, few researchers have investigated their antecedents. One study (Chonko, 1982) reported extremely high rank-order

correlations (.86–.87) between span of control (size of role set) and reported magnitude of role conflict and ambiguity among sales representatives. Role conflict and ambiguity have also been predicted by the organizational distance (vertical and horizontal) comprised by the role set and by the relative authority of the role senders (Miles, 1977). A more complex pattern of relationships was reported in a study of public utility employees that attempted to link attributes of supervisors' roles to stress experienced by their subordinates (Moch, Bartunek, & Brass, 1979). Although the context in which the supervisors as role senders performed their tasks had a substantial effect on the amount of stress reported by their subordinates as role receivers, the significant contextual factors were different for technical than for professional role sets. We conclude that the role set has been neglected as an explanatory level in stress research, but that it has been illuminating in the few studies that have utilized it.

Role Characteristics as Antecedents to Stress. A few studies have explored the relationship of role or positional location as a determinant of role stressors. Location in such studies has been measured either along a vertical axis, implying status and power, or in terms of proximity to an organizational boundary. Boundary-spanning among partners and managers in 14 public accounting firms was found to predict role conflict and overload among partners; it also predicted increased overload among managers but decreased conflict and ambiguity for reasons not readily apparent (Bartunek & Reynolds, 1983). Boundary-spanning and integration as a combined role requirement was also the best predictor of role conflict in a multiorganizational study of professionals (Miles, 1976; Miles & Perreault, 1976).

Data on hierarchical position as an antecedent to role stress are mixed, and it seems likely that the relative stressfulness of different hierarchical levels must be understood in the context of other organizational characteristics. In a study that compared upper-, middle-, and lower-level managers, a curvilinear relationship was reported, with stress highest among the middle-level managers (Ivancevich, Matteson, & Preston, 1982), a finding consistent with their reported satisfaction levels and their physiological measures. Other studies, usually conducted in single companies, have not replicated this pattern but have shown positive relationships between hierarchical level and both type and magnitude of reported stressors (Parasuraman & Alutto, 1981).

Occupation as Antecedents to Stress. Research findings based on occupation and on occupational clusters like blue collar or white collar jobs are sources of both information and frustration to the stress researcher. The information is substantial because such studies are numerous, and the frustration is considerable because most such studies report correlations between occupational categories and self-reported states without any explication of intervening processes.

There are, however, some important exceptions. Alfredsson and Theorell (1983) developed standardized occupational characteristics for 118 occupational groups in a nationwide (Swedish) interview survey. Occupations characterized by high levels of demand (e.g., lifting) and low levels of control (autonomy) were associated with elevated risks of myocardial infarction. For men in the 45 through 54 year age range, the risk was twice as high in these occupations as for all others. Studies of air traffic controllers, some involving comparison groups in other occupations and some involving comparisons across airports with different traffic densities, identified responsibility for the welfare of others in combination with heavy and variable work load and irregular work-rest cycles of occupation-determined stressors (Rose, Jenkins, Hurst, & Apple-Levin, 1978).

Russek (1973) demonstrated a marked gradient between independently rated occupation stressfulness and coronary disease among 25,000 professional men in 20 occupational categories. French, Caplan, and Harrison (1982), in a large-scale study of workers in 23 occupations ranging from machine-paced assembly workers to physicians and scientists, found consistent stressor patterns that differentiated blue collar from white collar occupations; the unskilled blue collar occupations scored lowest in complexity and responsibility, and people in those occupations reported greater discrepancies between preference and actuality on these dimensions. And the Framingham study showed women clerical workers who had nonsupportive supervisors to be at increased risk of developing coronary heart disease over an eight-year period (Haynes, Feinleib, & Kannel, 1980). The combination of supervisory behavior and occupation is not easily interpreted, but the link between occupation and stress is at least plausible.

On the other hand, an Israeli study of male kibbutz members showed virtually no differences between occupations in job stress or risk factors for coronary heart disease (Shirom, Eden, Silberwasser, & Kellermann, 1973). If these findings can be replicated, they imply that the occupational differences reported in most industrial societies reflect differences in status, rewards, and other sociocontextual factors rather than elements intrinsic to the occupations themselves, since material rewards do not differ across occupations in kibbutz communities.

Work-related Events. Stressful life events (SLE's) have figured prominently in health-oriented social research, at least since the initial work of Holmes and Rahe (1967), and job loss has always been prominent in the roster of such events. Whether we regard job loss as a stressor in itself or as an organizational antecedent to other stressors, such as economic deprivation and status reduction, is essentially a matter of definitional preference. In either case, job loss has been shown to initiate a cascade of negative psychological and physiological consequences. There is a half century of such research, beginning with the remarkable naturalistic study of Lazarsfeld-Jahoda and Zeisel (1933), and it has been reviewed by a number of researchers. See, for example, Kahn (1981) and Latack and Dozier (1986).

In combination, these studies show that, while work is often a source of stress, it is also a source of both material and psychological gratification. The importance of these gratifications becomes most apparent when work is denied. Ecological analyses like those reported by Brenner and his colleagues (Brenner, 1987a, 1987b; Brenner & Mooney, 1983); early case studies of plant closings like those of Sheppard, Ferman, and Haber (1960); and field experiments in intervention all demonstrate the stressfulness of job loss. The strength of this research consists partly in the considerable convergence of findings among studies conducted in different industries, in different localities, at different times, and with some variety of methods. The limitations of this work have to do with the dominance of cross-sectional designs, the absence of comparison groups in many studies, and for many of the case studies, the lack of independent quantitative measures.

The study of Michigan plant closings by Cobb and Kasl (1977) remains exceptional. Workers in plants that did not close were compared with those in plants that were marked for closing; five waves of data were collected over a two-year period, spanning the event sequence from rumor and threat to actual job loss and (in most cases) reemployment; and physiological measures were collected along with self-reported information. The research results show that the costs of unemployment are physical as well as economic and psychological. They also show that the threat of unemployment triggers some physiological changes long before actual job loss occurs and that most physical

indicators return to normal after new job stability is attained. Indeed, some people show net gains as a consequence of job loss. For most, however, involuntary loss of a job is an event that generates stressors and consequent strains, directly and indirectly. Recent field experiments by Vinokur, Price, and Caplan (in press) and their colleagues demonstrate the possibility of reducing such strains by means of counseling, role playing, and peer support.

Stressors in Organizational Life

We use the term stressors to designate stimuli generated on the job and having negative consequences, physical or psychological, for significant proportions of people exposed to them. The conceptualization and identification of specific job stressors is a major task for research workers in the domain of organizational stress. Their other tasks, broadly speaking, are to trace the causal paths by which such stressors have effects, to identify the organizational properties that create the stressors in the first place, and to identify also the individual and situational factors that mitigate or intensify their effects.

This view of the research task has explicit methodological implications: The stressors should be measured independently of their hypothesized effects, and the hypothesized causal sequence from stressors to perception/appraisal and consequent strains should be determined by means of longitudinal as well as cross-sectional research designs. These are obvious conclusions, and they have been frequently urged, perhaps most trenchantly, by Kasl (1978, 1983). They are nevertheless ignored in most research on organizational stress, which continues to rely on self-reported data, both for measurement of the stressor and its presumed effects.

A serious consequence of this persisting methodological deficiency is the confounding of hypothesized causes and effects through simultaneous self-reports of imposed stressors and experienced strains. For example, an employee may report that the work is monotonous and that he or she is bored, or that the work is too demanding and that he or she feels tense. A further problem with such reliance on individual self-report is the inability to make the distinction, urged by Lazarus and his colleagues (Lazarus, 1981; Lazarus & Folkman, 1984), between the external stimulus or stressor and its subjective appraisal by the individual.

In addition to these avoidable problems in identifying organizational stressors, there is a problem that is virtually unavoidable. Any array of identified stressors is a product not only of discovery but of what has been conceptualized and sought. Research workers seldom report things sought but not found (i.e., negative findings and insignificant relationships), and unlike geologists in search of oil, they cannot provide estimates of undiscovered reserves.

With these limitations in mind, we have found more than 250 research reports, almost all of them published since the 1976 *Handbook*, that measure job-generated stressors and specific associated strains or effects. We have included findings based on self-report but have excluded instances of obvious confounding of stressors and strains. The findings are heavily clustered around two conceptual categories:

- *Task content and its concomitants.* These include such dimensions as simplicity-complexity, variety-monotony, and physical conditions of work.

- *Role properties.* These refer primarily to the social aspects of the job, and include supervisory and peer relations, as well as the familiar concepts of role conflict, ambiguity, and overload.

In the following subsections we will review the research in these two categories

and provide specific citations for field studies and experiments typical of each.

Task Content and Concomitants. The dimension of variety-monotony is the aspect of task content that has been studied most frequently in stress research, and it has been studied in relation to physiological as well as psychological consequences. For example, a case-control study of 334 men who had experienced a myocardial infarction showed only two work-related factors associated with increased risk—monotony and shift work (Alfredsson, Karasek, & Theorell, 1982). A study of control room employees in power plants, based on self-report, showed monotony and understimulation to be associated with psychological strains (Agervold, 1983).

Additional studies implicate monotony as a stressor but are designed in a way that does not enable us to separate its effects from those of other job characteristics. Full-time microscope operators show various symptoms of visual strain in the performance of tasks that are clearly monotonous but that also require sustained vigilance (Soderberg, 1983). Assembly-line workers were shown to have higher catecholamine (epinephrine and norepinephrine) excretions, relative to their own baseline values as determined at home, than did workers in jobs rated as less monotonous and less physically constraining (Frankenhaeuser, 1976). Similar results were reported in a comparative study of workers in highly fragmented and repetitive jobs, in contrast to a control group of workers in jobs of greater variety and flexibility (Johansson, Aronsson, & Lindstrom, 1978).

Concomitant job characteristics (vibration, noise, heat, and the like) have been studied mainly in relation to performance and typically show decremental effects. Temperatures in the range of 20 to 38 degrees centigrade, for example, generated curvilinear patterns of performance at simulated tasks performed by nearly 1,000 workers, with performance peaking under conditions of mild heat stress—32 degrees centigrade for men and slightly higher for white women—and with significant reductions at higher and lower temperatures (Meese, Lewis, Wyon, & Kok, 1984). Other research on ambient temperature, typically carried out with small numbers of subjects under laboratory conditions simulating job content, shows reduced performance accuracy (Nunneley, Reader, & Maldonado, 1982) and significant loss of visual acuity (Hohnsbein, Piekarski, Kampman, & Noack, 1984).

Among the measures of increasing physical demand or stress, only the large-muscle requirements of work show associations with health criteria, and the associations are positive. Problems of self-selection in this research make interpretation difficult, however. For example, a large study of longshoremen ($N = 6,351$) showed a death rate among men doing heavy work of 5.6 per 10,000 man-years, as compared to 19.9 for moderate and 15.7 for light work (Paffenbarger & Hale, 1975). On the other hand, a 10-year follow-up study of young men in Sweden showed no such protective effect from working in occupations requiring frequent heavy lifting (Theorell, Knov, Svensson, & Waller, 1983). In fact, men in such occupations who had been classified in the upper third of the population (high, normal, low diastolic blood pressure) at the time of their military service examination 10 years earlier had higher diastolic pressure at the time of the follow-up study than others similarly classified.

Poulton (1978), in a chapter on blue collar stressors, summarizes a great deal of research on physical stressors—light, noise, vibration, heat, air pollution, and the like. For many such stressors, the relationship to strains of various kinds is curvilinear. For example, vertical vibration at frequencies of 4 to 6 Hz was found to help maintain vigilance, especially at dull routine tasks, while vibration at either greater or lesser rates tended to reduce alertness. Most such findings are based on laboratory research, but specificity of effects has also been determined for long-range exposures to some physical stressors. These will be discussed in the subsequent section on health and illness.

Role Properties. Research on job-related stress has long been dominated by concepts of role, especially role conflict, role ambiguity, and role overload. The last of these can be regarded as a special form of role conflict, in which the conflict is between quantity or time considerations on one hand, and quality on the other. At least 150 studies utilizing these concepts have been published since 1976. Another cluster of findings relating role requirements to strain involves control, sometimes measured as lack of autonomy on the job and sometimes as an excess of supervisory intervention. Finally, there is a set of studies in which social support in the work setting is a key variable, affecting job stress either directly or as a moderator of the relationship between stressors and resulting strains.

Since almost all studies of role conflict rely exclusively on self-reported data, those that are at least partly anchored in independent observations of some kind deserve special notice. A few such studies include measures of role conflict based on objective role requirements (Miles & Perreault, 1976) or plant differences in crisis exposure (Chisholm, Kasl, & Eskanazi, 1983), both of which were significant predictors of subjective role conflict and consequent symptoms of tension. A few other studies utilized physiological outcomes such as heart rate, respirations, and blood pressure in addition to self-reported strains and tensions. Orpen (1982) reported significant relationships between subjective role conflict and measures of physical strain among middle managers, especially those classified as Type A rather than Type B personalities. And at least one study (Manning, Ismail, & Sherwood, 1981) demonstrated physiological as well as subjective effects of role conflict among nurses engaged in an experimental simulation of hospital tasks.

The numerous cross-sectional studies based on self-report from convenience samples show considerable substantive convergence with respect to the effects of experienced role conflict on felt tension. Most such studies have found role conflict to occur wholly within the context of the job and to consist of perceptual differences regarding the content of the role or the relative importance of its elements. Such differences may occur directly between an individual and members of his or her role set or they may occur primarily between members of the role set, who attempt in effect to enforce different job descriptions for the person in question. Both such conflict configurations generate negative affect, tension, and, frequently, physical symptoms on the part of the focal person. Certain kinds of positions, especially those involving boundary spanning, are particularly vulnerable to role conflict. Kahn (1981) has summarized findings from this research.

Conflict between the demands of different roles enacted by the same individual is also a common subject of study. Such conflicts have been reported most often in occupations such as military service, police work, and teaching, where the compartmentalization of time between work and family cannot be easily or dependably arranged (Hageman, 1978; Kroes, Hurrell, & Margolis, 1974; Wisdom, 1984). Shift work, especially with rotating assignments, appears to generate similar problems (Jones & Butler, 1980). Finally, there is some evidence that crisis conditions at the group or organizational level are reflected in role conflict at the individual level (Duxbury, Armstrong, Drew, & Henly, 1984).

Although the concept of role ambiguity was introduced concomitantly with that of role conflict a generation ago, it has attracted much less empirical research. Nevertheless, role ambiguity emerges as a stressor consistently predictive of negative affect and somatic symptoms across a wide range of populations: managers in Dutch industries (Van Dijkhuizen & Reiche, 1980), teachers in Swedish elementary schools (Brenner, 1982), professional recreation workers in the United States (Rosenthal, 1983), and managerial employees in the mining industry (Gavin & Axelrod, 1977). In the Dutch study, job ambiguity was the factor with the most explicit negative consequences for such physiological indicators of strain as cholesterol level and mean arterial pressure.

Role overload was originally treated as a variant of role conflict, in which the conflict was experienced as a necessity to compromise either quantity, time schedule, or quality. In recent years, however, role overload has become a subject of research in its own right. Findings from many studies agree on the negative effects of overload at work, but most such research is based on cross-sectional designs and self-reported data, which means that respondents are simultaneously describing their work demands as excessive and their reactions as negative, the latter indicated by negative affect and feelings of tension.

A few studies, however, assess work load independently and measure physiological as well as psychological indicators of strain. These report findings are consistent with the more limited designs but extend our understanding of the stressor-strain causal sequence. For example, both British (Timio & Gentili, 1976) and Swedish (Frankenhaeuser & Gardell, 1976) studies report higher levels of adrenaline and noradrenaline among workers under machine-paced, assembly-line conditions, as compared to other wage and salary workers. Prospective research in Holland replicated the effects of elevated work load and catecholamine (adrenaline and noradrenaline) output and demonstrated an additional effect on hypertension (Falger, 1979).

Little is known of the relationship between objective and subjective stress, that is, a given stressor as measured independently and as reported by the person affected, and studies that make such measurements in comparable terms are much needed. The usual assumption is that subjective reports of stress will tend toward exaggeration, but individual, and perhaps cultural, differences are likely to be large. German research on postinfarction patients found that they reported the presence of many factors at work that we could consider stressors, but they did not regard them as stressors and denied, or did not perceive, strain (Borcherding, Michallik-Herbein, Langosch, & Frieling, 1984).

We also need research that includes performance measures as well as measures of strain under overload conditions. There is some fragmentary evidence that the effects of overload are very different for organizations than for individuals. For example, research on men and women in a variety of unionized white-collar jobs (drafting, mechanical, and technical-clerical) found role overload to be correlated positively with productivity and other organizationally valued outcomes, but to be also associated with three negative individual outcomes—job dissatisfaction, fatigue, and tension (Beehr, Walsh, & Taber, 1976).

Control has been sometimes measured as worker autonomy, especially over work pace and methods, and sometimes as closeness of supervision. It is clear that greater autonomy is a commonly expressed wish on the part of nonsupervisory employees and that the perception of unnecessarily close supervision is a consistent predictor of job dissatisfaction. Such findings have been reported over a period of several decades, and some 25 studies published during the past 10 years confirm them. Recent research, however, has extended that work by locating control in a larger pattern of prediction. For example, a study of nurses found that those characterized as Type A (hard-driving, competitive, time-sensitive, etc.) showed more signs of physiological strain than did the Type B nurses and that the stressors most responsible for those effects (role overload and role conflict) were also those over which the nurses had least control (Ivancevich, Matteson, & Preston, 1982). Another study of nurses found that the

self-reported need for control was directly related to the amount of subjective strain (Numerof & Abrams, 1984). And a Swedish study of men in a wide range of occupations found that quantitative overload (hectic work pace) was not itself associated with physiological strain (significant excess risk of myocardial infarction), but that overload in combination with lack of autonomy (low decision latitude) was so associated (Alfredsson, Karasek, & Theorell, 1982).

Perception and Cognition: The Appraisal Process

The acknowledgment of appraisal as an important cognitive element in the stress sequence has come about largely through the theoretical conviction and experimental research of Lazarus and Folkman (1984). Moreover, incorporation of the appraisal process into research and theories of stress is still incomplete, perhaps especially so in organizational studies. Except for that of Lazarus and Folkman (1984), none of the models we have examined emphasizes appraisal or other cognitive elements in stress. Ivancevich and Matteson (1980) and the early ISR model (French & Kahn, 1962) distinguish between stressors as objectively measured and as perceived but do not go beyond that. McGrath goes somewhat further. His model includes appraisal as an element that intervenes between the actual and the perceived situation. Moreover, his concept of perceived stressfulness is defined as the result of a cognitive process in which consequences of the event and the probability of successful coping are assessed. Perceived stressfulness increases with the importance of the event and the uncertainty of the outcome. French, Caplan, and Harrison (1982), in research utilizing objective and subjective goodness of fit between the individual and the job as predictors of strain, propose a model that has cognitive as well as perceptual implications. For example, goodness of fit between the objective and the perceived job situation is defined as contact with reality, and goodness of fit between objective attributes of the person and the same attributes as self-perceived is defined as accuracy of self-assessment. The cognitive processes are not specified, however, and we must go beyond the organizational literature to review the role of appraisal in the stress process.

The argument for its importance (Lazarus & Folkman, 1984) begins with the fact of individual differences; different people react differently to stressors that are objectively the same. Furthermore, the stressors encountered in real life are often embedded in complex situations, and successful coping requires analysis of both positive and negative situational aspects to reach some overall judgment of potential gain or loss and to decide upon a course of action.

Appraisal thus goes beyond perception; it is "the process of categorizing an encounter, and its various facets, with respect to its significance for well-being" (Lazarus & Folkman, 1984, p. 31). These authors further distinguish between primary and secondary appraisal, not on the basis of their relative importance, but of their temporal sequence. Primary appraisal consists of the initial determination that a stimulus (person, event, situation) is positive (benign), negative (stressful), or neither (irrelevant) in its implications for well-being. Secondary appraisal, which may follow very quickly, is a judgment about what might and can be done to minimize damage or maximize gain. Lazarus and Folkman (1984) recognize that the appraisal process may be iterative or cyclical as the individual takes into account a previous coping effort or some other new information; they therefore distinguish (initial) appraisal from reappraisal.

The importance of the appraisal process as a predictor of stress outcomes is well illustrated by a recent longitudinal study of 274 patients who had undergone surgery for breast cancer (Vinokur, Threatt, Vinokur-Caplan, &

Satariano, 1990). Neither the objective stage of the disease nor the extent of surgery predicted significantly the person's appraisal of threat, but that appraisal was a major predictor of subsequent anxiety, depression, and somatic complaints. Some other studies, while not specifically organizational, indicate that appraisal plays a similarly important role in predicting the outcome of job-generated stresses. The faulty appraisals so studied include the failure of trapped coal miners to recognize the importance of conserving water while they looked for alternative routes of escape (Lucas, 1969), the dysfunctional coping choice of a man passed over for promotion (Benner, 1982), and the effects on blood pressure of different employee responses to an angry manager (Harburg, Blakelock, & Roeper, 1979). In the last of these studies, the more reflective styles (reason with him, talk to him after he has cooled down) were associated with lower blood pressure than the more impulsive styles (ignore, deny, attack, or protest). The cognitive processes that evoked these differences in coping behavior are inferred rather than measured, however.

A thorough review of Lazarus's approach and an extension of it and related work to organizationally generated stress is provided by Beehr and Bhagat (1985) and the other contributors to their book, *Human Stress and Cognition in Organizations*. It includes a proposed three-stage model of appraisal that includes the following: (a) event redefinition; (b) judgment, in which the individual develops hypotheses about possible actions and outcomes; and (c) enactment, which involves the transition from cognition to behavior (Segovis, Bhagat, & Coelho, 1985). The model is specified in terms of ten propositions, which are appropriately stated as hypotheses to be tested rather than as summaries of research results that organizational scholars already have in hand.

To investigate adequately the role of cognitive processes in the stress sequence, we need studies that differentiate those processes from those that immediately precede and follow it, that is, from the mere subjective representation of the stressor and from the coping behaviors that follow cognitive appraisal. Measures capable of making such distinctions are not readily at hand, although some beginnings have been made. Latack (1986), in a methodological study of situation-specific coping with job stressors, identified two global dimensions, *control* and *escape*, each of them involving distinctive patterns of cognitive change as well as action.

Responses to Stress

Our model of stress distinguishes three major categories of possible responses to stress: physiological responses, psychological responses, and behavioral responses. This distinction is also found in the empirical studies on organizational stress; however, psychological responses and behavioral responses (especially burnout) have been investigated more frequently than physiological effects. In this section we will provide a concise overview of empirical studies in each of the three possible categories of stress responses.

Physiological Responses to Stress. In the medical sciences, the concept of stress is linked closely to physiological reactions by the individual. The inclusion of physiological responses to stress in organizational research, however, is relatively rare. In a review of research on physiological responses to stress in the work environment, Fried, Rowland, and Ferris (1984) cite 47 articles from organizational journals. From these he concludes that organizational researchers have investigated three major types of physiological responses to job stress. First, there are cardiovascular symptoms such as blood pressure, cardiac activity, and cholesterol level. Second are the biochemical measures: catecholamines (primarily epinephrine, norepinephrine, and dopamine), corticosteroids

(cortisol), and uric acid. Third, gastrointestinal symptoms, especially symptoms of peptic ulcer, have been measured in a number of empirical studies. Fried also classified these studies according to the temporal aspect of their design—cross-sectional, short-time-interval, and longitudinal.

Our own review of recent research reporting physiological responses to job stress shows partial agreement with Fried's. Heart rate, blood pressure, and catecholamine levels (epinephrine and norepinephrine) are the physiological responses for which we most often have independent assessment. Gastric symptoms, with or without the inference of peptic ulcer, have been studied less frequently, assessed from self-report rather than physician diagnosis or laboratory tests, and show less consistent results (Gardell, 1987).

Higher heart rates have been reported under conditions of role conflict, role ambiguity, ambiguity regarding future developments on the job, poor fit between person and job, and overall reported stress at work. Elevated blood pressure readings have been found in response to some of the same reported stressors—overall subjective stress at work, role ambiguity, and poor fit between properties of the person and the job. Examples of the research from which these findings emerged are presented in summary form in Tables 1 through 4.

Research that links job stress to catecholamine and cortisol levels has been summarized by Rose (1987), who explains that the catecholamines change very rapidly under stimulation and respond to a variety of stimuli. Frankenhaeuser, Gardell, Johansson, and their colleagues at the Karolinska Institute have been pioneers in studying catecholamine levels (epinephrine and norepinephrine) as affected by stressors encountered at work (Frankenhaeuser, 1979; Johansson, Aronsson, & Lindstrom, 1978; Gardell, 1987). Unpredictability at work, lack of control over pace and method, distracting noise, changes in method of pay from hourly wage to piece work, and intermittent demand for peak physical output have all been associated with increased levels of catecholamines.

Findings that link conditions at work to cortisol are fewer and less consistent. Rose (1987) suggests the possibility that cortisol, a product of the hypothalamic pituitary adrenal cortical system, is less influenced by objective conditions but more influenced by the individual's appraisal, anticipation, and previous experience with them. For example, novice parachute jumpers show elevations of both cortisol and catecholamines; after the third or fourth jump, however, cortisol levels revert to normal (Ursine, Baade, & Levine, 1978). Rose's own research with air traffic controllers shows significant associations between average daily level of cortisol secretion and work variables such as load and pace, and a Swedish study of bus drivers (Aronsson, Barklof, & Gardell, 1980) shows a clear relation between perceived time pressure and cortisol, as well as epinephrine.

An ambitious research project undertaken cooperatively by the Karolinska Institute and the Volvo Corporation involves comparisons of men and women, managers and non-supervisory workers, days at work and days at home, and time of day (two-hour intervals). Physiological measures included heart rate, catecholamines (epinephrine and norepinephrine), cortisol, and blood pressure. Results illustrate both the potentialities and the complications of using physiological indicators of stress in work situations. Epinephrine and norepinephrine levels were higher at work than at home, but the norepinephrine levels for women tended to persist into the evening, while those for men decreased more quickly. This effect was most marked for female managers. Men had higher cortisol levels and higher blood pressure than women, and this difference was also most marked for male managers. This project is a major example of the kind of work that must be undertaken to bring psychosocial and physiological variables together in organizational research.

Psychological Responses to Stress. When psychologists do research on the consequences of organizational stress, they concentrate on psychological effects. That is in part a reflection of disciplinary preference; psychologists tend to study psychological variables, and members of other disciplines are no less ethnocentric. That is not in itself objectionable, but it becomes so when it leads to the disregard of how psychological responses are expressed in behavior or reflected in physiological indicators. Such links are important both to reveal the full effects of stressors and to validate the self-reports of psychological effects. We will return to these issues in the concluding section of this chapter; for the present, let us consider the psychological effects of stress in their own right.

Since publication of the 1976 *Handbook*, comprehensive reviews of the psychological effects of organizational stress have appeared (Cooper & Payne, 1988; Holt, 1982). Table 1 is based on these sources and on our own review of recent publications. The variables (psychological responses, effects, strains) are listed in alphabetical order, and the terminology is that of the authors, except for very minor changes. For example, we have combined satisfaction and dissatisfaction, since the substantive findings show negative relationships between job stressors and satisfaction.

An inspection of the entries in this Table 1 tells us a good deal about the nature of research on psychological responses to stress at work. First, many different responses have been investigated. The table lists 43 responses, and it is not exhaustive.

Second, although many different responses have been measured, only a few have been measured in many studies and by different investigators. By far the most frequently cited response to job stress is job dissatisfaction. At its worst, this means that some set of respondents reported that their jobs were stressful and that they were dissatisfied with them, a correlation open to many interpretations, from

TABLE 1

Psychological Responses to Work Stress

Response to Stress	Reference	Response to Stress	Reference
Alienation from organization	Kahn, 1973	(Dis)satisfaction with job	Abdel-Halim, 1982 Bagozzi, 1978 Blau, 1981
Anxiety	Billings & Moos, 1982 Caplan et al., 1975 Caplan & Jones, 1975 Hurrell, 1985 Jayaratne et al., 1983		Caplan et al., 1975 Cooper & Roden, 1985 Davidson & Cooper, 1986 Fisher, 1985 Ford, 1985 Ford & Bagot, 1978
Anxiety (Job)	Abdel-Halim, 1981 LaRocco et al., 1980 Winnubst et al., 1982		Ganster et al, 1986 Howell et al., 1987 Ivancevich et al., 1982 Jackson, 1983
Boredom	Caplan et al., 1975 Kaufman & Beehr, 1986 LaRocco et al., 1980		Jayaratne et al., 1983 Karasek et al., 1981 Kaufman & Beehr, 1986 Keller, 1983
Burnout (Emotional exhaustion, depersonalization, reduced accomplishment)	Etzion, 1984 Ford, 1985 Gaines & Jermier, 1983		Kohli, 1985 LaRocco et al., 1980 LoRocco & Jones, 1978 Matteson & Ivancevich, 1982 Seers et al., 1983
Commitment (Organization professor)	Fisher, 1985 Vredenburgh & Trinkaus, 1983	(Dis)satisfaction with life	Ganster et al., 1986 Iris & Barrett, 1972 Karasek et al., 1981
Confusion	Hurrell, 1985	Dissatisfaction/work load	Kaufman & Beehr, 1986 LaRocco et al., 1980
Depersonalization	Jayaratne & Chess, 1984	Emotional arousal (Symptoms)	Dearborn & Hastings, 1987 Werbel, 1983
Depression	Billings & Moos, 1982 Caplan et al., 1975 Caplan & Jones, 1975 Fusilier et al., 1987 Hurrell, 1985 Jayaratne & Chess, 1984 Karasek et al., 1981 LaRocco et al., 1980 Winnubst et al., 1982	Emotional exhaustion	Jayarathne & Chess, 1984
		Fatigue	Beehr, Walsh, & Taber, 1976 Hurrell, 1985

TABLE 1

Psychological Responses to Work Stress (continued)

Response to Stress	Reference	Response to Stress	Reference
Frustration	Ford, 1985 Storms & Spector, 1987	Somatic complaints	Ford, 1985 Fusilier et al., 1987 Ganster et al., 1986 Jayaratne & Chess, 1984
Health (General)	Davidson & Cooper, 1986 Matteson et al., 1984 Matteson & Ivancevich, 1982		LaRocco et al., 1980 Winnubst et al., 1982
		Strain (Composite)	Halpin et al., 1985 Kittel, 1983
Health (Mental)	Cooper & Roden, 1985		Kobasa, 1982 Matteson et al., 1984
Health (Physical)	Dearborn & Hastings, 1987 Rhodewalt & Agustodottir, 1984		Nowack, 1986 Petrie & Rotheram, 1982
		Strain (Job)	Lasky et al., 1986
Health problems	Williams & Stout, 1985	Strain (Physical	Orpen, 1982
Hostility	Hurrell, 1985	Strain (Psychological)	Orpen, 1982
Illness	Kobacca, 1982 LaRocco & Jones, 1978 Schmied & Lawler, 1986	Strain (Emotional)	Jackson, 1983
		Stress (Job)	Ford & Bagot, 1978
Irritation	Caplan et al., 1975 Jayaratne & Chess, 1984 LaRocco et al., 1980 Winnubst et al., 1982	Tedium	Shamir & Drory, 1982
		Tension	Bagozzi, 1978 Kahn, 1973 Mossholder et al., 1982
Physical symptoms	Billings & Moos, 1982		
Resentment	Caplan & Jones, 1975	Tension (Job)	Abush & Burkhead, Hurrell, 1985
Self-confidence	Billings & Moos, 1982		Dailey et al., 1986 Matteson & Ivanevich
Self-esteem	Beehr, 1976 House, 1972 La Rocco & Jones, 1978		1982
		Turnover intent	Fisher, 1985
Sexual maladjustment	Mott, 1976	Vigor	Hurrell, 1985

causality to methodological artifact. At its best, the psychological response is located in the context of other variables, self-reported and independently assessed, as implied by the stress models described earlier in this chapter. As an example of research that makes such links explicit, see Frankenhaeuser et al. (1989).

The third characteristic apparent in Table 1 is the considerable conceptual overlap among the response categories that investigators have used. Boredom and tedium, for example, are synonymous. Dissatisfaction with the job seems to include dissatisfaction with some specific aspects of the job, such as work load. Health has been treated as an undifferentiated state in some studies, but others have asked more specifically about physical health, mental health, or health problems. Closely related, it would seem, to questions about health are those about symptoms, referred to in some studies as physical symptoms and in others as somatic complaints.

Less apparent in the table but very clear in the literature themselves is the variety of self-reported measures used to gauge psychological responses to stressors at work. In most cases we are not given enough information about questionnaire items and psychometric properties to make an informed judgment about combining measures or choosing among them.

We can, however, hazard some substantive, though tentative, conclusions from this body of research, with appropriate caution because of methodological reasons reiterated throughout the chapter.

Stress is a common aspect of the work experience. It is expressed most frequently as job dissatisfaction, but it finds expression also in more intense and aroused affective states—anger, frustration, hostility, and irritation. More passive, but perhaps no less negative, are such responses as boredom and tedium, burnout, fatigue, helplessness, hopelessness, lack of vigor, and depressed mood. Consistent with these feelings are the relationships between job stress and lowered self-confidence

and self-esteem. Complaints about health can be considered among psychological responses to stress or they can be treated as indicative of some illness; whichever interpretation we make, responses to job stress include somatic complaints and health symptoms. Finally, some of these responses suggest explicit consequent behavior. Alienation from the organization and lack of commitment to it, for example, are consistent with the reported intention to leave (intended turnover).

We believe that, even with due allowance for false positives and tautological measures, the psychological effects of work-related stressors have been plausibly established. Their implication for illness are not well established (Holt, 1982). The psychological effects themselves, however, are real, painful, and costly. Moreover, they extend to health behavior, job performance, and the enactment of other life roles.

Behavioral Responses to Stress.   The number of studies that have investigated behavioral responses of stress at work is fewer than those that have measured psychological responses. Table 2 summarizes the behavioral criteria used and the studies using them.

The 15 behavioral categories that appear in these studies can be grouped rather easily into five broader classifications. Three involve the work role itself, performance of the job, other behavior at work, and flight from work. One involves the disruption or degradation of roles other than work. And the fifth broad behavioral category, partly overlapping with the first, consists of self-damaging behaviors on and off the job. Arranged along these lines, the behavioral responses to stress appear as follows:

- *Degradation/disruption of the work role itself*
  Job performance
  Accidents and errors
  Alcohol use at work
  Drug use at work

TABLE 2

Behavioral Responses to Work Stress

Response to Stress	Reference	Response to Stress	Reference
Absence	Akerstedt, 1976 Jackson, 1983 Karasek et al., 1981 Keller, 1983 Matteson & Ivancevich, 1982	Disruptive performance Role as citizen Role as friend, dating partner	Gardell, 1976 Mott, 1976
Accidents and errors Harm to self Harm to self	 Theorell, 1974 Colquhoren, 1976	Drug use on the job	Davidson & Cooper, 1986 Mangione & Quinn, 1975
		Early retirement	Jacobson, 1972
Alcohol use on the job	Mangione & Quinn, 1975 Winnubst et al. 1952	Job performance	Bagozzi, 1978 Blau, 1981
Authoritarian punitiveness	Fodor, 1976		Davidson & Cooper, 1986 Kaufman & Beehr, 1986 Matteson et al., 1984 Mossholder et al., 1982 Vredenburg & Trinkaus, 1983
Caffeine intake	Caplan et al., 1975		
Counterproductive behavior on the job (Spreading rumors, doing inferior work on purpose, stealing, damaging property on purpose, not reporting accidental damage)	Mangione & Quinn, 1975	Smoking (rate)	Caplan et al., 1975 Howard et al., 1986 Kittel, 1983 Winnubst et al., 1982
		Strikes	Belbin & Stammers, 1972
		Turnover	Fisher, 1985 Jackson, 1983 Vredenburgh & Trinkaus, 1983

- *Aggressive behavior at work*
  Counterproductive acts (stealing, purposeful damage, spreading rumors, etc.)
- *Flight from the job*
  Absenteeism
  Turnover
  Early retirement
  Strikes

- *Degradation/disruption of other life roles*
  Spouse, including spouse abuse
  Friend, including dating
  Citizen
- *Self-damaging behaviors*
  Alcohol use
  Drug use
  Smoking
  Caffeine use
  Accidents

Most of these studies are cross-sectional, and most of the behaviors are based on self-report. They are thus subject to the methodological limitations we have noted in our discussion of psychological responses to stress. A further problem in assessing these behavioral responses is the relatively small number of studies and the consequent lack of replication. On the other hand, some of the findings seem adequately replicated—for example, those on job performance, absence and increased use of tobacco. And others—for example, stealing or damaging property and using alcohol or drugs at work—may well be underreported for reasons of social acceptability or the avoidance of punishment.

We are prepared to accept the general finding that work-generated stressors have behavioral effects, that those effects are manifest both on the job and away from it, and that they impose substantial costs on work organizations.

Ramifying Consequences of Stress

One can think of job stress as having potential consequences that go far beyond the immediate experience of stress and its associated response. Some such ramifications involve performance—performance of the individual on the job and in other life roles and, by extension, performance of the organization as a whole. Other ramifications involve the health of the individual, as affected by prolonged exposure to physical stressors or noxiants and through responses to prolonged or recurrent psychosocial stressors.

Much has been written about such ramifications in social space and time and, in the fields of toxicology and epidemiology, much has been done. In the related field variously referred to as ergonomics, human engineering, or (archaically) man-machine systems, evidence is accumulating that links specific physical job demands—postural constraint and prolonged work at video display terminals,

for example—to health complaints. With respect to the ramifying effects of psycho social stressors at work, however, empirical evidence is only beginning to accumulate, although the literature of accusation and advocacy is already large.

The effects of work-generated stress on individual health are best demonstrated with respect to coronary heart disease (myocardial infarction, angina pectoris, or abnormal electrocardiographic findings). Selye (1956) urged attention to these "diseases of adaptation" long ago, and research reviews have been published by Cooper and Marshall (1976) and by Matteson and Ivancevich (1987).

Job stressors of various kinds—cyclic overload, threat of job loss, and role conflict and ambiguity, for example—are associated with such risk factors as elevated cholesterol levels (Friedman, Rosenman, & Carroll, 1958), elevations in blood pressure (Kasl & Cobb, 1970), and increased heart rate (French & Caplan, 1970). Most of this work has been done with small samples of men selected from single establishments. Researchers in Sweden, however, developed standardized measures of job characteristics for 118 occupational groups on a nationwide basis (Alfredsson & Theorell, 1983) and used them in a case-control study in Stockholm County. Men in jobs characterized by high demand and low control (low autonomy) were at twice the risk for myocardial infarction, in comparison to men in the same age range (40–54) employed in all other occupations.

In combination, these studies suggest a research strategy that could be highly significant both for theory and practice. We need to identify stressful work settings (occupations, industries, etc.) and at the same time identify the characteristic stressors in those settings, as Alfredson and Theorell have begun to do. The next step, of course, should be field experiments and interventions to discover ways of reducing such sources of stress.

The relationship between work and the nonwork aspects of life has been the subject of more speculation than research. It is reasonably well established, however, that the feelings people have about their work extend to other domains of life. Life satisfaction correlates substantially with the prestige ordering of occupations (Quinn & Shepard, 1974), and work satisfaction is a major predictor of overall well-being (Campbell, Converse, & Rodgers, 1976).

Almost all such research is cross-sectional, leaving unsettled the extent to which work affects life off the job in comparison to the effects of nonwork stressors on attitudes and behavior at work. In the absence of longitudinal research, a few cross-sectional studies have shed some light on this question by including both objective and subjective measures of the work situation. For example, a comparison of abusive husbands with two groups of nonabusive husbands, one self-described as satisfied with marriage and the other dissatisfied, showed that abusive husbands experienced more objectively verifiable negative events on the job as well as more subjective job stress (Barling & Rosenbaum, 1986). A study of men working rotating shifts and their spouses showed some negative effects on family interactions from the structural (objective) properties of the situation—amount of required overtime, for example. Stronger effects were shown between the workers' reaction to shift work (emotional interference) and the quality of family interactions (Jackson, Zedeck, & Summers, 1985). Such findings demonstrate the value of distinguishing between the objective properties of a stressor and its properties as perceived and assessed by different individuals.

None of the research on the ramifying effects of work stress denies the plausible argument that nonwork stresses can affect attitudes and behavior at work. Such effects have long been assumed, and they have been reported by counselors. More recently, they have been demonstrated in research on single-parent families (Burden, 1986) and on families in which both parents are employed (Kelly & Voydanoff, 1985).

We need research that permits the examination of both effects—work on nonwork and vice versa. And we need research that shows the combined effects of work and nonwork stressors on health. Beginnings along these lines have been made by the development and validation of measures of total life stress (Bhagat, McQuaid, Lindholm, & Segovis, 1985) and by the measurement of work and nonwork stress in commensurate terms. For example, Frankenhaeuser and her colleagues showed that the characteristic elevation of catecholamines as the stresses of the work day accumulate are sharply reduced at the end of the work day for men, but for married employed women the elevation persists until the household responsibilities are also fulfilled (Frankenhaeuser, 1988).

Properties of the Person as Stress Mediators

The recognition of individual differences in resistance to stress must be among the oldest insights into the complexities of human behavior. Quantitative data about the moderating effects of individual characteristics on the relationship between job stress and strain are relatively recent, however. Kahn, Wolfe, Quinn, and Snoek (1964) reported that the effects of role conflict and ambiguity were moderated or conditioned by such personality characteristics as flexibility-rigidity, introversion-extraversion, and emotional sensitivity. Ganster (1987), in a review chapter, cites research demonstrating that the Type A behavior pattern intensifies the effects of various job stressors. Less work has been done with demographic characteristics as stress moderators, but an early study of managers by Christenson and Hinkle (1961) found that family background, socioeconomic status, and education reduced the effect of stress to the extent that they were congruent with the managerial role. Race and minority status have been largely ignored as stress moderators, although they would seem likely to have such effects. A 1985 review by Ford found only five such studies, and he was author or coauthor of three.

Our review of recent research shows three personal characteristics that have been studied as stress moderators, as well as for their main effects: (a) Type A behavior pattern, (b) self-esteem, and (c) locus of control. Research findings with respect to these three variables are summarized in Tables 3, 4, and 5. All three tables follow the same columnar format, presenting for each study the sample characteristics, the stresses (stressors) investigated, the strains measured, and the findings—main effects and moderating effects of the variable under investigation.

Type A Behavior.   Of the 18 studies cited in Table 3, six report consistent evidence for the expected moderating effect of Type A; that is, the Type A individuals (competitive, impatient, aggressive) showed greater evidence of strain than others (Type B) working under comparable conditions. Two studies reported mixed results, and one showed main effects but no moderating effect. Findings for a main effect of Type A behavior on strain are more consistent, as are findings for the relationship between Type A and psychosocial stressors such as poor interpersonal relationships.

We believe that the evidence for a moderating effect of Type A behavior, erratic as it is, justifies the continued exploration of this relationship. For such explorations to become more definitive, we require better measurement of the Type A behavior syndrome itself, the inclusion of objectively quantified measures of stressful stimuli, and the use of a wide range of outcome (strain) measures. It seems likely that the moderating effect of the Type A variable is operative in relation to some

stressors and strains and not others. We need research that will reveal such a pattern, if it exists.

Self-esteem.   Self-esteem and the closely related concept of self-efficacy have had an important place in social psychology for many years, and they have been prominent also in stress research and theory (Bandura, 1969; Moos & Billings, 1982). The basic idea is that self-esteem constitutes a resource for coping. Like any other resource, it can affect the appraisal of situations, the choice of coping behaviors, and the vigor with which a selected course of action is undertaken.

These are reasons why self-esteem might have been investigated extensively by researchers in the field of organizational stress, but they have given it relatively little attention. Moreover, the investigators who have used measures of self-esteem have tended to measure only its direct effects on strain, which in most cases they have found to be significant. Of eight recent studies of job stress that have included self-esteem as a variable and have reported quantitative results, six found significant main effects on job strain, and all were in the same direction—higher self-esteem was associated with lower job strain (see Table 4). Almost all these findings refer to self-reported strain, but Ivancevich and Matteson (1980) also found a negative relationship between self-esteem and risk factors for coronary heart disease (CHD).

In only three of the studies we reviewed was the moderating effect of self-esteem in the stress equation tested, and in only one of these studies (Mossholder, Bedeian, & Armenakis, 1982) was a significant moderating effect found in the stress-strain relationship. Several investigators have found that self-esteem moderates other relationships, however. For example, Inkson (1978) reported that self-esteem heightened the relationship between job satisfaction and job performance, and

TABLE 3

Type A Behavior: Main Effects and Moderating Effects on Job Stress and Strain

Study	Sample	Job Stress	Job Strain	Main Effects	Moderating Effects
Abush, R., & Burkhead, E. (1984). Job stress in midlife working women	$N = 161$ social service employees	Job characteristics	Job tension	Yes	
Caplan, R., & Jones, K. (1975). Effects of workload, role ambiguity, and Type A personality on anxiety, depression, and heart rate	$N = 122$ university computer users	Role ambiguity, Work load, Resentment, Heart rate	Anxiety, Depression	Yes	Yes for anxiety
Chesney, M. et al. (1981). Work environment, Type A behavior, and coronary heart disease risks	$N = 384$ managers	Composite stress, Peer cohesion, Autonomy, Physical comfort	Blood pressure, Heart rate	No	Yes for blood pressure
Cooper, C., & Roden, J. (1985). Mental health and satisfaction among tax officers	$N = 318$ tax officers	Quantitative load	Job satisfaction, Mental health	No for total sample, Yes for female subsample	
Dailey, R., Ickinger, W., & Coote, E. (1986). Personality and role variables as predictors of tension discharge rate in three samples	$N_1 = 116$ nurses, $N_2 = 60$ MBA executives, $N_3 = 46$ middle managers	Role conflict, Role ambiguity	Tension discharge rate	Yes for N_1 and N_2	
Davidson, M., & Cooper, C. (1986). Executive women under pressure	$N_1 = 696$ female managers, $N_2 = 185$ male managers	Composite stress, Management style	General health, Drug use, Job satisfaction, Job performance		

TABLE 3

Type A Behavior: Main Effects and Moderating Effects on Job Stress and Strain (continued)

Study	Sample	Job Stress	Job Strain	Main Effects	Moderating Effects
Dearborn, M., & Hastings, J. (1987). Type A personality as a mediator of stress and strain in employed women	$N = 136$ women	Tenure Hours/week Job stress	Smoking Overweight Exercise Blood pressure Physical health Emotional symptoms	No for health habits Yes for emotional symptoms Yes for smoking	Yes for stress and job satisfaction Yes for buffering Exercise
Evans, G., Palsane, M., & Carrere, S. (1987). Type A behavior and occupational stress	$N = 120$ bus drivers	Composite stress Accident rate Reprimands	Blood pressure Catecholamines		Yes for diastolic blood pressure No for catecholamines
Howard, J., Cunningham, D., & Rechnitzer, P. (1986). Personality as a moderator of job stress and coronary risk in Type A individuals	$N = 217$ managers	Role ambiguity	Smoking Blood pressure Cholesterol Triglycerides Uric acid	Yes for blood pressure and triglycerides	
Role ambiguity, Type A behavior, and job satisfaction					
Hurell, J. (1985). Machine paced work and Type A behavior pattern	Letter sorters $N_1 = 1,267$ $N_2 = 1,536$ paced $N_3 = 2,131$ $N_4 = 2,131$ unpaced	Life stress	Tension anxiety Depression Anger/hostility Fatigue Vigor Confusion	Yes for tension, anxiety, and confusion	No moderating effect

TABLE 3

Type A Behavior: Main Effects and Moderating Effects on Job Stress and Strain (continued)

Study	Sample	Job Stress	Job Strain	Main Effects	Moderating Effects
Ivancevich, J., Matteson, M., & Preston, C. (1982). Occupational faction stress, Type A behavior and physical well-being	N_1 = 339 managers N_2 = 50 nurses	Work load Career Role conflict	Job satisfaction Cholesterol Blood pressure Triglycerides	Yes for various relationships	
Keenan, A., & McBain, G. (1979). Effects of Type A behavior, intolerance of ambiguity, and locus of control on the relationship between role stress and work-related outcomes	N = 90 managers	Role stress	Job tension Job satisfaction	No	No
Kelly, K., & Houston, B. (1985). Type A behavior in employed women	N = 91 women	Work load Role conflict Skill under-utilization	Job tension	Yes for tension	
Kirmeyer, S., & Diamond, A. (1985). Coping by police officers: A study of role stress and Type A and Type B behavior patterns	N = 31 police officers	Role conflict Role ambiguity Role load		No differences between Type A and Type B on coping appraisal	Type A appraise more often and use more problem-focused and coping
Kittel, F. et al. (1983). Type A in relation to job stress, social and biochemical variables	N = 2,302 men	Composite stress Physical work conditions, pace, responsibilities	Composite strain Cholesterol Triglycerides Smoking habits Blood pressure	Yes for cholesterol, triglycerides, and smoking habits	
Matteson, M., & Ivancevich, J. (1982). Type A and Type B behavior patterns and self-reported health symptoms and stress	N = 315 medical technicians	No stressor specified	Health Job satisfaction Tension discharge Absenteeism		

TABLE 3

Type A Behavior: Main Effects and Moderating Effects on Job Stress and Strain (continued)

Study	Sample	Job Stress	Job Strain	Main Effects	Moderation Effects
Matteson, M., Ivancevich, J., & Smith, S. (1984). Relation of Type A behavior to performance and satisfaction among sales personnel	N = 355 life insurance agents	No stressor specified	Composite strain Health Job performance	Yes for strain and health	Yes for strain and health
Nowack, K. (1986). Type A, hardiness, and psychological distress	N = 189 university employees	Hours worked Daily hassles	Composite strain Burnout Hardiness	Yes for strain and burnout	
Orpen, C. (1982). Type A personality as a moderator for the effects of role conflict, role ambiguity, and role overload on individual strain	N = 91 middle managers	Role conflict Role ambiguity Role overload	Physical strain Psychological strain Heart rate Blood pressure Respiration rate	No	Yes for physical and psychological strain
Rhodewalt, F., Hayes, R., Chemers, M., & Wysocki, J. (1984). Type A behavior, perceived stress, and illness	N = 49 university administrators	Life events Job stress	Physical health Psychological well-being	Yes	
Schmied, L., & Lawler, K. (1986). Hardiness, Type A behavior, and stress-illness relation in working women.	N = 82 women	Life events	Illness	No	
Van Dijkhuizen, N., & Reiche, H. (1980). Psychosocial stress in industry: A heartache for middle management	N = 95 managers	Work load Interpersonal relations Job future ambiguity	Physical strain Psychosomatic strain Blood pressure Cholesterol	Yes	Yes, except for physical strain

TABLE 4

Self-esteem: Main Effects and Moderating Effects on Job Stress and Strain

Study	Sample	Job Stress	Job Strain	Main Effects	Moderating Effects
Bagozzi, R. (1978). Sales force performance and satisfaction as a function of individual difference, interpersonal, and situational factors	$N_1 = 123$ $N_2 = 43$ salespersons	Role ambiguity Work load	Satisfaction Performance Tension	Yes	
Bagozzi, R. (1980). Performance and satisfaction in an industrial sales force	$N_1 = 122$ salespersons	No stressors	Satisfaction Performance	Yes	
Byosiere, P. (1988). Effects of societal, organizational, and individual factors on job performance, job satisfaction, and job strain	$N = 255$ teachers	Role stress Organizational antecedents of stress	Job satisfaction Life satisfaction Somatic complaints Psychological strain	Yes	
Howell, R. et al. (1987). Self-esteem, role stress, and job satisfaction among marketing managers	$N_1 = 226$ $N_2 = 220$ $N_3 = 22$ managers	Role conflict Role ambiguity	Satisfaction	No	
Keller, R. (1983). Predicting from prior absenteeism, attitudinal factors, and nonattitudinal factors	$N = 190$ communication equipment plant personnel	No stressors Absenteeism	Satisfaction	Yes	
Kohli, A. (1985). Some unexplored supervisory behaviors and their influence on salespeople's role clarity, specific self-esteem, job satisfaction, and modification	$N = 114$ salespersons	Role clarity Supervisory behavior	Satisfaction	No	No

TABLE 4

Self-esteem: Main Effects and Moderating Effects on Job Stress and Strain (continued)

Study	Sample	Job Stress	Job Strain	Main Effects	Moderating Effects
Mossholder, K., Bedian, A., & Armenakis, A. (1982). Group process–work outcome relationships	N_1 = 206 nursing employees	Peer group interaction	Tension Propensity to leave Performance	No	No
Petrie, K., & Rotheram, M. (1982). Insulators against stress: Self-esteem and assertiveness	N = 106 firemen	No stressor	Composite strain	Yes	
Werbel, J. (1983). Job change: A study of an acute job stressor	N = 62 employees	Skill uncertainty	Emotional arousal	Yes	No

Mossholder et al. (1982) found that it had a similar effect on the relationship between peer group interaction and performance.

This scatter of findings raises questions about the concept of self-esteem itself. It can be regarded as an almost unvarying personality trait, and some investigators appear to treat it as that. We consider it to be a relatively stable property of the person, but one that is nevertheless subject to influence throughout the life course. Few studies have considered self-esteem as a dependent variable, but Byosiere (1988), in a longitudinal study of public school teachers, found that role conflict and role ambiguity in the work setting had significant negative effects on the self-esteem level of new teachers. Thus, self-esteem appears as an element of importance in understanding job stress, but an element that is not yet well understood. We need studies that will examine its main effects, its moderating effects, and the extent to which it is itself affected by properties of the work situation.

Locus of Control.   Like self-esteem, locus of control has been an influential concept in social psychology where it has been treated as an enduring individual characteristic (Rotter, 1966). It differentiates between people who believe that they themselves are primarily responsible for what happens to them and those who believe that major events in their lives are mainly determined by other people or forces beyond themselves. The distinction between internal and external locus of control thus characterizes people in terms of their beliefs, and these beliefs are assumed to be stable over time and across situations. We do not consider either of these assumptions to be justified in absolute terms, but we do consider locus of control to be sufficiently stable to be taken seriously as a property of the person that affects strain and the stress-strain relationship.

Locus of control, used in this sense, should not be confused with, nor should it displace, the concept as a situational property, that is, the extent to which a person is actually autonomous or subject to supervision and control at work. Control in this latter sense has been investigated extensively as a determinant of job strain, especially by Karasek (1979) and Karasek, Baker, Marxer, Ahlbom, and Theorell (1981), who refer to it as *decision latitude*. Their research builds on a great deal of earlier experimental work in the laboratory, both with animal and human subjects. Murphy (1986) has summarized this research as it applies to the domain of job stress.

Our present concern, however, is with locus of control as an enduring property of the person who enters into the stress-strain sequence. The underlying hypothesis in research taking this approach is that people whose locus of control is primarily internal will respond to stress differently from those whose locus of control is external. Those who are internally oriented in this respect are more likely to take action against the source of the stress itself or to mitigate its effects in other ways. Those who are externally oriented are more likely to see effective action as beyond their powers and thus to endure rather than act. These are undoubtedly oversimplifications. Locus of control is better regarded as multidimensional and topic specific (Payne, 1988). Moreover, at least one study has shown curvilinear relationships that call into question the usual hypothesis: Krause and Stryker (1984) found that stressful life events were handled with less strain by people whose scores were moderate on the internal-external dimension than by those whose scores were at either the internal or the external extreme. Their study was not specific to job stressors, however.

We reviewed 11 studies of job stress and strain in which the locus of control was also assessed, and the results are summarized in Table 5. In four of these studies, tests were made on the hypothesized moderating effect of internal locus of control, and in three of the four a significant moderating effect was found. Main effects of locus of control were assessed in

TABLE 5

Locus of Control: Main Effects and Moderating Effects on Job Stress and Strain

Study	Sample	Job Stress	Job Strain	Main Effects	Moderating Effects
Dailey, R., Ickinger, W., & Coote, E. (1986). Pesonality and role variables as predictors of tension discharge rate in 3 samples	$N_1 = 116$ nurses $N_2 = 46$ managers	Role conflict Role ambiguity	Tension discharge rate		Yes, buffering
Fusilier, M., Ganster, D., & Mayes, B. (1987). Effects of social support, role stress, and locus of control on health	$N = 312$ police officers	Role conflict Role ambiguity	Depression Somatic complaints Epinephrine	No	
Halpin, G., Harris, K., & Halpin, G. (1985). Teacher stress as related to locus of control, sex, and age	$N = 130$ teachers		Composite strain	Yes	
Lester, D. (1982). Perceived stress in police officers and belief in locus of control	$N = 73$ police officers	Role stress	Job strain	Yes	
Marino, K., & White, S. (1985). Departmental structure, locus of control and job stress	$N = 278$ health care professionals	Organizational structure Work load Pressure	No strains measured	Yes on stressor	Yes
Parasuraman, S. (1984). Sources and outcomes of stress in organizational settings	$N = 217$ food process industry personnel	Role stress Composite stress	Job satisfaction Commitment Turnover Performance	Yes for satisfaction and commitment	
Revicki, D., & May, H. (1985). Occupational stress, social support, and depression	$N = 210$ physicians	Occupational stress	Depression	Yes	Yes

TABLE 5

Locus of Control: Main Effects and Moderating Effects on Job Stress and Strain (continued)

Study	Sample	Job Stress	Job Strain	Main Effects	Moderating Effects
Storms, P., & Spector, P. (1987). Relationships of organizational frustration with reported behavioral reactions	N = 160 employees		Organizational frustration	Yes	Yes
Vredenburgh, D., & Trinkaus, R. (1983). An analysis of role stress among hospital nurses	N = 566 nurses	Role stress Technology Turnover	Commitment Performance	Yes	No
Williams, J., & Stout, J. (1985). The effect of high and low assertiveness on locus of control and health problems	N = 78 service workers	No stressor	Health problems	Yes	
Wolpin, J., & Burke, R. (1986). Occupational locking-in	N = 72 administrators	Locked-in			

eight studies and were found to be significant in seven, involving such stressors as role conflict, role ambiguity, and overload. We conclude that it is useful to include locus of control in studies of job stress, preferably in combination with measures of autonomy and decision latitude. In other words, we believe that control should be measured both as a property of the person and as a property of the situation.

Properties of the Situation as Stress Mediators

Our model of stress and strain stipulates the possibility that certain properties of the situation, as well as enduring characteristics of the individual, can moderate or buffer the effects of a stressor. In principle, the buffering effect can occur between any pair of variables in the stress-strain sequence; thus, the buffering variable can reduce the tendency of organizational properties to generate specific stressors, alter the perceptions and cognitions evoked by such stressors, moderate the responses that follow the appraisal process, or reduce the health-damaging consequences of such responses. Each of these possibilities, for each variable predicted to have such an effect, is a buffering hypothesis. Each predicts an effect of the relationship between some pair of variables in the main causal sequence of the stress model. Together they represent a set of testable interaction effects.

Of the many variables that might thus be tested for their potential buffering effects, only one—social support—has had much attention from researchers on organizational stress. Sutton and Kahn (1987), on the basis of research outside the organizational context, have proposed three other situational variables as potential buffers against stress—(a) the extent to which the onset of a stressor is predictable, (b) the extent to which it is understandable, and (c) the extent to which aspects of the stressor are controllable by the person who must experience it.

Lack of predictability at work has been studied as a stressor in its own right; its main effects are well established in the research literature on role ambiguity (Katz & Kahn, 1978; Pearce, 1981). Data from laboratory research, moreover, suggest that predictability can also act as a buffer. Seligman (1975), whose experimental work on the predictability of a stressor has been especially influential, explains its buffering effect in terms of the signal-safety hypothesis. If the occurrence of a stressful event can be predicted, its absence can also be predicted. Thus, the experimental subject, human or animal, knows when it is safe to relax and need not maintain a constant state of vigilance or anxiety. Empirical support for the signal-safety hypothesis has been provided by a number of laboratory studies with both human and animal subjects, but organizational researchers have not yet attempted to test it explicitly.

The situation is much the same with respect to control; organizational research has emphasized the main effects of control or autonomy at work but has had little to say about its potential as a buffer. An exception is the work of Karasek and his colleagues (Karasek, 1979; Karasek, Baker, Marxer, Ahlbom, & Theorell, 1981), based on national survey data in the United States and Sweden. A primary finding is that workers with heavy job demands showed signs of physiological and psychological strain if they also had low decision latitude. The relationship between job demands and strain did not hold, however, among workers with high decision latitude.

The idea that understandability—that is, the reasons for the presence of a stressor and one's exposure to it—might also act as a buffer comes from social psychology and cognitive science rather than organizational theory. The human propensity to seek causal explanations is so strong that experimental subjects tend to neglect information that does not fit their implicit theories about the causes of events (Nisbett & Ross, 1980; Tversky & Kahneman, 1981).

Research to test the buffering qualities of these variables in work settings remains to be done, and we believe that the leads are promising. For the present, however, social support is the one situational variable that has been repeatedly studied for its buffering effects. The results of that research were summarized in 1980 by LaRocco, House, and French in an article that included an attempt to reconcile some apparently conflicting findings by means of reanalysis. The authors concluded that the buffering hypothesis was supported for some strains but not others. Social support moderated (reduced) the relationship between various job stressors and indicators of mental and physical health (anxiety, depression, irritation, and somatic symptoms). Social support did not moderate the relationship between job stressors and such specific job strains as boredom, job dissatisfaction, and dissatisfaction with work load. A more recent review chapter (Beehr, 1985) notes the considerable evidence for both main effects and buffering effects of social support, but notes also the occasional finding of reverse buffering—that is, instances in which the presence of social support seems to heighten the stress-strain relationship. Possible explanations for these unexpected effects have been proposed but not tested.

Our review of research on social support is based on 22 studies, the results of which are summarized in Table 6. All but two of the studies report main effects of social support on strain, and in most cases the effect is present for support from both co-workers and supervisors. Support from sources away from the job, family, and friends was measured less frequently, but the effects were positive, that is, strain-reducing, in studies for which support from those sources was measured.

Buffering effects were as predicted in most studies where they were assessed, but the pattern is less consistent than for main effects. Two studies that found significant main effects tested for buffering effects and found none

(Jayaratne, Tripodi, & Chess, 1983; LaRocco & Jones, 1978). Two others that found significant main effects reported negative buffering effects (Ganster, Fusilier, & Mayes, 1986; Kaufman & Beehr, 1986). And one study found neither main effects nor buffering effects (Kobasa, 1982).

These studies include a variety of measures, occupations, and modes of analysis. None of these factors provides a definitive explanation of the differences in their findings. We conclude that social support is a demonstrably potent variable, that with only occasional exceptions it has significant main effects, and that it frequently has buffering effects as well. We need research that tests for both effects and differentiates both source of support and type of support (emotional, informational, tangible-instrumental, etc.).

Prevention and Intervention

Recent years have seen a great deal of activity directed at the management of stress and its ramifying effects on health. To organizational psychologists, however, the activity pattern is disappointing in several respects. First, it is concentrated disproportionately on reducing the effects of stress rather than reducing the presence of stressors at work. Second, perhaps as a consequence, the main target of intervention has been the individual rather than the organization; the effort has been directed at increasing individual resistance to stressors generated at work. Third, the surge of practitioner activity in the domain of stress management has not been accompanied by a commensurate increase in serious research; most programs have not been evaluated in that sense. Finally, the programs in stress management that are sold to companies show a suspicious pattern of variance; they differ more by practitioner than by company. When practitioners in any field offer sovereign remedies regardless of the presenting symptoms, patients should be wary.

TABLE 6

Social Support: Main Effects and Moderating Effects on Job Stress and Strain

Study	Sample	Stress Measure	Support Measure	Strain Measure	Main Effects			Buffering Effects		
					Co-worker	Supervisor	Off Job	Co-worker	Supervisor	Off Job
Abdel-Halim, A. (1982). Effects of role stress–job design technology interactions on employee work satisfaction	$n_1 = 89$ middle and lower managerial personnel in large heavy equipment manufacturing firm	Role conflict Role ambiguity Participation	Co-worker support Supervisor support	Job dissatisfaction Job anxiety	Yes	Yes (not significant for anxiety)		Yes	Yes (not significant for anxiety)	
Billings, A., & Moos, R. (1982). Stressful life events and symtoms: A longitudinal model	$n_1 = 115$ employed women $n_2 = 214$ employed men	Involvement Autonomy Work pressure Clarity (Role ambiguity) Control	Co-worker support Supervisory support Family resources	Depression Anxiety Physical symptoms Self-confidence	Yes (in female sample, only significant for depression)	Yes (not significant for female sample)		Yes (no distinction was made between type of support and type of stressor; buffering effects in the female sample were found for depression)	See previous column	Yes (no buffering effects were found in the female sample for anxiety and self-confidence)

TABLE 6

Social Support: Main Effects and Moderating Effects on Job Stress and Strain (continued)

Study	Sample	Stress Measure	Support Measure	Strain Measure	Main Effects			Buffering Effects		
					Co-worker	Supervisor	Off Job	Co-worker	Supervisor	Off Job
Blau, G. (1981). Organizational investigation of job stress, social support, service length, and job strain	n = 66 bus operators	Stress (factor analysis of pretested questionnaire; Physical danger; Passenger (intracompany) Scheduling (assistance))	Co-worker support Supervisor support Off-job support	Job dissatisfaction Job performance	Yes (not significant for performance)	Yes	Yes (not significant for performance)	No	Yes for intracompany performance relation only	No
Etzion, J. (1984). Moderating effect of social support on the stress-burnout relationship	n = 657 Israeli managers and human service professionals	Work stress Life stress	Support at work Off-job support	Burnout	Yes (no distinction was made between co-worker and supervisor support)	See previous column	Yes	Yes for men only	See previous column	Yes for women only

TABLE 6

Social Support: Main Effects and Moderating Effects on Job Stress and Strain (continued)

Study	Sample	Stress Measure	Support Measure	Strain Measure	Main Effects			Buffering Effects		
					Co-worker	Supervisor	Off job	Co-worker	Supervisor	Off job
Fisher, C. (1985). Social support and adjustment to work: A longitudinal study	n = 270	Unmet expectations	Supervisor Co-worker	Job satisfaction Organizational commitment Professional commitment Turnover Intention to leave organization Intention to leave profession	Yes	Yes		Yes for organizational commitment only	Yes for organizational commitment only	No
Ford, D. (1985). Job-related stress of the minority professional	n = 166 clerical and managerial personnel	Episodic stress Chronic job stress Role conflict	Structural, informational and emotional support	Job satisfaction Somatic complaints Job burnout Frustration	No distinction made between the sources of social support; study focused on the difference in type of social support; main effects found for emotional support on job strain					

TABLE 6

Social Support: Main Effects and Moderating Effects on Job Stress and Strain (continued)

Study	Sample	Stress Measure	Support Measure	Strain measure	Main Effects			Buffering Effects		
					Co-worker	Supervisor	Off Job	Co-worker	Supervisor	Off Job
Ford, D., & Bagot, D. (1978). Correlates of job stress and job satisfaction for minority professionals in organizations	n = 22 managerial, supervisory, technical, and clerical minority personnel	Task structure Role clarity Pressure	Supervisor support	Job dissatisfaction Job stress (= strain)		Yes				
Fusilier, M., Ganster, D., & Mayes, B. (1987). Effects of social support, role stress, and locus of control on health	n = 312 employees of police and fire department	Role conflict Role ambiguity	Supervisor support Co-worker support Off-job support	Depression Somatic complaints Epinephrine excretion	Yes	Yes	Yes	Yes	Yes	Yes
Gaines, J., & Jermier, J. (1983). Emotional exhaustion in a high stress organization	n = 169 officers and support personnel of police department	Physical danger Task motivating potential Formalization Rule inflexibility Promotion Pay equity	Supervisor support Co-worker support Off-job support (marital status)	Burnout	Yes	Yes	No			

TABLE 6

Social Support: Main Effects and Moderating Effects on Job Stress and Strain (continued)

Study	Sample	Stress Measure	Support Measure	Strain Measure	Main Effects			Buffering Effects		
					Co-worker	Supervisor	Off Job	Co-worker	Supervisor	Off Job
Ganster, D., Fusilier, M., & Mayes, B. (1986). Role of social support in the experience of stress at work	n = 326 employees of contracting firm	Role conflict Role ambiguity Quantitative load Lack of variability Skill under-utilization	Supervisor support Co-worker support Off-job support	Depression Job satisfaction Life satisfaction Somatic complaints	Yes	Yes	Yes	Negative buffering	Negative buffering	No
Jackson, S. (1983). Participation in decision making as a strategy for reducing job-related strain	n$_1$ = 95 n$_2$ = 70 nursing and clerical employees	Perceived influence Communications Role conflict Role ambiguity	Social support (composites)	Emotional strain Job dissatisfaction Absenteeism Turnover	Yes (not significant for the withdrawal behaviors)	See previous column				
James, S. A., Lacroix, A. Z., Kleinbaum, D. G., & Strogatz, D. S. (1984). John Henryism and blood pressure differences among Black men: II	n = 112 black male residents	Job security Unfair wages Race conflict	Supervisor support Co-worker support	Blood pressure (DBP, SBP)	No	No				
Jayaratne, S., Tripodi, T., & Chess, W. (1983). Perceptions of emotional support, stress, and strain by male and female social workers	n$_1$ = 229 male social workers n$_2$ = 312 female social workers	Role conflict Role ambiguity	Co-worker support Supervisor support	Job dissatisfaction Emotional exhaustion Depersonalization Anxiety Irritability Somatic	Yes (not significant for irritability and somatic complaints)	Yes (not significant for depersonalization anxiety, and irritability)		No	No	

TABLE 6

Social Support: Main Effects and Moderating Effects on Job Stress and Strain (continued)

Study	Sample	Stress Measure	Support Measure	Strain Measure	Main Effects			Buffering Effects		
					Co-worker	Supervisor	Off job	Co-worker	Supervisor	Off job
Jayaratne, S., & Chess, W. (1984). The effects of emotional support on perceived stress and strain.	(This study reports additional findings from preceding study.)									
Karasek, R., Triantis, K., & Chaudhry, S. (1982). Co-worker and supervisor support as moderator of associations between task characteristics and mental strain.	n = 1,016 male workers	Stressor (composite) Job demands Decision latitude	Supervisor support Co-worker support	Depression Life dissatisfaction Job dissatisfaction Job-related depressed mood Absenteeism	Yes (not significant for job-related depressed mood and absenteeism)	Yes (not significant for absenteeism)		Yes (distinction is made between slope and/or intercept differences)	See previous column	
Kaufman, G., & Beehr, T. (1986). Interactions between job stressors and social support: Some counterintuitive results	n = 103 nurses	Work load P–E fit Job future ambiguity Skill under-utilization	Dimension 1: Supervisor Co-worker Off job Dimension 2: Tangible Emotional Instrumental	Job satisfaction Work load satisfaction Boredom Pulse rate Blood pressure Absenteeism Performance	Yes	Yes	Yes	Negative buffering	Negative buffering	

TABLE 6

Social Support: Main Effects and Moderating Effects on Job Stress and Strain (continued)

Study	Sample	Stress Measure	Support Measure	Strain Measure	Main Effects			Buffering Effects		
					Co-worker	Supervisor	Off job	Co-worker	Supervisor	Off job
Kobasa, S. (1982). Commitment and coping in stress among lawyers	n = 157 lawyers	Stressful life events	Social support	Strain Illness	No (no distinction made in sources support; no significant main effects)	See previous column	See previous column	No	No	No
LaRocco, J., House, J., & French, J. (1980). Social support, occupational stress, and health	n = 636 men from 23 occupations	Quantitative work load Role conflict Participation Under-utilization of skills Job future ambiguity	Co-worker support Supervisor support Home support	Job dissatisfaction Work load dissatisfaction Boredom Somatic complaints Depression Anxiety Irritation	Yes	Yes	Yes	Yes (not significant for job dissatisfaction and boredom)	Yes - (not significant for job dissatisfaction, depression, and somatic complaints)	Yes - (not significant for job dissatisfaction and anxiety)
LaRocco, J., & Jones, A. (1978). Co-worker and leader support as moderators of stress-strain relationships in work situations	n = 3,725 enlisted Navy men	Role conflict and ambiguity (composite)	Co-worker support Supervisor support	Job dissatisfaction Navy satisfaction Illness Self-esteem	Yes (not significant for illness)	Yes for satisfaction only		No	No	

TABLE 6

Social Support: Main Effects and Moderating Effects on Job Stress and Strain (continued)

Study	Sample	Stress Measure	Support Measure	Strain Measure	Main Effects			Buffering Effects		
					Co-worker	Supervisor	Off job	Co-worker	Supervisor	Off job
Seers, A., McGee, G., Serey, T., & Graen, G. (1983). The interaction of job stress and social support	n = 104 employees of large federal government agency	Role ambiguity Role conflict	Co-worker support Supervisor support Family support	Job dissatisfaction	Yes for work satisfaction with promotions only	Yes for overall satisfaction and supervisory satisfaction only	Yes for overall satisfaction	Yes for supervisory satisfaction	Yes for overall satisfaction	Yes for overall satisfaction
Shamir, B., & Drory, A. (1982). Occupational tedium among prison officers	n = 201 custodial personnel	Role conflict Role ambiguity Role overload Danger perception Working conditions Job scope	Supervisor support Co-worker support Off-job support	Tedium	Yes	Yes	Yes	No	Yes	Yes
Winnubst, J., Marcelissen, F., & Kleber, R. (1982). Effects of social support in the stressor-strain relationship: A Dutch sample	n = 246 employees of 13 organizations	Role conflict Role ambiguity Role overload Responsibility Future uncertainty	Supervisor support Co-worker support	Irritation Depression Threat Smoking Drinking Heart complaints Somatic complaints SBP, DSP Cholesterol level	Yes (not significant for smoking, drinking, SBP, and cholesterol)	Yes (not significant for smoking, drinking, SBP, DBP, SNF, and cholesterol)		Yes (not significant for irritation, drinking, blood pressure, and cholesterol)	Yes for threat, irritation, and blood pressure only	

In spite of these weaknesses, there has been progress in the field of stress intervention since the earlier edition of the *Handbook* was published. More than 40 research studies have been conducted, many of them summarized in Table 7; four reviews of stress management approaches have been published in organizational journals (Cullen & Sandbergh, 1987; Ivancevich & Matteson, 1986; Murphy, 1984; Newman & Beehr, 1979); and two recent books include chapters on workplace interventions and their evaluation (Cooper & Payne, 1988; Quick, Bhagat, & Dalton, 1987).

Our review is based on the minority of programs for which persuasive empirical data are available. These are listed alphabetically by author in Table 7 and are described in terms of four properties—nature of study, strategy, target, and phase in model. *Nature* distinguishes between prevention and intervention. *Strategy* refers to the activity undertaken to reduce stress or strain—training, counseling, exercise, and the like. *Target* identifies the level at which the program was actually conducted, that is, with individuals, with work groups, or at' the level of organizational structure and policy. *Phase in model* is an attempt to locate the intended thrust of each stress reduction program in relation to the model of stress and strain proposed earlier in this chapter (Figure 9). In principle, a program of stress reduction could be directed at any of the major elements in that model, from organizational antecedents of stress through ramifying consequences for health and organizational effectiveness. In practice, we have not been able to make such precise determinations. We can, however, distinguish between four kinds of programs— (a) those that attempt to alter the stressors as perceived by the individual, (b) those that concentrate directly on reducing the strains evoked by perceived stressors, (c) those that aim to alter the stress-resistant properties of the person more generally, and (d) those that are intended to improve the stress-moderating properties of the interpersonal situation. In the last column of Table 7, these program aims are designated as stress inhibition, response extinction, properties of the person, and interpersonal relations.

As the emphasis on the individual level suggests, the locus of these programs in our stress model (Figure 9) is substantially toward the right-hand side; there is more concern with reducing the cognitive appraisal of stressors and their subsequent effects than with reducing or eliminating the stressors themselves. Even the programs that aim at stress inhibition tend to address subjective rather than objective aspects of the stress sequence; almost none consider the organizational antecedents (policy and structure) that intensify or reduce the presence of objective stressors.

Murphy (1986) reaches a similar conclusion in his review chapter. He describes three classes of intervention programs, which correspond to the epidemiological categories of primary, secondary, and tertiary preventing. Thus, employee assistance programs attempt to repair damage already done, usually by abuse of alcohol and other substances. Stress management programs train individuals in techniques for reducing their physiological and psychological responses to stress. Stress reduction programs are few and deal with aspects of control—increased participation in decision making, autonomy on the job itself, and control over one's work schedule.

The crucial question for all these programs is how well they work. The research evidence to answer that question is unfortunately meager and the methodological problems are serious. Nevertheless, there are indications of some success. Employee assistance programs report about a 50 percent return to work, on average, and some centers report rates of 70 to 80 percent. Even at 50 percent, employee assistance programs must be judged cost effective (Murphy, 1986). Those programs in stress management that have been evaluated by procedures more rigorous than short-term participant satisfaction show significant

TABLE 7

Prevention and Intervention Studies in Organizational Stress Research

Study	Nature	Strategy	Target	Phase in Model
Archer, J., & Probert, B. (1985). Wellness breaks	Intervention Prevention	Wellness break 10 minutes	Group level	
Ault, R. (1986). Draw on new lines of communication	Intervention Prevention	Art and visual perception	Group level	
Bair, J., & Greenspan (1986). Teams: Teamwork training for interns, residents, and nurses	Intervention	Team building	Group level	Stress inhibition
Black, J. et al. (1985). Social skills training to improve job maintenance	Intervention	Social skills, training	Individual	Response extinction
Blair, S. (1985). Review of health promotion program for school employees	Intervention	Medical screening Fitness assessment Exercising Feedback 10–13 weeks	Individual	Response extinction
Brown, D., & Brooks, L. (1985). Career counseling as a mental health intervention	Intervention	Career counseling	Individual	Response extinction
Bunker, K. (1985). Coping with the "mess" of stress	Intervention	Assessment	Individual	Response extinction
Clark, A. (1983). The relationship between family participation and health	Prevention	Family	Individual	Response extinction

TABLE 7

Prevention and Intervention Studies in Organizational Stress Research (continued)

Study	Nature	Strategy	Target	Phase in Model
Falkenberg, L. (1987). Employee fitness programs	Prevention	Employee fitness program	Group level	Response extinction
Fine, S. (1986). Before the trainer comes	Prevention	Lecture Small group discussion	Group level	Properties of person Response extinction
Firth, J., & Shapiro (1986). An evaluation of psychotherapy for job-related distress	Intervention	Prescriptive & exploratory therapy 8 sessions	Individual	Response extinction
Forman, S. (1983). Occupational stress management	Prevention	Cognitive-behavioral programs	Individual Organizational	Properties of person Response extinction
Freeberg, S. (1984). Effortness exercises to balance daily executive stress	Prevention	Quick exercises	Individual	Stimulus inhibition Properties of person Interpersonal relations Response extinction
Ganster, D. et al. (1982). Managing organizational stress	Intervention	Group exposure 16 hours in 8 weeks Cognitive interpretation Relaxation	Individual	Response extinction
Graham, R. (1982). Employee support systems in a psychosocial rehabilitation setting	Prevention	Employee support system Participation program Motivation program	Group level Individual	Interpersonal relations Response extinction

TABLE 7

Prevention and Intervention Studies in Organizational Stress Research (continued)

Study	Nature	Strategy	Target	Phase in Model
Hartman, C. (1982). Stress relief for transportation employees	Intervention	Group counseling	Group level	Interpersonal relations Properties of person Response extinction
Hayes, L. (1986). The superwoman myth	Intervention	Discussion group 8 weeks	Group level	Stimulus inhibition Interpersonal relations Response extinction
Hayes, L., & O'Connor, M. (1982). Emotional components of supervision	Intervention	Employee assistance program Problem-solving 4 weekly meetings	Group level	Stimulus inhibition Response extinction
Higgins, N. (1986). Occupational stress and working women	Intervention	Progressive relaxation and systematic desensitization time management 7 sessions	Individual	Response extinction
Jackson, S. (1983). Participation in decision making as a strategy for reducing job-related strain	Intervention	Participation in decision making	Organizational level	Stimulus inhibition Response extinction
Kanas, N. (1986). Support groups for mental health staff and trainees	Intervention Prevention	Three types of support groups		Literature review
Kindler, H. (1984). Time out for stress management training training	Prevention	Participation Reinforcement Organizational support	Organizational level	Stimulus extinction Interpersonal relations Response extinction

TABLE 7

Prevention and Intervention Studies in Organizational Stress Research (continued)

Study	Nature	Strategy	Target	Phase in Model
Kindler, H. (1985). Stress management training for professionals		(See previous study.)		
Mallinger, M. (1986). Stress management	Prevention	Time management Problem solving Career assessment Assertion	Individual Organizational	Stimulus inhibition Response extinction
Manuso, J. (1983). Health promotion through psychological services	Prevention	Employee counseling Stress management Health management	Individual Organizational	Properties of person
Murphy, L. (1984). Occupational stress management	Intervention Prevention		Literature review	
Orpen, C. (1984). Managerial stress, relaxation and performance	Intervention	Relaxation 3 weeks	Individual	Response extinction
Porras, J. & Hargis (1982). Precursors of individual change	Intervention	Behavioral modeling training 10 weeks	Individual	Stimulus inhibition Properties of person Response extinction
Starak, Y. (1984). Strategies for mind and body health in social work education	Prevention	Yoga Meditation Autogenic training	Individual Organizational	Properties of person Response extinction
Wertkin, R. (1985). Stress-inoculation training	Intervention	Cognitive behavioral program	Individual	Properties of person

reductions in subjective distress and psycho-physiological indicators. Their effects on job satisfaction and performance are contradictory and unclear.

Programs that attempt to reduce or eliminate organizational stressors are rare, and adequate research evaluations of such programs are rarer still. Murphy (1986) describes three (Jackson, 1983; Pierce & Newstrom, 1983; Wall & Clegg, 1981). All three involve some aspect of control, and all show positive results.

We conclude that the stress programs are probably cost effective, regardless of their mode. There is too little research to permit systematic comparisons of effectiveness by program type. The content of most programs, with their emphasis on individualized approaches and stress management, reflects the concerns of managerial and white collar employees rather than those of blue collar populations. The one study that makes such comparisons (Neale, Singer, Schwartz, & Schwartz, 1982) shows that blue collar workers, at least those who are members of labor unions, more often point to physical and technological aspects of work as sources of stress, and propose remedies that involve organizational policies, government actions, and labor contracts.

Conclusion: The Future of Research on Organizational Stress

When George Bernard Shaw was approaching his 94th year, a reporter who was conducting a filmed interview took note of Shaw's 50-year effort at social reform and asked him whether he had any message for the waiting world. Shaw looked straight at the camera and replied accusingly, "I've told you what to do and you haven't done it!"

That remark has some applicability to the state of research on organizational stress. Various scholars, in the course of writing handbook chapters or the final chapters of books on work-related stress, have undertaken to instruct themselves and their readers about the needs of the field (Bhagat & Beehr, 1985; Frese & Zapf, 1988; Kasl, 1978; McGrath, 1976). There is a considerable convergence in their assessments and in their advice, and it is well summarized in Kasl's (1978) trenchant critique, in which he describes the common reliance on cross-sectional designs and self-perceived measures as a "self-serving methodological trap which has tended to trivialize a good deal of the research on work stress" (p. 13).

Kasl went on to advocate three main changes in research on stress in the workplace. The first is to include measures of stressors and strains that are independent of self-report, as well as those based on self-report. The effect of introducing such measures would be to anchor both ends of the hypothesized stress process in reality beyond the perceptions of the individual subject. The extent to which perceived stressors correspond to independent assessment of the work situation, and the extent to which perceived strains correspond to physiological indicators and clinical diagnosis, then become ascertainable. Thereafter, scholars can act on the theoretical and methodological implications of these findings.

The second advice, which is common to virtually all authors who attempt this exercise in self-criticism, is that studies of organizational stress and strain must make greater use of longitudinal designs. The reason, of course, is to clarify causal relationships that are otherwise indeterminate. Moreover, many effects of work stressors must be expected to show complex patterns over time. Some effects will be brief and perhaps undamaging; some will persist; still others are likely to show the "sleeper" pattern familiar in toxicology, in which prolonged exposure to a stressor produces an illness that is apparent only after months or years.

The third course of action that Kasl urges, and with which we concur, is greater attention to contextual factors, such as the moderating variables in our model. Work is not all of life, especially for the many men and women whose work is limited in content and reward. If we want to understand the relationship of work to health, therefore, we must take account of the larger context in which the work role is enacted.

All these improvements suggest research that is interdisciplinary and designed more as natural experiments than surveys or laboratory studies. It could be objected with reason that such research is more difficult, more time-consuming, more expensive, and therefore perhaps less feasible than the kinds of designs that make up the bulk of our research literature. Yet the past decade has seen considerable progress, as Frese and Zapf (1988) point out. They cite the increased use of longitudinal designs (Frese, 1985; Karasek et al., 1981; Kohn & Schooler, 1982; Parkes, 1982), the more frequent use of moderator variables (Beehr, Walsh, & Taber, 1976; Frese & Semmer, 1986; House, 1981; Howard, Cunningham, & Rechnitzer, 1986a, 1986b; Karasek et al., 1981; Semmer, 1984) and the more numerous studies in which objective measures of work settings were obtained (Greiner, Leitner, Weber, Hennes, & Volpert, 1987; Jenkins, Nadler, Lawler, & Camman, 1975; Kannheiser, 1987; Volpert, Oestrreich, Gablenz-Kolakovic, Krogoll, & Resch, 1983; Zapf, 1987). These citations are encouraging, and they are examples rather than complete listings. The recent work of Frankenhaeuser et al. (1989) in a Volvo plant includes all three of the cited characteristics: (a) it is longitudinal, (b) it incorporates objective measures of job characteristics, and (c) it includes moderator variables. In addition, it uses physiological as well as self-reported indicators of strain and measures the demands of "nonwork roles" (home responsibilities) as well as the demands of the job.

The inclusion of family roles, which are so different for men and women, calls attention to another explanatory factor in organizational stress: sex. The Swedish research is rare in that all the basic analyses are reported separately for men and women, but the question of gender differences in work stress has not been entirely neglected. Several review chapters and one book report the relevant research (Giel, 1982; Gupta & Jenkins, 1985; Gutek, Repetti, & Silver, 1988; Handy, 1979; Nathanson & Lorenz, 1982; Silver, 1988; Terborg, 1985). Nevertheless, the reporting of research findings separately for men and women is not common in the literature of organizational stress, even when the designs and numbers would seem to allow it. It is a much needed development, especially in light of changes in women's work roles, in family composition, and perhaps in the allocation of family responsibilities. Three articles in a recent issue of the *American Psychologist*, all of them by women, document that need well (Matthews & Rodin, 1989; Repetti, Matthews, & Waldron, 1990; Scarr, Phillips, & McCartney, 1989).

Even in the domain of stress management, the number of intervention studies that include adequate research evaluation shows an encouraging increase. Ten such studies are cited as "a representative sample" in a current review by Ivancevich, Matteson, Freedman, and Phillips (1990). In addition, a recent successful randomized field experiment on coping with job loss reminds us that interventions to improve the management of work-generated stress need not be limited to organizational settings (Caplan, Vinokur, Price, & Van Ryn, 1990).

In short, research on the stresses of work, in spite of the deficiencies we have cited, is not only growing but improving. As for the future, the lines of improvement still needed are clear; models and methods good enough to enable improvement are available; and some excellent examples are already before us. There is reason for optimism.

References

Abush, R., & Burkhead, E. J. (1984). Job stress in midlife working women: Relationships among personality type, job characteristics, and job tension. *Journal of Counseling Psychology, 31*(1), 36–44.

Abdel-Halim, A. (1981). Effects of role stress-job design-technology interaction on employee work satisfaction. *Academy of Management Journal, 24*(2), 260–273.

Agervold, M. (1983). Process control and psychic strains. *Psykologisk Skriftserie Aarhus, 8*(5), 1–57.

Akerstedt, T. (1976). Shift work and health: Interdisciplinary aspects. In P. G. Rentos & R. D. Shepard (Eds.), *Shift work and health*. Washington, DC: U.S. Government Printing Office.

Alfredsson, L., Karasek, R., & Theorell, T. (1982). Myocardial infarction risk and psychosocial work environment. *Social Science and Medicine, 16*(4), 463–467.

Alfredsson, L., & Theorell, T. (1983). Job characteristics of occupations and myocardial infarction risk: Effect of possible confounding factors. *Social Science and Medicine, 17*(20), 1497–1503.

Archer, J., & Probert, B. S. (1985). Wellness breaks. *Journal of College Student Personnel, 26*(6), 558–559.

Aronsson, G., Barklof, K., & Gardell, B. (1980). *Report 16, Research Group for social psychological working life*. Sweden: University of Stockholm, University of Psychology.

Ault, R. E. (1986). Draw on new lines of communication. *Personnel Journal, 65*(9), 73–77.

Bagozzi, R. P. (1978). Salesforce performance and satisfaction as a function of individual difference, interpersonal, and situational factors. *Journal of Marketing Research, 15*(4), 517–531.

Bagozzi, R. P. (1980). Performance and satisfaction in an industrial sales force: An examination of their antecedents and simultaneity. *Journal of Marketing, 44*, 65–77.

Bair, J. P., & Greenspan, B. K. (1986). Teams: Teamwork training for interns, residents, and nurses. *Hospital and Community Psychiatry, 37*(6), 633–635.

Bandura, A. (1969). *Principles of behavior modification*. New York: Holt.

Barling, J., & Rosenbaum, A. (1986). Work stressors and wife abuse. *Journal of Applied Psychology, 71*, 346–348.

Bartunek, J. M., & Reynolds, C. (1983). Boundary-spanning and public accountant role stress. *Journal of Social Psychology, 121*(1), 65–72.

Basowitz, H., Persky, H., Korchin, S., & Grinker, R. (1955). *Anxiety and stress*. New York: McGraw-Hill.

Beehr, T. A. (1976). Perceived situational moderators of the relationship between subjective role ambiguity and role strain. *Journal of Applied Psychology, 61*, 35–40.

Beehr, T. A. (1985). Organizational stress and employee effectiveness: A job characteristics approach. In T. A. Beehr & R. S. Bhagat (Eds.), *Human stress and cognition in organizations* (pp. 57–82). New York: Wiley.

Beehr, T. A., & Bhagat, R. S. (Eds.). (1985). *Human stress and cognition in organizations*. New York: Wiley.

Beehr, T. A., & Franz, T. M. (1987). The current debate about the meaning of job stress [Special issue]. Job stress: From theory to suggestion. *Journal of Organizational Behavior Management, 8*(2), 5–18.

Beehr, T., Walsh, J., & Taber, T. (1976). Relationships of stress to individually and organizationally valued states: Higher order needs as a moderator. *Journal of Applied Psychology, 61*(1), 41–47.

Belbin, R. M., & Stammers, D. (1972). Pacing stress, human adaptation, and training in car production. *Applied Ergonomics, 3*, 142–146.

Benner, P. (1982). *A phenomenological study of mid-career men: Relationships between work meaning, work involvement, and stress and coping at work*. Unpublished doctoral dissertation, University of California, Berkeley.

Bhagat, R. S., & Beehr, T. A. (1985). An evaluation summary and recommendations for future research. In T. A. Beehr & R. S. Bhagat (Eds.), *Human stress and cognition in organizations*. New York: Wiley.

Bhagat, R. S., McQuaid, S. J., Lindholm, H., & Segovis, J. (1985). Total life stress: A multimethod validation of the construct and its effects on organizationally valued outcomes and withdrawal behaviors. *Journal of Applied Psychology, 70*, 202–214.

Billings, A. G., & Moos, R. H. (1982). Stressful life events and symptoms: A longitudinal model. *Health Psychology, 1,* 99–117.

Black, J. L., Muehlenhark, C. L., & Massey, F. H. (1985). Social skills training to improve job maintenance. *Journal of Employment Counseling, 22*(4), 151–160.

Blair, S. N. (1985). Review of health promotion program for school employees. *Special Services in the Schools, 1*(3), 89–97.

Blau, G. (1981). Organizational investigation of job stress, social support, service length, and job strain. *Organizational Behavior and Human Performance, 27*(2), 279–302.

Borcherding, H., Michallik-Herbein, V., Langosch, W., & Frieling, E. (1984). Psychological stress and demands at work: Results of empirical studies of myocardial infarct patients under 40 years of age. *Psychologie und Praxis, 28*(1), 11–15.

Brenner, M. H. (1987a). Economic change, alcohol consumption, and heart disease mortality in nine industrialized countries. *Social Science and Medicine, 25*(2), 119–132.

Brenner, M. H. (1987b). Relation of economic change to Swedish health and social well-being, 1950–1980. *Social Science and Medicine, 25*(2), 183–195.

Brenner, M. H., & Mooney, A. (1983). Unemployment and health in the context of economic change. *Social Science and Medicine, 17*(16), 1125–1138.

Brenner, S. (1982). Work, health, and well-being for Swedish elementary school teachers. *Reports from the Laboratory for Clinical Stress Research,* No. 158, 1–35.

Brown, D., & Brooks, L. (1985). Coping with the "mess" of stress: An assessment-based research project. *Professional Psychology: Research and Practice, 16*(6), 660–867.

Burden, D. S. (1986). Single parents and the work setting: The impact of multiple job and homelife responsibilities. The single parent family [Special issue]. *Family Relations: Journal of Applied Family and Child Studies, 35*(1), 37–43.

Byosiere, P. H. (1988). Effects of societal, organizational, and individual factors on job performance, job satisfaction, and job strain: Multiple structural equation modeling in a three wave longitudinal panel study of new teachers. *Dissertation Abstracts International, 48*(5), 2831–2832.

Campbell, A., Converse, P. E., & Rodgers, W. L. (1976). *The quality of American life.* New York: Sage.

Cannon, W. B. (1935). Stresses and strains of homeostasis. *American Journal of Medical Science,* 189:1.

Caplan, R. D., Cobb, S., & French, J. R. P., Jr. (1975). *Job demands and worker health.* Washington, DC: U.S. Department of Health, Education, & Welfare, National Institute for Occupational Safety and Health.

Caplan, R. D., & Jones, K. W. (1975). Effects of work load, role ambiguity, and Type A personality on anxiety, depression, and heart rate. *Journal of Applied Psychology, 60*(6), 713–719.

Caplan, R. D., Vinokur, S. D., Price, R. H., & Van Ryn, M. (1990). Job seeking, reemployment and mental health: A randomized field experiment in coping with job loss. *Journal of Applied Psychology, 74*(5), 759–769.

Chesney, M. A., Sevelius, G., Black, G., Ward, M., Swan, G., & Rosenman, R. (1981). Work environment, Type A behavior, and coronary heart disease risks. *Journal of Occupational Medicine, 23,* 551–555.

Chisholm, R., Kasl, S., & Eskenazi, B. (1983). The nature and prediction of job-related tension in a crisis situation: Reactions of nuclear workers to the Three Mile Island accident. *Academy of Management Journal, 26*(3), 385–405.

Chonko, L. B. (1982). The relationship of span of control to sales representatives' experienced role conflict and role ambiguity. *Academy of Management Journal, 25*(2), 452–456.

Christenson, W. N., & Hinkle, L. E., Jr. (1961). Differences in illness and prognostic signs in two groups of young men. *Journal of American Medical Association, 177,* 247–253.

Clark, A. W. (1983). The relationship between family participation and health. *Journal of Occupational Behavior, 4*(3), 237–239.

Cobb, S., & Kasl, S. V. (1977). *Termination: The consequences of job loss.* U.S. Department of Health, Education and Welfare. Washington, DC: U.S. Government Printing Office.

Colquhoren, W. P. (1976). Accidents, injuries, and shift work. In P. G. Rentos & R. D. Shepard (Eds.), *Shift work and health.* Washington, DC: U.S. Government Printing Office.

Cooper, C. L., & Marshall, J. (1976). Occupational sources of stress: A review of the literature relating to coronary heart disease and mental ill health. *Journal of Occupational Psychology, 49,* 11–28.

Cooper, C. L., & Payne, R. (1988). *Causes, coping and consequences of stress at work.* Chichester, England: Wiley.

Cooper, C. L., & Roden, J. (1985). Mental health and satisfaction among tax officers. *Social Science & Medicine, 21*(7), 747–751.

Cullen, J., & Sandbergh, C. G. (1987). Wellness and stress management programmes: A critical evaluation [Special issue]. Musculoskeletal injuries in the workplace. *Ergonomics, 30*(2), 287–294.

Dailey, R. C., Ickinger, W., & Coote, E. (1986). Personality and role variables as predictors of tension discharge rate in three samples. *Human Relations, 39*(11), 991–1003.

Davidson, M. J., & Cooper, C. L. (1986). Executive women under pressure. Occupational and life stress and the family [Special issue]. *International Review of Applied Psychology, 35*(3), 301–326.

Dean, R. (1966). Human stress in space. *Science, 2,* 70.

Dearborn, M. J., & Hastings, J. E. (1987). Type A personality as a mediator of stress and strain in employed women. *Journal of Human Stress, 13*(2), 53–60.

Dohrenwend, B. S. (1978). Social stress in the community. *American Journal of Community Psychology, 6*(1), 1–14.

Dohrenwend, B. S., & Dohrenwend, B. P. (Eds.). (1974). *Stressful life events: Their nature and effects.* New York: Wiley.

Dohrenwend, B. S., Krasnoff, L., Askenasy, A. R., & Dohrenwend, B. P. (1982). The Psychiatric Epidemiology Research Interview Life Events Scale. In L. Goldberger & S. Breznitz (Eds.), *Handbook of stress* (pp. 332–363). New York: Free Press.

Dohrenwend, B., Pearlin, L., Clayton, P., Hanburg, B., Riley, R., & Rose, R. M. (1982). Report on stress and life events. In G. Elliott & C. Eisdorfer (Eds.), *Stress and human health.* New York: Springer.

Duxbury, M., Armstrong, G. D., Drew, D. J., & Henly, S. J. (1984). Head nurse leadership style with staff nurse burnout and job satisfaction in neonatal intensive care units. *Nursing Research, 33*(2), 97–101.

Elliott, G. R., & Eisdorfer, C. (Eds.). (1982). *Stress and human health: Analysis and implications of research.* New York: Springer-Verlag.

Etzion, J. A. (1984). Moderating effect of social support on the stress-burnout relationship. *Journal of Applied Psychology, 69,* 615–622.

Evans, G. W., Palsane, M. N., & Carrere, S. (1987). Type A behavior and occupational stress: A cross-cultural study of blue-collar workers. *Journal of Personality and Social Psychology, 52*(5), 1002–1007.

Falger, P. (1979). Changes in work load as potential risk constellation for myocardial infarction: A concise review. *Tijdschrift Voor Psychologie, 7*(1–2), 96–114.

Falkenberg, L. E. (1987). Employee fitness programs: Their impact on the employee and the organization. *Academy of Management Review, 12*(3), 511–522.

Fine, S. F. (1986). Before the trainer comes: A group approach to technological change. *Journal for Specialists in Group Work, 11*(1), 42–47.

Firth, J., & Shapiro, D. A. (1986). An evaluation of psychotherapy for job-related distress. *Journal of Occupational Psychology, 59*(2), 111–119.

Fisher, C. D. (1985). Social support and adjustment to work: A longitudinal study. *Journal of Management, 11,* 39–53.

Flanagan, J. C. (1949). Critical requirements: A new approach to employee evaluation. *Personnel Psychology, 2,* 419–425.

Flanagan, J. C. (1954). The critical incident technique. *Psychological Bulletin, 1,* 327–355.

Fodor, E. M. (1976). Group stress, authoritarian style of control, and use of power. *Journal of Applied Psychology, 61*(3), 313–318.

Folkman, S., & Lazarus, R. S. (1980). An analysis of coping in a middle-aged community sample. *Journal of Health and Social Behavior, 21*(3), 219–239.

Ford, D. L. (1985). Job-related stress of the minority professional. In T. A. Beehr & R. S. Bhagat (Eds.), *Human stress and cognition in organizations.* New York: Wiley .

Ford, D. L., & Bagot, D. (1978). Correlates of job stress and job satisfaction for minority professionals in organizations: An examination of personal and organizational factors. *Group and Organization Studies, 3,* 30–41.

Forman, S. G. (1983). Occupational stress management: Cognitive-behavioral approaches. *Children and Youth Services Review, 5*(3), 277–287.

Frankenhaeuser, M. (1976). The role of peripheral catecholamines in adaptation to under-stim-ulation. In G. Serban (Ed.), *Psychopathology of human adaptation.* New York: Plenum.

Frankenhaeuser, M. (1979). Psychoneuroendocrine approaches to the study of emotion as related to stress and coping. In H. E. Howard & R. A. Dienstbier (Eds.), *Nebraska Symposium on Motivation, 1978.* Lincoln: University of Nebraska Press.

Frankenhaeuser, M. (1988). Stress and reactivity patterns at different stages of the life cycle. In P. Pancheri & L. Zichella (Eds.), *Biorhythms and stress in physiopathology of reproduction.* Washington, DC: Hemisphere.

Frankenhaeuser, M., & Gardell, B. (1976). Underload and overload in working life: Outline of a multidisciplinary approach. *Journal of Human Stress, 2*(3), 35–46.

Frankenhaeuser, M., Lundberg, U., Fredrikson, M., Melin, B., Tuomisto, M., Myrster, A., Hedman, M., Bergman-Losman, B., & Wallin, L. (1989). Stress on and off the job as related to sex and occupational status in white-collar workers. *Journal of Organizational Behavior, 10,* 321–346.

Freeberg, S. G. (1984). Effortless exercises to balance daily executive stress. *Journal of Rehabilitation Administration, 8*(4), 128–132.

French, J. R. P., Jr., & Caplan, R. D. (1970). Psychosocial factors in coronary heart disease. *Industrial Medicine, 39*(9), 383–397.

French, J. R. P., Jr., Caplan, R. D., & Harrison, R. V. (1982). *The mechanisms of job stress and strain.* Chichester, England: Wiley.

French, J. R. P., Jr., & Kahn, R. L. (1962). A programmatic approach to studying the industrial environment and mental health. *Journal of Social Issues, 18*(3), 1–47.

Frese, M. (1985). Stress at work and psychosomatic complaints: A causal interpretation. *Journal of Applied Psychology, 70*(2), 314–328.

Frese, M., & Semmer, N. (1986). Shiftwork, stress, and psychosomatic complaints: A comparison between workers in different shiftwork schedules, non-shiftworkers, and former shiftworkers. *Ergonomics, 29*(1), 99–114.

Frese, M., & Zapf, D. (1988). Methodological issues in the study of work stress: Objective vs. subjective measurement of work stress and the question of longitudinal studies. In C. L. Cooper & R. Payne (Eds.), *Causes, coping and consequences.* Chichester, England: Wiley.

Fried, Y., Rowland, K. M., & Ferris, G. R. (1984). The physiological measurement of work stress: A critique. *Personnel Psychology, 37*(4), 583–615.

Friedman, M., Rosenman, R., & Carroll, V. (1958). Changes in the serum cholesterol and blood clotting time in men subjected to cyclic variation of occupational stress. *Circulation, XVII,* 852–861.

Fusilier, M. R., Ganster, D. C., & Mayes, B. T. (1987). Effects of social support, role stress, and locus of control on health. *Journal of Management, 13*(3), 517–528.

Gaines, J., & Jermier, J. M. (1983). Emotional exhaustion in a high stress organization. *Academy of Management, 26*(4), 567–586.

Ganster, D. C. (1987). Type A behavior and occupational stress. Job stress: From theory to suggestion [Special issue]. *Journal of Organizational Behavior Management, 8*(2), 61–84.

Ganster, D. C., Fusilier, M., & Mayes, B. T. (1986). Role of social support in the experience of stress at work. *Journal of Supplied Psychology, 71,* 102–110.

Ganster, D. C., Mayes, B. T., Sime, W. E., & Tharp, G. D. (1982). Managing organizational stress: A field experiment. *Journal of Applied Psychology, 67*(5), 533–542.

Gardell, B. (1976). Reactions at work and their influence on nonwork activities. *Human Relations, 29,* 885–904.

Gardell, B. (1987). Efficiency and health hazards in mechanized work. In J. C. Quick, R. S. Bhagat, J. E. Dalton, & J. D. Quick (Eds.), *Work stress: Health care systems in the work place.* New York: Praeger.

Gavin, J., & Axelrod, W. (1977). Managerial stress and strain in a mining organization. *Journal of Vocational Behavior, 11*(1), 66–74.

Giel, J. Z. (Ed.). (1982). *Women in the middle years: Current knowledge and directions for research and policy.* New York: Wiley Interscience.

Graham, R. S. (1982). Employee support systems in a psychosocial rehabilitation setting. *Psychosocial Rehabilitation Journal, 6*(1), 12–19.

Greiner, B., Leitner, K., Weber, W. G., Hennes, K., & Volpert, W. (1987). RHIA—Ein Verfahren zur Erfassung psychischer Belastung. In Kh. Sonntag (Ed.), *Arvertsanalyse und Technident-wicklung* (pp. 145–161). Bachem, Köln: Wirtschaftsverlag.

Grinker, R., & Spiegel, J. (1945). *Men under stress.* Philadelphia: Blakiston.

Gunderson, E. K. E., & Rahe, R. H. (Eds.). (1974). *Life stress and illness.* Springfield, IL: Thomas.

Gupta, N., & Jenkins, G. D. (1985). Dual career couples: Stress, stressors, strains and strategies. In T. A. Beehr & R. S. Bhagat (Eds.), *Human stress and cognition in organizations* (pp. 141–175). New York: Wiley .

Gutek, B. A., Repetti, R. L., & Silver, D. L. (1988). Nonwork roles and stress at work. In C. L. Cooper & R. Payne (Eds.), *Causes, coping and consequences of stress at work.* Chichester, England: Wiley.

Hageman, M. (1978). Occupational stress and marital relationships. *Journal of Police Science and Administration, 6*(4), 402–412.

Halpin, G., Harris, K. R., & Halpin, G. (1985). Teacher stress as related to locus of control, sex, and age. *Journal of Experimental Education, 53*(3), 136–140.

Handy, C. (1979). The family: Help or hinderance. In C. L. Cooper & R. Payne (Eds.), *Stress at work.* Chichester, England: Wiley.

Harburg, E., Blakelock, E. H., & Roeper, P. J. (1979). Resentful and reflective coping with arbitrary authority and blood pressure: Detroit. *Psychosomatic Medicine, 51*(3), 189–202.

Hartman, C. (1982). Stress relief for transportation employees. *Social Work, 27*(5), 449–451.

Hayes, L. S. (1986). The superwoman myth. *Social Casework, 67*(7), 436–441.

Hayes, L. S., & O'Connor, M. R. (1982). Emotional components of supervision: An EAP workshop. *Social Casework, 63*(7), 408–414.

Haynes, S. G., Feinleib, M., & Kannel, W. B. (1980). The relationship of psychosocial factors to coronary heart disease in the Framingham study III. Eight-year incidence of coronary heart disease. *American Journal of Epidemiology, 111*(1), 37–58.

Higgins, N. C. (1986). Occupational stress and working women: The effectiveness of two stress reduction programs. *Journal of Vocational Behavior, 29*(1), 66–78.

Hinkle, L. E., Jr. (1974). The concept of stress in the biological and social sciences. *International Journal of Psychiatry in Medicine, 5*(4), 335–357.

Hohnsbein, J., Piekarski, C., Kampman, B., & Noack, T. (1984). Effects of heat on visual acuity. *Ergonomics, 27*(12), 1239–1246.

Holland, J. L. (1976). Vocational preferences. In M. D. Dunnette (Ed.), *Handbook of industrial and organizational psychology* (pp. 521–570). Chicago: Rand McNally.

Holmes, T. H., & Masuda, M. (1974). Life change and illness susceptibility. In B. S. Dohrenwend & B. P. Dohrenwend (Eds.), *Stressful life events: Their nature and effects.* New York: Wiley.

Holmes, T. H., & Rahe, R. H. (1967). The social readjustment rating scale. *Journal of Psychosomatic Research, 11*, 213–218.

Holt, R. R. (1982). Occupational stress. In L. Goldberger & S. Breznitz (Eds.), *Handbook of stress.* New York: Free Press.

House, J. S. (1981). *Social support and stress.* Reading, MA: Addison-Wesley.

House, R. J., & Rizzo, J. R. (1972). Role conflict and ambiguity as critical variables in a model of organizational behavior. *Organizational Behavior and Human Performance, 16*, 467–505.

Howard, J. H., Cunningham, D. A., & Rechnitzer, P. A. (1986a). Personality (hardiness) as a moderator of job stress and coronary risk in Type A individuals: A longitudinal study. *Journal of Behavioral Medicine, 9*(3), 229–244.

Howard, J. H., Cunningham, D. A., & Rechnitzer, P. A. (1986b). Role ambiguity, Type A behavior, and job satisfaction: Moderating effects on cardiovascular and biochemical responses associated with coronary risk. *Journal of Applied Psychology, 71*(1), 95–101.

Howell, R. D., Bellenger, D. N., & Wilcox, J. B. (1987). Self-esteem, role stress, and job satisfaction among marketing managers. *Journal of Business Research, 15*(1), 71–84.

Hudgens, R. W. (1974). Personal catastrophe and depression: A consideration of the subject with respect to medically ill adolescents, and a requiem for retrospective life-event studies. In B. S. Dohrenwend & B. P. Dohrenwend (Eds.), *Stressful life events: Their nature and effects.* New York: Wiley.

Hurrell, J. J. (1985). Machine-paced work and the Type A behavior pattern. *Journal of Occupational Psychology, 58*(1), 15–25.

Inkson, J. K. (1978). Self-esteem as a moderator of the relationship between job performance and job satisfaction. *Journal of Applied Psychology, 63*(2), 243–247.

Iris, B., & Barrett, G. V. (1972). Some relations between job and life satisfaction, anxiety-stress, and performance. *Administrative Science Quarterly, 56*, 301–304.

Ivancevich, J. M., & Matteson, M. T. (1980). *Stress and work: A managerial perspective.* Glenview, IL: Scott Foresman.

Ivancevich, J. M., & Matteson, M. T. (1986). Organizational level stress management interventions: Review and recommendations. *Journal of Organizational Behavior and Management, 8*, 229–248.

Ivancevich, J. M., Matteson, M. T., Freedman, S. M., & Phillips, J. S. (1990). Worksite stress management interventions. *American Psychologist, 45*(2), 252–261.

Ivancevich, J., Matteson, M., & Preston, C. (1982). Occupational stress, Type A behavior, and physical well-being. *Academy of Management Journal, 25* (2), 373–391.

Jackson, S. E. (1983). Participation in decision making as a strategy for reducing job-related strain. *Journal of Applied Psychology, 68*(1), 3–19.

Jackson, S. E., Zedeck, S., & Summers, E. (1985). Family life disruptions: Effects of job-induced structural and emotional interference. *Academy of Management Journal, 28*(3), 574–586.

Jacobson, D. (1972). Fatigue-producing factors in industrial work and preretirement attitudes. *Occupational Psychology, 46*, 193–200.

James, S. A., Lacroix, A. Z., Kleinbaum, D. G., & Strogatz, D. S. (1984). John Henryism and blood pressure differences among Black men: II. *Journal of Behavioral Medicine, 7*(3), 259–275.

Janis, I. L. (1951). *Air war and emotional stress.* New York: McGraw-Hill.

Janis, I. L. (1958). *Psychological stress.* New York: Wiley.

Jayaratne, S., & Chess, W. A. (1984). The affects of emotional support on perceived job stress and strain. *Journal of Applied Behavioral Sciences, 20*(2), 141–153.

Jayaratne, S., Tripodi, T., & Chess, W. A. (1983). Perceptions of emotional support, stress, and

strain by male and female social workers. *Social Work Research and Abstracts, 19*(2), 19–27.

Jenkins, G. C., Nadler, D. A., Lawler, E. E., III., & Camman, C. (1975). Standardized observations: An approach to measuring the nature of jobs. *Journal of Applied Psychology, 60*, 171–181.

Jick, T. D., & Payne, R. (1980). Stress at work. *Exchange: The Organizational Behavior Teaching Journal, 5*(3), 50–56.

Johansson, G., Aronsson, G., & Lindstrom, B. (1978). Social psychological and neuroendocrine stress reactions in highly mechanized work. *Ergonomics, 21*(8), 583–599.

Jones, A., & Butler, M. (1980). A role transition approach to the stresses of organizationally induced family role disruption. *Journal of Marriage and the Family, 42*(2), 367–376.

Kahn, R. L. (1973). Conflict, ambiguity and overload: Three elements in job stress. *Occupational Mental Health.*

Kahn, R. L. (1981). *Work and health.* New York: Wiley.

Kahn, R. L., Wolfe, D. M., Quinn, R. P., & Snoek, J. D. (1964). *Organizational stress: Studies in role conflict and ambiguity.* New York: Wiley.

Kanas, N. (1986). Support groups for mental health staff and trainees. *International Journal of Group Psychotherapy, 36*(2), 279–296.

Kannheiser, W. (1987). Neue Techniken und organisatorische Bedingungen: Ergebnisse und Einsatzmoglichkeiten des Tatigkeits-Analyse-Inventars (TAI). In Kh. Sonntag (Ed.), *Arbeitsanalyse und Technikentwicklung* (pp. 69–85). Bachem, Köln: Wirtschaftsverlag.

Karasek, R. A. (1979). Job demands, job decision latitude, and mental strain: Implications for job redesign. *Administrative Quarterly, 24*, 285–307.

Karasek, R. A., Baker, D., Marxer, F., Ahlbom, A., & Theorell, T. (1981). Job decision latitude, job demands, and cardiovascular disease: A study of Swedish men. *American Journal of Health, 71*, 694–705.

Karasek, R. A., Triantis, K. P., & Chaudhry, S. S. (1982). Co-worker and supervisor support as moderators of associations between task characteristics and mental strain. *Journal of Occupational Behavior, 3*(2), 181–200.

Kasl, S. V. (1978). Epidemiological contributions to the study of work stress. In C. L. Cooper & R.

Payne (Eds.), *Stress at work*. Chichester, England: Wiley.

Kasl, S. V. (1983). Methodological issues in stress research. In C. L. Cooper (Ed.), *Stress research: Issues for the eighties*. Chichester, England: Wiley.

Kasl, S. V., & Cobb, S. (1970). Blood pressure changes in men undergoing job loss: A preliminary report. *Psychosomatic Medicine, 32,* 19–38.

Katz, D., & Kahn, R. L. (1978). *The social psychology of organizations* (2nd ed.). New York: Wiley.

Kaufman, G. N., & Beehr, T. A. (1986). Interactions between job stressors and social support: Some counterintuitive results. *Journal of Applied Psychology, 71*(3), 522–526.

Keenan, A., & McBain, G. D. (1979). Effects of Type A behavior, intolerance of ambiguity, and locus of control on the relationship between role stress and work-related outcomes. *Journal of Occupational Psychology, 52*(2), 277–285.

Keller, R. T. (1983). Predicting absenteeism from prior absenteeism, attitudinal factors, and nonattitudinal factors. *Journal of Applied Psychology, 68*(3), 536–540.

Kelly, K., & Houston, B. K. (1985). Type A behavior in employed women: Relation to work, marital, and leisure variables, social support, stress, tension, and health. *Journal of Personality and Social Psychology, 48*(4), 1067–1079.

Kelly, R. F., & Voydanoff, P. (1985). Work/family role strain among employed parents. *Family Relations: Journal of Applied Family and Child Studies, 34*(3), 367–374.

Kindler, H. S. (1984). Time out for stress management training. *Training & Development Journal, 38*(6), 64–66.

Kindler, H. S. (1985). Stress management training for training professionals. *Consultation: An International Journal, 4*(2), 157–158.

Kirmeyer, S. L., & Diamond, A. (1985). Coping by police officers: A study of role stress and Type A and Type B behavior patterns. *Journal of Occupational Behavior, 6*(3), 183–195.

Kittel, F. (1983). Type A in relation to job-stress, social and bioclinical variables: The Belgian physical fitness study. *Journal of Human Stress, 9*(4), 37–45.

Kobasa, S. (1982). Commitment and coping in stress among lawyers. *Journal of Personality and Social Psychology, 42*(4), 707–717.

Kohli, A. K. (1985). Some unexplored supervisory behaviors and their influence on salespeople's role clarity, specific self-esteem, job satisfaction, and motivation. *Journal of Marketing Research, 22*(4), 424–433.

Kohn, M. L., & Schooler, C. (1982). Job conditions and personality: A longitudinal assessment of their reciprocal effects. *American Journal of Sociology, 87,* 1257–1286.

Krause, N., & Stryker, S. (1984). Stress and well-being: The buffering role of locus of control beliefs. *Social Science and Medicine, 18*(9), 783–790.

Kroes, W., Hurrell, J., & Margolis, B. (1974). Job stress in police administrators. *Journal of Police Science and Administration, 2*(4), 381–387.

LaRocco, J. M., House, J. S., & French, J. R. P., Jr. (1980). Social support, occupational stress and health. *Journal of Health and Social Behavior, 21,* 202–216.

LaRocco, J. M., & Jones, A. P. (1978). Co-worker and leader support as moderators of stress-strain relationships in work situations. *Journal of Applied Psychology, 63,* 629–634.

Lasky, G. L., Gordon, B. C., & Srebalus, D. J. (1986). Occupational stressors among federal correctional officers working in different security levels. *Criminal Justice and Behavior, 13*(3), 317–327.

Latack, J. C. (1986). Coping with job stress measures and future directions for scale development. *Journal of Applied Psychology, 71*(3), 377–385.

Latack, J. C., & Dozier, J. D. (1986, April). After the ax falls: Job loss as a career transition. The *Academy of Management Review, 11*(2), 375–392.

Lazarsfeld-Jahoda, M., & Zeisel, H. (1933). *Die arbeitslosen von Marienthal*. Leipzig, E. Germany: S. Hirzel.

Lazarus R. S. (1966). *Psychological stress and the coping process*. New York: McGraw-Hill.

Lazarus, R. S. (1974). Psychological stress and coping in adaptation and illness. *International Journal of Psychiatry in Medicine, 5,* 321–333.

Lazarus, R. S. (1981). The stress and coping paradigm. In C. Eisdorfer, D. Cohen, A. Kleinman, & P. Maxim (Eds.), *Models for clinical psychopathology* (pp. 177–214). New York: Spectrum.

Lazarus, R. S. (1983). The costs and benefits of denial. In S. Bresnitz (Ed.), *Denial of stress* (pp. 1–30). New York: Guilford.

Lazarus, R. S., Deese, J., & Osler, S. (1952). The effects of psychological stress on performance. *Psychological Bulletin, 48,* 293–315.

Lazarus, R. S., De Longis, A., Folkman, S., & Gruen, R. (1985). Stress and adaptational outcomes: The problem of confounded measures. *American Psychologist, 40*(7), 770–779.

Lazarus, R. S., & Folkman, S. (1984). *Stress, appraisal, and coping.* New York: Springer.

Lester, D. (1982). Perceived stress in police officers and belief in locus of control. *Journal of General Psychology, 107*(1), 157–158.

Levi, L. (1972). Stress and distress in response to psychosocial stimuli. Laboratory and real life studies on sympathoadrenomedullary and related reactions. *Acta Medica Scandinavica, 191* (Supplement No. 528), p. 14. Stockholm, Sweden. (Reprinted by Pergamon Press)

Levi, L. (1981). *Preventing work stress.* Reading, MA: Addison-Wesley.

Lucas, R. A. (1969). *Men in crisis.* New York: Basic Books.

Mallinger, M. A. (1986). Stress management: An organizational and individual responsibility. *Training and Development Journal, 40*(2), 16–17.

Mangione, B. L., & Quinn, R. P. (1975). Job satisfaction, counterproductive behavior, and drug use at work. *Journal of Applied Psychology, 63,* 114–116.

Manning, M., Ismail, A., & Sherwood, J. (1981). Effects of role conflict on selected physiological, affective, and performance variables: A laboratory simulation. *Multivariate Behavior Research,* 16(1), 125–141.

Manuso, J. S. (1983). Health promotion through psychological services. *New Directions for Mental Health Services, 20,* 49–56.

Marino, K. E., & White, S. E. (1985). Departmental structure, locus of control, and job stress: The effect of moderators. *Journal of Applied Psychology, 70*(4), 782–784.

Marshall, J., & Cooper, C. (1979). Work experiences of middle and senior managers: The pressure and satisfaction. *International Management Review, 19,* 81–96.

Mason, J. W. (1975). A historical view of the stress field. *Journal of Human Stress, 1,* 6–12 and 22–36.

Matteson, M. T., & Ivancevich, J. M. (1982). The how, what and why of stress management training. *Personnel Journal, 61*(10), 768–774.

Matteson, M. T., & Ivancevich, J. M. (1987). *Controlling work stress.* San Francisco: Jossey-Bass.

Matteson, M. T., Ivancevich, J. M., & Smith, S. V. (1984). Relation of Type A behavior to performance and satisfaction among sales personnel. *Journal of Vocational Behavior, 25*(2), 203–214.

Matthews, K. A., & Rodin, J. (1989). Women's changing work roles: Impact on health, family, & public policy. *American Psychologist, 44*(11), 1389–1393.

McGrath, J. E. (1976). Stress and behavior in organizations. In M. D. Dunnette (Ed.), *Handbook of industrial and organizational psychology.* Chicago: Rand McNally.

Meese, G. B., Lewis, M. I., Wyon, D. P., & Kok, R. (1984). A laboratory study of the effects of moderate thermal stress on the performance of factory workers. *Ergonomics, 27*(1), 19–43.

Miles, R. H. (1976). Role requirements as sources of organizational stress. *Journal of Applied Psychology, 61*(2), 172–179.

Miles, R. H. (1977). Role-set configuration as a predictor of role conflict and ambiguity in complex organizations. *Sociometry, 40*(1), 21–34.

Miles, R., & Perreault, W. (1976). Organizational role conflict: Its antecedents and consequences. *Organizational Behavior and Human Performance,* 17(1), 19–44.

Moch, M. K., Bartunek, J., & Brass, D. J. (1979). Structure, task characteristics, and experienced role stress in organizations employing complex technology. *Organizational Behavior and Human Performance, 24*(2), 258–268.

Monat, A., & Lazarus, R. S. (1985). Introduction: Stress and coping—some current issues and controversies. In A. Monat & R. S. Lazarus (Eds.), *Stress and coping: An anthology* (pp. 1–12). New York: Columbia University.

Moos, R. H., & Billings, A. G. (1982). Conceptualizing and measuring coping resources and processes. In L. Goldberger & S. Breznitz (Eds.), *Handbook of stress.* New York: Free Press.

Morris, J. H., Steers, R. M., & Koch, J. L. (1978). *Influence of organizational structure on role conflict and ambiguity for three occupational groupings* (Tech. Rep. Paper 16). University of Oregon Graduate School of Management.

Mossholder, K. W., Bedeian, A. G., & Armenakis, A. A. (1982). Group process-work outcome relationships: A note on the moderating impact of self-esteem. *Academy of Management Journal, 25*(3), 575–585.

Motowidlo, S. J., Packard, J. S., & Manning, M. R. (1986). Occupational stress: Its causes and consequences for job performance. *Journal of Applied Psychology, 71*(4), 618–629.

Mott, P. E. (1976). Social and psychological adjustment to shift work. In P. G. Rentos & R. D. Shepond (Eds.), *Shift work and health.* Washington, DC: U. S. Government Printing Office.

Murphy, L. R. (1984). Occupational stress management: A review and appraisal. *Journal of Occupational Psychology, 57*(1), 1–15.

Murphy, L. R. (1986). A review of organizational stress management research. *Journal of Organizational Behavior Management, 8*(2), 215–227.

Nathanson, C., & Lorenz, G. (1982). Women and health: The social dimensions of biomedical data. In J. Zollinger Giel (Ed.), *Women in the middle years: Current knowledge and directions for research and policy.* New York: Wiley Interscience

Neale, M. S., Singer, J., Schwartz, G. E., & Schwartz, J. (1982). *Conflicting perspectives on stress reduction in occupational settings: A systems approach to their resolution* (Report to NIOSH on P.O. No. 82–1058). Cincinnati, OH.

Newman, J. E., & Beehr, T. A. (1979). Personal and organizational strategies for handling job stress: A review of research and opinion. *Personnel Psychology, 32*, 1–44.

Nisbett, R. E., & Ross, L. D. (1980). *Human inference: Strategies and shortcomings of social judgement.* Englewood Cliffs, NJ: Prentice-Hall.

Nowack, K. M. (1986). Type A, hardiness, and psychological distress. *Journal of Behavioral Medicine, 9*(6), 537–548.

Numerof, R. E., & Abrams, M. N. (1984). Sources of stress among nurses: An empirical investigation. *Journal of Human Stress, 10*(2), 88–100.

Nunneley, S., Reader, D., & Maldonado, R. (1982). Temperature effects on physiology, comfort, and performance during hyperthermia. *Aviation, Space, and Environmental Medicine, 53*(7), 623–628.

Orpen, C. (1979). The effects of job enrichment on employee satisfaction, motivation, involvement, and performance: A field experiment. *Human Relations, 32*(3), 189–217.

Orpen, C. (1982). Type A personality as a moderator for the effects of role conflict, role ambiguity and role overload on individual strain. *Journal of Human Stress, 8*(2), 8–14.

Orpen, C. (1984). Managerial stress, relaxation, and performance. *Journal of Management Development, 3*(2), 34–47.

Osler, W. (1910). The Lumleian lectures on angina pectoris. *Lancet 1*, 696–700, 839–844, 974–977.

Paffenbarger, R., & Hale, W. (1975). Work activity and coronary heart mortality. *New England Journal of Medicine, 292*(11), 545–550.

Parasuraman, S., & Alutto, I. A. (1981). An examination of the organizational antecedents of stressors at work. *Academy of Management Journal, 24*(1), 48–67.

Parkes, K. R. (1982). Occupational stress among student nurses: A natural experiment. *Journal of Applied Psychology, 67*, 784–96.

Payne, R. L. (1988). Individual differences in the study of occupation stress. In C. L. Cooper & R. Payne (Eds.), *Causes, coping and consequences of stress at work.* Chichester, England: Wiley.

Payne, R. L., Jick, T. D., & Burke, R. J. (1982). Whither stress research? An agenda for the 1980s. *Journal of Occupational Behavior, 3*, 131–145.

Pearce, J. L. (1981). Bringing some clarity to role ambiguity research. *Academy of Management Review, 6*(4), 665–674.

Perkins, D. V. (1982). The assessment of stress using life-events scales. In L. Goldberger & S. Breznitz (Eds.), *Handbook of stress.* New York: Free Press.

Petrie, K., & Rotheram, M. J. (1982). Insulators against stress: Self-esteem and assertiveness. *Psychological Reports, 50*(3, Pt. 1), 963–966.

Pierce, J. L., & Newstom, J. W. (1983). The design of flexible work schedules and employee responses: Relationships and processes. *Journal of Occupational Behavior, 4*, 247–262.

Porras, J. I., & Hargis, K. (1982). Precursors of individual change: Responses to a social learning theory based on organizational intervention. *Human Relations, 35*(11), 973–990.

Poulton, E. C. (1978). Blue-collar stressors. In C. L. Cooper & R. Payne (Eds.), *Stress at work* (pp. 51–80). Chichester, England: Wiley.

Quick, J. C., Bhagat, R. S., & Dalton, J. E. (1987). (Eds.). *Work stress: Health care systems in the workplace.* New York: Praeger.

Quinn, R., & Shepard, L. (1974). *The 1972–73 Quality of Employment Survey.* Ann Arbor: University of Michigan, Survey Research Center.

Rabkin, J., & Struening, E. (1976). Life events, stress, and illness. *Science, 194,* 1013–1020.

Rahe, R. H., & Arthur, R. H. (1978). Life change and illness studies. *Journal of Human Stress, 4*(3), 15.

Reiche, H. M., & Van Dijkhuizen, N. (1979). Company size, hierarchy and personality: Do they influence feelings of stress and strain? *Tijdschrift voor Psychologie, 7*(1–2), 58–75.

Repetti, R. L., Matthews, K. A., & Waldron, I. (1990). Employment and women's health: Effects of paid employment on women's mental and physical health. *American Psychologist, 44*(11), 1394–1401.

Revicki, D. A., & May, H. J. (1985). Occupational stress, social support, and depression. *Health Psychology, 4*(1), 61–77.

Rhodewalt, F., & Agustsdottir, S. (1984). On the relationship of hardiness to the Type A behavior pattern: Perception of life events versus coping with life events. *Journal of Research in Personality, 18*(2), 211–223.

Rhodewalt, F., Hays, R. B., Chemers, M. M., & Wysocki, J. (1984). Type A behavior, perceived stress, and illness: A person-situation analysis. *Personality and Social Psychology Bulletin, 51*(6), 1218–1223.

Rizzo, J. R., House, R. J., & Listzman, S. I. (1970). Role conflict and ambiguity in complex organizations. *Administrative Science Quarterly, 15,* 150–163.

Rogers, D. L., & Molnar, J. (1976). Organizational antecedents of role conflict and ambiguity in top-level administrators. *Administrative Science Quarterly, 21*(4), 598–610.

Rose, R. M. (1987). Neuroendocrine effects of stress. In J. C. Quick, R. S. Bhagat, & J. E. Dalton (Eds.), *Work stress: Health care systems in the work place.* New York: Praeger.

Rose, R. M., Jenkins, C. D., Hurst, M. W., & Apple-Levin, M. (1978). *Air traffic controller health study* (Federal Aviation Authority Report FAA-AM 78,39). Washington, DC: U. S. Department of Transportation.

Rosenthal, D. (1983). The relationship between work environment attributes and burnout. *Journal of Leisure Research, 15*(2), 125–135.

Rotter, J. B. (1966). Generalized expectancies for internal versus external control of reinforcement. *Psychological Monographs, 80* (1, Whole No. 609).

Russek, H. I. (1973). Emotional stress as a cause of coronary heart disease. *Journal of the American College Health Association, 22*(2), 120–123.

Scarr, S., Phillips, D., & McCartney, K. (1989). Working mothers and their families. *American Psychologist, 44*(11), 1402–1409.

Schmied, L. A., & Lawler, K. A. (1986). Hardiness, Type A behavior, and the stress-illness relation in working women. *Journal of Personality & Social Psychology, 51*(6), 1218–1223.

Schmitt, N., Colligan, M. J., & Fitzgerald, M. (1980). Unexplained physical symptoms in eight organizations: Individual and organizational analyses. *Journal of Occupational Psychology, 53*(4), 305–317.

Schuler, R. S. (1981). Definition and conceptualization of stress in organizations. *Organizational Behavior and Human Performance, 25*(2), 184–215.

Seers, A., McGee, G. W., Serey, T. T., & Graen, G. B. (1983). The interaction of job stress and social support: A strong inference investigation. *Academy of Management Journal, 26*(2), 273–284.

Segovis, J. C., Bhagat, R. S., & Coelho, G. V. (1985). The mediating role of cognitive appraisal in the experience of stressful life events: A reconceptualization. In T. A. & R. S. Bhagat (Eds.), *Human stress and cognition in organizations.* New York: Wiley.

Seligman, M. E. P. (1975). *Helplessness.* San Francisco: Freeman.

Selye, H. (1936). A syndrome produced by diverse noxious agents. *Nature, 138,* 32.

Selye, H. (1956). *The stress of life.* New York: McGraw-Hill.

Selye, H. (1960). *The concept of stress in experimental physiology.* In J. M. Tanner (Ed.), *Stress and Psychiatric disorder.* Oxford: Blackwell.

Selye, H. (1971). The evolution of the stress concept: Stress and cardiovascular disease. In L. Levi (Ed.), *Society, stress, and disease.* London: Oxford Press.

Selye, H. (1973). The evolution of the stress concept. *American Scientist, 61,* 692–699.

Selye, H. (1975). Confusion and controversy in the stress field. *Journal of Human Stress, 2*, 36–44.

Selye, H. (1982). History and present status of the stress concept. In L. Goldberger & S. Breznitz (Eds.), *Handbook of stress* (pp. 7–17). New York: Free Press.

Semmer, N. (1984). *Strebbezogene Tatigkeitsanalyse.* Berlin: Beltz, Weinheim.

Shamir, B., & Drory, A. (1982). Occupational tedium among prison officers. *Criminal Justice and Behavior, 9*(1), 79–99.

Sheppard, H., Ferman, L., & Haber, W. (1960). *Too old to work, too young to retire: A case study of a permanent plant shutdown.* Washington, DC: U. S. Government Printing Office.

Shirom, A., Eden, D., Silberwasser, S., & Kellermann, J. (1973). Job stresses and risk factors in coronary heart disease among five occupational categories in kibbutzim. *Social Science and Medicine, 7*(11), 875–892

Soderberg, I. (1983). Investigation of visual strain experienced by microscope operators at an electronics plant. *Applied Ergonomics, 14*(4), 97–305.

Starak, Y. (1984). Strategies for mind and body health in social work education and practice. *Mental Health in Australia, 1*(13), 19–22.

Storms, P. L., & Spector, P. E. (1987). Relationships of organizational frustration with reported behavioral reactions: The moderating effect of locus of control. *Journal of Occupational Psychology, 60*(3), 227–234.

Sutton, R. I., & D'Aunno, T. (1989). Decreasing organizational size: Untangling the effects of people and money. *Academy of Management Review, 14,* 194–212.

Sutton, R. I., & Kahn, R. L. (1987). Prediction, understanding and control as antidotes to organizational stress. In J. W. Lorsch (Ed.), *Handbook of organizational behavior.* Englewood Cliffs, NJ: Prentice-Hall.

Terborg, J. R. (1985). Working women and stress. In T. A. Beehr & R. S. Bhagat (Eds.), *Human stress and cognition in organizations.* New York: Wiley.

Theorell, T. (1974). Life events before and after the onset of a premature myocardial infarction. In B. S. Dohrenwend & B. P. Dohrenwend (Eds.), *Stressful life events: Their nature and effects.* New York: Wiley.

Theorell, T., Knov, S., Svensson, J., & Waller, D. (1983). Work and blood pressure. *Stressforkningsrapporter (Stress Research Reports),* No. 196, 1–54.

Timio, M., & Gentili, S. (1976). Adrenosympathetic overactivity under conditions of work stress. *British Journal of Preventative and Social Medicine, 30*(4), 262–265.

Tversky, A., & Kahneman, D. (1981). The framing of decisions and the psychology of choice. *Science, 211*(4481), 453–458.

Ursine, H., Baade, E., & Levine, S. (1978). *Psychobiology of stress.* New York: Academic Press.

Van Dijkhuizen, N., & Reiche, H. (1980). Psychosocial stress in industry: A heartache for middle management? *Psychotherapy and Psychosomatics, 34*(2–3), 124–134.

Vinokur, A., Price, R. H., & Caplan, R. D. (in press). From field experiments to program implementation: Assessing the potential outcomes of an experimental intervention program for unemployed. *American Journal of Community Psychology.*

Vinokur, A. D., Threatt, B. A., Vinokur-Caplan, D., & Satariano, W. A. (1990). The process of recovery from breast cancer in younger and older patients. *Cancer, 65,* 1242–1254.

Volpert, W., Oestrreich, R., Gablenz-Kolakovic, S., Krogoll, T., & Resch, M. (1983). *Verfahren zur Ermittlung von Regulationserfordernissen in der Arbeitstatigkeit (VERA).* TUV-Rheinnland, Köln.

Vredenburgh, D. J., & Trinkaus, R. J. (1983). An analysis of role stress among hospital nurses. *Journal of Vocational Behavior, 22*(1), 82–95.

Wall, T. D., & Clegg, C. W. (1981). A longitudinal study of group work redesign. *Journal of Occupational Behavior, 2,* 31–49.

Werbel, J. D. (1983). Job change: A study of an acute job stressor. *Journal of Vocational Behavior, 23*(2), 242–250.

Wertkin, R. A. (1985). Stress-inoculation training: Principles and applications. *Social Casework, 66*(10), 611–616.

Williams, J. M., & Stout, J. K. (1985). The effect of high and low assertiveness on locus of control and health problems. *Journal of Psychology, 119*(2), 169–173.

Winnubst, J. A. M., Marcelissen, F. G. H., & Kleber, R. J. (1982). Effects of social support in the stressor-strain relationship: A Dutch sample. *Social Science and Medicine, 5*(3), 475–482.

Wisdom, B. (1984). Primary sources of hospital administrator stress. *Journal of Occupational Behavior, 5*(3), 229–232.

Wolpin, J., & Burke, R. J. (1986). Occupational locking-in: Some correlates and consequences [Special Issue]. Occupational and life stress and the family. *International Review of Applied Psychology, 35*(3), 327–346.

Zapf, D. (1987). Selbst-und-Fremdbeobachtung in der psychologischen Arbeitsanalyse. Methodische Probleme bei der Erfassung von Streb am Arbeistplatz. Dissertation an der Freien Universitat Berlin, Berlin.

CHAPTER 11

Conflict and Negotiation Processes in Organizations

Kenneth W. Thomas
Naval Postgraduate School

The primary purpose of this chapter is to develop an integrated overview of the complex fabric of variables involved in conflict and negotiation. The major parts of this fabric include (a) the sequence of events in the conflict/negotiation process, (b) structural variables which shape that process, (c) outcomes of the process, and (d) third-party interventions to manage conflict/negotiation. Separate models are developed for each of these parts, along with a more general model or paradigm that shows the interrelationships between them.

In writing this chapter, special attention has been given to topics that are central to conflict and its management but which have not received sufficient analysis. One involves the prevailing motivational/behavioral assumptions used to explain or predict conflict/negotiation behavior. The deficiencies of prevailing rational-economic assumptions are noted, and a more complex model of motivation is introduced that incorporates emotions and normative reasoning as well as rational-economic reasoning. A second topic involves the goals of conflict management. It is argued that much of the divergence in conflict management prescriptions within the literature is based on confusion among quite different goals. A framework is developed to categorize these goals, based on one's choice of beneficiary and time frame.

Introduction

SINCE THE FIRST edition of the *Handbook* was written, the field of organizational conflict has grown dramatically in both the size of its literature and in its acceptance as a legitimate field of study. Conflict is now recognized as one of the basic processes that must be managed within organizations. Chapters on conflict are almost universal in organizational behavior textbooks, for example. Likewise, it has become a cliché to say that conflict is inevitable in organizations, that it is frequent, and that it serves useful functions when managed properly. Managers have reported spending about 20 percent of their time dealing with some form of conflict (Baron, 1989; Thomas & Schmidt, 1976).

Like the chapter for the first edition (Thomas, 1976), the basic purpose of the present chapter is to synthesize the literature into an integrative theoretical framework for understanding and managing conflict. In contrast, many other reviews of this literature have been more comparative than integrative,[1] identifying different subtopics or paradigms within the literature and highlighting the differences between them. While extremely useful, these reviews also serve to reify and perpetuate the theoretical fractionation within the field. Thus, the emphasis in this chapter is on the larger fabric of conflict phenomena—attempting to show how the different theoretical pieces fit together and attempting to provide some of the missing pieces. This chapter is in many ways an attempt to accelerate theory development by going beyond the data to suggest new theory, research, and applications.

I have been particularly concerned that the theoretical framework in this chapter be useful (Kilmann, Slevin, & Thomas, 1983) or relevant (Thomas & Tymon, 1982) for the applied purpose of conflict management. Accordingly, this chapter attempts to incorporate the properties of relevant research identified by Thomas and Tymon (1982). In particular, the chapter

considers in some detail the goals of conflict management and the types of interventions available (for the sake of goal relevance and operational validity, respectively). Where possible, the chapter also draws more heavily on organizational studies than laboratory studies (for descriptive relevance) and attempts to capture the complexity of forces that shape conflict events.[2]

This chapter builds on the theoretical framework developed in the earlier chapter (Thomas, 1976). The basic outlines of that framework appear to have held up well. However, many additions, updates, and modifications have been required to reflect developments in the literature and in my own appreciation of these issues. Thus, although it builds on the earlier ideas, almost all of the text of this chapter is new.

There are several major themes in the changes from the earlier chapter. There is more discussion of the connections between the parts of the theoretical framework—the conflict process, structural variables, and conflict management. There is much more on negotiation, one of the primary growth areas within conflict research. A more explicit cognitive model of conflict behavior is also discussed as a foundation for conflict theory and research. In keeping with the relevance objective of this chapter, there is a more detailed consideration of the goals and interventions of conflict management. Finally, as the chapter took shape, there was also a rediscovery of the importance of normative dynamics—in creating conflicts, shaping behavior, and formulating the long-term goals of conflict management.

Definition of Conflict

In the behavioral sciences, the word *conflict* has two broad usages. The first usage denotes incompatible response tendencies *within* an individual—forms of individual dilemmas. For example, ambivalence may be called *approach-avoidance conflict* (e.g., Levinger, 1957).

Likewise, *role conflict* refers to competing response tendencies within an individual stemming from the requirements of different roles (e.g., Kahn, Wolfe, Quinn, Snoek, & Rosenthal, 1964). The second usage refers to the sort of conflict that occurs *between* two or more parties or social units. These parties may be individuals, groups, organizations, or other social units. It is this second usage that is the focus of this chapter and of the literature on organizational conflict.

Even with this restriction, there is still no consensus within the literature on a precise definition of conflict. The diversity of definitions has been summarized at different times by several authors (Fink, 1968; Lewicki, Weiss, & Lewin, 1988; Mack & Snyder, 1957). One of the key differences among definitions involves their scope. Pondy (1967) observed that early definitions, from a variety of social science disciplines, focused on a variety of specific concepts, including objective conditions, emotions, perceptions, and behaviors. Rather than adopt one of these definitions, Pondy argued for a broad working definition of conflict to include the entire process that included all these phenomena.

One fairly specific class of definitions still influential within the organizational conflict literature involves the deliberate interference or blocking of another party's goal attainment. The conceptual work of Schmidt and Kochan (1972) has provided support for this approach, which seems especially popular in the industrial relations literature, where the notion of conflict corresponds closely to the strikes and other job actions of central concern to many industrial relations researchers.[3]

With this major exception, however, there appears to have been a trend toward more general definitions following Pondy. In effect, the more general definitions move "upstream" in the conflict process to include psychological events—usually perceptions of the situation—that occur prior to a party's choice to engage in

behavior. Accordingly, these definitions also allow for other nonblocking types of strategies or behaviors to be used by parties to deal with conflict situations.

Putnam and Poole (1987) identify three general properties shared among these broader definitions: interdependence between the parties (in the sense that each has the potential to interfere with the other), perception by at least one of the parties that there is some degree of opposition or incompatibility among the goals (or other concerns) of the parties, and some form of interaction. There is some redundancy among these properties, so that the definitions of contemporary researchers have focused on different subsets of these properties, often treating the others as implicit.

Within this tradition of broad definitions, the objective here is to identify the beginning point (or "headwaters") of the conflict process, as an aid to modeling that process. Accordingly, conflict is defined in this chapter as *the process that begins when one party perceives that the other has negatively affected, or is about to negatively affect, something that he or she cares about.*[4]

Given the present purpose, this definition has several benefits. First, it is relatively simple (i.e., parsimonious). The notion of things which one cares about (concerns) being negatively impacted by the other party implies some form of interdependence and interaction, as well as a perceived likelihood of incompatible concerns. (These variables will be treated more explicitly later in the chapter.) Second, this definition seems to capture the point at which any other ongoing activity or process (e.g., decision making or discussion) "crosses over" to become experienced as an interparty conflict.[5] Finally, this definition is sufficiently broad to cover a variety of conflict issues and events. Thus, the very general notion of "something that [the party] cares about" (rather than goals or interests) allows for conflict issues involving a wide variety of types of concerns. Likewise, negative effects to a party's concerns can be perceived following actions ranging from violence to disagreement, or can be anticipated in a variety of situations.

A General Model of Conflict

Figure 1 shows the general, systemic model of conflict that provides a means of organizing this chapter.[6] This general model serves to identify the major components of conflict theory and to indicate the essential interrelatedness of these components. A brief description of the model here and an example will help to put the material in the remainder of this chapter in perspective.

The model is concerned with conflict at the interface between two parties within some larger system. In most cases of industrial and organizational psychology, that larger system will be an organization.[7] To illustrate, consider a hypothetical conflict between the sales and production managers of a manufacturing firm (from Thomas, 1976).

Conflict occurs as a *process*, or sequence of events. These events take place in conflict episodes between the parties. Such episodes have an internal logic, with each preceding event causing later events and outcomes. These events include the internal experiences of the parties as well as their externally visible behaviors. Consider the following scenario:

Sales has promised a major customer an early delivery date on a given item. When informed of this during a meeting, the production supervisor feels frustrated because that delivery date would throw off his whole production schedule. He has carefully planned his schedule in order to maximize the productive capacity of his equipment. Perceiving that covering the sales department's promise is incompatible with the efficiency of his own department, the production supervisor attempts

to make the sales supervisor change the promised delivery date. Annoyed at this response, and disturbed by the idea of disappointing the customer, the sales manager resists this influence attempt and tries to convince the production manager to meet the delivery date. In the resulting discussion, both parties become more hostile and argumentative. After an hour the parties remain deadlocked. (Thomas, 1976, p. 893)

These conflict processes, however, do not occur in a vacuum. Rather, they are shaped by structural parameters of the system—the relatively fixed or slow-changing conditions influencing events at the interface between the parties.[8] These *structural conditions* include properties of the parties as well as of the context in which they interact. We return to our sales/ production example for illustration:

Negotiations between the department heads are largely confined to biweekly meetings convened by the vice president of operations. This procedure shapes the behavior of both parties—complaints accumulate and smolder until meeting time. Social pressures from other department heads help to keep the competition from escalating uncontrollably, although the prevailing organizational norms do not encourage problem solving. The production manager tends to be somewhat more competitive than the sales manager. This difference is partly due to the production manager's personality: He is an older up-from-the-ranks manager who fought his way out of poverty. However, competitive behavior by both department heads is encouraged by social pressure from the members of their departments, each of which has come to view the other department as an enemy. Underlying many of the issues that arise between the two department heads is some very real conflict of interest

FIGURE 1

General Model of Conflict

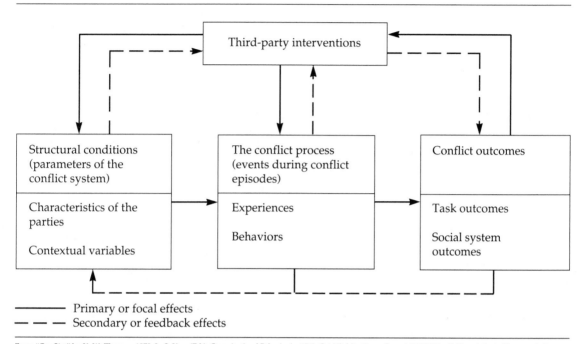

From "Conflict" by K. W. Thomas, 1979. In S. Kerr (Ed.), *Organizational Behavior* (p. 154). Grid Publications. Copyright 1979 by S. Kerr. Adapted by permission.

stemming from tight performance measures and tightening organizational resources. Both parties have high stakes in these issues, since their departmental performance evaluations depend heavily on production cost efficiency (for production) and meeting delivery dates (for sales). (Thomas, 1976, pp. 893–894)

Shaped by structural conditions, conflict episodes produce *conflict outcomes*—the primary consequences of conflict episodes. These outcomes include consequences for both task accomplishment and for the maintenance of the social system. Adding to the example:

The conflict between the sales and production managers has consumed an hour of the meeting, preventing the department heads from addressing a

number of important agenda items. The decision reached (more properly, the lack of decision) also appears to mean that the sales department will be unable to honor its promise to one of the organization's important customers. Moreover, relations between the two department heads have become even more antagonistic, and the sales manager seems to be even more frustrated and disenchanted with how the organization operates.

Because of the number of conflicts in any system, most conflicts are managed primarily by the principal parties of the conflict. However, one or more *third parties* may also play a role in managing the conflict. Depending on the system and the interface where the conflict occurs, the third party could, for example, be a manager, board of directors, organization development consultant, mediator, or government official. The third party is seen as exercising a control function in the system. Monitoring the current outcomes, the third party may occasionally choose to make an *intervention* to attempt to improve matters. The types of interventions available vary according to the third party's role, but in general there are two broad types of interventions. *Process interventions* occur when the third party becomes directly involved in the sequence of events of an ongoing conflict episode. These process interventions include such activities as those used in mediation or arbitration and tend to be directed at the short-term goal of managing or resolving the current conflict episode.

> The vice president of operations, the immediate supervisor of the two managers, is chairing the meeting in question. The VP suppresses the conflict for the remainder of the meeting to move on to other topics. He schedules a meeting with both department heads for later in the day, when he attempts to help the two clear the air and reach an agreement that will be acceptable to both departments and will not alienate the customer in question.

In contrast, third parties may also look beyond the current episode to make *structural interventions* in the social/organizational system in which the conflict occurs. These interventions alter the conditions that create conflicts or that shape the manner in which the parties deal with them. Structural interventions are, thus, typically intended to have a long-term, continuing impact on future episodes.

> The VP mandates regular meetings between the sales and production departments, requiring the sales and production managers, along with their immediate subordinates, to meet jointly at a fixed time each week to discuss the scheduling of major upcoming orders.

He also calls in a staff specialist to reexamine the performance evaluation systems for the two department heads.

The interrelationships among the components of the model are assumed to be highly complex. For simplicity, the preceding example has highlighted the causal relationships designated by the solid lines in Figure 1. These relationships will be treated as primary or focal for purposes of this chapter. For the sake of completeness, however, other relationships are also included in Figure 1, represented by broken lines. These relationships serve as a reminder of the fundamental interconnectedness of these variables—structural variables are also affected by conflict processes and their outcomes, third parties are also influenced by the conditions and events that influence the principal conflict parties, and third-party behavior will sometimes influence outcome variables directly, rather than through the conflict process.

Each of the major components of this general model will be considered in more detail, beginning with the conflict process.

The Conflict Process

As I've mentioned, the conflict process refers to the sequence of events that occurs during a conflict and the manner in which earlier events cause later events and outcomes.

Models of the conflict process necessarily incorporate a number of general assumptions about human behavior, although these assumptions are often implicit. Because of the strong influence of economics in the conflict/negotiation literature, prevailing assumptions have tended to be rational/instrumental in nature. That is, parties have been assumed to choose behaviors based on their perceived likelihood of attaining desired outcomes—as in the expected value calculations of economics. Moreover, the desirability of outcomes has tended to be based on rather narrow notions of self-interest. (See Etzioni, 1988, for a comprehensive critique of economic paradigms.)

Although these prevailing assumptions capture important causal dynamics, they are notable for what they appear to omit. First, they have a "sociopathic" flavor in their omission of internalized concerns about social/ normative issues (Thomas, 1989). Briefly, sociopaths are individuals who have a clear perception of reality except for their social or moral obligations (Merriam-Webster, 1986). Motivated exclusively by self-interest, they are concerned only with the personal consequences of their acts, not with the morality of the act itself. Just as sociopaths are regarded by society as dangerously deficient in this way, much of our theory has exhibited similar deficiencies. That is, in our explanations of behavior, we have tended to ignore the extent to which individuals consider the normative acceptability (morality, ethicality) of the means chosen to achieve a given end. Second, prevailing economic assumptions also tend to "sanitize" the conflict process by eliminating emotions and their potentially strong effects on thoughts and actions.

The process model developed here attempts to incorporate these neglected features into a more complex and explicit model of conflict behavior. Conceptually, the model draws heavily on the work of Fishbein (1963). Basically, the Fishbein model, which has been extensively tested in a variety of contexts (Ajzen & Fishbein, 1980; Fishbein & Ajzen, 1975), views behavior as resulting from intentions and sees intentions as shaped by the additive effects of two forms of reasoning—rational/instrumental reasoning and normative reasoning. Because the Fishbein model is basically cognitive, however, and because emotions are frequently an important feature of conflict phenomena (e.g., Pondy, 1967), the model presented in this chapter also attempts to incorporate recent work on the role of emotions (affect) in behavior. Unlike the Fishbein model, the model presented

here also allows for the dynamic effects of interaction on intention and behavior.

The process model that incorporates these features is shown in Figure 2. The unit of analysis is the conflict episode (Pondy, 1967; Walton, 1969). The model depicts the main sets of events within an episode, viewed from the perspective of one of the principal conflict parties.[9] Briefly, the episode begins with the party's *awareness* of the conflict. This awareness may be triggered by a threat to the party's self-interest but may also involve a variety of other types of concerns or issues. Awareness leads to various *thoughts and emotions* (cognition and affect) of the party concerning the conflict situation and possible responses to it. Here, thoughts include normative reasoning as well as rational/ instrumental (means/ends) reasoning. The thoughts and emotions result in the formulation of *intentions* with respect to coping with the conflict, which are then enacted in the form of observable *behavior*. The other party then reacts to this behavior (other's reaction). The loop in Figure 2 between behavior and thoughts and emotions represents the effects on the party of the other's reaction to his or her behavior. The party's initial behavior may initiate a more or less prolonged interaction with the other. During the course of this interaction, the party's thoughts and emotions may change, altering intentions and behavior accordingly. When the interaction on a given issue stops, some set of *outcomes* has occurred. As shown in the figure, the outcomes of a given episode set the stage for subsequent episodes on the same issue.

Let us now consider the events in the process model in more detail.

Awareness

Consistent with our definition of conflict, the conflict episode begins when one party becomes aware that another party has negatively affected, or is about to negatively affect, something which the original party cares about. Walton (1969) noted that this awareness often

FIGURE 2

Process Model of Conflict Episodes

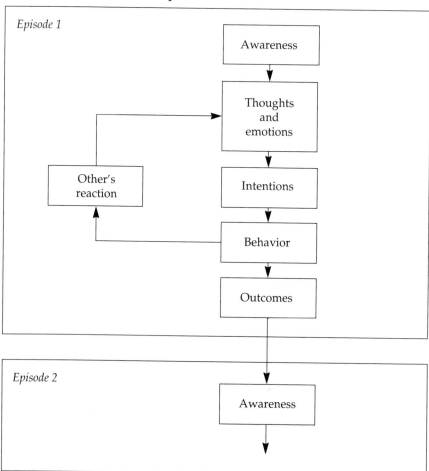

follows some sort of "triggering event," which makes this damage or danger salient to the party.

The word *concern* will be used here as a general term for the thing the party cares about.[10] It now appears that there are at least three elemental forms of conflict, based on the types of concerns which are at stake for the party: goals, judgments, and normative standards.[11] Each of these forms of conflict involves somewhat different dynamics and tasks for the conflict parties.

Goal conflicts involve divergent or apparently incompatible ends desired by the parties. These goals may, for example, take the form of satisfying personal needs, achieving delegated responsibilities or objectives, or obtaining scarce resources. Goal conflicts are prominent in negotiation models, where they are commonly called *interest conflicts* (e.g.,

Pruitt & Rubin, 1986). Here, each party's pursuit of his or her own goals threatens or obstructs the goal attainment of the other, and the key task is the reconciliation of the parties' aspirations for different goals.

Judgment conflicts involve differences over empirical or factual issues. These conflicts have also been called *cognitive conflicts* (Eiseman, 1978; Hammond, Todd, Wilkins, & Mitchell, 1966). Here, the party perceives that the other has drawn different (incorrect) conclusions about what is true in an empirical sense. The expression of judgment conflicts is called *controversy* by Tjosvold (1985). Judgment conflicts or controversies play a prominent role in a number of decision-making models.[12] In such conflicts, the key issue is how to combine the different information, insights, or reasoning of the two parties to form a conclusion that is more or less accurate.

Normative conflicts center on a party's evaluation of another party's behavior in terms of expectations of how the other *should* behave. These expectations may involve various kinds of standards regarding proper behavior: for example, ethics (Lewicki, 1982; Lewicki & Litterer, 1985, chap. 13), notions of equity (Vecchio, 1984) or justice (Thibaut & Walker, 1975), observance of status hierarchies (Kabanoff, 1985; Seiler, 1963), and various other norms of the social system. Some of these standards may also have become formal rules, as in the case of grievances (Bouwen & Salipante, 1986). When the party perceives a violation of these standards, such emotional reactions as disapproval, blame, and anger may be triggered, as well as sanctions intended to produce conformity to the standard. In such conflicts, key issues involve which standards should be applied, how a given behavior compares with a standard, and appropriate punishments (including apologies or reparation) for violations (e.g., Thomas & Pondy, 1977).

Some conflicts may involve only one of these elemental forms. For example, two managers with a shared goal may disagree over

the best way of achieving it—a judgment conflict. However, the elemental forms can also combine in various ways in a given conflict episode. During negotiations over divergent goals, for example, parties may also disagree in their judgments of the consequences of a possible settlement, and one may anger the other through negotiation tactics that are seen as unfair. In this manner, a number of different types of conflict issues may accumulate during the episode.

In turn, as shown in Figure 2, some residual perceptions of threat or loss to a party's concerns may remain after the episode ends. Follett (1941) argued that these residuals tend to spawn further episodes until a given conflict issue is truly *resolved*—that is, until some form of settlement or agreement is reached which leaves no significant dissatisfaction for either party on a given set of concerns.

Thoughts and Emotions

As the party becomes aware of a given conflict, that awareness is experienced in terms of the thoughts (cognitions) that help the party make sense of the conflict and consider ways of dealing with it, as well as by emotions (affect) interacting with the thoughts.

The party's thoughts and emotions are especially important elements of the process model. They define the party's subjective interpretation of reality and are presumed to be the immediate determinants of the party's intentions. Because they intervene in the causal relationship between so-called objective conditions and the party's behavioral reactions, they serve as a means of explaining and predicting the effects of different structural conditions on conflict phenomena.[13] Because of their key role, a party's thoughts and emotions are often the target of influence attempts during conflict episodes—by the other party, and by the process interventions of a third party. For these reasons, it seems extremely important to develop a more complete understanding of the

FIGURE 3

The Joint Outcome Space

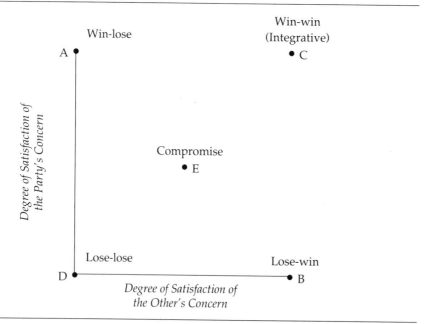

From "Conflict and Conflict Management" by K. W. Thomas, 1976. In M. D. Dunnette (Ed.), *Handbook of Industrial and Organizational Psychology* (1st ed., p. 898). Chicago: Rand McNally. Copyright 1976 by M. D. Dunnette. Adapted by permission.

manner in which thoughts and emotions shape a party's intentions.

Issues and Possible Settlements. The most basic aspect of a party's sense making appears to be defining the conflict issue (i.e., deciding what the conflict is about) and recognizing what general sorts of outcomes might be possible to settle it.[14] This definition of the issue is often called its *framing* (e.g., Sheppard, Lewicki, & Minton, 1986). Operationally, defining the conflict issue involves some interpretation or labeling of the primary concerns of the two parties—the party's own concern (that which is threatened or damaged by the other party) and the other party's concern (that which drives the other party).[15] Using a goal conflict, for example, the union members might say, "We want an additional dollar an

hour, but management only wants to give us fifty cents."

The party's definition of the issue, in turn, usually suggests a set of possible settlements. By *settlements* I mean the possible final actions of conflict episodes that represent dispositions of the conflict issue—possible decisions or agreements that can be reached by the parties (including the outcome of no agreement). At any given point, a party's reasoning is limited to a restricted set of possible settlements. The set of possible settlements of which the party is aware will be referred to as that party's set of *salient* possible settlements.

Within this salient set, the party is assumed to have some notion, however rough, of the degree to which each settlement would satisfy the primary concerns of the party and the other. Figure 3 represents a party's conceptualization

FIGURE 4

Modal Patterns of Salient Possible Settlements

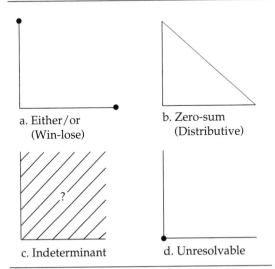

a. Either/or (Win-lose)

b. Zero-sum (Distributive)

c. Indeterminant

d. Unresolvable

From "Conflict and Conflict Management" by K. W. Thomas, 1976. In M. D. Dunnette (Ed.), *Handbook of Industrial and Organizational Psychology* (1st ed., p. 899). Chicago: Rand McNally. Copyright 1976 by M. D. Dunnette. Adapted by permission.

of salient settlements and their outcomes. The horizontal and vertical axes represent the degree to which the party perceives that the other's concern and the party's concern, respectively, would be satisfied by a given settlement.[16] Point C represents a settlement seen as satisfying the concerns of both parties—an *integrative* (Follett, 1941) or *win-win* (Filley, 1975) outcome. Point D represents a *lose-lose* settlement, with relatively complete frustration of both parties' concerns. At Point A, the party's concern is satisfied while the other's is frustrated (*win-lose*); the opposite is true at Point B. Point E represents a settlement that yields some, but incomplete, satisfaction to both parties—a *compromise* settlement.

Figure 4 depicts four common patterns for a party's set of salient possible settlements. Figure 4a represents an either/or

conceptualization of possible settlements. The only outcomes seen as possible are total satisfaction and total frustration of the parties' concerns, and each party's satisfaction is seen as occurring at the other's expense. This type of conceptualization is referred to by Blake, Shepard, and Mouton (1964) as *win-lose*.

The *zero-sum* conceptualization in Figure 4b is similar, but less extreme. This conceptualization is somewhat more sophisticated than the previous one—the party has identified a dimension rather than two points. For example, the issue may now involve the amount of time or money spent on a new product line rather than the decision of whether or not to develop it. Such issues were referred to by Walton and McKersie (1965) as *distributive*. A range of intermediate settlements or compromises is recognized as possible and some degree of satisfaction is seen as simultaneously possible for both parties, although increases in one party's satisfaction are still at the expense of the other.

In the *indeterminant* conceptualization in Figure 4c, the party is not immediately aware of a specific set of possible settlements. For example, in a dispute between sales and production, a conflict may be perceived to involve quickness of delivery versus efficient utilization of production facilities. Because there is no a priori relationship between these two concerns, identifying alternatives becomes a matter of analytic or empirical search. Thus, the indeterminate set, by not immediately suggesting either/or or distributive outcomes, facilitates the search for other possibilities.

Finally, Figure 4d represents a party's conceptualization of an *unresolvable* conflict. Unresolvable issues are depicted as frustrating to both parties.

In effect, the party's salient set represents alternative outcomes from which the party chooses his or her *strategic intentions* for the conflict episode. Here conflict researchers have been particularly concerned that parties often fail to recognize the possibility of integrative settlements (e.g., Bazerman, 1986, chap. 7; Filley,

1975; Fisher & Ury, 1981) and thus often pursue win-lose or distributive outcomes unnecessarily. Accordingly, attention has been directed toward cognitive processes that result in these oversights or omissions.

One factor that seems particularly influential in this regard is the manner in which the party defines the conflict issue. Based on a literature review, Thomas (1976) identified three important dimensions of issue definition: egocentricity, insight into underlying concerns, and size of the issue. *Egocentricity* refers to defining the issue solely in terms of one's own concern. For example: "We need another maintenance man, but the maintenance supervisor won't lend us one" (a *goal* conflict); "Frank should cooperate, but refuses to" (a *normative* conflict); or "We think sales would soar with this new marketing plan, but he won't agree" (a *judgment* conflict). By focusing entirely on a party's own concern, egocentric perceptions of an issue are particularly likely to generate either/or sets of alternatives: "Either my concern is satisfied or it isn't." In addition, they appear to minimize the perceived desirability of satisfying the other's concern and to make the other's behavior seem arbitrary (i.e., normatively questionable). Thus, egocentric perceptions appear especially likely to generate competitive (win-lose) intentions.[17]

The second dimension of issue definition, *insight into underlying concerns,* has received much recent attention by conflict theorists. At one extreme, the party may think rather superficially in terms of the *positions* taken on an issue—the settlements favored by the two parties. A deeper appreciation, in contrast, identifies the more basic concerns of the parties that have led them to take these positions. In the case of the goal conflicts discussed in the negotiations literature, positions are contrasted with the underlying interests of the parties (Fisher & Ury, 1981; Lax & Sebenius, 1986; Pruitt & Rubin, 1986). For example, a positional definition might be, "My boss wants me to adopt a new form for my reports, but I want to use the old one," while a deeper appreciation

of underlying interests might be, "I can't afford the time required to complete the new, longer form, but my boss needs information which wasn't on the old form." Likewise, in the case of judgment conflicts, one can define conflict issues in terms of the contradictory conclusions reached by the parties (their positions), or in terms of the different considerations (data, examples, insights, or reasoning) that have led them to those conclusions. An example would be, "I think this project is on schedule, but my boss doesn't," versus "I know that we have met every deadline on this project, but my boss is concerned that quality at the last stage was marginal." Several theorists have pointed out that the appreciation of underlying concerns encourages collaborative problem solving (Eiseman, 1978; Filley, 1975; Fisher & Ury, 1981; Follett, 1941; Pruitt & Rubin, 1986; Walton, 1969). In essence, deeper definitions tend to result in indeterminate sets of salient possibilities, which appear to facilitate the search for integrative or win-win settlements. Using the two examples above, for instance, the deeper definitions may suggest (a) the possibility of a shorter project that focuses on what is most useful to the boss and (b) a more complete judgment of the project that includes work quality as well as time schedules. Appreciating the underlying concerns of the other party as well as one's own also appears to increase the perceived desirability of an integrative outcome and to make the other party's behavior seem more reasonable.

The third dimension of issue definition, *size of the issue,* was originally discussed by Fisher (1964) in the context of international conflict. Issues are made larger when they are conceptualized as involving large numbers of people, a large number of instances or events, or abstract principles, or as setting precedents for future interaction. For example, instead of a sales manager negotiating with a production scheduler to rush order a product for a customer, the same issue could be defined as a conflict between two departments in which the production department's general inattention to customer service will be settled once and for all. Motivationally, very large issues appear to make integrative outcomes seem impossible, to raise the stakes dramatically, and also to arouse high levels of threat and defensiveness.

The combined effects of these three dimensions were studied experimentally by Magula (1977). Using an elaborate role-induction technique, individuals were given definitions of conflict issues that were high or low on each of the dimensions. The individuals were then shown the same brief descriptions of several conflict incidents and asked how they would respond. The dominant effects were produced by egocentricity and insight into underlying concerns. Consistent with the reasoning given earlier, egocentricity was strongly related to competitive (win-lose) intentions, while insight into underlying concerns was related to collaborative (win-win) intentions.

Given the party's definition of the issue a salient set of possible settlements, remaining elements of the party's thinking involve the sort of reasoning which leads to choice—selection of a strategic intention (a favored settlement or outcome from the salient set) and tactics to implement it. As mentioned earlier, two forms of reasoning seem to be involved: rational/instrumental reasoning and normative reasoning.

Rational/Instrumental Reasoning. This first type of reasoning is the familiar means/ends reasoning that is basic to economic notions of rationality (e.g., Simon, 1957) and is embodied in expectancy theories of motivation (Lawler, 1973; Vroom, 1964). This sort of reasoning considers the desirability of the likely outcomes of a course of action: A course of action is considered desirable (and its choice is considered rational) if and only if it is seen as instrumental in producing a desired outcome.

Using rational/instrumental explanations, a party's choice of a given settlement (outcome) as a strategic intention is presumed to be a function of the desirability (valence) of that settlement, together with the likelihood (expectancy) that the strategy could be successfully implemented if one tried. Within the negotiations literature, Pruitt (1983; Pruitt & Rubin, 1986) provides an especially detailed discussion of the role of outcome valences in the choice of strategic intentions. Paraphrasing Pruitt, a party's valence for a given settlement appears to be a function of the degree to which the settlement meets the party's own aspirations and his or her perceptions of the degree to which it meets the other's aspirations, together with the party's desire to satisfy his or her own and the other's concerns.

The party's valences for satisfying the party's and the other's concerns are the independent variables in a family of models that Pruitt (1983) has termed *dual concerns models*. These models, which build upon earlier work by Blake and Mouton (1964), are more fully described later in the section on strategic intentions. Essentially, a party's choice of strategy is presumed to be a joint function of the party's valences (desires or degrees of concern) for satisfying the party's own concern and the other's concern. Thus, collaborative or win-win strategies are more likely to be chosen when the party places a high valence on satisfying both his or her own and the other's concerns; competitive or win-lose strategies occur when the party places a high valence on satisfying his or her own concerns but a low valence on the other's concerns; avoiding or lose-lose strategies occur when the party places a low valence on satisfying either his or her own or the other's concerns; and this same reasoning applies to the other possible combinations.

In a series of laboratory experiments on negotiations (described in Pruitt, 1983), Pruitt and his colleagues have investigated the sources and consequences of a party's valence for satisfying his or her own and the other's concerns. Pruitt concludes that the party's valence for satisfying his or her own concern is determined by such considerations as the strength of the value or the need at stake, the importance of other issues competing for the party's attention, the party's fear of conflict, and the extent to which the party sees him or herself as representing the interests of (and being accountable to) a set of constituents. Likewise, the party's valence for satisfying the other's concern would depend on interpersonal bonds (e.g., identity or attraction) and on various forms of dependence by the party on the other. Pruitt and his colleagues have manipulated these variables and found the predicted effects on the instance of win-win and win-lose settlements.

In addition to the valence of a given settlement, a party's choice of strategy is also presumed to depend on the party's perceived likelihood (expectancy) that the settlement can be achieved—what Pruitt refers to as the *feasibility* of a strategy.[18] This perception essentially involves the party's assessment that tactics are available that would be likely to successfully implement a given strategy. These assessments, in turn, may involve a set of diverse tactical assumptions about the party's skills and the other's probable reactions to the party's tactics.[19] Some of these assumptions will be discussed later in the section on tactical intentions.

Normative Reasoning. This second type of reasoning is asserted by Fishbein and Ajzen (1975) to be qualitatively different from rational/instrumental reasoning. Whereas rational/instrumental reasoning evaluates any course of action on the basis of the desirability of its probable consequences, normative reasoning considers the *goodness* of the act itself—that is, its normative acceptability (propriety, morality, ethicality, or worthiness).

As social creatures, individuals are presumed to be inherently concerned with the social expectations that are the building blocks of groups and societies. In general, these expectations act to moderate the potential ruthlessness implicit in rational/instrumental reasoning (where the ends justify the means) by discouraging specific kinds of actions regarded as destructive to a social unit. As individuals come to identify with a given unit, its expectations regarding these actions become invested with a normative quality of good/bad that attaches to the actions themselves in different contexts. Normative reasoning, then, involves consideration by the party of how the normative expectations of individuals or groups with whom the party identifies apply to a given course of action. The party's own internalized normative standards are also assumed to be added into these considerations.[20] These normative assessments can be made at various levels to consider the acceptability of strategies, tactics, or specific behavioral acts.

To date, the most heavily researched normative issues in the conflict literature have involved justice, or fairness—the distributive justice of settlements (e.g., Deutsch, 1975) and the procedural justice of some conflict management procedures (e.g., R. Folger & Greenberg, 1985; Thibaut & Walker, 1975; Tyler, 1986). Some research has also been directed at ethical standards for negotiation tactics (Lewicki, 1982), as well as at the general social desirability of strategic intentions in conflict (Thomas & Kilmann, 1975). Nevertheless, the systematic investigation of normative forces in conflict and negotiation seems to be at a relatively early stage.

As in the Fishbein model, the motivational forces produced by rational/instrumental reasoning and normative reasoning are presumed to have a combined, additive effect on an individual's intentions. In tests of the Fishbein model in a number of contexts, interestingly, the normative portion of the model has explained most of the variance in behavior in some situations, while the rational/instrumental portion has dominated in others (Ajzen & Fishbein, 1980; Fishbein & Ajzen, 1975).

Briefly recapping, then, there seem to be three important elements of a party's cognition in a conflict episode—(a) an assessment of the conflict issue that suggests a salient set of possible settlements, (b) rational/instrumental reasoning about the likely consequences of different courses of action, and (c) normative reasoning about the propriety or acceptability of these courses of action. We will now turn our attention to the manner in which emotions interact with cognition to shape intentions in conflicts.

Emotions. Perhaps more than any other industrial and organizational phenomena, conflicts are often accompanied by strong emotions. Many of these emotions are generated during the conflict process and are presumed to be a by-product of the party's cognitions (e.g., Kumar, 1989). Other emotions, left over from other events, may enter the conflict episode as moods that influence the episode.

Based on a review of the larger literature on emotions, or *affect*, Kumar (1989) notes that emotions have two types of influences that are relevant here: their shaping of cognition and their introduction of additional motivational forces. With respect to shaping cognitions, Kumar notes that negative emotions, once aroused, feed back on cognition to produce cognitive simplification, reduce trust, and construe the other's behavior negatively. Among other things, cognitive simplification seems likely to produce either/or conceptualizations of conflict issues and, in general, to reduce a party's ability to think in an integrative fashion (Pruitt & Rubin, 1986). Carnevale and Isen (1986) conclude that positive affect, in contrast, increases a party's tendency to see potential relationships among the elements of a problem, to take a broader view of the situation, and to develop more innovative solutions.[21]

Motivationally, emotions appear to add additional forces to those produced by a party's rational/instrumental and normative reasoning. In the extreme, in fact, these urges may drive out (or very much simplify) normative and rational/instrumental reasoning so that the party's behavior is primarily understandable in terms of emotional venting. Different classes of emotions seem to add forces that push a party's behavior in different strategic directions. Anger and hostility, which tend to result from experienced frustration with the other, appear to add a motivational push for the party to behave in an aggressive manner (Baron, 1977; Kumar, 1989; Pruitt & Rubin, 1986, chap. 6) in attempting to thwart the other in win-lose fashion. The agitation emotions of anxiety and threat, on the other hand, appear to push the party in a withrawal or lose-lose direction (Kumar, 1989). In contrast, positive emotions appear to increase generosity and helpfulness, pushing the party in more cooperative directions (Carnevale & Isen, 1986).

Interestingly, several laboratory studies of positive emotion in conflict or negotiation have suggested the importance of humor. Baron and his associates (Baron, 1984; Baron & Ball, 1974) found that nonhostile humor tended to reduce aggression. Specifically, Carnevale and Isen (1986), as well as Pruitt, Carnevale, Ben-Yoav, Nochajski, and Van Slyck (1983), found that reading magazine cartoons prior to negotiations produced more integrative settlements.

Intentions

The combined motivational forces produced by rational/instrumental thinking, normative thinking, and emotions are presumed to result in the party's intentions, the next event in the conflict episode. An intention is the *conation*, or decision to act in a given way, that intervenes between the party's thoughts and emotions and the party's overt behavior. Although the earlier chapter (Thomas, 1976) treated intentions and behavior together, subsequent theoretical work (e.g., Thomas & Pondy, 1977) has underscored the importance of distinguishing between them.

Most terms ostensibly used to describe conflict behavior are in fact attributions of intent. For example, cooperation, collaboration, bargaining, self-defense, and competition are not themselves behaviors (in the sense of observable speech and movement), but are intentions or purposes that serve to explain patterns of observed behavior. The distinction is important for at least three reasons. First, a great deal of slippage occurs between intentions and behaviors, so that behavior does not always successfully implement one's intentions. Second, a party in conflict must infer the other's intent in order to know how to respond to the other's behavior. Thus, judgments of the other's intent play an important role during conflict episodes. Third, conflict researchers have often used questionable behavioral measures of intentional constructs—labeling a behavior as competition, for example, without directly checking on the subject's intentions in choosing it.

As Fishbein and Ajzen (1975) note, the content of an intention can be examined at various levels of specificity from "a general intention to cooperate...[to] a very specific intention" (p. 303). More general intentions, in effect, constitute the purposes or goals for more specific intentions. Here we will discuss two levels of intention: strategic intentions and tactical intentions.[22]

Strategic Intentions.   Strategic intentions are the more general intentions of a party in a given conflict episode. Until the mid-1960s, theorists tended to conceptualize these general intentions in unidimensional terms: for example, as cooperative versus competitive, or cooperative versus conflictful. In more recent organizational research, this unidimensional framework has been replaced by a family of two-dimensional models stemming from the work of Blake and Mouton (1964). Those models are summarized in Table 1.[23]

Each of the models in Table 1 identifies a set of strategic intentions, although these intentions have been variously labeled *orientations, approaches, styles, strategies, behaviors,* and *conflict-handling* modes. These sets of intentions are quite similar across the models.[24] The first model listed in Table 1 (from Thomas, 1979) is purely a classification or taxonomic scheme. That model, shown in Figure 5, classifies or defines each of the strategic intentions in terms of two more basic dimensions of intention, assertiveness, and cooperativeness. It will be used here to describe strategic intentions.

Although the remaining models in Table 1 include very similar strategic intentions, they are essentially *causal* models—variations of the dual concerns model mentioned earlier. That is, the two dimensions defining the axes of these models are independent variables asserted to interact to cause the strategic intentions. As noted earlier, these models essentially seek to explain the occurrence of the intentions in terms of a party's valences for satisfying different concerns. The causal models relevant to individual styles or traits shown in the tables seek to explain regularities in an individual's strategic intentions in terms of the individual's general values—one's general concern for people (or relationships or others) and one's general concern for production (or personal goals or self). The causal models relevent to situational intentions or states seek to explain specific instances of the strategic intentions in terms of the individual's valences for satisfying his or her own and others' concerns in a given situation.

Researchers using these models have often missed the distinction between taxonomies and causal models, using the dual concerns models as though they were only taxonomies. They have also confused the individual styles models with the situational models. Thus, the Blake and Mouton (1964) grid is still widely used as though it were only a classification scheme (taxonomy) for the strategic intentions by researchers who introduce independent variables that are quite different from Blake and Mouton's. The strategic intentions are also often called *styles,* even by researchers who discuss situational influences.[25] In general, there is a need for much greater precision in the use of these models (Thomas, 1988). In particular, it seems important to realize that the dual concerns

TABLE 1

Two-dimensional Models of Strategic Intentions

Sets of Models	Dimensions		Strategic Intentions	
	Names	*Interpretation*	*Names*	*Interpretation*
Taxonomic models				
Thomas (1979)	Cooperativeness (attempting to satisfy the other's concerns) Assertiveness (attempting to satisfy one's own concerns)	Intentions Collaborating Avoiding Accommodating Compromising	Competing	Intentions
Causal models, I: Individual styles (traits)				
Blake & Mouton (1964)	Concern for people Concern for production	Personal/ Cultural values	Forcing Confronting Withdrawing Smoothing over Compromising	Approaches (elements of managerial styles)
Hall (1969)	Concern for relationships Concern for personal goals	Personal values	Win-lose Synergistic Yield-lose Lose-leave Compromise	Styles
Rahim & Bonoma (1979)	Concern for others Concern for self	Motivational orientations	Dominating Integrating Avoiding Obliging Compromising	Styles
Causal models, II: Situational intentions (states)				
Thomas (1976)	Desire to satisfy the other's concerns Desire to satisfy one's own concern	Desires	Competitive Collaborative Avoidant Accommodative Sharing	Orientations (relationship specific)
Pruitt (1983)	Concerns about the other's outcomes Concerns about one's own outcome	Concerns	Contending Problem solving Inaction Yielding	Strategies (negotiation-specific)

FIGURE 5

Two-dimensional Taxonomy of Strategic Intentions

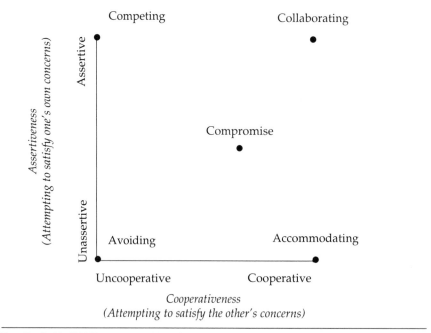

From "Conflict" by K. W. Thomas, 1979. In S. Kerr (Ed.), *Organizational Behavior* (p. 154). Grid Publications.
Copyright 1979 by S. Kerr. Adapted by permission.

models are distinctly causal models that capture only a subset of the independent variables that determine the strategic intentions of a conflict party. Accordingly, a more complex causal model of the psychological determinants of strategic intentions has been presented here, which, in addition to the outcome valences that are the focus of the dual concerns models, include other aspects of rational/instrumental reasoning, along with normative reasoning and emotions. The array of strategic intentions available to a party (as opposed to their causes) are discussed in terms of a purely taxonomic model.

Returning to the taxonomic model in Figure 5, the party's strategic intentions are classified and plotted along two basic orthogonal dimensions of intent: *assertiveness*—

the extent to which the party attempts to satisfy his or her own concerns; and *cooperativeness*— the extent to which the party attempts to satisfy the other's concerns. Five strategic intentions are classified in terms of these two dimensions: competing, collaborating, compromising, avoiding, and accommodating. These strategic intentions, in effect, correspond to salient regions of the joint outcome space (Figure 3) toward which a party may strive.

A *competing* intention (uncooperative, assertive) represents an attempt to prevail or win one's position—to satisfy one's own concerns at the other's expense. As shown in Table 1, this strategic intention has also been called *forcing, win-lose, dominating,* and *contending.* In goal conflicts, the intention is to achieve one's goal at the sacrifice of the other's goal. In judgment conflicts, one attempts to convince the other that one's conclusion is correct and the other's is mistaken. In normative conflicts, one tries to make the offending party accept blame for some perceived transgression, together with any responsibilities attached to blame (guilt, punishment, restitution, etc.).

The opposite of competing is an *accommodating* intention (cooperative, unassertive), which involves an attempt to satisfy the other's concerns at the neglect of one's own. Other terms for this intention include *smoothing over, yielding-losing, obliging,* and *yielding.* Depending on the type of concern involved, this intention may represent an attempt to attain the other's goals at the sacrifice of one's own, to support the other's opinion despite one's own reservations, or to forgive the other for a perceived transgression and to allow subsequent ones.

A *compromising* intention (intermediate in both cooperativeness and assertiveness) is understood as midway between competing and accommodating. Compromising is an attempt to attain moderate but incomplete satisfaction of both parties' concerns—giving up something but also holding out for something. Accordingly, Lewicki and Litterer (1985) argue that compromising is aimed at satisfying but not optimizing for the two parties. Since this intention seeks an outcome that is between the preferred outcomes (and positions) of both parties, it is also called *splitting the difference* and *sharing.* Depending on the nature of the conflict issue, compromising might mean seeking partial attainment of a goal (e.g., getting a raise of 50 cents an hour rather than a dollar), partial agreement on a conclusion ("Well, I suppose that's sometimes true"), or partial blame for an offense (e.g., pleading guilty to a lesser charge).

In contrast, a *collaborating* intention (cooperative, assertive) represents an attempt to *fully* satisfy the concerns of the two parties to achieve an integrative settlement. Other terms for this intention are problem solving, synergy,

integrating, and confronting (in the sense of confronting the conflict to work it through). In goal conflicts, one attempts to find a win-win solution that allows both parties' goals to be completely achieved. In judgmental conflicts, the goal is to achieve a *synthesis* (Hegel, 1964; Mason, 1969), a new conclusion or idea that incorporates the valid insights of both parties. In the case of normative conflicts, one might try to arrive at a shared set of expectations and an interpretation of the transgression in question that meets both parties' standards of what is proper in a given situation.

The remaining intention, *avoiding* (uncooperative, unassertive), reflects a desire to ignore or neglect the concerns of both self and other. Other terms for this construct in Table 1 are *withdrawing, lose-leave,* and *inaction* (although the latter is a more behavioral term). The terms *escapist, evasion, flight, lose-lose, fatalistic,* and *isolation* have also been used to refer to this intention. Basically, one seeks to avoid involving oneself in an issue, allowing events to take their own course without attempting to steer the outcome toward the concern of either party.

There is now relatively strong empirical evidence for the psychological validity of the basic features of this taxonomy. A series of studies using different methodologies has confirmed that individuals use two orthogonal dimensions to differentiate among the five intentions in the taxonomy, and that the relative positioning of the intentions along those two dimensions is basically in accordance with Figure 5 (Prein, 1976; Ruble & Thomas, 1976; van de Vliert & Hordijk, 1989).[26] Moreover, the results of Ruble and Thomas (1976) also support the assumption that the two underlying dimensions correspond to assertiveness and cooperativeness.

These strategic intentions provide a way of describing a party's general aims during a conflict. Without such steering mechanisms, the party's conflict behavior would merely be reactive or wandering. Nevertheless, there is a danger in viewing these strategic intentions in an oversimplified manner—in reifying them as "cast in concrete."[27] A strategic intention need not remain fixed during the course of a conflict and may change with a party's reconceptualizations and emotions. Likewise, there are times when a party may in fact lack a clear strategic intention and simply react to unfolding events.

Tactical Intentions.   These are more specific intentions that direct behavior and can be interpreted as the means of implementing or realizing the strategic intentions just discussed. Viewed differently, tactical intentions are the purposes that serve to explain observed bits of behavior during a conflict episode and are themselves explainable as ways of realizing broader strategic intentions.

With the growth of the negotiations literature, the subject of bargaining tactics has become one of the most developed areas in the conflict literature. Before discussing these tactics, however, it is important that they be placed in perspective. First, the bargaining or negotiation literature (following Lewicki and Litterer, 1985, these terms are used interchangeably) has focused primarily on goal conflicts. Tactics related to primarily judgmental and normative conflicts are less prominent in the negotiation literature and are less fully integrated into the mainstream organizational conflict literature. Second, negotiations are restricted to tactics that involve a search for agreement between the parties (Lewicki & Litterer, 1985). Thus, negotiation tactics exclude a variety of more escalated competitive tactics in which one attempts to defeat the other party through use of physical force or by coalition formation. Finally, the negotiations literature has tended to focus on more assertive attempts to reach agreement. In principle, tactics of avoidance and accommodating could also be described in some detail. For example, the artful avoidance of conflicts may involve a number of substeps, including the making of convincing excuses or the appointment of committees to camouflage inaction (e.g., see Lippitt & Mackenzie, 1979).[28] However, negotiations theorists have tended thus far to focus almost exclusively on tactics for competing, collaborating, and compromising.

Since the seminal work of Walton and McKersie (1965), negotiation tactics have been discussed in terms of *integrative* and *distributive* dimensions. In effect, these two dimensions provide another way of analyzing the array of strategic intentions shown earlier in Figure 5.[29] Figure 6 superimposes these two dimensions on that array. Roughly speaking, the *distributive* dimension represents a party's intentions with respect to the proportion of satisfaction going to each party's concern. It is a give-and-take, zero-sum dimension that involves relative shares of the pie. Thus, competing represents extreme taking, accommodating represents extreme giving, and the other intentions represent a more or less equal distribution between the parties. In contrast, the *integrative* dimension involves a party's intentions with respect to the total or joint degree of satisfaction of the two parties' concerns—the size of the total pie. Along this dimension, collaborating seeks to enlarge the pie by identifying an alternative that allows both parties to satisfy their concerns completely; avoiding reduces the size of the pie by neglecting both parties' concerns; and the remaining intentions are focused on a pie of intermediate size.

For ease of presentation, integrative and distributive tactics will be described separately here, as has been the trend in the negotiation literature (e.g., Lewicki & Litterer, 1985; Putnam & Poole, 1987). However, Walton and McKersie (1965) note that integrative and distributive bargaining are subprocesses that occur in various mixes in negotiations.[30]

Distributive tactics have been analyzed in terms of the kind of outcome range shown in Figure 7 (Lewicki & Litterer, 1985; Walton & McKersie, 1965). The focus of theorists has typically been on the allocation of some divisible commodity (e.g., money in labor-management negotiations), so that a more or less continuous

FIGURE 6

Integrative and Distributive Dimensions of Intent

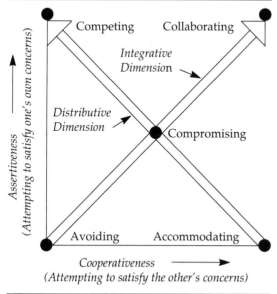

Reproduced with permission of authors and publisher from R. H. Kilmann and K. W. Thomas, "Interpersonal conflict-handling behavior as reflections of Jungian personality dimensions." *Psychological Reports*, 1975, *37*, 971–980.

range of possible decisions exists. Negotiations occur along the portion of this range that is anchored at either end by the aspirations (Pruitt & Rubin, 1986) or *target points* (Walton & McKersie, 1965) of the two parties. Each party is also assumed to have a *resistance point* (Walton & McKersie, 1965), which represents a minimally acceptable outcome for that party—the point at which the party would break off negotiations rather than accept a less favorable settlement. This resistance point is assumed to depend on the expected value of that party's "best alternative to a negotiated agreement," or BATNA (Fisher & Ury, 1981)—for example, finding another buyer, or calling for a strike. Each party, then, is assumed to be willing to consider only settlements that lie in the *aspiration range* between their target and resistance point. To the extent that the aspiration ranges of

the two parties overlap (as in Figure 7), some negotiated settlement is seen as possible along this length of overlap, or *settlement range*.

Against this backdrop, a party's distributive influence tactics are intended to motivate the other to agree to a settlement that is as close as possible to the party's own target—in effect to extend the other's resistance point toward the party's target, to get the other to abandon his or her target, and to accept a decision near the party's target. Specific distributive tactics for accomplishing this have been discussed by a number of authors. The reader is referred to them for more detail and supporting evidence.[31] Here we are concerned with a broad overview of these tactics in terms of the behavioral model presented earlier (see Table 2).[32] That is, the focus here is on the manner in which a party attempts to influence the other's intentions and behavior by shaping the other's rational/instrumental thinking, normative thinking, and emotions.

The first set of tactics in Table 2 is directed at the other's rational/instrumental reasoning. It is this set of tactics that has been most thoroughly analyzed in the negotiations literature. Essentially, the purpose of these tactics is to convince the other that there is no reasonable chance of obtaining the other's target and that the other would be better off accepting a settlement near the party's target. The first of these tactics, involving the *other's outcome valences*, is essentially aimed at convincing the other that the settlement range is near the party's target—that is, that any possible decision must be in that neighborhood. The party tries to move the other's resistance point northwest in Figure 7 by convincing the other that the other's alternatives to reaching an agreement are less desirable (or more costly or less feasible) than the other had believed. (Ideally, the other's resistance point is shifted far enough to include the party's target.) The other's old target is also devalued. At the same time, the party attempts to convince the other that the party's resistance point is also farther northwest because the party

FIGURE 7

**Range of Possible Outcomes in Distributive
Bargaining Projected Onto Joint Outcome Space**

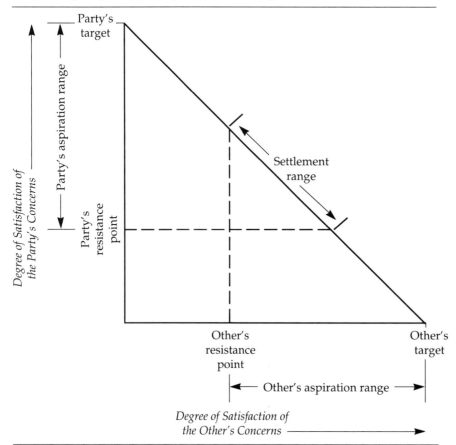

has other attractive alternatives. The party's valuing of his or her target is also stressed. These tactics, if successful, shift the other's target to a new position within the new settlement range, and discussion continues. The second type of rational/instrumental tactics, involving the *other's expectancies*, is then employed in an attempt to force acceptance of the party's target position rather than any other decision within the new settlement range. Essentially, the thrust of these tactics is to convince the other that he or

she must choose between the party's target position and breaking off negotiations. If successful, this means that the other will accept the party's target, since it is now seen as better than the other's alternatives to reaching an agreement (i.e., falls within the other's resistance point). The party attempts to force this choice by convincing the other that the party is unalterably committed to his or her target, so that the party would break off negotiations rather than abandon this position. At the same time,

TABLE 2

Distributive **Negotiation Tactics in Terms of Their Motivational Targets**

Motivational Targets	Tactical Objectives
Other's Rational/Instrumental Reasoning	
Other's outcome valences (moving settlement range toward the party's target)	Convince the other that breaking off negotiations would be costly for the other (the other has no satisfactory alternatives)
	Convince the other that the other's valence for his or her target should be lower
	Convince the other that breaking off negotiations would not be costly for the party (the party has other attractive alternatives)
	Convince the other that the party's valence for the party's target is high
Other's expectancies (managing feasibilities through commitments)	Convince the other that the party is unalterably committed to an outcome close to the party's target
	Prevent the other from making a firm commitment to an outcome near the other's target
	Allow the other to abandon his or her position without loss of face or other cost
Other's Normative Reasoning	
Other's consideration of general (societal) norms	Convince the other that the party's target would be a fair (equitable) outcome
	Convince the other that the other's target would be an unfair (inequitable) outcome
	Convince the other that the party is behaving fairly
	Convince the other that the other's distributive tactics are (or would be) unfair
Other's consideration of specific group expectations	Convince the other that groups important to him or her favor the party's target and tactics and disapprove of the other's
	Isolate the other from groups which would support the other's target and tactics
Other's Emotions	
Other's emotions toward the party or issue	Minimize the use of distributive tactics and behaviors that would anger the other toward the party
	Use nonhostile humor or other means to build positive affect in the other
Other's emotions toward extraneous matters (distractions)	Distract the other with irrelevant affect that impairs the other's ability to concentrate

the party seeks to prevent the other from making a similar commitment to the other's target and to allow the other to abandon any commitment already made without loss of face.

The second set of tactics in Table 2 is directed at the other's normative reasoning. The goal is to convince the other that the party's target would be a fair or proper outcome and that the party's distributive tactics are fair, while the other's target and distributive tactics would be unfair. The normative tactics labeled "Other's consideration of general norms" appeal to generally accepted norms of fairness or justice. These norms have been recently investigated in terms of distributive and procedural justice. *Distributive justice* (e.g., Deutsch, 1975; Leventhal, 1976) refers to normative standards for evaluating the fairness of the allocation of outcomes between the parties. Thus, one set of distributive tactics attempts to convince the other that the party's target would be a fair or equitable outcome and that the distribution resulting from the other's target would be unfair. (The party "deserves" more than that.) *Procedural justice* (e.g., Thibaut & Walker, 1975; Tyler, 1986) refers to normative standards for evaluating the manner in which a decision is reached. Here, some negotiation tactics (e.g., threats) may be seen as unfair and thus provoke retribution from the other (to give the party "what he deserves" in another sense). Thus, another set of tactics is aimed at convincing the other that the party's distributive tactics are fair, conforming to norms of fairness in order to invite fair treatment in return or appealing for fair behavior from the other to moderate the other's distributive tactics. For example, the party may attempt to justify distributive tactics by citing mitigating circumstances or other acceptable explanations for them.

In contrast, the normative tactics labeled "Other's consideration of specific group expectations" involve the normative beliefs of specific reference groups or individuals of importance to the other. Here the party attempts to convince the other that these groups (e.g., a common superior, constituents, a newspaper, or other stakeholders) approve of the party's target and tactics and disapprove of the other's. Likewise, the party may attempt to isolate the other from groups that would support the other's target or the other's strong distributive tactics during negotiations.

The third set of tactics in Table 2 attempts to influence the other's emotions during negotiations. The goal is to facilitate emotions that support reasonableness and generosity in the other but may also distract the other so that the other is not in top form as an adversary. The first two emotional tactics, labeled "Other's emotions toward the party or issue," address the other's negotiating mood toward the central features of the negotiation—the party and the central issue being negotiated with the party. The first tactic here is to avoid any unnecessary angering of the other toward the party, which would intensify the other's win-lose intentions and make the other less "reasonable," thus reducing the likely effectiveness of the first two sets of the party's tactics. The party may need to carefully moderate the use of rational/instrumental and normative tactics that would have that effect and to employ some sensitivity and tact in the phrasings of communications to the other. (See the discussion of behavior later in this chapter.) The second tactical objective is to facilitate positive emotions in the other when possible—not only to interfere with possible anger from the other, but also to place the other in a generous mood on the conflict issue. The same effect may also be achieved through timing—by waiting until the other is experiencing positive emotions from another source. The emotional tactic labeled "Other's emotions toward extraneous matters" is concerned with distractions. Here the party may attempt to distract the other with emotions that are irrelevant or peripheral to the issue at hand but may impair the other's ability to concentrate on distributive tactics.[33]

In contrast to distributive tactics, *integrative tactics* relate more to appealing to a potential ally than forcing the other to yield. These tactics must be understood against the background of the decision process required for the sort of problem solving required to arrive at an integrative outcome. The underlying concerns of both parties must be revealed in some detail, a list of possible alternatives must be generated and examined, and the most jointly satisfactory alternative must be agreed upon by the two parties.[34] This process imposes requirements on the parties that contrast sharply with distributive bargaining. The parties must candidly exchange accurate information about underlying concerns, probable outcomes of alternatives, and their satisfaction with those outcomes (in contrast to the slanted or distorted information presented in distributive tactics). They must also remain flexible and exploratory with respect to alternatives (in contrast to the commitment tactics of distributive bargaining). Considerable trust is also required—trust that the other party will not exploit this information or flexibility for competitive gain.

Table 3 provides an overview of integrative negotiation tactics and their motivational objectives. Again, the interested reader is referred to other works for more detailed discussion of these tactics.[35]

Briefly, rational/instrumental tactical objectives in integrative bargaining involve showing the other that an integrative outcome would be both instrumental to the other and feasible. The party can attempt to demonstrate the desirability of an integrative outcome in at least two ways, as shown under the label "Other's outcome valence" in Table 3. Assuming that the other already regards his or her concerns as important, the party can increase the other's valence for an integrative outcome by demonstrating that the satisfaction of the party's concern would also be instrumental to the other in some way. For example, both parties' concerns may involve a common objective or superordinate goal. Likewise, an integrative outcome may be instrumental to the other for maintaining a cooperative continuing

relationship with the party. Alternatively, the party may increase the other's valuing of an integrative outcome by demonstrating that the party will not compromise his or her concern, so that the other's concern can only be satisfied through an integrative outcome. Thus, although integrative problem solving requires a flexibility with respect to positions, it is also likely to require a firmness or assertiveness with respect to the pursuit of the party's underlying concerns. This stance has been referred to as being *hard on interests but soft on positions* (Fisher & Ury, 1981) or as *firm flexibility* (Pruitt, 1983; Pruitt & Rubin, 1986).

The second type of rational/instrumental integrative tactics, "Other's expectancies," is directed at showing the other that integrative problem solving is feasible. This feasibility involves both showing the other that an integrative solution is possible, and showing the other that the party could be trusted to engage in this process. The possibility of an integrative solution can be conveyed by defining the issue as an integrative problem and by showing that the parties have the ability to resolve it. Trust can be conveyed by demonstrating that one has collaborative intentions (e.g., by emphasizing the importance of the other's concerns as well as the party's) and by demonstrating flexibility with respect to solutions and positions.

The normative integrative tactics in Table 3 are aimed at the other's sense that integrative problem solving would be proper. The tactics labeled "Other's consideration of general norms" appeal to widespread social norms—those that are shared by society as a whole. Research suggests that collaborative intentions are regarded as more socially desirable than other conflict-handling intentions in our culture (Thomas & Kilmann, 1975). Thus, the party may appeal to this general norm to set a collaborative strategic tone. During the process of integrative problem solving, moreover, researchers have emphasized the importance of generally accepted criteria of fairness for choosing among the set of possible solutions

TABLE 3

Integrative Negotiation Tactics in Terms of Their Motivational Targets

Motivational Targets	Tactical Objectives
Other's Rational/Instrumental Reasoning	
Other's outcome valences (making an integrative outcome desirable)	Show the other that the party's concern is also instrumental to the other Show the other that the party's concern is too important to be compromised (signaling firmness with respect to interests)
Other's expectancies (making integrative problem solving feasible)	Show the other that an integrative outcome is a logical possibility (through framing of issue) Show the other that the parties have the skill to find an integrative solution Demonstrate that the party has collaborative intentions Demonstrate that the party is flexible with respect to positions
Other's Normative Reasoning	
Other's consideration of general (societal) norms	Make collaborative norms salient to the other Insist on fair criteria for deciding among possible solutions
Other's consideration of specific group expectations	Isolate the negotiations from groups that would exert distributive pressure
Other's Emotions	
Other's emotions toward the party or issue	Minimize use of behaviors or tactics that would produce negative emotions in the other toward the party Provide an emotionally supportive climate and generally build positive affect in other
Other's emotions toward extraneous matters (distractions)	Shield the other from emotional distractions

generated by the parties. Agreement on these criteria, especially if made operational at the beginning of the problem-solving process, reduces the need for distributive negotiations among alternatives, which might in turn interfere with the problem-solving process (Fisher & Ury, 1981; Walton & McKersie, 1965). The tactics labeled "Other's consideration of specific group expectations" are concerned with the normative beliefs of specific reference groups or individuals of importance to the other. Here the party attempts to isolate the negotiation process from any of these groups which might exert distributive pressures.[36]

Of the integrative tactics concerned with the other's emotions, the first group, "Other's emotions toward the party or issue," have objectives that are quite similar to those in distributive bargaining—preventing unnecessary negative emotions toward the party (e.g., anger and fear) and encouraging positive emotions in the other. Thus, the party may attempt to minimize the use of tactics or behaviors that would generate negative emotions toward the party and thereby prevent the other from recognizing integrative possibilities and/or add uncooperative (competitive or avoiding) motivational forces. Likewise, the party may try to facilitate positive emotions in the other as a means of interfering with negative emotions, increasing the other's ability to handle the cognitive demands of problem solving and adding cooperative forces. Theorists have sometimes discussed this objective in terms of providing a climate that is noncritical and supportive (e.g., Likert & Likert, 1976). Creating this climate has been asserted to depend in part on the party's own ability to "separate [the other] from the problem" (Fisher & Ury, 1981), treating the other as a potential ally in dealing with the conflict problem as opposed to *personalizing* the conflict by treating the other as part of the problem. The third tactical objective, however, addressing the "Other's emotions toward extraneous matters," is quite different from distributive tactics. While

distributive tactics may seek to distract the other with irrelevant affect, integrative objectives include shielding the other from extraneous emotional distractions. For example, the party may want to meet with the other away from a stressful work environment so that the other can better concentrate on problem solving.

Behavior

After the formation of intentions, the next event in the conflict episode is overt behavior. Behaviors here refer to statements or other observable actions performed by the party. To the extent that the party's behavior is reasoned, these behaviors are interpreted as overt attempts to implement the party's intentions. Once they are performed, however, these behaviors have a stimulus quality that is separate from the party's intentions, producing effects that may or may not achieve those intentions—through the party's miscalculations or unskilled enactment.[37]

Putnam and Poole (1987) summarize types of behaviors that factor analyses have shown to be generally associated with integrative and distributive strategic intentions.[38] Integrative strategies are typified by "acceptance statements, other-supporting arguments, and exploratory problem solving messages," while distributive strategies are accompanied by "threats, put-downs, irrelevant arguments, commitments, demands, and charge-fault statements" (p. 568).

While these results characterize types of behaviors commonly used by typical subjects, the Huthwaite research group (Huthwaite, Inc., 1985) attempted to discover behavioral patterns that were characteristic of skilled negotiators in real-world settings. The researchers identified a set of 51 individuals who met three criteria for successful negotiators: (a) being rated as effective by both sides, (b) having a track record of significant success over an extended time period, and (c) having a low incidence of

TABLE 4

Behaviors of Skilled Negotiators Relative to Average Negotiators

Less Use of:	*More Use of:*
Irritators (favorable statements about the party, unfavorable statements about the other)	Advanced labeling of behaviors other than disagreement (letting the other know what the party is doing)
Immediate counterproposals	Testing understanding and summarizing
Defending/attacking comments	Asking questions
Stating disagreement without first providing reasons	Giving information on the party's internal states (e.g., concerns, emotions, intentions)
Argument dilution (providing many reasons for each argument or case advanced, rather than the main reason)	

Summarized from Huthwaite, Inc. (1985).

implementation failures for their agreements. These successful negotiators, along with a group of average negotiators, were then observed during actual negotiations. Table 4 summarizes the observed behaviors of the successful negotiators in comparison with the average negotiators.[39]

Some of the behavioral tendencies of successful negotiators in Table 4 can be interpreted as aiding communications and (in the case of disclosing feelings) building trust. In terms of the influence tactics discussed earlier, however, most of these behavioral tendencies can also be interpreted as a means of reducing the arousal of negative emotions in the other and providing some elements of a supportive climate. Provocations, in the form of irritators and defend/attack comments, are reduced. Moreover, some elements of support appear to be provided, in effect, by slowing down the pace of give-and-take to give the other time to think before responding and by attending to what the other is saying.

Along similar lines, Baron (1988b) has identified constructive ways of giving performance criticism that arouse less negative emotion in the other. Constructive feedback was specific, considerate, and did not attribute poor performance to causes internal to the other. In comparison to those who received less constructive feedback, people receiving constructive feedback reported being less angry and tense and indicated that they would be more likely to respond toward the party with collaboration or compromise in the future.

Interaction

Following the party's behavior, the next event in the process model is the other's reaction. The other's reaction, in turn, is a cue to which the party will likely need to respond. The result is a more or less prolonged interaction between the two parties. During this interaction, each party's behavior is seen as a stimulus that provides additional input to the other's thoughts and feelings, leading to potential adjustments in tactical and/or strategic intentions that may change the course of the conflict episode.

Once the interaction phase of a conflict episode is under way, the episode becomes a dynamic process with many of the characteristics of a dance. The parties become involved in both leading and following each other while coordinating their behaviors. Beyond the initial moves, it becomes increasingly difficult to predict the precise course of activities ahead of time, and the episode takes on more of the quality of an emergent or dynamic process (Knapp, Putnam, & Davis, 1988; Putnam, 1990). Accordingly, the Huthwaite, Inc. (1985) study reported that skilled negotiators planned for negotiations in a relatively flexible manner, considering more possible outcomes and options, and making fewer assumptions about the sequence in which issues would be discussed.

Two broad ways of describing the changing or dynamic patterns that occur during conflict interaction have involved phase analysis and escalation.

Phase analysis, as Folger and Poole (1984) note, seeks to divide a conflict interaction into "recognizable, sequential periods marked by different behaviors and sequences of behaviors" (p. 20). To date, most descriptions of conflict phases have been based on bargaining over goal conflicts, although many descriptions seem more broadly applicable. To a large extent, the phases represent sequential subtasks of reaching agreement. For example, Sheppard (1984) has identified four main stages of interaction: (a) joint *definition* of the conflict issue (including the broad identification of possible settlements), (b) *discussion* of alternative settlements and their merits, (c) *alternative selection*, and (d) *reconciliation* of parties to the settlement. Several more specific activities are identified within each phase.

While Sheppard identified four broad phases, a number of other theorists have focused more narrowly on a particular change or evolution between two states. Thus, Ikle (1964) observed that agreement on a broad *formula* for agreement (including criteria for the fairness or justice of a settlement) was necessary before working out the *detail* of an agreement. For a more complete description and critique of stage models of negotiation, see Lewicki et al. (1988), Putnam (1990), and Putnam and Poole (1987).

Escalation/deescalation is a general way of referring to changes in the level or intensity of conflict. Escalation is reflected in such changes as increasing the number and size of issues disputed, increasing hostility, increasing competitiveness, pursuing increasingly extreme demands or objectives, using increasingly coercive tactics, decreasing trust, and enlisting other parties to take sides in the conflict. Escalation can be examined during the course of one episode or in the changes occuring from one episode to the next in an ongoing relationship.

Glasl (1982) has attempted to map the broad range of escalatory levels possible in a conflict. As shown in Table 5, three main phases of escalation are identified, each of which is divided into three stages. Conflicts are asserted to escalate from one stage to the next highest when the parties pass some threshold of progressively extreme tactics or behavior. Once a given threshold is passed, additional dynamics are introduced into the conflict that make it difficult to move back to the prior, less escalated level. Glasl notes that escalation beyond stage six is rarely encountered within organizations.

The dynamics of escalation have been discussed in detail by several authors (e.g., Glasl, 1982; Pruitt & Rubin, 1986; Thomas, 1976; van de Vliert, 1984). These dynamics appear to be consistent with the behavioral assumptions posited in the process model we have been discussing. First, the major phases of escalation seem to be accompanied by different definitions of what the conflict is about, as the parties' focus shifts from substantive issues (Phase I) to personalized focus on the other party (Phase II) to surviving combat (Phase III). These escalating definitions of the conflict situation give

TABLE 5

Glasl's Levels of Conflict Escalation

Phase 1: Rationality and Control

Parties are aware of tensions but try to handle them in a rational and controlled manner. Parties interact with some degree of cooperation and deal mostly with impersonal topics or issues.

Stage 1	Attempts to cooperate and incidental slips into tensions and frictions
Stage 2	Polarization and debating style
Stage 3	Interaction through deeds, not words

Phase II: Severing the Relationship

The relationship between the parties becomes the main source of tension. Distrust, lack of respect, and overt hostility evolve. The parties cannot imagine solving the conflict together and attempt to exclude each other.

Stage 4	Concern for reputation and coalition
Stage 5	Loss of face (and moral outrage)
Stage 6	Dominance of strategies of threat

Phase III: Aggression and Destruction

Confrontations become very destructive. The other party is viewed as having no human dignity, and any attempt to achieve positive outcomes is blocked. The parties risk their own welfare, or even existence, in order to damage or destroy the other.

Stage 7	Systematic destructive campaigns against the sanction potential of the other party
Stage 8	Attacks against the power nerves of the enemy
Stage 9	Total destruction and suicide

Note: Descriptions of phases are paraphrased for brevity. Names of phases have been added.

Summarized from Glasl (1982).

each party progressively fewer and less attrac-tive options to choose from.[40] Second, each party's decision to escalate is influenced by rational/instrumental considerations, norma-tive considerations, and by growing emotion-ality (in the form of hostility), which distorts reasoning in predictable ways and introduces additional drives to compete with, or harm, the other party. For example, rational/instrumen-tal considerations include the growing distrust of the other and the awareness that the other is not responding to reason, so that less escalated tactics are no longer seen as effective. Norma-tive considerations include the assessment that the other is behaving increasingly improp-erly (or is increasingly evil) and deserves to be punished. Distortions of reasoning include overestimates of the merits of one's own posi-tion and bargaining power, plus escalating commitment to one's position (largely distor-tions of rational/instrumental reasoning), as well as projection of undesirable characteristics onto the other and denial of personal blame for events (largely distortions of normative reasoning).[41]

In the negotiations literature, Bazerman (1986, chap. 7) has provided a detailed list of distortions in a party's rational/instrumental reasoning that can contribute to escalation. These include (a) assuming a *fixed pie* (i.e., that integrative outcomes are impossible), (b) fram-ing the party's judgments in terms of potential losses rather than gains, (c) nonrational com-mitment processes, (d) overconfidence, (e) un-dervaluing the importance of accurate infor-mation, and (f) failure to take the other's per-spective. Most of these dynamics have been investigated in a program of research by Neale and Bazerman (e.g., 1983, 1985; Bazerman, Magliozzi, & Neale, 1985).

Two additional perceptual dynamics that contribute to escalation deserve special men-tion here because they concern the strategic intentions central to the process model. First, there appears to be a strong tendency for a party to see the other as relatively competitive, while seeing oneself as relatively uncompetitive and cooperative. In one study, for example, 73 percent of managers who were asked to recall a recent conflict reported that the other party in the conflict had been predominately competi-tive, compared with only 21 percent who saw themselves as competitive (Thomas & Pondy, 1977). Second, a recent multidimensional scaling study by van de Vliert and Prein (1989) suggests that a party's interpretation of the other's competing differs from the party's interpretation of his or her own competing. This difference concerns the cooperativeness dimension of the two-dimensional taxonomy shown in Figure 5. Whereas the party sees his or her own competing as simply uncooperative (as in Figure 5), the party appears to see the other's competing as more negative—as inten-tionally harmful, hostile, or aggressive. These two perceptual biases, then, appear to combine to magnify the party's perception of hostile intent in the other, while reducing the party's awareness of the extent to which he or she may be signaling hostile intent to the other.

Researchers have noted that low levels of competitive escalation may serve a useful pur-pose by laying the groundwork for collabora-tion. Walton (1969) observed that competitive phases often help sharpen a conflict issue, which may be necessary before the parties can seek an integrative solution that combines their con-cerns. Pruitt and Rubin (1986) argue that prob-lem solving (collaboration) often emerges after a contentious (competitive) stage has resulted in stalemate, as equally matched parties learn that competition is unlikely to succeed.

Nevertheless, the costs and risks of escala-tion, especially at more advanced stages, have led a number of researchers to identify deescalating tactics and countermoves for han-dling potentially escalating behaviors by the other party. These include the blocking of de-structive cycles (see Putnam & Poole, 1987) and the clarification of the party's noncompetitive intentions (Thomas & Pondy, 1977). The nondestructive Eastern martial arts of jujitsu and akido have provided metaphors for some of these tactics (e.g., Fisher & Ury, 1981; Lee, Olson, & Swinth, 1987).[42]

Outcomes

The final element depicted in the process model involves the outcome(s) of the conflict episode. When interaction between the parties ceases, some set of outcomes is presumed to have occurred. The most obvious outcome involves the decision that has been reache regarding the conflict issue—or the lack of a decision. A variety of other consequences of the episode are also likely to be important to the principal parties and to the third party.

Because the conflict process is part of a system of interrelated variables (refer back to Figure 1), the consequences of conflict are considered to be widespread and complex. In the face of this complexity, different theorists have considered different subsets of these consequences. Considering different consequences, in effect, means that theorists have adopted different criteria for evaluating conflicts and have adopted different, often implicit, goals for conflict management. Much of the apparent contradiction in the literature regarding conflict management is based less on empirical issues than on the choice of outcome variables. The following section on the goals of conflict management will explore these outcome variables in more detail.

Criteria for Conflict Management Effectiveness

The remainder of this chapter contains much descriptive theory regarding conflict. From this point, however, discussion focuses on managing the conflict process and the applied issues related to goals and methods of conflict management. Since, by definition, conflict management is a purposeful or goal-directed

activity, the discussion begins with an examination of the goals or purposes that direct conflict management.

Early definitions of *conflict management* were nonspecific about its purpose, using such vague phrases as keeping conflict "productive or at least not destructive" (Deutsch, 1971, p. 53) or "creative and useful" (Kahn & Boulding, 1964, p. 76). Where more specific goals were identifiable, Pondy (1967) noted that theorists often seemed to assume those goals instead of stating and defending them. Although considerable progress has recently been made in theory development in this area (e.g., Sheppard, 1984), disagreement and ambiguity still exist. This section offers a conceptual framework for reconciling some of these differences.

As in the process model, two different types of reasoning are assumed to be involved in shaping purposes (intentions) in conflict management—normative reasoning and rational/instrumental reasoning. Thus, there are two different sets of goal dimensions or criteria—normative and rational/instrumental.

Normative Considerations

To date, the most explicitly considered normative criteria applied to conflict management have involved justice or fairness. As mentioned earlier, these criteria involve both distributive justice (the fairness of the settlement) and procedural justice (the fairness of the procedure for arriving at a settlement). Sheppard (1984) specifies that distributive justice involves such criteria as equitability, consistency of results with similar conflicts, the relative needs of the parties, and consistency with accepted rules or norms. Specific elements of procedural justice identified by Sheppard include (a) the neutrality of the third party, (b) the ability of the principal parties to control the process, and (c) the protection of the rights of the principal parties.[43]

Rational/Instrumental Considerations

Unlike the normative goals, rational/instrumental goals are concerned with outcomes that appear desirable because they will benefit some person, group, or system. These goals, then, take on value because they are seen as instrumental to the welfare of that person, group, or system.

Much of the diversity among conflict management recommendations in the literature appears to stem from two conceptually independent sets of choices in the rational/instrumental reasoning of researchers—the choice of a primary beneficiary and the choice of time horizon. As shown in Figure 8, these choices combine to define different broad goals for conflict management. These different goals, often chosen implicitly, can result in quite different recommendations. It is important to realize that much of the resulting disagreement has little to do with the effectiveness of a given intervention in achieving an objective (an empirical issue). Rather, it reflects the fact that different theorists and researchers are trying to solve different problems. That is, the interventions are directed at different ends.

Primary Beneficiary. The primary beneficiary of conflict management refers to the entity whose welfare is of focal concern. Most approaches to conflict management seem to fall within three categories in this regard: (a) partisan, (b) joint-welfare, and (c) systemic.[44] The choice among these approaches is equivalent to how broadly one defines the unit of analysis in a criterion function. In the order listed, the goals of each earlier approach are included as parts of the goals of each following (broader) approach.

Partisan approaches identify with *one* of the conflicting parties and with satisfying that party's concerns. Here typical objectives are to help the party identify his or her concerns, develop the skills or other resources needed to assertively pursue them, and protect the party from the other. Areas of the literature where partisan approaches have frequently been taken include assertiveness training (e.g., Smith, 1975) and group or class organizing (e.g., Alinski, 1971; Chesler, Crowfoot, & Bryant, 1978).

Joint-welfare approaches focus on satisfying the combined concerns of *both* conflicting parties. Economic analyses of negotiations (e.g., Raiffa, 1982) or conflict (e.g., Boulding, 1963), for example, often adopt this approach, equating the goodness of a settlement with the extent to which it is *Pareto optimal*—loosely speaking, the extent to which there is no possible settlement that would better satisfy the joint concerns of the two parties. This same approach is also widespread in psychological discussions of conflict management that emphasize the desirability of *win-win* (e.g., Filley, 1975), *synergistic* (e.g., Craig & Craig, 1974), or *integrative* (e.g., Thomas, 1976) outcomes for the two parties.

Systemic approaches focus on the welfare of the larger system, of which the conflicting parties are elements. Thus, in addition to the welfare or satisfaction of the two conflicting parties, who are only a part of the system, attention is directed to the consequences of their conflict for the functioning of the system as a whole.[45] This approach has been adopted by a number of organizational conflict theorists concerned with the need of administrators or managers to harness conflict to contribute to organizational survival and performance (e.g., Pondy, 1967; Robbins, 1978; Thomas, 1982).

In general, the systemic approach will be adopted in the remainder of this chapter because it appears most congruent with the applied, managerial/organizational concerns of industrial and organizational psychology.[46] As the broadest approach, however, it also allows elements of partisan and joint-welfare criteria to be incorporated as well.

Time Horizon. As shown in Figure 8, each of the approaches I've discussed can also be

FIGURE 8

Alternative Approaches to Conflict Management Goals Based on Beneficiary and Time Horizon

	Time Horizon	
Choice of Beneficiary	*Short-term*	*Long-term*
Partisan	Pursuing one party's concerns in the here and now	Improving conditions for one party over time
Joint welfare	Pursuing both parties' concerns in the here and now	Improving conditions for both parties over time
Systemic	Pursuing the larger system's concerns in the here and now	Improving conditions for the larger system over time

divided roughly into two time horizons—short-term and long-term.[47] For each choice of beneficiary, one can choose to focus on the short-term problem of managing the immediate conflict situation for the sake of that beneficiary and/or on the long-term problem of improving conditions so that more optimal situations and outcomes are possible for the beneficiary. These time horizons involve different assumptions and address different types of actions or interventions, as described in Table 6.[48] Both are regarded here as important, supplementary aspects of conflict management.

Short-term approaches focus on coping with the immediate conflict situation. Thus, the conditions surrounding the conflict are accepted as givens, and the goal is to achieve the best possible outcome for the beneficiary under those conditions. Recommendations tend to focus on process—what actions to take in the immediate situation. Prescriptive theories that adopt this approach tend to take the form of contingency theories, with intended outcomes contingent on constraints or opportunities that vary with the prevailing circumstances. This grounding in the realities of the immediate situation tends to give short-term approaches an especially pragmatic flavor.

The recognition and acceptance of present conditions, which gives the short-term approach the strength of pragmatism, necessarily restricts it to the search for a local optimum. To move beyond the limitations of the present situation requires addressing the long-term issue of how

TABLE 6

Comparison of Short-term and Long-term Approaches to Conflict Management

	Time Horizon	
Characteristics	*Short-term*	*Long-term*
Focus	Coping with the here and now	Building desirable futures
Context assumption	Contextual variables are given	Contextual variables are changeable
Goal	Local optimum: best achievable in present situation	Global optimum: excellence
Recommendations	What actions to take under present circumstances	What circumstances to create
Type of theory required	Contingency theory	Universalistic theory
Flavor	Pragmatic/realistic	Idealistic/visionary

Adapted by permission of Greenwood Publishing Group, Inc., Westport, CT, from "Norms as an Integative Theme in Conflict and Negotiations" by W. Thomas, 1989. In M. S. Rahim (Ed.), *Managing Conflict: An Integrative Approach.* Copyright 1989 by Praeger Publishers, Greenwood Publishing Group, Inc.

to *improve* conditions. The long-term approach focuses on this sort of improvement. Here situational variables are regarded as changeable, and the goal becomes the modification of these variables to enhance opportunities and reduce constraints—essentially to achieve a more globally optimal set of outcomes for the beneficiary. Because it deals with the changing of conditions, the long-term approach tends to be enacted through structural, as opposed to process, interventions. Moreover, theories that adopt this approach tend to be more universalistic, as opposed to contingent, in their intended outcomes.[49] That is, if one is concerned with improving conditions, there needs to be a more universal ideal or vision of perfection to strive toward that is not contingent on present conditions. This focus on what could be tends to give the long-term approach a somewhat more idealistic or visionary flavor.

Specific Criteria for Conflict Management

While the broad goals or purposes I have discussed provide general directions for conflict management, more specificity is required. This specificity involves identifying the more detailed, multidimensional subgoals of conflict management. In effect, these subgoals provide somewhat more operational outcome variables toward which to steer conflict episodes and also serve as criteria for assessing the effectiveness of conflict management (Sheppard, 1984; Thomas, 1982).

Table 7 displays the set of criteria that will be used here.[50] This list combines the normative criterion of justice or fairness with four systemic, rational/instrumental criteria. The rational/instrumental criteria include two variables related to task accomplishment

TABLE 7

A Set of Systemic Criteria for Conflict Management

Type of Criteria	Criteria
Normative	Perceived fairness (justice)
Rational/instrumental	Decision quality Resource consumption during episode Satisfaction of parties Effects on working relationship

(quality of the decision reached and time and other resources consumed during the conflict episode), as well as two variables related to the social maintenance of the system (satisfaction of the parties and any changes in the quality of their work relationship). These latter four criteria are conceptualized as dimensions of conflict outcomes (states existing at the end of a conflict episode) that contribute to system performance.

Although the criteria in Table 7 were derived theoretically, they overlap strongly with a more empirically based scheme developed by Sheppard (1984). Rather than criteria for desirable outcomes of conflict episodes, Sheppard focused on the more specialized issue of the criteria used by third parties (managers, parents, police officers) to select different third-party intervention procedures. Nevertheless, Sheppard identified four general factors that seem to parallel four of the five criteria in Table 7: (a) fairness, (b) effectiveness (involving decision quality and acceptance of the decision by the parties), (c) efficiency (resource consumption), and (d) participant satisfaction.[51] A recent factor analytic study of these criteria (Sheppard, Blumenfeld-Jones, Minton, Hyder, & Deeb, 1987) has provided partial support for this categorization of criteria.[52] (Sheppard's work will be discussed later in this chapter.)

Applying These Criteria to the Conflict Process

While the criteria in Table 7 can be used to direct third-party process interventions, it is important to realize that, of necessity, most conflict management in organizations is done by the principal parties themselves, unassisted by third parties. To the extent that the principal parties are effective in this, the need for third-party intervention is reduced. Thus, effective conflict management by the principal parties contributes to an organization's welfare in two ways—by directly producing more effective conflict outcomes for the organization, and by saving the organizational costs (in terms of man-hours and opportunity costs) of having to involve third parties extensively in ongoing conflicts.

In the remainder of this section, the criteria in Table 7 will be used to assess the effectiveness of different strategic intentions (conflict-handling modes) that can be adopted by the principal conflict parties. As indicated earlier, the parties' strategic intentions (as opposed to tactics or behaviors) appear to provide the most basic way of characterizing the direction of the conflict process. Consistent with the preceding discussion, effectiveness will be examined from the viewpoint of both long-term and short-term approaches.

The Long-term Approach. Briefly, available evidence appears strongly to support the value of a long-term goal of building high levels of collaboration for dealing with significant conflict issues in organizations.[53] This position has considerable intuitive appeal: An overall system will tend to benefit most when conflicts between its parts can be managed to produce integrative settlements that more fully meet the combined concerns of those component parts. The apparent advantages of collaboration are supported by a compelling body of theoretical analyses and empirical findings that relate collaboration to each of the criteria in Table 7.[54] The following is a brief overview of themes in this literature.

With respect to fairness or justice, Eiseman (1978) argued that collaboration (integration) enhances the sense of justice, since "all parties are vindicated" (p. 136). Fisher and Ury (1981), in fact, refer to more collaborative or integrative bargaining as *principled* negotiation. More generally, normative approval of collaboration is indicated by the fact that collaboration is typically rated as the most socially desirable of the strategic intentions (Thomas & Kilmann, 1975) and that ratings of collaboration load highly positive on the evaluation scale of the semantic differential (Ruble & Thomas, 1976).

The link between collaboration (as a search for integrative settlements) and decision quality is hardly surprising, since decision quality is often defined in terms of finding the most jointly optimal settlement. Nevertheless, studies do tend to document the linkage between collaborative intentions in a given conflict (or at least the conditions believed to produce collaborative intentions) and more integrative decisions (e.g., Pruitt & Rubin, 1986; Tjosvold, 1985). The supportiveness, open exchange of information, and investigation of underlying issues are also presumed to produce greater learning for the parties, which transfers to improved decision making on other cognitive tasks. Thus, an extensive review of relevant studies in the educational field (Johnson & Johnson, 1983)

concluded that collaboration (cooperation) tended to produce markedly greater learning and academic performance than competition.

In terms of resource consumption, collaboration will often take more time than compromise or other processes, since it requires digging into underlying issues. While it may extend a given episode, however, the overall issue of resource consumption or efficiency is considerably more complex. For example, integrative solutions tend to resolve a given conflict issue (Follett, 1941), saving the time and energy required to deal with the issue again and again as it recurs. Moreover, the efforts of the conflict parties appear to be directed relatively efficiently at the task of decision making, with less energy diverted into the posturing, increased psychological stakes, or psychological face-saving that tend to become involved in competition. Kohn (1986a), for example, concludes that "competition generally does not promote excellence because trying to do well and trying to beat others simply are two different things" (p. 28). Considering the higher overall quality of decisions, especially, the overall efficiency of collaboration (in terms of output per unit of input) may well prove to be higher than for the other processes.

Research is abundant linking collaboration to the increased satisfaction of the parties.[55] Again, this is hardly surprising, since collaboration tries to satisfy fully the parties' concerns and appears to provide a relatively supportive climate for the parties.

Finally, collaboration appears to contribute to the quality of working relationships in a number of ways. Ruble and Thomas (1976) conclude that perceptions that the other is collaborative are linked to forms of both liking and respect for the other (from the combination of the other's perceived cooperativeness and assertiveness, respectively). Collaboration is also believed to generate trust and to avoid the damage to working relationships frequently associated with distributive or power bargaining (e.g., see Fisher & Ury, 1981).

Broad evidence for the effectiveness of collaboration also comes from a number of studies that relate collaboration to individual and organizational success over time. Lawrence and Lorsch (1967) found that firms who were high performers in their industry (as judged by financial criteria) tended to be characterized by more collaborative interdepartmental relations. At the individual level, Blake and Mouton (1964, p. 238) presented evidence that managers who had been promoted more rapidly tended to be relatively more collaborative. In contrast, research by Spence and Helmreich (1983; summarized in Kohn, 1986a) on male scientists found that scientists cited most by colleagues scored low on competitiveness.

These apparent advantages imply that, on the whole, the organization will tend to benefit from high levels of collaboration in conflicts among its members on significant issues. It is important to clarify this conclusion. It does not mean that collaboration can *always* be effective or appropriate in a given instance. As noted below, short-term conditions often arise that make collaboration inappropriate. The long-term issue involves whether one can manage those conditions to make collaboration more often appropriate—to increase the "mix" of collaboration in significant organizational conflicts. Later, in the structural model, we will explore the kinds of conditions and structural interventions that contribute to this end.

The Short-term Approach. In the short term, then, the principal parties are likely to encounter a variety of conflict situations in which collaboration is not feasible. For example, there may be insufficient time, the conflict issue may not allow integrative solutions, the parties may not have sufficient skills, or the necessary trust and motivation may not exist. Even if they adopt the long-term approach of beginning to change these conditions, the parties must still deal with the present situation. That, in turn, is likely to force

the parties to choose among the other strategic intentions.

A number of theorists have noted that the short-term choice of strategic intentions needs to be based on consideration of various situational contingencies and that each of the strategic intentions is therefore likely to be appropriate in some circumstances.[56] This conclusion also seems to fit the opinions of experienced managers. Table 8 (from Thomas, 1977) presents a list of situations in which a group of 28 chief executive officers of organizations reported that it would be appropriate to adopt each of the strategic intentions. The list strongly suggests that the ability to implement each of the strategic intentions in appropriate situations is a useful managerial skill.

Combining Long-term and Short-term Approaches. Note that the uses of noncollaborative strategies in Table 8, even though they may be optimal under the short-term circumstances, often appear to involve some costs or risks in terms of the criteria in Table 7—especially the satisfaction of one or both parties, decision quality, relationships, and fairness. For example, although a manager may need to adopt a competitive strategy in a conflict with subordinates in an emergency or when trust does not exist, that strategy seems likely to put some strain on subordinates' satisfaction, relationships, and fairness, and may result in a sacrifice in decision quality. If one adopts the short-term approach exclusively, these costs may become rationalized or accepted as facts of life in an organization. There is also the risk that this short-term view will begin to alter structural variables in the organization—for example, as these facts of life become incorporated into the culture, and as rules and incentive systems evolve to cope with evolving levels of distrust. (Refer back to the feedback arrows from process and outcomes to structure variables in Figure 1.) Thus, this analysis suggests the importance of combining the short-term ability to adopt necessary strategies to

TABLE 8

Situations in Which to Adopt the Five Strategic Intentions, as Reported by 28 Chief Executives

Competing

When quick, decisive action is vital—i.e., emergencies
On important issues where unpopular actions need implementing—e.g., cost cutting, enforcing
    unpopular rules, discipline
On issues vital to company welfare when you know you're right
Against people who take advantage of noncompetitive behavior

Collaborating

To find an integrative solution when both sets of concerns are too important to be compromised
When your objective is to learn
To merge insights from people with different perspectives
To gain commitment by incorporating concerns into a consensus
To work through feelings that have interfered with a relationship

Compromising

When goals are important, but not worth the effort or potential disruption of more assertive modes
When opponents with equal power are committed to mutually exclusive goals
To achieve temporary settlements to complex issues
To arrive at expedient solutions under time pressure
As a backup when collaboration or competition is unsuccessful

Avoiding

When an issue is trivial, or more important issues are pressing
When you perceive no chance of satisfying your concerns
When potential disruption outweighs the benefits of resolution
To let people cool down and regain perspective
When gathering information supercedes immediate decision
When others can resolve the conflict more effectively
When issues seem tangential or symptomatic of other issues

Accommodating

When you find you are wrong—to allow a better position to be heard, to learn, and to show
    your reasonableness
When issues are more important to others than yourself—to satisfy others and maintain cooperation
To build social credits for later issues
To minimize loss when you are outmatched and losing
When harmony and stability are especially important
To allow subordinates to develop by learning from mistakes

cope with difficult conflict situations with the long-term ability to improve conditions for collaboration—for example, by planning ahead for likely emergencies and by building trust.

With this understanding of the criteria for conflict management effectiveness, we will now shift the discussion to the conflict management interventions used by third parties, beginning with third-party process interventions.

Third-party Process Interventions

As noted earlier, process interventions occur when a given third party (e.g., the supervisor of two conflicting parties) becomes directly involved in the sequence of events of an ongoing conflict episode. Because of the extra resource expenditures involved in committing the third party's time, third-party process interventions tend to occur on an exceptional basis. That is, these process interventions tend to occur when the principal parties appear not to be handling their own conflict well enough, or there is reason to believe that they will not be able to do so. Process interventions, then, are primarily attempts to improve on the efforts of the principal parties in a given episode in order to bring about conflict management that more closely meets the criteria of effectiveness discussed earlier (Table 7). Third-party roles and procedures vary greatly, often based on who the third party is—such as a manager, organizational consultant, or mediator.

Process Interventions by Managers

With their formal authority and responsibility for effectiveness, managers are obviously key third parties in the management of conflict in organizations. Recent empirical evidence regarding managerial process interventions has come from Sheppard and his colleagues (Lewicki & Sheppard, 1985; Sheppard, 1983, 1984; Sheppard et al., 1987).

Sheppard (1984) built on the earlier work of Thibaut and Walker (1975) to develop a more complex matrix for identifying the detailed ways in which a third party could exert control over different events (or substages) during the course of dispute resolution.[57] With four basic ways of exerting control (process control, content control, control in response to parties' request, and motivational control) and thirteen substages at which each type of control can theoretically be exerted, the resulting matrix is potentially enormously complicated. Necessarily, then, most subsequent work has involved simplifications of this matrix.

Thus far, the most widely used simplification is shown in Figure 9. In it, the resolution process is divided into two stages: (a) the process (all events before a decision is reached) and (b) the outcome (the decision itself). At both stages, the total amount of third-party control is aggregated across types of control and substages to establish dichotomous high or low ratings. In a study in which managers generated detailed descriptions of a recent conflict in which they had intervened, Sheppard (1983) identified three dominant styles or procedures, corresponding to the labels in three of the four cells in Figure 9. The most common style was *inquisitorial intervention,* in which managers actively controlled the discussion (such as asking questions to determine facts) and then invented and tried to enforce a decision. Second most common was *adversarial intervention* (named after U.S. courtroom procedures), in which the manager passively listened to the disputing parties' arguments and then issued a decision. The third most common style was *providing impetus,* which provided very little control over process or outcome. Rather, the manager briefly determined what the conflict was about and then communicated to the parties that they needed to work it out quickly themselves (with an implied threat). For completeness, Sheppard added *mediation* to the remaining cell, in which the manager controlled the interaction between the parties but allowed them to make their own

FIGURE 9

Sheppard's Taxonomy of Process Intervention by Managers

		Process Control	
		High	*Low*
Outcome Control	*High*	Inquisitorial intervention	Adversarial intervention
	Low	Mediation	Providing impetus

From "Choosing How To Interview" by R. J. Lewicki and B. H. Sheppard, 1985, *Journal of Occupational Behavior, 6,* p. 51. Copyright 1985 by John Wiley & Sons, Ltd. Reprinted by permission.

decision. He found little evidence of managers reporting this type of intervention. In general, then, managers reported using interventions in which they exercised strong control over the outcome (decision) of the conflict.

A subsequent study by Lewicki and Sheppard (1985), involving managerial responses to hypothetical conflict scenarios, suggested that a number of situational contingencies influenced managers' choice of the four procedures. In general, managers were more likely to say that they would exercise outcome (decision) control when there was significant time pressure, when disputants were not expected to be working together in the future, and when the resolution of the dispute would have a broad range of impact.

In a more recent study (Sheppard et al., 1987), managers were asked for a recent episode about the degree of control they had exerted in each of the thirteen substages of dispute resolution in Sheppard's (1984) model. Rather than collapse these ratings into the four styles just mentioned, they used factor analysis to identify underlying dimensions or substyles of intervention.[58] Four such dimensions resulted: *process consulting* (feeling out parties, defining the dispute, presenting arguments, and clarifying information and arguments), *fact finding* (identifying relevant information and presenting relevant information), *adjudicating* (identifying possible alternatives, evaluating information and arguments, and selecting the solution), and *impetus providing* (reconciling parties with the solution, enforcing the decision, and hearing appeals). Further analysis showed that the manager's use of each of these dimensions of intervention varied with the manager's goals or objectives (i.e., the criteria for conflict management effectiveness that were most operative for the manager in that situation), as well as with aspects of the manager's definition or *framing* of the dispute.

Process Interventions by Consultants

One of the central questions addressed by Sheppard and his colleagues has been why managers do not appear to engage in as much of the process consultation and/or mediation activities as the literature suggests would be helpful. Lewicki and Sheppard (1985), for example, speculated that managers might prefer to mediate, but that time pressure and concern with the effects of the outcome (decision) might inhibit that desire. It appears that an important additional factor is the skill level required for these sorts of interventions, which may relegate them to more specialized individuals.

In his model of escalation, Glasl (1982) makes the case that different types of third-party interventions are required to deal effectively with different stages of conflict escalation. From less escalated to more escalated stages, these intervention strategies are (a) moderation (acting as moderator), (b) process consultation, (c) sociotherapeutic process consultation, (d) mediation, (e) arbitration, and (f) power intervention. Of these strategies, Glasl observes that process consultation and sociotherapeutic process consultation involve the deepest interventions into negative emotions, stereotypes, and other psychological obstacles to trust.[59] Thus, these strategies are most likely to require specialized clinical or human relations skills. While mediation does not involve the same psychological depth of intervention, it also seems to require a great deal of interpersonal sensitivity and the building of trust between the principal parties and the third party.

In the organizational setting, these specialized skills are most likely to be possessed by internal or external consultants. Consultants, employed to supplement the skills of managers, appear to confine their efforts largely to these more skilled forms of process intervention. Evidence on this point comes from Prein's (1984) study of successful and unsuccessful conflict interventions by internal and external consultants. The interventions clustered into three types, corresponding to two kinds of process consultation plus mediation.

The first process consultation strategy, *confrontation*, was aimed at direct confrontation of underlying differences and the expression of emotions, with the goal of clarifying issues and improving the relationship. In this form of process consultation, the third party's role was relatively nondirective, placing high importance on the parties' own efforts (e.g., see Fisher, 1972; Walton, 1969).

In contrast, Prein's second form of process consultation, *procedural*, involved more active direction from the third party, including the use of more structured designs or procedures for identifying problems and for problem solving, together with substantive proposals by the third party. This strategy was thus concerned not only with improving relationships, but also finding a workable solution. The principal parties were free to choose their solutions, however, without manipulation or pressure tactics from the third party. (For examples, see the classic intergroup workshops used by Beckhard, 1969, and Blake, Shepard, & Mouton, 1964, as well as the application by D. A. Gray, Sinicropi & Hughes, 1982.)

Finally, the mediation form of process consultation focused much more directly on the content of the conflict, being far less concerned with improving work relations and more concerned with finding a workable compromise for a specific issue. Moreover, the third party did not hesitate to pressure the parties, sometimes bringing external pressures to bear on the parties and sometimes using "clandestine or manipulative ways of influencing behavior" (p. 85).

In general, Prein found that the *procedural* form of process consultation was more often successful than the other two strategies, as well as being effective across a broader range of conditions. The relatively unstructured confrontation procedure, in contrast, was most applicable to relatively uncomplicated conflicts at low levels of escalation. In comparison, mediation seemed most appropriate for conflicts that were not highly escalated or deadlocked, and dealt with negotiable, substantive issues.

Process Interventions by Mediators

Of the more formal, specialized third-party roles (e.g., mediator, arbitrator, fact finder, ombudsman), most study has been devoted to the process interventions of mediators in labor-management disputes.[60]

In comparison to the manager, and to a lesser extent the consultant, the greater specialization of the mediator's role is apparent in a more focused set of goals or criteria.[61] Within the labor relations system, the mediator's general goal is generally stated as preventing or minimizing the disruption of the larger system (i.e., the flow of goods and services) caused by strikes or lockouts. In terms of the criteria in Table 7, this translates into a concern with resource consumption, namely the minimizing of disruption through a timely settlement (Thomas, 1982).

While there have been a number of descriptions and lists of specific mediator tactics, there is no tested framework thus far for organizing them into general categories. Building upon Kressel's (1972) work, Carnevale and Pegnetter (1985) attempted to organize the mediator's tactics into three broad categories: (a) reflexive, (b) directive, and (c) nondirective.[62] *Reflexive* tactics involved the management of the emotional tone of the mediation through such activities as building trust and rapport, maintaining neutrality, and using humor. *Directive* tactics involved such substantive actions as suggesting settlements, applying pressure, clarifying needs, and reinforcing progress. *Nondirective* tactics involved such procedural or facilitative activities as controlling the agenda and timing of issues, educating the parties about impasse procedures, helping the parties save face, and controlling hostility.

Carnevale and Pegnetter found that mediators adapted specific tactics to different sources of dispute. For example, when mediators perceived unrealistic expectations, they reported attempting to change these expectations. When mediators believed impasses stemmed from negotiators having too many issues, they reported using such issue-reducing tactics as simplifying agendas, prioritizing issues, and suggesting tradeoffs. Likewise, mediators simplified the agenda and educated negotiators when negotiator inexperience was seen as a factor, and became more directive when hostility was perceived as a problem.

Nevertheless, Carnevale and Pegnetter report disappointment with the negative results of aggregating tactics to test the effects of each of Kressel's categories. They speculated that the categories are too heterogenous and concluded that further empirical work is necessary to identify meaningful clusters of tactics.

Structural Variables and Interventions

The final elements of the general model of conflict (Figure 1) involve the structural conditions that shape conflict episodes and structural interventions to change those conditions. In the negotiations literature, especially, third-party intervention has usually been equated with process interventions and with the short-term goal of obtaining desirable outcomes for a given negotiation. It is important to realize that these process interventions are only one class of intervention. There exists a whole other class of intervention—structural intervention—that is directed at the long-term goal of improving the way in which a system can handle conflict. While process interventions tend to take the current social/organizational system as fixed, structural interventions are attempts to reengineer or adjust aspects of that system to improve it. The term *structural* is used in a broad way, as in the general systems theory distinction between process and structure as aspects of any system.[63] Whereas *process* refers to the temporal sequence of events that occurs in a system, *structure* refers to the *parameters* of the system—the more or less stable (or slow-changing) conditions or characteristics of the system that shape the course of those events.

Structural variables can be used to explain different types of events within the conflict process.[64] Here we will consider structural variables that influence the use of different strategic intentions (or conflict-handling modes) during conflict episodes. Consistent with the earlier discussion of the long-term goals of conflict management, discussion will be focused more specifically on those structural variables fostering collaboration in a given system.

As in the remainder of the chapter, the goal here is to provide the outlines of an integrative theoretical framework. Structural theories of conflict have tended to involve only a small number of variables, or only a restricted class of variables—for example, individual values or incentives. Attempts at more comprehensive theoretical frameworks have tended simply to identify and list diverse classes of variables and their separate effects.[65] While useful, these more comprehensive frameworks have not been true integrations, since they have provided no underlying theory that would allow one to predict the combined effects of different classes of variables.[66]

A Locational/Theoretical Classification Matrix

A step toward an integrative structural framework is presented in Table 9. The framework of structural variables, while broad, is not regarded as complete, but rather as a partial framework to be filled in and revised with subsequent research.

Briefly, each structural variable is placed in a matrix of *locational* and *theoretical* classifications. (Some variables with multiple effects are listed in more than one theoretical category.) The locational categories, represented by columns, have become a common way of grouping structural variables (e.g., Putnam & Poole, 1987; Sheppard, 1984). Briefly, they classify variables according to their locus within the

social system—here, either as characteristics of a conflict issue, of the parties themselves, of the socioemotional relationship between the parties, of the broader informal organization of the system, or of the formal organization of the system. Among other things, it is useful to group variables in this manner for purposes of intervention, since different locational classes of variables tend to require different forms of interventions.

The theoretical categories, represented by rows in the matrix, describe the functional roles of the different variables within an overall theoretical framework—what effects they have. The present framework makes use of the theoretical assumptions at the core of the process model. That is, collaboration (as a strategic intention) is assumed to result from the additive effects of three sets of motivational forces in conflict parties, produced respectively by rational/instrumental reasoning, normative reasoning, and emotions. Structural variables, then, are seen as influencing the occurrence of collaboration only insofar as they tend to affect one or more of these forces, and are classified theoretically according to their manner of impact.

Now we will briefly review the variables by theoretical category.

Variables Shaping Rational/Instrumental Reasoning

As in expectancy theory, structural variables that tend to effect rational/instrumental reasoning about collaboration are classified according to their roles in either contributing to the valence of an intended outcome (in this case, an integrative outcome) or in contributing to the expectancy that such an outcome is attainable. The former variables are referred to as *integrative incentives* and the latter as *feasibility conditions*. Both incentives and feasibility are required in order for rational/instrumental forces to be operative.

TABLE 9

Structural Variables That Foster Collaboration

Theoretical Function	*Location*				
	Substantive Issue	*Individual Party*	*Relationship*	*Informal Organization*	*Formal Organization*
Variables shaping rational instrumental reasoning					
Integrative incentives	High stakes	Self-esteem Need for achievement	Positive mutual regard	Commitment to organiza- tion mission	Collaborative rewards system Task interdepen- dencies Likelihood of future interaction
Feasibility conditions	Low time pressure Clearly defined, substantive issues Low conflict of interest	Low dogmatism Self-esteem Internal locus of control Low fear of conflict Skills and knowledge High self- monitoring	Mutual trust Power parity	No positional commitments to constituents Discretion allowed rep- resentatives Organic climate	Absence of constraining rules and procedures Sufficiently organized interface
Variables shaping normative reasoning					
Collaborative norms and precepts		Collaborative moral/ ethical precepts	Shared collaborative expectations	Collaborative societal norms Collaborative organizational culture Collaborative group ideologies	

TABLE 9

Structural Variables That Foster Collaboration (continued)

Theoretical Function	Location				
	Substantive Issue	*Individual Party*	*Relationship*	*Informal Organization*	*Formal Organization*
Variables shaping normative reasoning (continued)					
Acceptance/ internalization factors		Internalization of precepts	Mutual attraction, identification	Social cohesiveness Organizational cohesiveness Group cohesiveness	
Variables shaping emotions					
Threat/ support factors		Self-esteem Self-insight Relational competence Sociability Type B behavior pattern	Supportive relationship	Supportive group and organizational	Formal support mechanisms

Integrative Incentives. Since integrative outcomes are those that satisfy the concerns of both parties, integrative incentives to a party are variables that contribute to the party's valence for the satisfaction of both his or her own and the other's concerns. This overall valence is presumed to be an additive effect of any intrinsic valence to the party of such an outcome, plus the degree to which such an outcome would be instrumental to the attainment of other outcomes of value to the party.[67]

The intrinsic valence to the party of an integrative outcome has sometimes been explained in terms of a characteristic motivational orientation that the party brings to each conflict—a characteristic desire (valence) for satisfying both his or her own and the other's concerns (e.g., Norem-Hebeisen & Johnson, 1981; Rahim & Bonoma, 1979).[68] While this approach describes central tendencies in an individual's valences, however, it does not serve to explain them. Thus, other research has sought to find personality variables that would tend to produce such valences. There is some indication, for example, that individuals with high self-esteem tend to place greater value upon the satisfaction of both own and others' concerns (Diamond & Allcorn, 1984; Thomas & Fried, 1986). Likewise, integrative orientations seem to be more characteristic of individuals with high need for achievement (Bell & Blakeney, 1977).[69]

Assuming that individuals do differ in their central tendencies to value integrative outcomes, these tendencies can be viewed as baseline values to which other situational incentives add (or subtract) additional valence. For example, two parties can derive additional intrinsic rewards from integrative outcomes to the extent that they identify with, or like, each other.[70] Likewise, these valences will tend to be larger or smaller to the extent that a given conflict involves issues that are especially important to the party and the other.[71] This latter variable is often referred to as the *stakes* involved for the party and the other.

Finally, additional valence can be added by variables that make integrative outcomes instrumental in achieving other outcomes of value to the party—that is, that introduce additional positive (or negative) consequences. For example, since integrative outcomes tend to improve the quality of work relationships, such outcomes appear to increase in valence as a given relationship increases in importance to the party—as mutual interdependencies and the likelihood of future interactions increase (e.g., Pruitt & Rubin, 1986). Some of the most compelling integrative incentives, however, take the form of *superordinate goals* (Sherif, 1958). Here, task-related concerns of both parties are instrumental in achieving a high-valence, common goal. Such goals can take various forms within an organization, including a shared commitment to the organization and its mission (e.g., London & Howat, 1978) as well as reward systems that provide incentives for group or organizational accomplishments.[72]

Feasibility Conditions. Feasibility conditions are variables that increase the expectancy that integrative outcomes can be achieved—

in other words, the likelihood that collaborative efforts would be productive. At this point, four types of feasibility conditions seem important: flexibility, opportunity, confidence, and trust.

Flexibility factors are variables that enable the parties to remain flexible with respect to positions—a requirement of the problem-solving process. More accurately, what is required is the absence of various *inflexibility* conditions that tend to commit the parties firmly to positions. Dogmatism (Rokeach, 1960) represents one individual difference variable that produces inflexibilities. Low self-monitoring is another. Baron (1989), for example, found that low self-monitoring individuals were less likely to report collaborating or compromising with peers or subordinates. In terms of the formal organization, inflexibility can also be created by an abundance of rules[73] and procedures that constrain the parties' options. In performance appraisal systems, for example, procedures commonly require a superior to commit to a rating of a subordinate (and to have that rating approved by his or her own superior) prior to meeting with the subordinate to discuss the subordinate's performance. Such procedures tend to put the superior in the inflexible position of having to defend a position (Thomas & Tymon, 1985). When the parties are serving as representatives for larger constituency groups, equivalent inflexibilities are introduced by positional commitments to constituencies or by the limited authority of representatives to exercise discretion.[74] Inflexibilities can also be introduced through the informal climate of an organization. In an experimental study, for example, Bigoness, Grigsby, and Rosen (1980) found that mechanistic climates (characterized as rigid, traditional, and autocratic) generated less collaboration than did more organic climates.

Opportunity factors provide the necessary time and interface for collaboration to take place. The effects of time pressures in discouraging collaboration have been discussed by several authors.[75] The notion of interfaces has been explored in detail by Brown (1983) for conflicts between groups. Brown argues that collaboration between such groups requires the establishment of interfaces (a set of representatives and an organized pattern of interaction among them) that are sufficiently organized to enable cumulative progress in negotiations.[76]

Confidence factors have to do with the abilities of the parties to handle the difficulties involved in resolving conflict issues. Confidence, then, is positively influenced by various skills and attitudes, and negatively influenced by various difficulties. With respect to general attitudes, confidence appears to be enhanced to some extent by such broad personality variables as self-esteem (often operationalized as self-confidence) and internal locus of control (e.g., Bigoness, Grigsby, & Rosen, 1980; Wall, 1977), and to be reduced by a generalized fear of conflict (Pruitt & Rubin, 1986). Although there is little systematic research on the topic, one would also expect that specific skills, such as· communication skills or problem-solving skills and depth of knowledge in substantive topics at issue, would contribute to collaborative confidence. With respect to difficulties, on the other hand, collaboration appears to be more problematic as issues become less clearly defined (e.g., Filley, 1975), more complex, less conscious (e.g., Walton, 1969), and more tied to strongly held values or personality clashes.[77] Finally, collaboration becomes more obviously difficult as a given issue appears to exhibit stronger conflict of interest—as it appears that no integrative outcomes exist for that issue.[78]

As used here, *trust* refers to each party's belief that the other party would reciprocate collaborative attempts. Of special concern is that the other not take competitive advantage of such attempts. This sort of trust reflects past experiences with the other, but is also presumed to be influenced by perceived

temptations. One important temptation includes perceived imbalances of power in the relationship. Thus, collaboration has been asserted to be most likely between parties of roughly equal power (e.g., Walton, 1969).[79]

Variables Shaping Normative Reasoning

The two parties are embedded in various overlapping normative systems. Each normative system is likely to include norms or precepts that cover different levels of abstraction—from concrete behaviors to more general attitudes and intentions. Here we are concerned with norms and precepts that bear upon the desirability of collaboration as opposed to other strategic intentions in conflicts. Strategic intentions in conflict situations are particularly likely to be an important part of normative systems, since issues of conflict or tradeoffs between the welfare of different social entities is at the very core of ethics, and since conflicts pose recurrent threats to the survival of individuals and groups.[80] Although the focus here is on norms and precepts, these phenomena may be embedded in ideologies that also provide meanings and beliefs (world views) to support them.

As in the Fishbein model (Fishbein, 1963), the force of each normative system on the individual's intention to collaborate is assumed to be a multiplicative product of (a) the degree to which that normative system prescribes collaboration and (b) the degree to which the party is motivated to comply with that normative system. In Table 9, these structural factors are referred to as "collaborative norms and precepts" and "acceptance/internalization factors," respectively.[81] The different normative systems of revelance to a party are presumed to have an additive effect on the party's intentions.

Collaborative Norms and Precepts. Table 9 shows five different kinds of normative systems that bear upon the parties, from the broad sociocultural context in which an organization is located to the individual parties' own moral/ethical systems. At the sociocultural level, there is abundant evidence that cultural norms affect negotiations (Adler, 1986, chap. 7). With respect to strategic intentions, collaboration is rated highly socially desirable in the American culture (Thomas & Kilmann, 1975), although Rosenstein (1985) reports that managers in American organizations are rewarded somewhat less for such behavior than are managers in Japan.

Despite some central tendencies in the norms of a society, recent studies document considerable variation among the cultures of organizations within the United States. Kotter (1982), in his description of general managers, concluded that excellent performers established strong cooperative cultures in their organizations. Tjosvold (1982, 1983) found that organization members were more likely to collaborate if they viewed their company's history as predominately collaborative (i.e., cooperative and confrontational).

Within a given organization, groups may differ significantly in their subcultures and ideologies. Not only may these ideologies endorse generally preferred conflict-handling modes, they may also serve to identify specific other groups as allies or foes and thus prescribe different strategic intentions for negotiations with those groups.[82] When a party is acting as a group representative, he or she is likely to be especially subject to such norms.

Over time, the two parties to a given relationship also tend to develop their own normative system of expectations—in effect, constituting their own small group. In fact, groups may commonly select their representatives to negotiate with another group on the basis of the nature of previously established relationships.

Finally, each party is likely to have some internalized moral/ethical standards that form a personal normative system. Kohlberg's (1969) stages of moral development provide one attempt to classify such systems. The precepts within Kohlberg's later stages seem generally to correspond to a movement away from competing for one's own needs toward a more collaborative emphasis on the needs of both parties and of the larger system.

Acceptance/Internalization Factors. The parties' tendencies to comply with their personal moral/ethical systems are presumed to depend on the degree to which they have been internalized. The parties' motivations to comply with the other normative systems are assumed to depend on each party's attraction to and identification with the social units in question (i.e., relationship, group, organization, society). This attraction is frequently described in terms of the cohesiveness of each social unit.

When normative systems provide contradictory recommendations, the parties may experience considerable internal conflict. Parties who serve in boundary-spanning roles (essentially as formal representatives of groups or organizations) are especially subject to these pressures, caught between loyalties to the constituents they represent and their relationships with other social units to whom they act as emissary (Adams, 1976; Carnevale, 1984; Fobian, 1987).

Variables Shaping Emotions

Threat and support are key factors in understanding the emotions produced in conflict episodes.[83] Conflict is a potential stressor. Stressors are events or conditions requiring responses that appear to be beyond one's capabilities, or at least taxing to them, and therefore threaten some aspect of one's self-concept (Thoits, 1984). Stress reactions appear to take the form of a generalized negative arousal, which can take the form of more specific emotions, depending on the individual's cognitive interpretations of the situation.[84]

Viewed from this perspective, the problem solving involved in collaboration appears to represent a form of *problem-focused coping* (Thoits, 1984). It is a *reality-based* form of coping with an external threat, rather than one that invokes cognitive distortions (defense mechanisms) to construct a psychological protection from the threat to self-concept. In the language of transactional analysis, this coping involves an "adult" ego state that does not respond to threat by blaming or otherwise demeaning either the self or the other, but rather regards both parties as "okay" (Berne, 1961).

With this background, Table 9 shows a number of threat/support variables that appear to facilitate this mental state by reducing psychological threat or by reducing the cognitive distortions produced by it. At the individual level, self-esteem has been found to buffer the individual from stress—in part by making the self-concept less vulnerable to threat.[85] Diamond and Allcorn (1984) argue more specifically that self-esteem reduces the need for various defense mechanisms that tend to generate noncollaborative intentions. Baron (1989) also notes that Type B individuals, in contrast to Type A's, are less likely to be irritable, impatient, lose their tempers, or demonstrate high levels of competitiveness. Louis (1977) argued that two other individual differences would also enable individuals to experience conflicts in a less defensive, more reality-based manner—self-insight and relational competence. *Self-insight* involves an accurate understanding and acceptance of oneself—making it less likely that one will project unacknowledged (threatening) parts of the self onto the other party.[86] *Relational competence* refers to the individual's range of nondefensive behavior—more specifically, the absence of unresolved issues (such as relations with authority) that tend to distort perceptions of such issues.

Remaining threat/support variables involve the degree of social threat or support received from others in the organization. Recent research indicates that social support is generally an important factor in buffering individuals from the effects of stressors (Rook, 1984; Thoits, 1984).

More specifically, social support appears to serve a number of functions in enabling collaboration. Support from others serves to reduce or offset the perceived threat to self-concept or self-esteem, and thus reduces the likelihood of defensiveness. Social support is also a major source of positive affect which, as discussed earlier, serves to block the expression of negative emotions and to provide a motivational force for cooperation. Finally, research shows that social support involves more than simple comforting of an individual. Thoits (1984) cites empirical studies demonstrating that colleagues also help individuals work through their emotions, steering individuals away from distorted interpretations of events that generate inappropriate or maladaptive negative emotions.[87]

Social support, in turn, requires that an individual be sociable (Hansson, Jones, & Carpenter, 1984; Rook, 1984) and that support be available from the other party in a relationship and/or from other members of the organization.[88] Support may be incorporated into an organizational climate that maintains the individual's "sense of personal worth and importance" (Likert, 1961, p. 103) as opposed to being evaluative and critical. It may also be institutionalized into more formal support mechanisms, including mentoring programs and peer support groups.

A Note on Complexity and Congruity

The framework in Table 9 serves to underscore the complex nature of the structural fabric that shapes strategic intentions. Different types of variables subject the conflict parties to a set of forces that are not always in total agreement. Emotions may challenge logic, ethical reasoning may be at odds with rational/instrumental considerations, and so on. In terms of descriptive theory, this complexity implies that relatively simple theories with few variables, although their propositions may be valid in a ceteris paribus way, will likely be confined to explaining relatively small proportions of variance. It also implies that collaboration will be a reliable occurrence in conflict episodes only when a relatively high degree of congruence is created between the sets of forces that are acting upon the parties.

Structural Interventions

Most, if not all, of the variables in Table 9 can be altered through structural intervention to help foster collaboration. For example, the characteristics of individuals in any given part of the organization can be controlled to some extent through the organization's personnel systems—recruitment, selection, placement, evaluation, and training.[89] Also, the characteristics of relationships can be altered through the kinds of interventions discussed earlier in the section "Process Interventions by Consultants." Characteristics of the informal organization can also be changed through a variety of techniques directed at the cultures of organizations and their parts. In addition, characteristics of the formal organization can be redesigned through formal organizational channels.

Two organization-wide change programs appear most widely associated with fostering collaboration—those developed by Likert (1961, 1967; Likert & Likert, 1976) and those developed by Blake and Mouton (1964). Rather than discussing specifics of these programs, I will discuss briefly how these two programs address structural forces to achieve congruence between forces acting upon the individual.

Both the Likert and the Blake and Mouton programs deal with structural changes affecting all three of the types of forces in Table 9. Both programs attempt to change a number of the variables associated with integrative incentives and feasibility factors and, thus, to make collaboration a more logical choice for conflict parties. In addition, both programs are built around strong ideologies (involving "System IV" and "9,9 Management"), which serve to justify explicit collaborative norms and to work at building strong organization-wide commitment to those norms. Finally, both programs attempt to provide emotional support to individuals through climates that emphasize both achievement and the importance of human resources or concern for people.

Both programs also incorporate specific interventions that are directed at individual, relationship, informal organizational, and formal organizational variables. The Blake and Mouton program, for example, is divided into phases aimed at different locations (Blake & Mouton, 1964, chap. 12). The first phases focus on individual skills and learning, on groups (including norm development), and on building collaborative intergroup relationships. Subsequent phases involve setting and getting commitment to organizationwide goals (which serve as superordinate goals), as well as addressing a number of specific issues in the formal organization (e.g., those that include reward systems, organization design, and performance appraisal). Together, the phases involve virtually all members of the organization and thus help create a set of collaborative norms that is congruent across levels, subgroups, and relationships.

Concluding Comments

This chapter has presented a general model of the overall fabric of conflict and its management within a system, along with more detailed theoretical frameworks for understanding the major parts of that fabric—the sequence of events in the conflict process, criteria (goals) for conflict management, process interventions by third parties, structural variables that shape the conflict process, and structural interventions. The major purpose has been to take integrative theory to the next step.

Areas for Further Research

Three themes of this chapter—normative phenomena, emotions, and criteria for conflict management—involve relatively underdeveloped parts of the conflict literature. Each involves a set of assumptions that appears to be basic to the literature and, therefore, to have widespread implications. I have tried to provide some additional theoretical structure for each of these topics and to incorporate them into the larger map of conflict phenomena. Nevertheless, much theoretical and empirical work needs to be done to develop more fully our knowledge in these areas.

In researching the chapter, I became particularly concerned about the shortcomings of the pervasive, rational-economic assumptions in the conflict literature. The first two themes, involving normative phenomena and emotions, incorporate important additions to those assumptions. There has been a growing body of research on both of these topics within the conflict literature. The findings, however, are hard to reconcile with the dominant, rational/instrumental paradigm. Perhaps for this reason, the findings seem to have taken on the status of "something else worth knowing," rather than becoming an integral part of bargaining strategy, third-party tactics, or other issues central to the field. Thus, I have tried to develop a foundation for a revised behavioral paradigm that systematically incorporates normative reasoning and emotions as well as rational/instrumental reasoning, and then to integrate that paradigm into discussions of major elements of conflict and conflict management.

Normative Phenomena. Once normative reasoning was included in the behavioral paradigm, it became apparent that normative phenomena are of greater centrality to conflict and its management than is reflected in the current literature. I tried to demonstrate, for example, that some conflicts are predominantly normative in origin, that normative tactics are important in negotiations, and that norms are important structural factors in shaping conflict episodes. My personal belief, in fact, is that the loyalties (cohesiveness) and normative structures within strong organizational cultures are often the dominant source of cooperative conflict intentions and behaviors.

It is my hope that more conflict researchers will explicitly include normative phenomena in their models to help balance the dominance of rational/instrumental assumptions. A corollary hope is that more empirical studies will use real-world settings or at least use laboratory situations that allow norms and cohesiveness to develop. The typical experimental laboratory study of conflict or negotiations, which uses strangers as subjects, may only be able to tap norms shared very broadly within a culture, such as justice norms. Although justice has become a more popular research topic recently, it taps only one aspect of the normative dynamics involved in conflict.

Emotions. It seems ironic that conflict, which is among the most emotion-arousing of phenomena, has been predominantly studied as though those emotions had no bearing on it. While this assumption may have been workable in dealing with some professional negotiators, it appears highly questionable in other contexts. In this chapter, I have tried to show how emotions feed back on both rational/instrumental and normative reasoning, how emotion-managing tactics are an important part of negotiation, and how some structural variables have a significant impact on the conflict process through their effects on emotions.

As Shaver (1984) states, emotion "was swept off center stage several decades ago, thanks to behaviorism, and then ignored a while longer when cognitivism captured the limelight" (p. 7). There seems little question, however, that it is now becoming a more popular research area for psychologists. It seems quite likely, therefore, that considerable theoretical/empirical progress will be made in this area in the future. It is my hope that conflict and negotiation researchers will be an important part of this progress.

Criteria for Conflict Management.   As I stated earlier, I am convinced that much of the prescriptive disagreement within the literature stems from different assumptions about conflict management goals rather than empirical assumptions about the relationships between variables. I have tried to develop a conceptual grid for identifying fundamental choice among these goals—involving the choice of beneficiaries (partisan, joint-welfare, or systemic) and choice of time frame (short-term or long-term). Using that grid, I have tried to develop the systemic approaches in some detail, showing how the short-term versus long-term distinction serves to reconcile some of the basic prescriptive issues that I and others have struggled with over the years. I believe that still other issues will be resolved as other (partisan and joint-welfare) perspectives are explicitly developed. There is a need, then, for researchers to become quite explicit about the perspectives they adopt and to explore their consequences further.

This chapter is dedicated to Lou Pondy, a gentle scholar. Preparation of this chapter was supported in part by the Graduate School of Business, University of Pittsburgh, and by the Foundation Research Program of the Naval Postgraduate School. I wish to thank Amy Fried and Betty Velthouse for their insightful help in reviewing the conflict literature, and Larry Boone, Young Doo Lee, and Sandra Milberg for their helpful comments on earlier drafts of these ideas. Special thanks go to Robert Baron, Roy Lewicki, Linda Putnam, and Walt Tymon for their insightful reviews of later drafts.

Notes

1   The distinction between comparative and integrative (or generalist) approaches to theory building in conflict was made by Beres and Schmidt (1982).

2   This complexity addresses the property of "nonobviousness." The remaining Thomas and Tymon (1982) property, timeliness, appears to be less crucial for integrative theory than for studies of specific phenomena, which may be in flux.

3   To be sure, the Schmidt and Kochan definition also applies to interfering actions outside industrial relations contexts, although their model is restricted to goal conflicts. (See the discussion of forms of conflict in the "awareness" portion of the conflict process model later in the chapter.) The point here, however, is that its focus on interfering behavior diverts attention from antecedent events in the conflict process and from other, noninterfering ways of dealing with those events.

4   This definition has been adapted from the earlier chapter (Thomas, 1976). Frustration has been replaced by the more general notion of negative effects. The word *frustration* is now used more precisely to denote a specific form of negative emotion, as discussed in the process model.

5   Contrast this definition with definitions that emphasize perceived incompatibility of concerns, for example. Such definitions appear particularly useful in capturing the situation faced by a conflict party who is about to choose a conflict strategy (e.g., Pruitt & Rubin, 1986; Thomas & Kilmann, 1974). However, they refer to an ongoing perception rather than a beginning point. Likewise, without the notion of at least potentially adverse behavior by the other party, these definitions appear to focus more on the party's internal dilemmas than on interparty conflict. For example, if the party is allocating scarce resources between self and other, but believes the other would not resist any possible allocation, then the party would seem to be experiencing a dilemma rather than an interparty conflict.

6   This model is adapted from a model of intraorganizational conflict management (Thomas, 1979), which was in turn derived from Walton and Dutton's (1969) model of interdepartmental conflict. The model serves to provide a more integrated treatment of conflict phenomena than the separate process and structural models of the previous chapter (Thomas, 1976).

7   The system can also be defined in smaller or larger terms, depending on the conflict. For example, the relevant system for analyzing interorganizational conflicts between unions and managements would often be society, while some interpersonal conflicts can be analyzed at the departmental or work group level. For a more detailed discussion of types of interfaces and levels of analysis, see Brown (1983).

8   For a more thorough discussion of the process versus structure distinction in conflict theory, see Kilmann and Thomas (1978) and Thomas (1976).

9   The model in Figure 2 is adapted from Thomas (1976), which built upon features of the process models of Pondy (1967) and Walton (1969). Frustration, an affective construct, has been replaced by the notion of awareness as the beginning point of the episode. The conceptualization stage has been broadened to include feelings as well as thoughts. Finally, intention has been added as a new, intervening stage.

10   The word *concern* has also been used to denote the magnitude of the party's caring (e.g., Pruitt & Rubin, 1986). There, it is essentially a valence construct, as discussed later in this process model.

11   Although derived independently, this scheme is in essence a condensation of the four-category scheme proposed by Schmidt and Tannenbaum (1960). Their *facts* and *methods* conflicts have been combined into the judgment category because of their common empirical content. Their *value* conflict has been relabeled *normative* to more clearly distinguish it from goal or interest conflict and to focus more clearly on the evaluation of behavior. Their *goals* category remains the same.

12   See, for example, dialectical decision-making models (e.g., Mason, 1969; Mitroff & Emshoff, 1979) as well as Cosier's (1981) treatment of the devil's advocate method and Hammond's "Brunswick lens" model of conflict (e.g., Hammond, Todd, Wilkins, & Mitchell, 1966). These models presume some shared goal (e.g., the pursuit of truth or the desire to do what is best for an organization). For a detailed discussion of the role of controversy in organizations, see Tjosvold (1985).

13   The ontological status of subjective interpretation versus "reality" is a somewhat controversial one. For *objectivists* (e.g., Deutsch, 1969), subjective

interpretation allows for slippage or errors between an objective reality and one's perceptions of it. However, for *subjectivists* (*social constructionists* or *interpretivists*), interpretation is the way in which reality is created from an inherently ambiguous world. Weick (1969), for example, argues that many social "facts" are inherently subjective and are *negotiated* among the parties in a social system. For more on the subjectivist/objectivist distinction, see Burrell and Morgan (1979). For discussions of the growing subjectivist perspective within conflict research, see Bouwen (1987) and Gray (1987).

14   This section is based on Thomas (1976). *Action alternatives* have been relabeled as *possible settlements* for greater precision.

15   For simplicity, this discussion focuses on simple dyadic conflicts—those involving one primary issue. For a detailed analysis of multiple-issue dyadic conflicts as well as multiple-party conflicts, see Raiffa (1982).

16   The joint outcome space is most commonly used for goal conflicts in the negotiations literature (e.g., Axelrod, 1967; Luce & Raiffa, 1957; Pruitt & Rubin, 1986; Raiffa, 1982), although it can also be used to represent perceived patterns of outcomes for judgmental and normative conflicts. In the negotiations literature, the axes have sometimes been anchored by the following reference points: *satisfaction* (points A and B) is defined as occurring at the two parties' levels of aspirations (e.g., Bazerman & Lewicki, 1983; Pruitt & Rubin, 1986), while the origin, point D, is set in terms of each party's "best alternative to a negotiated agreement" or resistance point (Lewicki & Litterer, 1985).

17   Egocentric definitions of a conflict issue may be one manifestation of low perspective-taking ability, or PTA (Davis, 1981)—an inability to see things from the other's point of view. Neale and Bazerman (1983) found that low PTA reduced concession rates and the likelihood of agreement in negotiation.

18   More precisely, Pruitt (1983; Pruitt & Rubin, 1986) notes that the feasibility of a strategy depends on the extent to which the strategy seems likely to succeed *plus* a consideration of any anticipated costs (outcomes other than the intended satisfaction of the parties' primary concerns) that might result from implementing the strategy.

19   For an excellent discussion of tactical assumptions involving competitive/compromising strategies in negotiations, see Bacharach and Lawler (1981).

For a thorough discussion of common biases or miscalculations in negotiations, see Bazerman (1986, chap. 7).

20 Fishbein and Ajzen (1975) have operationalized an individual's overall normative assessment of an act as the product of the perceived endorsement of the act by a given reference group and the individual's "motivation to comply" (identification) with that group's views, summed across reference groups. Other researchers (e.g., Pomazal & Jaccard, 1976; Schwartz & Tessler, 1972) have commented on the need to add the individual's own normative standards to this equation, as in the original Fishbein formulation. This is equivalent to the common practice in role theory of regarding the focal person as receiving a "sent role" from the self as well as the other members of one's role set.

21 See also observational studies of negotiation, which link the expression of positive affect during negotiations to the attainment of more creative solutions (McGrath & Julian, 1963) and consensus (Theye & Seiler, 1979).

22 The previous chapter (Thomas, 1976), in the section on behavior, posited three levels of constructs, all of which, in retrospect, involved intentions—orientations, strategic objectives, and tactical behaviors. The first two of these are collapsed here into *strategic intentions. Orientations* were in effect a kind of outcome preference, based on one's valence for his or her own and the other's concerns (in the tradition of the dual concerns models), while *strategic objectives* were also based on the perceived feasibility of different outcomes (in essence, the instrumentality of attempting to achieve those outcomes). Consistent with the Fishbein model, both *outcome valences* and *perceived instrumentalities* are now treated as partial determinants of one's strategic intentions. *Tactical behaviors* are more accurately labeled *tactical intentions*, and behavior is introduced as a distinct element of the conflict process.

23 For an extensive review of instruments designed to measure the two-dimentional models, critiqued from the point of view of communication, see Putnam (1988). For one more recent study, see Pickering (1989). For a description of simpler schemes, see Greenhalgh (1987), Mastenbroek (1980), and Norem-Hebeisen and Johnson (1981). In effect, these schemes appear to collapse or omit some of the strategic intentions in the two-dimentional models. In this connection, see Rahim and van de Vliert's (1989) suggestion that the strategic intentions available to a party may in fact simplify to trichotomies and dichotomies as a conflict escalates.

24 For an empirically based analysis of some differences between interpretations of the less assertive intentions, see Thomas and Kilmann (1978).

25 See, for example, the collection of articles on conflict "styles" in Putnam (1988).

26 There appear to be anomalies in the placement of two of the strategic intentions, however. The most consistent anomaly is that compromising is seen by the parties as more cooperative than its placement in the model. That is, even though compromising withholds something as well as offering something to the other, it is rated as cooperative, as is accommodating or collaborating. For possible explanations of this anomaly, see Kabanoff (1987) and Ruble and Thomas (1976). The other anomaly is restricted to the party's perception of the other's intentions. In ratings of the other's intentions, competing is seen as significantly lower on the cooperativeness continuum than the model suggests (van de Vliert & Prein, 1989). In other words, in ratings of the other's intentions, competing appears not to be perceived as merely uncooperative, but as more actively hostile. This is not the case in perceptions of one's own intentions.

27 For criticisms of the oversimplified uses of this taxonomy, see Knapp, Putnam, and Davis (1988) and Putnam (1990).

28 Negotiations theorists have considered in some depth the question of *when* to withdraw from negotiations (e.g., Fisher & Ury, 1981; Lewicki & Litterer, 1985), and have discussed the *threat* of withdrawal as a competitive tactic. However, tactics of *how* to avoid or withdraw seem of less focal interest.

29 Mathmatically, the two sets of dimensions merely represent alternative sets of axes and coordinates for describing the same space. However, the cooperativeness/assertiveness axes have thus far proven more useful in capturing the semantic-differential meaning of the strategies and the factors that shape the valences of outcomes, while the integrative/distributive dimensions have proven more useful in comparing tactics.

30 See also Lax and Sebenius (1986) and Putnam (1990) for more recent treatments of the manner in which these subprocesses combine.

31 For broad reviews and critical discussion of bargaining tactics, see Bacharach and Lawler (1981),

Greenhalgh (1987), Lewicki and Litterer (1985), Pruitt and Rubin (1986), and Walton and McKersie (1965). The review by Lewicki and Litterer is especially comprehensive and provides much of the background for the discussion of rational/instrumental and normative tactics. Of the three sets of tactical objectives considered here, those concerned with the other's emotions appear to be the least systematically developed in the negotiations literature at present.

32 The focus here is exclusively on distributive *influence* tactics. Bargaining theorists also discuss subsidiary tactics concerned with getting information about the other's preferences and with increasing the accuracy of communications (e.g., Lewicki & Litterer, 1985).

33 I am indebted to Roy Lewicki for pointing out this tactic.

34 See Pruitt and Rubin (1986) for discussion of a range of different types of integrative solutions that can be negotiated. Unlike the present theoretical framework, Pruitt and Rubin regard compromise as a "lazy" form of collaborative strategy, rather than as a separate strategic intention. Thus, their integrative solutions range from fully integrative (win-win) outcomes to compromises. Our concern here is with the most fully integrative solutions, which, as Pruitt and Rubin note, require the most sharing of information and more vigorous or intense problem solving.

35 See Filley (1975), Fisher and Ury (1981), Lewicki and Litterer (1985), Pruitt and Rubin (1986), and Walton and McKersie (1965). Again, Lewicki and Litterer's comprehensive review provides much of the background for this discussion. Attention is restricted here to *influence* tactics aimed at motivating the other to engage in collaborative problem solving. Other tactics, including those concerned with managing the technical/analytic aspects of finding an integrative solution, are not included.

36 Groups or individuals who are legitimate stakeholders in the conflict issue, however, will sometimes need to be involved in the negotiations in some fashion in order for a workable integrative solution to be found. Thus, the party may occasionally need to encourage explicit negotiations between the other and the other's constituents (e.g., see Walton & McKersie, 1965, on "intraorganizational bargaining") or to broaden the negotiation to include the interested groups (see Brown, 1983).

37 The systematic behavioral analysis of conflict or negotiation has tended to be of concern to communications researchers. For a comprehensive review of conflict and negotiation from the viewpoint of communication, see Putnam and Poole (1987). These authors argue, in part, that behavior has been understudied in comparison with strategic and tactical analyses.

38 Putnam and Poole describe these phenomena as tactics. However, given the distinction here between tactical intentions and overt behaviors, they seem to correspond more directly to overt behavior.

39 The Huthwaite study also included planning behaviors not summarized here. The negotiators studied included both union and management labor-relations negotiators, as well as contract negotiators and others. Unfortunately, the methodology of this study is not reported in detail, so the findings should be accepted with some caution. There is clearly a need for more research on the behavior of skilled negotiators.

40 See Rahim and van de Vliert (1989) for a discussion of the notion that strategic options diminish with phases of escalation from (a) the five strategic intentions discussed in the process model, to (b) Horney's (1945) trichotomy of movement toward, against, or away from the other party, to (c) the dichotomy of conflict versus cooperation. Note that Horney's trichotomy appears to correspond to the motivational forces added by the emotions discussed earlier in this process model, so that her scheme may be most useful for describing the choices perceived in emotionally charged situations (as in Phase II of Glasl's model where personalization has occurred), but before the parties have become locked into win-lose combat.

41 The reader is referred especially to Glasl (1982), who provides an especially comprehensive description of nonrational dynamics as well as rational/instrumental dynamics.

42 See also van de Vliert's (1984) description of prevention behaviors in conflict. Note that most of the tactics discussed in the literature on organizational conflict are only likely to be effective at relatively low levels of escalation. For an example of deescalatory tactics for more extreme (e.g., Phase III) levels of escalation, see Axelrod (1984) and Osgood (1969).

43 See also the empirical study of managerial fairness by Sheppard and Lewicki (1987), which suggests that procedural and distributive justice may not be exhaustive criteria for evaluating justice.

44 This classification of primary beneficiaries is adapted from Thomas (1982). For greater clarity, the *functionalist* approach has been relabeled *systemic*.

45 These approaches are analogous to choices of the beneficiary or client in counseling as well. In dealing with conflicts between a husband and wife, for example, individual counseling is a partisan approach, martial counseling is often a joint-welfare approach, and family counseling is a systemic approach. For a more detailed application of the framework in Figure 8 to counseling, see Hunt, Koopman, Coltri, and Favretto (1987).

46 For a quite different, partisan view of managerial behavior, see Marxist interpretations (e.g., Burrell & Morgan, 1979, chap. 10). From this latter viewpoint, organizations are arenas in which a larger class conflict is enacted, and managers are seen as using their power to retain their elitist positions.

47 Obviously, time horizon is a continuum, so that it could be divided into more than a dichotomy. One could look at short, intermediate, and long terms, for example, if that proved more useful.

48 This discussion is based on Thomas (1989). For greater precision, *normative* theory has been relabeled *universalistic* theory. Universalistic theories have often been referred to as normative within the conflict/negotiation literature, because they specify a single correct way of doing things and thus, if internalized, can lead to the formation of a norm. (See, e.g., Lewicki & Sheppard, 1985; Thomas, 1982.) However, the word *normative* is often used elsewhere simply as a synonym for prescriptive. Obviously, contingency theories and universalistic theories can both be used prescriptively. The word *normative* in this chapter is used in the more restrictive sense, pertaining to norms and norm-related reasoning.

49 More precisely, one must have a more universalistic notion of the end state one seeks to achieve. One can still have contingency notions of how to get to that state—since different interventions may be necessary to get there from different starting points.

50 The four rational/instrumental criteria in this list are adapted from Thomas (1982), which was in turn derived from a content analysis of different conflict theorists (Thomas, Jamieson, & Moore, 1978).

51 Initially, Sheppard (1984) applied these four general criteria separately to evaluations of the third party's procedure and evaluations of the outcome of the procedure, for a total of eight separate sets of criteria. In a more recent study (Sheppard, Blumenfeld-Jones, Minton, Hyder, & Deeb, 1987), this distinction has been collapsed, resulting in the set of four criteria as discussed here. The addition of improved work relationships as a fifth broad criterion is supported by Prein's (1984) analysis of process interventions by consultants (discussed later in the section on third-party process interventions).

52 In this study, specific questions concerning twenty-two objectives were answered by a heterogenous sample of academic managers, private sector managers, public sector managers, parents, and students. While four factors emerged, and were labeled with Sheppard's original categories, a large number of the objectives loaded on different factors than in Sheppard's original classifications. In particular, the effectiveness factor bears little resemblance to Sheppard's original category, and appears difficult to interpret. Other factors, including fairness, conform very well to expectations.

53 I have added the qualifier *significant* because issues that appear trivial to both parties may be handled more efficiently through avoiding or quick compromises. Note also that this discussion refers to conflict situations, in which the conflicting parties are relatively interdependent parts of a system and interact directly. (Refer to the earlier section on definition.) Thus, we are not concerned with the potential benefits of economic competition (*parallel striving,* without direct interaction) in markets.

54 For detailed analyses of the merits of collaboration, including reviews of relevant empirical studies, see Blake and Mouton (1984), Brown (1983), Eiseman (1978), Filley (1975), Fisher and Ury (1981), Kohn (1986a, 1986b), Likert and Likert (1976), Pruitt and Rubin (1986), and Thomas (1976). There are now too many separate empirical studies of the conflict-handling modes to summarize comprehensively here. For an overview of the results of studies using self-report measures, see Putnam (1988).

55 See, for example, Burke (1970, Kohn (1986a, 1986b), Phillips and Cheston (1979), and Thomas and Tymon (1985).

56 See, for example, Derr (1978), Rahim (1986), Robbins (1974), Thomas (1977), and Thomas, Jamieson, and Moore (1978).

57 Sheppard's framework, like the earlier Thibaut and Walker (11975) scheme, seems to highlight dispute *resolution*. For managerial process interventions that involve the deliberate stimulation or sharpening of conflict, see van de Vliert (1985). The most widely studied of such interventions involve the stimulation of dialectic debates or devil's advocacy roles among the principal parties to help third parties or groups reach higher quality decisions. As will be discussed, there are also important sets of process interventions directed not at the resolution of a given episode, but at improving a given working relationship. (Recall that Sheppard's list of criteria for conflict management does not include changes in the relationship between the parties.)

58 The sample included 60 parents and 60 students along with 180 managers in different types of organizations. The factors reported here were originally reported as *styles*, but appear more accurately to be relatively independent dimensions or *substyles* of process intervention.

59 Note that some of these process interventions shade into structural interventions, as the term is used in this chapter (see the following section on structural variables and interventions). That is, some of the "deeper" process interventions also have the effect of making lasting changes in individuals and/or relationships. In Walton's (1969) rich descriptions of third-party peacemaking, for example, the third-party uses data about ongoing conflict issues, but consistently steers discussion back to issues of parties' behavior and the resulting relationship. When the *primary* rationale for such interventions is to produce change in an individual's conflict-handling skills, to change a relationship, or even to change the culture of a system, these interventions can be thought of as structural—as attempts to change the parameters of the social/organizational system.

60 For a more detailed review of this literature, including the applications of mediation to arenas other than labor relations, see Lewicki et al. (1988). For one of the most often cited list of mediator tactics, see Wall (1981). For an exploration of the ways in which mediation may occur within organizations, see Kolb (1986). See also the general model of mediation strategies developed by Carnevale (1986), which generalizes across different arenas, and which uses the amount of *common ground* (commonality versus conflict of interest) between the parties as a contingency.

61 For a theoretical analysis and comparison of the rational/instrumental goals of managers versus mediators, see Thomas (1982).

62 Although Kressel's framework was based more broadly, the Carnevale and Pegnetter study used public sector disputes. Data were based on the self-report of 32 mediators.

63 This distinction between process and structural elements of conflict was introduced in Thomas (1976) and was further elaborated on in Kilmann and Thomas (1978).

64 For example, some structural models essentially attempt to explain the initiation of conflict episodes—to identify the causes of conflicts. See, for example, Schmidt and Kochan's (1972) model of the causes of goal conflicts. See also Seiler's (1963) explanation of the origin of normative conflicts, as caused by violations of the status structure in organizations. As noted earlier, these and other models differ significantly in their definitions of conflict so that they are predicting somewhat different kinds of events.

65 As examples of more comprehensive frameworks, see Brown (1983), Rahim (1976), and Thomas (1976).

66 The recent work of Pruitt and Rubin (1986) seems to come closest to providing an integrated theoretical treatment, using the rational/instrumental framework of expectancy theory as a way of predicting the combined effects of diverse variables. The present framework builds upon many of the Pruitt and Rubin insights, while also introducing normative reasoning and emotional dynamics in a more systematic fashion.

67 Pruitt and Rubin (1986), in referring to the party's valence for the satisfaction of the other's concern, refer to this distinction as *genuine* versus *strategic* concern.

68 As shown in Table 1 in the text, the earliest of the dual-concerns models explained collaborative intentions in terms of somewhat different motives or values—"concern for production" and "concern for people" (Blake & Mouton, 1964). See also Hall's (1969) explanation in terms of "concern for personal goals" and "concern for relationships."

69 Interestingly, competitive orientations were more closely associated with a high need for power (Bell & Blakeney, 1977).

70 See, for example, Thomas (1976) and the more extensive discussion of social bonds in Pruitt and Rubin (1986).

71 See, for example, Blake, Sheppard, and Mouton (1964), Gladwin and Walter (1980), Pruitt and Rubin (1986), and Thomas (1976). Each party's stakes also increase to the extent that the party is serving as representative for a constituent group that would hold the party accountable for the satisfaction of its concerns (e.g., Blake & Mouton, 1961; Pruitt & Rubin, 1986).

72 See Kohn (1986a, 1986b) for a review of integrative versus distributive incentives in organizational and other settings.

73 See Thomas (1976, pp. 923, 924) for a brief discussion of *decision rules* in conflict.

74 Note that positional commitments are different from commitments regarding the degree to which a concern will be satisfied. The latter can sometimes aid the achievement of integrative outcomes (Pruitt & Rubin, 1986). For examples of problems involving limited authority among representatives, see Burton (1969).

75 See, for example, Pruitt and Rubin (1986). See also the related literature on crises. Crises, which combine time pressures with high stakes, seem to produce greater assertiveness, but especially to make competing the dominant strategic intention (Kravitz, 1987). See also Carnevale and Conlon's (1988) finding that mediators are less likely to encourage integrating as time deadlines approach in negotiations.

76 Brown (1983) also discusses the effects of "overorganized" interfaces, which stifle dissent. Thus, collaboration is asserted to be facilitated by an intermediate degree of organization. Brown's book makes especially rich use of actual cases to illustrate the role of interfaces in different types of conflicts—between departments, hierarchical levels, cultures, and organizations. The cases are also helpful in describing the detailed roles of consultants in attempting to create and manage the structure of these interfaces.

77 For self-report data on which strategic intentions would most likely be used with different sorts of issues or sources of conflict, see Renwick (1975). See also the results of London and Howat (1978).

78 Conflict of interest has been generally asserted to encourage uncooperative behavior (Axelrod, 1967). More specifically, conflict of interest appears to interact with the stakes in an issue to shape strategic intentions (Gladwin & Walter, 1980; Pruitt & Rubin, 1986; Thomas, 1976). Thus, collaboration is more likely to occur when there are both less conflict of interest (more commonality of interest) and high stakes. In laboratory studies, conflict of interest tends to be treated in objectivist terms, as a factual constraint that makes integrative outcomes impossible. In real-world settings, on the other hand, conflict of interest is often largely a subjective assessment, based on a given definition of an issue and assumptions about possible solutions (see, e.g., Filley, 1975, 1978; Fisher & Ury, 1981). Thus, conflict of interest is treated here as a difficulty rather than an objective impossibility.

79 Power is treated here not in objectivist terms, but as a perception or socially constructed reality within a relationship. See Bacharach and Lawler (1981) for the notion that perceptions of power are themselves often negotiated between conflict parties. Thus, while power is to some extent based on realities, including formal rank, the relationship is often tenuous. See Pruitt and Rubin (1986) and Lax and Sebenius (1986) for descriptions of difficulties in the basic construct of power that led them to exclude it from their models. For mixed results on the effects of differences in formal rank on strategic intentions in conflict, see Putnam and Wilson (1982) and Rahim (1985).

80 See Feldman (1984) for a discussion of the kinds of issues that are likely to be covered by group norms. See also Thomas (1977) for alternative value systems emphasizing different strategic intentions.

81 For simplicity, other variables have been omitted. For example, collaborative norms existing in a given normative system may differ in their importance or relevance in comparison to the other norms in that system (Mudd, 1968). Moreover, a party's motivation to comply with the norm may also vary with factors that affect the salience of the norm (or the normative system), such as the presence of other members of the norm group.

82 See the discussion of group ideologies in Putnam and Poole (1987), including the work of Billig (1976).

83 This discussion focuses chiefly on the role of threat in producing cognitive distortions. High levels of threat also serve to reduce the flexibility listed earlier as a feasibility factor for collaboration. See Staw, Sandlelands, and Dutton (1981) for discussion of a threat-rigidity effect at various levels of analysis.

84 For the role of cognitive interpretation in the identification of specific emotions, see Roseman (1984) and Scherer (1984).

85 See Norem-Hebeisen and Johnson (1981) for an empirical study of the relationship between self-esteem and collaboration. For more personality variables related to buffering against stress, see Kobasa, Maddi, and Kahn (1982) on the "hardy" personality and Hansson, Jones, and Carpenter (1984).

86 Along these lines, see Linville's (1987) finding that individuals with a more finely differentiated view of their self-concept were more buffered from the negative effects of stressors.

87 See Newcomb's (1947) classic treatment of *autistic hostility* for the notion that persistant hate requires isolation from the target person and from neutrals. Thus, assassinations are frequently performed by loners, for example.

88 The concern here is primarily with variables within the organization. Individuals may also have important support systems outside the organization that serve the same function.

89 For summaries of conflict training in organizations and in universities, see Shockley-Zalabak (1984) and Wehr (1986), respectively.

References

Adams, J. S. (1976). The structure and dynamics of behavior in organizational boundry roles. In M. D. Dunnette (Ed.), *Handbook of industrial and organizational psychology* (pp. 1175–1199). Chicago: Rand McNally

Adler, N. J. (1986). *International dimensions of organizational behavior.* Boston: Kent.

Ajzen, I., & Fishbein, M. (1980). *Understanding attitudes and predicting social behavior.* Englewood Cliffs, NJ: Prentice-Hall.

Alinski, S. (1971). *Rules for radicals.* New York: Vintage.

Axelrod, R. (1967). Conflict of interest: An axiomatic approach. *Journal of Conflict Resolution, 11,* 87–99.

Axelrod, R. (1984). *The evolution of cooperation.* New York: Basic Books.

Bacharach, S. B., & Lawler, E. J. (1981). *Bargaining: Power, tactics, and outcomes.* San Francisco: Jossey-Bass.

Baron, R. A. (1977). *Human aggression.* New York: Plenum.

Baron, R. A. (1984). Reducing organizational conflict: An incompatible response approach. *Journal of Applied Psychology, 69,* 272–279.

Baron, R. A. (1988a). Attributions and organizational conflict: The mediating role of apparent sincerity. *Organizational Behavior and Human Decision Processes, 41,* 111–127.

Baron, R. A. (1988b). Negative effects of destructive criticism: Impact on conflict, self-efficacy, and task performance. *Journal of Applied Psychology, 73,* 199–207.

Baron, R. A. (1989). Personality and organizational conflict: Type A behavior pattern and self-monitoring. *Organizational Behavior and Human Decision Processes, 44,* 281–297.

Baron, R. A., & Ball, R. L. (1974). The agression-inhibiting influence of nonhostile humor. *Journal of Experimental Social Psychology, 10,* 23–33.

Bazerman, M. H. (1986). *Judgment in managerial decision making.* New York: Wiley.

Bazerman, M. H., & Lewicki, R. J. (1983). *Negotiating in organizations.* Beverly Hills, CA: Sage.

Bazerman, M. H., Magliozzi, T., & Neale, M. A. (1985). The acquisition of an integrative response in a competitive market. *Organizational Behavior and Human Performance, 34,* 294–313.

Beckhard, R. (1969). The confrontation meeting. *Harvard Business Review, 45*(2), 149–155.

Bell, E., & Blakeney, R. (1977). Personality correlates of conflict resolution modes. *Human Relations, 30,* 849–857.

Beres, M. E., & Schmidt, S. M. (1982). The conflict carousel: A contingency approach to conflict management. In G. B. J. Bomers & R. B. Peterson (Eds.), *Conflict management and industrial relations* (pp. 37–59). Boston: Kluwer-Nijhoff.

Berne, E. (1961). *Transactional analysis in psychotherapy.* New York: Grove Press.

Bigoness, W. J., Grigsby, D. W., & Rosen, B. (1980, August). *Effects of organizational climate, locus of control, and target of confrontation upon individual's willingness to confront conflict.* Paper presented at the annual meeting of the National Academy of Management, Detroit, MI.

Billig, M. (1976). *The social psychology of intergroup relations.* London: Academic Press.

Blake, R. R., & Mouton, J. S. (1961). Reactions to intergroup competition under win-lose conditions. *Management Science, 7,* 420–435.

Blake, R. R., & Mouton, J. S. (1964). *The managerial grid.* Houston, TX: Gulf.

Blake, R. R., Shepard, H. A., & Mouton, J. S. (1964). *Managing intergroup conflict in industry.* Houston, TX: Gulf.

Boulding, K. E. (1963). *Conflict and defense: A general theory.* New York: Harper.

Bouwen, R. (1987, August). *A multi-perspective view of social reality construction in organizational conflict.* Paper presented at the national meeting of the Academy of Management, New Orleans.

Bouwen, R., & Salipante, P. (1986, July). *A kaleidoscopic model of conflict formulation.* Paper presented at the 21st International Congress of Applied Psychology, Jerusalem, Israel.

Brown, L. D. (1983). *Managing conflict at organizational interfaces.* Reading, MA: Addison-Wesley.

Burke, R. J. (1970). Methods of resolving superior-subordinate conflict: The constructive use of subordinate differences and disagreements. *Organizational Behavior and Human Performance, 5,* 393–411.

Burrell, G., & Morgan, G. (1979). *Sociological paradigms and organisational analysis.* London: Heinemann.

Burton, J. W. (1969). *Conflict and communication: The use of controlled communication in international relations.* New York: Free Press.

Carnevale, P. J. D. (1984). Accountability of group representatives and intergroup relations. In E. J. Lawler (Ed.), *Advances in group processes: Theory and research* (Vol. 2, pp. 227–248). Greenwich, CT: JAI Press.

Carnevale, P. J. D. (1986). Strategic choice in mediation. *Negotiation Journal, 2,* 41–56.

Carnevale, P. J. D., & Conlon, D. E. (1988). Time pressure and strategic choice in mediation. *Organizational Behavior and Human Decision Processes, 42,* 111–133.

Carnevale, P. J. D., & Isen, A. M. (1986). The influence of positive affect and visual access on the discovery of integrative solutions in bilateral negotiation. *Organizational Behavior and Human Decision Processes, 37,* 1–13.

Carnevale, P. J. D., & Pegnetter, R. (1985). The selection of mediation tactics in public sector disputes: A contingency analysis. *Journal of Social Issues, 41*(2), 65–81.

Chesler, M. A., Crowfoot, J. E., & Bryant, B. I. (1978). Power training: An alternative path to conflict management. *California Management Review, 21*(2), 84–90.

Cosier, R. A. (1981). Dialectical inquiry in strategic planning: A case of premature acceptance? *Academy of Management Review, 6,* 643–648.

Craig, J. H., & Craig, M. (1974). *Synergic power.* Berkeley, CA: ProActive Press.

Davis, M. (1981). A multidimensional approach to individual differences in empathy. *JSAS Catalogue of Selected Documents in Psychology, 10,* 85.

Derr, C. B. (1978). Managing organizational conflict: Collaboration, bargaining, and power approaches. *California Management Review, 21*(2), 76–83.

Deutsch, M. (1969). Conflicts: Productive and destructive. *Journal of Social Issues, 25,* 7–41.

Deutsch, M. (1971). Toward an understanding of conflict. *International Journal of Group Tensions, 1,* 42–54.

Deutsch, M. (1975). Equity, equality and need: What determines which value will be used as the basis for distributive justice? *Journal of Social Issues, 31,* 137–149.

Diamond, M. A., & Allcorn, S. (1984). Psychological barriers to personal responsibility. *Organizational Dynamics, 12*(4), 66–77.

Eiseman, J. W. (1978). Reconciling "incompatible" positions. *Journal of Applied Behavioral Science, 14,* 133–150.

Etzioni, A. (1988). *The moral dimension: Toward a new economics.* New York: Free Press.

Feldman, D. C. (1984). The development and enforcement of group norms. *Academy of Management Review, 9,* 47–53.

Filley, A. C. (1975). *Interpersonal conflict resolution.* Glenview, IL: Scott, Foresman.

Filley, A. C. (1978). Some normative issues in conflict management. *California Management Review, 21*(2), 61–66.

Fink, C. F. (1968). Some conceptual difficulties in the theory of social conflict. *Journal of Conflict Resolution, 12,* 412–460.

Fishbein, M. (1963). An investigation of the relationship between beliefs about an object and the attitude toward that object. *Human Relations, 16,* 233–240.

Fishbein, M., & Ajzen, I. (1975). *Belief, attitude and behavior: An introduction to theory and research.* Reading, MA: Addison-Wesley.

Fisher, R. (1964). Fractionating conflict. In R. Fisher (Ed.), *International conflict and behavioral science: The Craigville papers* (pp. 91–109). New York: Basic Books.

Fisher, R. J. (1972). Third party consultation. *Journal of Conflict Resolution, 16,* 67–94.

Fisher, R., & Ury, W. (1981). *Getting to YES: Negotiating agreement without giving in.* Boston: Houghton Mifflin.

Fobian, C. (1987). *Interorganizational negotiation and accountability: An examination of Adam's paradox.* Teaching Materials Series. Washington, DC: National Institute for Dispute Resolution.

Folger, J. P., & Poole, M. S. (1984). *Working through conflict.* Glenview, IL: Scott Foresman.

Folger, R., & Greenberg, J. (1985). Procedural justice: An interpretive analysis of personnel systems. In K. Rowland & G. Ferris (Eds.), *Research in Personnel and Human Resources Management, 3,* 141–183.

Follett, M. P. (1941). Constructive conflict. In H. C. Metcalf & L. Urwick (Eds.), *Dynamic administration: The collected papers of Mary Parker Follett* (pp. 30–49). New York: Harper & Row.

Gladwin, T. N., & Walter, I. (1980). *Multinationals under fire: Lessons in the management of conflict.* New York: Wiley.

Glasl, F. (1982). The process of conflict escalation and roles of third parties. In G. B. J. Bomers & R. Peterson (Eds.), *Conflict management and industrial relations* (pp. 119–140). Boston: Kluwer-Nijhoff.

Gray, B. (1987, August). *Dispute resolution as reconstructed meaning.* Paper presented at the national meeting of the Academy of Management, New Orleans.

Gray, D. A., Sinicropi, A. V., & Hughes, P. A. (1982). From conflict to cooperation: A joint union-management goal-setting and problem-solving program. In B. A. Dennis (Ed.), *Proceedings of the thirty-fourth annual meeting* (pp. 26-32). Madison, WI: Industrial Relations Research Association.

Greenhalgh, L. (1987). Interpersonal conflicts in organizations. In C. L. Cooper & I. T. Robertson (Eds.), *International review of industrial and organizational psychology* (pp. 229–271). New York: Wiley.

Hall, J. (1969). *Conflict management survey: A survey of one's characteristic reaction to and handling of conflicts between himself and others.* Houston, TX: Teleometrics.

Hammond, K. R., Todd, F. J., Wilkins, M., & Mitchell, T. O. (1966). Cognitive conflict between persons: Application of the "lens model" paradigm. *Journal of Experimental Social Psychology, 2,* 343–360.

Hansson, R. O., Jones, W. H., & Carpenter, B. N. (1984). Relational competence and social support. *Review of Personality and Social Psychology, 5,* 265–284.

Hegel, G. W. F. (1964). *The phenomenology of mind* (2nd ed.), translated by J. B. Baillie. London: Allen and Unwin.

Horney, K. (1945). *Our inner conflicts: A constructive theory of neurosis.* New York: Norton.

Hunt, E. J., Koopman, E. J., Coltri, L. L., & Favretto, F. (1987). *Incorporating idiosyncratic client characteristics in the development of agreements: Toward an expanded understanding of "success" in the mediation of child custody disputes.* Unpublished manuscript, University of Maryland Graduate School, College Park.

Huthwaite, Inc. (1985). *The behavior of successful negotiators.* Purcellville, VA.

Ikle, F. C. (1964). *How nations negotiate.* New York: Harper and Row.

Johnson, D. W., & Johnson, R. T. (1983). The socialization and achievement crisis: Are cooperative learning experiences the solution? In L. Bickman (Ed.), *Applied social psychology annual 4* (pp. 119–164). Beverly Hills, CA: Sage.

Kabanoff, B. (1985). Potential influence structures as sources of interpersonal conflict in groups and organizations. *Organizational Behavior and Human Decision Processes, 36,* 113–141.

Kabanoff, B. (1987, August). *Why is compromise so favourably viewed?* Paper presented at the meeting of the Academy of Management, New Orleans, LA.

Kahn, R. L., & Boulding, E. (Eds.). (1964). *Power and conflict in organizations.* New York: Basic Books.

Kahn, R. L., Wolfe, D. M., Quinn, R. P., Snoek, J. D., & Rosenthal, R. A. (1964). *Organizational stress: Studies in role conflict and ambiguity.* New York: Wiley.

Kilmann, R. H., Slevin, D. P., & Thomas, K. W. (1983). The problem of producing useful knowledge. In R. W. Kilmann, K. W. Thomas, D. P. Slevin, R. Nath, & S. L. Jerrell (Eds.), *Producing useful knowledge for organizations* (pp. 1–21). New York: Praeger.

Kilman, R. H., & Thomas, K. W. (1975). Interpersonal conflict-handling behavior as reflections of Jungian personality dimensions. *Psychological Reports 37*, 971–980.

Kilmann, R. H., & Thomas, K. W. (1978). Four perspectives on conflict management: An attributional framework for organizing descriptive and normative theory. *Academy of Management Review, 3*, 59–68.

Knapp, M. L., Putnam, L. L., & Davis, L. J. (1988). Measuring interpersonal conflict in organizations: Where do we go from here? *Management Communication Quarterly, 1*, 414–429.

Kobasa, S. C., Maddi, S. R., & Kahn, S. (1982). Hardiness and health: A prospective study. *Journal of Personality and Social Psychology, 42*, 168–177.

Kohlberg, L. (1969). Stage and sequence: The cognitive-development approach to socialization. In D. Goslin (Ed.), *Handbook of socialization theory and research* (pp. 347–380). Chicago: Rand McNally.

Kohn, A. (1986a). How to succeed without even vying. *Psychology Today, 20*(9), 22–29.

Kohn, A. (1986b). *No contest: The case against competition.* Boston: Houghton Mifflin.

Kolb, D. M. (1986, June). *Organization mediation.* Paper presented at the meeting of the International Society of Political Psychology, Amsterdam.

Kotter, J. P. (1982). *The general managers.* New York: Free Press.

Kravitz, J. H. (1987). *Crisis management: A determination of management style preferences.* Unpublished doctoral dissertation, University of Pittsburgh.

Kressel, K. (1972). *Labor mediation: An exploratory survey.* New York: Association of Labor Mediation Agencies.

Kumar, R. (1989). Affect, cognition and decision making in negotiation: A conceptual integration. In M. A. Rahim (Ed.), *Managing conflict: An integrative approach* (pp. 185–194). New York: Praeger.

Lawler, E. E., III. (1973). *Motivation in work organizations.* Monterey, CA: Brooks/Cole.

Lawrence, P. R., & Lorsch, J. W. (1967). *Organization and environment: Managing differentiation and integration.* Boston: Division of Research, Harvard Business School.

Lax, D., & Sebenius, J. (1986). *The manager as negotiator.* New York: Free Press.

Lee, J. B., Olson, G. D., & Swinth, R. L. (1987, June). *Akido: An empowering model for conflict.* Paper presented at the First International Conference of the Association for Conflict Management, Fairfax, VA.

Leventhal, G. S. (1976). Fairness in social relationships. In J. W. Thibaut, J. T. Spence, & R. C. Carson (Eds.), *Contemporary topics in social psychology.* Morristown, NJ: General Learning Press.

Levinger, G. (1957). Kurt Lewin's approach to conflict and its resolution: A review with some extensions. *Journal of Conflict Resolution, 1*, 329–339.

Lewicki, R. J. (1982). Ethical concerns in conflict management. In G. B. J. Bomers & R. B. Peterson (Eds.), *Conflict management and industrial relations* (pp. 423–445). Boston: Kluwer-Nijhoff.

Lewicki, R. J., & Litterer, J. A. (1985). *Negotiation.* Homewood, IL: Irwin.

Lewicki, R. J., & Sheppard, B. H. (1985). Choosing how to intervene: Factors affecting the use of process and outcome control in third party dispute resolution. *Journal of Occupational Behavior, 6*, 49–64.

Lewicki, R. J., Weiss, S. E., & Lewin, D. (1988). *Models of conflict, negotiation and third party intervention: A review and synthesis* (Working Paper Series No. 88–33). Columbus: Ohio State University, College of Business.

Likert, R. (1961). *New patterns of management.* New York: McGraw-Hill.

Likert, R. (1967). *The human organization: Its management and value.* New York: McGraw-Hill.

Likert, R., & Likert, J. G. (1976). *New ways of managing conflict.* New York: McGraw-Hill.

Linville, P. W. (1987). Self-complexity as a cognitive buffer against stress-related illness and depression. *Journal of Personality and Social Psychology, 52*, 663–676.

Lippitt, M. E., & Mackenzie, K. D. (1979). A theory of committee formation. In K. Krippendorff (Ed.), *Communication and control in social processes* (pp. 389–405). New York: Gordon and Breach Science Publishers.

London, M., & Howat, G. (1978). The relationships between employee commitment and conflict resolution behavior. *Journal of Vocational Behavior, 13,* 1–14.

Louis, M. R. (1977). How individuals conceptualize conflict: Identification of steps in the process and the role of personal/developmental factors. *Human Relations, 30,* 451–467.

Luce, R. D., & Raiffa, H. (1957). *Games and decisions: Introduction and critical survey.* New York: Wiley.

Mack, R. W., & Snyder, R. C. (1957). The analysis of social conflict: Toward an overview and synthesis. *Journal of Conflict Resolution, 1,* 212–248.

Magula, M. M. (1977). *Toward a theory of conflict: Perceptions and preferred behaviors.* Doctoral dissertation, University of Washington. (University Microfilms No. 77–18, 381)

Mason, R. O. (1969). A dialectical approach to strategic planning. *Management Science, 15,* B403–B414.

Mastenbroek, W. F. G. (1980). Negotiating: A conceptual model. *Group & Organization Studies, 5,* 324–339.

McGrath, J. E., & Julian, J. W. (1963). Interaction process and task outcomes in experimentally created negotiation groups. *Journal of Psychological Studies, 14,* 117–138.

Merriam-Webster. (1986). *Webster's ninth new collegiate dictionary.* Springfield, MA.

Mitroff, I. I., & Emshoff, J. R. (1979). On strategic assumption-making: A dialectical approach to policy and planning. *Academy of Management Review, 4,* 1–12.

Mudd, S. A. (1968). Group sanction severity as a function of degree of behavior deviation and relevance of norm. *Journal of Personality and Social Psychology, 8,* 258–260.

Neale, M. A., & Bazerman, M. H. (1983). The effect of perspective taking ability under alternate forms of arbitration on the negotiation process. *Industrial and Labor Relations Review, 36,* 378–388.

Neale, M. A., & Bazerman, M. H. (1985). Perspectives for understanding negotiation: Viewing negotiation as a judgmental process. *Journal of Conflict Resolution, 29,* 33–55.

Newcomb, T. M. (1947). Autistic hostility and social reality. *Human Relations, 1,* 69–86.

Norem-Hebeisen, A. A., & Johnson, D. W. (1981). The relationship between cooperative, competitive, and individualistic attitudes and

differentiated aspects of self-esteem. *Journal of Personality, 49*(4), 415–424.

Osgood, C. E. (1969). Calculated de-escalation as a strategy. In D. G. Pruitt & R. C. Snyder (Eds.), *Theory and research on the causes of war* (pp. 213–216). Englewood Cliffs, NJ: Prentice-Hall.

Phillips, E., & Cheston, R. (1979). Conflict resolution: What works? *California Management Review, 21,* 76–83.

Pickering, G. (1989). *The reliability and validity of the Thomas-Kilmann "Management-of-Differences-Exercise" instrument when applied in negotiation situations at the organizational boundary.* Unpublished doctoral dissertation, University of Melbourne.

Pomazal, R. J., & Jaccard, J. J. (1976). An informational approach to altruistic behavior. *Journal of Personality and Social Psychology, 33,* 317–326.

Pondy, L. R. (1967). Organizational conflict: Concepts and models. *Administrative Science Quarterly, 12,* 296–320.

Prein, H. C. M. (1976). Stijlen van conflicthantering [Styles of conflict management]. *Nederlands Tijdschrift voor de Psychologie, 31,* 321–346.

Prein, H. C. M. (1984). A contingency approach to conflict management. *Group and Organization Studies, 9,* 81–102.

Pruitt, D. G. (1983). Strategic choice in negotiation. *American Behavioral Scientist, 27,* 167–194.

Pruitt, D. G., Carnevale, P. J. D., Ben-Yoav, O., Nochajski, T. H., & Van Slyck, M. R. (1983). Incentives for cooperation in integrative bargaining. In R. Tietz (Ed.), *Aspiration levels in bargaining and economic decision making* (pp. 22–34). Berlin: Springer-Verlag.

Pruitt, D. G., & Rubin, J. Z. (1986). *Social conflict: Escalation, stalemate, and settlement.* New York: Random House.

Putnam, L. L. (Ed.). (1988). Communication and conflict styles in organizations [Special issue]. *Management Communication Quarterly, 1*(3).

Putnam, L. L. (1990). Reframing integrative and distributive bargaining: A process perspective. In B. H. Sheppard, M. H. Bazerman, & R. J. Lewicki, *Research on negotiation in organizations, Volume 2* (pp. 3–30). Greenwich, CT: JAI Press.

Putnam, L. L., & Poole, M. S. (1987). Conflict and negotiation. In F. M. Jablin, L. L. Putnam, K. H. Roberts, & L. W. Porter (Eds.), *Handbook of organizational communication: An interdisciplinary perspective* (pp. 549–599). Newbury Park, CA: Sage.

Putnam, L. L., & Wilson, C. E. (1982). Communicative strategies in organizational conflicts: Reliability and validity of a measurement scale. In M. Burgoon (Ed.), *Communication yearbook 6* (pp. 629–652). Beverly Hills, CA: Sage.

Rahim, M. A. (1985). Referent role and styles of handling interpersonal conflict. *The Journal of Social Psychology, 126*, 79–86.

Rahim, M. A. (1986). *Managing conflict in organizations.* New York: Praeger.

Rahim, M. A., & Bonoma, T. V. (1979). Managing organization conflict: A model for diagnosis and intervention. *Psychological Reports, 44*, 1323–1344.

Rahim, M. A., & van de Vliert, E. (1989). Introduction to Part 5. In M. A. Rahim (Ed.), *Managing conflict: An integrative approach* (pp. 247–249). New York: Praeger.

Raiffa, H. (1982). *The art and science of negotiation.* Cambridge, MA: Belknap Press.

Renwick, P. A. (1975). Impact of topic and source of disagreement on conflict management. *Organizational Behavior and Human Performance, 14*, 416–425.

Robbins, S. P. (1974). *Managing organizational conflict: A nontraditional approach.* Englewood Cliffs, NJ: Prentice-Hall.

Robbins, S. P. (1978). "Conflict management" and "conflict resolution" are not synonymous terms. *California Management Review, 21*(2), 67–75.

Rokeach, M. (1960). *The open and closed mind.* New York: Basic Books.

Rook, K. S. (1984). Research on social support, loneliness, and social isolation: Toward an integration. *Review of Personality and Social Psychology, 5*, 239–264.

Roseman, I. J. (1984). Cognitive determinants of emotion: A structural theory. *Review of Personality and Social Psychology, 5*, 11–36.

Rosenstein, E. (1985). Cooperativeness and advancement of managers: An international perspective. *Human Relations, 38*, 1–21.

Ruble, T. L., & Thomas, K. W. (1976). Support for a two-dimensional model of conflict behavior. *Organizational Behavior and Human Performance, 16*, 143–155.

Scherer, K. R. (1984). Emotion as a multicomponent process: A model and some cross-cultural data.

Review of Personality and Social Psychology, 5, 37–63.

Schmidt, S. M., & Kochan, T. A. (1972). Conflict: Toward conceptual clarity. *Administrative Science Quarterly, 17*, 359–370.

Schmidt, W. H., & Tannenbaum, R. (1960). The management of differences. *Harvard Business Review, 38*, 107–115.

Schwartz, S. H., & Tessler, R. C. (1972). A test of a model for reducing measured attitude-behavior discrepancies. *Journal of Personality and Social Psychology, 24*, 225–236.

Seiler, J. A. (1963). Diagnosing interdepartmental conflict. *Harvard Business Review, 41*, 121–132.

Shaver, P. (1984). Editor's introduction. *Review of Personality and Social Psychology, 5*, 7–10.

Sheppard, B. H. (1983). Managers as inquisitors: Some lessons from the law. In M. Bazerman & R. J. Lewicki (Eds.), *Negotiating in organizations* (pp. 193–213). Beverly Hills, CA: Sage.

Sheppard, B. H. (1984). Third party conflict intervention: A procedural framework. In B. M. Staw & L. L. Cummings (Eds.), *Research in organizational behavior* (Vol. 6, pp. 141–190). Greenwich, CT: JAI Press.

Sheppard, B. H., Blumenfeld-Jones, K., Minton, J. W., Hyder, E., & Deeb, A. (1987, August). *Informal conflict intervention: A tale of two models.* Paper presented at the meeting of the Academy of Management, New Orleans.

Sheppard, B. H., & Lewicki, R. J. (1987). Toward general principles of managerial fairness. *Social Justice Research, 1*, 161–176.

Sheppard, B. H., Lewicki, R. J., & Minton, J. (1986). A new view of organizations: Some retrospective comments. In R. J. Lewicki, B. H. Sheppard, & M. Bazerman (Eds.), *Research on negotiation in organizations* (pp. 311–321). Stamford, CT: JAI.

Sherif, M. (1958). Superordinate goals in the reduction of intergroup conflict. *The American Journal of Sociology, 63*, 349–356.

Shockley-Zalabak, P. S. (1984). Current conflict management training: An examination of practices in ten large American organizations. *Group and Organization Studies, 9*, 491–507.

Simon, H. A. (1957). *Administrative behavior: A study of decision-making processes in administrative organization* (2nd ed.). New York: Macmillan.

Smith, M. J. (1975). *When I say no, I feel guilty.* New York: Bantam.

Spence, J., & Helmreich, R. (1983). Achievement related motives and behavior. In J. Spence (Ed.), *Achievement and achievement motives.* New York: W. H. Freeman.

Staw, B. M., Sandelands, L. E., & Dutton, J. E. (1981). Threat-rigidity effects in organizational behavior: A multi-level analysis. *Administrative Science Quarterly, 26,* 501–524.

Theye, L. D., & Seiler, W. J. (1979). Interaction analysis in collective bargaining: An alternative approach to the prediction of negotiated outcomes. In D. Nimmo (Ed.), *Communication yearbook 3.* New Brunswick, NJ: Transaction-International Communication Association.

Thibaut, J., & Walker, L. (1975). *Procedural justice: A psychological analysis.* Hillsdale, NJ: Erlbaum.

Thoits, P. A. (1984). Coping, social support, and psychological outcomes: The central role of emotion. *Review of Personality and Social Psychology, 5,* 219–238.

Thomas, K. W. (1976). Conflict and conflict management. In M. D. Dunnette (Ed.), *Handbook of industrial and organizational psychology* (pp. 889–935). Chicago: Rand McNally.

Thomas, K. W. (1977). Toward multi-dimensional values in teaching: The example of conflict behaviors. *Academy of Management Review, 2,* 484–490.

Thomas, K. W. (1979). Conflict. In S. Kerr (Ed.), *Organizational behavior* (pp. 151–181). Columbus, OH: Grid Publications.

Thomas, K. W. (1982). Manager and mediator: A comparison of third-party roles based upon conflict-management goals. In G. B. J. Bomers & R. B. Peterson (Eds.), *Conflict management and industrial relations* (pp. 141–157). Boston: Kluwer-Nijhoff.

Thomas, K. W. (1988). The conflict-handling modes: Toward more precise theory. *Management Communication Quarterly, 1,* 430–436.

Thomas, K. W. (1989). Norms as an integrative theme in conflict and negotiation: Correcting our "sociopathic" assumptions. In M. A. Rahim (Ed.), *Managing conflict: An integrative approach* (pp. 265–272). New York: Praeger.

Thomas, K. W., & Fried, A. (1986, July). *Constructive mind-sets in conflict: Lessons from the empowerment literature.* Paper presented at the 21st International Congress of Applied Psychology, Jerusalem, Israel.

Thomas, K. W., Jamieson, D. W., & Moore, R. K. (1978). Conflict and collaboration: Some concluding observations. *California Management Review, 21*(2), 91–95.

Thomas, K. W., & Kilmann, R. H. (1974). *The Thomas-Kilmann conflict mode instrument.* Tuxedo, NY: Xicom.

Thomas, K. W., & Kilmann, R. H. (1975). The social desirability variable in organizational research: An alternative explanation for reported findings. *Academy of Management Journal, 18,* 741–752.

Thomas, K. W., & Kilmann, R. H. (1978). Comparison of four instruments measuring conflict behavior. *Psychological Reports, 42,* 1139–1145.

Thomas, K. W., & Pondy, L. R. (1977). Toward an "intent" model of conflict management among principal parties. *Human Relations, 30,* 1089–1102.

Thomas, K. W., & Schmidt, W. H. (1976). A survey of managerial interests with respect to conflict. *Academy of Management Journal, 19,* 315-318.

Thomas, K. W., & Tymon, W. G., Jr. (1982). Necessary properties of relevant research: Lessons from recent criticisms of the organizational sciences. *Academy of Management Review, 7,* 345–352.

Thomas, K. W., & Tymon, W. G., Jr. (1985). Structural approaches to conflict management. In R. Tannenbaum, N. Margulies, & F. Massarik (Eds.), *Human systems development* (pp. 336–366). San Francisco: Jossey-Bass.

Tjosvold, D. (1982). Effects of approach to controversy on supervisors' incorporation of subordinates' information in decision making. *Journal of Applied Psychology, 67,* 189–191.

Tjosvold, D. (1983). Effects of supervisors' influence orientation on their decision making in controversy. *Journal of Psychology, 113,* 175–182.

Tjosvold, D. (1985). Implications of controversy research for management. *Journal of Management, 11,* 19–35.

Tyler, T. R. (1986). When does procedural justice matter in organizational settings? In R. J. Lewicki, B. H. Sheppard & M. H. Bazerman (Eds.), *Research on negotiation in organizations* (Vol. 1, pp. 7–23). Greenwich, CT: JAI Press.

van de Vliert, E. (1984). Conflict: Prevention and escalation. In P. J. D. Drenth, H. Thierry, P. J. Willems & C. J. de Wolff (Eds.), *Handbook of work and organizational psychology* (pp. 521–551). New York: Wiley.

van de Vliert, E. (1985). Escalative intervention in small-group conflicts. *Journal of Applied Behavioral Science, 21,* 19–36.

van de Vliert, E., & Hordijk, J. W. (1989). A theoretical position of compromising among other styles of conflict management. *Journal of Social Psychology, 129,* 681–690.

van de Vliert, E., & Prein, H. C. M. (1989). The difference in the meaning of forcing in the conflict management of actors and observers. In M. A. Rahim (Ed.), *Managing conflict: An integrative approach* (pp. 51-63). New York: Praeger.

Vecchio, R. P. (1984). Models of psychological inequity. *Organizational Behavior and Human Performance, 34,* 266–282.

Vroom, V. H. (1964). *Work and motivation.* New York: Wiley.

Wall, J. A. (1977). Intergroup bargaining: Effects of opposing constituent stances, opposing representative's bargaining, and representative's locus of control. *Journal of Conflict Resolution, 21,* 459–474.

Wall, J. A. (1981). Mediation: An analysis, review and proposed research. *Journal of Conflict Resolution, 25,* 157–180.

Walton, R. E. (1969). *Interpersonal peacemaking: Confrontations and third party consultation.* Reading, MA: Addison-Wesley.

Walton, R. E., & Dutton, J. M. (1969). The management of interdepartmental conflict: A model and review. *Administrative Science Quarterly, 14,* 73–84.

Walton, R. E., & McKersie, R. B. (1965). *A behavioral theory of labor negotiations: An analysis of a social interaction system.* New York: McGraw-Hill.

Wehr, P. (1986, April). Conflict resolution studies: What do we know? *Dispute Resolution Forum,* pp. 3-4, 12-13.

Weick, K. E. (1969). *The social psychology of organizing.* Reading, MA: Addison-Wesley.

CHAPTER 12

Organizational Development: Theory, Practice, and Research

Jerry I. Porras
Stanford University

Peter J. Robertson
University of Southern California

This chapter provides a comprehensive review of theory, practice, and research in the field of organizational development. An organizing theoretical framework is presented in the first section of the chapter. In the second section, the theoretical base of the field is analyzed. Implementation theory is distinguished from change process theory, and each is summarized and critiqued. A variety of organizational development interventions, organized into four categories drawn from the theoretical framework, are described in the third section. In the fourth section, findings from nearly 50 published evaluations of organizational development interventions are aggregated and used to evaluate predictions derived from the theoretical framework. The chapter concludes with a discussion of significant recent issues and trends in theory, practice, and research in the field.

> To him who devotes his life to science, nothing can give
> more happiness than increasing the number of discoveries.
> But his cup of joy is full when the results of his studies
> immediately find practical application. There are not two
> sciences. There is only one science and the application of
> science, and these two activities are linked as the fruit is to
> the tree.
> (Louis Pasteur)

Introduction

ORGANIZATIONAL DEVELOPMENT (OD) is the practical application of the science of organizations. Drawing from several disciplines for its models, strategies, and techniques, OD focuses on the planned change of human systems and contributes to organization science through the knowledge gained from its study of complex change dynamics. The field follows Kurt Lewin's two dicta, "In order to truly understand something, try changing it" and "There is nothing as practical as a good theory." The interplay between the development of scientific theory and its application makes OD an exciting and vibrant part of organizational studies.

Although a substantial number of important contributions have been made, the field has had its problems, some of which have plagued it from the beginning. Many of OD's problems relate to its relative newness as an academic field; it has been in existence slightly more than three decades. Some derive from the enormous complexity that exists in the processes OD attempts to map. Consequently, OD's theoretical base is unsettled; there are blurred conceptualizations of the process and inadequate understandings of its underlying change mechanisms. In addition, significant questions about the robustness of OD research methods cast doubt on the validity of many research findings. Moreover, the tendency to emphasize action over systematic evaluation of OD's effects results in a less than desired data base for the field. Finally, the field has, for some, a "messianic" rather than scientific flavor because of its normative humanistic value based roots. These factors make the field a difficult as well as challenging arena for both research and practice.

The purpose of this chapter is to capture some of the vitality and complexity of organizational development and to present its theory, practice, and research in such a way that the reader can better comprehend the essence of the field, where it is now, and where it is headed. We begin with brief introductory comments on organizational change as a construct and a definition of organizational development. We expand on this definition by presenting a perspective on organizational change based on Porras' (1986, 1987; Porras & Silvers, 1991) organizational framework. A discussion of OD theory follows, concentrating on two types: change process theory and change implementation theory. Next, we broadly describe the vast array of intervention techniques currently popular in the field and discuss a few in depth. Then we describe research findings on the effects of OD and discuss what OD does and does not accomplish. We conclude with some final comments on theory, practice, and research in the field.

The Concept of Organizational Change

Current views on organizational change come mainly from the organizational theory literature and from the organizational behavior literature, with a surprisingly smaller number coming from the OD literature. In this section, we outline four types of organizational change, based on the category of change and its order. By *category of change* we mean whether it is planned or unplanned, and by *order* we mean whether it is first or second order. Each of these dimensions is more precisely defined below.

- *Planned change* is change that "originates with a decision by the system to deliberately improve its functioning and (typically) to engage an outside resource to help in the processes of making these improvements" (Levy, 1986, p. 6). Planned change often focuses on developing the organization's general capabilities to deal with existing or anticipated environmental demands and typically affects many, often unforeseen, segments of the organization.

- *Unplanned change* is change whose impetus originates outside the organizational system and which is an adaptive response typically focused on the alteration of relatively clearly defined and often narrow segments of the organization. As Lippitt, Watson, and Westley (1958b) describe unplanned change, it is spontaneous, evolutionary, fortuitous, or accidental.

Change thus varies according to the mode in which it is initiated. If triggered primarily by something outside the organization that forces a coping response from within, the change tends to be unplanned and mainly adaptive. If, on the other hand, change is initiated from inside the organization based on a desire to improve system functioning, the result tends to be a change process that is planned, follows clearer strategies, uses more existing knowledge about how to consciously alter system dynamics, and is implemented with preexisting techniques for altering system performance.

- *First-order change,* linear and continuous in nature, involves alterations in system characteristics without any shift either in fundamental assumptions about key organizational cause-and-effect relationships (e.g., high pay causes people to work harder, poorly maintained machines won't negatively affect morale, orderly work spaces promote better quality work, or introduction of feelings into the work place will reduce effectiveness) or in the basic paradigm used by the system to guide its functioning.

- *Second-order change* is a "multidimensional, multilevel, qualitative, discontinuous, radical organizational change involving a paradigmatic shift" (Levy & Merry, 1986, p. 5).

Using this latter pair of concepts, change can also vary according to whether organizational conditions are altered in ways consistent with previously existing conceptions of possible changes, or whether radically different conceptualizations are created and used as the basis for creating new organizational characteristics. In the first case, the frames of reference used by members to define organizational phenomena are maintained, and the change process is viewed, along a previously defined continuum, as shifts in the degree to which a condition exists. In the second type, the original frames of reference are replaced by new ones, with the result that the new organizational condition is seen by members as conceptually quite distinct from the old.

To best understand the types of change that occur specifically as a consequence of OD intervention activity, we must assess the types of change implied by the combinations of these two dimensions (Table 1). Since both planned or unplanned change can result in either first- or second-order change, then in fact there are at least four different types of change processes that can occur in organizations.

Organizational development, first and foremost a planned process, deals with developmental and transformational change. As such, OD interventions can precipitate either first- or second-order organizational change, depending on the character, scope, and magnitude of the change interventions used and on the intensity and duration of the change process.[1] With this perspective on change as a background, let us now turn to a definition of organizational development as the beginning point of our review of this field.

Definition of Organizational Development

Organizational development can be very broadly described as the use of planned, behavioral science–based interventions in work settings for the purpose of improving organizational functioning and individual development. For a better sense of the breadth of views

TABLE 1

Types of Organizational Change

Order of Change	Change Category	
	Planned	Unplanned
First	Developmental	Evolutionary
Second	Transformational	Revolutionary

on OD and its fundamental characteristics, let us look at some of the many definitions that exist in the literature. A small sample of the more prominent of these, chronologically presented, is shown in Table 2.

These definitions embody several themes. The *purpose* of OD is improvement in the organization's effectiveness (Beckhard, 1969; Huse & Cummings, 1985; Margulies & Raia, 1978; Robey & Altman, 1982), its ability to adapt (Bennis, 1966), its self-renewing processes (French & Bell, 1984) or capacity (Beer, 1980), its health (Beckhard,1969), and its development of new and creative organizational solutions (Beckhard, 1969). Its *scope* is overall organizational or systemwide change (Beckhard,1969; Beer,1980; Huse & Cummings, 1985). Its *conceptual underpinnings* derive from behavioral science theory, research, and technology (Beckhard, 1969; Beer, 1980; Burke, 1982; French & Bell, 1984; Huse & Cummings, 1985). Its *process* is planned (Beckhard, 1969; Burke, 1982; Huse & Cummings, 1985; Margulies & Raia, 1978), value based (Margulies & Raia,1978; Robey & Altman, 1982), action research oriented (Beer, 1980; French & Bell, 1984; Margulies & Raia, 1978), technology driven (Margulies & Raia, 1978; Robey & Altman, 1982), consultant aided (Beer, 1980; French & Bell, 1984; Robey & Altman, 1982), and directed or supported by

top management (Beckhard, 1969; French & Bell, 1984). And finally, its *targets* are the organization's culture (Bennis, 1966; Burke, 1982; French & Bell, 1984), structure (Bennis, 1966; Huse & Cummings, 1985); strategy (Huse & Cummings, 1985), processes (Beckhard, 1969; Huse & Cummings, 1985), and congruence among the various key organizational factors (Beer, 1980).

Drawing from and expanding on these definitions, we define OD as follows:

> *Organizational development* is a set of behavioral science–based theories, values, strategies, and techniques aimed at the planned change of the organizational work setting for the purpose of enhancing individual development and improving organizational performance, through the alteration of organizational members' on-the-job behaviors.

This definition of OD is broader than the view derived from the definitions cited earlier in three key ways. First, we maintain that OD has two primary purposes. One is improvement in the organization's ability to perform. This would encompass all the purposes noted in our synthesis of the existing definitions. The second is improvement in the

TABLE 2

Definitions of Organizational Development

Bennis (1966) described planned change as involving "a *change-agent,* who is typically a behavioral scientist brought in to help a *client-system,* which refers to the target of change. The change-agent, in *collaboration* with the client-system, attempts to apply *valid knowledge* to the client's problems" (p. 82). Later, Bennis (1969) defined OD as "a response to change, a complex educational strategy intended to change the beliefs, attitudes, values, and structure of organizations so that they can better adapt" (p. 2).

Beckhard (1969) defined OD as "an effort (1) *planned,* (2) *organization-wide,* and (3) *managed* from the *top,* to (4) increase *organization effectiveness* and *health* through (5) *planned interventions* in the organization's 'processes,' using *behavioral-science* knowledge" (p. 9).

Margulies and Raia (1972) first described OD as a "body of knowledge concerning the ways in which organizations can better adapt" (p. ix). They later define it more specifically as "a value-based process of self-assessment and planned change, involving specific strategies and technology, aimed at improving the overall effectivenes of an organizational system"(Margulies & Raia, 1978, p. 24).

Beer (1980) described OD as "a system-wide process of data collection, diagnosis, action planning, intervention, and evaluation aimed at: (1) enhancing congruence between organizational structure, process, strategy, people, and culture; (2) developing new and creative organizational solutions; and

(3) developing the organization's self-renewing capacity. It occurs through collaboration of organizational members working with a change agent using behavioral science theory, research, and technology" (p. 10).

Burke (1982) viewed OD as "a planned process of change in an organization's culture though the utilization of behavioral science technology, research, and theory" (p. 10).

Robey and Altman (1982) defined OD as "a systematic process with an underlying value system which employs a variety of techniques introduced by a consultant to improve the effectiveness of complex organizations" (p. 1).

French and Bell (1984) described OD as a "top-management–supported, long-range effort to improve an organization's problem-solving and renewal processes, particularly through a more effective and collaborative diagnosis and management of organization culture—with special emphasis on formal work team, temporary team, and intergroup culture—with the assistance of a consultant-facilitator and the use of the theory and technology of applied behavioral science, including action research" (p. 17).

Huse and Cummings (1985) defined OD as "a system-wide application of behavioral science knowledge to the planned development and reinforcement of organizational strategies, structures, and processes for improving an organization's effectiveness" (p. 2).

---

development of the organization's members—that is, in their psychological well-being, their level of self-actualization or realization, and their capabilities. This second purpose is largely ignored in the definitions cited earlier.

A second key way that our view is more expansive is in the targets we see as appropriate for intervention. We believe that the focus

of change efforts must encompass more organizational variables than just culture, structure, strategy, and processes. As we discuss in greater detail later, OD can influence many variables, all of which collectively constitute the work setting of individual organizational members. As such, OD must take a broad view of all the organizational factors that have an impact on human behavior in the work setting.

Finally, and perhaps most importantly, we view change in the behavior of individual organizational members as a necessary prerequisite for meaningful and lasting organizational change. In other words, organizational change that results from OD interventions, whether it be improvement in organizational performance or enhancement of individual development, is mediated by change in members' work behavior. This premise leads to the conclusion that OD interventions need to be chosen according to the likelihood that they will promote appropriate changes in employee behavior.

These three ideas—the importance of individual behavior, the wide array of organizational variables that can be changed through OD interventions, and the dual focus on organizational performance and individual development—comprise the basic framework underlying our perspective of organizational development. This perspective is developed more completely in the next section.

A Perspective on Organizational Change

Changing an organization, normally a complex and fast-paced process, becomes even more problematic when those instituting change operate without the guidance of a clear perspective on organizations and how they change—that is, without an organizational model, what the key variables are and how they interrelate. Most of those who work in change settings have distinct views of the critical variables to target for change. However, few use as a guide a comprehensive and integrated framework, one that provides a more complete set of perspectives for more smoothly facilitating complex change (cf. Tichy, 1975). Indeed, the absence of a broad, widely accepted, usable, and change-based model of organizations is one of the important weaknesses in the field today.

This section addresses that weakness by providing a framework for understanding the effects of interventions on organizations.[2] It presents some underlying assertions and background concepts, as well as a description of the organizational framework (Porras, 1986, 1987) that guides our thinking about OD.

A basic assumption in this framework is that *change in the individual organizational member's behavior is at the core of organizational change and, therefore, any successful change will persist over the long term only if, in response to changes in organizational characteristics, members alter their on-the-job behavior in appropriate ways.* This assumption is rooted in the belief that behavior is significantly influenced by the nature of the setting in which it occurs. This leads to the conclusion that an individual's work behavior is best changed by changing aspects of his or her work setting. Therefore, we present a framework for conceptualizing organizational work settings and thus identify key leverage points for change. We conclude the section by exploring the relationships between changes in behavior and changes in organizational outcomes.

Centrality of Individual Behavior

As noted earlier, the purposes of organizational development are defined in terms such as "to increase organization effectiveness and health" (Beckhard, 1969, p. 9), "to improve an organization's problem-solving and renewal processes" (French & Bell, 1973, p. 15), "to make it possible for organizations to become or remain viable, to adapt to new conditions, to solve problems, to learn from experiences" (Lippitt, 1969, p. 1), to vitalize, energize, actualize, activate, and renew organizations (Argyris, 1971), or "to change the beliefs, attitudes, values, and structure of organizations" (Bennis, l969, p. 3).

In none of these views, however, is the full purpose of OD spelled out in operational terms—terms useful from the perspective of guiding specific intervention action. Change agents, with unique models for perceiving and intervening in organizations, have different ways of describing how a system's functioning is different following a successful change effort. Most describe it in terms of attitude change (Kimberly & Nielsen, 1975), some in terms of thinking patterns or problem-solving processes (Argyris, 1982), and only a few in terms of actual behavioral change of organizational members (Porras & Hoffer, 1986). In the end, unless attitudes and ways of framing problems result in different actions, the organization, over the longer run, will not behave in a significantly different way. Organizational members must do things differently for the system to change. Thinking or feeling differently is not enough; behavior must also change.

We propose, therefore, that the alteration of tangible on-the-job behaviors performed by individual organizational members are key effects of successful planned change efforts. All effective intervention activity must have as one important result the concrete alteration of human behavior. Over the long term, only when individual employees collectively change their behavior does the overall organization function in a new and different manner. Shifts in organizational setting variables are relatively meaningless unless people wind up doing something differently.

While the action-oriented OD literature has noted the need to affect behaviors in a change process, relatively little measurement of this type of change has actually been done (Liebowitz & DeMeuse, 1982; McLean, Sims, Mangham, & Tuffield, 1982; Nadler, Cammann, & Mirvis, 1980). Most often, behaviors are not even mentioned in reports of large-scale change projects (e.g., Boje, Fedor, & Rowland, 1982; Patterson, 1981; Paul & Gross, 1981). If behaviors are mentioned, they typically are outcome behaviors such as turnover, absenteeism, or grievances (Nicholas, 1982). Individual performance, which is not work behavior per se but

which can be viewed as a summary measure of work behavior, is also frequently assessed.

A few studies have attempted to identify and measure specific behaviors. Examples are (a) studies that count the frequency of occurrence of certain actions (Boss & McConkie, 1981; Harvey & Boettger, 1971; Moorhead, 1982; Porras, Hargis, Patterson, Maxfield, Roberts, & Bies, 1982); (b) studies that count certain verbal statements (Greenbaum, Holden, & Spataro, 1983; Keys & Bartunek, 1979; Manz & Sims, 1982; Rasmussen, 1982; Waldie, 1981); and (c) studies that record observed actions (Ketchum, 1984; Ottaway, 1983; Sargent, 1981). In general, however, the OD research has suffered from a lack of focus as to the *behaviors* that are critical to assess in any change process.

What is achieved when change agents successfully intervene into organizational systems? Most planned change practitioners would say that the system functions differently, solves its problems differently, makes decisions differently, treats its people differently, and so on. At the system level, these intentions seem well understood and, as indicated earlier, are generally regarded as important goals of OD.

However, the fundamental question is, how are these changes in processes achieved? Change agents attempt to accomplish them by intervening into various parts of the system— by changing various aspects of the work environment. This process of organizational design "requires a wide variety of organization members to agree to behave differently. Because organizations are designed to promote certain patterns of behavior, redesigning involves fundamental changes in how people behave and relate to one another" (Cummings, Mohrman, Mohrman, & Ledford, 1985, p. 275).

Whatever the actions taken to alter the work environment, the underlying purpose is to affect the behavior of organizational members, which in turn should alter the effectiveness of the overall system. This is because behavior is the crucial link between the organization's intentions and its outcomes (Beer, 1987). Since an organization's functioning is composed of the functioning of all its members, it can only change when its members' behaviors change (Tannenbaum, 1971). As indicated earlier, few OD efforts concentrate directly on individual behavior. Instead, they focus on altering the organizational conditions under which employees function. The result of these alterations is individual behavioral change, with the final outcome being changes in organizational outputs.

In summary, all successful planned organizational change efforts ultimately lead to organizational members changing the way they behave on the job, for example, the decisions they make, the tasks they carry out, the information they share, the care with which they do their work, the creativity they bring to their activities, and the initiatives they take. Changes in variables such as formal structure, cost control systems, budgetary systems, machinery, techniques for doing the job, policies and procedures, or job designs and responsibilities, will not have much impact on the outputs generated by the organization unless people behave differently as a result of these prescribed alterations. If aspects of the organization are changed, yet its members do not change their basic work-related behaviors, there will be no long-term organizational change.

Common Behavioral Change in Successful OD Interventions. If individual behavior is the intermediate factor linking change agent interventions and organizational outcomes, then questions arise about just which behaviors are of most concern in any planned change situation. Clearly, the number of critical behaviors can be quite large and can vary dramatically across organizational settings. Behaviors that might be important in one organization could well be less important in another. Some of these, of course, would be specific to the particular organization

and its unique problems. Nevertheless, we believe that a set of behaviors exists that is generalizable across different types of organizations and situations. These are the behaviors whose enactment in the organization might be most generally desirable from the point of view of both the organization and the individual.

Porras and Hoffer (1986) explored this issue to determine if there were a core set of behaviors that might be relatively constant across all organizational settings and, in addition, might be associated with successful organizational change efforts. They surveyed 42 leading OD scholars and practitioners in the United States, asking them to specify the behaviors that would change as a consequence of a successful planned change effort. Thirty-eight of the respondents believed that there were behavioral changes common to successful change efforts, and they were able to specify the ones they saw as most important.

The common behaviors identified were organized into two sets, one focused on behaviors appropriate to all organizational members, and one focused specifically on managers. In each of these sets, specific behaviors identified were grouped into categories based on similarity or common focus. For all levels, the categories of behaviors most frequently mentioned were (a) communicating openly, (b) collaborating, (c) taking responsibility, (d) maintaining a shared vision, (e) solving problems effectively, (f) respecting/supporting others, (g) processing/facilitating interactions, (h) inquiring, and (i) experimenting. For managers, in addition to the behaviors just mentioned, the following categories were also frequently mentioned: (a) generating participation, (b) leading by vision, (c) functioning strategically, (d) promoting information flow, and (d) developing others.

These behaviors, then, in the minds of the leaders in the field of organizational change, are associated with increased organizational effectiveness. They represent a core set of behaviors hypothesized to change across all successful change efforts in all types of change settings. The identification of these behavioral outcomes does not imply, however, that every behavior in the set is of equal importance for every setting or situation. Rather, in general, a greater frequency of these behaviors is linked to greater effectiveness and a lower frequency is linked to lesser effectiveness. The relative importance of the particular categories may vary across different change projects and different organizations.

Regardless of whether the list just presented is the most appropriate, the key finding from this study was that those individuals most knowledgeable in the field of organizational change believe that change in behavior is associated with system improvement.[3] We can infer from this that activities that lead to changes in on-the-job behaviors will also lead to improved organizational functioning, with its consequent improvement in organizational outputs. Given this conclusion, it would be useful to address briefly the issue of the determinants of behavior. Understanding the determinants of behavior is a prerequisite to being able to effectively change behavior.

Determinants of Behavior. We have argued that people and their behaviors are a key element in understanding organizations and how to change them. If one wishes to consciously improve the organization's outcomes, then the behavior of individual organizational members must first be changed in a desired direction. Given this assumption, it would be useful to address briefly the issue of how people learn new behaviors and change the way they act on the job.

The field of psychology has developed a number of theories and perspectives attempting to explain the bases of individual behavior. These include psychodynamic theory (Freud, 1955), trait theory (Allport, 1961; Cattell, 1966), need theory (Alderfer, 1972; Maslow, 1954;

McClelland, 1961), behaviorism (Skinner, 1953, 1969), expectancy theory (Porter & Lawler, 1968; Vroom, 1964), and social learning or social cognitive theory (Bandura, 1977, 1986). Because these perspectives focus on different determinants of human behavior, one result is that little widespread agreement exists concerning the most effective methods for bringing about change in behavior.

The earlier theories tended to focus on the internal needs, drives, and impulses of people. Therefore, management development in organizations has historically tried to teach managers to understand the needs and personalities of their subordinates. With this knowledge, the manager could take the actions necessary to influence subordinates, leading to increased motivation to work harder on the job. The success of this approach would be based on a manager's ability to correctly assess the needs of his or her employees and then either change those needs or do the things necessary to satisfy them. Later theories have recognized the important role of the situation as an influence on a person's behavior. While behaviorism focuses exclusively on the situation, the cognitive models of behavior (e.g., expectancy theory and social learning or social cognitive theory) maintain that individuals make conscious choices about their behaviors and that the information on which these choices are based comes largely from their environment.

It is beyond the scope of this chapter to argue for one or another model of how individuals learn and change behaviors. Suffice it to say that inherent in all cognitive models of behavioral change is the importance of the individual's environment as a source of information about appropriate behaviors. Through natural processes of perception and attribution, individuals form beliefs regarding the nature of their organizational environment. Such beliefs energize, direct, and regulate behavior (Bernstein & Burke, 1989). For example, Neumann (1989) explains how the level of participation in decision making is shaped by environmental factors. "People will do as the workplace requires of them," she maintains (p. 203).

In other words, based on cues received from their work setting, individuals form beliefs regarding which behaviors are appropriate and/or will be rewarded. Their perceptions of these cues are integrated with such factors as their particular sets of objectives, needs, and personalities, and they make choices regarding the nature of the behaviors in which they will engage. This notion of the work environment shaping behavior is central to our perspective on organizations and organizational change.

Summary. Organizational change—that is, improvements in organizational functioning —requires change in the behavior of individual organizational members. The behavior of individual members is influenced by the setting within which the behavior occurs. The work setting influences behavior by providing information to individuals that they use as inputs into their choices regarding which behaviors they will exhibit. An important means of inducing change in behavior, therefore, is to change aspects of individuals' work setting such that desired behaviors will be induced more frequently. Since organizational development can be viewed as the process by which the organizational work setting is changed, it is useful to delineate those aspects of organizations that can be changed in order to influence behavioral change. An organizational framework used to categorize those factors amenable to change is presented next.

Characteristics of the Work Setting

The purpose of this section is to identify those key factors in the internal organizational environment that shape and guide behavior of people on the job. The specific factors

constituting the work setting are divided into four basic categories.[4] These four categories are (a) organizing arrangements, (b) social factors, (c) technology, and (d) physical setting. Figure 1 contains a listing of the specific factors that constitute each of these four categories. Since the work setting is the environment in which people work, and since the environment plays a key role in determining the behavior of people, these factors define the characteristics that, if changed, will induce change in on-the-job behaviors of individual employees.

Organizing Arrangements. The organizing arrangements category contains the formal elements of the organization which are developed to coordinate the behavior of people and the functioning of various parts of the organization. As formal mechanisms, they usually exist in written form and represent a description of the way the organization is intended to work, not necessarily the way it actually does. Organizing arrangements include (a) goals, (b) strategies, (c) formal structure, (d) administrative policies and procedures, (e) administrative systems, (f) reward systems, and (g) ownership.

Goals. Goals can be defined as planned positions or results to be achieved (Richards, 1978). They are premises that serve as inputs to decisions (Simon, 1964) and immediate regulators of action (Erez & Kanfer, 1983). Thus, they are instrumental in the generation of and selection from alternative courses of action. Goals exist at all organizational levels, from top to bottom, and can be differentiated between official and operative goals (Perrow, 1961). The latter have a stronger impact on behavior, yet this impact may or may not be consistent with the official goals of the organization.

Strategies. Closely linked with goals are the strategies of the organization. Organizational strategies specify the means by which system goals are to be achieved (Ansoff, 1984). They

FIGURE 1

Factors Constituting the Organizational Work Setting

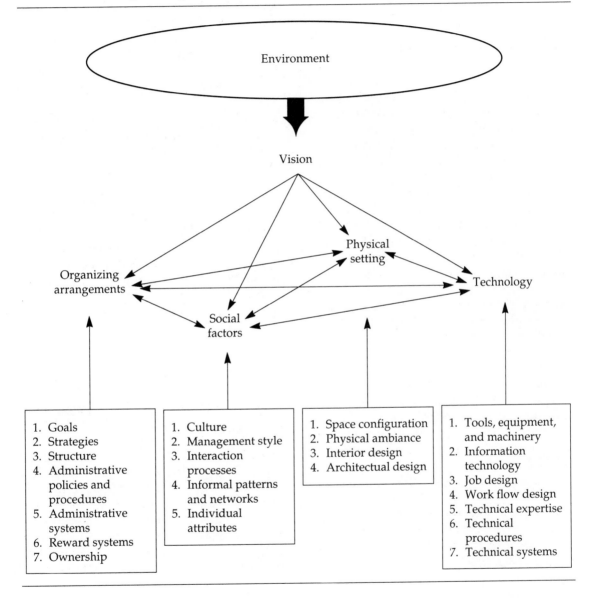

are patterns of resource deployments and environmental interactions that indicate how the organization will achieve its objectives (Hofer & Schendel, 1978).

Formal Structure.   Probably the most obvious element of the organizing arrangements category is the formal structure of the organization. Structure refers to the formal allocation of work roles and the administrative mechanisms to control and integrate work activities (Child, 1972) and the regularities in such activities as task allocation, the exercise of authority, and coordination of function (Pugh, 1966). It has also been defined as the distributions, along various lines, of people among social positions that influence the role relations among these people (Blau, 1974). Thus, an organization's structure defines the hierarchy—that is, the division of labor and the authority relationships in the organization (Hall, 1982)—and it specifies the formal lines of communication existing in the organization. It defines the broad roles of each organizational subsystem and how these subsystems are interrelated (Thompson, 1967).

Administrative Policies and Procedures.   Policies and procedures consist of the formal rules that define appropriate methods for carrying out various organizational activities. They are intended to help ensure that the formal structure operates as designed. Thus, Galbraith (1977) says that rules and procedures are simply decisions made in advance of their execution, and that if organizational members adopt the appropriate behavior, the resultant aggregate response is an integrated and coordinated pattern of behavior.

Administrative Systems.   The administrative systems in the organization are all of the formally designed and established systems focused on facilitating the coordination of the organization. These include such systems as financial accounting and control systems,

information systems, and personnel management systems.

Reward Systems.   Formal reward systems, technically a type of administrative system, are included separately because of their unique importance and the more direct impact they have on behaviors of individuals in organizations (Lawler, 1981). The reward systems include the compensation system (both pay and benefits) and the performance appraisal system. Finally, reward systems differ depending on the types of organizational positions to which they apply.

Ownership.   The patterns of ownership describe corporation situations that can vary greatly from all of the stock owned by one person to all of the stock owned by thousands of people; from all stock solely owned by people within the corporation to stock owned totally by outsiders; from each stock owner possessing one share to stock owners possessing numerous shares; from stockholders being able to vote their shares to stockholders not having the right to vote their shares; and so on (Rosen, Klein, & Young, 1986).

Summary.   These are the main features of the organizing arrangements category and the ones most typically the targets of planned change efforts. They are the formal aspects of the system that drive behavior. As such, they indicate to people what they should be doing and describe the way the system is supposed to work. These factors assume rationality and individual behavior consistent with rational choices. If all the components were consistent with each other, they would tend to reinforce the same behaviors.

While aspects of the organization such as the reward system and the formal structure do have a powerful impact on behavior, people do not always respond consistently with what the organizing arrangements tell them to do. This is because there are a variety of other factors that impact behavior, and thus organizational members respond in many different ways, some of them quite unpredictable.

Social Factors. The social factors encompass the characteristics of the people in the organization individually and in small groups, their patterns and processes of interaction, and many of their features as larger social groups. Specifically, they include (a) culture, (b) management style, (c) interaction processes, (d) informal patterns and networks, and (e) individual attributes. These factors have traditionally been referred to in the aggregate as the informal organization, in contrast to the organizing arrangements, which have been considered the formal organization.

Culture. The culture of organizations has been a popular topic in management literature over the past few years (Davis, 1984; Deal & Kennedy, 1982; Kilmann, Saxton, Serpa, & Associates, 1985; Schein, 1985). Many scholars and practitioners are focusing on culture as the key area for change activity, yet they are finding it a difficult and complex phenomenon to understand, much less change. A variety of the elements that comprise an organization's culture are described below.

Values are a basic element of organizational cultures (Deal & Kennedy, 1982; Peters & Waterman, 1982). Every organization has a set of values that influences the work behavior of its members. A distinction can be made between *espoused values*, those in which employees say they believe, and *inferred values*, those inferred from a variety of organizational activities as being the operational values of the employees (Argyris & Schön, 1978; Siehl, 1984). Values are translated into behavior in part through the development of *norms*. Norms are standards of conduct applicable to members of a group (Shaw, 1976), or the specification of values relating to behavior in interactions (Peterson, 1979). They are not written guidelines nor are they formal policies or procedures.

Values are transmitted to organizational members through artifacts (Schein, 1985) such as symbols, rituals, history, stories, and myths. *Symbols* are signs that express much more than their intrinsic content, in that they represent a wider pattern of meaning (Pondy, Frost, Morgan, & Dandridge, 1983). Any element of organizational life, including objects, actions, events, utterances, concepts, and images, can be symbols. *Rituals* or rites are systematic and programmed routines of day-to-day life that dramatize the company's values (Deal & Kennedy, 1982; Trice & Beyer, 1984). The *history* of the organization is the broad collection of facts about what the organization has accomplished (e.g., Clark, 1970). *Stories* recount incidents that appear to be drawn accurately from an oral history (Martin, 1982; Wilkins, 1978), but they tend to be more focused, contain more emotional undertones, and have a closer link to the value or values they are intended to convey. *Myths* or legends are like stories, but they take bits and pieces of factual data and weave them together. As such, they are fictitious but with a strong basis in the reality of the organization (Wilkins & Martin, 1980).

Management Style. The values and basic assumptions held by managers have a key impact on their behavior and decision making. Through their actions, managers strongly influence the behavior of employees. Management style helps to determine or create culture although, in our view, it is a separate construct (Schein, 1985).

Interaction Processes. In working together to perform the tasks of the organization, people interact in various social groupings. Interactions take place at the interpersonal, group, and intergroup level, and they can be described in terms of a number of processes, such as communication processes, conflict resolution processes, problem-solving processes, and decision-making processes.

Informal Patterns and Networks. While the organizational structure specifies formal patterns of communication, decision making, and authority, an informal set of patterns coexists with the prescribed patterns. They comprise what Scott (1970) calls the organization's behavioral structure. These informal patterns and networks either can be consistent with, and thus mutually reinforcing of, the prescribed patterns, or they may be inconsistent with the formal structure, in which case there will be some degree of inefficiency in the system.

Individual Attributes. The important attributes of the individual organizational members include their beliefs, attitudes, and feelings, which influence not only the way they perform but also the way others around them behave. A fourth important attribute of individual organizational members is the behavioral skills they possess. Behavioral skills reflect the ability an individual has to effectively interact with others.

Summary. These five social factors—culture, management style, interaction processes, informal patterns and networks, and individual attributes—describe the human and informal side of the organization. As such, they are the most intangible parts of the organization and are difficult to characterize precisely. As a result, they are also the most difficult to change. However, greater awareness of these factors, along with an ability to think about them systematically, increases the likelihood that they can be influenced, especially in concert with other changes made in the organization.

Technology. The technology of the organization encompasses all of the factors that directly enter into the transformation of organizational inputs into organizational outputs. The technology category includes: (a) tools, equipment, and machinery used in the transformation process, (b) designs of jobs required

to perform that transformation, (c) work flow design, (d) technical procedures, (e) technical systems, and (f) technical expertise of organizational members.

Tools, Equipment, and Machinery. The tools, equipment, and machinery required to produce the organization's output refer to any physical object that can be used to perform a function on something else in the creation of a product or service. This component of technology can range from equipment as large and complex as a mainframe computer or heavy machinery to a tool as simple as a pencil.

Job Design. Jobs are designed by combining a series of tasks, the performance of which are the responsibility of an organizational member. The design of a job reflects the nature of the set of tasks that are formally designated as comprising that job. According to Rousseau (1977), the job design perspective (e.g., Hackman & Oldham, 1975) and the sociotechnical systems perspective (e.g., McWhinney, 1972) have both focused on a set of properties of jobs thought to be important to individual outcomes such as attitudes and performance. These characteristics are meaningful work, control over work processes, performance feedback, use of a variety of skills, learning opportunities, and interaction with other people.

Work Flow Design. Jobs are grouped together to create a flow of work. The design of the work flow is guided by knowledge of the types of interdependence that exist in the process of producing a product or service. Three types of interdependence identified by Thompson (1967) are pooled, sequential, and reciprocal. In *pooled* interdependence, each part provides a discrete contribution to the whole and each is supported by the whole. *Sequential* interdependence is serial, such that the outputs of one part become inputs for the next part. The latter cannot act until the former properly carries out its activities. In *reciprocal* interdependence, the outputs of each become inputs for the other, such that each part poses a contingency for the other.

Technical Procedures. Technical procedures specify the prescribed methods for performing the tasks of transforming the system's inputs into its outputs. In contrast to the administrative procedures described in the organizing arrangements category, they are directly related to the transformation process and are not broadly organizational in nature. Like administrative procedures, however, the degree to which the prescribed methods are complied with depends in part on the extent to which they are supported by various norms and informal processes.

Technical Systems. The systems that provide information about the state of, or which control various aspects of, the transformation process are called technical systems. They provide the technical structure around which coordination and management of the transformation process can occur. Scheduling systems, parts control systems, procurement systems, inventory control systems, maintenance systems, and "just-in-time" systems are all examples of technical systems.

Technical Expertise. Organizational members' technical expertise includes their level of knowledge and physical skills, which allow them to carry out the concrete tasks necessary to perform their assigned jobs. If members do not possess the appropriate knowledge or skills, the technology will not operate as effectively as possible, regardless of how well the jobs and work flow are designed.

Summary. Technology has been a dominant element of organizational design since the inception of the modern industrial organization (Davis, 1971). The factors that comprise the organization's technology have direct effects on individual organizational members. The design and content of one's job has perhaps a more powerful impact on behavior than any other aspect of the organization. The more dominant the technology of a system, the more impact it has on individual behavior. Therefore, understanding the various aspects of technology and the ways in which they affect individuals is a necessary prerequisite for successful organizational change.

Physical Setting. The fourth and final category of organizational features is the physical setting. The physical setting describes the concrete structures and objects of the nonsocial/ nontechnical part of the environment, which influences the way people behave at work. The four main components of the physical setting are (a) space configuration, (b) physical ambiance, (c) interior design, and (d) overall architectural design.

Space Configuration. Space configuration refers to the amount of space, the shape of the space (both horizontal and vertical), traditional versus open office designs (Oldham, 1988; Zalesny & Farace, 1987), and the relative locations of offices or work areas (Brill, Margulis, Konar, & BOSTI, 1984; Steele, 1983). Office design and relative locations of offices or work areas are perhaps the two most critical factors in space configuration. The ease of contact, dictated by whether an office is traditional or open or where people are located, does much to determine patterns of interaction that eventually influence the effectiveness with which work gets done.

Physical Ambiance. Characteristics of the ambiance include such factors as the quantity and types of lights, the level of heat or cold, the levels and types of noise, the quality of air, and the cleanliness of the area in which they work (Brill et al., 1984). These factors may at times affect an individual's physical ability to perform on the job, while at others they may simply affect a person's attitudes about the job and/or his or her performance.

Interior Design.   The interior design includes the furniture, decorations, window and floor coverings, and colors of floors, walls, and ceilings (Brill, Margulis, Konar, & BOSTI, 1985; Steele, 1986). The quality, style, and design of settings in which people work can influence the way they perceive themselves and their roles, which in turn can affect the decisions they make as part of their job responsibilities (Brill et al., 1985).

Architectural Design.   The architectural design is the overall structural design of the buildings in which people work. While the architectural design influences individual behavior in a manner similar to the interior design, an important additional effect is felt because of the impact of the overall building design on a person's perceptions of the organization (Deasy, 1976).

Summary.   The physical setting within which people work can do much to block or facilitate effective organizational behavior. In and of itself, it does not appear to have a substantial motivational impact on people (Steele, 1986). In other words, it does not induce people to engage in specific behaviors, but it can make certain behaviors easier or harder to perform. In this way, the effectiveness of people may be enhanced or reduced. Space configuration is perhaps the most significant aspect of the physical setting and, as such, must be designed with an eye toward using it to support desired behaviors and inhibit undesired ones.

Interconnections Among the Four Categories.   Overall, then, these four broad categories of organizational components make up the internal work setting of the organization. To enhance effective organizational performance, they must be designed so as to create work

setting conditions that will best support effective on-the-job behaviors of organizational members. Although they have been dealt with separately, these components are inevitably interconnected. The four categories of factors affect each other such that the design of one influences the functioning of the others. Their interaction affects the behavior of organizational members. A high degree of interrelationship drives the need for congruence among the parts. If different components are congruent, they will complement each other. If they are not aligned well, they are likely to work at cross-purposes, resulting in inefficiency and ineffectiveness (cf. Beer, 1980; Kotter, 1978; Nadler & Tushman, 1977).

There is another implication of the interrelationships between components that is not as explicitly addressed in some other organizational models, however. Specifically, this is the fact that a change in one factor will usually require complementary changes in others. In other words, interdependence between organizational characteristics must be taken into account if programs of change are to be effective. If interventions that attempt to change certain aspects of the organization are used without also trying to support these changes by intervening on other, interdependent system variables, any change is likely to be resisted, constrained, or short-lived. Change attempts made without considering the implications for other relevant organizational characteristics are likely to be less effective than they otherwise might have been.

A third important implication of these interconnections reflects our focus on the behavior of individuals as a key determinant of organizational effectiveness. Organizational components need to be congruent in terms of the signals they send to organizational members regarding appropriate behaviors. Congruency in these signals is important, since otherwise there will be greater variance and less predictability in the behavior exhibited by organizational members. For example, recent research (Robertson, 1990) has demonstrated that inconsistency in job behavior is negatively related to the degree of congruency between a variety of work setting characteristics. Higher levels of variance in desired organizational behavior lead to less coordinated and effective behavior of individual organizational members and consequently lower levels of organizational effectiveness. Therefore, it is imperative that changes be made only after consideration is given to the signaling effect they have on individuals, to whether these signals are consistent or inconsistent with signals coming from other key variables, and to whether the resulting signal pattern is likely to promote desired behaviors.

From a design point of view, then, the key strategy for any person changing a system is to design, as much as possible, factors in each of the four variable categories such that they give consistent and congruent messages to people regarding desired behavior. To the degree that the messages are made consistent, more successful change will occur. In situations in which one area is changed and others are not, or in which they are changed in ways that deliver inconsistent messages, people will become confused and their responses difficult to predict. Some will change their behavior while others will not. Those who do change will do so in a variety of unexpected ways. Those who do not will often become even more fixed in their previous behaviors because of the anxiety caused by the risks they perceive in trying anything new. The end result is that the program of change is much less likely to produce improvements in overall organizational functioning.

Role of Organizational Vision. Vision is the force that guides the organization, for both the short and long term. Organizational vision is a complex concept comprised of four distinct, yet interdependent parts: (a) the core values and beliefs of the organization, (b) the organization's enduring purpose, (c) a highly compelling mission, and (d) the vivid description that brings the mission to life (Collins & Porras, 1991).

The core beliefs and values of the organization are the foundation around which vision develops. They are inveterate, are relatively few in number, tend not to change over time, are rarely compromised, and provide a basis for the organization's purpose.

Although purpose is an important organizational component, well-articulated theoretical conceptualizations of it are conspicuously missing from the literature on organizations. It has been given prominent attention by various management theorists (e.g., Barnard, 1938; Drucker, 1977; Selznick, 1957), yet a precise definition, distinguishing it from other, similar notions (e.g., mission, vision, strategic intent, and goals), has not emerged. Likewise, while systems theorists claim that a distinguishing characteristic of living systems is that they are purposive, these theorists' focus has been on defining the nature of purposive behavior (i.e., specifying the defining characteristics of a purposive system) rather than on defining purpose itself (cf. George & Johnson, 1985).

Without attempting to provide a more elaborate discussion of purpose here, it would be useful to indicate broadly what we mean by the concept. An organization's purpose is its fundamental reason for being or its collective reasons for existence. As such, it is an end state never attained. Like a distant star, purpose is an achievement the organization moves toward but never reaches. Operationally, it can be thought of as a major contribution the organization expects to make within 100 years.

This general view is similar to Vaill's (1982), who refers to purpose as the knowledge organizational members have as to why the organization exists. Without purpose, interdependent individuals cannot efficiently or effectively carry out organizational activities.

Although Selznick (1957) uses the terms *purpose* and *mission* interchangeably, we view purpose as more abstract and fundamental than mission. Mission is more tangible than purpose and is a representation of major shorter term accomplishments achieved by the organization if it were moving toward its purpose.

Mission, more precisely, is a major goal: bold, exciting, and energizing; achievable within a medium time span (5 to 20 years); stretching the organization's capabilities; more narrowly focusing its attention; and spurring it into dedicating all of its energies toward mission accomplishment. Specifically, mission provides strategic direction and guides day to day functioning of the organization (Barnard, 1938).

The final component of overall organizational vision, the vivid description of the mission, paints an elaborate and compelling picture of what mission accomplishment would look like for the organization. It communicates the excitement and sense of achievement that comes from attaining a highly challenging and difficult major goal.

Taken together, these four constructs form the vision of the organization. Together they provide the direction, focus, and motivation that guides the organization for both the short and long term. Core values and beliefs and purpose are enduring and relatively unaffected by environmental conditions. Mission and vivid description, on the other hand, are more short-term and highly influenced by the particular environment the organization expects to face over the shorter run.

Vision, if clearly developed, serves to integrate an organization's various interdependent elements into an effectively coordinated whole. Since purpose and mission provide most of that integrating force, we will elaborate more on their role.

Purpose and mission serve as an integrating mechanism because of two primary roles they play in organizational functioning. First, they provide a common criterion for decision making by the many organizational actors responsible for defining the nature of the various organizational components we have just specified. Without a common criterion, it is likely that many of the necessary decisions would be made independently, resulting in incongruence and inconsistency among them, with consequent decreased effectiveness. A well-defined purpose and mission help ensure that these decisions are made in such a way that all organizational factors contribute to the achievement of the organization's vision.

Second, purpose and mission help organizational members interpret environmental changes and guide their decisions regarding how to respond to these changes. Similar organizations may respond to the same environmental changes in drastically different ways. This can be, in large part, because they hold very different conceptions of what their fundamental purpose and mission are. Likewise, members of organizations without a clearly defined purpose and mission may make counterproductive decisions regarding the actions they wish to take to meet these environmental challenges. But, when clearly defined, purpose and mission serve to clarify what the most appropriate response is and enhance the likelihood that key actions, generated from a variety of individuals and/or organizational subunits, will be integrated and coordinated toward achievement of the same vision.

By guiding decisions regarding the design of the organization's internal characteristics and regarding the actions that will be taken to meet environmental challenges, purpose and mission permeate the entire existence of an organization and directly or indirectly influence many of the decisions and behaviors of the organization's members.

In summary, the organization exists in an environment that inevitably has an impact on the organization. As the environment changes, the organization must usually adapt to the new environmental conditions. The adaptations chosen are guided by decision makers' understanding of the organization's purpose and mission. To the extent that such adaptations require changes in organizational characteristics (i.e., those comprising the four categories described earlier), a well-defined purpose and mission enable these changes to be made such that organizational characteristics are congruent and consistent with one another. These elements, because they collectively define the work context of individual organizational members, have a significant impact on the nature of the behaviors exhibited by these members.

Figure 2 depicts the relationships described up to this point, along with three additional relationships not yet addressed. These relationships involve the outcomes generated by the behavior of individual members. Therefore, we turn now to a discussion of the impact of behavior on organizational outcomes and of the relationship between the two types of outcomes identified.

Impact of Individual Behavior on Organizational Outcomes

Organizations generate outcomes in two broad areas. Although highly interdependent, these two types of outcomes are conceptually distinct. One set relates to the performance of the system, while the second describes the personal development of each organizational member. Organizational performance consists of a variety of outcomes generated by organizations. Such factors as revenue, costs, market share, and market position are primary descriptors of economic performance; turnover, absenteeism, and grievances are the main indicators of human relations performance. In both cases, these factors all describe outcomes that are indicators of the performance of the organizational system.

The second set of organizational outcomes relates to the individual organizational member's personal development that occurs as a consequence of his or her involvement with the organization. Level of self-actualization,

psychological or mental health, and level of realization of personal abilities are all indicators of the impact organizations have on the personal development of their members. A final point to be elaborated on later is that performance outcomes and personal development outcomes are interdependent. In the long run, one cannot be achieved without the other, and emphasizing one at the expense of the other will yield neither. Each of these two organizational outcome sets will be discussed in relationship to the behavior change of individual organizational members.

Individual Behavioral Change and Organizational Performance.   Many factors contribute to the performance of an organization, but perhaps the most important one is the behavior of individual organizational members. While individual performance has received significant attention in the organizational literature, the primary focus has been on motivation, which has to do with the level of effort of organizational members (Staw, 1984). However, the issue may be not only one of level of effort, but also one of direction of effort—that is, whether individuals engage in effective or ineffective behaviors. Naylor, Pritchard, and Ilgen (1980) suggest that individuals have a reservoir of energy that can be allocated among a variety of activities, some of which are productive and some of which are not. Katerberg and Blau (1983) found that the direction of effort—the various activities into which effort is channeled—can contribute to organizational members' job performance.

While Naylor et al. and Katerberg and Blau do not attempt to explain the nature of the relationship between individual behavior and organizational performance, it seems obvious that the latter will be influenced by the former. If individuals were to exhibit such behaviors as working hard and smart, taking responsibility and initiative, learning their jobs well, being creative, cooperating with one

FIGURE 2

A Change-based Organizational Framework

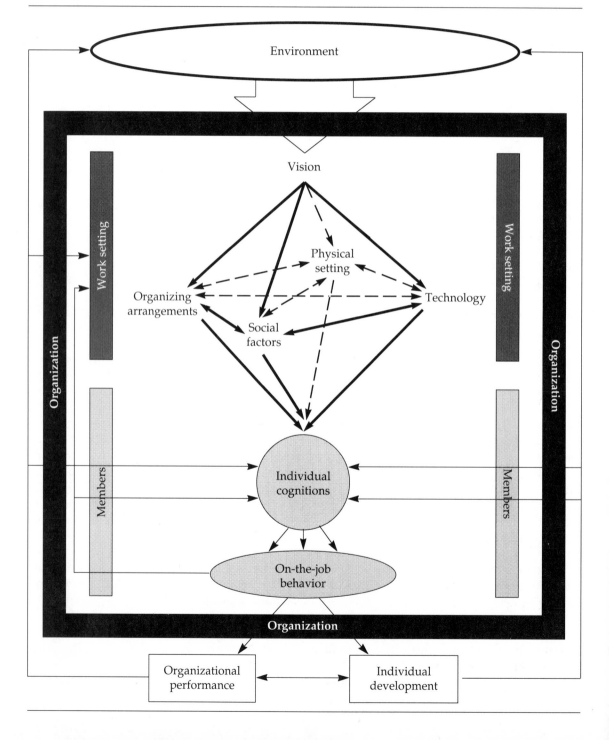

another, communicating what is important, listening to each other, facing conflict head-on, and committing themselves to their jobs, then the likelihood that the organization as a whole will perform well is enhanced (cf. Peters & Waterman, 1982). The organization may not turn out to be an economically successful system because of factors such as uncontrollable events in the environment or poor strategic choices made by its managers. But if individuals perform well, the system will also tend to perform as well as possible, given the context of its situation.

Hoffer (1986) investigated the relationship between the set of behaviors identified by Porras and Hoffer (1986) and the performance of a large real estate company. She used a variety of measures to assess the performance of 34 relatively autonomous and geographically dispersed sales offices, including such factors as profits per salesperson, market share, and costs. She found significant positive relationships between each of the performance measures and a composite index reflecting a behavior profile of each office. Based on the findings of this study, it appears that the behavior of organizational members can be associated with high levels of organizational performance. If this is the case, one can argue that a key goal of any change process must be to create work settings that will promote and facilitate the adoption of these behaviors by every organizational member.

Individual Behavioral Change and Personal Development. While one outcome of behavior in organizations is the overall level of organizational performance, a second type of outcome focuses on the level of the members' personal development. It has long been argued that people are psychologically affected by their involvement with traditional formal organizations (e.g., Argyris, 1957; Merton, 1957; Ouchi & Johnson, 1978). The essence of this argument is that the organization's need for control over the behavior of organizational

members results in various organizational characteristics which, because they restrict members' abilities to meet their higher level needs, limit their personal development and result in anxiety and/or alienation. Alternatively, such practices as decentralization, job enlargement, and participative management allow greater opportunities for the satisfaction of many of these needs (McGregor, 1960).

In summarizing this argument, Strauss (1963) describes some of the behavioral manifestations that are thought to result when organizations seek to program individual behavior and reduce discretion. When the organization demands conformity, obedience, and dependence, members

> may fight back through union activity, sabotage, output restriction, and other forms of rational or irrational (aggressive) behavior. Or they may withdraw and engage in regression, sublimation, childish behavior, or failure to contribute creative ideas or to produce more than a minimum amount of work.... They are apathetic and have settled for a low level of aspiration. They do as little work as they can get away with and still hold their job.... Organizational pressures, particularly being subjected to programmed work, may lead to serious personality disturbances and mental illness. (pp. 412–413)

A consequence of this type of organization is that its members would not be likely to experience much personal development as a result of their involvement in the organization. Instead, one could predict that the organizational members, as a group, would be relatively underdeveloped psychologically. They would not be growing in their ability to use whatever talents they possessed, nor would they be developing their confidence in themselves and in the contributions they could make to the success of the organization. They would be unlikely to learn how to further develop their capabilities, both behavioral and technical. In short, they would not be doing the many things that would lead to an actualization of their abilities and talents.

This line of thinking suggests that the nature of the organization in which a person works encourages some types of behavior and inhibits others, which in turn have an important influence on the person's psychological health and personal development. While the focus has been primarily on organizations that have a negative impact on their members, analyses of the characteristics of these organizations have yielded a variety of suggestions regarding how organizations should be designed to provide positive experiences for their members. Evidence indicates that such organizational qualities can have beneficial results (e.g., Likert, 1967). At present, however, we know of no research that specifically links either behavior of people on the job with level of personal development or changes in such behavior with personal growth.[5]

A final relationship in Figure 2 that should be amplified is the mutual effect between organizational performance and personal development. The assumptions here are that these two outcomes affect each other, that over the long run one cannot improve without the other, and that if an organization has placed great emphasis on one and virtually ignored the other, neither will occur. The interdependence of the two is reflected in a recent observation by Mirvis (1988): "In OD of the 1960s, it was assumed that by developing people we could create healthier and more effective organizations. Today many advocate that we must develop organizations to create healthier and more effective people" (pp. 17–18). In a similar vein, Weisbord (1988) asserts that "dignity and meaning are the 'bottom line' of bottom lines. Without them, technology can't be fully utilized, or organizations run economically" (p. 63).

Summary

Four main categories of organizational characteristics have been identified and described. Together, they constitute the work environment for each organizational member. This environment provides information to individuals concerning their ability to engage in particular behaviors and/or about the likely consequences of those behaviors. Individuals then make choices regarding which behaviors they will enact based in large part on this information. To change individuals' behavior, those engaging in programs of planned change should identify the appropriate changes to be made, in as many factors as are necessary, to clarify to individuals the types of behavioral change that are desired. In so doing, the interrelationships among organizational components must be taken into account. First, a variety of components, in all four categories, must be considered when planning the actions to be taken. Also, it must be recognized that changing some factors will have implications regarding necessary changes in others. The goal of these strategies is to achieve consistency and congruency in the signals sent to individuals regarding desired behaviors. The organization's purpose, if clearly defined, can serve as an important guide to those decision makers designing the various organizational characteristics, enabling them to achieve a greater degree of consistency and congruency among these factors.

The process of intervening into organizational systems, creating changes in organizational components that will in turn result in changes in the work behaviors of organizational members, constitutes the primary activity of organizational development. However, individual behavioral change is not the ultimate goal of OD. According to the perspective presented here, change in individual behavior is necessary to effect change in organizational outcomes. Two such categories of outcomes, defined as the end focus of OD efforts, are organizational performance and individual development. The behavior of organizational members is a key determinant of both of these types of outcomes. Therefore, to improve either or both, it is necessary for individuals to engage in more effective behaviors. Furthermore, we feel that these two types of outcomes are related to each other. We believe that it is not possible, over the long term, to maintain high levels of one without correspondingly high levels of the other.

The organizational framework presented in this section is an attempt at developing a theoretical model that can (a) guide the practice of OD by specifying potential change levers and identifying the basic causal relationships between key types of organizational variables and (b) guide research by suggesting testable hypotheses regarding the dynamics of change that can subsequently be tested in the field. Obviously, there are many complexities regarding the dynamics of organizational change that are left unaddressed in this framework. However, we believe that, as a starting point, this framework provides a useful contribution to the field of OD since theory of this type is, unfortunately, relatively undeveloped in the field. To provide evidence regarding this assertion, we shall provide an overview and assessment of the body of OD theory in the next section.

Organizational Development Theroy

Bandura (1986) has noted that "theories are interpreted in different ways depending on the stage of development of the field of study. In advanced disciplines, theories integrate laws; in less advanced fields, theories specify the determinants and mechanisms governing the phenomena of interest" (p. xii). As noted earlier, organizational development is a field in its earlier stages of development. It contains theory in which the specification of a comprehensive set of determinants and mechanisms has proceeded at a rather uneven pace. This is due in part because of the character of the phenomena under study. Social systems with the complexity of organizations have been very difficult to model from a static perspective, much less a dynamic one. Also contributing to the slow development of the field's theory base is the nature of OD as an applied field. While OD practice continues to expand, research literature, and thus theory development, has not kept pace (Bullock & Tubbs, 1987).

Over the last decade and a half, the quality of theory in organizational development has been criticized for its inadequacy in capturing the rich dynamics of planned change processes (Burke, 1982; Friedlander & Brown, 1974; Golembiewski, 1979; Lundberg, 1978; Margulies & Raia, 1978). Sashkin and Burke (1987) recently acknowledged that "we find no real coherence among the various theoretical contributions of the 1980s that would lead us to think that the field of OD is approaching a theoretical synthesis" (p. 401).

One reason for this may be that considerable confusion exists about what is meant by the term *theory* in OD. OD theory has been described as a specification of the steps to be followed in an action-research-oriented investigation into an organization's processes (e.g., Frohman, Sashkin, & Kavanaugh, 1976), as a statement of the mechanisms underlying a particular intervention approach (e.g., Hackman & Oldham, 1975), as a delineation of the variables targeted for change (e.g., White & Mitchell, 1976), or as an explanation of the dynamics through which interventions impact the system's outputs (e.g., Lawler, 1982). While each of these categories alone is insufficient to encompass the variety of concepts that constitute the body of theory in the field, all of them do contribute to our theoretical understanding of OD. Therefore, it would be useful to be more precise in defining categories of theory. Our categorization, and a description of the current state of theory development in each of the categories, is provided in this section.[6]

OD theory has evolved as two general types of theories rather than one—namely, theories of change and theories of changing (Bennis, 1966). Recently, Porras and Robertson (1987) labeled these two types *change process* theories and *implementation* theories, respectively.

- *Change process theory* describes the underlying dynamics of the planned change process within an organization by specifying (a) the variables that can be manipulated by the OD intervention, (b) the outcomes intended by the change effort, (c) the variables that mediate the effects of manipulable variables on the outcomes, (d) the causal relationships between manipulable, mediator, and outcome variables, and (e) the relevant moderator variables that affect the causal relationships specified.

- *Implementation theory,* on the other hand, focuses on the actions undertaken by change practitioners when effecting planned change. It describes what must be done, and in what general order, to trigger changes in organizational variables. Ideally, it should draw its guidance from change process theory that describes the dynamics of the intervention activity. Yet implementation theory has largely been driven by micro (e.g., theories of small group behavior) rather than macro theories of social system change and by concepts derived from the actual practice of planned organizational change rather than

a priori assumptions drawn from research-based theories.

With this background, we first turn to a discussion of change process theory, followed by an analysis of implementation theory. Comments on the strengths and weaknesses of both types of OD theory will be incorporated throughout the discussion.

Change Process Theory

As noted, change process theory explains the dynamics through which a system is altered by a program of planned change. It does so by specifying key variable sets and the relationships that exist among them. The generalized change process model used to analyze this set of theories is shown in Figure 3.

Planned change processes begin with OD interventions that alter a set of manipulable, or independent, variables (I) of the system. Changes in these variables in turn produce changes in a second class of variables, the mediating variables (M_i). One group of mediating variables can alter a second group, which can alter a third, and so on until a set of outcomes, or dependent variables (D), is impacted. Any of the links among manipulable, mediating, and outcome variable sets may be affected by one or more groups of moderating variables (m_j).[7]

The Porras and Robertson (1987) review of the planned change literature identified seven theories that fit this category, namely those described by Cartwright (1951), Dalton (1970), Goodman and Dean (1982), House (1967), Lawler (1982), Miles, Hornstein, Callahan, Calder, and Schiavo (1969), and Nadler (1977).[8] These theories were selected because they most clearly specified variables in the categories just identified as well as relationships between these variables. Clearly, the number of OD theories attempting to

FIGURE 3

A Generalized Change Process Model

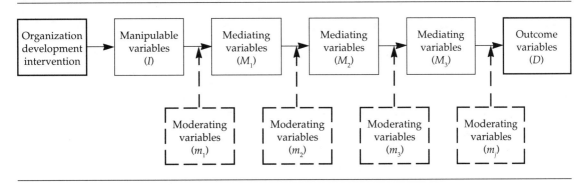

explicitly model the dynamics of change is rather small.[9]

In Figure 4, each theory is diagramed using the format given in Figure 3. The structural complexity of these theories ranges from relatively simple (e.g., Cartwright, 1951), with two mediating and one moderating variable sets, to fairly complex (Goodman & Dean, 1982; House, 1967), with four moderating and four or five mediating variable sets. Lawler (1982) presented a model with two unique sets of outcomes and, consequently, two separate causal chains leading from the intervention to the change outcomes. However, both of the chains in this theory were relatively simple, with two mediating variables proposed in one and only one in the other.

Range of Variables.   Table 3 shows the four variable categories—manipulable, mediator, moderator, and outcome—and the sets of variables included in each of the theories. The specific variables used in the theories have been classified into more general variable sets.

Manipulable Variables.   Three classes of manipulable variables have been included in OD theory: information, group characteristics, and organization design features. Information, the manipulable variable for five of the theories, is a broad and general construct. Moreover, it is not altogether clear that information can accurately be referred to as a variable, as the term is used here. It was designated as the manipulable variable when the impetus for change began with organizational members receiving, from one source or another, new information regarding particular aspects of the organization. However, according to the perspective of change presented earlier, new information can come to individuals as a result of a myriad of changes in organizational features. Therefore, an adequate change process theory needs to be much more precise in designating variables to be manipulated in the initial change intervention step.

Perhaps the weakest aspect of current change process theory is the paucity in the number of manipulable variables it defines as targets of intervention. Information is specified as the sole manipulable variable by most of the models. Clearly, available information is an important ingredient in all change efforts. However, OD models would be more useful if they first defined the organizational

FIGURE 4

Structural Complexity of OD Change Process Theory

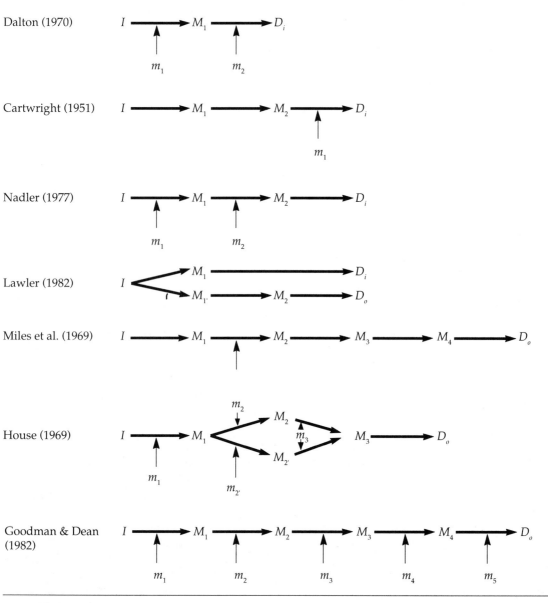

Dalton (1970)

Cartwright (1951)

Nadler (1977)

Lawler (1982)

Miles et al. (1969)

House (1969)

Goodman & Dean (1982)

I = Independent variables
M = Mediating variables
m = Moderating variables

D = Dependent variables
o = Organizational outcomes
i = Individual outcomes

TABLE 3

Variable Content of OD Change Process Theories

Variable Category	Variable	*Cartwright (1959)*	*Dalton (1970)*	*Goodman & Dean (1982)*	*House (1967)*	*Lawler (1982)*	*Miles et al. (1969)*	*Nadler (1977)*
Manipulable	Information		X	X	X		X	X
	Group characteristics	X						
	Organizational design features					X		
Mediator	Motivational factors	X				X	X	X
	Social influence factors	X		X			X	
	Individual attributes		X	X	X	X		
Moderator	Information generation and transmission	X	X	X	X		X	X
	Propensity to change		X	X	X			X
	Social influence	X		X	X			X
Outcome	Individual	X	X			X		X
	Organizational			X	X	X	X	

factors most important to manipulate, and then indicated the ways in which changes in these characteristics can differentially affect both information and other mediating variables in the causal chain. In this manner, the differences in operation of the causal change mechanisms could be hypothesized and empirically tested.

In this regard, Lawler (1982) is both the most specific and most comprehensive in laying out the variables initially affected by OD activities. He broadly labels them organizational design features and defines them as organizational structure, job design, information systems, career systems, selection and training policies, reward systems, personnel policies, and physical layout. More change process theories need to be similarly rich.

Mediator Variables. As shown in Table 3, the mediator variables linking manipulable variables to outcome variables can be clustered into three groups, namely motivational factors, social influence factors, and individual attributes. The first two groups of mediator variables focus primarily on the mechanisms through which various types of individual behaviors in the organization are unfrozen, changed, and refrozen (Lewin, 1951). The third emphasizes which behavior-related attributes of individuals must be changed.

Behaviors can be *unfrozen* in a variety of ways. Some examples of the mechanisms suggested are creating awareness and understanding of new behaviors (Goodman & Dean, 1982; House, 1967), disconfirming perceptions (Miles et al., 1969; Nadler, 1977), clarifying desired end states (Cartwright, 1951; Miles et al., 1969), or creating awareness of potential rewards through such methods as the use of performance-based rewards (Lawler, 1982), alteration of reward expectancies (Nadler, 1977), or exposure to rewarding success experiences (Miles et al., 1969).

Behaviors are *changed* through social influence processes such as pressures from a group to conform (Cartwright, 1951), developing a preference for and continuation of the new behavior (Goodman & Dean, 1982), or a combination of these two (Miles et al., 1969). New behaviors are *refrozen* when people's existence, social, and growth and control needs are met (Lawler, 1982), normative and value consensus occurs (Goodman & Dean, 1982), proposed changes are tested out (Dalton, 1970), or new change-supporting structures are implemented (Miles et al., 1969).

These factors comprise the motivational and social influence categories. Individual attributes constituted a third category of mediating variables. Important attributes identified are knowledge and attitudes (Goodman & Dean, 1982; House, 1967), technical skills (House, 1967; Lawler, 1982), and change-facilitating skills (Miles et al., 1969).

Moderator Variables. Moderator variables affect the relationship between any two sets of variables in the causal chain. The extent to which a moderator variable is present influences the nature of the causal relationship between two relevant manipulable, mediator, or outcome variables. The moderator variables proposed by this set of theories can also be divided into three groups. These are (a) characteristics of the information generation and transmission process, (b) individual propensity to change, and (c) social influence factors.

Since information was identified most often as the primary manipulable variable, the category of moderators specified most frequently as influencing the relationship between information and the first group of mediating variables focused on characteristics of the information generation and transmission process. Factors such as the perceived accuracy of diagnostic data fed back to the organization (Nadler, 1977), relevancy of information (Goodman & Dean, 1982), authority and prestige of individual(s) presenting data (Cartwright, 1951; Dalton, 1970), collaborative nature of the data collection process (Miles et al., 1969), and data discussion opportunities (House, 1967) were specified as key moderating variables.

Variables relevant to a person's propensity to change were also frequently specified as moderating variables. Factors influencing a person's ability to change (Goodman & Dean, 1982; House, 1967; Nadler, 1977) and desire to change (Dalton, 1970; Goodman & Dean, 1982; House, 1967; Nadler, 1977), as well as rewards for changing (Goodman & Dean, 1982; House, 1967; Nadler, 1977), were included in this category.

Finally, social influence factors were also specified in four of the theories as key moderating variables. Psychological safety (Nadler, 1977), social support (Dalton, 1970), top management philosophy and practices (House, 1967), group characteristics (Cartwright, 1951), and communication and persuasion (Goodman & Dean, 1982) were some of the social influence variables specified as moderating various relationships in the causal process. In two of these theoretical perspectives (Cartwright, 1951; Goodman & Dean,

1982), social influence factors were identified as both mediating *and* moderating variables.

In contrast to the limited range of manipulable variables, the theories reviewed proposed a relatively wide array of both mediator and moderator variables. Yet within each of these two classes of change variables, nearly all the variables specified could be placed into one of three categories, reflecting some degree of agreement on the general nature of the variables most likely to be consequential in planned change processes.

An additional aspect of the mediator and moderator variable sets defined by these theories is noteworthy. Substantial overlap exists between variables classified as mediators and those identified as moderators. For example, both classes contain social influence variables as one of the three categories specified, even though the actual variables constituting each are not identical. System norms, liking one's involvement in the system, and degree of system support for change were all factors included as both mediators and moderators. Also, motivational factors, such as performance-reward relationships, expectations regarding how changes will affect rewards, change motivation, perception of a need for change, and goal-setting effects, were mentioned as both mediators and moderators. One implication of this overlap is that while there is some agreement on the nature of the variables central to any OD process, confusion exists over how the causal mechanisms operate.

Outcome Variables.   These variables describe the ultimate targets of the OD process. Change targets prescribed by the theories clustered around two levels, the individual and the organization. Three theories focused on the individual. Cartwright (1951) specified individual behavioral and cognitive change as the target of planned change processes.

Dalton (1970), although pointing out that organizational change is the ultimate goal, focused on behaviors and attitudes as the immediate targets of change efforts. He proposed that organizational change occurs when the behavioral patterns of a large part of the organization's members are altered. Similarly, while Nadler (1977) prescribed behavioral change of individuals, groups, and the organization as the desired end result, he did not define the latter two in terms other than the aggregated change in behavior of all the organization's members.

For the remaining theories, the organization is the ultimate change target. Goodman and Dean (1982) describe individual behavioral change as a mediating variable for organization-level change. In contrast to Nadler (1977), they attempt to theoretically explain how individual behavior is institutionalized into organizational change. Behavior is institutionalized when it persists over time, two or more individuals perform it in response to a common stimulus, and it exists as a social fact (Goodman, Bazerman, & Conlon, 1980). Outcome variables other than behavior are prescribed by House (1967), who targets organizational performance; by Miles et al. (1969), who focus on organizational health; and by Lawler (1982), who emphasizes both organizational performance and quality of work life.

The outcome variables specified by the theories thus tend to focus on individual behavior or organizational performance. None targets individual psychological health, self-realization/self-actualization, or personal growth and development as one of the outcomes of OD. Lawler (1982) is perhaps the closest to focusing on this outcome as a variable of interest. He does include in his model the quality of work life of the individual member, which he specifies is a function of meeting people's existence, social, and *growth* (emphasis added) and control needs. Otherwise, however, this important outcome is left unaddressed by these theorists.

Overview of Change Process Theory. In general, the structure of these models was not overly complex. They tended to contain only two sets of mediating variables and two sets of moderating variables. Except for the Lawler (1982) and House (1967) models, all were linear and began with changes in one set of manipulable variables leading to changes in various sequential sets of mediating variables until a single set of outcome variables was affected. Each particular set of moderating variables was hypothesized to have an impact on one of the proposed causal links.

While none of the theories are particularly complex, variance does exist in the degree of specification of variables and interrelationships. Dalton (1970), for example, specifies one mediator and six moderator variables, while Miles et al. (1969) describe fifteen mediator variables clustered in four stages, and House (1967) identifies 21 variables moderating four causal links. The variance in the complexity of these OD theories therefore points to an inadequate understanding of planned change dynamics.

The generalizability of the theories is another dimension along which they can be evaluated. Most of the theories are limited in the degree to which they are generalizable because their underlying guiding framework is rooted in one particular intervention strategy. These include group-based interventions (Cartwright, 1951), management development interventions (House, 1967), increased worker involvement (Lawler, 1982), and the survey feedback approach (Miles et al., 1969; Nadler, 1977). Only two theories attempt to explain the change process without linking it to any particular intervention strategy (Dalton, 1970; Goodman & Dean, 1982).

A final characteristic of these theories is that they do not appear to build on each other. Arranging them in chronological order yields no indication of any evolution toward a more global and parsimonious change process theory. Part of the reason for this might be related to their close association with a particular intervention approach. But it may also be driven by the absence of any shared view of their more fundamental theoretical underpinnings. For instance, a theory of change dynamics will of necessity have to incorporate elements of motivation theory. If we assess the theories reviewed here, it is quickly apparent that various motivation theories are represented in them. Expectancy theory is the most prominent, but traces of need theory and theories of goal setting can be found as well. Agreement on the most useful underlying concepts is necessary before OD theorists can build on each other's work and develop a parsimonious and robust theory of planned organizational change processes.

Implementation Theory

Implementation theory is applied theory and as such guides practitioners by prescribing the sets of actions needed for effective intervention. The Porras and Robertson (1987) review of the OD theory literature yielded three categories of implementation theory, each corresponding to a different level of specificity. The most general theories are labeled strategy theories, followed by what we refer to as procedure theories, with technique theories being the most specific type of implementation theory.

Strategy Theories. This type of implementation theory is at the most general level of specification and describes the broad strategies that can be used to change human systems. For example, one set of approaches emphasizes the role of power in the implementation of change (Bennis, 1966; Chin & Benne, 1969; Greiner, 1967). A second focuses on the broad organizational factors targeted for change (Hornstein, Bunker, Burke, Gindes, & Lewicki, 1971; Margulies & Raia, 1978). A third prescribes targeting the individual's cognitive mechanisms as the key method for bringing

TABLE 4

Procedure-oriented OD Implementation Theories

Authors	Year of Study
Lippitt, Watson, & Westley	1958
Likert	1967
Blake & Mouton	1968
Beckhard	1969
Lawrence & Lorsch	1969
Argyris	1970
Bowers & Franklin	1972
Bowers, Franklin, & Pecorella	1975
Beckhard & Harris	1977
Cummings & Srivastva	1977
French & Bell	1978
Margulies & Raia	1978
Beer	1980
Nadler	1981
Burke	1982
Tichy	1983

about alterations in behaviors (Chin & Benne, 1969; Walton, 1965).

In each case, the focus is on a broad strategy for implementing change. These strategic approaches, as Margulies and Raia (1978) point out, are "descriptive methods for categorizing either approaches to change or in some global sense methods for bringing about change.... (They) do not appear to adequately provide a functional model for implementing and directing change in organizations" (pp. 44–45). However, they do circumscribe to some extent the different activities that change agents might use to bring about change. For example, a specific intervention action might be consistent with a particular strategy while another would not. In this manner, they do provide some guidance for change activity, albeit the direction provided is quite general.

Procedure Theories. A higher level of specificity in prescribing change actions is provided by this second category of implementation theory. Procedure theories include descriptions of the major steps that must be taken in executing a complete change process. As a consequence, these theories are more specific than strategy theories because they outline the actual procedures that should be carried out and, in some cases, provide recommendations on how best to implement them. In this way, procedure theories conform most closely to what we mean by implementation theory, and thus our discussion of them goes into somewhat greater detail than do our discussions of the other two categories of implementation theory.

To discuss procedure theory, we will present an overview of the information found in 16 representative theories (listed in Table 4) pertaining to the five following categories: (a) prescribed intervention steps, (b) diagnostic variables identified, (c) criteria for choosing which specific intervention to use, (d) conditions for effective change, and (e) characteristics of effective change agents.

Intervention Steps. A consolidated list of the various steps proposed by each of the 16 procedure theories was created as a means for analyzing the degree of agreement existing in the field. A total of 11 steps in a complete OD process were identified. Table 5 indicates which of these steps were included in each of the 16 theories.

Table 6 indicates the frequency with which each of the steps was included in the theories, the percentage of the theories that included each step, and the ranking of each step in terms of its frequency. It is clear that diagnosis, planning, action/intervention, and monitoring and evaluation are the phases of the OD implementation process most frequently recognized in these theories. This finding appears quite reasonable since these would be part of any

TABLE 5

Intervention Steps Contained in Procedure-oriented OD Implementation Theories

Stages in Implementation Procedure	Lippitt, Watson, & Westley (1958)	Likert (1967)	Blake & Mouton (1968)	Beckhard (1969)	Lawrence & Lorsch (1969)	Argyris (1970)	Bowers & Franklin (1972)	Bowers, Franklin, & Pecorella (1975)	Beckhard & Harris (1977)	Cummings & Srivastva (1977)	French & Bell (1978)	Margulies & Raia (1978)	Beer (1980)	Nadler (1981)	Burke (1982)	Tichy (1983)
Client selection										X			X			
Entry													X		X	
Contracting	X									X		X	X		X	
Formulation of an ideal model			X				X									
Diagnosis	X	X		X	X	X	X	X	X	X	X	X	X	X	X	X
Designing alternatives										X			X			X
Goal selection	X					X	X			X	X					
Planning			X	X	X					X			X	X	X	X
Action/intervention	X	X	X	X	X	X	X	X	X	X	X	X	X	X	X	X
Monitoring and evaluation			X	X	X		X			X	X	X	X		X	X
Institutionalization/stabilization	X									X	X		X			

From "Organizational Development Theory: A Typology and Evaluation" by J. I. Porras and P. J. Robertson, 1987. In R. W. Woodman and W. A. Pasmore (Eds.), *Research in Organizational Changes and Development*, Greenwich, CT: JAI Press. Copyright 1987 by JAI Press. Reprinted by permission.

rationally designed change process. It is interesting to note, however, that only one of these steps was described by all the theories. One might have expected that since, for instance, diagnosis, planning, and action/intervention are the logical steps to take when trying to change an organization in a planned manner, all the theories would have contained them.

It is possible that this finding may simply be a problem of semantics since some of the adjacent categories in the table have more or less the same meaning. For example, designing alternatives might be considered synonymous with planning. To explore this possibility, seemingly synonymous categories were combined into entry, diagnosis, planning, intervention, and monitoring stages. The three columns at the right of the table contain the data regarding the condensed categories. Even under these conditions, however,

TABLE 6

**Patterns of Steps Prescribed by
Procedure-oriented OD Implementation Theories**

Steps in Implementation Process	Full Model			Condensed Model		
	N	*Percent*	*Rank*	*N*	*Percent*	*Rank*
1. Client selection	2	12.5	9			
2. Entry	2	12.5	9	4	25.0	5
3. Contracting	5	31.3	5			
4. Formation of ideal model	2	12.5	9	16	100.0	1
5. Diagnosis	15	93.8	2			
6. Designing alternatives	3	18.8	8			
7. Goal selection	5	31.3	5	12	75.0	3
8. Planning	8	50.0	4			
9. Action/intervention	16	100.0	1	16	100.0	1
10. Monitoring and evaluation	10	62.5	3	11	68.8	4
11. Institutionalization/stabilization	4	25.0	7			

Note: *N* = number of theories including each step in the implementation process

only diagnosis and action/intervention are specified 100 percent of the time.

Tables 5 and 6 yield other observations regarding the amount of agreement as to which steps are important in the OD process. First, only 4 of the 16 theories reviewed included one half or more of the steps (Beckhard & Harris, 1977; Beer, 1980; Burke, 1982; Cummings & Srivastva, 1977). The theories included an average of 4 of the 11 steps, and the number included in any one particular theory ranged from 3 (Argyris, 1970; Bowers, Franklin, & Pecorella, 1975; Likert, 1967) to 9 (Beer, 1980). Client selection, entry, and formulation of an ideal model were the least frequently mentioned (2 times), while diagnosis was the most frequently included (15 times).

In sum, although there is reasonable agreement around the core of the intervention process, much less agreement exists about other less fundamental but nevertheless important steps in the process.

Diagnostic Variables. A second area of interest concerns the variables specified as critical to diagnosing an organization. Since the 16 theories yielded a rather diverse set of diagnostic variables, they were classified as one of the eight types of variables that comprise the

TABLE 7

Frequencies of Diagnostic Variables in
Procedure-oriented OD Implementation Theories

Diagnostic Variable	N	Percent	Rank
Environment	6	37.5	4
Vision	1	6.3	7
Organizing arrangements	15	93.8	1
Social factors	15	93.8	1
Technology	9	56.3	3
Physical setting	1	6.3	7
Individual behavior	2	12.5	6
Outcomes	4	25.0	5

Note: N = number of theories that included each diagnostic variable

organizational framework presented in the previous section. These eight variables are (a) the external environment of the organization, (b) the organization's vision, (c) organizing arrangements, (d) social factors, (e) technology, (f) physical setting, (g) individual behavior, and (h) outcomes in relation to both organizational performance and individual development.

Table 7 summarizes the diagnostic variables included in the 16 procedure theories reviewed. Organizing arrangements and social factors variables were the most common targets of diagnostic activities, with each included in 94 percent of the implementation theories surveyed, while technology was third with 56 percent. These three variable sets were the only ones to appear in over half of the 16 theories and seem to comprise the core diagnostic variables of OD. The remaining variable sets (environment, vision, physical setting, individual behavior, and outcomes) were included in substantially less than half of the perspectives, with vision (purpose) and

physical setting each part of only one diagnostic model (Tichy, 1983, and Bowers et al., 1975, respectively).

Of particular interest in these findings is the fact that outcomes were included in only 4 of the 16 theories (Beer, 1980; Likert, 1967; Nadler, 1981; Tichy, 1983). This may indicate the degree to which OD emphasizes process over outcomes. An implicit assumption in many views has been that improvements in organizational processes will automatically lead to improvements in system outcomes. The content of the field's diagnostic models is consistent with this perspective.[10]

Only 8 of the 16 theories included 4 or more of the variable sets, with the average 3 and the median 4. One approach did not include any (Bowers et al., 1975), while Tichy (1983) included 6, which was the most included by any of the theories. It appears, then, that substantial diversity exists in the field over what constitutes an important set of diagnostic variables.

Although Table 7 indicates that there has not been a high degree of agreement about key diagnostic variables in OD, the raw data from which the table was derived show an even greater disparity. Furthermore, when assessing the evolution of OD diagnostic models over time, there is little evidence that a coalescence around a common set of variables is occurring. When contrasting the pre- to post-1970s time periods, there is also no evidence of any expansion in diagnostic variable sets. Variables proposed in the later period are not much more varied than those emphasized in the earlier period. In sum, there has been neither a narrowing of focus on a few key variable sets nor a proliferation of new variables to consider in diagnosing organizational systems. Instead, there seems to be stagnation in the evolution of our understanding of the most fundamental factors to assess prior to implementing planned change interventions.

Intervention Selection.   Ten of the 16 theories suggested criteria for choosing which particular intervention to implement once a diagnosis has been made. Collectively, these criteria suggest that the decision regarding which intervention to use may involve a two-stage process. In the first stage, delineation of an appropriate set of interventions occurs by assessing the general problem areas, defined in terms of either the gap between actual and desired organizational states or a lack of congruency among relevant organizational characteristics. In the second stage, selection of the specific interventions to use is based on readiness of the target system, available leverage points for change, and skill of the change agent.

Gaps between states are determined by initially pinpointing the particular organizational variables that require attention, determining their present state, identifying their desired future state, and assessing the gaps between actual and desired. The variables upon which attention is focused are the strategic change levers in the organization (Tichy, 1983) or the set of change precursors (Bowers et al., 1975).

After assessing the present state of these factors, the next step is to develop an ideal model (Blake & Mouton, 1968), a desired end state (Bowers et al., 1975), or the change goals and objectives (French & Bell, 1978; Margulies & Raia, 1978). Identification of these desired futures provides the basis for assessing the gaps between the actual and desired end states and determining which intervention sets are most appropriate to implement.

An alternative approach to the identification of an appropriate intervention set focuses on the congruence among various key factors (e.g., external environment, formal structure, reward systems, culture, job design, and individual needs) in the organization. This view is based on the assumption that effective organizational functioning occurs when these factors are consistent with each other. Thus, intervention sets are selected based on their ability to develop congruence between factors such as environmental demands and organizational characteristics, or between organizational needs and individual needs (Lawrence & Lorsch, 1969), or between any of the organizational components listed earlier (Beer, 1980; Nadler, 1981).

Once an appropriate set of interventions is identified, the second stage in the process is to choose the particular interventions needed. The readiness of the target system for a particular intervention is of primary importance. Each intervention must be assessed in light of such factors as the availability of key organizational members to be involved in the change process (Argyris, 1970; Margulies & Raia, 1978), available resources in the system to support a particular change activity (Burke, 1982; French & Bell, 1978), consistency of the intervention with the current organizational culture and management philosophy (Margulies & Raia, 1978), health of the organization (Argyris, 1970), degree of intervention depth the organization can tolerate (Tichy, 1983), and the organization's experience with self-assessment (Margulies & Raia, 1978).

The selection of a particular intervention is also influenced by the identification of the leverage points for change—that is, those aspects of the organization that are (a) both amenable to change and concretely linked to the change objectives (Lippitt, Watson, & Westley, 1958a), (b) the power points in the organization (Burke, 1982), or (c) the causal rather than intervening variables in the organization's processes (Likert, 1967). Decisions on specifically where and how to intervene and on the sequencing of intervention activity are guided by a knowledge of these leverage points.

Finally, the selection of a specific intervention activity should be based on the competence (Argyris, 1970) and orientation (Margulies & Raia, 1978) of the change agent and on his or her understanding of intervention possibilities (Tichy, 1983). Change agents must know their capabilities and limitations and should carry out interventions that match their skills. This would imply that additional resources would often need to be brought into a change project to implement necessary activity that was beyond the ability of the change agents currently working with the system.

In summary, while the specific criteria for selecting interventions specified by these theories initially appears diverse, it is possible to group them into five categories that correspond to a two-stage process for the selection of interventions. These five categories of criteria can potentially serve as a useful guide to change agents for choosing the interventions they will use in their attempts to improve an organization. To the extent that they can lead change agents to more thoughtfully choose the interventions they will use, these criteria are an important strength of the procedure theories.

Conditions for Effective Change. In the 11 procedure theories specifying conditions crucial for successful organizational development, the most commonly mentioned factor focused on the degree and quality of organizational member involvement in the change process. Top management leadership (Beckhard, 1969) or support (French & Bell, 1978; Lawrence & Lorsch, 1969), lower level employee involvement (Cummings & Srivastva, 1977), or commitment and involvement of the entire target system (Argyris, 1970; Blake & Mouton, 1968) were all considered central to any effective change process. The key theme in all these perspectives is that the organization's members must be the key sources of energy for the change process, not the external change agent or consultant. To the degree that this happens, the effectiveness of the change process will be enhanced.

The second most commonly mentioned factor was the necessity for key members of the target system to recognize the need for change or to be attracted by the positive nature of an improved situation. For the former, this could be situations such as a dissatisfaction with the status quo (Beer, 1980), an awareness that important organizational problems exist (French & Bell, 1978), a high degree of personal or system discomfort (Argyris, 1970), or environmental pressure for change (Beckhard, 1969). For the latter, it could simply be the desire to be more effective, even though the current level might be relatively satisfactory.

A third factor is also based primarily on the attitudes and behaviors of key organizational members. Willingness to deviate from existing norms (Argyris, 1970) and to take risks (Beckhard, 1969), alteration of binding operating procedures (Likert, 1967), and creation of an open, experimental, risk-taking, and high trust climate (Cummings & Srivastva, 1977) are all considered important preconditions for the success of OD efforts.

While these three categories of conditions for effective change were each identified in a few of the theories, a wide diversity of factors were delineated with not a substantial degree of agreement among the theorists as to which are most important. This suggests that adequate systematic knowledge regarding the factors that facilitate or inhibit the change process has yet to be obtained.

Characteristics of Effective Change Agents. In the 12 theories that specified important change agent qualities, four main sets of characteristics were most commonly mentioned. The first included various aspects of interpersonal competence (Lawrence & Lorsch, 1969) such as relational skills (Lippitt et al., 1958a), ability to support and nurture others (Burke, 1982), listening and empathy (Margulies & Raia, 1978), group process facilitation (Bowers & Franklin, 1972), awareness and sensitivity (Margulies & Raia, 1978), and ability to influence others (Burke, 1982).[11] The second related to theory-based problem-solving capabilities. Examples of these include knowledge of theory and methods of change (Lippitt et al., 1958a), the ability to link this knowledge with organizational realities (Bowers & Franklin, 1972), the ability to conceptualize (Burke, 1982) and diagnose (Lawrence & Lorsch, 1969), and the ability to present a range of options to the client system (French & Bell, 1978).

The third set of characteristics prescribes the change agent's role as educator (Lawrence & Lorsch, 1969), one who needs to be able to create learning experiences (Burke, 1982), who can invest the environment with growth experiences (Argyris, 1970), and who can accomplish this by modeling discrepant behavior (Beer, 1980) and developing effective behavior in others (French & Bell, 1978). The final set of effective change agent characteristics focuses on self-awareness, namely awareness of one's own assumptions and models (Beer, 1980), the ability to quickly recognize one's own feelings and intuitions (Burke, 1982), and the ability to have a clear understanding of one's own needs and motivations (Lippitt et al., 1958a).

As with the conditions for effective change, there was marginal agreement concerning four categories of characteristics important for change agents to be effective. Again, however, the diversity that exists beyond these four categories is greater than the similarity apparent in these theories. No individual could hope to develop the vast array of qualities suggested in these theories. Weisbord (1988) warns of the problems that may result from specifying too many qualities and skills necessary for change agents, namely "fragmentation, alienation from knowledge, feelings of hopelessness in the face of complexity, a sense that I'll never know enough to be able to cope" (p. 94). Thus, it would be useful to begin to identify the most important of these characteristics. This would enable individuals interested in becoming change agents to better assess their capabilities and thus their likelihood of success, and it would provide guidance regarding the training and career development of those already in the field.

Finally, of critical importance to the field is a theoretical understanding of the interactive effects of the particular problems being addressed in a change program, the conditions present within the situation and the change process, and the characteristics of the change agent. Better specification both of the conditions for effective change and of the characteristics of effective change agents is necessary to develop a more comprehensive understanding of how these various factors affect each other during the course of a complex process of planned organizational change.

Technique Theories. This group of theories, the final and most specific category of implementation theory, consists of perspectives that focus primarily on one of the core steps identified in procedure theory. The four types of technique theories are (a) diagnostic theories, (b) planning theories, (c) micro-intervention theories, and (d) evaluation theories. Most of the theories in this category are either diagnostic or micro-intervention theories, with the other two types existing in smaller numbers.

Diagnostic Theories. Diagnostic theories present models that can be used to diagnose organizational functioning. Diagnostic models proposed by Beer (1980), Kotter (1978), Nadler and Tushman (1977), and Weisbord (1976) appear to be some of the more comprehensive in the OD literature. Table 8 presents a comparison of the diagnostic variables contained in each of these models. The table is set up with the components of the organizational model as the basic framework around which the diagnostic variables of the other models are organized.

As with the procedure theories discussed earlier, the most commonly agreed-upon variables in all the diagnostic models were the environment, organizing arrangements, social factors, and technology. Only Weisbord (1976) included vision (purpose), and none of the models included the physical setting. Individual behavior/cognition and the two types of outcomes were all mentioned in at least three theories. In general, these models display a reasonable level of consistency on a broader array of diagnostic factors than were included in the procedure theories. The latter could therefore benefit by integrating more fully these diagnostic models into their frameworks.

These models also stress the fact that important organizational variables are all interrelated. Kotter (1978) points out that, in the short run, the primary interrelationships are the impact of structural elements on organizational processes and vice versa. Over a longer time period, however, he indicates that relationships between structural elements are key, with organizational effectiveness depending on the degree to which they are aligned. Nadler and Tushman (1977) likewise point out that incongruence between the four interactive components they specify will result in less than optimal organizational and individual performance. Beer (1980) acknowledges that any of the eight primary components of organizational

systems he identifies can affect any other part, indicating also that congruence between them is important for organizational effectiveness.

A recent diagnostic model by Bernstein and Burke (1989) focuses not on the relationships between organizational variables themselves, but on members' beliefs about these variables and the relationships between them, as well as the relationships between the beliefs of various organizational subgroups. Their model focuses on beliefs about variables that have been identified through previous research as correlates or causes of individual behavior and organizational performance. These are the external environment, mission and strategy, leadership, organization culture, structure, management practices, formal policies and procedures, task requirements, work unit climate, and individual needs and values. Bernstein and Burke argue that "understanding the distinction between the organizational system itself and the beliefs about the organizational system is absolutely basic for OD practitioners and their clients" (p. 118). They view OD methods as designed to facilitate changes in beliefs that will in turn lead to individual and organizational improvement. This perspective is congruent with the framework we presented in the previous section.

Planning Theories. Although planning is a key part of most OD intervention procedures, the field contains relatively few planning theories. The more prominent ones—open systems planning (Jayaram, 1976), open systems redesign (Krone, 1975), and stream analysis (Porras, 1987)—draw their basic concepts from open systems theory. Open systems planning and open systems redesign are heavily oriented toward developing a clear perspective of desired future states and establishing plans to attain them. Stream analysis emphasizes the interconnections among actions and arrays plans in a PERT chart format.

TABLE 8

Content of Diagnostic OD Implementation Theories

Organizational Dimension	Beer (1980)	Kotter (1978)	Nadler & Tushman (1977)	Weisbord (1976)
Environment	Environment (social, market, technological)	Environment	Environment (resources and history)	Environment
Vision				Purpose
Organizing arrangements	Structures	Formal organizational arrangements	Formal organizational arrangements	Structure
		Key organizing processes	Strategy	Rewards
Social factors	People/culture	Social system	Informal organization	Relationships
	Dominant coalition	Dominant coalition		Leadership
	Processes	Key processes		Helpful mechanisms
Technology		Technology	Task	
		Key processes		
Physical setting				
Individual cognitions		People	Employees	
Individual behavior	Behavior	Behavior		
Outcomes— organizational	QWL and economic outcomes	QWL and economic outcomes	Organizational outputs	
Outcomes— individual	Human outcomes	Human outputs	Individual and group outputs	

Each of these approaches recognizes the fact that planned change is organic—that it grows in such a manner that actions at any point in time are based on the success or failure of any previous action. Change often involves an uncertain implementation process requiring considerable experimentation, and adjustments are frequently necessary in light of new information and unanticipated consequences (cf. Cummings & Mohrman, 1987). Therefore, plans cannot be created to cover excessively long time periods. Broad, more general plans can be long-term, but specific action plans must cover shorter time periods. This reality of planned organizational change processes is perhaps one reason that few planning models have been developed for the field.

Micro-intervention Theories. Micro-intervention theories guide the implementation of specific interventions. These theories define most of OD practice and as such will be described in detail in the next section of this chapter. Suffice it to say here that this rather large group of theories, which describe concrete intervention techniques, are all minitheories that focus on a relatively small and circumscribed part of an overall planned change process.

Evaluation Theories. In the last 15 years, an important theoretical approach to the evaluation of organizational change has been developed. Golembiewski, Billingsley, and Yeager (1976) identified three types of change that might occur in a planned change effort. Labeled alpha, beta, and gamma change, they correspond to behavioral change, scale recalibration, and concept redefinition, respectively. These types of change were defined by Golembiewski et al. as follows:

> *Alpha change* involves a variation in the level of some existential state, given a constantly calibrated measuring instrument related to a constant conceptual domain. (p. 134)

Alpha change occurs when reality has changed and that shift is accurately represented in the survey instruments used to measure it. The scale dimensions remain constant and, after a change process, there is no shift in the mapping of a particular reality to a particular point on a rating scale.

> *Beta change* involves a variation in the level of some existential state, complicated by the fact that some intervals of the measurement continuum associated with a constant conceptual domain have been recalibrated. (p. 135)

Beta change occurs when not only reality has changed, but the scaling properties of the measurement instruments become stretched or contracted as well and as a consequence do not accurately reflect the degree of change obtained. For example, a response of 3 on a pretest measuring the level of trust in a group might be scaled a 4 on the posttest measure after a team-building intervention. The instrument would indicate that the level of trust had improved (a shift from 3 to 4). However, the change process may also have stretched the scale, such that the same level of trust that was rated a 4 after the team-building exercise would have been rated a 5 had the respondent not experienced the recalibration of the scale. Under these circumstances, the level of trust actually improved more than it appeared because of the concurrent recalibration of the scale. The reverse can also occur in that the responses on the pretest and posttest measures may be very different, yet the reality has changed only marginally. In this case, the scale has contracted, and the shift in the respondent's perception of reality leads him or her to give responses indicating that more change has occurred than actually has.

> *Gamma change* involves a redefinition or reconceptualization of some domain, a major change in the

perspective or frame-of-reference within which phenomena are perceived and classified, in what is taken to be relevant in some slice of reality. (p. 135)

Gamma change is the most complex type of all. It occurs when participants in a change process totally reconceptualize a phenomenon, rendering meaningless the scales used to measure it. So, for example, if a variable such as superior-subordinate relationships was being measured, the way a respondent might conceptualize this construct on an *after* measure could change, making the meaning of his or her responses on the scales used to measure it different than the *meaning* attached to the same scales on the before measure.

The evaluation problems posed by the presence of beta and gamma change result from the use of "soft" (i.e., behavioral) criteria for evaluating organizational change, measured through survey research methods. It is when organizational members' perceptions are used to assess such factors as communication, decision-making processes, and control processes that scale recalibration and concept redefinition can occur. The presence of beta and gamma change make it difficult to determine the extent to which survey data actually assess change in the organizational system. Therefore, a number of methodologies have been proposed for identifying the presence of and distinguishing between alpha, beta, and gamma change.

Armenakis (1988) recently reviewed the evaluation literature for the various procedures that have been used. He differentiates between statistical and design approaches. Statistical approaches rely on a comparison of factor structures or covariance structures at different measurement periods. A comparison of factor structures uses the transformation method (Ahmavaara, 1954; Golembiewski et al., 1976), which involves factor-analyzing responses to a pretest and posttest survey and comparing the resulting factor structures. Alternatively, the coefficients of congruence method (Armenakis, Feild, & Wilmoth, 1977; Armenakis & Smith, 1978) could be used. An analysis of covariance structures through LISREL V (Jöreskog & Sörbom, 1981), proposed by Schmitt (1982), tests the homogeneity of the variance-covariance structures across time. Unfortunately, while these three methods are similar to each other, the degree of convergent validity among them is questionable; different mathematical computations can yield different conclusions (Armenakis, Randolph, & Bedeian, 1982).

Design approaches have utilized the retrospective procedure (Terborg, Howard, & Maxwell, 1980), the ideal scale approach (Armenakis & Zmud, 1979; Zmud & Armenakis, 1978), or the criterion approach (van de Vliert, Huismans, & Stok, 1985). Using the retrospective procedure, respondents are asked at the posttest to reassess their earlier pretest perceptions. If the reassessments are different than the original pretest assessment, then respondents have changed their measurement scales. In the ideal scale approach, respondents are asked to assess the actual state and the ideal state at both the pretest and posttest measurements. Comparisons of changes in actual scores, ideal scores, and difference scores (between actual and ideal) provide evidence regarding scale recalibration. Finally, the criterion approach uses pretest and posttest measures of the target variable of the change program and a variable that will signal scale recalibration. Dynamic correlations between changes in these two variables provide evidence regarding beta change.

Strengths and weaknesses exist in each of these methods, and the merits of the various approaches have been debated in the OD evaluation literature. Armenakis (1988) reviews the empirical tests of these approaches, but no firm conclusions can be drawn yet regarding their relative efficacy. Until more compelling evidence is available, the best strategy may be to rely on the use of multiple methods—interviews, observation, and archival records, in addition to surveys—as a means of minimizing the errors resulting from unintended scale recalibration and concept redefinition.

Summary

Two types of theory in OD have been identified: change process theory and implementation theory. The former is a theory of change and the latter a theory of changing. At present, implementation theory is the better developed of the two, as change process theory is quite fragmented and underspecified. Change process theory most urgently needs a conceptual framework of organizations from which to begin specifying the dynamics of change that would unfold as a consequence of OD activities. It is a major weakness of the field that, as a group, the theories supposed to define the dynamics of the planned change process are so vague.

The most severe weakness in both types of theory is that they are based on uncertain or unspecified models of organizations. In other words, in all cases we found, the model of organization upon which the theory was based was not clearly specified. Therefore, it appears that theories are being developed without an explicit understanding or awareness of the fundamental theoretical base from which the theories are derived.

Both types of theory are needed because the field is an applied one and must bridge the gap from theory to action. Each type should draw from as well as feed the other. A synergistic relationship between these two types of OD theory would do much to enhance the field. Woodman (1989b) argues that the goal should not be a grand, unified theory of organizational change. "There is no shortage of theories and models of change and changing," he says.

What is needed is more comprehensive frameworks, categorization schemes, or models that will allow us to make sense of the theory and knowledge that already exists. Or, put another way, we have plenty of theories; what the field needs is more theorists—or at least, more effort by theorists to integrate existing knowledge. (p. 211)

From a research point of view, the theory base in OD needs to be sufficiently defined so as to guide research activity. From a practice point of view, the theories should be rich and robust enough to comprehensively specify which variables might be targeted for diagnosis and action. The current theory base and the present mode of theory development are not likely to facilitate more effective practice. "The more complicated and diverse the models, technologies, and typologies of OD become, the more fragmented, uneven, and confusing is the practice" (Weisbord, 1988, p. 94). In fact, instead of theory guiding practice, it could be that "practice leads theory and that the OD movement is lagging developments in client organizations and the community of practice" (Mirvis, 1988, p. 36). With this in mind, we turn to a discussion of organizational development practice.

Organizational Development Practice

While organizational development theory remains rather underdeveloped, the field does not suffer from a lack of techniques available to change agents in their attempts to improve organizational functioning.[12] Table 9 shows the major OD change techniques classified according to the target or recipient each most closely affects—that is, the individual, interpersonal, group, intergroup, or overall organization. It also cross-classifies OD technology according to the category of organizational characteristics

TABLE 9

Classification of OD Interventions by Organizational Unit of Analysis and System Variable Impacted

System Variable Impacted

	Organizing Arrangements	Social Factors	Technology	Physical Setting
Individual	Diagnostic task force Employee stock ownership plans Employee ownership Flexible benefits programs Flexible working hours Goal setting MBO Open job posting Pay systems design Performance appraisal design Recruitment and selection Scanlon plan	Assessment centers Career planning Behavioral education and training Grid OD—Phase I Life planning Modeling-based training Personal consulting Personal coaching Responsibility charting Sensitivity training Stress management T-groups Transactional analysis	Job design Technical education and training	Space design
Interpersonal	Job expectations technique Role analysis technique Role negotiation	Job expectations technique Role analysis technique Role negotiation Third-party consultation	Job expectation technique Role analysis technique Role negotiation	Space design
Group	Quality circles	Family group diagnostic meeting Gestalt team building Goal confrontation meetings Goal-setting group development Grid OD—Phase II Management diagnostic meeting Process consultation Sensing meetings Tavistock conference Team building	Autonomous work groups Self-managing work groups Self-regulating work groups	Space design
Intergroup	Contingency organizational design	Grid OD—Phase III Intergroup conflict resolution Intergroup relations meetings Organizational mirroring		Space design

TABLE 9

Classification of OD Interventions by Organizational Unit of Analysis and System Variable Impacted (continued)

System Variable Impacted

	Organizing Arrangements	*Social Factors*	*Technology*	*Physical Setting*

Organizational	Collateral organization
	Management information systems
	Grid OD—Phases IV & V
	Human resources accounting
	Information processing-based
	  organizational design
	MAPS
	Organizational structure design
	Multilevel planning
	Open systems planning
	QWL
	Strategic planning
		Confrontation meetings
		Communication network redesign
		Likert—system 4 management
		Sociometric network analysis
		Survey feedback
			Information technology design
			Sociotechnical organizational
			  design
				Space design

Note: Information in this table was derived from Beer (1980), Burke (1982), French and Bell (1984), Huse and Cummings (1985), Tichy (1983), and the authors.

(from the framework presented earlier) most affected by each approach. As space prohibits a thorough discussion of every intervention approach, only a subset of techniques will be described in enough detail to provide an overview of the breadth and character of the OD process. Using Table 9 as the basis for discussion, a prominent approach in each cell of the table will be described.

Organizing Arrangements Interventions

In general, this set of interventions focuses on altering the formalized coordinating mechanisms of a system. We will now describe five different OD interventions, each aimed primarily at affecting the organizing arrangements of one of the organizational levels.

Individual Level. One prominent change technique affecting organizing arrangements at the individual level is the use of flexible working hours (Cohen & Gadon, 1978). A flexible working hours program gives employees an opportunity to schedule when they want to be at work (within some broad parameters) and gives them the opportunity to choose how to allocate their time between work and nonwork activities. In the flexible working hours approach, a representative workday is defined as consisting of core hours during which all employees must be present at the work site, and flexible hours during which employees may choose for themselves whether they want to be present. The sum of these two sets of hours represents a band width of time which is, in effect, the maximum length of the workday (Cohen & Gadon, 1978).

A total workday may be established, for example, as consisting of the hours between 6:00 A.M. and 7:00 P.M. Core time could be the period between 10:00 A.M. to 12:00 noon and 1:00 P.M. to 3:00 P.M. During those four hours, all employees must be present in their work setting. The remaining part of the individual's workday is left up to the person to determine.

One employee might choose to come to work at 6:00 A.M. and leave at 3:00 P.M. (eight working hours, plus an hour for lunch), while another could work between 10:00 A.M. and 7:00 P.M. In either case, both employees would be present during the core time, work eight hours per day, yet be working dramatically different hours. The choice would be up to each employee to be made according to his or her own needs.

A series of variations to this basic theme exists. For example, core time could be established for the entire organization or for each work unit individually. In addition, employees' hours each day could vary or be fixed for a given time period. For example, employees could be allowed to carry forward hours from day to day rather than be required to work eight hours each day. An employee might work six hours one day and ten the next, or twelve hours one day and four the next, the constraints being that they total the number of hours required for the pay period (such as 40 hours per week) and that the person be present during the core hours each day.

This technique might be used in situations in which a key problem is that people frequently arrive late to work or tend to leave early whenever they can get away with it. For example, this intervention is commonly used when outside factors such as rush-hour traffic, daycare, or school schedules result in excessive employee tardiness, absenteeism, or time off from work. Flexible working hours allow people to make better choices about when to be at work and when to be involved with personal activities.

Interpersonal Level. The job expectation technique and role analysis technique are two techniques influencing the interpersonal level of the organizing arrangements stream (Dazal & Thomas, 1968; French & Bell, 1984).

Fundamentally, these two are the same technique, with both designed to establish clarity around the formal roles of members in any work team (from first level to top management). This technique, therefore, applies most directly to those situations, especially managerial teams, characterized by ineffective definitions of individual roles in a work group. Problems often arise in management teams because responsibilities are not explicitly assigned to a team member, because people disagree over who is responsible for what, or because one team member expects another to be responsible for a set of activities that are not perceived by the latter as being part of his or her role. These are all appropriate reasons for using this technique.

The specific procedure involves bringing the work team together, preferably away from the work situation and having each member list on a flip chart, in the presence of the other team members, all of his or her perceived job duties and responsibilities. As the listing progresses, other group members add comments, agree, disagree, or discuss until a job definition evolves that everyone understands and can support.

By requiring every group member to engage in this process, all the tasks of the group get assigned to someone, everyone knows to whom he or she is assigned, and typically the recipient of each job responsibility agrees to accept it as defined. This process leads to increased smoothness in operations, with group members minimally encroaching on each other's functions. It also often results in increased levels of commitment to both the individual job and the management team.

Group Level. The quality control circle is an intervention activity that focuses on the structure of group problem solving and decision making by providing new techniques for the inclusion of first-level work group members. The overall purpose of quality control circles is to improve the productivity of the

organization (Steel & Shane, 1986). Quality control circles first gained prominence in Japan before their recent popularity in the United States. They are typically used in situations warranting increased employee participation in solving manufacturing types of problems, although they are increasingly occurring in white collar settings (Yager, 1981).

Quality control circles consist of small groups of employees, all volunteers from the same section or department, who meet on a regular basis to identify problems in their work environment and propose solutions for them. Usually circles are led by the unit supervisor, but nonsupervisorial team members often coordinate specific meeting activities. Immediately after the formation of a quality control circle, its participants are trained in specific problem-solving techniques, such as brainstorming, Pareto analysis, and Gantt charting, and also in presentation skills.

Procedurally, a quality control circle first identifies a problem of interest, analyzes it, generates alternative solutions, then presents recommended actions to the management team overseeing the group's activities. The management team then decides whether or not to implement the recommended solution. If it does, then all resources necessary to carry out chosen actions are made available and a solution is implemented. The quality control circle then goes on to identify another problem and the cycle repeats itself.

Use of this form of structured problem solving for first-level employees provides an important opportunity for them to make significant contributions to the solution of problems negatively affecting organizational performance. As a consequence, the use of quality control circles has increased rapidly in the United States, with many companies creating large numbers of the circles throughout their organizations (Yager, 1981).

Intergroup Level. A common problem in organizational functioning concerns the formal coordinative arrangements governing relationships between groups. These often break down, resulting in substantial losses in efficiency and group performance. The contingency approach (Lawrence & Lorsch, 1967) to organizational design is a useful technique for organizing intergroup relationships. Although typically used for overall organizational design, contingency theory is especially appropriate for laying out the interfaces between groups.

Contingency theory assumes that there is no one best way to design all organizations and that, in fact, many highly effective configurations do exist for any one particular system. The key task is to identify the demands placed on the organization by its environment and to design the system to best fit these demands. Consequently, two dimensions of design become most critical: the degree of system differentiation required to meet environmental demands and the amount of system integration needed to pull together the differentiated organizational parts.

System differentiation refers to the differences in orientations that exist among various departments. These orientation differences typically occur along four dimensions: (a) the degree of formality managers create in their organizational structure, (b) the degree of concern for people as opposed to concern for the task, (c) the degree of time urgency or rapidity of feedback from system actions, and (d) characteristics of unit goals.

Integration describes the degree of collaboration that exists among departments that must work together to achieve their goals. Integration can be achieved through a variety of structural mechanisms. These include the organizational hierarchy, cross-functional teams, formal control systems, direct managerial contacts, and individuals or departments that serve as integrators. Intergroup relationships must be designed to provide a sufficient amount of integration across groups, especially if they are very different.

An organizational design using the contingency approach is developed based on the degree of task environment diversity facing the organization. The greater the diversity, the more differentiated organizational units need to be. The greater the number of specialized units in the organization, the more integration required to keep the overall system moving in the same direction. Therefore, both differentiation and integration are needed in any organization. The amount of each depends on the diversity of the task environment in which the organization functions.

Organizational Level. One organizing arrangements intervention affecting the organizational level focuses on developing plans and the strategies for achieving these plans. Most appropriate for situations in which the intention is to change the overall organization, open systems planning (Jayaram, 1976) helps an organization assess itself and develop plans for its future.

The open system planning process, conducted over a three-day period, consists of five steps. The key management team is most typically the organizational group involved with this technique. Open system planning begins with the creation of a view of the current organizational situation. This present scenario consists of all expectations perceived by the managers as placed on the organization by its external environment, its internal environment, and the transactions, across the boundaries of the organization, between the internal parts and the external domains, and it includes the value system underlying all the expectations identified.

A realistic future scenario is created next. The scenario described is based on the assumption that no deliberate activity will be taken by the organization to alter the direction in which it is headed. It also assumes that nothing is done to alter the evolution of the environment in which the organization operates. This realistic future scenario identifies sets of expectations and values that are analogous to those generated for the description of the present scenario.

The third step in the open system planning process is the development of an idealistic future scenario that attempts to describe what the organization would be like in the future if the management team had the power to change anything it wanted. The key to this step is not to be inhibited by uncertainties about how this ideal future might be achieved, but rather to fantasize without restraint.

The next step is a comparison of the idealistic future scenario with both the realistic future scenario and the present scenario. The purpose here is to identify broad areas of agreement, uncertainty, and disagreement. During the discussion which ensues, the managers clarify their values and views on what is worth trying to change and the reasons why.

In the last step, each discrepancy noted in the fourth step is analyzed, and an attempt is made to decide what actions should be taken in three time frames: tomorrow, six months from now, and two years from now. In some areas, agreement will have been reached about the issues and possible actions the organization might take. For these areas, concrete plans (with assigned responsibilities and timetables) are made. For areas in which broad disagreement exists, plans for dealing with that disagreement are developed. Finally, there will always be some areas in which an unacceptable level of uncertainty exists. For these, more data must be gathered before proceeding further.

The open systems planning process generally results in a clear understanding of the organization's current state, where it wants to go and why, and how to get there. At times a difficult and tedious process, open systems planning has the potential for generating true involvement and support for the goals and strategies developed.

Social Factors Interventions

Organizational development interventions focusing on changing the social factors in the organization are both the most numerous and most frequently used. OD's roots are based on group techniques for changing individual behavior, and consequently a large number of approaches have evolved with a focus on the organization's culture, interaction processes, social patterns, informal networks, and human attributes.

Individual Level. Training groups (T-groups) were the most common form of OD intervention in the early days of the field (late 1950s to middle 1960s). We have chosen to highlight them because of their historical prominence and because they have provided the basis for many other, more organizational, task-related change techniques, such as team building, process consultation, and intergroup conflict resolution.

T-groups consist of approximately 12 participants and one or two trainers/facilitators. No formal structure exists in the group except for the one that develops out of the interactions among its participants. In fact, the lack of a traditional group structure, in which the trainer or "leader" sets the agenda and directs the group's efforts toward accomplishing concrete goals, provides the greatest impetus for group activity. Ambiguity resulting from the uncertainty about what to do provides an important stimulus for group members to engage each other interpersonally. Individual actions create reactions in fellow group members that get shared in the group. The sharing is called feedback, and it describes to a person how the other perceived the behavior and what effect it had on him or her.

Since one seldom receives this sort of information in an honest and clear way, the process leads to an increased awareness of self, the dimensions of one's behavior and its effects.[13]

Often, out of this awareness comes experimentation with different behaviors—that is, behaviors more consciously selected for increased effectiveness. These experiments also result in reactions which are shared, and the cycle thus repeats itself.

One outcome of a successful T-group experience is increased participant awareness of their own behaviors, the forces driving what they do, the effects they have on others, alternatives to frequently used behaviors, and perhaps most importantly, a process for continued learning about the self and interactions with others. This last outcome, learning how to learn about one's own self and behavior, is intended to help the participant change ineffective behaviors in the "back-home" job setting. Proponents of this technique assume that eventually the changed organizational behaviors of individuals will lead to organizational change.

Although many organizations in the early 1960s were doing massive, in-house T-group training, this is not the case today. By the middle to late 1960s, it had become apparent that merely sending large numbers of managers to T-group training would not necessarily precipitate change back on the job. As a result, T-groups today are used more judiciously as only one component of a more comprehensive change process.

Interpersonal Level. Interventions focused specifically on the interpersonal dynamics occurring in an organization overlap considerably with individual and group-oriented activities. Yet in the area of conflict resolution, a clear example of an interpersonal social factors intervention exists.

Conflicts between two people—rather common occurrences in most organizations—are often open and apparent to everyone who comes in contact with the conflicting parties. Sometimes, however, conflicts move "underground" and are not very obvious.

This latter type of conflict, insidious and potentially quite damaging to both the conflicting parties and the organization, can be dealt with using the techniques of third-party consultation (Walton, 1969, 1987).

Walton notes that interpersonal conflict occurs in cycles, beginning with issues over which people disagree, leading to behaviors occurring in reaction to these issues, with consequences that then create more issues for disagreement. This cycle gets repeated over and over again as various events trigger behaviors that are related to preexisting issues.

Conflict can be based on either substantive or emotional issues, or both. In any case, the third-party consultation technique begins with a diagnosis of the conflict cycle to determine the basis for the conflict as seen by the warring parties and to clarify the barriers to potential action for resolution. Strategies for resolution either escalate or deescalate the conflict, depending on what the diagnosis has yielded. Specific strategies include (a) preventing the ignition of further conflictful interchange; (b) constraining the form of the conflict (i.e., defining the limits and the tactics that are acceptable); (c) coping differently with the consequences of the conflict (e.g., ventilating feelings to other parties, using sources of emotional support and reassurances, and making one's future less dependent on the party with whom the conflict is occurring); and finally, and most obviously, (d) eliminating the issues upon which the conflict has been based (Walton, 1969).

Third parties help those in conflict resolve their differences by using the concepts just described and by acting to help them confront these differences under conditions that maximize the probability of resolution. Conflict resolution processes are tedious and frustrating to work through but, depending on how important the conflicting persons are to the effective functioning of the organization, can result in significant returns to the system.

Group Level.   Team building or team development, perhaps the most commonly used change intervention in OD, targets the improvement of a work team's ability to solve problems and make decisions (Dyer, 1977; Patten, 1981). As a consequence, a relatively large number of approaches to building a work team exist, each differing in a variety of ways. Time invested in the process and location of the activity are two typical dimensions around which there is substantial variation. For example, at one extreme are extensive team-building efforts, carried out over a three- to five-day period, away from the work setting, in a hotel or retreat facility. At the other end of the spectrum are more "quick-fix" team activities, taking but a few hours, done during the group's regular meeting time, in the organizational setting.

The procedure for building a team's problem-solving and decision-making competence typically begins with gathering information from its members about the team's functioning.[14] This information may be collected by a variety of means. The particular approach used will depend on such factors as how much trust exists in the group, how interpersonally competent group members are, how much experience they have had in examining interpersonal processes, and what the group's relationship is with its manager. Some common data-gathering techniques are: (a) interviews of individual group members by an outside consultant, held prior to the team-building activity, with the data reported to the group without disclosure of the source; (b) open sharing of views by group members at the beginning of a team-building session; (c) detailed questionnaires administered prior to a session with the resulting data reported in aggregated form; and (d) relatively brief questionnaires, completed at the beginning of a session, with the data tabulated by the group and then reported either anonymously or with disclosure of their source.

Whatever the method of data generation, the information about the team's functioning is shared with the team members and discussed in detail. Out of this discussion, a diagnosis of the team's malfunctionings is generated by the group members. Actions to deal with identified problems are planned, responsibilities for their implementation are assigned, and deadlines for accomplishment are agreed upon.

Since the main purpose of team-building activities is to improve the group's problem-solving and decision-making capabilities, the issues discussed are generally limited to those related to task accomplishment. Unlike a T-group, in which any group member behavior is relevant for the group to focus on, the emphasis in team-building activities is only on those issues that directly impact the team's work goals.

Team-building interventions are most appropriate under the following conditions:

- When a legitimate organizational need for a team exists (i.e., there is formal or informal interdependence among team members)

- When the manager clearly wants to improve team functioning; when team members themselves feel a strong desire to be more effective in their work relationships

- When the team has expressed a willingness to look at itself, its performance, and how it functions

- When there is sufficient time to engage in the process

- When there is both an openness among team members to accept new data about themselves and a willingness to do something about the information they receive (Dyer, 1977)

Team-building interventions are less effective when these conditions do not exist, especially the first one. Without any real or perceived interdependence among group members, motivation to participate in what is often an emotionally painful process simply will not be there. When this happens, the team-building activity lacks substance and results in relatively little improvement in group functioning.

Intergroup Level. Conflict between groups in organizations is a pervasive and particularly difficult problem to solve. A strategy for managing intergroup conflict was developed in the early 1960s (Blake, Shepard, & Mouton, 1964) and has been systematically refined in the interim period. Burke (1974) presents a particularly useful and well-planned two-day off-site design for dealing with conflict of this nature.

Prior to the off-site meeting, the person in the hierarchy to whom both of the conflicting groups report calls a meeting of all group members. The purposes of this meeting are for the boss to legitimize the conflict resolution meeting, share expectations of outcomes, and define the limits of potential actions. This premeeting is critical because it sets the stage for the off-site activity by clarifying its importance and relevance for the responsible manager.

The off-site meeting consists of five phases spread out over two days. In the first phase, image exchange, the two conflicting groups develop and exchange their lists of responses to the following questions:

- How do we see ourselves?

- How do we see the other group?

- How do we think the other group sees us?

This information is then exchanged in a manner that maximizes the flow of information. Specifically, discussion aimed only at clarifying the information is allowed at this stage.

Phase two, problem identification, begins with each individual group member identifying problems existing at the interface between the two groups. Individual lists are consolidated within each group and then presented to the other group. Finally, the two groups work together to create one overall consolidation of the two group lists. Two representatives from each group work on consolidating the lists, while the remaining members observe the process but are not allowed to intervene in it.

Phase three, organizing for problem solving, involves organizing the two groups for problem solving. Each person selects and rank-orders, on the basis of how important a particular problem is to him or her, a small number of the issues previously listed. Rankings are consolidated across the two groups and one rank-ordered master list of problems is generated. Each person then selects two problems from the consolidated list that he or she would like to work on. This leads to the formation of problem-solving groups focused on each problem, with membership based on interest and representation (one half of each group needs to come from each of the two conflicting teams).

Phase four, problem solving, involves each problem-solving group working on its target problem and developing proposed solutions. In phase five, these solutions then get shared with the other group members. After presentation of proposed solutions, all group members critique the ideas presented and give suggestions for alterations to proposed plans. Agreements then are reached defining all concrete actions to be taken.

This approach does not immediately solve all the problems inherent in any long-standing intergroup conflict. However, it does initiate a process for collaboration that seems to reduce the mistrust and antagonism inherent in any conflict situation. The reduced tension then allows conflicting teams to focus on accomplishing their assigned tasks rather than winning battles with the other group.

Organizational Level. Interventions focusing on purely social factors at the broad organizational level are relatively rare. Recently, culture change approaches (e.g., Kilmann et al., 1985) have attempted to focus on altering an entire organization's corporate culture. Because these techniques are enormously complex and difficult to capture in a short synopsis, we will focus on a more bounded technique affecting the social factors of the overall organization. This technique, called the confrontation meeting (Beckhard, 1967), was developed to provide a process whereby all the managers of an organization could be gathered in one place at the same time to sort out the key issues facing the organization and devise actions for dealing with the problems identified.

The confrontation meeting is most appropriate when the total management group needs to examine its own functioning yet only has a limited time to do so, when enough cohesion and commitment exists at the top to execute large-scale change, when top management wishes to improve the situation quickly, and when the organization may have just experienced a major change of another sort, such as a merger.

The approach involves assembling all of the organization's managers—the number could reach as high as 100—for approximately an eight-hour period (one full workday; an evening and the following morning; or one afternoon and evening) to meet with the top management team. The process consists of seven phases, five of which are accomplished during the meeting. The sixth and seventh phases are accomplished a few days to six weeks later.

Phase one consists of climate setting, in which the top manager communicates his or her goals for the meeting and strongly encourages honest sharing of views, assuring people that they will not be punished for anything they might say. Most importantly, the top manager must establish a perspective in which the importance of wide-ranging commitment for problem solving and action is emphasized.

Phase two involves collecting information through the formation of seven- or eight-person heterogeneous (i.e., cutting across all levels) groups whose responsibility is to identify obstacles to high performance and the conditions that, if they existed, would make the organization more effective.

Phase three consists of reports from each group, which are written down and posted on the meeting room walls. After the reporting process has been completed, the top manager suggests six or seven major categories under which most of the items can be grouped. Once completed, the overall group then takes a break and all the written information is duplicated for general distribution.

In phase four, the managers form into their natural work units and discuss all the previously identified problems and issues that affect their particular area. They define actions that they themselves should take and the problems the top management team should deal with immediately. Finally, they decide how the results of the meeting will be communicated to their subordinates.

Phase five involves reconvening the large group and having each functional area report its own plans and what it wishes top management to deal with first. The top manager reacts and makes commitments where appropriate. Each unit also then shares its plans for communicating the outcome of the meeting to subordinates.

The sixth phase occurs a few days later and is a follow-up to the decisions and requests for actions surfaced in the meeting. The top management team meets immediately after the meeting and plans its courses of action, which then become the substance for a follow-up report to the management group at large.

Finally, a progress review is held four to six weeks later to discuss the actions taken and all that remain and to get new input on issues.

This follow-up is important because it demonstrates to the managers below the top team that they were listened to and that something is happening in response to their concerns.

The confrontation meeting can generate widespread awareness and consensus concerning problem identification. It can also create support for top management action. Finally, it can result in increased morale and sense of involvement on the part of middle- and lower-level managers.

Technology Interventions

OD interventions focusing on changes in the organizational technology have their roots in industrial engineering concepts of job design. However, in the OD tradition, these concepts have been substantially modified to take into account the human and social needs of the people who must operate the machinery, equipment, and other aspects of the technical system. The techniques presented in this section all focus on technology-based interventions that emphasize the human perspective.

Individual Level. The design of an individual's job is one of the more important determinants of individual productivity in the organization. As a consequence, work redesign with a focus on the psychological interface of individuals with technology has gained increased prominence in recent years. Physiological bases for job design have been around for about 80 years (Gilbreth, 1912; Taylor, 1911), but it has not been until recently that designs of jobs based on the psychological characteristics of individuals achieved prominence.

Hackman and Oldham (1975) proposed a framework for looking at jobs and designing them around an analysis of their core attributes. In Hackman and Oldham's view, jobs have certain basic or core characteristics that create critical psychological states in an employee, leading to certain behavioral and attitudinal outcomes. Core job characteristics consist of: (a) the variety of skills needed to do a job (skill variety), (b) the degree to which a job consists of an identifiable or whole piece of the overall work (task identity), (c) the degree to which a job affects others (task significance), (d) the degree to which an individual is relatively free to make decisions relevant to accomplishment of the job (autonomy), and (e) the degree to which an individual receives meaningful feedback on the effectiveness of his or her performance.

According to Hackman and Oldham (1975), there are three psychological states or reactions that occur when a person performs the set of tasks constituting a job. Skill variety, task identity, and task significance of a job generate some level of experienced meaningfulness in the work. Job autonomy results in experienced responsibility for the outcomes of work, and feedback from the job leads to knowledge of the actual results of the work activities. These three psychological states—experienced meaningfulness, experienced responsibility, and knowledge—can lead to four personal and work outcomes: (a) high internal motivation, (b) high-quality performance, (c) high work satisfaction, and (d) low absenteeism and turnover. The level of these outcomes depends on the level of the psychological states created by the job. Finally, the strength of an individual employee's growth needs will moderate the relationships just described. Those with high growth needs should respond positively to jobs with these features, while those who do not value personal growth and accomplishment may be uncomfortable with such jobs.

The intervention process of individual job design begins with a diagnosis of the present situation to determine current job characteristics and the resultant psychological states of employees performing them. With this as a basis, work can then be redesigned using the following principles: (a) combine highly fractionalized tasks into larger, more challenging combinations; (b) combine group tasks into logical, more inherently meaningful modules; (c) link employees to the clients receiving the output of their work; (d) give employees more responsibility over areas previously reserved for management; and (e) create processes for feeding back information on employee performance in such a manner that timely corrective action can be taken.

Through use of these design principles, work can be reconfigured so as to fit both the needs of individual employees and, through their improved performance, the needs of the organization. The redesign of work has always been an important strategy for changing the performance of an organization. The approach described here expands work design concepts to include the important human dimensions historically omitted in earlier change approaches.

Interpersonal Level. The technology of many organizations often demands that jobs be designed with a high degree of interdependence. In this case, the particular tasks assigned to each job incumbent typically cannot be grouped in such a manner so as to avoid overlap with the job definition of others while at the same time assuring that no necessary tasks are left undone. A technique called role negotiation (Harrison, 1972a) focuses on situations such as these and helps organizational members clarify their roles vis-à-vis each other so as to maximize the effectiveness of the overall work unit.

In this approach, work team members meet together in a group and list the things that each of the other members should start doing, do more of, do less of, and continue to do as they have been doing. These requests are made to specify how the other person can help make an individual more effective in his or her job. Once completed, these lists are exchanged, with each person receiving a list from every other group member. Time is given for group members to privately study the information they received

and to decide which requests they can respond to readily, which they are unclear about, and which they do not find agreeable. The work group reassembles and discusses each member's reactions to the lists. Once a clear understanding of the exchanged information is achieved, then a negotiation process occurs in which differences are ironed out and uncertainties clarified. The end result is a clear definition of each work group member's role, one affected by the needs and perceptions of the other team members.

This procedure leads to substantial clarity about both the formal and informal roles of work group members. Interdependencies are clarified through the redefinitional process, leading to specification of the behaviors needed to enhance the effectiveness of the overall work group.

Group Level. Interventions that focus on technology factors at the work group level generally emphasize the match between technological requirements of the work to be done by the group and human needs of group members. These interventions, called autonomous or self-regulating work group designs,[15] are characterized by a variety of factors. Cummings (1978) has identified these as

> a relatively whole task, members who each possess a variety of skills relevant to the group task, worker discretion over such decisions as methods of work, task schedules, and assignments of members to different tasks, and compensation and feedback about performance for the group as a whole. (p. 625)

Technological systems requiring substantial interdependence across tasks performed by different people are most suitable for an autonomous work group design. In other words, if the task performed by one person is heavily dependent on or strongly influences the tasks performed by another, and if this is common across a group of people, then a very important technical condition for this type of work group design exists. Technical interdependence can be based on such factors as a requirement that the input to one person's job is the direct and immediate output of another's job, or on a need for two or more group members to share the same materials or equipment. In either case, the resulting interdependence makes the situation ideal for autonomous work groups.

If *groups* of interdependent tasks can be identified and differentiated from each other, creating an opportunity for subproducts to be produced by an autonomous group, then a second ideal condition for this type of design exists. An example of this occurs in the automobile industry. At Volvo's Kalmar plant in Sweden, a car's important subcomponents include its engine, transmission, electrical system, exhaust system, axles, interior, and exterior body. Using an autonomous work team design, Volvo has assigned responsibility for building each of these components to a separate work team. The machinery and equipment have also been designed to be compatible with the concept of having an autonomous team building a unique subsystem of the overall automobile (Gyllenhammar, 1977).

An important characteristic of autonomous work groups is that they perform many of the functions previously assigned to first-line supervisors. One result is that the role of managing these groups is drastically different from the way a traditional work group is managed. The differences are most apparent in two areas: the responsibilities of the supervisor vis-à-vis the work team, and the role of the supervisor in the larger organizational context.

Supervisors of autonomous work groups have two main functions vis-à-vis their work team (Cummings & Srivastva, 1977; Susman, 1976). First, they assist the group in managing its exchanges with the larger organizational setting, for example, assuring that the group always has the raw materials it needs, negotiating schedules for finished products, and developing relationships with other groups so that shared resources can be used collaboratively. Second, they find ways to develop the capabilities of the group members, for example, by building up their technical expertise, by helping them to be more interpersonally effective, and by imparting problem-solving and decision-making skills for more effective group functioning.

Since the supervisors are not needed to direct the day-to-day activities of the autonomous work group, they can focus more of their efforts on understanding the larger organizational context in which the group operates and how the group fits within it. Supervisor time is thus freed up for more attention to planning and dealing with broader organizational demands. And, as noted, it also makes possible more effort directed at helping team members plan their own careers and develop the skills necessary to achieve both personal and group goals (Porras, 1986).

Intergroup Level.   There do not appear to be any technology-based interventions that have as their primary target the intergroup level of the organization. Although the sociotechnical systems approach to be described in the next section does have some impact on this level, its primary focus is the wider organization.

Organizational Level.   Sociotechnical system views permeate all of the approaches described in the technology interventions category. As such, we have presented only portions of this perspective in discussing individual and group intervention approaches. In this section, we will define sociotechnical systems ideas more precisely and present them in the context of an organizational design approach that more fundamentally takes technological requirements into account.

The sociotechnical view begins with the assumption that any system that produces a product consists of two subsystems, a social system and a technical system. The social system requires a structure that defines how the people in it should be configured role-wise so as to effectively operate the technical system used to produce the organization's product and get the job done. The technical system consists of such instruments as the tools, equipment, machines, methods, and process layout—the actual instruments used for converting raw materials into end product or service.

Production systems, often designed primarily with the technical system in mind, only secondarily take into account the requirements of the social system. Sociotechnical system design principles are based on the joint optimization of both social and technical designs rather than the predominance of one over the other. In other words, sociotechnical designs attempt to develop organizations that result in the best possible social design concurrent with the best possible technical design. Designing social systems requires special attention to the needs of individuals as well as to the dynamics associated with task-related interaction. Optimally designed social systems, however, are typically incompatible with optimally designed technical systems. Therefore, both the social and technical designs may well be suboptimal when considered independently. However, with joint optimization they represent the ultimate in overall system design. Substantial evidence on the effectiveness of sociotechnically designed systems shows that both organizational performance and human satisfaction improve as a result of shifting to these forms (Pasmore, Francis, Haldeman, & Shani, 1982).

Sociotechnical system design, originally developed on subsystems such as manufacturing plants, departments, offices, and so on, has been expanded to include design of the overall organization (Davis, 1980). Using this approach,

the broad steps to follow in designing a large organization begin with an analysis of what the future organization might look like given the organization-environment set in which it finds itself and the development of an organizational philosophy as a statement of a shared set of values and purposes of the organization. (p. 218)

In defining the organization-environment set, one must first consider the organization as embedded in an environmental context. As such, it is subjected to ever-changing demands from its technology, market preferences, government, competitors, and so on. As it is dealing with these external demands, it must continue satisfying the needs of its employees, who are also continually in a state of flux. Specifying these two groups of demands (external and internal) establishes the foundation for all subsequent design work.

The values and philosophy of the organization, a second step in the development of a sociotechnically designed system, are determined by the status of the development of the science underlying the organization's technology, the various governmental constraints, societal work values, and the designer's values. These factors are all inputs into the definition of organizational philosophy and play significant roles in the final value statement.

Once the organization-environment set and organizational values and philosophy have been specified, a series of sociotechnical design principles are used to develop an operational organization design. These principles lead to specific designs for the organization's systems, structure, functions, support systems, and approaches to maintaining organizational continuity in the transition from the present to future designs. The concrete steps used to actually develop a specific organizational design involve first creating a temporary design organization consisting of all staff members who possess needed expertise or who are key managers in terms of their support for the new organization. The temporary design organization establishes its mission and a design process, defines the roles of any consultants to be used, appoints the manager of the future organization, and negotiates the sanction, support, and protection needed by the new organization.

Once the temporary design organization is in place, the basic preliminary data that will be needed for the new design are developed. These data are acquired by assessing the internal environment of the parent organization, scanning the community in which the new organization will reside, and scanning the local labor market. Analyses of these data yield some of the general parameters around which the new organization can be created.

A series of design efforts follow, all occurring at more or less the same time in a somewhat iterative process. These include design of the technical system, the social system, the sociotechnical system, the jobs, the social support system, and finally, the overall organization. Concurrent efforts undertaken in each of these areas are so interdependent that, in fact, design processes do not proceed linearly but instead occur in a holistic fashion. Once completed, implementation of the newly developed organizational design requires the formation of a transitional organization with the responsibility of taking the new design and making it a reality. Once the design is in place, the final step is to evaluate and redesign as appropriate (Davis, 1980).

From this description, it should be clear that an organizational design process of this magnitude requires much time and many resources. However, if done thoughtfully, it can be extremely effective in producing a sound, useful organizational design.

Physical Setting Interventions

Although a variety of scholars and practitioners have done a reasonable amount of work

to develop approaches to designing more effective work spaces, OD-based technology focusing on the physical setting in organizations is quite limited in both scope and quantity. As a consequence, with the exception of Steele's work (1971, 1973, 1980, 1981, 1986; Steele & Jenks, 1977), no approaches drawn from *traditional* OD technology are available to classify into each one of the cells of Table 9. A second problem leads to additional difficulties in making such assignments. The very nature of organizational physical settings creates problems in categorizing interventions according to which of the five organizational target groups they primarily affect. Physical settings are such that they influence individuals in various combinations as they work alone, with others one-on-one, or within groups. It is therefore quite difficult to separate out the main thrusts of a particular approach to physical setting change and say that it only impacts one level of the organization. For these reasons, we will discuss the major approaches to physical setting design as a group and not attempt to subcategorize them. Our discussion of these approaches will therefore be organized according to the key principles guiding the design of physical work settings and the stages involved in creating them.

Key Principles of Physical Setting Design. Concepts of work-setting design can be organized into two general categories: (a) design and layout generalizations and (b) social processes for design development and implementation. Each category will be discussed in turn.

Design and Layout Generalizations. Steele (1986) asserts that there is "no single 'best' design for factory or office layouts—what is appropriate depends on the mix of people, the tasks being done, the resources available, and the stage of development of the system" (p. 190). Within that context, the key factors to take into account are the amount of visibility needed or desired; degree of decor integration; personalization of workplaces; promotion of privacy and sense of community; existence of centers where people can find out what is happening; manner in which traffic patterns, entrances, and exits affect people's experiences; necessity for effective orientational elements (signs and other graphics telling people where they are in relation to where they want to go); avoidance of creating "no-person's lands"; allocation of scarce resources (e.g., windows, views) to the community rather than to top managers only; minimization or control of status symbols; support for quick personalization of workplaces; maintenance of flexibility in space design; provision of forums (places where people can gather and see and hear one another discuss shared issues); use of graphics to tie settings together and create patterns of experience for users; consideration of functional distances (accessibility of getting from one point to another, regardless of physical distance); permeability or fixedness of boundaries; sizes of areas and spaces; and consideration of the particular materials chosen for such elements as walls, floors, and furniture (pp. 190–195).

Brill et al. (1985) propose a set of principles with a somewhat different emphasis. They suggest that all large areas should be subdivided so they are experienced as a collection of "places"; that each work group be designed so it is recognized as a separate "place"; that some walking is good for people and the organization; that horizontal connections are better than vertical ones; that connections with the fewest directional and other changes are desirable; that long, straight corridors are undesirable; that major, fixed horizontal circulation should be designed as "main streets" and that these should differ in many qualities from nonfixed paths; that certain types of work groups should be located so that many colleagues pass near or through them each day;

and finally, that consideration should be given to providing the space at the windows as a resource for everybody by using it as a main circulation with access to a band of services and amenities across from the window wall (pp. 119–120).

Deasy (1974) emphasizes more the relationship of the design to human needs over organizational needs. His basic principles include a primary concern for using the human values that would be derived from the participants of the physical setting as the basis for design, a focus that would provide a degree of freedom for each participant to adapt his or her personal environment to his or her own needs, a building exterior that expresses the human activities contained in it (the real texture of human diversity), and a building that communicates what people need to know in a language they can understand (pp. 136–138).

Social Processes for Design Development and Implementation. The physical setting change process is implemented through a variety of social processes intended to be consistent with the general tone of the basic design principles just described. Steele (1986) describes important tasks and orientations in the implementation process. He suggests that top leadership should first clarify for themselves the different classes of decisions that go into creating new or improved workplaces and decide how comfortable they are with unilateral as opposed to shared decisions in each class; that regular data collections and diagnoses of the match between human system needs and physical settings should occur; that the organization should capitalize on the potential of settings by creating policies and evaluations that promote using settings with gusto; that the setting not be maintained in its "move-in" state but that full use be gotten out of it; that open resolution of conflicts in spatial decision areas be encouraged; that social norms be periodically assessed to determine how well they match the physical setting; that social structures be designed that support and encourage individual problem solving of and adaptations to work environments, especially right after moving into the new setting; and that when designing organizational events, the choice of a setting and how it can be used should always be kept consciously in mind as making a difference (pp. 190–195).

Becker (1981) emphasizes the personal development aspect of the social processes used to implement physical setting change. He proposes that the process should support employees' feelings of competence and expertise by drawing on them as a basis for design, that the process should provide opportunities to develop a better understanding of the organization's overall operation, that the process should permit employees to tap skills and abilities that are relatively dormant, that the process should permit employees to develop skills and abilities that may improve their chances of job and career advancement, and that the process should indicate that the organization is aware of employees and values them (p. 173).

Deasy (1974) further emphasizes the relationship of design to human needs. He asserts that user participation is vital in defining architectural problems and establishing positive motivation for acceptance of any solutions developed.

With these key design principles and social process characteristics as a basis, let us now turn to a description of several approaches to the actual creation of new physical settings.

Stages in Creating New Physical Settings. Approaches to the actual implementation of physical setting change are relatively few and, of these, three stand out as being the most complete yet different from each other. For purposes of contrast, we will briefly describe all three to give the reader a clearer understanding of the available options.

Steele (1986) provides a perspective that emphasizes the top management's role in the change process and attempts to clarify the decision-making process. He suggests five main steps:

- *First pass at defining the project.* The top management group specifies the size, style, shape, importance of options, technology needs, budget, and location of the new physical setting.

- *Structuring of the new workplace project.* Top management still takes leadership at this stage and addresses the tasks to be done, the different phases the project will go through, rough timing estimates, and what the organizational structure will be to support the project.

- *Defining the program.* Top management, with the involvement of other key players in the organization, specifies what the new setting should be like, what problems it should solve, how it should contribute to the goals of the organization and its members, how it fits with the organization now, and what it will become in the future.

- *Defining the classes of decisions.* Top management and other key organizational members identify the different classes or types of decisions that need to be made and state clearly who has the final authority to make each type.

- *Refining the program and structure.* In this stage, the executive group reviews the building program as a whole and the social structures that will carry it out and, based on all that has been generated up to this point, defines in detail the overall goals of the program; the location, nature, and size of the facility to be built; the major organizational, behavioral, and task parameters that the new facility should support; the time schedules as they can now be estimated, including major milestones; and finally, the overall budget figures, cost estimates, and financial guidelines.

As one can see from the steps proposed by Steele, his main emphasis is on the decision-making and tangible characteristics of the process and much less on the degree of participation of all segments of the organization in the design and development of the new setting. In contrast, Brill et al. (1985) emphasize more the involvement of the direct users of the physical space. They specify three broad steps in the change process:

- *Environmental evaluation*, in which a "deliberate, detailed, and purposeful examination of the office as an environment for work" is undertaken (p. 216). This type of evaluation can be diagnostic, emphasizing data on what's wrong and permitting quantification of the pervasiveness and severity of the situation; predesign programming, exploring what's right and what's wrong and asking what's needed in the new facility; postoccupancy, emphasizing both how well the new office works and what still needs to be done; and finally, yearly monitoring, emphasizing both what's wrong and what's right, permitting quantification of the pervasiveness and severity, and becoming part of an ongoing program of change. The procedures used to accomplish the evaluation involve examining the physical traces (unintentional residues of past actions) and formal records (intentionally created records) of the organization, and/or collecting information through group interviews, walk-through interviews, or questionnaire-based surveys.

- *User orientation and training*, which is a process that acquaints workers with their physical environments so that they can use them more effectively.

- *Participation of workers in the key design decisions made about their offices.* The objective of involving users of space in its design and implementation is to get more productive and satisfying offices by improving the fit between the physical environment and workers' activities; to use the collective experience and knowledge of the work force about work and workplace in this process; to increase interest in and concern with the work environment as a tool; to increase acceptance of newly designed environments; to have employees feel they have participated in an appropriate and satisfactory manner and that they were heard; and to keep environmental expectations of employees at levels that the organization expects to meet.

The possible roles employees can play in this process are as unstructured designers, designers using preselected systems, selectors from among alternative designs presented to them, reviewers of and commentators on designs presented to them, or sources of information. From this list, one can see that the role of the user can vary from very involved and responsible for the key dimensions of the final design, to merely providing information about his or her physical setting needs and desires. Clearly, the degree to which employees will support and agree with the new design will be strongly influenced by the level to which they are able to participate in its development.

The third distinct approach to implementation of physical setting change is proposed by Dunn (1985). Her perspective involves the implementation of three phases in the change process:

- *Phase One: Prework for project support.* Approval for the project is received from the top executives, a steering committee for the project is selected, and the change is communicated to all employees affected.

- *Phase Two: Prework to develop the steering committee.* This involves the development of individual steering committee members, team development of the steering committee as a group, establishment of objectives for the steering committee, approval of the objectives by top executives, intergroup development (executive committee with steering committee), and the creation of a regular meeting schedule for the steering committee.

- *Phase Three: The intervention process itself.* This includes the administration and feedback of a space questionnaire, training on space design concepts for the steering committee, a company meeting to communicate plans to all affected employees, training on space design for all employees (conducted by the steering committee), employee involvement in planning and designing new space configurations, the actual move into the new space, and finally, the postmove administration of the new space.

In summary, there appears to be no one correct way to design the physical setting. The best way should be determined by the organizational members and the particular organizational situation. Yet, even though the principles and approaches described here provide some guidance on how to more effectively deal with the proper integration of physical settings and other organizationa dimensions, factoring space design into the change equation appears often to be a neglected step in most OD efforts.

Recent Developments

Most of the OD interventions currently available have been in use for quite some time. The majority were developed in the 1960s and 1970s, and except for techniques designed to implement culture change, little new intervention technology has been generated in the last decade. There are a few exceptions, however, and a brief overview of some of the more recent developments are presented below.

In the organizing arrangements category, a new structural form called the *circular organization* has been developed by Ackoff (1981, 1989) and applied in a number of private and public organizations. This new organizational form was designed to enhance organizational democracy, adaptability, and quality of working life. The defining element of this structure is that each manager is provided with a board, comprised of (at least) the manager whose board it is, his or her immediate superior, and his or her immediate subordinates. The responsibilities of a board are to develop plans and policies for the unit whose board it is, coordinate the plans and policies of the next lower level, integrate its own plans and policies with those made at higher levels, and make decisions regarding the quality of working life of the board members. In this way, organizational members have substantial input into relevant organizational decisions, and quality of working life considerations are guaranteed to be taken into account in these decisions.

A second type of structural innovation is a race relations advisory group (Alderfer, Tucker, Alderfer, & Tucker, 1988). This intervention involves the formation of a group of approximately equal numbers of black and white organizational members, with balanced membership by gender within race, and reflecting a representative cross-section of hierarchical levels and functional departments. The objectives of the group are to eliminate racism and improve race relations among black and white managers. It participates in all major decisions and programs affecting race relations in the organization. Change in the behavior of group members both reflects and serves to generate changes in the larger organization. Woodman (1989b) suggests that this intervention is related to the growing use of OD techniques and strategies in social movements.

Three new social factors interventions or approaches to intervening have recently been outlined. First, Mitchell (1986) reports the use of a new type of team-building intervention. Of course, team building is not new to OD, but this intervention adopts a somewhat novel approach as a result of its grounding in the theoretical work of Culbert and McDonough (1980). In essence, it is based on the idea that disclosure of internal frames of reference can improve group members' working relationships. Sharing information about work orientations, backgrounds and past experiences, and present attitudes about their jobs and other aspects of their lives helps group members develop a better understanding of what others seek to accomplish through their work behavior. Greater awareness of how others attempt to balance the external demands of their jobs with their internal needs and interests enables more accurate attributions regarding others' intentions when observing their work behavior. Outcomes for the team include improved communication, reduced conflict, and enhanced respect for one another.

Understanding frames of reference is also important to a new approach proposed by Bernstein and Burke (1989). Arguing that OD efforts are designed to facilitate changes in beliefs that will lead to performance improvements, they point out that diagnosing organizational belief systems and feeding this information back to organizational members are important steps in generating such change. Multivariate analysis of organizational survey data is utilized to identify (a) the set of beliefs used by most individuals to understand organizational events and (b) the relationships between the belief systems of various organizational subgroups. By helping to make implicit assumptions explicit, this intervention enables members to examine their own belief systems and can create pressures that lead to the development of beliefs that are more congruent with reality, values, and goals.

Finally, an intervention approach recommended by Eden (1986a, 1988) also focuses directly on the beliefs of organizational members. In this case, the beliefs of interest are members' performance expectations. Eden points out that client expectations can have a significant impact on the effectiveness of OD interventions. Thus, he suggests that change agents should intentionally raise expectations in order to capitalize on the creation of productive self-fulfilling prophecies. Various interventions are identified that can be used to raise expectations. Of course, Eden acknowledges that expectancy-raising is not feasible as a stand-alone program, but that it can conveniently supplement other interventions with little effort or cost.

Summary

A variety of OD intervention techniques exist, ranging from the simple to the highly complex, from a short-term to a long-term duration, from affecting one individual to affecting an entire organization, and from impacting only one organizational variable within one category to impacting several variables across all four categories. Effective OD intervention involves identifying and selecting the best change technique or combination of techniques to apply to any given situation.

Since present OD theory does not provide sufficient guidance for determining the best techniques to use in particular situations, it is important to evaluate change efforts to ascertain which interventions have the greatest impact on which organizational variables, and thus which interventions are most useful given the intended outcomes. The accumulated findings from such evaluations will enable further development of a theory base that can be used to guide intervention in the future. In turn, improvements in the effectiveness of OD intervention itself will become more possible. As one step in this process, the results of evaluations of OD interventions from the last 14 years will be reviewed in the next section.

Organizational Development Research

This section reviews recent research on the impact of organizational development interventions, focusing on the findings that have been generated regarding the relationships between interventions (i.e., changes in work setting characteristics) and changes in relevant organizational variables. Empirical evidence regarding these relationships has been reviewed previously. For example, Friedlander and Brown (1974) summarized the early OD literature, dividing a variety of interventions into two categories: human-processual and technostructural. Margulies, Wright, and Scholl (1977) divided interventions into three categories: human system, technical system, and management system interventions.

These reviews assessed the impact of OD interventions without categorizing the dependent variables that were targets of change. To do this, Porras and Berg (1978) divided dependent variables into process and outcome variables, reflecting a distinction between human interactive processes and individual and system outputs, both of which can change as the result of OD interventions. Distinguishing between "soft" measures of attitudes and perceptions and "hard" measures of job behavior and system performance, Nicholas (1982) evaluated the differential impact of human-processual, technostructural, and multifaceted interventions on four classes of behavior measured with "hard" criteria, specifically work force behavior, monetary or financial performance, productivity, and output quality.

This review examines the relationships between interventions and dependent variables using categories for each drawn from the organizational framework presented earlier. In so doing, we are able to improve on previous reviews in two ways. First, the classification provides a broader and more complete differentiation of the interventions and dependent variables. Second, because the classification is based on a theoretical framework and is not simply an emergent, descriptive taxonomy, we are able to compare results found in the literature to a variety of hypotheses, derived from the framework, regarding the relationships between variables.

We compiled the results of empirical evaluations of change programs published in the literature from 1975 to 1988 to assess the impact of interventions on dependent variables.[16] We selected only those studies that were conducted with an acceptable degree of methodological rigor, to enhance the validity and generalizability of the conclusions drawn from the aggregate set of studies. Only studies meeting the following criteria were included in our analysis:

- The researchers provided detailed information describing the participants of the project, the research design, and methods of evaluation.

- Quantitative data on dependent variables were collected and reported, along with the results of the statistical analyses performed on the data. Any studies reporting only anecdotal or subjective data were eliminated, as were those that did not perform tests of significance.

- Only field studies were included, as laboratory experiments and simulations limit generalizability (Miller & Monge, 1986; Tubbs, 1986). Thus, the OD intervention occurred, at a minimum, in an intact work group in an existing organization, if not in larger organizational units or in the entire organization.

The 63 studies listed in Table 10 were found to meet these criteria.[17]

The following information from each study was coded. First, the category of the primary intervention employed in the change project was determined. Again, the possible categories are organizing arrangements, social factors, technology, and physical setting.[18] Second, the dependent variables measured in the study were classified into seven categories. Since interventions may have an impact on any of the work setting variables, the first four dependent variable categories are the same as the four primary intervention categories. In addition to these four, dependent variables could be classified as individual behavior, organizational outcomes, and individual outcomes. Third, within each of the seven categories of dependent variables, the percentages of variables demonstrating positive change, negative change, and no change were determined. This was done by counting the number of separate dependent variables in that category measured in that study, and calculating the percentages of that total that corresponded to the three levels of change.[19] As an example of this classification, Adams and Sherwood (1979) measured four individual outcome variables. Three of these variables experienced no change, and one experienced negative change. Thus, 75 percent of the variables demonstrated no change, and 25 percent exhibited negative change.[20]

The discussion that follows is based on the data coded from the 72 studies. We first provide a descriptive overview of the studies as a set, focusing on the types of interventions used and the dependent variables assessed. Next, we examine the nature of the change occurring in the various dependent variables and the impact of the different categories of interventions on these variables. Finally, we draw upon the findings from this research to explore hypotheses, derived from the framework presented earlier, regarding the relationships between work setting variables, individual behavior, and individual and organizational outcome variables.

Overview of Interventions and Dependent Variables

Interventions. Thirty-one of the 72 studies (43%) reported using organizing arrangements interventions. Formal structure interventions, such as setting up new committees, task forces, or quality circles, were the most common interventions in this category. Social factors interventions were employed in 29 (40%) of the studies. The most commonly used social factors intervention was team building. Eleven (15 percent) of the studies reported technology interventions, the most common of which was job redesign. Finally, nine (13%) of the studies reported physical setting interventions. Three of these changes were from a closed-office to an open-office layout, three involved other types of changes in work space (e.g., a nonterritorial office), and three involved relocations.[21]

The fact that organizing arrangements interventions were the most commonly used in this set of studies reflects a recent trend toward greater use of structural interventions. Half of the studies using organizing arrangements interventions were published in 1986 or later. The high frequency of social factors interventions is not particularly surprising, as it reflects the historical roots of OD in laboratory training, team building, and process consultation. Likewise, it does not seem unusual that physical setting interventions were the least frequently used, since there has been an underutilization in OD of this organizational variable as a mechanism for creating change. The relatively infrequent use of technology interventions is somewhat surprising, given the popularity of job redesign and the sociotechnical systems approach to organizational change. It is not clear whether the small number of studies with technology interventions indicates

TABLE 10

Empirical Studies Used for Analysis of OD Research Impact

1.	Adams & Sherwood, 1979	33.	Kimberly & Nielsen, 1975
2.	Allen & Gerstberger, 1973	34.	Locke, Sirota, & Wolfson, 1976
3.	Arvey, Dewhirst, & Brown, 1978	35.	Luthans, Kemmerer, Paul, & Taylor, 1987
4.	Bartunek & Keys, 1982	36.	Marks, Mirvis, Hackett, & Grady, 1986
5.	Bhagat & Chassie, 1980	37.	Mathieu & Leonard, 1987
6.	Bocialetti, 1987 (2)	38.	Meyer & Raich, 1983
7.	Boss, 1979	39.	Mitchell, 1986
8.	Boss & McConkie, 1981	40.	Morrison & Sturges, 1980
9.	Buller & Bell, 1986 (3)	41.	Nadler, Cammann, & Mirvis, 1980 (2)
10.	Bushe, 1987	42.	Narayanan & Nath, 1984 (2)
11.	Cohen & Turney, 1978	43.	Oldham, 1988 (2)
12.	Conlon & Short, 1984	44.	Oldham & Brass, 1979
13.	Cooke & Coughlan, 1979	45.	Ondrack & Evans, 1986
14.	Crawford, Thomas, & Fink, 1980	46.	Orpen, 1979
15.	Cummings & Srivastva, 1977	47.	Pasmore & King, 1978
16.	Dalton & Todor, 1984	48.	Pasmore, Petee, & Bastian, 1986 (2)
17.	Donaldson, 1975	49.	Pate, Nielsen, & Mowday, 1977
18.	Eden, 1986b	50.	Paul & Gross, 1981
19.	Frye, Seifert, & Yaney, 1977	51.	Pearson, 1987
20.	Golembiewski, Hilles, & Daly, 1987	52.	Porras, Hargis, Patterson, Maxfield,
21.	Golembiewski, Yeager, & Hilles, 1975		Roberts, & Bies, 1982
22.	Griffin, 1988	53.	Porras & Wilkins, 1980
23.	Hackman, Pearce, & Wolfe, 1978	54.	Scarpello, 1983
24.	Hautaluoma & Gavin, 1975	55.	Schuster, 1984
25.	Head, Molleston, Sorenson, & Gargano, 1986	56.	Steel & Lloyd, 1988
26.	Hicks & Klimoski, 1981	57.	Steel, Mento, Dilla, Ovalle, & Lloyd, 1985 (2)
27.	Hughes, Rosenbach, & Clover, 1983	58.	Sundstrom, Herbert, & Brown, 1982
28.	Jordan, 1986	59.	Szilagyi & Holland, 1980
29.	Joyce, 1986 (2)	60.	Terpstra, Olson, & Lockeman, 1982
30.	Keller, 1978	61.	Wall, Kemp, Jackson, & Clegg, 1986
31.	Keys & Bartunek, 1979	62.	Woodman & Sherwood, 1980
32.	Kim & Campagna, 1981	63.	Zalesny & Farace, 1987

Note: Numbers in parentheses reflect the number of substudies contained in the research study.

that they are not being used very often in change programs, or that these interventions are simply not being evaluated and/or reported in the literature.

The small number of studies with multifaceted, multicategory interventions is also notable, although here too there is some ambiguity as to what the reasons for this might be.

First, it could be that comprehensive programs of change are simply not carried out with any degree of regularity. Second, it could reflect the difficulty of getting studies that use a diverse set of interventions published, since it would be hard to ascertain just which changes produced any results that might be found. On the other hand, since single interventions may not produce desired results very often, it would be useful to start examining the efficacy of multi-intervention programs of change, instead of being concerned about which particular interventions were most powerful (e.g., Bowers, 1973; Pasmore, 1978). Finally, since in practice multiple interventions are frequently implemented sequentially and thus over a long time period, various pressures to publish quickly and frequently may inhibit evaluating the long-term effects of a comprehensive change effort. Thus, it is not clear whether such efforts rarely occur in practice or whether their evaluations are just infrequently published.

Dependent Variables.   Social factors variables were measured the most often of all the dependent variables, in 52 (72%) of the studies. Technology variables were measured in 24 studies (33%), organizing arrangements variables were measured in 16 (22%), and physical setting variables were measured in 7 (10%). Thirty-three (46%) of the studies measured individual behaviors. Organizational outcomes were measured in 39 (54%) of the studies, and 42 (58%) of the studies measured individual outcomes.

  As with the use of social factors interventions, the fact that social factors variables were measured most often is not surprising since OD traditionally has had a more human-processual emphasis. Many OD researchers and practitioners are still heavily influenced by this orientation. Also, the fact that organizational outcomes were measured frequently is consistent with a tendency, noted elsewhere (Porras & Berg, 1978), for OD researchers to measure hard criteria in addition to the soft, human-processual variables.

  Organizing arrangements and physical setting variables were measured rather infrequently. It could be that these variables are often manipulated, but then not measured. For example, if the intervention is to change the formal structure or to redesign the

workspace, there is no need to measure these changes. The change is apparent. It is more interesting to assess the changes in, for example, the interaction processes or informal power structure (social factors variables) that result from the change in structure or workspace. Furthermore, these variables may be less likely to change on their own as a result of changes in other types of variables. If they are changed, it is usually at the intervention stage. Thus, it may seem unnecessary to measure them as dependent variables.

  It is worth noting that over 60 (83%) of the studies measured either organizational or individual outcomes, with 21 (29%) measuring both. It is encouraging that researchers recognize that changes in organizational processes (i.e., social factors variables) or individual behavior are not the ultimate objective of OD efforts. Only 12 (17%) studies relied on social factors or individual behavior change as a measure of the success of the change program.

Impact of Interventions on Dependent Variables

Table 11 presents data regarding the nature of the changes that occurred in the dependent variables in these studies. Column 1 presents the average percentage change in these variables across all the studies, while Columns 2 through 5 indicate the average percentage change across the studies that employed the type of intervention identified at the top of the column. The bottom rows in the table specify the average percentage change in all the variables combined, across all studies (Column 1) and broken down into intervention types (Columns 2 through 5).[22]

Dependent Variable Change.   The average percentage of positive, negative, and no change experienced in each of the work setting variables is given in Column 1 of Table 11 and

TABLE 11

The Impact of OD on Key Organizational Variable Sets

		Intervention Category				
Target Variables	Change Direction	Overall (Percent)	Organizing Arrangements (Percent)	Social Factors (Percent)	Technology (Percent)	Physical Setting (Percent)
Organizing arrangements	+	42.7	29.2	50.0		
	0	50.0	62.5	44.4		
	−	7.3	8.3	5.6		
Social factors	+	44.0	39.2	56.4	40.7	22.7
	0	48.0	55.6	39.8	36.7	52.6
	−	8.0	5.2	3.8	22.6	24.7
Technology	+	23.2	12.8	38.9	20.0	14.6
	0	69.2	79.5	61.1	70.0	52.5
	−	7.6	7.7	0.0	10.0	32.9
Physical setting	+	47.6	0.0	0.0	0.0	66.7
	0	45.2	100.0	100.0	100.0	23.3
	−	7.2	0.0	0.0	0.0	10.0
Individual behavior	+	35.0	16.3	65.8	19.6	0.0
	0	51.0	81.2	18.8	60.7	66.7
	−	14.0	2.5	15.4	19.7	33.3
Organizational outcomes	+	48.3	52.8	56.8	27.8	0.0
	0	46.6	47.2	43.2	38.9	100.0
	−	5.1	0.0	0.0	33.3	0.0
Individual outcomes	+	28.4	25.0	17.8	31.5	27.8
	0	57.5	64.6	65.6	61.4	32.2
	−	14.1	10.4	16.6	7.1	40.0
Total	+	38.0	30.6	50.7	27.8	27.8
	0	52.5	63.6	43.1	54.8	44.0
	−	9.5	5.8	6.2	17.4	28.2

depicted graphically in Figure 5. Physical setting variables experienced the most positive change overall, with an average of 48 percent changing significantly in the desired direction.[23] On the average, 44 percent of the social factors variables and 43 percent of the organizing arrangements variables showed positive change. Technology variables changed positively an average of 23 percent of the time. Table 11 and Figure 6 show the percentage change in individual behavior and in each of the outcome variables. While an average of 48 percent of the organizational outcomes were reported as changed, individual behavior and individual outcomes changed in a positive direction much less frequently, 35 percent and 28 percent, respectively.

As can be seen at the bottom of the first column in Table 11, the combined impact on all dependent variables is 38 percent positive change, 53 percent no change, and 9 percent negative change. In other words, on the average, just over half of the dependent variables measured did not change as a result of the OD intervention or interventions used. The overall percentage change in these studies is thus somewhat lower than the rates of change found in earlier reviews (e.g., Nicholas, 1982; Porras & Berg, 1978). The overall general pattern of results—no change occurring most frequently, negative change occurring least frequently, and positive change occurring with medium frequency—holds for all the individual variables except for physical setting and organizational outcomes, in which case positive change was the most common outcome.

The fact that a lack of change in the dependent variables occurred more frequently than any change did can potentially be explained in one of three ways. First, and most pessimistically, it could simply be that OD, in general, is not very effective, with desired results being achieved less than half the time. Second, it could be that the interventions used in these studies cannot achieve results consistently. The problem may not be with any

specific intervention, but that too frequently there was only one intervention, or interventions of one type, used. Only six cases existed in which a multifaceted, multicategory program of intervention took place. The lack of positive change may be a result of the lack of comprehensiveness of the change effort.

Finally, it could be that beta change was involved in the measurement of many of the dependent variables. As discussed previously, beta change involves a psychological recalibration of the measurement instrument used to measure a stable dimension of reality (Golembiewski et al., 1976, pp. 135–136). In other words, as a result of the OD intervention or interventions, organizational members' perceptions of various aspects of their work environment can be altered such that the measures used to assess these characteristics do not maintain their calibration over time. Consequently, while the characteristics being measured may in fact undergo change, such change may not be demonstrated because of the psychological recalibration of the measure. An apparent lack of change can thus mask an actual change in the variable measured.[24]

While the dominant result in these studies was a lack of change, it is encouraging that positive change did occur almost as frequently in organizing arrangements and social factors variables. On the other hand, it is somewhat disheartening that individual behavior and individual outcomes changed positively only slightly more than one-third and one-fourth of the time, respectively. Furthermore, these variables changed in a negative direction more than any other category of variables. Even though these rates of negative change are relatively low, it is still worth noting that the impact of OD interventions on individual behavior and individual outcomes appears somewhat unpredictable.

All in all, as Table 11 and Figures 5 and 6 verify, little negative change was observed in the variables. The average amount of negative change ranged from five percent in the

FIGURE 5

OD-induced Change in Key Organizational Work Setting Variables

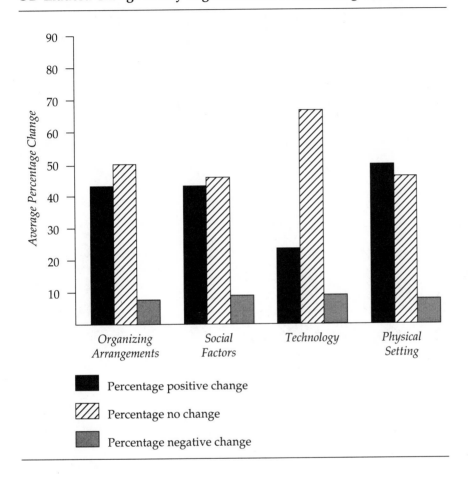

Percentage positive change

Percentage no change

Percentage negative change

organizational outcomes to 14 percent in the individual behavior and individual outcomes variables. Obviously, this low rate of negative change is a positive finding, since otherwise it would imply that OD interventions can easily have the opposite effect of that intended. A word of caution, however, is that the low rate of negative change might reflect more the fact that researchers have a tendency to find what they are looking for and fail to find what they do not want to find (Bass, 1983) than it does the actual effectiveness of the OD interventions.

Additionally, it could simply be a result of the fact that negative results may be less likely to get published (Woodman & Wayne, 1985).

Differential Impact of Interventions. Table 11 also presents data on the impact of the four categories of interventions assessed in these studies. The impact of each type of intervention on all variables combined is given at the bottom of Columns 2 through 5. Overall, the social factors interventions resulted in the most frequent positive change, physical

FIGURE 6

OD-induced Change in Individual Behavior, Organizational Outcomes, and Individual Outcomes

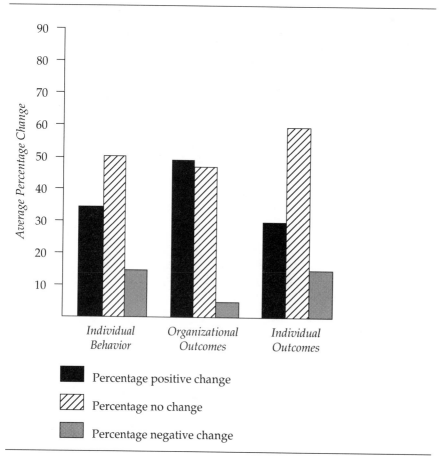

- ■ Percentage positive change
- ▨ Percentage no change
- ▧ Percentage negative change

setting interventions had the most frequent negative impact, technology interventions also demonstrated a relatively high frequency of negative change, and organizing arrangements interventions resulted most frequently in no change.

A close examination of Columns 2 through 5 of Table 11 reveals some interesting trends that deserve mention. First, there is little impact of organizing arrangements interventions on technology variables and no impact on

physical setting variables.[25] This may not be unusual in that the structural changes that comprised most of the interventions in this category will not yield changes in either the organization's technological or physical characteristics. It also appears that these interventions have little impact on individual behaviors. Since organizing arrangements are the formalized aspects of the organization, this points out the fact that simply making changes in the more prescriptive elements of the work setting is not necessarily going to result in behavior change. On the other hand, organizing arrangements interventions have their greatest impact on organizational outcomes, which demonstrate more than twice as much positive change as individual outcomes.

Second, social factors interventions have a positive impact on an average of 50 percent of the organizing arrangements variables. They also have basically an equivalent impact on social factors variables and on organizational outcomes, with positive change occurring over half the time. While consistent with the findings of Nicholas (1982), this contradicts the claim by Woodman and Wayne (1985) that process interventions (i.e., social factors types) are most likely to produce change in process variables and that evidence for their impact on outcome variables is sparse. The greatest positive impact of social factors interventions is on individual behavior. Combined with the frequency of negative change in these variables, social factors interventions seldom leave individual behavior unaffected. Finally, these interventions have a mixed impact on individual outcomes. When the latter do change, it is almost as often in the negative direction as in the positive direction. This pattern suggests that the effects of social factors interventions alone on individual outcomes may be rather arbitrary, or at least unpredictable. Thus, consistent positive change may depend on using other types of interventions such as technology ones (e.g., as in a sociotechnical intervention) along with social factors interventions.

Technology interventions produce the greatest total change in social factors variables and organizational outcome variables. However, in both cases there are relatively large amounts of negative change, especially in the latter, where there is more negative than positive change. All in all, the relationship of technology interventions to organizational outcomes appears somewhat random, as the results are fairly evenly split between the three change categories. Technology interventions also produce equal negative and positive change in individual behavior, and more negative change across all variables than either organizing arrangements or social factors interventions. Combined, these findings suggest that interventions of this type have a significant potential to impact many other organizational variables. However, this impact can easily be in the wrong direction and thus, if technology is to be changed, it is important to make sure that other elements of the organization are in place or changed to help ensure that desired results are obtained.

Finally, it is notable that the physical setting interventions result in very little positive change in any of the variables except for physical setting variables themselves. It could be that the lack of use of physical setting interventions in organizational development has prevented the accrual of much information regarding the most appropriate changes to make or the most effective method of implementing them, and that as a result these interventions are less effective than other types. For example, instead of simply focusing on the decision of whether an office design should be an open-office or a closed-office format, more attention may need to be placed on aspects such as who should be located where, or what kind of workspace would be most beneficial given the nature of the tasks that must be accomplished by the people using it. The fact that physical setting interventions result in negative changes more frequently than other types of interventions supports this contention as well.

Focusing now on the rows of Table 11, a few additional trends can be noted. First, social factors variables show better than average positive change from organizing arrangements, social factors, and technology interventions. This suggests either that these variables may be the most amenable to positive change or, alternatively, that they may be more susceptible to measurement and interpretation error (cf. Woodman & Wayne, 1985). On the other hand, technology and physical setting interventions create relatively high amounts of negative change in social factors variables. Because the nature of an organization's technology and physical setting can place important constraints on, for example, the interaction patterns that can occur among individuals, any changes must be made carefully to ensure that they do not result in undesirable consequences in the social factors variables.

Second, there were consistently high frequencies (greater than 50%) of no change in the technology variables no matter what type of intervention was utilized. This may indicate that these variables typically will not change as a result of interventions targeting other types of variables. Thus, if technological change is desired, it may have to be the explicit target of the intervention. An alternative explanation is that technological change that occurs in response to other interventions could potentially take a relatively long time to obtain, and thus the time span of these studies may just have been too short to be able to monitor it.

In looking at the individual behavior variables, social factors interventions result in a very high frequency of positive change, while no other type of intervention yields very much positive change at all. Furthermore, with one exception,[26] the impact of social factors interventions on individual behaviors is greater than the impact of any other type of intervention on any other variable. These data indicate that social factors interventions, while not being either a necessary or sufficient condition for individual behavior change to occur, are very closely related to change in these variables.

Overall, individual behaviors also changed in a negative direction more frequently than any other variable (except individual outcomes). This may be because behavior is rather unpredictable and influenced by numerous organizational factors, and thus changes in one set of these factors is not guaranteed to produce the desired consequences and in fact may result in the opposite. Therefore, it is important

to plan and implement multiple types of interventions, such that organizational characteristics will consistently affect behavior in desired directions.

The high rate of positive change in organizational outcomes was primarily a result of organizing arrangements and social factors interventions. These interventions both produced positive change over half the time, and neither of them resulted in any negative change. All of the negative change in these outcomes were the result of technology interventions as physical setting interventions yielded neither positive nor negative change. In contrast, the organizing arrangements and social factors interventions yielded the lowest rates of positive change in individual outcomes and higher rates of negative change than technology interventions. The negative impact of physical setting interventions on individual outcomes was the highest of any intervention on any category of dependent variables. Although a cautionary note regarding the validity of this finding is again necessary, it suggests that a change in individuals' physical workspace may be a rather risky means to improve individual outcomes.

Findings Regarding Hypothesized Relationships

We turn now to a discussion of data that provide evidence regarding relationships among various sets of variables in the organizational framework presented earlier. Specifically, we will look at the relationships between (a) work setting variables and individual behavior, (b) behavior and outcomes, and (c) the two types of outcomes, organizational and individual. In each case, we examine only those studies that measured both types of variables in the relationship.

In each study, each of the seven variables was coded for change using the following algorithm: A variable was recorded as demonstrating positive change only if there was positive change in 50 percent or more of the specific variables[27] of that type measured in that study. For example, Keys and Bartunek (1979) measured five specific social factors variables, four (80%) of which changed positively. Thus, their social factors variable was rated as showing positive change. On the other hand, Woodman and Sherwood (1980) measured two specific individual outcome variables, neither of which showed any change. Therefore, the individual outcome variable was rated as not changing positively.[28]

The number of studies in each of four categories was then determined. These four categories were: (a) positive change in both variables, (b) positive change in neither variable, (c) positive change in the first but not the second variable, and (d) positive change in the second but not the first variable. The pattern of changes in each pair of variables, as represented by the number of studies in each of these categories, provides some information, albeit indirect, about the degree to which changes in the two variables are related. In other words, it suggests whether or not change in one variable is associated with change in the other.

Figure 7 presents an example of the 2 x 2 matrix used to indicate, for the pair of variables being discussed, the pattern of distribution of studies into the four categories just listed. Each cell of the matrix represents one of the categories, and for ease of discussion these will be referred to by cell number as identified in the figure.

Work Setting and Individual Behavior. The first set of relationships to be considered are those between the work setting variable changes and individual behavior change. As discussed previously, the organizational framework hypothesizes that behavior is a function of the work setting in that individuals receive cues from their environment, process these cues, and make decisions about how to behave. Therefore, to change behavior it is necessary to change the environment so that

FIGURE 7

Sample Analytical Matrix

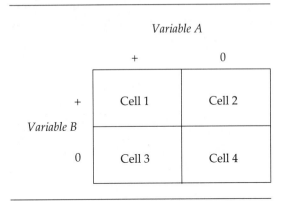

individuals receive different cues about appropriate behavior. According to the framework, then, there must be change in work setting variables if there is to be change in behavior. Without change in work setting variables, the likelihood of behavior change is considerably reduced.

Twenty-six studies measured at least one of the work setting variables as well as individual behavior. All but 2 measured social factors, and 12 of these also considered one or more of the remaining three work setting variables. Seven looked at organizing arrangements, 11 included technology, and 1 measured physical setting. The remaining 2 studies measured only physical setting variables. Fourteen of the studies had positive change in at least one work setting variable. As Figure 8 indicates, 6 of these also had positive behavior change (Cell 1), while 8 did not (Cell 3). Of the 12 without positive change in a work setting variable, 1 did show positive behavior change (Cell 2), and 11 did not (Cell 4).

Of the four types of outcomes represented in Figure 8, two are supportive of the framework (Cells 1 and 4), one contradicts the framework (Cell 2), and one is neither consistent nor inconsistent (Cell 3). Overall, the data are quite compatible with the framework. In two-thirds of the cases (17 out of 26), change either occurred in both the work setting and behavior or it occurred in neither. Only one case contradicts the framework by exhibiting behavioral change without corresponding change in the work setting. In eight cases (Cell 3), there was change in the work setting and no change in behavior. This does not contradict the framework but suggests instead that work setting change is not a sufficient condition for change in behavior.[29]

The framework predicts that behavioral change is a function of change in the work setting, yet these results indicate that even when the work setting changes, behavior is just as likely not to change as it is to change. However, another hypothesis implied by the framework is that the greater the amount of change in the work setting, the more likely it is that behavioral change will follow. To test this hypothesis, the studies that measured work setting change could be categorized according to how many of the four variables underwent positive change. The hypothesis would be supported if the percentage of specific behavior variables showing change in a study increased as the number of work setting variables showing change increased.

There were 12 studies in which none of the work setting variables changed. In these studies, a total of 34 specific behavior variables were measured. Four of these (12%) changed positively. In the 11 studies in which one work setting variable changed, the rate of change in specific behavior variables was 44 percent (8 out of 18). And the rate of change was 92 percent (12 out of 13) in the three studies that had change in two work setting variables. According to these data, then, the greater the number of work setting variables that changed, the more frequently behavioral change occurred.

This analysis concentrated only on the number of work setting variables that changed. However, one could also predict from the

FIGURE 8

Number of Studies Showing Change in Work Setting and Individual Behavior Variables

framework that as more of the specific work setting variables changed, behavior would be more likely to change. To consider this possibility, the 14 studies that did in fact demonstrate work setting change were examined. Out of the 11 studies in which there was positive change in one work setting variable, there were 4 studies in which behavior changed as well and 7 in which behavior did not change. In the former group, the percentage of specific work setting variables (across all four variables) that changed positively was 67 percent (10 out of 15). In contrast, in the latter set the percentage of specific variables undergoing change was 58 percent (15 out of 26). When the three studies that had change in two work setting variables were added into this comparison (two had behavioral change and one did not), these numbers are 85 percent (28 out of 33) and 59 percent (19 out of 32), respectively.

These numbers suggest that more behavioral change is associated with greater rates of change among the specific work setting variables. Together with the findings concerning the work setting variables themselves, there seems to be considerable support for the hypothesis that the greater the amount of change in the work setting, the more likely it is that behavioral change will be exhibited as well. The link between the work setting and individual behavior appears to be fairly strong.

However, a caveat is in order here. In examining these patterns of change, it is not clear to what extent the individual behavior variables measured should in fact be expected to change, given positive change in the particular work setting variables measured. The causal relationships between particular interventions, work setting variables, and particular behaviors are not well understood. Therefore, while the results demonstrated in this set of studies suggest that, broadly speaking, behavioral change is related to work setting change, more compelling evidence would require testing specific hypotheses concerning the relationships between changes in particular work setting characteristics and the changes expected in particular behaviors.

Individual Behavior and All Outcomes. The second set of relationships to consider are those between individual behavior and the outcome variables. According to the framework, improvements in outcomes, both organizational and individual, are the result of changes in individuals' behaviors. When there is no behavioral change, there is not likely to be outcome change, either. To examine the evidence regarding these relationships, the same procedure as described earlier was implemented. There were 27 studies that measured both behavior and at least one of the two types of outcomes. Figure 9 shows the number of studies that fell into each of the four categories. As long as either of the two outcome variables changed, the study was regarded as demonstrating positive outcome change.

FIGURE 9

Number of Studies Showing Change in Individual Behavior and All Outcome Variables

	Individual Behavior	
	+	0
+	7	10
All Outcomes		
0	1	9

Once again, this pattern can be assessed for the degree to which it is compatible with the framework. The 16 studies in Cells 1 and 4 are consistent with the framework's predictions. Either behaviors and outcomes both change, or neither changes. That Cell 3 only contains one study is also compatible with the framework. When behaviors do change, outcomes almost always change as well. However, Cell 2 exhibits a definite incongruity. In ten studies, there were positive outcome changes even when no behavioral change was recorded. In other words, in situations where behaviors did not demonstrate positive change, outcome change was more likely to occur than not to occur. Furthermore, outcome change occurred more often when behavior did not change than when it did.

Because the patterns of change are somewhat different, it would be useful to consider organizational and individual outcomes separately. Figures 10 and 11 exhibit the distributions of the studies for these two variables, respectively.

FIGURE 10

Number of Studies Showing Change in Individual Behavior and Organizational Outcome Variables

Individual Behavior

	+	0
+	2	7
0	2	8

Organizational Outcomes (rows: + , 0)

FIGURE 11

Number of Studies Showing Change in Individual Behavior and Individual Outcome Variables

Individual Behavior

	+	0
+	2	7
0	2	8

Individual Outcomes (rows: + , 0)

Individual Behavior and Organizational Outcomes. Looking at Figure 10, it is clear that the pattern of incompatible findings is not eliminated completely. When no behavioral change occurred, there were still positive organizational outcomes one-third of the time. And almost half of the occurrences of outcome change took place when there was no change in behavior. However, the overall pattern is basically in the direction predicted by the framework.

Individual Behavior and Individual Outcomes. The relationship between behavioral change and individual outcome change (Figure 11), on the other hand, is more confusing. For example, two studies demonstrated both behavioral change and outcomechange. Yet there were also two studies in which behavior changed and outcomes did not change. When behavior did not change, there was again nearly an equal frequency of outcome change and no outcome change. Ten of the 19 studies were consistent with the

framework, but the 8 cases in which neither behavior nor outcomes changed can hardly be considered support for the framework in light of the entire pattern of results. Overall, these findings suggest that there is no relationship between behavioral change and improvements in individual outcomes.[30]

It is possible that these findings are in part the result of the predominant focus on satisfaction as the individual outcome of interest. Because satisfaction is such a broad concept, and because there can be more or less satisfaction with a number of facets of the entire work context, it is particularly difficult to specify and verify empirically all of the influences on satisfaction. Therefore, the results presented here are not that surprising. Furthermore, while they certainly do not support the framework, the evidence is not enough to negate the framework, either. To assess the framework's validity regarding the link between changes in behavior and changes in individual outcomes, a broader range of individual outcomes must be incorporated into research on change.

Organizational Outcomes and Individual Outcomes. The final relationship to be investigated is between organizational and individual outcomes. The framework proposes that the two are interrelated in that (a) they both result from change in behavior and (b) each is enhanced by the other so that, in the long run, increases in one will be associated with increases in the other. The evidence regarding this hypothesis comes from 21 studies measuring both organizational and individual outcomes. Although not presented in the table format, the 21 studies provide no support for the framework. In fact, the 21 studies were evenly distributed across the four cells. Thus, 10 studies were congruent with the hypothesis while 11 contradicted it, indicating that there is no clear relationship between these two variables.

These results do not take into account the effects of time, however. The prediction was that, in the long run, organizational and individual outcomes would be related. This suggests that studies completed over a longer time period might show a stronger relationship between these two variables than those done in a shorter time frame. To investigate this possibility, the length of time of the intervention period was determined for each of the 21 studies that provided sufficient data. The intervention period was defined as the length of time between the start of the intervention and the date of the postmeasure. The average length of the intervention period of the studies in each cell was then calculated. Based on the hypothesis that the relationship between individual and organizational outcomes should be more apparent after longer intervention periods, the prediction would be that the average intervention period is longer when both types of outcomes change than when only one type changes. (Since a lack of change in both types of outcomes could be either a long-term or a short-term phenomenon, it is more difficult to predict the relative

average length of intervention of these studies.)

The data do not support this hypothesis. Ten months was the average length of the intervention of the five studies in which both organizational and individual outcomes changed as well as of the five studies in which only individual outcomes changed. For the six studies in which only organizational outcomes changed, the average length of the intervention was 18 months. (For the five studies in which no outcome change occurred, the average was 9 months.) One possible interpretation of this pattern is that change in individual outcomes alone can occur more quickly than change in organizational outcomes alone, and that the latter can occur more quickly when accompanied by change in the former. However, these studies provide no clear evidence of a direct relationship between individual outcomes and organizational outcomes.

Work Setting, Individual Behavior, and Outcomes. Up to this point we have been considering each link in the framework separately. However, it is possible to use a similar method to evaluate the extent to which the framework as a whole is supported. Specifically, a hypothesis that reflects the overall theoretical perspective of the framework is that outcome change is related to work setting change only as mediated by change in individuals' behavior. To examine the data relevant to this hypothesis, a three-dimensional table is needed, incorporating work setting change, individual behavior change, and outcome change. Figure 12 provides these data. This figure is similar to the previous figures, but it includes the third variable as well. Cells 1 through 4 are in the top row, while Cells 5 through 8 comprise the bottom row, as identified by the number in the upper left-hand corner. As before, a study was coded as demonstrating work setting change if there was significant positive change in any of the variables measured.

FIGURE 12

Number of Studies Showing Change in Work Setting, Individual Behavior, and Outcome Variables

		Work Setting			
		+		0	
		Individual Behavior		*Individual Behaivor*	
		+	0	+	0
Organizational Outcomes	+	**1** 4	**2** 7	**3** 1	**4** 3
	0	**5** 1	**6** 1	**7** 0	**8** 7

Likewise, if either organizational or individual outcomes had significant positive change, the study was coded as demonstrating outcome change.

Twenty-four studies were distributed among the eight cells representing the possible combinations of change in the three variables. In this matrix, Cells 1, 6, and 8 are consistent with the framework, Cell 5 is ambiguous (it does not support but it is not inconsistent with the model), and Cells 2, 3, 4 and 7 contradict the framework. In the overall pattern, then, 12 studies are consistent, eleven are contradictory, and 1 neither supports nor contradicts.

This distribution does not provide much support for the framework. The framework predicts that when there is change in the work setting, there will not be any outcome change unless there are changes in behavior. Thirteen studies demonstrated a change in the work setting. Eleven of these had positive changes in

outcomes, only four of which also had change in behavior. Therefore, outcome change apparently does not need to be mediated by behavioral change. Even when there was no change in the work setting, outcome change was preceded by behavioral change in only one out of four studies with positive change in outcomes.

On the other hand, the likelihood of positive outcome change apparently is greater when there is behavioral change than when there is not. When work setting changed, four out of the five studies with behavioral change resulted in positive outcome change. When the work setting did not change, the only study with behavioral change also had positive outcome improvements. In all, then, 83 percent (5 out of 6) of the studies with behavioral change had outcome change. In contrast, only 56 percent (10 out of 18) of the studies without behavioral change ended up with outcome change.

While outcome change seems to be related to behavioral change, it also seems to be associated with work setting change. Eight-six percent of the studies with work setting change resulted in outcome improvements (regardless of whether or not there was behavioral change), compared to only 36 percent of studies without work setting change. Of course, with data of this nature, any definitive conclusions are not possible. But based on the data in Figure 12, the trends would suggest that work setting change is more of a necessary, and less of a sufficient, condition for outcome change, while behavioral change is more of a sufficient, and less of a necessary, condition for outcome change.

Drawing on the last two findings, then, it is clear that changes in outcomes are much more likely when there is positive change at least in either the work setting or individual behavior. When neither work setting nor individual behavior change occurred, 70 percent of the studies did not result in any outcome change. When either work setting or individual behavioral change did occur, outcome change was demonstrated in 87 percent of the cases.

Summary

Evaluations of OD interventions from the past ten years were analyzed to assess the impact of different types of interventions on various organizational variables and to see if there were supportive evidence for predictions generated from the organizational framework regarding relationships between changes in various sets of these variables. In total, the interventions assessed resulted in positive change in the dependent variables, on the average, less than 40 percent of the time. Also, the four types of interventions demonstrated varying degrees of overall effectiveness, the seven dependent variables changed in a positive direction with varying degrees of frequency, and the different types of interventions showed varying patterns of relationships with the set of dependent variables.

As for the predictions from the organizational framework, (a) individual behavior change does appear to be related to change in the work setting variables, (b) there is some ambiguity regarding the relationship between individual behavioral change and change in outcome variables, and (c) there is little support for the hypothesized relationship between organizational and individual outcomes. Overall, these studies provide mixed support for the organizational framework.

Conclusion

In this chapter, we have attempted to present an overview of the field of organizational development by evaluating the current state of development of the field's theory base, describing a variety of the prominent interventions used to promote organizational change, and analyzing the results of 14 years' worth of empirical research exploring the impact of OD on organizations. In so doing, we have organized much of the material according to a framework we have found to be, and which we believe can continue to be, useful to the field for theoretical, practical, and empirical purposes. To conclude the chapter, then, we briefly offer a few additional observations on the nature of theory, practice, and research in organizational development.

Theory

Our evaluation of the state of theory development in the field concluded that, on the whole, OD theory is considerably underdeveloped. Confusion over what constitutes theory in the field and the field's relative youth and complexity may contribute to the present state of OD theory. In addition to these factors, however, we question whether everything of which we are capable is being done to develop as good a theoretical base as possible. As pointed out earlier, it appears that this is not the case. Change process theories do not demonstrate that they build on previous theoretical formulations; diagnostic models are not integrated into implementation procedure theories; change process theories do not draw from either diagnostic models or from the myriad of micro-intervention theories to specify potential manipulable variables; and the evaluation theory of Golembiewski et al. (1976) has been largely ignored in all other types of theoretical work. Therefore, regardless of the quality of theory ultimately available, the present level of development suffers from an apparent lack of effort to build upon previously developed theory and integrate it into new formulations.

An inattention to theory building may be attributable in part to the separation of theory and practice that is characteristic of the discipline of action-research (Cooperrider & Srivastva, 1987). Descriptions of action-research strategies focus primarily on the process of action-research and only secondarily, if at all, on the potential theoretical contributions of the research (Bartunek, 1983; Friedlander & Brown, 1974). In turn, according to Argyris (1983), practice-oriented scholars tend to accept their clients' definition of a problem and thus are unable to develop theories and testable propositions that are rooted in their experience of the change process. In short, then, an overemphasis on the practice of OD is seen as another factor responsible for the lack of theoretical development.

Of course, underlying the statement that OD theory is underdeveloped is a set of assumptions regarding the nature of theory and the characteristics of an adequately developed theory base. Traditionally, the standards for good theory are derived from a logical positivist approach to science. According to Cooperrider and Srivastva (1987), theory development in this tradition has as its goals the ability to understand, predict, and control the domain of interest by discerning general laws or principles governing the relationships between units of observable phenomena.

These principles are viewed as stable, enduring, reliable, and replicable. A primary criterion of a good theory is its correspondence with fact, and thus it is necessary for the theory to be verified through the testing of empirically disconfirmable hypotheses.

It has been argued that the rigor associated with the process of developing theory of this type may actually preclude development of theory that is useful (Argyris, 1983). Useful theory, from a social science perspective, is theory that can contribute to the change and development of social systems. This link between theory and action is a fundamental premise of action-research (Lewin, 1951), a discipline upon which OD is founded. Yet Cooperrider and Srivastva (1987) argue that, to the extent that social science conceives its role in the logical positivist sense, it stifles creative theorizing, unintentionally serves the interests of the status quo, underestimates the power and usefulness of theory, and thus reduces "the constructive role science can have in the *development* of the groups and organizations that make up our cultural world" (p. 137; italics in original).

Cooperrider and Srivastva go on to point out that since good theory is a powerful means for helping social systems evolve, adapt, and creatively alter themselves, theory should be judged not in terms of its predictive capacity, but in terms of its generative capacity—that is, its ability to generate new alternatives for social action. Good theory accomplishes this by opening dialogue regarding that which has previously been taken for granted, by generating new meanings and understandings, by expanding the realm of what is conventionally understood as possible, and by generating provocative new alternatives for social action.

Toward this end, Cooperrider and Srivastva argue for a reconceptualization of the action-research process. They propose that action-research move from a discipline that attempts to solve typical, organizationally defined problems by following the standardized rules of problem solving to one that promotes social innovation as it "decides to expand its universe of exploration, seeks to discover new questions, and rekindles a fresh perception of the extraordinary in everyday organizational life" (p. 159). Appreciative inquiry, as they call this process, is intended to awaken the desire to create and discover new social possibilities that can enrich our existence and give it meaning. More recently, Vaughan (1989) provided thoughtful support for this same perspective when he wrote that "applied social scientists should play a greater role in shaping the future by serving not merely as technical problem solvers, but also as developers of theoretical alternatives for the future" (p. 291).

One critique of these perspectives might be that they contain too much social activism, are too value laden and philosophical, and therefore are inappropriate for "true science." Our opinion is that these views on the way theory development in OD should occur are laudable and we hope that their recommendations are heeded.

Practice

Our earlier discussion on OD practice described interventions that have been developed for use by practitioners, many of them designed to address particular types of problems or issues. Not many new intervention methodologies have been developed as of late (Beer & Walton, 1987), which may indicate that insufficient new theory exists to drive the development of new change techniques. One implication of the lack of development of new change techniques is the apparent satisfaction with the types of organizational factors being addressed by the current set of interventions. However, we believe that OD should not remain stagnant in terms of the types of issues addressed. In particular, we wish to

encourage greater attention to two facets of organizations that have been largely ignored in the past, by planned change practitioners as well as by organizational scholars.

The first of these facets is the organization's physical setting. As this chapter has indicated, the physical setting has received very little attention by those theorizing about OD (e.g., those specifying organizational frameworks, diagnostic models, or change process), by those implementing change, and by those researching the impact of changes in key organizational elements. Little is known about how individual behavior, group or organizational processes, organizational performance, and individual development are related to the nature of the physical environment within which they work. Greater attention to these relationships is undoubtedly warranted.

The second facet worthy of greater attention revolves around the issue of organizational ownership. Specifically, it would be useful to begin exploring the consequences, for organizations and their members, of various forms of employee ownership. Employee ownership seems to us to be a logical extension of the principle of increased employee participation in organizations. Since this is perhaps the most fundamental principle underlying the various efforts that comprise the practice of OD (cf. Mohrman, Ledford, Lawler, & Mohrman, 1986), going a step further to address the issue of ownership seems both natural and highly desirable. While a literature on this topic is beginning to develop (e.g., Hammer & Stern, 1980; Klein, 1987; Long, 1980; Rosen, Klein, & Young, 1986; Toscano, 1983), considerably more research on the benefits, to both organizations and individuals, of providing greater ownership opportunities for all employees is highly recommended.

Greater attention to the physical setting and the issue of employee ownership would contribute to the most prominent trend noticeable in the practice of OD over the past decade. This trend is that OD in general is becoming increasingly more system oriented (cf. Woodman, 1989b). Brown and Covey (1987) point out that a comparison of the OD texts of the 1970s and 1980s reveals increasing attention to an organizational level of analysis. Sashkin and Burke (1987) view this trend as a more complete integration of the technostructural and human-processual approaches to OD. This greater systemic approach to planned change is evident in five relatively recent shifts in the field.

The first shift reflects an emphasis on what can be labeled high performance–high commitment work systems (Woodman, 1989b). Development of these organizations requires implementation of a constellation of changes designed to support and reinforce each other to produce systemwide change. This approach contrasts with a tendency in OD to address specific organizational concerns with the use of one or a small number of interventions or by changing a limited number of factors. Perhaps the best examples of this approach are new high-involvement plants in which new practices and innovative changes are installed more or less simultaneously (Lawler, 1978, 1982; Walton, 1980). The organizational elements that must be designed to effectively support the intended principle of high involvement include management philosophy and core values, organizational structure, job design, problem-solving groups, information systems, physical and technical design, reward systems, personnel policies, career systems, selection systems, training orientation, leadership style, and labor relations (Lawler, 1986).

Another example is that of self-designing organizations (Cummings & Mohrman, 1987; Mohrman & Cummings, 1989). This approach involves multiple stakeholders at all levels of the firm and focuses on continual organizational improvement through ongoing adjustments of all features of the organization—for example, strategy, structure, human resource practices, and technology. Continual, ongoing improvement is often necessary, since many organizations are confronted with rapid and ongoing transitions in their environments (Weisbord, 1988). Although systemic redesign of existing organizations toward high involvement or self-designing systems is more complex and difficult than creating new organizations in this manner, continued efforts in this direction are to be encouraged.

A second shift in the field is the adoption of a cultural metaphor of organizations. Although OD historically has recognized that cultural aspects of organizations are important (e.g., Bennis, 1966; Burke & Hornstein, 1972; French & Bell, 1978; Harrison, 1972b), it has never fully developed the concept (Beer & Walton, 1987). In the last decade, however, new and extensive focus has been given to the notion of organizational culture. This shift was ushered in by analyses of Japanese management by Ouchi (1981) and by Pascale and Athos (1981). Yet it was given its greatest impetus by the immense popularity of *In Search of Excellence* (Peters & Waterman, 1982), in tandem with the specific treatment of the subject of corporate cultures by Deal and Kennedy (1982). Since that time, management literature has been inundated with books and articles focusing on the process of managing or changing an organization's culture (e.g., Barney, 1986; Bate, 1990; Davis, 1984; Drake & Drake, 1988; Kerr & Slocum, 1987; Kilmann et al., 1985; O'Reilly, 1989; Sathe, 1985; Schein, 1985; Wilkins & Dyer, 1988). This focus on culture is consistent with the larger scale, systemic orientation toward change discussed earlier (Sashkin & Burke, 1987).

Although the renewed interest in culture was instigated primarily by those who might not consider themselves part of the field of OD, the practice of OD has been influenced by the implications of a focus on culture. A frequent recommendation derived from this perspective is that it is necessary to make sure that the culture is aligned with other organizational features (e.g., Kilmann, 1984; Tichy, 1983). This may entail changing other features to be congruent with the culture, but probably more often the focus is on changing the culture. While it is not clear to what extent culture can be consciously and proactively changed or managed (cf. Fitzgerald, 1988; Frost, Moore, Louis, Lundberg, & Martin, 1985; Robertson, 1986), many suggestions focus on intervening into the symbolic aspects of organizational life, using myths (Boje et al., 1982), symbols (Dandridge, 1985), metaphors (Krefting & Frost, 1985; Srivastva & Barrett, 1988; Sackmann, 1989), rites (Trice & Beyer, 1985), stories (Siehl, 1985; Feldman, 1990), and humor (Kahn, 1989). The notion underlying these approaches is that the organization's beliefs and values are reflected in a variety of symbols, and thus, by changing the symbolic elements, the beliefs and values will come to change as well. New intervention technologies for creating cultural change provide an important addition to the repertoire of tools available for creating organizational change.

While the cultural perspective has so far prompted greater attention to the symbolic aspects of organizational life, we believe its greatest potential contribution to OD practice can come from its explicit focus on the underlying assumptions and values that permeate organizations and all facets of their design. More specifically, this perspective can more effectively facilitate systemwide change to the extent that it provides the justification and the tools for surfacing deeply held and not always obvious beliefs, for examining the various ways in which these beliefs are enacted and reinforced, and for identifying the conflicts between values and assumptions that are espoused and those that are enacted (cf. Wilkins, 1983). To the extent that values and assumptions of key organizational decision makers can be confronted and changed, resulting in organizations that are more effective for all its constituents, OD practice

will have undoubtedly benefited from the adoption of a cultural metaphor of organizations.

Third, there has been increasing interest over the last few years in OD becoming more strategically based (Jelinek & Litterer, 1988). For example, efforts have been made to integrate the concepts and practices of strategic management with those of OD (e.g., Buller, 1988). This interest was generated as managers attempting to implement their strategic plans frequently found that their organizations did not change as intended. A greater focus on the requirements of effective implementation of strategy resulted in the use of OD techniques to help with the process of strategic change (Buller, 1988). Such change, often necessary to meet changing environmental demands, seeks to align an organization's strategy with such characteristics as its structure, human resource practices, and technology. It requires "significant alterations in the firm's design features to channel behaviors in the desired directions" (Cummings & Huse, 1989, p. 431). Thus, Jelinek and Litterer (1988) argue that OD should be strategically based because the systemic changes facing organizations require systemic diagnoses and systemic remedies.

The emphasis on organization culture discussed above has helped to forge the link between OD and strategic change. This is because, in addition to various design features, effective strategic change requires an alignment between the organization's strategy and its culture (Bourgeois, 1986). An organization's present culture can be either a strength or a weakness as the organization attempts to implement a new strategy (Schwartz & Davis, 1981). Organizations have found that it is difficult to implement a new strategy that is inconsistent with the organization's culture (e.g., "Corporate Culture," 1980). Thus, effective management of the organization's cultural system is a fundamental aspect of strategic change (Tichy, 1983). As concepts and techniques for assessing and changing cultures developed in OD, this expertise became increasingly useful to those interested in implementing strategic change.

A fourth trend emerging in the field is an increased focus on organizational transformation. Transformation entails a second-order, fundamental alteration of the qualitative nature of the organization (Cummings & Huse, 1989; Torbert, 1989).[31] It involves a change in the organizational paradigm, which can be defined as the fundamental set of beliefs or organizing principles that are unquestioned and unexamined assumptions about the nature of reality (Adams, 1984), or the system's metarules that unnoticeably shape perceptions, procedures, and behaviors (Levy, 1986). Thus, transformation can be viewed as consisting of a radical shift in the typical ways individuals perceive, think, and act, for example, through schema change (Poole, Gioia, & Gray, 1989), or through reframing perceptions of reality or raising consciousness about the transformation process (Levy & Merry, 1986). The goal is a "learning organization" (Porras & Silvers, 1991), with the capability for continuous self-diagnosis and change. This is similar to what Bartunek and Moch (1987) refer to as third-order change.

Transformational change is induced primarily through a change in the organization's vision (Frame, Nielsen, & Pate, 1989; Porras & Silvers, 1991), although other approaches have begun to surface in the literature (e.g., transformation through the use of metaphors; Sackmann, 1989). In an example of transformation through vision change, Beer (1987) evaluates three cases in which the development of a future vision for the organization was an element critical to successful change.

Typically, a redefinition of an organization's vision comes in response to drastic environmental or internal disruptions, crises, or life cycle changes (Bartunek & Louis, 1989; Cummings & Huse, 1989; Tushman, Newman, & Romanelli, 1986).[32] However, because the organizational vision provides the logic for all other system factors, these factors will have to be altered as well if the vision shifts. Thus, organizational transformation will necessarily entail changes in the core processes used by the organization (Levy, 1986). Historically, changes in these factors have been facilitated by traditional OD interventions. In the future, in addition to cultural change, an alignment of culture, strategy, and organizational processes and structures must also occur.

As indicated earlier, the renewed interest in organizational culture and the recent focus on strategic management and change are yielding methods for bringing about these new alignments. However, Levy (1986) points out most of the efforts developed by OD practitioners to change the organizational culture do not go deeply enough to facilitate second-order change. Instead, it is necessary to change the system metarules, or underlying assumptions, which have been defined by some to be the core of a culture (e.g., Schein, 1985). This is equivalent to a change in the organization's paradigm.[33]

By itself, change in core processes and structures is similar to what Lundberg (1989) refers to as organizational change. Alignment of strategy, culture, structures, and processes is similar to what he calls organizational development. A shift in the organizational paradigm is consistent with what he also labels organizational transformation. The point is that these three types of organizational change processes are nested, such that in Lundberg's terms, organizational development implies the necessity of organizational change, and organizational transformation implies the necessity of organizational development and organizational change. Torbert (1989) suggests that, despite the number of consultants and writers who have claimed to promote and document transformational changes, "intentional transformational action leading to second-order change is very rare" (p. 89).

The final trend in the field of OD we wish to identify is the growing use of OD applications to help implement change in increasingly broader-scaled contexts; specifically, in interorganizational domains and in multinational corporations. Interorganizational domains are groups of organizations that collaborate to address problems or issues that are too complex for a single organization to resolve (Trist, 1983). Recently, Gray (1990) conceptualized a model for understanding the process of interorganizational alliance development and identified arenas in which OD interventions could be useful. Programs of planned change are being used more often in these domains.

Interorganizational or transorganizational development (Cummings, 1984; Motamedi, 1985; Schermerhorn, 1979; Trist, 1985) attempts to improve the ability of these interdependent organizations to effectively accomplish their mission. Recent examples of interorganizational development include efforts to reshape community leadership networks in a large metropolitan area (Brown & Detterman, 1987), and the development of mechanisms for regulating information exchange and handling the resolution of conflict between the members of a domain of community groups (Gricar & Brown, 1981).

Brown and Covey (1987) point out that efforts such as these are good examples of applied behavioral science interventions that shape societal changes through interorganizational cooperation partnerships among diverse organizations. They stress that it is important for OD consultants to adopt a societal perspective that recognizes the external impacts and long-term consequences of their work. Otherwise, success at the domain level can produce unintended and dysfunctional consequences at the broader societal level. With this caution in mind, it is clear that increased attention to problems at the interorganizational level, and efforts to improve the functioning of the interorganizational domains that are chartered with addressing these issues, can make important contributions to societal development as well.

Multinational corporations are another arena in which OD has been utilized. Multinationals are similar to interorganizational domains in that they are often loosely coupled "network organizations" (Woodman, 1989b, p. 216). Evans (1989) provides an historical overview of the role of OD in multinationals. He points out that OD has not always been entirely relevant to multinational firms because of its traditional focus on the internal system of the firm (cf. Heenan & Perlmutter, 1979) and because many of its values and technologies are culture bound (cf. Jaeger, 1976). Evans argues that the task of OD is to help multinationals develop their organizational capabilities through (a) building critical dualistic properties (e.g., differentiation–integration; loose–tight; planned–opportunistic; vision–reality) into their organizational cultures and (b) building the appropriate degree of global integration while allowing for sufficient differentiation to achieve necessary local responsiveness.

These five trends, then, reflect a move in the field to a more systemic orientation. This shift has resulted in OD becoming less person-centered and more organization-centered. "OD work is increasingly defined, managed, and controlled by client organizations in the 1980s" (Mirvis, 1988, p. 36). A strategic orientation puts OD in service of larger organizational goals, encompassing the key concerns of managers (Jelinek & Litterer, 1988). For example, OD is now frequently linked to the human resource management function in organizations, with a growing emphasis on operational and financial matters (Mirvis, 1988). Yet in this movement can be seen a potential reason for some concern. It may be that OD is no longer "different enough" and that it may have been co-opted by the system (Sashkin & Burke, 1987, p. 410). More pointedly, Mirvis (1988) suggests that it "raises the important question of whether or not OD has 'sold out' " (p. 42). The extent to which OD maintains its perspective regarding the importance and interdependence of both organizational effectiveness *and* personal development must be monitored carefully as the field heads into the 1990s and beyond.

Research

Our discussion of OD research in this chapter focused on the results of evaluations of the impact of OD interventions. It would be useful, therefore, to briefly address the quality and nature of research in the field. It appears that, in general, there is a greater quantity of higher quality research being performed. For example, our review found 63 studies, from the period 1975 to 1988, which met a set of methodological criteria. These criteria were not overly stringent, yet a useful comparison can be made to a review from a decade earlier. Porras and Berg (1978), searching the entire OD literature that existed up until 1975, found 35 studies that met an even more lenient set of criteria. If the present criteria were applied to the set of studies they evaluated, only 20 would meet all of them. Thus, the number of studies meeting this basic level of methodological rigor is apparently on the rise.

There are other indications that improvements in OD research are being made. Roberts and Porras (1982) concluded that progress was being made in four areas: (a) the operationalization of the concept of change, (b) the development of research designs, (c) measurement processes and procedures, and (d) the design of statistical procedures used to analyze intervention data. Vicars and Hartke (1984) found, relative to an earlier study (Morrison, 1978), an increase in validity criteria and in the use of controls. Nicholas and Katz (1985) found that, since 1977, there have been substantial increases in the use of both quasi-experimental designs and statistical analyses. And Beer and Walton (1987) concluded that investigators are increasingly using quantitative data, sophisticated research

designs, and statistical procedures aimed at accurate measurement of change.

In addition to these methodological improvements, there have also been recent developments geared toward evaluating what can be learned from OD research. Meta-analysis has begun to be used as a tool for assessing the pattern of findings across a group of studies regarding the relationship between OD interventions and outcome variables (Beekun, 1989; Guzzo, Jette, & Katzell, 1985; Neuman, Edwards, & Raju, 1989; Robertson, Roberts, & Porras, 1991) or between relevant organizational characteristics and outcomes (Carsten & Spector, 1987; Farrell & Stamm, 1988; Fried & Ferris, 1987; Miller & Monge, 1986; Spector, 1986; Tubbs, 1986; Wagner & Gooding, 1987; Wood, Mento, & Locke, 1987). Some of these analyses examine the influence of moderator variables on these relationships as well. These meta-analyses typically have used traditional techniques (e.g., Glass, McGaw, & Smith, 1982; Hunter, Schmidt, & Jackson, 1982). However, a recommendation has been made for greater use of case meta-analyses (Bullock, 1986; Bullock & Tubbs, 1987), since much of the OD evaluation literature consists of case studies.

The validity of OD research is being evaluated through attempts to determine whether methodological rigor is associated with the likelihood of positive findings. Terpstra (1981) found evidence of a positive-findings bias—that is, an inverse relationship between positive findings and the methodological rigor of evaluation studies. Further analyses (Barrick & Alexander, 1987; Bullock & Svyantek, 1983; Golembiewski & Sun, 1990; Guzzo et al., 1985; Neuman et al., 1989; Woodman & Wayne, 1985) have found mixed results. A recent study by Roberts and Robertson (1991) indicated that the rigor measure typically used in research on positive-findings bias—an equally weighted sum of scores on various rigor dimensions—is of questionable validity. Continued efforts to aggregate research findings and to monitor the validity of these findings would be useful.

OD research is thus demonstrating improvements in the use of methods that are more rigorous according to the traditional criteria derived from a logical positivist approach. However, related to the reactions discussed earlier regarding the process of theory development, greater recognition is being given to the potential problems inherent in the use of traditional methods to study and assess organizational change (e.g., Argyris, 1980; Carnall, 1982; Legge, 1984). For example, two problems identified by Argyris (1980) are (a) the requirements of precision and quantification may result in instruments whose meanings are not rooted in the context experienced by subjects in their everyday life, and which thus may be confusing, unclear, and ambiguous; and (b) the axiom that the purpose of science is to understand and explain, with prediction and control being tests of the degree to which this is achieved, leads to a social science of the status quo.

Beer and Walton (1987) summarize additional problems. First, research relying on traditional science, since it attempts to isolate causation, often focuses on identifying the results of a single intervention while overlooking the systemic nature of organizations. However, since a constellation of causes, including exogenous variables and intervening events, is likely to produce changes, it is nearly impossible to identify the precise effect of a given action. Second, reliance on traditional methods may prevent gathering the extensive qualitative data that would describe in depth the nature of the intervention process and the situation in which it occurs. Lack of such data can inhibit full understanding of the numerous influences operating to produce or prevent change from occurring. Research combining quantitative and qualitative methods would be beneficial to the evaluation of change (Woodman, 1989a). Third, the use of control groups may produce problems for the change program being assessed—for example, if they resent the changes being made for the experimental group and

take action to prevent further change (e.g., Blumberg & Pringle, 1983). In any event, true experimental designs with random assignment of experimental and control groups are incompatible with OD change processes (Bullock & Svyantek, 1987).

One consequence of doing research of this nature is that the knowledge produced is often not very useful to those wanting to implement organizational change or to enhance organizational effectiveness (Beer & Walton, 1987; Lawler, 1985). Therefore, new approaches, using new methodologies and/or applying new criteria for good research, are being recommended with increasing frequency (e.g., Argyris, Putnam, & Smith, 1985; Kilmann, Thomas, Slevin, Nath, & Jerrell, 1983; Lawler, Mohrman, Mohrman, Ledford, Cummings, & Associates, 1985). A comprehensive list of the specific suggestions offered by researchers such as these would be lengthy, and in fact not all of the recommendations are compatible with each other. In light of this, the conclusion drawn by Lawler (1985) seems very appropriate:

> This is not to argue that traditional research is to be discontinued or that there is only one right way to do research; rather, there are multiple valid ways to do research in organizations, and the field needs to be eclectic in the approaches it includes. In short, the argument is that there is more than one way of establishing theory and fact. There are multiple ways, and these all need to be used if research that contributes to both theory and practice is to be conducted. (p. 15)

Summary

To conclude this chapter, we wish to make explicit a final, although probably rather obvious, point implicit in Lawler's advice. Specifically, although we have addressed the topics of

OD theory, practice, and research separately in this chapter, these three aspects are inevitably and inextricably intertwined. By its very nature, OD requires a constant and thorough interaction between these three facets. Although the specific activities required for theory development, research, and change implementation may at times be different, those engaging in any of the three should strive to ensure that their efforts can make a contribution to either or both of the other two. Furthermore, they should draw on work done in other areas to facilitate their own efforts. For example, theory can help to create change by "expand[ing] the realm of what is conventionally understood as possible" (Cooperrider & Srivastva, 1987, p. 138); studying the process of implementing change can help build a theory base (e.g., Gray, 1985); meta-analysis of research results can also enhance theory development (Bullock & Tubbs, 1987); and finally, involvement in the process of implementing change yields benefits to the research that cannot be gained from remaining in simply an observational role (Cummings et al., 1985).

Since its inception as a field, the impact of environmental change on organizations has been given as a preeminent justification and rationale for OD's value to organizations. In the 25 years since Emery and Trist (1965) warned of the impact of turbulent environments, the one thing that has remained constant (if not gotten worse) is environmental turbulence. Events of the last decade have left many organizations fighting a constant battle for survival, with no smooth roads in sight. As a result, many organizations have been, and are likely to continue to be, willing to take more drastic steps to adapt to new environmental conditions and to ensure that they are able to continue to adapt as new changes emerge.

Helping organizations with this process of development is a primary element of OD's charter. Therefore, OD seems to have arrived at a new threshold of opportunity. It is thus critical that those in the field strive to enhance OD's usefulness to organizations. This can be achieved by developing theory that is pertinent to organizations and that enables them to view their realities in a new light; by implementing change that is systemic in nature and that addresses fundamental characteristics such as underlying assumptions, beliefs, and values; by engaging in research that produces knowledge and information that can be translated into new insights, methods, and possibilities that are directly useful to organizations; and by ensuring that these activities all contribute to and build on each other. Together, these tasks provide a challenging and exciting agenda for the field in the decade to come.

We would like to express appreciation to Lisa Goldman for her help with data collection and analysis, and to Darryl R. Roberts for his help with the literature search.

Notes

1   At present, there is disagreement in the field over whether OD can be used to describe transformational types of change activities. A new label called *organizational transformation* has recently surfaced (Adams, 1984; Levy & Merry, 1986) and is purported by its proponents to describe a uniquely different approach to change, and, as such, to merit a new name. For our purposes, we will use *organizational development* to describe all theory, practice, and research focused on both developmental and transformational change.

2   Substantial portions of this section are drawn from Porras (1987).

3   An additional key finding of this study related to whether differences in the change agent's conceptual approach affected the behaviors identified as most important in a change process. An analysis of responses grouped according to whether the subject focused primarily on altering the human-processual variables or the technostructural variables in the organization yielded no significant differences between the two groups. The authors concluded that selection of organizational variables does not affect the composition of the set of behaviors viewed as essential for effective change.

4 The factors we describe here are not new and are in fact well known to all who have worked in or studied organizations. Furthermore, the categories into which we group these factors have also been identified previously. However, they have been defined differently than they are here, and thus the particular combination of factors comprising each category is new and we believe more parsimonious than previous formulations.

5 Up to now, we have proposed that the connections between behavior on the job and both organizational performance and personal development are unidirectional—that is, that behavior influences performance and development but the influence does not also go in the opposite direction. Clearly, this is not the case, for there are times that both the performance of the organization and the level of personal development affect behavior on the job. We believe, however, that the dominant direction of the forces at work is from behavior outward, especially from the point of view of planned change. In the planned change situation, the outcomes of the organization cannot be changed directly. They are altered as a consequence of the behavioral changes that occur, which are also a consequence of the change efforts going on in the system. Thus, it is more consistent with our discussion to consider the forces in the direction shown in Figure 2, although we recognize that they may also go in the other direction.

6 Substantial portions of this section are drawn from Porras and Robertson (1987).

7 We should note that a more complex set of relationships than the ones depicted here actually occurs in planned change processes. Feedback of effects normally occurs (e.g., changes in M_1 may in turn impact I, changes in M_2 may impact both M_1 and I, etc. Unfortunately, at this point in the development of OD theory, we are forced to assume rather simplistic change models.

8 This review, upon which the following analysis is based, covered the period from 1950 to 1985 and included a search of (a) the more prominent academic journals in the field (*Academy of Management Journal, Academy of Management Review, Administrative Science Quarterly, Group and Organization Studies, Human Relations, Journal of Applied Behavioral Science,* and *Journal of Occupational Behavior*), (b) the leading

OD textbooks (Beer, 1980; Burke, 1982; French & Bell 1984; Huse & Cummings, 1985; Tichy, 1983), and (c) prominent books of OD reading (Bennis, Benne, & Chin, 1985; French, Bell, & Zawacki, 1983; Tannenbaum, Margulies, & Massarik, 1985; and Warrick, 1985).

9 A few additional theories focusing on change dynamics were found (e.g., Kinberly & Nielsen, 1975; Schein, 1969). but they were insufficiently specified in that causal mechanisms were not adequately identified. Therefore, they were not included in the analysis.

10 Porras (1979) and Porras and Wilkins (1980) have presented findings that tend to discount this assumption. Outcome improvements were found to occur without concomitant improvement in organizational processes, implying that the relationship between these two variables is more complex than has been assumed.

11 In recent research, Hamilton (1988) identified additional interpersonal competence factors associated with change agent effectiveness, namely openness and responsiveness to the needs and concerns of others, comfort with oneself in relation to others, and comfort with ambiguity and the ability to make sense of it.

12 Substantial portions of this section are drawn from Porras (1986).

13 One basic assumption of a T-group is that although on the surface it may appear to be an artificial environment, in fact it is a microcosm of situations encountered in everyday life, both work and nonwork.

14 Examples of diagnostic questions are: "What are the things that help us work more/less effectively together? What facilitates/blocks better communication between us? Do we know what our goals are? Are there conflicts between us that remain unresolved?" (Dryer, 1977).

15 In the discussion that follows, the term *autonomous work groups* will be used to describe self-regulating work groups also. The distinction between the two is more semantic than substantive.

16 We systematically reviewed six journals that contain articles pertaining to organization development: *Academy of Management Journal, Administrative Science Quarterly, Group and Organization Studies, Human Factors, Human Relations,* and *Journal of Applied Behavioral Science.* Articles were also obtained from a number of additional sources, including

Academy of Management Proceedings, Environment and Behavior, Journal of Applied Psychology, Journal of Management Studies, Organizational Behavior and Human Performance, Personnel Psychology, and Cummings and Srivastva (1977). The 1975 to 1988 time period was chosen because Porras and Berg (1978) reviewed the literature up through 1975.

17　Eight of these reported more than one set of results (i.e., different results for two or more target groups). As a consequence, we counted each of these substudies as a separate study. Of the eight studies, seven reported two sets of results and one reported three sets. Therefore, a total of 72 studies provide the data for discussion.

18　A single intervention was used in many studies, and thus these studies were classified according to the typology of interventions given in Table 9. Other studies, however, reported using more than one type of intervention. In those cases in which the interventions were all from the same category, the studies were classified into that category. Many of the studies that used organizing arrangements, technology, or physical settings interventions also used survey feedback, a social factors intervention. In these cases, the survey feedback was considered supplementary, while the other intervention was viewed as the primary intervention, and thus the studies were classified according to the category of the latter. Six studies used primary interventions from more than one category, and these have been classified into multiple categories, one for each of the primary interventions.

19　To be considered positive change, there had to be a significant ($p < .05$) increase/improvement in the variable. For negative change, there had to be a significant ($p < .05$) decrease. If a variable did not show significant change in either direction, it was considered no change.

20　We chose to use percentages rather than the actual frequencies so that in determining average rates of change across studies, each of the studies would be counted equally in the analysis. Using raw frequencies would result in an unequal weighting based on the number of variables measured in the study. For example, many of the studies measured satisfaction. Some of the studies reported an overall assessment of this individual outcome variable. Others reported changes in many subscales of satisfaction, such as job satisfaction, satisfaction with supervisor, and satisfaction with co-workers. If

frequencies were used in the analysis, rather than percentages, studies that reported the results of seven subscales of satisfaction would weight seven times more heavily than those which only reported the overall change in satisfaction. Therefore, it is more appropriate to use percentages than raw frequencies.

21　The preceding numbers add up to more than 72 because, as indicated earlier, six of the studies reported multifaceted, multicategory interventions and were thus classified into more than one category.

22　These overall averages are weighted averages of the average percentage changes of the seven individual variables, with the weights being the number of studies that measured the particular variable. (For Columns 2 through 5, the weights are the number of studies, from among only that used the relevant type of intervention, that measured the variable of interest.) In other words, the average percentage change in each variable was multiplied by the number of studies measuring that variable. The resulting seven products were summed and divided by the number of studies employing that type of intervention that measured that particular variable.

23　As a caveat, all of the positive change in physical setting variables occurred as a result of physical setting interventions. Furthermore, only 15 such variables were measured in the entire set of studies, compared to 69 technology variables, which were the next least frequently measured. Thus, as will be discussed more later, the high rate of positive change in physical setting variables is rather misleading.

24　While beta change is a phenomenon relevant only to variables measured through reports of organizational members, sufficient number of the variables in these studies were measured in this manner that we believe beta change cold be partly responsible for the frequent occurrence of a lack of change in the dependent variables.

25　There was actually only one physical setting variable measured as a dependent variable for each of the organizing arrangements, social factors, and technology intervention categories. Thus the "100 percent no change" found in these cells in Table 11 simply reflects the fact that, in each case, the one variable measured did not demonstrate any change.

26　The exception is the impact of physical setting interventions on physical setting variables which, because of the small number of variables involved, is not a strong finding.

27 Herein, the term *variables* will refer to the seven variables in the framework, while the phrase *specific variables* will refer to the particular variables of that type measured in a given study.

28 For the following analyses, negative change and nonsignificant change are combined into a single category that represents the lack of significant positive change.

29 Although the data are not presented here, there is little difference among the four individual work setting variables regarding the associations between work setting change and behavioral change. For each work setting variable, most of the data either support the framework or at least do not contradict it.

30 The particular variables measured in these studies were examined to see whether different patterns of relationships were associated with different kinds of variables. However, in looking for any trends that might explain the pattern of results described here, none could be found. Regardless of the type of individual behaviors measured, different studies with similar variables would demonstrate different results—that is, the results would fall into different cells in the table. Furthermore, since in most of the studies the only individual outcomes measured were various satisfaction variables, the entries in the various cells cannot be explained as a function of the type of outcome variable measured, either.

31 Leifer (1989) discusses an innovative approach to understanding organizational transformation though the use of the dissipative structure model.

32 Cummings and Huse (1989) point out that transformational change is not always developmental in nature, in that the organization may undergo transformation without developing its capacity to solve problems, to achieve high performance as well as quality of work life, and to develop human resources by involving members in problem solving, communication, and innovation.

33 The emphasis on organizational transformation in the field of OD has undoubtedly been motivated in part by the recent trends focusing on cultural and strategic change in organizations. Indeed, many writers seem to equate cultural or strategic change with organizational transformation (e.g., Cummings & Huse, 1989, chap. 16;

Jelinek & Litterer, 1988, pp. 155–156; Tichy, 1983, p. 17; Woodman, 1989b, pp. 214–215). Whether cultural change is equivalent to transformation depends on the conceptualization of culture utilized and the degree to which the change focuses on underlying assumptions and meanings rather than simply on norms and values. Whether strategic change is transformational depends on the extent to which it involves a paradigmatic shift in culture, structures, and processes to support the implementation of a new strategy rather than simply on a change in strategic direction.

References

Ackoff, R. L. (1981). *Creating the corporate future.* New York: Wiley.

Ackoff, R. L. (1989). The circular organization: An update. *Academy of Management Executive, 3,* 11–16.

Adams, J. D. (Ed.). (1984). *Transforming work: A collection of organizational transformation readings.* Alexandria, VA: Miles River Press.

Adams, J., & Sherwood, J. J. (1979). An evaluation of organizational effectiveness: An appraisal of how army internal consultants use survey feedback in a military setting. *Group & Organization Studies, 4,* 170–182.

Ahmavaara, Y. (1954). Transformation analysis of factorial data. *Annals of the Academy of Science Fennicae,* Series B, *881*(2), 54–59.

Alderfer, C. P. (1972). *Human needs in organizational settings.* New York: Free Press.

Alderfer, C. P., Tucker, R. C., Alderfer, C. J., & Tucker, L. M. (1988). The race relations advisory group: An intergroup intervention. In W. A. Pasmore & R. W. Woodman (Eds.), *Research in organizational change and development* (Vol. 2). Greenwich, CT: JAI Press.

Allen, T. J., & Gerstberger, P. G. (1973). A field experiment to improve communications in a product engineering department: The nonterritorial office. *Human Factors, 5,* 487–498.

Allport, G. W. (1961). *Pattern and growth in personality.* New York: Holt, Rinehart and Winston.

Ansoff, H. I. (1984). *Implanting strategic management.* Englewood Cliffs, NJ: Prentice-Hall.

Argyris, C. (1957). *Personality and organization: The conflict between the system and the individual.* New York: Harper and Row.

Argyris, C. (1970). *Intervention theory and method.* Reading, MA: Addison-Wesley.

Argyris, C. (1971). *Management and organizational development.* New York: McGraw-Hill.

Argyris, C. (1980). *Inner contradictions of rigorous research.* New York: Academic Press.

Argyris, C. (1982). *Reasoning, learning, and action: Individual and organizational.* San Francisco: Jossey-Bass.

Argyris, C. (1983). Action science and intervention. *Journal of Applied Behavioral Science, 19,* 115–140.

Argyris, C., Putnam, R., & Smith, D. M. (1985). *Action science.* San Francisco: Jossey-Bass.

Argyris, C., & Schön, D. (1978). *Organizational learning: A theory of action perspective.* Reading, MA: Addison-Wesley.

Armenakis, A. A. (1988). A review of research on the change typology. In W. A. Pasmore & R. W. Woodman (Eds.), *Research in organizational change and development* (Vol. 2.). Greenwich, CT: JAI Press.

Armenakis, A. A., Feild, H. S., & Wilmoth, J. N. (1977). An algorithm for assessing factor structure congruence. *Educational and Psychological Measurement, 37,* 213–214.

Armenakis, A. A., Randolph, W., & Bedeian, A. G. (1982). A comparison of two methods for evaluating the similarity of factor analytic solutions. *Proceedings of the Southwest Academy of Management Meeting.*

Armenakis, A., & Smith, L. (1978). A practical alternative to comparison group designs in OD evaluations: The abbreviated time series design. *Academy of Management Journal, 21,* 499–507.

Armenakis, A. A., & Zmud, R. W. (1979). Interpreting the measurement of change in organizational research. *Personnel Psychology, 32,* 709–723.

Arvey, R. D., Dewhirst, H. D., & Brown, E. M. (1978). A longitudinal study of the impact of changes in goal setting on employee satisfaction. *Personnel Psychology, 31,* 595–608.

Bandura, A. (1977). *Social learning theory.* Englewood Cliffs, NJ: Prentice-Hall.

Bandura, A. (1986). *Social foundations of thought and action: A social cognitive theory.* Englewood Cliffs, NJ: Prentice-Hall.

Barnard, C. I. (1938). *The functions of the executive.* Cambridge, MA: Harvard University Press.

Barney, J. B. (1986). Organizational culture: Can it be a source of sustained competitive advantage? *Academy of Management Review, 11,* 656–665.

Barrick, M., & Alexander, R. A. (1987). A review of quality circle efficacy and the existence of positive-findings bias. *Personnel Psychology, 40,* 579–592.

Bartunek, J. M. (1983). How organization development can develop organizational theory. *Group & Organization Studies, 8,* 303–318.

Bartunek, J. M., & Keys, C. B. (1982). Power equalization in schools through organization development. *Journal of Applied Behavioral Science, 18,* 171–183.

Bartunek, J. M., & Louis, M. R. (1989). The interplay of organization development and organizational transformation. In R. W. Woodman & W. A. Pasmore (Eds.), *Research in organizational change and development* (Vol. 3). Greenwich, CT: JAI Press.

Bartunek, J. M., & Moch, M. K. (1987). First-order, second-order, and third-order change and organization development interventions: A cognitive approach. *Journal of Applied Behavioral Science, 23,* 483–500.

Bass, B. M. (1983). Issues involved in relations between methodological rigor and reported outcomes in evaluations of organizational development. *Journal of Applied Psychology, 68,* 197–199.

Bate, P. (1990). Using the culture concept in an organization development setting. *Journal of Applied Behavioral Science, 26,* 83–106.

Becker, F. D. (1981). *Workspace: Creating environments in organizations.* New York: Praeger.

Beckhard, R. (1967). The confrontation meeting. *Harvard Business Review, 45,* 149–153.

Beckhard, R. (1969). *Organization development: Strategies and models.* Reading, MA: Addison-Wesley.

Beckhard, R., & Harris, R. T. (1977). *Organizational transitions: Managing complex change.* Reading, MA: Addison-Wesley.

Beekun, R. I. (1989). Assessing the effectiveness of sociotechnical interventions: Antidote or fad? *Human Relations, 42,* 877–897

Beer, M. (1980). *Organization change and development: A systems view.* Santa Monica: Goodyear.

Beer, M. (1987). Revitalizing organizations: Change process and emergent model. *Academy of Management Executive, 1,* 51–55.

Beer, M., & Walton, A. E. (1987). Organization change and development. *Annual Review of Psychology, 38,* 339–367.

Bennis, W. G. (1966). *Changing organizations.* New York: McGraw-Hill.

Bennis, W. G. (1969). *Organization development: Its nature, origins, and prospects.* Reading, MA: Addison-Wesley.

Bennis, W. G., Benne, K. D., & Chin, R. (Eds.). (1985). *The planning of change* (4th ed.). New York: CBS College.

Bernstein, W. M., & Burke, W. W. (1989). Modeling organizational meaning systems. In R. W. Woodman & W. A. Pasmore (Eds.), *Research in organizational change and development* (Vol. 3). Greenwich, CT: JAI Press.

Bhagat, R. S., & Chassie, M. B. (1980). Effects of changes in job characteristics on some theory-specific attitudinal outcomes: Results from a naturally occurring quasi-experiment. *Human Relations, 33,* 297–313.

Blake, R. R., & Mouton, J. S. (1968). *Corporate excellence through grid organization development.* Houston, TX: Gulf.

Blake, R. R., Shepard, H. A., & Mouton, J. S. (1964). *Managing intergroup conflict in industry.* Houston, TX: Gulf.

Blau, P. M. (1974). *On the nature of organizations.* New York: Wiley.

Blumberg, M., & Pringle, C. D. (1983). How control groups can cause loss of control in action research: The case of Rushton Coal Mine. *Journal of Applied Behavioral Science, 19,* 409–425.

Bocialetti, G. (1987). Quality of work life: Some unintended effects on the seniority tradition of an industrial union. *Group & Organization Studies, 12,* 386–410.

Boje, M., Fedor, D. B., & Rowland, K. M. (1982). Myth making: A qualitative step in OD interventions. *Journal of Applied Behavioral Science, 18,* 17–28.

Boss, R. W. (1979). It doesn't matter if you win or lose, unless you're losing: Organizational change in a law enforcement agency. *Journal of Applied Behavioral Science,* 15, 199–220.

Boss, R. W., & McConkie, M. L. (1981). The destructive impact of a positive team-building intervention. *Group & Organization Studies, 6,* 45–56.

Bourgeois, L. J. (1986). Strategic management: From concept to implementation. In G. E. Germane (Ed.), *The executive course: What every manager needs to know about the essentials of business.* Reading, MA: Addison-Wesley.

Bowers, D. G. (1973). OD techniques and their results in 23 organizations: The Michigan ICL Study. *Journal of Applied Behavioral Science, 9,* 21–43.

Bowers, D. G., & Franklin, J. L. (1972). Survey-guided development: Using human resource measurement in organizational change. *Journal of Contemporary Business, 1,* 43–55.

Bowers, D. G., Franklin, J. L., & Pecorella, P. A. (1975). Matching problems, precursors and interventions in OD: A systemic approach. *Journal of Applied Behavioral Science, 11,* 391–409.

Brill, M., Margulis, S. T., Konar, E., & BOSTI. (1984). *Using office design to increase productivity* (Vol. 1). Buffalo, NY: Workplace Design and Productivity.

Brill, M., Margulis, S. T., Konar, E., & BOSTI. (1985). *Using office design to increase productivity* (Vol. 2). Buffalo, NY: Workplace Design and Productivity.

Brown, L. D., & Covey, J. G. (1987). Development organizations and organization development: Toward an expanded paradigm for organization development. In R. W. Woodman & W. A. Pasmore (Eds.), *Research in organization change and development* (Vol. 1). Greenwich, CT: JAI Press.

Brown, L. D., & Detterman, L. (1987). Small interventions for large problems: Reshaping urban leadership networks. *Journal of Applied Behavioral Science, 23,* 151–168.

Buller, P. F. (1988). For successful strategic change: Blend OD practices with strategic management. *Organizational Dynamics, 16,* 42–55.

Buller, P. F., & Bell, C. H. (1986). Effects of team building and goal setting on productivity: A field experiment. *Academy of Management Journal, 29,* 305–328.

Bullock, R. J. (1986). A meta-analysis method for OD case studies. *Group & Organization Studies, 11,* 33–48.

Bullock, R. J., & Svyantek, D. J. (1983). Positive-findings bias in positive-findings bias research: An unsuccessful replication. *Academy of Management Proceedings, 221–224.*

Bullock, R. J., & Tubbs, M. E. (1987). The case meta-analysis method for OD. In R. W. Woodman & W. A. Pasmore (Eds.), *Research in organizational change and development* (Vol. 1). Greenwich, CT: JAI Press.

Burke, W. W. (1974). Managing conflict between groups. In J. D. Adams (Ed.), *Theory and method in organization development: An evolutionary process.* Arlington, VA: NTL Institute for Applied Behavioral Sciences.

Burke, W. W. (1982). *Organization development.* Boston: Little, Brown.

Burke, W. W., & Hornstein, H. A. (Eds.). (1972). *The social technology of organization development.* Fairfax, VA: NTL Learning Resources.

Bushe, G. R. (1987). Temporary or permanent middle-management groups? *Group & Organization Studies, 12,* 23–37.

Carnall, C. A. (1982). *The evaluation of organizational change.* Brookfield, VT: Gower.

Cartwright, D. (1951). Achieving change in people: Some applications of group dynamics theory. *Human Relations, 4,* 381–392.

Carsten, J. M., & Spector, P. E. (1987). Unemployment, job satisfaction, and employee turnover: A meta-analytic test of the Muchinsky model. *Journal of Applied Psychology, 72,* 374–381.

Cattell, R. B. (1966). *The scientific analysis of personality.* Chicago: Aldine.

Child, J. (1972). Organizational structure, environment and performance: The role of strategic choice. *Sociology, 6,* 1–22.

Chin, R., & Benne, K. D. (1969). General strategies for effecting changes in human systems. In W. G. Bennis, K. D. Benne, & R. Chin (Eds.), *The planning of change* (2nd ed.). New York: Holt, Rinehart, and Winston.

Clark, B. (1970). *The distinctive college: Antioch, Reed and Swarthmore.* Chicago: Aldine.

Cohen, A. R., & Gadon, H. (1978). Changing the management culture in a public school system. *Journal of Applied Behavioral Science, 14,* 61–78.

Cohen, S. L., & Turney, J. R. (1978). Intervening at the bottom: Organizational development with enlisted personnel in an army work setting. *Personnel Psychology, 31,* 715–730.

Collins, J. C., & Porras, J. I. (1991). *Organizational vision and visionary organizations.* Unpublished manuscript, Stanford University, Graduate School of Business, Stanford, CA.

Conlon, E. J., & Short, L. O. (1984). Survey feedback as a large-scale change device: An empirical examination. *Group & Organization Studies, 9,* 399–416.

Cooke, R. A., & Coughlan, R. J. (1979). Developing collective decision-making and problem-solving structures in schools. *Group & Organization Studies, 4,* 71–92.

Cooperrider, D. L., & Srivastva, S. (1987). Appreciative inquiry in organizational life. In R. W. Woodman & W. A. Pasmore (Eds.), *Research in organization change and development* (Vol. 1). Greenwich, CT: JAI Press.

Corporate culture: The hard-to-change values that spell success or failure (1980, October 27). *Business Week,* 148–160.

Crawford, K. S., Thomas, E. D., & Fink, J. J. (1980). Pygmalion at sea: Improving the work effectiveness of low performers. *Journal of Applied Behavioral Science, 16,* 482–505.

Culbert, S. A., & McDonough, J. J. (1980). *The invisible war: Pursuing self-interests at work.* New York: Wiley.

Cummings, T. G. (1978). Sociotechnical experimentation: A review of sixteen studies. In W. A. Pasmore & J. J. Sherwood (Eds.), *Sociotechnical systems: A sourcebook.* San Diego: University Associates.

Cummings, T. G. (1984). Transorganizational development. In B. M. Staw & L. L. Cummings (Eds.), *Research in organizational behavior* (Vol. 6). Greenwich, CT: JAI Press.

Cummings, T. G., & Huse, E. F. (1989). *Organization development and change.* St. Paul, MN: West.

Cummings, T. G., & Mohrman, S. A. (1987). Self-designing organizations: Toward implementing quality-of-work-life innovations. In R. W. Woodman & W. A. Pasmore (Eds.), *Research in organizational change and development* (Vol. 1). Greenwich, CT: JAI Press.

Cummings, T. G., Mohrman, S. A., Mohrman, A. M., Jr., & Ledford, G. E., Jr. (1985). Organization design for the future: A collaborative research approach. In E. E. Lawler et al. (Eds.), *Doing research that is useful for theory and practice.* San Francisco: Jossey-Bass.

Cummings, T. G., & Srivastva, S. (1977). *Management of work: A socio-technical systems approach.* San Diego: University Associates.

Dalton, D. R., & Todor, W. D. (1984). Unanticipated consequence of union-management cooperation: An interrupted time series analysis. *Journal of Applied Behavioral Science, 20,* 253–264.

Dalton, G. W. (1970). Influence and organizational change. In *Organizational behavior models* (Comparative Administration Research Institute Series No. 2). Kent, OH: Kent State University, Bureau of Economic and Business Research.

Dandridge, T. C. (1985). The life stages of a symbol: When symbols work and when they can't. In P. J. Frost et al. (Eds.), *Organizational culture.* Beverly Hills, CA: Sage.

Davis, L. E. (1971). The coming crisis for production management: Technology and organization. *International Journal of Production Research, 9,* 65–82.

Davis, L. E. (1980). Organization design. Source unknown.

Davis, S. M. (1984). *Managing corporate culture.* Cambridge, MA: Ballinger.

Dazal, I., & Thomas, J. (1968). Developing a new organization. *Journal of Applied Behavioral Science, 4,* 473–506.

Deal, T., & Kennedy, A. (1982). *Corporate cultures: The rites and rituals of corporate life.* Reading, MA: Addison-Wesley.

Deasy, C. M. (1976). *Design for human affairs.* New York: Wiley.

Donaldson, L. (1975). Job enlargement: A multidimensional process. *Human Relations, 28,* 593–610.

Drake, B., & Drake, E. (1988). Ethical and legal aspects of managing corporate cultures. *California Management Review, 30,* 107–123.

Drucker, P. F. (1977). *Management.* New York: Harper's College Press.

Dunn, M. T. (1985). *The effects of organization development on physical setting changes: An empirical assessment.* Unpublished thesis, Pepperdine University, Malibu, CA.

Dyer, W. G. (1977). *Team building: Issues and alternatives.* Reading, MA: Addison-Wesley.

Eden, D. (1986a). OD and self-fulfilling prophecy: Boosting productivity by raising expectations. *Journal of Applied Behavioral Science, 22,* 1–13.

Eden, D. (1986b). Team development: Quasi-experimental confirmation among combat companies. *Group & Organization Studies, 11,* 133–146.

Eden, D. (1988). Creating expectation effects in OD: Applying self-fulfilling prophecy. In W. A. Pasmore & R. W. Woodman (Eds.), *Research in organizational change and development* (Vol. 2.). Greenwich, CT: JAI Press.

Emery, F. E. & Trist, E. L. (1965). The causal texture of organizational environments. *Human Relations, 18,* 21–31.

Erez, M., & Kanfer, F. H. (1983). The role of goal acceptance in goal setting and task performance. *Academy of Management Review, 8,* 454–463.

Evans, P. A. L. (1989). Organizational development in the transnational enterprise. In R. W. Woodman & W. A. Pasmore (Eds.), *Research in organizational change and development* (Vol. 3). Greenwich, CT: JAI Press.

Farrell, D., & Stamm, C. L. (1988). Meta-analysis of the correlates of employee absence. *Human Relations, 41,* 211–227.

Feldman, S. P. (1990). Stories as cultural creativity: On the relation between symbolism and politics in organizational change. *Human Relations, 43,* 809–828.

Fitzgerald, T. H. (1988). Can change in organizational culture really be managed? *Organizational Dynamics, 17,* 5–15.

Frame, R. M., Nielsen, W. R., & Pate, L.E. (1989). Creating excellence out of crisis: Organizational transformation at the Chicago Tribune. *Journal of Applied Behavioral Science, 25,* 109–122.

French, W. L., & Bell, C. H. (1973). *Organization development: Behavioral science interventions for organization improvement.* Englewood Cliffs, NJ: Prentice-Hall.

French, W. L, & Bell, C. H. (1978). *Organization development: Behavioral science interventions for organization improvement* (2nd ed.). Englewood Cliffs, NJ: Prentice-Hall.

French, W. L., & Bell, C. H. (1984). *Organization development: Behavioral science interventions for organization improvement* (3rd ed.). Englewood Cliffs, NJ: Prentice-Hall.

French, W. L., Bell, C. H., & Zawacki, R. A. (1983). *Organization development: Theory, practice, and research* (rev. ed.). Plano, TX: Business Publications.

Freud, S. (1955). *The complete psychological works of Sigmund Freud.* (J. Strachey, trans.). London: Hogarth.

Fried, Y., & Ferris, G. R. (1987). The validity of the job characteristics model: A review and meta-analysis. *Personnel Psychology, 40,* 287–322.

Friedlander, F., & Brown, L. D. (1974). Organization development. *Annual Review of Psychology, 25,* 313–341.

Frohman, M., Sashkin, M., & Kavanaugh, M. (1976). Action-research as applied to organization development. *Organization and Administrative Sciences, 1,* 129–161.

Frost, P. J., Moore, L. F., Louis, M. R., Lundberg, C. C., & Martin, J. (1985). *Organizational culture.* Beverly Hills, CA: Sage.

Frye, N., Seifert, G., & Yaney, J. P. (1977). Organizational change through feedback and research (OD) efforts. *Group & Organization Studies, 2,* 296–309.

Galbraith, J. (1977). *Organization design.* Reading, MA: Addison-Wesley.

George, F. H., & Johnson, L. (Eds.). (1985). *Purposive behaviour and teleological explanations.* New York: Gordon and Breach Science Publishers.

Gilbreth, F. B. (1912). *Primer of scientific management.* New York: Van Nostrand.

Glass, G. V., McGaw, B., & Smith, M. L. (1982). *Meta-analysis in social research.* Beverly Hills, CA: Sage.

Golembiewski, R. T. (1979). *Approaches to planned change.* New York: Marcel Dekker.

Golembiewski, R. T., Billingsley, K., & Yeager, S. (1976). Measuring change and persistence in human affairs: Types of change generated by OD designs. *Journal of Applied Behavioral Science, 12,* 133–157.

Golembiewski, R. T., Hilles, R., & Daly, R. (1987). Some effects of multiple OD interventions on burnout and work site features. *Journal of Applied Behavioral Science, 23,* 295–213.

Golembiewski, R. T., & Sun, B. C. (1990). Positive-findings bias in QWL studies: Rigor and outcomes in a large sample. *Journal of Management, 16,* 665–674.

Golembiewski, R. T., Yeager, S., & Hilles, R. (1975). Factor analysis of some flexitime effects: Attitudinal and behavioral consequences of a structural intervention. *Academy of Management Journal, 18,* 500–509.

Goodman, P. S., Bazerman, M., & Conlon. E. (1980). Institutionalization of planned organizational change. In B. M. Staw & L. L. Cummings (Eds.), *Research in organizational behavior* (Vol. 2.). Greenwich, CT: JAI Press.

Goodman, P. S., & Dean, J. W., Jr. (1982). Creating long-term organizational change. In P. S. Goodman and Associates (Eds.), *Change in organizations.* San Francisco: Jossey-Bass.

Gray, B. (1985). Conditions facilitating interorganizational collaboration. *Human Relations, 38,* 911–936.

Gray, B. (1990). Building interorganizational alliances: Planned change in a global environment. In W. A. Pasmore & R. W. Woodman (Eds.), *Research in organizational change and development* (Vol. 4). Greenwich, CT: JAI Press.

Greenbaum, H. H., Holden, E. J., Jr., & Spataro, L. (1983). Organization structure and communication processes: A study of change. *Group & Organization Studies, 8,* 61–82.

Greiner, L. E. (1967). Patterns of organization change. *Harvard Business Review, 45,* 119–130.

Gricar, B. G., & Brown, L. D. (1981). Conflict, power and organization in a changing community. *Human Relations, 34,* 877–893.

Griffin, R. W. (1988). Consequences of quality circles in an industrial setting: A longitudinal assessment. *Academy of Management Journal, 31,* 338–358.

Guzzo, R. A., Jette, R. D., & Katzell, R. A. (1985). The effects of psychologically based intervention programs on worker productivity: A meta-analysis. *Personnel Psychology, 38,* 275–291.

Gyllenhammar, P. G. (1977). *People at work.* Reading, MA: Addison-Wesley.

Hackman, J. R., & Oldham, G. R. (1975). Development of the job diagnostic survey. *Journal of Applied Psychology, 60,* 159–170.

Hackman, J. R., Pearce, J. L., & Wolfe, J. C. (1978). Effects of changes in job characteristics on work attitudes and behaviors: A naturally occurring quasi-experiment. *Organizational Behavior and Human Performance, 21,* 289–304.

Hall, R. H. (1982). *Organizations: Structure and process* (3rd ed.). Englewood Cliffs, NJ: Prentice-Hall.

Hamilton, E. E. (1988). The facilitation of organizational change: An empirical study of factors predicting change agents' effectiveness. *Journal of Applied Behavioral Science, 24,* 37–59.

Hammer, T. H., & Stern, R. N. (1980). Employee ownership: Implications for the organizational distribution of power. *Academy of Management Journal, 23,* 78–100.

Harrison, R. (1972a). Role negotiation: A tough–minded approach to team development. In W. W. Burke & H. A. Hornstein (Eds.), *The social technology of organization development.* La Jolla, CA: University Associates.

Harrison, R. (1972b). Understanding your organization's character. *Harvard Business Review, 50,* 119–128.

Harvey, M. J., & Boettger, C. R. (1971). Improving communication within a managerial work-group. *Journal of Applied Behavioral Science, 7,* 164–179.

Hautaluoma, J. E., & Gavin, J. F. (1975). Effects of organizational diagnosis and intervention on blue-collar "blues." *Journal of Applied Behavioral Science, 11,* 475–496.

Head, T. C., Molleston, J. L., Sorenson, P. F., Jr., & Gargano, J. (1986). The impact of implementing a quality circles intervention on employee task perceptions. *Group & Organization Studies, 11,* 360–373.

Heenan, D. A., & Perlmutter, H. V. (1979). *Multinational organization development.* Reading, MA: Addison-Wesley.

Hicks, W. D., & Klimoski, R. J. (1981). The impact of flexitime on employee attitudes. *Academy of Management Journal, 24,* 333–341.

Hofer, C. W., & Schendel, D. (1978). *Strategy formulation: Analytical concepts.* St. Paul, MN: West.

Hoffer, S. J. (1986). *Behavior and organizational performance: An empirical study.* Unpublished doctoral dissertation, Stanford University, Stanford, CA.

House, R. J. (1967). *Management development.* Ann Arbor, MI: University of Michigan.

Hornstein, H. A., Bunker, B. B., Burke, W. W., Gindes, M., & Lewicki, R. J. (Eds.). (1971). *Social intervention: A behavioral science approach.* New York: Free Press.

Hughes, R. L., Rosenbach, W. E., & Clover, W. H. (1983). Team development in an intact, ongoing work group: A quasi-field experiment. *Group & Organization Studies, 8,* 161–186.

Hunter, J. E., Schmidt, F. L., & Jackson, G. B. (1982). *Meta-analysis: Cumulating research findings across studies.* Beverly Hills, CA: Sage.

Huse, E. F., & Cummings, T. G. (1985). *Organization development and change* (3rd ed.). St. Paul, MN: West.

Jaeger, A. M. (1976). Organization development and national culture: Where's the fit? *Academy of Management Review, 11,* 178–190.

Jayaram, G. K. (1976). Open systems planning. In W. G. Bennis, K. D. Benne, R. Chin, & K. Corey (Eds.), *The planning of change* (3rd ed.). New York: Holt, Rinehart & Winston.

Jelinek, M., & Litterer, J. A. (1988). Why OD must become strategic. In W. A. Pasmore & R. W. Woodman (Eds.), *Research in organizational change and development* (Vol. 2). Greenwich, CT: JAI Press.

Jordan, P. C. (1986). Effects of an extrinsic reward on intrinsic motivation: A field experiment. *Academy of Management Journal, 29,* 405–412.

Jöreskog, K. G., & Sörbom, D. (1981). *Analysis of linear structural relationships by maximum likelihood and least squares methods.* Sweden: University of Uppsala.

Joyce, W. F. (1986). Matrix organization: A social experiment. *Academy of Management Journal, 29,* 536–561.

Kahn, W. A. (1989). Toward a sense of organizational humor: Implications for organizational diagnosis and change. *Journal of Applied Behavioral Science, 25,* 45–63.

Katerberg, R., & Blau, G. J. (1983). An examination of level and direction of effort and job performance. *Academy of Management Journal, 26,* 249–257.

Keller, R. T. (1978). A longitudinal assessment of a managerial grid seminar training program. *Group & Organization Studies, 3,* 343–355.

Kerr, J., & Slocum, J. W., Jr. (1987). Managing corporate culture through reward systems. *Academy of Management Executive, 1,* 99–107.

Ketchum, L. (1984). Sociotechnical design in a third world country: The railway maintenance depot at Sennai in the Sudan. *Human Relations, 37,* 135–154.

Keys, C. B., & Bartunek, J. M. (1979). Organization development in schools: Goal agreement, process skills, and diffusion of change. *Journal of Applied Behavioral Science, 15,* 61–78.

Kilmann, R. H. (1984). *Beyond the quick fix: Managing five tracks to organizational success.* San Francisco: Jossey-Bass.

Kilmann, R. H., Saxton, M. R., Serpa, R., & Associates (1985). *Gaining control of the corporate culture.* San Francisco: Jossey-Bass.

Kilmann, R. H., Thomas, K. W., Slevin, D. P., Nath, R., & Jerrell, S. L. (1983). *Producing useful knowledge in organizations.* New York: Praeger.

Kim, J. S., & Campagna, A. F. (1981). Effects of flexitime on employee attendance and performance: A field experiment. *Academy of Management Journal, 24,* 729–741.

Kimberly, J. R., & Nielsen, W. R. (1975). Organization development and change in organizational performance. *Administrative Science Quarterly, 20,* 191–206.

Klein, K. J. (1987). Employee stock ownership and employee attitudes: A test of three models. *Journal of Applied Psychology, 72,* 319–332.

Kotter, J. P. (1978). *Organizational dynamics: Diagnosis and intervention.* Reading, MA: Addison-Wesley.

Krefting, L. A., & Frost, P. J. (1985). Untangling webs, surfing waves, and wildcatting: A multiple-metaphor perspective on managing organizational culture. In P. J. Frost et al. (Eds.), *Organizational culture.* Beverly Hills, CA: Sage.

Krone, C. G. (1975). Open systems redesign. In J. D. Adams (Ed.), *Theory and method in organization development: An evolutionary process.* Arlington, VA: NTL Institute for Applied Behavioral Sciences.

Lawler, E. E., III. (1978). The new plant revolution. *Organizational Dynamics, 6,* 2–12.

Lawler, E. E., III. (1981). *Pay and organization development.* Reading, MA: Addison-Wesley.

Lawler, E. E., III. (1982). Increasing worker involvement to enhance organizational effectiveness. In P. S. Goodman & Associates (Eds.), *Change in organizations.* San Francisco: Jossey-Bass.

Lawler, E. E., III. (1985). Challenging traditional research assumptions. In E. E. Lawler et al. (Eds.), *Doing research that is useful for theory and practice.* San Francisco: Jossey-Bass.

Lawler, E. E., III. (1986). *High-involvement management.* San Francisco: Jossey-Bass.

Lawler, E. E., III, Mohrman, A. M., Jr., Mohrman, S. A., Ledford, G. E., Jr., Cummings, T. G., & Associates (1985). *Doing research that is useful for theory and practice.* San Francisco: Jossey-Bass.

Lawrence, P. R., & Lorsch, J. W. (1967). *Organization and environment: Managing differentiation and integration.* Boston: Graduate School of Business Administration, Harvard University.

Lawrence, P. R., & Lorsch, J. W. (1969). *Developing organizations: Diagnosis and action.* Reading, MA: Addison–Wesley.

Legge, K. (1984). *Evaluating planned organizational change.* Orlando, FL: Academic Press.

Leifer, R. (1989). Understanding organizational transformation using a dissipative structure model. *Human Relations, 42,* 899–916.

Levy, A. (1986). Second-order planned change: Definition and conceptualization. *Organizational Dynamics, 15,* 4–20.

Levy, A., & Merry, U. (1986). *Organizational transformation: Approaches, strategies, theories.* New York: Praeger.

Lewin, K. (1951). *Field theory in social science.* New York: Harper.

Liebowitz, S. J., and DeMeuse, K. P. (1982). The application of team-building. *Human Relations, 35,* 1–18.

Likert, R. (1967). *The human organization.* New York: McGraw-Hill.

Lippitt, G. L. (1969). *Organization renewal.* Englewood Cliffs, NJ: Prentice-Hall.

Lippitt, R., Watson, J., & Westley, B. (1958a). *Dynamics of planned change.* New York: Harcourt, Brace, and World.

Lippitt, R., Watson, J., & Westley, B. (1958b). *Planned change: A comparative study of principles and techniques.* New York: Harcourt, Brace, and World.

Locke, E. A., Sirota, D., & Wolfson, A. D. (1976). An experimental case study of the successes and failures of job enrichment in a government agency. *Journal of Applied Psychology, 61,* 701–711.

Long, R. J. (1980). Job attitudes and organizational performance under employee ownership. *Academy of Management Journal, 23,* 726–737.

Lundberg, C. C. (1978). *Organization development theory: A strategic and conceptual appraisal.*

Unpublished manuscript, Oregon State University, Corvallis, OR.

Lundberg, C. C. (1989). On organizational learning: Implications and opportunities for expanding organizational development. In R. W. Woodman & W. A. Pasmore (Eds.), *Research in organizational change and development* (Vol. 3.). Greenwich, CT: JAI Press.

Luthans, F., Kemmerer, B., Paul, R., & Taylor, L. (1987). The impact of a job redesign intervention on salespersons' observed performance behaviors. *Group & Organization Studies, 12,* 55–72.

Manz, C. C., & Sims, H. P. (1982). The potential for "group think" in autonomous work groups. *Human Relations, 35,* 773–784.

Margulies, N., & Raia, A. P. (1978). *Conceptual foundations of organizational development.* New York: McGraw-Hill.

Margulies, N., Wright, P. L., & Scholl, R. W. (1977). Organization development techniques: Their impact on change. *Group & Organization Studies, 2,* 428–448.

Marks, M. L., Mirvis, P. H., Hackett, E. J., & Grady, J. F., Jr. (1986). Employee participation in a quality circle program: Impact on quality of work life, productivity, and absenteeism. *Journal of Applied Psychology, 71,* 61–69.

Martin, J. (1982). Stories and scripts in organizational settings. In A. Hastorf & A. Isen (Eds.), *Cognitive social psychology.* New York: Elsevier-North Holland.

Maslow, A. H. (1954). *Motivation and personality.* New York: Harper and Row.

Mathieu, J. E., & Leonard, R. L., Jr. (1987). Applying utility concepts to a training program in supervisory skills: A time-based approach. *Academy of Management Journal, 30,* 316–335.

McClelland, D. C. (1961). *The achieving society.* Princeton, NJ: Van Nostrand.

McGregor, D. M. (1960). *The human side of enterprise.* New York: McGraw-Hill.

McLean, A. J., Sims, D., Mangham, I., & Tuffield, D. (1982). *Organization development in transition.* New York: Riley.

McWhinney, W. H. (1972). *Open systems and traditional hierarchies.* International Conference on the Quality of Working Life, Arden House.

Merton, R. K. (1957). *Social theory and social structure* (2nd ed.). Glencoe, IL: Free Press.

Meyer, H. H., & Raich, M. S. (1983). An objective evaluation of a behavior modeling training program. *Personnel Psychology, 36,* 755–761.

Miles, M. B., Hornstein, H. A., Callahan, D. M., Calder, P. H., & Schiavo, R. S. (1969). The consequence of survey feedback: Theory and evaluation. In W. G. Bennis, K. D. Benne, & R. Chin (Eds.), *The planning of change* (2nd ed.). New York: Holt, Rinehart and Winston.

Miller, K. I., & Monge, P. R. (1986). Participation, satisfaction, and productivity: A meta-analytic review. *Academy of Management Journal, 29,* 727–753.

Mirvis, P. H. (1988) Organization development: Part 1: An evolutionary perspective. In W. A. Pasmore & R. W. Woodman (Eds.), *Research in organizational change and development* (Vol. 2.). Greenwich, CT: JAI Press.

Mitchell, R. (1986). Team building by disclosure of internal frames of reference. *Journal of Applied Behavioral Science, 22,* 15–28.

Mohrman, S. A., & Cummings, T. G. (1989). *Self-designing organizations: Learning how to create high performance.* Reading, MA: Addison-Wesley.

Mohrman, S. A., Ledford, G. E., Lawler, E. E., & Mohrman, A. M., Jr. (1986). Quality of worklife and employee involvement. In C. L. Cooper & I. T. Robertson (Eds.), *International review of industrial and organizational psychology 1986.* Chichester, England: Wiley.

Moorhead, G. (1982). Group think: A hypothesis in need of testing. *Group & Organization Studies, 7,* 429–444.

Morrison, P. (1978). Evaluation in OD: A review and assessment. *Group & Organization Studies, 3,* 42–70.

Morrison, P., & Sturges, J. (1980). Evaluation of organization development in a large state government organization. *Group & Organization Studies, 5,* 48–64.

Motamedi, K. (1985). Transorganization development: Developing relations among organizations. In D. D. Warrick (Ed.), *Contemporary organization development: Current thinking and applications.* Glenview, IL: Scott, Foresman.

Nadler, D. A. (1977). *Feedback and organization development: Using data-based methods.* Reading, MA: Addison-Wesley.

Nadler, D. A. (1981). Managing organizational change: An integrative perspective. *Journal of Applied Behavioral Science, 17,* 191–211.

Nadler, D. A., Cammann, C. T., & Mirvis, P. H. (1980). Developing a feedback system for work units: A field experiment in structural change. *Journal of Applied Behavioral Science, 16,* 41–62.

Nadler, D. A., & Tushman, M. L. (1977). A diagnostic model for organization behavior. In J. R. Hackman, E. E. Lawler, & L. W. Porter (Eds.), *Perspectives on behavior in organizations.* New York: McGraw-Hill.

Narayanan, V. K., & Nath, R. (1984). The influence of group cohesiveness on some changes induced by flexitime: A quasi-experiment. *Journal of Applied Behavioral Science, 20,* 265–276.

Naylor, C., Pritchard, R. D., & Ilgen, D. R. (1980). *A theory of behavior in organizations.* New York: Academic Press.

Neuman, G. A., Edwards, J. E., & Raju, N. S. (1989). Organizational development interventions: A meta-analysis of their effects on satisfaction and other attitudes. *Personnel Psychology, 42,* 461–483.

Neumann, J. E. (1989). Why people don't participate in organizational change. In R. W. Woodman & W. A. Pasmore (Eds.), *Research in organizational change and development* (Vol. 3). Greenwich, CT: JAI Press.

Nicholas, J. M. (1982). The comparative impact of organization development interventions on hard criteria measures. *Academy of Management Review, 7,* 531–542.

Nicholas, J. M., & Katz, M. (1985). Research methods and reporting practices in organization development: A review and some guidelines. *Academy of Management Review, 10,* 737–749.

Oldham, G. R. (1988). Effects of changes in workspace partitions and spatial density on employee reactions: A quasi-experiment. *Journal of Applied Psychology, 73,* 253–258.

Oldham, G. R., & Brass, D. J. (1979). Employee reactions to an open-plan office: A naturally occurring quasi-experiment. *Administrative Science Quarterly, 24,* 267–284.

Ondrack, D. A., & Evans, M. G. (1986). Job enrichment and job satisfaction in quality of working life and nonquality of working life work sites. *Human Relations, 39,* 871–889.

O'Reilly, C. (1989). Corporations, culture, and commitment: Motivation and social control in organizations. *California Management Review, 31,* 9–25.

Orpen, C. (1979). The effects of job-enrichment on employee satisfaction, motivation, involvement, and performance: A field experiment. *Human Relations, 32,* 189–217.

Ottaway, R. N. (1983). The change agent: A taxonomy in relation to the change process. *Human Relations, 36,* 361–392.

Ouchi, W. G. (1981). *Theory Z: How American business can meet the Japanese challenge.* Reading, MA: Addison-Wesley.

Ouchi, W. G., & Johnson, J. B. (1978). Types of organizational control and their relationship to emotional well being. *Administrative Science Quarterly, 23,* 293–317.

Pascale, R. T., & Athos, A. G. (1981). *The art of Japanese management.* New York: Simon & Schuster.

Pasmore, W. A. (1978). The comparative impacts of sociotechnical system, job-redesign, and survey feedback interventions. In W. A. Pasmore & J. J. Sherwood (Eds.), *Sociotechnical systems: A sourcebook.* San Diego: University Associates.

Pasmore, W. A., Francis, C., Haldeman, J., & Shani, A. (1982). Sociotechnical system: A North American reflection on empirical studies of the seventies. *Human Relations, 35,* 1179–1204.

Pasmore, W. A., & King, D. C. (1978). Understanding organizational change: A comparative study of multifaceted interventions. *Journal of Applied Behavioral Science, 14,* 455–468.

Pasmore, W., Petee, J., & Bastian, R. (1986). Sociotechnical systems in health care: A field experiment. *Journal of Applied Behavioral Science, 22,* 329–339.

Pate, L. E., Nielsen, W. R., & Mowday, R. T. (1977). A longitudinal assessment of the impact of organization development on absenteeism, grievance rates and product quality. *Academy of Management Proceedings,* 353–357.

Patten, T. (1981). *Organizational development through team building.* New York: Wiley.

Patterson, K. J. (1981). The failure of OD success. *Group & Organization Studies, 6,* 5–15.

Paul, C. F., & Gross, A. C. (1981). Increasing productivity and morale in a municipality: Effects of organization development. *Journal of Applied Behavioral Science, 17,* 59–77.

Pearson, C. A. L. (1987). Participative goal setting as a strategy for improving performance and job satisfaction: A longitudinal evaluation with railway track maintenance gangs. *Human Relations, 40*, 473–488.

Perrow, C. (1961). The analysis of goals in complex organizations. *American Sociological Review, 26*, 854–866.

Peters, T. J., & Waterman, R. H., Jr. (1982). *In search of excellence: Lessons from America's best run companies.* New York: Harper and Row.

Peterson, R. A. (1979). Revitalizing the culture concept. *Annual Review of Sociology, 5*, 137–66.

Pondy, L. R., Frost, P. J., Morgan, G., & Dandridge, T. C. (Eds.). (1983). *Organizational symbolism.* Greenwich, CT: JAI Press.

Poole, P. P., Gioia, D. A., & Gray, B. (1989). Influence modes, schema change, and organizational transformation. *Journal of Applied Behavioral Science, 25*, 271–289.

Porras, J. I. (1979). The comparative impact of different OD techniques and intervention intensities. *Journal of Applied Behavioral Science, 15*, 156–178.

Porras, J. I. (1986). Organization development. In G. E. Germane (Ed.), *The executive course: What every manager needs to know about the essentials of business.* Reading, MA: Addison-Wesley.

Porras, J. I. (1987). *Stream analysis: A powerful way to diagnose and manage organizational change.* Reading, MA: Addison-Wesley.

Porras, J. I., & Berg, P. O. (1978). The impact of organization development. *Academy of Management Review, 3*, 249–266.

Porras, J. I., Hargis, K., Patterson, K. J., Maxfield, D. G., Roberts, N., & Bies, R. J. (1982). Modeling-based organizational development: A longitudinal assessment. *Journal of Applied Behavioral Science, 18*, 433–446.

Porras, J. I., & Hoffer, S. J. (1986). Common behavior changes in successful organization development. *Journal of Applied Behavioral Science, 22*, 477–494.

Porras, J. I., & Robertson, P. J. (1987). Organization development theory: A typology and evaluation. In R. W. Woodman & W. A. Pasmore (Eds.), *Research in organization change and development* (Vol. 1). Greenwich, CT: JAI.

Porras, J. I., & Silvers, R. C. (1991). Organization development and transformation. *Annual Review of Psychology, 42*, 51–78.

Porras, J. I., & Wilkins, A. (1980). Organization development in a large system: An empirical assessment. *Journal of Applied Behavioral Science, 16*, 506–534.

Porter, L. W., & Lawler, E. E., III (1968). *Managerial attitudes and performance.* Homewood, IL: Irwin.

Pugh, D. S. (1966). Modern organization theory: A psychological and sociological study. *Psychological Bulletin, 66*, 235–251.

Rasmussen, R. V. (1982). Team training: A behavior modification approach. *Group & Organization Studies, 7*, 51–66.

Richards, M. S. (1978). *Organizational goal structures.* St. Paul, MN: West.

Roberts, D. R., & Robertson, P. J. (1991). Positive-findings bias in organization development evaluation research: An expanded investigation. *Academy of Management Proceedings*, 199–203.

Roberts, N. C., & Porras, J. I. (1982). Progress in organization development research. *Group & Organization Studies, 7*, 91–116.

Robertson, P. J. (1986). *The excellence framework: A review and discussion.* Paper prepared for the Conference on Organizational Excellence in the U.S. and Europe, London.

Robertson, P. J. (1990). *The relationship between work setting characteristics and employee job behavior: An exploratory study.* Paper presented at the annual meeting of the Academy of Management, San Francisco.

Robertson, P. J., Roberts, D. R., & Porras, J. I. (1991). *A meta-analytic review of the impact of planned organizational change interventions.* Unpublished manuscript, University of Southern California, School of Public Administration, Los Angeles, CA.

Robey, D., & Altman, S. (1982). *Organization development: Progress and perspectives.* New York: Macmillan.

Rosen, C., Klein, K. J., & Young, K. M. (1986). *Employee ownership in America: The equity solution.* Lexington, MA: Lexington Books.

Rousseau, D. M. (1977). Technological differences in job characteristics, employee satisfaction, and motivation: A synthesis of job design research and sociotechnical systems theory. *Organizational Behavior and Human Performance, 19*, 18–42.

Sackmann, S. (1989). The role of metaphors in organization transformation. *Human Relations, 42,* 463–485.

Sargent, A. G. (1981). Training men and women for androgynous behaviors in organizations. *Group & Organization Studies, 6,* 302–311.

Sashkin, M., & Burke, W. W. (1987). Organization development in the 1980s. *Journal of Management, 13,* 393–417.

Sathe, V. (1985). *Culture and related corporate realities.* Homewood, IL: Irwin.

Scarpello, V. (1983). Who benefits from participation in long-term human process interventions? *Group & Organization Studies, 8,* 21–44.

Schein, E. H. (1969). *Process consultation: Its role in organization development.* Reading, MA: Addison-Wesley.

Schein, E. H. (1985). *Organizational culture and leadership.* San Francisco: Jossey-Bass.

Schermerhorm, J. (1979). Interorganizational development. *Journal of Management, 5,* 21–38.

Schmitt, N. (1982). The use of analysis of covariance structures to assess beta and gamma change. *Multivariate Behavioral Research, 17,* 343–358.

Schuster, M. (1984). The Scanlon Plan: A longitudinal analysis. *Journal of Applied Behavioral Science, 20,* 23–38.

Schwartz, H., & Davis, S. M. (1981). Matching corporate culture and business strategy. *Organizational Dynamics, 10,* 30–48.

Scott, W. R. (1970). *Social processes and social structures: An introduction to sociology.* New York: Holt, Rinehart and Winston.

Selznick, P. (1957). *Leadership in administration.* New York: Harper and Row.

Shaw, M. E. (1976). An overview of small group behavior. In J. W. Thibaut, J. T. Spence, & R. C. Carson (Eds.), *Contemporary topics in social psychology.* Morristown, NJ: General Learning Press.

Siehl, C. (1984). *Cultural sleight-of-hand: The illusion of consistency.* Unpublished doctoral dissertation, Stanford University, Stanford, CA.

Siehl, C. (1985). After the founder: An opportunity to manage culture. In P. J. Frost et al. (Eds.), *Organizational culture.* Beverly Hills, CA: Sage.

Simon, H. A. (1964). On the concept of organizational goal. *Administrative Science Quarterly, 9,* 1–22.

Skinner, B. F. (1953). *Science and human behavior.* New York: Free Press.

Skinner, B. F. (1969). *Contingencies of reinforcement.* New York: Appleton-Century-Crofts.

Spector, P. E. (1986). Perceived control by employees: A meta-analysis of studies concerning autonomy and participation at work. *Human Relations, 39,* 1005–1016.

Srivastva, S., & Barrett, F. J. (1988). The transforming nature of metaphors in group development: A study in group theory. *Human Relations, 41,* 31–64.

Staw, B. M. (1984). Organizational behavior: A review and reformulation of the field's outcome variables. *Annual Review of Psychology, 35,* 627–666.

Steel, R. P., & Lloyd, R. F. (1988). Cognitive, affective, and behavioral outcomes of participation in quality circles: Conceptual and empirical findings. *Journal of Applied Behavioral Science, 24,* 1–17.

Steel, R. P., Mento, A. J., Dilla, B. L., Ovalle, N. K., & Lloyd, R. F. (1985). Factors influencing the success and failure of two quality circle programs. *Journal of Management Studies, 11,* 99–119.

Steel, R. P., & Shane, G. S. (1986). Evaluation research on quality circles: Technical and analytical implications. *Human Relations, 39,* 449–468.

Steele, F. (1971). Physical settings and organization development. In H. A. Hornstein, B. B. Bunker, W. W. Burke, M. Gindes, & R. J. Lewicki (Eds.), *Social intervention: A behavioral science approach.* New York: Free Press.

Steele, F. (1973). *Physical settings and organization development.* Reading, MA: Addison-Wesley.

Steele, F. (1980). Defining and developing environmental competence. In C. Alderfer & C. Cooper (Eds.), *Advances in experiential social processes* (Vol. 2). Chichester, England: Wiley.

Steele, F. (1981). *The sense of place.* Boston: CBI.

Steele, F. (1983). The ecology of executive teams: A new view of the top. *Organizational Dynamics, 11,* 65–78.

Steele, F. (1986). *Making and managing high-quality workplaces: An organizational ecology.* New York: Teachers College Press.

Steele, F., & Jenks, S. (1977). *The feel of the workplace.* Reading, MA: Addison-Wesley.

Strauss, G. (1963). The personality-versus-organization hypothesis. In H. J. Leavitt (Ed.), *The social science of organizations: Four perspectives.* Englewood Cliffs, NJ: Prentice-Hall.

Sundstrom, E., Herbert, R. K., & Brown, D. W. (1982). Privacy and communication in an open-plan office: A case study. *Environment and Behavior, 14,* 379–392.

Susman, G. I. (1976). *Autonomy at work.* New York: Praeger.

Szilagyi, A. D., & Holland, W. E. (1980). Changes in social density: Relationships with functional interaction and perceptions of job characteristics, role stress, and work satisfaction. *Journal of Applied Psychology, 65,* 28–33.

Tannenbaum, R. (1971). Organizational change has to come through individual change. *Innovation, 23,* 36–43.

Tannenbaum, R., Margulies, N., & Massarik, F. (1985). *Human systems development: New perspectives on people and organizations.* San Francisco: Jossey-Bass.

Taylor, F. W. (1911). *The principles of scientific management.* New York: Harper.

Terborg, J. R., Howard, G. S., & Maxwell, S. E. (1980). Evaluating planned organizational change: A method for assessing alpha, beta, and gamma change. *Academy of Management Review, 5,* 109–121.

Terpstra, D. E. (1981). Relationship between methodological rigor and reported outcomes in organization development evaluation research. *Journal of Applied Psychology, 66,* 541–543.

Terpstra, D. E., Olson, P. D., & Lockeman, B. (1982). The effects of MBO on levels of performance and satisfaction among university faculty. *Group & Organization Studies, 7,* 353–366.

Thompson, J. D. (1967). *Organizations in action.* New York: McGraw–Hill.

Tichy, N. M. (1975). How different types of change agents diagnose organizations. *Human Relations, 28,* 771–799.

Tichy, N. M. (1983). *Managing strategic change: Technical, political and cultural dynamics.* New York: Wiley.

Torbert, W. R. (1989). Leading organizational transformation. In R. W. Woodman & W. A. Pasmore (Eds.), *Research in organizational change and development* (Vol. 3.). Greenwich, CT: JAI Press.

Toscano, D. J. (1983). Toward a typology of employee ownership. *Human Relations, 36,* 581–602.

Trice, H. M., & Beyer, J. M. (1984). Studying organizational cultures through rites and ceremonials. *Academy of Management Review, 9,* 653–669.

Trice, H. M., & Beyer, J. M. (1985). Using six organizational rites to change culture. In R. H. Kilmann, M. J. Saxton, R. Serpa, & Associates (Eds.), *Gaining control of the corporate culture.* San Francisco: Jossey-Bass.

Trist, E. L. (1983). Referent organizations and the development of interorganizational domains. *Human Relations, 36,* 269–284.

Trist, E. L. (1985). Intervention strategies for interorganizational development. In R. Tannenbaum, N. Margulies, F. Massarik, & Associates (Eds.), *Human systems development: New perspectives on people and organizations.* San Francisco: Jossey-Bass.

Tubbs, M. E. (1986). Goal setting: A meta-analytic examination of the empirical evidence. *Journal of Applied Psychology, 71,* 474–483.

Tushman, M., Newman, W., & Romanelli, E. (1986). Convergence and upheaval: Managing the unsteady pace of organizational evolution. *California Management Review, 29,* 29–44.

Vaill, P. (1982). The purposing of high-performing systems. *Organizational Dynamics, 11,* 23–39.

van de Vliert, E., Huismans, S., & Stok, J. (1985). The criterion approach to unraveling beta and alpha change. *Academy of Management Review, 10,* 269–274.

Vaughan, T. R. (1989). Validity and applied social science research: A theoretical reassessment. *Journal of Applied Behavioral Science, 25,* 291–305.

Vicars, W. M., & Hartke, D. D. (1984). Evaluating OD evaluations: A status report. *Group & Organization Studies, 9,* 177–188.

Vroom, V. H. (1964). *Work and motivation.* New York: Wiley.

Wagner, J. A., III, & Gooding, R. Z. (1987). Shared influence and organizational behavior: A meta-analysis of situational variables expected to moderate participation-outcome relationships. *Academy of Management Journal, 30,* 524–541.

Waldie, K. F. (1981). The learning potential of the dominant personality within small intensive training groups. *Group & Organization Studies, 6,* 456–468.

Wall, T. D., Kemp, N. J., Jackson, P. R., & Clegg, C. W. (1986). Outcomes of autonomous workgroups:

A long-term field experiment. *Academy of Management Journal, 29,* 280–304.

Walton, R. E. (1965). Two strategies of social change and their dilemmas. *Journal of Applied Behavioral Science, 1,* 167–179.

Walton, R. E. (1969). *Interpersonal peacemaking: Confrontations and third party consultation.* Reading, MA: Addison-Wesley.

Walton, R. E. (1980). Establishing and maintaining high commitment work systems. In J. R. Kimberly & R. H. Miles (Eds.), *The organizational life cycle.* San Francisco: Jossey-Bass.

Walton, R. E. (1987). *Managing conflict: Interpersonal dialogue and third-party roles* (2nd ed.). Reading, MA: Addison-Wesley.

Warrick, D. D. (1985). *Contemporary organization development: Current thinking and applications.* Glenview, IL: Scott, Foresman.

Weisbord, M. R. (1976). Organizational diagnosis: Six places to look for trouble with or without a theory. *Group & Organization Studies, 1,* 430–447.

Weisbord, M. R. (1988). Toward a new practice theory of OD: Notes on snapshooting and moviemaking. In W. A. Pasmore & R. W. Woodman (Eds.), *Research in organizational change and development* (Vol. 2). Greenwich, CT: JAI Press.

White, S. E., & Mitchell, T. R. (1976). Organization development: A review of research content and research design. *Academy of Management Review, 1,* 57–73.

Wilkins, A. L. (1978). *Organizational stories as an expression of management philosophy: Applications for social control in organizations.* Unpublished doctoral dissertation, Stanford University, Stanford, CA.

Wilkins, A. L. (1983). The culture audit: A tool for understanding organizations. *Organizational Dynamics, 12,* 24–38.

Wilkins, A. L., & Dyer, W. G. (1988). Toward culturally sensitive theories of culture change. *Academy of Management Review, 13,* 522–533.

Wilkins, A. L., & Martin, J. (1980). *Organizational legends.* Unpublished manuscript, Stanford University, Graduate School of Business, Stanford, CA.

Wood, R. E., Mento, A. J., & Locke, E. A. (1987). Task complexity as a moderator of goal effects: A meta-analysis. *Journal of Applied Psychology, 72,* 416–425.

Woodman, R. W. (1989a). Evaluation research on organizational change: Arguments for a "combined paradigm" approach. In R. W. Woodman & W. A. Pasmore (Eds.), *Research in organizational change and development* (Vol. 3). Greenwich, CT: JAI Press.

Woodman, R. W. (1989b). Organizational change and development: New arenas for inquiry and action. *Journal of Management, 15,* 205–228.

Woodman, R. W., & Sherwood, J. J. (1980). Effects of team development intervention: A field experiment. *Journal of Applied Behavioral Science, 16,* 211–227.

Woodman, R. W., & Wayne, S. J. (1985). An investigation of positive findings bias in evaluation of organization development interventions. *Academy of Management Journal, 28,* 889–913.

Yager, E. G. (1981). The quality control circle explosion. *Training and Development Journal, 35,* 98–105.

Zalesny, M. D., & Farace, R. V. (1987). Traditional versus open offices: A comparison of sociotechnical, social relations, and symbolic meaning perspectives. *Academy of Management Journal, 30,* 240–259.

Zmud, R. W., & Armenakis, A. A. (1978). Understanding the measurement of change. *Academy of Management Review, 3,* 661–669.

CHAPTER 13

Behavior Change: Models, Methods, and a Review of Evidence

Lowell W. Hellervik
Joy Fisher Hazucha
Robert J. Schneider
Personnel Decisions, Inc.

This chapter addresses the topic of adult behavior change. The principal thesis is that significant behavior change is far more possible than those who postulate "People don't change" have believed. However, creating and measuring change requires thoughtful interventions and careful attention to measurement issues. A second thesis is that researchers' and practitioners' beliefs about change are important, as they influence the science and practice of behavior change. The discussion begins with a summary of the magnitude and permanence of change, as indicated by psychotherapy and training outcome studies. These studies indicate that the magnitude of change resulting from an intervention is typically about half a standard deviation. However, moderators of the effect include individual differences (motivation, ability, personality, age), the type and duration of the intervention, and the characteristic targeted for change. Next, recommendations are made about how to improve change measurement by increasing validity, reliability, and statistical power. Several important theories, models, and methods of behavior change are then described. Based on these models, theories, and methods, a general behavior change framework is proposed. This framework implies threats to change, some of which emanate from the individual, others from the organization. Finally, a behavior change program, which was carefully designed to minimize the threats to change, is described, illustrating the applicability of our framework as well as issues in outcome research.

Introduction

IN OUR OPINION, industrial and organizational psychologists and organizational decision makers need to change the way they think and the way they talk about individual change issues. Most psychologists and managers have probably been involved in discussing the question, Can people change? Most of the time, though, this is one of those questions that isn't really a question, but is instead a statement. And that statement is, People don't change.

A derivative of the question is, Do people *really* change? And the statement implied by that question is, People *don't really* change. This implies that change efforts are doomed to *ultimate* failure—that any observed change is merely cosmetic, that it will disappear overnight, or that the change is somehow being faked by modifying external behavior without changing more fundamental internal qualities. When discussing mature adults, the added implication is that such persons' behavior patterns are deeply ingrained and virtually impossible to change. The impossiblity of change is even embedded in our folk culture through adages such as, "You can't teach an old dog new tricks."

This is not a trivial matter; nor are we setting up a straw person to demolish. We have listened to presentations by industrial and organizational psychologists where the theme "People don't change" was driven home time and again; and we've observed human resource development professionals formally and informally express the same sentiments with great frustration. When pressed, such persons will express a more balanced view of change potential. However, the fundamental attitudes and statements have already done their damage.

We believe, however, that this pessimism is premature and unjustified. Moreover, we are concerned about the outcomes of such thinking at both the individual and the organizational level. At the individual level, people's beliefs

about the possibility of change may dramatically affect the success of change attempts through their effect on the types of goals people pursue. They may also serve to inhibit the change attempts of others and may distort perceptions of whether those who have been through behavior change interventions achieved their goals.

At the organizational level, we expect that such beliefs will promote resistance to change and change efforts throughout the organization. When senior executives state flatly that people do not change, others are likely to accept such maxims without thinking deeply enough about them to offer an effective challenge. The human resource consequences of this philosophy include:

- Weak support by management for human resource development activities

- Shallow and erratic commitment on management's part to their own development

- Unwillingness to expend time and effort in executive coaching

- Expenditure only on selection and outplacement, to the exclusion of human resource development

Elements of the same lack of belief in the possibility of change appear in many branches of psychology. The psychoanalytic tradition assumes that the first five years of life largely determine one's behavior in the remaining years. Behavior genetics research tells us that human characteristics are largely accounted for genetically (e.g., Tellegen, Lykken, Bouchard, Willcox, Segal, & Rich, 1988). And an early article on psychotherapy outcome (Eysenck, 1952) concluded that treatment for behavior disorders made no difference in recovery rates. Costa and McCrae (1986) concluded from their review of longitudinal studies of personality that "naturally occurring events of a lifetime seem to have little impact on the personalities of most people; why should a few hours a week of psychotherapy for a year or two have much more success?" (p. 420).

Inadequate research also contributes to an implicit theory of no change. When the question, Has change occurred? is asked, sample sizes are often small because of practical constraints, and effect sizes are modest because an intervention may not take into account all of the complexities inherent in achieving substantial behavior change. Both of these factors—small samples and small effect sizes—as well as measurement unreliability, result in low statistical power and a propensity not to find statistically significant differences attributable to an intervention.

Claims by research psychologists that people don't change are also based on longitudinal findings of stability on psychological test scores. Because the test-retest reliabilities and predictive validities are high, many researchers infer that change has not occurred. However, this conclusion disregards several relevant facts. First, many psychological tests are explicitly designed to do the best possible job of measuring stable, relatively unchanging human characteristics. Second, the test-retest correlations for an entire group across all of the characteristics may mask substantial individual changes on particular scales.

We propose that psychologists state their conclusions more carefully. To say that people don't change is, in our opinion, intellectually indefensible. On the other hand, it is also important not to join the extremists of the human potential movement who often seem to believe that *any* change is possible. We believe that much change is very difficult to achieve. Almost always, though, a prepositional phrase or other modifier needs to be added to make the phrase accurate. Thus, "People don't change..." should become "People don't change...on IQ scores" or "...easily," for example.

Researchers could also express their findings more precisely. They should not call the amount of change *large* or *small* (especially if this corresponds to significant or nonsignificant)

but should instead describe the magnitude of change relative to change occurring via other methods. For example, Smith, Glass, and Miller (1980) compared effect sizes for psychotherapy to the effects of nine months of elementary school reading instruction, providing much-needed context. Such increased specificity should replace the global and simplistic overstatements that are common, especially in everyday communications.

Just as behavior genetics has gotten away from questions of heredity *or* environment, and personality theory from state *or* trait, the areas of psychology concerned with adult change must no longer ask simply, Can adults change? Rather, they must ask:

- Who can change?
- How much can they change?
- What characteristics can be changed?
- By what methods can change take place?
- How much time and effort does it take?
- How can change be maintained?
- What prevents people from changing?
- How can people best facilitate change?
- What environmental variables are important?

Leadership by the industrial and organizational psychology profession in articulating that people do, of course, change would be helpful in shaping opinions by executive opinion molders and decision makers. Researching and articulating what changes to what degree under what conditions would be helpful to all concerned.

We intend to address important issues in adult behavior change, drawing on diverse psychological disciplines. We will begin with a discussion of general findings regarding the magnitude of change and its moderators. We will then provide recommendations for addressing the major issues in measuring change. Next, we will integrate these findings with major theories and paradigms of behavior change. This integrative review of the literature includes a general behavior change framework, which we have formulated to provide a context for our discussion and to guide future research and practice. The framework is illustrated with a description of a coaching program designed to maximize long-term behavior change in managers and executives. We conclude the chapter with a research agenda designed to fill in some of the missing pieces of the framework.

The Magnitude of Adult Change and Stability

It is our intention in this section to show that people can indeed change. We briefly review various studies that document the magnitude of change and stability. Change and stability are usually measured using mean differences and/or correlations. The former can be standardized and expressed as an effect size for ease of comparison across studies.[1]

Effect Sizes

Effect sizes can be computed to compare either (a) the mean of a group that has experienced an intervention with a control group mean or (b) pretest and posttest means. Two of the major literatures that deal with the effects of interventions are psychotherapy outcome research and management development research. Two representative meta-analyses have summarized the results reported in these literatures. According to these meta-analyses, the median effect sizes for control group designs were .78 for psychotherapy (Lambert, Shapiro, & Bergin, 1986) and .43 for managerial training (Burke & Day, 1986). From their data, the authors drew favorable conclusions: "Psychological treatments are, overall and in general, beneficial" (Lambert et al., 1986, p. 158), and overall, different methods of "managerial

training are, on the average, moderately effective in improving learning and job performance" (Burke & Day, 1986, p. 243).

While these summary figures mask important variables contributing to differences among studies (e.g., patient diagnosis, intervention method, criterion), they are nevertheless impressive compared with the effects of nine months of elementary school reading instruction (.67) and the impact of computer-based instruction on mathematics achievement (.40) reported by Smith, Glass, and Miller (1980).

While of respectable magnitude, the detection of such effect sizes requires more statistical power than that of a typical small sample training outcome study (Arvey, Cole, Hazucha, & Hartanto, 1985). In such a study, the low power frequently results in an erroneously pessimistic conclusion of no effect. For example, a study with the median sample size for training evaluation found by Arvey et al. ($n = 43$) and a true underlying effect size of .50 would have power ranging from .50 to .93, depending on the statistical design. This means that using the traditional alpha level of .05, the researcher would erroneously conclude that the intervention had no effect between 7 and 50 percent of the time.

It is interesting to contrast the effect sizes obtained across many psychotherapy and managerial training studies (.78 and .43) with those obtained in certain organizational behavior modification (OB Mod) and behavior modeling studies. In one OB Mod study, Komaki, Heinzmann, and Lawson (1980) found that an operant-based behavioral safety intervention achieved effect sizes of .60 and 1.0 for training only, and 1.51 and 1.23 for training plus feedback. A second OB Mod example is a study by Luthans, Paul, and Baker (1981) who applied contingent reinforcement to salespersons' performance, resulting in effect sizes of 4.85 for absence from the work station and idle time, and 4.87 for aggregate retailing behavior.

There are also examples of sizable effect sizes in the behavior modeling literature. Latham and Saari's (1979) classic behavior modeling study yielded effect sizes of .76 for learning measures, 1.92 for behavioral measures, and .72 and 1.06 for job performance measures. Hogan, Hakel, and Decker (1986) compared trainer-provided coding and trainee-generated coding in behavior modeling training and found between-group effect sizes of 4.23 for coaching and 2.78 for employee-initiated complaints. Decker (1983) investigated the effects of group size and video feedback on the effectiveness of behavior modeling training and found effect sizes between the observer/video and large group/no video groups of .62, 1.46, and 2.92 for various outcomes.

These studies represent a variety of designs and outcome measures, but the effect sizes are consistently larger than the average (.43) reported by Burke and Day (1986). Given the intensity and length of these interventions, this difference is reassuring and indicates that some interventions can produce dramatic change. In percentile terms, we may conclude that standard training results in moving the group from the 50th to the 66th percentile of the untrained group, while the most effective interventions may result in *virtually no overlap* between the scores of the trained and untrained groups: The lowest score in the trained group is higher than the highest score in the untrained group.

Correlations

Another common measure of behavior change, most frequently used in developmental research, is the correlation between scores obtained at two different points in time. This is an index of stability in rank-ordering within a group, which ignores any changes in the group mean.

An example of this type of research is a paper by Costa and McCrae (1986) in which they reported results for seven longitudinal studies (10 samples) with test-retest intervals ranging from 10 to 20 years. The median stability coefficients ranged from .46 to .71 for the various samples. They concluded from these results that attempts to change people, as with psychotherapy, are futile. However, while Costa and McCrae's results indicate some stability across a substantial time period, they also imply that a substantial proportion of the variance remains to be explained by other factors. These may include maturation, life events, work experiences, or even psychotherapy, in addition to measurement unreliability.

Howard and Bray's (1988) results from a 20-year study of managers illustrate this juxtaposition of stability and change. In addition to reporting correlations between measures taken at two points in time, they also reported the percentages of individuals who changed by half a standard deviation or more on various *Edwards Personal Preference Scale* scores. These ranged from 32 percent to 46 percent on the various scales over a 20-year period, despite the high correlations across the 20-year interval.

Similar results have been found by Hazucha, Schneider, and Gentile (1992). Over a two-year period, they found a median correlation of .58 across 19 skills (and each correlation was significant), yet several of the paired *t*s also differed significantly from zero. These findings further illustrate the coexistence of stability and change and the importance of simultaneously looking for both. Failing this approach, one is likely to find only what one is looking for at the risk of drawing erroneous conclusions.

These summaries provide some needed perspective. Yes, people can change both their mental health and their managerial skills (among other areas), and the change measured by these instruments is at least moderate and at times quite substantial. Not many illiterate adults will eventually give public readings, not many tone deaf people will become great musicians, but twenty-year high-school reunions will likely bring both surprises and exclamations of "You haven't changed a bit!"

But even moderate change can be highly meaningful to individuals, organizations, and society. Costa and McCrae (1986) acknowledged that, despite their pessimistic conclusion, therapy may prolong the period between bouts of depression or may keep prisoners out of trouble for a little longer. Hunter and Schmidt (1983) showed the substantial economic impact (utility) of even small effects when multiplied across an organization. The utility of the larger effect sizes obtained with more intensive interventions may therefore turn out to be substantial.

The Permanence of Change

Those who may reluctantly grant that some initial change can occur are often skeptical about its permanence (e.g., Georgenson, 1982). Some of this skepticism is due to the scarcity of research on the persistence of change. Baldwin and Ford (1988) found evidence of training transfer (defined as generalizability of the changed behavior to other situations and maintenance of that behavior over time) to be sparse and uninformative because most studies have focused on simple memory and motor tasks with immediate learning and retention.

However, two meta-analyses of the durability of psychotherapy outcome reached optimistic conclusions. Andrews and Harvey (1981) found the benefits of psychotherapy to show only a slight decrease over a two-year period after therapy, and Nicholson and Berman (1983) found that, for most diagnoses, the magnitude of posttreatment and follow-up effect sizes did not differ. However, in the latter study, diagnosis moderated outcome durability. Patients with phobias tended to become slightly worse over time, while patients with social problems (i.e., assertiveness, dating, and public speaking) improved between posttreatment and follow-up.

There are also examples of durable change in the organizational literature. Latham and Saari (1979) found that one year after training the gains in job performance were equal to those obtained on a learning measure six months earlier. There have even been cases of gains from immediate posttest to later periods in time. For example, Hand, Richards, and Slocum (1973) found no change in behavior three months after completing a human relations training program, but they did find changes 18 months after training. This situation is especially likely with complex behaviors that require practice and that may take longer to develop.

Some moderators of generalizability and maintenance have also been investigated. For example, Smith (1975) found that intact groups were more likely than stranger groups to maintain their gains after sensitivity training. There is also some sparse evidence in the training literature implicating boss feedback, involvement, and support in the effectiveness of transfer. A recent study (Hazucha et al., 1992), for example, has found that some specific boss behaviors are related to managerial skill development, while others are not. In this study, developing managers rated the extent to which their boss performed a number of supportive behaviors, and change was measured via co-workers' ratings obtained two years apart.[2] "Provides encouragement and support" had no effect on change, but "provides coaching and feedback" was associated with dramatic change. Interestingly, boss support behaviors that were related to change tended to be less common than those that were not.

A few studies have found relationships between perceptions of transfer climate (e.g., appreciation for innovation, encouragement of risk taking) and effort to apply training (Baumgartel & Jeanpierre, 1972; Baumgartel, Reynolds, & Pathan, 1984; Baumgartel, Sullivan, & Dunn, 1978; Huczynski & Lewis, 1980). Hazucha et al. (1992) also found significant relationships between two perceived organizational support items ("managers are rewarded for training and development," and "managers' skills are routinely assessed") and skill development as viewed by others.

As Baldwin and Ford (1988) pointed out, one of the problems in the transfer literature is that these proposed moderator constructs (boss support, organizational support) and their components have not been operationalized very clearly, despite widespread agreement that they are important. However, several of the researchers above have made positive steps in the direction of understanding and measuring those constructs.

In conclusion, some encouraging evidence of the durability of change exists. However, there have been few long-term follow-up studies. This area deserves more attention, and moderators (e.g., what was learned, environmental support) should also be investigated.

Individual and Subgroup Differences in Change

Individual differences have received inconsistent attention in outcome studies. Change method (e.g., lecture, behavior modeling) is a more typical focus, with individual differences in response included as an afterthought. Yet it is apparent from the research that the characteristics of the individuals receiving the treatment have a strong impact on the magnitude of change. Cronbach described the differential response to a similar treatment as an *aptitude-treatment interaction* in 1957. Early tests of this proposition were clumsy, but interest has recently been revived, as indicated by two recent books (Ackerman, Sternberg, & Glaser, 1989; R. Kanfer, Ackerman, & Cudeck, 1989). The studies described below show that cognitive, motivational, and personality variables, when combined with various interventions, affect various types of change, including

learning process and outcome, psychotherapy, and management development. Individual differences also appear to affect the maturation process and career outcomes, and we will review studies that have examined these phenomena as well.

Individual Differences in Learning and Training Outcomes

Over a period of several decades, numerous researchers have found differences in *trainability*. The most common findings have been the relationship between ability and training or learning outcome (e.g., Gordon & Kleiman, 1976; Robertson & Downs, 1979; Taylor, 1952; Taylor & Tajen, 1948). More recent work has begun to investigate the influence of personality and motivational variables on learning and training outcomes. Researchers have also begun to examine interactions between cognitive, noncognitive, and contextual variables in predicting such outcomes.

Fleishman (e.g., 1972) and Ackerman (1988) have both found that proficiency at various points in the learning process is related to different types of abilities. In addition, Ackerman found that the consistency of the task affects the abilities required to perform it.[3] Early in the process of learning consistent tasks and throughout the performance of inconsistent tasks performance depends on general intelligence, that is, on assimilating the new information and deducing strategies. However, in the case of consistent tasks, the intellectual demands are reduced, and performance begins to depend on perceptual speed and psychomotor abilities.

Summarizing various research, Snow and Lohman (1984) made a strong case for an interaction between general ability and the degree of structure present in the learning environment. They concluded that for more able learners, less structure provides challenge, but more structure inhibits their natural learning process. For less able learners, less structure produces anxiety because of the difficulty of the task, and more structure brings the task closer to their "zone of tolerable problematicity" (Snow, 1989).

Motivation and personality have received less attention in the literature than ability variables. However, several studies have found pretraining motivation to play a role in outcome. These include motivation to succeed in training (Ryman & Biersner, 1975), belief in the value of training (Baumgartel et al., 1984), and perception of a choice to attend (Hicks & Klimoski, 1987). Noe and Schmitt (1986) found that job involvement and career planning were antecedents of learning and behavior change. Interestingly, negative motivators such as feelings of need (Porras & Hargis, 1982) and job insecurity (Hazucha, 1990a) have not been shown to moderate training outcome.

R. Kanfer and Ackerman (1989) found interactions between motivational and ability variables during the learning process. They found that a goal-setting manipulation inhibited performance during the early phases of learning, especially for low-ability subjects. However, goal setting enhanced this group's performance during the later phases of skill acquisition.

There is also some evidence for a relationship between training outcome and stable personality traits. In a study investigating the relationship between pretraining trainee characteristics and the outcome of an intensive coaching program that took place over six months, Hazucha (1990) found several strong predictors of training outcome (as rated by two training staff). In addition to tested mental ability ($r = .32$ to $.51$) and initial skill levels ($r_s \sim .40$), several personality variables including adjustment, achievement orientation, and acceptance of social norms ($r_s \sim .20$) were related to training outcome.

In summary, individual differences in learning and training outcomes have been found with some regularity. Abilities have received

the most attention, but there is also evidence that motivation and personality variables moderate the impact of training. In addition, ability and motivation have been found to interact with treatment variables (e.g., degree of task structure, goal setting) in their effects on learning.

Individual Differences in Psychotherapy Outcome

Several person variables have been found to moderate the effectiveness of psychotherapy. Landman and Dawes (1982) reported effect sizes of .68 for patients with severe problems (e.g., schizophrenia, depression, and alcoholism) and 1.11 for those with more circumscribed problems (e.g., specific phobias). Shapiro and Shapiro (1982) found similar results in their meta-analysis: Target problem had a larger impact on effect size than did type of treatment. Specifically, simple phobias seemed to be much more amenable to treatment than anxiety or depression, and physical and performance problems and performance anxieties were intermediate in their tractability. Note, however, that meta-analyses are less sensitive to individual differences because they treat the group, rather than the individual, as the unit of analysis.

Nathan and Skinstad (1987) reported that younger, married, and employed persons with a shorter history of abusive drinking fare better in alcohol treatment. They noted that while there is agreement on the importance of motivation, there is less agreement on how to measure it. They also supported Miller's (1985) recommendation not to rely on trait models of motivation but to search for ways to increase client motivation.

Several studies have found moderators of the maintenance of therapeutic gains. Brownell, Marlatt, Lichtenstein, and Wilson (1986) identified several individual factors that affect the likelihood of lapse and relapse into addictive behavior. These include negative emotional states, inadequate motivation, initial response to treatment, physiological factors, and coping skills, including those associated with self-efficacy. Lambert, Shapiro, and Bergin (1986) reported that patients who view their own efforts as causing the change and who have been helped to anticipate future events and their reactions to them are most likely to maintain the gains they achieved. In contrast, those who attribute their improvement to external factors, such as medication, were unable to maintain improvement.

In summary, several person variables have been found to moderate the effectiveness of psychotherapy and the maintenance of therapeutic change. People with more circumscribed problems, better social supports, higher self-efficacy, and who attribute their gains to internal factors responded better to psychotherapy and maintained their gains.

Individual Differences in Maturation

There also appear to be individual differences in maturational change. We define maturation broadly as changes that occur over time, and that are *not* the result of a specific intervention (such as training or psychotherapy) common to a group, but which may result from specific life events.

A study by Swanson and Hansen (1988) investigated stability and change in vocational interest over a 12-year period. To better understand individual differences in stability, they computed individual stability coefficients. Consistent with similar longitudinal studies, they found a median stability coefficient of .72, which indicates substantial stability for the group. However, the range of individual stability coefficients was quite broad (−.04 to .96). This indicates that while some individuals' responses remained nearly identical from Time 1 to Time 2, others' patterns bore no relation to one another over this period. Unfortunately, the study did not include potential moderator variables that might serve to explain the variation in stability, such as exposure

to different occupations or disabling accidents. However, the methodology they used to compute individual stability coefficients is a contribution to the measurement of individual differences in stability.

Other researchers have attempted to explain the differences between those who changed more and those who changed less over time. For example, Plant and Minium (1967) found that young adults of higher aptitude exhibited more change in personality over two- to four-year periods compared to their lower aptitude counterparts. In addition, the personality changes experienced by the higher aptitude group tended to be in a more psychologically positive direction. Whitbourne (1986) found that personality (openness to experience), social resources, and to some degree age and education predicted flexibility and life change over a 12-month period.

Stokes, Mumford, and Owens (1989) collected biodata from a large group of college freshmen and followed them up six to eight years after graduation. At each point in time (college freshman year and six to eight years following graduation), the researchers clustered individuals into subgroups based on the similarity of their responses. This procedure yielded 23 male subgroups and 15 female subgroups from the freshman data, and 10 male and 14 female subgroups from the young adult data. Stokes et al. then charted the progression between adolescent and young adult subgroups. They found that individuals from a given adolescent subgroup were more likely to move to certain young adult subgroups. They called the most common trajectories between groups "pathways," and an example is shown in Figure 1. They also compared individuals who followed a trajectory common to their initial subgroup (path followers) and those who adopted a more unusual path. For men, academic and intellectual factors discriminated between path followers and nonfollowers. For women, the two groups differed in concern for relationships, self-esteem, and emotionality.

FIGURE 1

Selected Pathways for Males and Females

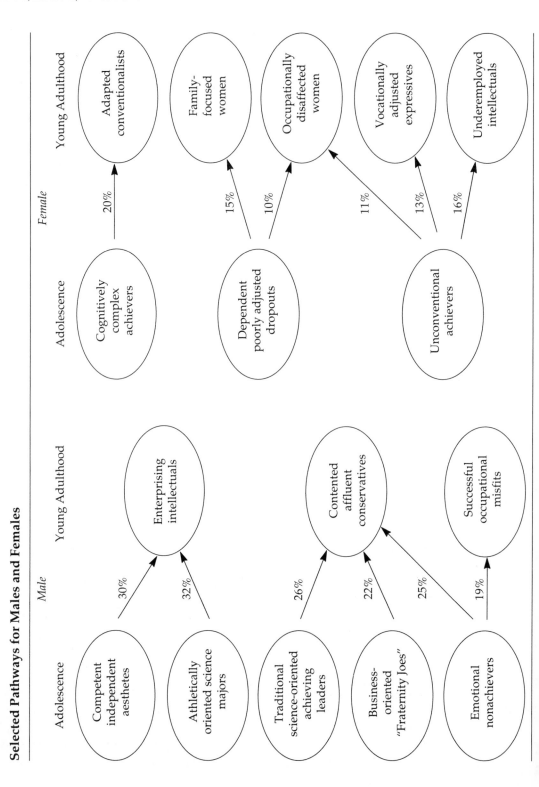

Other researchers have found interactions between personality and life events. Elder and Clipp (1989) studied the long-term effects of combat experience on personality and found dramatic individual differences in response to combat. The men who were less resilient (according to Q-sort data and clinical ratings) as adolescents experienced significantly more postwar problems compared to the initially more resilient group (83% vs. 17%). Differences due to combat experience were also apparent: Relative to the light and no combat groups, the heavy combat veterans showed more marked changes between adolescence and midlife in goal orientation and assertiveness as measured by clinical ratings of psychological functioning. There was also an interaction effect between combat experience and clinically measured ego resilience: Heavy combat veterans who were least resilient in adolescence were more likely to have experienced behavioral and emotional problems after the war compared to the high precombat resilience group.

Mortimer, Finch, and Kumka (1982) found that adolescent self-concept and postcollege life experiences each contributed to later self-concept. Their analyses indicated that the relationship between life experiences and self-concept seemed to be reciprocal: Early self-concept was related to later career outcomes, and early personal outcomes to later self-concept. They found that while 70 percent maintained a stable self-concept (either high or low) ten years after college graduation, the remaining group either decreased or increased due to life events that were at odds with their initial self-concept. Compared to "stable lows," "increasers" had improved their relations with their father and attained higher incomes and work autonomy. "Stable highs" and "decreasers" also differed: The decreasers' relations with their father worsened, and they experienced more employment insecurity, lower income, and less work autonomy.

In summary, despite the long-term stability of personality and interests, great variability exists in the extent to which different people change. Several researchers have found the search for moderators of stability to be fruitful. These moderators include mental ability, personality (e.g., openness to experience), relationship quality (e.g., relations with father), and life events (e.g., combat experience). These findings suggest that individuals may play an active role in shaping their own maturational change. In addition, individuals seem to play an active role in responding to events not of their choosing; some may grow, whereas others may be set back by the same event. These data further illustrate how asserting that people don't change vastly oversimplifies reality.

Individual Differences in Career Progress

In the organizational arena, several studies of change have examined individual potential and experience together. Bray, Campbell, and Grant (1974) found that first job challenge and overall assessment rating both accounted for management progress. There was no direct confounding between assessment rating and job challenge since initial jobs were assigned before assessment and results were kept secret. It is remotely possible that the few weeks or months of high challenge before assessment honed the skills of the high challenge group before assessment. However, assessed potential and challenge seem to have exerted independent effects. In fact, their contribution seems almost equal and compensatory: Low potentials with challenging early assignments progressed almost as well as high potentials with low challenge assignments.

Vicino and Bass (1978) studied the incremental validity of experience variables beyond an early test battery in predicting managerial success. They found that the manager's perceived first job challenge, life stability, personality match with first supervisor, and success of first supervisor (which they called *lifespace variables*) accounted for a significant amount of unique variance, raising the cross-validated multiple R from .63 with the test battery alone to .79 with tests and lifespace variables. The multiple R for lifespace variables alone was .58.

Wakabayashi and Graen (1984) followed the careers of a group of Japanese management recruits to examine the effects of assessed potential and relationships with one's early supervisors on career progress. They found that a strong relationship with one's early supervisors (vertical exchange) seemed to compensate for low assessed potential (and vice versa) in the prediction of promotion and merit bonuses. There also seemed to be a cumulative effect over time: The best got better, the others lagged further and further behind.

Howard (1989) contrasted managers whose skills dramatically increased (*developers*) and those whose skills decreased (*decliners*) over a 20-year period. These distinct groups of "prediction defiers" were discernible despite the good prediction for the overall group. Howard was unable to isolate entry-level individual differences variables that separated these "misses" from the two groups of "hits," which indicates that experience may have played a role.

Grabow (1989) found relationships between assessment center results and self-reported developmental events 12 years later. Developmental events are important events or episodes in a manager's career that, in the mind of the manager, led to lasting change in his or her managerial behavior. Several of the correlations exceeded .30, including seven assessment center ratings (Desire to Lead, Desire to Advance, Long-range Goal Orientation, Verbal Intelligence, Knowledge of Current Events, Achievement Orientation, and Work Orientation), and four CPI scales (higher Dominance, Sociability, and Social Presence, and lower Self-control were associated with more developmental events). Developmental

events were, in turn, highly related to career progress.

Another study (Hazucha et al., 1992) illustrated the relative impact of formal training and self-management on managerial skill development. To assess skill development, managers were rated by an average of seven coworkers in nineteen different skill areas using the *Management Skills Profile* (MSP; Sevy, Olson, McGuire, Fraser, & Paajanen, 1985). Two years later they were rated again using the same instrument. At Time 2, participants also completed a questionnaire describing the development steps they had taken, including training programs and other self-development steps from the development planning guide they received when they received their Time 1 feedback. The dependent variable skill development was the residual of the correlation between the average Time 1 and Time 2 ratings. While attendance at training programs had a small effect on skill development, specific actions taken by the individual, such as reviewing development plans and progress at least quarterly, were related to much larger differences in skill development over this two-year period.

In summary, these studies indicate that both individual differences (e.g., assessment center ratings) and work experience factors (e.g., job challenge) affect career outcomes. In addition, each seems to account for some unique variance in management development and career progress, and they may have compensatory effects.

Age Effects

In addition to the findings described above, age seems to moderate change in at least three areas: psychotherapy (Dobson, 1989), managerial skills training (Hazucha, 1990a), and test-retest correlations (Bentz, 1985). In all cases, changeability seems to decrease with age.

As Glenn (1980) pointed out, these age effects may be due to (a) the decline in exposure to influences for change, (b) the increasing *incumbency advantage* of existing attitudes, or (c) decreases in inherent changeability. The first point means that more major life changes (e.g., marriage, parenthood, moving to a new house, promotion into management) tend to occur in early adulthood than later. These changes may break the inertia in self-concept, causing a reexamination and steps toward change. The second—the increasing incumbency advantage of existing attitudes—is another way of describing psychological inertia: Longer-standing attitudes are supported by more evidence and contradictory evidence will therefore carry less weight than would evidence contrary to attitudes that are still being formed. Several processes operate to maintain the existing self-concept, and these are largely adaptive. The processes that inhibit change will be described in the later section, "The Self and Behavior Change."

The third possibility—decreases in inherent changeability—is consistent with the decrease in *fluid intelligence* (G_f), the ability to process novel stimuli, and the increase in *crystallized intelligence* (G_c), the ability to draw on specific, learned knowledge that occurs over the lifespan (Horn & Donaldson, 1980). This divergence may influence the relative weight given to new information (processed by G_f) versus cumulative experience and knowledge (G_c). A better understanding of the dynamics involved in these age differences is critical to designing effective training programs for older workers.

Summary

The evidence cited in this section on individual differences and change indicates that different people change in different ways. On average, change is moderate, but some individuals change a lot, others hardly at all. The sum of the evidence indicates that personality, motivation, ability, age, and readiness to change may have at least as great an impact on subsequent change as which course or technique is chosen

to induce the intended change. Aptitude-treatment interactions have been demonstrated in several domains, although few have been consistently replicated across studies. In addition, the direction of change may vary across subgroups, and it has proven fruitful to contrast those whose scores move in opposite directions.

The relative importance of ability, personality, self-management, and motivation to change is probably related to what is being changed. For example, highly cognitive tasks will be strongly related to ability, but those with more behavior and noncognitive components will also be a function of noncognitive predictors.

Unfortunately, our outcome research designs, with their emphasis on the intervention effect and group means, have not often enough investigated the moderators of change or the dynamics that underlie them. But it is plausible that individual differences should impact changeability, and more systematic investigation is indicated.

Characteristics and Their Changeability

Human characteristics appear to vary in their degree of long-term stability. What Conley (1984) called a *hierarchy of consistency* has been proposed by several researchers over the past several decades. A better understanding of the relative changeability of human characteristics would have several applications. For example, individuals could increase the payoff of their development efforts by targeting characteristics with a reasonable chance of success, and organizations could select people on the basis of qualifications that are less trainable.

Evidence for constructing such a hierarchy may come from two sources: (a) meta-analyses of the impact of interventions on various characteristics and (b) stability coefficients over a period of years. Unfortunately, with the exception of psychotherapy research, little evidence exists for differential impact of interventions across characteristics, as meta-analyses typically investigate method of intervention as the primary moderator. However, we will discuss some evidence of differential stability.

Differential Stability

Conley (1984) made a major contribution to documenting the relative stability of intelligence, personality, and self-opinion (with the latter defined as a variety of state measures of satisfaction and well-being). Drawing on studies that spanned intervals of 6 months to 50 years, he separated the obtained test-retest reliabilities into period-free reliability and annual stability. *Period-free reliability* is the reliability that would be obtained across a very short period of time, and is a property of the test. *Annual stability* is a measure of the predictable change in test-retest coefficients that is attributable to the time elapsed between test administrations. Conley found the annual stabilities of intelligence, personality, and self-opinion to be .99, .98, and .94, respectively. While these are quite high and quite similar at one year, for a ten-year interval the resulting correlations would be .90, .82, and .54 (assuming perfect reliability). These coefficients indicate how much of the change between Time 1 and Time 2 is due to factors other than measurement error and offers hope for their identification and measurement.

While Conley's (1984) work provided a useful starting point for understanding the relative changeability of the three characteristics he investigated, we could benefit from an extension of the methodology to include other characteristics and subgroups. For example, while Conley found no differences between the personality groupings of Extraversion, Neuroticism, and Psychoticism, both theoretical and empirical work by others indicates that some personality constructs are more stable

than others over time. On the theory end, Schaie and Parham (1976) suggested that personality traits fall into three groups: biostable (most stable), acculturated, and biocultural (most changeable). Unfortunately, it has not yet been determined which traits fall into each group. On the empirical side, Howard and Bray (1988) found that Need for Order was the most stable, and Need for Affiliation the most changeable over a 20-year time span. Kelly (1955) found that the retest correlation for Conventionality approached its reliability, while self-ratings of Physical Energy, Voice Quality, and Modesty showed more change in rank ordering of individuals over time.

There is also preliminary evidence of differential changeability of management skills (Hazucha et al., 1992). As viewed by others, the mean rating for Occupational and Technical Knowledge increased substantially over a two-year period, but Communication Skills (oral and written) did not change at all. All of these findings are intriguing, but they do not fit neatly into a theory.

Other evidence for a hierarchy of changeability was provided by Kelly (1955), who contrasted the stability of values, interests, and personality over a 20-year period. He found more cross-time stability in values and vocational interests than in personality measures and very little stability in attitudes.

We also note that people may differ in the extent to which a given characteristic is elaborated and organized in their self-structure (Baumeister & Tice, 1988; Tellegen, 1988). Although more empirical evidence is needed to validate this notion of individual differences in *traitedness*, if such differences do in fact occur, one could reasonably hypothesize that *the same characteristics could be differentially changeable for different people.* The more highly *traited* a person is on a given characteristic, the more difficult it would be to change the person's standing on it. This is, we believe, a fascinating and important area for future research on change.

A Research Framework for Constructing a Hierarchy of Changeability

Clearly, the research on hierarchies of changeability has not progressed very far as yet. Because we believe that the construction of such hierarchies is so important to the field of behavior change, and because prior research has yielded so little, we want to take this opportunity to offer our own preliminary hierarchy and, in so doing, to suggest some directions for systematic future research.

Our conceptualization of a hierarchy of changeability is based largely on the concept of *complexity*. Within the domain of mental abilities, complexity has been defined as the extent to which an ability correlates with general intelligence (Marshalek, Lohman, & Snow, 1983; Snow & Lohman, 1984). And, recently, Ackerman and Humphreys (1990) tied the concept of complexity to changeability: "The more complex the ability as determined by the location of that ability in the hierarchy of abilities, the less plastic the ability is" (p. 260).

The reasonableness of hypothesizing that greater complexity may be associated with less changeability can be seen by looking at the cognitive substrates of various abilities. It seems reasonable to suggest that the more highly correlated an ability is with general intelligence, the more highly elaborated and organized it is in some superordinate cognitive structure. This hypothesis is consistent, for example, with the work of Ferguson (1954, 1956) who argued that general intelligence is built up via transfer into a progressively more extensive ability structure. The implication of the foregoing is that a specific skill, such as learning to operate a new word processing software package, would be more changeable than a broad ability, such as verbal ability.

Complexity may also be associated with a greater capacity for the adaptation of one's existing store of declarative and procedural knowledge to accommodate a given task (see Snow & Lohman, 1984). Such adaptation may occur in certain recurrent ways—through analogy or inductive reasoning, for example. Such flexible adaptation and reassembly of existing knowledge and skill structures to perform a complex task appear to characterize Horn and Cattell's (1966) fluid intelligence construct, which Snow and Lohman see as the essence of general intelligence. Changing one's capacity for flexible adaptation and reassembly and (nontrivially) changing one's standing on a cognitive structure that has been built up for years would not seem to be very likely outcomes.

Of course, a complete hierarchy of changeability would need to be broadened beyond mental abilities alone. Ackerman and Humphreys (1990) noted that individual differences variables have historically been divided into three categories: *cognitive* (mental abilities), *affective* (temperament, personality), and *conative* (motivation). We therefore suggest that a preliminary hierarchy of changeability would be comprised of two axes. One axis would be *complexity* and would be continuous. The other axis would be discrete and would consist of mental ability, personality, and motivational characteristics. The kind of hierarchy of changeability that we are contemplating, together with a proposed mapping of various characteristics within the hierarchy, is shown in Table 1. The working hypothesis is that greater complexity would be defined in the case of all three classes of variables as degree of overlap with the highest level variable(s) in the hierarchy.[4] In the case of mental abilities, the highest level would be general intelligence; in the case of personality variables, the highest level would be the Norman 5 (e.g., Digman, 1990) or Tellegen's (1982, 1985) constructs of Positive Emotionality, Negative Emotionality, and Constraint. In the motivational domain, taxonomic work is still in its infancy, and it is currently difficult to speculate as to what higher-order motivation-related traits might be. Need for Achievement is a possible candidate.

TABLE 1

**Tentative Mapping of the Changeability
of Various Personal Characteristics**

	Cognitive (Mental Ability) Variables	Conative (Motivational) Variables	Affective (Personality, Temperament) Variables
More complex ↑	General intelligence Verbal ability Spatial ability	Need for achievement	Extraversion
Complexity (Difficulty of Change)	Reading comprehension	Mastery and performance orientation	Talkativeness Abrasiveness
↓ *Less complex*	Basic arithmetic skill	Basic self-management skills (e.g., monitoring one's performance against goals)	Basic interpersonal skills (e.g., listening attentively, being polite in meetings)

While work of this sort on the changeability of individual differences variables is important and interesting, we are cognizant that the bottom line for most industrial and organizational psychologists is job performance. We therefore want to extend our proposed hierarchy of changeability to include job performance behaviors. Noting the paucity of research on the criterion side of the traditional validity model, Campbell (1990, pp. 708 ff.) recently proposed a useful taxonomy of job performance components, together with a model that delineates the determinants of those components. This taxonomy can be conveniently adapted to extend our changeability hierarchy to the job performance domain. The components in Campbell's taxonomy are the following:

- Job-specific task proficiency
- Non–job-specific task proficiency
- Written and oral communication tasks
- Demonstrating effort
- Maintaining personal discipline
- Facilitating peer and team performance
- Supervision
- Management/administration

According to Campbell's model, each performance component is a function of three things: declarative knowledge, procedural knowledge, and motivation. In Campbell's model, declarative knowledge consists of facts, principles, goals, and self-knowledge; procedural knowledge consists of cognitive, psychomotor, physical, self-management, and interpersonal skills; and motivation consists of choices to expend effort, exert effort at a given level, and persist in applying that effort.

Since many (and probably all) of the determinants of Campbell's performance components are encompassed by characteristics that can be embedded in a hierarchy of changeability of the sort that appears in Table 1, it seems reasonable to assume that Campbell's taxonomy of performance components can also be embedded in a changeability hierarchy.

A representation of what such a job performance hierarchy might look like appears in Table 2. As with the characteristics depicted in Table 1, one dimension of the job performance hierarchy of changeability is complexity, defined as before. The other dimension includes the components of Campbell's performance taxonomy. This seems appropriate, since Campbell has speculated that his performance components are relatively independent and "are meant to be the highest order structures that can be useful" (Campbell, 1990, p. 710). In Table 2, we have again tried to suggest where different kinds of job performance behaviors might be placed within the hierarchy. In most cases, our placement of traits and behaviors in Tables 1 and 2 is rational, rather than empirical. Systematic research to fill in Tables 1 and 2 would, we strongly believe, represent a significant advance in the science and practice of behavior change.

Summary

The possibility that human characteristics and behaviors may vary in their changeability is an old idea that has a certain amount of theoretical and empirical support. The establishment of empirically based hierarchies of changeability would have important training and selection applications and would represent a significant advance for the science and practice of psychology.

It is suggested that more systematic research is needed to establish a sound hierarchy of changeability, and a framework for such research is proposed in the foregoing section. Hierarchies for three categories of characteristics and eight categories of job performance behaviors are proposed. Complexity is suggested as a unifying construct to indicate the level of changeability of variables within each of the categories.

We also noted that the same characteristics may be more changeable for some people than for others. If this idea is ultimately shown to

TABLE 2

Tentative Mapping of the Changeability of Various Job Performance Behaviors

Job-specific Task Proficiency	Non-job-specific Task Proficiency	Written and Oral Communication Tasks	Maintaining Personal Discipline	Demonstrating Effort	Facilitating Peer and Team Performance	Supervision	Management/ Administration
Prepare a scientific treatise	Chair a committee whose task is to select a new president for a major university	Persuasively present a controversial plan to a large audience	Overcome a serious chemical dependency problem	Make a habit of working Saturdays to increase the chances of making long-term career goals	Emerge as the de facto leader of a cross-organizational task force that goes on to achieve a goal of great significance to the organization	Take over a large unproductive department and inspire and coach its employees to the point where it becomes highly productive	Plan and oversee a major overseas expansion for a Fortune 500 multinational corporation
Prepare a legal brief		Write a lengthy technical report					
Prepare a high school physics lecture		Brief a group of one's peers about a new product	Eliminate chronic fatigue at work by partying and drinking substantially less	Meet a tough long-term deadline by working 70 to 80 hours per week over six weeks		Turn a problem subordinate into a productive one through effective coaching	Prepare an annual operating budget for a large department
Operate a drill press				Work an extra hour each day for a week or do an especially good job on a report	Inspire a dejected colleague not to give up on a project	Conduct a competent performance review	
	Administer basic first aid	Write a short transmittal letter/memo	Cut absences from work by 10 percent	Turn down an offer to go out for a beer to finish an important memo	Become a more active listener	Periodically ask subordinates how their work is going	
Mow a lawn		Write a grammatical sentence, free of spelling errors					Complete a purchase requisition for ten new personal computers

More complex ← Complexity (Difficulty of Change) → Less complex have validity, then the generality of change-ability hierarchies would be somewhat reduced. At that point, subgroup moderator variables should be investigated.

Recommendations for Measuring Change

Perhaps the most daunting aspect of change research is the measurement of change. The issues encountered in other measurement contexts (i.e., reliability, validity, and statistical power) are exacerbated when change is considered. Unfortunately, recognition of the problems associated with measuring change, which was crystallized by Cronbach and Furby's (1970) classic discussion, has resulted in a decrease in poor research, but not an increase in good research. Yet change and its measurement are important and fascinating, and we need to find ways around the problems. Therefore, we would like to make some recommendations for people who wish to measure change. Most of these recommendations will be illustrated with studies that have been discussed earlier.

Assumption and Interpretation Issues

The detection of change—even when it has occurred—is not always easy. The proper design and analysis of change research represents a substantial challenge in and of itself. The following section was written with this set of difficulties in mind and is intended to reduce the changes that useful interventions may fail to be so identified due to inadequately designed and/or misinterpreted research.

Do not assume that stability and change are incompatible. This assumption is a dangerous one. Research should investigate the magnitude of both. For example, look at Time 1–Time 2 correlations (to assess stability in rank ordering), mean differences (to assess average change), *and* residuals (to assess individual variance in Time 2 unexplained by Time 1 standing). Several researchers have looked for and found *both* stability *and* change, thereby avoiding erroneous conclusions. For example, Howard and Bray (1988) found that, despite the high correlation between *Edwards Personal Preference Scale* scores across a 20-year interval, a substantial proportion of individuals changed by half a standard deviation or more on each scale. Swanson and Hansen (1988) found wide variability across individuals in their stability coefficients over a 12-year interval, despite the median stability coefficient of .72. And Hazucha et al. (1992) concurrently found fairly high correlations and mean differences over a two-year interval.

Make realistic predictions about the magnitude and the timing of change expected from an intervention. The amount of change detected in outcome studies will vary depending on (a) the length and intensity of the intervention, (b) the complexity of what is being targeted for change, (c) the source of the information (e.g., trainee, supervisor, spouse), and (d) the measures used.

As an example, the change resulting from a two-day human relations training program is likely to be small relative to an intensive six-month coaching program targeted at improving overall interpersonal skills. In addition, management development programs typically cover complex issues (such as communication and interpersonal skills) that require practice, and visible changes should not be expected before six months after training. Immediately after the intervention, the amount of change observed may be small.

Whether measured change is self-rated or not may also affect the amount of change detected. The finding of differences between ratings by self and others is robust (e.g., Borman, 1974; Harris & Schaubroeck, 1988; Mabe & West, 1982), and similar differences are expected in the measurement of change. Such differences may be caused by differing expectations about change and opportunity to observe.

Consider multiple types of Time 1–Time 2 statistical analyses. Data analysis options for the analysis of Time 1 and Time 2 data include the use of raw gain scores and covariance models or residuals. Cronbach and Furby (1970) recommended the use of residualized gain scores as a solution to the problems associated with gain scores (e.g., unreliability, regression to the mean).[5] However, Cohen and Cohen (1975) showed that the residual from the covariance model is simpler to calculate and is equivalent to the residualized gain score.[6] Rogosa, Brant, and Zimowski (1982) defended the use of raw gain scores with reliable measures and nonnegligible change. They argued that how much person A changed (represented by a gain score) is much more interesting and interpretable than how much person A would have changed if she or he started out at X (represented by a residual). The use of residuals also assumes that any correlation between Time 1 and Time 2 minus Time 1 is spurious, yet there are cases where one would expect such a correlation.

Make sure that your experimental design will yield adequate statistical power. Statistical power is the probability of detecting a true effect. Low power may result in a false conclusion of no change. Power is always an important consideration, given the typical sample sizes available in change measurement. It is a function of true effect size, error of measurement, sample size, and alpha level. Researchers usually use the largest sample size possible, and alpha levels can be chosen carefully. However, steps can and should also be taken to optimize the other parameters, as follows:

- The most important way to maximize power is through attention to true effect size. Effect sizes can be maximized by using high-quality interventions and by measuring their impact at a reasonable time. Collaboration between experts on both the intervention and the measurement sides is likely to produce the largest effect sizes.

- Arvey et al. (1985) showed that another way to minimize error is through the choice of statistical design: The analysis of covariance design is always more powerful than posttest only or gain score designs (unless the correlation between Time 1 and Time 2 is negligible, causing the unnecessary loss of a degree of freedom).

- In addition, reliability can be increased (and error decreased) with multiple raters and/or measures, as discussed below.

Do not view perceptions of change as useless. Scientists are trained to be skeptical, and they consistently request more evidence with statements such as, Well, people think it worked, but did it *really* work? While it is true that perceptions are only one type of change measurement (others are learning, behavior, and performance), this does not diminish their importance. In fact, in some cases, it is precisely the perception of change that is important, regardless of whether *real* change occurred. For example, for an individual whose job is on the line if changes do not occur, what matters is whether the supervisor perceives the change, regardless of the individual's learning or behavior when the boss is not around.

An example with encouraging findings is a study conducted by Sloan, Schneider, and Hazucha (1990), which used ratings by both participants and their co-workers to assess the impact of a management development program. One measure was a *reaction* type questionnaire, which listed the objectives of the program and asked participants for ratings at two points in time—when the program started, and "now," which represented a span of 18 months. The second was the *Management Skills Profile* (MSP; Sevy et al., 1985), which elicited behavioral ratings from the participants and seven of their co-workers. They found that (a) self-reported perceptions indicated more change than skills change reported by others and (b) within the self-report instrument, raters distinguished between the areas most directly targeted by the intervention (self-development) and those which were targeted indirectly, leading the researchers to conclude raters could be quite perceptive about subtle changes.

Describe conclusions in terms that accurately and specifically reflect the magnitude of the findings. It is helpful to discuss the magnitude of the effect size in the context of other effect sizes familiar to the reader. For example, Smith, Glass, and Miller (1980) compared effect sizes associated with psychotherapy to those obtained from nine months of elementary school reading instruction. These types of comparisons are much more helpful than general terms such as *large, significant,* or *nonsignificant.* As Cohen (1990) recently pointed out again, *highly significant* means only *quite certainly not zero,* rather than *quite different from zero,* as it is commonly interpreted.

Validity

Our next set of recommendations concerns the validity of change measures. In the case of change measurement, the validity of the measure is defined as the extent to which the measure detects the nature and degree of change that actually occurred. In this section we offer recommendations to help maximize the validity of the inference about the magnitude of change.

Use measures that match the intervention in content and specificity. For example, ratings or behavioral counts of the specific areas targeted by the intervention are more likely to detect change than is a personality scale, which may be deficient and/or contaminated relative to the intervention.[7] Use personality or intelligence measures only if the intervention is designed to change personality or intelligence. Too often, measures are chosen because of their availability rather than because of their relevance. For example, a measure of interpersonal behavior and an empathy scale both measure content covered in a human relations course. However, the former is more targetable to the intervention and is therefore more likely to detect any change that occurred.

In their meta-analysis of therapy outcome, Shapiro and Shapiro (1982) found smaller effect sizes for achievement and personality trait measures than for measures more specifically targeted to the therapy (e.g., fear/anxiety, physiological stress). In the Hazucha et al. (1992) study, the instrument used to detect change was designed to measure management skills rather than long-standing personality traits. In this case, there was a perfect match between the intervention and the measure because the intervention was feedback on the management skills measure at Time 1.

It is especially difficult to target the outcome measurement to the intervention when each individual receives a different treatment. This has been a long-standing dilemma in counseling research, and it is also an issue in individualized training programs. As discussed by Peterson (1990), units of change may not be comparable across objectives, nor may they all be equally susceptible to the influences of the intervention. This issue, and an example of how to deal with it, will be discussed further in a later section.

Be creative about the use of comparison groups. Finding a control group that is directly comparable to the group experiencing the intervention is especially difficult in organizations. In fact, it is practically impossible for unique interventions and groups, such as team building for the top management group or coaching for people at risk of losing their job. One way of dealing with this problem is to assess both targeted and nontargeted skills within the targeted group to document the discriminant validity of the intervention (e.g., Peterson, 1990). A second option is to contrast subgroups who have experienced different levels of the intervention (e.g., partial versus complete training;

Thompson, 1986). A third option is to use the premeasure as the control group, as did Howard and Bray (1988), reporting Time 2 scores against Time 1 norms. Thus, the Time 1 norms serve as a baseline against which to compare the scores of the treated group. A fourth option is to use standardized measures with established norms, although this is only appropriate when they match the content and specificity of the intervention, as described above.

Be wary of standardizing pre- and posttest scores. Rogosa, Brandt, and Zimowski (1982) cautioned against standardizing the measures used in pre- and posttest designs when the variance changes dramatically from Time 1 to Time 2. Because correlations are standardized, this would also make their use inappropriate in such cases. Effect sizes may still be used, but only with careful consideration of which standard deviation is most appropriate.

An example of increasing variance over time would involve a group of beginners who all score at chance levels (with very little variance) on a pretest, but who learn at different rates and show large variance on the posttest (shown in Figure 2). An example of decreasing variance (shown in Figure 3) would involve a group that begins at different points and is measured at the end of training with a criterion-referenced test (which is designed not to spread people out but to assess who has passed a critical hurdle). In statistical terms, the first example has a *floor effect* on the pretest; the second has a *ceiling effect* on the posttest. There would also be artifactual correlations in both groups because of the ceiling and floor effects: A positive correlation between Time 2 minus Time 1 and Time 2 for the first group, and a negative correlation between Time 2 minus Time 1 and Time 1 for the second group. In addition, reduced variance at either end would make the use of the Time 1/Time 2 correlation inappropriate (the correlation would be spuriously low), and the determination of a standard deviation for computing effect size problematic. Therefore, properties of the measures

and of the expected change need to be explicitly considered when choosing data analysis methods.

Reliability

Reliability has received the most emphasis in the change measurement literature, and, indeed, it is important not to sacrifice reliability in the pursuit of specificity and sensitivity. There are several ways to do this, most of which require collecting more measurement points.

Use multiple items per construct at each point in time. For example, if the intervention is a motivation-to-manage course, operationalize the construct with several statements and collect observations or performance measures on each one, rather than obtaining only a single observation.

Use multiple rater types. Although research shows that different rater types (e.g., trainee, peers, and trainee's supervisor) do not necessarily agree with each other (e.g., Harris & Schaubroeck, 1988), each type of rater provides important information. For example, Hazucha (1990) found that boss ratings of the outcome of an individualized coaching program were strongly related to the trainee's pretraining success and job jeopardy (lower level trainees who were also *not* in jeopardy received better training outcome ratings). Higher ratings of training outcome provided by the boss were in turn related to lower risk of involuntary termination. On the other hand, staff psychologists' ratings of training outcome were essentially unrelated to pretraining organizational level and jeopardy, but they were strongly related to initial management skill level (especially in interpersonal and administrative areas), mental ability, and personality. These findings suggested that bosses seemed to be equating training outcome with absolute skill level at the end of training, whereas staff psychologists defined outcome as the degree to which participants improved during training.

FIGURE 2

**Chance Levels on Pretest;
Large Variance on Posttest**

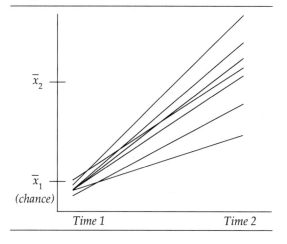

FIGURE 3

**Different Levels on Pretest;
Criterion-referenced Posttest**

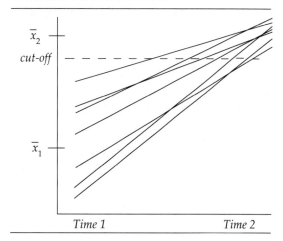

Use multiple types of measures. In general, change can be measured using trainee perceptions (e.g., How effective was this program?), learning, behavior, and performance measures (Kirkpatrick, 1967). A prominent example of a research study which assessed behavior change at all four of Kirkpatrick's levels is Latham and Saari's (1979) behavior modeling study. Latham and Saari assessed perceptions using a five-item questionnaire with a five-point Likert scale. It asked the trainees to indicate the extent to which their training improved their on-the-job skills relevant to the training program. Learning was assessed using a situational judgment test consisting of 85 items. The items were developed from critical incidents and possible responses, and the response options for each situation were given weights (indicating the quality of the response) by supervisors. Behavioral measures were obtained by obtaining ratings of role plays in which the trainees were asked to resolve problems relevant to the training they had received. The participants were rated on the learning

points they had been given during training. The participants were given a rating on each of nine role plays that operationalized the nine topics covered during training. Finally, Latham and Saari measured job performance by obtaining supervisory ratings on five-point behavioral observation scales (before and after training). The scales were developed from a job analysis of effective and ineffective performance. Learning measures assess the knowledge acquired in training (declarative knowledge); behavior is how well a person can apply that knowledge (procedural knowledge); and performance refers to more global job performance criteria. The last three criteria are generally assumed to be cumulative: Knowledge is a prerequisite to behavior, which in turn impacts performance. Within the area of perception, options include collecting similar measures at Times 1 and 2, asking directly about degree of change (e.g., Peterson, 1990), or concurrently asking about *then* and *now* (e.g., Sloan, Schneider, & Hazucha, 1990). As Peterson pointed out, asking several questions at once provides insight into how change is viewed from several vantage points. For example, a number of factors may influence the differences among (a) *objective* change as measured at Times 1 and 2, (b) *perceptions* measured at both times, and (c) *retrospective judgments* of change at Time 2.

Distinguish between stability and reliability. When researchers observe a high Time 1–Time 2 correlation, they often tend to assume that the residual is random error and fail to try to explain additional variance. However, there is an important distinction between variance in Time 2 unexplained by Time 1 and error of measurement. Conley (1984) addressed this distinction by partitioning the residual of stability over time (i.e., 1 minus the stability coefficient) into two components: *period-free reliability*, which represents random measurement error, and *annual stability*, which represents true variability between Time 1 and Time 2 scores and may therefore be explained by other factors. Failing to distinguish between stability and reliability results in choosing instruments to measure change based on their high *test-retest* reliability, which will *reduce* the likelihood of finding change. It is instruments with high period-free reliability and lower annual stability that are most useful in change research.

The Hazucha et al. (1992) study is an example of a case where both relatively high test-retest correlations and a predictable residual were found. Hazucha et al. observed moderately high correlations (median *r* = .58) between management skills as rated by others across a two-year interval, yet significant portions of the residuals were explained by development activities performed by the developing manager in the interim. It was possible to find these effects because the dependent measure used at both points in time, the *Management Skills Profile* (Sevy et al., 1985), was highly reliable (alpha > .90).

Measure early and often. Frequent measurement during learning of the sort done by R. Kanfer and Ackerman (1989) in their study of the acquisition of air traffic control skill is optimal in change research. Many learning situations do not lend themselves to such continous data collection, but obtaining measurements throughout a course rather than simply at the end, for example, would be helpful. Moreover, Baldwin and Ford (1988) recommended plotting curves both during *and* after the intervention to measure not only learning but also retention and transfer.

Summary

Despite the challenges inherent in change research, steps can be taken to increase the chances of finding true change when it occurs. These involve increasing validity, reliability, and statistical power. Obviously, the basic principles are the same as for measurement at one point in time. However, their implementation is more complex in the case of change measurement. The complexity inherent in the accurate measurement of change is an indication that experts from both the intervention and measurement sides should collaborate more in future change research.

A Proposed Framework for Behavior Change

In this section, we will describe a behavior change framework to help guide future research and practice. That framework appears as Table 3. Although there is nothing particularly new about this framework, it does serve to unify diverse literatures which, together, converge on the process of behavior change. Moreover, different theories and methods contribute differentially to various components of the change process, and we

TABLE 3

An Integrated Behavior Change Framework

Change Method, Model, or Theory	Assessment/ Needs Analysis	Assignment of Behavioral Standards	Intention Formulation and Protection	Behavioral Expression in Change Environment	Generalization and Maintenance of New/Changed Behaviors
Organizational behavior modification	Functional analysis Baseline performance measurement	Change in antecedents (goals, instructions, rules)		Behavioral standards Feedback Rewards	Keep new behavioral standards, feedback, and rewards in place
Behavior modeling	Organizational analysis Task analysis Person analysis (skill deficits identified)	Specification of desired behaviors Learning points Modeling	Self-efficacy increased by observation and successful performance Public rehearsal Instrumentality made clear	Behavioral standards Rehearsal Feedback Reinforcement	Train supervisor to reinforce Overlearning Identical elements Identify behavior components General principles taught Variety of stimuli used in change environment
Self-management	Self-assessment	Self-set goals	Self-efficacy increased by developing self-management skills in the past Commitment to self-development goal	Self-set goals Self-monitoring Self-evaluation Self-reaction Self-administered reinforcers and punishers	Maintain self-created antecedents and consequences and self-monitoring Identify potentially threatening situations Learning coping skills

TABLE 3

An Integrated Behavior Change Framework (continued)

Change Method, Model, or Theory	*Assessment/ Needs Analysis*	*Assignment of Behavioral Standards*	*Intention Formulation and Protection*	*Behavioral Expression in Change Environment*	*Generalization and Maintenance of New/Changed Behaviors*
Kuhl's action control theory and Heckhausen & Kuhl's model of intention formulation and protection			Expectancy check OTIUM (future) check Metavolitions Induce action orientation Self-regulatory strategies	OTIUM (now) Action launching impulse	OTIUM (ongoing)
Control theory		Behavioral standard assigned (externally or internally)	Expectancy evaluation Valuing of standard	Behavioral output Feedback (perceptual input) Sensed discrepancy Adaptive discrepancy-reducing behavior (or disengagement) Self-focused attention	Accurate, clear, timely feedback continually provided or available Behavior standards remain in place Other mechanisms of negative feedback loop not disrupted
Social-cognitive work on the self	Possible selves Undesired selves		Expectancy (possible selves) Value (possible selves) Implicit theory or self change OTIUM (future) for possible selves	OTIUM (now) for possible selves	OTIUM (ongoing) for possible selves Self-verification

Note: OTIUM = opportunity, time, importance, urgency, and means

TABLE 3

An Integrated Behavior Change Framework (continued)

Change Method, Model, or Theory	Assessment/ Needs Analysis	Assignment of Behavioral Standards	Intention Formulation and Protection	Behavioral Expression in Change Environment	Generalization and Maintenance of New/Changed Behaviors
Campbell's (1988) training model	Analyzing goals and job design Determining training needs	Specifying training (behavioral) objectives Specifying training content learning	Accounting for individual differences	Accounting for individual differences Specifying learning methods and learning Specifying the conditions for learning	Specifying the conditions for learning
Noe's (1986) training model			Motivation to learn Environmental favorability (perceived) Self-efficacy Job involvement Locus of control Trainee reaction to skills assessment Career exploration behavior		Environment favorability Motivation to transfer

believe our framework will show how they can inform and strengthen one another.

It is also our intent to use our framework to indicate in greater detail than has previously been provided what may threaten an otherwise successful change intervention (see Table 4). Threats to change are implied by each step in our framework. It is our hope that this list of threats will serve as a guide both to practitioners and researchers. Research on various threats is needed because some have not been empirically tested and need to be placed on an empirical footing. Practitioners should be guided by our list of threats in that (a) empirically grounded threats to change should be heeded and (b) speculative threats to change should be considered if they seem sound under the circumstances. The framework, which abstracts and combines key elements from diverse theories and methods relevant to behavior change, is meant to be normative and has implications for a variety of behavior change interventions. The number of steps and conceptualizations attests to the complexity of achieving lasting change, and implies a range of possible obstacles to a successful intervention.

Although it is presented in a linear, sequential fashion, with each step in the behavior change sequence leading to the next step, the framework also allows for the possibility of reciprocal influence among certain steps in the sequence. For example, Behavioral Expression in the Change Environment may increase the strength of one's intention by enhancing self-efficacy and thereby feed back into the Intention Formulation and Protection stage. Likewise, if trainees are unable to formulate a strong intention to complete their training goals because the goals proved too difficult, then this is an indication that an error was made in the Assessment/Needs Analysis portion of the framework. Perhaps most importantly, transfer issues should be attended to throughout an intervention. Waiting until the

end of the Behavioral Expression in the Change Environment step to address transfer issues is likely to jeopardize the success of the entire intervention.

According to our framework, the first step in the change process involves an assessment of training needs—the organization (or other change agent) must determine the general nature of the behavior change that it seeks to bring about. Once the Assessment/Needs Analysis phase has been completed, the next step involves the Assignment of Behavioral Standards. This step takes the general training needs identified in the previous step and converts them into more concrete behavioral objectives and, subsequently, into training content (Campbell, 1988).

It is possible that a trainee may be assigned a behavioral standard and yet not be committed to attaining it. He or she may consider the standard too difficult or, perhaps, not worth attaining (particularly after a failed attempt or two). It is vitally important, therefore, that trainees form strong intentions to achieve the behavioral standards of the training programs, particularly if the standards are challenging. Thus, Intention Formulation and Protection is included as the next step in our framework.

The step following Intention Formulation and Protection is Behavioral Expression in the Change Environment. The change environment may be carefully designed and quite different from the ultimate transfer environment, as in many behavior modeling interventions, or it may be identical to the transfer environment, as is usually the case in operant organizational behavior modification interventions. Finally, the changed behaviors must be generalized to the transfer environment, and steps must be taken to ensure that they are maintained without relapse. We have termed this step in the behavior change process Generalization and Maintenance of New/Changed Behaviors.

In the next section, we demonstrate the capacity of our framework to encompass a

TABLE 4

Threats to Change Implied by Integrated Framework

	Assessment/Needs Analysis	Assignment Behavioral Standards	Intention Formulation and Protection	Behavioral Expression in Change Environment	Generalization and Maintenance of New/Changed Behaviors
Change/Transfer Environment Variables	Poor needs analysis (e.g., task analysis, job analysis, organizational analysis, person analysis) Incongruity between training goals and organizational goals	Goal too difficult Goal too vague Incorrect standards assigned No standard assigned Poorly modeled behaviors Undesirable personal characteristics in model Failure to specify behavioral objectives Failure to specify knowledge and skills to be learned and proper learning sequence	OTIUM support not in place	Behavioral confirmation effects OTIUM support not in place Inaccurate, ambiguous, distorted, or delayed feedback Failure to reinforce trainee successes Failure to promote trainee success in change environment Improper learning methods and media used Failure to properly incorporate principles of learning (e.g., production of behaviors to be learned)	Behavior confirmation effects OTIUM support not in place Insufficient attention paid to normative TOT principles during training New/changed behaviors not periodically reinforced Inaccurate, ambiguous, distorted, or delayed ongoing feedback Change-inhibiting role set or interpersonal standards

TABLE 4

Threats to Change Implied by Integrated Framework (continued)

	Assessment/Needs Analysis	Assignment Behavioral Standards	Intention Formulation and Protection	Behavioral Expression in Change Environment	Generalization and Maintenance of New/Changed Behaviors
Person Variables	Trainees react negatively to skills assessment	Low need achievement (for self-set goals/standards only) Conflicting possible selves (for self-concept change only) Low self-knowledge (for self-concept change only) Low self-knowledge (for self-concept change only)	State orientation Low job involvement External locus of control Entity theory of attitude to be changed Low self-efficacy Low expectancy evaluation Low perceived instrumentality Trainees don't value rewards Lack of career exploration behavior history Poor self-regulatory skills OTIUM (future) not satisfied (a.k.a. low perceived environmental favorability)	General intelligence too low Insufficient prerequisite knowledge and skill to perform desired behaviors Attention not self-focused OTIUM (now) not passed Rewards not valued Self-related expertise that inhibits change (e.g., cognitive conservatism) Failure to self-monitor, self-evaluate, and self-react	All person variables applicable to behavioral expression in change environment Low motivation to transfer OTIUM (ongoing) not passed (a.k.a. low perceived opportunity) Environmental unfavorability

wide variety of theories, models, and methods relevant to behavior change. In so doing, we explicate the tenets of each and give examples of how they have been tested, where empirical support is available. Threats to change implied by each theory, model, and method are also discussed.

Theories, Models, and Methods Relevant to Behavioral Change

Industrial and organizational psychologists interested in designing behavior change interventions have a much larger theoretical and empirical arsenal to draw on than they did at the time the first edition of this *Handbook* was published. Much useful research testing the principles of organizational behavior modification has appeared (Komaki, 1986). The theoretical base of OB Mod was broadened to encompass internal cognitive events by Bandura (1977a) in his social learning theory, which led to a steady stream of practical behavior modeling applications (Decker & Nathan, 1985). The topic of self-regulation has gained considerably in status within the clinical (e.g., F. H. Kanfer & Hagerman, 1987; F. H. Kanfer & Schefft, 1988) and motivational (Heckhausen & Kuhl, 1985; Kuhl, 1984, 1985, 1986; Kuhl & Kraska, 1989) domains, resulting in a substantial body of theory and research with much relevance to issues of behavior change. Control theory has been imported into industrial and organizational psychology as a way of explaining, in more microanalytic detail, certain results predicted by other theories (Campion & Lord, 1982; Lord & Hanges, 1987). Recent work by cognitively oriented social psychologists appears to have great promise in helping to elucidate potential intrapsychic inhibitors and facilitators of change, as well as the processes by which external agents can facilitate or threaten the process (e.g., Schlenker, 1985). And industrial and organizational

psychologists have formulated training models that encompass diverse theories, methods, and results from other psychological disciplines (Campbell, 1988; Noe, 1986) in an effort to provide greater theoretical and empirical support to the training and development field.

In the following sections, we review various theories and methods of behavior change that fall into each of these areas. Some are well known to industrial and organizational psychologists, while others, taken from other psychological disciplines, are not. However, we believe that all of these theories and methods have the potential to contribute to our understanding of the behavior change process.

Operant Organizational Behavior Modification

Within the past 20 years or so, OB Mod has become a popular method for change interventions in organizations. It has been used successfully to change a variety of employee behaviors, including productivity, absenteeism, tardiness, safety, and sales behavior (Luthans & Kreitner, 1985). Rooted in B. F. Skinner's operant conditioning techniques, OB Mod attempts to

> make specific, on-the-job behavior occur more or less often by systematically managing *antecedent conditions* (that serve to cue the target behavior) and/or by managing *contingent consequences* that serve to encourage or discourage repetition of the target behavior. (Luthans & Kreitner, 1985, p. 184)

Antecedents include instructions, rules, and goals; consequences include recognition, feedback, and incentives (Komaki, 1986). Although OB Mod places emphasis on consequences in accord with the principles of operant conditioning, it seems apparent now that the coupling of antecedents and consequences is necessary to cause and maintain maximum behavior change (Erez, 1977; Locke, 1980; Locke, Shaw, Saari, & Latham, 1981). The general procedure suggested by the OB Mod approach is summarized by Goldstein (1986):

1. An assessment is performed to specify where problems exist and to help in the determination of precise behaviors that require elimination, modification, or development.

2. Reinforcers appropriate to the situation and to the individual are selected.

3. The implementation of the actual program consists of a variety of different procedures dependent on the behavior of the trainees.

4. Desired responses are immediately and continuously reinforced. Once the behavior is established, intermittent programs of reinforcement are instituted.

5. Evaluation procedures are employed to determine the degree of change. (pp. 220–221)

Although there are few carefully designed evaluations of OB Mod interventions (Goldstein, 1986), a series of research studies performed by Komaki and her colleagues are an exception. Komaki's studies investigated not only the effectiveness of OB Mod as a general technique, but also the relative contributions of antecedents and consequences to that overall success. Moreover, Komaki's studies allow us to rule out certain threats to internal validity such as history, maturation, and regression to the mean (see Komaki, 1986, for a discussion of her methodology).

An intervention by Komaki, Barwick, and Scott (1978) was designed to improve employee safety in a bakery. As part of this intervention, employees were given information regarding appropriate and inappropriate safety-related behaviors, agreed to a goal of 90 percent safe behaviors, and were given both baseline and intervention period feedback. The intervention caused a substantial improvement in safety-related performance, which reverted to baseline levels following the withdrawal of the intervention.

In a follow-up study using similar methodology, Komaki, Heinzmann, and Lawson (1980) attempted to assess the relative contribution of antecedents (in the form of information via modeling and related discussion) versus antecedents plus consequences (with information and specific goals functioning as antecedents and graphed safety observations by supervisors functioning as consequences). The investigators found that feedback was a necessary condition for behavior change, with antecedents alone proving insufficient.

Komaki, Collins, and Penn (1982) noted that Komaki, Heinzmann, and Lawson's (1980) findings could also have been explained by the greater frequency of stimulus changes and/or amount of supervisory attention in the antecedent-plus-consequences condition. They therefore designed a study to assess more rigorously the effects of antecedents and consequences on employee performance by holding supervisor involvement and stimulus change constant across experimental conditions. Komaki et al. (1982) found that while the antecedent control condition produced significant improvement in two of the four departments in which the intervention was implemented, the consequence condition resulted in significant improvement for all four departments, both from baseline performance and from antecedent control condition performance.

Luthans and Kreitner (1985) described the results of other OB Mod–based interventions in a variety of organizations. One example from the management development domain involved a medium-sized manufacturing plant where first-line supervisors received OB Mod training for the purpose of helping them manage their subordinates better. Training sessions were held over the course of ten weeks, with each session lasting 90 minutes. The trainees were taught to (a) focus on objective target behaviors rather than on unobservable internal states; (b) chart the frequency of the behaviors they observed; (c) perform functional analysis—that is, identify antecedents and consequences operating in the work environment in order to better predict, understand, and control behavior; (d) apply the results of the functional analyses to strengthen desirable and weaken undesirable subordinate behaviors; and (e) monitor the results of their interventions to evaluate whether the desired change had in fact occurred. The emphasis of the training course was on facilitating transfer of these techniques so that the supervisors would be able to use them regularly after the course had ended. To accomplish this, the supervisors applied their training to solve existing problems in their departments, such as chronic complaining or high scrap rates. In both of these cases, interventions jointly planned by the supervisors and trainers resulted in substantial behavior change in the desired directions. To assess the effectiveness of the OB Mod training intervention, departments whose supervisors had received training were compared to control departments whose supervisors had not received training. It was found that the mean productivity of the experimental departments exceeded that of the control departments both during and after the intervention.

How does OB Mod fit into our framework? At the Assessment/Needs Analysis stage, dysfunctional behaviors are identified and baseline performance data are collected, which will be used both to provide feedback to the employees after the intervention is implemented and to assess the effectiveness of the intervention. The functional analysis, whereby the antecedents and consequences that maintain the existing ineffective behaviors are identified, is also performed at this early stage of the change process. The next step in our change framework involves Assignment of Behavioral

Standards. Within the OB Mod paradigm, this usually involves applying new antecedents to replace the old maladaptive ones identified by the functional analysis. New antecedents may involve both a quantitative goal (e.g., 80% safe behaviors) and instructions and rules to facilitate the achievement of that goal.

In the OB Mod paradigm, the Behavioral Expression in the Change Environment is largely the same as Generalization and Maintenance of New/Changed Behaviors. There is nothing artificial about the learning environment in an OB Mod intervention. Behavior change occurs as a result of changes in antecedents and consequences based on functional analysis of the employees' behaviors within the organization. Since behavior change occurs *on the job*, transfer is not an issue. The changed behavior should be maintained as long as the new antecedents and consequences stay in place.

The Intention Formulation and Protection part of the framework has not typically been very well addressed within OB Mod. With the emphasis on overt, clearly measurable behaviors, this is not very surprising. However, as a result of OB Mod's failure to focus on employee intentions, some individuals may resist such interventions (Mawhinney & Fellows, 1990). Although the data indicate that OB Mod interventions are generally successful even without attending to employee intentions, it may be that they would be even more successful if intention formulation and protection became part of those interventions.

Despite the general neglect of Intention Formulation and Protection within the OB Mod paradigm, at least one group of investigators recently incorporated an intention formulation component into an OB Mod intervention. In this study (Siero, Boon, Kok, & Siero, 1989), the investigators attempted to change employee attitudes regarding targeted behaviors so that solid intentions to behave in desired ways could be formed, in accord with Fishbein's theory of reasoned action (Fishbein, 1979). The purpose of the intervention was to change the driving behavior of mail-van drivers to produce greater energy efficiency. Employees participating in the intervention (a) were shown an instructional film and given a booklet containing information about energy-efficient driving, (b) were provided with stickers reminding them about proper driving procedures on the dashboards of their vans, (c) attended a meeting where a driving expert answered questions about energy-saving driving procedures (which served as the attitude change portion of the manipulation), (d) were given a goal of five percent savings on fuel consumption, and (e) were given group fuel consumption feedback on a weekly basis. Siero et al. found that fuel consumption was significantly lowered as a result of the intervention and that attitudes and subjective norm perceptions also changed in the expected directions.[8]

Whether employee attitudes and social norm perceptions, and therefore their intentions, would have changed had attitude change not been specifically designed into the intervention is, of course, an open question. Another question is whether the results would have been the same had attitude change not been targeted, and the results of a pilot study reported by Siero et al. indicate that they probably would not have been. However, a direct empirical test of the incremental validity of a typical OB Mod intervention versus an OB Mod intervention plus attitude change (or, more generally, an intention-strengthening) intervention would be a useful test of the utility of our framework.

Our framework implies several threats to a successful OB Mod intervention. The baseline measurement or functional analysis may be faulty (perhaps because of organizational unwillingness to expend the necessary time and resources), resulting in the misidentification of behaviors to be changed; assigned goals may be vague or perceived by employees as unrealistic; feedback may be inaccurate, ambiguous, distorted, or delayed; there may be a discrepancy between what the organization

perceives as rewarding and what the employees perceive as rewarding; or the antecedents and consequences introduced as part of the intervention may be removed.

Behavior Modeling

In the original operant OB Mod paradigm, antecedents lead to behaviors that, in turn, lead to consequences (A–B–C). One criticism leveled against this paradigm is that the mediating role of cognitive processes is ignored (Kreitner & Luthans, 1987). While acknowledging the substantial impact that the environment has on human behavior, Bandura (1977a) formulated a social learning theory that integrated cognitive processes into the operant paradigm, thus dealing with this sort of criticism. According to Bandura's theory, people are neither deterministically controlled by their environments nor entirely self-determining. They exist instead in a state of reciprocal determinism with their environments whereby they and their environments influence one another in a perpetual dynamic interplay.

An important consequence of Bandura's reciprocal determinism is that people can acquire certain skills by watching other people perform them. Although the theoretical underpinnings and methodology needed to effectively implement a behavior modeling intervention are complex, the process can be summarized as follows: Once an organization has determined that a behavior modeling intervention is feasible and desirable (a decision that should, ideally, be made only after a series of questions has been asked and answered in the affirmative—see Robinson & Graines, 1980, cited in Decker & Nathan, 1985, p. 134), a training needs analysis should be done. This would include an organizational analysis, a person analysis, and a task analysis. If the training needs analysis identifies a remediable skill deficit, the resolution of which would be consistent with organizational goals, the next step involves identifying key behaviors to be learned, learning points to facilitate the acquisition of desired behaviors, and choosing an effective model for the trainees to observe.

Once the observational phase of learning has been completed, trainees are given an opportunity to rehearse what they have learned through observation. This may be done one-on-one with a trainer or in groups of varying size. During rehearsal, trainees are given feedback and reinforcement where appropriate, which serves both the informational function of providing knowledge of results and the motivational function of encouraging the trainees to apply the newly learned behaviors in the future. Finally, transfer of training is facilitated by (a) training the supervisor to reinforce behaviors in the transfer environment, (b) making the training environment as similar as possible to the transfer environment (identical elements), (c) causing the trainees to rehearse the new behaviors beyond the point where they have been performed correctly once (overlearning), (d) using a variety of stimuli in the training environment to show trainees how the key behaviors can generalize, (e) labeling the crucial components of the training content through the use of learning points, (f) making sure the trainees understand the general principles that underlie the training content through discussion of the modeled behavior and the learning points, and (g) making it clear to the trainees that the training intervention will help them perform better on their jobs through improved skills and increased self-efficacy.

A substantial number of research studies testing the effectiveness of behavior modeling were reviewed by Decker and Nathan (1985), leading them to conclude that

the consistent results of these studies indicate the efficacy of the technique [behavior modeling] for changing behavior, maintaining that change over time, generalizing new behaviors to different contexts, and transferring the training content to the job or other transfer contexts. (p. 10)

The first such studies were reported at a behavior modeling symposium held in 1976 (Kraut, 1976). The symposium made it clear that behavior modeling applications to organizational training had promise, but it was also clear that further research was needed. A number of threats to internal validity, which were present in these early studies, needed to be ruled out, and the psychological processes underlying behavior modeling interventions needed to be investigated.

Latham and Saari (1979) implemented a behavior modeling study that was much more rigorous than its predessors and remains one of the best studies of behavior modeling. In this study Latham and Saari trained first-line supervisors in various interpersonal skills required of managers. The training procedure involved an introduction of the topic by two trainers, presentation of a film depicting a model performing the target behaviors effectively, a set of learning points that were shown in the film before and after the model was presented, group discussion about the effectiveness of the model, participants role playing the modeled behaviors, and feedback from the training class on each participant's effectiveness in role-playing the modeled behaviors. Transfer of training was facilitated by instructing the trained subjects to use their newly learned behaviors within one week of learning that particular behavior. The subjects were then instructed to report successes and failures to the training class the following week. To provide the necessary reinforcement of the subjects' newly trained behaviors, their supervisors were trained to praise the subjects whenever they displayed the desired behaviors. Reaction measures, learning measures, behavioral measures, and job performance measures were used to assess the outcome of the intervention.

Latham and Saari found that the intervention was successful based on measurements at all four training outcome levels.

Despite the generally encouraging findings, not all behavior modeling results have been positive. Russell, Wexley, and Hunter (1984), for example, noted that Byham, Adams, and Higgins (1976) reported positive results, but not statistical significance, and also pointed to a finding reported by Burnaska (1976) that although trainees outperformed trained control subjects on a behavioral measure, the trainees' subordinates reported no significant differences in the trainees' pre- and postintervention target behaviors. Russell et al. also noted the general methodological weakness of many of the empirical studies that had been done up to that time, echoing a similar observation made by McGhee and Tullar (1978) some years earlier. We would hasten to add, however, that Russell et al.'s conclusions overlook some of the issues reviewed at the beginning of this chapter. The Byham et al. (1976) results may be due to low statistical power, and the perceived lack of change reported in Burnaska (1976) may be due to systematically inaccurate perceptions of change by subordinates that do not reflect the true state of affairs.

One line of recent behavior modeling research has begun to explore the cognitive processes of trainees in behavior modeling interventions. A study that exemplifies this line of research was done by Hogan, Hakel, and Decker in 1986. These investigators evaluated different encoding processes to explore ways to fine-tune the behavior modeling method. In the Hogan et al. study, subjects attended a one-day (eight-hour) behavior modeling workshop to learn skills relating to coaching problem employees and handling employee-initiated complaints. The skills were modeled on a film that was displayed after a live introduction. The film was followed by group discussion, role playing, and feedback via examination of videotaped role plays. The importance of rule coding (acquisition of learning points) was also explained to the subjects.

Two experimental groups were created. For the first group, the coding rules were given to the subjects by the trainers. In this manipulation, trainees identified and applied learning points that had been given to them after viewing a film containing models performing the targeted behaviors in two subsequent viewings of the same film. In the other group, the subjects were asked to develop their *own* rule codes in whatever way they felt would enhance their retention of the modeled behavioral skills. Both experimental groups were shown the modeling film a total of three times, with time in between to review and rehearse the learning points/rule codes. Reaction and performance ratings (not on-the-job performance, though) were obtained to assess the training outcomes.

Hogan et al. found that (a) trainee-generated rule coding substantially improved the subjects' performance and (b) the improved trainee performance that was found when the trainees were allowed to generate their own rule sets occurred despite the fact that the quality of the rules that they generated was judged inferior to the rules given to the trainees by the trainers. This implies that the improved trainee performance was caused not by better rules, but by the greater depth of processing that likely resulted from the trainees' more active cognitive role in the learning process. One caveat: Hogan et al. noted that the smallness of their sample size ($n = 15$) necessitates replication of their findings.

The behavior modeling process can be readily incorporated into our framework. The needs analysis fits under the Assessment/Needs Analysis category, and the specification of desired behaviors and learning points and the modeling itself correspond to the Assignment of Behavioral Standards category. Intention Formulation and Protection includes making the applicability of the training intervention to the employees' job clear and rehearsing the newly learned behavior publicly (which may enhance commitment because the behavior cannot later be disowned). Increments of self-efficacy that occur by observing the model performing the desired behaviors successfully should also contribute to Intention Formulation and Protection.

The Behavioral Expression in Change Environment component of a behavior modeling intervention involves the provision of antecedents (in the form of the behavioral standards mentioned previously) and consequences (in the form of feedback and reinforcement following rehearsal of the target behaviors by the trainees). Generalization and Maintenance of New/Changed Behaviors encompasses such components as training supervisors and other co-workers to reinforce desired behaviors and the other transfer of training principles discussed earlier (such as identical elements, overlearning, identification of important behavioral components, teaching of general principles, and using a variety of stimulus situations in the rehearsal environment).

Given the complexity of a good behavior modeling intervention, it should not seem too surprising that there are a number of ways to do it wrong or, at least, nonoptimally. One might begin with the obvious observation that a faulty needs analysis will ruin an otherwise well-implemented intervention. Other threats to change involve poorly modeled behaviors, a model who is not reinforced for performing the desired behaviors, a model with nonoptimal personal characteristics (e.g., not an expert, or not the same age, sex, or race as the trainee), inaccurately specified target behaviors or learning points, uninformative feedback, failure to praise the trainees during rehearsal, failure to make it clear to the trainees how the new behaviors will help them on the job, failure to set up a training environment where the trainees are likely to be able to perform the

target behavior successfully, and failure to utilize the transfer of training principles set forth above.

Intention Formulation, Self-regulation, and Behavioral Change

The investigation of self-regulatory processes is receiving increased research attention. Clearly, such theories have much relevance for behavior change, although their applicability to the workplace has only recently begun to be explored in earnest (e.g., see R. Kanfer & Ackerman, 1989; R. Kanfer & F. H. Kanfer, 1991; Lord & Hanges, 1987). In the following sections, we will first briefly review theory and research on self-management based on work by F. H. Kanfer and Bandura, and will then look at some primarily theoretical work by Heckhausen and Kuhl on intention formulation and protection.

Self-management Approach. One consequence of Bandura's (1977a) reciprocal determinism is that human beings can exercise some control over their thoughts, feelings, and behavior. To argue that people are entirely controlled by external stimuli is to present a "truncated image of human nature," according to Bandura (1986, p. 335). Somewhat counterintuitively, Bandura (1986) noted that such personal agency occurs not through acts of *willpower*, where one grits one's teeth and "just does it," but through specific psychological processes. These processes have collectively become known as *self-regulation*. Most work on self-regulation in the United States is based on the theories of F. H. Kanfer (e.g., see F. H. Kanfer & Hagerman, 1987; F. H. Kanfer & Schefft, 1988) and Bandura (1986). According to these theories, self-regulation includes self-monitoring, whereby people attend to their own behavior; self-evaluation, whereby people judge the discrepancy between their current behavior and the behavioral standards they have accepted; and self-reactions, whereby people respond to their self-evaluations both affectively and with an adjustment in their self-efficacy expectations. See Bandura (1986) and F. H. Kanfer and Schefft (1988) for detailed descriptions of these self-regulatory processes.

A consequence of not viewing self-regulation as *willpower* but as specific cognitive and affective processes is a movement from a static traitlike conceptualization to a more dynamic, learning-based conceptualization. Although the identification of cognitive and affective processes certainly does not preclude the possibility that one or more traits may be involved, the identification of such processes (regardless of whether or not traits are involved) is crucial if change agents are to begin to develop self-regulatory skills in their clients. Moreover, even if one or more traits is implicated, change is still possible and is most likely to be effected if the psychological processes underlying the traits are understood.

Researchers have recently begun to test interventions designed to train self-regulatory skills, with encouraging results (Frayne & Latham, 1987; Latham & Frayne, 1989). Basing their work on F. H. Kanfer's self-management theories and methods, Frayne and Latham (1987) attempted to train employees in self-management to improve their attendance. Their intervention consisted of eight weekly one-hour sessions and eight 30-minute one-on-one sessions to tailor the training to individual employee's needs. During the sessions, topics such as identification of problem behaviors, personal goal setting, self-monitoring, self-reinforcement and self-punishment, and maintenance of self-management skills were covered. Frayne and Latham (1987) found that on both a learning measure and an attendance measure, the trained employees exceeded control group employees at a statistically significant level. They also found that the self-management training received by the experimental group significantly increased their self-efficacy with respect to being able to come to work, given certain attendance obstacles.

In a follow-up study, Latham and Frayne (1989) assessed whether the employees retained their gains in attendance and self-efficacy following self-management training. They found that the training group had significantly higher attendance than the control group when they measured attendance nine months after the training had been completed. They also found that after training the control group, there was no significant difference in attendance between the two groups. In their self-efficacy analysis, Latham and Frayne found that the employees' self-efficacy increased over time after self-management training and that self-efficacy correlated significantly with job attendance at each point in time when measurements were taken (three, six, and nine months after training). Finally, there were no significant differences in the self-efficacy of the training and control groups following the exposure of the control group to self-management training.

The function of this type of self-regulatory skill training appears to be to teach trainees to go through the various steps in our framework on their own. They are taught (a) to assess their current standing on some performance dimension and then to attempt to identify the conditions that cause and maintain their current performance on the dimension (Assessment/Needs Analysis), (b) to set their own performance goals based on their self-assessment (Assignment of Behavioral Standards), (c) to monitor their ongoing performance and to self-administer rewards and punishments depending on whether they have met their self-set goals (Behavioral Expression in Change Environment and Generalization and Maintenance of New/Changed Behaviors), and (d) to proactively identify situations that might result in relapse and develop coping skills to deal with those situations (Generalization and Maintenance of New/Changed Behaviors). According to Frayne and Latham (1987), one effect of training in self-management is to increase the self-efficacy of the trainees in the area on which the self-management skills are focused. In this way, the successful application of one's newly learned self-management skills also results in the strengthening of one's intentions to continue to perform successfully the new behaviors.

Threats to change within the self-management training paradigm include the following. First, trainees must be committed to the training program because otherwise they will neither adequately monitor their ongoing behavior nor provide consequences appropriate to their performance. Second, inadequate self-assessment may also constitute a threat to change. The wrong goals may be set and maladaptive behaviors may remain in place due to the resulting misregulation. Finally, the trainee's achievement motivation may play a role in threatening an otherwise successful change intervention. Although the goals will typically be set in conjunction with a trainer, the trainees must be committed to them if they are to serve as true behavioral standards. Individuals low in achievement motivation may be both unwilling to commit to challenging goals and willing to commit themselves only to goals that are too difficult (Geen, Beatty, & Arkin, 1984).

Kuhl's Theory of Action Control. Other important work in the area of self-regulation has been done by Kuhl and his colleagues, who have focused on intention protection. Kuhl (1984, 1985, 1986; Kuhl & Kraska, 1989) has formulated an elaborate theory of action control that specifies various processes underlying effective self-regulation. According to Kuhl, these processes are initiated when a person perceives that (a) an intention will be difficult to act on, (b) his or her current level of state orientation (defined below) exceeds a critical threshold, and (c) he or she can successfully act on the intention.

Kuhl discussed in detail the processes by which intentions are transformed into behavior. One process is *attentional selectivity*, which involves paying greater attention to information that supports a current intention and then encoding this selected information in ways that are likely to further protect the existing intention from falling prey to competing action alternatives. Another action control process is *emotion control*, which involves inhibiting emotions that could jeopardize the enactment of an intention. A third strategy, *motivation control*, is similar to the selective attention strategy. However, the two strategies differ: While the selective attention strategy serves to maintain the strength of an existing intention in the face of competing action alternatives, the motivation control strategy serves to change a weak intention into a stronger one; put another way, it changes the existing queue of action tendencies (Atkinson & Birch, 1970).

To illustrate what he meant by motivation control, Kuhl (1985) gave the example of an individual who does not want to mow his lawn but manages to increase his motivation to do so by thinking about the social consequences of not doing so. This strategy may be very important to changing behavior because many behaviors that people want to change require them to commit to actions that are undesirable, at least in the short term: the dieter avoiding desired foods, for example. In cases such as this, one must strengthen the intention to perform the less desirable behaviors by considering their beneficial long-term consequences (in the dieter's case, becoming more physically attractive).

A fourth action control process is called *environmental control* and involves manipulating one's environment to create motivational and emotional conditions likely to protect an existing intention. An example would be staying away from old drinking buddies if one's intention is to stop drinking. A final action control process proposed by Kuhl is *parsimonious information processing*, which involves optimizing the length of the decision-making process. According to Kuhl, an individual should cease mulling over various ways of acting on an intention when it appears that further processing may undermine the intention by yielding information that casts doubt on its desirability.

Kuhl has suggested that an individual differences variable, action versus state orientation, may account for how effectively people act on their intentions. According to Kuhl, *action-oriented* persons focus their attention on a "fully-developed action structure," which enables them to bring about desired change. *State-oriented* persons, however, typically focus their attention on some past, present, or future state. Such a focus is posited to inhibit action and, therefore, change. State orientation may be caused by a "perceived incongruence between any two pieces of information processed" (Kuhl, 1985, p. 108) or the *degeneration* of an intention. Degeneration could be the result of relaxing one's commitment to an intention, feeling less personally involved in the previously formulated intention, or developing a belief that the desired action cannot be performed as initially thought.

According to Kuhl, state orientation can occur in various forms, depending on the type of degeneration that has occurred. An individual may ruminate over repeated failures to achieve a desired goal, may wish for the consequences associated with the goal so much that the desired end-state is attended to at the expense of the performance necessary to achieve it, or may lower his or her commitment to an intention, resulting in vacillation and a general inability to make a decision to act.

Kuhl has hypothesized that the existence of a state orientation will have a detrimental effect on how effectively an individual performs the action control processes discussed above. For example, Beckmann and Kuhl (1983; cited in Kuhl, 1984) looked at the differential effects of action versus state orientation

on motivation control. In that study, students who were seeking an apartment were provided a list of various apartments that varied in their desirability. They were asked to review the list twice and to rate the attractiveness of the various apartments both times. In addition, they were asked to tentatively choose an apartment they would like to live in after their first review of the list. Consistent with action control theory, Beckmann and Kuhl (1983) found that for action-oriented subjects, the difference in mean attractiveness between the tentatively chosen apartment and the rejected alternatives increased between the first and the second reviews of the list, whereas this increasing difference did not occur for state-oriented subjects. Other empirical research cited by Kuhl (1984, 1985) showed that action versus state orientation affects other action control processes as well.

Although Kuhl has developed a scale to assess the extent to which a person is action- or state-oriented, the precise nature and psychometric structure of this instrument (and the construct) is still under investigation (R. Kanfer, Dugdale, & McDonald, in press; Klinger & Murphy, in press; Kuhl, in press). Nevertheless, Kuhl's action control theory, and the action/state orientation construct that it encompasses, provides a useful framework for studying the mechanisms that facilitate and impede the execution of desired change-related intentions.

Heckhausen and Kuhl's Intention Formulation and Protection Model.   Heckhausen and Kuhl (1985) elaborated on the intention formulation and protection process in an insightful paper that integrated Kuhl's theory of action control and Vroom's (1964) expectancy theory of motivation (as elaborated by Heckhausen, 1977). This allowed them to develop a theory that encompassed both preintention and postintention psychological processes. According to Heckhausen and Kuhl (1985), intentions begin as wishes, which must pass through several hurdles before they can be acted on. First, the actor must have an expectancy that the desired wish can be successfully transformed into action and, usually, that the action will lead to desired outcomes and consequences. Moreover, if such an expectancy exists, the wish must pass additional *relevance checks* hypothesized to exist by Heckhausen and Kuhl (called OTIUM checks). OTIUM stands for opportunity, time, importance, urgency, and means. Thus, to form an intention, an actor must perceive that (a) there will be an opportunity to act on the wish, (b) there will be time to carry out the behaviors necessary to make the wish reality, (c) it is important to accomplish the action goal, (d) the accomplishment of the action goal bears some urgency, and (e) the means exist to act on the wish.

Heckhausen and Kuhl (1985) believed that wishes must go through two OTIUM checks before they can be acted on. Prior to forming an intention to act, the actor must believe that the criteria specified by the OTIUM check can be satisfied at some future time (OTIUM Future). At this point, the actor will have formed an intention to perform the desired action(s); however, in order to actually *perform* the action, the actor must believe that the five OTIUM criteria can be satisfied at the *present* time (OTIUM Now). If the OTIUM criteria cannot be satisfied, then the intention to act is hypothesized to be transferred to long-term memory and the actor must then wait until the criteria can be satisfied.

If the OTIUM criteria can be satisfied, then self-regulatory processes such as those hypothesized to exist by Kuhl (and discussed earlier) will be elicited. If they are successful in protecting the intention from competing action tendencies, the wish will be transformed into action. If the self-regulatory processes are unsuccessful, then the individual may postpone acting on the intention or attempt to reinitiate self-regulatory processes. If an individual repeatedly fails to act successfully on an intention,

then that intention may degenerate due to uncertainty about the feasibility of the initial action plan. According to Heckhausen and Kuhl (1985), degenerated intentions occupy space in working memory even when an individual attempts to formulate and act on other more productive intentions. This may be experienced phenomenologically as rumination about an unobtainable goal state or past failures. For example, a person who has failed to quit smoking after repeated attempts may dwell on those failures and the possibility of dying of lung cancer as the result of those failures. The probability of developing degenerated intentions is increased by forming what Heckhausen and Kuhl (1985) referred to as a *defective intention*, that is, an intention that has been formed without passing all of the requisite relevance checks.

Although the Heckhausen and Kuhl paper is predominantly theoretical, it does yield some preliminary implications for change agents. For example, does the client habitually commit to impractical goals (i.e., form defective intentions bound to degenerate)? Perhaps this kind of thinking has become automatized and the client needs to be made aware of it. Intention formation training could then be instituted. This would involve teaching the client to routinely perform the relevance checks whenever they are attempting to act on a desire. To the extent that the OTIUM criteria are not satisfied, clients could be trained to manipulate those criteria to create nondefective intentions that can be acted on.

For example, the client might be trained to make time for regular exercise if lack of time was preventing the formation of an intention to do so. Or the change agent might train the client to increase the importance of forming and acting on an intention by constantly reminding him or herself of the consequences of acting versus not acting. For instance, lack of exercise may lead to unfortunate consequences such as obesity, unrelieved stress, or increased probability of a coronary. The change agent might suggest that the client make a list of these consequences and put them in a conspicuous place to make them more salient.

Another implication of Heckhausen and Kuhl's (1985) paper is that wishes will not become intentions as long as a person believes that he or she cannot perform a desired act (or that the act will lead to undesired outcomes and consequences of those outcomes). For example, a middle manager who is trying to become less autocratic may believe that although it is feasible for him or her to adopt a more participative leadership style, such a leadership style would reduce the productivity of his or her department, which would, in turn, jeopardize future personal rewards such as salary increases, promotions, and prestige within the organization. In such cases, it is likely that training in self-regulatory strategies would not be effective. A preferable intervention would be to change the consequences associated with a given action or to challenge client's low expectations if they do not seem warranted.

Research cited in Kuhl (1984) indicates that state orientation has a general inhibitory effect on the enactment of intentions. This suggests that change agents should attempt to induce action orientation in their clients, perhaps by training them to keep their behavior change goals in the forefront of their minds. If future research shows action versus state orientation to be a broad and stable personality disposition, then more long-term change interventions may be needed to induce an action orientation, since a change in personality structure would be implicated. Finally, Heckhausen and Kuhl (1985) noted that the likelihood of enacting an intention may be enhanced if clients know which self-regulatory processes work best for them. They refer to this knowledge as *metavolition*. Such knowledge can best be gained by providing clients with training in a broad range of self-regulatory methods and allowing them to discover which are most effective.

The theories and research of Kuhl and Heckhausen and Kuhl have important implications for the intention formulation and protection portion of our framework. Together they suggest that change interventions may be enhanced by training clients (a) to perform relevance checks for intention formulation, (b) to apply self-regulatory strategies, (c) to acquire and apply metavolitional knowledge, and (d) to focus their attention on current change-related intentions to induce a change-promoting action orientation. Threats to change implied by the Kuhl and the Heckhausen and Kuhl approaches include failure to perform requisite relevance checks, dispositional or situationally induced state orientation, failure by the organization (or other aspects of the postintervention environment) to help ensure that the OTIUM criteria continue to be met, and inadequate use of self-regulatory and neutralization strategies.

Clearly, further research is needed to test these theories. Nevertheless, these approaches appear to be potentially useful to change agents. By exploring the anatomy of intention formulation and protection in more detail, these investigators have paved the way for further research that will address a vitally important, yet poorly understood, portion of our behavior change framework.

Self-efficacy and Behavior Change

Bandura's (1977b, 1986) construct of self-efficacy has a good deal of relevance to behavior change and is mentioned throughout this chapter. It therefore seems appropriate to pause and discuss it at greater length. Self-efficacy is defined as one's belief about one's capacity "to organize and execute courses of action required to attain designated types of performances" (Bandura, 1986, p. 391). Note that within the Heckhausen and Kuhl (1985) model, an expectation that one can accomplish a desired result is a necessary condition for the formation of a nondefective intention. And while an expectancy is subtly different from self-efficacy (R. Kanfer, 1990b), one might plausibly suggest that self-efficacy can contribute substantially to an individual's ability to formulate strong intentions. A study by Locke, Frederick, Lee, and Bobko (1984) provided evidence that indirectly supports this hypothesis. Locke et al. found, through path analysis, that higher self-efficacy affected the specificity of self-set goals, which may indicate greater commitment and more reality-based intention formulation.

People with higher self-efficacy also appear to set more challenging goals (Bandura, 1989; Locke et al., 1984) and to engage in more "venturesome" behavior, among other consequences (Bandura, 1989). Moreover, Bandura (1986) stated that "perceived self-inefficacies that lead people to shun enriching environments and activities retard development of potentialities and shield negative percepts from corrective change" (p. 393). It appears, then, that increasing a client's self-efficacy in crucial behavior domains would be an important tool in the change agent's arsenal.

Bandura (1977b) discussed four ways in which self-efficacy can be developed in people: performance accomplishments, vicarious experience, verbal persuasion, and feedback regarding their physiological state. The first method of developing self-efficacy, experiencing performance accomplishments, is easily understood: Successes breed self-efficacy and failures breed self-inefficacy, particularly in areas where an individual has had little experience. According to Bandura (1977b), therapies designed to develop self-efficacy via the performance accomplishment strategy include (a) *participant modeling*, where the change agent induces the client to perform the desired behavior in an environment structured to ensure the client's success; (b) *performance desensitization*, in which clients are exposed to progressively more threatening activities; and (c) *performance exposure*, which involves inducing intense anxiety by exposing an

individual to a very aversive activity and maintaining that high level of anxiety until emotional reactions are extinguished.

The second method of developing self-efficacy is through vicarious experience. Bandura (1977b) noted that vicarious experience is less effective than direct performance accomplishments in building self-efficacy because the experience is less direct. Modeling can, however, have a positive effect. To ensure maximum impact, change agents should ideally use a variety of models who are as similar to their clients as possible (Bandura, 1977b).

A third method of inducing self-efficacy simply involves attempting to persuade people that they can do what they seek to do. Verbal persuasion works best when the therapist is realistic; raising false hopes will only create failures on the part of the client that will undermine both the client's self-efficacy and the change agent's credibility with the client (Bandura, 1986). Bandura (1977b) suggested that while verbal persuasion *alone* is not a terribly powerful change intervention, verbal persuasion can bolster performance interventions by inducing individuals to put forth more effort in their practice performances than they would without the verbal encouragement.

The fourth method of building self-efficacy involves treatments that reduce aversive emotional arousal. Bandura (1977b) theorized that by convincing individuals that their reactions to aversive situations are not as physiologically negative as they expected (through false feedback, for example), they will experience a temporary decrease in anxiety and negative thinking, which will make them less susceptible to aversive emotional states and their corresponding physiological reactions. This, in turn, will enable them to perform successfully in those situations and increase their self-efficacy naturally.

The development of self-efficacy in clients is important to the success of most change interventions. In addition to its effect on intention formulation, the development of self-efficacy likely plays an important role in self-management training, particularly in enabling trainees to set challenging goals for themselves. Several techniques for increasing a client's self-efficacy have been described. An interesting area of potential research involves the extent to which change agents can induce self-efficacy about one's ability to protect already formulated intentions.

Implicit Theories and Behavior Change

Self-efficacy refers to people's beliefs that they can successfully perform certain behaviors in specific performance domains. And if, as has been suggested, self-efficacy can contribute powerfully to the success of change interventions, then what about more global beliefs about changeability? In a provocative paper, Dweck and Leggett (1988) recently addressed this question. They proposed that people's implicit theories of ability and personality exert powerful effects on the change-related goals they pursue and the behavior that results from pursuing those goals.

More specifically, Dweck and Leggett proposed that people have either *entity* theories, meaning that they believe that an attribute is fixed, or *incremental* theories, meaning they believe that a personal attribute can be developed. According to Dweck and Leggett (1988), entity theories produce performance goals, and incremental theories produce *learning* goals. People who set *performance* goals do so to obtain positive evaluations from others on the attribute in question. People who set learning goals, on the other hand, seek to increase their competence on a given attribute.

A person's behavior will vary depending on whether they typically set performance or learning goals. Performance goals will not be maintained in the presence of negative feedback, and challenging (potentially diagnostic) tasks will be avoided in favor of tasks where successful performance is practically assured

(at the expense of learning). Learning goals, however, are hypothesized to produce a more adaptive behavior pattern. Here, individuals seek out challenging tasks that are likely to help them develop on a given attribute and likely to persist even in the face of negative feedback.

Dweck and Leggett's (1988) model is hypothesized to apply to both social and academic achievement situations. Thus, people who believe that social/personality attributes are fixed (an entity theory) should adopt *social performance* goals, leading to the avoidance of social risk and a lack of persistence in challenging social tasks, whereas those who believe that social/personality attributes are *malleable* (an incremental theory) will adopt *social learning* goals, leading them to seek out challenging social tasks that will facilitate learning and will persist even in the face of short-term failures on those social tasks.

R. Kanfer (1990a) noted, however, that Dweck and Leggett's (1988) model was based on research done with children and that adults may have a more differentiated view of personal attributes such that their implicit intelligence theories, for example, "are likely to involve a blend of controllable and fixed components" (p. 231). R. Kanfer suggests that for adults, characteristics of the learning environment may play a much larger role in determining whether mastery or performance goal orientations are adopted. She suggests that implicit intelligence theories may influence motivation only indirectly by affecting self-efficacy beliefs, which then determine choices of goal difficulty level.

The clear implication of Dweck and Leggett's (1988) model, particularly when superimposed on R. Kanfer's (1990a) ideas, is that some attempt should be made to induce incremental theories on the attributes that the training program is seeking to develop in the trainees (Campbell, 1988; R. Kanfer & F. H. Kanfer, 1991). The extent to which this can, in fact, be done for different attributes and the best means for inducing incremental theories in trainees is not yet clear. These questions represent intriguing areas for future research.

In terms of our framework, people's implicit theories of changeability should influence the same stages of the change process as self-efficacy; that is, they should primarily influence the Intention Formulation and Protection stage and should also influence certain other portions of the framework within the self-management training paradigm.

Control Theory and Behavioral Change

As noted by Ilgen and Klein (1988), cybernetic control theory has recently been imported into industrial and organizational psychology (Campion & Lord, 1982; Lord & Hanges, 1987) from motivational psychology (Carver & Scheier, 1981, 1982; see also Scheier & Carver, 1988), and it appears to have substantial utility in explaining several behavior change findings. The basic unit of control theory is the negative feedback loop, the function of which is to reduce discrepancies between current behavior and a behavioral standard. An input function senses a present condition, and the presence and amount of the negative discrepancy is assessed by a so-called comparator function. If a discrepancy exists, people attempt to reduce it through adaptive behavior. If the discrepancy is too large, Carver and Scheier (1981) hypothesize that people will disengage from the task. Carver and Scheier also proposed that attention must be self-focused in order for discrepancies to be detected and acted on. They view the tendency to focus chronically on oneself or on the external environment as an individual differences variable.

The usefulness of control theory for explaining and predicting various change-related findings within the industrial and organizational literature was initially argued by Campion and Lord (1982). For example, they noted that in order for the comparator to work properly, both goals *and* feedback are necessary, which converges with the findings of Erez (1977), Komaki, Collins, and Penn (1982), and Locke et al. (1984) that neither goals nor feedback alone is as effective as goals plus feedback. In addition, Campion and Lord explain the robust finding that specific goals produce better performance than "do your best" goals (e.g., R. Kanfer, 1990a) by creating more specific, informative feedback, resulting in a more effective reduction of an existing negative discrepancy. Likewise, they explain that difficult goals produce better performance because difficult goals engage discrepancy-reducing responses more often than easy goals do. Of course, if the task is too difficult, the individual will exit from the task out of frustration.

Lord and Hanges (1987) proposed some interesting extensions of control theory, particularly in the interpersonal domain. For example, they noted that in social interactions, a person or a role set can serve as a standard against which another person can self-regulate. From the perspective of behavior change, this proposition provides a theoretical basis for worrying about regression to original maladaptive behavior patterns following a change intervention if the environment that the client returns to after the intervention has not changed. This sort of social or interpersonal standard will likely compete for dominance with new possible selves (Hyland, 1988; Markus & Nurius, 1986) that the client may have incorporated into his or her existing self-concept (Carver & Scheier, 1985).

This suggests implications for the generation and maintenance of new behaviors. If a client's role set is preventing him or her from achieving and/or maintaining desired change, then the change agent may have to work with the client's organization to modify certain aspects of the client's postintervention environment. For example, the employee's role set may have to be modified or the client may have to be transferred to a job in which the former role constraints no longer exist. A less intrusive change strategy, of course, might simply be to make the client aware of the ways in which his or her role may influence his or her behavior, which may be sufficient to avoid jeopardizing progress achieved during the intervention. In terms of role models, change agents may wish simply to make the client's organization aware of the potential adverse effects that such models may have on the clients' newly changed behavior in order to minimize the risk of regression, or they may wish to take the more extreme step of including certain members of the client's immediate work group (particularly immediate superiors) in the training.

Although empirical research based on control theory has been scarce (Lord & Hanges, 1987), studies have recently begun to appear in industrial and organizational psychology journals. Hollenbeck (1989) assessed the hypothesized moderating effect of self-consciousness on the relationship between perceived current and future negative discrepancies and job satisfaction, organizational commitment, and turnover. Control theory suggests that the larger the perceived negative discrepancy, the lower one's satisfaction should be. Hollenbeck found that self-consciousness did indeed moderate the relationship between perceived future negative discrepancies and various indices of job satisfaction and withdrawal. However, he also found that self-consciousness did *not* moderate the relationship between perceived *current* negative discrepancies and the satisfaction and withdrawal indices. The difference in these findings, however, might be explained by differences in the perceived chronicity of the discrepancy.

In another recent study, illuminating the chronicity issue, Frone and McFarlin (1989) tested a cybernetic model of stress. Noting conflicting findings in the literature regarding whether private self-consciousness buffers or exacerbates the relationship between stressors and experienced strain (where strain is defined as the discrepancy between one's current state and a desired physical or emotional condition), these investigators hypothesized that the extent to which stressors are perceived as controllable will determine if there is an interaction between private self-consciousness and the stress-strain relationship. The hypothesis was that if a self-focused person experienced a *nonchronic* stressor, he or she would be more likely than a non–self-focused person to take steps to ameliorate the perceived strain by instituting coping mechanisms (i.e., discrepancy reduction). However, if the stressor was perceived to be chronic and uncontrollable, self-focused individuals would be more aware of it and therefore would experience more intense negative affective and somatic symptoms, along with *reduced* coping capacity. In accord with this hypothesis, Frone and McFarlin found that individuals high in private self-consciousness experienced greater work distress and somatic symptoms in the presence of chronic work-related stressors (e.g., noxious physical environment, work overload, lack of praise from boss) than persons low on private self-consciousness. The interaction was more pronounced when the dependent variable was somatic symptoms as opposed to work distress.

The latter study has interesting implications for stress management interventions. Aside from the obvious suggestion that organizational development interventions should be designed to remove chronic stressors from the work environment, it is also clear that training employees to self-monitor will only be an effective self-management strategy when they are able to exert some control over their environment. In work environments where chronic stress is unavoidable from the perspective of the organization, the indicated coping strategy is to direct employee attention away from the perceived stress to the extent possible.

This might, for example, involve visual imagery training (Flanagan, 1990) or informal competitions. In cases where the chronicity of a stressor is only *subjectively* present, it may be that interventions designed to increase employees' self-efficacy with regard to their ability to exercise some personal agency over their work environments would be useful. After reducing the perceived chronicity of work-related stressors, self-monitoring and other self-management strategies could be taught to improve clients' skills in coping with job stress.

Control theory seems to fit into many of the categories of our framework. A behavioral standard is assigned, one's commitment to it is determined by an expectancy/value process resulting in something roughly equivalent to an intention, and negative feedback loop mechanisms facilitate change in both the change and transfer environments. The initiation and maintenance of a changed behavior then depends on the creation and operation of a negative feedback loop. By implication, then, threats to a successful intervention derive from malfunctions in the control process. These malfunctions are discussed by Carver and Scheier (1981, chap. 9) under the separate headings of "Absence of Regulation" and "Misregulation."

Absence of regulation means that the regulation of behavior is not occurring due to a break in the flow of the negative feedback loop. Such breaks may occur in several places. One scenario is that the behavioral standard may be either missing or so vague as to be useless (consider the implications for delegation and clear performance goals). The feedback loop would also break down if one were unable to produce the desired behavior to be compared against the standard. Likewise, the negative feedback loop requires clear and accurate feedback from the environment regarding how one's current behavior compares with an existing standard. Finally, absence of regulation will occur if the comparator function breaks down, which occurs when one's attention is no longer self-focused. Strong emotions can also cause the comparator to malfunction.

Misregulation, unlike absence of regulation, occurs while the negative feedback loop system is up and running. But self-regulation under these conditions is based on information that is either of low quality or is just plain wrong. One source of misregulation involves applying the wrong behavioral standards. Within the behavior modeling paradigm, for example, the wrong learning points may be modeled due to a poor needs analysis. Alternatively, the right learning points may have been identified, but the model may have done a poor job of translating them into behavior. Feedback may also be a source of misregulation. It may be inaccurate, as when potentially harsh criticisms are "sugar coated"; it may be mistimed, as when feedback is provided only once a year in a formal performance review; it may be ambiguous; or it may be distorted by the perceiver (Fiske & Taylor, 1984; Greenwald, 1980). Ilgen, Fisher, and Taylor (1979) summarized many of the ways in which feedback can fail to be effectively communicated.

A final threat to change implied by control theory derives from people's beliefs about whether they can achieve the behavioral standard against which they are self-regulating. If the discrepancy between a current behavior and a behavioral standard is large, an individual's expectation may be especially low, causing a potential withdrawal from the self-regulatory process. This would seem to again implicate self-efficacy, although Carver and Scheier (1982) refer only to an *expectancy-assessment process*. Possessing an *entity* rather than an *incremental* theory of the attribute targeted for change would therefore jeopardize a change intervention within the control theory paradigm by making relevant self-efficacy beliefs less malleable (R. Kanfer, 1990a).

The Self and Behavior Change

Many behavior change interventions, particularly those involving interpersonal skills training in psychotherapy and management development contexts, are directed at modifying some aspect of the self. Therefore, a brief review of the large and growing body of basic research on the self conducted by social/personality psychologists will help facilitate a deeper understanding of the processes and problems associated with behavior change.

The Self as Inhibitor of Change.   Within the past 15 to 20 years, there has been a paradigm shift in the psychology of the self (Greenwald & Pratkanis, 1984). Prior to this shift, the self was conceived as a passive entity containing whatever thoughts and feelings one had about oneself. However, current cognitive theories posit a more active entity that include passive self-conceptions but contain mechanisms that actively process incoming information as well (Greenwald, 1980; Greenwald & Pratkanis, 1984; Markus, 1977; Schlenker, 1985). As a consequence of its active nature, the self appears to act as *distortor* as well as *assimilator* of incoming information. Greenwald (1980) has summarized much of the literature dealing with ways in which the self can distort incoming information and, based on his review, likened the cognitive processes of the self to those of a totalitarian government. The cognitive biases seemed disturbingly similar to the "thought control and propaganda devices that are considered to be defining characteristics of a totalitarian political system" (Greenwald, 1980, p. 603).

Of the cognitive biases identified by Greenwald, the one most directly relevant to the issue of behavior change is the so-called cognitive conservatism bias. *Cognitive conservatism* is the "disposition to preserve existing knowledge structures, such as percepts, schemata (categories), and memories" (Greenwald, 1980, p. 606). Cognitive conservatism is posited to be necessary to preserve the organization and integrity of personality. Closely related to the cognitive conservatism bias is the

confirmation bias, which occurs when people attend selectively to data that confirms their expectations and make judgments that tend to preserve their existing beliefs.

There is also evidence that people tend to *create* social environments that preserve their self-concepts (Swann, 1985, 1987). Swann posited three general strategies by which this is done (collectively referred to as *self-verification strategies*). One strategy is fairly obvious: Interact on a regular basis only with those who act in ways that tend to provide you with self-confirmatory feedback. Swann (1987) cited evidence that people prefer to have as friends and intimates those who "see them as they saw themselves" (Swann, 1987, p. 1039). More ominously, Swann cited evidence that people with negative self-images tend to avoid those who see them positively even as those with positive self-images will tend to avoid those who see them negatively. Another strategy discussed by Swann for maintaining an existing self-concept is to display physical cues that inform others about what kind of person one is. For example, people who see themselves as conservative in their views may dress conservatively to help convey that philosophy. A final strategy for obtaining self-confirmatory feedback is to interact with others in ways calculated to obtain such feedback. For example, Swann summarized research that found that dominant individuals, when presented with feedback that they did not seem very dominant, behaved in a *particularly* dominant fashion (more so than they did under normal circumstances).

Swann (1985) suggested that these self-verification strategies can be interpreted in the context of control theory's negative feedback loop. He suggested that "people's self conceptions influence their actions [i.e., self-verification strategies] which channel the reactions of others, which in turn serve as a basis for people's subsequent inferences about themselves, and so on" (Swann, 1985, p. 103). The standard of behavior here is the *existing* self-concept and, according to Swann's theory, it operates to drive behavior to bring social reality closer and closer into synch with the self-concept.

An important reason why it has proved so difficult for people to change is that some of the change-preventing psychological mechanisms operate outside of conscious awareness in the form of automatized procedures (Cantor & Kihlstrom, 1987; Showers & Cantor, 1985). Cantor and Kihlstrom (1987) argued that "efforts at corrective change stand on a foundation of insight into the self, one's declarative and procedural expertise" (p. 217) and noted that it is especially difficult to make people aware of procedural self-expertise, such as self-verification strategies and cognitive conservatism.

Cantor and Kihlstrom (1987) conceived of this self-related declarative and procedural expertise in terms of individual differences, meaning that certain individuals may be more resistant to change than others. For example, some people may significantly distort incoming information to confirm an existing self-concept, while others may be quite objective in their evaluation of self-relevant data and are, therefore, more open to change. In any event, existing change-preventing procedures need to be identified and interrupted in order for people to improve themselves. Some methodology currently exists to assess self-related (and social) expertise (Cantor & Kihlstrom, 1987), but more work is needed to develop sensitive tests of these individual differences constructs.

The Adaptiveness of Change-inhibiting Mechanisms. Although the change-inhibiting mechanisms identified in the preceding section might appear to be negative given this chapter's focus on change, we want to emphasize that the stability they cause is not a negative human characteristic. Indeed, it is essential to the survival of the psyche. This point has also been made by Costa and McCrae (1986), who argued that the stability of personality is neither the result of inertia nor a sign of psychopathology, but is rather a fundamental attribute of personality and an active psychological process. Without stability, we would be without identity and (unless the change followed a regular pattern) would behave randomly, a state of affairs that no one (least of all psychologists!) wants.

Greenwald (1980) noted that biases such as cognitive conservatism and egocentricity serve to protect the core self from disorganization. He analogized to scientific methodology, where auxiliary hypotheses are formulated to protect a core theory in order to prevent unwarranted immediate disconfirmation. Indeed, scientific progress is most likely to occur when existing theoretical structures are allowed to stand even in the face of a certain amount of empirical attack.

Likewise, growth in the self seems best achieved within the context of the self-maintaining processes discussed earlier. Disruption of those processes *should be* a difficult process; if it were not, then change agents would rightfully worry about the permanence of any change that might be achieved in training.

The Creation of Possible Selves. Markus and her colleagues have begun to explore the effects that conceptualizing possible selves can have on changing a person's self-concept (Markus & Nurius, 1986; Markus & Ruvolo, 1989; Markus & Wurf, 1987). *Possible selves* are "specific representations of oneself in future states and circumstances that serve to organize and energize one's actions" (Markus & Ruvolo, 1989, p. 212). They are posited to be part of the self-schemata, and it is suggested that through the self-knowledge embedded in such schemata one is able to envision concrete examples of one's self as it may exist in some future state. Possible selves are thought to derive from values and affect (Markus & Nurius, 1986) and to be vital to acting on self-related desires.

According to Markus and Ruvolo (1989), positive possible selves will motivate organized behavior, leading to effective performance, and negative possible selves will create disorganized, ineffective performance. However, negative possible selves have an important motivational function as well. According to Markus and Ruvolo (1989), positive possible selves are most motivating when matched with a feared possible self in the same domain. For example, a possible self of "being less abrasive at work" would be less motivating than the same possible self in the context of the undesired self of "failing to obtain a desired promotion because of my abrasiveness."

It is important to note that the development of motivating possible selves is not a trivial task, for self-knowledge is hypothesized to be a necessary condition for the creation of possible selves. And because of various defenses, chronic lack of self-focus, or any number of other reasons, people may lack the necessary self-knowledge to formulate possible selves that can be made a reality. Once formulated, possible selves appear to function as broad goals and, in accord with the tenets of expectancy theory (Mitchell, 1982; Vroom, 1964), the extent to which they will be enacted into behavior will likely depend on the perceived likelihood of their being achieved and the extent to which they are valued (Markus & Ruvolo, 1989).

Part of the motivational power of possible selves is that they may function as behavioral standards against which people can self-regulate. The concept of a possible self can speculatively be embedded in Carver and Scheier's (1981) control theory as a very high level (abstract) behavioral standard (Hyland, 1988). This would allow for the achievement of the same possible self through distinct sets of behaviors (which certainly happens in real life), and also for the organization of behavior that Markus and Ruvolo (1989) believed results from the existence of possible selves.

Such organization results from having a high-level behavioral standard against which to self-regulate and involves smooth transitions from task to task. Such transitions are made possible because they are linked to a common superordinate goal at a high level in Carver and Scheier's hierarchy. For a more complete description of the hierarchical organization of behavioral standards posited by Carver and Scheier and its effect on behavior, the interested reader is referred to Carver and Scheier (1981).

One might suggest that accurate self-knowledge is so necessary to formulating possible selves because, as with other intentions, possible selves may degenerate on the way to action (Heckhausen & Kuhl, 1985) if appropriate relevance checks are not performed. One may have as a possible self a picture of "me becoming president of my company next year." However, one may not have the opportunity or the means to achieve that possible self unless one already has a high position in the company hierarchy. Presumably, the more accurate a person's store of self-knowledge, the more likely one is to commit to possible selves that are realistic and, therefore, less bound to degenerate due to defective formulation.

The foregoing discussion suggests three points where change agents could intervene to help a client. One would be to attempt to persuade a client of the value and possibility of achieving a new possible self so that he or she would be able to commit to and focus time and energy on making the new possible self a reality.

Possible selves may conflict. Thus, a second way a change agent could help a client is by identifying a conflicting set of possible selves (Cantor & Kihlstrom, 1987). Cantor and Kihlstrom discussed a conflict grid that might enable the change agent to assess the extent to which a client's progress in achieving one possible self would serve to inhibit progress on another possible self. For example, suppose an employee has a well-elaborated high-level corporate executive possible self and an equally well-elaborated world-famous ballet dancer possible self. The change agent's job in cases like this would be to help the client see the incompatibility of these two competing possible selves and perhaps to help the client prioritize his or her existing possible selves. In the case of the example just cited, perhaps the world-famous ballet dancer possible self could be downgraded a bit to the level of avocation—dancing in local exhibitions, for example.

A third way that a change agent could help a client is to either (a) achieve a possible self to which the client is already committed or (b) achieve a possible self that has been formulated as a part of the change intervention. For example, suppose that a change agent encounters a client who professes to be anxious over her inability to get along with others on the job, but cannot understand why people do not like her and generally consider her abrasive. In a case like this, part of the change agent's job will be to help the client understand why others consider her abrasive, perhaps by videotaping a simulated interaction with a co-worker and then reviewing the videotape with the client and pointing out those behaviors that most others would find offensive.

If the client is able to accept this illustration and acknowledge that it would be valuable to create a new, less abrasive self (and assuming that the change agent is able to convince the client that creating this new self is achievable), then the next step would be to help the client achieve the desired change. This might involve any number of possibilities, depending on the person's store of self-related and social knowledge (Cantor & Kihlstrom, 1987). Examples might include being less defensive in social interactions, training certain basic interaction skills, or controlling negative emotions aroused by certain types of co-workers (e.g., secretaries, bosses, techies).

Identity Negotiation.   One of the crucial problems facing change agents is that even when change interventions are successful, clients must often return to environments that retard or simply negate the change. One explanation for this effect has become known as behavioral confirmation. *Behavioral confirmation* occurs when other people inadvertently cause the client to behave in ways consistent with their expectations that, of course, are based on the client's preintervention behavior. Swann (1984) has hypothesized that the

> tendency for targets to strive to behave in ways that confirm their self-concepts…might compete with the tendency for them to behave in ways that confirm the expectancies of perceivers. If target self-conceptions and perceiver expectancies differ, then a battle is likely to occur, with perceivers struggling to elicit behavioral confirmation for their expectancies and targets striving to verify their self-conceptions. (p. 466)

Swann and Ely (1984) have shown that greater self-certainty attenuates the ability of perceivers to elicit confirmatory behavior from targets. Unfortunately, this should not hearten change agents, since people in the midst of change interventions can hardly be certain of newly minted self-concepts and are therefore likely to be extremely vulnerable to the behavior confirmation effect. Thus, it may be necessary for a change agent to work somehow to either (a) modify a client's environment by making those people that he or she interacts with regularly aware of the behavioral confirmation effect and how it can jeopardize an otherwise successful change intervention (Swann, 1987), or (b) inoculate the client against the behavior confirmation effect by making him or her aware of how he or she may be affected by others.

To summarize and elaborate, the foregoing discussion suggests that possible selves (perhaps coupled with their complementary undesired selves) may serve as behavioral standards against which people can self-regulate

(Assignment of Behavioral Standards). If the client expects that the possible self can be achieved, values that achievement, and perceives that the requisite OTIUM (Future) criteria can be satisfied (Intention Formulation and Protection), then the individual will expend effort to attempt to attain it (as long as the OTIUM criteria continue to be satisfied). If this new possible self has become part of the individual's existing self-concept, self-verification strategies should operate to increase the likelihood of attaining and maintaining that new possible self (Behavioral Expression in the Change Environment and Generalization and Maintenance of New/ Changed Behavior).

Several threats to successful change interventions were also identified. If possible selves conflict, the achievement of both may be threatened. Low self-efficacy and implicit entity theories of the self may intefere with the formulation of nondefective intentions to achieve possible selves, along with failure to satisfy various relevance checks. Within the change environment, the confirmation bias, the behavioral confirmation effect (where the latter is caused by the change agent), and other maladaptive self-related "expertise" may all threaten behavior change. Finally, behavioral confirmation effects can threaten an otherwise successful modification of a client's self-concept by forcing the client to negotiate his or her new identity rather than allowing him or her simply to express it without challenge.

Industrial and Organizational Training Models

Behavior change within the field of industrial and organizational psychology is generally thought about and researched under the category of training and development. And just as we have attempted to extract a generic change process from relevant literatures, other industrial and organizational psychologists (Campbell, 1988; Noe, 1986) have attempted

to extract a generic training process (in Noe's case, a portion of the training process) from the existing training and development (and other relevant) literatures. It therefore makes sense for us to review these two training models and integrate them with our own behavior change framework.

Campbell's Training Design Model. Campbell (1988) proposed a training design model built around the question, What is to be learned? The model specifies a series of questions and guidelines that Campbell believes training designers must consider when they put together a training program. The first two components of Campbell's model, analyzing goals and job design and determining training needs, appear to fit into the Assessment/Needs Analysis component of our framework. The former seems to correspond to the organizational analysis portion of training needs analysis and refers in Campbell's model to determining the organization's operating goals. Determining training needs in Campbell's model involves identifying the components of effective performance, establishing those dimensions of performance that would benefit from training, and prioritizing them to determine what the most critical training needs are. Campbell noted that the identified training needs must not conflict with the organization's operating goals identified as part of the first step in his model.

The next two steps in Campbell's model, specifying training (behavioral) objectives and specifying training content, fit under our Assignment of Behavioral Standards category. The former involves specifying what the trainees are supposed to learn and "include[s] some indication of the conditions under which the individual should be able to perform them (the behavioral objectives) and the level of proficiency the individual should be able to exhibit" (Campbell, 1988, p. 194). The specification of training content requires the identification of the knowledge and skills that underlie the successful performance of the objectives identified in the previous step in the model. According to Campbell, the specification of training content must include the proper sequence in which the knowledge and skills are to be learned and may be obtained from expert judgment, formal theory regarding effective performance within a given domain, or from protocol analysis.

The next two components in Campbell's model, specifying learning methods and learning media and specifying the conditions for learning, fit under the Behavioral Expression in Change Environment portion of our framework. Learning methods, according to Campbell, are generic and include such things as simulation and question-and-answer discussion. Once selected, learning methods may then be executed through various media such as videotapes or reading materials. The specification of the appropriate conditions of learning draws on principles of learning theory hypothesized to apply to everyone. In this phase, the trainer must attempt to ensure that such principles are incorporated into the training program to the maximum extent possible. According to Campbell, the current literature indicates that the following learning principles would be good candidates for inclusion in training programs: "stimulating learner interest, using learning events that require 'productive' behavior, providing appropriate feedback, and providing opportunities for practice under conditions that promote transfer" (1988, pp. 204–205).

Another component of Campbell's model is accounting for individual differences (actually, he places this component between specifying learning methods and media and specifying the conditions for learning). This part of his model seems to fit under both the Intention Formulation and Protection and the Behavioral Expression in Change Environment portions of our framework. His individual differences component fits with Intention Formulation and Protection to the extent that

it includes motivational variables such as self-efficacy, expectancy, instrumentality, valence, and performance versus learning goals, all of which seem relevant to the formulation of strong, nondefective intentions. Campbell's accounting for individual differences component relates to Behavioral Expression in the Change Environment because of its incorporation of aptitude-by-treatment interactions—that is, the hypothesis that, depending on an individual's personal attributes, some treatments may facilitate learning better than others.

The final component of Campbell's model is evaluating training outcomes. Although behavior change evaluation is not explicitly included in our framework, we will discuss some aspects of outcome research in a later section of this chapter.

Because Campbell's model encompasses so many complex training techniques and literatures, it is difficult to summarize the threats to change (and ways to maximize the likelihood of change) that it implies. For the purposes of this chapter, we will simply note in Table 4 the more obvious threats to change implied by his model. These include (a) incongruity between training goals and organizational operating goals, (b) failure to specify behavioral objectives, (c) failure to specify knowledge and skills to be acquired in training and the proper sequence in which they are to be learned, (d) improper use of learning methods and media, and (e) failure to incorporate normative learning principles into one's training design. Interested readers are referred to Campbell (1988) for more detailed discussion of various training design issues and prescriptions that derive from his model.

Noe's Motivational Model. Whereas Campbell's training design model looks at training largely from the perspective of the training designer (i.e., what questions must be addressed in order to design a sound training program), Noe (1986) synthesized a model that focused

FIGURE 4

Noe's (1986) Model of Trainee Readiness

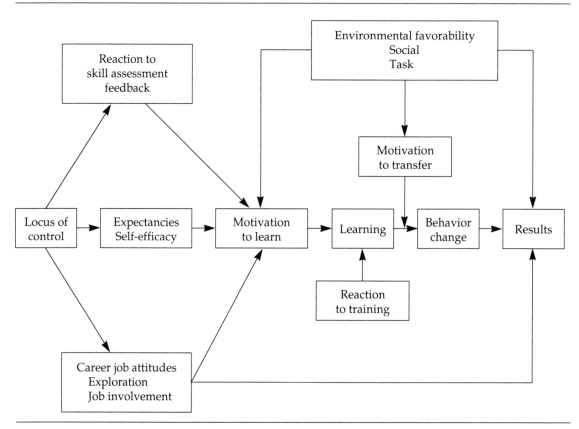

From "Trainees' Attributes and Attitudes: Neglected Influences on Training Effectiveness" by R. A. Noe, 1986, *Academy of Management Review*, 2, pp. 736–749. Copyright 1986 by *Academy of Management Review*. Reprinted by permission.

more on the change process. More specifically, it focused on the way that individual and organizational variables affect trainee motivation, which, in turn, is posited to affect training outcome. Noe's (1986) model is shown in Figure 4.

In several ways the model is consistent with other theories we have discussed that deal with the motivational aspects of the change process, although in certain cases variables that seem similar possess different names in the different models. For example, Noe's motivation-to-learn variable seems somewhat similar to an intention. It follows an expectancy check and is dependent on self-efficacy (both of which Noe hypothesized are caused by an internal locus of control), and in that way has antecedents that are similar to the hypothesized antecedents of intentions within the Heckhausen and Kuhl (1985) model. Note also that motivation to learn is hypothesized to be directly influenced by environmental favorability. According to Noe, environmental favorability has both a task component and a social component. The task component involves the trainee's perception of whether the requisite tools, supplies, and monetary support (among other necessities) will be available to facilitate the use of newly acquired knowledge and skills. The social component of environmental favorability involves the trainee's perception regarding "opportunities to practice skills or use knowledge acquired in the training program and receive reinforcement and feedback from supervisors and peers" (Noe, 1986, p. 744).

Based on these definitions, perceived environmental favorability sounds quite similar to Heckhausen and Kuhl's (1985) OTIUM (Future), particularly the opportunity and means. And just as both an expectancy evaluation and an OTIUM (Future) check must be passed successfully for a wish to become an intention in the Heckhausen and Kuhl (1985) model, so an expectancy evaluation and a perceived environmental favorability evaluation directly influence one's motivation to learn within Noe's model. The structural similarity between the two models suggests similar psychological processes with slightly different terminology. Noe hypothesized that motivation to learn is also influenced by one's perception about the accuracy of the training needs assessment, by one's job involvement, and by one's career exploration behavior history.

An interesting aspect of Noe's model is the fact that the relationship between learning in the training environment and actual behavioral change is moderated by motivation to transfer, which in turn is directly influenced by perceived environmental favorability. As its name implies, motivation to transfer refers to the desire of a trainee to use what was learned in training on the job. Noe's inclusion of the motivation to transfer variable indicates that it

is possible to formulate two distinct intentions regarding training—one to learn the training content and another to transfer the learned content to the job environment. In the former case, it seems likely that the environmental favorability (or OTIUM) check relates simply to the feasibility and desirability of learning the training content rather than both to learn and to transfer the content.

The implications of Noe's model for minimizing threats to change both echo other work we have discussed and provide new food for thought. According to his model, low self-efficacy and perceptions on the part of the trainees that effort will not cause them to learn the training content satisfactorily or that learning the training content will not lead to valued organizational outcomes should threaten an otherwise well-designed training program. And as also implied by the Heckhausen and Kuhl (1985) model, failure to provide conditions within the organizational environment that will facilitate positive OTIUM-like perceptions may also threaten positive change. Finally, low trainee job involvement or negative trainee reactions to either the training program or the training needs analysis may also threaten the success of a training program. The links between the variables in Noe's model imply that training program designers should make an effort to measure variables that affect training outcomes prior to the interventions to determine the readiness of the trainees to benefit from the training program. For those trainees who are not ready, techniques will have to be devised to create both in trainees and in the training and transfer environments those conditions that will maximize the impact of the training intervention. Such techniques include attempting to induce greater self-efficacy, using more face-valid methods for assessing the trainees' pretraining skill level, or increasing the organization's commitment to training programs.

An Example of Behavior Change in the Workplace

At Personnel Decisions, Inc. a large part of our professional experience is with behavior change, especially in the form of management development. Among a variety of behavior change techniques we use to help managers develop, we have designed a unique program called Individual Coaching for Effectiveness (ICE) to help managers and professionals with more serious skill deficits achieve significant changes in their work behavior. Its design reflects the complexity of a successful change intervention and serves to illustrate other points made throughout this chapter. We will first describe the program and then discuss how it addresses threats to change and transfer. We will also present some preliminary findings regarding its effectiveness.

The Individual Coaching for Effectiveness Program

We drew on various literatures as well as our own expertise in behavior change to design the program, which was initiated in 1981 as a result of a client request.[9] The intervention serves a variety of important purposes, but most often it is used to help an otherwise successful person deal with a problem behavior that is proving to be an Achilles' heel. Those who are referred to us for coaching typically are having trouble in the leadership, interpersonal, or communication domains, and in many cases there are indications that the person's career may be in jeopardy if changes are not made (Thompson, 1986). Two prototypical cases are (a) a bright, highly skilled manager who is interpersonally abrasive, overly aggressive, and autocratic in her leadership style, and (b) a good problem-solver who is unable to influence those around him and is, therefore, lacking in leadership skill. Other common problems include inability to be a team player, lack of conflict

management skills, lack of sensitivity, and poor social skills. There are three major phases in the ICE process: diagnosis, coaching, and maintenance/support. Each is intensive, organizationally sponsored, and tailored to each individual participant. At each step, care is taken to minimize threats to change originating either in the person or the organization and to address transfer considerations.

The Diagnosis Phase. The first step is to diagnose the ICE candidate. A great deal of information is collected, including standardized psychological measures (e.g., mental ability tests, personality and interest inventories), skills ratings from behavioral simulations, interview and work history data, and information from people in the client's organization (e.g., the immediate boss, the boss' boss, the human resources department, subordinates, peers). The specific assessment battery is tailored to the presenting problem. Because of the complexity inherent in diagnosing ICE participants (and in many other aspects of the ICE process), only experienced and highly trained psychologists are given primary responsibility for handling a participant's case. Most psychologists who work in PDI's coaching programs have a Ph.D. in industrial and organizational psychology, counseling, or clinical psychology.

The first outcome of the assessment phase is a decision about whether or not ICE is an appropriate intervention for the candidate. One question is whether the desired changes are among those that a cognitive-behavioral-educational intervention like ICE is designed to produce. A second question is whether program success is probable, given individual and organizational factors. Possible reasons for turning a person down include chemical dependency, family problems, or serious emotional problems. In cases like these, people are often referred to other professionals, including psychotherapists or chemical dependency counselors. In other cases, the underlying problem may be a poor person-job fit, and the most appropriate intervention is simply to redesign the position or move the ICE candidate into a different assignment—that is, to change the environment rather than the person. In yet other cases, there may be insufficient organizational support for change, or the problem has gone on too long and too many bridges have been burned.

If the assessment indicates to the coaching staff that ICE is an appropriate intervention, the individual and organization are encouraged to proceed to the next (coaching) phase. If all parties (i.e., the participant, the organization, and PDI staff) agree to proceed to the coaching phase, the program continues. If all cannot agree to proceed, efforts are made to resolve the issue through other channels.

The next step in the assessment phase, which serves as a lead-in to the coaching phase, is the development of specific training objectives. This brings necessary focus to the intervention.

The diagnosis phase includes the first two steps in our framework and addresses the threats to change implied by these steps. In the first step, Assessment/Needs Analysis, the threats to change are (a) poor needs analysis, (b) incongruity between training and organizational goals, and (c) negative trainee reaction to skills assessment. As described above, the diagnosis process includes steps that ensure accuracy, congruity, and acceptance as viewed by all three parties—the participant, the coaching staff, and an organizational representative (typically the participant's supervisor). Accuracy is obtained by using multiple sources of information in the assessment; congruity with organizational goals is achieved by maintaining communication with organizational representatives about their goals and objectives; and acceptance of the diagnosis is obtained by soliciting input on the coaching objectives. In addition, individual characteristics that may threaten later steps are screened for during diagnosis.

These include low general intelligence and extreme defensiveness.

In the second step of our framework, Assignment of Behavioral Standards, the threats to change are improper behavioral standards (e.g., too difficult, too vague) and lack of acceptance by the participant. The behavioral standards on the coaching plan are developed by skilled clinical, counseling, and/or industrial and organizational psychologists who attend to specificity and achievability in developing the plan. Acceptance is addressed by requiring that the participant buy into the diagnosis results and training plan as a condition of proceeding with coaching.

The Coaching Phase. The second phase of the intervention, coaching, typically takes place over a period of at least six months. The spacing of coaching over this length of time allows participants to apply what they are learning on the job between sessions. They are encouraged to report back on their efforts to apply their new skills. The specific techniques used depend on the coach and the nature of the behavior to be changed, but several elements are common to all ICE training programs. These include traditional didactic instruction on the basic information participants need to perform the new skills; coaching, which encompasses facilitation, modeling, and encouragement; and short-term counseling to overcome perceptions or beliefs that may block effective learning and transfer.

The didactic portion involves communicating the knowledge that is prerequisite to performing new behaviors. This knowledge may include (a) the kinds of behaviors that are most effective in the participant's organization, (b) principles of effective communication, (c) the nature of supervisor/subordinate relationships, (d) basic principles of teamwork, (e) how personal power and influence are created, (f) the concept of toleration of individual differences, or (g) how to conduct effective meetings.

Increasing a client's knowledge base is not enough, however. The core of the coaching phase is behavioral skills coaching, where clients are taught to produce the behaviors targeted for change during the assessment phase. Such behavioral skills training relies heavily on the principles of behavior modeling. By watching a PDI psychologist model the targeted behaviors, rehearsing the behaviors themselves, and then receiving feedback, participants are helped to better understand their strengths and weaknesses, how they are perceived by others, and the need for change on their part.

ICE training also involves short-term counseling to change maladaptive beliefs that are incompatible with the targeted skills. Such maladaptive beliefs assume many forms. It may be that the person does not believe that (a) she or he is deficient in the areas targeted for change (recall Noe's point about how disagreement with the assessment process affects participant readiness), (b) the new behaviors are important and will be rewarded (i.e., have valence), (c) they will have the opportunity or time to practice their newly learned skills on the job (recall the discussion on the role of Heckhausen & Kuhl's OTIUM relevance checks in facilitating change), (d) people in general can change (recall the discussion on implicit theories), or (e) he or she, in particular, can change the targeted behaviors (recall the discussion on self-efficacy).

The coaching phase of ICE encompasses steps three through five of our framework. Intention Formulation and Protection is addressed throughout coaching by (a) clarifying the instrumentality of the behavioral change, (b) challenging negative implicit theories of change and external locus of control, (c) enhancing self-efficacy through observation and Performance, (d) teaching the participant self-management skills, and (e) arranging for OTIUM support. The Opportunity and Time are made available by the organization's decision to refer a participant to the program, and the work supervisor is encouraged to clarify the Importance and Urgency of the change as well as to provide the Means to change.

These Intention Formulation and Protection actions are prerequisites to change, and their importance is highlighted by the long list of threats to change associated with this step. These threats to change, and those in the Generalization and Maintenance of New/Changed Behaviors step, tend to be largely motivational and volitional, in contrast to the skill and ability threats in the intermediate step (Behavioral Expression in Change Environment). In many cases, the coaching staff spends at least as much time working to overcome these threats as imparting the new skills.

The Behavioral Expression in the Change Environment step involves imparting new skills in a number of ways. These include (a) communicating the behavioral standards through didactic instruction and modeling, (b) having the participant practice the skills, (c) providing feedback, and (d) adapting our methodology to each individual. These steps serve to overcome the threats to change that originate in the coaching environment (e.g., delayed or inaccurate feedback, lack of reinforcement, lack of success in the coaching environment) and those that come from the person (e.g., insufficient prerequisite skills, attention not self-focused).

The last step, Generalizability and Maintenance of New/Changed Behaviors, is also embedded in the coaching phase. PDI's approach is to attend carefully to basic transfer of training principles in designing its coaching programs. This is accomplished by (a) teaching the participant the principles underlying the new behaviors, (b) identifying situations that may threaten the maintenance of the new behaviors and developing strategies to cope with them, (c) encouraging the supervisor to reinforce the new behaviors even while the skills to perform them are being acquired, (d) enhancing motivation, and (e) rehearsing *identical elements*—using real work situations and behaviors.

The Maintenance and Support Phase. The final phase of the intervention is the maintenance and support phase, which further insulates the participant from slippage. If the participant has relapsed, refresher coaching sessions may be necessary. The maintenance and support phase is important because it provides the participant with support in applying the new behaviors. In addition, the knowledge that someone will be checking their progress may also make clients more self-aware and, in that way, may serve to stimulate self-regulation (Carver & Scheier, 1981).

This phase continues to address Generalizability and Maintenance of New/Changed Behaviors. The focus is on (a) monitoring the maintenance of the new behavioral standards, feedback, and rewards and (b) providing refresher coaching if necessary.

Transfer Considerations. Transfer of the participants' new skills to the workplace is attended to in several ways throughout the program. One way involves ensuring frequent communication with the participant's organization, which is accomplished by formally incorporating such communication into the structure of the intervention. Thus, the participant's progress against his or her training objectives is frequently discussed.

The coaching phase of the program involves the use of actual work situations (either recent or upcoming) provided by the participant, which also helps to facilitate transfer. Coach and participant also work together to identify those situations in the participant's work environment that may evoke old behavior patterns and to formulate strategies to cope with them (or avoid them altogether, if that is feasible). In addition, the participant is able to try the new behaviors at work between coaching sessions. The participant and coach then work together to analyze the results. This technique parallels portions of the self-management training methodology utilized by Frayne and Latham (1987).

Another critical transfer tactic is to work with the participant's supervisor to (a) ensure that his or her expectations are realistic, (b) keep him or her informed of the participant's progress, and (c) provide suggestions about how she or he can support the change. Unrealistic expectations about both rate of change and final outcome have an important effect: If a person expects change to happen overnight, or in a core personality attribute, she or he is likely to be disappointed and may discount the change that *is* occurring. This ongoing communication with the supervisor also provides the participant with an environment supportive of the new, rather than the old, behavior patterns.

Summary. The ICE program is an example of a systematic, intensive, individualized, state-of-the-art behavior change process that draws on a variety of models, methods, and theories. Woven throughout the design of the assessment, coaching, and maintenance and support phases are numerous steps that minimize individual and organizational threats to change. In addition, great care is taken throughout the process to enhance transfer of the new skills to the work environment by (a) using real work situations in role plays, (b) involving the participant's supervisor in the change process, (c) challenging beliefs held by the participant and supervisor that may inhibit change, and (d) teaching the participants to observe, critique, and adapt their own behavior. These steps require time and effort from all parties beyond what is necessary in a standard training program. It is important not to short-circuit the change process by cutting corners in these areas. For example, moving ahead to the coaching phase without agreement from the participant and the supervisor jeopardizes the achievement of lasting change.

The ICE Population

Thompson (1986) surveyed the first 166 ICE participants, their supervisors, and their coaching staff, asking questions about background, ICE process, ICE outcome, and career outcome. He found that (a) 75 percent of the participants were in some degree of job jeopardy at the time they began the program, (b) over 90 percent were referred by either their work supervisor or a human resource manager, and (c) motives for participation were more likely to be remedial (e.g., to decrease negative perceptions at work) than simply to polish skills (e.g., to prepare for a possible promotion).

Hazucha (1991) compared the same sample to a comparison management group with more common development needs. Based on test data (mental ability, personality, and interest), management skills ratings (using the MSP; Sevy et al., 1985), and demographics, this ICE group showed both similarities to and differences from the comparison management group. As a group, the participants were equally bright, less interested in people, more ambitious, and more rebellious than the comparison group. They were also less interested in management and altruism. Others viewed them as having weaker management skills, especially *person-oriented* skills (e.g., informing, human relations, coaching), but also problem analysis and decision-making skills. Perhaps their distance from people kept them from obtaining input from others for decisions. The participants rated themselves lower on the person-oriented skills, but they rated themselves *higher* than the norm in several other skill areas. Thus, the gap between their self-perceptions and the perceptions of others was larger than it was for the norm group. As a whole, the ICE group was more successful (as indicated by salary and organizational level), but also poorer-performing than the comparison groups.

Peterson (1990) compared a more recent ICE sample with managers undergoing an assessment for other purposes (e.g., selection, promotion, development). As a whole, the ICE group received lower ratings in several areas (interpersonal skills, leadership skills, and adjustment), but ratings in judgment and decision-making and administrative skills did not differ for the two groups.

Empirical Data on the Success of ICE

The success of the ICE program has been evaluated using several different criterion variables. These include satisfaction, behavior, performance, and career outcomes (e.g., involuntary termination, change in compensation). Unfortunately, few objective and reliable measures of performance are available at the managerial and professional level (see Campbell, 1990), so most of our measures are ratings. To ameliorate problems associated with ratings, however, we collect ratings at multiple times, on multiple scales, from multiple raters, each of which provides a different vantage point on change. When all of these vantage points are synthesized, we believe we have a fairly complete picture of the change that has occurred.

As Peterson (1990) argued, using a control group design to assess change is not feasible due to several factors, including the uniqueness of the population, the intensity and duration of the intervention, and the ethical problems associated with providing purposely ineffective services. However, each of the designs we have used attempts to address concerns of internal validity in some other way: (a) by contrasting targeted and nontargeted objectives, (b) by comparing people who completed the program with those who did not, or (c) by using standardized measures for which we have general management norms.

In the following sections, we will discuss findings from research we have done to evaluate the success of ICE in an attempt to (a) demonstrate empirical support, (b) illustrate issues in behavior change outcome research, and (c) indicate how such issues can be addressed.

An Early Follow-up Study. Thompson (1986), Marsh (1990), and Hazucha (1990) described an early follow-up study. In 1986, questionnaires were sent to 166 current and former ICE participants, their work supervisors, and PDI staff. As described earlier, they were asked to provide three types of information: organizational background/work history, ICE program evaluation, and demographics. Thompson contrasted three subgroups. The first consisted of people who were assessed but not admitted; the second group included people who were diagnosed, admitted, and began coaching, but who did not complete the coaching phase of the program; and the third group was diagnosed, admitted, and completed the coaching phase.

The dependent variables of greatest interest were initial jeopardy (sense of job insecurity), satisfaction with the changes achieved in the program, frequency of use of the skills acquired, effectiveness of skill use, changes in the frequency of use since the end of the coaching phase of the program, and continued tenure with the organization. The independent variables included program status (i.e., whether or not the individual completed the coaching phase of the program), initial jeopardy and success, and various other individual differences variables.

Marsh (1990) summarized some of the major results of the Thompson (1986) study. Compared to the "partial training" group, the "completed training" group received higher ratings on all outcomes (number of skills demonstrated, effectiveness of skills use, frequency of skills use, satisfaction with changes achieved, job effectiveness) from all rater types (PDI staff, self, work supervisor). The one exception was self-ratings of frequency of skills use. In addition, for participants whose coaching had ended at least one year earlier, "80 percent of both participants and supervisors perceived little or no decay in frequency or effectiveness of skill use" between the end of the coaching phase and follow-up. In fact, "half of the supervisors and

two thirds of the participants believed skills usage had *increased* in effectiveness since the end of training" (Marsh, 1990, p. 6, emphasis added).

Because 75 percent of the participants were in some degree of job jeopardy at the beginning of the coaching phase, continued tenure with the organization was an important indicator of program success. Here, too, there were differences between the "completed training" and "partial training" groups, although these failed to reach statistical significance because of diminishing sample sizes. Ninety-five percent of those who completed training were still employed by the same organization after one year; 85 percent were still there after two years. By contrast, for the group comprised of those receiving partial training and those who were not admitted to the program, 80 percent were on the job after one year, and 64 percent and 75 percent, respectively, were still employed after two years. Note also that there was some contamination: Some participants left the program *because* they were terminated.

Hazucha (1990a) looked at the relationship between precoaching variables and ratings of coaching outcome. Outcome ratings by the participants' boss were almost completely explained by initial jeopardy, initial success, and staff outcome ratings. Participants who were initially in less jeopardy at lower organizational levels (success) and who received higher outcome ratings from the coaching staff were also rated higher by the work supervisor. On the other hand, ratings by the coaching staff were unrelated to initial success and jeopardy, but were strongly related to a number of individual differences variables and management skills ratings. The predictors included CPI results (including Achievement via Conformance, Well-Being, and Work Orientation), ability test scores (especially verbal reasoning and critical thinking), and ratings of interpersonal and administrative skills. In all cases, those who performed better during diagnosis also performed better in coaching, as rated by PDI staff. This contrast between supervisor and coaching staff perceptions of coaching outcome is interesting. One possible explanation is that while people who were in jeopardy before the intervention were as able as those in less jeopardy to actually learn the skills, they were nevertheless unable to change the negative perceptions that others had about their behavior back on the job. In addition, it seems that the coaching staff may have viewed outcome as the degree to which individuals learned the skills, while bosses focused more on the negative perceptions.

The Ongoing Evaluation Program.   Because the program is tailored to each participant, the more recently instituted ongoing evaluation program has drawn heavily on psychotherapy outcome research. As described by Peterson (1990), the similarities between ICE and counseling interventions include:

- Focus on one particular individual and his or her needs

- A one-to-one relationship between the participant and the psychologist

- An ongoing relationship, typically including six months of coaching and an additional six months of follow-up

- Presenting problems, interventions, and goals that vary across individuals

These features contrast with more typical interventions, where assessment is performed at the group level, the relationship between the trainer and the group is shorter-term and less personal, and the entire group receives the same intervention.

As pointed out by Mintz and Kiesler (1982), there is an important tradeoff in psychotherapy outcome research between measures that are comparable across individuals and those that are tailored to training objectives. If everyone is evaluated on the same criteria, these criteria will not match individual goals.

If the outcome measures are targeted to individual goals, the comparability across persons is lost. With PDI's approach, there are goals that are common across individuals (e.g., improving job performance and promotability, satisfaction with training outcome), as well as goals targeted to specific participants. Therefore, in an attempt to tailor the outcome measurement to the individual's objectives *and* to maintain comparability across participants, the evaluation instrument includes both unique and common content. The individually tailored components are the participant's coaching objectives, developed at the end of the diagnosis phase. The common portions include global evaluations of performance, promotability, and outcome, and several standard items that are described in a similar format to the objectives but are very unlikely development needs for this group (e.g., administrative skill). This type of evaluation allows us to (a) evaluate progress on the targeted objectives, (b) assess the program's impact on more global criteria, and (c) contrast the objectives targeted by the coaching with those which are not targeted, as a test of discriminant validity.

The instrument currently used to evaluate ICE interventions is called the *Coaching Plan Rating Form,* which is used to collect data at three points in time. Time 1 is between diagnosis and the beginning of coaching, Time 2 is on completion of the coaching phase, and Time 3 is at the end of the formal follow-up (usually six months after the end of coaching). At all three points in time, raters evaluate the individual's current effectiveness on the tailored coaching objectives and the standard comparison objectives. At Times 2 and 3, raters are also asked to rate the participants' degree of change on each of these objectives (providing data on retrospective judgments of change by raters). In addition, raters are asked to evaluate the participants' (a) overall progress, (b) current effectiveness on the job, (c) effort expended to implement changes, and (d) advancement potential, and also to rate the impact of the intevention on current job effectiveness.

At each point in time, ratings are obtained from at least three people: the participant, his or her boss, and the PDI staff member who is responsible for coaching. Additional raters may include the boss' boss, the human resources contact person, the participants' direct reports, and any other key parties.

This evaluation design will allow us to investigate a broad array of questions, including the following:

- How do ratings change over time?

- How are changes in specific behaviors related to more global outcomes, such as job performance and promotability?

- How do coaching objectives differ in their tractability?

- What individual differences variables are related to change?

- How is rater type related to the ratings?

- What affects retrospective judgments of change?

Peterson (1990) presented preliminary data regarding the impact of the program on the participants' individually tailored coaching objectives. On a seven-point scale, with four defined as "average effectiveness," mean initial ratings ranged from 2.2 by human resources raters to 3.9 as rated by participants. Following coaching, the range was smaller, with a low of 4.9 by boss and coaching staff, and a high of 5.9 by human resources raters. Needless to say, these results are very encouraging. The HR ratings are an example of a case where all of the initial ratings are low, and the pre- and posttraining ratings do not overlap. As Peterson pointed out, this fits the two criteria set forth by Carver (1970) for an ideal change measurement scale, which (a) minimizes initial scale variability (because everyone scores low) and (b) is capable of showing a difference between pre- and posttest. Finer grained analyses (e.g., by type of objective, rater type, time since training) are planned within the next year.

Summary. While preliminary, these results are quite encouraging. They indicate that the ICE program is effective, at least in the minds of the participant, the coaching staff, the work supervisors, and human resources staff. In general, all parties are satisfied with the participants' general progress, with the frequency with which they use their new skills, with the effectiveness of those skills when they are used, and with the maintenance of the changes achieved by the participants during coaching. In addition, mean ratings on the coaching objectives are much higher after coaching than before. However, there is also variability across partipants in how well they do in training. Future research will elucidate other important questions about the dynamics and outcomes of changes in behavior and perceptions in the workplace.

Recommendations for Further Research

Although an enormous number of useful research questions are implied by the material in this chapter, we would like to close by identifying several streams of research that we view as most important.

First, further work on the relative malleability versus stability of various individual differences variables is needed. Questions in this area include:

- What characteristics are most changeable? least changeable?

- What psychological processes underlie relative malleability?

- Are there individual differences in malleability itself (e.g., due to "traitedness")?

Results from this line of research would help individuals concerned with changing behavior (their own or others') to target more malleable characteristics.

Environmental variables that influence change and transfer constitute another important research area. Questions include:

- What is the nature of the constructs of "boss support " and "organizational support"?

- How can boss and organizational support be enhanced?

- How can individuals influence their environment to make it more supportive?

- How can people be inoculated against environmental factors that inhibit change?

The investigation of these questions would yield answers useful to human resource professionals and supervisors interested in creating an environment that is conducive to developing employees.

A third important research area is the study of the motivational and volitional abilities and skills that underlie self-regulation. Researchers have just begun to scratch the surface here. Relevant questions include:

- Is there a unitary trait of self-regulatory ability?

- Could a useful taxonomy of self-regulatory skills be created? Could such skills be trained?

- Is it possible to train people to formulate strong intentions?

- Can people's implicit theories of behavior change be modified so that they more routinely adopt mastery rather than performance goals?

- What are the most crucial personality correlates of self-regulatory ability and skill?

The answers to such questions will suggest strategies for teaching people to manage their own development, and to maintain the gains they have achieved.

Fourth, investigations of the effectiveness of interventions should go beyond mode of presentation (e.g., lecture, videotape) to include important contextual variables such as needs assessment, change agent, and transfer issues. Questions here include:

- What affects the face validity (and therefore the credibility) of a needs assessment?

- What is the impact of choice to attend a program on acceptance and effectiveness?

- What change agent characteristics affect self-efficacy, beliefs about change, and success of change?

- What is the effect of including self-management and relapse prevention topics into the intervention?

Such research would yield results that could guide the designers of organizational interventions in maximizing the benefits of the programs.

Fifth, perceptions of change are an important topic area. Questions include:

- How do people make judgments about whether change has occurred in themselves? In others?

- What kind of evidence do they require to believe the change?

- Is the process for changing a negative impression similar to or different from what is required to change a positive impression?

This stream of research would yield suggestions for how to manage others' perceptions of one's change.

Finally, the still vexing issue of how to best measure change deserves continuing attention.

It is our position that change can be measured substantially more reliably and validly provided the research is rigorously designed. However, additional work is needed to improve our understanding of the impact of methodology on results. Suggested topics include:

- How do ratings of change compare with "hard" Time 1 minus Time 2 data?

- How do instrument and rater type, statistical design, and other spurious factors affect the results obtained?

- How does the density of multiwave data affect the reliability of change scores?

- What is the optimal number and spacing of waves of data?

Because the detection of change requires considerable psychometric sophistication, and because research addressing these and other questions will undoubtedly substantially improve change research, we would like to call for collaborative efforts between intervention experts and measurement experts. Such collaboration would be fruitful (a) because the interventions would be effective in producing change, and (b) because change would be validly measured.

Conclusion

It is clear from the evidence we have presented that it is indeed possible for people to change. To say otherwise, as many persons flippantly do, flies in the face of considerable contrary evidence, and builds barriers to effective change interventions.

Significant behavior change is often complex and sometimes can be difficult both to induce and to detect psychometrically. But, when interventions are done properly, taking into account the principles we have described, attempts at change can be highly successful. Further, when the changes are measured carefully, they are detectable psychometrically. We have therefore argued that assertions that people don't change are intellectually indefensible, and that such claims must be modified to become accurate; for example, "People don't change... much on IQ scores" or, "People can't change...easily on nontrivial characteristics."

We have presented evidence that the effectiveness of change interventions depends on (a) the characteristic or behavior targeted for change, (b) the person, (c) the intervention, and (d) the transfer environment. Yet only a few aspects of these parameters (e.g., method of presentation, ability-by-learning interactions) have received much research attention. In addition, the change agent and the relationship between the agent and the participant may be a factor, although we are not aware of research in industrial and organizational psychology dealing with this area.

Because of the complexity of behavior change, many threats to change exist, and they must be dealt with carefully. Many of those threats exist both before and after the intervention. Needs assessment, intention formulation and protection, and transfer concerns are just as important as the more salient problems associated with actually teaching participants new behaviors, and these steps should receive as much consideration in designing the intervention process as the actual intervention. In sum, there is much to be excited about in the science and practice of behavior change, yet much remains to be done in mapping out what characteristics can be changed to what degree under what conditions.

We thank Ruth Kanfer, Marcia Sytsma, Cindy Marsh, David Peterson, and Katherine Holt for their helpful comments on portions of this chapter, and gratefully acknowledge the research assistance of Gaye Gilliand.

Notes

1   The formula for effect size is $(\bar{x}_1 - \bar{x}_2) / sd_{12}$. Thus, the effect size represents the magnitude of the difference expressed in standard deviation units.

2   The change measure was the residual of the correlation between the Time 1 and Time 2 average *Management Skills Profile* ratings (Sevy et al., 1985).

3   The term *consistency* has acquired a precise technical meaning in the literature. Generally speaking, consistency refers to "invariant rules for information processing, invariant components of processing, or invariant sequences of information processing components that may be used by a subject to attain successful task performance" (Ackerman, 1987, p. 4).

4   If there is more than one variable at the highest level of the hierarchy, then complexity would be defined as the correlation between the variable of interest (i.e., the variable whose complexity level one is trying to assess) and the variable at the highest level in the hierarchy that the variable of interest is "descended" from.

5   Residualized gain score = $(T_2 - T_1) \cdot T_1$.

6   Residual of covariance model = $T_2 \cdot T_1$.

7   A *deficient* criterion measures only part of the construct of interest; a *contaminated* criterion includes additional constructs beyond the construct of interest.

8   In Fishbein's (1979) theory, social norm perceptions are a function of so-called normative beliefs and of one's motivation to comply. *Normative beliefs* refer to an individual's beliefs that certain people think he or she should or should not perform a specific behavior. *Motivation to comply* simply refers to the extent to which one will be swayed by one's normative beliefs. An *attitude*, in Fishbein's theory, is a function of one's belief that a behavior will lead to various outcomes and of one's evaluations of those outcomes. See Fishbein (1979) for a complete discussion of his theory.

9   Significant portions of this section are taken from Thompson (1986) and Marsh (1990).

References

Ackerman, P. L. (1987). Individual differences in skill learning: An integration of psychometric and information processing perspectives. *Psychological Bulletin, 102,* 3–27.

Ackerman, P. L. (1988). Determinants of individual differences during skill acquisition: A theory of cognitive abilities and information processing. *Journal of Experimental Psychology: General, 17,* 299–329.

Ackerman, P. L., & Humphreys, L. G. (1990). Individual differences theory in industrial and organizational psychology. In M. D. Dunnette & L. M. Hough (Eds.), *Handbook of industrial and organizational psychology* (2nd ed., vol. 1, pp. 223–282). Palo Alto, CA: Consulting Psychologists Press.

Ackerman, P. L., Sternberg, R. J., & Glaser, R. (Eds.). (1989). *Learning and individual differences: Advances in theory and research.* New York: Freeman.

Andrews, G., & Harvey, R. (1981). Does psychotherapy benefit neurotic patients? *Archives of General Psychiatry, 38,* 1203–1208.

Arvey, R. D., Cole, D. A., Hazucha, J. F., & Hartanto, F. M. (1985). Statistical power of training evaluation designs. *Personnel Psychology, 38,* 493–508.

Atkinson, J. W., & Birch, D. (1970). *The dynamics of action.* New York: Wiley.

Baldwin, T. T., & Ford, J. K. (1988). Transfer of search. *Personnel Psychology, 41,* 63–105.

Bandura, A. (1977a) *Social learning theory.* Englewood Cliffs, NJ: Prentice-Hall.

Bandura, A. (1977b). Self-efficacy: Toward a unifying theory of behavior change. *Psychological Review, 84,* 191–215.

Bandura, A. (1986). *Social foundations of thought and action: A social cognitive theory.* Englewood Cliffs, NJ: Prentice-Hall.

Bandura, A. (1989). Human agency in social cognitive theory. *American Psychologist, 55,* 1175–1184.

Baumeister, R. F., & Tice, D. M. (1988). Metatraits. *Journal of Personality, 56,* 571–598.

Baumgartel, H., & Jeanpierre, F. (1972). Applying new knowledge in the back-home setting: A study of Indian managers' adoptive efforts. *Journal of Applied Behavioral Science, 8,* 674–694.

Baumgartel, H., Reynolds, M., & Pathan, R. (1984). How personality and organizational-climate variables moderate the effectiveness of management development programmers: A review and some recent research findings. *Management and Labour Studies, 9,* 1–16.

Baumgartel, H., Sullivan, G. J., & Dunn, L. E. (1978). How organizational climate and personality affect the pay-off from advanced management training sessions. *Kansas Business Review, 5,* 1–10.

Bentz, V. J. (1985). Research findings from personality assessment of executives. In H. J. Bernardin & D. A. Bownas (Eds.), *Personality assessment in organizations.* New York: Praeger.

Borman, W. C. (1974). The rating of individuals in organizations: An alternate approach. *Organizational Behavior and Human Decision Processes, 12,* 105–124.

Bray, D. W., Campbell, R. L., & Grant, D. L. (1974). *Formative years in business: A long-term A T & T study of managerial lives.* New York: Wiley.

Brownell, K. D., Marlatt, G. A., Lichtenstein, E., & Wilson, G. T. (1986). Understanding and preventing relapse. *American Psychologist, 41,* 765–782.

Burke, M. J., & Day, R. R. (1986). A cumulative study of the effectiveness of managerial training. *Journal of Applied Psychology, 71,* 232–245.

Burnaska, R. F. (1976). The effects of behavior modeling training upon managers' behaviors and employees' perceptions. *Personnel Psychology, 29,* 329–335.

Byham, W. C., Adams, D., & Higgins, A. (1976). Transfer of modeling training to the job. *Personnel Psychology, 29,* 345–349.

Campbell, J. P. (1988). Training design for performance improvement. In J. P. Campbell, R. J. Campbell, & Associates (Eds.), *Productivity in organizations: New perspectives from industrial and organizational psychology* (pp. 177–215). San Francisco: Jossey-Bass.

Campbell, J. P. (1990). Modeling the performance prediction problem in industrial and organizational psychology. In M. D. Dunnette & L. M. Hough (Eds.), *Handbook of industrial and organizational psychology* (2nd ed., pp. 687–732). Palo Alto, CA: Consulting Psychologists Press.

Campion, M. A., & Lord, R. G. (1982). A control systems conceptualization of the goal-setting and changing process. *Organizational Behavior and Human Performance, 30,* 265–287.

Cantor, N., & Kihlstrom, J. F. (1987). *Personality and social intelligence.* Englewood Cliffs, NJ: Prentice-Hall.

Carver, C. S., & Scheier, M. F. (1981). *Attention and self-regulation: A control theory approach to human behavior.* New York: Springer-Verlag.

Carver, C. S., & Scheier, M. F. (1982). Control theory: A useful conceptual framework for personality-social, clinical, and health psychology. *Psychological Bulletin, 92,* 111–135.

Carver, C. S., & Scheier, M. F. (1985). Aspects of self, and the control of behavior. In B. R. Schlenker (Ed.), *The self and social life* (pp. 146–174). New York: McGraw-Hill.

Carver, R. P. (1970). Special problems in measuring change with psychometric devices. In *Evaluative research: Strategies and methods.* Pittsburgh, PA: American Institutes for Research.

Cattell, R. B. (1980). The heritability of fluid, g_f, and crystallised g_c, intelligence, estimated by a least squares use of the MAVA method. *The British Journal of Educational Psychology, 50,* 253–265.

Cohen, J. (1990). Things I have learned (so far). *American Psychologist, 45,* 1304–1312.

Cohen, J., & Cohen, P. (1975). *Applied multiple regression/correlation analysis for the behavioral sciences.* Hillsdale, NJ: Erlbaum.

Conley, J. J. (1984). The hierarchy of consistency: A review and model of longitudinal findings on adult individual differences in intelligence, personality and self-opinion. *Personality and Individual Differences, 5,* 11–25.

Costa, P. T., Jr., & McCrae, R. R. (1986). Personality stability and its implications for clinical psychology. *Clinical Psychology Review, 6,* 407–423.

Cronbach, L. J. (1975). Beyond the two disciplines of scientific psychology. *American Psychologist, 30,* 116–127.

Cronbach, L. J., & Furby, L. (1970). How should we measure change—or should we? *Psychological Bulletin, 74,* 68–80.

Decker, P. J. (1983). The effects of rehearsal group size and video feedback in behavior modeling training. *Personnel Psychology, 36,* 763–773.

Decker, P. J., & Nathan, B. R. (1985). *Behavior modeling training: Principles and applications.* New York: Praeger.

Digman, J. M. (1990). Personality structure: Emergence of the five-factor model. In M. R. Rosenweig & L. W. Porter (Eds.), *Annual review of psychology* (Vol. 41, pp. 417–440). Palo Alto, CA: Annual Reviews.

Dobson, K. S. (1989). A meta-analysis of the efficacy of cognitive therapy for depression. *Journal of Consulting and Clinical Psychology, 57*(3), 414–419.

Dweck, C. S., & Leggett, E. L. (1988). A social-cognitive approach to motivation and personality. *Psychological Review, 95,* 256–273.

Elder, G. H., Jr., & Clipp, E. C. (1989). Combat experience and emotional health: Impairment and resilience in latter life. *Journal of Personality, 57,* 311–341.

Erez, M. (1977). Feedback: A necessary condition for the goal setting-performance relationship. *Journal of Applied Psychology, 62,* 624–627.

Eysenck, H. J. (1952). The effects of psychotherapy: An evaluation. *Journal of Consulting Psychology, 16,* 319–324.

Ferguson, G. A. (1954). On learning and human ability. *Canadian Journal of Psychology, 8,* 95–112.

Ferguson, G. A. (1956). On transfer and the abilities of man. *Canadian Journal of Psychology 10,* 121–131.

Fishbein, M. (1979). A theory of reasoned action: Some applications and implications. In H. E. Howe, Jr. (Ed.), *Nebraska symposium on motivation* (pp. 65–116). Lincoln: University of Nebraska Press.

Fiske, S. T., & Taylor, S. E. (1984). *Social cognition.* New York: Random House.

Flanagan, C. M. (1990). *People and change: An introduction to counseling and stress management.* Hillsdale, NJ: Erlbaum.

Fleishman, E. A. (1972). On the relation between abilities, learning, and human performance. *American Psychologist, 27,* 1017–1032.

Frayne, C. A., & Latham, G. P. (1987). Application of social learning theory to employee self-management of attendance. *Journal of Applied Psychology, 72,* 387–392.

Frone, M. R., & McFarlin, D. B. (1989). Chronic occupational stressors, self-focused attention, and well-being: Testing a cybernetic model of stress. *Journal of Applied Psychology, 74,* 876–883.

Geen, R. G., Beatty, W. W., & Arkin, R. M. (1984). *Human motivation: Physiological, behavioral, and social approaches.* Boston: Allyn and Bacon.

Georgenson, D. L. (1982). The problem of transfer calls for partnership. *Training and Development Journal, 36*(10), 75–78.

Glenn, N. (1980). Values, attitudes, and beliefs. In O. G. Brim, Jr., & J. Kagan (Eds.), *Constancy and change in human development* (pp. 596–640). Cambridge, MA: Harvard.

Goldstein, I. L. (1986). *Training in organizations: Needs assessment, development, and evaluation.* Monterey, CA: Brooks/Cole.

Gordon, M. E., & Kleiman, L. S. (1976). The prediction of trainability using a work sample test and an aptitude test: A direct comparison. *Personnel Psychology, 29,* 243–253.

Grabow, K. M. (1989). *The roles of developmental events and individual differences in managerial success.* Unpublished doctoral dissertation, University of Minnesota, Minneapolis.

Greenwald, A. G. (1980). The totalitarian ego: Fabrication and revision of personal history. *American Psychologist, 35,* 603–618.

Greenwald, A. G., & Pratkanis, A. R. (1984). The self. In R. S. Wyer & T. K. Srull (Eds.), *Handbook of social cognition* (pp. 129–178). Hillsdale, NJ: Erlbaum.

Hand, H. H., Richards, M. D., & Slocum, J. W., Jr. (1973). Organizational climate and the effectiveness of a human relations training program. *Academy of Management Journal, 16,* 185–195.

Harris, M. M., & Schaubroeck, J. (1988). A meta-analysis of self-supervisor, self-peer, and peer-supervisor ratings. *Personnel Psychology, 41,* 43–62.

Hazucha, J. F. (1990). *Individual differences in the learning of managerial skills.* Unpublished manuscript. Minneapolis, MN: Personnel Decisions Inc.

Hazucha, J. F. (1991). *Success, jeopardy, and performance: Contrasting managerial outcomes and their predictors.* Unpublished doctoral dissertation, University of Minnesota, Minneapolis.

Hazucha, J. F., Schneider, R. J., & Gentile, S. (1992). The impact of self-managed development, boss support, and organizational support on skill development. In W. Tornow (chair), *Employees' reactions to alternative sources of developmental feedback.* Symposium conducted at the 7th Annual Conference of the Society of Industrial and Organizational Psychology, Montreal.

Heckhausen, H. (1977). Achievement motivation and its constructs: A cognitive model. *Motivation and Emotion, 1,* 283–329.

Heckhausen, H., & Kuhl, J. (1985). From wishes to action: The dead ends and shortcuts on the long way to action. In M. Frese & J. Sabini (Eds.), *Goal-directed behavior: Psychological theory and research on action* (pp. 134–159). Hillsdale, NJ: Erlbaum.

Hellervik, L. W. (1989, June). *Can executives change?* Paper presented at the meeting of the American Society for Training and Development, Boston.

Hicks, W. D., & Klimoski, R. J. (1987). *Academy of Management Journal, 30*, 542–552.

Hogan, P. M., Hakel, M. D., & Decker, P. J. (1986). Effects of trainee-generated versus trainer-provided rule codes on generalization in behavior modeling training. *Journal of Applied Psychology, 71*, 469–473.

Hollenbeck, J. R. (1989). Control theory and the perception of work environments: The effects of focus of attention on affective and behavioral reactions to work. *Organizational Behavior and Human Decision Processes, 43*, 406–430.

Horn, J. L. (1968). Organization of abilities and the development of intelligence. *Psychological Review, 75*, 242–259.

Horn, J. L., & Cattell, R. B. (1966). Refinement and test of the theory of fluid and crystalized general intelligences. *Journal of Educational Psychology, 57*, 253–270.

Horn, J. L., & Donaldson, G. (1980). Cognitive development in adulthood. In O. G. Brim, Jr., & J. Kagan (Eds.), *Constancy and change in human development* (pp. 445–529). Cambridge, MA: Harvard.

Howard, A. (1989). *When does assessment not predict?* Paper presented at the 1989 National Assessment Conference, Minneapolis.

Howard, A., & Bray, D. W. (1988). *Managerial lives in transition: Advancing age and changing times.* New York: Guilford Press.

Huczynski, A. A., & Lewis, J. W. (1980). An empirical study into the learning transfer process in management training. *Journal of Management Studies, 17*, 227–240.

Hunter, J. E., & Schmidt, F. L. (1983). Quantifying the effects of psychological interventions on employee job performance and work force productivity. *American Psychologist, 38*, 473–478.

Hyland, M. E. (1988). Motivational control theory: An integrative framework. *Journal of Personality and Social Psychology, 55*, 642–651.

Ilgen, D. R., Fisher, C. D., & Taylor, M. S. (1979). Consequences of individual feedback on behavior in organizations. *Journal of Applied Psychology, 64*, 349–371.

Ilgen, D. R., & Klein, H. J. (1988). Organizational behavior. In M. R. Rosenweig & L. W. Porter (Eds.), *Annual review of psychology* (Vol. 40, pp. 327–351). Palo Alto, CA: Annual Reviews.

Kanfer, F. H., & Hagerman, S. (1987). A model of self-regulation. In F. Halisch & J. Kuhl (Eds.), *Motivation, intention and volition* (pp. 293–307). Berlin: Springer.

Kanfer, F. H., & Schefft, B. K. (1988). *Guiding the process of therapeutic change.* Champaign, IL: Research Press.

Kanfer, R. (1990a). Motivation and individual differences in learning: An integration of developmental, differential and cognitive perspectives. *Learning and Individual Differences, 2*, 221–239.

Kanfer, R. (1990b). Motivation theory and industrial and organizational psychology. In M. D. Dunnette & L. M. Hough (Eds.), *Handbook of industrial and organizational psychology* (2nd ed., vol 1, pp. 75–170). Palo Alto, CA: Consulting Psychologists Press.

Kanfer, R., & Ackerman, P. L. (1989). Motivation and cognitive abilities: An integrative/aptitude-treatment interaction approach to skill acquisition [Monograph]. *Journal of Applied Psychology, 74*, 657–690.

Kanfer, R., Ackerman, P. L., & Cudeck, R. (Eds.). (1989). *Abilities, motivation and methodology: The Minnesota symposium on learning and individual differences.* Hillsdale, NJ: Erlbaum.

Kanfer, R., Dugdale, B., & McDonald, B. (in press). Empirical findings on the Action Control Scale in the context of complex skill acquisition. In J. Kuhl & J. Beckmann (Eds.), *Volition and personality: Action- and state-oriented modes of control.* Gottingen, West Germany: Hogrefe.

Kanfer, R., & Kanfer, F. H. (1991). Goals and self-regulation: Applications of theory to work settings. In M. L. Maehr & P. R. Pintrich (Eds.), *Advances in motivation and achievement: Vol. 7. Goals and self-regulatory processes.* Greenwich, CT: JAI Press.

Kelly, E. L. (1955). Consistency of the adult personality. *American Psychologist, 10*, 659–681.

Kirkpatrick, D. L. (1967). Evaluation of training. In R. L. Craig & L. R. Bittel (Eds.), *Training and development handbook* (pp. 87–112). New York: McGraw-Hill.

Klinger, E., & Murphy, M. D. (in press). Action orientation and personality: Some evidence on the construct validity of the action control scale. In J. Kuhl & J. Beckmann (Eds.), *Volition and personality: Action- and state-oriented modes of control.* Gottingen, West Germany: Hogrefe.

Komaki, J. (1986). Applied behavior analysis and organizational behavior: Reciprocal influences of the two fields. In B. M. Staw & L. L. Cummings (Eds.), *Research in organizational behavior: An annual series of analytical essays and critical reviews* (No. 8). Greenwich, CT: JAI Press.

Komaki, J., Barwick, K. D., & Scott, L. R. (1978). A behavioral approach to occupational safety: Pinpointing and reinforcing safe performance in a food manufacturing plant. *Journal of Applied Psychology, 63,* 434–445.

Komaki, J. L., Collins, R. L., & Penn, P. (1982). The role of performance antecedents and consequences in work motivation. *Journal of Applied Psychology, 67,* 334–340.

Komaki, J., Heinzmann, A. T., & Lawson, L. (1980). Effective training and feedback: Component analysis of a behavioral safety program. *Journal of Applied Psychology, 65,* 261–270.

Kraut, A. I. (1976). Developing managerial skills via modeling techniques: Some positive research findings: A symposium. *Personnel Psychology, 29,* 325–328.

Kreitner, R., & Luthans, F. (1987). A social learning approach to behavioral management: Radical behaviorists "mellowing out." In R. M. Steers & L. W. Porter (Eds.), *Motivation and work behavior* (4th ed., pp. 184–199). New York: McGraw-Hill.

Kuhl, J. (1984). Volitional aspects of achievement motivation and learned helplessness: Toward a comprehensive theory of action control. In B. A. Maher (Ed.), *Progress in experimental personality research* (Vol. 13, pp. 99–171). New York: Academic Press.

Kuhl, J. (1985). Volitional mediators of cognitive-behavior consistency: Self-regulatory processes and action vs. state orientation. In J. Kuhl & J. Beckmann (Eds.), *Action control: From cognition to behavior* (pp. 101–128). New York: Springer-Verlag.

Kuhl, J. (1986). Motivation and information processing: A new look at decision-making, dynamic change, and action control. In R. M. Sorrentino &

E. T. Higgins (Eds.), *Handbook of motivation and cognition* (pp. 404–434). New York: Guilford.

Kuhl, J. (in press). Action versus state orientation: Psychometric properties of the Action Control Scale (ACS-90). In J. Kuhl & J. Beckmann (Eds.), *Volition and personality: Action versus state-oriented modes of control.* Gottingen, West Germany: Hogrefe.

Kuhl, J., & Kraska, K. (1989). Self-regulation and metamotivation: Computational mechanisms, development, and assessment. In R. Kanfer, P. L. Ackerman, & R. Cudeck (Eds.), *Abilities, motivation, and methodology: The Minnesota symposium on learning and individual differences* (pp. 343–374). Hillsdale, NJ: Erlbaum.

Lambert, M. J. (1983). Introduction to assessment of psychotherapy: Historical perspective and current issues. In M. J. Lambert, E. R. Christensen, & S. S. DeJulio (Eds.), *The assessment of psychotherapy outcome* (pp. 3–33). New York: Wiley.

Lambert, M. J., Shapiro, D. O., & Bergin, A. E. (1986). The effectiveness of psychotherapy. In S. L. Garfield & A. E. Bergin (Eds.), *Handbook of psychotherapy and behavior change* (3rd ed.). New York: Wiley.

Landman, J. T., & Dawes, R. N. (1982). Psychotherapy outcome: Smith and Glass' conclusions stand up under scrutiny. *American Psychologist, 37,* 504–516.

Latham, G. P., & Frayne, C. A. (1989). Self-management training for increasing job attendance: A follow-up and a replication. *Journal of Applied Psychology, 74,* 411–416.

Latham, G. P., & Saari, L. M. (1979). The application of social learning theory to training supervisors through behavior modeling. *Journal of Applied Psychology, 64,* 239–246.

Locke, E. A. (1980). Latham versus Komaki: A tale of two paradigms. *Journal of Applied Psychology, 65,* 16–23.

Locke, E. A., Frederick, E., Lee, C., & Bobko, P. (1984). Effect of self-efficacy, goals, and task strategies on task performance. *Journal of Applied Psychology, 69,* 241–251.

Locke, E. A., Shaw, K. N., Saari, L. M., & Latham, G. P. (1981). Goal setting and task performance: 1969–1980. *Psychological Bulletin, 90,* 125–152.

Lord, R. G., & Hanges, P. J. (1987). A control systems model of organizational motivation: Theoretical development and applied implications. *Behavioral Science, 32,* 161–178.

Luthans, F., & Kreitner, R. (1985). *Organizational behavior modification and beyond: An operant and social learning approach.* Glenview, IL: Scott, Foresman.

Luthans, F., Paul, R., & Baker, D. (1981). An experimental analysis of the impact of contingent reinforcement on salespersons' performance behavior. *Journal of Applied Psychology, 66,* 314–323.

Mabe, P. A., III, & West, S. G. (1982). Validity of self-evaluation of ability: A review and meta-analysis. *Journal of Applied Psychology, 67,* 280–296.

Markus, H. (1977). Self-schemas and processing information about the self. *Journal of Personality and Social Psychology, 35,* 63–78.

Markus, H., & Nurius, P. (1986). Possible selves. *American Psychologist, 41,* 954–969.

Markus, H., & Ruvolo, A. (1989). Possible selves: Personalized representations of goals. In L. Pervin (Ed.), *Goal concepts in personality and social psychology* (pp. 211–241). Hillsdale, NJ: Erlbaum.

Markus, H., & Wurf, E. (1987). The dynamic self-concept: A social psychological perspective. In M. R. Rosenzweig & L. W. Porter (Eds.), *Annual Review of Psychology* (Vol. 38, pp. 299–337). Palo Alto, CA: Annual Reviews.

Marsh, C. M. (1990, April). Factors affecting managerial and executive development in an individualized coaching program. In V. Arnold (Chair), *Executive and management development: Who changes and under what conditions?* Symposium conducted at the meeting of the Society for Industrial and Organizational Psychology, Miami.

Marshalek, B., Lohman, D. F., & Snow, R. E. (1983). The complexity continuum in the radex and hierarchical models of intelligence. *Intelligence, 7,* 107–127.

Mawhinney, T. C., & Fellows, C. (1990, April). *The effects of trainee participation on motivation and training outcomes.* Paper presented at the meeting of the Society for Industrial and Organizational Psychology, Miami.

McGhee, W., & Tullar, W. L. (1978). A note on evaluating behavior modification and behavior modeling as industrial training techniques. *Personnel Psychology, 31,* 477–484.

Miller, W. R. (1985). Motivation for treatment: A review with special emphasis on alcoholism. *Psychological Bulletin, 98,* 84–107.

Mintz, J., & Kiesler, D. J. (1982). Individualized measures of psychotherapy outcome. In P. C. Kendall & J. N. Butcher (Eds.), *Handbook of research methods in clinical psychology.* New York: Wiley.

Mitchell, T. R. (1982). Expectancy-value models in organizational psychology. In N. T. Feather (Ed.), *Expectations and actions: Expectancy-value models in psychology* (pp. 293–312). Hillsdale, NJ: Erlbaum.

Mortimer, J. T., Finch, M. D., & Kumka, D. (1982). Persistence and change in development: The multidimensional self concept. *Life-span Development and Behavior, 4,* 263–313.

Nathan, P. E., & Skinstad, A. (1987). Outcomes of treatment for alcohol problems: Current methods, problems, and results. *Journal of Consulting and Clinical Psychology, 55,* 332–340.

Nicholson, R. A., & Berman, J. S. (1983). Is follow-up necessary in evaluating psychotherapy? *Psychological Bulletin, 93,* 261–278.

Noe, R. A. (1986). Trainees' attributes and attitudes: Neglected influences on training effectiveness. *Academy of Management Review, 11,* 736–749.

Noe, R. A., & Schmitt, N. (1986). The influence of trainee attitudes on training effectiveness. Test of a model. *Academy of Management Review, 39,* 497–523.

Peterson, D. B. (1990, April). Measuring and evaluating change in executive and managerial development. In V. Arnold (Chair), *Executive and management development: Who changes and under what conditions?* Symposium conducted at the meeting of the Society for Industrial and Organizational Psychology, Miami.

Plant, W. T., & Minium, E. W. (1967). Differential personality development in young adults markedly different at the two levels. *Journal of Educational Psychology, 58,* 141–152.

Porras, J. I., & Hargis, K. (1982). Precursors of individual change: Responses to a social learning theory based on organizational intervention. *Human Relations, 35,* 973–990.

Prioleau, L., Murdock, M., & Brody, N. (1983). An analysis of psychotherapy versus placebo studies. *The Behavioral and Brain Sciences, 6,* 275–310.

Robertson, I., & Downs, S. (1979). Learning and the prediction of performance: Development and trainability testing in the United Kingdom. *Journal of Applied Psychology, 64,* 42–50.

Rogosa, D., Brandt, D., & Zimowski, M. (1982). A growth curve approach to the measurement of change. *Psychological Bulletin, 92,* 726–748.

Russell, J. S., Wexley, K. N., & Hunter, J. E. (1984). Questioning the effectiveness of behavior modeling training in an industrial setting. *Personnel Psychology, 37,* 465–481.

Ryman, D. H., & Biersner, R. J. (1975). Attitudes predictive of diving training success. *Personnel Psychology, 28,* 181–188.

Schaie, K. W., & Parham, I. A. (1976). Stability of adult personality traits: Fact or fable? *Journal of Personality and Social Psychology, 34,* 146–158.

Scheier, M. F., & Carver, C. S. (1988). A model of behavioral self-regulation: Translating intention into action. In L. Berkowitz (Ed.), *Advances in experimental social psychology* (Vol. 21, pp. 303–346). New York: Academic Press.

Schlenker, B. R. (Ed.). 1985). *The self and social life.* New York: McGraw-Hill.

Sevy, B. A., Olson, R. D., McGuire, D. P., Fraser, M. E., & Paajanen, G. (1985). *Management Skills Profile research report and technical manual.* Minneapolis: Personnel Decisions, Inc.

Shapiro, D. A., & Shapiro, D. (1982). Meta-analysis of comparative therapy outcome studies: A replication and refinement. *Pscyhological Bulletin, 92,* 581–604.

Showers, C. J., & Cantor, N. (1985). Social cognition: A look at motivated strategies. In M. Rosenzweig & L. W. Porter (Eds.), *Annual review of psychology* (Vol. 36, pp. 275–305). Palo Alto, CA: Annual Reviews.

Siero, S., Boon, M., Kok, G., & Siero, F. (1989). Modification of driving behavior in a large transport organization: A field experiment. *Journal of Applied Psychology, 74,* 417–423.

Sloan, E. B., Schneider, R. J., & Hazucha, J. F. (1990). Unpublished manuscript. Personnel Decisions, Inc., Minneapolis.

Smith, M. L., Glass, G. V., & Miller, T. I. (1980). *The benefits of psychotherapy.* Baltimore, MD: The John Hopkins University Press.

Smith, P. B. (1975). Controlled studies of the outcome of sensitivity training. *Psychological Bulletin, 82*(4), 597–622.

Snow, R. E. (1989). Aptitude-treatment interaction as a framework for research on individual differences in learning. In P. L. Ackerman, R. J. Sternberg, & S. R. Glaser (Eds.), *Learning and individual differences: Advances in theory and research* (pp. 13–59). New York: Freeman.

Snow, R. E., & Lohman, D. F. (1984). Toward a theory of cognitive aptitude for learning from instruction. *Journal of Educational Psychology, 76,* 347–376.

Sternberg, R. J. (1985). *Human abilities: An information-processing approach.* New York: Freeman.

Stokes, G. S., Mumford, M. D., & Owens, W. A. (1989). Life history prototypes in the study of human individuality. *Journal of Personality, 57,* 509–545.

Swann, W. B., Jr. (1984). Quest for accuracy in person perception: A matter of pragmatics. *Psychological Review, 91,* 457–477.

Swann, W. B., Jr. (1985). The self as architect of social reality. In B. Schlenker (Ed.), *The self and social life* (pp. 100–125). New York: McGraw-Hill.

Swann, W. B., Jr. (1987). Identity negotiation: Where two roads meet. *Journal of Personality and Social Psychology, 53,* 1038–1051.

Swann, W. B., Jr., & Ely, R. J. (1984). A battle of wills: Self-verification versus behavioral confirmation. *Journal of Personality and Social Psychology 46,* 1287–1302.

Swanson, J. L., & Hansen, J. C. (1988). Stability of vocational interests over 4-year, 8-year, and 12-year intervals. *Journal of Vocational Behavior, 33,* 185–202.

Taylor, C. W. (1952). Pre-testing saves training cost. *Personnel Psychology, 5,* 213–239.

Taylor, E. K., & Tajen, C. (1948). Selection for training: Tabulating equipment operators. *Personnel Psychology, 1,* 341–348.

Tellegen, A. (1982). *Brief manual for the Multidimensional Personality Questionnaire.* Unpublished manuscript.

Tellegen, A. (1985). Structures of mood and personality and their relevance to assessing anxiety, with an emphasis on self-report. In A. H. Tuma & J. Maser (Eds.), *Anxiety and the anxiety disorders* (pp. 681–706). Hillsdale, NJ: Erlbaum.

Tellegen, A. (1988). The analysis of consistency in personality. *Journal of Personality, 56,* 621–663.

Tellegen, A., Lykken, D. T., Bouchard, T. J., Jr., Wilcox, K. J., Segal, N. L., & Rich, S. (1988). Personality similarity in twins reared apart and together. *Journal of Personality and Social Psychology, 54,* 1031–1039.

Thompson, A. D. (1986). *A formative evaluation of an individualized coaching program for business managers and professionals.* Unpublished doctoral dissertation, University of Minnesota, Minneapolis.

Vicino, F. L., & Bass, B. M. (1978). Lifespace variables and managerial success. *Journal of Applied Psychology, 63,* 81–88.

Vroom, V. H. (1964). *Work and motivation.* New York: Wiley.

Wakabayashi, M., & Graen, G. B. (1984). The Japanese career progress study: A 7-year follow-up. *Journal of Applied Psychology, 69,* 603–614.

Whitbourne, S. K. (1986). Openness to experience, identity flexibility, and life change in adults. *Journal of Personality and Social Psychology, 50,* 163–168.

Organization Design and Strategy

The next three chapters of this volume of the *Handbook* share a common theme in their emphasis on the art of designing, developing, and implementing the structures and systems within which organizations and members of organizations operate. Obviously, comprehensive coverage of such a diverse topic cannot be accomplished in only three chapters; and in fact, previous chapters in the present volume capture many aspects of the strategic issues that are relevant to organizing for carrying out productive endeavors. The following three chapters simply focus more thoroughly on design and strategy and are therefore grouped together as a separate section of this volume.

Accordingly, chapters in this section focus specifically on organization design (chapter 14), decision making (chapter 15), and strategic reward systems in organizations (chapter 16).

In chapter 14 [Alternative Metaphors for Organization Design], D. McKenna and P. Wright employ metaphor to capture the essence of much that is central to an understanding of the backdrop formed by the *ground* of organizational structure—a backdrop that both influences and is influenced by individual and group behavior within the organizational context. After discussing the use of metaphor and detailing specifications for a good abstract metaphor,* the authors discuss *organization as machine, organization as organism, organization as brain, organization as family,* and *organization as political arena.*

The authors' strategy in this chapter is stunningly successful as a means of effectively communicating important insights about differential strengths, weaknesses, and dangers implicit in various organizational forms. Each of the five metaphors explored here illuminates distinctly different facets of organizations.

In closing their discussion, the authors challenge their readers to explore additional metaphors for organization design as an important

---

* A *good* abstract metaphor must (a) be sufficiently specific and concrete to call up a visual image, (b) draw on a common experience shared by many persons, and (c) be fresh and engaging, even surprising.

way of gaining new insights and understanding about the constantly changing interplay between organizational members and the structures within which they are asked to perform.

R. Taylor, in chapter 15 [Strategic Decision Making], describes the roots, scope, current focus, and research methods in *strategic decision making* (SDM). Many models of decision making are reviewed and explored: *rational-analytic, cognitive/perceptual, incremental adjustment, strategic planning, bureaucratic, collective, interpretive,* and *contingency.* Taylor's purpose in exploring these several models is to examine both their descriptive and normative implications as they relate to each component of strategic decision making. The state of the art in SDM theory development and research methods is presented with the intention of stimulating further discussion and research on processes involved in strategic decision making.

E. Lawler III and G. Jenkins, Jr., in chapter 16 [Strategic Reward Systems], present theory and research on the role of pay systems in complex organizations. In particular, the authors focus on how pay systems may impact a number of aspects of an organization's effectiveness: *performance motivation, skill development motivation, attraction and retention, organizational structure, culture,* and *costs.* In the process of exploring the above elements of effectiveness, Lawler and Jenkins discuss several specific pay system practices, including *job-based pay, person-based pay, individual-based pay for performance, organization-level pay for performance,* and *executive compensation practices.* The authors place a particular emphasis on the link between strategy, structure, and pay systems in relation to evidence showing the impact between pay systems and organizational effectiveness.

They conclude by commenting on the uneven nature of research on pay in organizations. They mention the need for studying pay practices and their effects in the context of the nature of the organizations in which specific types of systems are found. In particular, such factors as managerial style, organization size, work design, and so forth need to be studied more fully as potential moderators of the nature of the impact shown by different types of pay systems. Lawler and Jenkins predict that such research will lead to useful theories that are more at the organizational level in contrast to the currently most useful theories of impact of pay, which focus mostly on individual behavior.

−Marvin D. Dunnette
−Leaetta M. Hough

CHAPTER 14

Alternative Metaphors for Organization Design

D. Douglas McKenna
Seattle Pacific University

Patrick M. Wright
Texas A & M University

In this chapter, we examine how ways of thinking about organizations influence the science and practice of industrial and organizational psychology. We suggest that these ways of thinking are guided, constrained, tested, and stretched by metaphors. By thinking of an organization as if it were a machine, for example, our attention is directed to the machinelike features and events of organizational life. Consequently, our research and practice then focus on learning about and improving the efficiency of the organization as machine. This focus on the machinelike aspects of organizations, however, can cause us to overlook other features that are not machinelike. An organization's capacity to adapt and change, which is characteristic of biological organisms but not of machines, may be deemphasized or ignored. By arbitrarily limiting our thinking to a few common organizational metaphors, we limit our ability to study, understand, and influence organizations in new and creative ways. To show and explore the implications of such metaphors, we present five metaphors that have influenced or could influence industrial and organizational psychology. These include the organization as machine, organism, human brain, family, and political arena. We conclude the chapter with a demonstration of how these metaphors can be used in combination to enrich, refresh, and strengthen our research and interventions in organizations.

LET'S GO TO the theater. Our destination is City Repertory Theater, which for more than 60 years has been dedicated to "excellence in all the great traditions of the theater." The theater's past is a story of continuing success and its future looks bright. It enjoys a steady stream of financial support from the community and is consistently able to attract talented actors and actresses to its company.

Entering the building, we see lofty ceilings, a polished gray marble floor, ornate gold and crystal chandeliers, and massive stone pillars. The people milling about seem to fit the theater itself: well-aged, affluent, proper, and comfortable with themselves and the setting. Like a clock ticking in a thunderstorm, the theater appears to have kept its own time and pace in a world swirling with change.

When the houselights dim and the curtain rises, a spotlight opens the darkness, illuminating a lone figure at center stage. Our thoughts about the theater, its history and mission, the building, and the audience fade as the play begins. Soon other members of the cast join the main character on stage, and they move in and out of the spotlight as the drama unfolds.

Suddenly, midway through the first act, a mischievous stagehand turns up the houselights. As our eyes adjust to the light, we see activity that had been hidden in darkness moments before—actors waiting just offstage for their cues, stagehands hustling around moving props and backdrops, a prompter holding the script whispering lines to the star from stageright, and the director frantically waving her arms at the lighting crew. The theater itself becomes visible again, as do the people in the audience around us.

Notice what happened when the houselights came on. Our focus on what was happening on stage, so essential to enjoying the play, was lost. But we gained—or regained—an appreciation for the organizational context that both shapes and is shaped by the play.

Messages in the Metaphor

This story using the theater as a metaphor contains the two messages driving this chapter. The first message is that industrial and organizational psychology has contributed much to our understanding of organizational behavior by focusing its "spotlight" of inquiry on individuals and their immediate work environment. While we have no intention of asking industrial and organizational psychologists to become macro-organization theorists, sociologists, or economists, we believe it is critically important that we be aware of how what we see determines what we don't see (Weick, 1969). We need to become aware of our organizational tunnel vision. Specifically, by focusing on the individual as figure, we fail to notice and appreciate the ground of the organization, which both influences and is influenced by individual and group behavior. The first premise of this chapter, then, is that industrial and organizational psychologists need to turn up the houselights to see the organizational context in which the individuals or work groups are embedded.

Organizational Tunnel Vision

What specifically are we missing because of our individual focus? The first consequence of our inattention to organizational context is that we have failed to consider seriously the possibility that not all organizations are the same, that there may be fundamentally different organizational types, species, or configurations that affect and are affected by individual behavior in different ways (Mintzberg, 1979). Overlooking this possibility, we may be unknowingly muddling our results and making inappropriate generalizations. Even a cursory review of our journals suggests that the majority of field research in industrial and organizational psychology has been done in large, bureaucratic organizations. Most of what we know about the validity of assessment centers, for example, comes from a handful of large companies (cf. Dreher & Sackett, 1983; Klimoski & Strickland, 1977). Is what we know about prediction of managerial performance generalizable to other kinds of organizations, such as professional service organizations like CPA firms, law firms, and hospitals; to young, small, fast-growing entrepreneurial organizations; or to complex, dynamic, innovative, matrix-structured organizations? These questions can be answered only by systematically including different types of organizations in our research.

The second consequence of our constricted view of the organizational "stage" is that we have limited our effectiveness in developing and implementing human resource systems and programs. Assuming that what works in large hierarchical organizations will work anywhere, we try to force-fit systems and programs into fundamentally different types of organizations. Following our theater metaphor, this is like trying to stage a colossal grand opera such as *Aida*, with hundreds of performers and live elephants, in a neighborhood dinner theater. As Hakel, Sorcher, Beer, and Moses (1982) have so ably noted, successful implementation of any significant change in the way we select, train, or reward people requires an understanding of and ability to influence the organization's political system, which lies mostly outside industrial and organizational psychology's spotlight. By not considering an organization's political dynamics, we doom our most sophisticated efforts to operational failure.

The third consequence of our narrow focus on individuals and jobs is that it can lull us into taking what we see "on stage" at face value (cf. Argyris, 1976). Our typical approaches to job analysis, for example, provide us with a clear view of jobs as they are currently being performed and perceived by those who know them (usually supervisors and incumbents). But such job analysis methods are not well-suited to discovering that (a) what is being done now will either not be done or will be done differently in the future or (b) what is being done now is not necessarily what should be done.

We really have no excuse for this form of myopia. More than 25 years ago, Dunnette (1966) warned that a job analysis should include consideration of job dynamics (ie., time-, person-, and situation-determined changes in the behaviors required by the job) and the link between the job and broader organizational goals and structures. As he explained, unanticipated changes in the job may have significant consequences for individual and organizational effectiveness:

> If a job changes due to situational factors and we have been able to anticipate them, our selection strategies will obtain people who respond successfully to the changes. On the other hand, failure to anticipate such changes can result in hiring persons whose behavioral repertoires are too sparse for successful response. (Dunnette, 1966, p. 72)

While it may be difficult to anticipate how a job may change in the future, it is surely a mistake to ignore the possibility of such change. When a job is poorly designed or likely to change, a purely descriptive job analysis may lead to the development of selection, appraisal, training, and compensation policies and programs that perpetuate a less than optimal status quo (cf. Argyris, 1969). However, by factoring an awareness of the organization's overall strategy, goals, and direction into the job analysis process, we stand a better chance of "doing the right thing" as well as "doing things right" (cf. Bennis & Nanus, 1986). Attempts to redesign jobs to improve their motivating potential (Hackman & Oldham, 1980), to create more effective work systems or groups (Hackman, 1987), and to forecast the skill requirements of future jobs (Arvey, Salas, & Gialluca, 1988; Schein, 1978) are steps in the direction of doing the right thing.

The fourth argument for increasing the scope of our perspective is that a large number of industrial and organizational psychologists are directly involved in planning, designing, and helping to implement changes in entire organizations, business units, and departments. For the practitioners among us, an understanding of organization-level issues is important in its own right. We suspect, however, that few industrial and organizational psychologists were well-prepared by their academic training to deal with such problems. More likely, they have had to learn these skills and perspectives on the job. Since the problems we face in organizations cut across levels of analysis, so should our graduate preparation and our perspective.

Implicit Organizational Perspectives

The second message in the theater metaphor is more subtle. Please take a moment to reread our description of the theater at the beginning of the chapter in preparation for this question: Why did we describe some things about the theater and not others? For example, why did we describe the theater in terms of its mission and history, its relationship to the community and its successes, its physical facility, its customers traits, and its rhythm or pace? Why focus on these aspects of the theater and not others, such as the fact that the theater has gone through three creative directors in the past three seasons, each complaining of a lack of artistic freedom? Why didn't we tell you about the unwritten expectation that the theater's leadership will cater to the whims of the Smith family, the major benefactor to the theater since its inception? Why didn't we mention that the plumbing in the theater is old and needs to be replaced?

The point is that while there are many ways of describing something as complex as a theater, we selected a particular subset of all the possibilities. Both the things we see and the things we do not see reflect our point of view or perspective on organizations. There is

a Sufi story about a group of blind men who all touched the same elephant, but at different parts. Consequently they described it in mutually exclusive ways. So too does our perspective on organizations have a profound—and limiting—effect on how we think about and interact with them. Perrow (1970) states this well:

> No matter what you have to do with an organization—whether you are going to study it, work in it, consult for it, subvert it, or use it in the interest of another organization—you must have some view of the nature of the beast with which you are dealing. This constitutes a perspective on organizations. (p. 1)

There is no alternative to having a perspective on organizations. But failure to be aware of one's perspective sets the stage for dogmatism and stagnation and brings down the curtain on tolerance and creativity. It is interesting that as industrial and organizational psychologists we are fairly open to different perspectives on the nature of individuals (e.g., cognitive, behavioral, psychoanalytic). Yet when we move up to the level of the organization as a whole, many of us are not even aware that we have a perspective or implicit theory of organization that affects what we study and how we try to intervene in them. We believe that this limited awareness of our organizational perspectives is cramping the creativity of industrial and organizational psychology as a discipline and as a practice. It is a problem that merits our immediate attention.

Dominant Organizational Metaphors

How then can we become more aware of our implicit theories of organization? In his book, *Images of Organization*, Morgan (1986) argues persuasively that the ways we think about and understand organizations are forged from metaphors. To comprehend something as abstract and complex as a human organization,

Morgan says that we think of it in terms of something more concrete, familiar, and comprehensible; that is, we find and use metaphors to bridge the gap between what we know and don't know.

What then are the metaphors used by industrial and organizational psychologists to think about organizations? We believe that a strong argument can be made that this thinking is dominated by two metaphors: the "machine" and the "organism" (Morgan, 1986). A third, the organization as "political arena," has received some attention (Hakel, Sorcher, Beer, & Moses, 1982), but is best described as an *emerging* metaphor at this point.

We maintain that the machine has been and continues to be the most dominant organizational metaphor in industrial and organizational psychology. Following closely in the footsteps of Frederick Taylor (1915), we measure jobs and people for the purpose of "finding" (recruiting and selecting) or "building" (training and development) the "right part" (person) to perform a necessary machine "function" (job). Recognizing that parts can break down or go out of alignment, we develop preventive maintenance procedures to provide "lubrication" (compensation and reward systems) and systems for detecting and correcting "performance deviations" (performance appraisal). Particularly on the industrial side of industrial and organizational psychology, we think and act as if we are engineers assigned with the responsibility of designing and maintaining the human parts of the organizational machine.

Those of us on the organizational side of industrial and organizational psychology often prefer a different metaphor: the organization as a biological organism. Rather than a machine designed by engineers to perform an unchanging task, the organization as organism is seen as a living, growing, dynamic entity, its development and behavior driven by "genetic" endowments and the demands of an environment to which it must adapt to survive.

The organism metaphor suggests an organization cannot be understood as a stand-alone entity, but must be viewed as a system within a more encompassing system composed of other organisms—an ecosystem, if you will. This system-within-a-system principle also holds true inside the organizational organism itself. The metaphor reveals that an organization is composed of many subsystems, one of which is the human subsystem (Katz & Kahn, 1986).

Like the machine metaphor, the organism metaphor draws our attention to the interdependence of parts or subsystems, but it adds at least two key ideas to our thinking about organizations. First, it adds the idea that organizations learn, change, and grow in response to both internal and external pressures. But what does it mean to say that an organization learns and changes? Does the organism metaphor provide us with ideas for investigating this question? Perhaps we need an alternative metaphor.

This brings us to the second key idea added by the organism metaphor. People are not simply parts to be engineered into the machine. They are whole, living organisms with their own capabilities, commitments, goals, needs, and opinions. This was the message delivered so forcefully by the Hawthorne studies (Roethlisberger & Dickson, 1939) and by Lewin and his intellectual offspring (e.g., McGregor, Trist, Emery, Argyris, Bennis). The organism metaphor brings to light the possibility that the best-designed organizational machine from a technical perspective may not work very well from a human or social perspective. We will return to this issue later in a more detailed examination of these dominant metaphors and their implications for industrial and organizational psychology.

Purpose of the Chapter

We can summarize the two premises for this chapter as follows. First, we maintain that industrial and organizational psychology's focus on the individual and his or her immediate work environment obscures our view of an array of potent organization-level variables that influence and are influenced by the individual. Second, we argue that industrial and organizational psychology is not indifferent to organizational issues, but that its organizational perspective and assumptions are largely unexamined and grounded in two dominant but implicit metaphors: the machine and the organism.

Our purpose in this chapter is to challenge the reader to turn up the houselights on his or her perspective on organizations. But as Morgan (1986) says, "Any realistic approach to organization analysis must start from the premise that organizations can be many things at one and the same time" (p. 321). So a single or even a pair of houselights will not do. We need different sets to see different aspects of an organization, and we also need ways of creating new houselights when our existing ones do not provide us with additional insights.

In this chapter, we will turn on five different houselights, each one a metaphor for organization. In order, we will look at organization as: machine, organism, brain, family, and political arena. We will turn on the houselights separately, considering how each has influenced or could influence industrial and organizational psychology. We have selected this particular set of metaphors to illuminate a full range of possibilities, from the overworked machine metaphor to the fresh but potentially controversial family metaphor. Our hope is that this will stimulate the reader's interest in challenging dominant metaphors, in looking further into emerging metaphors, and in creating new metaphors.

Before turning to the five metaphors, we begin with a brief discussion of metaphor itself. Some metaphors, as we shall see, are more interesting and useful than others. If we are to realize the full potential of metaphorical thinking for organizational analysis, we must be able to create and recognize meaningful metaphors and pass by those that are strained, stale, or confusing.

Metaphor

Philosopher Ortega y Gasset once said, "The metaphor is the most fertile power possessed by man." Yet it seems that we have underutilized this power in industrial and organizational psychology. Let us take a closer look at the meaning of metaphor, characteristics of good and bad metaphors, and finally, why we need metaphors in industrial and organizational psychology.

What Is a Metaphor?

A metaphor is a type of figurative language. We use figurative language when we use words to communicate anything other than their literal meaning. When we describe an organization as a machine, we are speaking figuratively (and metaphorically) because we do not mean literally that the organization *is* a machine. Rather, we are talking *as if* the organization were a machine; we are speaking of its *machine-likeness*. While this may seem a trivial point, we make it to draw attention to our tendency to treat metaphors as statements of fact rather than as rhetorical devices. Embler (1966) notes:

> Homer does not say that men *are* gods but only that in certain respects they resemble gods. Wordsworth does not say that nature *is* a teacher, but only that nature is *like* a teacher. Yet when metaphor is new, those who find their attitudes implicit in the metaphor construe the metaphor to be a statement of identity, that is a statement of fact...prescribing certain kinds of behavior. (p. vii)

This reminds us of Argyris' (1976) charge against industrial psychology in the first edition of this *Handbook*: "A field that tends to ignore theory, but uses it implicitly, may unwittingly become tied to this implicit theory" (p. 164). Have we become unwittingly tied to our implicit organizational metaphors?

While there are three different types of metaphors (Marius, 1991), it is the *abstract metaphor* with which we are concerned in this chapter. All metaphors involve making comparisons—comparisons designed to help us see or understand the characteristics of one thing in terms of the characteristics of another. The abstract metaphor helps us to understand an abstraction (e.g., organization) by comparing it to something more concrete, familiar, and graspable (e.g., a machine). When we speak of an organization as if it were a machine, we draw attention to those qualities of the organization that are machinelike; for example, its function, energy source, operating procedures, parts, maintenance needs, and so forth. Referring again to the basic perceptual organizing principle of figure-ground, the metaphor pulls forth the organization's machinelike qualities so they become figure, while its non-machinelike qualities (e.g., interactions with the environment, creativity, conflict between people and groups, cultural legends and symbols, roles and interaction patterns) recede into ground. In this way, the metaphor can help us to see the organization in a new way. When held unconsciously or too rigidly, however, the metaphor can also become the source of blind spots.

What Is a Good Metaphor?

George Orwell (1945) said, "The sole purpose of a metaphor is to call up a visual image" (p. 165). In the case of the abstract metaphor, one end of the comparison—the abstraction—is by definition hard to visualize or grasp. For the abstract metaphor to do its work, the other end of the comparison needs to be concrete, vivid, and familiar to the audience. The more vivid the visual image evoked in the audience

by the metaphor, the more clearly and creatively they will be able to think about the abstraction.

This brings to light three specifications for a good abstract metaphor. First, the concrete end of the metaphor should be sufficiently specific and concrete so as to call up a visual image. Consequently, "organization as machine" is probably not as interesting a metaphor as would be "organization as automobile" or "organization as windmill."

Second, a metaphor only works when it draws on a common experience of the author and the audience. Good metaphors are like good jokes: They make a sudden and graphic impression and do not have to be explained to the listener. But what seems to one person to be a great joke may be lost on another. Consequently, the "organization as an 80486 microprocessor" metaphor will only evoke a visual image for those with this particular technical familiarity. Pushing this point a bit, we suspect that this may be one of the reasons we—as a field—have been inconsistently effective in communicating the accomplishments of industrial and organizational psychology as a science to executives in organizations. They do not "get it" because we fail to explain our theories or findings using metaphors or images that are familiar to and therefore capable of evoking a visual image in an executive audience.

Third, metaphors should be fresh and engaging, even surprising, if they are to spur new insights into organizations. For example, our favorite metaphors for organization—machine and organism—have provided and continue to provide us with useful insights into organizations, if for no other reason than that we have believed in them strongly enough to create organizations that emphasize their qualities.

But our metaphors can and should do more for us. The modern French poet, Pierre Riverdy (quoted in Dickey, 1968) said, "Insofar as the juxtaposition of entities be separated by the greater distance, and yet be just, the metaphor will be thereby stronger" (p. 4). In other words, the higher the negative correlation between the apparent characteristics of the organization and the concrete side of the metaphor, the stronger and more powerful the metaphor will be, provided the connection between the two is capable of evoking interesting or useful thoughts or feelings in the audience. Clearly, what's "just" varies from reader to reader. Our concern is that industrial and organizational psychology has become conformed to a few safe metaphors (i.e., high positive correlation) that are, therefore, not particularly powerful or creative. "The true metaphor orients the mind toward freedom and novelty; it encourages the mind to be daring" (Dickey, 1968, p. 12). It is time to stretch ourselves with fresh, new metaphors.

What Is a Bad Metaphor?

Metaphors lose their power when they fail to evoke a clear visual or emotionally charged image in the audience. When this happens, they become clichés—dead or stale metaphors. Orwell (1945) attacks our attachment to dying metaphors:

> A newly invented metaphor assists thought by evoking a visual image, while on the other hand, a metaphor which is technically "dead" (e.g., *iron resolution*) has in effect reverted to being an ordinary word and can generally be used without loss of vividness. But in between these two classes there is a huge dump of worn-out metaphors which have lost all evocative power and are merely used because they save people the trouble of inventing phrases for themselves. (p. 165)

Perhaps our affinity for the machine and the organism as organizational metaphors is based in part on our greater concern for analytical efficiency than for creative effectiveness.

Mixed metaphors can be a more serious problem than dead or stale metaphors because they bring confusion rather than clarity. Here is a good example from *The New Yorker*, spoken in all seriousness:

> Perhaps I am only flogging a straw herring in midstream, but in light of what is known about the ubiquity of security invulnerabilities, it seems vastly too dangerous for university folks to run with their heads in the sand. (Quoted in Marius, 1991, p. 186)

Orwell (1954, p. 86) argues that when images clash, it is certain that the writer is not seeing a mental image of the objects he or she is naming; in other words, he or she is not really thinking. This happens frequently in articles and texts concerned with models for organizational analysis and diagnosis. Environment ("organism"), strategy ("brain"), policy and procedures ("machine"), conflict management ("political arena"), norms ("culture"), and many other aspects of organization are spoken in the same breath without any apparent thought to the distinctively different organizational metaphors from which they are drawn. We need multiple metaphors for organizations, but we cannot throw them into a mishmash without losing the clarity and integrity available in each separate metaphor.

Why Do We Need Metaphors?

We need metaphors to catalyze the creative process. Marius (1991) observes:

> As aids to thinking, metaphors are important—perhaps necessary—to modern science. Some might argue that without metaphor some current scientific thinking could scarcely go on. Albert Einstein's theory of relativity

deals with phenomena so removed from commonsense experience that most people can scarcely begin to understand it. Indeed the *London Times* once called Einstein's theory "an affront to common sense." (p. 179)

We need metaphors in industrial and organizational psychology to open up new paths for research and practice. We also need them to communicate our ideas clearly to each other and to the world outside our discipline. And finally, we need metaphors for organizations because they are inherently complex, ambiguous, paradoxical, multifaceted entities. Metaphorical thinking is a method that allows us to respond flexibly to the "many-sided character of organizational life" (Morgan, 1986, p. 321), rather than resorting to unabashedly oversimplified images of organization found in management bestsellers or scholarly theories so abstract, complicated, and confusing that they generate light and heat only for an elite and isolated audience.

Now we are ready to turn on five metaphorical houselights in sequence. As we reflect on each metaphor, we will be attempting to address four basic questions:

- What are the characteristics of the entity we wish to compare to organizations (e.g., machine)?

- What characteristics of an organization does this metaphor bring to our attention?

- How has this metaphor influenced industrial and organizational psychology?

- What creative possibilities does this metaphor suggest for theory, research, or practice in industrial and organizational psychology?

Organization as Machine

In his 1936 film, *Modern Times*, Charlie Chaplin portrays the plight of a bumbling, insubordinate factory worker on an assembly line. One of the most potent images in the movie shows Charlie caught up in and virtually becoming part of a giant cogwheel that drives the line. This image symbolizes what can happen when organizations are designed and operated as if they were machines composed of human and physical parts. In this section, we will examine how the organization as machine metaphor dominates much of management science and practice, including industrial and organizational psychology.

Characteristics of Machines

A machine is "an arrangement of fixed and moving parts for doing work, each part having something special to do" or "any device for applying or changing the direction of power, force, or motion" (*World Book Dictionary*, 1989, p. 1249). Machines, therefore, can be as simple as a crowbar or as complex as the human brain. Orwell would undoubtedly shudder at the thought of using such a broad and abstract concept as a metaphor for another abstraction—the organization. Nevertheless, machines share common features that provide an interesting and useful perspective on human organizations.

Machines transform or redirect energy for a given purpose. Lurking just below the surface of this statement is the notion of a designer of the machine who created, selected, and arranged its parts so that when energized, some purpose is realized. When we think of machines, we think of a designer with a purpose.

Second, machines cannot create energy; they simply convert it to another form or change its direction. Machines depend, therefore, on a consistent flow of energy being imported from outside. When its energy source dries up or is blocked, a machine stops functioning. The most efficient machine in the world is useless without imported energy.

A primary measure of a machine's ability to do work is efficiency—that is, the ratio of energy put into the machine to the useful energy it puts out. Some machines, such as a lever, are almost 100 percent efficient. By contrast, a car or truck is only about 25 percent efficient because much of the heat it generates is lost in the conversion process. Inefficiency is caused primarily by friction, which in turn can usually be traced back to poor machine design or maintenance. Since all machines are subject to the effects of friction, no machine is capable of operating at 100 percent efficiency. So unless you have an unlimited or cheap energy source, finding ways to reduce friction beween the parts of your machine is a major concern.

Fourth, an interesting distinction can be made between machines that are *prime movers* and those that run on the energy transformed by prime movers. Prime movers, such as the mainsail on a sailboat or a water wheel on a mill in a stream, convert energy directly into mechanical energy. We mention this distinction because the organizational parallels are so intriguing. For example, the language of CPA firms identifies three different types of employees—*finders, minders,* and *grinders*—to distinguish those who find new business, those who mind the work and the firm, and those who actually grind out tax returns and audits.

Finally, while machines can be extremely complex, all machines that do mechanical work are based on six types of simple machines: the lever, the wheel and axle, the pulley, the inclined plane, the wedge, and the screw. A complex machine, then, is basically just a system of interconnected, simpler machines. We can understand the machine as a whole by studying the functions of the parts and their connections. The machine is nothing more than the sum of its parts. The fact that all machines are made up of simpler machines has also led to the creation of common parts that can be used in many different machines performing different functions. Ball bearings, gears, pistons, connecting rods, and valves are examples of such common parts. This allows design engineers to create new machines by arranging common parts into new sequences of connections. Again, the correspondence of common machine parts to organizational parts should be obvious.

Machines, Organizations, and Industrial and Organizational Psychology

It would be difficult to overestimate the significance of machinelike organizations to human society. Satisfaction of the world's growing appetite for inexpensive, mass-produced goods and services depends heavily on organizations capable of efficiently harnessing and coordinating the efforts of large numbers of people. As Mintzberg (1983a) has so aptly noted: "When an integrated set of simple, repetitive tasks must be performed precisely and consistently by human beings, the Machine Bureaucracy is the most efficient structure—indeed, the only conceivable one" (p. 76). Without such large organizational machines, the pyramids of Egypt, the Egg McMuffin, and the Boeing 747 simply would not exist.

Our familiarity and comfort with machines makes it easy to apply the machine metaphor to organizations. Assuming that an organization has a primary mission or purpose, organizational "engineers" (i.e., executive management and key staff groups such as strategic planning, finance, industrial engineering, and human resources) can then define the activities necessary to achieve this purpose. Human parts are selected and trained to perform the activities within tolerances defined by formal rules and procedures. The organizational machine is fueled and energized by capital provided by investors. Friction between the parts of the machine—and therefore inefficiency—is minimized through a variety of planning and control systems including budgets, supervision, formal work rules and procedures, performance goals, and information gathering and reporting. When the organizational machine breaks down, an expert design or maintenance engineer (i.e., a staff expert or external consultant) can be called on to troubleshoot the problem and repair or replace the broken parts of the organizational machine.

Frederick Taylor's (1915) *The Principles of Scientific Management* could be called the Holy Grail of the machine approach to organization and management. Taylor's principles included (a) scientific analysis of jobs to determine the one most efficient way to perform them; (b) job specialization to maximize worker efficiency and minimize training and personnel replacement costs; (c) selection of a *first class man*, that is, the person most suited for the job; (d) training of the person in the "best way" to do the job; and (e) the use of work standards and monetary incentives to motivate productive behavior.

The parallels with modern industrial and organizational psychology are obvious. We stress the need to analyze jobs into their more fundamental parts, test and select the right person for a given job, grind the rough edges off or add new functions to people through indoctrination and training, and find ways to use the organization's primary energy resource—money—to persuade people to work hard and follow the rules. When the organizational machine's efficiency breaks down, we stand ready with our job design tools and employee opinion surveys. The bold-print slogan in the Booz, Allen, and Hamilton, Inc. advertisement that appears regularly on the back cover of *Personnel Psychology* (e.g., 1991, vol. 44, no. 2) sums it up well: The right people, the right jobs. Furthermore, the ad goes on to list many of the tools that industrial and organizational psychologists have so capably developed and used to help design and maintain organizational machines: personnel selection design/validation, recruiting programs, executive assessment/evaluation, staffing requirements, employee relations,

compensation/benefit design, position classification, and so on. We are reminded of Cascio's (1982) comment that job analysis is the industrial and organizational psychologist's "wrench." Clearly, the machine metaphor is alive and well in industrial and organizational psychology. Several specific examples from employee selection and performance appraisal will illustrate both the strengths and limitations of this metaphor.

Employee Selection and the Machine Metaphor. Our approach to employee selection has been heavily influenced by the machine metaphor. A specific example is the way in which we assume that the machine can be broken down into separate job-person unit parts that can be isolated and changed without consideration of the machine as a whole. In the words of Schmidt, Pearlman, Hunter, and Hirsch (1985):

> What situational aspect of work would be relevant to the prediction of job performance from the knowledge, skills, abilities, and other traits of the worker? We believe the obvious answer to this question is the nature of the work itself. (p. 773)

There are several problems with this perspective. First, it begs questions about the appropriate scope of an analysis of "the nature of the work." This problem is illustrated by Brown's (1981) meta-analysis of the criterion-related validity of a biodata form used in selection by a large number of insurance companies. He found that biodata validities were moderated by the quality of management practices—measured at the organizational level. While an assessment of managerial effectiveness could be done at the job level (e.g., of managers with whom the incumbent is likely to work), this is not the sort of information one typically gathers when doing a job analysis for selection purposes. Where does the "nature of the work" end and the organization begin? Even a novice auto mechanic understands that the cause of a malfunction in an engine system—a misfiring spark plug, for example—may not be found in the immediate proximity of the symptom and that replacing the spark plug itself may not solve the problem. Yet many industrial and organizational psychologists have consistently attacked selection problems from such a narrow, nonsystemic point of view.

Another problem with Schmidt et al.'s (1985) perspective is that it may lead us to overlook organization-level indicators that the purpose and tasks of the organizational machine, and therefore the job, may change in the future. In other words, the machine will need to be modified if it is to continue to function successfully in the future. The best sources of information about the job as it exists today—usually incumbents and supervisors—may not be aware of organizational plans and strategies that will significantly change the nature of the job. By questioning higher-level managers or executives about organization plans and how they may affect the jobs in question, we may avoid developing selection systems that will quickly become obsolete. Bentz (1968) demonstrated this approach more than 25 years ago in developing the *Sears Executive Battery*. By forecasting where the company was headed and how it was likely to change and grow (which machines do not do), Bentz was able to identify and measure the executive traits and abilities needed to support the company's emerging strategy. Bentz's methodology is nicely summarized by Schein's (1978) *strategic job analysis,* which is a useful step-by-step approach to developing a future-oriented selection process.

Schmidt et al.'s (1985) perspective also focuses too narrowly on the technical problem of developing selection methods (e.g., tests, interviews, work samples, or combinations) that will validly predict job performance. Even the most valid selection tools are useless when their predictions are ignored or misinterpreted by those making hiring

decisions. An understanding of how the organization goes about making selection decisions is essential to figuring out ways to ensure that the utility of our selection tools is realized. How formalized is the selection process? Who is involved? How is information from various sources integrated and used in making a hiring decision? Who has the authority to make that decision? Are there organizational norms concerning what personal characteristics should or should not be assessed in selection (cf. Rynes & Gerhart, 1990) These kinds of questions call for organization-level analysis and organizational metaphors other than the machine.

Performance Appraisal and the Machine Metaphor.   Performance appraisal systems also provide good examples of the influence of the machine metaphor. Latham and Wexley's (1981) behavior observation scale (BOS) format has strong mechanistic roots. It begins with identifying critical behaviors associated with effective and ineffective performance. Then, observers rate the frequency with which an individual performs each of the critical behaviors. In some applications of BOS, complex algorithms developed by system designers are then used to combine the frequency ratings into an overall performance rating that is then mechanically fed into the employee's personnel file (e.g., McKenna & Latham, 1987). Supervisors may use a salary increase chart to translate these mechanically determined composite ratings into recommendations (evaluated subjectively by their managers) regarding employee pay raises for the coming year. While it is important to point out that Latham and Wexley endorse a more organic, interactive implementation of their methodology, its design lends itself to mechanical misuse, particularly in large, bureaucratic organizations such as government agencies that place a premium on treating all employees equally, or at least in making it appear so.

As in employee selection, our typical approaches to performance appraisal have reflected a reductionistic and mechanical perspective on organizations. When asked, for example, what type of performance appraisal system would be most effective for motivating performance, many of us would propose a process in which clear behavioral expectations are communicated; challenging, specific goals are set; regular feedback is given; and valued outcomes are made contingent on the level of performance achieved (Latham & Wexley, 1981). Our answer is based on explicit and systematic theories of individual learning, motivation, and performance. If we view the organization as nothing more than a collection of individual-job parts, then this point of view would be sufficient.

But practitioners concerned with implementing our recommendations are likely to ask additional questions that will be hard to answer from this limited perspective. How will this approach to performance appraisal be received and supported by various stakeholders in the organization such as top management, supervisors, employees, and unions? More concretely, how will supervisors feel about monitoring employee performance closely enough to give specific feedback when the organizational norm may be for supervisors to stay in their offices and wait for employees to come to them? Or how will managers who've always done performance reviews but never had much contact with employees feel about delegating this responsibility to supervisors who are better positioned to give credible feedback? We might also be asked if it's appropriate to set precise behavioral expectations for employees in an organization where success depends on innovation and creativity. How specific should expectations be in an organization where things change so fast that employees must continually redefine their own jobs and roles? Answers to questions like these require that our perspective include more than the "right person–right job" engineering; they require that we understand the broader issues of organizational politics, culture, strategy, and

structure. Again, the machine metaphor is insufficient.

Limitations of the Machine Metaphor

Morgan (1986) cites four general limitations of the machine metaphor. First, machinelike organizations are designed for efficiency, not for adaptation. When environmental conditions change, the finely tuned and highly efficient machine is likely to misfire or grind to a halt.

Second, the machinelike organization's control system is designed to correct deviations from its planned equilibrium as quickly as possible. As Mintzberg (1983a) puts it, "The implicit motto of Machine Bureaucracy seems to be 'when in doubt, control.' All problems are to be solved by the turning of technocratic screws" (p. 180). Any disruption to the machine's planned activity—dissent, personal problems, conflict, even innovative ideas—are quickly corrected and banished by the machine's control processes. Double-loop learning as a source of adaptive ideas and energy is ruled out (Argyris, 1982).

Third, the machine view of organizations depends on a unifying mission and goal structure. Imagine three engineers trying to design a car with different ideas about what the machine is to do. One wants the car to be the most fuel efficient in the world. Another wants it to be the fastest. The third wants it to be the most luxurious. If they are successful in actually building a prototype, we could expect some sort of compromise product that would not appeal to any particular market segment.

Most organization theorists would argue that organizations are in a continuous process of negotiating purposes and goals (Daft, 1986). At the individual level, each person has his or her own goals, which are rarely in perfect congruence with the organization's goals. Individuals seek career and salary progression, increased job security, and other goals, many of which can and must be achieved at the expense of organizational goals. The implication here is that industrial and organizational psychologists need to be more aware of these conflicting goals and to be prepared to help address them. As we shall see, the political arena metaphor provides insight into just this sort of problem.

Finally, the machine view of organizations can result in policies and programs that are dehumanizing. Given their obsession with control (Mintzberg, 1983a) and recognition that human beings are essentially the wild card in the system, designers of organizational machines created jobs so narrow, specialized, and repetitive that (a) little or no training was involved, thus making the individual worker easily replaceable, and (b) individual performance deviations could be quickly detected and corrected by supervisor intervention. Such jobs "treat people as means...as categories of status and function rather than as individuals," thus undermining the meaning of work, the dignity of the individual, and the productivity of organizations (Worthy, 1959, p. 70).

In closing this section on the organization as machine, we would call industrial and organizational psychologists to take a hard look at the human impact of our work and the moral dilemmas it raises. Is it true, as Braverman (quoted in Mintzberg, 1979, p. 338) argues, that "Taylorism dominates the world of production; the practitioners of 'human relations' and 'industrial psychology' are the maintenance crew for the human machinery"? Given our tacit acceptance of the machine view of organizations and the fact that our work in industry is largely supported by those who stand to gain the most from exploitative systems, we believe the question merits careful consideration. It is also a good reason to explore other organizational metaphors.

Organization as Organism

In 1917, the Lake Washington Ship Canal was constructed in the city of Seattle to allow large ships to pass from Puget Sound inland to Lakes Union and Washington. To compensate for the effects of tide changes in the Sound and differences in elevation between the Sound and the inland lakes, two locks were constructed at the mouth of the canal. Anticipating that the locks would be a serious obstacle and threat to the salmon run through the waterway, engineers built a fish ladder adjacent to the locks to provide a way for the salmon to make their annual round trip between the Sound and their upstream spawning ground.

All was well until the late 1980s, when a California sea lion—nicknamed Herschel by the press—and his friends discovered the steelhead salmon congregating on the Puget Sound side of the fish ladder. The sea lions began feasting on the salmon at an alarming rate, drastically reducing the size of the run over several years and putting it in jeopardy. Although Herschel and friends were doing exactly what one would expect of any animal in its struggle to survive, it was apparent that the sea lions were taking "unfair" advantage of an unnatural, man-made situation. Something had to be done; human intervention in the natural order had created the problem, and human intervention would be necessary to correct it.

A variety of options were considered, but the situation was complicated by the protected species status of the California sea lion. Harming the sea lions in any way was forbidden by federal law. Attempts to scare them away with underwater explosions and rubber bullets failed. Finally, exasperated fisheries officials obtained special permission to trap and transport Herschel and friends over 1,000 miles south to the California coast. Within weeks, the sea lions had returned, obviously hungry from their long swim back north to the sea lion paradise at the foot of the fish ladder.

Characteristics of Organisms

The story of Herschel concretely illustrates a number of characteristics of living organisms that can be metaphorically useful in understanding organizations. Focusing first on Herschel, we see a living entity whose basic problem is to obtain from his environment resources needed to survive (e.g., air, food, water). Because of his mobility, Herschel is able to seek out environments that provide him with the most steady supply of food. At the bottom of the fish ladder, he found an environmental niche that was perfectly suited to his needs. With all he could eat and legislation to protect him from his most powerful predator, Herschel held nature's equivalent of a monopoly—a ready supply of resources and no competition. This part of the story is instructive in that it highlights the fundamental importance of the dynamic, interactive, and adaptive relationship between an organism and its environment.

Seeing how Herschel and his behavior allow him to adapt to his environment is one way of thinking systemically. We can also go the other direction. If we were to study Herschel himself, we would discover that he is also a system composed of related subsystems (e.g., digestive system, nervous system), which are composed of related subsystems (e.g., organs in the digestive system), and so on. The important point here is that each system within the hierarchy of systems must not only be aligned to fit with its environment (i.e., its supersystem), but it must also maintain the alignment or fit among its own subsystems. A problem in Herschel's diet (e.g.,

too much of one kind of food) may create problems for another of his subsystems (e.g., he becomes too overweight to maneuver away from nets).

A third characteristic of organisms brought to light by the Herschel story is that there are different species of organisms (e.g., sea lions, people, salmon), each of which has evolved, and is evolving, in ways that enhance its ability to survive in its environment. Understanding similarities and differences between species has advanced both pure and applied biological science. With the latter in mind, we would simply note: What's good for a sea lion may not be good for a salmon.

The story also points to the importance of developmental process and life cycles in organisms. The salmon in particular illustrate this. Salmon are spawned, they grow and mature, they reproduce, they return to the ocean, and they die. Although there are many interesting aspects of this process that could be noted, we will mention three. First, only a very low percentage of salmon spawned ever reach maturity. Second, salmon in different stages of development are physically different and they face different challenges from their environment. Third, if you want to catch an adult salmon, it is probably sufficient to understand only what and where it eats. But if you are interested in ensuring that there are salmon available for future generations to catch, you will need to understand its full life cycle.

Finally, when we follow the story through time, we see how Herschel is just one element in a web of interconnected elements and events. Salmon, sea lions, people, and countless other organisms are all participants in an intricate group dance in which a change in step by one causes changes in the movement of all. Herschel, for example, may be his own worst enemy. Failing to recognize how his welfare (and that of his species) is related to that of the salmon, Herschel acts in his own short-term best interests, tipping the balance of nature and doing irreparable damage to his future food source.

Failure to think systemically is also reflected in the legislation that protected Herschel. While singling out particular animals or plants for placement on endangered or threatened species lists can protect them from extinction in the short term, the only long-term solution is to protect the ecosystem within which they live. Many ecologists are now arguing that protecting Herschel without protecting the salmon, the streams, and so forth, that make up his ecosystem may well be futile. The lesson: Failure to think systemically and to anticipate how actions or events may alter the balance in a system can have tragic consequences.

Organisms, Organizations, and Industrial and Organizational Psychology

If we think about organizations as if they were biological organisms, five different characteristics come to light. First, organizations live and die depending on how successful they are in coping with the demands of their environments. Second, an organization that is effective in one environment may not be effective in another. Third, the interaction of organizations and environments gives rise to different species of organizations. Fourth, organizations can be thought of in terms of a developmental life cycle. Fifth, organizations are not alone with their environment but participate in a supersystem or ecosystem with other organizations and institutions.

Together, these ideas based on the organism metaphor form the conceptual foundation for most of the current thinking, research, and practice in the fields of business strategy, organization theory, and organizational development. We will look at each idea in turn, presenting examples of how they have influenced our thinking and research.

Organization-Environment Relations. Like a biological organism, a human organization is an open system that imports resources (e.g., informational, physical, financial, and human resources) from its environment, transforms them into products or services, and then exports its products or services back into the environment. From an organismic perspective, the central problem of an organization is how to position itself and conduct transactions vis à vis its environment to obtain the resources it needs to function and survive.

Like biological organisms, organizations appear to vary in the degree to which they are mobile or position-bound relative to their environments. As organization theorists have moved away from thinking of organizations as essentially passive machines or plants with limited mobility, the notion of *strategic choice* has risen in importance. According to Child (1972) and Miles and Snow (1978), an organization can create, select, and influence environmental conditions in hopes of increasing its viability. Like Herschel moving to the base of the fish ladder or like a person with arthritis who moves to Arizona for its warm, dry climate, an organization may be able to move to or create an environment that is better suited to its particular strengths and weaknesses. With the capacity for strategic choice, however, comes the risk of choosing an environment to which the organization is not well suited.

Different environments place different demands on organizations. To conceptualize these demands, Mintzberg (1979) proposed that environments vary along four dimensions: *stability, complexity, diversity,* and *hostility.* Organizations in unstable environments have a hard time predicting what actions will be needed to survive in the future. This places limits on their ability to plan ahead and places a premium on having flexible systems, processes, and people. By contrast, organizations in stable environments can predict what is likely to be required for future success and can create detailed plans for executing those actions. And by doing the same things again and again, organizations in stable environments have the opportunity to design highly efficient work systems and processes.

Environments also vary in the complexity of their demands. Simple environments are those that present organizations with problems for which there are readily available solutions (e.g., how to cook fast food). In complex environments, organizations must deal with unique, unusual, or complicated problems. These are problems for which there may be no currently available solution (e.g., how to cure a disease) or that require highly specialized expertise (e.g., how to develop a valid employee selection system). It is important to point out that environmental complexity is relative: Problems that may be simple for one organization may be completely insurmountable for another. The critical question is whether a given organization has the knowledge or expertise needed to solve the problems posed by the environment in which it has chosen to compete.

Diversity is the environmental characteristic that describes the range of customers, markets, or clients an organization attempts to serve. For example, Microsoft Corporation's environment is highly diverse in that it sells different products (e.g., applications and systems software) to different customers (e.g., weekend personal computer users and software developers) in almost every part of the world. By contrast, Alpine Data Systems sells project management software to small to medium-sized architectural engineering firms—a fairly integrated or homogeneous environment. Generally speaking, environmental diversity requires that an organization differentiate itself into subsystems, each specialized in dealing with a segment of the environment (cf. Lawrence & Lorsch, 1986).

Finally, environments vary in the degree to which they are munificent or hostile.

Competition from other organizations and relationships with key external groups (e.g., government, unions) are the key factors in determining the amount of hostility in a given environment. As Mintzberg notes, hostile environments are also typically unstable environments. An organization in an extremely hostile environment—like an antelope being chased by a lion— must be capable of reacting very fast to the moves of its competitors.

Organizational Design and Internal Congruence.   Through the evolutionary process, biological organisms develop characteristics that allow them to function effectively in their environment. Similarly, research has demonstrated that organizations in different environments often have different characteristics and that organizational effectiveness is related to the "fit" between these characteristics and the demands of the environment (Burns & Stalker, 1966; Woodward, 1965). Furthermore, since an organization's environment is often composed of subenvironments or sectors with varying characteristics (e.g., stability, complexity), units within the organizations must be created to deal with these differing demands (Lawrence & Lorsch, 1986). And because these subunits must cope with different subenvironments, significant differences in structure and process across subunits should be expected.

What are these characteristics of organizations that arise from the adaptation process? Morgan (1986) proposes that there are five essential subsystems of an organization— essential in that each fulfills a basic requirement for the organization's survival. These subsystems include (a) a *strategic* subsystem, which manages relationships with the environment and determines the organization's overall direction and design; (b) a *technological* subsystem, which includes the technical system (e.g., machines, work processes) and the knowledge or skills used to transform resources acquired from the environment into products or services; (c) a *human/cultural* subsystem, which seeks to align the capabilities and interests of employees with the needs and goals of the organization; (d) a *structural* subsystem, which divides up the organization's work and provides formal structural mechanisms (e.g., task forces, liaison positions, dual reporting lines) to coordinate work across departments or work units; and (e) a *managerial* subsystem, which plans, monitors, and controls the flow of resources, work, and people in and through the organization.

According to contingency theories of organizational design (cf. Burrell & Morgan, 1979; Daft, 1986), these subsystems must be designed such that they are congruent with each other and with the environment. Figure 1 graphically portrays this congruence hypothesis in terms of environment and subsystem alignment in four different organizations, labeled A through D.

Organization B, for example, might be a company in the biotechnology industry. As the figure shows, this company faces a highly turbulent and unpredictable environment, primarily because of the unpredictability of technology development and financial support. To cope with this high level of uncertainty, B needs (a) a strategic subsystem designed for continuous monitoring of the environment; (b) a technological subsystem that gives its scientists the autonomy necessary to pursue fruitful paths of research and development; (c) a human/cultural subsystem that supports creativity, flexibility, cooperation, and individual growth within the context of company goals; (d) a structural subsystem that provides for functional specialization (e.g., research, product development, manufacturing) and cross-functional collaboration; and (e) a managerial subsystem that ensures high levels of employee and manager involvement in decision making. Figure 1 shows that organization B has achieved a high degree of alignment externally with its environment and internally with its subsystems. This is also true

of organizations A and C, but at different points along the subsystem dimensions. Organization D, however, is portrayed as having four of its subsystems out of alignment with the environment and with its human/cultural subsystem. Contingency theorists would predict that this incongruence would create tension within the organization and reduce its effectiveness compared to more well-aligned competitors.

This hypothesized need for internal congruence is one of the more obvious implications of the organism metaphor for industrial and organizational psychologists. Training specialists in particular have shown interest in aligning training with other organizational subsystems through the process of organization analysis. Goldstein (1986), for example, views organization analysis as one aspect, along with task (or job) and person analysis, of the process of identifying training needs. He defines organization analysis as

> an examination of the system-wide components of the organization that may affect a training program's factors beyond those ordinarily considered in task and person analysis.... It involves an examination of organizational goals, resources of the organization, climate for training, and internal and external constraints present in the environment. (p. 28)

Failure to do such an analysis, according to Goldstein, can result in training programs that become prematurely obsolescent, are difficult to implement, or do not fit well with other human resources management (HRM) programs or systems (e.g., selection, appraisal, compensation). Despite the alleged importance of organization analysis, Goldstein presents a discouraging picture of our ability to do it well: "To be perfectly candid, it is only recently that industrial/organizational psychologists have begun to realize how important these issues [i.e., organization-level factors] are in the

FIGURE 1

Congruence and Incongruence Between Organizational Subsystems

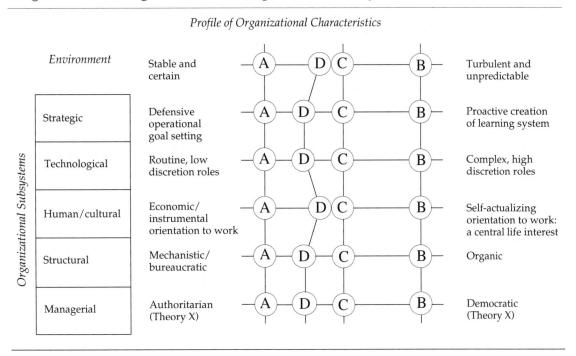

Profile of Organizational Characteristics

Environment		
Strategic	Defensive operational goal setting → ... →	Proactive creation of learning system

Note: Lines Ⓐ, Ⓑ, and Ⓒ illustrate congruent, and line Ⓓ incongruent, relations between subsystems.

From *Images of Organizations* by G. Morgan, 1986, Newbury Park, CA: Sage. Copyright © 1986 by Sage Publications, Inc. Reprinted by permission.

implementation of their programs. Thus, the procedures are not completely understood" (p. 30).

He goes on to suggest, however, a list of "self-diagnostic" questions that can be used to determine whether "training is really ready to begin." These questions can be mapped, as we have done below, to the five basic organizational subsystems described earlier (Goldstein, 1986, p. 36).

- Are there unspecified organizational goals that should be translated into training objectives or criteria? (strategic subsystem)

- Are the various levels of the organization committed to the training objectives? (managerial and human/cultural subsystems)

- Have the various levels and/or interacting units participated in the development of the program beginning at the end assessment? (human/cultural subsystems)

- Are key personnel ready both to accept the behavior of trainees and to serve as models of the appropriate behavior? (managerial and human/cultural subsystems)

- Will trainees be rewarded on the job for the appropriate learned behavior? (managerial and human/cultural subsystems)

- Is training being used as a way of overcoming other organizational problems or organizational conflicts that require other types of solutions? (problems in the strategic, technological, structural subsystems)

- Is top management willing to commit the necessary resources to maintain work organizations while individuals are being trained? (strategic subsystem)

To this list we can add two questions proposed by Wexley and Latham (1982) in their discussion of organization analysis:

- How does the organization relate to its external environment and what are the training and development implications of these relationships? (environment and strategic subsystem interaction)

- What are the organization's current and future human resource needs (e.g., size of work force, skill mix) and how can the training function help meet those needs? (human/cultural subsystem)

Looking back over this list of questions and their relationships to the five subsystems of organization design, we can identify potential blind spots in the current approaches to organization analysis. For example, we see few questions about how the organization's structural subsystem is likely to interact with a given training program (e.g., how are work units grouped together? How are jobs structured? How rigid or flexible are organization policies and procedures?).

In sum, the concept of external and internal congruence of organizational design that flows from the organism metaphor calls our attention to the need for HRM policies and programs that are well coordinated with organization environment, strategy, technology, structure, people, culture, and management philosophy. To ignore these organizational variables could be fatal—like transplanting a heart from a person with type O blood into a person with type A blood!

Evolution of Organizational Species or Configurations. Pursuing the organism metaphor even further, researchers have discovered that organizations are not simply random combinations of characteristics. Rather, they have determined that certain characteristics (e.g., complex technology, organic structure, democratic management philosophies) tend to cluster together to form the organizational equivalents of different species of organisms.

The most basic framework for differentiating organizational species was proposed by Burns and Stalker (1966). They discovered that organizations successful in stable, predictable environments tended to have a mechanistic design, characterized by hierarchical, centralized authority structures; narrow, clearly defined jobs and responsibilities; and extensive rules and procedures. By contrast, successful organizations in unstable environments tended to have an organic design with nonhierarchical, decentralized authority systems; broadly defined, dynamic jobs and responsibilities; and few rules or procedures. The importance of this finding should not be underestimated. Their research demonstrated the existence of two fundamentally different types of organizations, each adaptive and effective in a particular type of environment. Given the clarity of their scheme and its empirical support, it is puzzling that this basic distinction of mechanistic and organic organizational types has only recently begun to be incorporated into the thinking and research of industrial and organizational psychologists.

Latham and Fry (1986), for example, have criticized appraisal systems and research studies that fail to take into consideration macro-level organizational variables such as strategy, structure, technology, and design. More specifically, however, they propose that different types of appraisal systems will be differentially effective in mechanistic and organic work systems.

Carroll and Schneier (1982) pursued this same hypothesis in more depth. While they offer no empirical evidence for their propositions regarding how performance appraisal systems should be designed and administered in mechanistic versus organic structures, they did generate a number of interesting ideas that, if substantiated by research, could significantly enhance our understanding of and ability to implement performance appraisal systems. For example, they hypothesize that:

- Goals and directions in organic structures can change rapidly; performance appraisal systems must, therefore, be flexible and accommodate shifts in employee responsibilities, changes in performance criteria, and so forth.

- Supervisors will be viewed as the most legitimate source of appraisals in mechanistic organizations with their hierarchical authority structures.

- Since people in organic systems are more accustomed to working in project teams, they are more likely to accept the use of peer ratings in appraisal than are people working in mechanistic systems.

- Appraisal formats with more detailed standards calling for structured responses by raters may be more appropriate in mechanistic systems.

- Management by objectives (MBO) systems are easier to use in mechanistic systems because goals are relatively stable and performance criteria are more easily quantified.

- Group-based performance measures may be more appropriate in organic, highly interdependent project team–based organizations or work units.

In the area of recruiting and selection, Olian and Rynes (1984) have also made a commendable effort to develop propositions linking differences in organizational species with differences in staffing policies and practices. They used Miles and Snow's (1978) three strategic types of organizations in their analysis. These species are characterized by fundamentally different strategies and designs. *Defender* organizations operate in narrow, stable markets, use efficient technology and production to keep costs low, invest few resources in research and development, develop highly specialized managers and promote them from within, and have dominant power coalitions comprised of financial and production experts. *Prospector* companies seek new product and market opportunities, reinforce the importance of innovation and adaptability through organic structures and processes, hire managers from outside to handle new businesses, and have dominant coalitions made up largely of experts from marketing or product research and development. *Analyzers* operate in stable and dynamic markets, behave like defenders in stable markets and like prospectors in dynamic markets, coordinate these different businesses through matrix structures, hire managers from outside or promote from within depending on the needs of each business unit, and have dominant coalitions comprised of marketing, applied research, and production experts.

Olian and Rynes developed propositions about how these different species are likely to proceed differently through the five stages of the staffing process: choice of selection criteria, choice of recruiting method, development of marketing strategy, choice of selection techniques, and final decision making. Comparing defenders and prospectors, for example, they proposed that a defender's selection criteria will emphasize aptitude (or potential), specialized skills, and personality traits like need for security and need for structure. By contrast, Olian and Rynes predict that prospectors will select more for past achievement, broad skills, traits of independence, risk taking, and tolerance for ambiguity. In terms of selection techniques, they also hypothesize that defenders will be more likely to use formal, standardized selection devices (e.g., psychological tests) than will prospectors. And consistent with the more organic, less specialized, more collaborative subsystems needed by the prospector, Olian and Rynes suggest that more people will be involved in selection decisions in prospector than in defender organizations.

One of the most interesting propositions in this article is that organizations use secondary selection criteria that are not obviously job-related. The authors contend that when candidates are similarly well qualified on primary selection criteria, an organization will prefer candidates with experience or skills in that organization's dominant function. Defenders, for example, will prefer candidates with experience or background in production and/or finance, the dominant functions in such organizations. Presumably, these secondary skills will allow the individual to communicate and build relationships more easily with those in the dominant functions. One could argue, of course, that such communication requirements should be revealed in the job analysis, that an understanding of the organization's overall strategy is not needed to detect them. Nevertheless, awareness of strategy could guide the job analyst to investigate aspects of the job that might otherwise be overlooked. Although not a direct test of this particular hypothesis, Rynes and Gerhart (1990) were able to demonstrate that assessments of general employability differ from firm-specific employability (i.e., assessments of

suitability for employment in a particular firm) and that there is a firm-specific component to interviewer evaluations of applicants. This study represents an empirical step that supports the claim that organizational variables beyond immediate job requirements have an impact on selection decisions.

Olian and Rynes' proposals regarding selection criteria in prospector organizations also challenge traditional approaches to developing selection procedures from detailed job analyses. The prospector organization's preference for people who are independent, creative, risk taking, and tolerant of ambiguity reflects the fact that jobs in such organizations are continually changing. Trying to do a detailed, task-oriented job analysis in such an organization is often a waste of time and money. In prospector organizations, "other duties as assigned" is not just a catchall phrase used by those who don't want to spend any more time writing job descriptions. It reflects a fundamental reality of life in organic organizations: People do what needs to be done, whether it is in their job description or not.

Perhaps the most elegant and comprehensive taxonomy of organizational species is that of Mintzberg (1979). He identifies four basic species or configurations. The four basic species include *simple structure, machine bureaucracy, professional bureaucracy, and adhocracy.* Mintzberg differentiates these species in terms of the situations in which they are found (i.e., age, size, technical system, and environment), the ways in which they coordinate their activity (i.e., mutual adjustment, direct supervision, standardization of work, outputs, or skills), the part of the organization that is most important (i.e., strategic apex, middle line, operating core, technostructure, support staff), and their structural design (e.g., type of decentralization, mechanistic or organic structure). We will briefly describe these four species, commenting on the possible implications of their differences for research and practice in industrial and organizational psychology.

The *simple structure* species operates in simple, dynamic environments and is typically a young, small organization with an unsophisticated technical system. Work within the *simple structure* is coordinated through direct supervision, often by the CEO or owner of the small business. All significant strategic and even tactical decisions are centrally made at the top, thus making the *strategic apex* the critical part of the simple structure. An informal organic structure is maintained to maximize the organization's ability to respond quickly to a changing environment. This responsiveness is the competitive strength of the simple structure. Its Achilles heel, however, is that its strategic apex, usually one person, may not be able to process all the information needed to make key decisions, particularly if the environment becomes more complex.

For industrial and organizational psychology, the critical question posed by the simple structure species is simply this: When will we get around to studying them? Such organizations lack both the number of people typically desired for quantitative research and the financial resources to support research or consultation by industrial and organizational psychologists. Nevertheless, small businesses provide the vast majority of jobs in the U.S. economy.

The *machine bureaucracy* is the incarnation of the machine metaphor. It is typically an older, large organization operating in a simple, stable environment. The technical system of the machine bureaucracy is highly routinized, regulated, and not automated. Work is coordinated through the application of detailed standard operating procedures, decision rules, budgets, and policies created by experts in the organization's technostructure (e.g., finance, human resources, industrial engineering). As long as all the parts of the machine stay within the tolerances of this detailed design and customers continue to buy the organization's products or services, the machine bureaucracy hums efficiently along like a well-tuned engine. The machine bureaucracy's strength lies in its efficiency in doing routine things in large volume. When the environment becomes more unstable or complex, however, the machine bureaucracy is like a supertanker—it takes a very long time to change course. More than any of the other species, however, the large, established machine bureaucracies wield significant economic and political clout. This enables them to influence and control their environments more than other types of organizations. By influencing their environment, the machine bureaucracies are able to slow the pace of change that would threaten their survival. For example, because of its economic and political influence, Chrysler was able to survive under conditions that would have put smaller, less powerful companies out of business.

Though the most familiar, machine bureaucracies are the dinosaurs of organizational species—unable to adapt to a rapidly changing environment, they are becoming extinct. Here, then, are some important questions to consider. Will industrial and organizational psychologists be capable of helping machine bureaucracies become more adaptive and flexible? Will we be able to adapt our thinking and methods—fine-tuned in the stable, laboratorylike conditions of this species—for use in more fluid and organic organizational species? If not, will we be pulled into extinction along with our patron species?

Universities, law firms, CPA firms, management consulting firms, architectural engineering firms, and medical clinics are all examples of the species Mintzberg calls the *professional bureaucracy*. Professionals in the operating core form the key part of this configuration because they have specialized and standardized skills developed through advanced education that are necessary for the organization to deal with the complex but fairly predictable set of problems posed by its environment. The configuration's design emphasizes ongoing training and specialized jobs providing a high degree of autonomy and decision-making authority to the professionals. The professional bureaucracy's adaptive strength lies in the knowledge and skill of its professionals. But the primary allegiance of professionals to their professional guilds and associations creates an almost inherent conflict of interest with management. Raelin (1986) describes this as a "clash of cultures," which is never far from the surface in professional bureaucracies and often threatens their viability.

For industrial and organizational psychology, this is another neglected species that holds a number of challenges and opportunities. For those concerned with traditional personnel issues, research on the design and implementation of performance appraisal systems for professionals is a critical need because it lies at the heart of the clash of the management-professional cultures. The performance management system developed by Hough, Russell, Keyes, and Zaugg (1990) for attorneys in the U.S. General Accounting Office provides an outstanding example of what can be achieved when careful attention is paid to both content (e.g., job analysis, selection criteria and methods, performance appraisal format) and process (e.g., attorney involvement in system development, training, management attention to system performance and integrity).

The *adhocracy* is the organizational species that populates environments that are both complex and unstable. To cope with rapid changes in a highly complex environment, the adhocracy brings together experts from different fields in an informal, organic, communication-rich environment. Matrix structures that provide employees with a dual focus on markets and functional specialties are common.

The adaptive strength of the adhocracy is its ability to create innovative solutions to complex problems in a rapidly changing environment. We like to refer to the adhocracy as the "James Dean of organizations" because it lives continually on the edge. Its state-of-the-art technical capabilities can be made obsolete overnight and its loose organic structure is often only one-step removed from total chaos.

Unlike scholars in organization theory and practitioners in organizational development, industrial and organizational psychologists have not shown much interest in the adhocracy's torrid pace, high-energy culture, and kaleidoscopic structure. Considering the enormous economic, political, and social impact of high-technology organizations in contemporary society, it is time for industrial and organizational psychology to test its mettle in the crucible that these organizations provide. Interestingly, it is in the adhocracy where our traditional measures of cognitive abilities and personality may prove most useful. The inherent fluidity of the adhocracy requires people with high capacities for learning, behavioral flexibility, and interpersonal skills. But although these individual difference variables are readily assessed with psychological tests, the authors' experience with high-technology organizations is that they are highly resistant to formal selection procedures such as tests (an observation that is consistent with Olian and Rynes's hypothesis regarding the informality of selection procedures in prospector organizations). Persuading these technologically sophisticated organizations to use psychologically sophisticated assessment technologies represents an important challenge for industrial and organizational psychologists in the area of selection.

Organizational Life Cycles.   Like biological organisms, organizations can be seen as proceeding through life stages. Based on their longitudinal study of 36 corporations, Miller and Friesen (1984) proposed a developmental model with five stages: (a) birth, (b) growth, (c) maturity, (d) decline, and (e) revival. Although organizational death, or more accurately, dissolution, is a possibility, Miller and Friesen found in their sample that decline was most often succeeded by revival rather than death.

Miller and Friesen also noted changes in organizational structure that coincided with different stages in the life cycle. In organizational newborns, structure is simple and centralized. They tend to take risks and aggressively pursue new market opportunities. Firms in the growth stage move to a more complex organizational structure with functional (e.g., marketing, manufacturing) departments and begin to push decision making down to middle managers. At maturity, increasing organizational size and stable environments push the firm toward more elaborate financial controls to control costs and increase efficiency. Mature companies become more internally focused on efficiency and less focused on innovation and market responsiveness.

Organizations go into decline for both external and internal reasons. First, the market for their products or services may change, shrink, or even disappear. Failure to recognize and respond to such fundamental market changes will send the organization into decline. Second, organizations decline when management fails to recognize that organizations must be structured and managed differently at different stages in the life cycle. Greiner's (1972) model of organizational growth identifies specific crises associated with each stage in the life cycle. For example, newborn organizations are characterized by high energy, creativity, and little or no structure. Growth, however, brings the organization to its first crisis: the *crisis of leadership*. A leader must step forward or be designated to set direction and coordinate decisions and actions.

Unless a leader is found, Greiner predicts the organization will move into decline. As the organization continues to grow, however, the leader's ability to make informed decisions is swamped. Delegation is needed to resolve the *crisis of autonomy*.

From a psychological and HRM perspective, the individual and group-level effects of organizational decline are particularly significant. Robey (1986) proposes that stress, conflict, and turnover are common problems in declining organizations. These are all topics that have received considerable research attention from industrial and organizational psychologists, but not usually in a specific organizational context such as the declining organization. Given the number of organizations either in or threatened by decline, we believe such work is of great theoretical and practical importance.

Organizations in revival are characterized by efforts to refocus product/market strategies (e.g., developing new products, raising product quality, changing price or positioning) and increase efficiency (e.g., cutting costs, divesting nonproductive assets; Robey, 1986). From an organizational design standpoint, the revival stage produces some of the most sophisticated and demanding organizational structures, such as the matrix. Looking at the matrix from a psychological perspective, we see that it requires individuals who can analyze and solve problems, make decisions, communicate clearly, work cooperatively, identify with the organization and the task, and remain flexible under highly ambiguous and stressful circumstances. Not surprisingly then, Greiner (1972) says that the revival stage sends the organization headlong into what he calls the *crisis of psychological saturation*. Here again is an opportunity for industrial and organizational psychologists to conduct interesting and practical research by studying psychological issues in the context of a specific stage in the organizational life cycle.

Organizational Ecosystems. A final insight from the organism metaphor is that organizations are not alone in their environment but are elements of an ecological web or network composed of similar and dissimilar organizations. Just as Herschel's voracious feeding on salmon affected other sea lions, people, and creatures (especially the salmon), so the actions of one organization have consequences—both intended and unintended—on other organizations. This idea forms the basis for the social ecology perspective on organizations.

Social ecology focuses attention on the communal arrangements created by organizations functioning in the same environment (Emery & Trist, 1973). It differs from the population ecology view of organizations (Aldrich, 1979; Hannan & Freeman, 1977) in that population ecology focuses on the environment as the primary determinant of organizational activity. The environment is hypothesized to affect organizations by requiring certain activities for survival. Organizations that do not meet the demands of the environment die. So population ecology views the organization as having little or no freedom to maneuver or control its fate (Astley & Fombrun, 1983).

By contrast, the social ecology perspective emphasizes how organizations link together to form a larger community that collectively provides a degree of independence and protection from environmental pressures and threats. Astley and Fombrun (1983) describe four different types of organizational collectives. *Agglomerate collectives* are clusters of organizations of the same species that compete for a limited supply of similar resources. *Confederate collectives* are found in highly concentrated industries where direct interactions are made possible by the small number of organizations. *Conjugate collectives* involve symbiotic relationships where the output of one organization is the input of another. And finally, *organic collectives* exist where resources flowing between apparently distant but symbiotically related organizations create a giant corporate web.

While this perspective may seem far removed from most of the activities of industrial and organizational psychologists, it nevertheless offers some potentially important implications for our programs and interventions. First, most organizational participants view other organizations on the environmental landscape in a fairly binary way. Other organizations are seen as either a threat to their business (e.g., a direct competitor, federal regulatory agencies) or irrelevant to their business (e.g., other organizations in different industries in the same community). This type of thinking, which characterizes other organizations as either competitors or not competitors, has been widely encouraged in many companies. For example, consider Lee Iacocca's consistent pounding of the Japanese automobile industry in company meetings, newsletters, and press conferences. What were employees to think when Chrysler entered into strategic alliance with Mitsubishi, first to buy cars from them to be sold under the Chrysler name, and then later to produce cars jointly? Chrysler employees will need to undergo significant changes in attitude and behavior if this alliance is to be successful.

Similarly, the recently announced alliance between IBM and Apple will require the convergence of groups of employees who have learned through years of competition that the other company is the enemy. This new alliance presents even more interesting problems for Microsoft, the world's largest software company, which markets software for both IBM and Apple Computer. Although its long-term alliance with IBM in systems software launched Microsoft to its current status as the major player in the software industry, the relationship between the two companies soured in their attempt to develop the next generation operating system on a joint basis. And despite its long-standing cooperative relationship with Apple in the development and of applications software for the Macintosh computer, Microsoft is now locked in a high-stakes legal battle with Apple over whether its Windows product violates Apple's proprietary rights to the graphical user interface found on the Macintosh. As strategic alliances become more common, employees are likely to find themselves wondering again and again, who's the friend and who's the foe?

This new focus on interorganizational cooperation and alliance has other implications for industrial and organizational psychology. Because cooperation among organizations has become increasingly important (Astley, 1984), the types of skill required of high-level executives may also change. Future selection of executives may place more emphasis on identifying individuals who can think cooperatively about their industry and community as a whole. They will also need skills in communicating and negotiating with executives in other organizations with which they must compete on one level and cooperate on a higher level.

Finally, the social ecology view also draws our attention to the likelihood of an increased level of personnel flow between organizations within a collective. This flow of people across organizations will require investment in training, appraisal, and reward systems that ensure that behavior is in concert with both organizational and collective goals.

Limitations of the Organism Metaphor

Both theoretically and empirically, the organism metaphor has proved much more fruitful than the machine metaphor. In particular, the organism metaphor captures the dynamic, adaptive, and developmental character of human organizations that is missing from the machine perspective. Like all metaphors, however, the organism metaphor breaks down when carried too far.

The most critical difference between a human organization and a biological organism is that the latter is physically connected. Our hearts and lungs cannot decide to pack up and leave for another body, but employees can. Katz and Kahn (1986) strongly emphasis this difference, arguing that social systems must invest far more energy than physical systems in system maintenance, that is, in simply holding themselves together. Max DePree (1989, personal communication), former chairman and CEO of Herman Miller Furniture, described this problem well: "The primary task of the leader is to intercept entropy." We will examine this problem of social systems and their maintenance later in the sections on the organization as family and as political arena.

Another important and related limitation of the organism metaphor is that organisms are limited in their capabilities by their genetic endowments. By contrast, organizations can, and do change their employees quite readily. Indeed, over time all of an organization's employees will eventually die and need to be replaced. This raises the possibility that organizations have a greater capacity for radical change than do biological organisms, and therefore perhaps greater adaptive fitness.

A final limitation of the organism metaphor is that organizations function only through the thoughts and actions of the people who create and maintain them. Given the cognitive abilities of humans, we should expect that our organizations will reflect the use of these abilities. Although we may certainly gain insights by comparing organizations to less cognitively capable organisms like Herschel the sea lion, the biological organism with the greatest likeness to human organization is probably a human being. Accordingly, our next metaphor for organization is the human brain.

Organization as Brain

The human brain is the most complex and unique structure in the discovered universe (Eccles, 1973). Its range of functions is awe inspiring. The same structure that caused Einstein's heart to beat and his eyes to blink also allowed him to construct the theory of relativity and to experience deep regret over his decision to encourage Franklin Roosevelt to initiate the research program that led to Hiroshima. Although the intellectual and creative capacities of Einstein's brain were unique, brains capable of sensing, perceiving, thinking, feeling, acting, learning, and self-reflection are not. They come with every person who participates in a human organization. It seems quite natural, then, to think about the organization as human brain.

When we recognize the presence and potential of human brains in organizations, some of the limitations of the machine and organism metaphors become readily apparent. While tremendous advances are being made in the area of artificial intelligence, it remains true that machines lack the creative, affective, adaptive, and self-reflexive capabilities of the human brain. Consequently, organizations designed as machines create conditions that not only fail to tap into available brain power but discourage its use (cf. Worthy, 1959).

Although the organism metaphor moves us closer to the idea that organizations are capable of brainlike functions such as adaptation to environmental conditions through learning processes, it falls short of the human brain metaphor in two ways. First, the organism metaphor can refer to any level of organism—from an amoeba to a human being. Since organizations are not made up of amoebas or sea lions, using such organisms as metaphors could cause us to overlook important characteristics of organizations composed of human beings. Second, the organism metaphor draws our attention to the organism as a whole in its struggle with the environment. The brain is viewed as that part of the organism that integrates and interprets incoming information, makes the key decisions, and directs the actions of the body. Applied to organizations, the metaphor may lead us to think that

every organization needs a single brainlike structure or function to direct everything else. Even though this may be true of hierarchical organizations such as Mintzberg's (1979) simple structure and machine bureaucracy, it does not seem to fit the other organizational species such as the professional bureaucracy or adhocracy. A different metaphor is needed to capture the decentralized, flexible, and innovative character of these types of organizations and to guide us in thinking about how to create them. The human brain metaphor holds promise for meeting these needs.

Characteristics of the Human Brain

The human brain's development, structure, and functioning provide an almost unlimited source of rich metaphors for understanding organizations. Our main interest, however, is to identify characteristics that provide the brain with its remarkable ability to learn, create, adapt, and self-organize. In an environment of turbulent change, these are precisely the abilities needed by organizations if they are to survive. The human brain may answer some of our questions about how to develop them. We describe four characteristics of brains that underlie these abilities: interconnectivity, dynamic patterns of brain activity, specialization and generalization, and self-organization.

Interconnectivity. Neuroscientists estimate that the human brain contains somewhere between 10 and 100 billion neurons. While this is an impressive number of parts, the number of connections between these parts is astounding. Each neuron has more than 1,000 synapses connecting it to other neurons. This means that there are somewhere between 10 and 100 trillion synapses packed in a structure that weighs about 3.5 pounds. This incredible level of interconnectivity is a hallmark of the human brain, differentiating it from the brains of lower animals. The elephant's brain, for example, is larger but much less richly interconnected.

Although the computer is commonly used as a metaphor for the brain, the two are wired quite differently. In fact, the neurons in the brain are not cabled together at all. Rather, they are biologically independent entities that communicate with each other via electrochemical transmissions at their synapses (Eccles, 1973).

All neurons have both excitatory and inhibitory synapses. The latter are particularly critical given the level of interconnectivity in the human brain. It is also interesting to note that the number of inhibitory synapses is correlated with brain complexity and capability, humans having the most inhibitory synapses. Without inhibitory transmissions, the simplest stimulus would create a tidal wave of excitation that would throw the brain into a prolonged epileptic seizure. This system of inhibition is also important because individual neurons often fire spontaneously without external stimulation. As Restak (1984) says, "the passage of neuronal impulses is a mixture of predictable and unpredictable, stable and unstable" (p. 40). Could this be a parallel to the actions of human beings in organizations?

Patterns of Brain Activity. Activation of the brain leading to even the most simple experience involves a "100-millionfold democracy" of neurons (Eccles, 1973, p. 202). Sherrington (1940, quoted in Eccles, 1973) was even more poetic in describing the active brain as "an enchanted loom, weaving a dissolving pattern, always a meaningful pattern, though never an abiding one, a shifting harmony of subpatterns" (p. 202). Eccles goes on to assert that the patterns of brain activity are so rich and complex that new forms of mathematics and physics may be required to make sense of them. Certainly, linear models of the sort we are so attached to in industrial and organizational psychology cannot begin to capture what happens in the brain.

These dynamic and complex patterns provide the brain with the flexibility needed for dealing with an environment that presents it with a broad spectrum of stimuli requiring a wide-ranging repertoire of responses. For example, the brain can be equally capable of pulling our hand quickly away from a hot stove, threading a needle, and working on a difficult problem for many years (e.g., a dissertation or a handbook chapter). As Restak (1984) observes, our environment is characterized by gradients of force, power, delicacy, and savvy. Our brains must be ready to respond in kind.

The important message here is that an understanding of the brain requires more than static snapshots of its anatomy or structure. As with any living system, it is the process of interaction or relationship among structures that is most revealing. And in the human brain, this process is one of continuously changing, almost infinitely complex patterns of neuron activity.

Specialization and Generalization. Research by brain scientists has identified specialized areas of the brain that are responsible for certain functions. For example, lesions in the region called Broca's area interfere specifically with a person's ability to speak. Damage to the limbic system affects emotional expression. But the kind of specialization found in the brain is different from that of machines.

In machines, specialized parts perform their functions, receiving input from preceding parts and sending output to the next parts in the causal chain. In the brain, however, specialized parts perform their roles in concert with many other parts of the brain. This is made possible by the dense network of synaptic connections described above. The result is simultaneous specialization and generalization of brain activity. Coordinated patterns of neuron activity between many areas of the brain make integrated experience possible; for example, we can carry on a conversation while walking with a friend. This comes easily and even automatically for those without disabilities. At the level of brain functioning, however, talking and walking at the same time require an incredibly complex and simultaneous integration of specialized brain functions such as seeing, smelling, hearing, understanding speech, thinking, feeling, speaking, and walking. The parts and their activities are so dynamically and richly connected with the whole that they can perform their specialized roles in harmony.

Studies of hemispheric lateralization (Sperry, 1968) provide another example of the brain's specialized/generalized character. The brain is composed of two hemispheres that in many ways are mirror images of each other. Connecting the two hemispheres is the corpus callosum, which is composed of 200 million callosal fibers. The level of communication across this hemispheric bridge is extraordinary—around 4 billion impulses per second. Differences in specialization or capabilities of the two hemispheres were discovered by Sperry through the study of "split-brain" patients whose corpus callosum had been severed to control epileptic seizures. The findings of these studies are well known. We mention them to reinforce the point that while the hemispheres may be specialized, the interconnectivity provided by the corpus callosum allows them to function in a generalized, fully integrated manner.

Self-organization. Another remarkable thing about the brain is its capacity for self-organization. Essentially, this means that the brain is capable of locally (i.e., at the point of need) changing its structure and process to increase or maintain its effectiveness in dealing with internal or external demands. At the microstructural level, there is evidence that changes in the patterns of transmission to a neuron stimulate structural changes in the size and number of its synapses. Increased activation such as that caused in the visual cortex by enriched visual stimuli can result in an increase in the number of dendritic

spines and synapses on the affected neurons, thus increasing complexity at the synaptic level. Reduced activation can cause atrophy and thus reduction of the number of synapses on a neuron. The resulting structural changes at the synaptic level are thought to be the physiological correlates of learning (Eccles, 1973).

A related example of the brain's capacity for changing itself to cope more effectively with incoming information occurs during the early stages of cortical development. Restak (1984) describes the process of maturation of cortical neurons and circuits as *competitive*. He states that "the competition of organisms for survival in the external world mirrors a competition in the inner world among neurons to fashion the circuits that will be most effective in the external world" (p. 47). Thus, it is the *fitness* of cortical circuits for coping with information presented by the internal or external environment that determines their survival. Again, this represents a learning process at the microstructural level of the brain.

A final example of the brain's learning and self-organizing capabilities is the well-known experiment by George Stratton in 1896 (cf. Restak, 1984). Seeking to answer the question of whether vision instructs touch or vice versa, Stratton wore prism glasses that inverted his visual world. Objects dropped to the floor would seem to fly up and vice versa. To pick up an object from the floor required looking up while bending down. After three days, Stratton had overcome his initial vertigo and total lack of coordination for performing even simple actions. More recently, H. Dolezal (1982) repeated Stratton's experiment, wearing the glasses for 17 days. By the end of the experiment, he was able to swim, ride a bike, and shake hands correctly. Although we cannot give an account here of how this adaptation process was accomplished at the level of brain physiology, we present Stratton and Dolezal's experiences to demonstrate the brain's capacity to suspend its assumptions about the nature of the physical world, make corrections based on sensory feedback, and reorganize its functioning around new assumptions. As we shall see, these capacities are more and more frequently being mentioned as critical to organizational survival and effectiveness in turbulent environments.

Brains, Organizations, and Industrial and Organizational Psychology

Before considering the organizational implications of the four specific characteristics described in the preceding section, it is important to note the significant contributions of March and Simon (1958) and Galbraith (1977) that have focused on organizations as information processing systems. This work is clearly founded on the brain metaphor and has contributed enormously to our understanding of how information processing requirements influence organizational structure and design. Because their work is so well known, we will not review it here but will pursue a somewhat different path within the same metaphor. What new insights into organizations can be gleaned from looking at them as if they were human brains with the characteristics we have described?

Interconnectivity in Organizations. If an organization is to be brainlike, it would have to be characterized by an incredibly rich and intricate network of interconnections among its people and groups. Turning back for a moment to Burns and Stalker's (1966) distinction between mechanistic and organic work systems, we can see significant differences in their interconnectivity. Because of their extensive and detailed rules and procedures prescribing how things are to be and who they are to be done with, mechanistic organizations would seem to be less brainlike than organic organizations. The latter are characterized by broad and flexible roles and open communications vertically and horizontally. The open-door policy, collaborative decision making processes, and informal gatherings of people from different departments at lunch or after work are specific examples of how interconnectivity is encouraged in organic structures.

It is important to remember, however, that the human brain is not simply a wide-open system of communication among neurons. Rather, it is dominated by inhibitory as opposed to excitatory synapses. This inhibitory capability is critical in creating effective patterns of information and preventing the "brainstorms" that would result if all the neurons began chattering with each other at once. There are lessons here for both mechanistic and organic organization designs. Mechanistic organizations, like the brain, are dominated by inhibitory responses. But while the brain's rich interconnectivity leaves many communication paths open, communication paths in mechanistic organizations tend to be rigid and severely constrained. As a result, information needed in different parts is not communicated directly and efficiently. Selective elimination of these inhibitory synapses—whether they be policies, rules, people, or norms—may increase the effectiveness of the system as a whole.

The prevalence of inhibitory synapses in the brain has a different message for organic organizations. Too much communication can create problems. It may be possible to go too far in encouraging wide-open communications and interconnections within an organization. When applied to organizations, Eccles' (1973) comment that even the simplest experience is based on the chattering of a "100-millionfold democracy" in the brain can strike fear into the heart of a CEO under pressure to improve a firm's financial results over the short-term.

The Microsoft Corporation provides an outstanding example of an organization that manifests the brainlike interconnectivity through its use of intraorganizational electronic mail. With this system, an entry-level software development engineer or field sales representative in Austria can send messages in real time 24 hours a day to Chairman Bill Gates or vice versa—and they do. Just how interconnected by e-mail are people in the company? A director level (about 3 levels removed from the chairman) manager can expect to receive from 100 to 250 e-mail messages per day. Not surprisingly, many regard the e-mail system as the company's greatest strength and its greatest weakness. As the company continues to grow at a phenomenal pace, there is continuing discussion about the need to teach people to write concise e-mail messages, to control "flame-mail" (i.e., messages in which people express anger and frustration on others without having to face them in person), and to discourage unnecessary "cc'ing" of messages, which is as easy as typing in a person or group's e-mail alias. Note that all of these prescriptions for making the company's e-mail system more efficient and effective have to do with introducing inhibition into the system. Nevertheless, few if any companies have been as successful as Microsoft in developing the brain-like quality of interconnectivity.

Briefly, what are the implications of organizational interconnectivity for industrial and organizational psychology? From a selection and development standpoint, it is clear that richly interconnected organizations will need employees with the cognitive ability to comprehend and benefit from information coming in from widely varying parts of the company. They will also need communication skills—both oral and written—that will allow them to pass information effectively to people and groups with expertise and interests different from their own. From a personality perspective, we speculate that at least one of the "big five" (Digman, 1989) will be related to performance in the highly interconnected organization: openness to experience. Our reasoning is that people will need to be broad-minded and curious about what is

happening in other parts of the organization and in the environment.

In addition to reinforcing individual job performance, the reward system, including performance appraisal and compensation, in the richly interconnected organization will need to support behaviors related to these same abilities, skills, and traits. In particular, the reward system will need to focus employee attention on and provide positive consequences for broad identification with the organization as a whole, willingness to share information and express opinions, and discernment and selectivity over what is shared.

Finally, if industrial and organizational psychologists are to function effectively in highly interconnected organizations, we will need to become more interconnected and less functionally isolated ourselves. Whether as internal managers or external consultants, we will need to become more well integrated with organizations at the strategic (cf. Golden & Ramanujam, 1985) and at the operational level. Isolation from the brainlike organization will drive us into obsolescence—we will be perpetually behind the wave of action in the organization.

Patterns of Activity in Organizations. In many respects, organizational activity is much like that of the brain. It involves complex patterns of interaction between many different people and groups, patterns with rhythms and melodies that exhibit both continuity and change when studied over-time. Some organizational scholars are adamant in their insistence that organization is process and that we have seriously overlooked this fact in our "empirical snapshots" (Burrell & Morgan, 1979, p. 54) approach to organizational research. Katz and Kahn (1986) criticize this approach as follows:

> A social system is a structuring of events or happenings rather than of physical

parts and it therefore has no structure apart from its functioning. A social system has no anatomy which can be identified when it is not functioning. When a social system ceases to function, there is no longer an identifiable structure. There has been no more pervasive, persistent, and futile fallacy handicapping the social sciences than the use of the physical model for the understanding of social structures.... So long as writers are committed to a theoretical framework based on the physical model, they will miss the essential social-psychological facts of the highly variable, loosely articulated character of social systems.... They will see social organizations in terms of machine theory, or they will go to the opposite extreme of interpreting social outcomes as individual decisions and behavior in organizational roles as the mere expression of individual personality. (p. 36)

We will examine the issue of organizational process in some detail in the next section dealing with organization as family. The most obvious implication of brain activity as patterned process for industrial and organizational psychologists is that we need to pay more attention to patterns of interaction over time among organizational members. This raises several issues. First, do we have and are we willing to use research methods capable of measuring and tracking interaction patterns in real time? Second, do we have theoretical models that tell us what aspects of interaction between members are significant in terms of individual, team, and organizational effectiveness? Third, are we willing to step in to the stream of organizational activity and observe it in a qualitative fashion long enough to develop such methods and models?

Simultaneous Specialization and Generalization in Organizations. This characteristic of the organization as brain flies directly in the face of scientific management principles and mechanistic approaches to organization design. It is quite consistent, however, with prescriptions for participative management and high-involvement work systems (Lawler, 1986). Both encourage employees to identify with their tasks *(specialization)*, with their work group *(first-order generalization)*, and the organization as a whole *(second-order generalization)*. In the brain, simultaneous specialization and generalization is achieved through highly efficient learning processes at the local level *(creating specialization)* and rich interconnectivity at the whole brain level *(creating generalization)*.

In organizations, the same thing can be accomplished by providing employees with the means and incentives to (a) develop special skills for dealing with their local task environments, (b) become more broadly aware of the activities of other areas of the organization, and (c) put that information to use in coordinating their own activities with others for the benefit of the whole. Implications for the types of people to be selected, skills to be developed, and behaviors to be appraised and rewarded flow directly from these prescriptions.

Morgan (1986) has suggested that self-directed work teams (Orsburn, Moran, Musselwhite, & Zenger, 1990) represent an attempt to put the "whole into the parts"—that is, to create simultaneous specialization and generalization like that found in the brain. The character of the teams in terms of specialization and generalization depends, however, on the organization's approach to building such teams. One approach is to build a team such that it contains all the varied, specialized skills needed for production and adaptation. Team members bring different specialized skills to the team and are encouraged to maintain their specialization. At the same time, they are asked to generalize by learning other specialized skills needed by the team and by involving themselves in the management of the team's business as a whole. The more common approach to creating self-directed work teams, however, involves identifying groups of people who perform the same specialized task (e.g., answering customer questions over the phone, assembling electronic components) and organizing them into work teams. Generalization occurs primarily in terms of the involvement of each individual in the management of the team and its business, not from developing additional specialized skills.

The split-brain research also has organizational implications. Looking back at these studies, it is interesting to note that the functional differences between the two hemispheres went undiscovered until patients with split-brains were studied. In those of us with an intact corpus callosum, the two hemispheres communicate so continuously and integrate their activities so effectively that their differences never become apparent. With this in mind, how would we expect an organization made up of individuals with intact corpus callosums to describe itself? Since the left hemisphere is typically responsible for speech and verbal expression, an organization's public self-descriptions are most likely to be expressed in the mode with which the left hemisphere is most conversant—that is, verbal, convergent, analytical, and linear thinking. Notice that this is precisely what we find in annual reports, recruiting brochures, and employee handbooks. As in the brain, however, this does not mean that the organization's "right hemisphere" is not active. It is just expressed in different ways. Tracy Kidder's (1981) book, *The Soul of a New Machine*, is an exquisite description and reminder of the creative capabilities of organizations. We will leave it to you, the reader, to ponder how an organization with a "split-brain" might act and express itself.

Self-organization in Organizations. While all brain characteristics we have discussed are impressive and important, self-organization may be the most so. Essentially, the brain is able to change its structure and processing on the fly as new information and problems present themselves. Furthermore, it is able to do this without the need for a central processing unit or executive function to guide the design changes. The areas most affected by the new information change on their own. Interconnectivity ensures, of course, that local changes are communicated to and represented in other parts of the brain that are less affected.

This sounds very much like the kind of organization that management gurus (e.g., Peters, 1988) and organizational consultants/researchers (e.g., Mohrman & Cummings, 1989) have been prescribing as the answer to today's turbulent, complex, diverse, and often hostile business environment. As Argyris and Schön (1978) have said, "there has probably never been a time in our history when members, managers, and students of organizations were so united on the importance of organizational learning" (p. 9). Since the topics of organization self-design and learning have been discussed by many writers, we will focus specifically on what insights are to be gained from the use of the brain metaphor. We have four.

First, learning in the brain is reflected in changes in its *structure* (synaptic complexity) and *process* (patterns of transmission). Similarly, we should expect and look for the effects of organizational learning and self-organization to be reflected in changes in the ways people think and in their patterns of interaction with others inside the organization. The latter are particularly important because it is changes in the pattern of activity and interaction that increase effectiveness. For industrial and organizational psychology, this implication again draws attention to our need to become more adept at describing dynamic interactive processes in organizations. When these processes are better understood, we will need to align our selection, training, and reward systems with those that are effective.

Second, learning in one area of the brain is shared with other brain areas. We would say this happens selectively, but given the importance of integration across most of the activities of the brain, we suspect that its threshold for assessing whether information is pertinent to other parts of the brain is much lower than what we observe in organizations. The *need to know*, we believe, is still too narrowly defined in most organizations.

Argyris and Schön (1978) cogently argued that individual learning is a necessary but not sufficient condition for organizational learning. Too often organizations seem to know less than their individuals and individuals seem to be unaware of relevant learning that has taken place in another part of the organization. Argyris and Schön (1978) define organizational learning as having occurred when effective changes in norms, strategies, and assumptions are encoded in the organization's "theory-in-use" and represented in the mental models (Senge, 1990) of most, if not all, organization members. The implication: Organizations learn only when they, like the brain, disseminate local learning in ways that have an adaptive effect on their working norms, strategies, and assumptions. The challenge for industrial and organizational psychology here is to develop ways of assessing an organization's theory-in-use and mapping its changes so the "living" theory can be disseminated most effectively through training and reinforced by the reward system. We also need to become more skilled at diagnosing and helping to break down barriers to organizational learning (Argyris, 1982, 1985).

Third, learning in the brain is decentralized. As the "competition" of cortical neurons to form the most effective circuits for dealing with the environment shows, the brain derives its plasticity and responsiveness by putting minimal constraints on local and specialized brain areas as they try to adapt to challenges of their specific environment. Morgan (1986) describes this design characteristic of brain as *minimum critical specifications*. Applied to organizations, this means that optimal flexibility for learning is created when an organization places only essential (for the good of the whole) constraints on the actions of local units.

This has particular implications for one of industrial and organizational psychology's most favored interventions: goal setting. The traditional view, which has received much empirical support, is that specific, difficult goals that are acceptable to employees lead to a maximizing of performance (Locke, Shaw, Saari, & Latham, 1981). By contrast, the brain's *minimal critical specifications* strategy provides only general parameters within which local brain elements are free to act. Research by Wood and his associates (Wood, Mento, & Locke, 1987) has questioned whether specific difficult goals should be used on complex tasks. Furthermore, Earley, Connolly, and Ekegren (1989) found that specific difficult goals can be less effective and possibly even detrimental to performance when people are learning a task. Using much the same logic, Morgan (1986) argues that designation of *noxiants*—those conditions we want to avoid at all costs—may be more effective in stimulating learning and creativity than designation of specific goals. Clearly, there are new theoretical and research challenges here.

Finally, brains have the capacity to think about what they have learned and how they have learned it. This makes it possible for organizations to use their experience to develop more effective learning strategies. A very simple example of this is the postmortem or lessons learned analysis conducted by many organizations following the completion of a major project. Such projects may involve *single-loop learning* (how could we have accomplished our goal more effectively?), *double-loop learning* (was this an appropriate goal?), or *deutero-learning* (How could we adjust our work process to increase our rate of learning during projects?). Argyris and Schön (1978) is an essential reference for those interested in understanding organizational learning processes. More recently, Senge (1990) has added a systemic perspective to Argyris's approach in building a view of what he calls the *learning organization.*

Limitations of the Brain Metaphor

The brain metaphor breaks down in at least three ways. First, the brain's capacity for simultaneous differentiation and integration is made possible by its fundamental unity of purpose—that is, the survival and adaptation of the individual. Despite the rhetoric of organizational mission, it seems unlikely that an organization could ever achieve the level of unity of purpose characteristic of the individual brain. Organizations are made up of individual human beings, each having different goals, values, needs, and interests. Thus, we need another metaphor to frame the organizational structures and processes through which individual differences of purpose and interest are mediated. The final two sections of this chapter deal with metaphors that assume the existence of separate but interdependent human beings in organizations.

A second limitation with this metaphor is that while the structures of the brain are well adapted to perform their specific functions, some (perhaps many) people are not well suited for life in the brainlike organization. A brainlike organization would require significant behavioral and attitudinal changes of many

employees. Morgan (1986) describes the difference this way: "Learning and self-organization generally call for a reframing of attitudes, emphasizing the importance of activeness or passiveness, autonomy over dependence, flexibility over rigidity, collaboration over competition, openness over closedness, and democratic inquiry over authoritarian belief" (p. 109).

For many people, these requirements run directly against the grain of their personalities and attitudes. So efforts to create a brainlike organization may run head-on into two problems: (a) resistance from those who cannot or will not adapt and (b) a shortage of people with the needed aptitude, traits, and attitudes.

The third weakness of the brain metaphor is that it can quickly become too technical for those of us who are not physiological psychologists. The best abstract metaphors are those that compare something with which the audience is very familiar to that which it would like to understand better. Frankly, without a great deal more study than the authors care to undertake, we can become more hopelessly lost in the brain than in organizations. For this reason, our next metaphor deals with something with which we are all intimately familiar: the family.

Organization as Family

Family is the stuff of good metaphor. For each of us, a moment's reflection on family surfaces a rich stream of creative ideas for thinking about other types of organizations. Consider, for example, how the following family-related images and concepts might be applied to work organizations: adopted child, blended families, arranged marriage, divorce, abusive family, family feuds, skeletons in the family closet, problem child, love and hate, growing family, empty nest, elderly parents, and death. Family is an organizational metaphor ripe with potential. Although we cannot explore all its possibilities here, we can take some first steps along the path.

Family Characteristics

What is a family? Poets, philosophers, social scientists, self-help experts, our parents, and even our children would be willing to answer this question. One perspective that we have found particularly useful in thinking about organizations, however, is that of family systems therapy.[*] Family systems therapy is based on open systems thinking and consequently has much in common with the organizational perspective described in our earlier section on organization as organism. There is a subtle and significant difference, however. Family systems therapy views the family as a fundamentally *social* system that is held together and defined by the process and patterns of interaction among its members. From this perspective, a family system can only be understood by observing it in action and identifying the principles by which action is organized within the system.

Because of their systems orientation, family systems therapists see families differently than do laypersons or individual-oriented therapists. For our purposes here, we will present five important characteristics or principles that family systems therapists look for in their work with families. These include: (a) a systems perspective and homeostasis, (b) subsystems and boundaries, (c) triangles and triangulation, (d) symmetry, and (e) family adaptation.

Systems Perspective and Homeostasis.
At the core of family systems therapy are two basic assumptions or principles. The first is a radical adherence to a systems perspective—that is, to viewing the family as an interdependent system of relationships. From this perspective, individual behavior can only be understood by examining how it fits into a broader pattern of interaction within the family as a whole. Generally speaking, the family systems therapist sees no individual saints or sinners. Saintly or sinful behaviors of individuals are seen as elements in a pattern of family interaction.

The second principle is that a family system is oriented toward self-preservation. As an open system, the family is subject to continuously changing inputs from both internal and external sources. Attempts by family members to cope with these changes will be perceived as either consistent with or in violation of the system's current transaction rules. Because of the family's instinct for self-preservation, behaviors that violate the rules trigger a homeostatic or balance-restoring response from the family system to bring the deviant behaviors back in line. The ways in which families restore homeostasis and avoid change are amazingly varied and creative. These detours or escape routes often become the presenting problems in therapy.

Adaptation of a family system to new circumstances requires an often painful, temporary disabling of the family's homeostatic mechanisms. This is necessary for family members to try out new behaviors and create more adaptive transaction rules. Paradoxically, the family must risk its integrity to maintain its integrity. It must live through the anxiety and confusion that accompany the release of old rules to search for and find new ones.

These principles are clearly exemplified in the concept of the *identified patient* or IP. When families come to therapy, they frequently identify one family member as the source of their discomfort and unhappiness: a spouse having an affair, a child in trouble at school, a depressed or substance abusing parent, and so on. If the therapist can "fix" this person, the family says, their problems will be solved.

---

[*]We recognize that the field of family systems therapy is comprised of many different theoretical and therapeutic schools. Our presentation is admittedly oversimplified and eclectic, but our intention is simply to stimulate the reader's interest in pursuing the family metaphor by delving deeper into the family systems literature (cf. Bowen, 1978; Friedman, 1985; Minuchin, 1974, 1981; Nichols & Everett, 1986).

The family systems therapist, however, resists this individual-focused diagnosis. The troublesome behavior of the IP is viewed as an effort by the family to maintain homeostasis and preserve its current rules. For example, a family presents its teenage son who is using drugs as the IP. Rather than focusing on the son as the problem, the family systems therapist reframes the son's behavior as an expression of the whole family system. This leads to questions about how the son's behavior is linked to the behavior of other family members. By looking at the problem from this perspective, the therapist may discover, for example, that the son's drug use is often preceded by periods of stony silence between his parents. When he gets in trouble, his parents start talking again long enough to focus on his problem. Observing this pattern, the family systems therapist might interpret the son's drug problem as providing the parents with a way of deflecting their marriage-related tension onto their son, thus allowing them to avoid dealing directly with their own conflict. This process may work to keep the couple's current transaction rules in effect; for example, they may have implicit rules dictating that negative feelings about each other are wrong and therefore should not be discussed. Although the son's drug abuse clearly introduces a whole new set of problems into the family, it "works" in that the rules governing the parent's marital subsystem are protected and perpetuated. In this case, treating the son's drug problem without addressing the three-way interaction pattern is like trying to cure strep throat with a lozenge rather than an antibiotic.

Subsystems and Boundaries. Another important principle of family systems therapy is concerned with subsystems and boundaries. Minuchin (1974) argues that families differentiate themselves into subsystems, each of which has its own functions to perform. The primary subsystems within the family are the spousal, parental, sibling, and individual subsystems. Observing these subsystems in action, the family systems therapist is concerned with the ways in which subsystem boundaries are and are not maintained. Do the different subsystems allow each other to work independently to perform their tasks or do they interfere with each other? For example, can spouses spend time alone with each other without being constantly interrupted by children? Are siblings allowed to work through their arguments or disagreements without immediate intervention by a parent at the first sign of trouble? Are individuals given the opportunity to express their personal opinion or make an independent decision without being criticized, attacked, or made to feel guilty by others in the family? Do parents fail to negotiate their disagreements about limits for children, thus ending up siding with one or more of the children rather than with each other?

The boundaries between family subsystems are, in fact, transaction rules about who interacts with whom, how, when, and on what topics. Minuchin (1974) describes boundaries between subsystems as being diffuse, open, or closed. Families with diffuse internal boundaries are enmeshed, meaning that it is difficult or impossible for one subsystem or individual to think, feel, or act independently of the others. Emotions and information are transmitted from person to person, quickly activating the whole family.

Closed boundaries between family members or subsystems are the result of transaction rules that reinforce autonomy at the expense of togetherness. A child crying for help, for example, might be ignored by its brothers and sisters in a sibling subsystem with closed boundaries. Relationships between family members and across subsystems are cool and distant.

If we make the assumption that the tasks of family life vary in the degree to which they require separateness and togetherness, family or subsystem boundaries that are inflexibly and nonnegotiably closed or diffuse will, depending on the task, create performance problems. The alternative is open boundaries. Families with open, flexible boundaries have transaction rules that reinforce open and honest communication, compassion without overidentification, and recognition of individual needs for both independence and involvement. When family members or subsystems need to function separately, the transaction rules support firmer boundaries. When the task requires cooperation or togetherness, transaction rules allow a relaxing of the boundaries.

Triangulation and Triangles. Dyads in families are viewed by family systems therapists as inherently unstable. When two family members find themselves embroiled in a conflict that cannot be resolved using their existing transaction rules, there is a powerful tendency for one or both to draw a third person into the fray. This process of triangulation resulting in a structural triangle manifests itself in many different forms. All triangles, however, serve the purpose of reducing the tension or anxiety between the original pair and restoring homeostasis to the system. One kind of common triangle develops when the dyad detours their own conflict by focusing on the problems of a third person. The father–mother–drug-abusing-son triangle described earlier is an example.

Triangles represent one way in which the family tries to keep itself together—that is, to preserve its transaction rules or organizing principles even when these rules have become obsolete. Paradoxically, in using triangles to hold itself together, a family may sow the seeds of its ultimate destruction. When the family's life space (Lewin, 1935) changes in fundamental ways, old transaction rules no longer work. Something will eventually give, either the rules or the family itself. By providing the family with temporary relief from conflict-generated anxiety, triangles redistribute energy within the family such that the heat needed to produce change within a dyad or subsystem is never concentrated enough to catalyze the needed transformation of the family's transaction rules.

Symmetry. We have seen that the process and structure of a family is defined by unique transaction rules. But the rules themselves can be seen as adhering to higher level principles characteristic of all systems: entropy, equifinality, law of requisite variety, and so on. One such general systems principle that is helpful in understanding family process is the principle of symmetry.

Symmetry in family process refers to the idea that homeostasis is maintained in a family system because all behavioral or emotional forces are balanced out or neutralized by opposing forces of equal intensity. This is the *parity or complementarity* principle that has allowed scientists to predict the existence of unseen particles or forces in a physical system from calculations of what forces must be present in order to hold the observed system in balance (cf. Friedman, 1985).

The principle of symmetry is crucial in moving away from an individual-focused understanding of family life toward a systems perspective. A couple comes into therapy with the wife complaining that her husband is emotionally distant and nonexpressive. The individual-oriented therapist might diagnose the husband's personality as introverted and analytical. The systems therapist, by contrast, might ask why the husband isn't even more distant and nonexpressive than he appears to be. What forces are maintaining his behavior at the observed level of distance from his wife? The principle of symmetry leads us to assume that the husband's behavior is being balanced by other unarticulated, countervailing forces in the family system. For example, the unarticulated force may be the wife's pursuit of her husband with an intensity equal to that with which he distances, thus cancelling out the effects of the two forces and maintaining the current balance or distance between them. This leads the therapist to ask the following question: What would happen if she stopped pursuing him? The reduction of her pursuing force would immediately alter the balance of the system, increasing the distance between them. Would he then stop retreating and move back toward her to restore the balance? Note that application of the symmetry principle in this case suggests that intervention could focus on coaching the wife, who is presumably the one with the most interest in changing the relationship, to change her behavior. The success of this strategy may depend on the wife's capacity for what Bowen (1978) describes as self-differentiation, which we will discuss momentarily as a key aspect of the family adaptation process.

Wherever we see a family member behaving· in an extreme manner, the symmetry principle predicts that other family members are doing something—perhaps subtle—that maintains homeostasis or balance in the system as a whole. In addition to pursuer and distancer, other common forms of symmetry that are seen in families are responsible and irresponsible, giver and taker, spendthrift and tightwad, optimist and pessimist, anxious one and reassuring one, symptomatic one and healthy one, good cop (permissive) and bad cop (strict), favorite and black sheep.

Family Adaptation and Change.   The proximal goal of family systems therapy is to help families develop new interaction patterns and rules that will allow them to accommodate internal and external changes such that the family as a whole and as individuals can perform their life tasks in a more effective and satisfying way. Beyond this proximal goal of helping the family deal with their immediate situation, family systems therapists also try

to help families become more capable of learning and adaptation on their own. There are several principles that are particularly useful in helping families achieve both these goals.

First, learning and adaptation require that the family take steps outside the comfort zone circumscribed by their existing transaction rules. To do so is to experience anxiety, fear, and confusion. This predictably sends the family scurrying back into their comfortable but ineffective interaction patterns. When one member of the family dares to challenge the rules, the other family members will step up the pressure on him or her to "support the family" or "stop being so self-centered." If the family member persists in violating the rules, the family's behavior can be expected to deteriorate over the short-term but improve in the long-term as the system reorganizes itself around the new movements (often characterized in the family systems literature as a "dance") of the pattern-breaker. Helping the family understand that the discomfort and anxiety during this transition period is essential to improvement is a key task of the therapist. Many families terminate therapy when change-related pain increases, blaming the therapist for making them even more miserable than they were before they began therapy. Termination thus enables them to escape from their anxiety, restabilize the family system, and preserve their dysfunctional transaction rules.

A second principle that is helpful in facilitating family system adaptation is that stress typically increases a family's tendency to create linear explanations for their problems. Often this explanation comes in the form of a diagnosis scapegoating one family member as the problem (i.e., the identified patient), thus reducing their ability to see the systemic nature of their current difficulties. To deal with this tendency to diagnose individual behaviors as the cause of the problem, the therapist will attempt to shift the family's focus away from the IP and toward previously overlooked behavior patterns or reactions of other family members. This defocusing effort will often involve consideration of the extended family system of the spouses and the ways in which this extended family may be influencing current nuclear family interactions and rules (Nichols & Everett, 1986).

To this point, our description of family adaptation has focused on system principles and processes. There is, however, an individual difference variable that some family therapists regard as critical to assessing a family's capacity for change and to developing an intervention strategy. Bowen (1978) argues that a family's capacity for change is determined by the degree of self-differentiation of its members. *Self-differentiation* is the degree to which a family member is capable of nonanxiously defining and asserting his or her own goals and values in the face of pressures for togetherness or conformity. Moreover, a highly self-differentiated family member is able to assert his or her individuality without disconnecting or distancing him or herself from others in the family. This ability to be simultaneously separate and connected under stress allows the individual to: (a) behave in ways that violate the family's existing, nonadaptive rules, (b) withstand homeostatically driven pressures from other family members to change back, (c) remain in the system, making it impossible for other family members to continue behaving in accordance with the old rules, and (d) encourage or even force others to try out new behaviors and to create new rules.

For these reasons, maximum leverage for change lies with the most self-differentiated member of the family. Following this principle, Bowen advocates an intervention strategy organized around coaching and supporting this individual in how to change his or her behavior to precipitate transformation of the family's transaction rules. In a family that lacks such members, Bowen believes there is a definite limit on capacity for change—a limit that should be considered in setting therapeutic goals and expectations. We mention this here because it parallels important questions about capacity for change and transformation in work organizations—questions that we examine in the following section.

Families, Organizations, and Industrial and Organizational Psychology

Since both families and work organizations are social systems, it is not a long stretch to identify similarities between the two. Nevertheless, the emphasis in family systems therapy on dynamic family process differs significantly from the machine and organism metaphors that dominate the organizational perspective of most industrial and organizational psychologists. Consequently, this metaphor holds the promise of fresh ideas to stimulate our theory, research, and practice.

Organization as Process. Like Katz and Kahn (1986), Burrell and Morgan (1979) have criticized much of contemporary organizational research for its tendency to ignore the process-based character of social systems. In their words, most of our research consists of "a host of empirical snapshots of reified social structures" (p. 54). With its strong emphasis on family as process, family systems therapy calls us back to a dynamic and interactive view of organizations. We can only begin to speculate on how such a shift in point of view might affect industrial and organizational psychology, but we believe that the effects could be interesting and even profound. For example, if we were to view organizations as transactions over time between participants, how would we think differently about selection, training, performance appraisal, and compensation systems? Would we begin to understand why, for example, Dunnette (1985, personal communication) would speculate that performance appraisal systems have a half-life of two years? Would we gain insights into why the half-life of many training programs is even shorter? Would we be better positioned to facilitate the successful implementation of our state-of-the-art HR systems that often end up on the shelf gathering dust with other expensive technical reports? Perhaps.

Organizations as Homeostatic Systems. The idea of work organizations as systems is hardly new to industrial and organizational psychologists. But our bias toward the individual prevents us from seeing the full implications of the systems perspective.

Management assessment and development is one area in which we might do things differently from a systems perspective. Industrial and organizational psychologists spend significant time and money in the creation and study of assessment and development centers for managers and executives. Using a full toolbox of psychometric and behavioral diagnostic instruments, we inspect a manager for personological or skill-based strengths and defects. Then we assist this person in creating an individualized development plan. An underlying assumption of this process is, of course, that it is the traits, aptitudes, and skills of the individual that lead to varying degrees of success or effectiveness. All this occurs with very little, if any, attention paid to the characteristics of other individuals in the manager's work system and the transaction patterns and rules by which that system currently functions. For example, how would we do assessment and coaching for a problem manager differently if we were to think like a family systems therapist about work organizations?

Consider the possibility that a manager referred to an industrial and organizational psychologist for his "abrasive personality" may be acting as the identified patient on behalf of his work group to help preserve the group's homeostasis and existing transaction rules. Where this is the case, assessment and coaching may be effective in stimulating and supporting the manager's individual development in general, but any change in the manager's behavior is likely to be resisted in overt or covert ways by the group.

Interestingly, the systems perspective also suggests an alternative approach to dealing with the problem manager. Rather than coaching the manager to change, we could coach or otherwise induce other members of the system to change their behavior vis à vis the manager. Assuming that all behavior in the system is connected, we would expect that changes in the behavior of the manager's boss, peers, or direct reports will elicit changes in the manager's behavior.

As consultants, we have dealt with a number of situations in which subordinates are virtually obsessed with their manager's shortcomings: interpersonal insensitivity, technical or managerial incompetence, poor communication skills, lack of vision, and so on. The family systems concept of the IP suggests different questions than would typically be asked by the individual-oriented industrial and organizational psychologist in this situation. From a systems perspective, for example, we might ask any of the following questions: If we were to fix this manager today, what problems or challenges would remain for this group? How would your manager say that your behavior contributes to this perception? Besides changing your manager's skills or personality, what could you or the group do to overcome the problems that appear to be created by her behavior? These questions often help the members of the group to focus less on their manager and to begin to see that he or she is only one piece of the puzzle and that their own behavior plays a contributing role in keeping the organization stable and often dysfunctional.

The homeostatic systems and identified patient concepts can also be helpful at a higher level in understanding why some departments or divisions are viewed by others in the organization as chronic problems. Human resource departments, for example, often become scapegoats for problems that are systemically maintained. In growing organizations, the recruiting function may be under almost continuous attack by line departments for its inability to attract strong candidates for open positions. If the line department—product development, for example—has a reputation on the street for burning out and underpaying its scientists and engineers, no amount of recruiting sophistication or effort is likely to produce quality candidates for this department. Human resources is virtually condemned to fail. Consider though how blaming HR for the problem could be functional for the organization and its existing transaction rules. If the company's transaction rules dictate that (a) product development is king, (b) 80-hour work weeks for scientists is expected, and (c) the opportunity to develop state-of-the-art products is its own reward, then blaming HR for recruiting problems makes eminent sense. Without HR as the identified patient in this case, the organization would be forced to confront the fact that the transaction rules that made it successful in its early years have become obsolete as the company has grown. Indeed, a family system therapist looking at this situation would predict that if HR were exonerated of its alleged incompetence, the system would find another culprit to replace it. Thus, the organization's stability would be preserved, but at the expense of its long-term viability.

Subsystems and Boundaries. It is interesting to note how the issue of system boundaries has been investigated by industrial and organizational psychologists, but primarily as an individual-oriented question; that is, what are the personality characteristics of more or less effective "boundary-spanning" individuals? True to the family systems tradition, we consider some of the more organizational or systemic implications of these ideas.

For industrial and organizational psychologists working either in or through the HR department in an organization, boundary issues are critical in the design and implementation of HR policies and programs. Cascio (1982), in describing the low status of HR departments 20 or so years ago, suggested that the HR director could be identified by looking for the person carrying the watermelon at the company picnic. Although this view of HR appears to be changing, imagine the difficulties of having a significant impact on HR policy and practice through the HR channel in an organization that has transaction rules (and therefore boundaries) dictating that HR can only become involved with line organizations with regard to personnel record keeping and mechanical implementation of procedures. We believe that this disengagement between HR and line organizations can be and has been a significant obstacle to disseminating and putting into practice the sound ideas that the field of industrial and organizational psychology has to offer.

Internal HR departments may also suffer from the opposite problem: enmeshment with line organizations. In an effort to break away from the isolation and paper-pushing of the past, HR departments have moved quickly toward a more client-service orientation. But an attitude of responsiveness and service can easily give way to overwhelming workload and reactivity unless HR leadership is able to define its boundaries by communicating its mission, priorities, and expertise to other groups in the organization. It is the creation and maintenance of well-defined yet open boundaries that allows a group such as HR to achieve both efficiency (i.e., stability) and effectiveness (ie., adaptability).

Industrial and organizational psychologists involved in team building interventions and team research could find the concepts of boundaries and subsystems useful. The idea that subsystems in families (e.g., spousal, parental, sibling) are formed to perform different tasks or functions has direct implications for work team development. Most family therapists would maintain that in "healthy" families, a primary function of the parental subsystem is to provide leadership in the form of family goals, values, norms, and ground rules. When this function is abdicated by parents or children are invited in as equal partners in the leadership of the family, many family systems therapists would predict problems for the family. To what extent does this hypothesized need for a subsystem set apart to provide leadership generalize to work teams as well? Research on the relationship of boundary-maintaining transaction rules between team leaders and members and team effectiveness would be most interesting and practically helpful. Answers to this question would also be relevant to the development of self-directed work teams (Orsburn et al., 1990).

Organizational Triangles. Family systems therapists maintain that the triangle is the elementary unit of interpersonal systems (Lerner, 1989). In our experience, triangles are like politicos in organizations—once you begin to look for them, they're everywhere. Here are just a few of the ways in which triangles develop and operate in work systems.

One of the most common types of triangles in organizations is the *detouring* triangle. Such triangles are readily observable in the halls, cafeteria, restrooms, and parking lots of virtually any organization. It is there that many of the things people wish they would have said in a meeting actually get said. When conflict or tension between two people rises beyond what is currently tolerable, one or both of them will disengage and triangulate a third party (e.g., a favored peer, a subordinate, a spouse, or best friend). By expressing my frustrations and fears about Sue (my boss) indirectly to Joe (my confidante), I reduce the level of tension in my relationship with Sue. This short-circuits a direct confrontation with Sue, which I fear might lead to negative and unpredictable results. It also keeps the transaction rules of my relationship with her intact (e.g., tell the boss

only what she wants to hear and never disagree with her). Triangling Joe into the system works to preserve the stability of the system, but it prevents potentially healthy changes in my relationship with my boss.

Industrial and organizational psychologists can easily become the unwitting third leg of such triangles. Suppose there is growing tension between a group's manager and its staff. One way to temporarily relieve this pressure is to call in a consultant to do an opinion survey or to implement team-building. The simple introduction of the consultant into the system creates a triangle that allows the manager and the staff to redistribute the anxiety resulting from their conflict. They may welcome the consultant with open arms and proclaim their desire to work through the problems. But unless the consultant recognizes and deals with the triangulation process, he becomes a stabilizing factor in the system, helping the group preserve its homeostasis and avoid the pain associated with direct confrontation of its problem.

Symmetry in Organizations and Work Groups. Symmetry or balance can be a powerful, often unseen, force affecting behavior in work systems. A rule of thumb in family systems therapy is that wherever there are observable extremes of behavior or emotion, one should look into the system for opposite, counterbalancing behaviors or emotions. While the deviant behavior is being presented at center stage in a work group, the symmetry principle suggests that we look behind the scenes for behavior of a stagehand that prevents the system from flying completely out of control.

At the organizational level, we can observe symmetries in the relationship between HR departments and line organizations. A marketing organization's "irresponsible and self-serving" decisions regarding staff compensation may be balanced by HR's position as the organization's "responsible and organization-serving" guardian of its compensation system.

Would marketing really run amok on compensation if it weren't for HR's counterbalancing efforts? In manufacturing, would employees send defective assemblies on down the line (i.e., be irresponsible) if there were no quality assurance department to audit their work?

System symmetries are often revealed when organizations try to move toward a more participative, high-involvement culture. Overfunctioning, proactive, fully responsible supervisors and underfunctioning, reactive, "I just do my job" employees must learn that they each play a role in preserving a hierarchical, bureaucratic, machinelike workplace. From family systems theory, we should also expect that breaking up this symmetry confuses and threatens everyone involved, not just employees or supervisors. And, as many consultants to this process have observed, not everyone is comfortable with the new symmetry of high-involvement workplaces, which calls for more equal distribution of responsibility among supervisors and employees.

Facilitating Organizational and Team Transitions. There is much to be learned from family systems therapy about individual, group, and organizational change. One of the most important of these lessons is that significant change always involves a process of renegotiating transaction rules. Groups or organizations must not only have transaction rules—both formal and informal—appropriate for its immediate task, but they must have a process by which the effectiveness of the rules can be raised quickly and adjustments can be made efficiently. Satir (1972) calls the latter a family's "freedom to comment" rules. A family or a work organization in which only a handful are free to comment and only on some rules but not others will have tremendous difficulty remaining viable in a changing environment. We need more research on the social psychology of dissent in organizations and the impact of "freedom to comment" rules on organizational adaptation and effectiveness.

Another important lesson from family systems for industrial and organizational psychology is that things often get worse in a group before they get better. Whether introducing a new selection system or job redesign program, we should expect that the resultant disruption of system transaction rules will create a backlash from managers and employees. Expecting this resistance, providing opportunities for those affected to participate in system design and implementation, and helping the group to reinterpret confusion as a sign of movement and progress are all important in assisting the client group through this difficult period. We might also be on the alert for underreactions or uniformly positive reactions to our proposals and programs. If our objective for a new performance appraisal system is a significant change in the way managers and employees interact on performance and development issues, then no reaction or a completely positive reaction may be a bad sign. It may be that people are not clear about how the system will actually affect their transaction rules, therefore they are not threatened at all by what we are proposing. Or it may be that the group has learned that the best way to neutralize a potentially disruptive HR program is to voice full support for everything it entails—then ignore it. Like many of the other implications of family systems for our work in industrial and organizational psychology, this one calls for us to take a closer look at how our ideas are implemented over time in organizations.

The final implication of family systems theory for organizational and group change brings us back to an individual differences variable. As noted earlier, Bowen argues that a family's capacity for change hinges on the degree of self-differentiation among its members. We strongly suspect that this is equally true in work systems.

Weisbord (1987) cites three factors as key to assessing a group or organization's *potential for action:* (a) a leader who is committed to the need for change and who is willing to put him or herself at risk to make it happen, (b) people in the organization or group who recognize the need for change and who, like the leader, are willing to put their interests at risk, and (c) a significant business opportunity—either economic or technological. The first two factors seem consistent with Bowen's notion of self-differentiation. Again, however, it is apparent that wisdom from the organizational trenches has gone beyond our research base. Given the practical and theoretical significance of the organizational adaptation process, the opportunity to assess the potency of an individual differences variable with direct theoretical implications for system change should be seized by industrial and oganizational psychologists.

Limitations of the Family Metaphor

The comparison of families to work organizations breaks down at several points. First, families function primarily through informal structure—their unwritten transaction rules. Work organizations, particularly larger ones, have in addition a formal, public structure. Organizational charts, policy manuals, job descriptions, planning and budgeting systems, and work rules are some of the formal ways in which organizations attempt to channel employee behaviors and transactions in a consistent and coordinated manner. It seems likely that what we know about family dynamics will be most applicable to younger, smaller organizations that do not yet have a powerful formal structure. We could also argue that professional organizations (e.g., CPA firms, law firms, management consulting firms) that depend heavily on internal qualities of professionals (e.g., skills, interests, values, ethical standards) for coordination will also be more "familylike" than will large, bureaucratic, formal organizations. One interesting side

question here is the extent to which a company founder's values regarding the nature of the company-employee relationship and bureaucratic controls affects the importance of the firm's informal structure. The Boeing Company, for example, despite its huge size and strong formal structure, is still referred to by many employees as "Boeing's," a reference to the Boeing family that started and led the company for many years. In many respects, Boeing is still a family company with a powerful informal structure that dictates values, behavior, and boundaries.

A second limitation of the family metaphor is that which gives rise to the need for more formal structure in work organizations. People join and leave organizations more frequently and easily than they do their family. Explicit transaction rules and formal structure are therefore needed to assimilate changing participants as efficiently as possible. The fact that people can come and go in work organizations more easily than in families reflects an even more significant limitation of the metaphor. A basic reason for the existence of the family as a human institution is that human beings must be protected and nurtured through a much longer period of dependency than other animals. We live our early years in a state of almost complete dependency on our parents. This level of dependency—particularly emotional dependency—of individual on organization is rarely found in work organizations. Thus, the work organization is likely to be more loosely coupled than is the family. Our greater freedom to engage or disengage from our work organizations probably weakens the emotional and behavioral force of system effects such as triangling, symmetry, and disorientation during periods of organizational change. At the same time, there are organizations that consciously lure employees into a familylike identification with and dependency on the company. Schaef and Fassel's (1989) *The Addictive Organization* is an attempt to describe this phenomena.

The applicability of family systems concepts to work organizations seems to hinge on at least two key variables: the degree of task and emotional interdependency in the system and the relative potency of formal and informal structures in the organization. Furthermore, in situations where these factors make family systems concepts less applicable at the organization level, it still seems likely that the concepts will be helpful in understanding the dynamics of work groups within the organization. Clearly, we believe that family is a metaphor that can do much to inform and invigorate research and practice in industrial and organizational psychology.

Organization as Political Arena

In the presidential election of 1860, Abraham Lincoln soundly defeated Stephen Douglas, his long-time political rival, and southern democrat John C. Breckinridge by carrying every northern state. Lincoln won the election even though his name did not even appear on ballots in the South. Before his inauguration, however, South Carolina seceded from the Union to protest the election of the "Black President" and to protect the institution of slavery within its borders. In the weeks that followed, Congress tried but failed to prevent further secessions by working out a compromise on slavery. The central problem was that senators from the southern states were committed not only to the preservation of slavery, but to its extension into new territories. By February, 11 southern states had formed the Confederate States of America and were preparing to go to war against the Union. On April 12, 1861, the American Civil War began in Charleston Habor when Confederate forces fired on Fort Sumter.

Lincoln's primary objective in taking military action against the South was "to save the Union, and...not either to save or to destroy slavery." Lincoln continues: "What I do about slavery and the colored race, I do because I believe it helps to save the Union" (Basler,

1953–1955, vol. 4, p. 439). Lincoln's personal opposition to slavery was unequivocal: "I am naturally anti-slavery. If slavery is not wrong, nothing is wrong" (Basler, 1953–1955, vol. 4, p. 438). But as president, his responsibility to the Constitution and the nation came first. His priorities were founded upon his deep-rooted commitment to the principles on which the United States was founded and on his belief that an issue larger than slavery was at stake in this war.

> This issue embraces more than the fate of these United States. It presents to the whole family of man, the question, whether a constitutional republic, or a democracy...can, or cannot, maintain its territorial integrity. Nor is the struggle altogether for today; it is for a vast future.... On the side of the Union it is a struggle for maintaining in the world that form and substance of government whose leading object is to elevate the condition of men...to afford all an unfettered start, and a fair chance in the race of life. (Basler, 1953–1955, vol. 5, p. 53)

Lincoln's overriding concern for the preservation of the Union was the basis for protracted negotiations with the slaveholding border states of Kentucky, Maryland, Delaware, and Missouri, which had remained loyal to the Union. The president realized that an "anti-slavery war" could easily push at least three of these states over to the Confederate side. When it was suggested to him that the Union needed God on its side, Lincoln replied that he would like to have God on his side, but that he *must* have Kentucky. So in the spring and summer of 1862, Lincoln tried to persuade the border states to phase out slavery on a gradual, voluntary basis in return for federal compensation for their "property" losses. Their repeated refusals to compromise and Lincoln's growing awareness that freeing the slave population in the South was essential to the Union war effort led him, as commander in chief of the Union forces, to issue the Emancipation Proclamation on New Year's Day, 1863. While many rejoiced at this historic decision, northern democrats were furious, calling the proclamation unconstitutional and Lincoln a tyrant. To control growing opposition and dissention within the Union, Lincoln also invoked his military authority as commander in chief to suspend the constitutional right of *habeas corpus*, thus allowing the military to arrest and detain agitators suspected of undermining Union war efforts. Voices condemning Lincoln as a tryrant were raised again.

From a military standpoint, the first two years of the war went badly for the Union. Although the North's industrial capabilities and population far exceeded those of the South, the military brilliance of Confederate president Jefferson Davis and his generals exacted a bloody toll on the Union army. Lincoln's own lack of military expertise left him at a disadvantage when evaluating the performance of his own generals. General McClelland, for example, continually frustrated the president with his never-ending excuses and requests for more time and troops. True to his lifelong pattern of self-education, Lincoln worked to overcome this problem by reading extensively on military strategy and becoming directly involved in both strategic and tactical direction of the Union forces. Nevertheless, he was greatly relieved when, after hiring and firing general after general, he discovered General Ulysses S. Grant. He declared: "Grant is the first general I have had. You know how it has been with all the rest. They wanted me to be the general. I am glad to find a man who can go ahead without me" (quoted in Freedman, 1987, p. 108). The rest is history.

Characteristics of the Political Arena

In this illustration, we see an itinerant President Lincoln moving from one tension-filled and explosive situation to another, from the White House to the Capitol to McClelland's tent on the battlefield. Under scrutiny, each scene reveals itself to be a "political arena"—that is, a place where individuals or groups with differing beliefs or interests engage each other in a struggle to influence events and outcomes such that their own beliefs and interests are served. We will use Lincoln's political arenas to highlight the major characteristics of this metaphor.

Divergent Interests and Conflict.   First, as our definition states, political arenas are places or contexts in which interdependent people or groups disagree about the ends they will jointly pursue or the means by which they will pursue them. They dis-agree because they perceive themselves to have different interests. The political arena in which the North and the South clashed in 1860 was founded on their disagreement over slavery, a disagreement that was based on clear differences of interest between the two sides. For the southern states, slavery was a cornerstone of their economy and culture. Its abolition would cause an almost complete redefinition of the lives and fortunes of slave owners and slaves alike. By contrast, people in the North did not have a similar economic or cultural stake in slavery. Many did have an interest, however, in breaking up the South's dominance of Congress. As often happens in political arenas, however, these underlying and conflicting interests were kept in the background by the rhetoric of both sides. Defenders of the South's position argued that private property rights—including the right to own slaves—were guaranteed under the constitution. Abolitionists countered that slavery was a violation of the principle that "all men are created equal," as stated in the Declaration of Independence and that men so created could not be regarded as property. In this way, both sides were able to take what they believed to be "high moral ground" in this political arena.

Choice. A second characteristic of political arenas is choice. In human political arenas, the contestants have three alternative paths of action when conflict arises. First, like the northern states, they can choose *loyalty* by acceding to the interests and goals of the existing authority or power structure (i.e., the Federal government). Second, participants can choose to *exit* the arena to protect their interests or values. The secession of the southern states exemplifies this alternative. Third, participants can choose to *voice* their interests, concerns, needs, goals, and so forth by engaging in debate or negotiations with each other to determinewhat decisions are made and what actions are taken. This was the choice made by the slave-holding border states and by Lincoln's vocal critics in the North.

Power. Political arenas can also be characterized by the weapons of power or influence that are used by participants. Lincoln, for example, used four major weapons in his political arenas. First, he wielded the power of *authority* vested in the office of the president when he suspended *habeas corpus* and made the Emancipation Proclamation. Second, in presenting his case for the Union to the people and setting his priorities, Lincoln used the weapon of *ideology.* The opening lines of his Gettysburg address are a direct appeal based on the power of ideology: "Four score and seven years ago, our forefathers brought forth a new nation, conceived in liberty and dedicated to the proposition that all men are created equal." Third, in developing his own military *expertise,* Lincoln gained a weapon that increased his ability to influence the decisions and actions of the Union army while at the same time reducing his vulnerability to misinformation from his supposedly expert generals. Later on, though, the President was willing to give this power away when he deferred to the greater expertise of the loyal

General Grant. Finally, Lincoln was willing and able to *play politics*—that is, he did not hesitate to work in the gray areas of government to build strategic alliances or coalitions with those from whom he needed support. His understanding of the importance of the political process is illustrated in his negotiations with the border states.

Change Over Time. The fourth characteristic of political arenas is that the conflicts they contain change over time. Fierce battles are balanced by periods of calm and rest. An advantage at one time may be lost at a later time as protagonists bring new weapons, resources, or strategies into play. The dynamic quality of political arenas is illustrated by the early advantage of the southern states in the war due their greater military prowess. But the balance of power shifted as Lincoln used new weapons and made strategic moves (e.g., appointing Grant, recruiting liberated southern slaves to serve in the Union army) that the South could not counter. The shifting nature of the conflict within this arena is also illustrated by the growing opposition of northern democrats to Lincoln's war policy. This opposition peaked with the Emancipation Proclamation. In sum, we need videotape rather than snapshots to capture the action in political arenas.

External Stakeholders. The fifth characteristic of a political arena is that it usually involves and affects more than just the immediate and visible contestants. While our Lincoln illustration focuses on the political arenas in which the president was directly engaged, it is obvious that the American people were more than just spectators at the arena. Through the electoral process they had selected the president and the other government officials to represent them in the political arena of government. Consequently, the decisions made in this arena preserved the Union but cost over 620,000 citizens their lives.

Political Arenas, Organizations, and Industrial and Organizational Psychology

The political arena metaphor draws our attention to a number of facets of organizations that are not revealed by the metaphors we have examined so far. As we shall see, each of the five characteristics of organizations as political arenas has interesting and significant implications for industrial and organizational psychology.

Interests and Conflict in Organizations.   First and foremost, organizations as political arenas are places in which individuals pursue their own interests—some of which are common and some are not. In our efforts to understand an organization, then, we must inquire about the unique and shared interests of the different participants in the organizational arena. Furthermore, we should expect conflict to be an inherent feature of organizational life because, taking the political arena perspective, organizations are "arbitrary focuses of interests, marketplaces whose structures and processes are the outcomes of the complex accomodations made by actors exchanging a variety of incentives and pursuing a diversity of goals" (Georgiou, 1973, p. 291).

One implication of this point of view concerns the common prescription that HR programs should be aligned with organizational goals. The political arena metaphor suggests that this may be easier said than done. In a political arena, whose goals are the organization's goals? Where there is disagreement over goals, how do we decide which ones to align our programs with? While the machine, organism, and brain metaphors would have us continue to search for the "real" or "true" values of the organization, the political arena metaphor suggests that such a search may come up empty-handed. Following this metaphor, we should expect disagreement, conflict,

and ongoing negotiation over which goals and means the organization should pursue.

What then does *organizational alignment* of HR programs mean? If it means gaining the resources and support necessary to make the program work as intended, then alignment involves ensuring that HR programs serve the interests of those who have the power and influence needed for program success. Since these influential people or groups may have divergent interests, industrial and organizational psychologists should be prepared to step into the arena as facilitators and, indeed, as contestants (we have our own interests that are relevant) to negotiate agreements needed to ensure support from those in the arena. While the technical or scientific purity of the program may be reduced in the course of such negotiations, its impact on the organization will be enhanced.

Choices in Response to Conflicting Interests.   Loyalty of the parts to the whole is assumed in machines, organisms, and brains. And although family members can try to change or even leave the family, the psychological ties that remain are often strong and enduring (but not necessarily positive). In the organization as political arena, however, we can expect to see a fluid, dynamic pattern of choices with respect to loyalty, exit, and voice. These choices can be assumed to move in concordance with changing perceptions of the costs and benefits of organizational membership.

The meaning of *exit* from organizations is self-evident. Like the Southern states in 1861, people choose to leave organizations when they perceive that their interests are not being well served, that their efforts to change the situation will not be effective, and they believe their interests will be better served elsewhere. By contrast, to choose *loyalty* in an organization is to submit to the interests or demands of the organization, presumably because it is in one's perceived interest to do so. To be loyal is to accede to the interests of those currently in power. This was the choice of the slaves who served their masters without protesting or running away. Loyal members provide an organization with the essential quality of stability and continuity over time. Finally, organizational participants choose *voice* when they attempt to change the system to make it more responsive to their interests or desires. As we mentioned earlier, this was the choice of those who protested Lincoln's policies. Loyalty is a conservative choice; voice is a radical choice. Exit is the most radical choice of all.

These alternative responses of participants to the organization's political processes raise several interesting questions for industrial and organizational psychologists. In designing new HR policies and programs, for example, could it be valuable to consider how these changes are likely to affect the interests of loyal employees? Could a new compensation or performance appraisal program radicalize this silent majority? Would the organization be more effective if these employees were to speak up rather than remain passively loyal?

We might also consider studying exit (i.e., turnover) as a political process. Presumably, people leave an organization because their interests are not being sufficiently satisfied and they see exit as a more attractive alternative than loyalty or voice. Careful consideration of the unmet interests of those choosing to leave the organization may provide significant insights into whose interests are being served by the organization. If exiting employees complain of a lack of challenge in their jobs, for example, it may be an indication that the challenging tasks are being monopolized by those who remain.

Finally, we need more research on employee voice and its relationship to organizational change. Without people who are willing to stay to try to change the organization, adaptation to changing conditions simply will not occur. Too often, though, managers and HR practitioners regard employee voice as a force to be controlled and minimized. While employee voice can certainly be disruptive, it is also essential to the survival of organizations in turbulent environments.

Sources of Power and Systems of Influence in Organizations. As contestants in the political arenas of organizations, organization members try to satisfy their own interests and avoid discomfort by influencing the actions and decisions of others. To influence others effectively, Mintzberg (1983b) asserts that three things are necessary: (a) a source of power, (b) the will to use it, and (c) skill in using it. As we showed earlier, President Lincoln influenced others by drawing on each of four sources of power that are commonly found in political arenas: authority, ideology, expertise, and politics. His actions in the situations we described are evidence that Lincoln had the will to use his available power to achieve his objectives. Nevertheless, he also demonstrated an awareness of the dangers of using more power than necessary to influence others. To paraphrase Ury (1991), political skill involves using power to bring others to their senses, not to their knees. Lincoln's understanding of this principle was illustrated by his repeated efforts to compromise with the border states. Although these efforts eventually failed, Lincoln only used his power to free the slaves in the South with the Emancipation Proclamation—thus violating the interests of the border states—when his other less potent options had run out. In fairness, however, it would be difficult to call Sherman's march through Georgia an exercise in political moderation.

Thinking of an organization as a political arena draws us inevitably to two questions: (a) Where does power come from in this organization? and (b) who has how much of this power? In answering the first question, it is helpful to think of the four sources of power mentioned above as wells that vary in depth from one organization to another or even across subunits in a single organization.

For example, in many organizations, the well of authority runs very deep. Hierarchical position and the formal authority vested in that position are the primary factors in determining who can get whom to do what. Mintzberg (1983b) has observed that authority is an integrative force in organizations. It puts the most power in the hands of the priveleged few at the top of the organization, thus allowing them to channel member behavior along a common path. It is also a conservative force in the organization because those with the power to change things may not want to risk the loss of power that radical changes can bring.

Ideology is an important source of power in many organizations. In such organizations, influence over others is gained by convincing them that one's favored action or decision is dictated by the shared values, beliefs, or principles of the organizations members. Like authority, ideology is an integrative and conservative force. Appeals and influence attempts based on ideology are usually calls to unity under the organization's ideological banner. It channels behavior within the boundaries of the ideology. Ideology is a conservative force in that the organization's structure and process must remain consistent with its basic tenets and traditions. Radical change of an organization with a long-standing ideology is likely to be difficult. Unlike the authority-dominated organization, however, those dominated by ideology distribute power widely. All "true believers" can call upon the power of the organization's ideology to prevail in its political arenas.

Expert power is dominant in organizations whose survival and effectiveness depend on their ability to deal with complex, specialized problems that only experts can solve. In the political arenas of high-tech organizations or hospitals, for example, engineers and doctors have tremendous influence because their skills are essential, unique, and nonsubstitutable (Mintzberg, 1983). Unlike authority or ideology, expertise tends to be a disintegrative force in organizations. It distributes power horizontally to those with the skills needed at a particular point in time. Since the loyalties of these experts are often divided between their discipline and the organization, actions and decisions influenced by expert power may not be good for the whole. In this way, power scattered meritocratically around an organization can create a centrifugal force which, if not balanced by some degree of authority or ideology, can tear it apart.

In organizations dominated by politics, the arena becomes a "few holds barred" scramble for personal influence. Furthermore, since authority, ideology, and expertise are weak sources of power in such organizations, a different group of contestants may enter the arena. The only eligibility requirements are that one have the will and the skill to play a variety of political games whose rules lie outside the "legitimate" systems of authority, ideology, or expertise.

The *insurgency game*, for example, occurs when employees (often at lower levels) find ways to sabotage the instructions, rules, and needs of those in authority over them. By working to rule, withholding information, or flooding management with useless information, workers can bring those ostensibly with more power to their knees, often in short order. Other common political games include *alliance building games* (e.g., Lincoln's efforts to compromise with the border states), *empire building games* (e.g., McClelland's requests for more and more troops and more budget for training them), *expertise games* (e.g., Lincoln's generals discounting his queries because of his lack of military experience), *rival camps games* (e.g., the North vs. South), and the *young Turks game* (e.g., those in the North who protested Lincoln's "tyranny"). Mintzberg (1983b) has insightfully described these games, who plays them, and their relationship to the other three power systems in organizations.

Like expertise, politics is a disintegrative force in organizations. For this reason, it is unreasonable to expect a highly politicized organization to move quickly or efficiently in any one direction. In the extreme, the politically dominated organization is an anarchic bazaar of self-serving deal-merchants. We should not be too quick to condemn such organizations, however, because they may also be organizations in transition. As Mintzberg (1983b) so aptly points out, political action outside or between the boundaries of authority, ideology, and expertise is the primary recourse of those who see the need for radical organizational change. Such political action is necessary to break up existing power blocks so that power and influence can be redistributed to those who are more capable of dealing with the new challenges posed by a changing environment. So the politically dominated organization may be one that is en route to a more effective power configuration.

For industrial and organizational psychologists, the concepts of power source, distribution, and configuration offer a wealth of ideas, particularly for practice. Most simply, this aspect of the political arena metaphor suggests that those with power and the will and skill to use it will influence how, when, where, and with whom our programs are designed and implemented. We cannot afford to be politically naive if we want our science to make a positive difference in organizations. The first author learned this lesson the hard way in an interaction with the CEO of a fast-growing, high-tech company. After a quick run through a three-page job description for a new, executive-level marketing position, the CEO testily wadded it up and threw it in the wastebasket exclaiming, "This is no way to run a lean company!" The job description, which was bare-bones by industrial and organizational psychology standards, was too long and detailed for this executive who was determined to prevent bureaucracy from creeping

in and destroying the company's flexibility, creativity, and responsiveness. Failure to pay sufficient attention to the organization's ideology—of which the CEO was the high priest—resulted in wasted time and reduced credibility for the consultant.

Changing Power Distributions in Organizations. Our Lincoln illustration shows how the balance of power in political arenas can change over time. We see at least three direct implications of this idea for organizations. First, we should assume that organizational analysis from a political perspective must be ongoing—a process rather than a conclusion. Unless we assume that the contestants, their interests, their power, and their political will and skill are continually changing, we may overlook or ignore changes in any of the four that could have a significant impact on our strategies and tactics for intervening in an organization's HR system.

Second, we need to understand that changing organizations are often highly politicized organizations. Viewed only at a single point in time, we might be tempted to introduce stabilizing interventions in the HR system to "clean things up" (e.g., clearer job descriptions, tightly linked pay-for-performance systems, performance appraisal forms reinforcing the organization's traditional values). These interventions could become obstacles to necessary change. The implication is that we should not be too quick to put the HR house in order. It may be evolving toward a new structure and process that will prove more effective in meeting environmental demands. Only a dynamic view of the organization will allow us to recognize this evolution.

Third, this aspect of the metaphor should serve to remind us that we are inevitably contestants in our client organizations' political arenas. The knowledge and tools we bring can affect the distribution of power and influence in the organization. For example, training line managers in how to do structured interviewing can demystify these skills and reduce the power of those who were previously the unique bearers of these talents, namely the HR organization. We must anticipate the impact of our interventions on the organization's political structure as well as on its task structure. Only in this way will we be able to understand and deal with the almost inevitable resistance of those who perceive our work as a threat to their source or sources of power.

Organizational Stakeholders.   As we have said, the American people were far more than passive observers of the events occuring in Lincoln's political arenas. Similarly, in organizations there are often a number of stakeholders who are heavily invested in the actions, decisions, and performance of the contestants in the center ring. Without an analysis of the interests and power of these stakeholders, events in the arena may be difficult to understand because part of the picture is missing.

The political arena metaphor, then, leads us directly to a process of identifying an organization's key stakeholders—that is, key individuals or groups who have an interest or stake in its performance (e.g., stockholders, suppliers, customers, employees, regulatory bodies). Next, we need to assess "how the interests of various stakeholders differ, how much weight those distinct interests should be given, and the mechanisms by which those various stakeholders can exercise influence over the enterprise" (Beer, Spector, Lawrence, Mills, & Walton, 1985, p. 11). Each of the key stakeholder's own goals, strategies, interests, concerns, sources of power, and perceptions relevant to the organization must be determined. This leads to the identification of criteria that are used or are likely to be used by each constituency in evaluating the effectiveness of the organization. Because the nature of their investment differs, constituencies often use different criteria to evaluate effectiveness (e.g., stockholders are likely to be most interested in the firm's financial performance, customers are likely to be interested in product/service price and/or quality, employees may be most interested in compensation and the quality of work life afforded by the company). Only by identifying these various criteria can we begin to anticipate the response of the various constituencies to organizational strategies, policies, programs, decisions, and so on.

For the industrial and organizational psychologist developing a specific HRM program (e.g., a management training course), the organizational analysis process should identify the interests and goals of each stakeholder likely to be affected by a proposed program or policy. Only in so doing can we anticipate and address resistance or lack of support from certain groups or individuals because of differences in goals and priorities.

Limitations of the Political Arena Metaphor

A key assumption of this chapter is that the metaphors we use play a major role in determining what we see in organizations. Rigid adherence to a single metaphor cannot only cause us to overlook interesting and important events, but can also create self-fulfilling prophecies. That is, we reinforce those aspects of organizational life that are consistent with our metaphor.

This seems to be particularly true with the political arena metaphor. Once we start looking for political behavior in organizations, we see it virtually everywhere we turn. Assuming that everyone is seeking to maximize their own interests, we become overly suspicious of their intentions. Looking Out for Number One becomes our motto, potentially blinding us to the cooperative and altruistic motives of others. Similarly, we may become so aware of the possibility of political games that we actually encourage their development by pointing them out. Our tendency, then, to cling too tightly to the political arena metaphor is one of its dangers and limitations.

A second limitation of this metaphor is that while most of us can immediately see its implications at the interpersonal level (e.g., employee and supervisor, employee and employee), fewer seem to understand its expression at the organizational or societal level. As industrial and organizational psychologists with individual and small-group biases, we may be particularly vulnerable to this oversight. It is tempting, and even appropriate at times, to try to explain political processes in terms of individual differences and interpersonal relations. But we should not overlook the impact of organization-level structures (e.g., external control of the organization, how tasks are allocated to departments, formal structures for coordinating work across departments), and how processes (e.g., budgeting, strategic planning) affect the layout of the arena and the rules of the game (cf. Mintzberg, 1983b; Pfeffer, 1981).

Metaphors and Organization Analysis

We began this chapter by inviting you into an imaginary theater. Our purpose was to use the images and activities of the theater to draw your attention to two ideas. First, we asked you to consider how the theater's spotlight was like industrial and organizational psychology's spotlight—both illuminate individual actors and their immediate environment while leaving the rest of the theater in the dark. We then asserted our opinion that it is time for industrial and organizational psychologists to turn up the houselights and take a closer look at the organizational context in which individuals and groups work.

Second, we asked you to think about why our initial description of the theater included some things, such as the theater's financial condition and age of its audience, but not others. In doing so, we intended to draw your attention to the subtle effects of implicit theories of organization. Then we

argued that industrial and organizational psychologists do have ideas about what is going on offstage but have not given them much thought. Consequently, our perspectives on organization have been heavily influenced and limited by two dominant metaphors for organization: the machine and the organism.

To take a look at the organization as a whole and to describe different ways of seeing that organization, we turned on five different metaphorical houselights in sequence. In addition to the machine and the organism, we turned on three alternative houselights— the brain, the family, and the political system.

Having presented the five metaphors in sequence, it is now time to mix them together as we would in using them to gain a more comprehensive understanding of a given organization. As Morgan (1986) says, different metaphors provide alternative lenses on the same organizational reality. When used together, our perspective gains texture and depth. Our ideas for research and intervention become more insightful and creative. Let's briefly look at the theater through the five metaphors.

The Theater as Machine

When the machine houselight is turned on in the theatre, our attention is drawn to its formal structure and design. Since this theater has been around for many years, we might see a stable organizational chart showing a clear chain of command from the executive director to the janitor. We would also see clearly written job descriptions for all administrative staff, along with detailed planning and operational procedures. We see a steady supply of monetary fuel that allows the theater to crank out its plays efficiently and within its budget.

The machine houselight also reveals a disillusioned and dispirited creative staff. They feel that the administration's concerns for following procedure, containing costs, and doing "safe" plays undermines their ability to be creative and grow as professionals.

The Theater as Organism

The organism houselight reveals several things we missed with the machine houselight. First, we notice that the theater's relationship with the community has been stable and favorable for many years. Unfortunately for the theater, that is about to change. The organism houselight shows a change in the demographics of the community and in the theater-going population. The percentage of baby boomers in that population has grown immensely, and they are looking for a more creative, status-quo-challenging theater experience than City Repertory has traditionally provided. Moreover, two new avant-garde theaters have recently opened, challenging City Repertory's corner on the market. It appears that the theater's design and subsystems may have been a good fit for a stable environment, but they are rapidly becoming too mechanistic and unresponsive for the unstable and hostile environment the organization now faces.

Second, the organism houselight calls our attention to the fact that the theater is a different species from the frozen dinner factory on the edge of town. We recognize it to be a member of the professional bureaucracy species (Mintzberg, 1979). Now we recognize that the clash between administrators and the creative professionals in the theater is endemic to this species, like the ongoing battle between disease and white blood cells in the human body.

Third, we see that the theater is well along in its life cycle, perhaps suffering from the "crisis of red tape" described by Greiner (1972) as common in mature organizations. Greiner's life cycle model, which is built into this houselight, also suggests that the key to resolution of this crisis and reviving the organization will be growth through collaboration, probably between the theater's administrators, professional staff, and even its patrons.

The Theater as Brain

The brain houselight directs our attention to the interconnections among the theater's employees. Looking at the theater as a brain, we immediately suspect that we may be dealing with a split-brain patient. There is an administrative (probably the left) hemisphere, and a professional (undoubtedly the right) hemisphere with only limited and heavily censored communication passing between them. Within the professional hemisphere, the creative staff appear to be highly interconnected. Information of both a personal and professional nature is widely and openly shared. In fact, some of the professionals think that too much is shared within this hemisphere. In the administrative hemisphere, there is substantial interconnectedness among employees, but most of the interactions are formal and could be predicted by looking at the administrative organizational chart.

The two hemispheres are also differentiated by their learning capabilities. In the administrative hemisphere, only the executive director has responsibility for monitoring changes in the environment. He is close to retirement, however, and has frequently been heard to say that you can't teach an old dog new tricks, especially when the old tricks still work pretty well. Because of their lack of contact with the environment and the routine nature of their jobs, other administrative employees show little interest in learning or trying new things.

In the professional hemisphere, almost the opposite is true. The director and actors travel extensively and spend time with others in the theatrical community. Learning and professional growth are primary motivators for these people. When it comes to learning how to interact more effectively with the administration, however, this group and its administrative counterpart appear to have a severe learning disability. The family houselight may offer some clues on how to stimulate change in this system.

The Theater as Family

With the brain houselight turned on, we began to see patterns of interaction among the various members of the theater organization. The family houselight provides some insight for understanding those patterns. For example, we notice that this conflict between administration and professionals has persisted for a long time. The family systems principle of homeostasis or balance suggests that this conflict is functional in preserving the transaction rules that govern this social system. One such implicit rule may be, When intragroup tensions mount, vent them on the other group. This relieves pressure inside each subgroup and helps prevent intragroup conflict from getting out of hand. Of course, family systems theory would predict that this venting process also prevents resolution of conflicts within each group.

Several years ago, the theater's board engaged a consultant to help bridge the gap between the administrative and professional staffs. Many meetings and several retreats were held. Though everyone seemed to like the consultant, the effects of team building were short-lived. The consultant eventually faded out of the picture. Without the benefit of the family houselight, no one knew that the consultant had been triangled into the "family" process, thus stabilizing rather than changing the situation.

Because the family houselight probes the theater organization in greater detail than the other houselights, it reveals many more insights than we can talk about here. It is time to turn on the fifth and final houselight—the political system.

The Theater as Political Arena

This houselight shows that the conflict between the administration and the professionals is based on significant differences in interests and values. The executive director's primary concern is job security, due to his impending retirement. Having served the theater for many years, he understands that his job depends on satisfying the theater's dominant coalition, which is its board of trustees. The board is largely composed of older members of wealthy families who have provided the lion's share of support to the theater through the years. The board likes the theater just as it is—conservative, polished, traditional, and efficient. The board is self-perpetuating in that nominations to the board can only come from the board. Membership is for five-year terms with no limit on the number of terms a member can serve. Clearly, the board has a disproportionate share of power relative to the other players.

Frustrated by their lack of success in negotiating with the administration, the professionals have tried—playing the insurgency game—to overthrow the executive several times without success. As a result, relationship between administration and professional staff are sorely strained and characterized by an ongoing rival camps game. Since the family houselight is still on, we cannot help but notice the recurring triangulation pattern involving the board, the executive director, and the professional staff.

Political change in this system could come in at least two ways. First, without significant changes in its format, the theater is likely to lose its audiences in the future, thus forcing the board to contribute more and more financial support at the same time the theater is losing stature in the community. This may eventually create a financial crisis sufficient to catalyze changes in the board, redistribute power, and create degrees of freedom for organizational change.

Change could also come with the retirement of the executive director and the subsequent search for a replacement. This might present a window of opportunity for the remaining administrative staff, the professional staff, and new community leaders to form a coalition strong enough to influence the selection process, thus breaking free of the board's chokehold and bringing needed change to the theater.

Encore

Each of the five metaphors presented illuminates distinctly different facets of organizations. Our primary goal for this chapter is to stimulate new ways of thinking about research and practice in industrial and organizational psychology. Also, we hope it arouses your interest in metaphor as a highly productive way of generating creative ideas about organizations. In the spirit of our theater metaphor, we invite you to perform the encore by creating and exploring new metaphors for organizations.

References

Aldrich, H. (1979). *Organizations and environments.* Englewood Cliffs, NJ: Prentice-Hall.

Argyris, C. (1969). The incompleteness of social-psychological theory. *American Psychologist,* 24(10), 893–908.

Argyris, C. (1976). Problems and new directions for industrial psychology. In M. D. Dunnette (Ed.), *Handbook of industrial and organizational psychology.* Chicago: Rand McNally.

Argyris, C. (1982). *Reasoning, learning, and action: Individual and organizational.* San Francisco: Jossey-Bass.

Argyris, C. (1985). *Strategy change and defensive routines.* Boston: Pitman.

Argyris, C., & Schön, D. (1978). *Organizational learning: A theory of action perspective.* Reading, MA: Addison-Wesley.

Arvey, R. D., Salas, E., & Gialluca, K. A. (1988). *Using task inventories to forecast skills and abilities.* Unpublished manuscript, University of Minnsota, Minneapolis.

Astley, W. G. (1984). Toward an appreciation of collective strategy. *Academy of Management Review, 9,* 526–535.

Astley, W. G., & Fombrun, C. J. (1983). Collective strategy: The social ecology of organizational environments. *Academy of Management Review, 9,* 576–586.

Beer, M., Spector, B., Lawrence, P., Mills, Q., & Walton, R. (1985). *Human resource management: A general management perspective.* New York: Free Press.

Bennis, W., & Nanus, B. (1986). *Leaders.* New York: Harper and Row.

Bentz, V. J. (1968). The Sears experience in the investigation, description, and prediction of executive behavior. In J. A. Myers, Jr. (Ed.), *Predicting managerial success.* Ann Arbor, MI: Foundation for Research on Human Behavior.

Bowen, M. (1978). *Family therapy in clinical practice.* New York: Jason Aronson.

Brown, S. H. (1981). Validity generalization and situational moderation in the life insurance industry. *Journal of Applied Psychology, 66,* 664–670.

Burns, T., & Stalker, G. M. (1966). *The management of innovation,* (2nd ed.). London: Tavistock.

Burrell, G., & Morgan, G. (1979). *Sociological paradigms and organizational analysis.* London: Heinemann.

Carroll, S. J., & Schneier, C. E. (1982). *Performance appraisal and review systems.* Glenview, IL: Scott Foresman.

Cascio, W. (1982). *Applied psychology in personnel management* (2nd ed.). Reston, VA: Reston.

Child, J. (1972). Organizational structure, environment, and performance—the role of strategic choice. *Sociology, 6,* 1–22.

Daft, R. L. (1986). *Organization theory and design* (2nd ed.). St. Paul, MN: West.

Dickey, J. (1968). *Metaphor as pure adventure.* A lecture delivered at the Library of Congress, December 4, 1967, Washington, DC: Library of Congress.

Digman, J. M. (1989). Five robust trait dimensions: Development, stability, and utility. *Journal of Personality, 57,* 195–214.

Dolezal, H. (1982). *Living in a world transformed: Perceptual and performatory adaptation to visual distortion.* New York: Academic Press.

Dreher, G. F., & Sackett, P. R. (1983). *Perspectives on employee staffing and selection.* Homewood, IL: Irwin.

Dunnette, M. D. (1966). *Personnel selection and placement.* Belmont, CA: Wadsworth.

Earley, P. C., Connolly, T., & Ekegren, G. (1989). Goals, strategy development, and task performance: Some limtis on the efficacy of goal setting. *Journal of Applied Psychology, 74,* 24–33.

Eccles, J. C. (1973). *The understanding of the brain.* New York: McGraw-Hill.

Embler, W. (1966). *Metaphor and meaning.* DeLand, FL: Everett/Edwards.

Emery, F. E., & Trist, E. L. (1973). *Toward a social ecology.* Harmondsworth: Penguin.

Freedman, R. (1987). Lincoln: A photobiography. New York: Scholastic.

Friedman, E. H. (1985). *Generation to generation: Family process in church and synagogue.* New York: Guilford.

Galbraith, J. (1977). *Organization design.* Reading, MA: Addison-Wesley.

Georgiou, P. (1973). The goal paradigm and notes towards a counter paradigm. *Administrative Science Quarterly,* 291–310.

Golden, K., & Ramanujam, V. (1985) Between a dream and a nightmare: On the integration of the human resource management and strategic business planning processes. *Human Resource Management, 24,* 429–451.

Goldstein, I. L. (1986). *Training in organizations: Needs assessment, development, and evaluation* (2nd ed.). Pacific Grove, CA: Brooks-Cole.

Greiner, L. E. (1972). Evolution and revolution as organizations grow. *Harvard Business Review, 50,* 37–46.

Hackman, J. R., & Oldham, G. R. (1980). *Work redesign.* Reading, MA: Addison-Wesley.

Hakel, M. D., Sorcher, M., Beer, M., & Moses, J. L. (1982). *Making it happen: Designing research with implementation in mind.* Beverly Hills, CA: Sage.

Hannan, M. T., & Freeman, J. H. (1977). The population ecology of organizations. *American Journal of Sociology, 82,* 929–964.

Hough, L. M., Russell, T. L., Keyes, M. A., & Zaugg, L. B. (1990). *Development of human resource management systems for OGC attorneys at the U.S. General Accounting Office* (Institute Report No. 184). Minneapolis, MN: Personnel Decisions Research Institutes.

Katz, D., & Kahn, R. L. (1986). *The social psychology of organizations.* New York: Wiley.

Kidder, T. (1981). *The soul of a new machine.* New York: Avalon.

Klimoski, R. J., & Strickland, W. J. (1977). Assessment centers—valid or merely prescient? *Personnel Psychology, 30,* 353–361.

Latham, G. P., & Wexley, K (1981). *Increasing productivity through performance appraisal.* Reading, MA: Addison-Wesley.

Latham, G. P., & Fry, L. W. (1986). Measuring and appraising employee performance. In S. Gael (Ed.), *Job analysis handbook.* New York: Wiley.

Lawler, E. E. (1986). *High involvement management.* San Francisco: Jossey-Bass.

Lawrence, P. R., & Lorsch, J. W. (1986). *Differentiation and integration in complex organizations.* Cambridge, MA: Harvard Graduate School of Business Administration.

Lerner, H. G. (1989). *The dance of intimacy.* New York: Harper and Row.

Lewin, K. (1935). *A dynamic theory of personality: Selected papers of Kurt Lewin.* New York: McGraw-Hill.

Locke, E., Shaw, K., Saari, L., & Latham, G. (1981). Goal setting and task performance: 1969–1980. *Psychological Bulletin, 90,* 125–152.

March, J. G., & Simon, H. A. (1958). *Organizations.* New York: Wiley.

Marius, R. (1991). *A writer's companion* (2nd ed.). New York: McGraw-Hill.

McKenna, D., & Latham, G. P. (1987). *Development and implementation of a behavior-based performance appraisal in the Water Pollution Control Department.* Technical report prepared for the municipality of Metropolitan Seattle, Seattle, WA.

McPherson, J. M. (1991). *Abraham Lincoln and the second American revolution.* New York: Oxford.

Miles, R. E., & Snow, C. C. (1978). *Organizational strategy, structure, and process.* New York: McGraw-Hill.

Miller, D., & Friesen, P. H. (1984). *Organizations: A quantum view.* Englewood Cliffs, NJ: Prentice-Hall.

Mintzberg, H. (1979). *The structuring of organizations.* Englewood Cliffs, NJ: Prentice-Hall.

Mintzberg, H. (1983a). *Structure in fives: Designing effective organizations.* Englewood Cliffs, NJ: Prentice-Hall.

Mintzberg, H. (1983b). *Power in and around organizations.* Englewood Cliffs, NJ: Prentice-Hall.

Minuchin, S. (1974). *Families and family therapy.* Cambridge, MA: Harvard University Press.

Minuchin, S. (1981). *Family therapy techniques.* Cambridge, MA: Harvard University Press.

Mohrman, S. A., & Cummings, T. G. (1989). *Self-designing organizations: Learning how to create high performance.* Reading, MA: Addison-Wesley.

Morgan, G. (1986). *Images of organization.* Newbury Park, CA: Sage.

Nichols, W. C., & Everett, C. A. (1986). *Systemic family therapy: An integrative approach.* New York: Guilford Press.

Olian, J., & Rynes, S. (1984). Organizational staffing: Integrating practice with strategy. *Industrial Relations, 23*(2), 170–183.

Orsburn, J. D., Moran, L., Musselwhite, E., & Zenger, J. H. (1990). *Self-directed work teams: The new American challenge.* Homewood, IL: Business One Irwin.

Orwell, G. (1954). Politics and the English language. In G. A Orwell (Ed.), *Collection of Essays by George Orwell.* Garden City, NY: Doubleday.

Perrow, C. (1970). *Organizational analysis: A sociological view.* Belmont, CA: Wadsworth.

Pfeffer, J. (1981). *Power in organizations.* Marshfield, MA: Pitman.

Raelin, J. A. (1986). *The clash of cultures: Managers and professionals.* Cambridge, MA: HBS Press.

Restak, R. M. (1984). *The brain.* Toronto: Bantam Books.

Robey, D. (1986). *Designing organizations* (2nd ed.). Homewood, IL: Irwin.

Roethlisberger, F. J., & Dickson, W. J. (1939). *Management and the worker.* Cambridge, MA: Harvard University Press.

Rynes, S., & Gerhart, B. (1990). Interviewer assessments of applicant "fit": An exploratory investigation. *Personnel Psychology, 43,* 13–34.

Satir, V. (1972). *Peoplemaking.* Palo Alto, CA: Science and Behavior Books.

Schaef, A., & Fassel, D. (1989). *The addictive organization.* New York: Harper and Row.

Schein, E. H. (1978). *Career dynamics: Matching individual and organizational needs.* Reading, MA: Addison-Wesley.

Schmidt, F. L., Pearlman, K., Hunter, J. E., & Hirsch, H. R. (1985). Forty questions about validity generalization and meta-analysis. *Personnel Psychology, 38*(4), 697–798.

Senge, P. (1990). *The fifth discipline: The art and practice of the learning organization.* New York: Doubleday Currency.

Sperry, R. W. (1968). Hemisphere deconnection and unity of conscious awareness. *American Psychologist, 23,* 723–733.

Taylor, F. W. (1915). *Principles of scientific management.* New York: Harper and Row.

Ury, W. (1991). *Getting past no: Negotiating with difficult people.* New York: Bantam.

Weick, K. E. (1969). *The social psychology of organizing.* Reading, MA: Addison-Wesley.

Weisbord, M. (1987). *Productive workplaces.* San Francisco: Jossey-Bass.

Wexley, K. N., & Latham, G. P. (1982). *Developing and training human resources in organizations.* Glenview, IL: Scott Foresman.

Wood, R., Mento, A., & Locke, E. (1987). Task complexity as a moderator of the goal difficulty-performance relationship. *Journal of Applied Psychology, 73,* 416–425.

Woodward, J. (1965). *Industrial organization: Theory and practice.* London: Oxford University Press.

Worthy, J. C. (1959). *Big business and free men.* New York: Harper and Row.

CHAPTER 15

Strategic Decision Making

Ronald N. Taylor
Rice University

Strategic decision making (SDM) has its roots in business policy and strategic management and is concerned with understanding and improving decisions about the strategies organizations use. The scope of SDM is necessarily broad, drawing theories and techniques from a number of disciplines, such as psychology, economics, operations research, and management. The broad focus of SDM offers potential strength since it is not limited to a single established research paradigm, but rather has the opportunity to adopt and adapt methods of theory development and research from many fields. Rather than providing a detailed analysis of a limited set of developments, the approach taken in this chapter is to consolidate literature from a number of fields for a broad review of SDM. Models of decision making are examined, and the implications of these models for making strategic decisions are explored. The decision models included in our review are the following: rational-analytic, cognitive/perceptual, incremental adjustment, strategic planning, bureaucratic, collective, interpretive, and contingency. Each model of decision making can be viewed as a lens that offers valuable insights into SDM, and debate among writers favoring various decision models has made a healthy contribution to understanding the processes involved in strategic decisions. Following a critique of these models of decision making, the major components of SDM are identified by drawing upon the psychological processes involved in making strategic decisions. The component steps of SDM examined in this chapter are the following: identify values, assess internal and external environment, develop strategic alternatives, choose strategy, and execute and control strategy. Our purpose is to examine the nature of the decision-making models and to explore both the descriptive and normative implications of the decision models for each component of SDM and for strategic decisions in general. Following this, the state of the art in SDM theory development and research methods is discussed, and suggestions for advancing this field are made. Contributions of decision models to SDM are painted with a broad brush in this chapter, with the intention of stimulating further discussion and research on the processes involved in making strategic decisions.

Introduction

POLICY ANALYSIS AND strategic decision making (SDM) have evolved rapidly since 1976, when the chapter on "Problem Solving and Decision Making" (MacCrimmon & Taylor, 1976) appeared in the first edition of this *Handbook*. Many advances have been made during the past decade and a half.[1] Business policy and strategic management have produced some promising models and techniques for making strategic decisions—yet they have tended to neglect an underpinning of behavioral science theory and empirical research. Increasingly, however, behavioral science theories and research methods have been used in studies of SDM, and the result has been progress in the field.

This chapter examines behavioral and organizational models of decision making and explores the implications of these models for strategic decisions. The analysis emphasizes behavioral and organization decision-making literature, with an emphasis on strategic decisions made on behalf of business firms or other organizations.

The focus on deriving implications from models of decision making for strategic decisions requires several caveats. The first is that strategic decisions are viewed as being made by individual decision makers and by decision-making groups; therefore, understanding strategic decisions requires a study of the psychology of decision makers as individuals and as groups. This focus does not intend to denigrate contributions made to SDM by disciplines other than psychology. Indeed, many other fields of study, including economics, political science, operations research, and decision

support systems theory, make valuable contributions to SDM, but these lie beyond the scope of this chapter. The second caveat is that it is impossible to examine every model in detail. Thus, this chapter highlights only models that link decision making to strategic decisions. References to more complete treatments of other relevant contributions are provided throughout. The third caveat is that this chapter does not distinguish between problem solving and decision making in discussing the implications of the models for SDM. While these two processes differ in important features (e.g., Smith, 1988), the distinction only complicates our efforts to draw insights from psychology to better understand strategic decisions. Hence, in this chapter the term *decision making* also encompasses aspects of problem solving.

Definitions and Origins

Strategic decision making is essentially a process by which information flows through various highly integrated stages of analysis and is directed toward attaining the objectives of an organization (Pearce & Robinson, 1988). It is a decision process that can be modified to reflect the contingencies in the firm and its environment. The information flow is data (e.g., forecasts) about the business, operations, and the environment. Strategic decision making can also be viewed as a series of decision-related activities that firms undertake to determine appropriate future thrusts. These activities do not always occur in the same sequence. Also, the amount of attention each component requires varies over time and with the conditions facing a company. Rapidly changing environments may force a firm to make more frequent situation assessments compared to firms in stable environments. Units competing in a mature and slow growth products industry may require less frequent reviews than do company units competing in rapidly growing industries.

The strategic decision-making processes are interconnected, and any change in one stage will affect other stages. For example, feedback from early diagnosis of decision problems is likely to influence strategy selection. Many of the techniques used to assess a company's situation focus only on current conditions. Hence, SDM is a dynamic process, and changes in the firm and its environment necessitate adjustments in the processes used to make strategic decisions.

Strategic decision making is a behavioral and organizational activity and is subject to the same pitfalls as other activities in which people are involved; SDM is sensitive to human frailties. Indeed, advancing SDM requires greater understanding of the role of behavioral and organizational aspects involved in the decision-making process. Research on some behavioral aspects of SDM are reviewed in this chapter, but many others need to be studied in order to more thoroughly understand the behavioral aspects.

Strategic decision making has its roots in the fields of business policy and strategic management, beginning with the pioneering efforts of Chandler (1962) and Andrews (1971) to define organizational strategy. Andrews' (1971) definition of corporate strategy appears central to the field. This definition of strategy refers to a pattern of decisions made over time and across conditions in a company. Nonetheless, no clear consensus on a definition of strategy exists (e.g., Bourgeois, 1980; Gluck, Kaufman, & Walleck, 1982; Hambrick, 1983). Hambrick (1983) suggested two reasons for lack of agreement: (a) Strategy will vary from one industry to another, and (b) strategy is multidimensional. Chaffee (1985) pointed out another reason for disagreement about a unitary

concept of strategy: Strategy refers to different mental models rather than a single model, as most writers assume.

Despite the many ways in which strategy is viewed in the field of strategic management, many business strategy researchers would probably agree with Hofer and Schendel (1978) in defining strategy in terms of a fit or match between an organization and its environment. The inseparability of organization and environment is a key feature in most definitions of strategy. Strategy enables an organization to deal creatively with complex, dynamic environments and involves decisions that affect the long-term welfare of an organization (e.g., Hambrick, 1983; Mason & Mitroff, 1981; Narayanan & Fahey, 1982).

Decision-based Perspective

Some theorists (Kudla, 1980; Leontiades & Tezel, 1980) view strategy formulation as planning. Others, however, argue that decision making should replace strategic planning as the dominant focus for investigations of strategy formulation (e.g., Bourgeois, 1981; Mintzberg, 1978; Quinn, 1980). Not all firms use formal planning, but all are engaged in strategic decision making by individuals and/or groups. The role of formal planning systems should not be ignored, but it is important to determine how decisions are made in planning systems, as well as in other strategic choice contexts.

Fredrickson (1983) has argued for a decision-making view of strategy formulation, advocating research on how individual strategic decisions are made and combined. Indeed, a number of researchers (e.g., Carter, 1971; Mintzberg, Raisinghane, & Theoret, 1976) have taken a decision-based approach to investigating strategic choice and attempting to discover how individual strategic decisions are made and how they are integrated into more complex strategies.

A frequent discussion is whether the term *choice* accurately describes the processes that precede a strategic action (e.g., Fredrickson, 1983). Further model and theory development is needed to answer this type of question. Nevertheless, decision-based perspective to strategy formulation seems more fruitful than the other approaches suggested in the literature. For example, a decision-based orientation encourages the study of both the content and the process of strategy. Studies of decision *content* can analyze what decisions are made and the conditions under which they are made. Studies of decision *process* can identify the decision requirements upon which certain types of behavior are based.

In taking a decision-based approach to conceptualizing strategic choice, decision making is considered to be the act of choice with all its associated processes. No attempt is made to distinguish between decision making and problem solving. Meaningful distinctions between these concepts can be made—in which problem solving is directed toward the resolution of a problem by achieving some goal and decision making implies a choice among alternative courses of action (e.g., Smith, 1988)—but in our focus on applied decisions, this distinction is less useful. While logical distinctions can be made between these terms by considering decision making to be a component of problem solving (e.g., Kepner & Tregoe, 1965), this confines decision making to simply choosing among alternative courses of action, and in practice decision making generally implies a greater range of activities.

What are strategic decisions? Shirley (1982) identified them as choices that (a) specify an organization's relationship to its environment, (b) consider an organization as a single unit, (c) are influenced by inputs from multiple organizational functions, (d) determine actions in both administration and operations, and (e) are necessary for an organization's success. Pearce and Robinson (1988) described strategic decisions as (a) being top management decisions, (b) involving considerable company resources, (c) committing the firm with implications for its profitability far into the future, (d) requiring coordination of many businesses or many functional areas of the firm, and (e) requiring the involvement of factors external to the firm. Clearly, strategic decisions are seen as having important implications for the firm or organization in which they are made and involve novel, ill-structured, and complex sets of interdependent decision problems. As Thomas (1984) defined them, strategic decisions have little initial structure, long time horizons, political implications, sensitivity to environmental dynamics, and affect many units within an organization. Strategic decision problems are generally characterized as "messy" (e.g., Ackoff, 1974) and "ill-structured" (e.g., Mintzberg et al., 1976).

Organization of the Chapter

The chapter is organized into three sections. In the first section, strategic decision-making models are discussed. An examination of the typologies of SDM models reported in the literature is made, a taxonomy is proposed, and the major models are described. In the second section, the basic components of SDM are examined, along with the contributions of the various SDM models to understanding each component of strategic decision making. Finally, suggestions are made for advancing SDM theory and research.

Models of Strategic Decision Making

Many models (representations) have been proposed to depict how decisions are made, or should be made, in strategic decision situations. Strategic decision-making models can be either descriptive or normative, and represent various approaches that can be taken in making decisions that provide strategic direction for business organizations.

In this I will section examine some of the typologies that have been used to describe the decision-making models. After examining typologies of decision-making models reported in the literature, I will discuss the major decision-making models with relevance for strategic decisions.

Discussion of Typology and Proposed Taxonomy

A number of systems or typologies have been developed in attempts to map the models of SDM processes and activities. An intriguing psychoanalytic taxonomy explained strategic decision making in terms of the neuroses of top executives as revealed by their fantasies (Kets de Vries & Miller, 1984). In this taxonomy the pathological conditions that affect strategy making included paranoid, compulsive, histrionic, depressive, and schizoid behaviors. What follows is a discussion of some more traditional taxonomies of decision models.

The range of strategies available for making strategic decisions may be depicted by postulating types of strategic responses that organizations may use. Such typologies of SDM responses are either logically or empirically derived. Two of the earliest and best-known typologies of strategies are set forth by Miles and Snow (1978) and by Mintzberg (1973). The Miles and Snow (1978) types—*defenders, analyzers, prospectors,* and *reactors*—were developed to explain how organizations approach product development and marketing new products, but the typology has also been used to identify psychological models of strategy development (e.g., Hambrick, 1983). Mintzberg's (1973) three types—*entrepreneurial, adaptive,* and *planning*—refer directly to decision making.

Mechanistic (machine-based) and *organismic* (organism-based) models are two traditional types of models. Gharajedaghi and Ackoff (1984) reviewed the literature on them and found they were inadequate guides for decision and action in modern organizations. These two traditional types of models have been criticized because they were designed to help decision makers acquire more information but not more knowledge of the problem, and they seek to understand the functions of subparts but not the whole problem situation. A third model type, a *social system* model, was proposed to overcome the inadequacies of the models based on machines and organisms and to better understand social systems. Decision making based on a social systems model requires a focus on resolution of conflict within the system, its parts, and the environment of the system in order to encourage system development. Planning in an ideal system, then, would require designing a desirable future and inventing ways to attain this future, while retaining maximum freedom of choice for those affected by the plan (Gharajedaghi & Ackoff, 1984).

Shrivastava and Grant (1985) developed an empirically derived taxonomy of strategic decision-making process models. They studied 32 firms that were in the process of deciding to adopt a new computer system. Personal interviews and questionnaires were used to gather information about their strategic decision-making processes from 61 managers. Descriptions of decision-making processes were coded and then subjected to thematic analysis to develop a generalized model of the decision process. Four patterns or types of strategic decision making processes were revealed by repeated within-case and across-case comparisons.

- The *managerial autocracy* model, in which a single manager made the decision based on his or her preferences and took responsibility for the outcomes. Intuitive judgmental evaluation was used, and the main motive was to improve the organization by computerization.

- The *systemic bureaucracy* model, in which decisions about activities, information flows, and interactions were largely determined by organizational systems and official rules and procedures. Solution development was guided in this model by existing, and frequently inadequate, operating procedures involving cost-benefit analysis of each alternative, implementation planning, and top management approval of the choice. This model was found most frequently in large and old firms in mature industries and in state-owned organizations.

- The *adaptive planning* model, in which long-range strategic plans are used to make the computerization decision. Professional planning staff or management information systems personnel were generally used in a formal planning cycle. Decision making was supported by thorough assessment of information needs and analysis of options.

- The *political expediency* model, in which groups of decision makers formed coalitions around the computerization issue. Decision making was managed by knowledgeable individuals and by using conflict-reducing negotiations among the groups to protect the interests of all the groups.

Anderson and Paine (1975) have suggested a perceptual model of strategy formulation. In this model, the main inputs are managerial perceptions of environmental uncertainty and need for change. The four quadrants that result from the cross-classification of these two dimensions specify the appropriate manner of mission (e.g., fixed and well-defined), objectives (e.g., optimization), strategies (process planning), organization form (e.g., open, adaptive, organic), and role performance of the policy maker (e.g., adaptive planner, information gathering).

Chaffee (1985) reviewed the literature and proposed three types of strategic decision-making models: linear, adaptive, and interpretive. The *linear* model has a planning focus and connotes the methodological, directed, and sequential actions of planning. This appears similar to Chandler's (1962) view that strategy involves determining a firm's basic long-term goals, choosing courses of action, and allocating resources needed to achieve goals. The *adaptive* model attempts to develop a good fit between the threats and opportunities in the external environment and an organization's own capabilities and resources. The *interpretive* model assumes that reality is socially constructed and that the social contract is the basis for organizing. These interpretations can take the form of orienting metaphors (frames of reference) that permit organizational stakeholders to understand the organization and its environment. The interpretive model is based on the notion of strategy making as a cultural phenomenon (e.g., Weick & Daft, 1983) and stresses the role of cooperative actions of individuals based on shared meanings of relevant symbols.

There is some overlap among the three models. For instance, Weick and Daft (1983) argue that affective interpretation can be based on processes central to the adaptive model (i.e., interpretive context based on in-depth knowledge of the environment). Another way to link these three models is to see them as representing stages that an organization moves through as it becomes more experienced and adept at strategy making. An organization may begin at the stage of financial forecasts (linear model), then progress to strategic analysis (adaptive model), and on to strategic management (interpretive model).

Management by information and management by ideology have been identified as two major themes in strategy formulation (Cummings, 1983), and effective organizations would be expected to integrate these two themes. Management by information implies a linear or adaptive approach to strategy making; management by ideology appears similar to the notion of interpretive strategy making.

So far, however, little is known about the nature of this integration and how these themes relate to developing and implementing organizational strategies.

Allison (1971) developed an approach that provides a taxonomy for understanding important, ill-structured, and complex organizational and political decisions. He identified three model, or levels of analysis: rational actor/individual, organizational, and societal/governmental. Two of the three levels of analysis are directly relevant to the psychology of strategic decision making. The *rational actor/individual level* model focuses on the components of individual decision making, such as goals, alternatives, consequences, and choices. Decision makers are expected to behave so as to maximize the payoff. The *organizational level* model expands the rational actor analysis to include various organizational processes that appear likely to affect a decision. The *societal/governmental model* makes the taxonomy more complete by including various sociopolitical processes that influence complex decisions.

The psychological processes involved in Allison's individual and organizational models are important to understanding strategic decision making. Since strategy formulation is a decision-making process, investigators should study how strategic decisions are made in organizational contexts and how these decisions are integrated into an overall strategy.

MacCrimmon (1973) has built on Allison's framework to produce a very useful taxonomy of collective decisions. In this typology, a logic tree describes types of decisions in terms of Allison's three levels. The nodes in the logic tree represent (a) rationality (comprehensive or bounded), (b) a decision unit (multiple or single decision makers), (c) an information unit (yes or no), and (d) an action unit (yes or no). This model assumes that individuals are either comprehensively rational (the classic view of rational choice models) or bounded rational (the satisficing model). Also, the model assumes that individuals engage in decision making activities, either individually or in groups, and that these individuals will interact with information units, decision units, and action and implementation units as they make and implement decisions. The single decision maker acting in a comprehensively rational manner corresponds to Allison's rational actor/individual level of analysis. Allison's organizational level corresponds to a bounded rational decision maker—acquiring information through separate information units, but retaining responsibility for carrying out decisions. The societal/governmental level is represented in MacCrimmon's tree as a bounded rational and multiple person, with separate decision, information, and action/implementation units. The logic tree effectively illustrates the sources of problem "ill-structuredness" and links modeling and process approaches for representing decision-making activities.

Stein (1981) developed and tested a system of strategic decision approaches in which several decision models in addition to the rational model were investigated to identify their main elements or themes. Other models, such as Allison's organizational-level, incrementalism, and political-bureaucratic models (i.e., Allison's level three), were also included. The items were listed in a questionnaire that was answered by the top managers in 64 firms. Managers' descriptions of their own behavior on the questionnaire items were factor analyzed, yielding four dimensions that appeared to be the most important: analysis (i.e., evaluation of courses of action), search (i.e., generating alternative solutions), flexibility (i.e., stability of problem definition), and group behavior (i.e., activities of decision-making groups). Cross-classification of two levels of each of these four dimensions yielded 16 decision modes. For example, the rational mode involves explicit analysis, extensive search, rigid problem definition, and homogeneous group behavior. While these factor-analytic–based decision modes are helpful in identifying the range of possible approaches to decision making, it is difficult to cleanly fit the research literature into these modes. Some theories and strategies can be classified into more than one decision mode (are not mutually exclusive), and other theories and strategies are omitted from the taxonomy (are not collectively exhaustive).

One of the more thorough taxonomies for classifying organizational decision models was developed by Nutt (1976). He derived six types of organizational decision making models from a review of the literature. These models are (a) the *bureaucratic* model (e.g., Weber, 1947), where decision making is conducted by competent and powerful people using master plans, (b) *normative decision* theory (e.g., operations research), in which decisions attempt to maximize subjective expected utility, (c) *behavioral decision* theory (e.g., Simon, 1967), or satisficing decisions, (d) *group decision making* (e.g., Collins & Guetzkow, 1964; Delbecq, Van de Ven, & Gustafson, 1975), where decisions are based on group dynamics and processes, (e) *conflict-equilibrium* theory (e.g., March & Simon, 1958; Thompson, 1967), in which decisions result from resolution of conflict through group consensus, and (f) *open system* theory (e.g., Lindblom, 1965), where acceptable decisions are developed by incremental adjustment. Arguments for stipulating the decision conditions under which each model should optimally be used were developed through a series of propositions, but no empirical test of the propositions was reported for the study.

Nutt (1976) also suggested that different stages of decision making call for different models. This notion of using different decision models at various stages of a decision process (e.g., making the model of decision making contingent upon the stage in the decision process) has been proposed by a number of writers (e.g., Lorange & Vancil, 1977; Mintzberg, 1973).

Despite many attempts to develop taxonomies of strategic decision-making models, none are sufficiently complete to be used to organize an analysis of psychological approaches to making strategic decisions. Nevertheless, the typologies I have just describe do provide useful insights into the diversity of models that need to be incorporated into a useful taxonomy. A formal and noncontroversial taxonomy of decision making models that encompasses all SDM models is impossible. Nonetheless, organizing a discussion of the contributions and research on strategic decision making around general approaches facilitates understanding and highlights similarities and differences between models and between types of models. The logical groupings reflect the various schools of thought among those who have studied strategic decisions. These types of models are *rational-analytic, cognitive/perceptual, incremental adjustment, strategic planning, bureaucratic, collective, interpretive,* and *contingency.* Each type of model will be described here only as it relates to SDM. Suggestions drawn from the critique of potential contributions of SDM models for advancing SDM will be discussed later in the chapter.

Rational-analytic Models

Rational-analytic models of decision making represent a highly constrained and rigorous approach to decision making based on theories of economic decision making. This viewpoint also has been called *synoptic* or *calculated rationality.* Classic SDM models have been based on the notion of rationality or some variant of this concept and typically present the rational model as the ideal approach and one that should be followed as closely as possible (e.g., Etzioni, 1968; Janis & Mann, 1977; Raiffa, 1968).

Rational-analytic models assume that all important aspects of a decision can be adequately analyzed by specifying a limited range of variables using objective quantitative measures. The decision maker is assumed to be a unitary entity, and even decision-making groups are considered to be in agreement on all values pertaining to the decision. According to this approach, decisions are highly purposive and actions are consciously chosen as calculative solutions to problems. Also assumed is that behaviors represent the intentions and purposes of a decision maker and that it is possible to understand actions by knowing a decision maker's economic purposes. From the perspective of process rationality, this means that decisions can be understood by demonstrating that a decision maker is pursuing goals, and that the actions taken as a result of making a decision are reasonable considering the nature of these goals. Decision makers demonstrate procedural rationality in terms of the methods they consistently use in reaching a decision.

Thompson (1967) has described a model of the rational operation of organizations that contains two types of rationality—*technical* and *organizational*. The production aspects of an organization operate by technical rationality. Technical production decisions are assumed to proceed by a process of ranking various production methods in terms of how well the expected consequences of a given production method will correspond to organizational objectives. Selecting a production system that efficiently leads to desired results is a technically rational decision. Systems are organizationally rational to the extent that technical rationality is efficiently linked to other activities of the organization (e.g., acquiring production inputs such as manpower and raw materials and distributing the outputs of production).

Maintaining both technical and organizational rationality requires an organization to shield itself from the constraining influences of nonrational aspects of the organization's social environment. Status, social cliques, sentiments, and other social influences introduce uncertainty into the organizational system; thus, the rational organization attempts to limit nonrational behavior of its members. To protect the rational operation of an organization, individuals who violate the organization's norms of rationality are sanctioned by reducing their power and spheres of action.

In Thompson's view, the rational model of organizational functioning is a rather direct extension of human rationality.

A rigorous form of rational-analytic decision making, such as maximizing expected utility, requires complete specificity of the underlying decision model. In practice, expected value models are generally used in which subjective probabilities specify the degree of uncertainty that exists regarding events and outcomes. Decision makers must specify the goals they wish to obtain as a result of making a decision. Criteria must be specified to represent each goal, and the merits of alternative courses of action are judged in light of these criteria. It is important that all significant courses of action be listed and that the consequences of choosing each course of action be known. While rigorous forms of rational-analytic models demand considerable information to fully specify the decision problem for a maximizing solution, this type of solution is seldom possible in strategic decisions (Taylor, 1981).

Mintzberg (1990) has challenged the traditional approach to strategy formulation as being of a "design school" that attempts to design a fit between external threats and opportunities and the internal distinctive competencies of a firm. He questions the use of a simple model to assess a firm's competitive position, much less its decision-making strategies. He questions whether a decision maker is in conscious control of the decision-making process. He also questions the premise that strategies must first be determined, then implemented. He has proposed a more fluid and realistic model of strategy formulation. Bateman and Ziethaml (1989) extended this approach to develop and empirically test a model that provided an explicit psychological context for strategic decisions.

Satisficing (Simon, 1967) is frequently used as a descriptive model of how decisions in organizational contexts are actually made. *Satisficing* is a form of rational-analytic decision making in which some assumptions of the more rigorous rational-analytic models are relaxed to permit decision makers to deal with more realistic information processing and decision-making demands (Taylor, 1975b). Rather than searching for all information pertaining to a problem, a decision maker seeks only enough information about decision alternatives to permit a good enough course of action to be found and chosen.

Rationality-based models of decision making generally are associated with normative models, but attempts have been made to describe how decision makers tend to depart from the rational prescriptions in practice (e.g., MacCrimmon, 1968). An active research area has involved efforts to describe to what extent actual decision makers—mostly in simulated decisions—depart from the calculated rational view of decision making. A general conclusion from this line of research is that decision makers tend to be overconfident about the quality of their judgments and choices (e.g., Dawes, 1976; Lichtenstein, Fischhoff, & Phillips, 1982). Management students and presidents of firms have been found to share this overconfidence in predicting inordinate success for their firms (e.g., Larwood & Whittaker, 1977).

Bounded rationality has been suggested as the basis for a more accurate description of how decisions are made in the context of a firm (Simon, 1957, 1976). It appears that decision makers exhibit rationality only within the constraints of their perception of the decision problem (March & Simon, 1958; Simon, 1957). These perceptually imposed constraints tend to be very narrow compared to the complexities of most organizational problems (Cyert & March, 1963). This limitation has been linked to "cognitive strain" for decision makers (e.g., Taylor, 1975b) and has been observed to affect decisions made in business (e.g., Katona, 1951), in natural resource management (e.g., Kates, 1962), and in setting governmental policy (e.g., Lindblom, 1965). March (1978) discussed the idea of rationality in decision making as an attempt to rationalize apparent abnormalities in intelligent behavior. Two basic approaches to defining rationality are using either *calculated rationality* (explicit calculation of consequences of actions in terms of objectives) or *systematic rationality* (following sensible rules) to evaluate decision-making behavior.

Calculated Rationality. Calculated rationality is generally used in defining rational decision making, but this view can be criticized as inadequate either because it inaccurately characterizes preferences or because it uses the wrong unit of analysis. March (1978) described four types of calculated rationality: *limited, process, contextual,* and *game.*

Limited Rationality. Limited rationality considers the degree of problem simplification needed to enable decision makers to deal with sufficient alternatives and information to reach a sound decision (e.g., Lindblom, 1965; March & Simon, 1958). Those who adopt this view tend to use simple search rules, work backward, and use organizational slack, uncertainty avoidance, incrementalism, and muddling through as ways to overcome limits on rational decision making (March, 1978).

Process Rationality. Process rationality emphasizes making sense of decisions in terms of the processes used in making decisions, rather than in terms of decision outcomes (e.g., Cohen & March, 1974). The focus is on ways people act while making decisions and on the symbolic content of the choice and the procedures used in choosing. The primary intent is to make sense of the way choices are orchestrated (March, 1978).

Contextual Rationality. Contextual rationality is concerned with the degree to which choices are mingled with other demands for a decision maker's attention (e.g., Cohen,

March, & Olsen, 1972; Schelling, 1971). Rationality of choice is determined by opportunity costs of attending to the choice situation and by the apparent randomness with which people, problems, choices, and solutions become joined together (March, 1978).

Game Rationality. Game rationality deals with the degree to which individuals in various social institutions calculate their self-interests and combine those calculations as the group pursues joint goals (e.g., Brams, 1975). Rationality is expressed through forming coalitions, developing mutual incentives, attending to goals sequentially, manipulating information, and interpersonal gaming. Common to the calculated rationality theories is the view that intelligent decision makers calculate the extent to which their actions will attain desired objectives and act sensibly to achieve the objectives. Actions have consequences that are intended, are conscious, and relate to personal goals (March, 1978).

Systematic Rationality. While calculated rationality theories are most frequently used to guide organizational decision making, March (1978) reported that some research interest had been shown in systematic rationality (e.g., Becker, 1976). According to this view, knowledge accumulates across time, people, and organizations within a system, with no one having complete access to this knowledge. Hence, actions are taken by sensible people but without understanding of the full body of knowledge. Systematically rational theories produce difficulties for those interested in engineering improved decision making. Systematically rational behavior is not viewed as following from calculation of consequences based on objectives. In fact, proponents of these theories suggest either that calculation is not performed, or that calculated rationality has value only as a long-surviving social rule of behavior or as an experientially learned tendency. March (1978) described three types of

systematic rationality: *adaptive rationality, selected rationality,* and *posterior rationality.*

Adaptive Rationality. Adaptive rationality refers to learning through experiences by either individuals or groups (e.g., Day & Groves, 1975). Generally, these theories assume that behavior will approach rational behavior based on complete knowledge if the experience lasts long enough and if preferences and the decision situation remain stable (March, 1978).

Selected Rationality. Selected rationality considers the processes through which individuals or organizations are selected for growth or survival (e.g., Winter, 1975). These theories assume that rational behaviors are those actions that enable the social institution to grow or to survive. Choice is identified with standard operating procedures and social regulation of roles (March, 1978).

Posterior Rationality. Posterior rationality looks at decisions as intentional, after-the-fact interpretations of events, rather than at intentions as leading to decisions and on to decision consequences (e.g., Hirschman, 1967; Weick, 1969). Actions should be consistent with preferences, but actions produce experiences that are later given meaning—that is, a decision may be assumed to have caused certain consequences (March, 1978).

Conclusion. Viewing rationality from the various perspectives described can sharpen and extend our understanding of decision making. Yet these viewpoints also challenge the classical views of rational decision making. If behaviors that appear to deviate from calculated rationality are seen to be intelligent, then models of calculated rationality may be considered deficient, both as descriptions of how decisions are made and as prescriptions about how decisions should be made. Systematic views of rationality may provide insights to more realistically cope with some of the observed deficiencies of calculated rationality (March, 1978).

Cognitive/Perceptual Models

Cognitive/perceptual models of decision making draw on the work of cognitive psychologists in the areas of evaluative and predictive judgments and choice. These processes underlie the intuitive thinking activities (e.g., Simon, 1987) that appear so important to strategic decision making. Hogarth (1987) described two major conclusions drawn from the research on intuitive thinking. First, a great many studies have confirmed that even simple laboratory tasks require more information processing capacity than humans have. Slovic (1972) contrasted the limited abilities of humans, based on research concerning human information-processing capacity, with Shakespeare's view of human infinite ability. The contrast between the literary view and actuality is indeed striking. Hogarth's (1987) second conclusion stated that cognitive research has revealed that people misperceive information content, process information sequentially to accommodate their poor integrative capacity, and have very limited memory.

An ongoing discussion in the field concerns the extent to which these findings are due to the artificiality of research tasks and setting. Similar findings about errors in judgment, however, have occurred with expert judges (professionals in the various fields involving judgments) and in a variety of settings and tasks outside the laboratory that range from gambling in casinos to buying theater tickets.

There are strategies and techniques to help people overcome their limitations in judgmental ability. Some of these techniques are designed to help people represent the consequences of the courses of action they are considering (e.g., consider a goal hierarchy and consequences at each level) as they engage in decision analysis (e.g., Howard, 1988). Other techniques help in assessing uncertain aspects of a decision (e.g., to more accurately elicit subjective probabilities from decision makers [Speltzer & Stael von Holstein, 1975]). Still other techniques help decision-making groups combine their opinions, possibly by using the Delphi approach (Linstone & Turoff, 1975). In making repetitive judgments (e.g., personnel selection decisions), the decision maker may want to "bootstrap" by building a linear regression model. Such a strategy reduces the inconsistency found in clinical, case-by-case decisions (e.g., Dawes, 1979).[2]

Incremental Adjustment Models

Incremental adjustment models are examples of March's adaptive rationality classification and also have been described as myopic-existential experiments that involve taking sequential, iterating steps away from the existing state—both to learn more about what is effective in the decision problem and its context and to generate new experiences (Taylor & Vertinsky, 1981). Examples in the decision-making literature of incremental adjustment are *disjointed incrementalism* (Lindblom, 1959), *logical incrementalism* (Quinn, 1980), *unfolding rationality* (Pondy, 1983), and *management learning* (Mintzberg, 1977). Incrementalism was developed to describe decisions made in a political context. As such, it is mainly a descriptive model reflecting how decisions are made in groups in which members may have conflicting preferences. More recently, this approach has formed the basis for a normative model (Quinn, 1980).

A distinction has been made between rational-analytic (calculated rational or synoptic) and incremental models of decision making. Rational-analytic and incremental strategic decisions differ in the following ways: (a) how decision making is initiated, (b) how goals are used, (c) how means are linked to ends, (d) how choice is made, (e) how comprehensive or analytically complete the decision making is, and (f) how comprehensively decisions are integrated into strategy

(Fredrickson & Mitchell, 1984). A controversial point concerning rationality is just how comprehensive decisions should be. Too much comprehensiveness leads to the difficulties I've mentioned that are inherent in classical models of rationality—it is impossible to process the complete information base required for maximizing types of strategic decisions.

Johnson (1988) linked incrementalism with a cognitive process of enactment in an attempt to explain a long-term change in a firm's strategy. In this organizational action view of strategy formulation, strategy develops incrementally as the product of political, programmatic, cognitive or symbolic aspects of administration. Incremental approaches to decision making are more dynamic and interactive with the problem during the process of deciding than is the relatively static rational-analytic model.

The disjointed incrementalism approach to strategy making does not require that parties to the decision agree about objectives. Decision environments are tested, and based on feedback from the tests, either criteria or alternatives are adjusted. Lindblom (1959) argued that the most politically feasible action is usually a strategy that differs only slightly from the current strategy. Agreement among decision makers is sought in incrementalizing rather than high goal attainment, and it is generally easier to get agreement on marginal changes in strategy than to get agreement on organizational goals.

In this approach, decision makers take only small, incremental moves away from the existing state in the direction they desire to take, making successive limited comparisons. The steps, however, do not have to reach a precisely stated goal desired by the decision makers. When the small step has been achieved, the group reassesses the situation and decides if further steps should be taken. The incremental steps and evaluation points can be viewed as small experiments used by decision makers to learn about themselves and their decision environment as decision making progresses (Taylor & Vertinsky, 1981).

A financial strategy development approach based on incrementalism was proposed by Wu (1981). Integrating incrementalism into the financial planning model was intended to overcome the limitations imposed by the traditional, rational-analytic approach to planning financial strategies. The limitations pertain to the limited problem-solving ability of humans, the cost and inadequacy of information, the openness of systems for which financial analysis is done, and the many forms in which policy problems appear.

The steps developed for decision making using incremental adjustment (Wu, 1981, pp. 135–136) are:

1. Define problem and general goals.

2. Appraise the incremental adjustments needed to deal with problem.

3. Assess consequences of the incremental steps and decide if this is acceptable.

4. Implement incremental adjustments if consequences are acceptable; if not, go back to the second step.

5. Assess consequences of implementing the incremental adjustments.

6. If the total problem is not solved, initiate a further incremental adjustment with step one .

The features of this method include the following: (a) there is no necessity to identify all decision alternatives, (b) incremental adjustments are in line with the decision maker's values and should improve the situation, and (c) by evaluating the outcomes of each incremental step, it is possible to move toward an acceptable solution.

Berlin (1978) has structured the muddling-through approach of incrementalism through administrative experimentation in organizational contexts. In this approach, administrators systematically make small changes in the organization and receive feedback from this trial-and-error process. Reorganizing a health department permitted an administrator to conduct time-series experiments to determine the effect on cost per unit of service produced by assigning a health manager to each district health center. He suggested that this approach to administrative experiments would be useful under the following conditions: (a) organizational subunits are unable to readily communicate with each other (e.g., geographically separate), (b) an administrator is able to change some subunits but not others, (c) measures of the results of the experimental changes are available, (d) there is sufficient lead time to permit a time-series experiment to be conducted, and (e) the administrator is able to get timely feedback regarding the effects of the administrative experiments. Relatively few objectives need to be considered, and alternatives considered generally are available through local search. There is no requirement for an exhaustive assessment of the problem environment (Berlin, 1978).

When decisions can develop through a series of limited, discrete steps representing sequential subdecisions, and when a good deal of disagreement exists among decision makers regarding goals, incremental adjustment suggests that subproblems may be treated more effectively as new and separate problems. Also, instead of attempting to anticipate and prepare for adverse consequences, it may be more effective to wait for them to occur. Incrementalizing tends to overlook important values, outcomes, and decision alternatives. When agreement among decision makers is essential, they may choose to stress agreement and acceptance of a decision by the group rather than high-level goal attainment. This technique is well suited to the political decision environment that it was originally intended to describe. Strategic decisions also involve a good deal of politics, so incrementalism seems useful in this context as well. The greatest limitation of using incrementalism in strategic decisions is that solutions reached by this procedure tend to be conservative, since the method uses small steps. Adjustments also tend to be slow, due to the need to reevaluate the decision situation after each step.

Strategic Planning Models

Starr (1965) includes planning as a form of decision making. The link between planning and decision making has also been emphasized by Ackoff (1970), who concluded that while not all decision making is planning, planning is clearly decision making. Planning is a special type of decision making that is performed in advance of the planned actions, involves a system of decisions, and is motivating in that it focuses activity on things to be done. The strategic planning model possesses some of the logic and systematic and comprehensive elements of rational-analytic models. Yet planning is adaptive in the sense that the typical five-year plan is reviewed and adjusted each year by most firms. It is subject to cognitive and perceptual influences (e.g., Taylor, 1976, 1982) and involves collective decision making, since an entire organization may engage in this form of decision making.

The strategic planning model of decision making is the dominant model used in strategic management and business policy, and at times the strategic planning model and strategic management have been viewed as nearly synonymous (e.g., Pearce & Robinson, 1988). Not surprisingly, strategic planning models are widely used by business firms. Ramanujam, Camillus, and Venkatraman (1987) studied trends in using strategic planning that were revealed by the responses of more than 200 corporate executives to a survey questionnaire. They found a trend toward increased use of planning (81% reported increased use) and an increased assessment of its value to the firm (82% reported seeing an increased value in planning). They also reported a 75 percent increase in the amount of time the chief executive spent planning and a 74 percent increase in executives' acceptance of the outputs of planning. Resistance to planning was reported to decrease for 58 percent of the respondents.

Not all firms use the same processes, nor do they all have the same level of formality in their planning approaches. Nevertheless, planning is an essential activity in the usual conceptualization of strategic management. Generally, strategic management approaches involve (a) setting the firm's missions, (b) assessing the firm itself and its external environment to identify the nature of the firm's competitive situation, (c) devising an appropriate strategy to compete successfully, and (d) implementing and controlling the execution of the strategy (e.g., Chakravarthy & Lorange, 1984). These steps represent strategic planning. Planning may proceed from top management downward in a firm. First, the business is studied as a whole and its environment is assessed; then lower operating units of the firm are included in the planning process. The top-down approach to planning may be unrealistic and may ignore special situations in the lower units. Another approach to planning, the tactical approach, is to initiate planning activities in the lower operating units of a firm and to proceed upward. After an initial analysis of the situation facing the operating units, the overall environment of the situation is analyzed. Frequently, some combination of these two approaches to planning is used in which an initial overall assessment of the firm's situation engages both the operating managers and the lower operating units in providing valuable information and critique of the planning outputs.

Strategic planning has generated a large volume of published research. Research on strategic planning has examined the effectiveness of this approach (e.g., Herold, 1972; Karger & Malik, 1975; Schoeffler, Buzzell, & Heaney, 1974), but the wide variety of planning systems used from one firm to another tends to confound conclusions. Among the planning issues investigated are the cognitive processes involved in strategic planning (e.g., Barnes, 1984), the relationship between participation in planning and the effectiveness of the strategic plan (e.g., Dyson & Foster, 1982), the organizational processes of managing a strategic planning effort (e.g., Lyles & Lentz, 1982), and methods for selecting Delphi panels for strategic planning purposes (Preble, 1984).

Bureaucratic Models

The bureaucratic decision model limits decision-making responsibilities to people in positions of authority in an organization (e.g., Weber, 1947). Typically, these people prepare detailed master plans for the direction the organization should take and organize a structured set of standard operating procedures for people lower in the organizational hierarchy to follow. Military organizations and government agencies tend to be organized for making decisions in a bureaucratic manner, and under highly stable environments this approach can be efficient. Routine decisions can be anticipated and made in a standardized way to reduce the demand on the decision-making capability of an organization. The efficiency attained by standard programs in organizations has been pointed out in the literature (e.g., Cyert & MacCrimmon, 1968; Cyert & March, 1963; March & Simon, 1958). Most firms handle some of their decisions using this approach, and frequently firms detail these decisions in the form of a policy manual. Most professions tend to standardize certain procedures with formal rules of conduct. For example, certification in a trade or profession generally is based on evidence that the individual knows the rules (e.g., building codes, accounting standards, rules of evidence).

The difficulty with bureaucratic decision models is that seldom do decision contexts in organizations remain stable. Consequently, strategic decisions under this model challenge the capability of an organization to anticipate all the events that may occur and to prepare standard decision protocols to cope with these events. Even if all situations an organization may face are anticipated, the individual or organizational unit may misperceive the situation and apply the incorrect response. A commercial aircraft entering the airspace of a country may be incorrectly judged to be an enemy military aircraft, with disastrous consequences. While there are some appropriate uses for the bureaucratic decision models in organizations, rarely is an entirely bureaucratic decision model an effective approach for making strategic decisions.

Collective Models

Much of the literature on group or collective decisions (e.g., Levine & Moreland, 1990; McGrath & Kravitz, 1982; Zander, 1979) is applicable to strategic decisions made by firms. A top management team or a board of directors is typically a small group of decision makers and subject to the dynamics that affect any group. Small groups may also be involved in strategic decisions from the perspective of strategic business units within a firm. Strategies typically are evaluated by small groups at various levels of an organizational hierarchy and implemented by small groups of employees representing organizational units.

There are three types of collective decision models: *group dynamics, game theory,* and *devil's advocate and dialectical inquiry.* I will describe each type, emphasizing aspects most relevant to SDM.

Group Dynamics Models. Group dynamics models recognize that organizational and political forces heavily influence the decision-making process and attempt to incorporate these types of forces into decisions. This approach may reduce conflict, increase conflict, or simply model and utilize the degree of conflict that exists in a decision situation. It thus reflects the level of conflict that typically exists in the decision situation that it was developed to understand: decisions made in organizations. Organizational decisions generally are not made by single individuals or by groups acting in unison. There may be no internal consensus among the parties to a decision concerning goals and objectives of a firm. Multiple goals may not only exist, they may be incompatible with one another. The parties to a decision may disagree about preferred goals. Generally, organizational decision makers focus on solving immediate problems instead of long-term problems and frequently rely on standard operating procedures, formal plans, industry standards, or officially stated policies.

Much research on collective decisions has taken place in large organizations, generally on work groups within business corporations (e.g., Alderfer & Smith, 1982; Ancona, 1987; Krantz, 1985). Research on collective behavior in business firms has tended to focus on topics such as links between the small group and the corporation. Among the topics investigated are the dependence of the group on the firm and the attempts by the small group to adapt to the corporation (Ancona & Caldwell, 1988; Tichy, 1981). For example, it has been argued that successful work groups relate to their corporate settings through scanning for information, maintaining a profile that will impress others, negotiating, and providing a group defense buffer (Ancona & Caldwell, 1988). Group members perform roles corresponding to these activities (e.g., guard or scout).

An important topic for research on groups is how group members relate to one another. The goals of all members of a group cannot be simultaneously met. Conflict results. Occasionally, conflict may produce creativity and innovation (e.g., Nemeth & Staw, 1989), but it is more likely to result in negative consequences for the group and the containing organization. Among the negative consequences of group conflict are lowered productivity, hostility among group members, and disbanding of the group (Levine & Moreland, 1990).

How influence attempts shape behavior in groups is another central theme addressed in group studies. It is apparent that influence attempts figure importantly both in the choice process and in the nature of the choice itself. A normative approach to strategic management suggests that consensus is an important outcome of the strategy formulation process, but Preim (1990) found that a curvilinear relationship existed between group consensus and performance, moderated by environmental dynamism.

Game Theory Models. Game theory (Shubek, 1987) is a mathematical model of decision making. As is the case in rational-analytic decision models, game theory attempts to define the decision problem space in a formal manner and to propose an optimal decision. Unlike the rational-analytic models, game theory outcomes reflect joint decisions made by more than one decision maker. In some formulations, the nature of the decision outcomes may produce conflicts among the players as they try to reach their conflicting goals. Most game theory formulations require each player to choose a course of action, but players cannot communicate with other players. All players state their decision simultaneously, and outcomes for each player are prescribed by a payoff matrix.

Bargaining Games. Bargaining games or mixed-motive games, such as the prisoner's dilemma (Rapoport & Chammah, 1965), permit communication, persuasion, and deception to have an impact on the choices made by players. A player may gain an advantage in this game through having information about the preferences of other players. Since both cooperation and competition are involved in organizational contexts, mixed-motive games appear highly relevant to strategic decisions. Mixed-motive games involve a cooperative solution that is of benefit to both players but does not yield the greatest gain to either player. Many strategic decisions involve elements of mixed-motive games. A firm may be dealing with a supplier who can provide the lowest cost of all potential suppliers, but the suppliers' product fails to meet the exacting standards specified by the firm. Rather than giving the order to another supplier, the firm may work with the first supplier to improve the quality of its product and find a quality/price position that is of mutual advantage to both the firm and the supplier. Murray (1978) has described a process by which the strategic plan of an electric utility company was developed through negotiation with external parties.

Zero-sum Games. Zero-sum games involve pure competition. Each player can win only the amount that another player loses. No combination of choices that benefit both players exists in zero-sum games. This form of game is also determinate—the rational player will always receive the same outcome. In a typical game, both players will choose the outcome that results in no gain or loss for either player. Hence, the outcomes of zero-sum games, unlike the mixed-motive games, cannot be influenced by persuasion and negotiation.

Competitive situations in strategic management may contain either type of game formulation. Though game theory is conceptually valuable as a way to describe payoffs in a competitive strategic situation, it cannot be used to fully model most strategic business situations. Nevertheless, the heuristic value of game theory as a way to understand the nature of strategic competitive situations is great. MacDonald (1975) discussed a number of business situations, ranging from the development of J. Paul Getty's oil empire to Walt Disney's negotiations with bankers to fund the film *Fantasia*. Schelling (1963) drew upon game theory concepts to discuss the use of threats and counterthreats in high-conflict situations.

Devil's Advocate and Dialectical Inquiry Models.   Devil's advocate and dialectical inquiry are both techniques that represent collective decision models because they are designed to create a level of conflict among group members that will facilitate decision making. The devil's advocate method requires that some group member point out weaknesses or flaws in solutions to problems favored by the group. This technique has been investigated to determine how effective it is in encouraging high-quality solutions and the conditions under which it would be most useful (e.g., Schwenk, 1984).

The dialectical inquiry method (e.g., Mason, 1969; Mitroff & Emshoff, 1979) is more structured than the devil's advocate method in that it prescribes the nature of the positions to be taken by group members speaking for and against a course of action. It is a debate format in which each position is presented by its supporters, with both sides having equal access to all available information about the decision. After both sides have presented the arguments for their favorite position, the group works together to synthesize the best features of each course of action into a new action that should be superior to either of the original actions. A major difference between the two methods is that the dialectical method requires an alternative action to be analyzed, whereas the devil's advocacy method focuses only on what is wrong with the original decision alternative. Research with dialectical inquiry suggests that it tends to control conflict in a planning group, but may not lead to more effective planning decisions (e.g., Chanin & Shapiro, 1985; Cosier, Ruble, & Aplin, 1978).

Several researchers have examined tests of propositions about whether groups using dialectical inquiry or devil's advocacy make better decisions and whether these approaches are superior to use of control treatments (e.g., Chanin & Shapiro, 1985; Schweiger & Sandberg, 1989; Schweiger, Sandberg, & Ragan, 1986). A general finding from this line of research is that groups using dialectical inquiry or devil's advocacy tend to make better decisions than do control groups, but dialectical inquiry proved to be superior to devil's advocacy only in the validity of the assumptions used and not in quality of recommendations (Schweiger & Sandberg, 1989).

Collective Model Concepts.   Many concepts are important in the collective models. Among the most important to strategic decision making and understanding behavior in groups are the concepts of *power, coalitions,* and *groupthink.*

Power.   The concept of power figures importantly in describing how conflict among group members may influence group decision making. Strategic decision making cannot be explained without knowing the relative degrees of power held by the stakeholders involved. Power not only affects choices and outcomes, it also influences other behaviors of decision makers (e.g., Shaw, 1981). Pfeffer (1977) clearly demonstrated how power can shape decisions made by universities. Scarce resources are the rule, and power influences the outcome as organizational members compete with each other and with forces outside the organization for the limited resources. One line of research with direct implications for strategic decision making deals with tactics used by group members in their influence attempts (e.g., Ford & Zelditch, 1988; Steckler & Rosenthal, 1985). Another research thrust with implications for strategic management is the development and validation of an inventory to measure French and Raven's five sources of power for CEOs of large firms (Pearce & Robinson, 1976). Power is an important concept in understanding coalition formation.

Coalitions. Coalitions are central to understanding group decision making from the perspective of collective decision models (e.g., Cook & Gilmore, 1984). Conflicts within a strategic decision making context may be resolved by coalitions made up of individuals or groups who have been drawn into a coalition to further the goals of coalition members. Competition for limited resources of a firm may take the form of coalition behavior. Power and politics are likely to have significant influences on strategic decision making when there are many conflicts among decision makers and when allocation of resources can be influenced by bargaining and negotiation.

Two types of coalitions that appear relevant to strategic decision making are minimum-winning-size coalitions and stable coalitions. The *minimum-winning-size coalition* is advantageous for its members in that each member will gain more from this form of coalition than any other type of coalition would yield. Winning by the smallest margin possible means that the winnings will be shared by the smallest number of players. In minimum resource theory, winnings are shared among the members of a winning coalition in direct proportion to the resources each member has committed to the coalition. There is no advantage to a player for committing more resources than necessary to win; to do so would only make each coalition member's resources of less value. *Stable coalitions* offer a decision maker a choice situation that can be anticipated. Faced with changes in the decision situation that cause a coalition to no longer yield the greatest gain for a player, the player would be expected to either form a more advantageous coalition or go it alone. Stable coalitions are important to many aspects of SDM—such as selecting joint actions that would be of mutual advantage or considering the duration of contractual

agreements used by a coalition (such as treaties for mutual defense or trade). Also, stable coalitions are valuable in anticipating the consequences of withdrawing from a coalition.

Researchers from both game theory (e.g., Kahan & Rapoport, 1984) and social psychology (e.g., Komorita, 1984) have devoted considerable effort to understanding bargaining and coalitions. The majority of coalition formation studies involve experiments performed in the laboratory. This type of research on coalition formation has been criticized for ignoring relationships among the subjects before and after the coalition situation, as well as neglecting the social environment of the game (Cook & Gilmore, 1984). Research limitations such as these tend to reduce the relevance of bargaining and coalition research for SDM applications (Levine & Moreland, 1990).

Several researchers, however, have studied coalition formation in more natural settings. For example, Lawler (1983) studied the influence of leader behavior on coalitions formed by subordinates. Thompson, Mannix, and Bazerman (1988) studied how decision rules affect coalitions in real negotiating groups. Miller and Komorita (1986) examined the influences of communication and information restrictions, uncertainty of a coalition actually winning, the ability to win without forming a coalition, and earned rewards (rather than assigned rewards) on coalition behavior. This trend toward conducting coalition research in more natural settings has and will contribute to our understanding of coalitions.

The use of power in an organization is likely to be influenced by coalitions. Coalitions made up of many members, or coalitions in which members hold about the same amount of power, present a situation in which preferences of many people need to be reflected in a decision. Also, resources of coalition members are likely to affect decision formulation, range of alternatives considered, and the way in which a decision is implemented (e.g.,

Komorita, 1984; Luce & Raiffa, 1957). It has been proposed that coalitions may also influence decision making in organizations by altering the goals and objectives of a firm, or even by causing a firm to be redesigned (e.g., Pfeffer, 1977).

Groupthink.   Groupthink has important implications for strategic decisions made by groups of people, such as boards of directors, task forces, or management teams. Stress applied to groups appears to produce tendencies to lessen external conflict and seek consensus. Some high-status groups have been found to yield to conformity when they feel they must resort to quick action to deal with a crisis. Groupthink may occur as they attempt to avoid the minority opinions of some group members, as well as the opinions of outsiders who do not agree with the group's majority viewpoint (Janis & Mann, 1977). Cohesiveness, defined as attraction to a group, appears to be the most logical way to explain groupthink. In fact, a high degree of group cohesiveness seems to be necessary for groupthink.

Groupthink can be viewed as a collective pattern of defensive bolstering used by a decision-making group to shield itself from negative information and criticism. Bolstering can be produced by processes such as (a) exaggerating favorable outcomes, (b) minimizing unfavorable outcomes, (c) denying aversive feelings associated with unfavorable outcomes, (d) exaggerating the time lag before action will need to be taken on a decision, (e) minimizing the degree of social surveillance needed to enforce the decision, and (f) minimizing personal responsibility for the decision. It should be noted that bolstering can be useful when a thorough search and appraisal has been made and the best choice has been reached; then bolstering may help to increase commitment to the choice as it is implemented.

Generally, groupthink is likely to have a negative influence on decision-making effectiveness. If critical evaluation of as many alternatives as possible in the time available and within information processing constraints is most likely to lead to good decisions, then groupthink can be expected to inhibit decision making. Being unrealistically optimistic, failing to heed warnings, and misperceiving the opponent are not likely to contribute to high-quality decisions. Isolation of decision-making groups from outside opinions, statement by a leader of a preferred solution at the beginning of a discussion, exertion of strong group pressures by group members against those who do not agree with the majority, and use of mind guards by group members are all likely to contribute to poor-quality decision making.

Summary and Extension.   Collective models are highly relevant to strategic decision making because they focus on decision making by groups. Group influences are pervasive in the organizational contexts in which strategic decisions are made—groups within an organization and groups in an organization's environment (e.g., stakeholders may influence decisions made by boards of directors, competitors may influence strategies chosen by a firm, customers may influence a firm's marketing decisions). Each of the collective decision models examined in this section approach group influence on strategic decisions from different perspectives.

The group dynamics model yields insights into social and political forces that shape decisions made by groups of organizational members. Power and influence are central concepts from group dynamics, and groupthink is generally viewed as a threat to effective group decisions. Devil's advocate and dialectical inquiry models are designed to assist decision-making groups to accurately evaluate the decision alternatives they are considering. Game theory models focus on understanding how competition for scarce resources shapes bargaining among those involved in competitive decisions. Here, influence is generally determined by economic power, and coalitions enable those involved in the game to increase their share of economic gains from the competition.

Fredrickson (1986) reviewed the literature on the strategic decision-making process and integrated it with the literature on organizational structure. He developed propositions to explain how the characteristics of an organization's strategic decision processes are affected by its structure. Another extension of collective decision models is represented by the development of a decision-making paradigm of organizational design in which organizations are designed primarily to facilitate decision making (Huber & McDaniel, 1986). As Huber (1990) points out, developments in the areas of management information systems, decision support systems, and advanced information technologies are making contributions to understanding how organizational decision makers use information to make decisions.

Interpretive Models

Interpretive models of decision making refer to a decision maker's subjective interpretation of the decision problem space. Perspectives of problem space may be distorted by social constructions in a false sense of orderliness, and causal relationships may be inferred where none exist. The two approaches to decisions that can be classified as interpretive models are *enactment* and *illusory* decision models.

Enactment Models. Some approaches to understanding organizational decision making take the general position that the problem space is not an entity that can be observed objectively, but is the subjective creation of people involved in the decisions. Enacted models of organizational decisions (Weick, 1977; Weick & Daft, 1983) and strategic management (Pfeffer & Salancik,

1978) are derived from a world view in which an organization's environment is formed through the social construction and interaction processes of actors in the organization. In this view, events are assumed to occur, and later, decisions are identified to which these events can logically be attributed.

A model of the organization as an interpretation system has been proposed (Weick & Daft, 1983) in which four interpretation modes are described (enacting, discovering, conditional viewing, and undirected viewing). Use of each mode depends on how much the organization intrudes into its environment and the beliefs management holds about the extent to which the external environment can be analyzed.

Smircich and Stubbart (1985) described organizational environments as enacted through the social constructions and interaction processes of organized actors. They suggest that it is important to abandon the conventional prescription that organizations should adapt to their environments. Such conventional wisdom, they claim, obscures a good deal of the complexity, ambiguity, and abstraction in the strategic management process. Executives do not merely react to the environment—they also direct future outcomes. It is important to rethink the role of constraints, threats, and opportunities in analyzing strategic position. Managers face an overwhelming tide of situations, events, pressures, and uncertainties, and they must negotiate decisions and find acceptable ways to explain their social world. As Huff (1982) suggested, one prominent sensemaking mechanism is the industry group.

The enacted view also challenges one to think differently about the role of the strategic manager (Smircich & Stubbart, 1985). In the enacted model, a strategist's task is to create meaning from the chaotic world of continuous streams of ecological changes and discontinuities. Relevant and irrelevant categories of events must be interpreted, and people must make sense of situations by engaging in an interpretative process that includes both intellectual and emotional realms. Managers can strategically influence this process by providing a vision that explains the streams of events and actions, thus making sense of their chaotic world (Davis, 1982; Pondy, 1976).

Illusory Decision Models. In illusory decision models, outcome events are viewed as unintended outcomes of organizational processes (Olsen, 1976). Observers merely retrospectively reconstruct events and their causes. Illusory decision approaches differ from other models of decision making in that the illusory approaches do not assume that events represent the realization of an organizational members's purposes.

Illusory decision models make use of goals very differently than other approaches (Olsen, 1976). Most approaches, such as rational-analytic models, assume choice behaviors are purposive. Hence, in these models (a) beliefs and attitudes precede attention and behavior, (b) beliefs and attitudes are sufficiently stable that attention will stay at a constant level during the choice process, and (c) the content of a choice can be predicted based on knowledge of the existing level of attention. Organizational members will continue to engage in decision-making behavior as long as they find the resources available to them attractive (Olsen, 1976). In contrast, illusory decision models view goals as misleading constructs that impart a false sense of order and purpose to choice processes.

Cohen, March, and Olsen (1972) proposed an illusory decision model, the *garbage can* model, to describe how decisions are made in organizations. In the garbage can model, people have limited energy and time to act on their beliefs and attitudes, and may not find decision making an attractive activity. Moreover, organization members direct their efforts to the choice situations they find most appealing.

According to the garbage can model, it is erroneous to suggest that organizational choice activities follow an orderly sequence from problem recognition to decision implementation. Instead, organizational decisions are viewed as the chance convergence of four streams of forces—representing choice situations, organizational members, decision problems, and decision solution—each of which is relatively independent of the other.

Yet the observation reported by Cohen et al. (1972) implied that the garbage can model also exhibits some orderliness. As organizational members move about the organization, they seem to identify similar problems and apply similar solution methods. One contribution of illusory decision models for advancing decision making is that reducing the emphasis on the importance of goals in directing decision making may advance understanding of how choices are actually made in complex organizations. Though illusory models are intriguing, they hold limited promise for efforts to improve decision making in a normative sense.

Contingency Models

Contingency models focus on contingencies that affect strategic decisions and can be viewed as hybrid SDM models, since contingency variables can be incorporated with other models of SDM described in this chapter. Beach and Mitchell (1978) identified two types of contingency variables: *task* and *decision maker*. According to Beach and Mitchell, there are two task contingency variables and three decision maker contingency variables. The task contingency variables are (a) the decision problem (unfamiliarity, ambiguity, complexity, and instability) and (b) the decision environment (irreversibility, significance, accountability, and time and/or money constraints). The decision maker contingency variables are (a) knowledge, (b) ability, and (c) motivation.

Beach and Mitchell (1978) also identified three decision-making strategies: aided-analytic, unaided-analytic, and nonanalytic. *Aided-analytic strategies* require the decision maker to apply a prescribed procedure using tools (e.g., a computer) in a guided systematic attempt to analyze the decision and evaluate the components. A major example of this strategy is decision analysis. In *unaided-analytic strategies,* the decision maker is limited to mental activities performed in his or her head. Examples are elimination by aspects (Tversky, 1972) and the large body of research on subjective expected utility analysis in which subjects attempt to do the calculations in their heads (e.g., Shanteau & Anderson, 1969; Tversky, 1967). The third strategy, *nonanalytic,* consists of simple, preformed rules that subjects apply by rote to decision tasks in which little information is acquired and decisions are not decomposed (e.g., flipping a coin). Use of these strategies is moderated by characteristics of the decision task and characteristics of the decision maker.

The model relating these strategies and contingency variables is rather complex, but in essence, the model identifies the strategy that may be used by decision makers in dealing with different types of problems. The decision maker is expected to choose a strategy that requires the lowest investment for a satisfactory solution, and that choice would depend on the problem type, the environment, and the attributes of the decision maker (Beach & Mitchell, 1978). This approach effectively describes the major variables that should serve as contingency variables for strategic decisions.

A more quantitative approach to modeling the contingencies related to organizational structure has been described by Lee, Luthans, and Olson (1982). In this approach, a goal programming model was developed to analyze and determine the optimal relationships for goal attainment between environmental variables and organizational structure variables for military organizations. In this model, nine organizational structure variables were used (such as size—the number of people in each organization, and level—squad, platoon, etc.). For demonstration of goal programming, a simplified model was described that appears useful for operationalizing a contingency approach to organizational theory. This model can be operationalized by (a) obtaining appropriate environmental and structural variables from organization theory, (b) using quantitative modeling techniques to obtain the logical relationships between these variables, (c) developing a model to optimize structural variables, given environmental variables, and (d) using the model in applied settings (Lee et al., 1982). This approach appears flexible in analyzing various relationships and holds promise for developing more effective organizations.

Components of Strategic Decision Making

This section describes the major components involved in making strategic decisions. Many different sets of strategic decision-making components have been proposed in the literature, but most contain the processes of (a) stating the mission, (b) assessing internal and external environments, (c) developing strategy, (d) choosing strategy, and (e) implementing and controlling execution of strategy. These components provide a focus for our discussion of implications of the psychological models of SDM processes.

Stating the Mission

Development of a company mission can be viewed as similar to goal setting in psychological research. These are the goals or standards used in identifying problems (e.g., gap analysis, which identifies problems as discrepancies between existing and desired states) and in setting priorities for their solution. Policy analysis and strategic management have tended to focus on recommending features of good mission statements in terms of the effect the statement may have on the firm and on its competitors. Little formal research has been conducted on mission setting, probably because of the difficulty of using conclusive research designs with real organizations. Nonetheless, one may empirically examine the effect of various mission statements on competitors' strategies, on morale of company employees, on the firm's performance, or on activities of other stakeholders of the firm (e.g., Pearce & David, 1987). These studies could be performed in real organizations or in the laboratory. Research may take the form of market research or simulated organizational contexts. Also, themes developed by content analysis of mission statements could be related to performance of firms. Another potential line of research would be to focus on the extent to which missions are effectively communicated to employees and others and how best to communicate these missions.

A simulation experiment by Neave and Petersen (1980) found that one way to attain good organizational performance was for firms with high aspiration levels to use adaptive decision processes. It appears that the high internal standards held by a firm may drive the firm to improve its decision rules and to reduce its slack. Other observed methods to achieve good performance were to use optimal decision processes, in an efficiently operating firm, to use optimal decision processes, and to incrementally adapt decision procedures in a highly competitive environment.

A major advantage of incremental adjustment models is that they do not require explicitly stated, detailed missions or goals. Other decision making models would view the strategic mission of a firm in a way very different from the incremental adjustment perspective. A few examples may illustrate this point. In bureaucratic decision models, well-informed authorities are likely to choose the missions for a firm, and organizational

members would yield to authority. Planning models require missions that are operationally defined, both to provide direction to the firm's strategic efforts and to gather measurable feedback about progress in attaining strategic objectives. Planning programs may also benefit from adopting a program involving separate goal setting, budgeting, and performance evaluation for operating and strategic activities of the firm. Collective decision models stress stakeholder acceptance of strategic missions and use of power, negotiation, coalitions, and consensus regarding goals.

**Assessing Internal
and External Environments**

This component of strategic decision making refers to strategic analysis involving examining the company profile and assessing the external environment. Simultaneous assessment of the company profile and the external environment enables the firm to identify potentially attractive strategic opportunities. But these opportunities must be screened in light of the company mission to develop alternative strategies that are both feasible and attractive. Selecting strategies to act on is at the heart of strategic choice, and much SDM literature has dealt with this process. This component of SDM involves the psychological decision-making processes of (a) problem diagnosis, (b) problem specification, and (c) problem formulation or reformulation. I shall discuss the process of strategic analysis in light of relevant concepts and research drawn from the SDM models we have examined.

Problem Diagnosis. Problem diagnosis refers to identifying problems and determining their problem space. One important issue is to determine the cause of a strategic problem in terms of changes in competitor strategy, production system or materials, consumer preferences, and so forth. The Kepner and Tregoe (1965) approach is suitable for a broad range of strategic problems but is best suited for simpler functional-level problems that can be described as a system having temporarily gone out of an equilibrium state. This approach can be extended, however, to cover problems in which goals are idea states rather than customary standards of performance. The problem analysis stage of Kepner and Tregoe is similar to the gap analysis of SDM.

Both consultants and organizational members generally arrive at a firm with education, experiences, and values that predispose them to find certain types of problems. Even in the garbage can model, decision makers tended to find the same types of problems as they moved about in an organization, and tended to apply the same solutions (Cohen, March, & Olsen, 1972). An argument may be made for a general diagnostician consulting function to determine the nature of a problem, supported by consultants with various specialties to solve the diagnosed problems (i.e., the medical model). Large consulting firms may, in fact, approximate this approach. But problem diagnosis is not an exact science, and the test of the effectiveness of a consulting intervention is generally, "Do things get better?"

Strategic planning models emphasize this stage and formalize it with techniques to assess the situation. Similar to rational-analytic models, the gap model defines a problem and initiates problem-solving activity. Most strategic decision-making approaches use some form of situation analysis, such as SWOT (assessment of strengths, weaknesses, opportunities, and threats in a firm's environment). Scanning the problem space frequently involves forecasts to deal with uncertainty. These involve probabilistic estimates, risk analysis, or sensitivity analysis, as well as preference analysis (e.g., risk preferences). While rational-analytic and cognitive models view these issues differently, both contribute heavily to our understanding of the process of situation analysis.

Decision analysis can be used to determine likely scenarios of future events. It also provides both a framework based on subjective expected utility calculations and techniques for assessing the probabilities of uncertain events, measuring risk-taking propensities for decision makers,[3] and judging decision-maker values relevant to the strategic decision under consideration.

Problem Specification. Problem specification determines the nature of a problem in terms of solution strategies (e.g., techniques in the field, such as JIT [Just in Time] for inventory control, or a matrix structure for adaptive behavior required for an organizational dysfunction or a functional area to which a problem may be assigned (e.g., a control problem, a morale problem, or a production problem). In either instance, a specialist is normally called in to solve the problem by applying one or more techniques. Smith (1988) has proposed a model of problem definition and structuring that defines problems in terms of the availability of solution strategies. This model structures problems by decomposing them into basic types of problem attributes (e.g., goals, solution alternatives, transformations) and suggests ways to structure problems so as to relate them to existing solution techniques.

Problem Framing. Problem framing relates to problem specification (Kahneman & Tversky, 1984; Tversky & Kahneman, 1974). Cognitive/ perceptual models have identified heuristic cognitive processes that provide frames of reference for perceiving problems, including *representativeness* (how likely it is that an object belongs to a given class), *viewability* (an event is viewed as likely if it is easy to recall examples), and *anchoring and adjustment* (setting a starting point and revising the judgment from there). Often these heuristics cause people to misperceive the true nature of a problem and violate accepted rules of probability in making judgments. Apparently, the way in which problems are presented to people tends to predispose them to make faulty judgments. Judgments in SDM appear likely to exhibit these biases, but some evidence has suggested that, at least for a complex and dynamic medical diagnosis decision problem, these biases are less likely to occur (e.g., Kleinmuntz, 1985).

Problem Formulation and Reformulation. Problem formulation and reformulation refer to restructuring the problem into a form that is easier to solve with existing techniques. The importance of creativity in the problem formulation process has been examined by Taylor (1975a), who concluded that problems requiring creative solutions can be formulated or reformulated in a manner that facilitates creative solutions. Knowledge of solutions is needed in order to know how to reformulate decision problems. For example, it may be necessary to decompose large, complex problems to make them easier to solve using decision analysis techniques (e.g., developing a lighter weight air cleaner is a subproblem of reducing size and weight of a car). The potential difficulty one must guard against is that suboptimal decisions may be made that lead to satisfactory solutions for subproblems, but not for the larger problem when the subdecisions are recombined.

One may also restructure problems in other ways to make them easier to solve, such as introducing assumptions into the problem formulation. This is frequently done to simplify a problem for solution techniques such as decision analysis, but invalid assumptions may lead to a problem formulation that produces faulty solutions. For instance, leaving an important variable out of the decision analysis can result in misleading recommendations. Howard, Matheson, and North (1972), in discussing the feasibility of seeding hurricanes, points out that leaving out an important variable such as the legal implications of seeding a hurricane could seriously distort the recommendation. Also, faulty estimates regarding variables included in a decision analysis can be misleading. Lawsuits resulting from Ford's decision to locate the Pinto gas tank behind the rear axle generally involved awards in cases involving deaths that

greatly exceeded the estimated cost of fatalities used by Ford to make the initial decision about gas tank location (Davidson & Goodpaster, 1983). The result may be interpreted as an inaccurate and misleading analysis of the problem.

Frost and Taylor (1985) used Allison's (1971) three-level analysis model to analyze the strategies used by professional journal editors to accept or reject manuscripts for publication. In the *rational actor* level of analysis of manuscript review, they concluded that the editor behaved like a normative scientist who objectively judges the worth of manuscripts and publishes those of greatest value. The decision is primarily determined by the values, standards, and actions of the journal editor as he or she seeks to accomplish one or more purposes (e.g., to maintain journal reputation or advance knowledge).

The *organizational* level of analysis of decision making appears to assume that organizations make decisions according to established conventions, frequently using standard operating procedures (Frost & Taylor, 1985). Organizational processes provide the context of choice and constrain the actions that editors may take. Most journal editors, for example, inherit a set of routines for choosing reviewers and judging manuscripts when they become editors. Editors are further constrained by customary routines imposed, for example, by editorial review boards, managing editors, and publication schedules. While standard operating procedures may add to the efficiency of the publication process, they also serve to constrain an editor's decision making freedom.

The *governmental* level of analysis emphasizes the political results of bargaining among parties to the decision (e.g., authors, reviewers, editors), as well as the perceptions, power, and maneuvers of players involved in this political game. Nepotism, professional affiliation, friendship, and other factors of this nature were observed by Mahoney (1977) to play a greater role in social science than in physical science editorial decisions. Also, reviewers were found to be biased against manuscripts that reported results opposed to the reviewer's point of view. Decision-making strategies based on the governmental political model have been found to feature use of power, subjective judgment, and compromise (e.g., Pfeffer, 1981). An important source of editorial power appears to reside in freedom to select reviewers. For example, selecting reviewers who are either hostile or sympathetic toward a controversial or a marginal manuscript is likely to strongly influence the decision about publishing it (Frost & Taylor, 1985).

The *rational actor* level, organizational, and governmental level of analysis models are all relevant in analyzing the decision-making process. Each model provides valuable perspectives in examining journal editorial decisions and the decision-making process. Based on their analysis of the decision-making process, Frost and Taylor (1985) made recommendations for improving editorial decisions and decision-making strategy.

Developing Strategy

Developing strategies involves the psychological processes of generating alternative problem solutions. Two types of solutions need to be considered in developing strategies: standard solutions and creative solutions. The general rule is the following: If an acceptable standard solution is available to a decision maker, then it should be used instead of spending time and resources reinventing a solution; if no appropriate solution is available, then it is necessary to engage in creative generation of alternatives. Each model of decision making would be expected to take a different view of creativity in strategic decision making.

Standard Solutions. Bureaucratic decision models suggest that standard operating procedures are efficient ways to make strategic decisions. These standardized procedures are decided in advance by an authority and made available to members of the organization. For example, the U.S. Forest Service prepared the seven-volume *Forest Service Manual* detailing their standard procedures (Kaufman, 1960). Kaufman reported that four of the seven volumes (i.e., *General Administration, Fiscal Control, National Forest Protection,* and *Management*) were issued to rangers. The more than 3,000 pages contained in the manuals describe what is to be done, who is to do it, how it is to be done, when and where each action should be taken, and the objectives the actions are designed to attain. The manual is continually updated as new situations arise. The intent of these manuals is to prescribe for rangers appropriate and standardized actions for any situation they face on the job. Standardized accounting practices serve the same function of ensuring that procedures are applied uniformly throughout the profession. Bureaucratic decision approaches see creativity as the province of those people in positions of authority; most organizational members, like the forest ranger, carry out standard orders.

Creative Solutions. Difficult problems often require a solution that is original (infrequent) and feasible (effectively solves the problem). An important consideration for applied creativity stimulation techniques is that creativity must result in a solution that is feasible. For example, a novel tax shelter program developed by a tax accountant would solve the problem only if it conforms to the relevant IRS tax code. A number of techniques are available in the psychological literature to stimulate the creativity of decision makers and help them to develop creative solutions to decision problems. Among the most useful methods to stimulate creativity in firms are *brainstorming, morphological analysis, nominal group technique,* and *synectics.* Taylor (1984) described the relative effectiveness of these methods and others for stimulating creative decision making.

Cognitive/perceptual decision models focus on ways to present decision problems or provide techniques to enable individual decision makers to be more creative by reformulating decision problems to more familiar structures or by using morphological analysis. Collective decision models attempt to marshal the forces of the group to achieve creative solutions through use of brainstorming, nominal group technique, or synectics. Planning decision models stress the allocation of resources to research and development to encourage the development of creative technologies or products.

One of the most promising methods for developing creative strategies is the *strategy table* (Howard, 1988). This table shows how an overall strategy can be defined by identifying many aspects of substrategies, then combining the substrategies to form the best overall strategy. These strategic options are then combined into grand strategies (described below) that represent the most promising means for attaining the desired results. Each grand strategy is then evaluated and compared to other grand strategies to determine which will have the best overall and long-term benefits for the firm.

Generic Business Strategies. Generic strategies—general types of strategies useful in many situations—are widely used in strategic decision making. These include basic strategies such as being the low cost producer, focus, or differentiation (e.g., Porter, 1980). A firm's comprehensive plan for reaching its long-term objectives is called its grand strategy. Twelve grand strategies have been identified: concentration, product development, market development, innovation, joint venture, concentric diversification, divestiture, liquidation, retrenchment, turnaround, and horizontal and vertical integration strategies (Pearce & Robinson, 1988).

Initiated in part by Hofer's (1975) discussion of a contingency view of strategy, attention has been devoted by Porter (1980, 1985) and by others (e.g., Abell, 1980; Hofer & Schendel, 1978; Miles & Snow, 1978) to developing typologies for classifying generic business strategies. For example, strategy types were empirically derived by a two-stage principal component and cluster analysis of a profit impact of marketing strategies (PIMS) data base for consumer products and an industrial data base (Galbraith & Schendel, 1983). This study found six types of strategies for consumer products (continuity, niche, climber, cash out, harvest, and build) and four types of strategies for industrial products (niche, maintenance, growth, and low commitment). Porter's contributions to understanding the nature of industry competition are among the most visible advances in strategic management and represent an analytical framework to be used to suggest appropriate generic strategy choices (Porter, 1980, 1985, 1990).

More recently, a system for classifying business strategies was proposed to overcome some of the limitations of the Abell and the Porter taxonomies (Chrisman, Hofer, & Boulton, 1988). Several weaknesses in the Porter taxonomy have been noted. Wright (1987) theorized that some successful firms use both differentiation and cost leadership simultaneously, whereas Porter's approach limits a firm to one strategy or the other. Also, Porter excluded the stuck-in-the-middle strategy from his scheme and tends to misclassify firms that try to differentiate through something other than a single industrywide difference (i.e., firms using different strategies in different market segments vs. firms using the same strategies in all market segments [Sandberg, 1986]). Porter does mention the possibility of simultaneous use of differentiation and cost leadership where being stuck in the middle may occur but excludes these considerations from the formal model.

The taxonomy proposed by Abell (1980) considers generic strategies to be based on the scope of a firm's goods and/or services, the extent of competitive differentiation, and whether these goods and/or services are differentiated across markets. Scope and differentiation can refer to technologies, customer groups, and customer functions. Three generic strategies result from this taxonomy: *focus* (e.g., narrow scope and one competitive weapon), *undifferentiation* (e.g., broad scope and one competitive weapon for all segments), and *differentiation* (e.g., broad scope and different weapons to compete in each segment). Abell's scheme fails to include some types of competitive weapons firms actually use, and the terms used to name the strategies are confusing. The Chrisman et al. (1988) classification scheme combines the competitive weapons of cost, utility, benefit, and shortage (just being at the right place at the right time) to yield 16 generic business strategies that are theoretically possible. This taxonomy combines some of the best features of the Porter and the Abell schemes while overcoming the major limitations of these schemes, and represents an important advance in developing generic business strategy classifications.

Choosing Strategy

Strategic decisions involve making choices; models of decision making view choices from various perspectives. Cognitive/perceptual models focus on the psychological aspects of choice (e.g., judgment of uncertainty, risk, and problem framing), and this topic has received a good deal of attention in the decision making literature. From the perspective of the planning, rational-analytic, and collective models that traditionally have dominated SDM, making a strategic decision involves evaluating each of the possible strategy options available to the firm in light of goals and objectives. Bureaucratic models follow much the same process, but the strategic choice activities are likely to be limited to those people in positions of authority. In incrementalizing, the primary consideration is that those involved in the decision-making process must accept each incremental

step. An ultimate solution of the larger problem is of secondary importance. Interpretive models are useful in suggesting that a decision maker's perception of the decision problem space is prone to subjective impressions, and approaches other than simply asking decision makers about their view of the problem situation may be needed to adequately answer SDM research questions.

Criteria. Many criteria are typically used to assess alternative actions in strategic choices. Decision makers may choose strategies on the basis of their own risk-taking propensity and opinions regarding profitability, growth, security, stability, and flexibility, as well as their willingness to adopt changes and their concerns about possible reactions to the strategy chosen by stakeholders and competitors.

Evaluating the quality of decisions can be improved by using a checklist appropriate to the decision (Howard, 1988). The checklist asks decision evaluators to systematically consider how well each element in the decision process was handled (e.g., specify how well the decision was framed; indicate any biases in information quality, values, or creativity; indicate the commitment to action, etc.). Influence diagrams have facilitated communication between decision maker and analyst by improving problem representation (e.g., Schachter, 1986).

Criteria for judging alternative strategies also may reflect the volatility of the firm's environment, the nature of competition in an industry, the organizational structure used by the firm, the life cycle stage of the firm's products, and the availability of resources to carry out the chosen strategy. Strategic decisions generally are based on the assessment of the decision situation by a relatively formal analysis in terms of the strengths, weaknesses, opportunities, and threats facing the firm, as described earlier.

In addition to choosing grand strategies, functional strategies may be developed by operating managers who specify in detail how the grand strategies will be made operational. Standard operating procedures may next be developed to more efficiently carry out routine and repetitive tasks, but use of these procedures may serve to limit the use of discretion by organizational members in carrying out the operating strategies. Contingency plans for strategic decisions have been adopted by many firms. Since conditions may turn out to be different from those expected, a sensitivity analysis is needed to identify the critical contingencies (e.g., an increase in interest rates, a technological advance, a labor strike). Under these contingency conditions, a firm would implement alternate strategies that are likely to be more effective in the new circumstances.

Hofer (1975) proposed a contingency theory of business strategy in which the content of various types of strategies is examined and appropriate strategies for each situation are suggested. Generic strategies such as those I've described earlier guide strategic decisions, but more specific direction can be given if the contingency variables—which moderate the effects of the independent on dependent variables in SDM research—are considered. Hence, the contingency model identifies conditions under which a given strategy is likely to be most effective. It appears that substantial advances in strategic decision-making theory and research can be made by more complete development of the contingency approach (Hofer, 1975).

Risk-taking Propensity . Tendencies to take or avoid risk influence strategic choices by predisposing a decision maker to prefer certain types of actions. Managers in highly uncertain and dynamic industries must live with greater overall levels of risk than would their counterparts in more stable industries. Risk-prone managers would be expected to prefer high-risk alternatives and would find attractive the opportunistic courses of action that offer high returns but involve risks. More conservative strategic alternatives would be more attractive

to risk-averse managers—courses of action that offer a greater margin of safety, even when they also promise lower returns. Gupta and Govindarajan (1984) studied risk-taking tendencies of decision makers, finding a link between risk-taking and choice of strategies. They showed the important aspect of risk-taking propensities was that the managers' risk preference should fit the mission assigned to the strategic business unit that they managed. Managers of high-performance units whose units were assigned star or build missions (growth of a business) were risk-prone. Conversely, the most successful managers of units assigned missions of harvesting (moving out of a business) tended to be risk-averse.

Decision makers also demonstrate a preference for strategies that are familiar to them. Current, familiar strategies affected choice of future strategies, particularly when the decision maker had a hand in selecting the current strategies (Carter, 1971). Incremental adjustments in strategy, which are more likely to be accepted by their bosses, appear to be attractive to those people responsible for charting future strategies of a firm. Staw's research (1976) suggested a disturbing tendency for decision makers faced with failing strategies to redouble their efforts in an attempt to make the strategies succeed, rather than to abandon the failing strategies for courses of action that may have a greater chance of success.

Power and Influence. Power in organizations can have several bases. For example, either charisma or expertise in skills valued by other members of an organization are important power bases (e.g., French & Raven, 1960). Also, power may be determined by organizational positions held by participants. Pfeffer (1977) studied power that resides in the formal authority structure of organizations. Power has also been observed to be linked to holding information others value (Mechanic, 1967). As strategic decisions are made, decision makers attempt to reduce uncertainty by striving to obtain more power than others in the organization hold. Decision makers with greater power have more discretion in influencing outcomes to reflect their preferences. This is central to the concept of uncertainty reduction common both to collective and rational-analytic approaches to decision making.

No single decision maker can possess all the information required, so strategic decisions typically require that many people contribute to decision making. Support of others would be required to carry out a decision, even if one person could make it unilaterally. Uncertainty generally is defined as possessing insufficient information to make a sound decision, and decision makers would be expected to seek information to reduce high levels of uncertainty. Similarly, information dependency is evident in the common expression that "knowledge is power." A form of uncertainty reducer that has direct implications for strategic decisions is communicating information needed by other people (e.g., Galbraith, 1973). Messages, including influence attempts, are transmitted through communication channels. Laboratory experiments have demonstrated consistently that information networks greatly influence decisions made by groups and that problem-solving groups frequently alter communication channels to facilitate the solution.

Formal organization hierarchy can be offset by information dependency, since lower-level members of an organization may seek to increase their power and influence on collective decisions by limiting access to information desired by higher-ranking members. One approach to accomplishing this is to attain a central position in organizational communication networks; another is to acquire expertise desired by an organization (Mechanic, 1967). Also, a powerful member may gain control over resources another person desires (Hickson et al., 1971). Balance of power can be shifted to gain mutually agreeable ends by providing resources needed by others or by making joint agreements to share the resources held by other people.

Compliance with group norms exerts considerable influence over a group to move toward consensus. An early research study by Thomas and Fink (1961) observed that the majority of groups made unanimous decisions and that groups reaching a consensus exhibited greater satisfaction with their decisions than groups failing to reach a consensus. Surprisingly, even when the group decision was incorrect, groups that reached a consensus tended to be satisfied with their decisions. Group pressure for consensus may benefit decision making under some conditions (e.g., when a solution is urgent and alternative choices are similar). However, group-generated pressure toward consensus may severely hamper decision making when valuable minority opinions are ignored or when complex decisions are being made and ideas need to be freely exchanged (Hoffman, 1965). Also, when groupthink intrudes into collective decisions (Janis & Mann, 1977), strategic choice would be expected to suffer.

Politics. Politics within an organization may affect strategic choices, and frequently these decisions in business firms appear to be based on collective decision models and use of power instead of the analytical choice processes suggested by other models (e.g., Stagner, 1969). Fahey and Naroyanan (1983) investigated which stages of strategic decision making are influenced by politics and found that political activities tend to emerge at every stage of SDM, from problem finding to implementation and control. Informal bargaining among subunits of a firm or coalitions represents essential coordination devices (e.g., Murray, 1978; Wright, 1974). Strategic choice seems to be particularly vulnerable to political influences, since selecting criteria to judge strategies and evaluating information about strategies involve value judgments. It is important for decision makers to be aware of potential political influences on strategic choices. An approach to SDM that recognizes political influences and takes them into account is likely to be more realistic and effective in making strategic decisions. This approach may, of course, be less efficient. To influence members and coalitions of an organization, it is likely that more time must be spent in reaching strategic decisions and that resulting decisions may tend to be conservative, incremental adjustments of a firm's existing strategies.

Collective decision models can be used to analyze influences on decisions that are external to the organization. Hence, governmental influences, the influence of consumers of the firm's goods or services, or the attempts of public groups advocating special interests to influence choices made in organizations can be identified. Major coalitions in society may exert significant influences through their political activities (Allison, 1971). Gouldner (1976) discussed in depth the influence of societies and governments on organizational decisions. Collective decision theories permit an analysis of organizational decision problems involving social and political features.

Competition.   Competitive reactions also have strong implications for choosing strategies. Perceptions of likely competitors' reactions weigh heavily in models of strategic choice. If a firm adopts a strategy that directly confronts a competitor, that competitor can be expected to use an aggressive strategy to counterattack. The competitive nature of strategic decisions requires that consideration be given to reactions of groups external to the firm, as well as to the competitive strength of other firms and the likely competitive consequences of the chosen strategy. For example, a previously weak Miller Brewing Company, after being acquired by Philip Morris, challenged the three leaders in the industry by aggressive advertising. Since Miller was not viewed as a threat by the leading brewers, their counteradvertising campaigns

were delayed. Meanwhile, Miller had substantially increased its market share.

Power held by external agents over strategy execution can influence strategic choice. Porter's (1980) model of structural determinants of intensity of competition in an industry examines the firm's power relative to their suppliers, customers, and others in the environment. Whirlpool's dependence on Sears, its major customer, shows the power Sears has over Whirlpool. The flexibility of a firm is reduced as environmental dependency is increased. One strategy for dealing with this restriction is to bring external parties, such as governmental agencies or labor unions, into the SDM process.

Decision Analysis.   Decision analysis has been used successfully in a great many well-specified and well-structured situations, including such decisions as oil and gas exploration, introducing new products, and locating airport sites (e.g., Brown, 1970; Brown, Kahr, & Peterson, 1974; Grayson, 1960). In addition, decision analysis has been increasingly applied to more complex and ill-structured strategic problems (e.g., Kaufman & Thomas, 1977; Keeney, 1982; Ulvila & Brown, 1982). Thomas (1984) has provided a useful critique of the contributions decision analysis appears capable of making to strategic decisions.

Decision analysis typically involves a series of actions taken to recommend a solution to a problem (Raiffia, 1968). The stages of the decision analysis feature six processes. First, the problem needs structuring by defining the alternative courses of action that may be taken, the criteria used to judge the quality of these courses of action, and the key uncertainties in the decision. Second, consequences are assessed to specify the impact or consequences of choosing a given course of action. Third, probabilities and preferences are assessed by key uncertainties and utilities regarding outcomes. Fourth, alternatives are evaluated in terms of a criterion to use for choosing among various courses of action (e.g., maximization of subjective expected utility). Fifth, sensitivity analysis is applied to the course of actions that appears optimally to identify any undesirable consequences that may result from taking this action. Finally, the course of action judged to be the best in view of the analysis and managerial judgment is chosen and implemented.

A common method for simplifying very complex problems for applying decision analysis is to decompose them into simpler subproblems, but it is important to avoid suboptimization as the subproblems are recombined to solve the original problems. Decision analysis typically employs quantitative techniques in making decision recommendations.

Many useful techniques for applied utility assessment have been advanced both for multiattribute utility assessment (e.g., Farquhar, 1980; Huber, 1974; Johnson & Huber, 1977; Keeney & Raiffa, 1976; MacCrimmon & Wehrung, 1977; Schoemaker, 1982) and for single-attribute utility functions (e.g., Farquhar, 1984). Methods used to assess utilities of decision makers have been classified as: (a) ranking methods (e.g., paired comparisons), (b) category methods (e.g., rating scales), (c) direct methods (e.g., direct assignment of values), (d) gamble methods (e.g., standard gamble), and (e) indifference methods (e.g., making tradeoffs [Johnson & Huber, 1977]). Although other researchers (e.g., Farquhar, 1984) have described additional methods for assessing utilities, these five approaches have been most widely used in decision analysis and appear to offer the greatest potential for other strategic decisions.

Strategic decision problems that can be simplified to focus on precise and quantitative analysis of a few key variables are analyzed effectively by rational-analytic decision models. However, leaving important factors, such as political or social aspects, out of a rational-analytic decision analysis can seriously mislead decision makers.

Seldom do rational-analytic models completely model the multitude of variables that influence strategic decisions. The computational decision methods that underlie rational-analytic decision making can lead to precise and quantitative maximizing decisions if there is little uncertainty regarding outcomes and if decision makers are in sufficient agreement about the desirability of decision outcomes. When these conditions are not present (i.e., decision makers disagree about outcomes or outcomes are highly uncertain), then decision makers would be expected to negotiate among themselves or make compromises to reach a mutually acceptable decision (Thompson, 1967). The diversity of preferences that typically exist in the contexts of strategic decision making presents a major challenge for rational-analytic models.

Rational-analytic models do, however, make valuable contributions to strategic decision making by providing relatively precise and frequently quantitative input to the strategic decision-making process through related forecasting models (e.g., multiple regression-based forecasts) and decision analysis solutions to more limited subproblems within strategic decisions. Indeed, rational-analytic decision models offer several advantages over other models. In this approach, values and preferences of decision makers are explicitly stated, social and political influences on a decision are identified, and a systematic approach is provided for combining information and preferences held by decision makers. Moreover, the rational-analytic approaches are extremely effective in routine and in highly structured choice situations that may be embedded within strategic decisions. Also, extremely complex problems that include a multitude of variables and highly uncertain outcomes, yet require very precise solutions in terms of permissible error, rely heavily on rational-analytic-based decision making. It would be impossible to design complex production systems or weapons systems without using these approaches to decision making. Clearly, rational-analytic approaches, although limited, make important contributions to SDM.

In addition to the effectiveness of decision analysis, increased attention has been devoted to efficiency of decision analysis. Further advances in decision analysis foreseen for the near future include greater use of expert systems to describe decision making and computerized intelligent decision systems to provide normative aids for improving decision making on an even broader scale (Howard, 1988).

Despite its many impressive contributions, decision analysis still is not widely used even in important decisions. Howard (e.g., 1968, 1988) has periodically assessed the state of development of applied decision analysis over the prior two decades. Howard's (1988) latest assessment concludes that major advances have been made in procedures for eliciting, formulating, and evaluating decision problems. Thomas (1984) predicted that applied decision analysis will play an important role in assisting future strategy makers to deal with the challenges of formulating and analyzing the complex, ill-structured problems that characterize strategic decisions.

Implementing and Controlling Execution of Strategy

Implementing and controlling strategies involve making them part of everyday life and require attention to culture, leadership, and structure of the firm. Relatively little research has been done on implementation and control of strategic decisions (for a thorough discussion, see Yavitz & Newman, 1982), although nearly every textbook in business policy and strategic management devotes a good deal of attention to describing logical ways to carry out and control strategies.

Conceptualizing SDM as a control process, as opposed to the planning orientation that it has traditionally taken, has been proposed to more effectively link long-term plans with short-term operational objectives (Ruefli & Sarrazin, 1981). For bureaucratic models of strategic decisions, implementation is similarly dominated by control processes. Control may involve either internalized willingness of subordinates to carry out the plans of those people in positions of authority or use of rewards and sanctions to guarantee that strategic decisions will be efficiently carried out. In either event, progress of strategic implementation must be monitored to determine if corrective actions or contingency plans are needed.

Collective models suggest that implementation and control require attention to group and organizational processes to ensure that those entrusted with implementing strategic decisions are able and motivated to do so. Participation in the strategic decision-making process by subordinates is a frequently used method to enlist the cooperation of subordinates in implementing decisions. In addition, techniques for structuring the involvement of subordinates (and possibly other stakeholders) in strategic decisions may take the form of Delphi panels to assist in setting policies, suggestion boxes, participation of subordinates in strategic planning, or other methods to elicit input into the SDM process and, it is hoped, assistance in implementing plans.

Planning models generally contain specific provisions to facilitate implementation and control, and rather than viewing implementation and control as something that happens after planning is completed, these provisions are in place throughout the planning process. For incremental adjustment models, implementation and control is an ongoing activity that involves the monitoring of results attained by each incremental step. Other decision-making models (e.g., cognitive/perceptual, rational-analytic) make relatively little contribution to implementation and control of strategic decisions. The greatest usefulness of the latter models is to the choice process, where they have made considerable gains.

Advancing Theory and Research in Strategic Decision Making

Understanding the behavioral processes involved in strategic decision making still eludes us. Indeed, there is no shortage of research questions involving important issues in strategic decision making. Given the importance of SDM in our society, there is an urgent need to find answers; competitive strategies are essential to the U.S. and world economies. Porter (1990) makes a strong case for the competitive advantages that accrue to nations in a world economy and the importance of competitive strategies at that level as well as for individual companies within a single nation. The great number of multinational firms that require global perspectives gives strategic decision making far-ranging impact.

Taylor (1984) proposed that behavioral aspects of decision making could be advanced both by developing alternative behavioral models of choice in organizations and by further developing empirical research methods used in the study of behavioral aspects of decision making (to include grounding both individual and collective choice theories firmly within behavioral science theories). More attention to these issues is needed to fulfill the promise SDM holds.

Developing Alternative Behavioral Models of Choice in Organizations

Among the most important developments in the strategic decision-making literature is identifying, often independently and in various fields of study, a number of models of SDM. The models of decision-making examined in this chapter reflect the variety of models available. While sometimes these models compete in arguments regarding the best approach to SDM, they can be viewed as complementary perspectives for viewing decision processes. These models of decision making appear to hold important implications for advancing the state of knowledge regarding strategic decisions. Unfortunately, only limited advances have been made in the extent to which SDM theories are related to more fundamental theories from various disciplines.

Behavioral Research. Developing ways to more accurately describe strategic problems, to more thoroughly assess the strategic situations, to create more effective strategic alternatives, and to specify the conditions under which they are most appropriately used all appear to hold great potential for advancing strategic decision making. In addition to investigating the influence of the decision task and situation, further attention needs to be given to investigations of behavioral influences on strategic decisions. Both types of research are needed, and SDM can be advanced significantly by greater understanding of the impact of behavioral aspects of the strategic decision process situation. Developing alternate models for representing strategic decision problems is likely to yield useful insights into the SDM process, as well as suggesting methods to improve strategic decisions. Problem finding, diagnosing, and formulating are important processes in strategic decision making, and they need additional research.

Processes used by decision makers to judge the uncertain aspects of a choice situation are important and have received considerable research attention. Some of these processes appear to represent serious and pervasive limitations in effective human judgments. Availability, representativeness, anchoring and adjustment, and the tendency toward overconfidence in judgments all reveal shortcomings in human decision-making abilities (Hogarth, 1987) that are likely to affect strategic decisions. It would be useful to place heuristic phenomena more clearly within psychological theories of choice. Ideally, theories of the psychological processes underlying these phenomena will guide the search for other factors that affect human judgment and choice. Prospect theory (Kahneman & Tversky, 1979) and other theoretical developments represent important steps in this direction.

Decision Making and Decision Aids. The preponderance of research has shown that human decision makers are not very adept at statistical thinking. Even though decision makers appear to want to make good decisions, they seem to have great difficulty in making high-quality decisions under conditions of either uncertainty or risk. Several explanations have been advanced to account for these difficulties—cognitive abilities may be overwhelmed by the problem's information processing demands, probabilistic processes may be counterintuitive, and training in decision making may be needed (Kahneman, Slovic, & Tversky, 1982).

Books on quantitative decision making such as decision analysis generally discuss methods for overcoming a decision maker's resistance or reluctance to using these methods. In a recent review, Howard (1988) pointed out that, despite its successes and potential, decision analysis is still not widely used for making important decisions. Why? Do the tasks or contexts used in these studies make judgments seem unnatural or difficult to human decision makers? Various explanations have been given in the literature: (a) the challenge of task, (b) poor training of decision makers, (c) people avoiding the hard work of thinking systematically and quantitatively, (d) the types of judgment tasks used in these studies appear artificial or limit the ability of a decision maker to apply his or her full ability to the judgment, or (e) difficulties in accurately eliciting probabilities

and values from subjects (e.g., Ravinder, Kleinmuntz, & Dyer, 1988; Wallsten & Budescu, 1983).

These difficulties could be overcome by training people to make decisions using quantitative methods and/or by designing and developing methods that are more natural and acceptable to human subjects. Both approaches require that more be known about the nature of human judgment. Some combination of these methods is most likely to be effective.

In the face of evidence of departures from the assumptions of rationality in actual decision making behavior, at least two ways to improve the accuracy of decision-making explanations may be considered. One may try to improve the models based on the assumptions of rationality—as Lynn (1986) suggested for the field of public policy-making. On the other hand, one could abandon the a priori postulates of neoclassical economics and substitute empirically based postulates developed from cognitive psychology and other behavioral fields. The gain in the latter course of action would be a greater descriptive accuracy in the behavioral models (Lynn, 1986).

Developing Empirical Research Methods

Little (1986) reported an attempt sponsored by the National Science Foundation to identify research opportunities in the applied decision and management sciences. Among the promising research areas noted were cross-disciplinary research on development of measurement-based models for operational processes (including organizational and managerial activities), choice theory Z (including risk behaviors, values, and judgments) for individuals and groups, decision support, and treatment of complexity in decisions. The mission stated for this program suggests that research should be generalizable, be capable of empirical testing, incorporate behavioral processes, and use research paradigms appropriate for operational decisions. It appears likely that these suggestions may help to direct SDM research.

Better Research Designs. Harrigan (1983) described business strategy research along a dimension of fine-grained to coarse-grained methodologies. Fine-grained studies (e.g., case studies) are highly relevant to business practices and give attention to important details that are involved in complex business policy issues. But they have long been criticized as lacking generalizability. Coarse-grained methodologies (e.g., PIMS cross-sectional studies of Buzzell, Gale, and Sultan, 1975) involve large samples that yield statistically significant results, but many of the unexplained variables that could yield richer insights into business strategy are lost in their error terms.

Harrigan (1983) further suggested that hybrid research methodology is needed to examine contingencies in business strategy—one involving multiple sites and sources and incorporating features of both fine- and coarse-grained research methods. Coarse-textured studies alone do not handle the competitive aspects of intraindustry competition well, and fine-textured single sites may not be generalizable. This weakness is particularly troublesome if industry aberrations or strategies of maverick firms are involved. A merger of these research streams, however, may yield a much more useful approach. Such hybrid methods could use multiple sites, multiple sources of data, and intricate sampling designs. Appropriate research topics for hybrid methodologies are investigations of variances in strategies and effectiveness of firms as each competitor takes the actions it chooses for coping with industry change. Such research requires a small design that permits the investigator to hold important aspects of the industry environment constant, and at the same time vary other aspects to see how the strategic decisions of different firms in the industry cope with the changes.

E. E. Lawler (1977) has described a series of adaptive experiments for organizational behavioral research in which features of an organization are systematically modified to determine the impact of these changes on behaviors of organizational members. A combination of laboratory and field research was advocated by Schwenk (1982) in which the rigor of the laboratory and the relevance of field research are both attained. The simultaneous use of laboratories and field methodologies counters the usual assumption that field research is only useful in an emerging field and that laboratories become appropriate only after a field has evolved to a fair degree of development. By this viewpoint, researchers should focus on in-depth field and case studies rather than laboratory research (Mintzberg, 1977). However, Schwenk (1982) argued that laboratory research is neither artificial nor premature in strategy research.

In fact, strategic decision making represents many topics at various stages of development, and many are appropriate for laboratory research. For example, research on the effectiveness of techniques such as devil's advocacy and dialectical inquiry have generally been conducted in laboratory settings with business school students (e.g., Schweiger et al., 1986). The stages of research on dialectical inquiry can be traced from the initial conceptual work (e.g., Churchman, 1971; Mason, 1969), through laboratory research (e.g., Cosier & Rose, 1977; Schwenk & Cosier, 1980), and field research (e.g., Cosier & Aplin, 1980; Elmsdorf & Finnel, 1979). Schwenk (1982) suggested an alternate approach for programmatic research in strategic management in which laboratory and field research are used simultaneously to develop a research topic.

Multiple Research Sites. Research using multiple sites can be expensive in travel costs and time unless existing data sources are used. An example may help to illustrate the challenges of research involving multiple sites. A landmark study of risk-taking behaviors of executives conducted by MacCrimmon and Wehrung (1986) is one of the most extensive studies of risk taking that has been conducted. This research spanned 12 years and investigated risk-taking by 509 top-level executives representing 189 Canadian firms and 52 American firms.

The initial study was done by mail and used multiple measures of risk-taking tendencies included in a risk portfolio consisting of six booklets, each containing from 4 to 16 pages. The risk portfolio contained a risk in-basket and questionnaires presenting investment gambles, risk-return rankings, and money wagers. In addition, the research used questionnaires to assess attitudes toward risk and self-reports of risky behaviors (e.g., amount of insurance held, hazardous recreational activities, gambling). A follow-up study required further questionnaires and structured interviews with a subsample of 128 executives who lived in 7 Canadian cities. Research efforts that involve extensive measurements of subjects in multiple sites can present difficulties for researchers, but this type of research is critically important in identifying the limits of generalizability of our models and theories.[4]

Multiple Data Sources. Multiple data sources are also important in contingency approaches to strategic decision research. Possible data sources for research include archive data, data banks, field interviews, questionnaires, surveys, and Delphi panels. Although not frequently used in SDM research, experimental and quasi-experimental research designs used in organizational behavior field studies seem potentially useful in SDM research, particularly in research investigating behavioral aspects of strategy.[5]

Stahl and Zimmer (1984) modeled strategic acquisition policies of executives in simulated decisions, finding that the executive decision makers showed remarkably little insight into their own decision processes. This result suggests that multiple decisions need to be observed and criterion importance calculated.

Use of multiple data sources and multiple measures of phenomena enriches conclusions, provides cross-checks on data accuracy, and permits the use of techniques to test for convergence of the various data sources. Miller and Friesen (1982) have also argued for longitudinal analysis of organizations and have described ways to perform such research.

Conceptualizing Theoretical Constructs and Measurement. Many attempts have been made to investigate the impact of strategic planning on organizational effectiveness (e.g., King, 1983; Ramanujam, Venkatraman, & Camillus, 1986; Sinha, 1990). However, it has been difficult to demonstrate the effectiveness of strategic planning since a variety of planning methods typically are used by the firms investigated in these studies. Ramanujam and Venkatraman (1987) identified nine widely used planning methods, including portfolio models, financial models, zero-based budgeting, profit impact of marketing strategy models, value-based planning (using financial market indicators), stakeholder analysis, using Delphi panels or scenarios, forecasting and trend analysis, and project management methods such as PERT (program evaluation and review technique) or CPM (critical path method).

Strategic planning programs used by firms may use various combinations of these or other methods. Yet determining which approach to strategic planning is most effective ideally requires controlled studies in which a strategic planning method used in common by a number of firms is investigated to assess its effectiveness, or several planning methods may be included in a research study to provide evidence about the relative effectiveness of the planning methods. Further attention to contingencies in theory and research may help solve this problem since one could investigate which types of firms benefited the most from using each type of strategic planning. Measurement of the effectiveness of strategic planning methods is another problem area: The criteria and measures used to judge effective strategic planning may be different across studies.

Considerable advances have occurred in strategic decision-making theory and research. Yet much more remains to be done before the field of SDM comes of age. More rigorous and conclusive theories tested by methodologically sound research designs and measures are needed. Nevertheless, SDM research has demonstrated considerable progress in theoretical and methodological sophistication in recent years.

Conclusion

This chapter surveyed models and research relevant to strategic decision making drawn from a wide range of disciplines. Each model offers valuable insights into strategic decisions. The debate among writers favoring various decision models has made a healthy contribution to understanding the processes involved in SDM. Review of even a small portion of the research literature related to these decision models demonstrates how rich they are in terms of important potential research topics. Research on SDM is, of necessity, broad because SDM processes and activities subsume many topics traditionally studied by behavioral science, operations research, economics, and other scholarly fields. A strength of SDM is the varied perspectives of researchers who have entered

this field. Rather than being limited by a single established research paradigm, SDM has the opportunity to adopt and adapt research methods from many fields and to conduct interdisciplinary research without being constrained by disciplinary boundaries. While the strategic planning model clearly is the dominant approach to strategic decisions in business policy and strategic management, other decision models have a great many things to contribute regarding how strategic decisions are made and how they should be made.

Theories and research studies from a variety of fields related to strategic decision making have been juxtaposed here in the hope that this approach may stimulate debate and further advancement of SDM. It is evident that SDM has made substantial progress toward understanding both underlying decision models and important issues for business policy and strategic management that can be derived from these models. In an era of concern about national productivity and competitiveness, SDM can figure importantly in accomplishing national objectives. In addition, an increasingly international focus of multinational enterprises and other business firms offers potential opportunities for research that may advance international health and stability (e.g., La Force & Novelli, 1985). Porter's (1990) book clearly points to the central position held by strategic management and business policy in contributing to world economic health. The challenge facing SDM is to contribute to realizing this potential.

The author wishes to thank L. M. Hough and M. D. Dunnette for their careful reading of the manuscript and many helpful suggestions.

Notes

1   See Anderson and Paine (1978) on profit impact of marketing strategies (PIMS); Bracker (1980) on

historical development of strategic management; Hofer (1976) on strategic planning; Howard (1988) on decision analysis; Kahneman, Slovic, and Tversky (1982) on heuristics and uncertainty; Mintzberg (1978) on paradigms of strategic management; Porter (1980, 1985, 1990) on industrial competition; Shubek (1987) on social science game theory; and Snow and Hambrick (1980) on measuring strategies.

2   For a thorough treatment of cognitive/perceptual models, the reader is referred to the chapter by Stevenson, Busemeyer, and Naylor (1991) in Volume I of this *Handbook*; to a summary by Hogarth (1987); and to *Annual Review of Psychology* chapters by Einhorn and Hogarth (1981) and Pitz and Sachs (1984).

3   MacCrimmon and Wehrung (1986) provide a thorough discussion of how risk taking can be assessed in managerial decision-making situations.

4   See Taylor and Vertinsky (1981) for suggestions regarding experimental or quasi-experimental designs for use in multiple research site studies.

5   See Romanelli and Tushman (1986) for a quasi-experimental study using a comparative-longitudinal design to study inertia, environments, and strategic choice.

References

Abell, D. F. (1980). *Defining the business: The starting point of strategic planning.* Englewood Cliffs, NJ: Prentice-Hall.

Ackoff, R. L. (1970). *A concept of corporate strategy.* New York: Wiley.

Ackoff, R. L. (1974). *Redesigning the future.* New York: Wiley.

Alderfer, C. P., & Smith, K. K. (1982). Studying intergroup relations embedded in organizations. *Administrative Science Quarterly, 27,* 35–65.

Allison, G. T. (1971). *Essence of decision: Explaining the Cuban missile crisis.* Boston: Little, Brown.

Ancona, D. G. (1987). Groups in organizations: Extending laboratory models. In C. Hendrick (Ed.), *Review of personality and social psychology* (Vols. 8, 9). Newbury Park, CA: Sage.

Ancona, D. G., & Caldwell, D. F. (1988). Beyond task and maintenance: Defining external functions in groups. *Group and Organizational Studies, 13,* 468–494.

Anderson, C. R., & Paine, F. T. (1975). Managerial perceptions and strategic behavior. *Academy of Management Journal, 18,* 811–823.

Anderson, C. R., & Paine, F. T. (1978). PIMS: A reexamination. *Academy of Management Review, 3,* 602–612.

Andrews, K. R. (1971). *The concept of corporate strategy.* Homewood, IL: Dow Jones-Irwin.

Barnes, J. H., Jr. (1984). Cognitive biases and their impact on strategic planning. *Strategic Management Journal, 5,* 129–137.

Bateman, T. S., & Zeithaml, C. P. (1989). The psychological context of strategic decisions: A model and convergent experimental findings. *Strategic Management Journal, 10,* 59–74.

Beach, L. R., & Mitchell, T. R. (1978, July). A contingency model for the selection of decision strategies. *Academy of Management Review,* 439–449.

Becker, G. S. (1976). Altruism, egoism, and genetic fitness: Economics and sociobiology. *Journal of Economic Literature, 14,* 817–826.

Berlin, V. N. (1978). Administrative experimentation: A methodology for more rigorous "muddling through." *Management Science, 24*(8), 789–799.

Bourgeois, L. J., III. (1980). Strategy and environment: A conceptual integration. *Academy of Management Review, 5.* 25–39.

Bourgeois, L. J., III. (1981). On the measurement of organizational slack. *Academy of Management Review, 6,* 29–39.

Bracker, J. (1980). The historical development of the strategic management concept. *Academy of Management Review, 5,* 219–224.

Brams, S. J. (1975). *Game theory and politics.* New York: Free Press.

Brown, R. V. (1970, May). Do managers find decision analysis useful? *Harvard Business Review,* 78–89.

Brown, R. V., Kahr, A. S., & Peterson, C. R. (1974). *Decision analysis for the manager.* New York: Holt, Rinehart and Winston.

Buzzell, R. D., Gale, T., & Sultan, R. (1975). Market share—Key to profitability. *Harvard Business Review, 53*(1), 97–106.

Carter, E. E. (1971). The behavioral theory of the firm and top level corporate decisions. *Administrative Science Quarterly, 16,* 413–428.

Chaffee, E. E. (1985). Three models of strategy. *Academy of Management Review, 10*(1), 89–98.

Chakravarthy, B. S., & Lorange, P. (1984). Managing strategic adaptation: Options in administrative systems design. *Interfaces, 14,* 34–46.

Chandler, A. D. (1962). *Strategy and structure: Chapters in the history of the American enterprise.* Cambridge: MIT Press.

Chanin, M. N., & Shapiro, M. N. (1985). Dialectical inquiry in strategic planning: Extending the boundaries. *Academy of Management Review, 10*(4), 663–675.

Chrisman, J. J., Hofer, C. W., & Boulton, W. R. (1988). Toward a system for classifying business strategies. *Academy of Management Review, 13*(3), 413–428.

Churchman, C. W. (1971). *Design of inquiring systems.* New York: Basic Books.

Cohen, M. D., & March, J. G. (1974). *Leadership and ambiguity: The American college president.* New York: McGraw-Hill.

Cohen, M. D., March, J. G., & Olsen, J. P. (1972). A garbage can model of organizational choice. *Administrative Science Quarterly, 17,* 1–25.

Collins, B., & Guetzkow, H. (1964). *A social psychology of group processes for decision making.* New York: Wiley.

Cook, K. S., & Gilmore, M. R. (1984). Power, dependence, and coalitions. In E. J. Lawler (Ed.), *Advances in group processes* (Vol. 1, pp. 27–58). Greenwich, CT: JAI Press.

Cosier, R. A., & Aplin, J. C. (1980). A critical view of dialectical inquiry as a tool in strategic planning. *Strategic Management Journal, 1,* 343–356.

Cosier, R. A., & Rose, G. L. (1977). Cognitive conflict and goal conflict effects on task performance. *Organizational Behavior and Human Performance, 19,* 378–391.

Cosier, R. A., Ruble, T. L., & Aplin, J. C. (1978). An evaluation of the effectiveness of dialectical inquiry systems. *Management Science, 28*(14), 1483–1490.

Cummings, L. L. (1983). The logics of management. *Academy of Management Review, 8,* 532–538.

Cyert, R. M., & MacCrimmon, K. R. (1968). Organizations. In G. Lindsey & E. Aronson (Eds.), *The handbook of social psychology.* Reading, MA: Addison-Wesley.

Cyert, R. M., & March, J. G. (1963). *A behavioral theory of the firm.* Englewood Cliffs, N J: Prentice-Hall.

Davidson, D. L., & Goodpaster, K. E. (1983). *Managing product safety: The Ford pinto* (No. 383-129). Cambridge, MA: Harvard Business School.

Davis, S. M. (1982). Transforming organizations: The key to strategy is context. *Organizational Dynamics, 3*(10), 65–80.

Dawes, R. M. (1976). Shallow psychology. In J. Carroll & J. Payne (Eds.), *Cognition and behavior.* Potomac, MD: Erlbaum.

Dawes, R. M. (1979) The robust beauty of improper models in decision making. *American Psychologist, 34,* 571–582.

Day, R. H., & Groves, T. (Eds.). (1975). *Adaptive economic models.* New York: Academic Press.

Delbecq, A., Van de Ven, A., & Gustafson, D. H. (1975). *Group techniques for program planning.* Glenview, IL: Scott, Foresman.

Dyson, R. G., & Foster, M. J. (1982). The relationship of participation and effectiveness in strategic planning. *Strategic Management Journal, 3,* 77–88.

Einhorn, H. J., & Hogarth, R. M. (1981b). Behavioral decision theory: Processes of judgment and choice. *Annual Review of Psychology, 32,* 53–88.

Elmsdorf, J. R., & Finnel, A. (1979, Spring). Defining corporate strategies: A case study using strategic assumption analysis. *Sloan Management Review,* 41–52.

Etzioni, A. (1968). *The active society.* New York: Free Press.

Fahey, L., & Naroyanan, V. K. (1983). The politics of strategic decision making. In K. J. Albert (Ed.), *The strategic management handbook* (pp. 18–21). New York: McGraw-Hill.

Farquhar, P. H. (1980). Advances in mulitattribute utility theory. *Theory and Decision, 12,* 381–394.

Farquhar, P. H. (1984, November). Utility assessment methods. *Management Science, 30*(11), 1283–1300.

Ford, J. B., & Zelditch, M., Jr. (1988). A test of the law of anticipated reactions. *Social Psychology Quarterly, 51,* 164–171.

Fredrickson, J. W. (1983). Strategic process research: Questions and recommendations. *Academy of Management Review, 8*(3), 5.

Fredrickson, J. W. (1986). The strategic decision process and organizational structure. *Academy of Management Review, 11*(2), 280–297.

Fredrickson, J. W., & Mitchell, T. R. (1984). Strategic decision processes: Comprehensiveness and performance in an industry with an unstable environemnt. *Academy of Management Journal,* 27(2), 399–423.

French, J. R. P., & Raven, B. (1960). The bases of social power. In D. Cartwright & A. F. Zander (Eds.), *Group dynamics* (2nd ed., pp. 607–623). Evanston, IL: Row Peterson.

Frost, P. J., & Taylor, R. N. (1985). Partisan perspectives: A multiple level interpretation of the manuscript review process. In L. L. Cummings & P. J. Frost (Eds.), *Publishing in the organizational sciences* (pp. 35–62). Homewood, IL: Irwin.

Galbraith, J. R. (1973). *Designing complex organizations.* Reading, MA: Addison-Wesley.

Galbraith, C., & Schendel, D. (1983). An empirical analysis of strategic types. *Strategic Management Journal, 4,* 153–173.

Gharajedaghi, J., & Ackoff, R. L. (1984). Mechanisms, organisms and social systems. *Strategic Management Journal, 5,* 189–300.

Gluck, F., Kaufman, S., & Walleck, A. S. (1982). The four phases of strategic management. *Journal of Business Strategy, 2*(3), 9–21.

Gouldner, A. W. (1976). *The dialectic of ideology and technology.* New York: Seaburg.

Grayson, C. J. (1960). *Decisions under uncertainty: Oil and gas drilling decisions.* Cambridge, MA: Harvard University Press.

Gupta, A. K., & Govindarajan, V. (1984, March). Build, hold, harvest: Converting strategic intentions into reality. *Journal of Business Strategy,* 34–47.

Hambrick, D. C. (1983). Some tests of the effectiveness and functional attributes of Miles and Snow's strategic types. *Academy of Management Journal, 26,* 5–25.

Harrigan, K. R. (1983). Research methodologies for contingency approaches to business strategy. *Academy of Management Review, 8,* 398–405.

Herold, D. M. (1972, March). Long-range planning and organizational performance: A cross validation study. *Academy of Management Journal,* 91–102.

Hickson, D. J., Hinings, C. R., Lee, C. A., Schunk, R. E., & Pennings. J. M. (1971). A strategic contingency theory of intraorganizational power. *Administrative Science Quarterly, 16,* 216–224.

Hirschman, A. O. (1967). *Development projects observed.* Washington, DC: The Brookings Institution.

Hofer, C. W. (1975). Toward a contingency theory of business strategy. *Academy of Management Journal, 18,* 784–810.

Hofer, C. W. (1976). Research on strategic planning: A survey of past studies and suggestions for future efforts. *Journal of Economics and Business, 28,* 261–286.

Hofer, C. W., & Schendel, D. E. (1978). *Strategy formulation: Analytical concepts.* St. Paul, MN: West.

Hoffman, R. L. (1965). Group problem solving. In L. Berkowitz (Ed.), *Group processes.* New York: Academic Press.

Hogarth, R. (1987). *Judgement and choice* (2nd ed.), New York: Wiley.

Howard, R. A. (1968). The foundations of decision analysis. *IEEE Transactions in Systems Science and Cybernetics, SSC-4,* 211–219.

Howard, R. A. (1988). Decision analysis: Practice and promise. *Management Science, 34*(6), 679–695.

Howard, R. A., Matheson, J. E., & North, D. W. (1972). The decision to seed hurricanes. *Science, 176,* 1191–1202.

Huber, G. P. (1990). A theory of the effects of advanced information technologies on organizational design, intelligence, and decision making. *Academy of Management Review, 15*(1), 47–71.

Huber, G. P. (1974). Multiattribute utility models: A review of field and fieldlike studies. *Management Science, 20,* 1393–1402.

Huber, G. P., & McDaniel, R. R. (1986). The decision-making paradigm of organizational design. *Management Science, 32*(5), 572–598.

Huff, A. S. (1982) Industry influences on strategy reformulation. *Strategic Management Journal, 3,* 119–131.

Janis, I., & Mann, L. (1977). *Decision making: A psychological analysis of conflict, choice, and commitment.* New York: Free Press.

Johnson, E. M., & Huber, G. P. (1977). The technology of utility assessment. *IEEE Transactions in Systems, Man, and Cybernetics, SMC-7*(5), 311–325.

Johnson, G., (1988). Rethinking incrementalism. *Strategic Management Journal, 9,* 75–91.

Kahan, J. P., & Rapoport, A. (1984). *Theories of coalition formation.* Hillsdale, NJ: Erlbaum.

Kahneman, D., Slovic, P., & Tversky, A. (Eds.). (1982). *Judgment under uncertainty: Heuristics and biases.* New York: Cambridge University Press.

Kahneman, D., & Tversky, A. (1979). Prospect theory: An analysis of decision under risk. *Econometrica, 47*, 263–291.

Kahneman, D., & Tversky, A. (1984). Choices, values, and frames. *American Psychologist, 39*(4), 341–350.

Karger, D. W., & Malik, Z. A. (1975, December). Long-range planning and organizational performance. *Long-Range Planning,* 60–64.

Kates, R. W. (1962). *Hazard and choice perception in flood plain management.* Chicago: University of Chicago, Department of Geography.

Katona, G. (1951). *Psychological analysis of economic behavior.* New York: McGraw-Hill.

Kaufman, G. M., & Thomas, H. (1977). *Modern decision analysis.* London: Penguin.

Kaufman, H. (1960). *The forest ranger.* Baltimore, MD: Johns Hopkins University Press.

Keeney, R. L. (1982). *Decision analysis: State of the field* (Tech. Rep. No. 822). San Francisco: Woodward-Clyde Consultants.

Keeney, R. L., & Raiffa, H. (1976). *Decisions with multiple objectives: Preferences and value tradeoffs.* New York: Wiley.

Kepner, C. H., & Tregoe, B. B. (1965). *The rational manager.* New York: McGraw-Hill.

Kets de Vries, M. F. R., & Miller, D. (1984). Neurotic style and organizational pathology. *Strategic Management Journal, 5*, 35–55.

King, W. R. (1983). Evaluating strategic planning systems. *Strategic Management Journal, 4*, 263–277.

Klienmuntz, D. N. (1985, June). Cognitive heuristics and feedback in a dynamic decision environment. *Management Science, 31*(6), 680–702.

Komorita, S. S. (1984). The role of justice and power in reward allocation. In G. M. Stephenson & J. H. Davis (Eds.), *Progress in applied social psychology* (pp. 185–206). Chichester, England: Wiley.

Krantz, J. (1985). Group process under conditions of organizational decline. *Journal of Applied Behavioral Science, 21*, 1–17.

Kudla, R. J. (1980). The effects of strategic planning on common stock returns. *Academy of Management Journal, 23*, 5–20.

La Force, J. C., & Novelli, R. J. (1985). Reconciling management research and practice. *California Management Review, 27*(3), 74–81.

Larwood, L., & Whittaker, W. (1977). Managerial myopia: Self-serving biases in organizational planning. *Journal of Applied Psychology, 62*, 194–198.

Lawler, E. E., III. (1977, October). Adaptive experiments: An approach to organizational behavior research. *Academy of Management Review,* 576–585.

Lawler, E. J. (1983). Cooptation and threats as "divide and rule" tactics. *Social Psychological Quarterly, 46*, 89–98.

Lee, S. M., Luthans, F., & Olson, D. L. (1982). A management science approach to contingency models of organizational structure. *Academy of Management Journal, 25*(3), 553–566.

Leontiades, M., & Tezel, A. (1980). Planning perceptions and planning results. *Strategic Management Journal, 1*, 65–75.

Levine, J. M., & Moreland, R. L. (1990). Progress in small group research. *Annual Review of Psychology, 41*, 585–634.

Lichtenstein, S., Fischhoff, B., & Phillips, L. D. (1982). Calibration of probabilities: The state of the art to 1980. In D. Kahneman, P. Slovic, & A. Tversky (Eds.), *Judgement under uncertainty: Heuristics and biases* (pp. 306–334). New York: Cambridge University Press.

Lindblom, C. E. (1965). *The intelligence of democracy: Decision making through mutual adjustment.* New York: Free Press.

Lindblom, C. E. (1959). The science of muddling through. *Public Administration Review 19*, 79–88.

Linstone, H. A., & Turoff, M. (1975). *The Delphi method: Techniques and applications.* Reading, MA: Addison-Wesley.

Little, J. D. (1986). Research opportunities in the decision and management sciences. *Management Science, 32*(1), 1–13.

Lorange, P., & Vancil, R. F. (1977). *Strategic planning systems.* Englewood Cliffs, NJ: Prentice-Hall.

Luce, R. D., & Raiffa, H. (1957). *Games and decisions.* New York: Wiley.

Lyles, M. A., & Lentz, R. T. (1982). Managing the planning process: A field study of the human side of planning. *Strategic Management Journal, 3*, 105–118.

Lynn, L. E., Jr. (1986). The behavioral foundations of public policy making. *Journal of Business, 59*(94), 379–384.

MacCrimmon, K. R. (1968). Descriptive and normative implications of the decision theory postulates. In J. L. Cochrane & M. Zeleny (Eds.), *Risk and uncertainty.* Columbia, SC: University of South Carolina Press.

MacCrimmon, K. R. (1973). *Theories of collective decision.* Paper presented at the Fourth International Research Conference on Subjective Probability and Utility, Rome.

MacCrimmon, K. R., & Taylor, R. N. (1976). Problem solving and decision making. In M. D. Dunnette (Ed.), *Handbook of industrial and organizational psychology* (1st ed., pp. 1397–1453). Chicago: Rand McNally.

MacCrimmon, K. R., & Wehrung, D. A. (1977). Trade-off analysis: The indifference and preferred proportion approaches. In D. E. Bell, R. L. Keeney, & H. Raiffa (Eds.), *Conflicting objectives in decisions* (pp. 123–147). New York: Wiley.

MacCrimmon, K. R., & Wehrung, D. A. (1986). *Taking risks.* New York: Free Press.

MacDonald, J. (1975). *The game of business.* New York: Doubleday.

Mahoney, M. J. (1977). Publication prejudices: An experimental study of confirmatory bias in the peer review system. *Cognitive Therapy and Research, 1,* 161–175.

March, J. G. (1978). Bounded rationality, ambiguity, and the engineering of choice. *The Bell Journal of Economics, 9*(2), 587–608.

March, J. G., & Simon, H. A. (1958). *Organizations.* New York: Wiley.

Mason, R. O. (1969). A dialectical approach to strategic planning. *Management Science, 15*(8), B-403–B-414.

Mason, R. O., & Mitroff, I. I. (1981). *Challenging strategic planning assumptions.* New York: Wiley.

McGrath, J. E., & Kravitz, D. A. (1982). Group research. *Annual Review of Psychology, 33,* 195–230.

Mechanic, D. (1967). Sources of power of lower participants in complex organizations. *Administrative Science Quarterly, 7*(3), 349–364.

Miles, R. E., & Snow, C. C. (1978). *Organizational strategy, structure, and process.* New York: McGraw-Hill.

Miller, D., & Friesen, P. H. (1982). The longitudinal analysis of organizations: A methodological perspective. *Management Science, 28*(9), 1013–1034.

Miller, C. E., & Komority, S. S. (1986). Coalition formation in organizations: What laboratory

studies do and do not tell us. In R. J. Lewicki, G. H. Sheppard, & M. H. Bazerman (Eds.), *Research on negotiation in organizations* (Vol. 1, pp. 117–137). Greenwich, CT: JAI Press.

Mintzberg, H. (1973). Strategy-making in three modes. *California Management Review, 16*(2), 44–54.

Mintzberg, H. (1977). Strategy formulation as a historical process. *International Studies of Management and Organization, 2,* 28–40.

Mintzberg, H. (1978). Patterns in strategy formation. *Management Science, 24,* 934–949.

Mintzberg, H. (1990). The design school: Reconsidering the basic premises of strategic management. *Strategic Management Journal, 11,* 171–195.

Mintzberg, H., Raisinghane, E., & Theoret, A. (1976). The structure of "unstructured" decision processes. *Administrative Science Quarterly, 21,* 246–275.

Mitroff, I. I., & Emshoff, J. R. (1979). On strategic assumption-making: A dialectical approach to policy and planning. *Academy of Management Review, 4*(1), 1–12.

Murray, E. A., Jr. (1978). Strategic choice as a negotiated outcome. *Management Science, 24*(9), 960–972.

Narayanan, V. K., & Fahey, L. (1982). The micropolitics of strategy formulation. *Academy of Management Review, 7,* 25–34.

Neave, E. H., & Petersen, E. R. (1980). A comparison of optimal and adaptive decision mechanisms in an organizational setting. *Management Science, 26*(8), 810–822.

Nemeth, C. J., & Staw, B. M. (1989). The tradeoffs of social control and innovation in groups and organizations. *Advances in Experimental Social Psychology, 22,* 175–210.

Nutt, P. C. (1976, April). Models for decision making in organizations and some contextual variables which stipulate optimal use. *Academy of Management Review,* 84–98.

Olsen, J. P. (1976). Choice in an organized anarchy. In J. G. March & U. P. Olsen (Eds.), *Ambiguity and choice in organizations.* Bergen, Germany: Univesitetsforeaget.

Pearce, J. A., II, & David, F. R. (1987). Corporate mission statements: The bottom line. *Academy of Management Executive, 1*(2), 109–116.

Pearce, J. A., II, & Robinson, R. B., Jr. (1976). A measure of CEO social power in strategic decision making. *Strategic Management Journal, 8,* 297–304.

Pearce, J. A., II, & Robinson, R. B., Jr. (1988). *Strategic management: Strategy formulation and implementation* (3rd ed.). Homewood, IL: Irwin.

Pfeffer, J. (1977). Power and resource allocation in organizations. In B. M. Staw & G. R. Salancik (Eds.), *New directions in organizational behavior* (pp. 235–265). Chicago: St. Clair Press.

Pfeffer, J. (1981). *Power in organizations.* Marshfield, MA: Pitman.

Pfeffer, J., & Salancik, G. R. (1978). *The external control of organizations.* New York: Harper & Row.

Pitz, G. F., & Sachs, N. J. (1984) Judgment and decision: Theory and application. *Annual Review of Psychology, 35,* 139–163.

Pondy, L. R. (1976). Leadership is a language game. In M. McCall & M. Lombardo (Eds.), *Leadership: Where else can we go?* (pp. 87–98). Durham, NC: Duke University Press.

Pondy, L. R. (1963). Union of rationality and intuition in management action. In S. Srivastva (Ed.), *The executive mind.* San Francisco: Jossey-Bass.

Porter, M. E. (1980). *Competitive analysis.* New York: Free Press.

Porter, M. E. (1990). *The competitive advantage of nations.* New York: Free Press.

Porter, M. E. (1985). *Competitive advantage: Creating and sustaining superior performance.* New York: Free Press.

Preble, J. F. (1984). The selection of Delphi panels for strategic planning purposes. *Strategic Management Journal, 5,* 157–170.

Preim, R. L. (1990). Top management team group factors, consensus, and firm performance. *Strategic Management Journal, 11,* 469–478.

Quinn, J. B. (1980). *Strategies for change: Logical incrementalism.* Homewood, IL: Irwin.

Raiffa, H. (1968). *Decision analysis.* Reading, MA: Addison-Wesley.

Ramanujam, V., Camillus, J. C., & Venkatraman, N. (1987). Trends in strategic planning. In W. R. King & D. I. Cleland (Eds.), *Strategic planning and management handbook.* New York: Van Nostrand Reinhold.

Ramanujam, V., & Venkatraman, N. (1987, May–June). Planning and performance: A new look at an old question. *Business Horizons,* 19–25.

Ramanujam, V., Venkatraman, N., & Camillus, J. (1986). Multi-objective assessment of effectiveness of strategic planning: A discriminant analysis approach. *Academy of Management Journal, 29*(2), 347–372.

Rapoport, A., & Chammah, A. M. (1965). *Prisoner's dilemma.* Ann Arbor: University of Michigan Press.

Ravinder, H. V., Kleinmuntz, D. N., & Dyer, J. S. (1988). The reliability of subjective probabilities obtained through decomposition. *Management Science, 34*(2), 186–199.

Romanelli, E., & Tushman, M. L. (1986). Inertia, environments, and strategic choice: A quasi-experimental design for comparative-longitudinal research. *Management Science, 32*(5), 608-621.

Ruefli, T., & Sarrazin, J. (1981). Strategic control of corporate development under ambiguous circumstances. *Management Science, 27*(10), 1158–1170.

Sandberg, W. R. (1986). *New venture performance: The role of strategy and industry structure.* Lexington, MA: Lexington Books.

Schachter, R. D. (1986). Evaluating influence diagrams. *Operations Research, 34*(6), 871–882.

Schelling. T. C. (1971). On the ecology of micromotives. *Public Interest, 25,* 59–98.

Schelling, T. C. (1963). *The strategy of conflict.* Cambridge, NJ: Harvard University Press.

Schoeffler, S., Buzzell, R. D., & Heaney, D. F. (1974, March–April). Impact of strategic planning on profit performance. *Harvard Business Review,* 137–145.

Schoemaker, P. J. H. (1982). The expected utility model: Its variants, purposes, evidence, and limitations. *Journal of Economic Literature, 20,* 529–563.

Schweiger, D. M., & Sandberg, W. R. (1989). The utilization of individual capabilities in group approaches to strategic decision-making. *Strategic Management Journal, 10,* 31–43.

Schweiger, D. M., Sandberg, W. R., & Ragan, J. W. (1986). Group approaches for improving strategic decision making: A comparative analysis of dialectical inquiry, devil's advocacy, and consensus. *Academy of Management Journal, 29*(1), 51–71.

Schwenk, C. R. (1982). Why sacrifice rigor for relevance? A proposal for combining laboratory and field research in strategic management. *Strategic Management Journal, 3,* 213–225.

Schwenk, C. R. (1984). Effects of planning aids and presentation media on performance and affective responses in strategic decision making. *Management Science, 30*(3), 263–272.

Schwenk, C. R., & Cosier, R. A. (1980). Effects of the expert, devil's advocate, and dialectical inquiry methods on prediction performance. *Organizational Behavior and Human Performance, 26,* 409–424.

Shanteau, J., & Anderson, N. H. (1969). Test of a conflict model for preference judgment. *Journal of Mathematical Psychology, 6,* 312–325.

Shaw, M. E. (1981). Group dynamics: The psychology of small group behavior (3rd ed.). New York: McGraw-Hill.

Shirley, R. C. (1982). Limiting the scope of strategy: A decision based approach. *Academy of Management Review, 7,* 262–268.

Shrirvastava, P., & Grant, J. H. (1985). Empirically derived models of strategic decision-making processes. *Strategic Management Journal, 6,* 97–113.

Shubek, M. S. (1987). *Game theory in the social sciences.* Cambridge, MA: MIT Press.

Simon, H. A. (1957). *Models of man: Social and rational.* New York: Wiley.

Simon, H. A. (1967). A behavioral model of rational choice. In M. Alexis & C. Wilson (Eds.), *Organizational decision making.* Englewood Cliffs, NJ: Prentice-Hall.

Simon, H. A. (1976). *Administrative behavior* (3rd ed.). New York: Free Press.

Simon, H. A. (1987, February). Making management decisions: The role of intuition and emotion. *Academy of Management Executive,* 57-64.

Sinha, D. K. (1990). The contribution of formal planning to decisions. *Strategic Management Journal, 11,* 1990, 479–492.

Slovic, P. (1972). From Shakespeare to Simon: Speculations—and some evidence—about man's ability to process information. *Oregon Research Institute Bulletin, 12*(2).

Smircich, L., & Stubbart, C. (1985). Strategic management in an enacted world. *Academy of Management Review, 10*(4), 724–736.

Smith, G. F. (1988, December). Toward a heuristic theory of problem structuring. *Management Science, 34*(12), 1489–1506.

Snow, C. C., & Hambrick, D. C. (1980). Measuring organizational strategies: Some theoretical and methodological problems. *Academy of Management Review, 5,* 527–538.

Speltzer, C. S., & Stael von Holstein, C. A. S. (1975). Probability encoding in decision analysis. *Management Science, 22,* 340–358.

Stahl, M. J., & Zimmer, T. W. (1984). Modeling strategic acquisition policies: A simulation of executives' acquisition decisions. *Academy of Management Journal, 27*(2), 369–383.

Stagner, R. (1969). Corporate decision making. *Journal of Applied Psychology, 53*(1), 1–13.

Starr, M. K. (1965). Commentary. *Management Science, 12,* 30–35.

Staw, B. M. (1976, June). Knee-deep in the big muddy: A study of escalating commitment to a chosen course of action. *Organizational Behavior and Human Performance, 27*–44.

Steckler, N. A., & Rosenthal, R. (1985). Sex differences in nonverbal and verbal communication with boses, peers, and subordinates. *Journal of Applied Psychology, 70,* 157–163.

Stein, J. (1981). Strategic decision methods. *Human Relations, 3*(11), 917–933.

Stevenson, M. K., Busemeyer, J. R., & Naylor, J. C. (1991). Judgment and decision-making theory. In M. D. Dunnette & L. M. Hough (Eds.), *Handbook of industrial and organizational psychology* (2nd ed., vol. 1, pp. 283–374). Palo Alto, CA: Consulting Psychologists Press.

Taylor, R. N. (1984). *Behavioral decision making.* Glenview, IL: Scott, Foresman.

Taylor, R. N. (1975a). Perception of problem constraints. *Management Science, 22*(1), 22–29.

Taylor, R. N. (1975b). Psychological determinants of bounded rationality: Implications for decision-making strategies. *Decision Sciences, 6,* 409–429.

Taylor, R. N. (1976). Psychological aspects of planning. *Long Range Planning, 9,* 24–35.

Taylor, R. N. (1981). Planning and decision making in managing organizations. In H. Meltzer & W. Nord (Eds.), *Making organizations humane and productive* (pp. 159–178). New York: Wiley.

Taylor, R. N. (1982). Organizational and behavioral aspects of forecasting. In S. Makridakis & S. C. Wheelwright (Eds.), *The handbook of forecasting* (pp. 519–534). New York: Wiley.

Taylor, R. N., & Vertinsky, I. (1981). Experimenting with organizatinal behavior. In P. Nystrom & W. Starbuck (Eds.), *Handbook of organizational design* (Vol. 1, pp. 139–166). New York: Oxford University Press.

Thomas, E. J., & Fink, C. E. (1961). Models of group problem-solving. *Journal of Abnormal Social Psychology, 63,* 53–63.

Thomas, H. (1984). Strategic decision analysis: Applied decision analysis and its role in the strategic management process. *Strategic Management Journal, 5,* 139–156.

Thompson, J. D. (1967). *Organizations in action: Social science bases of administrative theory.* New York: McGraw-Hill.

Thompson, L. L., Mannix, E. A., & Bazerman, M. H. (1988). Group negotiation: Effects of decision rule, agenda, and aspiration. *Journal of Personality and Social Psychology, 54,* 86–95.

Tichey, N. M. (1981). Networks in organizations. In P. C. Nystrom & W. H. Starbuck (Eds.), *Handbook of organizational design* (Vol. 2, pp. 225–249). New York: Oxford University Press.

Tversky, A. (1967). Additivity, utility, and subjective probability. *Journal of Mathematical Psychology, 4,* 175–202.

Tversky, A. (1972). Elimination by aspects: A theory of choice. *Psychological Review, 79,* 281–299.

Tversky, A., & Kahneman, D. (1974). Judgment under uncertainty: Heuristics and biases. *Science, 11,* 1124–1131.

Ulvila, J. W., & Brown, R. V. (1982). Decision analysis comes of age. *Harvard Business Review, 60*(5), 130–141.

Wallsten, T. S., & Budescu, D. V. (1983). Encoding subjective probabilities: A psychological and psychometric review. *Management Science, 29*(2), 151–173.

Weber, M. (1947). *The theory of social and economic organization.* New York: Oxford University Press.

Weick, K. E. (1969). *The social psychology of organizing.* Reading, MA: Addison-Wesley.

Weick, K. E. (1977). Enactment processes in organizations. In B. M. Staw & G. R. Salancik (Eds.), *New directions in organizational behavior* (pp. 267–300). Chicago: St. Clair Press.

Weick, K. E., & Daft, R. L. (1983). The effectiveness of interpretation systems. In K. S. Cameron & D. A. Whetten (Eds.), *Organizational effectiveness: A comparison of multiple models* (pp. 71–93). New York: Academic Press.

Winter, S. G. (1975). Optimization and evolution in the theory of the firm. In R. H. Day & T. Groves (Eds.), *Adaptive economic models.* New York: Academic Press.

Wright, P. (1974). The harassed decision maker: Time pressures, distractions and the use of evidence. *Journal of Applied Psychology, 59,* 555–561.

Wright, P. (1987). A refinement of Porter's strategies. *Strategic Management Journal, 8,* 93–101.

Wu, F. H. (1981). Incrementalism in financial strategic planning. *Academy of Management Review, 6*(1), 133–143.

Yavitz, B., & Newman, W. H. (1982). *Strategy in action.* New York: Free Press.

Zander, A. (1979). The psychology of group processes. *Annual Review of Psychology, 30,* 417–451.

CHAPTER 16

Strategic Reward Systems

Edward E. Lawler III
University of Southern California

G. Douglas Jenkins, Jr.
University of Arkansas

This chapter presents theory and research on the role of pay systems in complex organizations. It first looks at the relationship between pay systems and the business strategy and structure of organizations. It then focuses on the impact of pay systems on six important determinants of organizational effectiveness: performance motivation, skill development motivation, attraction and retention, organizational structure, culture, and costs. Different approaches to pay are reviewed with a focus on their impact on these six determinants of organizational effectiveness. The specific pay system practices reviewed include job-based pay, person-based pay, individual pay for performance, organizational pay for performance, and executive compensation. Overall the evidence indicates that pay systems have a strong impact on organizational effectiveness, and there is a link between strategy, structure, and pay systems.

Introduction

REWARDS SYSTEMS AND their role in organizations have been studied from many perspectives and by multiple disciplines. Psychology, sociology, anthropology, and economics all have contributed to the literature. This chapter will focus on the design features of the major organizational reward system, the pay system, and its relationship to organizational behavior. Since this topic is not the province of a single discipline, the literature will be drawn from a range of sources. The underlying assumption is that reward systems have a wide-ranging impact on organizations and that their impact is greatly affected by their design and by the organizational context in which they operate. Thus, to understand pay systems in organizations, it is necessary to focus on the characteristics of both the organization and the pay system.

Pay systems are one of the most prominent and important features of any organization. There is an extensive literature in psychology on the effects of rewards on human behavior that can help the understanding of the impact of reward systems. There is also considerable research on the impact of pay systems on individual behavior in organizations and on the behavior of organizations. Some areas, such as the design of job evaluation systems and the impact of merit pay plans, have been extensively researched, but many others have received little attention. The discussion in this chapter is intended to accomplish two purposes: first, to provide an overview of the research that has been done and, second, to identify those areas that are important but have been neglected by researchers.

This chapter looks first at the relationship between pay systems and the business strategy and structure of organizations. It then focuses on the impact of pay systems on six determinants of organizational effectiveness: performance motivation, skill development motivation, attraction and retention, organizational structure, culture, and costs. The specific pay system practices reviewed include job-based pay, person-based pay, individual pay for performance, organizational pay for performance, executive compensation, and flexible benefits. Two process issues, communication and participation, are also considered.

Reward Systems and Strategy

There is a growing body of literature on the relationship between organizational strategy and human resource management systems (e.g.,

see Lawler, 1986a; Ulrich & Lake, 1990). It typically suggests that once its strategy is developed, an organization needs to focus on the kind of human resources, culture, and behavior that is needed in order to make it effective. The next step is to design reward and other human resource management systems that will motivate the right kind of performance, attract the right kinds of people, and create a supportive climate and structure (e.g., see Balkin & Gomez-Mejia, 1987b; Hambrick & Snow, 1989; Lawler, 1986b).

Much of the writing on strategy is conceptual and descriptive in nature. It starts from a competitive advantage framework and focuses on how human resource management practices can enhance an organization's performance by supporting particular kinds of behavior (e.g., see Porter, 1985, 1990; Ulrich & Lake, 1990). Depending on the actual practices that are recommended, there may or may not be evidence that the practices are used and can produce the desired results. For example, if an organization is trying to become a low-cost producer, it is often argued that incentive plans and other pay for performance plans are called for. Missing is evidence that companies in fact are using plans with particular strategic agendas in mind. One exception to this concerns the area of management compensation where there are studies showing its relationship to strategy (e.g., see Hambrick & Snow, 1989; Kerr, 1985).

There is another way in which the reward system may need to be taken into consideration in the strategy area. Before the strategic plan is developed in an existing organization, it may be important to assess a number of things, including the current reward systems, and to determine what kind of behaviors, climate, and structure they are supportive of. This step is needed so that when the strategic plan is developed, it is based on a realistic assessment of the current condition of the organization and the changes likely to be needed to implement the new strategy. This point is particularly pertinent to organizations that are considering going into new lines of business, developing new markets, and acquiring new divisions. Often new lines of business require a different behavior and therefore a different reward system. Simply putting the old reward system in place in the new business is often not good enough and indeed can lead to failure. On the other hand, developing a new reward system for one part of an organization can cause problems in other parts because of the comparisons made between the different parts.

At this point it is impossible to go beyond the conceptual level in discussing reward systems and strategy. There are some useful typologies or menus available. These typically identify different strategies and then match them to reward system practices (e.g., see Galbraith & Kazanjian, 1986; Lawler, 1990). These are useful from an organizational design point of view but are largely untested. Until more research is done in this area, it is impossible to make any definitive statements. This is likely to be an increasingly important area for practitioners, if not for researchers. The field of strategy is developing and companies are increasingly focusing on how they can gain a competitive advantage (Porter, 1990). There is good reason to believe that human resource management practices in general and reward systems in particular are central to the implementation and effective operationalization of strategies. Thus, it is important to determine how reward system practices fit with different business strategies.

Reward Systems and Organizational Design

The literature on organizational design increasingly uses systems theory and fit models that stress the importance of congruence between the different subsystems of the organization (e.g., see Galbraith, 1973, 1977; Nadler & Tushman, 1988). Most of these approaches in turn identify the reward system as one of the major systems in an organization that needs to be driven by the strategy and aligned with the other systems. The other systems mentioned usually include the information system, the decision structure, the approach to work design, and the human resource management system. The literature usually goes on to argue that it is the degree of alignment that determines how effective an organization actually is. This raises the issue of what constitutes good alignment, not to mention the issue of what data exist to support this assertion.

At this point there is little research evidence to support the congruence or fit argument. Nevertheless, it is an attractive notion and one that has high face validity, particularly if system thinking is accepted. It is easy, for example, to argue that an approach to organizing that centers all decisions at the top may need a different reward system than one based on pushing decisions to lower levels (Lawler, 1990). In addition, it is easy to accept the argument that the organization probably also needs a different approach to information and control.

A substantial literature does exist that focuses on the relationship between reward systems and the degree to which participative management is practiced (e.g., see Lawler, 1981, 1990, 1992). A brief examination of the literature will serve to help focus on some of the organizational design issues that arise with reward systems. This literature argues that if an organization wishes to operate in a participative manner, it needs to change more than just its decision structure and information system flow. It needs to change all its systems, including its reward system. This line of reasoning goes back to the early writings on the Scanlon plan (e.g., Lesieur, 1958) and the writings of McGregor (1960). They argue rather convincingly that for participative management to be practiced effectively, a different approach to pay for performance is required. They go on to suggest that the correct approach is to pay bonuses based on group- or plantwide performance. The argument for this essentially rests on the point that traditional pay plans support individual excellence at the cost of team performance and that for participation to work, team performance needs to be rewarded. The evidence on the impact of gainsharing plans (e.g., Graham-Moore & Ross, 1983, 1990) tends to support this point and will be reviewed later in this chapter. At this point it is cited merely to establish the link between reward system design and organizational design.

The more recent writings on participative management have gone considerably beyond the argument that it requires a different approach to paying for performance. It argues that all the major features of a reward system need to be changed (e.g., Lawler, 1990). For example, it is argued that pay needs to be based more on the skills of the individual than on the jobs that they do, that fringe benefit programs should allow choice, and that pay information should be public. Later, each of these practices will be looked at separately. The important point to remember, however, is that part of the argument in favor of them rests on systems thinking; thus, to a degree, they cannot be evaluated without studying them in their proper context.

There is little direct evidence supporting the argument that reward systems need to be structured differently for participative management to be effective. There is some evidence about the actual reward system practices of companies that appears to be supportive, however. It tends to show that participative management is being more widely practiced and that reward system practices are changing in ways that are consistent with participative management (Lawler, Ledford, & Mohrman, 1989; Lawler, Mohrman, & Ledford, 1992; O'Dell, 1987). For example, gainsharing has become increasingly popular in the last decade, and skill-based pay plans have replaced job-based plans in many manufacturing locations practicing participative management (Gupta,

Jenkins, & Curington, 1986; Lawler, Mohrman, & Ledford, 1992).

In summary, a substantial literature focuses on the organizational systems issues affecting the impact that reward system practices have. The problem with it is that it lacks a substantial empirical basis. Some research has looked at the effect of certain reward system practices on individuals and organizations. This is important work and will be reviewed later, but it is not entirely satisfying because it provides limited information on how the impact of reward systems is affected by the organizational context.

Impact of Pay System

The first step in a detailed discussion of the impact of reward systems is to consider what behaviors they can affect in organizations. The theoretical research and work on reward systems has focused on six factors that are influenced by reward systems and that in turn influence organizational effectiveness.

Attraction and Retention of Employees

Research on job choice, career choice, and turnover clearly shows that the kind and level of rewards an organization offers influence who is attracted to work for an organization and who will continue to work for it (e.g., see Mobley, 1982; Mobley, Hand, Meglino, & Griffeth, 1979). Overall, those organizations that give the most rewards tend to attract and retain the most people (Lawler, 1971). This seems to occur because high reward levels lead to high satisfaction, which in turn leads to lower turnover and more job applicants. Individuals who are presently satisfied with their jobs expect to continue to be satisfied and, as a result, want to stay with the same organization. This interpretation is generally consistent with the work on equity theory as well as the work on expectancy theory and goal setting (Adams, 1965; Lawler, 1973; Locke & Latham, 1990).

The best performers represent a particularly interesting retention problem. To retain them a reward system must distribute rewards in a way that will lead them to feel equitably treated when they compare their rewards with those received by individuals performing similar jobs at a similar level of performance in other organizations. The emphasis here is on external comparisons because turnover means leaving an organization for a better situation elsewhere. One way to accomplish this is to reward everyone at a level that is above the reward levels in other organizations. This strategy has two drawbacks, however. In the case of some rewards, such as money, it can be very costly. It can also cause feelings of intraorganizational inequity—better performers are likely to feel inequitably treated when they are rewarded at the same level as poor performers in the same organization, even though they are fairly treated in terms of external comparisons. Faced with this situation, the better performers may not quit, but they are likely to be dissatisfied, complain, look for internal transfers, and mistrust the organization.

The answer may lie in basing rewards on performance. This should cause the better performers to be satisfied and to stay with the organization. It is important to note, however, that to be satisfied not only must the better performers receive more rewards than poor performers, they must receive significantly more rewards because, as equity theory points out, they are likely to feel they deserve much more.

Research has shown that absenteeism and pay satisfaction are related (e.g., Baumgartel & Sobol, 1959; see Steers & Rhodes, 1978, for a full review), although the relationship is not as strong as the one between pay satisfaction and turnover. When the workplace is satisfying and high paying, individuals come to work regularly; when it is not, they do not.

Several studies have shown that absenteeism can be reduced by tying pay bonuses and other rewards to attendance (Lawler, 1981; Pedalino & Gamboa, 1974; Schlotzhauer & Rosse, 1985). This approach can be costly, but sometimes it is less costly than absenteeism. It is a particularly useful strategy in situations where both the work content and the working conditions are poor and do not lend themselves to meaningful improvements. In situations where work content or conditions can be improved, such improvements are often the most effective and cost efficient way to deal with absenteeism (Hackman & Oldham, 1980). Reward system policies are only one of several ways to influence absenteeism, but they are potentially effective if an organization is willing to tie important rewards to coming to work. Often this is easier to do than tying rewards to performance because attendance is easily measurable and visible.

Motivation of Employee Performance

When certain specifiable conditions exist, reward systems have been demonstrated to motivate performance (Blinder, 1990; Lawler, 1971; Nalbantain, 1987; Vroom, 1964). What are those conditions? They are rather clearly articulated in the extensive literature on expectancy theory: Important rewards must be perceived to be tied in a timely fashion to effective performance. In essence, the argument is that organizations get the kind of behavior that leads to the rewards their employees value (Kerr, 1975). This occurs because people have their own needs and mental maps of what the world is like. They use these maps to choose those behaviors that lead to outcomes that satisfy their needs. They are inherently neither motivated nor unmotivated to perform effectively; performance motivation depends on the situation, how it is perceived, and the needs of people.

Expectancy theory is made up of a series of fairly straightforward observations about behavior. Three concepts serve as the key building blocks of the theory.

- *Performance-outcome expectancy.* Every behavior has associated with it, in an individual's mind, certain outcomes (rewards or punishments). In other words, individuals believe or expect that if they behave in a certain way, they will get certain things. For example, individuals may have an expectancy that if they produce 10 units they will receive their normal hourly rate, while if they produce 15 units they will receive their hourly pay rate plus a bonus. Similarly, individuals may believe that certain levels of performance will lead to approval or disapproval from members of their work group or their supervisor. Each performance level can be seen as leading to a number of different kinds of outcomes.

- *Outcome attractiveness.* Outcomes have differential attractiveness for different individuals. This is true because outcome values result from individual needs and perceptions, which differ because they reflect other factors in an individual's life. Some individuals may value an opportunity for promotion or advancement because of their needs for achievement or power, while others may not want to be promoted and leave their current work group because of needs for affiliation with others. Similarly, a fringe benefit such as a pension plan may have great value for older workers but little value for younger employees on their first job.

- *Effort-performance expectancy.* Each behavior also has associated with it a certain expectancy or probability of success. This expectancy represents the individual's perception of how hard it will be to achieve the behavior and the probability of his or her successful achievement of that behavior (Locke & Latham, 1990). For example, employees may have a strong expectancy (e.g., 90–10) that if they put forth the effort, they can produce 10 units per hour, but that they only have a 50–50 chance of producing 15 units per hour if they try. This expectancy is based on the characteristics of the task as well as such individual differences factors as an individual's sense of efficacy (Bandura, 1986).

Putting these concepts together, one can make a basic statement about motivation. In general, an individual's motivation to behave in a certain way is greatest when:

- The individual believes that the behavior will lead to certain outcomes (performance-outcome expectancy)

- The individual feels that these outcomes are attractive

- The individual believes that performance at a desired level is possible (effort-performance expectancy)

Given a number of alternative levels of behavior (e.g., 10, 15, or 20 units of production per hour), an individual will choose the level of performance that has the greatest motivational force associated with it, as indicated by a combination of the relevant expectancies, outcomes, and values. This combining process is theoretically defined as the multiplicative combination of these components such that if any one is zero there is no motivation. In other words, when faced with choices about behavior, an individual goes through a process of considering questions such as: Can I perform at that level if I try? If I perform at that level, what will happen? and How do I feel about those things that will happen? The individual then decides to behave in a way that seems to have the best chance of producing positive, desired outcomes.

The expectancy model also suggests that satisfaction is best thought of as a result of performance rather than as a cause of it (Locke & Latham, 1990; Porter & Lawler, 1968). Strictly speaking, it does influence motivation in some ways. For instance, when it is perceived to come about as a result of performance, it can increase motivation because it strengthens people's beliefs about the consequences of performance. Also, it can lead to a decrease in the importance of certain outcomes, and as a result, decrease the motivation for those performances that are seen to lead to whatever reward becomes less important.

In many ways, the expectancy model is a deceptively simple statement of the conditions that must exist if rewards are to motivate performance. It is deceptive in the sense that it suggests all an organization has to do is relate pay and other frequently valued rewards to obtainable levels of performance. Not only is this not the only thing an organization has to do, as is obvious from the research on pay for performance systems, it can be difficult to accomplish.

In order for employees to believe that a pay for performance relationship exists, the connection between performance and rewards must be visible, and a climate of trust and credibility must exist in the organization. The reason why visibility is necessary should be obvious; the importance of trust may be less so. The belief that performance will lead to rewards is essentially a prediction about the future. For individuals to make this kind of prediction they have to trust the system that is promising them the rewards. Unfortunately, it is not always clear how a climate of trust in the reward system can be established. As will be discussed later, some research suggests that a high level of openness and the use of participation can contribute to trust in the pay system.

Motivation of Employee Self-development

Just as reward systems motivate performance, they can motivate the learning of skills and the development of knowledge (Lawler, 1990). The key here is the same as it is with performance motivation. Individuals need to see a connection between learning specific skills and a valued reward. Pay for performance systems may motivate learning and development because individuals perceive that they must develop their skills in order to perform effectively. However, if individuals feel they already have the skills, then a pay for performance system may not have this impact.

Sometimes pay for performance systems may discourage individuals from learning new skills or motivate them to learn the wrong skills. This can happen when the skills that should be learned are not directly related to present performance and, as a result, are not likely to lead to a reward and indeed may decrease the chances of receiving a performance-based reward.

The reward systems in most organizations are extremely hierarchial. In major U.S. corporations, for example, executives often make more than 100 times as much as lower-paid employees (Crystal, 1991). As a result, strong motivation is created to learn those skills that are perceived to lead to promotion. To counter this tendency some organizations are using skill-based pay when they want individuals to add new skills that do not involve promotions. They also use them when they want employees to develop a broader understanding of how the organization operates (Jenkins & Gupta, 1985; Lawler & Ledford, 1985).

Organizational Culture

Reward systems are one feature of organizations that contributes to the overall culture and climate (Whyte, 1955). Depending on how reward systems are developed, administered, and managed, they may cause the culture of an organization to vary quite widely. For example, they may influence the degree to which it is seen as a human resources–oriented culture, an entrepreneurial culture, an innovative culture, a competence-based culture, and a participative culture.

Reward systems have the ability to shape culture precisely because of their important influence on motivation, satisfaction, and membership (Kerr & Slocum, 1987). The behaviors they elicit become the dominant patterns of behavior in the organization and lead to perceptions and beliefs about what an organization stands for, believes in, and values.

Perhaps the most obvious link between pay system practice and culture concerns the practice of performance-based pay. The absence or presence of this policy, as well as how well it is implemented, can have a dramatic impact on the culture of an organization because it so clearly communicates to organization members what the performance norms are in the organization. Many other features of the reward system may also influence culture. For example, having relatively high pay levels may produce a culture in which people feel they are an elite group working for a top-flight organization, while introducing such innovative pay practices as flexible benefits may produce a culture of innovativeness. Finally, having employees participate in pay decisions may produce a participative culture in which employees are generally involved in business decisions and as a result are committed to the organization and its success (Lawler, 1981).

Organizational Structure

The reward system of an organization can help reinforce and define the organization's structure (Lawler, 1981, 1990). Often this feature of reward systems is not fully considered in the design of reward systems. As a result, their impact on the structure of an organization is unintentional. This does not mean, however, that the impact of the reward system on structure is necessarily minimal. Indeed, it can help define the status hierarchy and the degree to which people cooperate with people from other departments and within their work area. It can also strongly influence the kind of decision structure that exists.

The decision to cover a group of people with a pay for performance system is an important structural decision that causes both integration and differentiation (Lawrence & Lorsch, 1967). It can have a particularly strong impact on the degree to which people feel they share a common fate with others in the organization. It can set them off or differentiate them from others, thereby creating a kind of structural boundary that reduces cooperation and sharing with individuals and groups outside the boundaries of the pay system. If the system pays them the same, based on a measure of their collective performance, it can integrate them and cause them to cooperate and work as a team. On the other hand, if the reward system asks individuals to compete among themselves for a fixed amount of money that has been allocated for raises or bonuses, it can serve to differentiate them from each other and cause them to compete among themselves.

Organizational Cost

Reward systems are often a significant cost factor in organizations. Indeed, the pay system alone may represent over 50 percent of an organization's operating cost. Pay systems involve direct pay and benefit costs, as well as the costs associated with managing and operating the system. In the case of some pay systems, these operating costs can be quite high. Thus, it is important in considering the impact of the reward system to focus on how high these costs are.

Recently, some economists have argued that it is important to consider how costs vary as a function of the organization's ability to pay (Weitzman, 1984). For example, a reasonable outcome of a well-designed pay system might be an increased cost when the organization has the money to spend and a decreased cost when it does not. This can help an organization avoid layoffs and provide individuals with greater job security. An additional objective for an organization might be to have lower overall reward system costs than its business competitors.

Establishing Base Pay

Most pay systems are founded on the idea of paying individuals based on the job they hold (Rock & Berger, 1991). The question then becomes, How does one begin to establish a basis for the compensation of different jobs. This will be discussed next, as will an alternative of paying individuals based on what their skills are worth.

Job Evaluation

Job evaluation is a formal procedure for ordering a set of jobs or positions in an organization with respect to their inherent value or worth in achieving the organization's objectives. This procedure is usually then linked to a rate of pay prescribed for that job. While the origins of job evaluation are variously attributed to the U.S. Civil Service Commission in 1871 (Patton, Littlefield, & Self, 1964) or to the work of Frederick W. Taylor in the 1880s (Pasquale, 1969), the earliest significant applications were found in the late 1930s with the growth of the labor movement (Patten, 1988). Its use in the private sector became widespread during World War II, when the National War Labor Board permitted wage increases only to correct demonstrated "inequities" in wage structure (Livy, 1975). At about the same time, most government jobs were being classified using some form of job evaluation system (Suskin, 1977). Generally, by the

mid-1970s, estimates of the percentage of U.S. firms using some form of job evaluation ranged from 70 to 80 percent (Bureau of National Affairs, 1976).

Regardless of the specific type of job evaluation procedure used, almost all share a similar methodology. First, the jobs to be evaluated are carefully described using a thorough job analysis. Second, based on the description of the job, each job is evaluated with respect to its value or *worth* to the organization, and the jobs are then arranged hierarchically with respect to this evaluation. Finally, these results are used to set wage rates within the organization. The remainder of this section will focus on the second step in that process, since it is the area that has been the subject of the most research.

Methods. There are four major methods of job evaluation: job ranking systems, job classification systems, factor comparison systems, and point systems. The first two of these methods are generally referred to as qualitative techniques, the second two as quantitative techniques.

Job Ranking. Job ranking systems are the crudest of the job evaluation techniques. Based on their relative worth to the organizations, jobs are ranked as a whole from the highest to the lowest. Because the rankings are based on job descriptions, not specific job facts, they are highly subjective. This procedure can be difficult to implement in a large organization where many jobs are to be evaluated.

Job Classification. This approach involves developing a set of job grades or classes and then fitting the jobs in the organization into these classes. First, comprehensive grade descriptions are written. These descriptions must be written generally so that many different types of jobs can be classified. Evaluators then examine job descriptions as a whole and match them to the appropriate grade description. Two difficulties with this approach are immediately obvious. The level of generality at which grade descriptions are written may encourage individuals to exaggerate and aggrandize their duties and responsibilities to obtain higher classifications and hence higher base pay. Second, most jobs will have some duties that are contained in one grade description and some in another. The evaluator is then forced to average or to pick the closest match to the job.

Factor Comparison Approaches. Factor comparison job evaluations compare jobs with respect to job dimensions or job requirements that the organization has deemed deserve compensation. The skeleton of the system is formed by selecting *key* or *benchmark* jobs that have relatively stable content, are found in many organizations, and for which a prevailing wage is known. Some systems use the current wage rate for the benchmark jobs rather than the prevailing wage. These jobs are then ranked along each compensable factor, and based on these rankings, the prevailing wage is apportioned across the compensable factors. Once the skeleton of the system is assembled, other jobs in the organization are compared factor by factor to the key jobs and given the dollar value thought to be appropriate for that factor. The dollar values assigned for each factor are then summed to reflect the worth of the non–key jobs.

While cumbersome to develop and explain, this approach is relatively easy to administer as long as prevailing wage rates are constant. There are two serious weaknesses in this approach, however. First, wage rates for the key jobs must be equitably aligned both internally and externally to produce useful assessments of relative worth. Second, the apportionment of the wage of the key jobs across factors must be valid since they constitute the foundation for the entire system.

Point Systems. The point system is the most widely used of the job evaluation approaches.

Estimates are that over 95 percent of major U.S. corporations use this approach to evaluate at least some of their jobs (Lawler, 1990). Like the factor comparison approach, compensable factors are first determined. They are given weights or points reflecting the relative importance of each factor in determining job worth. The factors are then divided into degrees and the points associated with that factor allocated across them. The upper end of each factor scale represents the maximum points associated with that factor, the lower end either zero or some "base." Detailed descriptions of the job content and requirements of each degree are written. Using job descriptions and/or task inventories, job evaluators then assess each job with respect to how much of each factor the job contains, match that assessment to the degree descriptions, and award the number of points associated with that degree. The relative worth of the job is then reflected in the sum of the points awarded for each factor.

Criticisms of Job Evaluation Systems. While job evaluation approaches are probably the most prevalent methods of establishing base pay, their usefulness, like the usefulness of any management system, depends on how well they achieve their objectives (Lawler, 1990). They have been increasingly subject to criticism. For example, Belcher (1969) characterized them as based on "untested assumptions," and Mahoney (1991) described them as increasingly anachronistic. The criticisms discussed next address three different but related areas: the reliability and validity of job evaluation techniques, the unintended consequences likely to accompany them, and the congruence between these techniques and other organizational systems.

Psychometric Properties. The reliability of job evaluation instruments has been challenged because the evaluation process is inherently subjective (Beatty & Beatty, 1984). Investigations of the reliability of job evaluations appear in two clusters (Welbourne & Gomez-Mejia, 1991): research in the late 1940s when job evaluation systems were achieving prominence as compensation tools (e.g., Ash, 1948; Chesler, 1948; Jones, 1948; Lawshe & Farbro, 1949; Lawshe & Wilson, 1947), and research in the 1980s as questions of equal pay for work of comparable worth were raised (e.g., reviews by Arvey, 1986; Madigan, 1985; Milkovich & Broderick, 1982; Schwab, 1980; Snelgar, 1983). The earlier studies generally report high reliabilities for the total scores and somewhat lower reliabilities for individual factor ratings. In addition, systems using few factors tend to have higher reliabilities than those using many factors. The later studies are more likely to report mixed results (Arvey, 1986). For example, Gomez-Mejia, Page, and Tornow (1982) examined seven different job evaluation methods and reported reliabilities of .44 to .80.

With respect to the validity of job evaluation techniques for producing assessments of the organizational value of jobs, Arvey (1986) characterizes the evidence as "sparse." Generally, the validation studies that do exist approach the validation process from either a convergent or a predictive validity perspective. In the first approach, a set of jobs are subjected to varying job evaluation techniques and the results compared (e.g., Gomez-Mejia, Page, & Tornow, 1982; Madigan & Hoover, 1986). In the second approach, job evaluation results are used to predict either the organization's existing wage structure or the prevailing wage rate as defined by wage and salary surveys (e.g., Dertien, 1981; Schwab & Grams, 1985). Even if the results of both approaches are consistent and supportive (which they are not), this does not establish the construct validity of job evaluation as a measure of relative worth (Gupta & Jenkins, 1991).

The first approach that looks at multiple job evaluation approaches simply demonstrates that different job evaluation techniques are measuring the same thing. Whether that "thing" is the value of the job to the organization remains to be seen. It may simply reflect the shared stereotypes, biases, training, or experience of the evaluators (Gupta & Jenkins, 1991).

Rynes and Milkovich (1986) have argued that the "going rate" for jobs does not exist. Rather, it is the sum of a series of subjective judgments on the part of those who conduct and use salary surveys. Similarly, the hierarchy of wage rates within a firm is a product of history, negotiation, stereotypes, convenience, and rationalization. Thus, the predictive approach to validation cannot prove that a job evaluation technique actually captures the "true" value a job adds toward meeting the organization's objectives. All it establishes is that the job evaluation approach reflects the subjective judgments and biases that have been institutionalized either in the marketplace or internally in the organization.

In summary, the evidence to date leaves the construct validity of job evaluations in question. Reliability evidence is abundant, but the convergent and predictive validity data are less convincing. They are not sufficient to establish that the "true" worth or value of a job has been captured (Gupta & Jenkins, 1991).

Unintended Consequences. A job evaluation system is a control system. Control systems are designed to influence and direct employee behavior (Lawler & Rhode, 1976). The behaviors they influence and direct, however, are not necessarily those that are intended or those that are functional for the organization (Kerr, 1975). Job evaluation systems are no different in this respect. Lawler (1986c) has highlighted a number of unintended and organizationally undesirable employee behaviors that are often associated with the use of job evaluation systems.

First, because job evaluation systems tie pay to those activities included in the employee's responsibilities, they necessarily highlight those activities that are outside that purview. "That's not my job" and "I'm not paid to do that" are common refrains for not doing things that further the organization's objective.

Second, because the intent of job evaluation is establishing internal equity, these systems direct employee attention to the internal relationships among jobs. Rather than paying attention to the competition in the marketplace, employees concentrate on how the pay for their jobs differs from the pay of others and how they can improve their relative pay positions.

Third, employees quickly realize that creatively written and aggrandized job descriptions and exaggerated task inventories can sometimes lead to pay increases more easily than actual changes in job duties. Thus, they produce inflated descriptions that raise their pay and the organization's costs.

Fourth, job evaluation systems implicitly or explicitly assign a heavy weight to responsibility, reinforcing the idea of a management hierarchy. Promotion, therefore, becomes the surest way to increase one's pay. In many modern organizations that require technical excellence or a broad-based understanding of the organization, the *linear career orientation* engendered by job evaluation approaches works at cross-purposes with organizational objectives (Fuller, 1972). The development of career ladders and maturity curves for scientists as alternative base pay structures for some groups of employees attests to the failure of traditional job evaluation methods to reward employees for electing career paths where they could only look forward to static or potentially declining levels of compensation.

System Congruence. Mahoney (1991) argues that the notion of work is undergoing a fundamental shift. Viewing work as a set of standardized, programmed tasks appropriate to the industrialization of the early 20th century is inappropriate in a time of internationalized markets, rapid technological and product developments, and emphases on quality and timeliness. The demands of this new environment require new organizational systems for designing work, authority structures, and organizations. The compensation system must be congruent with these new systems.

Job evaluation systems that reinforce power relationships and pecking orders based on pay may impede the success of organizations that need technical knowledge and innovation often found at the bottom of the organizations (Lawler, 1986c). Similarly, successfully managing organizations that require flexibility and adaptability from their employees to meet changing environments is at odds with job evaluation systems based on prescriptive job descriptions.

Job evaluation systems that reinforce organizational hierarchies also make the use of participative management systems more difficult (Lawler, 1990). Employee participation has an inherent dimension of equality. To the extent that the job evaluation system forces differences in pay and, by implication, worth, the success of a participative system is jeopardized.

Organizations are adopting team-based approaches to organizing to meet the new organizational realities (Lawler, Mohrman, & Ledford, 1992). The unit of management in these organizations is the team. Tasks, duties, and responsibilities are assigned to a team, not an individual. While they are performed by individuals, individual responsibility shifts among team members as internal needs and external demands shift. Traditional job evaluation, with its focus on the job performed by an individual, is fundamentally incompatible with this organizational design. In theory, the logic of job evaluation could be applied to a team as a whole rather than to the individual team member with all team members paid at the same rate. But this leads to the same problem discussed earlier with respect to job evaluation plans that focus on individuals: evaluating the relative importance of the contribution of one team versus another (Gupta & Jenkins, 1991). Whatever the strategy taken, the end result bears little resemblance to the original notion of job evaluation as conceived by Taylor and others.

Organizations using traditional job evaluation techniques leave little room for rewarding individual variations in behavior. The jobs for which individuals are paid are clearly specified, as are the ways the jobs are to be performed. Mahoney (1991) notes that job evaluation systems are appropriate where jobs are standardized and unvarying and where differences in performance are difficult to attribute to individuals. In many organizations, however, differences among individuals and teams are large and observable. Rewarding these differences means focusing on the individual, which is in fundamental opposition to the basic tenet of job evaluation systems, that of paying the job.

Conclusion. There is always likely to be a role for job evaluation in the administration of compensation. It can provide an internally justifiable wage structure for organizations that are structured around relatively stable collections of tasks. As organizations restructure to meet the new demands of a rapidly changing environment, however, it is less likely to be used because it fails to recognize differences in individual capability and it reinforces a hierarchial approach to management.

Skill-based Compensation Systems

The classic works of Katz and Kahn (1966) and Emery and Trist (1965), which apply the logic of open-systems theory and sociotechnical-systems theory to organizations, focus attention on the way work is designed and arranged. They focus particularly on the role of groups and on the design of work for groups or teams

that are given the responsibility for the production of a whole product (Lawler, 1978; Walton, 1980). In these self-managing teams, members are expected to function interdependently to accomplish this end. The rotation of individuals among tasks or jobs within a team is expected to be frequent, each team member assuming responsibilities as needed and as he or she is able. Thus, team members are expected to become flexible members of the group by becoming skilled in all or most of the tasks that fall within the group's purview.

The self-managing team approach was first used in a number of new plants, but it is now widely used (Lawler, Mohrman, & Ledford, 1992). When combined with other management practices and a management style that stresses employee participation, growth, and development, it can produce a high-involvement work culture (Lawler, 1986a, 1992).

Given the underlying premises of the job evaluation approaches and the problems associated with their use, a different approach to establishing base pay is needed in organizations that use teams and high-involvement management. Skill-based pay or pay-for-knowledge compensation systems seem to be the preferred approach (Lawler, 1990). Rather than paying individuals for the specific job they are performing, they are paid at a rate based on the repertoire of jobs or tasks they can perform—that is, their knowledge and mastery of different jobs in the organization.

Pay-for-knowledge or skill-based compensations systems can be grouped into two broad types: *multiskill-based* or *breadth systems*, where pay levels are linked to the number of different skills a worker learns and can perform in the organization; and *increased knowledge* or *depth-based systems*, where pay levels are linked to increased knowledge and skill within the same general job category.

Under a multiskill-based pay system, a new employee is paid a starting rate when first hired. When the employee masters a skill or task, a pay increase is awarded. As new skills or tasks are mastered, additional pay increases are given until the individual masters all the tasks required in the work team or all the tasks in the plant.

Organizations have tried a number of variations on this basic theme. Sometimes the pace at which employees can learn new skills is restricted. In some instances, the proficiency with which a mastered skill is performed is used as a basis for awarding the increment associated with learning that skill. Sometimes the increments associated with all tasks are the same; sometimes the increments vary with the complexity of the task or the average time required to learn the task. Whatever the particular details, multiskill-based pay plans tie individual pay levels to the number of skills or tasks the individual employee can perform.

Increased-knowledge-based systems, on the other hand, base individual pay on the depth of knowledge in a particular skill area. As individuals specialize in one skill area and acquire greater knowledge or proficiency in that area, increases in pay are awarded. Technical ladders in R & D organizations and organizations with apprenticeship systems in the skilled trades represent familiar forms of these systems. Less familiar are the depth-based systems in high-involvement organizations, where a worker chooses to specialize in a particular skill area, gaining expertise in that particular job and then acting as a trainer, a resource to others learning that skill, and as the technical expert when problems arise.

While no experimental evidence on the impact of skill-based approaches to base pay exists, a number of recent empirical case studies (Gupta et al., 1986; LeBlanc, 1990; Ledford, 1985; Ledford & Bergel, 1990; Ledford, Tyler, & Dixey, 1990; Tosi & Tosi, 1986) and theory pieces (Jenkins & Gupta, 1985; Lawler & Ledford, 1985; Ledford, 1991; Tosi, 1986)

suggests they can offer advantages over traditional job-evaluation approaches for both employers and employees.

Advantages for the Organization. The single biggest advantage of skill-based pay systems in a production setting is increased flexibility (Jenkins & Gupta, 1985). Because workers know more than one job, they can move with ease from one task to another as the need arises. As market and product demands change, workers can move from one set of jobs to another. As employees are absent, their roles can be filled temporarily by other team members, reducing the need to overstaff for absenteeism, fluctuations of supply and demand, and day-to-day uncertainties. Because in skill-based pay systems human resources tracks organizational needs more closely, organizations can enjoy leaner staffing and reduced overall labor costs.

Organizations using skill-based pay systems also report higher quality output (Gupta, Jenkins, & Curington, 1986). Because workers are multiskilled, they have a better idea of how the different tasks fit together, and thus they have a greater understanding of the importance of quality in their performance. In addition, because one of the skills frequently learned in multiskill systems is quality assurance, workers know the quality-assurance requirements for the task and can distinguish between acceptable and unacceptable products. Furthermore, as Jenkins and Gupta (1985) note, because of the frequent movement and rotation among jobs, operators producing low-quality output today may find they produced tomorrow's headaches when they move to quality assurance or to rework and repair.

Absenteeism and turnover tend to be lower in organizations using skill-based pay. For example, in a study of plants using skill-based pay systems (Gupta et al., 1986), 74 percent of the companies in the sample believed that their absenteeism rates were lower than they would have been without the skill-based pay system, and 69 percent reported that their voluntary turnover rates were lower. Many employees are more satisfied under these systems because they have a greater degree of control over their own lives and rates of pay. Also, because employees have a greater understanding of the entire operation in their organization, their intrinsic satisfaction may increase, and they are better able to see the importance of their attending work regularly. Turnover is decreased in part by the increased satisfaction experienced by employees in these organizations and in part because, in March and Simon's (1958) terms, the ease of movement has been decreased with the addition of firm-specific training (Becker, 1975; Oi, 1983). Finally, these systems often produce higher than market pay rates.

As employees become more broadly knowledgeable about the operations of the organization by working in different parts of it, the potential for them to become more self-managing is enhanced. They are in a position to control their own behavior, cooperate with others in the organization, solve problems, and participate in decisions about how the organization operates. The more self-managing employees become, the fewer the levels of management that are needed and, in fact, the fewer managers, supervisors, staff, and support personnel that are needed. In the Gupta et al. (1986) study, 61 percent of the companies responding said they would need more first-line supervisors without a skill-based pay system; 63 percent said they would need more skilled trades employees; 32 percent said they would need more managers.

Advantages for Employees. From the perspective of employees, a number of advantages may be gained from skill-based pay systems. Perhaps the most noticeable is an increase in satisfaction. Research has shown that employee satisfaction levels are generally higher in skill-based pay companies than they are in similar companies using traditional pay systems (Lawler, 1990; Ledford, 1991). Because employees in skill-based pay plans are generally paid more than they would be under traditional compensation systems, this may reflect the strong correlation between pay satisfaction and pay level (Lawler, 1971). It is also possible that the increase in satisfaction derives from a feeling by employees that they are being treated as individuals.

Increases in the intrinsic motivation to perform undoubtedly result from the enhanced job enrichment inherent in skill-based pay systems (Jenkins & Gupta, 1985). As individuals rotate through different jobs in the organization, either learning new skills or exercising the increased flexibility in assignment they possess, there is a natural increase in job variety, autonomy, task identity, and task significance, with a consequent increase in motivation (Hackman & Oldham, 1980).

Another employee benefit of these systems is increased feelings of self-worth and self-esteem. The organization is demonstrating its regard for employees by investing resources in them and providing them the opportunity to learn and grow. As people's talents develop, they feel better about themselves.

The increased flexibility and leaner staffing that skill-based pay plans promote may also create increased job security for employees. The organization is able to maintain a more stable work force, redeploying people in times of low or shifting demand.

Costs. The advantages of skill-based pay systems do not come without costs. First, the pay rates that these systems produce tend to be higher on average than they would be under a traditional pay system. By rewarding skill acquisition, these systems encourage employees to become more valuable to the organization by mastering new skills. As employees master new skills, their average hourly pay increases.

Second, because the systems encourage employees to learn multiple skills, the organization must make a larger investment in employee training than is the case in traditional systems. This investment can be substantial, involving hiring and paying trainers, lost time from work during training, and costs of less than fully competent individuals performing tasks. To some extent the training costs are mitigated because training is often provided by members of the work team as a normal part of the job, but the performance losses are real, at least in the short-run. In addition, because the work force is in flux, additional burdens are placed on the human resource management system, which must coordinate the movement of employees from job to job and insure a proper balance between production and employee skill acquisition. It is especially important that the planning system support the goals of the pay system. The human resource planning systems must encourage movement of employees across jobs and emphasize job rotation. Otherwise, employees quickly become frustrated and distrustful when they are ready to master a new skill and the opportunity to do so is not available to them.

Third, skill-based pay systems place extra demands on the performance appraisal system. Employees must be evaluated more frequently than in traditional systems, they must be evaluated for their ability to do multiple jobs, and at times they must be evaluated by multiple appraisers. Because of the increased empowerment of employees, inadequacies in the performance appraisal system are likely to become obvious, and pressure is likely to be brought by employees to rectify these inadequacies. Deficiencies in the performance appraisal system will also have the effect of certifying less than fully skilled individuals, producing well paid jacks-of-all-trades but masters-of-none.

Fourth, the administrative burden is greatly increased with skill-based pay systems. The pay rates change much more frequently and less predictably in skill-based pay systems than in traditional systems. Records must be maintained to keep track of which employees can do which jobs so that full advantage of the system can be realized.

Fifth, because the system abandons the traditional notion of paying the job and focuses on paying the individual, market comparisons become more difficult. When individuals perform jobs only part of the time and in different combinations, it is often impossible to find benchmark jobs in other organizations in order to peg pay rates. Furthermore, as multiskilled employees are worth more to the organization than are single-skilled employees, simple market comparisons are inappropriate on their face.

As skill-based pay systems mature, another difficulty develops. When a skill-based pay system is young, there are many skills for employees to learn. But as the system matures, the more ambitious employees may have mastered all available skills, with no place to go. While *topping out* occurs in traditional pay systems when individuals reach the top of their pay grades, it generally occurs much later in an employee's career. This problem is exacerbated by the fact that in skill-based pay systems employees may learn to expect more frequent pay raises than in traditional pay systems.

Ensuring that employees remain proficient in the skills they learn can also present problems for the organization. When organizations are faced with pressure to produce, employees may not be allowed to move as freely from job to job. Skills that are not used for extended periods of time may atrophy, and the organization thus may compensate individuals for skills they either no longer possess or cannot perform as effectively as when originally learned.

Finally, when organizations introduce technological innovations or other changes that make previously acquired skills no longer valuable to the organization, they must fashion fair and equitable methods to adjust employees' wages without penalizing them for decisions made by management. One approach is to freeze the employee's rate until new skills are acquired to replace the obsolete skills.

Development and Implementation. Setting up a skill-based pay system is not easy. There is very little institutionalization of these programs. Traditional job evaluation systems such as the point system or the Hay plan are more or less the same from one organization to the next and share a well-understood technology for their development and installation. Each skill-based pay plan is specific to the organization that uses it. Jenkins and Gupta (1985) note that there are probably as many variations of skill-based pay systems as there are organizations using them. While no handbook exists specifying the "correct" way to design a skill-based pay system, Ledford (1990) and Lawler (1990) have enumerated a set of issues potential adopters must address and have designed steps to make a successful plan more likely.

The first issue to be considered is how the skill-based pay system will fit with the organization's culture, its other management and technological systems, and its business objectives. Generally, skill-based pay systems are most effective when organizations have or are moving toward a participative organizational culture. The breadth of experience and skill that skill-based pay systems produce in employees provides them a perspective for organizational decision making. This perspective enhances employee problem-solving skills and cooperation, an important advantage where technological interdependence is high and teams are used.

Second, the organization must identify the skills required for effective operation through careful analysis of the tasks needing to be performed in the organization. These tasks are then grouped or clustered into sets of skills (often called *skill blocks*) for which the organization is willing to pay more money. This step is critical to the ultimate success of the plan; the structure of the skill blocks determines (a) how well the pay plan fits the organization's technology and (b) the skeletal structure that provides the basis for most of the plan's detail (e.g., pay levels, certifications, training modules, etc).

Third, the organization must identify the optimal skill profiles for all employees in the organization. The organization must specify how many employees with what combination of skills are needed to accomplish the organization's business objectives. In so doing, the organization must consider its technological constraints. For example, manufacturing cells that are self-contained units making a set of products for a specific market require employees who possess all the skills used within the cell, but not necessarily those in other cells. In contrast, workers in continuous process technologies (such as those used in food processing and pharmaceutical production) are highly interdependent and must respond quickly to problems that may appear anywhere in the process. Thus, the organization needs employees who possess skills to work throughout the facility.

Fourth, the organization must develop a mechanism for pricing each skill and skill block. In some cases, the skills can be identified and priced by going to the labor market and determining the hiring rate for individuals with specific skills. In others, the *value added* by the skill can serve as a guide. Regardless of the specific details of pricing the skill, this is one issue that cannot be sidestepped because it will form the basis for both internal and external equity assessments on the part of the employees.

Fifth, the organization must develop a set of rules about the sequence in which skills can be learned and the rate at which they can be learned by employees. Because employees' wages are determined by the number of skills they possess, they are naturally concerned with what they must do to acquire additional skills. Having too many employees learning new skills at the same time necessarily means that the organization is operating at a sub-standard level. Having too few employees learning new skills reduces the flexibility that organizations want from these systems. These access rules also have implications for the kinds, amounts, and timing of the training needed to impart the skills.

Sixth, the organization must develop methods and procedures to determine when and whether an employee has acquired a new skill. This is often the most contentious issue in skill-based pay systems. The criteria and methods used to determine skill assessment must be developed in light of the nature of the job that is under consideration. It is generally believed that a work sample test in which the employee performs the tasks relevant to the skill is the best approach to skill certification. On the other hand, some skills, particularly those involving cognitive skills (e.g., reporting and logging procedures), may be assessed more effectively using paper-and-pencil tests.

When the testing of employees for skill certification is conducted (on demand or at set intervals) and how long employees must wait to be retested if they fail the certification must also be determined ahead of time. In addition, the organization must make a determination of who conducts these skill assessments and certifications. In traditional pay systems, the responsibility for pay decisions usually lies with management. In high-involvement organizations, however, the responsibility may reside with co-workers and teams as well.

Finally, the organization must develop policies and procedures for decertification, that is, for situations in which individuals will no longer be paid for skills they previously mastered. This could occur, for instance, if

there were changes in the technology the organization used to produce its goods. It could also occur if the organization's product or service became obsolete. It could occur with the move of individuals from one work area to another, eliminating the need to posses those skills. Furthermore, some skills may atrophy or be lost if they are not used regularly. Since it is not in the organization's interests to pay for unneeded skills, procedures for decertification must constitute integral components of the pay system design.

Overall, developing a pay system that pays employees for the skills they possess requires considerable thought and system development. If properly done, however, pay can be used to reward individuals for developing the skills that help the organization function effectively, while at the same time furthering employee growth, development, and satisfaction. Compared to the amount of research on job evaluation, relatively little research has been done on skill-based pay. It is clearly an area where more research is needed.

Pay for Individual Performance

The idea of paying for performance is so widely accepted that almost every organization says that it pays for performance. A survey of 557 large U.S. corporations found that 80 percent of them rate pay for performance as a very important compensation objective (Peck, 1984). The major reason for the popularity of paying for performance is the belief that it can motivate job performance and increase organizational effectiveness. The research evidence clearly supports this view.

There has been, and continues to be, considerable evidence that pay can be a particularly powerful incentive (Blinder, 1990; Jenkins, 1985; Lawler, 1971; Locke et al., 1980; Nalbantian, 1987). Studies show productivity increases of between 1 and 35 percent when pay for performance systems are put into place

TABLE 1

Characteristics of Individual Pay for Performance Approaches

	Incentive Pay	*Merit Pay*
Payment Method	Bonus	Changes in base pay
Frequency of Payout	Weekly	Annually
Measures	Output, productivity, sales	Supervisor's appraisal
Coverage	Direct labor	All employees

(Lawler, 1990). Although pay for performance is often treated as a single approach, there are, in fact, many different approaches to paying for performance (e.g., see Blinder, 1990; Jenkins & Gupta, 1982; Lawler, 1990) that have very different consequences. They can be easily classified based on the level of performance on which they focus: individual, organizational subunit, or total organization. Within each of these general approaches, there are literally hundreds of different approaches to relating pay to performance.

The focus in looking at the different approaches to paying for performance will be on their impact on individual and organizational behavior. Pay for performance systems are not stand-alone systems; their impact is partially determined by the organizational context in which they operate. Thus, as different approaches to pay for performance are reviewed, consideration also will be given to how they fit with different management styles and organizational designs.

There are two common approaches to paying for individual performance. One, *incentive pay*, has been declining in popularity for decades; the other, *merit salary increases*, remains very popular (e.g., see Lawler, Ledford, & Mohrman, 1989; O'Dell, 1987). They are similar in that they measure and reward individual performance. They are different in how they measure performance and in how they

adjust an individual's pay according to performance. This is shown in Table 1, which summarizes the characteristics of the two approaches.

Incentive Pay

Incentive plans pay employees bonuses based on the number of units produced. They are perhaps the most direct way to relate pay to performance. There is a great deal of evidence that incentive pay can motivate individual behavior; indeed, much of this research is decades old (e.g., see Lawler, 1971). There is also good reason to believe it can attract and selectively retain good performers because they end up being paid more.

The literature on pay incentive plans is full of detailed descriptions of the counterproductive behaviors that piece-rate incentive plans produce (e.g., see Whyte, 1955). Most of the earlier accounts are from the manufacturing world, but the same kind of issues arise when salespersons and other service personnel are put on incentive pay (e.g., Babchuck & Goode, 1951). In many respects, these behaviors are caused not so much by the concept itself, but by the way it is managed. Nevertheless, it is difficult to separate the practical problems with particular plans from the general idea of incentive pay. A brief review of the major problems with incentive plans follows.

Beating the System.   Numerous studies have shown that when piece rate plans are put in place an adversarial relationship frequently develops between system designers and employees (Lawler, 1971). Employees engage in behaviors to get rates set so as to maximize their financial gains relative to the amount of work they have to do. They work at slow rates to mislead the time-study expert studying their jobs. They hide new work methods or new procedures from the time study so the job will not be restudied. In addition, informal norms develop about productivity, and employees set limits on their production. Anyone who goes beyond this limit is socially ostracized and even physically punished. Unfortunately for the organization, this limit often is set far below what people are capable of producing.

Other forms of gaming include producing at extremely low levels when the rates are set at levels that the employees consider too difficult to reach and using union grievance procedures to eliminate rates that are too difficult (Whyte, 1955). Another version involves doing only what is measured. In the case of production workers, this may mean not doing clean-up and material-handling work. In the case of salespersons, it may mean not doing customer service activities and tying up customers so that other salespersons cannot get the sale.

Divided Work Force.   Since many support and nonproduction jobs do not lend themselves to incentive pay, a typical organization with incentive pay has only part of the work force on it. This often leads to a counterproductive we/they split that can lead to noncooperative work relationships (Lawler, 1990). This split is not a management-worker split, but a worker-worker split that horizontally divides the organization. It can lead to incentive employees complaining about materials handling, maintenance, and other employees on whom they depend for support. This split can also influence the kind of career paths people choose.

Often, individuals will bid for and stay on incentive jobs even though they do not fit their skills and interests. The higher pay of incentive jobs may additionally cause individuals to be inflexible when asked to change jobs temporarily, and cause them to resist a new technology that calls for a rate change.

Maintenance Cost.   Because incentive plans by themselves are relatively complicated and need to be constantly updated, a significant number of people are needed to maintain them. Maintaining incentive systems is further complicated by the adversarial relationship that develops between workers and management. Since employees try to hide new work methods and avoid changes in their rates (unless, of course, it is to their advantage), management must be extremely vigilant in determining when new rates are needed. In addition, when a technological change is made or a product is introduced, new rates must be set. While no good estimates exist of how expensive it is to maintain an incentive pay plan, it is likely that the costs vary widely from situation to situation, and in some cases are high.

Organizational Culture.   The combined effects of dividing the work force into those who are and are not on incentive pay and the adversarial process of rate setting can create a hostile, differentiated organizational culture (Whyte, 1955). In particular, they produce a culture of low trust, lack of information sharing, conflict between groups, minimal support for joint problem solving, and employee inflexibility because individuals want to protect their pay rates. Overall, incentive pay generally works against creating a climate of openness, trust, joint problem solving, and commitment to organizational objectives.

Small Group Incentive Plans.   Closely related to individual incentive plans, but much less popular, are small group incentive plans (Lawler, Mohrman, & Ledford, 1992). They differ in that small group plans tend to fit situations where outcomes are based on the performance of small employee groups and individual performance is not easily measurable. They are usually less effective in motivating performance because pay is less directly related to the performance of individuals. They can, however, be quite effective if the groups are kept small (Lawler, 1971). In general, they suffer from all the same problems as the individual incentive plans do because they too are based on a top-down management process, engineered standards, and adversarial relationships.

Conclusion. The decades of research on incentive pay clearly demonstrates its strengths and weaknesses. It makes it clear that the installation of incentive pay is, at best, a mixed blessing. Although incentive pay may improve productivity, the counterproductive behaviors, maintenance costs, division of the work force, and poor culture it leads to may make it a poor choice. Many organizations have dropped it or decided not to put it in place simply because they have decided that the negative effects and maintenance costs outweigh the potential advantages that come from the increases in performance it typically produces.

Incentive pay clearly fits some organizational situations better than others. It best fits situations (a) where the work is designed for individuals or, in some cases, for small groups; (b) where the work is simple, repetitive, and easy to measure comprehensively; (c) where the nature of the work is stable, so that the work can be carefully studied, and there is rarely the need to revise standards and payment approaches; and (d) since more than any other system, it differentiates the organization to create isolated individuals or small groups who often feel in competition with each other,

where the need for integration is negligible or where other mechanisms can be used to produce it (Lawler, 1981).

Finally, incentive pay has usually been associated with the control approach to management, and it may be this fact that it has produced so many problems. It is possible that if it is used with a more involvement-oriented management style that stresses fairness, due process, and participation, incentive pay might be more effective (Lawler, 1990). It clearly has the power to motivate performance when individuals believe a fair and clear relationship exists between pay and performance.

Merit Pay

Merit pay is the most widely used approach to paying for performance (e.g., see Lawler, Ledford, & Mohrman 1989; O'Dell, 1987). Merit pay systems typically give salary increases to individuals based on their supervisor's appraisal of their performance. Their purpose is to affect motivation and to retain the best performers by establishing a clear performance-reward relationship. In light of their popularity, it is surprising that so few studies have examined their impact on performance experimentally. Of the 77 studies reviewed by Heneman (1990), only 6 looked at the performance impact of the installation or removal of a merit system. Despite the widespread adoption of merit pay, there is considerable evidence that in most organizations merit pay systems fail to create a clear relationship between pay and performance (see Heneman, 1984, 1990; Milkovich & Wigdor, 1991). As a result, they also fail to produce the positive motivational effects that are expected of them. There are a number of reasons why merit pay systems often do not effectively relate pay and performance.

Poor Performance Measures. Fundamental to an effective merit pay system are credible comprehensive measures of performance.

Without these, it is impossible to relate pay to performance in a way that is motivating. Considerable evidence suggests that in most organizations performance appraisal is not done well and as a result, good measures of individual performance do not exist (e.g., see Devries, Morrison, Shullman, & Gerlach, 1981; Meyer, Kay, & French, 1965; Milkovich & Wigdor, 1991; Mohrman, Resnick-West, & Lawler, 1989). There is also substantial evidence that even if good measures of performance exist, they often are distorted, ignored, or misused to accomplish other ends (Longnecker, Sims, & Gioia, 1987; Mohrman & Lawler, 1983; Murphy & Cleveland, 1991). In the absence of good objective measures of individual performance, most organizations rely on the judgments of managers. These judgments are often seen by subordinates as invalid, unfair, and discriminatory (Mohrman, Resnick-West, & Lawler, 1989). Because the performance measures are not trusted, when they are the basis for pay little is done to create the perception that pay is based on performance (Lawler, 1981).

Several studies have found that when pay is related to performance appraisal results the nature of the appraisal is changed for the worse (e.g., see Meyer, Kay, & French, 1965). Particularly troublesome is the finding that pay discussions tend to inhibit the discussion of development and learning. There is one study by Prince and Lawler (1986), however, that suggests that discussing salary during a performance appraisal has either no negative effects or small positive effects on how well the appraisal is done and how satisfied the participants are with it. It too, however, concludes that discussing pay makes it difficult to discuss development and suggests a separate meeting to consider it.

Poor Communication.   The salaries of most individuals in organizations are kept secret (Lawler, 1981). In addition, some organizations keep many of their pay practices secret. For example, it is common for organizations to keep secret such things as the amount of salary increases and what the highest and lowest raises are. Thus, the typical employee is often in the position of being asked to accept as an article of faith that pay and performance are related. Given pay secrecy, it is simply impossible to determine if they are. In situations of high trust, employees may accept an organization's statement that merit pay exists. Trust, however, depends on the open exchange of information; with secrecy, it is not surprising that many individuals are skeptical.

Poor Delivery Systems.   The actual policies and procedures that make up a merit pay system often lead to actions that do little to relate pay to performance (Lawler, 1990). In addition, the policies and procedures are often so complex that they do more to obfuscate than to clarify the relationship between pay and performance. The typical merit salary increase is particularly poor at actually relating pay and performance because it allows for only small changes in total pay to occur in one year. All too often only a few percentage points separate the raises given good performers and those given poor performers. This is particularly likely to be true in periods of low inflation because salary increase budgets are usually small.

Employees view pay increases as motivating only if they are large enough to be perceived as meaningful (Lawler, 1981). How large is large enough? The idea of a pay raise threshold has been of interest for over two decades (see Zedeck & Smith, 1968) and has drawn heavily on psychophysical concepts, most notably Weber's law (Gescheider, 1976).

Eleven studies have attempted to investigate the notion of a pay raise threshold (Bowen, Worley, & Lawler, in press; Champlin & Kopelman, 1991; Corbett & Potocko, 1969; Futrell & Schul, 1980; Futrell & Varadarajan, 1985; Heneman & Ellis, 1982; Hinrichs, 1969; Krefting & Mahoney, 1977; Rambo & Pinto, 1989; Varadarajan & Futrell, 1984; Zedeck & Smith, 1968). These studies have produced estimates of just noticeable pay raises ranging from 1.8 percent to 11.5 percent. Peck (1984) reported that in 1982 merit increases ranged from 5.0 percent to 14.3 percent, with a median increase of 8.8 percent. If the value of a just meaningful pay raise is estimated at the midpoint of the range of values in the empirical investigations it comes out to 6.7 percent. This suggests that in many years, large numbers of employees receive merit increases that are not noticed or significant psychologically.

While there have been no empirical investigations of the impact of less than noticeable pay raises on employee motivation, it is reasonable to assume that they do not serve to enhance pay for performance perceptions. Furthermore, when organizational pay policies dictate that pay increases be based on factors other than performance, differences in increases between employees at different performance levels may be further reduced, again weakening pay for performance perceptions.

Salary increase systems further compound the problem of relating present pay levels to present performance by making past merit payments part of the individual's base salary so that it becomes an annuity. Indeed, employees' current salary levels seem to be viewed by supervisors and employees as entitlements. An individual can be a poor performer for several years after being a good performer and still be highly paid. The less senior good performer, on the other hand, has to perform well for a number of years in order to achieve a relatively high pay level. Furthermore, as Schwab and Olsen (1988) demonstrated in a Monte Carlo simulation, the unreliability of the performance measure weakens the relationship between actual pay and actual performance over time when the merit payments become part of the employee's base salary. This can have disastrous effects for retaining outstanding performers. Because they are unable to increase their pay quickly, they often find it best to look for jobs elsewhere.

The annuity feature leads to one other problem, topping out. After a long period on a job, individuals often reach a point where they are at the top of the pay range for their job. The effect is to eliminate pay as a motivator because it cannot be adjusted to reflect performance.

Poor Managerial Behavior. Managers do a number of things that adversely affect the perceived and actual connection between pay and performance. Perhaps the most serious is the failure to recommend widely different pay increases for their subordinates when large performance differences exist (Kopelman, Rovenpor, & Cayer, 1991). Some managers are unwilling to recommend very large and very small pay changes, even when they are warranted (Heneman, 1984). One reason for this seems to be the unpleasant task of explaining why someone got a low raise.

Conclusion

The impact of tying the pay levels of individuals to performance is a complex one that has been the subject of considerable research. Table 2 highlights the advantages, disadvantages, and fit issues involved in both incentive and merit pay.

The existence in most organizations of any one of the common problems that plague the administration of merit pay programs, however, is usually enough to destroy the belief that pay is related to performance and, as a result, eliminate the motivational impact of merit pay. In reality, the merit pay systems of most organizations typically suffer from all or most of these problems. As a result, the policy of merit fails to improve performance.

The problems with merit pay raise the question of whether it should be used. A number of the leading figures in the Total Quality movement have concluded that it should not (e.g., see Deming, 1986; Mohrman, 1990). They list many criticisms, but perhaps the most telling is that merit pay focuses

TABLE 2

Individual Pay for Performance

	Incentive Pay	Merit Pay
Performance Motivation	Clear performance-reward connection	Little relationship between pay and performance
Attraction	Pays higher performers more	Overtime pays better performers more
Culture	Divides work force, adversarial	Competition within work groups
Organizational Structure	Many independent jobs	Helped by measurable jobs and work units
Management Style	Control	Some participation desirable
Type of Work	Stable, individual easily measurable	Individual unless group appraisals are done
Measures	Maintenance of measures costly	Requires well-developed performance appraisal system

attention on individual performance when, in fact, poor performance is often the result of poor organizational systems and processes. There is evidence that merit pay can have a positive impact when it fits the situation and is properly administered (e.g., see Heneman, 1984; Kopelman, Rovenpor, & Coyer, 1991). Like incentive pay, it focuses on individuals and, as a result, does little to integrate the members of the work force. Indeed, the typical approach of allocating a salary increase budget to be divided among a small group of employees clearly sets up a competition among them for the larger raises. This can be a serious problem if the organization needs employees to cooperate in order for it to be effective.

The research on individual incentive systems suggests they should be approached with a great deal of caution. As shown in Table 2, they can be a positive motivator but they do not fit most situations. Thus, they are likely to be used less in the future and ultimately may be applied only to individual sales jobs, repetitive clerical jobs, and simple, repetitive manufacturing jobs.

Pay for Organizational Performance

Bonus payments based on the performance of an organization and stock ownership are old

TABLE 3

Characteristics of Organizational Pay for Performance Approaches

	Gainsharing	*Profit Sharing*	*Ownership*
Payment Method	Bonus	Bonus	Equity changes
Frequency of Payout	Monthly or quarterly	Semiannually or annually	When stock is sold
Measures	Production or controllable costs	Profit	Stock value
Coverage	Production or service unit	Total organization	Total organization

and potentially quite effective ways to improve organizational performance. Proponents argue that they can improve motivation, build a work culture in which people are committed to and care about the organization's effectiveness, and finally, adjust the labor cost of an organization to its ability to pay (Weitzman, 1984). There is no question that in some instances, organizations have been able to accomplish just these outcomes as a result of tying the pay levels of individuals to organizational performance.

Approaches

It is far from simple, however, to design an effective approach. There are literally thousands of approaches to paying for organizational performance, and there are many complex organizational issues that must be dealt with if any plan is to be successful (Lawler, 1990). Historically, there have been three major approaches to paying for organizational performance. The oldest is the approach of paying bonuses based on the profitability of the organization. This is undoubtedly the most widely accepted approach worldwide and, as will be discussed later, has important advantages as well as very important limitations. Closely related to profit sharing are stock ownership plans that give individuals all or part

of the ownership of the organizations for which they work. They are similar in that they use existing measures of performance. They treat employees like investors, rewarding them when the organization does well in equity markets and reducing their wealth when the organization does poorly (Rosen & Young, 1991).

Less common but increasingly popular is gainsharing (Lawler, Ledford, & Mohrman, 1989; Lawler, Mohrman, & Ledford, 1992; O'Dell, 1987). Gainsharing differs from profit sharing in two respects. First, it is combined with a participative approach to management, and second, it typically measures controllable costs or units of output, not profits or stock price, in its approach to calculating a bonus (Lawler, 1990). Table 3 gives an overview of the characteristics of the three major organizational pay for performance systems. In the discussion that follows, consideration will first be given to what is known about gainsharing, then profit sharing and ownership plans will be considered.

Gainsharing. Gainsharing, a term originally coined by F. W. Taylor (Graham-Moore & Ross, 1990), has been used successfully for at least 50 years in hundreds of organizations (Bullock & Lawler, 1984; General Accounting Office, 1981; Graham-Moore & Ross, 1990;

O'Dell, 1981, 1987). Companies and employees have profited from gainsharing—companies in the form of reduced costs and employees in the form of bonus payments and improved job satisfaction. The original and best known gainsharing plan is the Scanlon Plan. Other gainsharing plans include Improshare and the Rucker Plan (for detailed descriptions of these plans, see Graham-Moore & Ross, 1983, 1990). In addition to these plans many companies have their own custom-designed gainsharing plans.

In the typical gainsharing plan, financial gains in organizational performance are shared on a formula basis with all members of the organization. A historical base period is established and is used as the basis for determining whether gains have occurred; hence the name *gainsharing*. Typically, only costs controllable by employees are measured for the purpose of computing the gain. Unless a major organizational change takes place, the historical base stays the same during the entire history of the plan; thus, performance is always compared to the time period before starting the gainsharing plan. When performance is better than in the base period, a bonus pool is funded. When it falls short, no bonus pool is created. In a typical plan, at least half of the bonus pool is paid out to the employees, while the rest is retained by the company. Payments are typically made on a monthly or quarterly basis, with all employees getting equal percentages amounts.

No one has an accurate estimate of how many gainsharing plans there are in the United States and Europe. There are probably at least a thousand, and there seems to be little doubt that their popularity has increased tremendously in the last 10 years. One recent survey in the United States indicated that about 13 percent of all firms have them and over 70 percent were started in the last 5 years (O'Dell, 1987).

Until 10 years ago, gainsharing was used primarily in small manufacturing organizations. Much has been written in the United States about the success of older gainsharing programs in smaller companies such as Herman Miller, Lincoln Electric, and Donnelly Mirrors (Graham-Moore & Ross, 1983; Moore & Ross, 1978). All three of these plans are over 30 years old. During the 1970s, large companies such as General Electric, Motorola, Rockwell, TRW, Dana, and Firestone began installing gainsharing plans in some manufacturing plants. The trend of large corporations defining organizational units that have their own gainsharing is continuing and resulting in the adoption of more gainsharing plans (Lawler, Mohrman, & Ledford, 1992). The increased popularity of gainsharing is significant and relates to an important feature of most gainsharing plans. They are more than just pay incentive plans; they are both a way of managing and an organizational development technology. To be specific, they are a participative approach to management and are often used as a way to install participative management (Frost, Wakeley, & Ruh, 1974; Lawler, 1986b, 1990).

The Participative System.   From the beginning, Joe Scanlon, the creator of the Scanlon Plan, emphasized that gainsharing fits a participative management style. In the absence of a change in employee behavior, there is no reason to expect a payout from the kind of formula that is typically developed in gainsharing plans. A payout requires an improvement in performance, and that improvement requires more effective behavior on the part of employees. Some improvement may be gained simply from the motivation that is tapped by tying pay to performance. This is particularly true in situations where the work is not highly skilled or interdependent and, as a result, effort is directly related to performance. In other situations, however, there are several reasons why a gainsharing plan without a participative system is unlikely to produce an appreciable improvement in performance.

First, the motivational impact of the plan may not be large because most gainsharing plans aggregate the performance of a number of people. As a result, the plan has only a small impact on the perceived relationship between individual performance and pay. The formula used is relevant here. Some plans use very simple formulas that focus on the relationship between labor input and productivity (e.g., Improshare); others use a more comprehensive set of cost measures (e.g., the Rucker plan). Simple labor-based plans are more likely to affect motivation directly because with them employees can see a more direct relationship between their efforts and their bonuses.

Second, in many cases, simple effort and good intentions are not enough to improve the operating results. What is needed is a combination of people working harder, working more effectively together, sharing their ideas, and working smarter. For this to happen, it often takes a formal participative system that converts the motivation to improve performance into actual changes in the operating procedures of an organization. In the absence of new procedures or systems to accomplish theses changes, they rarely seem to occur.

In traditional gainsharing plans such as the Scanlon Plan, the key to the participative system is a formal suggestion system with written suggestions and shop floor committees to review the suggestions (Frost, Wakeley, & Ruh, 1974). Often there is also a higher level review committee that looks over those recommendations that involve several parts of the organization and/or large expenditures. This system of committees is one way of trying to assure that new ideas will be seriously considered and, where appropriate, implemented.

Recently, some organizations have combined gainsharing with self-managing teams and other participative management practices to produce an approach that is best called high-involvement management (Lawler,

1986a, 1992). In this approach, employees make the most of the operating decisions and get rewarded for their organization's effectiveness through the gainsharing plan. This approach gives employees a chance to influence the things that determine the operating results of the organization, which is necessary if bonuses based on operating results are to influence motivation.

Research Results. The most important thing that research has shown about gainsharing plans is that they usually work (GAO, 1981). We know something about the frequency with which they work: There is evidence to suggest that they work in a relatively high percentage of cases (about 70% according to Bullock & Lawler, 1984). Lawler (1971, 1990) has summarized some of the common results that have been found in research studies of gainsharing plans:

- Coordination, teamwork, and sharing of knowledge are enhanced at lower levels.

- Social needs are recognized via participation and reinforcing group behavior.

- Attention is focused on cost savings, not just quantity of production.

- Acceptance of change due to technology, market, and new methods is greater because higher efficiency leads to bonuses.

- Attitudinal change occurs among workers, and they demand more efficient management, better planning, and good performance from their co-workers.

- Employees try to reduce overtime—to work smarter.

- Employees produce ideas as well as effort.

- When unions are present, more flexible administration of union-management relations occurs.

- When unions support the plan, they are strengthened because better work situations and higher pay result.

- Unorganized locations tend to remain nonunion.

There are also things that gainsharing plans do not do as well as other approaches to paying for performance. Perhaps the most important is differentially attracting and retaining the best performers. Because gainsharing plans do not pay better performers more, they do not necessarily motivate them to stay. Gainsharing plans do vary pay costs somewhat with the organization's ability to pay, but not as effectively as profit sharing since a gainsharing plan can produce a bonus even when the organization is not profitable. Finally, gainsharing plans contribute to both integration and differentiation. They integrate the units they cover in both a vertical and horizontal respect since they treat everyone the same. On the other hand, they tend to differentiate them from the rest of the organization.

Much is known about structuring gainsharing plans. There are a number of books and articles that describe in some detail how to put together formulas, introduce plans, and manage the process side of operating a gainsharing plan (e.g., Belcher, 1991; Graham-Moore & Ross, 1983; Moore & Ross, 1978). As a result, there is quite a bit of how-to-do-it knowledge. This is particularly true with respect to the Scanlon Plan. Indeed, a careful reading of the literature on this plan can make it possible for an organization to develop and install a plan without the help of a consultant. The research evidence also shows that certain situational factors favor gainsharing plans (Lawler, 1981). They include:

- *Organization size.* The plan is based on employees seeing a relationship between what they do and their pay. As organizations get larger, this is harder to accomplish. Most successful gainsharing plans cover fewer than 500 employees. They also tend to cover operating units that can operate relatively independently of other organizational units.

- *Performance measurement.* In some organizations, a good performance measure and a reasonable performance history simply do not exist and cannot be established. This is often true in organizations where rapid technological and market changes occur. For these organizations, gainsharing plan formulas are difficult to develop.

- *Measurement complexity.* Often performance can be measured only in very complex ways. The more true this is, the more difficult it is to make a plan work, because no clear, easily understood connection between an individual's behavior and rewards can be established.

- *Worker characteristics.* Gainsharing depends on employees wanting to participate and wanting to earn more money. Most individuals have these goals, but not all do. Unless a substantial majority in organizations want the benefits the plan offers, it cannot succeed.

- *Communication.* For gainsharing to work, employees must understand it and trust it enough to believe that their pay will increase if they perform better. For this belief to exist, a great deal of open communication and education is needed. If an organization does not have these already, they must be started if the plan is to succeed.

- *Management attitudes.* Unless managers are favorably disposed to the idea of participation, gainsharing is unlikely to fit the management style of the organization. In some organizations, the plan has been tried simply as a pay incentive plan without regard to management style, and it has failed because of a poor fit.

- *Supervisory skills.* Gainsharing requires supervisors to change. They are forced to deal with many suggestions and their competence is tested and questioned in new ways. Unless supervisors are prepared for and accept theses changes, the plan can fail. This point goes along with the general point that management must be prepared to manage in different ways.

As this list demonstrates, gainsharing does not fit every situation. Since they often have most of these favorable conditions, it is easy to see why for so long the installation of gainsharing plans was limited to manufacturing situations. Although much remains to be learned about how such plans should be installed in nonmanufacturing environments and in the public sector, it appears there are ways they can be designed to work in these settings (Graham-Moore & Ross, 1983; Schlesinger & Heskett, 1991). Indeed, it may be a more broadly applicable approach than has been assumed.

Profit Sharing.   Profit sharing is better known, older, and more widely practiced than gainsharing (Lawler, Ledford, & Mohrman, 1989). In the United States, for example, data indicate that at least one-third of all organizations have some form of profit sharing (O'Dell, 1987). Some definitions of profit sharing include it as a form of gainsharing; it is different, however, in two respects. It often does not have a participative management component, and it does not use formulas that only measure increases in employee-controlled financial or productivity-related performance.

Given its popularity, it is surprising that so little psychological research has been done on profit sharing. Gainsharing, despite being less popular, has been much more extensively researched. This may reflect the fact that profit sharing is associated with participative management theories. What evidence there is suggests that profit-sharing plans typically are much less effective than gainsharing plans in influencing motivation and in producing the kind of social and cultural outcomes that were listed earlier as resulting from gainsharing plans (e.g., see Blinder, 1990). This is particularly true in large organizations where the line of sight and line of influence from individual performance to corporate profits is virtually nonexistent. Large size often compounds the problem of tying present rewards to controllable performance to the point where it is hard to see that there can be any impact on motivation. In the typical profit-sharing plan, the line of influence problem is further compounded because most firms (estimates are about 85%) defer profit-sharing bonuses by putting them into retirement plans (Blinder, 1990; Lawler, 1990; Metzger, 1964).

Before dismissing profit sharing as totally useless from an organizational effectiveness point of view, it is important to note that there are three things even a deferred profit-sharing plan in a large corporation can accomplish. First, there is the potential symbolic and communication value of paying employees based on organizational performance. It can effectively point out to employees that they are part of a larger organization and that cooperative effort is needed. Since corporate executives are often rewarded on the basis of profit sharing, it can also help to assure that there is an alignment between the rewards received by top management and those received by people throughout the organization (Foulkes, 1991). This can help avoid the all-too-common problem of executives getting large bonuses while lower level employees receive none, thus creating a counterproductive vertical differentiation in the organization (Crystal, 1991).

Second, some companies, most notably Hewlett-Packard, have effectively used their profit-sharing plans as vehicles for educating employees about the financial performance of the business. When employees understand the financial performance of the business and are actually sharing in the profits, it brings alive for them the issue of what profits mean and how they are calculated. This in turn can increase their interest in learning about profits and organizational effectiveness and have an effect on the organization's culture.

Third, perhaps the most important advantage profit sharing offers is that it makes the labor costs of an organization variable and adjusts them to the organization's ability to pay (Weitzman, 1984). When profits go down, labor costs go down; and thus, rather than being fixed, labor costs, at least in part, become variable. This is a particularly desirable feature for organizations that are in cyclical or seasonal businesses. In most western countries, changes in labor costs are handled through increases and decreases in the size of the work force. This is a necessity when wages are high and fixed because there is no other way to control labor costs to reflect the company's ability to pay. With profit sharing, it is possible to reduce costs significantly without reducing the number of employees. Most Japanese firms have used this approach to adjusting labor costs for decades. As is the case in Japan, it can allow an organization to make a much stronger commitment to employment stability and help it gain the advantages that are inherent in having a stable work force.

Employee Ownership.   A number of plans exist that help get some or all of the ownership of a company into the hands of employees. These include stock option plans, stock purchase plans, and employee stock ownership plans (ESOP's). There is little question that stock ownership plans are increasingly popular and are being researched more. According to one study, some 11 million

employees in over 8,000 businesses now own at least 15 percent of the companies employing them (Quarrey, Blasis, & Rosen, 1986; Rosen, Klein, & Young, 1986). It is difficult to generalize about the impact of ownership plans because they vary widely in how much ownership employees receive, and their impact is likely to depend on the organizational situation.

Much of what has been said about the impact of profit sharing and gainsharing plans is relevant to the impact of ownership. In some situations there is reason to believe that ownership can have much the same impact as an effective gainsharing plan (Klein, 1987). In small organizations in which participative management is practiced it has a good chance of increasing organizational performance (Blinder, 1990; O'Toole, 1979; Rosen, Klein, & Young, 1986). The key is combining it with employee involvement since it typically produces a weaker line of influence than does gainsharing (Blinder, 1990; Conte & Tannenbaum, 1980).

In a large organization with little employee ownership it may positively impact the structure by creating integration across the total organization if, of course, all employees are included in the ownership plan. Unlike profit sharing, it does not adjust costs to reflect the organization's ability to pay unless it includes an approach in which stockholders directly share in profits. It can help organizations raise capital and finance themselves. Indeed, most plans are probably installed because of the tax and financing advantages they offer (Blasis, 1988). Ownership can have a more positive impact on attraction and retention than does profit sharing. In particular, if ownership is not easily saleable, it can help to lock someone into the organization both financially and psychologically.

Overall, based on the limited available research, there is reason to believe that ownership strategies can have a positive effect in a number of situations. Their usefulness, however, is likely to be highly situationally determined. For instance, in the case of small organizations, they might make profit sharing and gainsharing unnecessary, and if combined with an appropriate approach to employee involvement, they can contribute substantially to employee motivation. In a large organization they may contribute to a positive culture and to the integration of the organization. There is a need for considerable additional research on a number of issues, including the impact of the many different approaches to structuring ownership and how the impact of ownership is affected by characteristics of the organization.

Theory and Predictions

Existing theory and research can be combined to make some testable predictions about the impact of any pay for performance system (Lawler, 1988b). As mentioned earlier, congruence theory assumes that an organization's effectiveness is related to the degree to which the different systems in an organization fit or are congruent with each other (e.g., see Galbraith, 1973). This calls for a congruence among the way information, power, knowledge, and rewards are distributed in the organization (Lawler, 1986a).

Organizational pay for performance plans move rewards for organizational performance downward so that part of all employees' rewards depend on it. The implicit assumption is that this will change employee behavior in ways that will increase organizational performance. The major way it can change behavior is by affecting motivation since it does little to reward training and developing new skills. It follows from what was discussed earlier about motivation that organizational plans will increase organizational performance to the degree that they do the following:

- Establish the belief that rewards are based on organizational performance

- Provide communication about organizational performance to all employees

- Establish ways for employees to influence organizational performance as it is measured by the reward system

- Create opportunities for employees to learn how to contribute to organizational performance and how to interpret measures of performance

These four conditions can best be viewed as combining multiplicatively and varying from zero to one. Viewing them as combining in this way is critical because it means that if any of them is completely absent, organizational performance will not improve as a result of installing gainsharing, profit sharing, or stock ownership plans. As is frequently noted, they work only when individuals are motivated to perform differently. If one or more of these is missing, a pay change will not affect motivation because no link or line of sight and influence will exist between the reward and the inputs (i.e., effort, ideas) that most employees in an organization can control.

Working harder can improve individual performance, but it may have no or a relatively small impact on organizational performance unless the organization already has good work methods and systems. Often improvements in organizational performance require major system and method improvements; without them, increased effort may be wasted and employees frustrated. It is also important to note again that organizational pay for performance systems may not have a major impact on effort. Particularly in large organizations, they do little to increase the relationship between effort and rewards; thus, their impact on motivation may be small or nonexistent.

As has been shown by research, gainsharing, profit sharing, and ownership are more effective when combined with participative management (Blinder, 1990; Hammer, 1988). This follows from motivation and congruence theory because in the absence of a participative management approach that gives employees a chance to increase organizational performance in ways other than working harder, it is difficult for them to see how they can influence organizational performance.

Participative management can put into place two key elements: the ability to influence organizational performance in ways other than putting more effort into immediate job performance, and an understanding and trust of the relationship between improved organizational performance and a bonus or the value of stock. In the absence of these, it is unlikely that a perceived connection between improved individual performance and a pay reward will exist. The one exception to this may be the case of a very small organization. There a relationship between individual effort and organizational performance may be evident in the absence of a participative management style. In the case of a small organization, an organizational pay for performance plan might establish a line of influence and work as an incentive much like small group pay incentive plans do.

Turning to the specifics of particular plans, the congruence argument suggests that the type of participative approach used needs to be matched to the type of pay plan used. Most gainsharing plans advocate suggestion programs of some type. Although suggestion approaches give employees some additional power, they are very limited in the amount of power, knowledge, and information they move downward in the organization. They are, in essence, a parallel structure that does little to change the core operating style of the organization (Lawler, 1986a, 1988a, 1992). In this respect they differ appreciably from such approaches as work teams or semiautonomous work groups that push a considerable amount of power and knowledge to the lowest levels of the organization (Hackman & Oldham, 1980). Teams can give employees a chance to influence a number of the decisions that directly influence organizational performance (Lawler, 1986a).

The combined congruence-expectancy theory argument leads to some interesting predictions about which approach to participative management is needed to support different pay for organizational performance approaches. The Improshare formula is the simplest gainsharing formula since it looks only at hours of work relative to units produced. Because it is simple and straightforward, it is not difficult to establish a line of sight: Employees know if they produce more product by either working smarter or harder they will earn more. Little extra communication and education are needed. Further, individuals do not need to influence many of the decisions that are made in organizations in order to reduce the amount of labor that goes into a product—they can simply work harder or smarter. In short, the Improshare plan has a chance of working as an incentive plan in the absence of a great deal of participation if there is a reasonable level of trust, the organization is relatively small, and the production process is relatively simple. Therefore, the use of quality circles or some other suggestion programs can provide a reasonable vehicle for reducing labor hours through better work methods.

The situation is quite different for gainsharing formulas that look at multiple costs and involve complex computations and for profit-sharing and ownership plans. Like profit-sharing plans, these plans cover a number of costs, and the payments they produce are influenced by a wide range of factors, often including such things as purchasing and pricing decisions. If employees are to influence their rewards, a level of participation that goes far beyond quality circles and written suggestions is needed. They require at least the kind of participation that is present in self-managing teams and high-involvement plants. Profit-sharing plans and stock-ownership plans are a simple extension of this argument. For them to be effective as motivators, a high level of employee involvement is essential.

Other congruence issues come into play with respect to plan choice. The plan needs to fit the type of work the organization does. A labor-only gainsharing formula, for example, fits only those operations where labor costs are dominant and can be reduced. Situations where other costs are important need more complex formulas that reflect other key operating costs. In the absence of a more complex formula, there is the real danger that employees will focus only on reducing the measured costs and that unmeasured costs will increase.

In summary, the congruence approach does not argue for a particular approach to relating pay to organizational performance. Instead it suggests that the plan must measure and reward those things that employees influence, understand, and receive communications about. The prediction is that a pay plan will work best when the approach matches the participative management approach used. Simple plans will work with suggestion programs, while profit-sharing and ownership plans require the use of more participative approaches such as teams. This point is consistent with the finding that gainsharing plans generally have more impact than profit-sharing plans (Lawler, 1981; O'Dell, 1987). The latter are typically based on difficult-to-influence measures and often are not combined with an appropriate level of participative management. This point may also help explain the success of the Scanlon Plan and the Improshare Plan. These plans tend to combine a limited amount of participation with a formula that typically measures only one or a few costs directly controllable by the employee.

The arguments so far suggest that an organization's decision to adopt a particular approach to paying for organizational performance needs to be based on a contingency model. It seems clear that the type of plan that is adopted needs to fit the kind of technology and effectiveness issues that the organization faces. For example, organizations that

use relatively simple manufacturing technologies and need to reduce their labor costs probably can accomplish a great deal by adopting a simple gainsharing plan. On the other hand, a complex-knowledge work organization that needs to focus on customer satisfaction and on a number of costs is in a different situation. It may need a complex gainsharing plan, a profit-sharing plan, an ownership plan, or some combination of the three. It may need to use a participative management approach that combines teams, open information, and task forces to study major business issues.

The congruence argument also suggests some predictions about the process of developing and installing these plans. The effectiveness of the plan should increase if an organization uses a process that is congruent with the way the organization should operate after the plan is installed. This means it should be a participative process with open communication and an emphasis on education in most cases. This type of process should help the plan be effective for a number of the reasons mentioned earlier. In addition, it should help the organization learn how to manage participatively. The development of the pay plan in effect becomes a learning experience abut how to manage participatively. Participation in the design process probably is not as important in the case of the Improshare Plan as it is for more complex plans. With ownership, for example, participation in the design would seem to be necessary in order to develop both understanding and trust.

Conclusion

The research evidence suggests that employee ownership, gainsharing, and profit sharing can all be useful practices for many organizations. Table 4 summarizes the major advantages and limitations each approach. They ought not to be looked at as competing approaches, but as often compatible approaches that accomplish different objectives (Lawler, 1990). Profit

TABLE 4

Organizational Pay for Performance

	Gainsharing	Profit Sharing	Ownership
Performance Motivation	Some impact in small unit	Little pay-performance relationship	Very little pay-performance relationship
Attraction	Helps with all employees	Helps with all employees	Helps lock in employees
Culture	Supports cooperation, problem solving	Knowledge of business	Sense of ownership
Organization Structure	Fits small stand-alone work units	Fits any company	Fits most companies
Management Style	Some participation	Works best with participation	Works best with high levels of participation
Type of Work	Helps most with interdependent types	All types	All types
Costs	Ongoing maintenance needed, operating costs variable	Relates costs to ability to pay	Cost not variable with performance

sharing can have the desirable effect of creating variable costs for an organization, thus allowing it to adjust its costs to its ability to pay. Stock ownership can help with organizational financing and help retain employees. Ownership and profit sharing can also affect the communication pattern and culture of an organization in ways that emphasize the performance of the total organization. Gainsharing, on the other hand, if correctly designed, can provide motivation and produce a culture in which people are committed to seeing their organizational unit operate effectively.

The ideal combination for many large corporations would seem to be a corporate-wide profit-sharing plan, a stock ownership program, and gainsharing plans in major operating plants or units. The combination of gainsharing and profit sharing deals directly with the need to have variable costs and the need to motivate employees. Gainsharing

alone does not do this because it tends to be based on subunits of the organization and measures that do not include all the operating costs of the firm. Thus, the possibility exists for a gainsharing plan to pay out a bonus when the organization is performing poorly or for no bonuses to be paid even when the organization as a whole is performing well. From the motivational point of view, this is quite acceptable if the employees are performing well against the things they are measured on and can control. It fails, however, to integrate the total organization in the way an effective profit-sharing plan or an effective stock ownership plan can; employees may erroneously feel that the organization is in good shape if they are receiving a bonus. The addition of a profit-sharing plan and/or an ownership plan can help the organization call attention to the organization's ability to pay, something a gainsharing plan may not always do.

Executive Compensation

The reward practices at the top levels of an organization often differ from those at other levels. Senior managers are not only paid much more than others, they are also paid differently (Crystal, 1978, 1984, 1991; Ellig, 1982). This has led to some research and theory concerning what determines executive compensation, but relatively little research on what difference it makes with respect to individual and organizational performance (Finkelstein & Hambrick, 1988; Gerhart & Milkovich, 1990).

Executive compensation is a potentially important area of research simply because of the importance of the individuals it affects—executives. Their potential impact on the overall performance of an organization is great, and there is reason to believe that how they are treated can broadly affect the organization because it helps establish the culture and performance objectives for the organization. Executive compensation has been a research focus for economists, organizational theorists, and psychologists, although a limited amount of research has been done. Indeed it is one area where true multidisciplinary research can be done since disciplines approach the topic from very different theoretical perspectives.

Determinants

A number of studies have explored the relationship between type of firm, type of industry, and characteristics of executives and compensations amounts. The research has found some predictable relationships (see Gomez-Mejia & Welbourne, 1988, 1989, for reviews). There is abundant research linking firm size to CEO compensation levels. The larger the firm, the higher the level of executive compensation (Finkelstein & Hambrick, 1988). No definite explanation exists for this relationship, but a good guess is that it is due at least partially

to the widespread use of job evaluation and salary survey data that considers the size of jobs as an important factor. It may also be due to the desire of firms to have different pay levels for different management levels, which in turn leads to higher pay for individuals at the top of taller, larger organizations.

Research has also looked at the relationship between firm performance and amount of executive compensation. It has been argued that there should be relationships since executives are responsible for firm performance. They also often have compensation packages that include bonuses and stock plans that are tied to company performance (O'Reilly, Main, & Crystal, 1988). Although the case for a relationship seems compelling, the evidence shows only a very weak relationship between total compensation levels and firm performance (Finkelstein & Hambrick, 1988; Gerhart & Milkovich, 1990). Typically the relationship is higher between year to year changes in compensation and performance than it is between total compensation level and performance. No simple explanation for this low relationship exists. It is probably the consequence of a number of factors, including the fact that a good deal of an executive's pay is not dependent on performance, the problems with measuring performance, and the unique power position of executives. Because of their power in the organization, executives may well be able to create their own favorable compensation packages (Crystal, 1991).

Compensation levels have been found to be related to industry (Crystal, 1984). Some industries simply pay better than others. No good theoretical explanation exists for these differences. Some research has focused on the relationship between the personal characteristics of executives and compensation levels. The logic is that individuals with greater experience, tenure, education, and skills should have a higher market value. Overall the evidence does not show a strong relationship between personal characteristics and pay level (Gomez-Mejia, Tosi, & Hinkin, 1987).

Several studies have shown that an organization's approach to executive compensation may be related to its structure (Balkin & Gomez-Mejia, 1987b; Kerr, 1985; Napier & Smith, 1987). In general, studies have found weak relationships between types of compensation and organizational characteristics. Kerr (1985) did find that firm growth orientation is related to type of compensation—more growth-oriented firms seem to use greater amounts of risk-oriented compensation and to base it more on economic performance. The diversity of the businesses of a firm has also been considered as a predictor of compensation approach. Some support has been found for the argument that diversity makes a difference, as is predicted by some organization theorists (Galbraith & Kajzanjian, 1986).

Overall, the research on executive compensation provides some information on which executives are likely to be paid the most. It generally fails, however, to provide an explanation for the very large differences that exist between the pay of executives and the pay of other organization members. Finkelstien and Hambrick (1988) have offered some reasons for this, as have O'Reilly, Main, and Crystal (1988). There seems to be no single factor that accounts for it; rather, it is the historical product of a number of factors, some of which are unique to the United States. The uniqueness of the United States is particularly noticeable, as executive compensation levels are particularly high in the United States.

Executive compensation in the United States is public by law, and it is typically set by the board of directors. Because of these two factors, the issues of social comparison and power over the board must be considered in any analysis of executive compensation levels. Because pay is public, comparisons are easy to make and market rates are well known. Given the competitive nature of those individuals in executive positions, it follows that they would place great importance on how their pay compares to that of other executives (O'Reilly, Main, & Crystal, 1988).

Comparisons do not inherently lead to high levels of executive compensation, but when combined with executive power, they can. Power is where corporate boards come into play. They control pay but may be strongly influenced by the senior executives of the firm. Many senior executives sit on the boards of their firms and influence which outsiders sit on the board. In addition, they sit on the boards of those firms whose executives sit on the board of their firm (Schoorman, Bazerman, & Atkins, 1981). Thus, boards end up with overlapping memberships such that it can be hard for them to say no to higher and higher pay levels (Crystal, 1991; Hill & Phan, 1991; O'Reilly, Main, & Crystal, 1988). In the absence of government regulations and stockholder activism, there is little effective pressure toward reducing the level of executive compensation.

Consequences

Executive compensation, like compensation at other levels in the organization, is predicted to have an effect on individual behavior (Finkelstein & Hambrick, 1988). In particular, it should affect membership behavior, motivation, and skill development. There has been little research on how it affects behavior. In some respects, this is not a serious problem because there is so much general research on the effects of rewards on motivation and behavior. There are, however, some unique pay practices at the executive level, and thus the possibility exists for interesting research to be done at this level. For example, executives often are paid in special ways that are designed to prevent turnover (e.g., golden parachutes), and of course they are given unusual forms of incentive pay (e.g., phantom stock).

Perhaps most interesting at the executive level is how different forms of compensation influence the direction of effort. There is some evidence that type of executive compensation influences such things as how much executives invest in long-term research and development (Rappaport, 1978). Studies have found that long-term pay incentive plans lead to increases in capital expenditures and that contingent pay can reduce nonpecuniary expenditures (Larcker, 1983).

Little attention has been paid to the impact of executive pay practices on groups other than the executives themselves. Potentially, it has a significant impact on stockholders as well as on the rest of the organization. There is some evidence that stock prices react positively to executive compensation packages that tie pay to firm performance (Brickley, Bhagat, & Lease, 1985).

Lawler (1990) has argued that because of the visibility, symbolic importance, and direct effect on executive behavior, executive rewards can have a significant impact throughout an organization. In addition to influencing how much effort individuals invest in trying to obtain an executive position, reward levels can influence how much social distance exists between executives and others in the organization. Lawler also argues that how executive compensation is structured and administered can influence the credibility of executives, their ability to lead the organization, and how effectively pay for performance systems operate at other levels in the organization.

Overall it is surprising how little is known about the impact of executive rewards. The research has focused more on what causes the reward levels and reward systems than on their consequences. This is understandable since executive compensation levels routinely exceed several million dollars a year. However, perhaps more important and less frequently studied is the issue of what, if any, difference it makes.

Type of Reward

The kind of financial rewards that organizations give to individuals can vary widely. Pay comes in many forms varying from stock to medical insurance. Organizations can choose to reward people almost exclusively with cash, downplaying fringe benefits, perquisites, and status symbols—or they can do just the opposite.

The major advantage of paying in cash is that the value of cash in the eyes of the recipient is universally high. When the cash is translated into fringe benefits, perquisites, or other trappings of office, it may lose its value for some people and, as a result, be a poor investment if the intention is to give a valued reward (e.g., see Lawler, 1971; Nealey, 1963). However, certain status symbols and perquisites may be valued by some individuals beyond their actual dollar cost to the organization and thus represent good buys. Finally, there often are climate and organizational structure reasons for paying people in the form of perquisites, and status symbols. Unfortunately, there is relatively little research on the overall value and impact of nonfinancial status rewards; this clearly is an underresearched area.

Certain benefits, such as health care, can best be obtained through mass purchase, and therefore individuals may want the organization to provide them. Organizations increasingly have done just this over the last 40 years. One estimate is that benefits increased from 19 percent to 43 percent of cash compensation between 1950 and 1980 (Bloom & Trahan, 1986). No research has been conducted to determine the impact of this increase on issues of organizational culture, membership, and performance. It clearly represents, however, a significant increase in an organization's cost of doing business. From a cultural point of view, it may well have contributed to a more paternalistic culture since it makes individuals more dependent on their work organizations for important benefits in addition to cash compensation.

One interesting development in the area of compensation is the flexible or cafeteria style benefit program (e.g., see Fragner, 1975; Lawler, 1981). The potential value of this approach was established in early work by Nealey (1963), but it was not adopted by organizations until about a decade later (Lawler, Mohrman, & Ledford, 1992). In a flexible benefits plan, individuals are allowed to choose their own reward package so that it is sure to fit their needs and desires. The theory is that this will lead to organizations getting the best value for their money because they will give people only those things that they desire. It also has the advantage of treating individuals as mature adults rather than as dependent people who need their welfare looked after in a structured way.

The flexible approach has been tried in a number of organizations. Lawler, Ledford, and Mohrman (1989) found that 34 percent of the Fortune 1000 had plans in 1987. While little research has been done on flexible plans, the results so far have been favorable in several respects (Gifford & Seltz, 1988). It seems to offer a strategic cost benefit advantage in attracting and retaining employees (Bloom & Trahan, 1986). It does so because it gives employees the benefits they want, while relieving companies of buying benefits that are not cost effective from an attraction and retention point of view.

In addition to cost effectiveness considerations, the choice of what form of rewards to give individuals probably should be driven by a clear sense of what type of culture the organization wishes to have. For example, the idea of a flexible compensation package is congruent with a participative and open organizational culture that treats individuals as mature adults and wants to attract talented mature individuals (Lawler, 1990). A status symbol, non–cash-oriented approach may, on the other hand, appeal to people who are very status oriented, value position power, and need a high level of visible reinforcement for their position. This would seem to fit best a relatively bureaucratic organization that relies on position power and authority in order to carry out its actions.

Process Issues

A useful dichotomy in thinking about the design of reward systems is the process/content one. All organizational systems have a content or structural dimension as well as a process dimension (Lawler, 1981). The structural or content dimension of a reward system refers to the formal mechanisms, procedures, and practices (e.g., salary structure, performance appraisal forms), in short, the nuts and bolts, of the system that have already been discussed. The process side refers to the communication and decision process parts of the system. One key process issue involves the degree of openness with respect to information about how the reward system operates and how people are rewarded. A second issue involves the degree of participation allowed in the design of the reward system and the ongoing administration of it.

Communication Policy

Organizations differ widely in how much information they communicate about their reward systems. At one extreme, some organizations are very secretive, particularly in the area of pay. They forbid people from talking about their individual reward levels, give minimal information to individuals about how rewards are decided upon and allocated, and have no publicly disseminated policies about such things as market position, approach to gathering market data, and potential increases for individuals. In the middle are organizations in which pay ranges and median pay levels are shared and the budgets for pay raises are given. At the other extreme, some organizations are so open that everyone's pay is a matter of public record, as is the overall organization pay approach (Burroughs, 1982; Lawler, 1981). In addition, all promotions are subject to open job posting, and in some instances, peer groups discuss the eligibility of people for promotion. This is true of some government organizations and many new high involvement plants (e.g., see Lawler, 1978; Walton, 1980).

The arguments that are mounted in favor of secrecy tend to be very similar to those that argue in favor of openness. Both claim that communication affects satisfaction and motivation; they disagree, however, on whether openness has a positive or negative effect on them. There has been some research on the issue of how communication affects satisfaction. This research has focused on secrecy's impact on the accuracy of the pay comparison process. Lawler (1972) found that when secrecy exists, individual managers tend to overestimate the pay of their peers and subordinates but underestimate the pay of their bosses. He uses this finding to argue that secrecy may lead to lower satisfaction because it leads to misperceptions that make pay comparison less favorable for the receiver. This follows from the finding that pay satisfaction is, in part, based on how one's pay compares to that of similar others.

The arguments in favor of secrecy tend to reason that if pay is secret, unfavorable comparisons cannot be made, and thus satisfaction will be high. The problem with this argument is that there is no evidence that secrecy prevents comparison. At this point there is not much direct research on how secrecy affects satisfaction. One field experiment by Futrell (1978), however, provides some data. One year after moving from a closed to an open pay system, workers reported higher levels of pay satisfaction than before the change. The best answer to the ques-

tion of how communication affects pay satisfaction probably is that it depends on such things as the actual pay rates in the organization, the basis of the pay system, and the general management style of the organization.

The issue of how secrecy affects motivation is a complex one. The argument in favor of openness essentially reasons that it is necessary in order to establish a clear performance-reward relationship. There is evidence that individuals overestimate the amount of the merit pay rewards received by other individuals, which makes their own merit pay rewards look smaller (Lawler, 1972). Although there is no conclusive evidence, it can be argued that this misperception is harmful to both satisfaction and motivation. It has been argued that secrecy leads to more willingness among managers to base pay on performance because they do not have to offer an explanation to the person who gets a low payment. For example, in two laboratory investigations, Leventhal, Michaels, and Sanford (1972) and Peters and Atkin (1980) manipulated pay secrecy. Both studies found that the differences in merit increases between high and low performers were smaller in open pay systems than in systems with pay secrecy. Although this result makes some sense, little field research has been done that directly bears on it.

Research on individual preferences with respect to making pay public generally supports the view that individuals do not want to have pay completely in the open. For example, managers in one organization favored having everything made public about their performance-based bonus payments except the actual amount received by individuals (Lawler, 1981). It appears that individuals want to know everything except who got what amount of money. Overall, the evidence is so sparse that it is difficult to reach an empirically based conclusion concerning the effects of communication on employee motivation and satisfaction.

Participation in Pay System Design

Two of the original studies on participation in pay system design provide clear evidence that participation can make a difference in the impact of a pay plan. In the first study, two work groups were observed. In one group, productivity was very high and had continued to go up for more than ten years (Cammann & Lawler, 1973; Lawler & Cammann, 1972). In the other group, productivity was low and had remained relatively stable for years. Both groups did the same kinds of jobs, and both had similar pay incentive plans. In the second study, identical incentive plans designed to motivate attendance were installed in a number of work groups (Lawler & Hackman, 1969; Scheflen, Lawler, & Hackman, 1971). In some groups, the plan was highly successful in reducing absenteeism, but in others it was only moderately successful.

In the attendance-bonus study, the one characteristic that distinguished the groups where the plan worked from those where it did not was decision making. The plan was designed and developed by the employee groups where it worked, but it was imposed on those groups where it was less effective. In the incentive study, the group where the plan worked had a long history of employee participation in decision making, and employees had actually voted on the plan when it was put into effect years earlier. In the other group, no history of participation existed, and the plan had simply been designed by management and imposed on the employees.

Lawler (1981) and Jenkins and Lawler (1981) provide evidence on the use of employee task forces to design pay systems. In three cases, task forces successfully designed and implemented a plan. Thus, it seems that, like direct participation, participation through task forces can have a positive impact on pay plans.

The success of participative design efforts raises the question of why participation makes a difference. In some situations, it may lead to the design of a better plan because it involves a high level of information exchange. In some of the studies, however, this cannot account for the differences because similar plans produced different results. In these studies it must be because participation contributed to the amount of information employees have about the plans and to their feelings of control over and commitment to what was decided (Vroom, 1964).

Participation in System Administration

The logical extension of the practice of having individuals participate in the design of performance-based pay systems is to have them participate in the making of day-to-day pay decisions. There has been some experimentation with having peer groups and low-level supervisory people handle the day-to-day decision making about who should receive pay increases and how jobs should be evaluated and placed in pay structures (Jenkins & Lawler, 1981). There also have been isolated instances of peer executives assessing each other allocating pay (Lawler, 1981).

The most visible examples of peer group decision making are in the new participative plants that use skill-based pay (e.g., see Gupta et al., 1986; Walton, 1980). In these plants, typically the work group reviews the performance of the individual and decides whether he or she has acquired the new skills. Interestingly, the little evidence there suggests that this has gone very well. In many respects this result is not surprising since the peers often have the best information about performance and thus are in the best position to make performance assessments. Peer ratings are often valid and have been the subject of considerable research (Kane & Lawler, 1978). The problem in traditional organizations is that peers may lack the motivation to give valid feedback and to behave responsibly; thus, their expertise is of no use. In more participative systems, this motivational problem seems to be less severe, and as a result, involvement in decision making seems to be more effective.

Overall, there is evidence that some participative approaches to reward system design and administration can be effective. The key seems to be articulating the practices in the area of reward systems with the general management style of the organization. In more participative settings, there is good reason to believe that participative approaches to reward-system decision making can be effective because of their congruence with the overall management style and because the skills and group norms to make them effective are already in place. In more traditional organizations, the typical top-down approach to reward-system design and administration probably is better. Much more research is needed in this area before we can begin to sort out the impact of participation and understand when, where, and how it is best used.

Future Research

The research on pay in organizations can best be described as uneven. Some topics are extremely well researched, while others are barely touched upon. Some studies are well done, while others are not. Particularly noticeable by their absence are well-executed studies that look at the impact of pay practices while taking into consideration the nature of the organization in which the practices operate. The existing literature allows some general conclusions about the impact of a wide variety of pay systems, but it also suggests strongly that their impact depends on a number of key organizational factors. Management style, organization size, and work

design, for example, all appear to moderate the impact of a variety of pay systems.

Hopefully, future research will be more likely to study those pay practices that are relatively underresearched, and it will be more sensitive to issues of organizational context. This in turn could, and should, lead to the development of theories that are more organizational in their orientation. Most of the useful current theories concerning pay systems focus on individual behavior and the impact of pay on it. More theories are needed that focus on the relationship between pay systems and organizational behavior and performance. These theories are likely to develop only if more attention and research is focused on the organizational context in which pay and reward systems operate.

References

Adams, J. S. (1965). Injustice in social exchange. In L. Berkowitz (Ed.), *Advances in experimental social psychology* (Vol. 2, pp. 267–299). New York: Academic Press.

Arvey, R. D. (1986). Sex bias in job evaluation procedures. *Personnel Psychology, 39,* 315–335.

Ash, P. (1948). The reliability of job evaluation ranking. *Journal of Applied Psychology, 32,* 313–320.

Babchuck, N., & Goode, W. J. (1951). Work incentives in a self-determined group. *American Sociological Review, 16,* 679–687.

Balkin, D. B., & Gomez-Mejia, L. R. (1987a). *New perspectives on compensation.* Englewood Cliffs, NJ: Prentice-Hall.

Balkin, D. B., & Gomez-Mejia, L. R. (1987b). Toward a contingency theory of compensation strategy. *Strategic Management Journal, 8,* 169–182.

Bandura, A. (1986). *Social foundations of thought and action: A social-cognitive view.* Englewood Cliffs, NJ: Prentice-Hall.

Baumgartel, H., & Sobol, R. (1959). Background and organizational factors in absenteeism. *Personnel Psychology, 12,* 431–443.

Beatty, R. W., & Beatty, J. R. (1984). Some problems with contemporary job evaluation systems.

In H. Remick (Ed.), *Comparable worth and wage discrimination*. Philadelphia, PA: Temple University Press.

Becker, G. S. (1975). *Human capital* (2nd ed.). New York: National Bureau of Economic Research.

Belcher, D. W. (1969). The changing nature of compensation administration. *California Management Review, 4*, 225–235.

Belcher, J. G. (1991). *Gainsharing*. Houston, TX: Gulf.

Blasis, J. R. (1988). *Employee ownership*. Cambridge, MA: Ballinger.

Blinder, A. S. (1990). *Paying for productivity*. Washington, DC: Brookings.

Bloom, D. E., & Trahan, J. T. (1986). *Flexible benefits and employee choice*. New York: Pergamon.

Bowen, D. E., Worley, C., & Lawler, E. E., III. (in press). What laws govern the size of meaningful pay increases? *Journal of Organizational Behavior*.

Brickley, J. A., Bhagat, S., & Lease, R. C. (1985). The impact of long-range managerial compensation plans on shareholder wealth. *Journal of Accounting and Economics, 7*, 115–129.

Bullock, R. J., & Lawler, E. E. (1984). Gainsharing: A few questions and fewer answers. *Human Resource Management, 23*, 23–40.

Bureau of National Affairs. (1976, June). Job evaluation policies and procedures. *Personnel Policies Forum*, Survey No. 113.

Burroughs, J. D. (1982). Pay secrecy and performance. *Compensation Review, 14*, 44–54.

Cammann, C., & Lawler, E. E. (1973). Employee reactions to pay incentive plans. *Journal of Applied Psychology, 58*, 163–172.

Champlin, F. C., & Kopelman, R. E. (1991). Hinrichs revisited: Individual evaluations of income increments. *Journal of Psychology, 125*, 359–373.

Chesler, D. J. (1948). Reliability and comparability of different job evaluation systems. *Journal of Applied Psychology, 32*, 465–475.

Conte, M., & Tannenbaum, A. (1980). *Employee ownership*. Ann Arbor, MI: Institute for Social Research, University of Michigan.

Corbett, W., & Potocko, R. (1969). Economic and psychological determinants of the comparability of pay. *Proceedings of the 77th Annual Convention of the American Psychological Association, IV* (Pt 2, pp. 711–712).

Crystal, G. S. (1978). *Executive compensation*. New York: Amacom.

Crystal, G. S. (1984). *Questions and answers on executive compensation*. Englewood Cliffs, NJ: Prentice-Hall.

Crystal, G. S. (1991). *In search of excess*. New York: Norton.

Deming, W. E. (1986). *Out of the crisis*. Cambridge, MA: MIT.

Dertien, M. G. (1981, July). Accuracy of job evaluation plans. *Personnel Journal*, 566–570.

DeVries, D. L., Morrison, A. M., Shullman, S. L., & Gerlach, M. L. (1981). *Performance appraisal on the line*. New York: Wiley-Interscience.

Ellig, B. R. (1982). *Executive compensation: A total pay perspective*. New York: McGraw-Hill.

Emery, F. E., & Trist, E. L. (1965). The causal texture of organizational environments. *Human Relations, 18*, 21–32.

Finkelstein, S., & Hambrick, D. C. (1988). Chief executive compensation: A synthesis and reconciliation. *Strategic Management Journal, 9*, 543–558.

Foulkes, F. R. (1991). *Executive compensation*. Boston: Harvard Business School.

Fragner, B. N. (1975). Employees' "cafeteria" offers insurance options. *Harvard Business Review, 53*(6), 2–4.

Frost, C. F., Wakeley, J. H., & Ruh, R. A. (1974). *The Scanlon plan for organization development: Identity, participation, equity*. East Lansing, MI: Michigan State University Press.

Fuller, L. E. (1972). Designing compensation systems for scientists and professionals in business. In M. L. Rock (Ed.), *Handbook of wage and salary administration*. New York: McGraw-Hill.

Futrell, C. M. (1978). Effects of pay disclosures on pay satisfaction for sales managers: A longitudinal study. *Academy of Management Journal, 21*, 140–144.

Futrell, C. M., & Schul, P.L. (1980). Marketing executives' perceptions of salary increases. *California Management Review, 22*, 87–93.

Futrell, C. M., & Varadarajan, P.R. (1985). Marketing executives' perceptions of equitable salary increases. *Industrial Marketing Management, 14*, 59–67.

Galbraith, J. R. (1973). *Designing complete organizations*. Reading, MA: Addison-Wesley.

Galbraith, J. R. (1977). *Organization design*. Reading, MA: Addison-Wesley.

Galbraith, J. R., & Kazanjian, R. K. (1986). *Strategy implementation: Structure, systems and process* (2nd ed.). St. Paul, MN: West.

General Accounting Office. (1981). *Productivity sharing programs: Can they contribute to productivity improvement?* Washington, DC: U.S. General Accounting Office.

Gerhart, B., & Milkovich, G. T. (1990). Organizational difference in compensation and financial performance. *Academy of Management Journal, 33,* 663–691.

Gescheider, G. A. (1976). *Psychophysics: Methods and theory.* Hillsdale, NJ: Erlbaum.

Gifford, D. L., & Seltz, C. A. (1988). *Fundamentals of flexible compensation.* New York: Wiley.

Gomez-Mejia, L. R., Page, R. C., & Tornow, W. W. (1982). A comparison of the practical utility of traditional, statistical, and hybrid job evaluation methods. *Academy of Management Journal, 25,* 790–809.

Gomez-Mejia, L. R., Tosi, H., & Hinkin, T. (1987). Managerial control, performance, and executive compensation. *Academy of Management Journal, 30,* 51–70.

Gomez-Mejia, L. R., & Welbourne, T. M. (1988). Compensation strategy: An overview and future steps. *Human Resource Planning, 11,* 173–189.

Gomez-Mejia, L. R., & Welbourne, T. M. (1989). The strategic design of executive compensation programs. In L. R. Gomez-Mejia (Ed.), *Compensation and benefits* (pp. 216–260). Washington, DC: Bureau of National Affairs.

Graham-Moore, B. E., & Ross, T. L. (1983). *Productivity gainsharing.* Englewood Cliffs, NJ: Prentice-Hall.

Graham-Moore, B. E., & Ross, T. L. (1990). *Gainsharing.* Washington, DC: Bureau of National Affairs.

Gupta, N., & Jenkins, G. D., Jr. (1991). Practical problems in using job evaluation systems to determine compensation. *Human Resource Management Review, 1,* 133-144.

Gupta, N., Jenkins, G. D., & Curington, W. P. (1986). Paying for knowledge: Myths and realities. *National Productivity Review, 29,* 441–464.

Gupta, N., Jenkins, G. D., Jr., Curington, W. P., Clements, C., Doty, D. H., Schweitzer, T. P., & Teutsch, C. H. (1986). *Exploratory investigations of pay-for-knowledge systems.* Washington, DC: U.S. Government Printing Office.

Hackman, J. R., & Oldham, G. R. (1980). *Work redesign.* Reading, MA: Addison-Wesley.

Hambrick, D. C., & Snow, C. C. (1989). Strategic reward systems. In C. C. Snow (Ed.), *Strategy, organization design and human resource management* (pp. 929–964). Greenwich, CT: JAI.

Hammer, T. (1988). New developments in profit sharing. In J. Campbell, R. Campbell et al., *Productivity in organizations.* San Francisco: Jossey-Bass.

Heneman, H. G., III, & Ellis, R. A. (1982). Correlates of just noticeable differences in pay increases. *Labor Law Journal, 33,* 533–538.

Heneman, R. L. (1984). *Pay-for-performance: Exploring the merit system* (Work in America Institute Studies in Productivity No. 38). New York: Pergamon.

Heneman, R. L. (1990). Merit pay research. *Research in Personnel and Human Resources Management, 8,* 203–263.

Hill, C. W. L., & Phan, P. (1991). CEO tenure as a determinant of CEO pay. *Academy of Management Journal, 34,* 707–717.

Hinrichs, J. R. (1969). Correlates of employee evaluations of pay raises. *Journal of Applied Psychology, 55,* 481–489.

Jenkins, G. D., Jr. (1985). Financial incentives. In E. A. Locke (Ed.), *Generalizing from laboratory to field settings.* Lexington, MA: Lexington.

Jenkins, G. D., Jr., & Gupta, N. (1982). Financial incentives and productivity improvement. *Journal of Contemporary Business, 11*(2), 43–56.

Jenkins, G. D., Jr., & Gupta, N. (1985). The payoffs of paying for knowledge. *National Productivity Review, 4,* 121–130.

Jenkins, G. D., Jr., & Lawler, E. E. (1981). Impact of employee participation in the development of a base pay plan. *Organizational Behavior and Human Performance, 28,* 111–128.

Jones, A. M. (1948). Job evaluation of nonacademic work at the University of Illinois. *Journal of Applied Psychology, 32,* 15–19.

Kane, J., & Lawler, E. E. (1978). Methods of peer assessment. *Psychological Bulletin, 85,* 555–586.

Katz, D., & Kahn, R. L. (1966). *The social psychology of organizations.* New York: Wiley.

Kerr, J. L. (1985). Diversification strategies and managerial rewards: An empirical study. *Academy of Management Journal, 28,* 155–179.

Kerr, J. L., & Slocum, J. W. (1987). Managing corporate culture through reward systems. *Academy of Management Executive, 1,* 99–108.

Kerr, S. (1975). On the folly of rewarding A, while hoping for B. *Academy of Management Journal, 18,* 769–783.

Klein, K. J. (1987). Employee stock ownership and employee attitudes: A test of three models. *Journal of Applied Psychology, 72,* 319–332.

Kopelman, R. E., Rovenpor, J. L., & Cayer, M. (1991). Merit pay and organizational performance: Is there an effect on the bottom line? *National Productivity Review, 10,* 299–307.

Krefting, L. A., & Mahoney, T. A. (1977). Determining the size of a meaningful pay increase. *Industrial Relations, 16,* 89–93.

Larcker, D. F. (1983). The association between performance plan adoption and corporate capital investment. *Journal of Accounting and Economics, 5,* 3–30.

Lawler, E. E. (1971). *Pay and organizational effectiveness: A psychological view.* New York: McGraw-Hill.

Lawler, E. E. (1972). Secrecy and the need to know. In M. Dunnette, R. House, & H. Tosi (Eds.), *Readings in managerial motivation and compensation* (pp. 362–371). East Lansing, MI: Michigan State University Press.

Lawler, E. E. (1973). *Motivation in work organizations.* Monterey, CA: Brooks/Cole.

Lawler, E. E. (1978). The new plant revolution. *Organizational Dynamics, 6,* 2–12.

Lawler, E. E. (1981). *Pay and organization development.* Reading, MA: Addison-Wesley.

Lawler, E. E. (1986a). *High involvement management.* San Francisco: Jossey-Bass.

Lawler, E. E. (1986b). Reward systems and strategy. In J. R. Gardner, R. Rochlin, & H. W. Sweeney (Eds.), *Strategic planning handbook* (pp. 10.1–10.24). New York: Wiley.

Lawler, E. E. (1986c). What's wrong with point-factor job evaluation. *Compensation and Benefits Review, 18*(2), 20–28.

Lawler, E. E. (1988a). Choosing an involvement strategy. *Academy of Management Executive, 2*(3), 22–27, 197–204.

Lawler, E. E. (1988b). Gainsharing theory and research: Findings and future directions. In W. A. Pasmore & R. Woodman (Eds.), *Research*

in organizational change and development (Vol. 2, pp. 323–344). Greenwich, CT: JAI.

Lawler, E. E. (1990). *Strategic pay.* San Francisco: Jossey-Bass.

Lawler, E. E. (1991). Paying the person: A better approach to management? *Human Resource Management Review, 1,* 145–154.

Lawler, E. E. (1992). *The ultimate advantage: Creating the high-involvement organization.* San Francisco: Jossey-Bass.

Lawler, E. E., & Cammann, C. (1972). What makes a work group successful? In A. J. Marrow (Ed.), *The failure of success* (pp. 122–130). New York: Amacom.

Lawler, E. E., & Hackman, J. R. (1969). The impact of employee participation in the development of pay incentive plans: A field experiment. *Journal of Applied Psychology, 53,* 467–471.

Lawler, E. E., & Ledford, G. E. (1985). Skill based pay. *Personnel, 62*(9), 30–37.

Lawler, E. E., Ledford, G. E., & Mohrman, S. A. (1989). *Employee involvement in America.* Houston, TX: American Productivity and Quality Center.

Lawler, E. E., Mohrman, S. A., & Ledford, G. E. (1992). *Employee involvement and total quality management: Practices and results in Fortune 1000 companies.* San Francisco: Jossey-Bass.

Lawler, E. E., & Rhode, J. G. (1976). *Information and control in organizations.* Santa Monica, CA: Goodyear.

Lawrence, P. R., & Lorsch, J. W. (1967). *Organization and environment: Managing differentiation and integration.* Homewood, IL: Irwin.

Lawshe, C. H., Jr., & Farbro, P. (1949). Studies in job evaluation VIII: The reliability of an abbreviated job evaluation system. *Journal of Applied Psychology, 32,* 118–129.

Lawshe, C. H., Jr., & Wilson, R. F. (1947). Studies in job evaluation VI: The relationship of two point rating systems. *Journal of Applied Psychology, 31,* 355–365.

LeBlanc, P. V. (1990). Skill-based pay case number 2: Northern Telecom. *Compensation and Benefits Review, 23*(1), 39–56.

Ledford, G. E., Jr. (1985). *Skill based pay: Some implementation issues in new high involvement plants*. Paper presented at the annual meeting of the Academy of Management, San Diego, CA.

Ledford, G. E., Jr. (1990). The design of skill-based pay plans. In M. L. Rock & L. A. Berger (Eds.), *The compensation handbook: A state-of the art guide to compensation strategy and design*. New York: McGraw-Hill.

Ledford, G. E., Jr. (1991). Three case studies on skill-based pay: An overview: *Compensation and Benefits Review, 23*(1), 11–23.

Ledford, G. E., Jr., & Bergel, G. (1990). Skill-based pay case number 1: General Mills. *Compensation and Benefits Review, 23*(1), 24–38.

Ledford, G. E., Jr., Tyler, W. R., & Dixey, W. B. (1990). Skill-based pay case number 3: Honeywell Ammunition Assembly Plant. *Compensation and Benefits Review, 23*(1), 57–77.

Lesieur, F. G. (1958). *The Scanlon plan: A frontier in labor-management cooperation*. New York: Wiley.

Leventhal, G. S., Michaels, J. W., & Sanford, C. (1972). Inequity and interpersonal conflict: Reward allocation and secrecy about reward as methods of preventing conflict. *Journal of Personality and Social Psychology, 23*, 88–102.

Livy, B. (1975). *Job evaluation: A critical review*. New York: Wiley.

Locke, E. A., Feren, D. B., McCaleb, V. M., Shaw, K. N., & Denny, A. T. (1980). The relative effectiveness of four methods of motivating employee performance. In K. D. Duncan, M. M. Gruneberg, & D. Wallis (Eds.), *Changes in working life*. London: Wiley.

Locke, E. A., & Latham, G. P. (1990). *A theory of goal-setting and task performance*. Englewood Cliffs, NJ: Prentice-Hall.

Longnecker, C. O., Sims, H. P., & Gioia, D. A. (1987). Behind the mask: The politics of employee appraisal. *Academy of Management Executive, 1*, 183–193.

Madigan, R. M. (1985). Comparable worth judgments: A measurement properties analysis. *Journal of Applied Psychology, 70*, 137–147.

Madigan, R. M., & Hoover, D. J. (1986). Effects of alternative job evaluation methods on decisions involving pay equity. *Academy of Management Journal, 29*, 84–100.

Mahoney, T. A. (1991). Job evaluation: Endangered species or anachronism? *Human Resource Management Review, 1*, 155–162.

March, J. G., & Simon, H. A. (1958). *Organizations*. New York: Wiley.

McGregor, D. (1960). *The human side of enterprise*. New York: McGraw-Hill.

Metzger, B. L. (1964). *Profit sharing in perspective*. Evanston, IL: Profit Sharing Research Foundation.

Meyer, H. H., Kay, E., & French, J. R. P., Jr. (1965). Split roles in performance appraisal. *Harvard Business Review, 43*(1), 123–129.

Milkovich, G. T., & Broderick, R. (1982). Pay discrimination: Legal issues and implications for research. *Industrial Relations, 21*, 309–317.

Milkovich, G. T., & Wigdor, A. K. (Eds.). (1991). *Pay for performance: Evaluating performance appraisal and merit pay*. Washington, DC: National Academy Press.

Mobley, W. H. (1982). *Employee turnover: Causes, consequences, and control*. Reading, MA: Addison-Wesley.

Mobley, W. H., Hand, H. H., Meglino, B. M., & Griffeth, R. W. (1979). Review and conceptual analysis of the employee turnover process. *Psychological Bulletin, 86*, 493–522.

Mohrman, A. M. (1990). Deming versus performance appraisal: Is there a resolution? In G. N. McLean, S. R. Damne, & R. A. Swanson (Eds.), *Performance appraisal perspectives on a quality management approach* (pp. 3–23). Alexandria, VA: American Society for Training and Development.

Mohrman, A. M., & Lawler, E. E. (1983). Motivation and performance appraisal behavior. In F. Landy, S. Zedeck, & J. Cleveland (Eds.), *Performance measurement and theory*. Hillsdale, NJ: Erlbaum.

Mohrman, A. M., Resnick-West, S. A., & Lawler, E. E. (1989). *Designing performance appraisal systems*. San Francisco: Jossey-Bass.

Moore, B. E., & Ross, T. L. (1978). *The Scanlon way to improved productivity*. New York: Wiley-Interscience.

Murphy, K. R., & Cleveland, J. N. (1991). *Performance appraisal: An organizational perspective*. Boston: Allyn and Bacon.

Nadler, D., & Tushman, M. (1988). *Strategic organization design*. Glenview, IL: Scott, Foresman.

Nalbantain, H. (1987). *Incentives, cooperation and risk sharing*. Totoway, NJ: Rowman and Littlefield.

Napier, N. K., & Smith, M. (1987). Product diversification, performance criteria and compensation at the level. *Strategic Management Journal, 8,* 195–201.

Nealey, S. (1963). Pay and benefit preferences. *Industrial Relations, 8,* 17–28.

O'Dell, C. (1981). *Gainsharing: Involvement, incentives, and productivity.* New York: American Management Association.

O'Dell, C. (1987). *People, performance and pay.* Houston, TX: American Productivity Center.

O'Reilly, C. A., Main, B., & Crystal, G. S. (1988). CEO compensation as tournament and social comparison: A tale of two theories. *Administrative Science Quarterly, 33,* 257–274.

O'Toole, J. (1979). The uneven record of employee ownership. *Harvard Business Review, 57*(6), 185–197.

Oi, W. Y. (1983). The fixed employment costs of specialized labor. In J. E. Triplett (Ed.), *The measurement of labor cost.* Chicago: University of Chicago Press.

Pasquale, A. M. (1969). *A new dimension to job evaluation.* New York: American Management Association.

Patten, T. H. (1988). *Fair pay?* San Francisco: Jossey-Bass.

Patton, J. A., Littlefield, C. L., & Self, S. A. (1964). *Job evaluation: Text and cases* (3rd ed.). Homewood, IL: Irwin.

Peck, C. (1984). *Pay for performance: The interaction of compensation and performance appraisal* (No. 155). New York: The Conference Board.

Pedalino, E., & Gamboa, V. V. (1974). Behavior modification and absenteeism: Intervention in one industrial setting. *Journal of Applied Psychology, 59,* 694–698.

Peters, R., & Atkin, R. (1980). The effect of open pay systems on allocation of salary increases. *Proceedings of the Academy of Management, 40,* 293–297.

Porter, L. W., & Lawler, E. E. (1968). *Managerial attitudes and performance.* Homewood, IL: Irwin-Dorsey.

Porter, M. E. (1985). *Competitive advantage.* New York: Free Press.

Porter, M. E. (1990). *The competitive advantage of nations.* New York: Free Press.

Prince, J. B., & Lawler, E. E. (1986). Does salary discussion hurt the developmental performance appraisal? *Organizational Behavior and Human Decision Processes, 37,* 357–375.

Quarrey, M., Blasis, J. R., & Rosen, C. (1986). *Taking stock: Employee ownership at work.* Cambridge, MA: Ballinger.

Rambo, W. W., & Pinto, J. N. (1989). Employees' perceptions of pay increases. *Journal of Occupational Psychology, 62,* 135–145.

Rappaport, A. (1978). Executive incentives vs. corporate growth. *Harvard Business Review, 56*(4), 81–88.

Rock, M. L., & Berger, L. A. (1991). *The compensation handbook* (3rd ed.). New York: McGraw-Hill.

Rosen, C., & Young, K. M. (1991). *Understanding employee ownership.* Ithaca, NY: ILR Press.

Rosen, C., Klein, K. J., & Young, K. M. (1986). *Employee ownership in America: The equity solution.* Lexington, MA: Lexington.

Rynes, S., & Milkovich, G. T. (1986). Wage surveys: Dispelling some myths about the "market wage." *Personnel Psychology, 39,* 71–91.

Scheflen, C., Lawler, E. E., & Hackman, J. R. (1971). Long-term impact of employee participation in the development of pay incentive plans: A field experiment revisited. *Journal of Applied Psychology, 55,* 182–186.

Schlesinger, L. A., & Heskett, J. L. (1991). The service-driven company. *Harvard Business Review, 69*(5), 71–81.

Schoorman, F. D., Bazerman, M. H., & Atkins, R. S. (1981). Interlocking directorates: A strategy for ordering environmental uncertainty. *Academy of Management Review, 6,* 243–251.

Schwab, D. P. (1980). Job evaluation and pay setting: Concepts and practices. In E. R. Livernash (Ed.), *Comparable worth: Issues and alternatives.* Washington, DC: Equal Opportunity Advisory Council.

Schwab, D. P., & Gram, R. (1985). Sex related errors in job evaluation: A "real world" test. *Journal of Applied Psychology, 70,* 533–539.

Schlotzhauer, D. L., & Rosse, J. G. (1985). A five-year study of incentive absence control program. *Personnel Psychology, 38,* 575–585.

Schwab, D. P., & Olsen, C. A. (1988). Pay-performance relationship as a function of pay for performance policies and practices. *Academy of Management Best Papers Proceedings, 48,* 287–291.

Snelgar, R. J. (1983). The comparability of job evaluation methods in supplying approximately similar classifications in rating one job series. *Personnel Psychology, 36,* 371–380.

Steers, R. M., & Rhodes, S. R. (1978). Major influences on employee attendance: A process model. *Journal of Applied Psychology, 63,* 391–407.

Suskin, H. (1977). *Job evaluation and pay administration in the public sector.* Chicago: International Personnel Management Association.

Tosi, H., & Tosi, L. (1986). What managers need to know about knowledge-based pay. *Organizational Dynamics, 14*(3), 52–64.

Ulrich, D., & Lake, D. (1990). *Organizational capability.* New York: Wiley.

Varadarajan, P., & Futrell, C. M. (1984). Factors affecting perceptions of smallest meaningful pay increases. *Industrial Relations, 23,* 278–285.

Vroom, V. H. (1964). *Work and motivation.* New York: Wiley.

Walton, R. E. (1980). Establishing and maintaining high commitment work systems. In J. R. Kimberly, R. H. Miles, et al. (Eds.), *The organizational life cycle.* San Francisco: Jossey-Bass.

Weitzman, M. L. (1984). *The share economy.* Cambridge, MA: Harvard.

Welbourne, T. M., & Gomez-Mejia, L. R. (1991). *Job evaluation: Rational or political?* (Faculty Working Paper Series, No. 91-13). University of Colorado at Boulder, College of Business Administration, Boulder.

Whyte, W. F. (Ed.). (1955). *Money and motivation: An analysis of incentives in industry.* New York: Harper.

Zedeck, S., & Smith, P. C. (1968). The psychological determination of equitable payment: A methodological study. *Journal of Applied Psychology, 52,* 343–347.

Credits

Acknowledgment is made to the following authors and publishers for their kind permission to reprint material from the copyrighted sources as follows:

Chapter 1 Lubinski and Dawis

Page 6 From "Fads, Fashions, and Folderol in Psychology" by M. D. Dunnette, 1966, *American Psychologist, 21*, pp. 343–352. Copyright 1966 by *American Psychologist*. **7** From *Contingencies of Reinforcement: Theoretical Analysis* (p. 183) by B. F. Skinner, 1969, New York: Appleton-Century-Crofts. Copyright 1969 by Julie Vargas. **15** From *Human Ability* (p. 143) by C. Spearman and L. L. Jones, 1950, London: Macmillan. Copyright 1950 by Macmillan. **24** From "Exploratory Factor Analysis: A Tutorial" by J. B. Carroll in *Current Topics in Human Intelligence: Vol. 1* (p. 30), D. K. Detterman, Ed. (1985), Norwood, NJ: Ablex. Copyright 1985 by Ablex. Reprinted by permission of Ablex Publishing Corporation. **27** From "Content–Construct Confusion" by M. L. Tenopyr, 1977, *Personnel Psychology, 30*, pp. 47–54. Copyright 1977 by *Personnel Psychology*. Reprinted by permission. **34a** From *Aptitudes and Instructional Methods: A Handbook for Research on Interactions* (pp. 496–497) by L. J. Cronbach and R. E. Snow, 1977, New York: Irvington. Copyright 1977 by Irvington. **34b** From *Learning and Individual Differences: Advances in Theory and Research* by P. L. Ackerman. Copyright © 1989 by Scientific American Library. Reprinted with permission of W. H. Freeman and Company. **36a** From *Personnel Testing* (p. 415) by R. M. Guion, 1965, New York: McGraw-Hill. Copyright 1965 by R. M. Guion. Reprinted by permission. **36b** From *Standards for Educational and Psychological Testing*. Copyright © 1985 by the American Psychological Association. Reprinted with permission. Further reproduction without the express written permission of the APA is prohibited. **41** From *The Work of the Counselor* (p. 120) by L. E. Tyler, 1953, Needham Heights, MA: Allyn & Bacon. Copyright 1953 by Allyn & Bacon. Reprinted by permission. **49** "Reinforcing Stimulus Properties of Drugs: Interpretations II" by K. MacCorquodale in *Stimulus Properties of Drugs* (pp. 215–217), T. Thompson and R. Pickins, Eds. (1971), Needham Heights, MA: Appleton-Century-Crofts. Copyright 1971 by Appleton-Century-Crofts. Reprinted by permission. **51a** From *The Structure of Human Abilities* (2nd ed., pp. 122, 128) by P. E. Vernon, 1961, New York: Methuen London, Ltd., a subsidiary of Routledge, Chapman, and Hall, Inc. Reprinted by permission. **51b** From "Gender Differences on 86 Nationally Standarized Aptitude and Achievement Tests" by J. C. Stanley in *Proceedings of H. B. and J. Wallace National Research Symposium on Talent Development* (1991), N. Colangelo (Ed.), Iowa City: University of Iowa Press. Copyright 1991 by University of Iowa Press. Reprinted by permission.

Chapter 4 Hackman

Page 215 From *A Thousand Days* by A. M. Schlesinger, Jr. Copyright © 1965 by A. M. Schlesinger, Jr. Reprinted by permission of Houghton Mifflin. All rights reserved. **217** From "Social Structure and Behavior" by W. E. Moore in *The Handbook of Social Psychology* (2nd ed., p. 289), G. Lindzey and E. Aronson , Eds. (1969), New York: McGraw-Hill. Copyright 1969 by McGraw-Hill. Reprinted by permission. **243** From *Victims of Group Think* (pp. 41–42) by I. L. Janis, 1972, New York: Houghton Mifflin. Copyright 1972 by Houghton Mifflin. Reprinted by permission. **253** From "Rough Justice" by L. Morrow, April 1991, *Time*, pp. 16–17. Copyright 1991 by Time. Reprinted by permission.

Chapter 5 Guzzo and Shea

Page 293 From "Progress in Small Groups Research" by J. M. Levine and R. L. Moreland, 1990, *Annual Reviews, 40*, p. 620. Copyright 1990 by *Annual Reviews*. Reproduced, with permission from the *Annual Review Psychology, 41*, 1990, by *Annual Reviews*.

Chapter 6 Davis and Powell

Page 322 From *The External Control of Organizations: A Resource Dependence Perspective* (p. 68) by J. Pfeffer and G. R. Salancik, 1978, New York: Harper & Row. Copyright 1978 by Harper & Row. Reprinted by permission. **328** From "The Economics of Organization: The Transaction Cost Approach" by O. E. Williamson, 1986, *American Journal of Sociology, 87,* p. 559. Copyright 1981 by University of Chicago Press. Reprinted by permission. **348** From "Niche Width and the Dynamics of Organizational Populations" by J. Freeman and M. T. Hanna, 1983, *American Journal of Sociology, 88,* pp. 1118–1119. Copyright 1983 by University of Chicago Press. Reprinted by permission.

Chapter 9 Gerhart and Milkovich

Page 550 From "Information Sharing and Collective Bargaining in Japan: Effects on Wage Negotiation" by M. Moroshima, 1991, *Industrial and Labor Relations Review, 44,* 469–485. Copyright 1991 by *Industrial and Labor Relations Review.* Reprinted by permission.

Chapter 12 Porras and Robertson

Page 805 From "Challenging Traditional Research Assumptions" by E. E. Lawler III in *Doing Research That Is Useful for Theory and Practice* (p. 15) , E. E. Lawler III et al., Eds. (1985), San Francisco: Jossey-Bass. Copyright 1955 by Jossey-Bass. Reprinted by permission.

Chapter 14 McKenna and Wright

Page 906 From *Metaphor and Meaning* (p. vii) by W. Embler, 1966, DeLand, FL: Everett/Edwards. **908a** Excerpt from "Politics and the English Language," copyright 1946 by Sonia Brownell Orwell and renewed 1974 by Sonia Orwell, reprinted from *Shooting an Elephant and Other Essays* by permission of Harcourt Brace Jovanovich. **908b and c** From *A Writers Companion* (pp. 186, 179) by R. Marius, 1991, New York: McGraw-Hill. Copyright 1991 by McGraw-Hill. Reprinted by permission. **932** From *The Social Psychology of Organizations* (p. 36) by D. Katz and R. L. Kahn, 1986, New York: Wiley. Copyright © 1986 by John Wiley & Sons. Reprinted by permission of John Wiley & Sons. **947** From *The Collected Works of Abraham Lincoln* (Vol. 4, pp. 439, 438; vol 5, p. 53), R. P. Basler, Ed. (1953–1955), New Brunswick, NJ: Rutgers University Press. Copyright © 1953 by Rutgers University, The State University of New Jersey.

Name Index

Subject Index